Church of England Record Society

Volume 19

THE LETTERS OF
THEOPHILUS LINDSEY (1723–1808)

VOLUME II: 1789–1808

The letters of Theophilus Lindsey (1723–1808) illuminate the career and opinions of one of the most prominent and controversial clergymen of the eighteenth and early nineteenth centuries. His petitions for liberalism within the Church of England in 1772–3, his subsequent resignation from the Church and his foundation of a separate Unitarian chapel in London in 1774 all provoked profound debate in the political as well as the ecclesiastical world. His chapel became a focal point for the theologically and politically disaffected and during the 1770s and early 1780s attracted the interest of many critics of British policy towards the American colonies. Benjamin Franklin, Joseph Priestley and Richard Price were among Lindsey's many acquaintances.

The second and final volume of this edition covers the period from the regency crisis and the early stages of the French Revolution to Lindsey's death nineteen years later, at the height of the Napoleonic War. His letters from this period reveal in depth Lindsey's central role in the formation of Unitarianism as a distinctive denomination, his involvement in movements for religious and political reform, his close friendship with Joseph Priestley and the tribulations of dissenters during the 1790s. From his vantage point in London, Lindsey was a well-informed and well-connected observer of the responses in Britain to the French Revolution and the war of the 1790s, and he provides a lucid commentary on the political, literary and theological scene.

As with Volume I, the letters are fully annotated and are accompanied by a full contextual introduction.

G. M. DITCHFIELD is Professor of Eighteenth-Century History, University of Kent at Canterbury.

THE LETTERS OF THEOPHILUS LINDSEY (1723–1808)

VOLUME II: 1789–1808

EDITED BY

G.M. Ditchfield

THE BOYDELL PRESS

CHURCH OF ENGLAND RECORD SOCIETY

First published 2012

A Church of England Record Society publication
Published by The Boydell Press
an imprint of Boydell & Brewer Ltd
PO Box 9, Woodbridge, Suffolk IP12 3DF, UK
and of Boydell & Brewer Inc.
668 Mt Hope Avenue, Rochester, NY 14620–2731, USA
website: www.boydellandbrewer.com

ISBN 978–1–84383–742–8

ISSN 1351–3087

Series information is printed at the back of this volume

A CIP catalogue record for this book is available
from the British Library

The publisher has no responsibility for the continued existence or accuracy
of URLs for external or third-party internet websites referred to in this book,
and does not guarantee that any content on such websites is,
or will remain, accurate or appropriate.

Papers used by Boydell & Brewer Ltd are natural, recyclable products
made from wood grown in sustainable forests

MIX
Paper from
responsible sources
FSC   FSC® C013604
www.fsc.org

Printed and bound in Great Britain by
CPI Group (UK) Ltd, Croydon, CR0 4YY

Contents

To the memory of my maternal grandparents

James Walpole McClure
Miriam McClure

Acknowledgments

As with Volume I of this edition, I thank the owners and custodians of the manuscript letters of Theophilus Lindsey for permission to print those letters. Of those which are privately owned, I am grateful to Dr John Scott for making available to me his valuable unitarian collection. Through the kindness of Mark Goldie and Barry Kingston of Churchill College, Cambridge, I was able to consult the letterbook of William Davy, which contains four letters from Lindsey, as well as several references to him. Dr Goldie helped to arrange for the deposit of this remarkable document in the highly appropriate setting of Dr Williams's Library, London. Thanks to Captain H. F. Pipe-Wolferstan of Statfold Hall, Staffordshire, and Staffordshire Record Office, I was able to make use of the diary of Samuel Pipe-Wolferstan. Higgs and Sons and Harward and Evers, solicitors, Stourbridge, allowed me to read James Scott's manuscript 'History of Cradley'. Carlisle Public Library granted me access to the manuscript diary of James Losh. Mr George Cockman generously provided me with photocopies of manuscript letters to Lindsey from Frances, duchess of Somerset, which are in his possession.

I thank the following archives and libraries for permission to consult and reproduce letters of Lindsey in their custody: the Historic Society of Pennsylvania; the William L. Clements Library, Ann Arbor, Michigan; the James Marshall and Marie-Louise Osborn Collection, Beinecke Rare Book and Manuscript Library, Yale University; Cambridge University Library; Norfolk Record Office; North Yorkshire Record Office; the Literary and Philosophical Society of Newcastle upon Tyne; Liverpool University Library; University College London; and the Bodleian Library, Oxford. Letters of Lindsey in the Royal Society are reproduced by permission of the President and Council of the Royal Society. I am particularly indebted to the Unitarian Collection, formerly housed at the Unitarian College, Victoria Park, Manchester, and now in the keeping of the John Rylands University Library, Manchester. This collection contains the largest single group of Lindsey's letters and it is a pleasure to record my gratitude to those who have so liberally allowed me access to its contents. The letters are reproduced here by courtesy of the University Library and Director, the John Rylands University Library, the University of Manchester. In particular, I thank the late Fred Kenworthy; Ann Peart; John Hodgson; Graham Johnson and Peter Nockles.

I owe a similar debt to my fellow-trustees of Dr Williams's Library, who have once again granted me permission to print the letters of Lindsey in their keeping. The Library stands high among the leading depositories of nonconformist archives and its resources have been indispensable in the preparation of this edition. Since 2005, moreover, the Library's collaboration with Queen Mary College London in the Centre for Dissenting Studies has been of enormous benefit to historians of post-Reformation British religious history. Under the leadership of its co-directors, Isabel Rivers and David Wykes, the Centre has sponsored a series of conferences and publications, together with a regular seminar series, secured the award of major Arts and Humanities Research Council grants, engaged the services of some of the ablest post-doctoral scholars and launched several valuable electronic resources. I have benefited in particular from the on-line edition of Joseph Priestley's letters to Lindsey between 1769 and 1794, prepared by Simon Mills, and the highly informative Hackney College website of Stephen Burley, which in 2011 reached a second edition. At the Library my particular thanks are due to Alice Ford-Smith, Jane Giscombe and the late Jonathan Morgan, for professional advice. David Powell has once again placed at my disposal his knowledge of classical languages, and I hope that my annotations of Lindsey's letters do justice to his erudition.

I thank the staff of many libraries and archives for access to their resources and for helpful responses to queries. I thank the National Archives, Kew; London Metropolitan Archives; the City of Westminster Archives Centre; the Institute of Historical Research, London; the Guildhall Library, London; Tyne and Wear Archives; the Centre for Research Collections, University of Edinburgh (particularly Rona Morrison); the Special Libraries and Archives, King's College, University of Aberdeen (particularly June Ellner); Cambridge University Library; Gloucestershire Archives; Suffolk Record Office (Bury St Edmunds and Ipswich); Dundee Public Library; Canterbury Cathedral Archives; Cheshire Archives and Local Studies; and the Manuscript and the Rare Books and Music Rooms of the British Library. At the University of Kent, I have been able to draw upon the wise counsel of my colleagues John and Kathleen Court, Kenneth Fincham, Tim Keward, Emma Long, Judi Mayland, David Shaw and Jackie Waller, while the Templeman Library, not least by means of its subscription to ECCO and the Burney Collection of eighteenth-century newspapers, has greatly facilitated the research for this volume. Linda Randall has been characteristically efficient with the copy-editing, and at Boydell I owe a great deal to the support of Vanda Andrews.

For help and encouragement I am grateful to Beryl and Jim Anderson; Nigel Aston; Michael and Margaret Bee; Jeremy Black; Jerome Bowers; James E. Bradley; Brian and Jean Cogger; Edna Cooper; William Gibson; John Goodchild; Stephen Harbottle; Roger Hayden; Robin Hutton; Joanna Innes; Geraint Jenkins; William McCarthy; the late John McLachlan; Anthony Page; Julian Pooley; the late Leslie Pressnell; Wilf Prest; John Seed; Jeffrey Teagle; the late D. O. Thomas; Gina Luria Walker; John Walsh; Timothy Whelan; Frances Willmoth (Jesus College, Cambridge); and Duncan Wu. I have been fortunate enough to be able to consult Andrew Hill and Alan Ruston, two of the foremost authorities in the field of unitarian history, and they both have been very patient, as well as prompt with expert guidance, in dealing with my questions. To Peter Godfrey, I owe my introduction to the unitarian archives at Essex Hall (and from 2004 at Dr Williams's Library) and advice as to their use and interpretation. Martin Fitzpatrick, as always, has been generous with his time as well as with his unrivalled knowledge of dissenting history and through his editorship of *Enlightenment and Dissent* has been an inspiration to other scholars. The friendship, learning and hospitality of David Wykes have been indispensable throughout the entire project. The patience of Stephen Taylor in awaiting the completion of this volume has been monumental, and I am very much in his debt.

As with its predecessor, this volume has been supported by research grants from the British Academy, for which I express my gratitude. And, as before, my most profound obligation is to my late parents, George and Winifred Ditchfield.

G. M. Ditchfield

Abbreviations used in Volume II

In addition to the abbreviations listed in Volume I, pp. ix–xv, the following are used in Volume II

**	Signifies a joint letter from Theophilus and Hannah Lindsey.
APS	American Philosophical Society.
Birm. MS 281	Birmingham University Special Collections, MS 281, 'A view of academical institutions founded by protestant dissenters in the 17th, 18th, and 19th centuries'.
Bowers, *Priestley and English unitarianism in America*	J. D. Bowers, *Joseph Priestley and English unitarianism in America* (University Park, PA, 2007).
Brooks, 'Priestley's plan'	Marilyn Brooks, 'Priestley's plan for a "continually improving" translation of the Bible', *E & D*, XV (1996), 89–106.
Clarke, *Answer to the question*	John Clarke, *An answer to the question, why are you a Christian*? (Boston, MA, 1795).
Committees for repeal	*Committees for repeal of the Test and Corporation Acts. Minutes 1786–90 and 1827–8*, ed. T. W. Davis (London Record Society, 14, 1978).
COPAC	Copac National, Academic, and Specialist Library Catalogue.
Davy letterbook	Letterbook of William Davy, Dr Williams's Library.
Dinwiddy, *Wyvill and reform*	J. R. Dinwiddy, *Christopher Wyvill and reform 1790–1820* (Borthwick paper no. 39, York, 1971).
Ditchfield, 'Lindsey–Wyvill	G. M. Ditchfield, 'The Lindsey–Wyvill correspondence', *TUHS*, XX, 3 (Apr. 1993), 161–76.
Ditchfield, 'Quaker–unitarian encounter'	G. M. Ditchfield, 'A quaker–unitarian encounter in 1801', *TUHS*, XIV, 4 (Oct. 1970), 209–17.
Ditchfield, 'Unitarianism after the French Revolution'	G. M. Ditchfield, 'Unitarianism after the French Revolution: some later letters of Theophilus Lindsey, 1791–1801', *TUHS*, XXV, 1 (Apr. 2011), 35–44
Dyer, *Inquiry into the nature of subscription*	George Dyer, *An inquiry into the nature of subscription to the thirty-nine articles* (?London, ?1789; 2nd edn, London, 1792).

Eaton, *Scripture the only guide* — David Eaton, *Scripture the only guide to religious truth. A narrative of the proceedings of the society of baptists in York, in relinquishing the popular systems of religion, from the study of the scriptures. To which is added, a brief account of their present views of the gospel, in a series of letters to a friend* (York, 1800).

ECCO — Eighteenth-Century Collections On-line.

Ehrman, *The Younger Pitt. The consuming struggle* — John Ehrman, *The Younger Pitt. The consuming struggle* (London, 1996).

Ehrman, *The Younger Pitt. The reluctant transition* — John Ehrman, *The Younger Pitt. The reluctant transition* (London, 1983).

Evans, *Vestiges* — G. Eyre Evans, *Vestiges of Protestant dissent* (Liverpool, 1897).

Extracts from books and other small pieces — *Extracts from books and other small pieces; in favour of religious liberty and rights of dissenters. Number II* (Birmingham, ?1790).

Fasti Ecclesiae Scoticanae — Hew Scott, *Fasti Ecclesiae Scoticanae. The succession of ministers in the Church of Scotland from the Reformation* (new edn, 7 vols., Edinburgh, 1915–28).

Grafton, *Hints* — [Duke of Grafton] *Hints &c. submitted to the serious attention of the clergy, nobility and gentry, newly associated, by a layman* (London, 1789).

Graham, *Revolutionary in exile* — Jenny Graham, *Revolutionary in exile. The emigration of Joseph Priestley to America 1794–1804* (American Philosophical Society, Philadelphia, Vol. 85, part 2, 1995).

Graham, 'Unhappy country' — Jenny Graham, 'This unhappy country of ours: extracts of letters, 1793–1801, of Theophilus Lindsey', *E & D*, XVIII (1999), 124–62.

Hanway, *Advice from Farmer Trueman to his daughter Mary* — Jonas Hanway, *Advice from Farmer Trueman to his daughter Mary, upon her going to service, in a series of discourses, designed to promote the welfare and true interest of servants: with reflections of no less importance to masters and mistresses: abridged by consent of the author from the works of Jonas Hanway Esq* (Edinburgh, 1789).

Issitt, *Jeremiah Joyce* — John Issitt, *Jeremiah Joyce. Radical, dissenter and writer* (Aldershot, 2006).

JEH — *Journal of Ecclesiastical History.*

Jenkins, "Horrid affair" — Geraint H. Jenkins, '"A very horrid affair": sedition and unitarianism in the age of revolutions', in *From medieval to modern Wales. Historical essays in honour of Kenneth O. Morgan and Ralph A. Griffiths*, ed. R. R. Davies and Geraint H. Jenkins (Cardiff, 2004), pp. 175–96.

Jeyes, *The Russells of Birmingham*	S. H. Jeyes, *The Russells of Birmingham in the French Revolution and in America 1791–1814* (London, 1911).
Kenrick, *Memoir of Wellbeloved*	John Kenrick, *A biographical memoir of the late Rev. Charles Wellbeloved* (London, 1860).
Lindsey, *Conversations on Christian idolatry*	Theophilus Lindsey, *Conversations on Christian idolatry in the year 1791* (London, 1792).
Lindsey, *Conversations on the divine government*	Theophilus Lindsey, *Conversations on the divine government: shewing that every thing is from God, and for good, to all* (London, 1802).
Lindsey, *List of the false readings*	Theophilus Lindsey, *A list of the false readings of the scriptures, and the mistranslations of the English Bible, which contribute to support the great errors concerning Jesus Christ* (London, 1790).
Lindsey, *Second address*	Theophilus Lindsey, *A second address to the students of Oxford and Cambridge, relating to Jesus Christ, and the origin of the great errors concerning him: with a list of the false readings of the scriptures and the mistranslations of the English Bible, which contribute to support those errors* (London, 1790).
Losh diary	The manuscript diary of James Losh, Carlisle Library (Local Studies Collection).
Mather, *High church prophet*	F. C. Mather, *High church prophet. Bishop Samuel Horsley (1733–1806) and the Caroline tradition in the later Georgian church* (Oxford, 1992).
Memorials of the Old Meeting House	*Memorials of the Old Meeting House and burial ground, Birmingham. Copied, corrected and illustrated by Catherine Hutton Beale* (Birmingham, 1882).
MM	*The Monthly Magazine and British Register*,
Palmer, *Narrative*	Thomas Fyshe Palmer, *A narrative of the sufferings of T .F .Palmer and W. Skirving, during a voyage to New South Wales, 1794, on board the Surprise transport* (2nd edn, Cambridge, 1797).
Pipe-Wolferstan diary	The diary of Samuel Pipe-Wolferstan, Staffordshire RO, D1527/1–45 (typescript).
Priestley, *Answer to Mr Paine's Age of reason*	Joseph Priestley, *An answer to Mr Paine's Age of reason, being a continuation of letters to the philosophers and politicians of France, on the subject of religion; and of the letters to a philosophical unbeliever. With a preface by Theophilus Lindsey A.M.* (Northumberland Town, 1794; J. Johnson, London, 1795).
Priestley, *Appeal to the public*	Joseph Priestley, *An appeal to the public, on the subject of the riots in Birmingham. To which are added, strictures on a pamphlet intitled 'Thoughts on the late riot at Birmingham'* (Birmingham, 1791).

Priestley, *Appeal to the public* (2nd edn)

Joseph Priestley, *An appeal to the public, on the subject of the riots in Birmingham. To which are added, strictures on a pamphlet intitled 'Thoughts on the late riot at Birmingham'* (2nd edn, Birmingham, 1791)

Priestley, *Appeal to the public. Part II*

Joseph Priestley, *An appeal to the public, on the subject of the riots at Birmingham, Part II. To which is added, a letter from W. Russell, Esq. to the author* (London, 1792).

Priestley, *Appeal to the serious and candid*

Joseph Priestley, *An appeal to the serious and candid professors of Christianity* (Leeds, 1770).

Priestley, *Comparison of the institutions*

Joseph Priestley, *A comparison of the institutions of Moses with those of the Hindoos and other ancient nations; with remarks on Mr Dupuis's origin of all religions, on the allegorizing talents of M. Boullanger, the laws and institutions of Moses methodized, and an address to the Jews on the present state of the world, and the prophecies relating to it* (Northumberland, 1799).

Priestley, *Discourses relating to the evidences of revealed religion. Part I*

Joseph Priestley, *Discourses relating to the evidences of revealed religion, delivered in the church of the universalists at Philadelphia, and published at the request of many of his hearers. Part I* (Philadelphia, 1796).

Priestley, *Discourses relating to the evidences of revealed religion, Vol. 2*

Joseph Priestley, *Discourses relating to the evidences of revealed religion, delivered in Philadelphia. Volume 2* (Philadelphia, 1797).

Priestley, *Discourses relating to revealed religion. Vol. I*

Joseph Priestley, *Discourses relating to the evidences of revealed religion. Vol. I. Delivered at Hackney in 1793, 1794* (London, 1794).

Priestley, *Familiar letters ... to the inhabitants of Birmingham*

Joseph Priestley, *Familiar letters, addressed to the inhabitants of Birmingham, in refutation of several charges, advanced against the dissenters and unitarians by the Rev. Mr Madan. Also, letters to the Rev. Edward Burn, in answer to his on the infallibility of the apostolic testimony concerning the person of Christ* (Birmingham, 1790).

Priestley, *General history of the Christian church to the fall of the western empire*

Joseph Priestley, *A general history of the Christian church, to the fall of the western empire* (2 vols., Birmingham, 1790).

Priestley, *General history of the Christian church from the fall of the western empire*

Joseph Priestley, *A general history of the Christian church from the fall of the western empire to the present time* (4 vols., Northumberland, PA,1802–3).

Priestley, *Index to the Bible*

Joseph Priestley, *Index to the Bible, in which the various subjects which occur in the scriptures are alphabetically arranged* (London, 1805).

Priestley, *Present state of Europe*

Joseph Priestley, *The present state of Europe compared with antient prophecies; a sermon, preached at the Gravel Pit meeting in Hackney, February 28, 1794, being the day appointed for a general fast; with a preface, containing the reasons for the author's leaving England* (London, 1794).

Priestley, *Unitarianism explained and defended*

Joseph Priestley, *Unitarianism explained and defended, in a discourse delivered in the church of the universalists at Philadelphia* (Philadelphia, 1796).

Representation of the nature of true religion

A representation of the nature of true religion. Addressed to a lady. First published in the year 1697. To which is added, a short explanation of the end and design of the Lord's supper (London, 1793).

Robinson, *History of baptism*

Robert Robinson, *The history of baptism* (London, 1790).

Royal calendar

Royal calendar and court and city register (127 vols., London, 1767–1893).

Schofield, *Enlightened Joseph Priestley*

Robert E. Schofield, *The enlightened Joseph Priestley. A Study of his life and work from 1773 to 1804* (University Park, Pennsylvania, 2004)

State trials

A complete collection of state trials and proceedings for high treason and other crimes and misdemeanours from the earliest period to the ... present time, ed. W. Cobbett, T. B. Howell and T. J. Howell (34 vols , London, 1809–28).

Thorne, *Hist. Parl.*

The history of parliament. The house of commons 1790–1820, ed. R. G. Thorne (5 vols., London, 1986).

Toulmin, 'Descendants of Priestley'

Priestley Toulmin, 'The descendants of Joseph Priestley, LL.D, F.R.S. (a progress report)', *Proceedings of the Northumberland County Historical Society*, XXXII (1994), 1–126.

UH

Unitarian Herald.

Unitarian Society

The Unitarian Society for Promoting Christian Knowledge and the Practice of Virtue by the distribution of books

Unitarian Society ... 1791

Unitarian Society ... rules [a sixteen-page

Unitarian Society ... 1794

Unitarian Society. MDCCXCIV... rules [a twenty-page pamphlet setting out the rules of the society, with lists of members and publications] (London, 1794).

Unitarian Society ... 1813

Rules, &c. of the Unitarian Society [a twenty-two page pamphlet setting out the rules of the society, with lists of members and publications] (London, 1813).

Unitarian Society minute book

The minute book of the Unitarian Society, part of the Essex Hall Archives housed at DWL.

Universal British directory (1791)	*The universal British directory of trade and commerce* (5 vols., London, 1791).
Universal British directory (1793)	*The universal British directory of trade, commerce and manufacture* (London, 1793).
Wakefield, *Translation of the New Testament*	Gilbert Wakefield, *A translation of the New Testament* (3 vols., London, 1791).
Watson, *Apology for the Bible*	Richard Watson, *An apology for the Bible, in a series of letters, addressed to Thomas Paine, author of a book entitled, The age of reason, part the second* (London, 1796).
Western Unitarian Society	The Society of Unitarian Christians, Established in the west of England
Wykes, '"A finished monster"'	David L. Wykes, '"A finished monster of the true Birmingham breed": Birmingham, unitarians and the 1791 Priestley riots', in *Protestant nonconformists and the west midlands of England*, ed. Alan P. F. Sell (Keele, 1996), pp. 43–69.
Wykes, 'Priestley at Hackney'	David L. Wykes, '"We have lived very quietly and comfortably here": Joseph Priestley at Hackney, September 1791 – April 1794', *TUHS*, XXIII, 2 (Apr. 2004), 513–27.
Wykes, '"Spirit of persecutors"'	David L. Wykes, '"The spirit of persecutors exemplified": the Priestley riots and the victims of the church and king mobs', *TUHS*, XX, 1 (Apr. 1791), 17–39.
Wyvill, *Defence of Price*	Christopher Wyvill, *A defence of Dr Price and the reformers of England* (London and York, 1792).
Wyvill, *Political papers*	Christopher Wyvill, *Political papers, chiefly respecting the attempt of the county of York, and other considerable districts, commenced in 1779 and continued during several subsequent years, to effect a reformation of the parliament of Great Britain* (6 vols., York, 1794–1802).

The Later Career of Theophilus Lindsey, 1789–1808

The letters of Theophilus Lindsey during his early and middle years, published in Volume I of this edition, recorded a substantial change in the writer's mentality. From an aspiring fellow of his Cambridge college, the assiduous client of the aristocracy, the court whig and the dutiful parish priest, Lindsey became a committed unitarian minister, outside the church and increasingly critical of the establishment in which he had been reared. By contrast, the letters in Volume II, although often considerably longer, present a much more uniform and consistent record. There is none of the courtly gossip with which he had been wont to favour the earl of Huntingdon, and none of the theological self-doubt which he had confided to the earl's evangelical mother. By January 1789, the date of the first letter in this volume, Lindsey was sixty-five. His doctrinal and political ideas were firmly set, and his active ministerial career was approaching its end. There was far less personal information to record; among the main events in his later years were his retirement from the pastorate Essex Street in 1793, his declining health and the deaths – and emigrations – of some of his closest friends. At the same time, however, Lindsey's interest and involvement in public affairs remained intense and during the 1790s even increased. Until their deaths, he and his wife continued to live at Essex House, retaining a base at the centre of London, close to important sources of information. He followed developments in the world of publishing, read newspapers and monthly journals regularly and, particularly in the early 1790s, attended and sought to influence parliamentary debates. The state trials of 1794, which directly affected some of his fellow-unitarians, stimulated him to an even more energetic bout of letter writing than before. He remained intellectually active, published further theological works, extended his *rôle* as an editor to bring the work of others, notably Joseph Priestley, before the public and contributed more than any other individual to the formation of unitarianism as a distinctive denomination, or, as Lindsey's twenty-first-century unitarian successors would prefer to call it, a distinctive movement.

In 1801, he suffered the first of the paralytic strokes which were to afflict his later years and although he made a partial recovery, he was no longer able to write after 1803. His last surviving letter in his own hand is dated 18 January of that year (Letter 746). However, his mind remained alert almost until his death in November 1808, and his wife Hannah Lindsey, who took over his epistolary initiatives, emerges from these letters as an important figure in her own right.[1] There is every indication that she shared Lindsey's opinions and exceeded him in vehemence when expressing them. Certainly in his post-1789 letters, Lindsey himself was at his most embittered, angry and at times almost despairing over developments in Britain and elsewhere. He deplored the hostile response in much of Britain to the French Revolution, strongly criticized the British involvement in war with France after 1793 and came to regard the administration of Pitt the Younger with a detestation comparable

---

[1]   See G. M. Ditchfield, 'Hannah Lindsey and her circle: the female element in early English unitarianism', in *Intellectual exchanges: woman and rational dissent*, ed. Gina Luria Walker and G. M. Ditchfield, *E & D*, XXVI (2010), 54–79.

to that of many whose opinions were far more radical than were his. Immediately on its appearance in November 1790, he read – or at least scanned – Edmund Burke's *Reflections on the revolution in France* (Letter 428) and predictably excoriated its author. Yet, disillusioned as he was, Lindsey never completely abandoned his fundamental whiggish optimism, while his Socinian rejection of original sin left him with a continuing belief in the long-term potential for human political, moral and material improvement.

Letters remained one of Lindsey's highest priorities in his later life and he placed a high value upon his correspondence. He went to considerable lengths to encourage his correspondents to continue to write and to keep him informed. He took full advantage of the availability to members of the house of lords and commons during parliamentary sessions of the privilege of franking letters. Regularly, his friends in parliament dispatched his letters through their franks and thus saved him the cost of postage; the duke of Grafton, together with several MPs, notably John Lee, Benjamin Hobhouse and James Martin, obliged in this respect.[2] 'Postage is by no means an article we mind', he told William Turner of Newcastle in December 1789 (Letter 399), while in January 1791, Priestley assured Richard Price of the simplicity of communicating with him by letter, since Lindsey 'easily gets carriers for me'.[3] In 1792, when directing the collection of signatures for the unitarian petition to parliament he offered to pay the postage of at least one of his provincial correspondents (Letter 486), and in January 1800, he informed his Scottish friend Robert Millar that 'We are in such circumstances that the postage of a letter is nothing to us' (Letter 687). This was no modest claim. The expansion of the postal services in this period, with separate penny posts operating in many towns, and the availability from 1784 of the first mail coach (between London and Bristol), helped to bring about sharp increases in the costs of sending letters, as well as greater speed in their delivery.[4]

In January 1789, when this volume begins, the British political world was dominated by the regency crisis and the possibility that the death or permanent incapacity of George III would lead to a change of ministry as well as to a change of monarchical authority. There was a brief prospect that Pitt might be displaced by a new administration led by Charles James Fox and his friends, a group of politicians whom Lindsey much admired. Significantly, perhaps, Lindsey made no mention in his surviving letters of the king's recovery and the attendant celebrations in the spring of 1789. Although he seems not to have been present when Richard Price preached his celebrated 'Discourse on the love of our country' at the Old Jewry chapel on 4 November 1789, it is likely that Lindsey shared Price's condemnation of what he perceived to be the excessive adulation and sycophancy of the public celebrations of the king's recovery.[5] The outcome was that Pitt's ministry emerged from the crisis in a strengthened condition, with the prime minister's reputation and authority enhanced, a development which had profound consequences for the 1790s. The impeachment of Warren Hastings in Westminster Hall was about to enter its

---

[2] See K. L. Ellis, *The Post Office in the eighteenth century. A study in administrative history* (Oxford, 1958), pp. 39–43. It has been estimated that between 1790 and 1810 the annual number of parliamentary franks increased from 1,600,000 to 2,000,000 letters; Ellis, *Post Office*, p. 43. The system of franking was abolished in 1840.

[3] *Price corr.*, III, 336.

[4] See Frank Staff, *The Penny Post 1680–1918* (London, 1964), chs. 3 and 4.

[5] Price, *A discourse on the love of our country*, in *Richard Price. Political writings*, ed. D. O. Thomas (Cambridge, 1991), pp. 185–7.

second year. In France, a financial crisis of increasingly extreme proportions occasioned the summoning of the states-general at Versailles, opened by Louis XVI on 5 May. The Tennis Court Oath (20 June), the union of the three estates (27 June) and the fall of the Bastille (14 July) ensured that developments across the channel and their repercussions in Britain featured strikingly in and at times dominated Lindsey's letters, as they did the London and the expanding provincial newspaper press in Britain.

By 1789, Lindsey's chapel in Essex Street had been in existence for fifteen years. Its immediate future had been secured by the appointment six years earlier of John Disney as his co-minister, and designated successor, and it was a growing attraction for sympathetic visitors to London, and for the curious. There is even hearsay evidence that the prime minister had heard Lindsey preach.[6] Lindsey himself was becoming better known nationally. His published works were reviewed, sometimes favourably, in the *Gentleman's Magazine*, which in 1788 gave particular attention to his *Vindiciae Priestleianae*,[7] and received friendly treatment in the pro-dissenting *Monthly Review*, which in the later 1790s, had a sales figure of some 5,000.[8] There was also hostile treatment of his efforts. In 1784, Samuel Horsley, archdeacon of St Albans and soon to become a powerful high church bishop, had questioned whether Essex Street chapel had been licensed as required by the Toleration Act of 1689; he described it as a 'conventicle' and thus potentially vulnerable to prosecution.[9] Horsley, moreover, was the author or co-author in 1790 of a defence of the Church of England which referred in sardonic terms to Lindsey's enterprise: 'The reverend gentleman, in hopes of restoring "the truth of the Divine unity, now almost lost beyond recovery", has opened a shop in Essex Street, where he retails his new discoveries in divinity to all who are disposed to come and buy.'[10] The anxiety as to the unitarian doctrines which Lindsey preached and published was widespread. 'I can send you an extract from a Sermon preach'd in Essex street Chapel which if you are not harden'd [will] make your hair stand on end – I have long been harden'd', wrote John Randolph, regius professor of divinity at Oxford and a future bishop, to his brother-in-law in Kent in 1790.[11] In 1792, the *Gentleman's Magazine*, reviewing Lindsey's *Conversations on Christian idolatry*, expressed a more cautious, but nonetheless real, unease:

> It is not easy to conceive what end can be answered by annexing to the worship of the majority of Christians an appellation which, according to Mr. L's own construc-

---

[6]   'G. G. [George Greaves, vicar of Stanton, Derbyshire] in Polesworth – Pitt auditor of Lindsey – silent on his 1st. saying this but thought myself wrong and on his repeating said I wondered much Lindsey had never told me an auditor and acquaintance'; Pipe-Wolferstan diary, 20 Dec. 1788. Pitt's friend Wilberforce certainly attended Essex Street chapel; *The life of William Wilberforce by his sons Robert Isaac Wilberforce and Samuel Wilberforce* (5 vols., London, 1838), I, 76.

[7]   *Gent. Mag.*, LVIII, ii (1788), 909–10.

[8]   See Antonia Foster, 'Ralph Griffiths (?1720–1803), *ODNB*, XXIII, 999.

[9]   Samuel Horsley, *Letters from the archdeacon of St Albans, in reply to Dr Priestley. With an appendix, containing short strictures on Dr Priestley's letters by an unknown hand* (London, 1784), p. 169. He referred in sardonic vein to the 'miserable *unprotected* state' of unitarian places of worship.

[10] *An apology for the liturgy and clergy of the Church of England: in answer to a pamphlet, entitled Hints, &c. Submitted to the serious attention of the clergy, nobility and gentry, newly associated: by a layman. In a letter to the author, by a clergyman* (London, 1790), pp. 72–3. For a note on the authorship of this work, see Mather, *High church prophet*, p. 84.

[11] Bodl., MSS Top Oxon. D. 353–6 (John Randolph papers, John Randolph to Thomas Lambarde, 7 Feb. 1790).

tion, is harmless; but, being used in a more obnoxious sense, may embitter the minds of men, and particularly of religious disputants.[12]

On the other hand, there was much respect for Lindsey's scrupulous decision to resign from the Church of England rather than violate his conscience by remaining within it on an insincere basis. The evangelical Hannah More expressed this opinion, while Charles Hawtrey, vicar of Bampton, Oxfordshire, tempered his denunciation of Socinian theology with a word of recognition of the principled withdrawal from the church of those who espoused it. Naming Lindsey directly, he concluded 'If we think they have acted unwisely, still we think they have acted like honest men; and if we lay any blame on their judgment, we still allow greatly for them as having acted conscientiously.'[13] A reviewer for the *Gentleman's Magazine* in 1790 similarly praised Lindsey, Disney, John Jebb and Gilbert Wakefield for following their consciences out of the church, rather than hypocritically enjoying its emoluments.[14] Even Samuel Horsley, by this time bishop of St David's, conceded in his *Charge* to his diocesan clergy in 1790 that 'A man may be irreproachable in his moral conduct, and at the same time perfectly irreligious and profane ... And History, in some future day, may have to record the same of PRIESTLEY and LINDSAY.'[15] And recognition of a more positive kind was accorded by the unitarian minister William Enfield of Norwich who noted in 1789 that 'A young man, who was brought up at Hoxton, has just opened a Lindseian place of worship' in that city.[16] Perhaps, then, the *Gentleman's Magazine* was not engaging in irony when, in reporting the death in June 1790 of Philip Lloyd, dean of Norwich, it pointed out that Lloyd had 'succeeded the celebrated Mr. Lindsey as vicar of Piddletown in 1765'.[17]

I

Lindsey's whole purpose – indeed, the central concern of his remaining life – after 1789 was the advancement of anti-trinitarian thought and the extension of the legal and broader conventional boundaries within which it could be expressed. He was convinced that an important method by which he could achieve that aim involved the maintenance of his links with the anglican latitudinarian tradition from which he came. Lindsey never forgot or completely abandoned his roots in the established church. He retained a latitudinarian mentality, evident in his continued preference

---

12 *Gent. Mag.*, LXX, ii (1793), 639.
13 Charles Hawtrey, *Various opinions of the philosophical reformers considered; particularly Pain's* [sic] *Rights of man* (London, 1792), p. 88. For Hannah More's opinion, see *The Yale edition of Horace Walpole's correspondence*, ed. W. S. Lewis (48 vols., London and New Haven, 1927–83), XXXI, 329.
14 *Gent. Mag.*, LX, ii (1790), 727–8, reviewing the pseudonymous *Considerations on the expediency of revising the liturgy and articles of the Church of England ... by a consistent protestant* (London, 1790) The author of the book was Richard Watson, bishop of Llandaff.
15 *The charge of Samuel* [Horsley], *bishop of St David's to the clergy of his diocese, delivered at his primary visitation in ... 1790* (London, 1791), p. 27.
16 JRUL, Unitarian College Collection, B13. William Enfield to Nicholas Clayton, 15 Mar. 1789. I am grateful to Graham Johnson for this reference. The 'young man' was Thomas Drummond of Norwich; see Vol. I, Letter 356, n. 9.
17 *Gent. Mag.*, LX, i (1790), 575. In fact Lloyd succeeded Lindsey at Piddletown in 1763; see Vol. I, pp. xxxii–xxxviii.

for a non-trinitarian form of the church's liturgy over the dissenting tradition of extempore prayer. In 1793, he edited the fourth edition of his *Book of Common Prayer reformed*, built upon Samuel Clarke's version, which he had first published in 1774, and encouraged its use in those dissenting congregations which had adopted unitarian opinions.

Lindsey still hoped for reformation within the Church of England. In 1793, he described his chapel as 'founded on the principle of the worship of the church established being directed to wrong objects'.[18] His ministerial successor in 1793, John Disney, was not a dissenter, but a fellow-anglican seceder. Not until the appointment of Thomas Belsham as Disney's successor in 1805 did Essex Street chapel have a minister who had been raised as a dissenter. Admittedly, Lindsey, perhaps with some affectation, had taken to describing himself as a dissenter shortly after his resignation of the vicarage of Catterick (Vol. I, Letters 137, 294), and it is a measure of his vehemence that in 1790, he refused to subscribe to a work of Nehemiah Nisbett, perpetual curate of Ash, Kent, because he thought Nisbett had been a dissenter who conformed to the established church (Letters 428 and 429).[19] Indeed, Lindsey seems to have believed that criticisms of the church from him, with his long experience as a parish priest, would be more telling and would carry more authority than attacks upon it from dissenters. His *Conversations on Christian idolatry*, published in 1792, complained of the persistence of trinitarian formulations within the established church. Forwarding copies to his friend William Tayleur in 1792, he claimed 'perhaps I could censure the church of England with more propriety than many others' (Letter 492). When in 1810 the only collected edition of his sermons appeared, Lindsey was described on the title page not as a dissenter, but simply as 'Formerly Fellow of St John's College, Cambridge, and founder of the Congregation in Essex Street, Strand.'[20]

In this respect, Lindsey's two most important works were his *Historical view of the state of the unitarian doctrine and worship, from the Reformation to our own times*, published in 1783, and his *Vindiciae Priestleianae* five years later. In these carefully argued books, Lindsey had constructed a lineal narrative of a latitudinarian tradition which extended from Benjamin Whichcote, John Tillotson and John Locke through Gilbert Burnet, William Whiston and Benjamin Hoadly, to John Jones's *Free and candid disquisitions*, Francis Blackburne, Edmund Law and William Paley, and led directly to unitarianism.[21] In seeking to identify himself and his cause with this tradition, Lindsey sought legitimacy from, and asserted his continuity with, the past. He was also holding out for a day – albeit repeatedly postponed – when the church itself would return to this latitudinarian ethos, instead of pushing it towards the margins. His *Historical view* included a series of biographical essays of clergymen who were sympathizers with this ideal, most of whom were known to him personally. They were William Robertson, John Jebb, Edward Evanson, Paul Henry Maty, John Disney and Edward Harries – all of whom were seceders from the established church – together with William Chambers and Robert Tyrwhitt, who had remained within the church in a discreetly discontented way. Significantly, the series

---

18 Lindsey, *A discourse addressed to the congregation at the chapel in Essex Street, Strand, on resigning the pastoral office among them* (London, 1793), p. 38.
19 Lindsey quickly regretted this uncompromising attitude.
20 *Sermons, with appropriate prayer annexed, by the late Rev. Theophilus Lindsey* (2 vols., London, 1810).
21 A point made effectively by Isabel Rivers, 'John Tillotson 1630–1694', *ODNB*, LIV, 800.

of essays did not include any dissenters.[22] John Disney was working towards the same end with his editions of the works of the seceder John Jebb and his memoirs of the latitudinarian clergymen Arthur Ashley Sykes and John Jortin.[23]

Secessions of clergymen from the Church of England on unitarian grounds after 1788 were very few indeed.[24] But Lindsey still cherished any indications that clerical and lay members of the church might be adopting his ideas and, instead of withdrawing from its embrace, working quietly to bring about change from within. The anglican squire William Tayleur of Shrewsbury, who since the 1770s had arranged for unitarian worship in his own house, continued to be his most frequent correspondent. It was apparently through Tayleur's example that Lindsey learned of the unitarian 'conversion' of James Martin, MP for Tewkesbury, member of an eminent banking family and a supporter of the parliamentary opposition. His meeting with Martin in 1791 gave Lindsey an exaggerated hope that his example would 'put the church upon reforming itself' (Letter 436). Similarly, when thanking his friend Christopher Wyvill for his *Defence of Dr Price and the reformers of England* in 1792, he admitted that he had teased Wyvill for remaining a (non-resident) parish priest in spite of his criticisms of the church hierarchy. But, he added, 'I now see the hand of good and of providence in it' (Letter 494). And prominent among his friends were the Cambridge-educated gentry Richard Reynolds of Little Paxton, Lindsey's contemporary at St John's, and John Hammond, a former fellow of Queens' College, who relinquished his church living and gave unobtrusive support to unitarian sympathizers from his estate at Fenstanton. Church reform might still be a realistic aspiration as long as men such as these, together with latitudinarians in senior positions such as Richard Watson, John Hey and William Paley – all senior office-holders in Cambridge University – continued to exert influence within the establishment.

During the 1790s and thereafter, as before, those who attended Lindsey's chapel continued to include sympathetic members of the established church. A good example is the gentleman and landowner Samuel Pipe-Wolferstan of Statfold Hall, Staffordshire, who regularly worshipped there when visiting London, while continuing to attend anglican services in his own county. His diary is an important source for the chapel, its ethos and its membership. Another example is that of Bertie Greatheed (1759–1826), a landowner and close friend of the latitudinarian (and anti-war) John Henry Williams, vicar of Wellesbourne, Warwickshire.[25] Lindsey welcomed to his chapel William Frend, to whose struggles at Cambridge he gave warm support; he hoped that the proceedings would not lead to Frend's exclusion from the university, where Lindsey wanted him to remain (and remain influential). Frend became one of the most important correspondents of his later years, especially between 1788 and 1791, and his family came to be among Lindsey's closest

---

22 Lindsey, *Historical view*, pp. 477–551.
23 *The works, theological, medical, political and miscellaneous of John Jebb ... with memoirs of the life of the author by John Disney* (3 vols., London, 1787); John Disney, *Memoirs of the life and writings of Arthur Ashley Sykes* (London, 1785); John Disney, *Memoirs of the life and writings of John Jortin* (London, 1792).
24 A rare exception was Theophilus Browne (1763–1835), a Cambridge graduate, who was vicar of Cherry Hinton before adopting unitarian opinions and resigning his living. From 1800, he held a succession of dissenting pastorates, at Warminster, Norwich, Congleton and Gloucester; he was briefly (1807 to 1809) a tutor at Manchester College, York.
25 See Colin Haydon, *John Henry Williams (1747–1829) 'Political clergyman'. War, the French Revolution, and the Church of England* (Woodbridge, 2007), p. 68.

associates. When in Yorkshire, Lindsey preserved and improved his connexions with the family of Archdeacon Francis Blackburne. For all their disagreements in the 1770s and early 1780s, Lindsey honoured the memory and intellectual legacy of his father-in-law, whom he rightly regarded as a leading spokesman of the anti-dogmatic tradition within the church. He was probably wrong in supposing that Blackburne in his last years had mellowed in his strong objections to his resignation of Catterick and to Socinianism (Vol. I, Letter 352).[26] He nonetheless remained on the warmest of terms with Blackburne's family. The archdeacon's widow was the mother of Lindsey's wife, and until her death in 1799 the couple visited her regularly at Richmond. The archdeacon's eldest son, also named Francis Black-burne, was vicar of Brignall from 1780 to 1816, and Lindsey and his wife stayed with him during their northern sojourns. His younger brother William Blackburne, a physician who gained his medical qualifications at Edinburgh University, lived in London and frequently attended Lindsey's friends in his professional capacity. The connexions with Lindsey's circle became closer through the marriage of Archdeacon Blackburne's daughter Jane to John Disney, and that of his grand-daughter Sarah to William Frend. On at least one occasion, he stayed with the family of Christopher Wyvill at Constable Burton, Yorkshire (Letter 673). The family of Lindsey's Cambridge friend William Chambers regularly made available to Lindsey and his wife their summer retreat at Morden during the hottest and most odoriferous months of the London year. Hannah Lindsey's friendship with the gentry family of Clifford at Perrystone made possible an agreeable visit to Herefordshire in 1794 (Letter 588).

These and other latitudinarian friendships enabled Lindsey to preserve many of the aristocratic, parliamentary and other elite connexions to which he had become accustomed as a young man. Although their letters have not survived, he still corresponded with his former pupil Hugh Percy, formerly Lord Warkworth, and, from 1786, 2nd duke of Northumberland; he referred to letters from the duke in 1796 (Letter 622) and although not a frequent attender at the house of lords Northumberland pleased Lindsey by his hostility to Pitt's ministry. When Thomas Belsham approached him for a contribution to a subscription for the support of Lindsey's widow, Northumberland's response was prompt. 'The sincere regard, & affection, which I always entertained for my late Friend, with the many excellent qualities of whose heart I was well acquainted, & whose religious firmness I ever admired, will certainly induce me to lend my aid', he declared.[27] MPs such as Thomas Whitmore, Robert Smith, Benjamin Hobhouse and James Martin – in addition to the handful of MPs from dissenting backgrounds such as John Lee, Richard Slater Milnes and William Smith – helped to ensure that Lindsey was well informed in terms of inside political news and rumour, as well as national events, and reinforced his oppositional predilections.

A noteworthy aspect of the latitudinarian theme is Lindsey's link with Augustus Henry, 3rd duke of Grafton, an ally of Chatham, prime minister 1768 to 1770, whose final term of office as a cabinet minister ended in February 1783 – and who

---

[26] Shortly before his death in 1787, Blackburne composed a short paper entitled 'Answer to the question, why are you not a Socinian' which was only published after his death; *The works, theological and miscellaneous of ... Francis Blackburne* (7 vols., Cambridge, 1804–5), I, cxx–cxxvi.

[27] HMCO, Misc. 3, fo. 89r, Northumberland to Belsham, 24 Feb. 1809. Possibly his friendship with Lindsey was enhanced by his (second) marriage in 1779 to Frances Julia Burrell, the sister of Sir Peter Burrell, Baron Gwydir, and the niece of Lindsey's friend and supporter Elizabeth Rayner; see Letter 698.

was chancellor of Cambridge University from 1769 until his death in 1811. Grafton hardly appears in Lindsey's pre-1788 letters. But following his pseudonymous publication of *Hints &c. submitted to the serious attention of the clergy, nobility and gentry, newly associated, by a layman* in 1789, a work which advocated a liberal reform of the anglican liturgy, he and Lindsey came into regular contact. As Grafton's unitarian convictions grew, he became a frequent attender at Essex Street chapel. Although he was no longer in a position to exercise substantial patronage within the church, he became a consistent subsidizer of unitarian causes. On 4 June 1789, he wrote to Lindsey in the third person, requesting what he called 'the Liberty of calling on him *now* & *then* for half an hour's Conversation, on serious subjects'.[28] From that time – and we may assume that the request was immediately granted – he features quite considerably in Lindsey's later letters and those of his wife. He used his parliamentary franking privilege for Lindsey's letters, and marked his friend's eightieth birthday in 1803 with a gift of 'three bottles of super excellent wine' (Letter 753). His pious wish 'May the day soon arrive, when all that is not scriptural shall cease to be supported by the sanction of fallible men'[29] could have been penned by Lindsey himself. It is not surprising that Grafton was on terms of even closer friendship with Thomas Belsham, Lindsey's successor but one as minister of Essex Street chapel from 1805.[30] It was understandable that the baptist minister Robert Hall, in his sour review of Belsham's *Memoirs of Lindsey*, complained bitterly that Lindsey was no genuine dissenter, that he persisted with an anglican view of the world and that his association with the aristocracy marked him off from the humbler way of life that was the lot of most dissenters.[31]

II

For all his hopes of an internal reformation of the established church, Lindsey devoted most of his energy after 1788 to the formation and consolidation of unitarianism as a separate denomination. This had not been his original objective in 1774. As Martin Fitzpatrick puts it neatly, 'If he failed in his intention to create a reformed church of England, he succeeded in institutionalizing liberal heterodox dissent.'[32] By 1789, Lindsey implicitly accepted the increasing remoteness of the former possibility; the second possibility was a second choice. How, then, did he seek to bring about this institutionalization? His letters reveal in some depth the methods by which he promoted the interests of the heterodox dissent which was the immediate precursor of organized unitarianism.

Fundamental to his purposes was the survival and success of his chapel, 'the head-quarters of Unitarianism, the great mother-church', as Priestley had termed it in 1787.[33] Strategically placed and with its immediate prospects secured, it served as a metropolitan inspiration to the heterodox in the country as a whole. Lindsey's first

---

[28] DWL, MS 12.80, opp. p. 19.

[29] *Autobiography and political correspondence of Augustus Henry, 3rd duke of Grafton*, ed. Sir William R. Anson (London, 1898), p. 269.

[30] See DWL, MS 12.58 (14), Grafton to Belsham, 1 Aug. 1798; Williams, pp. 491ff.

[31] *The works of Robert Hall* (6 vols., London, 1831–2), IV, 188–225.

[32] Martin Fitzpatrick, 'Theophilus Lindsey', in *Britain in the Hanoverian age 1714–1837. An encyclopedia*, ed. Gerald Newman (New York and London, 1997), p. 412.

[33] Rutt, I, 410.

duty was to conduct services, to preach and to assure the chapel's financial viability. All of this he accomplished, with Hannah Lindsey as his advisor, partner and, in effect, his accountant. Two large collections of Lindsey's manuscript sermons (at Dr Williams's Library and at Harris Manchester College, Oxford) survive, the over-whelming majority of them written for and preached at Essex Street chapel. As with his published sermons, they leave the impression of a preacher intent on textual analysis, on the expounding of morality, the importance of education, the duty of benevolence and the elevation of human reason, all characteristic of eighteenth-century latitudinarianism, and on the avoidance of the sharpest forms of doctrinal controversy.[34] As his letters make plain, Lindsey believed strongly in the regularity of public worship to encourage piety and devotion, and he had no time for those who, such as Gilbert Wakefield in 1791, dismissed the value of public worship altogether, or who, such as Edward Evanson the following year, questioned the utility of Sunday observance.[35] One of his more partisan utterances was his sermon published but not preached at the time of his retirement in July 1793, where he urged his readers to avoid the corrupting effects of attendance at trinitarian worship.[36] His invitations, and those of Disney, to dissenting ministers to preach at Essex Street chapel show a similar doctrinal edge. On two successive Sundays in April 1791 Priestley preached 'to the largest audiences that were ever seen in our chapel' (Letter 451).[37] On other occasions, Joshua Toulmin of Taunton, George Walker of Nottingham and Thomas Belsham all delivered sermons there.[38] All four were active in campaigns for dissenting political rights as well as for unitarian theology.

An observer of Lindsey's preaching who frequently noted his impressions of what he heard was Samuel Pipe-Wolferstan.[39] He first recorded his presence on 7 June 1778, and he continued to attend, often at the afternoon as well as the morning service, during his annual visits to the capital throughout the 1780s and 1790s. He quickly came to admire the preacher, noting on 12 November 1786 'Lindsey's mode of preaching (on Zaccheus) so strikingly proper that I conceived the idea of getting copies of some discourses from him to read in house (or church possibly) at Statfold'.[40] Such a possibility of domestic worship under the leadership of a member of the established church who was prominent among his local elite was entirely to Lindsey's satisfaction. Pipe-Wolferstan became a subscriber to the chapel, and was listed as a contributor of fifteen guineas to the new building in c. 1785.[41] He became friendly with Lindsey, who presented him with copies of several of his

---

[34] There is a valuable account of Lindsey as a preacher by Russell E. Richey, 'Theophilus Lindsey: some manuscript sermons and an intellectual vignette', *TUHS*, XIV, 3 (Oct. 1969), 134–46, although Richey did not draw upon the manuscript sermons at HMCO.

[35] Gilbert Wakefield, *An enquiry into the expediency and propriety of public or social worship* (London, 1791); Edward Evanson, *Arguments against and for the sabbatical observance of the Sunday* (Ipswich, 1792).

[36] Lindsey, *A discourse addressed to the congregation at the chapel in Essex Street*, pp. 31–3.

[37] John Adams, the future president of the United States, heard Priestley preach at Essex Street chapel in 1786; Schofield, *Enlightened Joseph Priestley*, p. 318 n. 5.

[38] See Vol. I, Letter 198 (Walker); Letter 564 (Joshua Toulmin). For Belsham's sermon at Essex Street, see Pipe-Wolferstan diary, 8 July 1792.

[39] See John Money, 'Provincialism and the English "ancien regime": Samuel Pipe-Wolferstan and the "confessional state", 1776–1820', *Albion*, 21, 3 (1989), 389–425.

[40] Pipe-Wolferstan diary, 12 Nov. 1786.

[41] See Vol. I, Appendix I, p. 568.

books.[42] Like Lindsey, he began to call himself a dissenter and took a keen interest in the unitarian petition to parliament, of which Lindsey was the main organizer, in 1792. He shared the political views of many of the chapel's members, joining the Revolution Society and attending several of its public functions.[43] Having heard George Walker preach at the chapel, he decided to send his young son Stanley to be a pupil at the Manchester Academy, founded in 1786, when Walker became its theological tutor and principal twelve years later.[44] It must be acknowledged that on occasion, he found that Lindsey's preaching induced somnolence; on 20 June 1790, his other preoccupations led him to 'doze' at times during Lindsey's sermon; on 30 September 1792, he confessed: 'heard Lindsey in morning and in afternoon & slept on both occasions'; on 5 May 1793, he 'dozed as usual during Lindsey's sermon'.[45] Admittedly, Lindsey was by this time almost seventy and probably past his best as a pulpit performer; and Pipe-Wolferstan was equally prone to slumber during sermons preached by John Disney.[46] In the later 1790s and after 1800, however, he became a much closer friend of Disney, whose homes in Knightsbridge and subsequently in Essex he visited.

A feature of services at Essex Street chapel was, of course its use of the successive editions of Lindsey's revisions of Samuel Clarke's non-trinitarian version of the *Book of Common Prayer*. Its use was an attraction to those who, like Pipe-Wolferstan, were accustomed to anglican worship. One of Lindsey's most important moves at the end of his ministry was his superintendence of a new edition, the fourth, of his reformed *Book of Common Prayer* in 1793. It took his revisions a stage further by omitting the apostles' creed and the threefold invocations in the litany; he would have liked also to have excluded the references to the king and the royal family.[47] He set out his rationale for these changes, and his hopes for further revisions in what he thought a progressive direction, in a sermon entitled *On prayer; and forms of prayer, their defects, and remedy*, published immediately beforehand.[48] His aim, as before, was the purging from his chapel's worship of every tincture of polytheism (as he depicted trinitarianism) and of idolatry (as he labelled the worship of Christ). Lindsey's letters reveal his efforts to persuade provincial dissenting congregations to adopt it, or a variant thereupon. Although achieving very limited success in the short term, his prayer book was more widely adopted in later years and, according to a historian of the subject, became known as 'the liturgy of the Unitarians'.[49] A further, more predictable, characteristic of his services was the singing of hymns. All four editions of his revised *Book of Common Prayer* included the psalms and a collection of hymns. Lindsey took a considerable interest in hymnology, as Priestley

---

[42] Pipe-Wolferstan diary, 27 June 1788, 17 July 1793.

[43] BL, Add. MS 64814, fo. 62.

[44] G. M. Ditchfield, 'The early history of Manchester College', *Transactions of the Historic Society of Lancashire and Cheshire*, 123 (1972), 81–104.

[45] Pipe-Wolferstan diary, 20 June 1790, 30 Sept. 1792, 5 May 1793.

[46] 'Came at 5 from Disney's sermon without knowing a sentence from drowsiness'; 'dozed, notwithstanding a light dinner, under Disney's pulpit'; Pipe-Wolferstan diary, 20 June 1790, 12 Feb. 1792.

[47] *The Book of Common Prayer, reformed according to the plan of the late Dr Samuel Clarke* (4th edn, London, 1793). For the omission of the apostles' creed and the three invocations, see Belsham, *Memoirs*, pp. 223–4; for Lindsey's wish to exclude the references to the royal family, see Letter 527.

[48] Lindsey, *On prayer; and forms of prayer, their defects, and remedy. A sermon* (London, 1793).

[49] A. E. Peaston, 'The revision of the Prayer Book by Samuel Clarke', *TUHS*, XIII, 1 (Oct. 1959), 27.

noted in 1790.[50] In 1822, Thomas Belsham edited for publication A *Collection of hymns and psalms for public worship* originally made by Lindsey. For all that, however, his letters do not indicate that he took a detailed interest in music, and in 1793, Catharine Cappe, a more than sympathetic witness, described the singing at the chapel as 'execrable'.[51]

As a result of Lindsey's efforts, the (short-lived) *Christian Miscellany* could write in 1792, in an article entitled 'A view of the progress of unitarian sentiments and worship':

> Mr. Lindsey has had the peculiar happiness of seeing his resignation and his Apology drawing on them such notice and attention, as to be the cause of his beholding a Society in every view respectable, forming and rising under him, on the scriptural plan of offering up prayers and praises to the one only God of the universe, the God and Father of our Lord Jesus Christ.[52]

Social respectability, indeed, was one of Lindsey's priorities. The chapel received visits from provincial dissenters during professional or social engagements in London. Those provincial sympathizers whose sons attended the Inns of Court, such as the families of Benyon, Heywood and Shore, encouraged them to attend the chapel and contact Lindsey directly. The Liverpool cotton merchant Thomas Nicholson and his wife were favourably impressed by a service there in July 1791.[53] His wife Mary wrote in her diary on 24 July 1791:

> We went to Essex Street to hear Mr. Lindsay [*sic*] we were very much pleased by a discourse from the 16 chapter in St. John, 'These things they do not knowing the Father nor me!' Doctor Priestley and Mr. Scholefield were both present. The sermon was very applicable and very comfortable to them in their situation, after the great trouble they have had at Birmingham.[54]

Members of William Turner's Hanover Square chapel in Newcastle upon Tyne, Catharine Cappe from York, friends of Russell Scott of Portsmouth, dissenters from the west country, Suffolk and Shropshire were among those whose presence at the chapel Lindsey noted in his letters. In June 1791, Lindsey also recorded that 'Our chapel ... is always filled in the forenoons with foreigners, if our own members are absent' (Letter 457); the previous November he met two French protestant ministers (Letter 430). This level of interest, reinforced by the continuing financial succour provided by its wealthier members, meant that the endurance of the chapel through the 1790s – hardly the most comfortable decade for heterodox dissent – was his single most substantial contribution to the emergence of unitarianism. All his other efforts hinged on that.

In 1776, the eminent dissenting minister Andrew Kippis described Lindsey as 'a worthy and learned Man, but an indifferent writer'.[55] At that time, Lindsey had

---

[50] CUL, Add. MS 7886 (Frend papers), no. 189, Priestley to Frend, 11 [?] Aug. 1790.

[51] DWL, MS 24.81 (32), Cappe to Charles Wellbeloved, 1 May 1793.

[52] *Christian Miscellany*, Jan.–June 1792, p. 288.

[53] Ditchfield, 'Early history of Manchester College', p. 83.

[54] *Memorials of the family of Nicholson of Blackshaw, Dumfriesshire, Liverpool and Manchester*, ed. Ernest Axon (Kendal, 1928), p. 93. Mary Nicholson wrote in the immediate aftermath of the Birmingham riots, in which Priestley and Radcliffe Scholefield, minister of the Old Meeting, were among those whose chapels and houses were attacked.

[55] BL, Add. MS 28104, fo. 52, Kippis to Peter Emans of Coventry, 27 May 1776.

published only his *Apology on resigning the vicarage of Catterick* and its *Sequel*, together with his *Farewel address* to his parishioners, the first edition of his *Book of Common Prayer revised* and his sermon preached at the opening of Essex Street chapel in 1774. Between then and 1789, however, he published his two most substantial and important works, the *Historical view of the state of the unitarian doctrine* and his *Vindiciae Priestleianae*. In these works, he set out his fundamental principles – that unitarianism was sanctioned by scripture, that the church at the time of Christ and the apostles had been unitarian and that trinitarianism was a corrupt, human imposition upon the purity of original Christianity. His primary purpose was to locate unitarianism firmly within the Christian tradition, to persuade others that such inclusion was appropriate and to resist attempts to exclude it from that tradition on the ground that it was 'heretical'. An expression he used repeatedly in his publications and letters was 'Unitarian Christian'.[56] There is no doubt that Lindsey was not a 'popular' or particularly accessible writer, unlike Kippis, whose range was extremely wide and whose literary polish was well known. Lindsey deliberately appealed to educated opinion – especially educated clerical opinion – in the belief that this was the source of authority, where changes of attitudes would be most effective and, from his point of view, most beneficial. Such targeting, moreover, was consistent with his lingering hope that the Church of England might reform itself.

Lindsey's publications after 1789 were all extensions of the themes of these central works. Between 1789 and 1802, he published seven separate volumes, including the fourth edition of his revised *Book of Common Prayer*. He had the advantage of a friendly and sympathetic publisher in Joseph Johnson, a long-standing supporter of his chapel and, with his premises in St Paul's Churchyard, almost a neighbour. Despite Lindsey's occasional complaints about his tardiness (Vol. I, Letter 370; Letter 644), Johnson was a crucial figure in the printing and dissemination of unitarian propaganda. In 1788, he added to the range of dissenting periodical literature by founding the *Analytical Review*, a monthly which lasted until his imprisonment ten years later. Lindsey's letters amount to a principal source for Johnson's career.[57] In 1790, Lindsey followed up his *Vindiciae Priestleianae* with *A second address to the students of Oxford and Cambridge*; Priestley deemed it 'masterly and scholar-like'.[58] A supplement to this work was his *List of the false readings of the scriptures and the mistranslations of the English Bible, which contribute to support the great errors concerning Jesus Christ*, published in the same year. Lindsey's *Conversations on Christian idolatry* (1792), with its provocative title, was directed at those of his supporters who objected to the Socinian dogmatism set out in the preamble to the rules of the Unitarian Society, a topic which came to dominate his letters in 1791 and early 1792. His retirement from his pastorate in 1793 led to the publication of two sermons, *On prayer; and forms of prayer*, and his 'farewell' *Discourse*. His last work, *Conversations on the divine government; shewing that every thing is from God, and for good, to all* in 1802, reaffirmed his optimism as to the divine benevolence and the *rôle* of reason in sustaining human intellectual advancement. Hannah Lindsey believed that he had 'overplied'

---

[56] For example, Lindsey referred to his own congregation as 'the church of Unitarian christians assembling at the chapel in Essex-street'; *Historical view*, pp. 473–6.

[57] There are two biographies of Joseph Johnson: Gerald P. Tyson, *Joseph Johnson: a liberal publisher* (Iowa City, 1979); Helen Braithwaite, *Romanticism, publishing and dissent. Joseph Johnson and the cause of liberty* (Basingstoke, 2003).

[58] Rutt, I, 92.

himself in completing this final book and that his efforts had led directly to his para-lytic stroke (Letter 732). Several of his earlier works were re-issued in this period, including *An examination of Mr. Robinson of Cambridge's plea for the divinity of our Lord Jesus Christ* in 1789 and *The Catechist* in 1791. At the same time, Lindsey was quite capable of using his publishing contacts to defend his cause by placing in leading journals his own view of a controversial question, as he did with the *Gentleman's Magazine* in 1790 (Letter 414). Indeed, Lindsey had acquired the reputation as a kind of literary facilitator or middleman, who could be approached for practical advice by those seeking to publish or to launch new publishing ventures (Letters 391, 505, 681). His letters, especially those to William Frend between 1789 and 1791, show him to have been an essential promoter of Priestley's proposal for a new translation of the Bible. Although the project was effectively aborted by the destruction of many of the latter's manuscripts in the riots of July 1791, it gave rise to Lindsey's *List of the false readings of scripture* noted above. And he lived just long enough to witness the launch of the 'improved' version of the New Testament, published by the Unitarian Society in 1808, in which, as the ever-loyal Thomas Belsham related, he took particular pleasure.[59] Throughout the period, he edited the series of *Commentaries and essays*, begun by the SPKS, which ran to ten separate numbers between 1783 and 1800.

During the 1790s, the content and tone of Lindsey's publications reveal a second purpose. He was anxious to oppose theological 'infidelity', partly because he feared that association with it would damage unitarianism, but mainly because he genu-inely saw it as a threat to scriptural authority during what in 1790 he called 'the greater inquisitiveness and discernment of the times we live in' (Letter 429). He was particularly concerned by the attacks on revealed religion propounded by deists and unbelievers. Priestley commented: 'I had flattered myself that unitarianism would be the best barrier against infidelity',[60] and he, in his *History of the corruptions of Christianity* in 1782 and Lindsey in his *Historical view* had pointed to what they thought were perversions of 'primitive', apostolic, Christianity. They believed that these 'corruptions' of Christianity had left it open to attack and ridicule from scep-tics such as Edward Gibbon, and that the best means of warding off such attacks was to restore Christianity to its 'true', original, uncorrupted (i.e. unitarian) form. They both believed that Paine's *Age of reason*, published in two parts in 1794 and 1795, presented a particularly serious danger, which necessitated a counter-attack.[61]

This purpose is evident in Lindsey's extension of his publishing career from that of author to that of editor. To some extent it was a move necessitated by Priestley's emigration in 1794, and the latter's need to ensure the publication of his works in Britain as well as in America. However, Lindsey had already published (in 1790) a new edition of Hopton Haynes's *Scripture account of the attributes and worship of God* (Letter 406), with a biographical introduction, and in 1792 and 1793 had prepared the sermons of George Rogers for publication by the Unitarian Society (Letter 521). But he gave the highest priority to the dissemination of the work of Priestley. In 1794, he edited and provided a substantial preface to Priestley's *An answer to Mr. Paine's Age of reason*, which was first published in Northumberland,

[59] Belsham, *Memoirs*, p. 311.
[60] DWL, MS 24.86 (2), Priestley to Thomas Belsham, 27 Oct. 1795.
[61] See G. M. Ditchfield, 'Theophilus Lindsey and the uses of progressive religion', *Faith & Freedom. A Journal of Progressive Religion*, 62, 1 (Spring and Summer 2009), 17–22.

Pennsylvania, and which Johnson brought out in London. After the Birmingham riots, Lindsey was anxious – perhaps over-anxious – to protect Priestley's reputation from what he perceived to be the calumnies of his many critics, and in this preface he upheld the integrity of Priestley's character, his lack of malignity towards his opponents and his commitment to the exercise of reason in the pursuit of truth.[62] And, recognizing Paine's 'talent, perhaps above all other writers, of arresting the attention of his readers, and making them pleased and desirous of going on with him', he asserted that Priestley, by his defence of revealed religion, had 'most thoroughly confuted' his antagonist.[63] As a further counter-measure against 'infidelity', in 1796 and 1797, he arranged for the reprinting in London and elsewhere of *An answer to the question, why are you a Christian*, by the American minister John Clarke (Letter 625), and contributed a short introduction. This short but powerful work passed through many editions and was particularly successful in Massachusetts and New York.[64] His last significant editorial contribution was his preparation of, and preface to, Priestley's *Inquiry into the knowledge of the antient Hebrews, concerning a future state* in 1801. As a further sign of devotion to Priestley, he and his wife took the lead in raising subscriptions for the final volumes of his *General history of the Christian church* and his *Notes on the scriptures*. On 24 September 1803, Priestley wrote to Belsham:

> I have seen the list of the subscribers to my two works. It far, very far, exceeds my expectation, both with respect to the number of names and the generosity of many of them. Yourself and Mr. Lindsey, as well as some others, have gone far beyond your proportion.[65]

And Lindsey subscribed to a considerable number of works published by unitarians and those whose liberal thinking he approved in years after 1789, including those of Robert Robinson, William Hazlitt, Joshua Toulmin, William Enfield, George Walker and the liberal catholic Alexander Geddes.

III

Until his illness in 1801, Lindsey was a prime mover in several enterprises designed to further the interests of unitarianism. Chief among them was that of the dissenting academy, since the training of a new generation of ministers and lay supporters was fundamental to the survival and transmission of unitarian beliefs. Lindsey's letters after 1789 are particularly valuable as a source for the history of the short-lived but high-profile Hackney College, all the more so as the minutes of the governing committee come to an abrupt halt on 15 September 1791, almost five years before the college's closure.[66] On 21 May 1789, Lindsey was nominated as a member of

---

[62] Priestley, *An Answer to Mr. Paine's Age of Reason; being a continuation of letters to the philosophers and politicians of France, on the subject of religion; and of the letters to a philosophical unbeliever* (2nd edn, London, 1796), 'preface by the editor', pp. xix–xxi.

[63] Lindsey, 'preface by the editor', p. xiv, to Priestley's *Answer to Paine*.

[64] Conrad Wright, *The beginnings of unitarianism in America* (Boston, 1976; Archon Books reprint of the 1966 edition; originally published 1955), pp. 247–8.

[65] Rutt, I, 517.

[66] DWL, MS 38.14, pp. 159–60.

the committee of thirteen for examining the students,[67] and through his physical proximity to Hackney could attend committee meetings regularly thereafter. He was thus in a position to comment in an informed way on the administration, tutors, finances and students of the college, especially during its latter years, and hence to provide substantial compensation for the relative paucity of the college's own records. Although in June 1790 he declined, for reasons of health, an invitation from the committee to address the students at the close of the session, he persuaded an initially reluctant Priestley to deliver the college's anniversary sermon in April 1791 (Letters 440 and 445), and agreed to introduce the service himself.[68] In June 1794, he wrote vivid (and entertaining) descriptions of the orations delivered by some of the students (Letters 580 and 581) as they neared the completion of their studies. His letters record his distress at the financial decline and disciplinary problems of the college, although he is not recorded as protesting about the cost of the over-ambitious building programme which led directly to the demise in 1796. He contributed his moiety to the college through an annual subscription of five guineas, and on 13 September 1791 a grateful committee noted that he had waived the two years' interest arising from his initial gift of £100.[69] The closure of the college after only ten years not only deprived heterodox dissent of one of its most imposing seminaries, but also underlined the official and broader public hostility to radical dissent in the mid- and later 1790s of which Lindsey was all too well aware. But in the same year as the opening of Hackney College, the less-imposing but far more durable Manchester College was founded; although Lindsey had some initial reservations, fearing that it would compete with Hackney, he subsequently gave it genuine, if distant, support. He expressed consistent admiration in his letters for Charles Wellbeloved, a former Hackney student, who became principal of the college when it moved from Manchester to York in 1803, where it evolved into a major source of inspiration for many of the leading ministerial and lay unitarians of the nineteenth century.[70] Among other gestures of encouragement, in 1805 he presented it, via his wife, with £20.[71]

Lindsey's most formal and enduring contribution to the institutionalization of heterodox dissent was the Unitarian Society for Promoting Christian Knowledge, and the Practice of Virtue, by Distributing Books, usually known as the Unitarian Society, founded in February 1791. The preamble to its rules, for which he was largely responsible, made clear its purpose in a manner which combined boldness and over-optimism:

> Rational christians have hitherto been too cautious of publicly acknowledging their principles, and this disgraceful timidity hath been prejudicial to the progress of truth and virtue. It is now high-time that the friends of genuine christianity

---

[67] DWL, MS 38.14, p. 114.

[68] DWL, MS 38.14, pp. 138, 151.

[69] DWL, MS 12.90 (1) (list of subscribers), DWL, MS 38.14, p. 158.

[70] See *Truth, liberty, religion. Essays celebrating two hundred years of Manchester College*, ed. Barbara Smith (Manchester College, Oxford, 1986), especially chs. 1 and 2.The college was distinguished, among other characteristics, for its endurance. It moved to Oxford in 1889, educated generations of unitarian ministers, secured external sponsorship in the 1990s, prefixed 'Harris' to its title, was granted the status of a full Oxford college and became the university's designated institution for mature students. By contrast, the academy set up at Exeter by Lindsey's friend Timothy Kenrick lasted only for a few years and did not survive Kenrick's death in 1804.

[71] HMCO, MS WOOD, 1, fos. 32, 38, 75, 77.

should stand forth and avow themselves. The number of such, it is hoped, will be found to be much greater than many apprehend.[72]

Showing many of the signs of exuberance characteristic of the early British response to the French Revolution, Lindsey took the initiative in launching the society in the belief that it could serve as a pressure group to campaign for full toleration for those who denied the doctrine of the Trinity. Such a relief measure, if enacted, would remove any lingering threat of a prosecution of his chapel and its ministers, or other heterodox places of worship. Given cause to hope, moreover, by the passage of the Catholic Relief Act of 1791, he used the society to organize a petition to the house of commons for the removal of all legal restrictions upon unitarian belief and expression. The society's numbers were not high; although the Worcestershire unitarian and banker Samuel Kenrick wrote in June 1791 that it 'gains ground amazingly',[73] its membership list in 1791 consisted of 144 named individuals, with 11 others identified only by their initials; in 1794 the respective figures were no more than 153 and 14.[74] Nonetheless, immediately after the society's first meetings, Lindsey, in collaboration with sympathetic dissenting ministers in several parts of the country, secured approximately 2,000 signatures for a petition claiming legislative relief for unitarians, and used his connexions with the opposition whigs to persuade Charles James Fox to introduce it in the house of commons on 11 May 1792. He described Fox as 'our noble leader' (Letter 498). The decisive rejection of the petition, accompanied (although not caused) by a strong attack on unitarianism from Edmund Burke, seems, for all its apparent predictability, to have been a shock to Lindsey.[75] This setback, the Birmingham riots of 1791 and the outbreak of war with revolutionary France in 1793 brought home to him the realization that the 1790s would be a decade of disillusionment and apprehensiveness for dissenters in general and heterodox dissenters in particular. An indication, perhaps, of the odium attached to personal identification with unitarianism – flatly contradicting the hope expressed in the society's preamble – can be seen in the numbers of diners after the annual meeting each April. On 14 April 1791, fifty members and friends dined; on 12 April 1792, thirty-nine; on 11 April 1793, twenty-nine; on 14 April 1796, twenty-three and in 1799, twenty-one. Only in 1808 and the following years did the society's dining list exceed fifty.[76]

Fear and more subtle forms of pressure, however, do not alone explain this relative paucity. The Unitarian Society carefully defined itself in an exclusive manner, and made an immediate, stark and dogmatic statement of Socinian doctrine which was bound to deter those whose non- or anti-trinitarianism took other, mainly Arian, forms. Noting what it dismissed as perversions of true, or primitive, Christianity, the preamble stated:

> While therefore many well-meaning persons are propagating with zeal opinions which the members of this society judge to be unscriptural and idolatrous, they think it their duty to oppose the farther progress of such pernicious errors, and

---

[72] *Unitarian Society ... 1791*, p. 3.
[73] DWL, MS 24.157 (163), Samuel Kenrick to James Wodrow, 10 June 1791.
[74] *Unitarian Society ... 1791*, pp. 9–14; *Unitarian Society ... 1794*, pp. 9–15.
[75] See two articles by G. M. Ditchfield, 'Antitrinitarianism and toleration in late eighteenth-century British politics: the unitarian petition of 1792', *JEH*, XLII, 1 (1991), 39–67; 'Public and parliamentary support for the unitarian petition of 1792', *E & D*, XII (1993), 28–48.
[76] Unitarian Society minute book, pp. 16, 35, 41, 58, 106, 108, 112.

publicly to avow their firm attachment to the doctrines of the UNITY of GOD, of his UNRIVALLED and UNDIVIDED authority and dominion, and that Jesus Christ, the most distinguished of the prophets, is the CREATURE and MESSENGER of GOD, and not his EQUAL, nor his VICEGERENT, nor CO-PARTNER with him in divine honours, as some have strangely supposed.[77]

The description of the worship of Christ as 'idolatrous' was deliberately provocative and divisive. As Lindsey himself wrote, it was 'not our view to induce men of very discordant opinions to join us' (Letter 442). Objections to this terminology led to the withdrawal from the society of several sympathizers from Cambridge University, and Lindsey's letters in 1791 show that he went to considerable lengths to retain their support. Their loss was potentially serious, since they were exactly the types of clergymen and educators to whom he looked to bring about reform of the established church. Some members from the old dissenting sects also cancelled their membership; one of them was John Prior Estlin, minister of the Lewins Mead chapel, Bristol, who set out his reservations about the preamble in a lengthy letter to Thomas Belsham.[78] Richard Price joined the society on its foundation but it is unlikely that, with his Arian opinions, he would have remained a member had he lived beyond April 1791.

Lindsey's response to these concerns reveals his determination and extreme reluctance to compromise. He would not accept changes to the preamble and in particular refused to abandon the word 'idolatrous' (Letter 499), even though he recognized its deterrent effect – and (belatedly) the damage which it inflicted on the parliamentary prospects of the unitarian petition. His approach bore nothing of the personal mildness and gentleness with which he has often been credited, or the emollient tone of much of his preaching. His *Conversations on Christian idolatry* in 1792 amounted to a defiant reaffirmation of his intentions. In providing unitarianism with a central focus for identity and organization, he also in effect purged it of those whom he saw as less than wholeheartedly committed to the sole worship of God and the acceptance of the simple humanity of Christ. To many, such an aggressive dogmatism was a strange departure from someone who had been strongly opposed to clerical or lay subscription to articles of faith, although of course the Unitarian Society was a voluntary organization, not a state church with a near-monopoly of public life. The *Monthly Review*, while recognizing that 'mildness and benevolence' had characterized Lindsey's earlier works, took him to task for his application of the term 'idolatry' to orthodox Christians:

> It would surely be much more consistent with that Christian candour, which we are persuaded Mr. Lindsey is, in all possible cases, disposed to exercise, if the use of so doubtful and obnoxious a term were discontinued in the censures which one set of Christians think it necessary to cast on another.[79]

Nonetheless, Lindsey was unrepentant, and his actions were decisive in the evolution of unitarianism and although the Arian element in heterodox dissent remained significant (and is too easily overlooked), the institutionalization of heterodoxy took a firmly Socinian direction. Lindsey, of course, was not alone. He was supported in

---

[77] *Unitarian Society ... 1791*, p. 2.
[78] DWL, MS 12.48 (12), Estlin to Belsham, 27 Feb. 1791.
[79] *Monthly Review*, NS, VIII (1792), 580–1.

his adherence to Socinianism by Thomas Belsham, by the treasurer of the society Michael Dodson, by Priestley and by its first secretary, John Disney, although there is some evidence that he and Lindsey did not always see eye to eye over this and other issues (Letters 434, 461).[80] From his letters it is clear that Lindsey was closer to Belsham, his successor but one, and also to Jeremiah Joyce, the afternoon preacher at Essex Street chapel from 1793 to 1804, than to Disney.

In the event, the society weathered the storms of the 1790s and by the early nineteenth century was in a much healthier condition. It ensured that unitarian works regularly appeared in print, and re-published key unitarian tracts, including some of Lindsey's own, in its series of thirteen volumes between 1791 and 1802. Its publication of the improved version of the New Testament in 1808 was a substantial material achievement, illustrative of a considerable ability to raise subscription income, although one more recent unitarian scholar has derided the improved version as 'an embarrassment to Unitarians for more than 30 years'.[81] By 1813, the society's membership had increased, modestly, to 229.[82] With hindsight, the society can be seen as the forerunner of subsequent unitarian organizations – the unitarian fund (1805), the Christian Tract Society (1809), the association for the protection of the civil rights of unitarians (1819), and the British and Foreign Unitarian Association, into which these separate bodies were consolidated in 1825.

The Unitarian Society was based in London, with a committee and officers drawn from the metropolitan area. Lindsey himself was a committee member and although he was never its secretary or treasurer, he and his wife dealt with its subscriptions, correspondence and publications. It gradually developed provincial offshoots, which Lindsey was anxious to encourage. In 1792, the 'Society of Unitarian Christians, Established in the West of England' was founded in Exeter, with Lindsey's friend Timothy Kenrick as secretary and Lindsey as a life member. Its initial membership list numbered thirty-one (including fourteen ministers); by 1802 it had grown to ninety-seven.[83] A similar society of 'Unitarian Christians, established in the south of England' was founded in 1801; two years it listed fifty members (including Lindsey).[84] The names listed suggest a mainly clerical leadership, with sufficient support from propertied laymen drawn mainly from the professions to ensure continuity and the ability to finance publications, although not to reach a popular readership.

Lindsey, however, sought to stimulate the growth of unitarianism beyond London by personal contact as well as through institutions. Although reluctant to preach at dissenting chapels (he was still, at least nominally, in anglican orders), he preached

---

[80] For Disney's subsequent critical comments on Lindsey, and extremely harsh characterization of Hannah Lindsey, see Ditchfield, 'Hannah Lindsey and her circle', pp. 68–70.

[81] H. L. Short, *The founding of the British & Foreign Unitarian Association* (*TUHS* supplement to vol. XVI, 1, 1975), p. 5s [supplement]. Short had in mind the way in which Belsham, who was the main inspiration behind the new translation, treated any New Testament statement which was inconsistent with his Socinian convictions as a corruption of the biblical text.

[82] *Unitarian Society ... 1813*, pp.11–19.

[83] *Society of Unitarian Christians, Established in the West of England* (?Exeter, 1792), p. 8; list of members appended to Theophilus Browne, *The necessity of a new version of the sacred writings. A discourse delivered at Bath, July 7, 1802, before the Society of Unitarian Christians, Established in the west of England* (Warminster, 1802), pp. 33–6.

[84] List of members, appended to Thomas Belsham, *The study of the scriptures recommended in a discourse. Delivered at Newport, in the Isle of Wight, July 13, 1803, before the Society of Unitarian Christians established in the south of England* (London, 1803), pp. 33–6.

for Priestley at New Meeting, Birmingham, in September 1789, while in 1782 he considered seriously, although he did not take up, an invitation to preach at the High Street chapel, Shrewsbury.[85] He gave much succour to provincial unitarians through his letters, reinforced in some cases by personal visits and in most by small financial gifts. He was particularly gratified when, as happened in a few cases, a presbyterian or general baptist congregation adopted a form of liturgy, inspired directly or indirectly by his own. The High Street chapel, Shrewsbury, introduced a version of Lindsey's *Book of Common Prayer reformed* at its morning service in 1779 and at its evening service the following year.[86] On 10 February 1790, Lindsey reported that he had raised £160 towards the construction of the new chapel at Plymouth Dock (Letter 406) and was seeking further contributions; the chapel was opened in April 1791 with a prayer book compiled by Lindsey's friend John Kentish and the Plymouth dissenting minister Thomas Porter (Letters 408, 454). He took a detailed interest in the ministerial appointments to these and similar congregations, seeking, for example, to secure nominations as assistant minister at Shrewsbury for Russell Scott and for Jeremiah Joyce. Although William Tayleur of Shrewsbury died in 1796, he remained until then Lindsey's most regular correspondent and the one in whom Lindsey felt most free to confide. Tayleur was Lindsey's ideal lay supporter: a member of the Church of England who supported unitarian worship without formally abandoning the established religion, a wealthy and generous benefactor of unitarian causes and a highly respectable and respected figure in his own county. As Tayleur's health declined in the early 1790s, Lindsey wrote frequently to John Rowe, the scion of a dissenting family in Devon, who became assistant minister at the High Street chapel, Shrewsbury, in 1787 and sole minister in 1789; their correspondence continued after Rowe's move to Bristol in 1798, although only Lindsey's side of it survives. He was a dispenser of advice to Rowe and to other young unitarian ministers, notably Russell Scott of Portsmouth (Letters 516, 599, 602) and Timothy Kenrick of Exeter (Letter 518). He presented Scott with manuscript copies of his sermons, with permission to use them for any purpose he wished (Letters 630, 633), suggested which published sermons were most worthy of emulation (Letter 516) and urged him (successfully) to persevere when distracted by disputes within his congregation (Letter 597).

While the main thrust of unitarian affirmation and persuasion was directed at the educated, Lindsey was aware of, though far from intimate with, the potential for a non-elite readership. 'We want much to have the common people applied to', he wrote in 1789 (Letter 396). He seized eagerly upon unitarian autodidacts, such as the shoemaker David Eaton of York, just as he had lauded the efforts of the society of Attercliffe in the 1780s (Vol. I, Letters 313, 315, 319). He helped Eaton to publish his account of the York society, provided him with gifts, and met him during his last visit to Yorkshire in 1799 (Letter 686). Eaton regarded Lindsey with deferential devotion and composed a series of adulatory verses on his death.[87] When the self-educated Carmarthenshire weaver Thomas Evans (Tomos Glyn Cothi) published a Welsh translation of Priestley's *Appeal to the serious and candid professors of Christianity*, proposed to open a unitarian meeting house at Cwn Cothi, and

---

[85] Schofield, *Enlightened Joseph Priestley*, p. 197 n. 6; Vol. I, Letter 246.

[86] Hugh Owen, *A history of Shrewsbury* (2 vols., London, 1825), II, 480.

[87] *Lines sacred to the memory of the Rev. Theophilus Lindsey, founder of Essex Street chapel, for the worship of one God* (London, 1808).

approached Lindsey for financial support, Lindsey was delighted to help. He was successful in his encouragement of others, including William Tayleur, and subsequently the duke of Grafton, to do so (Letters 501, 505, 668). As Geraint Jenkins has shown, there was a powerful unitarian element within the bardic tradition of South Wales, which involved itself in radical activity (and Evans in gaol) in the 1790s. One of the most prominent representatives of that tradition was Edward Williams (Iolo Morganwg), 'a phenomenally well-read autodidact' who worshipped at Essex Street chapel in 1793 and 1794 and who wrote admiringly to Lindsey.[88] Another member of that tradition who was attracted to the heterodoxy and radicalism of unitarianism was Williams's friend, the naval surgeon David Samwell (Dafydd Ddu Feddyg), who admired Lindsey's revised *Book of Common Prayer*.[89] The Unitarian Christian Society of South Wales was founded at Gelli-gron on 8 October 1802, under the leadership of Williams and David Davis (1778–1846) of Neath.[90] Although one motive behind its foundation was an aspiration to assert the autonomy of Welsh unitarianism and avoid the necessity to seek external subsidies,[91] the principles of the Welsh society bear many traces of Lindsey's influence.

In *A list of the false readings of the scriptures*, published in 1790, Lindsey wrote: 'There is happily a spirit of inquiry gone forth, upon the momentous subject, in many parts of England and Scotland; though it be chiefly confined to the lower and middle classes.'[92] Some of his most important post-1789 letters were addressed to the Dundee merchant and unitarian lay preacher Robert Millar. Lindsey had also been in correspondence (apparently lost) with heterodox ministers in the Church of Scotland, including William Dalrymple of Ayr (Letter 411), and with William Christie of Montrose, the founder (in 1781) of the first avowedly unitarian meeting in Scotland. He followed in detail the prosecution and partial recantation of William M'Gill, Dalrymple's ministerial colleague at Ayr, in 1789 and 1790 (Letters 413, 444, 448, 454) as disturbing evidence of an increasingly intolerant attitude towards trinitarian unorthodoxy in the established church north as well as south of the border. The original development of unitarianism in Scotland, however, had very little directly to do with Lindsey. Only five of the original members of the Unitarian Society in 1791 were listed with addresses in Scotland, while the following year Samuel Kenrick of Worcester, drawing on information supplied by his friend James Wodrow of Stevenston, Ayrshire, noted in a letter that 'The Unitarian Society goes on flourishᵍ at Glasgow. They appointed a weekly meeting for debate or public disputation. But they became so noisy they were obliged to discontinue it.'[93] However, Lindsey's foundation of Essex Street chapel was duly acknowledged as a source of encour-

---

88 Geraint H. Jenkins, *Facts, fantasy and fiction: the historical vision of Iolo Morganwg* (Aberystwyth, 1997), p. 3; NLW MS 21285E, no. 861, Iolo Morganwg to Lindsey, 10 Feb. 1797. For the background, see Jenkins, '"Horrid affair"', and the same author's 'The unitarian firebrand, the Cambrian Society and the Eisteddfod', in *A rattleskull genius. The many faces of Iolo Morganwg*, ed. Geraint H. Jenkins (Cardiff, 2005), pp. 269–92.

89 Martin Fitzpatrick, 'The "cultivated understanding" and chaotic genius of David Samwell', in *A rattleskull genius*, ed. Jenkins, p. 389, and n. 33.

90 Jenkins, '"Horrid affair"', p. 195; Thomas Oswald Williams, 'David Davis', *The dictionary of Welsh Biography down to 1940* (London, 1959), pp. 163–4.

91 Jenkins, '"Horrid affair"', p. 195.

92 Lindsey, *List of the false readings* , 'Advertisement', p. v.

93 *Unitarian Society ... 1791*, pp. 9–14; UCL Sharpe (Kenrick) papers, 178/36, Samuel Kenrick to Timothy Kenrick, 30 Oct. 1792.

agement and Christie in particular acknowledged his debt to Lindsey's published work.[94]

The Scottish town where Lindsey became most continuously supportive of unitarianism was Dundee. One reason was the presence there of Thomas Fyshe Palmer, a Cambridge-educated Englishman in anglican orders, like himself. Palmer's involvement in radical theology and politics occasioned the loss of his fellowship at Queens' College. Dundee was at the forefront of radical activity in Scotland; Robert Millar told Lindsey in 1791:

> A great reformation has been brought about in the minds of people here of late on the Subject of liberty – And its astonishing the execution Mr Paine's Pam. has done on this head – To hear people who a few years ago revered Religious Establishments, – now reason against them nay reprobate them, is such an internal sort of revolution as must please every friend of truth & the human race.[95]

An anonymous pamphlet of 1793 claimed that 'It has been attempted to plant the Tree of Liberty in Dundee by a mob of six hundred persons.'[96] Palmer's relatively mild involvement in the Scottish Convention in 1792–3 led to his arrest, conviction and transportation to Botany Bay. It was characteristic of Lindsey that when he heard of Palmer's likely return in 1800, he expressed the hope that he 'had found any means of teaching the knowlege [*sic*] of the one true God, and of his goodness to Mankind by Jesus Christ' (Letter 708). Palmer's transportation left the small and harassed unitarian congregation in Dundee without a trained minister. Millar, largely self-educated in theology, although with the advantage of a fairly prosperous mercantile background, took over the leadership of his flock and sustained it through difficult and demoralizing times. Lindsey, and from 1803 Hannah Lindsey, used every possible means of improving his morale, providing him with unitarian literature, paying his subscription to the Unitarian Society when his sail-cloth business underwent financial difficulties and even seeking to win orders for that business in London (Letter 773). That there was still a small unitarian congregation in Dundee by the time the travelling unitarian preacher and organizer Richard Wright undertook a Scottish missionary tour in 1811[97] was largely due to Millar's determination, and Lindsey's efforts in prompting him when his prospects were at their bleakest.

Lindsey's letters in the 1790s show beyond doubt that he and many of his fellow-unitarians perceived themselves to be part of an unpopular and persecuted minority. Socinianism was under attack from politicians, high churchmen, evangelicals and numerous orthodox dissenters. These attacks went beyond the standard denunciations of Socinianism as a heretical deviation from fundamental Christian doctrines. It was also held up as a form of subversion of conventional morality and of political

---

[94] L. Baker Short, *Pioneers of Scottish unitarianism* (Narberth, n.d.), pp. 42–57, and the same author's 'William Christie and the first unitarian church in Scotland', *TUHS*, XIV, 1 (Oct. 1967), 10–27; Archibald MacWhirter, 'Unitarianism in Scotland', *Records of the Scottish Church History Society*, XIII (1959), 101–43; and an important article by Andrew M. Hill, 'The successors of the remnant: a bicentenary account of St Mark's unitarian church, Edinburgh, I: before 1776 until 1822', *TUHS*, XVI, 3 (Sept. 1977), 101–23.

[95] DWL, MS 12.46 (78), Robert Millar to Lindsey, 18 June 1791 (copy).

[96] *Opinions delivered at a numerous and respectable meeting in the country, lately held for the purpose of signing a declaration for the support of government in the present alarming crisis* (London, 1793), p. 3.

[97] *MR*, VII (1812), 121.

loyalty. The particular baptist Andrew Fuller noted in his diary in 1791: 'I have lately been reading several Socinian writers; viz. *Lindsey, Priestley, Belsham &c.*, and have employed myself in penning down thoughts on the moral tendency of their system. I feel an increasing aversion to their view of things.'[98] His published attacks drew him into controversy with Lindsey's friends Joshua Toulmin and John Kentish, who, recognizing the danger posed by the spread of such a perception, replied to Fuller in a series of sometimes acrimonious exchanges during the 1790s and beyond. Fuller's 'aversion' was widely shared, as was the belief that Socinians paid no regard to moral or social obligation, and were accordingly unreliable citizens. On Monday 7 January 1793, the *World* printed this denunciation:

> The Friends of Reform, those loudest in calling out for a change, are public men, better known than trusted, of descriptions that follow:

Arians,	Infidels
Socinians,	Greeks
Dissenters,	Swindlers, and
Atheists,	Stock-jobbing Gamesters;

> A very proper groupe to purify or renovate any government.

Fuller's friend Samuel Greatheed welcomed attacks of this kind: 'I am provoked at the impudence of the Socinians in assuming that Scriptural Criticism is on their Side.'[99] George Pretyman, bishop of Lincoln and a close advisor of Pitt, told his diocesan clergy in 1794 that 'We, who live at the end of the eighteenth century, have seen the Disciples of Socinus amongst the most zealous abettors of Republican Principles.'[100] Samuel Horsley's tone became more violent than it had been in the 1780s. In his *Charge* to his clergy of the diocese of Rochester in 1800, he denounced the 'Socinian heresy', which 'openly disowns the Son of God', adding, with premature triumphalism in the aftermath of Priestley's emigration and Lindsey's retirement, 'The advocates for that blasphemy have preached themselves out of all credit with the people. The patriarch of the sect is fled, and the orators and oracles of Birmingham and Essex Street are dumb; or if they speak, speak only to be disregarded'.[101] Many similar examples could be adduced.[102] The bitterness was of long duration. As late as 1849, John Andrew Jones, introducing his book *Bunhill Fields*, where Lindsey, Belsham and other unitarians were buried, could write:

> I have not acknowledged, as Christian brethren, those, who in their day, have denied the Divinity of my Lord, who have rejected Redemption through Jesus' atoning blood, and Justification by his righteousness. I have inserted verbatim what is inscribed on their Grave Stones, having promised to do so, but I have no

---

98 Quoted in Alan P. F. Sell, 'Andrew Fuller and the Socinians', *E & D*, XIX (2000), 92, an article which is essential reading for Fuller's controversy with Joshua Toulmin and John Kentish.

99 JRUL, English MS 370, fo. 54, Samuel Greatheed to Mr Williams, 30 Oct. 1798.

100 George Pretyman, *A charge delivered to the clergy of the diocese of Lincoln at the triennial visitation of that diocese in May and June 1794* (London, 1794), p. 14.

101 *The charge of Samuel* [Horsley] *lord bishop of Rochester, to the clergy of his diocese, delivered at his second general visitation, in the year 1800* (London, 1800), p. 18.

102 See, for example, *The footman's pamphlet: or, the footman's arguments against the unitarians, &c: and in defence of the divinity of Christ; is humbly offered to the public* [by James Saunders] (Falkirk, 1793); James Ramsay, *A clear scriptural detection of Satan transformed into an angel of light. Or the Socinian creed, as held by Drs M'Gill and Dalrymple, ministers of Ayr, exhibited in distinct articles, illustrated by extracts from their own works* (Glasgow, 1793).

sympathy with what is there inscribed. God forbid that *I* should acknowledge a *Belsham*, to be a 'diffuser of the knowledge of the *pure religion of Jesus*'.[103]

Even before the Birmingham riots, some of the first members of the Unitarian Society expressed unease at the prospect of the society's adopting some of Priestley's theological works (Letter 434), fearing association with such a heresiarch. After the destruction of Priestley's chapel, laboratory and house in July 1791, and less widespread but nonetheless disturbing attacks elsewhere, such as that upon Henry Toulmin at Chowbent in 1793 (Letter 516), the sense of persecution understandably deepened.

One response was sardonic self-referral as heretics. Lindsey, writing to William Hazlitt in 1790, complained ironically that 'sermons of known heretic Socinians, and their works in general, are soon mere old drugs that never get off' (Letter 401). Anna Letitia Barbauld lampooned their critics in verse:

> The Birmingham Apostle then,
> And Essex Street Apostate,
> Debarred from paper and from pen
> Should both lament their lost state.[104]

In 1794, Samuel Pipe-Wolferstan found himself chaffed by an anglican clergyman and his wife for patronizing the 'arch tabernacle of heresy'.[105] In much the same spirit, when writing on Lindsey's behalf to Belsham in 1805, Hannah Lindsey referred to Essex Street chapel as 'this theatre of great notoriety' (Letter 770). This was the period in which it could be said of dissenters, and particularly heterodox dissenters, 'this sect, we know that every where it is spoken against'.[106] It seemed, moreover, particularly after July 1791, that the hostility was not confined to words.

Lindsey had been a critic of government during the 1770s and 1780s. However, the period of 'reaction' in the early 1790s intensified his oppositional mentality and strengthened his involvement with extra-parliamentary radicalism. In his letters, he frequently declared that he would not discuss politics (Letters 617, 723) but then proceeded to do so, or apologized for having done so (Letter 650). In his published works, he made few explicit references to political events, although running through all of those works is a plea for greater religious and civil freedom, as well as the duty to exercise human reason without restriction. A rare example of a direct political observation which he made in print may be found in his *Conversations on Christian idolatry*, when he expressed pleasure at the fall of the Bastille and the ending, as he saw it, of absolutism. With hope triumphing over experience, he welcomed 'the pleasing prospect of a constitution settled, where liberty will be secured, where the sound of offensive war will no more be heard, and where religion will become placed on its only just and solid basis, that of free and rational inquiry'.[107] Statements of this

---

103 John Andrew Jones, *Bunhill Fields. Sacred reminiscences of three hundred ministers and other persons of note, who are buried in Bunhill Fields* (London, 1849), p. vi.

104 'The apology of the bishops, in answer to "Bonner's ghost", *c.* 1791'; see *The poems of Anna Letitia Barbauld*, ed. William McCarthy and Elizabeth Kraft (Athens, GA, and London, 1994), pp. 120, 287–9.

105 Pipe-Wolferstan diary, 23 Nov. 1794.

106 Acts xviii. 22. Valentine Cunningham incorporated this text into the title of his book, *Everywhere spoken against. Dissent in the Victorian novel* (Oxford, 1975).

107 *Conversations on Christian idolatry*, p. 161. Lindsey drew particular encouragement from the news that protestant chapels had been opened in Paris and Dunkirk.

kind, although rare in his publications, occur frequently in his letters; he rejoiced at the recapture of Louis XVI and his family after their brief escape from Paris in June 1791, applauded the new French constitution and hoped that Jacobin extremism would not undermine it (Letters 459, 474, 502). It is clear that he took a detailed and well-informed, albeit unashamedly partisan, interest in politics in Britain, on the European continent and in North America. Had Jeremiah Joyce not destroyed many of his letters in 1808 'because they were chiefly political', the impression of Lindsey as a committed follower of, and at times participant in, political affairs would be even stronger.[108] He remained a keenly interested observer of, and at times participant in, the advancement of reforming causes. Indeed, the need, as he perceived it, to defend and promote religious liberty intensified during the late 1780s and early 1790s. His letters in 1789 and 1790 describe in detail the public campaigns and parliamentary debates over the repeal of the Test and Corporation Acts, and the disillusionment which followed the emphatic defeat of the latter application by the house of commons on 2–3 March 1790. In 1791 and 1792, he played the central part in organizing a parliamentary campaign when he collected signatures for the unitarian petition, encouraged others to do so and approached sympathetic politicians. The rejection of the petition had the effect of drawing public attention to the fact that denial of the doctrine of the Trinity was one of the legal disabilities not indemnified by the Toleration Act of 1689, and thus made vexatious prosecutions, at least theoretically, more likely to be made.

The failures to enact religious reform through parliament between 1787 and 1792 pushed Lindsey and others to the conclusion that such reform would never be brought about until parliament itself had been reformed and rendered, in however limited a manner, more representative of the propertied sections of the nation. Professor J. C. D. Clark has rightly warned of the dangers of anachronism in applying the term 'radicalism' to opinions and organizations critical of the existing regime during the 1790s.[109] Lindsey himself did not use the noun 'radicalism' to denote a species of political opinion. But he referred to 'radical reform' in 1797 (Letter 657) and he may be described accurately, and in a way which he would have recognized, as one who held radical opinions. Admittedly, his opinions were not as thoroughgoing as those of more extreme critics of the British state. Lindsey never openly advocated a republican form of government, despite his disapproval of George III and his family, and did not contemplate any kind of social or economic redistribution. His preference was for the achievement of change in a 'quiet legal way' (Letter 616). However, he associated with whig and radical critics of Pitt; the Foxite *Morning Chronicle* was his favourite newspaper. He read and recommended to others Benjamin Flower's *Cambridge Intelligencer*, which began publication in 1793 (Letter 649). In June 1792, he noted that he had read four Parisian newspapers (Letter 501). He was a member of a club, or, rather, a succession of clubs, which consisted of dissenting ministers and sympathetic laymen whose theological opinions were predominantly heterodox and whose political opinions were almost all oppositional. In 1799, he referred to a club in Paternoster Row, to which he, Priestley and Richard Price had belonged (Letter 681). From 1791, he was a member of the 'Quarterly Club', of which some details were preserved in a notebook of Joseph Towers; Andrew

---

[108] See Vol. I, pp. lxxiii–lxxiv.
[109] J. C. D. Clark, *English society 1688–1832. Ideology, social structure and political practice during the ancien regime* (Cambridge, 1985), ch. 5.

Kippis, Abraham Rees, John Disney and Michael Dodson were also among its thirty members. Its rules specified that its members should gather four times each year, in March, June, October and December; the membership fee was half a guinea.[110] Although Towers himself died in 1799, this was probably the club to which Lindsey referred when writing to John Rowe in January 1800 (Letter 688). On 24 June 1789, he was elected the fifty-fourth member of the Revolution Society, which, although short-lived, encompassed many leading unitarians, including several members of Essex Street chapel,[111] and where Lindsey found himself in the company of John Horne Tooke (Letter 430). The laconic entries in the diary of William Godwin reveal that he and Lindsey were on fairly informal social terms, particularly between 1789 and 1791, although Lindsey came, understandably enough, to suspect Godwin and his circle of atheism.[112] And to complete this catalogue of radical connexions, Lindsey on several occasions in the early 1790s met Thomas Paine, of whose *Rights of man*, part one, he wrote 'It is indeed an admirable work, and Burke a very child in his hands' (Letter 445). Significantly, however, he also described Paine, in a letter to William Tayleur, as 'the most inveterate declared unbeliever I ever conversed with' (Letter 430). Three and a half years later he recalled of Paine, who by then had prudently removed himself to France, that 'The few times I was in company with him, he commonly took occasion [to] shoot his bolt against the Bible' (Letter 560). Paine's *Age of reason*, with its scornful dismissal of the authenticity of scripture, alienated many of his erstwhile admirers among the dissenters. Lindsey feared that Paine, Godwin, Thomas Holcroft, John Thelwall and their associates, by attacking revealed religion and the moral values of Christianity, were damaging the far more important objective of parliamentary reform, which they should have made a priority (Letter 606).

IV

Two of the most decisive events of Lindsey's later career were the Birmingham riots of July 1791 and the emigration of their principal victim, Joseph Priestley, to America in April 1794. Detailed investigations of the Priestley riots, notably those of Dr David Wykes, have demonstrated the fundamentally religious motivation behind the attacks on Priestley's house and laboratory, the Old and New Meetings in the town and the property of other leading sympathizers with unitarianism.[113] Lindsey's letters record his horrified response in some detail, especially when he received news that the riots, with dissenters among their main targets, had spread to other towns in the west midlands. He described Priestley's arrival in London immediately after his escape from the conflagration (Letter 464), followed closely the trials of the rioters and the claims for compensation mounted by Priestley and his fellow-sufferers and wrote solicitously to William Tayleur in Shrewsbury, who,

---

[110] Bodl., MS Eng. Misc. 3. 334, pp. 49–54. I owe this reference to Dr John Seed.

[111] BL, Add. MS 64814, fo. 59v.

[112] See Letter 560, n. 3.

[113] See in particular Wykes, '"Spirit of persecutors exemplified"'; '"A finished monster"'. A further recent contribution is Harry Smith, '"The blessedness of those who are persecuted for righteousness sake": the *rôle* of "candour" and the Priestley riots in Birmingham unitarian identity, 1791–1815', *Midland History*, 35, 2 (Autumn, 2010), 174–90.

he feared, might be caught up in the disturbances. He soon came to ascribe the riots to the malevolence of high churchmen, to the influence of Burke's *Reflections* (Letter 469), to the 'church and king' sentiment which was beginning to take a more organized form, and – a view shared by many contemporaries and later historians – to the connivance of the local authorities in Birmingham itself. He took comfort from the calmness of Priestley's response to the 'great calamity' (Letters 462, 464) and bravely hoped for better times. The minister of the Octagon chapel in Norwich, William Enfield, wrote 'But let us persevere in well doing: every meritorious exertion has its effect – a phoenix will rise out of the ashes of our Birmingham conventicles.'[114]

For all this rather forced optimism, the Birmingham riots dismantled, at least temporarily, much of the optimism and the expectation of uninterrupted human improvement which had been an essential feature of heterodox dissenters' perception of British, and indeed European, society. They brought to an end the hope that the French Revolution would lead to a widening of religious freedom (manifested, for example, in the enhanced status of protestants in France) and improvements in the fortunes of religious minorities. The extent of the breakdown of order at Birmingham and elsewhere helped to produce a more baleful perception among unitarians of the mass of the population, who, they thought, were too easily inflamed by propaganda from high churchmen and Tories, and who clearly were in need of much more education before they could be considered suitable for enfranchisement. Lindsey had witnessed civic unrest at close quarters in June 1780, when his own chapel had been worryingly close to the Gordon rioters. Two years later he noted in his chapel's accounts the payment of a 'Riot tax' and expressed the unfulfilled hope that such a measure would never be needed again (Vol. I, Letter 255).[115] Signs of the insecurity which were the legacy of the Priestley riots included William Tayleur's relief that the main victim had not experienced any trouble on the first anniversary in 1792,[116] and in Lindsey's advice to Timothy Kenrick to proceed with caution when refusing to preach a fast day sermon in 1793 (Letter 518). Priestley himself, writing in Hackney, observed: 'On the 14th of July, 1792, it was taken for granted by many of my neighbours, that my house was to come down, just as at Birmingham the year before.'[117] In 1798, Lindsey wrote to Thomas Belsham: 'Your account of Birmingham … was very acceptable, as we are much interested in respect of many of its inhabitants, tho' for my part I never wish to see the place again and would go some miles out of my way to avoid it' (Letter 674).

Priestley himself never returned to Birmingham. Instead, as Lindsey recorded, he was elected as minister of the Gravel Pit Meeting, Hackney, in November 1791, as the successor to Richard Price – but only after significant reluctance on the part of a section of the congregation to accept as their pastor so controversial a figure who might attract mob violence (Letter 478). Nonetheless, he was able to resume his scientific work, to lecture on theology and natural science at Hackney College, and to continue his preaching ministry. But a combination of growing public hostility

---

114 Bodl., MS Add. C.89, 'Letters to Ralph Griffiths Monthly Review', Enfield to Griffiths, 5 Aug. 1791. Enfield's use of the work 'conventicles' was presumably ironical.

115 The additional rate levied by act of parliament in 1793 (33 Geo. III, c. 39) upon the hundred of Hemlingford, to provide compensation to the victims of the Birmingham riots was in effect a 'riot tax'.

116 JRUL, C2¹³, Tayleur to Lindsey, 26 July 1792.

117 Priestley, *Present state of Europe*, p. v.

to dissenters and the emigration of his sons to America led Priestley to follow them across the Atlantic.[118] A few days after his departure, Lindsey wrote plaintively: 'How much we feel Dr Priestley's separation, in this house, where we comonly were happy in seeing him once or twice a week or oftner, is not to be described, for with all his other powers, he excelled eminently in the private virtues of a friend and chearful, social converse' (Letter 566). It is possible that Lindsey even contemplated the option of going to America himself, perhaps for an extended visit rather than emigration; he seems to have received an offer to go there on his resignation of Catterick (Vol. I, Letter 117). On 13 October 1794, Hannah Lindsey wrote to Catharine Cappe: 'The rage for going to America is like another rage which would continue the war. The first go for a freedom which exists no where, to live well without trouble, care, or disappointment; the latter would beat the French, because we have always done it.'[119] Writing from Northumberland, Pennsylvania, on 13 August 1800, Priestley told Lindsey: 'The longer I live in this country, the more I like it. Your spending a year with me in this place, of which you dropped something like a hint in a late letter, would make it a paradise.'[120] If this was a remote possibility, Lindsey clung to the sanguine expectation that Priestley would return to England, and believed that only the continuation of the war obstructed such a desirable outcome. As late as 1799, he expressed this hope to Russell Scott (Letter 679). He sought to compensate for Priestley's absence by editing his works for publication in Britain, as we have seen, and by preserving his memory and reputation at every possible opportunity. When the unitarian minister William Shepherd of Gateacre visited Lindsey at Essex Street in 1797, he found that Lindsey had recently received two letters from Priestley and that in his drawing room were two pictures of Priestley's house near the Susquehanna.[121] Although Lindsey's letters to Priestley after, as well as before, his emigration have been destroyed, just over 100 of Priestley's letters to him have survived. Just as Lindsey's letters to other correspondents form a vital biographical source for Priestley, so Lindsey's continued presence in England – he outlived Priestley by more than four years, even though he was ten years older – inspired Priestley to write at length, and informatively, about his life in America and his last major theological works.

The possibility that Lindsey, who reached the age of seventy-one in July 1794, might tear up his English roots and seek a new life across the Atlantic seems remote. Yet it was not entirely without plausibility. He was in correspondence with several unitarian sympathizers in New England, notably James Freeman, the minister of King's chapel, Boston. Although only one letter from Lindsey to Freeman appears to have survived (Letter 603), seventeen letters from Freeman to Lindsey, written between 1786 and 1801, do survive in some form. Lindsey reported that he sent Freeman tracts 'two or three times a year' (Letter 582). Freeman's detailed accounts of the growth of unitarianism in America, although excessively optimistic, were of considerable interest to Lindsey, not least because they offered hopes of greater religious freedom at a time when he feared the opposite in Britain; there was nothing

---

[118] See David L. Wykes, '"We have lived very quietly and comfortably here": Joseph Priestley at Hackney September 1791–April 1794', *TUHS*, XXI, 2 (Apr. 2004), 513–27.
[119] Cappe, *Memoirs*, p. 263.
[120] Rutt, I, 441.
[121] HMCO, Shepherd MS, Vol. IV, William Shepherd to his wife Frances, née Nicholson, 3 July 1797.

new in dissenting admiration for the independent United States.[122] Lindsey probably enjoyed the irony whereby Freeman's chapel in Boston had until 1776 been an episcopalian stronghold, with a minister – Henry Caner, now an exile in England – who had been a strong supporter of the British government's policies, but which had become one of the first avowedly unitarian churches in North America. It gave Lindsey particular pleasure to learn that Freeman's congregation used a version of his own *Book of Common Prayer reformed*. And Lindsey followed the career of Henry Toulmin, with whom he had been in correspondence while Toulmin had been minister at Chowbent (Vol. I, Letter 338; Letters 392, 397). Although Henry Toulmin turned from a ministerial to a political and judicial career, as he became the secretary of state for the commonwealth of Kentucky and subsequently a judge in Alabama, Lindsey regarded him as an important source of information, and as a promising young man. As late as June 1804 Henry's father Joshua Toulmin wrote to William Davy: 'The excellent Mr Lindsey, who regards my Son with a most partial attachment & nearly paternal affection wishes to convey to him, thro' your very friendly services a box of books, which a friend here is so obliging as to enclose in a Cask.'[123] Davy himself, an English merchant from a dissenting family in Devon, spent several years in America at the turn of the century and was one of the last of Lindsey's new correspondents. Similarly, the exiled Dutch patriot preacher Francis Adrian Van der Kemp, while appearing to flatter Lindsey, adopted heterodox religious, as well as republican, sentiments. He wrote to Hannah Lindsey on 5 November 1807: 'It must fill Mr. Lindsey's heart with gladness that his labours are blessed here in the wilderness, through the means of those whom he enlightened and confirmed in the gospel doctrine by his writings.'[124] Among those 'labours' was the gift of his own works and those of Priestley to the library of Harvard College, for which he received an appreciative acknowledgment from the president and fellows of the college.[125]

For the historian of the tribulations of dissenters during the 1790s, however, Lindsey's decision – surely not a difficult one – to remain in Britain has conferred one major benefit. The fifty-one surviving letters written by him in the single year of 1794 are highly informative about Priestley's emigration and of the trials of leading reformers. Lindsey himself was not personally involved, or ever likely to be involved, as a defendant, or even as a witness. Nonetheless, he was directly affected by the trials and was physically as well as emotionally close to those held in London. Several of his friends experienced arrest and prosecution, and in some cases conviction and imprisonment. The young unitarian minister Jeremiah Joyce, whom Lindsey regarded as a man of considerable promise, was interrogated by the privy council and incarcerated in the Tower of London, and subsequently in Newgate, from 14 May to 1 December before the charges of treason against him were dropped. Joyce had been a leading member of the Society for Constitutional Information and the London Corresponding Society, was the tutor to the children of the eccentric radical Charles, third Earl Stanhope and a kind of political agent to the

---

122   See Anthony Page, '"Liberty has an asylum": John Jebb, British radicalism and the American Revolution', *History*, 87 (2002), 204–26.

123   Davy letterbook, p. 84, Joshua Toulmin to William Davy, 27 June 1804. In this letter, Joshua Toulmin referred to an apparently non-surviving letter from Lindsey to Henry Toulmin, dated 12 Apr. 1804.

124   Belsham, *Memoirs*, p. 174.

125   *Ibid.*, p. 157.

earl himself.[126] Four years later, Lindsey's publisher Joseph Johnson, a committed unitarian, was convicted of publishing a seditious pamphlet, Gilbert Wakefield's *Reply* to Bishop Watson's *Address to the people of Great Britain*. Johnson was sentenced to imprisonment for six months, in addition to detention in the king's bench prison before trial and judgment. Although his treatment was relatively mild, his conviction brought to an end the publication of his monthly, the *Analytical Review*. Gilbert Wakefield, a far more outspoken critic of the government, was less fortunate. He was put on trial for sedition in 1799 – 'Would that I were one of his jury! His liberty should be inviolate', wrote Lindsey (Letter 676) – and on conviction sentenced to two years' imprisonment in Dorchester gaol, from which he emerged with broken health. That Joyce, Johnson and Wakefield were all high-profile sympathizers with unitarianism as well as political reform was of especial concern to Lindsey. In 1799, moreover, the unitarian Benjamin Flower, the co-owner and editor of the *Cambridge Intelligencer*, a newspaper which during its brief existence opposed the war against France and advocated reform, was imprisoned for six months for a libel upon Bishop Watson. In 1792 and 1793, Lindsey feared that his Suffolk friend William Alexander would be prosecuted for teaching his pupils in an unlicensed school, and it was to Alexander that Lindsey expressed his suspicion that his outgoing and incoming letters were intercepted and opened by the Post Office (Letter 511).

The trials of 1793 in Scotland and 1794 in London conveyed to Lindsey a particularly sharp sense that his world had changed. Hannah Lindsey undoubtedly represented their joint opinion when writing to her half-brother in Yorkshire in October 1794, immediately before the trials of Thomas Hardy, John Horne Tooke and John Thelwall:

> The approaching trials of the State prisoners excite great attention in the Capital, & the first processes are not favorable in their aspect: How blind are our Governors not to see the tendency of these things upon the lower classes of w[ch]. rank most of the prisoners are: They are sowing the seeds of that resistance & commotion, w[ch]. they mean to crush.[127]

Lindsey followed the proceedings very closely, by means of the newspaper press, especially the sympathetic *Morning Chronicle*, through information provided by the extensive legal and political contacts of his chapel members, and possibly through attendance at some of the trials themselves. He collected the published accounts of those trials (Letter 593).[128] And although he derived comfort from the acquittals of Hardy, Horne Tooke and Thelwall at the end of 1794, his main concern was for the fate of the leaders of the reform movement in Scotland, and particularly Thomas Fyshe Palmer. Having preached and written on behalf of unitarianism in Scotland and served as minister to small unitarian communities in Montrose and Dundee, Palmer was charged with sedition, after taking a small part in the production of

---

[126] John Issitt, *Jeremiah Joyce*, chs. 4–6.

[127] DWL, MS 12.80, opp. p. 278, Hannah Lindsey to her half-brother Francis Blackburne, Oct. 1794 (postmarked 20 Oct.).

[128] According to McLachlan, 'Lindsey to Scott', 128 n. 22, the published volumes of state trials bought by Lindsey 'are still on the shelves of his collection of books in Dr Williams's Library'. There is indeed a Lindsey room at DWL where many of Lindsey's books are preserved. However, I have not been able to confirm that the volumes in question were acquired by Lindsey himself. I am grateful to Jane Giscombe for advice on this point.

a pamphlet on behalf of the Dundee 'Friends of Liberty'. He was convicted in September 1793 and imprisoned successively at Perth, on the hulks in the Thames, and then on board ship at Portsmouth. At the beginning of May 1794, he was transported to Botany Bay. In his company were the Scottish reformers Thomas Muir, William Skirving and Maurice Margarot.

Amid hopes of reprieve, or commutation of sentence, for Palmer and his associates, Lindsey believed that the best contribution he could make to their welfare lay in personal visits to preserve their morale, in sending them books (as he did for Palmer; Letter 540), raising funds for their support, and encouraging others to do the same. His letters to Robert Millar, who, because of its implications for unitarianism in Dundee, was vitally interested in Palmer's fate, contain details of his efforts on behalf of the prisoners, while his letters to Russell Scott at Portsmouth reveal a constant solicitude for their future, as well as outrage at their treatment. Palmer kept up a correspondence with Lindsey during his exile, and although hardly any of his letters to Lindsey have survived, it is clear that he regarded Lindsey with gratitude.[129] Lindsey fully expected Palmer's return to Britain at the end of his seven-year term of transportation (Letter 729), and his letters in 1800 and 1801 expressed anticipation, then concern, before the news reached London of Palmer's death in 1802 after a hazardous voyage from Australia to Guam. It is not entirely certain from his letters whether Lindsey actually met Thomas Muir, although it is likely that he paid Muir at least one visit in the hulks. After his dramatic escape from Botany Bay in 1796, Muir wrote of Lindsey and the portrait painter Richard Shields as his 'dearest friends forever'.[130] Lindsey visited Joseph Johnson in prison in 1798 and three years later wrote (Letter 718) to the imprisoned Gilbert Wakefield, who requested an unnamed friend that 'When you call in Essex-Street, do not fail of giving my affectionate respects to Mr. Lindsey. It is scarcely possible for man to live a more liberal, and conscientious life than he.'[131] And Lindsey took a particular interest in the case of the baptist minister William Winterbotham of Plymouth, who was imprisoned in New Prison, Clerkenwell and subsequently in Newgate, for two years after preaching sermons sharply critical of the government. Lindsey visited him in gaol (Letter 636) and maintained cordial relations with him after his release.[132]

The experience of the 1790s for many political reformers and religious dissenters was one of disillusionment, and in some instances of vexation, demoralization, loss of liberty or enforced emigration. Lindsey's letters in this decade reveal an acute sense of the vulnerable position of heterodox dissent, under attack from a hostile political establishment and at the same time incurring the hostility of much of the press and popular opinion. In the circumstances, it is not surprising that Lindsey

---

[129] Two letters from Palmer to Lindsey, written from Botany Bay and dated 5 Aug. and 16 Sept. 1796, may be found in HMCO, Shepherd MS, Vol. X, nos. 11 and 12. Palmer also wrote several letters to John Disney from Botany Bay; see Michael T. Davis, '"A register of vexations and persecutions": some letters of Thomas Fyshe Palmer from Botany Bay during the 1790s', *E & D*, XXIII (2004–7), 148–66. On at least one occasion, Disney printed a letter of Palmer and circulated it to sympathetic friends; NYRO, ZFW 7/2/124/1, Disney to Wyvill, 18 Feb. 1799.

[130] Quoted in Christina Bewley, *Muir of Huntershill. A Scottish patriot's adventures around the world* (Oxford, 1981), p. 151.

[131] *Memoirs of the life of Gilbert Wakefield*, ed. J. T. Rutt and A. Wainwright (2 vols., London, 1804), II, 196.

[132] See Belsham, *Memoirs*, pp. 237–8 n. *, for Winterbotham's letter to Lindsey of 31 Aug. 1802. Interestingly, Winterbotham was an orthodox dissenter and a Calvinist, not a unitarian.

adopted an aggrieved tone, anxious about the possibility of repression, and a belief that he and those of his opinions were, like the earliest Christians, a small, uncorrupted and enlightened minority in a depraved age. Such a consciousness of insecurity was consistent with, and probably helped to facilitate, the moves towards the formal institutionalization of unitarianism over which Lindsey presided. However, although civil liberties were indeed curtailed under the legislation of Pitt's ministry in the 1790s, the same was not the case with the freedom of religious worship or publication. Account must be taken of the impact of constant attacks in the official and semi-official organs of the state and in the public prints. Such attacks, moreover, as so often with repressive regimes, encouraged and were intended to encourage self-censorship. However, proposals for legislative restrictions upon worship and preaching, notably Michael Angelo Taylor's bill of 1800 to curb the licensing of evangelical itinerant preachers, which was a clear blow at dissent, were not enacted into law. Pitt himself was no ideological Tory and had no commitment to an anglican political agenda; his reasons for opposing the repeal of the Test and Corporation Acts in 1787–90 and the unitarian petition in 1792 were pragmatic, not doctrinal.[133] Lindsey and his fellow-ministers were still able to preach and to publish; age and infirmity, not repression, explain the decline of Lindsey's publishing output after 1792. Jeremiah Joyce was able on his release to publish an account of his arrest, and to edit Thomas Fyshe Palmer's *Narrative* of the tribulations of his voyage to Botany Bay.[134] And although there were local instances of harassment of individual dissenters, some of which – such as that of William Alexander – came directly to Lindsey's attention, political repression was not matched by religious repression on a national scale. To Lindsey cases of this kind were individual tragedies, which he felt directly and personally. Yet among many heterodox dissenters there was a want of consistency between a serious concern over the trials of Palmer, Muir, Wakefield and Winterbotham, and the much more distant and impersonal way in which they responded to the evidence of mass, government-directed terror in France in and after 1792. William Cobbett was not the only writer to reproach Priestley for condemning public violence when directed against him, while condoning, or even welcoming, the violence of the Jacobins as a lesser evil potentially leading to a greater good.[135] Not fully sharing Priestley's millenarianism, Lindsey never went quite so far as to express such a view in pulpit or print, but it is implicit throughout his letters.

---

[133] See G. M. Ditchfield. 'Ecclesiastical legislation during the ministry of the Younger Pitt, 1783–1801', in *Parliament and the church 1529–1960*, ed. J. P. Parry and Stephen Taylor, *Parliamentary History*, special number (Edinburgh, 2000), pp. 64–80.

[134] Jeremiah Joyce, *A sermon preached on Sunday, February the 23d, 1794. By Jeremiah Joyce. Twenty-three weeks a close prisoner in the Tower of London. To which is added an appendix, containing an account of the author's arrest for treasonable practices; his examination before his majesty's most honourable privy council; his commitment to the Tower, and subsequent treatment* (London, 1794); Palmer's *Narrative* was published in 1796, with a second edition in 1797.

[135] William Cobbett, *Observations on the emigration of Dr. Joseph Priestley, and on the several addresses delivered to him on his arrival at New York* (Philadelphia, 1794), pp. 6–28. The contrast is drawn very effectively by David A. Wilson in his perceptive review of Graham, *Revolutionary in exile, E & D*, XV, 15 (1996), 107–11.

V

Lindsey retired from his ministry at Essex Street chapel in July 1793, immediately after his seventieth birthday. The succession of his co-minister John Disney had been long prepared. He conducted his last service on 14 July, and his letters record his nervousness on the occasion (Letters 531–2). Perhaps his retirement was timely. Samuel Pipe-Wolferstan certainly thought so, noting on 12 May that he was 'ill satisfied' with Lindsey's sermon.[136] Having attended Lindsey's last service and received a copy of his final sermon, he added:

> A present came from Lindsey of a Farewell which was originally meant for pulpit last Sunday – as it was a Farewell, read it while in hand – and so passed morning over what he has printed twenty times before – I perceive my estimation of his abilities much lowered; for I remember I used to describe him as the best preacher I knew.[137]

This sermon was indeed a measured re-assertion of some of Lindsey's most fundamental beliefs, insisting on the scriptural integrity of unitarianism and the authority conferred upon it by a series of distinguished theological writers. The *Monthly Review* commented, predictably, 'The whole is written with that mild and candid spirit which has marked the author's former publications.'[138] In fact, the content, as well as the style, marked Lindsey's previous work. This was the case, too, with Lindsey's last book, *Conversations on the divine government*, published in 1802. It was written in the form of a series of six conversations among a small group of friends with imagined names, in which Lindsey's own voice (through the character 'Photinus') is easily detected. The discussions concluded with an endorsement of the ultimate happiness of humanity, a denial of the notion of eternal punishment and an implicit rejection both of original sin and the death of Christ as an atonement for human sin.

Lindsey remained an influential figure among heterodox dissenters after his retirement. He regularly attended, and sometimes chaired, committee meetings of the Unitarian Society. Together with his wife he intervened decisively to ensure the succession of his friend Thomas Belsham as minister of Essex Street chapel on the retirement of John Disney in 1805.[139] He continued to be a devoted letter-writer. Although Hannah Lindsey told Russell Scott in April 1796 that 'even writing letters are not so easy to him as formerly except upon pressing occasions' (Letter 630), his correspondence only declined in volume after his illness in 1801–2 and more so after the death of Priestley in February 1804. Only Priestley's side of his correspondence with Lindsey survives, but it provides ample evidence of Lindsey's ability to sustain his absent friend, to supply him with books and newspapers and at times to comment critically on his work. As we have seen, it was through Lindsey's agency that some of Priestley's later works found their way to a British readership. 'I cannot express what I feel when I receive and read your letters', wrote Priestley to him in March

---

136   Pipe-Wolferstan diary, 12 May 1793.

137   *Ibid.*, 17 July 1793. In 1796, the diarist even found Lindsey's presence at the chapel to be something of an irritant; 'Old Lindsey ... who, good! is generally absent himself in afternoon'; *ibid.*, 28 Feb. 1786.

138   *Monthly Review*, NS, XII (1793), 236–7, reviewing Lindsey's *A discourse addressed to the congregation at the chapel in Essex Street*.

139   Williams, pp. 543–57.

1799, 'I generally shed many tears over them, but by no means from sorrow or any unpleasant feeling.'[140] The ability to encourage others was one of Lindsey's most important epistolary qualities, as with his efforts to succour, in despondent circumstances, his friend Robert Millar in Dundee. He solicited from his 'more opulent friends' numerous 'contributions … for the support of unitarian ministers' (Letter 659). Above all, by the late 1790s the financial condition of his retirement became increasingly comfortable. He and his wife continued to live in the house adjoining Essex Street chapel, while he benefited from the legacies left to him by several of his lay supporters.[141] In 1800, his devoted admirer, the widowed Elizabeth Rayner, bequeathed to him £1,000 in government annuities and the remainder of the lease of her house in Clapham, which yielded a useful annual rent (Letter 698).[142] He gave modest contributions to other unitarian causes, such as the chapel of Thomas Evans in Carmarthenshire and the academy of Timothy Kenrick at Exeter (Letter 746).

In this final phase of his life, Lindsey and his wife spent the winter months in Essex Street, their 'Winter quarters' (Letter 677). Until 1799, they made regular summer visits to Yorkshire, usually in alternate years, to visit Hannah Lindsey's mother, Hannah Blackburne, and to meet friends at York, notably Newcome and Catharine Cappe, and, in 1799, David Eaton (Letter 686). The death of Hannah Blackburne in the latter year, and their own increasing infirmity, meant that this was their last northern excursion. Thereafter, they continued and extended their practice of spending much of the summer in the Surrey countryside at Morden with their loyal friends Sophia and Frances Chambers, to whom Lindsey dedicated his *Conversations on the divine government*. in 1802.[143] In December 1802, Hannah Lindsey, recording that she and her husband had stayed there for twelve weeks during the previous summer, described Morden as their 'second home' (Letter 744). Eight years earlier she had described to her half-brother Francis Blackburne, vicar of Brignall, Yorkshire, the pattern of their year:

> Your parish School is the best service that can be done to the rising generation, there is a debasing ignorance thro' the want of being able to read, & wch. is of greater extent in the south, than the North: Mr Lindsey who rides about amongst the Cottagers upon the Skirts of Epsom downs laments every-day the total neglect of the poor, both by their Ministers & rich Neighbors: There is a whole Hamlet of very decent orderly people in wch. there is not one man, woman, or child that know their letters.
>
> We shall now in a week or two settle at home for the Winter, as the Season is fine and our friends wish it, we are benefited by the air, exercise, & comfort of this retreat: And it shortens the Winter to us all, being grown past those active imployments which the last twenty years have made necessary: Besides we have lost so many friends, particularly D^r. Priestley that M^r. Lindsey is more indifferent

---

[140] Rutt, I, 415.
[141] See G. M. Ditchfield, 'Testaments of faith: a comment on some unitarian wills in the age of Theophilus Lindsey', *TUHS*, XXII, 2 (Apr. 2000), 130–41.
[142] Elizabeth Rayner's will may be found in TNA: PRO PROB 11/1345, fos 264r–274v.
[143] The visitation return of the parish of Morden (diocese of Winchester) in 1788, under 'question 7: Dissenters' yielded the response 'No professed papists. No meetings. 3 followers of Mr. Lindsey'; *Parson and parish in eighteenth-century Surrey*, ed. W. R. Ward (Surrey Record Society, XXXIV, 1994), 125. Two of the followers of Lindsey were almost certainly the Chambers sisters; possibly the third was their cousin Christopher Chambers. I owe this reference to Dr David Wykes.

to London than he was: As the center of information it has its attractions, & in Winter is the best place of residence.[144]

Lindsey maintained these and other latitudinarian connexions until his death, through his correspondence with Christopher Wyvill and his interest in the fortunes of his former college companion Richard Reynolds of Paxton.

In the summer of 1801, Lindsey suffered a slight stroke, and in December of that year, a severe one. It deprived him for some weeks of the ability to write, and it was not until May 1802 that he was able to write to his correspondents in his own hand again (Letter 735). Shortly before that, he added a few lines in his own hand in a (non-surviving) letter to Priestley, most of which was written by Hannah Lindsey.[145] He wrote the full text of most of his remaining letters which survive from 1802; Priestley received a letter from him, dated 7 December 1802, which was 'written almost wholly' in his own hand.[146] His last surviving letter fully in his own hand was that to Timothy Kenrick of Exeter in January 1803 (Letter 746) and after that, Hannah Lindsey took over the *rôle* of correspondent completely. On 10 February and 14 July 1803 Lindsey was well enough to be present at, and indeed to chair, meetings of the Unitarian Society; the latter occasion was his last recorded attendance.[147] On 1 December 1804, Belsham wrote that Lindsey's death had been expected very soon, but that he had recovered.[148] In October the following year, after it had been closed for repairs in August and September, Essex Street chapel was re-opened with the fifth edition of Lindsey's liturgy, which was used 'at the express desire of the Duke of Grafton'. Lindsey attended the morning service, 'which he had not done for four years'.[149] But reading, 'his principal source of amusement & comfort', was becoming more difficult for him (Letter 772), although in April 1805, Hannah Lindsey told Belsham that he had 'conned again and again' one of the latter's sermons (Letter 771). On 28 July 1806, Lindsey, although enfeebled, could still read, enjoy visits from friends and could be carried from his house to the chapel (Letter 775). As late as August 1808, Hannah Lindsey could report to Belsham that Lindsey's hearing was still 'acute' (Letter 782). One result of his debility means that he could not make clear in his letters his opinions of Napoleonic, as distinct from revolutionary, France. There is every indication from Hannah Lindsey's letters, however, that while lamenting the renewal of the French war in 1803, they both held increasingly patriotic opinions, regarded Bonaparte as a tyrant and criticized the British government for lack of military and naval preparation. 'We trust that a merciful Providence will preserve us from the fangs of French despotism', wrote Hannah Lindsey to Wyvill on 8 August 1803 (Letter 753). There was, without doubt, an inner consistency in this attitude, which accorded with Lindsey's view of the Seven Years War, and the danger at that time of invasion from Bourbon despotism and a possible overthrow of British protestant liberties.

By the later 1790s, the image of Lindsey as a patriarch was already being fashioned. Many unitarians were anxious to meet him. On 14 April 1804, Hannah Lindsey recounted that they had numerous visitors at their London home: 'Our

---

[144] DWL, MS 12.80, opposite p. 278, Hannah Lindsey to Francis Blackburne, 20 Oct. 1794.
[145] Rutt, I, 482.
[146] *Ibid.*, 507.
[147] Unitarian Society minute book, pp. 84, 88–9.
[148] Williams, p. 539.
[149] *Ibid.*, pp. 561–2.

house is often like a fair, regret for our friend [i.e. Priestley, who had died on 6 February], and solicitude for Mr Lindsey brings us many inquirers, who all learn something from the aged Saints calm and chearing fortitude' (Letter 759). John Towill Rutt recollected:

> It was during the latter years of Mr. and Mrs Lindsey's exemplary lives that I had the pleasure and advantage of sharing their society. The evening hours passed in the library at Essex House, still provide some of the most agreeable recollections of former years; not, I am persuaded, *dum memor ipse mei*, will they be easily forgotten.[150]

That library passed to Lindsey's wife, who in turn bequeathed its contents to the trustees of the chapel, for the use of its minister and his successors. For this purpose, David Eaton had compiled a catalogue of Lindsey's books and pamphlets.[151]

Another visitor was the barrister, reform campaigner and unitarian James Losh of Newcastle upon Tyne, whose account of his meeting with Lindsey in March 1802 leaves the same impression of patriarchal serenity:

> Breakfast Mr Lindsey's – It is a pleasing thing to observe the calmness and even chearfulness which this good man displays in the midst of illness and approaching dissolution – he expressed to me his full and undoubted confidence in the universal providence of God, and of the future prevalence of happiness in all his rational creation ... Mrs Lindsey is a clear headed acute woman.[152]

Over several days in March and April 1813, Losh read with considerable care Belsham's *Memoirs of Lindsey*, which prompted him to remember Lindsey as 'a gentleman like and very excellent person of competent learning and talents, and a sincere disciple of the blessed Jesus'.[153] The Yorkshire dissenting antiquary Joseph Hunter, curious to see Lindsey, was brought into his presence in 1808, but found him 'but the ruin of a man', whose 'power of utterance seemed nearly gone'. Lindsey was able, however, to pronounce a 'benediction' over his visitor.[154] Immediately after his death on 3 November 1808, Hannah Lindsey wrote to William Alexander a rather touching account of his last moments, which suggests that, though physically enfeebled, he retained a coherence of mind.[155] Lindsey was buried, as he had directed, in Bunhill Fields, the traditional place of interment for dissenters, a symbolic gesture which re-affirmed his affinity with nonconformity together with his failure to achieve his hopes for the internal reform of the established church. His tomb, already shared with his friend and benefactress Elizabeth Rayner, was also to be the burying-place of Hannah Lindsey and Thomas Belsham.[156]

---

[150] Rutt, I, 81–2, n. ‡.
[151] TNA: PRO PROB 11/1529, fo. 235v.
[152] Losh diary, 9 Mar. 1802.
[153] Losh diary, 15 Mar. to 18 Apr. 1813; quotation from 20 Apr. 1813.
[154] BL, Add. MS 36527, fo. 77 (Joseph Hunter, 'Biographical notices of some of my contemporaries').
[155] This letter, dated 12 Dec. 1808, was published in *UH*, 25 Jan. 1862, p. 32. See also DWL, MS 12.46 (60), Hannah Lindsey to Robert Millar, 15 Nov. 1808.
[156] For the inscription, see Williams, pp. 775–6.

VI

The typically laconic entry in the diary of William Godwin on 3 November 1808 simply read 'Lindsey dies'.[157] Others who had known Lindsey were more fulsome. 'I feel my loss: but I reflect with gratitude on the Providence, to which I owe the blessing of his regards & friendship', wrote Joshua Toulmin four days later.[158] The duke of Grafton declared that 'His memory will be revered by us to our latest breath, as having done more than any one to spread genuine Christianity.'[159] Christopher Wyvill was equally generous:

> At last our worthy Friend M^r. Lindsey has finished his course; & finished it, as all would wish to finish theirs, preserving his accustomed benignity & serene reliance on the good tidings of the Gospel, under the gradual loss of almost every other comfort. In Christian Virtue, Utility to his Fellow-Men, & consequent Felicity, I believe, his superior is not left behind Him.[160]

Public obituary notices of Lindsey were generally complimentary; almost all regarded his most important act as his resignation of the vicarage of Catterick exactly thirty-five years previously.[161] When the *Gentleman's Magazine* claimed that 'he might have risen to the first stations within the pale of the Church', it gave added emphasis to the theme of self-sacrifice.[162] So did the flattering obituary in the sympathetic *Morning Chronicle*, which was the work of William Frend.[163] The geographical range of the provincial newspapers which reported his death suggests that he had acquired some form of national status.[164] There were published funeral sermons on Lindsey's death, all of them preached by dissenters.[165] The process of memorializing was already beginning. Catharine Cappe continued it in her memoir of Lindsey, and her further eulogy on the death of Hannah Lindsey in 1812.[166] Her own *Memoirs*, first published in 1822, drew on her family recollections of Lindsey in Yorkshire in the 1760s and early 1770s, and depicted him as a sacrificial martyr for truth.[167] In 1812, Thomas Belsham, with privileged (and enviable) access to Lindsey's papers, published the 'official' biography, which has remained the single most important repository of information about his life. A second edition appeared in 1820 and on the centenary of Lindsey's resignation of Catterick a third,

---

157 Bodl., Abinger collection, reel 12: diary of William Godwin, 3 Nov. 1808.

158 DWL, MS 12.80 (between pp. 190 and 191), Joshua Toulmin to Hannah Lindsey, 7 Nov. 1808.

159 *Ibid.*, opp. p. 54, Grafton to Belsham, 11 Nov. 1808.

160 NYRO, ZFW 7/2/203/17, Wyvill to Samuel Shore III, 17 Nov. 1808.

161 See *Gent. Mag.*, LXXVIII, ii (1808), 1044; *Scots Magazine*, LXX (1808), 879; *The Athenaeum*, V, 25 (1 Jan. 1809), 41–54.

162 *Gent. Mag.*, LXXVIII, ii (1808), 1044.

163 *Morning Chronicle*, 5 Nov. 1808.

164 See, for example, *Hull Packet*, 8 Nov. 1808; *Kentish Gazette*, 11 Nov. 1808; *Shrewsbury Chronicle*, 11 Nov. 1808; *York Herald*, 12 Nov. 1808; *Jackson's Oxford Journal*, 12 Nov. 1808; *Lancaster Gazette and General Advertiser*, 19 Nov. 1808; *Bury and Norwich Post*, 23 Nov. 1808.

165 Robert Aspland, *The duty and reward of sacrificing temporal interests on the altar of truth* (London, 1808); James Hews Bransby, *The Christian hero* (Birmingham, 1808); Thomas Belsham, *A sermon occasioned by the death of the Rev. Theophilus Lindsey, preached at the chapel in Essex Street, Strand* (London, 1808).

166 *MR*, III (1808), 637–42, IV (1809), 1–6. Cappe's memoir of Hannah Lindsey may be found in *MR*, VII (1812), 109–18.

167 *Memoirs of the life of the late Mrs Catharine Cappe. Written by herself* (London, 1822), chs. 14–20. There were further editions in 1823 and 1826.

commemorative, edition was commissioned in 1873. These works were consistent in the impression which they created of Lindsey as a man of conscience, principled and incorruptible, whose commitment to what he conceived to be religious truth was matched equally by the calm and emollient manner in which he expressed himself.

Already, however, there were doubts as to the extent of this idealization. Several readers of Belsham's biography thought that it carried admiration to excess. James Losh was 'struck with the overcharged Epithets applied to the good and amiable M^r. Lindsey – such as "venerable Patriarch", "eminent Confessor" and even "Prophet" – Epithets more calculated to produce a smile than to inspire respect.'[168] John Disney scrawled sardonic, derogatory comments over these 'epithets' in Belsham's work and thought the biography had, by its absurd exaggerations, wasted an excellent opportunity of commemorating Lindsey in a realistic and convincing way. Robert Hall's dismissal of Lindsey and his biographer have already been noted; but these critiques among Lindsey's fellow-unitarians were more serious. And indeed, Lindsey was a divisive figure within nineteenth-century unitarianism. There was tension between those who, like James Martineau, abandoned Lindsey's enlightenment coolness for a greater degree of spirituality inspired by romanticism, and those who, like Robert Spears, continued to regard Lindsey as a courageous pioneer to whose doctrinal principles his successors should remain faithful. The former almost completely overlooked Lindsey in their published work; the latter undertook pilgrimages to Catterick in his honour.[169]

Since 1900, perhaps slightly earlier, however, the unitarian movement in Britain and elsewhere has recognized Lindsey as its most important individual progenitor. If Priestley was its most original thinker, Lindsey was primarily responsible for its organizational existence and its doctrinal identity. When the congregation of Essex Street chapel, responding to the demographic changes which turned the area adjacent to the Strand into a commercial rather than a residential area, removed in 1887 to Kensington, where it joined a small existing unitarian congregation, it retained the name of Essex chapel. The original chapel building became Essex hall, the headquarters of what became the General Assembly of Unitarian and Free Christian Churches. Restored to full use after severe damage in the Second World War, it now houses a Lindsey room, and a plaque to Lindsey's memory adorns the entrance foyer.[170] In 2008, the bicentenary of Lindsey's death was commemorated with a service at Bunhill Fields, a study pack for unitarian congregations and a series of lectures.[171] Beyond unitarianism itself, increasing academic recognition of the importance of religion in eighteenth-century British society, led by scholars such as J. C. D. Clark, Jeremy Gregory, Colin Haydon, Peter Nockles, Anthony Page, Gina Luria Walker and David Wykes, has led to a revival of interest in Lindsey as a pivotal figure.[172] A recent historian of unitarianism has noted, justly, that 'Theophilus Lindsey was a religious pioneer and the unequivocal founder of Unitarianism in England'.[173] Yet he would not have been awarded this title had he not seceded

---

[168] Losh diary, 20 Apr. 1813.
[169] For a discussion of this theme, see G. M. Ditchfield, 'A unitarian saint? Theophilus Lindsey 1808–2008', *TUHS*, XXIV, 2 (Apr. 2008), 81–99.
[170] Mortimer Rowe, *The story of Essex Hall* (London, 1959). The publisher was the Lindsey Press.
[171] See *The Herald. The Journal of the Unitarian Christian Association*, LXVIII (Summer 2009).
[172] See also the article by Martin Fitzpatrick and John Stephens on Lindsey in *The Dictionary of Eighteenth-Century British Philosophers* (2 vols., Bristol and Sterling. VA, 1991), II, 554–7.
[173] Bowers, *Priestley and English unitarianism in America*, p. 25.

from the Church of England. A remark of a unitarian minister of the later nineteenth century enshrined a conclusion that was both accurate and succinct: 'it was for *his honestly coming out* that we honoured such a man as Lindsey'.[174] With or without the honour, it was his 'coming out' that gave historical significance to the man and to his letters.

---

[174] Marmaduke Charles Frankland (1815–88), minister of Chowbent chapel, Atherton, Lancashire, from 1852 to 1885, quoted in J. J. Wright, *The story of Chowbent chapel 1645–1721–1921* (Manchester, 1921), p. 87.

Short Biographies of Recipients of Lindsey's Letters in Volume II

Alexander, William (1763–1858)
He was born at Woodbridge, Suffolk, on 5 January 1763. His father was a shoe-maker and he was brought up to the same trade. He formed an early friendship with Samuel Say Toms, dissenting minister at Framlingham, who was evidently his first mentor and who probably encouraged him to contact Lindsey (Letter 546). In 1789, by which time he was a committed unitarian, Alexander opened a small school at Yoxford and his first surviving letter to Lindsey dates from that year. His refusal to teach the church catechism in his school, together with his lack of a licence as a dissenting schoolmaster, exposed him to the danger of prosecution. His letters to Lindsey do not survive, but it is evident that Lindsey advised him as to the best methods of proceeding. On 1 January 1793 (Letter 511), he warned Alexander against a tendency to 'simplicity and vehemence of expression against what you esteem wrong', and urged him 'to be cautious what you say and what you write'. It appears that Alexander heeded this advice. In 1794, he returned to Woodbridge, where he opened another school and a small bookshop. He remained in epistolary contact with Lindsey until at least 1801. In later life, he circulated unitarian publications and, according to his obituary in the *CR* (NS, XIV (1858), 189–90), he 'occasionally corresponded with some of the more eminent Unitarians at home and abroad'. He died at Great Yarmouth, to which town he had removed in 1809, on 28 January 1858, at the age of ninety-five. In 1830, the *MR* (2nd series, IV, 132) printed a short obituary notice of his elder daughter Anne Lindsey Alexander, describing her as 'a decided and unwavering Christian Unitarian'. It is likely that she was named after Theophilus Lindsey.

Astley, Thomas (1738–1817)
A student at Daventry and Warrington academies, Astley was a dissenting minister at Congleton, Cheshire, before undertaking the pastorate of a chapel at Chesterfield, where he remained from 1773 until 1813. There is one surviving letter from Lindsey to Astley in 1802 (Letter 736), but on 25 March 1804, Hannah Lindsey wrote to Astley's wife, Phoebe, née Wilkinson (*c*. 1774–1829) from Essex House about a possible meeting in London (Bodl., MS Eng. lett. c. 352, fos. 29–30). This was Phoebe Astley, of Chesterfield, who died at Chesterfield in 1829; Astley himself died on 15 October 1817 and there are biographical notices in *MR*, XII (1817), 688, and XIII (1818), 81.

Belsham, Thomas (1750–1829)
Although not mentioned in any of Lindsey's surviving letters before 1789, Belsham became one of his most important correspondents thereafter and his work became a vital source of information for Lindsey's life. He had access to many of Lindsey's papers and included extracts from his letters in *Memoirs of the late Reverend Theophilus Lindsey, M.A.*, which he published in London in 1812; a second edition

followed, and a centenary edition appeared in 1873, 100 years after Lindsey's resignation of Catterick. Belsham belonged to a dissenting family and was educated at Kibworth and Daventry academies, served briefly as a minister to a dissenting congregation at Worcester (1778–81) and was tutor and professor of divinity at Daventry, before becoming resident tutor and professor of divinity at Hackney College in 1789. He gradually developed doubts over the doctrine of the Trinity and described in his *Memoirs of Lindsey* (p. 93) how in January 1779 on a visit to London he attended evening worship at Essex Street chapel, presumably on his first visit there. Lindsey's sermon on that occasion, and some of Priestley's works, helped to convince him 'that it was *possible* for a Socinian to be a good man'. In 1794, he was nominated the successor to Priestley as minister to the Gravel Pit meeting at Hackney and in 1805, succeeded Disney as minister of Essex Street chapel, where he remained, with assistance, until his death on 11 November 1829. His brother William Belsham (1750–1829) was a noted historian. His sister Elizabeth became the second wife of Timothy Kenrick. Belsham shared Lindsey's theological and political opinions and was a member of the Revolution Society. 'What an excellent creature is he, and of what use likely to be in his station!', declared Lindsey in January 1790 (Letter 400).

Belsham was a prolific writer in defence of unitarianism and regarded himself as a custodian of Lindsey's heritage and memory. He became a friend of Augustus Henry, 3rd duke of Grafton, and won his support for several unitarian ventures, including the new translation of the New Testament, for which Belsham was the prime mover, in 1808. John Williams, in his *Memoirs of the late Reverend Thomas Belsham* (London, 1833), quotes extensively from his diaries. In September 1802, Priestley wrote to him: 'Now that Mr. Lindsey and myself are going off the stage, you will be looked up to as the principal support of the Unitarian cause' (Rutt, I, 491). Indeed, as R. K. Webb has observed, Belsham 'dominated the second generation of Unitarianism as a continuous denomination' (*ODNB*, V, 43), just as Lindsey had dominated the first.

Bretland, Joseph (1742–1819)
Born and raised in Exeter, Bretland became a leading presbyterian minister and teacher in that city. After studying at the Exeter Academy, he served as minister of the Mint meeting from 1770 to 1772, before devoting himself completely to teaching at his own school. Gradually adopting unitarian principles, he returned to the pastorate of the Mint meeting in 1789, and in 1794, left to become the co-minister of Timothy Kenrick at the George's meeting. In 1797, he retired from ministry altogether, after a series of disputes with his congregation. Although only one letter (dated 26 July 1790) from Lindsey to Bretland survives for the post-1788 period (Letter 420), and Lindsey referred to him relatively infrequently thereafter, he was widely respected for the breadth of his learning, and from 1799 until its closure in 1805, he was a tutor at the third Exeter Academy, in partnership with Kenrick.

Cadell, Thomas (1742–1802)
Usually known as Thomas Cadell the elder, Cadell, initially in partnership with Andrew Millar, to whom he was apprenticed in 1758, became one of London's leading booksellers in the later eighteenth century. Operating from premises at 141 The Strand, he worked, at various times, in partnership with Andrew Millar, William and Andrew Strahan and Thomas Davies. Although he did not publish any of Lind-

sey's works, he was a sympathizer with unitarianism and in 1783 he became one of the first trustees of Essex Street chapel and contributed £50 to the new building in *c.* 1785 (Vol. I, p. 568). He published the work of authors of markedly differing opinions, including those of Edward Gibbon, Samuel Johnson, Adam Smith and Tobias Smollett. Hence, Lindsey wrote in 1787 (Vol. I, Letter 346) that Cadell 'values books of all kinds according to their vent'. The historian John Whitaker commented of him 'Cadell is a true Swiss in publications, and fights only for pay' (R. Polwhele, *Reminiscences in prose and verse* (3 vols., London, 1836), I, 97). Hannah Lindsey recorded that he always referred to Lindsey as 'the Apostle John' (Letter 766). In 1793, Cadell retired and relinquished the business to his son Thomas Cadell the younger (1773–1836), who ran the firm as Cadell and Davies from 1793, in partnership with William Davies (d. 1820). The standard history of the firm is Theodore Besterman, *The publishing firm of Cadell & Davies. Select correspondence and accounts 1793–1836* (Oxford, 1938). There is only one, very brief, undated, surviving note from Lindsey to Cadell (Letter 783); it is likely that other letters between them have been lost.

Chadwick, Joseph (1751–1841)
From a west country family with general baptist connexions, Chadwick studied for the dissenting ministry at South Petherton and at Bridport, and for a short time was a pupil of Joshua Toulmin of Taunton. He was assistant minister, then sole minister, at Wellington, Somerset, between 1778 and 1785, and minister at Sherborne, Dorset, from 1785 to 1790. His final pastorate was that of a dissenting chapel at Oundle, Northamptonshire, and it was to Oundle that Lindsey addressed his three surviving letters to Chadwick (Letters 509, 541, 714). In 1818, Chadwick contributed to the *MR* a letter setting out the details of his nonconformist ancestry; his great-grandfather, Joseph Chadwick, MA, of Emmanuel College, Cambridge, had been ejected in 1662 from Winsford, Somerset; *MR*, XIII (1818), 233–5.

Davy, William (1757–1827)
Born at Crediton, Davy was the son of a woollen cloth manufacturer, and a member of an old dissenting family in Devonshire. In 1780, at Kidderminster, he married Susanna Broome, the daughter of a carpet manufacturer; they had seven children between 1786 and 1800. He emigrated to the United Sates and settled at Philadelphia in 1794, where he established himself as a merchant engaged in shipping goods across the Atlantic. In Philadelphia was soon on friendly terms with Priestley. In 1796, he became an American citizen. To Lindsey he was a useful contact and a conduit for the letters and unitarian literature which he forwarded to his friends in America. In 1816, Davy returned to England and served as United States consul at Hull and at Leeds. He died at Leeds in 1827. There is a letter from him to Timothy Kenrick, dated 22 May 1795, in W. Byng Kenrick, *Chronicles of a nonconformist family* (Birmingham, 1932), pp. 100–5.

Eaton, David (1771–1829)
Born at Brechin to a Scottish family, Eaton worked as a shoemaker in York, where he became the leading figure in a group of general baptists at York who adopted unitarian opinions. Eaton told their story in his *Scripture the only guide to religious truth* (1800). As a largely self-taught author, he quickly came to the attention of prominent unitarians, notably Charles Wellbeloved, minister of the St Saviourgate

congregation in York, and of Lindsey, both of whom gave him material and intellectual support. Subsequently, he set himself up as a bookseller in Holborn, and worked with other unitarians with general baptist origins, notably William Vidler and Robert Aspland. On Lindsey's death, he published *Lines sacred to the memory of the Rev. T. Lindsey, founder of Essex Street chapel, for the worship of one God* (London, 1808). There is a short account of his career, with particular respect to his years at York and his connexions with Charles Wellbeloved, in John Kenrick, *A biographical memoir of the late Rev. Charles Wellbeloved* (London, 1860), pp. 117–27, and an obituary appeared in *MR*, NS, III (1829), 357–8.

Evans, Thomas (1764–1833)

Born in Carmarthenshire, and from a family of weavers whose occupation he followed, Evans adopted the bardic name of Tomos Glyn Cothi, became friendly with Edward Williams (Iolo Morganwg) and adopted anti-trinitarian opinions through the preaching of David Davis of Castellhywel, which, as a young man, he would walk from Brechfa to Alltyblaca to hear. An admirer of Priestley, whose works he translated into Welsh, he himself was nicknamed 'Priestley bach', and named his son Joseph Priestley Evans. The spread of unitarianism in the area led to the application to Carmarthen of the label 'Y Smotyn Du' (the black spot). On 6 June 1792, Lindsey described Evans as 'a self taught unitarian in Wales, who had instructed many in the village he lived in, and brought them on so much, that … they were desirous and solicited assistance towards building them a place to assemble in' (Letter 501). It is apparent that Evans had approached Lindsey for funds for this purpose, and equally apparent that Lindsey had been very pleased to oblige. Evans's religious radicalism merged into his association with the bardic tradition and his theological radicalism. In 1801, he was imprisoned for two years on rather dubious evidence for allegedly singing a seditious song. Lindsey was sympathetic to his plight, although Hannah Lindsey in 1802 referred to his 'unsubdued resentful mind' and his 'high conceit of himself his talents, & title to distinction' (Letter 741). However, he achieved his ambition to become a unitarian minister, and from 1811, was pastor of the Old Meeting House in Aberdare. He died there on 29 January 1833. A key source for his career is Geraint H. Jenkins, '"A very horrid affair": sedition and unitarianism in the age of revolutions', in *From medieval to modern Wales. Historical essays in honour of Kenneth O. Morgan and Ralph A. Griffiths*, ed. R. R. Davies and Geraint H. Jenkins (Cardiff, 2004).

Freeman, James (1759–1835)

Born in Charlestown, Massachusetts, on 22 April 1759 and educated at Harvard, Freeman became reader, then minister, at King's chapel, Boston, where he served until his retirement in 1826. His appointment there was highly symbolic, since the King's chapel had been a pillar of episcopalianism and support for the British government during the War of American Independence. By the mid-1780s Freeman, although brought up in the Congregationalist tradition, had begun to adopt unitarian opinions, and at the same time began to correspond with Lindsey. He used an adaptation of Lindsey's *Book of Common Prayer reformed* in his chapel's worship. Only one letter from Lindsey to Freeman survives (Letter 603), but there are seventeen letters from Freeman to him, all highly informative as to early American unitarianism, in Dr Williams's Library, and in some cases published in Belsham, *Memoirs*. Lindsey was sufficiently impressed by Freeman's letters to forward one of them to

William Tayleur (Letter 456) and to quote extensively from another (Letter 582). Visiting Boston in 1795, Martha Russell, the daughter of Lindsey's friend William Russell, attended Freeman's chapel in Boston with her family and described it as 'a handsome, neat building', where Freeman 'has a very numerous and genteel congregation' (quoted in S. H. Jeyes, *The Russells of Birmingham in the French Revolution and in America 1791–1814* (London, 1911), p. 184). In 1804, Lindsey hoped to solicit support for his chapel from the duke of Grafton (Letter 761). As a Socinian and admirer of Lindsey and Priestley, Freeman was in a minority among liberal Christians in New England, but he has a strong claim to be regarded as one of the first, if not the first, of unitarian ministers in the United States.

Frend, William (1757–1841)

Born in Canterbury on 22 November 1757, Frend retained many connexions in Kent throughout his life. His father was an alderman, and twice mayor, of Canterbury and Frend himself was educated at the King's School in that city, before his entry to Christ's College, Cambridge, in 1776. He was ordained as deacon and priest in the Church of England, was nominated to two small livings near Cambridge and became a fellow of Jesus College in 1781. Frend first came to Lindsey's notice in 1787, when he attended Essex Street chapel, and a correspondence between them began the following year. His critique of subscription to the thirty-nine articles, while predictably attracting Lindsey's admiration, led to his deprivation from his college tutorship in 1788, and Lindsey's letters contain much information about his case. He and Lindsey were also collaborators in Priestley's proposal for a new translation of the Bible. They held different opinions, however, of the preamble to the Unitarian Society's rules in 1791, and Frend and several of his fellow anti-trinitarians in Cambridge withdrew from the society. Frend did not accept Lindsey's definition of the worship of Christ as 'idolatrous', although in political terms he went further than Lindsey in his association with the London Corresponding Society. In 1793, he published *Peace and union*, a strong attack on the British involvement in the war with revolutionary France, which resulted in his expulsion from Cambridge University (although not the loss of his college fellowship). To Lindsey, whose letters have much to say about Frend's 'trial' by the university authorities, this was a severe blow, since he looked to Frend and others of his type to be the leaders of reform within the church. After 1793, Frend, who had resigned his church livings in 1787, worked as an independent teacher in London, published on political and mathematical subjects and from 1806, was employed as actuary at the Rock Life Assurance Company. In later life, he was a close friend of the family of Lord Byron, and a supporter of the libertarian campaigns of Sir Francis Burdett. In 1808, he married Sara Blackburne, the grand-daughter of Archdeacon Francis Blackburne, and the niece of Hannah Lindsey. He died on London on 21 February 1841.

Hays, Mary (1759–1843)

The work of Gina Luria Walker has transformed our knowledge of the career and writings of Hays, and particularly the importance of heterodox dissent in her intellectual formation. See in particular *The idea of being free. A Mary Hays reader* (Toronto, 2006), *Mary Hays (1759–1843). The growth of a woman's mind* (Aldershot and Burlington, VT, 2006), and 'Energetic sympathies of truth and feeling: Mary Hays and rational dissent', in *Intellectual exchanges: women and rational dissent*, ed. Gina Luria Walker and G. M. Ditchfield, *E & D*, XXVI (2010). Hays soon established herself as one of the most significant female proponents of dissenting values. Lindsey admired her defence of social worship, under the pseudonym 'Eusebia', in reply to Gilbert Wakefield, and wrote to her in appreciation of her gift of a copy of her *Letters and essays* in 1793 (Letter 520). It appears, however, that he, and even more Hannah Lindsey, rather disapproved of her novel *Emma Courtenay*, published in 1796, which 'retails too much of the principles of Helvetius and other french writers, as well as Mr Godwin, all of whom she frequently quotes' (Letter 648). Although only one letter from Lindsey to Hays survives, Dr Williams's Library holds collections of correspondence between her and John Disney and Hugh Worthington. M. L. Brooks has edited *The correspondence of Mary Hays (1779–1843), British novelist* (Lewiston, 2004).

Hazlitt, William, senior (1737–1820)
He was minister at Noble Street, Wem, Shropshire, from 1787 until 1820, after a varied career as a dissenting minister at Wisbech and Maidstone, as well as in Ireland and in New England. Even before his ministry at Wem, his opinions were firmly unitarian, and it seemed for a short time in the later 1790s that his son of the same name, a former student at Hackney College and subsequently a distinguished author, would follow in his footsteps. Lindsey respected the elder Hazlitt and helped to secure the publication of his sermons (Letter 401), although he seems to have retained some doubts as to his temperament. Hazlitt senior died at Crediton, Devon, on 16 July 1820.

Kenrick, Timothy (1759–1804)
Kenrick's family were landowners in North Wales, with an estate at Wynn Hall, Denbighshire, and retained a long-standing commitment to nonconformity. Timothy Kenrick was educated at the Daventry Academy, and spent his entire ministerial career in Exeter, where he became assistant minister at George's meeting in 1784. He shared the unitarianism of Priestley and Belsham, and was instrumental in the foundation of the Western Unitarian Society, of which he was the first secretary, in 1792. Two years he married, as his second wife, Belsham's sister Elizabeth. He became involved in controversy in Exeter when some members of his congregation objected to his discussion of political subjects in his sermons, and when he declined to preach a fast sermon at the beginning of the war with revolutionary France in 1793. In each case, Lindsey endorsed his course of action, but suggested caution as to its implementation. Together with Joseph Bretland, he revived the Exeter Academy in 1799, but the enterprise did not long survive his sudden death on 22 August 1804. His eldest son John Kenrick became one of the most eminent of nineteenth-century unitarian ministers.

Lee, John (1733–93)
He continued his support and subscription to Essex Street chapel until the end of his life, although declining health limited his attendance there and in the house of commons. MP for Clitheroe from 1782 to 1790, he was unable to retain his seat at the general election of 1790 through the loss of his patron's influence. But in December 1790, he was returned for Earl Fitzwilliam's pocket borough of Higham Ferrers, and remained its MP until his death at his country estate of Staindrop, County Durham, on 5 August 1793. He was a consistent supporter of the parliamentary opposition and an admirer of Fox. Lee had been a friend of Priestley and

Lindsey from their years in Yorkshire during the later 1760s. In 1793, Lindsey described him as 'one from whose pleasant conversation you always rose up pleased and satisfied with so much that you wished to remember more than of any one I ever conversed with: and so says always Dr Priestley' (Letter 534). He published tributes to Lee in *Conversations on the divine government* (1802), p. 140, and in his preface (p. xvii) to Priestley's *Answer to Mr. Paine's Age of reason* (2nd edn, London, 1796). A portrait of Lee by Sir Joshua Reynolds is reproduced in E.K. Waterhouse, *Reynolds* (London, 1941), plate 262. There is a monument to him in Staindrop church; it is reproduced in Robert Surtees, *The history and antiquities of the county palatine of Durham*, IV (London, 1840), opp. p. 132. An informative and entertaining source for Lee's career as an attorney is *Lord Eldon's anecdote book*, ed. Anthony L. J. Lincoln and Robert Lindley McEwen (London, 1960). There is an appreciation of his unitarian commitment in *CL*, 26 Aug. 1876, p. 190. A former solicitor-general and attorney-general in 1782–3, he was one of Lindsey's most important political contacts.

Millar, Robert (1761–1841)
Born on 27 July 1761, Millar, the son of a farmer, developed a mercantile business in Dundee which specialized in the export of linen and sail-cloth; he evidently had interests and property in Russia (Letter 723). Although raised in the established Church of Scotland, he developed unitarian opinions through the influence of William Christie of Montrose, to whom he had been apprenticed in 1776. Lindsey's first surviving letter to him, dated 16 November 1793 (Letter 538), was clearly not the start of their correspondence, and they seem to have met in London some time earlier than that (Letter 413). In his letter to Lindsey of 4 December 1790, Millar expressed appreciation for Lindsey's 'kind attention shewn me when in London'. In Dundee, he assisted Thomas Fyshe Palmer in the formation of a small Unitarian Society, and after Palmer's arrest in 1793, the burden of leading the society fell upon him, even though he had no ministerial qualifications. His few extant letters to Lindsey have much to say about religious and political radicalism in his region of Scotland. Lindsey wrote frequently to Millar, as did Hannah Lindsey after 1801, and their main purpose was to bolster his morale in difficult times. Hannah Lindsey referred to his 'natural diffident temper' in 1804 (Letter 756). The letters appear to have succeeded; Millar survived near disaster in his business in the first few years of the nineteenth century and continued to preach to the Dundee congregation until the appointment of a full-time minister. In 1812, the unitarian missionary Richard Wright noted: 'At *Dundee*, there is still a small, but pious, liberal and affectionate congregation, which has been preserved for many years by the labours, and steady exertions of our worthy and respectable friend Mr. *R. Millar*. I preached four times in *Dundee* to full, and most of them crowded, congregations, who were deeply attentive. I was told that so many people never attended Unitarian preaching before in that town' (*MR*, VII (1812), 121). In 1817 Thomas Belsham told him 'I have often heard from my venerable friend Mr Lindsey of your meritorious & unwearied exertions to support the interest of christian truth in the populous town of Dundee' (DWL, MS 12.46 (4)). For all his financial vicissitudes, Millar possessed considerable status in Dundee: a commissioner of the property tax in 1804 (Letter 764), he was probably the Robert Millar who is listed in the *Caledonian Mercury* of 18 June 1801 as one of the managers of the Dundee infirmary. He died at Dundee on 12 June 1841, aged seventy-nine.

Neville, Sylas (1741–1840)

Best known as a diarist and man about town in the 1760s, with a series of radical dissenting connexions, Neville studied for his qualification as a physician at the University of Edinburgh in the early 1770s, although it seems that he never took a patient, let alone practised regularly. His one surviving letter to Lindsey (Letter 387), seeking an introduction to the duke of Norfolk, was characteristic of his place-seeking and social climbing. Among his dissenting friends was Caleb Fleming (1698–1779), the minister of the independent congregation at Pinner's Hall, London, and he was a close friend also of his fellow-physician Thomas Blackburne, the son of Archdeacon Francis Blackburne. See *The diary of Sylas Neville 1767–1788*, ed. B. Cozens-Hardy (Oxford, 1950), and G. M. Ditchfield, '"All truth, all righteous things"; the correspondence of Caleb Fleming and Sylas Neville, 1769–1776', *E & D*, XVIII (1999).

Priestley, Joseph (1733–1804)

Priestley was Lindsey's closest colleague in the evolution of unitarianism, and it is a matter for considerable regret that only one letter – and that a letter of which Lindsey was not sole author – from him to Priestley survives (Letter 555). Important clues about Lindsey's opinions, however, may be drawn from Priestley's letters to Lindsey, which survive in considerable quantities and which are frequently cited in this edition; and Lindsey's letters to other correspondents provide much biographical information about Priestley. Revealingly, Lindsey was interested only in Priestley's theological and historical writings, and took virtually no interest in his scientific researches.

Born at Fieldhead, in the parish of Birstall, near Leeds, Yorkshire, on 13 March 1733 (old style), Priestley was educated at Caleb Ashworth's academy at Daventry. On leaving Daventry his first ministerial appointment was as assistant minister to a small dissenting congregation at Needham Market, Suffolk, where his annual stipend was £30. In 1758, Priestley moved from Needham Market to a congregation at Nantwich, Cheshire; in 1761, he moved to Warrington Academy as tutor in languages and belles-lettres. In 1762, he married Mary Wilkinson, the sister of the iron merchants John and William Wilkinson. In 1767, he left Warrington to be minister of the prosperous dissenting congregation at Mill Hill, Leeds. In Yorkshire, he made acquaintance with Archdeacon Francis Blackburne, and met Lindsey, John Lee and William Turner of Wakefield. In June 1773, he became librarian and literary companion to Lord Shelburne, through the good offices of Richard Price. In June 1780, he left Shelburne and settled at Birmingham, where he became joint minister at the unitarian New Meeting. He usually spent one month each year in London (Rutt, I, 55) and thus could keep up his friendship with Lindsey. 'One is never tired of being with him', wrote Lindsey on 24 April 1784 (Vol. I, Letter 290).

After the destruction of Priestley's house, laboratory and chapel in the Birmingham riots of July 1791, Lindsey and his wife supported him in London, as he became the minister of the Gravel Pit meeting, Hackney, and gave lectures at Hackney College. Lindsey's letters describe his preparations for emigration to America in April 1794, and thereafter Lindsey supplied him with books and newspapers, edited his work for publication in London and retained, albeit with declining confidence, the hope that his friend would ultimately return to Britain. Instead, after residences at Philadelphia, Priestley made his home at Northumberland, Pennsylvania, and although his ambitious scheme for a unitarian college there came to nothing, he continued writing and publishing almost up to his death on 6 February 1804. The best summary of his career is that by David L. Wykes, 'Joseph Priestley, minister and teacher', in *Joseph Priestley. Scientist, philosopher and theologian*, ed. Isabel Rivers and David L. Wykes (Oxford, 2008). For aspects of his career which are particularly relevant to this edition, see J. D. Bowers, *Joseph Priestley and English unitarianism in America* (University Park, PA, 2007), and G. M. Ditchfield, '"The preceptor of nations": Joseph Priestley and Theophilus Lindsey', *TUHS*, XXIII, 2 (Apr. 2004). Among many tributes paid by Priestley to Lindsey was that of 19 June 1800: 'Your friendship is a balance to almost every thing, the most adverse' (Rutt, I, 441).

Rathbone, William (1757–1809)
The son of a prominent mercantile family in Liverpool, Rathbone was brought up as a member of the society of friends. He associated himself with liberal causes, notably the campaign for the abolition of the British slave trade, and he opposed the war with revolutionary France in the 1790s. By the beginning of that decade, he questioned several quaker teachings and forms of discipline, and gradually developed unitarian opinions. In 1792, he joined the Unitarian Society, and Lindsey's only surviving letter to him (Letter 500) expressed appreciation of his support for the unitarian petition of that year. Shortly thereafter he employed the former anglican clergyman Theophilus Houlbrooke, who, like Lindsey had resigned his church living because of his rejection of trinitarian theology, as the tutor to his sons. In 1804, Rathbone published a *Narrative* of the events surrounding the schism within the society of friends which had been occasioned by the views of Hannah Barnard; he strongly sympathized with her case.

Rowe, John (1764–1832)
The scion of an old dissenting family in the west country, Rowe was educated at the Hoxton and Hackney academies before his appointment as assistant minister at the High Street chapel, Shrewsbury, in 1787. Lindsey took a keen interest in his appointment and from 1790, wrote to him frequently; in 1788, he was impressed by Rowe's 'pious dispositions, his good sense, and zeal to be useful in the cause of divine truth' (Vol. I, Letter 374). He became Lindsey's correspondent in Shrewsbury after the death of William Tayleur, before moving to Bristol in 1798, where he became joint minister of Lewin's Mead chapel, Bristol, with John Estlin. He spent the remainer of his ministerial career there. He was a leading figure in the Western Unitarian Society, founded in 1792. He retired in 1832 and died on 2 July 1834, at Siena. He published several sermons. There is an informative memoir of Rowe by Robert Aspland in *CR*, NS, I (1834).

Scott, Russell (1761–1833)
By 1789, Scott had been minister at the High Street chapel, Portsmouth, for one year. His unitarian opinions suited the congregation well, despite some internal disagreements, over which Lindsey advised him. His congregation included the important family of Carter (a branch of which became Bonham-Carter). Lindsey regarded him as a particularly important correspondent, partly because his was an important voice in the west country, and partly because of his proximity to Thomas Fyshe Palmer and other reformers on board ship at Portsmouth immediately prior to their enforced departure for Australia in May 1794. None of Scott's letters to Lindsey is

extant, although it is clear from Lindsey's reply to them that he regarded Scott as something of a protégé, for example by providing him with copies of his manuscript sermons. His confidence in Scott was demonstrated by the latter's *rôle* as a witness to Lindsey's will, dated 17 June 1801. Although he published relatively little, he was much respected among unitarians well into the nineteenth century, and his grandson was C. P. Scott (1846–1932), of *Manchester Guardian* fame.

Scott, Sophia, née Hawes (1761–1828)
She was the daughter of the physician and eminent humanitarian reformer William Hawes (1736–1808), of Spital Square, London, the founder of the Humane Society. Her sister Maria (d. 1849) married the barrister John Gurney, to whom Lindsey referred frequently at the time of the treason trials in 1794. Sophia Scott married Russell Scott on 4 May 1790 and thereafter lived in Portsmouth, where she died on 24 April 1828. Lindsey knew her father's family, and met her and her husband during their visits to London. The letter which Hannah Lindsey wrote to her on 17 July 1793 (Letter 533), though brief, indicates that Sophia Scott was a committed unitarian who gave the fullest support to Russell Scott's long ministry at Portsmouth.

Shore, Samuel, III (1738–1828)
The eldest son of Samuel Shore II (1707–85), he was numbered the third Samuel Shore in a family which confusingly christened many of its male members Samuel. Lady Stephen's article 'The Shores of Sheffield and the Offleys of Norton Hall', *Transactions of the Hunter Archaeological Society*, V, i (Jan. 1938) helpfully sets out these and other details of the family. Through his marriage to Urith, daughter of Joseph Offley of Norton Hall, he acquired the Norton Hall estate, near Sheffield. His family were wealthy patrons of dissenting causes, particularly of unitarianism. Lindsey had regarded him as a valuable friend since the 1770s (Vol. I, Letter 205); he was one of the first trustees of Essex Street chapel in 1783, and a contributor of £100 in c. 1785 (Vol. I, p. 567). Lindsey came to know him well in the 1790s, when he acquired a residence at Clapham in addition to his Yorkshire estate. Although at times Lindsey thought him too cautious, as over the wording of the Unitarian society's preamble in 1791 and over the unitarian petition the following year (Letters 461, 497), the two remained on excellent terms. Shore spent his later years at Meersbrook House, Derbyshire, to which location Lindsey addressed letters to him during this period. His sister Hannah married the Manchester merchant Thomas Walker, whose reforming activities resulted in an indictment for treason (and acquittal) in 1794.

Simons, Thomas
Simons is the correspondent of Lindsey of whom least is known. Lindsey wrote to him on 4 May 1792, in reply to a letter from Simons, but otherwise seems never to have mentioned him. He is listed as a vintner, at Henrietta Street, Cavendish Square, in the parish of St Marylebone, in the *Universal British Directory* in 1791 (Letter 495, n. 1). He was the author of a pamphlet entitled *A letter to every housekeeper in London, on behalf of parochial industry schools, for every child who has no other opportunity of receiving any instruction in the several duties of life. From a citizen of the world* (London, 1792), and sent a copy to Lindsey. This occasioned Lindsey's only surviving letter to him. It is possible that he was the Thomas Simons who published *Moral education the one thing needful. Briefly recommended in four letters to a friend* (London, 1802).

Tayleur, William (1712–96)

Tayleur had been Lindsey's most frequent and confidential correspondent since 1775, and continued to be so until his death at his residence near Shrewsbury on 6 May 1796. To John Rowe, Lindsey wrote: 'I was happy in taking every opportunity of pouring out my mind and conversing with a friend of such wisdom, and candour and goodness and of so exact a judgment, cultivated with such general knowlege, as well as of the world he lived in' (Letter 637). Tayleur remained a benefactor of unitarian enterprises, to whom Lindsey knew he could always turn. In 1791, he made a substantial donation to the newly formed Unitarian Society, and Lindsey cited his authority when seeking to persuade members of the society to be bold in their theological radicalism (Letter 442). Tayleur was much respected for his withdrawal from the Church of England, for holding unitarian worship in his own home, and for sponsoring the use of Lindsey's *Book of Common Prayer reformed* at the High Street unitarian chapel in Shrewsbury. The survival of a set of his letters, some of them in draft form, to Lindsey, which form part of the Unitarian College Collection at John Rylands University Library, offer an interesting illustration of the elite lay support which helped to facilitate the emergence of unitarianism in the later eighteenth century.

Toulmin, Henry ('Harry') (1766–1823)

The eldest son of Joshua Toulmin, he was born at Taunton on 7 April 1766, and educated by his father and at Hoxton Academy, although subsequently he did not share his father's denial of the validity of infant baptism. Trained for a ministerial career, he had charge of two small congregations in Lancashire, Monton, from 1786 to 1788, and Chowbent, from 1787 to 1793. In the latter year, he and his chapel were attacked, although without serious injury or damage, by a loyalist mob, an incident described by Lindsey (Letter 516). Partly for this reason, Henry Toulmin emigrated to America, where he pursued a legal and political career of some distinction. He was president of the Transylvania seminary in Lexington, Kentucky, secretary of state for the commonwealth of Kentucky in 1796 and was appointed to a judgeship in Alabama (at that time known as the Mississippi territory) by Thomas Jefferson. Lindsey retained a solicitous interest in his progress. J. J. Wright's *The story of Chowbent chapel 1645–1721–1921* (Manchester, 1921), has a silhouette (right-hand profile) of Henry Toulmin (opposite p. 55).

Toulmin, Joshua (1740–1815)

Toulmin was an important representative of the general baptist element in the evolution of British unitarianism. A leading writer on its behalf, he assisted Lindsey on garnering signatures to the unitarian petition of 1792. Lindsey hoped that he would be the successor to Andrew Kippis at Princes Street chapel, Westminster, in 1795, since '[Toulmin] in many respects resembles D^r K, but is an Unitarian with more decision' (Letter 613). In the event, he remained minister of the Mary Street congregation from 1765 until January 1804, when he intrepidly accepted a call to the pastorate of New Meeting, Birmingham, Priestley's former congregation. During the 1790s at Taunton, he experienced much of the hostility shown to heterodox dissenters, and the bookshop which he operated with his wife Jane was attacked on more than one occasion. Among his numerous publications was a series of defences of Socinianism in response to the strictures of the particular baptist Andrew Fuller, together with a history of the town of Taunton, to which Lindsey was a subscriber. In most cases, Lindsey's letters to him survive only in the excerpted form printed in Belsham, *Memoirs*. For an excellent analysis of his career, see David L. Wykes, 'Joshua Toulmin (1740–1815) of Taunton: baptist minister, historian and religious radical', *Baptist Quarterly*, XXXIX, 5 (Jan. 2002).

Turner, William, of Newcastle upon Tyne (1761–1859)

Lindsey had known his father, William Turner, minister of Westgate chapel, Wakefield, since 1769. His correspondence with the elder Turner had faded, due to the latter's declining health, after 1785, but he regarded Turner of Newcastle as one of his most important correspondents and a rising hope of unitarianism. From 1782 until his retirement in 1841, the younger Turner was minister of the Hanover Square chapel in Newcastle, and a leading promoter of civic improvement in that city. He was active as the founder of a Sunday school, in campaigns for the repeal of the Test and Corporation Acts and the abolition of the slave trade, and as a founder of the Literary and Philosophical Society of Newcastle in 1793. He published extensively on a variety of theological, political, social and medical subjects. His eldest son William Turner III (1788–1853) became a tutor at Manchester College, York, and unitarian minister at Halifax, continuing a remarkable family tradition. A most important primary source for Turner's later career is the manuscript diary of James Losh, available for consultation at Carlisle Public Library. See also Stephen Harbottle, *The Reverend William Turner: dissent and Reform in Georgian Newcastle upon Tyne* (Leeds, 1997), and Joan Knott, 'The vestry library of the Hanover Square unitarian chapel, Newcastle upon Tyne', *Library History*, I, 5 (Spring 1969).

Wakefield, Gilbert (1756–1801)

Like Lindsey, Wakefield was a Cambridge-educated anglican clergyman who had been a fellow of his college (Jesus). He served briefly as a curate in Stockport, but quickly abandoned the clerical profession, took up school teaching in Liverpool and established a reputation as a classical and biblical scholar. Rejecting trinitarian orthodoxy, he became classical tutor at Warrington Academy in 1779, and remained there until the academy closed four years later. Subsequently, he took pupils in Nottingham, where he became friendly with the minister of the High Pavement congregation, George Walker, and published a series of scriptural analyses. He acquired a reputation for acerbity in debate, and as early as October 1781, Lindsey thought that, though 'ingenious', Wakefield 'seems hasty in his publications, and to write with too confident an air, and with too much vehemence for me' (Vol. I, Letter 237). In 1792, he deplored Wakefield's 'high-conceit of himself' (Letter 491). By then, Wakefield had been classical tutor at Hackney College for one year (between 1790 and 1791) and had provoked a pamphlet controversy with his *Enquiry into the expediency and propriety of public and social worship* (London, 1791), which claimed that public worship was not sanctioned by scripture, an opinion to which Lindsey, along with most heterodox dissenters, strongly disapproved. However, Lindsey admired Wakefield's talents and on occasion succumbed to his undoubted personal charm (Letters 407, 438). When Wakefield was imprisoned on a charge of sedition, following his attack on Bishop Watson's *Address to the people of Great Britain* in 1798, Lindsey wrote to him in Dorchester gaol (Letter 718) and did his best to succour him. Wakefield died shortly after his release, on 9 September 1801.

Wood, William (1745–1808)

Educated for the dissenting ministry under David Jennings in London and at the Hoxton Academy, where his tutors included Andrew Kippis and Abraham Rees, Wood served as minister to congregations at Stamford, Lincolnshire, and Ipswich, before succeeding Priestley as minister to the Mill Hill chapel, Leeds, in 1773, where he remained until his death. He took a leading *rôle* in Yorkshire during the campaign for the repeal of the Test and Corporation Acts in 1789–90; and became a close friend of Charles Wellbeloved, whom he assisted when the latter became principal of Manchester College after its removal to York in 1803. Lindsey's one surviving letter to him (Letter 715) gave particular praise to two of his sermons, at the turn of the century. In addition to his preaching and publishing work, Wood was a gifted botanist. He died at Leeds on 1 April 1808; there is a published *Memoir* of him by Charles Wellbeloved (1809) and a tribute from Christopher Wyvill (Wyvill, *Politucal papers*, VI, 67). His eldest son, George William Wood (1781–1843), was elected MP for South Lancashire in 1832.

Wyvill, Christopher (1738–1822)

A member of a well-established landowning family in Yorkshire, Wyvill secured through marriage the estate of Constable Burton, near Bedale, and close to Lindsey's parishes of Kirkby Wiske and Catterick. Educated at Queens' College, Cambridge, Wyvill took holy orders and served as non-resident rector of Black Notley, Essex, until his resignation of the rectory in 1806. He was a signatory to the Feathers Tavern petition in 1772 and, although apparently assuring Lindsey that he would resign from the church in the event of its rejection, did not do so (Cappe, *Memoirs*, p. 150). From 1779 to 1780, he became the leading figure in the Yorkshire Association and the county-based movement for economical and parliamentary reform. In the 1790s, he argued strongly for moderate parliamentary reform as a prophylactic against revolution. He and Lindsey corresponded fairly frequently in that decade, and Wyvill drew upon some of Lindsey's ideas in his campaigns for 'universal toleration' after 1807. An essential source for his career in this period is John Dinwiddy, *Christopher Wyvill and reform 1790–1820* (Borthwick paper no. 39, York, 1971).

Wyvill, Sarah, née Codling (d. after 1822)

She was the second wife of Christopher Wyvill; they were married on 9 August 1787, four years after the death of Wyvill's first wife, his cousin Elizabeth Wyvill. There were no children from Wyvill's first marriage, but he and Sarah had three sons and three daughters. Lindsey referred more than once to their 'lovely family' (Letters 616, 661, 662). In December 1807, Hannah Lindsey wrote to thank her and her husband for an 'ample kind supply of Christmas fare' (Letter 780).

Editorial Note

As with the first volume of Theophilus Lindsey's letters, I have followed the editorial principles explained and applied in Dr Sarah Brewer's edition of *The early letters of Bishop Richard Hurd 1739–1762*, published in 1995, which formed volume III of the Church of England Record Society's series. I have done my best to emulate the very high scholarly standard set by Dr Brewer.

It is necessary to outline here four specific problems presented by the letters of Lindsey which appear in Volume II.

First, although before 1789 Hannah Lindsey occasionally wrote letters on her husband's behalf when he was ill or exceptionally busy, she did so much more frequently as his health deteriorated after 1800 and she took over the task completely after 1803. As with Volume I, I have included here letters from Hannah Lindsey which were written for him, often in his presence and incorporating his suggestions, and which clearly reflected their joint opinion. I have excluded the letters which she wrote independently to members of her family, although I have drawn upon them in the notes and in the introduction when they illuminate Lindsey's life, opinions and career. In common with all letter-writers, Hannah Lindsey had her own peculiarities of style, which in a few necessary cases are explained in the notes.

Secondly, an important correspondent of Lindsey after 1788 was William Alexander of Yoxford, Suffolk. The manuscripts of his letters to Lindsey have, it seems, not survived, but the thirty-three surviving letters from Lindsey to him are included in this edition. However, the only extant versions of these letters are those published in extract form in the *Unitarian Herald*. It is obvious that they have been heavily edited, although there is no indication as to the identity of the editor or editors. It is possible that they were edited by the unitarian historian Alexander Gordon, who prepared for publication in *Christian Life* several letters from Lindsey to William Tayleur, between 1784 and 1787, which are included in Volume I of this edition, but this must remain a conjecture. To some extent a similar reservation applies to the letters from Lindsey to William Hazlitt senior and to Henry Toulmin, which survive only in the form in which they appear in the *Christian Reformer*, but in these instances, there was almost certainly far less contraction of the original text than with the letters to William Alexander.

Thirdly, Appendix I contains letters of Lindsey which belong chronologically to Volume I. There is one complete letter (to Newcome Cappe, July 1788; Letter 374A), together with complete versions of letters which appeared only in part in Volume I (Letters 69 and 89). In each case, the only surviving text is a handwritten copy, and the editor, with what was probably an excess of fastidiousness, excluded them from Volume I because of doubts over the accuracy of the copies. For the sake of completeness, they are included in Appendix I of the present volume, together with an indication of the existence of accurate copies of two letters of Lindsey (Letters 155 and 244) which, from manuscripts in Lindsey's own hand, are printed in full in Volume I.

Fourthly, it is well known that many letters written by Lindsey were destroyed during his lifetime or immediately after his death. Reference has been made in

Volume I to the destruction of his letters to Joseph Priestley. Volume II includes only one letter to Priestley, written by Lindsey and colleagues among the Unitarian Society, in 1794. Indeed, in December 1791, Lindsey approved of the destruction of one of his more confidential letters to William Tayleur (Letter 480). A very large proportion of the letters to Lindsey suffered a similar fate. In December 1808, Jeremiah Joyce burned those of Lindsey's incoming letters which he deemed 'chiefly political'. The process of destruction seems to have been begun by Lindsey himself. Writing to Thomas Belsham on 24 July 1804, Hannah Lindsey, citing her husband's evident modesty, explained how,

> In looking over a mass of letters to find all we have of Dr Priestley a good job will be accomplished of committing to the flames many precious morsels, of various excellent men, correspondents of Mr Lindsey's most of them gone to sleep, and so peculiar to himself & detached from general use, that he chuses not to leave them behind him, least those who think better of him than he does of himself should give them to the public. (Letter 761)

Catharine Cappe took the process further when admitting that she destroyed many letters to Hannah Lindsey on the latter's death, and at her wish, in 1812. In some cases, letters to Lindsey were quoted in part by J. T. Rutt and Thomas Belsham, but the majority of them seem not to have survived – an expression which occurs too often in this edition. A significant exception, however, is the collection of letters from Priestley to Lindsey, together with a small number to Belsham. Most of these letters are held at Dr Williams's Library, in two large boxes, MS 12.12 and MS 12.13. It is necessary to point out that MS 12.12 is foliated and that the edition of the letters contained therein and available via the website prepared by Simon Mills for the Centre for Dissenting Studies takes full account of the folio numbers. By contrast, MS 12.13 (containing Priestley's letters to Lindsey and to Thomas Belsham written between 15 June 1794 and 23 December 1803) is unfoliated. Accordingly, when citing in notes letters from MS 12.13 I have been able to give the dates of the letters only. Consultation of them, however, is not a problem, since the letters in both MS 12.12 and 12.13 are arranged in chronological order.

List of Lindsey's Letters in Volume II (381–783)

No.	Date	Recipient	Source

1789

No.	Date	Recipient	Source
381.	29 Jan.	William Tayleur	JRUL
382.	31 Jan.	William Frend	CUL
383.	2 Feb.	William Turner of Newcastle	DWL
384.	6 Mar.	William Frend	CUL
385.	13 Mar.	William Frend	CUL
386.	11 Apr.	William Alexander	*UH*
387.	23 Apr.	Sylas Neville	Norfolk RO
388.	3 July	Russell Scott	Scott Coll.
389.	8 Aug.	William Alexander	*UH*
390.	10 Aug.	William Frend	CUL
391.	31 Aug.	William Hazlitt senior	*CR*
392.	5 Sept.	Henry Toulmin	*CR*; and *TUHS*
393.	12 Sept.	William Alexander	*UH*
394.	3 Oct.	William Turner of Newcastle	DWL
395.	17 Oct.	William Turner of Newcastle	DWL
396.	23 Oct.	Joshua Toulmin	Belsham, *Memoirs*
397.	27 Oct.	Henry Toulmin	*CR*
398.	14 Nov.	William Frend	CUL
399.	8 Dec.	William Turner of Newcastle	DWL

1790

No.	Date	Recipient	Source
400.	2 Jan.	William Frend	CUL
401.	2 Jan.	William Hazlitt senior	*CR*
402.	4 Jan.	Russell Scott	Scott Coll.
403.	14 Jan.	William Frend	CUL
404.	15 Jan.	William Turner of Newcastle	DWL
405.	7 Feb.	Russell Scott	Scott Coll.
406.	10 Feb.	William Tayleur	JRUL
407.	18 Mar.	William Frend	CUL
408.	31 Mar.	John Rowe	JRUL
409.	22 Apr.	William Frend	CUL
410.	1 May	William Alexander	*UH*
411.	4 May	William Turner of Newcastle	DWL
412.	7 May	William Tayleur	JRUL
413.	15 May	William Tayleur	JRUL
414.	27 May	Russell Scott	Scott Coll.
415.	29 May	William Alexander	*UH*
416.	31 May	William Frend	CUL

417.	9 June	William Frend	CUL
418.	14 July	William Frend	CUL
419.	19 July	William Frend	CUL
420.	26 July	Joseph Bretland	Rutt
421.	26 July	William Frend	CUL
422.	14 Aug.	Russell Scott	Scott Coll.
423.	15 Aug.	William Alexander	*UH*
424.	25 Aug.	William Frend	CUL
425.	13 Sept.	William Frend	CUL
426.	20 Sept.	William Tayleur	JRUL
427.	5 Oct.	William Tayleur	Royal Soc.
428.	2 Nov.	William Frend	CUL
429.	10 Nov.	William Frend	CUL
430.	10 Nov.	William Tayleur	JRUL
431.	23 Nov.	William Alexander	*UH*
432.	24 Dec.	William Tayleur	JRUL
433.	30 Dec.	William Frend	CUL

1791

434.	22 Jan.	William Tayleur	JRUL
435.	3 Feb.	William Tayleur	JRUL
436.	3 Feb.	William Tayleur	JRUL
437.	9 Feb.	William Tayleur	JRUL
438.	14 Feb	William Frend	CUL
439.	22 Feb.	Russell Scott	Scott Coll.
440.	23 Feb.	William Tayleur	JRUL
441.	1 Mar.	William Tayleur	JRUL
442.	12 Mar.	William Frend	CUL
443.	12 Mar.	William Tayleur	JRUL
444.	22 Mar.	William Tayleur	JRUL
445.	24 Mar.	Russell Scott	Scott Coll.
446.	26 Mar.	Thomas Belsham	DWL
447.	2 Apr.	William Tayleur	JRUL
448.	9 Apr.	William Tayleur	JRUL
449.	14 Apr.	William Tayleur	JRUL
450.	23 Apr.	William Frend	CUL
451.	27 Apr.	William Tayleur	JRUL
452.	7 May	William Tayleur	JRUL
453.	12 May	*Russell Scott	Scott Coll.
454.	12 May	William Turner of Newcastle	LPN
455.	13 May	Russell Scott	Scott Coll.
456.	21 May	William Tayleur	JRUL
457.	7 June	William Tayleur	JRUL
458.	18 June	William Tayleur	JRUL
459.	27 June	William Tayleur	JRUL
460.	11 July	Thomas Belsham	Williams
461.	15 July	William Tayleur	JRUL
462.	16 July	William Tayleur	JRUL

463.	19 July	Russell Scott	Scott Coll.
464.	19 July	William Tayleur	Royal Soc.
465.	20 July	William Tayleur	Royal Soc.
466.	21 July	*Russell Scott	Scott Coll.
467.	23 July	Samuel Shore III [copy]	DWL
468.	30 July	William Tayleur	JRUL
469.	4 Aug.	William Tayleur	Royal Soc.
470.	14 Aug.	Samuel Shore III [copy]	DWL
471.	16 Aug.	Samuel Shore III	DWL
472.	12 Sept.	William Tayleur	JRUL
473.	19 Sept.	William Tayleur	JRUL
474.	26 Sept.	Samuel Shore III	DWL
475.	15 Oct.	William Tayleur	JRUL
476.	15 Oct.	William Alexander	*UH*
477.	19 Oct.	William Tayleur	JRUL
478.	6 Nov.	William Tayleur	JRUL
479.	7 Nov.	Samuel Shore III	DWL
480.	3 Dec.	William Tayleur	JRUL
481.	31 Dec.	Russell Scott	Scott Coll.

1792

482.	5 Jan.	William Tayleur	JRUL
483.	7 Jan.	Samuel Shore III	NYRO
484.	4 Feb.	Russell Scott	Scott Coll.
485.	15 Feb.	William Tayleur	JRUL
486.	21 Feb.	Russell Scott	Scott Coll.
487.	27 Feb.	William Tayleur	JRUL
488.	6 Mar.	John Rowe	JRUL
489.	9 Mar.	Russell Scott	Scott Coll.
490.	26 Mar.	William Tayleur	JRUL
491.	26 Mar.	William Turner of Newcastle	DWL
492.	11 Apr.	William Tayleur	JRUL
493.	13 Apr.	William Frend	CUL
494.	19 Apr.	Christopher Wyvill	NYRO
495.	4 May	Thomas Simons	JRUL
496.	4 May	William Turner of Newcastle	DWL
497.	4 May	Christopher Wyvill	NYRO
498.	5 May	William Tayleur	JRUL
499.	29 May	Timothy Kenrick	UCL
500.	4 June	William Rathbone	Liverpool University Library
501.	6 June	William Tayleur	JRUL
502.	7 June	William Alexander	*UH*
503.	14 June	William Turner of Newcastle	DWL
504.	16 June	Timothy Kenrick	UCL
505.	25 June	William Tayleur	Royal Soc.
506.	26 June	Russell Scott	Scott Coll.
507.	25 Oct.	Russell Scott	Scott Coll.

508.	1 Dec.	John Rowe	JRUL
509.	5 Dec.	Joseph Chadwick	DWL
510.	11 Dec.	William Alexander	*UH*

1793

511.	1 Jan.	William Alexander	*UH*
512.	7 Feb.	William Alexander	*UH*
513.	7 Feb.	Christopher Wyvill	NYRO
514.	8 Feb.	William Tayleur	JRUL
515.	9 Mar.	Russell Scott	Scott Coll.
516.	26 Mar.	Russell Scott	Scott Coll.
517	30 Mar.	William Tayleur	JRUL
518.	6 Apr.	Timothy Kenrick	UCL
519.	13 Apr.	William Alexander	*UH*
520.	15 Apr.	Mary Hays	DWL
521.	15 Apr.	John Rowe	JRUL
522.	17 Apr.	Russell Scott	Scott Coll.
523.	1 May	*Russell Scott	Scott Coll.
524.	6 May	William Alexander	*UH*
525.	?May	Trustees of Essex Street chapel	Belsham, *Memoirs*
526.	7 May	John Rowe	JRUL
527.	10 May	William Tayleur	JRUL
528.	13 June	'A friend'	Belsham, *Memoirs*
529.	22 June	John Lee	William L. Clements Library, Ann Arbor, Michigan
530.	1 July	*Russell Scott	Scott Coll.
531.	8 July	William Tayleur	JRUL
532.	8 July	Joshua Toulmin	Belsham, *Memoirs*
533.	17 July	*Sophia Scott	Scott Coll.
534.	18 July	William Tayleur	JRUL
535.	5 Aug.	William Tayleur	JRUL
536.	9 Sept.	William Turner of Newcastle	DWL
537.	21 Oct.	William Alexander	*UH*
538.	16 Nov.	Robert Millar	DWL
539.	2 Dec.	William Tayleur	JRUL
540.	14 Dec.	Joshua Toulmin	Belsham, *Memoirs*
541.	17 Dec.	Joseph Chadwick	DWL

1794

542.	10 Jan.	Joshua Toulmin	Belsham, *Memoirs*
543.	post-10 Jan.	Joshua Toulmin	Belsham, *Memoirs*
544.	13 Jan.	Robert Millar	DWL
545.	16 Jan.	Christopher Wyvill	NYRO
546.	20 Jan.	William Alexander	*UH*
547.	24 Jan.	Russell Scott	Scott Coll.
548.	27 Jan.	Robert Millar	DWL

549.	8 Feb.	William Tayleur	JRUL
550.	8 Feb.	Joshua Toulmin	Belsham, *Memoirs*
551.	20 Feb.	Joshua Toulmin	Belsham, *Memoirs*
552.	8 Mar.	Joshua Toulmin	Belsham, *Memoirs*
553.	13 Mar.	Timothy Kenrick	UCL
554.	15 Mar.	William Alexander	*UH*
555.	18 Mar.	Joseph Priestley [from Lindsey and the Unitarian Society]	Rutt; and Unitarian Society minute book
556.	21 Mar.	William Alexander	*UH*
557.	24 Mar.	William Turner of Newcastle	DWL
558.	25 Mar.	**Russell Scott	Scott Coll.
559.	28 Mar.	Russell Scott	Scott Coll.
560.	30 Mar.	William Tayleur	JRUL
561.	4 Apr.	Russell Scott	Scott Coll.
562.	8 Apr.	Russell Scott	Scott Coll.
563.	10 Apr.	Russell Scott	Scott Coll.
564.	10 Apr.	William Tayleur	JRUL
565.	14 Apr.	Russell Scott	Scott Coll.
566.	17 Apr.	Robert Millar	DWL
567.	17 Apr.	Russell Scott	Scott Coll.
568.	19 Apr.	William Tayleur	JRUL
569.	22 Apr.	Russell Scott	Scott Coll.
570.	25 Apr.	Russell Scott	Scott Coll.
571.	1 May	Russell Scott	Scott Coll.
572.	2 May	Robert Millar	DWL
573.	3 May	?Joshua Toulmin	Belsham, *Memoirs*
574.	6 May	Russell Scott	Scott Coll.
575.	17 May	William Tayleur	JRUL
576.	29 May	William Tayleur	JRUL
577.	2 June	Russell Scott	Scott Coll.
578.	10 June	William Turner of Newcastle	DWL
579.	10 June	William Alexander	*UH*
580.	30 June	Russell Scott	Scott Coll.
581.	30 June	William Tayleur	JRUL
582.	1 Aug.	William Tayleur	JRUL
583.	13 Sept.	John Rowe	JRUL
584.	29 Sept.	William Tayleur	JRUL
585.	20 Oct.	William Alexander	*UH*
586.	8 Nov.	Joshua Toulmin	Belsham, *Memoirs*
587.	9 Nov.	William Turner of Newcastle	LPN
588.	27 Nov.	Russell Scott	Scott Coll.
589.	8 Dec.	William Tayleur	JRUL
590.	9 Dec.	Robert Millar	DWL
591.	10 Dec.	William Tayleur	JRUL
592.	15 Dec.	?Joshua Toulmin	Belsham, *Memoirs*
593.	16 Dec.	Russell Scott	Scott Coll.

1795

594.	7 Jan.	William Turner of Newcastle	LPN
595.	23 Jan.	John Rowe	JRUL
596.	26 Jan.	William Alexander	*UH*
597.	5 Feb.	Russell Scott	Scott Coll.
598.	7 Feb.	Robert Millar	DWL
599.	16 Feb.	Russell Scott	Scott Coll.
600.	3 Mar.	William Alexander	*UH*
601.	10 Mar.	William Tayleur	JRUL
602.	14 Mar.	Russell Scott	Scott Coll.
603.	23 Mar.	James Freeman	Historical Society of Pennsylvania
604.	30 Apr.	Russell Scott	Scott Coll.
605.	2 May	William Tayleur	*CL*
606.	23 May	Russell Scott	Scott Coll.
607.	25 May	William Tayleur	JRUL
608.	21 June	Russell Scott	Scott Coll.
609.	26 June	John Rowe	JRUL
610.	26 June	William Tayleur	JRUL
611.	27 June	William Alexander	*UH*
612.	16 Sept.	William Tayleur	JRUL
613.	26 Oct.	John Rowe	JRUL
614.	31 Oct.	Russell Scott	Scott Coll.
615.	4 Dec.	Russell Scott	Scott Coll.
616.	7 Dec.	Christopher Wyvill	NYRO
617.	14 Dec.	William Tayleur	JRUL
618.	19 Dec.	Robert Millar	DWL
619.	27 Dec.	William Tayleur	JRUL
620.	29 Dec.	William Alexander	*UH*
621.	30 Dec.	Russell Scott	Scott Coll.

1796

622.	4 Jan.	Christopher Wyvill	NYRO
623.	8 Jan.	To Russell Scott	Scott Coll.
624.	7 Mar.	William Tayleur	JRUL
625.	9 Mar.	John Rowe	JRUL
626.	23 Mar.	William Alexander	*UH*
627.	6 Apr.	John Rowe	JRUL
628.	7 Apr.	Christopher Wyvill	NYRO
629.	18 Apr.	William Tayleur	JRUL
630.	29 Apr.	*Russell Scott	Scott Coll.
631.	2 May	John Rowe	JRUL
632.	10 May	John Rowe	JRUL
633.	16 May	Russell Scott	Scott Coll.
634.	23 May	Christopher Wyvill	NYRO
635.	30 May	Robert Millar	DWL
636.	10 June	John Rowe	JRUL

637.	29 June	John Rowe	JRUL
638.	1 July	Russell Scott	Scott Coll.
639.	26 July	Thomas Belsham	DWL
640.	9 Aug.	Thomas Belsham	DWL
641.	11 Aug.	Robert Millar	DWL
642.	5 Oct.	Robert Millar	DWL
643.	7 Oct.	John Rowe	JRUL
644.	20 Oct.	William Turner of Newcastle	DWL
645.	12 Nov.	Russell Scott	Scott Coll.
646.	19 Nov.	Robert Millar	DWL
647.	10 Dec.	Robert Millar	DWL
648.	23 Dec.	John Rowe	Royal Soc.

1797

649.	27 Jan.	William Alexander	*UH*
650.	21 Feb.	Robert Millar	DWL
651.	3 Mar.	Robert Millar	DWL
652.	28 Apr.	William Alexander	*UH*
653.	29 Apr.	Russell Scott	Scott Coll.
654.	1 May	?William Turner of Newcastle	DWL
655.	17 May	Russell Scott	Scott Coll.
656.	1 June	William Davy	DWL
657.	12 June	Samuel Shore III	DWL
658.	1 July	Russell Scott	Scott Coll.
659.	25 July	Robert Millar	DWL
660.	12 Aug.	Russell Scott	Scott Coll.
661.	5 Nov.	Christopher Wyvill	NYRO
662.	9 Nov.	Christopher Wyvill	NYRO
663.	27 Nov.	John Rowe	JRUL
664.	13 Dec.	Christopher Wyvill	NYRO
665.	14 Dec.	John Rowe	JRUL

1798

666.	27 Jan.	William Alexander	*UH*
667.	13 Feb.	John Rowe	JRUL
668.	17 Feb.	Thomas Evans	*UH*
669.	22 Feb.	Russell Scott	Scott Coll.
670.	27 Feb.	Russell Scott	Scott Coll.
671.	21 May	William Alexander	*UH*
672.	2 July	William Turner of Newcastle	DWL
673.	1 Aug.	Thomas Belsham	DWL
674.	10 Sept.	Thomas Belsham	DWL
675.	15 Oct.	John Rowe	Yale
676.	22 Nov.	William Turner of Newcastle	LPN
677.	30 Nov.	*Russell Scott	Scott Coll.

1799

678.	14 Jan.	Russell Scott	Scott Coll.
679.	31 Jan.	Russell Scott	Scott Coll.
680.	22 Feb.	Thomas Evans	NLW
681.	1 Apr.	William Turner of Newcastle	DWL
682.	16 July	Thomas Belsham	DWL
683.	13 Aug.	Thomas Belsham	DWL
684.	5 Oct.	John Rowe	JRUL
685.	11 Nov.	John Rowe	JRUL

1800

686.	6 Jan.	David Eaton	Eaton, *Scripture, the only guide*
687.	7 Jan.	Robert Millar	DWL
688.	28 Jan.	John Rowe	JRUL
689.	22 Feb.	Russell Scott	Scott Coll.
690.	15 Mar.	Robert Millar	DWL
691.	18 Mar.	William Turner of Newcastle	DWL
692.	24 Apr.	Robert Millar	DWL
693.	1 May	William Alexander	*UH*
694.	10 May	Robert Millar	DWL
695.	18 June	William Davy	DWL
696.	30 June	Robert Millar	DWL
697.	7 July	William Turner of Newcastle	DWL
698.	17 July	Thomas Belsham	DWL
699.	30 July	Robert Millar	DWL
700.	31 July	Thomas Belsham	DWL
701.	7 Aug.	Thomas Belsham	DWL
702.	18 Aug.	Thomas Belsham	DWL
703.	26 Aug.	Thomas Belsham	DWL
704.	15 Sept.	Thomas Belsham	DWL
705.	3 Oct.	Thomas Belsham	DWL
706.	24 Oct.	William Frend	CUL
707.	10 Nov.	John Rowe	JRUL
708.	13 Nov.	Robert Millar	DWL
709.	23 Nov.	Christopher Wyvill	NYRO
710.	9 Dec.	William Alexander	*UH*
711.	12 Dec.	Robert Millar	DWL

1801

712.	2 Feb.	Robert Millar	DWL
713	3 Feb.	William Davy	DWL
714.	10 Feb.	Joseph Chadwick	DWL
715.	19 Feb.	William Wood	Wood
716.	21 Feb.	Robert Millar	DWL
717.	19 Mar.	Robert Millar	DWL

718.	14 Apr.	Gilbert Wakefield	DWL
719.	2 May	Russell Scott	Scott Coll.
720.	28 May	William Alexander	*UH*
721.	3 June	Robert Millar	DWL
722.	10 June	*William Alexander	*UH*
723.	16 June	Robert Millar	DWL
724.	16 June	Christopher Wyvill	NYRO
725.	30 June	William Davy	DWL
726.	30 July	Robert Millar	DWL
727.	9 Aug.	William Frend	CUL
728.	16 Aug.	Russell Scott	Scott Coll.
729.	26 Aug.	Robert Millar	DWL
730.	29 Sept.	Robert Millar	DWL
731.	21 Nov.	Robert Millar	DWL

1802

732.	20 Jan.	*Robert Millar	DWL
733.	25 Feb.	*Robert Millar	DWL
734.	27 Mar.	*Robert Millar	DWL
735.	20 May	Robert Millar	DWL
736.	11 June	Thomas Astley	Bodl.
737.	30 July	Christopher Wyvill	NYRO
738.	25 Aug.	Thomas Belsham	DWL
739.	28 Aug.	Robert Millar	DWL
740.	5 Sept.	Robert Millar	DWL
741.	27 Sept.	Thomas Belsham	DWL
742.	8 Oct.	Robert Millar	DWL
743.	26 Oct.	*Thomas Belsham	DWL
744.	4 Dec.	**Robert Millar	DWL

1803

745.	4 Jan.	*William Turner of Newcastle	LPN
746.	18 Jan.	Timothy Kenrick	UCL
747	12 Mar.	*Robert Millar	DWL
748.	5 July	**Thomas Belsham	DWL
749.	11 July	**Christopher Wyvill	NYRO
750.	16 July	**Thomas Belsham	DWL
751.	23 July	**Thomas Belsham	DWL
752.	29 July	**Robert Millar	DWL
753.	8 Aug.	**Christopher Wyvill	NYRO
754.	2 Sept.	**Thomas Belsham	DWL
755.	26 Dec.	**Robert Millar	DWL

1804

| 756. | 5 Mar. | **Robert Millar | DWL |
| 757. | 7 Mar. | *Robert Millar | DWL |

758.	31 Mar.	**Timothy Kenrick	UCL
759.	14 Apr.	**Robert Millar	DWL
760.	12 May	**Christopher Wyvill	NYRO
761.	24 July	**Thomas Belsham	DWL
762.	6 Aug.	**Thomas Belsham	DWL
763.	12 Aug.	**Thomas Belsham	DWL
764.	20 Aug.	**Robert Millar	DWL
765.	24 Aug.	**Thomas Belsham	DWL
766.	1 Sept.	**Thomas Belsham	DWL
767.	29 Nov.	**Robert Millar	DWL
768.	13 Dec.	**Robert Millar	DWL
769.	n.d., post- 7 Apr. 1804	**Robert Millar	DWL

1805

770.	5 Apr.	**Thomas Belsham	DWL
771.	15 Apr	**Thomas Belsham	Williams
772.	1 May	**Robert Millar	DWL
773.	20 Dec.	**Robert Millar	DWL

1806

774.	19 Feb.	**Robert Millar	DWL
775.	28 July	**Robert Millar	DWL
776.	8 Oct.	**Christopher Wyvill	NYRO

1807

777.	10 Apr.	**Robert Millar	DWL
778.	10 Aug.	**Robert Millar	DWL
779.	25 Nov.	**Robert Millar	DWL
780.	28 Dec.	**Sarah Wyvill	NYRO

1808

| 781. | 8 Mar. | *Russell Scott | Scott Coll. |
| 782. | 20 Aug. | **Thomas Belsham | DWL |

UNDATED LETTER

| 783. | 14 Sept. [no year] | Thomas Cadell | JRUL |

THE LETTERS

Text: JRUL, Lindsey Letters, vol. II, no. 28.
Addressed: Address missing.
Postmarked: Postmark missing.

London. Jany. 29. 1789

Dear Sir,

I was in hope to have had leisure to have written a longer letter than I shall now be able, but my cover confining me to this day, and visitors calling in, I have little time to say any thing. But the inclosed will make all amends.[1] It was through the neglect of one to whom I had intrusted a small pacquett and letter that Mr Watson did not hear from me again, of which he complains.[2] But I wrote to him again immediately on receiving his letter,[3] and have sent him;

100 Watts' Songs of Mr Buller's edition, w^h he prefers to D^r and Mrs Disneys[4]

30 Catechisms of young Mr Toulmins[5]

12 Economy of Charity[6]

25 Lessons &c for the poor[7]

3 dozen Servants friend[8]

3 dozen Farmers &[9]

I have generally sent him Dr Priestleys tracts, and have taken care to include his Defences for 1787.[10]

I sent him so many Watts's songs, because the small edition he prefers would soon be worn out and useless.

Mr Paley's I am told is a Spelling-book, but have not yet been able to get a sight of one of them, but am laying out for it.[11]

There are no books such as he[12] wishes to be had from the Society for promoting christian knowlege. I was a member of the Society, and was accustomed to get books annually, and could never get any which we could distribute without much gutting and altering which was generally my wife's province.[13] I have pressed him to write freely about any thing he may want, and he may be assured his letters shall be punctually attended to and his wants supplied: for a better creature, or more useful in his station cannot be.

When I write again, which I hope will be in about a weeks time, I shall desire Mr Rowe will let me know how you do. I have reason to be thankful in particular for being more free from head-achs, which I attribute to riding out thrice a week – though I murmur at it and with reason as a consumer of the whole of a winters day. My wife desires her most due and kind respects. I remain ever Dear Sir, Your most truly obliged and faithful affectionate servant

       T. Lindsey

I was in hope of enclosing a few lines to Mr Rowe, but cannot add a word more.

---

1   By 'the inclosed', Lindsey meant either this letter, which the cover contained, or a separate enclosure which has not survived.

2   Probably John Watson, tanner, of Selby, to whom Lindsey regularly supplied religious literature during the 1780s; see Vol. I, Letters 346, n. 2, and 347, n. 1. A more remote possibility is the dissenting minister Thomas Watson of Chichester (see Letter 388, n. 12), who was one of the first members of the Unitarian Society in 1791; Lindsey referred to him several times in his post-1788 letters. However, the reference to Watson's usefulness 'in his station' in the sixth paragraph of this letter is the kind of remark which Lindsey characteristically made about unitarian autodidacts, such as Watson of Selby, not about ministers with a formal education. Lindsey did not identify the neglectful person; a strong possibility is Joseph Johnson, to whose alleged neglect he referred on other occasions; see, for example, Vol. I, Letter 370.

3   Lindsey's letters to Watson, and Watson's letter of complaint to him, appear not to have survived.
4   For these editions, see Vol. I, Letter 353; for the carpet manufacturer William Buller of Wilton, near
    Salisbury, see Vol. I, Letter 354, n. 7.
5   According to the Toulmin family website, Henry Toulmin 'apparently had a catechism printed
    there [i.e. at Chowbent] about 1787'; see http://www.toulmin.family.btinternet.co.uk/Genealogy/
    dO/100000458.HTM. Although Lindsey evidently distributed this work, I have not been able to
    locate a copy. It is not mentioned in J. J. Wright, *The story of Chowbent chapel 1645–1721–1921*
    (Manchester, 1921).
6   This work was Sarah Trimmer (1741–1810), *The OEconomy of charity; or, an address to ladies
    concerning Sunday-schools; the establishment of schools of industry under female inspection; and
    the distribution of voluntary benefactions. To which is added an appendix, containing an account of
    the Sunday-schools in Old Brentford* (London, 1787).
7   Possibly this work was *Lessons of moral and religious instruction: for the benefit of the poor in
    general, and the use of Sunday schools in particular* (2nd edn, Derby, ?1780).
8   This was probably Sarah Trimmer, *The servant's friend, an exemplary guide*, first published in
    London in 1787, with a second edition, enlarged, later in the same year.
9   For a possible identification of this work of Jonas Hanway, see Vol. I, Letter 298, n. 9. It is also
    possible that Lindsey meant Hanway's *Advice from Farmer Trueman to his daughter Mary*, a work
    which was adopted by the Unitarian Society for its catalogue in 1792; see Letter 509, n. 6.
10 For Priestley's *Defences of unitarianism for the year 1787*, see Vol. I, Letter 353, n. 7.
11 This work was William Paley's *The young Christian instructed in reading and in the principles of
    religion; compiled for the use of the Sunday schools in Carlisle* (Carlisle, 1790). The year of publica-
    tion on the title page no doubt explains why Lindsey had not seen the book, although he was aware
    of its forthcoming appearance. Paley was archdeacon of Carlisle from 1782 to 1805. He was subse-
    quently accused of plagiarism by Joseph Robertson (1726–1802), vicar of Horncastle, from whose
    An introduction to the study of polite literature (London, 1782; 2nd edn, 1785) he allegedly lifted
    sections, without acknowledgment, for *The young Christian instructed*. See Robertson's complaints
    in *Gent. Mag.*, LXII, ii (1792), 131–2, 321–33, 408; Paley's reply may be found at pp. 297–8.
12 See n. 2, above.
13 Lindsey was a member of the Society for Promoting Christian Knowledge from 1764, the year
    after he became vicar of Catterick, until 1773, the year of his resignation of Catterick. He is listed
    as a member of the society in 1773, but not in 1774. See *An account of the Society for Promoting
    Christian Knowledge* (London, 1764), p. 48; *Account of the Society ...* (London, 1773), p. 28. For an
    example of Hannah Lindsey's 'gutting' of religious books at Catterick, see Vol. I, Letter 324.

382. To WILLIAM FREND   31 JANUARY 1789

Text: CUL, Add. MS 7886 (Frend papers), no. 145.
Addressed: Address missing.
Postmarked: Postmark missing.

London. Jan. 31. 1789

Dear Sir,

It is high time I should thank you for your *critique* on Mr Coulthurst, of which
I have received to Numb. iv, and should be highly both gratified and edified, were
it to go on without end.[1] So much good sense and such models of just criticism,
must do present local service to free inquiry and truth, and I trust will be spread for
general benefit.

I am also obliged to you, after the first, for your second Address to the Inhabitants
of Cambridge; and as I am in the habit of sending your publications to Dr Priestley,
I will transcribe what he says of it. "I like Mr Frends Second Address no less than
the first. I greatly admire his spirit and ability, and hope much from him["]²

As a mite of acknowlegement for what I have received in great abundance, and to
assist in the no small burden of what you have been and are carrying forwards and
circulating for the public good, I beg the inclosed bill may be put in your box; and
I would beg leave to tell you, that I should be sorry if *we* were such bad managers

(for my wife is most ardently interested in these matters) as not to be able to furnish this and more for the support of a good cause, especially since the demise of her uncle, which happened ab^t 2 years ago.³ But you will be so good as to let it rest with you only.

Some time since I wrote to Mr Hammond to acquaint him with some money that I had rec^d from different subscribers to Mr Dyers Discourses, wishing to know how to send it to him.⁴ I have since received two guineas for one copy, from that most excellent person Mr Tayleur of Shrewsbury.⁵ I should be much obliged to you to let me know how I may transmit it to him, or whether I may pay it for him to any one in Town.

You will be glad to hear that Dr Priestley has finished his Ecclesiastical History so far as to the end of the Western empire, and is going to the press with it. It will make 3 vol^s of the size of his history of early opinions.⁶ On a subject so worn, very much original as to the matter cannot be expected: but integrity and discernment in marking the progress of opinions, will I persuade myself please all candid men, and distinguish the Writer with advantage.

I should have rejoiced much to have been one of your audience upon a late occasion at St Mary's. But we who are at a distance, and cannot enjoy that satisfaction are not quite pleased that you should not go up so prepared as to let us profit by what is delivered, and we think this would be the best way to silence petulant cavil and misrepresentation, and furnish a natural call to lay the important subject before the Public.⁷ But indeed you have too much employ perhaps to exact this of You. When you see Mr Tyrwhitt, we should be obliged to you [to] make our comp^ts to him. How to express our respect and esteem, it w^d not be easy to furnish you with words. And I beg to be remembered with all respect to that worthy apostle Mr Hammond. I fear his bad state of health has prevented his writing.

Believe me at all times most truly and sincerely Yours
    T. Lindsey.

---

¹ For Frend's critique of William Henry Coulthurst, published in the form of six leaflets between Nov. 1788 and Mar. 1789 under the title *Mr Coulthurst's blunders exposed*, see Vol. I, Letter 380, n. 8. No. iv was dated 15 Jan. 1789. Coulthurst was a fellow of Sidney Sussex College, Cambridge.

² For Frend's *Address to the inhabitants of Cambridge* and its sequel, see Letter 383, n. 5. The quotation from Priestley may be found in his letter to Lindsey of 27 Jan. 1789; Rutt, I, 18.

³ Hannah Lindsey's uncle, John Elsworth, died on 25 Aug. 1786, and bequeathed to her a life interest in his estate; see Vol. I, Letter 352, n. 15. The 'inclosed bill' was no doubt a gift of money.

⁴ John Hammond of Fenstanton (d. 1830) was a former fellow of Queens' College, curate at St Botolph's, Cambridge, and (from 1783 to 1787) lecturer at Holy Trinity church, Cambridge. On adopting unitarian opinions he resigned his livings in the church and lived a scholarly life as gentleman and farmer at Fenstanton, where he provided hospitality to William Frend, George Dyer and other unitarian sympathizers in the Cambridge area. By 'Mr Dyer's Discourses', Lindsey almost certainly meant the first edition of George Dyer's *Inquiry into the nature of subscription*, a work which consisted of four essays. Dyer did not publish a separate volume of 'Discourses'. The 'advertisement' to Dyer's *Inquiry* acknowledged the encouragement provided by the subscriptions towards its publication, but did not include a list of subscribers. This first edition was circulated only among a small number of Dyer's friends; a second, enlarged, edition was published by Joseph Johnson in London in 1792. It, too, did not include a list of subscribers.

⁵ For Lindsey's first involvement in this subscription for Dyer's work, see Vol. I, Letter 376, n. 8.

⁶ Priestley's *A general history of the Christian church to the fall of the western empire* was published in two volumes in Birmingham in 1790, with a dedication to Samuel Shore III. The title page of volume I of the British Library's copy is inscribed 'D. of Grafton/1791.' A second edition was published in Northumberland, Pennsylvania, in 1802–3. Priestley's *An history of early opinions concerning Jesus*

Christ, compiled from original writers; proving that the Christian church was at first unitarian was published in four volumes in Birmingham in 1786 and sold in London by Joseph Johnson.

7   Frend preached a sermon at Great St Mary's, Cambridge, on 28 Dec. 1788. It provoked an immediate response in the form of *An address to the congregation at St. Mary's of the University and town of Cambridge on the subject of the sermon preached by the Rev. W. F ____ , M.A. on Sunday, Dec. 28, 1788. By a questionist of St. Joh. Coll.* (Cambridge, 1789). This pseudonymous tract was published by John Archdeacon (d. 1795), the printer to the university from 1766 to 1793, and was strongly critical of Frend, whom the author claimed (p. 30) never to have met. Frend did not accede to Lindsey's suggestion that he should publish his sermon.

383. To WILLIAM TURNER OF NEWCASTLE   2 FEBRUARY 1789

Text: DWL, MS 12.44 (48).
Addressed: Address missing.
Endorsed: Feb. 2. 1789
Postmarked: Postmark missing.

London. Feb. 2. 1789

Dear Sir,

Forgive my not having sooner acknowleged your obliging favour of the latter end of Sept.[1] As I become older, I grow like your worthy father, I would I was more like him in other things, in a reluctance to write as I was wont to do.

Tho' late, I must tell you I was greatly pleased with the new edition of your abstract, and the additions and especially the questions were much approved by one or two other friends no less than myself.[2] And I rejoice to hear from others of your labours and usefulness, and no one speaks more of your worthy character and especially of your invariable kindness to himself than the worthy person to whom I beg you will send the inclosed.[3] It is to offer him an imperfect, yet not very imperfect copy of D[r] Lardner's works, the last edition,[4] if he sh[d] not already be possessed of them. I mention this, because when I send them to him, or on hearing from him, I shall send you a small parcell of tracts to disperse for him and yourself. Among them will be some of the First Addresses – the Second of which, very lately printed I now send – and hope we shall by that time have an edition of this here that I may convey some of them to you.[5]

You see, I presume, the same worthy Confessor's – little, critical pieces addressed to M[r] Coulthurst, of which four are published.[6] I shall put in however one or two copies of each, lest you should not have gotten them all, and you can dispose of them, be that as it will.

M[r] Cadell is and has been waiting a month for the Regency to be settled in order to publish D[r] Campbell's two Vol[s]. of Theological pieces 4[to] and D[r] Leechmans posthumous Discourses w[h] those already printed and Memoirs of the most worthy Author. And certainly he judges right to wait, for no one w[d] purchase here any thing but what relates to the business of the day.[7]

You will be glad to hear that our friend at Birmingham is going to the press with his ecclesiastical history, which he has finished so far as to the end of the Western empire – and a most admirable work it will be. With respect to the facts and subject matter he cannot be expected to be original – but I am sure you will think him so, and will be much gratified, in that part in which he continually takes care to mark *the progress of opinions* at every stage as he goes along.

Your parcell was immediately conveyed to M[r] Christie. He is so immersed in his medical studies, that I have not seen him of two months.[8]

My wife desires to join with me in compt^s to Mrs Turner, who we hope enjoys tolerable health notwithstanding her late great loss of the most valuable parent.[9] Believe me always however tardy a correspondent –

Dear Sir most truly and sincerely yours

    T. Lindsey

---

[1]   This letter from William Turner of Newcastle to Lindsey seems not to have survived.

[2]   Turner's *An abstract of the history of the Bible for the use of children* was first published in Newcastle in 1785. There were several new editions thereafter and the Unitarian Society decided to reprint it, with Turner's alterations, in 1804; Unitarian Society minute book, p. 94. The *Abstract* reached a seventh edition in 1823. See Harbottle, *William Turner*, pp. 30–1.

[3]   Possibly the 'worthy person' was Edward Prowitt; see Letter 394.

[4]   This 'last edition' was *The works of Nathaniel Lardner* (11 vols., London, 1788), with a life of Lardner by Andrew Kippis prefixed to the first volume.

[5]   See Vol. I, Letter 377, n. 3. Frend published *An address to the inhabitants of Cambridge and its neighbourhood, exhorting them to turn from the false worship of three persons, to the worship of the one true God* (St Ives, 1788), with a second edition published in London by Joseph Johnson later in the same year. He republished it in London, also in 1788, with the same text but with the title *An address to the members of the Church of England, and to protestant trinitarians in general, exhorting them to turn from the false worship of three persons, to the worship of the one true God*. This version also reached a second edition in 1788. Frend then published *A second address to the inhabitants of Cambridge* (St Ives, 1789) and *A second address to the members of the Church of England, and to protestant trinitarians in general* (London, 1788). The texts of these two works were also identical, and although the title pages give different years of publication, they appeared almost simultaneously; both are dated Jesus College, 25 Dec. 1788. The first and second *Address to the members of the Church of England* were included in the volume entitled *Six tracts, in vindication of the worship of the one true God* (London, 1791), published by the Unitarian Society.

[6]   See Letter 382, n. 1.

[7]   During George III's illness in the last months of 1788 and the early months of 1789, a regency bill, conferring limited powers on the prince of Wales as regent, had been debated in the house of commons. But on 19 Feb. 1789 ,it was announced that the king was in a state of convalescence, the regency bill lapsed and normal political and commercial business was gradually resumed. George Campbell, *The four gospels, translated from the Greek. With preliminary dissertations, and notes critical and explanatory* (2 vols., London, 1789) was published by Andrew Strahan and Thomas Cadell; Campbell (1719–96) was principal and professor of divinity at Marischal College, Aberdeen. *Sermons, by William Leechman, D.D. ... to which is prefixed some account of the author's life, and of his lectures, by James Wodrow, D.D.* was published by Strahan and Cadell in London, and by two publishers in Edinburgh, in 1789. For Leechman, and for Lindsey's admiration for him, see Vol. I, Letters 244 and 276. Wodrow (1730–1810) was minister of Stevenston, Ayrshire, from 1759 to 1810 and a sympathizer with liberal theology.

[8]   Thomas Christie had studied medicine at Edinburgh University and at the Westminster dispensary. In 1789, he was in the process of preparing his MD thesis for publication.

[9]   This is a reference to Turner's first wife, Mary (1759–97), née Holland. She was the daughter of Thomas Holland (d. 1804) of Manchester, merchant, and his wife (and cousin) Anne Holland (d. 1785). Possibly her 'most valuable parent' who had died was her paternal grandmother Mary Holland, née Savage; see Harbottle, *William Turner*, pp. 45 and. 185. To Mr Harbottle I owe the suggestion that Lindsey's wording carries a slight air of detachment, signifying a lack of immediacy, but also respect for age. Perhaps Mary Turner's grandmother, who at that time would have been aged eighty-nine or ninety, had lived in William Turner's household after the death of her husband, Thomas Holland of Wem, the father of the Thomas Holland mentioned above.

384. To WILLIAM FREND   **6 MARCH 1789**

Text: CUL, Add. MS 7886 (Frend papers), no. 146.
Addressed: For the/The Rev^d M^r. Frend/fellow of Jesus college/Cambridge
Postmarked: Postmark missing.

London. March. 6. 1789.

Dear Sir,

I thank you for the present of your Appendix, in which you have clearly proved that Dr Beadon acted arbitrarily and unstatutably in dispossessing you of the Tutorship, but all the demonstration in the world would never have convinced your judge of the injustice done you; nor shall I be surprized if they proceed in a short time to eject you from your fellowship should the same favourable circumstances return as before the king's illness.[1]

I am glad to find that you are likely to be in Town the middle of April, as Dr Priestley tells me he shall make his annual visit at the same time, and I am sure will be very happy[?] and desirous to see you as he is continually inquiring about you. He does not begin to print his ecclesiastical history till after his return to Birmingham.[2]

I do not know whether you saw a pamphlet which came out the last summer, entitled *Hints &c* submitted to the attention of the clergy, nobility and gentry *newly* associated By a Layman, a true friend to the constitution in church and state. London, printed for Rivington, Dilly &c.[3] The new association was that formed to fulfill the object of the King's Proclamation.[4] It was sent me from the Author. I have very lately learned, that the Author is no less a person than the D. of Grafton himself, but was desired not to mention it so as to have it get into News-papers.[5] With or without a name, it is auspicious for such persons to stand forth for a reformation of the liturgy and estabilishment to the degree this author does. But unluckily, the same person that gave me this information, told me, there was not a single copy to be had in London, that upon their not being sold (Rivington would not promote the sale) they had been all returned to Ipswich, from whence it seems they had been sent to Town.[6]

This and Lord Stanhopes like movement in the house of Lords,[7] and the determination of the Dissenters to renew their application to Parliament this session, with a new case which I have seen in print, so strong that I think it must flash conviction in the face of every member of both houses[8] – all these things together will work out something – not to omit *your* recent movement of the waters to prevent stagnation, for we here in 15 years time are grown somewhat old and settled, tho' I trust we have our use.[9]

I was in hope of procuring you a Bank bill for the whole of what I have rec^d of Subscriptions to Mr Dyers book.[10] But it seems they descend not to fractions. I send therefore £15 in a bill and shall pay the odd money £1.15–0 when I have the pleasure of seeing you. If I can procure a frank to day, I shall inclose the names of those whose money I have received and of a few others who have sent in their names only.[11] Dr Disney and his family are all well. He has been the whole week on a visit to his brother in Essex,[12] but returns to day. I remain always very truly and sincerely Yours

T. Lindsey.

---

1   The subject of William Frend's *Appendix to thoughts on subscription* (St Ives, 1789) was his appeal to the visitor (James Yorke, bishop of Ely) of Jesus College, Cambridge, against the decision to deprive

him of his tutorship. Frend's appeal may be found at pp. 1–4; Richard Beadon's letter to the visitor defending the decision at pp. 5–17; Frend's reply to Beadon at pp. 18–28; and Yorke's dismissal of the appeal at pp. 29–30. Though deprived of his tutorship, Frend was not deprived of his college fellowship, which he retained until his marriage in 1808. Beadon (1737–1824) was master of Jesus College, Cambridge, from 1781 to 1789, when he became bishop of Gloucester; he was translated to Bath and Wells in 1802.

2   See Letter 382, n. 6.

3   Grafton, *Hints*. The author was the duke of Grafton and the publishers were John Rivington (St Paul's Churchyard), Charles Dilly (the Poultry), James Matthews (the Strand) and Thomas Hookham (New Bond Street). The second edition, revised and enlarged, was published in London in 1789 by Benjamin White & Son and by John Debrett, as were the third and fourth editions, both in 1790.

4   On 1 June 1787, George III issued a proclamation 'for the encouragement of piety and virtue, and for preventing and punishing of vice, profaneness and immorality'. The 'new association' was the Proclamation Society, founded in 1787 with Wilberforce as one of its leading figures. Grafton himself was a member of the society but argued that its priority should be the reform of the church's liturgy, rather than the prosecution of law-breakers from the lower orders. See Joanna Innes, 'Politics and morals. The reformation of manners movement in later eighteenth-century England', in *The transformation of political culture. England and Germany in the late eighteenth century*, ed. E. Hellmuth (Oxford, 1990), pp. 57–118.

5   Grafton's authorship of the *Hints* did not immediately get into the newspapers, but it soon became widely known.

6   In the 'Advertisement' to the second edition of the *Hints*, Grafton wrote 'A Public Affliction affecting all orders of People (but now most happily removed) caused the first Edition of this Pamphlet to be called in, when few Copies had been sold; for such a Publication would *then* have been ill-timed'. The 'public affliction' was the illness of George III. Possibly Lindsey's source of information as to the availability of the book was his correspondent William Alexander of Yoxford, or Edward Evanson, who purchased an estate at Great Blakenham, near Ipswich, in 1789, or possibly Evanson's friend George Rogers, rector of Sproughton, Suffolk, who was subsequently a member of the Unitarian Society; see Letter 427, n. 10.

7   In the house of lords on 17 Feb. 1789 Stanhope attacked the clause in the regency bill which would have restrained the regent from giving the royal assent to the repeal of the Act of Uniformity (1662) and of similar legislation of a fundamental character. On 18 May 1789, Stanhope introduced a general toleration bill into the lords; it was rejected without a division on its second reading on 9 June; see G. M. Ditchfield, 'Dissent and toleration: Lord Stanhope's bill of 1789', *JEH*, XXI, 1 (1978), 51–73.

8   On 16 Mar. 1788, the repeal committee of the protestant dissenting deputies resolved to make a further application to parliament for the repeal of the Test and Corporation Acts in 1789 rather than in 1788. This decision was reaffirmed at several further meetings, and on 18 Dec. 1788, the committee approved the publication of a new statement of the dissenters' case. It was entitled *A letter to the bishops on the application of the protestant dissenters to parliament for a repeal of the Corporation and Test Acts, including strictures on the bishop of Gloucester's sermon on January 30 1788*. See *Committees for repeal*, 22–3, 69. Samuel Hallifax, bishop of Gloucester, published *A sermon preached before the lords spiritual and temporal, in the Abbey church of Westminster, on Wednesday, January 30th, 1788, being the anniversary of King Charles's martyrdom* (London, 1788), in which (pp. 15–19) he asserted the need for a Test Law.

9   In Mar. 1789, almost fifteen years had elapsed since Lindsey first opened his unitarian chapel in Essex Street.

10   This is probably a reference to Dyer's *Inquiry into the nature of subscription*; see Letter 382, n. 4.

11   This list of names and subscriptions is not among the Frend MSS at CUL and appears not to have survived.

12   Lewis Disney (1738–1822), the eldest brother of John Disney, took the additional surname Ffytche on his marriage to Elizabeth Ffytche in 1775; he inherited Danbury Place, Essex, following his marriage into the Ffytche family.

385. To WILLIAM FREND   **13 MARCH 1789**

Text: CUL, Add. MS 7886 (Frend papers), no. 147.
Addressed: Address missing.
Postmarked: Postmark missing.

London. March. 13 1789

Dear Sir,

I am much gratified by your kind letter and shall be happy in any way to shew my sincere regards and esteem for the writer, as well as to be of any service hereafter to so valuable and worthy a confessor as Mr Dyer.

It remains to be shewn how far the D. of Grafton will come forth as a reformer. But I am pleased to see that Dr Symonds in his dedication to him has held him up as one that reads his bible, but much more pleased that the same gentleman in the preface of a work dedicated to the Chancellor [of] the university of Cambridge as his most intimate friend, has published the highest praises of a Dissenter, a most valuable person, with whom also he lived on terms of an intire friendship.[1] This will certainly not be relished by High-church, but I hope it may be reckoned one good sign of the times, and I confess it gives me an exceeding good opinion of Dr Symonds's heart and real christian temper and I hope I may add piety. I dwell upon it the more as I had been taught to look upon him as a polite gentleman who had travelled, and had balls and routs at Bury.[2]

Whatever I may think of N^r. vi I like N^r v. very much, both in its explications and in its hesitation, which latter is surely a juster way of proceeding than to make a point explaining every text. And many strongs [*sic*] remarks in it seem to be particularly calculated to strike the youth of the university. As to Cantabrigiensis I have long liked him so much, that I should be glad to know who he is, unless it be of the things not to be known.[3]

I shall however be glad to have a look at N^r. vi. tho' I must own that the little reading I have of the early X^n writers and many other considerations make me less favourable to the interpretation of John's introduction, to which you seem to incline. Nay, I must tell You, that as I have been hindred in preparing my second Address to the university youths, I had some thoughts this spring of throwing out one Section of it – with a new version and paraphrase of the first 18 or 19 verses, and I am not yet determined whether I shall not do it.[4]

As you mention Dr Priestley and Mr Gibbon together, I inclose a copy of their correspondence, with which if you have not seen it, you will be pleased, and you may keep it till we meet in Town. There is full liberty of comunicating it to any one, so that no copy get abroad – which I think sh^d not be, as Mr G. has entered his protest against it.[5]

I am sure the D^r. would be very happy in visiting our Alma Mater:[6] but I have never heard him speak of it, as she lies so much out of his way – whereas Oxford is his direct road to Birmingham.

Dr Disney and his family are all well. I made your *souvenirs* to him last night when he called here. My wife desires her respects and I am always most truly Yours

T. Lindsey

---

[1] John Symonds (1729–1807) was regius professor of modern history at Cambridge from 1771 until his death. He matriculated at St John's College, Cambridge, in 1747, the year in which Lindsey became a fellow of the college. The work which he dedicated to the duke of Grafton, the chancellor of Cambridge University and a neighbour and friend of Symonds, was *Observations upon the expe-*

diency of revising the present English version of the four gospels, and of the Acts of the Apostles (Cambridge, 1789). In the dedication (unpaginated), Symonds expressed appreciation for Grafton's recommendation for his professorship and for the duke's attention to scripture. The dissenter whom Symonds praised (in the preface, pp. iv–v) was Thomas Harmer (1714–88), Independent minister at Wattisfield, Suffolk, whose valuable manuscript accounts of dissenting congregations in Norfolk and Suffolk are now at Dr Williams's Library.

2   There is a short biographical account of Symonds in *Admissions to the College of St John the Evangelist. Part III*, p. 569; he had been recorder of Bury St Edmunds since 1772.

3   This refers to the fifth leaflet of Frend's *Mr Coulthurst's blunders exposed*; it was dated 18 Feb. 1789 (see Letter 382, n. 1). Frend cited letters from 'Cantabrigiensis' in the *Gent. Mag.* which exposed the key trinitarian text 1 John v. 7 as spurious; these letters may be found in *Gent. Mag.*, LVIII, ii (1788), 875–7 (Oct.) and 1063–4 (Dec.). 'Cantabrigiensis' was Richard Porson (1759–1808), a fellow of Trinity College, Cambridge, from 1782 to 1792. These letters were part of Porson's controversy with George Travis (1741–97), archdeacon of Chester from 1786 to 1797, who had asserted the authenticity of this text. Porson published four further letters as 'Cantabrigiensis' in this controversy; see *Gent. Mag.*, LIX, i (1789), 101–5, 297–300, 512–18, and LIX, ii (1789), 690–7. His letters were subsequently published in a single volume, entitled *Letters to Mr. Archdeacon Travis, in answer to his defence of the three heavenly witnesses, 1 John v. 7* (London, 1790).

4   This refers to the sixth leaflet of Frend's *Mr Coulthurst's blunders exposed*; it was dated 12 Mar. 1789. Frend cited (pp. 43–4) evidence from the first three chapters of St John's gospel to argue that the apostle regarded Christ as subordinate to God the father. In his *Second address*, section V, pp. 34–42, Lindsey did indeed set out what he called 'a new translation, and paraphrase, of the preface to St John's gospel, with remarks', followed (pp. 42–56) by 'corollaries and illustrations of the foregoing interpretations of John 1. 1–14'. Lindsey agreed with Frend in denying that the 'logos' in that chapter represented Christ, but went further than Frend in his insistence on the simple humanity of Christ and that worship of a human being amounted to idolatry. Here, perhaps, may be seen the origin of Lindsey's dispute with Frend and other Cambridge unitarians over the preamble to the Unitarian Society's rules in 1791. See also Lindsey's *List of the false readings*.

5   For Priestley's exchange of letters with Gibbon, following the publication of the former's *History of the corruptions of Christianity* and his attack on Gibbon's interpretation of the rise of Christianity in his *History of the decline and fall of the Roman empire*, see Paul Turnbull, 'Gibbon's exchange with Joseph Priestley', *British Journal for Eighteenth-century Studies*, XVI (1991), 139–58. Gibbon declined to enter a public controversy with Priestley, who did not publish their correspondence until after Gibbon's death; it may be found in Priestley's *Discourses relating to the evidences of revealed religion. Vol. 1*, pp. 412–19. Gibbon's letters to Priestley are printed in *The letters of Edward Gibbon*, ed. J. E. Norton (3 vols., London, 1956), II, 320–3. Probably Lindsey sent to Frend a manuscript or privately printed version of the correspondence.

6   Cambridge University. It is unlikely that Priestley visited Cambridge to meet Frend. In 1791, he was obliged to decline Frend's invitation; see Letter 450.

386. To WILLIAM ALEXANDER   11 APRIL 1789

Text: 'Letters of the Rev. Theophilus Lindsey. No. II',
                 UH, II, 45 (8 Mar. 1862), 84.

Note: For the identification of Lindsey as the writer of this and the other letters to William Alexander which are included in this volume, see *UH*, II, 40, 44 and 45, 84. This is the only section of this particular letter printed by the *UH*; the manuscript seems not to have survived.

April 11th, 1789.

When you are become settled in a school at Yoxford[1] or any other place, I desire you will look upon me as a subscriber, to pay for the education of a certain number of the poorer sort in the place and neighbourhood anonymously, as I know not any way in which a small matter may be better employed than in bringing up children under your tuition.

1   According to his own account, Alexander opened his school at Yoxford, Suffolk, in June 1789; see his contribution to the obituary of his friend Samuel Say Toms, *CR*, NS, I (1834), 817.

387. To SYLAS NEVILLE   23 APRIL 1789

Text: Norfolk RO, MC7/750 (Neville papers).
Addressed: To/D[r]. Neville/Norwich[1]
Endorsed: Rev[d] Theoph[s] Lindsey, the Minister of the Unitarian Chapel in
                 Essex S[t], Strand. Ap. 23rd. 1789
Postmarked: AP 23 89

London. April. 23. 1789

Dear Sir,

If it was in my power in any shape to serve you with the D. of Norfolk,[2] I would do it most gladly. I have formerly dined at his house[3] and met him at that of a common friend and he has also occasionally called here. But this was some years ago when he was Earl of Surrey, when also for a few years he had a pew in our chapel, and occasionally attended.[4] For some time before his father died[5] he ceased to frequent our worship, and I have since had no intercourse with him, so that I could not ask any favour of him. I have sent your letter to D[r] Blackburne whose address is, *New-Street, Spring Gardens*, London.[6] We hope he is getting forwards tolerably well. My wife desires her compt[s] and hopes we may congratulate you soon in the same way. M[r] Blackburne the Doctors and my wifes eldest brother is at present in Town from Yorkshire.[7] I am always very sincerely yours

T. Lindsey.

---

1   Sylas Neville graduated with the degree of MD from the University of Edinburgh in 1775.
2   Charles Howard (1746–1815), 11th duke of Norfolk.
3   Presumably Norfolk House, St James's Square, London.
4   For Charles Howard's attendance, when earl of Surrey, at Essex Street chapel in 1780–1, see Vol. I, Letters 218 and 228.
5   Charles Howard's father, Charles (1720–86), 10th duke of Norfolk, died on 31 Aug. 1786.
6   Neville had been a close friend of Thomas Blackburne (d. 1782), son of Archdeacon Francis Black-burne, and a medical practitioner at Durham. On 26 May 1781, he dined with Thomas Blackburne's younger brother, Dr William Blackburne, whom he described as 'a good sort of young man, though he falls short of the greatness of my friend at Durham'; *The diary of Sylas Neville 1767–1788*, ed. Basil Cozens-Hardy (Oxford, 1950), p. 269. Evidently, Neville was trying to re-establish a connexion with the Blackburne family.
7   Lindsey's wife's eldest (half-) brother was the Rev. Francis Blackburne, vicar of Brignall, Yorkshire.

---

388. To RUSSELL SCOTT   3 JULY 1789

Text: Scott Coll.
Printed: McLachlan, 'Lindsey to Scott', 117 (very brief summary
                 without quotation).
Addressed: To/The Rev[d]. M[r] Russell Scott/Portsmouth
Endorsed: July 5th 89
Postmarked: [JY] 4 89

Frend's Addresses, 1st & 2[d].[1] 3 dozen each
-------- Acc[t] of Proceedings &c[2] 2 dozen
General View &c[3] --- 3 dozen
Exhortation &c to refrain from Trinitarian worship[4] – 1 dozen
Examination of Robinson[5] 2 copies
Life of Biddle[6] – 2
-------- Mort[7] 3

Examination of M[r] Harrisons sermon[8] –
Appeals[9]

London. July. 3. 1789

Dear Sir,

The above tracts are put up for you, and will be sent the first opportunity, I believe from the White Hart and Ship in the Borough to,[10] whence our Book tells us, a Waggon goes daily to Portsmouth.[11]

Some of them I should be glad if you would communicate with M[r] Watson and our worthy friends, the physicians at Chichester.[12]

On monday next we set out on a long journey to Richmond in Yorkshire by way of Bristol, Birmingham &c. What carries us so far west is to see my wifes sister at Chew-magna, who is in a very precarious state of health,[13] After which we very naturally make a halt with our friends at Birmingham.[14] I suppose we shall be absent from Town a month or 5 weeks.[15] And at the expiration of that term I shall be glad to know how you do and go on. When I must beg you to inform me how to direct a parcell to your worthy brother in law, for whom I shoud have made up one now, had I known his address.[16]

It will give you pleasure to know that M[r] Belsham is engaged absolutely as resident Tutor at the college at Hackney.[17] I have a full hope, that by the blessing of divine providence, science, virtue and true religion will be promoted for ages to come and to a wide extent by means of that Seminary.

D[r] Price meets M[r] Belsham towards the end of August at Cicester to ordain M[r] Cogan.[18] After this the D[r] sets out for Wales to pass 6 weeks or two months,[19] and M[r] Belsham will be at Hackney in August to settle himself &c.

D[r] Kippis hopes M[rs] Kippis will be able to reach Brighthelmstone, and to spend his time there and in frequent returns to London, whence he cannot this year be absent for a long time together. We have heard nothing from M[r] Frend, since he left England.[20] He proposed to return in October. D[r] Disney and his family are all well, have been absent for a week in Essex, and I suppose will make some excursion when we come back from the North. I thought you woud be glad to know these particulars of the movem[ts] of y[r] friends for the summer. My wife sends you her sincere regards and good wishes. I remain always most truly Yours

T. Lindsey.

---

1   See Letter 383, n. 5.

2   This was a short pamphlet published in Canterbury by William Frend in 1789 with the title *An account of some late proceedings of the 'Society for promoting Christian Knowledge'; addressed to the members thereof, particularly those who are resident in the country* (London, 1789). The pamphlet recorded the resolutions of the society, at a meeting on 12 May 1789, that Frend be expelled from the society because of the views expressed in his *Address* and *Second address to the inhabitants of Cambridge*. It concluded with Frend's indignant reply, which reiterated his 'heretical' opinions.

3   This was probably the third edition of Priestley's *A general view of the arguments for the unity of God; and against the divinity and pre-existence of Christ: from reason, from the scriptures, and from history* (London, 1788).

4   *An exhortation to all Christian people to refrain from trinitarian worship* was published (without an author's name) by Joseph Johnson in London in 1789. The 'Advertisement' to the book, opposite p. 3, stated 'In the following address, great use is made of a tract entitled, '"A free and serious address to the Christian laity, especially those, who, being of Unitarian Sentiments, conform to Trinitarian Worship", which is ascribed to Mr. Toulmin of Taunton.' The *Exhortation* (p. 36) advocated private, family, unitarian worship and pointed out that liturgies such as Lindsey's were available for that purpose.

5   I.e. Lindsey's *Examination of Robinson*.

6   This work was Joshua Toulmin's *A review of the life and writings of the Rev. John Biddle, M.A.* (London, 1789); the book was re-issued by the Unitarian Society in London in 1791.

7   Henry Toulmin, *A short view of the life, sentiments and character of Mr John Mort* (Warrington, 1789). See Vol. I, Letter 338, n. 8.

8   *Examination of a sermon, preached in the cathedral-church of St. Paul, London … on Sunday, May 25, 1788, being the first Sunday in Trinity term. By the Rev. Richard Harrison* (London, 1789). The author was Robert Edward Garnham. Richard Harrison (1736–93) was minister of Brompton chapel, and chaplain to the lord mayor of London (John Burnell). The full title of his work was *A sermon, preached in the cathedral-church of St. Paul, London, before the right honourable the lord-mayor, the judges, aldermen, and sheriffs, on Sunday, the 25th of May, 1788, being the first Sunday in Trinity term* (London, 1788). He used the occasion to re-affirm the doctrine of the Trinity and the divinity of Christ, and denounced Socinianism (p. 3) as guilty of denying biblical truth.

9   Probably Lindsey referred here to his distribution of copies of William Frend's *Appendix to thoughts on subscription* (see Letter 384, n. 1), which consisted of the various stages of its author's appeal against his removal from his tutorship. It is conceivable that he referred to Priestley's *Appeal to the serious and candid* (see Vol. I, Letter 199, n. 14), of which Priestley had published a further edition at Birmingham in 1788. But Lindsey's reference to' the Appeals' in the context of Frend's other work in Letter 397 renders *Appendix to thoughts on subscription* the more likely allusion.

10 Lindsey omitted a word – probably 'Portsmouth' – at this point.

11 The White Hart inn and the Ship inn, both in the Borough, were departure points for Portsmouth. From the White Hart a coach departed for Portsmouth at six o'clock each evening; from the Ship inn a waggon departed for Portsmouth at nine o'clock each morning. 'Our book' was a London trades directory.

12 Thomas Watson (d. 1836) was minister to the dissenting congregation at Treville Street, Plymouth, from 1785 to 1788 and to the Baffins Lane congregation at Chichester from 1788 to 1803. He retired in the latter year and moved to Bath; see Jerom Murch, *A history of the presbyterian and general baptist churches in the west of England; with memoirs of some of their pastors* (London, 1835), p. 504; *CR*, NS, III (1836), 909. There is a short note on Watson in Joseph Hunter's 'Biographical notices of some of my contemporaries', BL, Add. MS 36527, fo. 88. By 'the physicians at Chichester', Lindsey meant Dr John Bayly (1735–1815) and Dr Thomas Sanden (1752–1840), both of whom were listed (with Sanden rendered incorrectly as 'Sandon') as members of the Unitarian Society, living in Chichester, in 1791. Bayly, who was related to the Carter family of Portsmouth, had been educated at Thomas Amory's dissenting academy at Taunton before taking his medical degree at Edinburgh University. According to his obituary in *MR*, X (1815), 764, 'during the last twenty-five years of his life he was a firm and zealous Unitarian' and 'one of the earliest members of the Essex Street Society'. He was also listed as a 'governor for life and benefactor' of Hackney College in 1786; DWL, MS 12.90 (1). Sanden was also educated at a dissenting academy (that of Samuel Merivale at Exeter) and took his medical degree at Edinburgh University. Like Bayly, he practised medicine at Chichester for most of his career. His obituary described him as a unitarian, adding that 'he agreed in nearly all the philosophical and theological opinions of Priestley, for whose character he entertained great esteem; but for many years before his death he had ceased to think highly of that great and excellent man'. It noted also that 'he was a decided but moderate whig'; *CR*, NS, VII (1840), 627. He published a tribute to Bayly in 1816, and *Unitarianism, old and new exemplified* (Chichester, 1817).

13 Lindsey's wife's half-sister was Sarah (1753–1811), the youngest child of Archdeacon Francis Blackburne and his wife Hannah. She was baptized at Richmond on 12 Feb. 1753; NYRO, PR/PM 1/7, Richmond parish registers. In 1782, she married John Hall (d. 1841), from 1784 vicar of Chew Magna, Somerset; she died on 8 May 1811; *Gent. Mag.*, LXXXI, i (1811), 502. The youngest of their three daughters was christened Theophila, after Lindsey; *Familiae min. gen.*, II, 770.

14 Priestley described the recollection of this visit by Theophilus and Hannah Lindsey to Birmingham as 'a pleasant dream'; see his letter to Lindsey of 22 July 1789, Rutt, I, 26.

15 Lindsey and his wife returned to London in the first week of Aug. 1789; see Letter 390.

16 Scott's 'worthy brother in law' was John Taylor; he married Scott's sister Mary in May 1788.

17 Thomas Belsham was resident tutor and professor of divinity at Hackney College from the summer of 1789 until the college's closure in 1796. From 1781 to 1789 he had been divinity tutor at the Daventry Academy.

18 Eliezer Cogan (1762–1855), a former pupil of Thomas Belsham at Daventry, was minister to a presbyterian congregation at Gosditch Street, Cirencester, from 1787 to 1789. He subsequently served congregations at Ware, Cheshunt and Walthamstow. See *Price corr.*, III, 337–8, and the memoir of Cogan in *CR*, NS, XI (1855), 237–59.

19 Price spent much of Aug. and early Sept. 1789 at Southern Down, near Bridgend; see *Price corr.*, III, 251–2, 255–7.

20 Frend left England early in June 1789 and returned in Oct, having travelled extensively in the low countries and north-west Germany; see Knight, *William Frend*, ch. 5.

389. To WILLIAM ALEXANDER   8 AUGUST 1789

Text: 'Letters of the Rev. Theophilus Lindsey. No. II', *UH*, II, 45 (8 Mar. 1862), 84.

Note: This is the only section of the letter printed by the *UH*; the manuscript seems not to have survived.

August 8th, 1789.

And now for the anxieties that you are under, the result of the peculiar situation of your mind, and your own honest inquiries after Divine truth; I have no doubt but that Divine Being whose favour you seek, and whom alone you esteem the object of your devout and highest regards, will, in the use of your own endeavours, supply the disadvantages you will labour under at times that you cannot attend public worship, by such employment of your hours at home as you mention.[1] And I am not without hope that a modest, unostentatious example of this kind, attended with a suitable Christian deportment, and the reason of your absenting yourself from the Church service, never introduced by you but when inquired into, may have a good effect in exciting sober inquiry, and so bring others to see the truth.

1   This appears to refer to the difficulties which Alexander encountered in connexion with the school which he opened at Yoxford in June 1789; see Letter 386, n. 1.

390. To WILLIAM FREND   10 AUGUST 1789

Text: CUL, Add. MS 7886 (Frend papers), no. 148.
Addressed: A Monsr./Monsr. Frend/chez Monsr. Bergstraesser/Hanau, pres de/Frankfort sur Maine./Allemagne
Endorsed: [In pencil] Theophilus Lindsey
Postmarked: Postmark missing.

London Aug. 10. 1789

Dear Sir,

Our return to Essex-street was only at the end of the past week, and I take the first opportunity of writing again to you.[1] The last stage of our journey was at Mr Reynoldss at Paxton,[2] with whom I rode over to visit our common friend at Fenstanton,[3] and was filled with surprise to see his mansion so beautiful and improved and its master so perfectly well, the latter circumstance I believe in some measure owing to the former, the gentle exercise and amusement out of doors which it has given him, added to a flannel shirt which he continues to wear next the skin. He was still in brick and mortar and very busy, but we spent a couple of hours very agreeably with him, and I fortunately happened to have your letter about me with a sight of which he was much gratified, as he had not heard of you since you left Dover.[4]

I find Dr Disney very well, though he has been much disturbed with the affair you know of relating to his brother, which has turned out most favourably respecting the judges and the whole court, but the jury unaccountably, tho they acquitted him of the accusation brought in their verdict, *guilty of an assault in general*; which in such a business is a most unpleasing thing.[5]

M[r] Lambert was in town for a few days when we were away, but has not yet got rid of his feverish complaint that had hung for such a long space about him. M[r] Hammond had heard that he was in a very low way with it, but Disney says he is rather better. The new B[p] of Chester, D[r] Clever, is going round his diocese, thro Lancashire, Westmoreland, and the 3 northern deaneries in Yorkshire,[6] charging against Socinianism, whose growth he complains of, especially among the Dissenters by name, for which he has very great cause in Lancashire in particular.[7] D[r] Pearce is your new master of Jesus, not Kiplin [*sic*] as was apprehended.[8] The latter certainly harangued away against any new translation of the bible; perhaps having got scent of a certain design, or moved by D[r] Symonds's work and tending towards it.[9] All these movements are good signs. When M[r] Garnham was in Town, I had the pleasure of seeing him frequently, and you will believe, liked him very much, as did also M[r] Dodson; and being persuaded that he would be an excellent coadjutor in *our design*, have mentioned it to him, and he came into it very willingly.[10] He has quitted intirely all connexion with the church, with his old father's acquiescence, for which he had long waited; and as I find he intends to reside much in the university, and is with all most indefatigable, he will be of great service.[11]

A good ingenious hand has animadverted on the popular orator, M[r] Harrison's orthodox sermon before the L[d] Mayor last year, which was exhibited also at Bury;[12] and the B[p] of Norwich is about to be asked in print on what grounds he took upon him to assert in his first charge to his clergy, that a Critic[?] and Divine of the first eminence, ostensibly intending B[p] Lowth, was of opinion that a new english version of the bible was not at all wanted.[13]

I do not at present recollect any more intelligence of our common friends or concerning what is passing among us at home. Abroad great and most important changes are coming in, which I trust will have the best effect in the moral state not of one country only but of the who[le] world.[14] Our parliament is still sitting to the great mortification of the members who are *constrained* to attend it, and the murmuring of many that things of moment are brought forward when it is known so few can or will attend. It is generally believed this will be its last session.[15] My wife and D[r] Disney and M[r] and M[rs] Dodson[16] with D[r] Priestley desire to be most kindly remembered to you. I remain always with the sincerest attachment and esteem most truly Yours
　　　　T. Lindsey.

1　Lindsey had travelled to Richmond (Yorkshire), Chew Magna (Somerset), Shrewsbury and Birmingham: see Letters 388 and 391.
2　Richard Reynolds, Lindsey's contemporary and friend at St John's College, Cambridge, whose estate was at Little Paxton, near St Neots, Huntingdonshire.
3　This 'common friend' was John Hammond; see Letter 382, n. 4.
4　See Letter 388, n. 20.
5　On 24 July 1789, Disney's eldest brother, Lewis Disney Ffytche (see Letter 384, n. 12) was tried at the assizes at Chelmsford for an alleged assault upon a waiter, William Ford, at the Cock and Bull hotel, Romford. He was accused of 'an assault with an attempt to commit an unnatural crime, and an assault'; the jury convicted him of the latter (hence Lindsey's reference to 'an assault in general'); *The World*, 27 July 1789. On 19 Nov. 1789, in the court of king's bench, he was fined £100 for this offence; *Morning Post and New Daily Advertiser*, 20 Nov. 1789.
6　By 'the three northern deaneries in Yorkshire', Lindsey meant the deaneries of Richmond, Catterick and Boroughbridge, all of which were in the diocese of Chester.
7　William Cleaver (1742–1815) was consecrated as bishop of Chester 20 Jan. 1788, in succession to

Beilby Porteus. He was translated to Bangor in 1800 and to St Asaph in 1806. He conducted his visitation of the diocese of Chester in Aug. 1789. His attacks on Socinians were published in *A sermon on the sacrament of the lord's supper* (Oxford, 1789) and *A sermon on a discourse of our lord's in the sixth chapter of St. John's gospel* (Oxford, 1789). Cleaver preached both of these sermons before the University of Oxford on 25 Nov. 1787, and repeated them in his diocesan visitation of 1789. They were published together with the title *Two sermons by William lord bishop of Chester. Addressed to the clergy of the diocese* (Oxford, 1789). Robert Edward Garnham replied to Cleaver's strictures in his anonymously published *A letter to the Right Rev. Dr William Cleaver, lord bishop of Chester. On the subject of two sermons addressed by him to the clergy of his diocese; comprehending also a vindication of the late Bishop Hoadly* (London, 1790).

8 William Pearce (1744–1820) was master of Jesus College, Cambridge, from 1789 to 1820, and twice thereafter vice-chancellor; from 1797 to 1820 he was dean of Ely. For Thomas Kipling (1745–1822), deputy regius professor of divinity at Cambridge, 1787–1802, and dean of Peterborough, 1798–1822, see Vol. I, Letter 374, n. 3.

9 As a vehement opponent of heterodoxy and (in 1793) one of the leading university prosecutors of William Frend, Kipling shared the growing orthodox anxiety that a new translation of the Bible would be 'hijacked by heretics' and motivated by a determination to complete the Reformation, especially as most initiatives for biblical translations after 1780 emanated from nonconformists of various types. The 'certain design' of which he had probably 'got scent' was almost certainly the proposed new translation of the Bible; see n. 10, below. For the background to this question, see Neil Hitchin, 'The politics of English Bible translation in Georgian Britain', *Transactions of the Royal Historical Society*, 6th series, IX (1999), 67–92, quotation at p. 92. For Symonds's *Observations upon the expediency of revising the present English version of the four gospels*, see Letter 385, n. 1.

10 'Our design' was a new translation of the Bible; see Letter 394. The idea came from Priestley and had warm support from Lindsey. It occupied much of Lindsey's time, and even more of Priestley's, before the loss of most of Priestley's papers in the Birmingham riots of July 1791 effectively ended the scheme. See Brooks, 'Priestley's plan', 89–106. Priestley's 'A proposal for correcting the English translation of the Scriptures' was published in the *Theological Repository*, IV (1784), 187–8 and is reproduced in Brooks, 'Priestley's plan', 103–6.

11 Robert Edward Garnham did not formally resign from the church, but ceased to officiate as a priest. He had been curate to his father's parishes of Nowton and Hargrave, Suffolk. His father was Robert Garnham (d. 1798), scholar of Trinity College, Cambridge, headmaster of Bury (St Edmunds) school from 1745 to 1767 and rector of Hargrave and of Nowton from the mid-1750s until his death. See *Gent. Mag.*, LXVIII, ii (1798), 999.

12 For Harrison's 'orthodox sermon before the Ld Mayor', see Letter 388, n. 8. Possibly he preached it also at Bury St Edmunds, Suffolk. The 'good ingenious hand' was that of Garnham.

13 The bishop of Norwich from 1783 until his translation to St Asaph in 1790 was Lewis Bagot (1740–1802). The work to which Lindsey referred was *A letter to the Right Rev. Lewis, by divine permission lord bishop of Norwich, requesting his lordship to name the prelate, to whom he referred, as 'contending strenuously for the general excellence of our present authorised translation of the Bible'* (London, 1789). The author, who was not named, was Robert Edward Garnham, and the publisher was Joseph Johnson. Bagot's work, entitled *A charge delivered to the clergy at the primary visitation of Lewis, lord bishop of Norwich*, was published in Norwich in 1784; Garnham, in the title of his *Letter*, was quoting from p. 33.

14 The manuscript is slightly torn at this point. Lindsey's optimism about 'great and important changes' abroad may be explained by the news of developments in the French Revolution; in early Aug. 1789 the National (Constituent) Assembly, formed as a result of the initiative of the Third Estate in June 1789, abolished a large number of feudal privileges, including tithe payments.

15 The parliamentary session ended on 11 Aug. 1789. This was not its last session; there was a further session, from Jan. to June 1790, before its dissolution and the general election in June 1790.

16 Elizabeth (d. 1811), née Hawkes, who married Michael Dodson in 1778; see *Gent. Mag.*, LXXXI, ii (1811), 197.

391. To WILLIAM HAZLITT SENIOR   31 AUGUST 1789

Text: 'The Hazlitt papers', *CR*, NS, V (1838), 756.
Addressed: To Rev. Mr. Hazlitt, Wem, Shropshire

London, Aug. 31, 1789.

DEAR SIR,

Dr. Priestley's and my visit to our venerable friend at Shrewsbury was so uncertain, that it was not possible to give any notice of it. We left Birmingham in the morning, dined and passed the evening at Mr. Tayleur's, and were in our chaise to return at five o'clock the next morning. And though I am forced to refrain from writing to you, as to many other friends, I retain the same sincere regards for you.

I have been this morning with Mr. Johnson, and talked to him much, when I recommended to him your MS. Sermons to publish by subscription. His advice is to desist for the present, as he has several publications of the kind for the next winter, and they go on very heavily.[1] As to myself, I would do my endeavour, but am afraid I could not assist you much in procuring many names, though for such a trifling sum. You would be surprised to hear how little this way I have been able to serve a much-esteemed, learned and ingenious friend, whose Sermons are nearly printed and will come forth early in the winter.[2]

I hope your son is well, and that he has changed his condition agreeably and with good prospects.[3]

I am always, dear Sir, very sincerely yours,

T. LINDSEY.

Dr. Disney and my wife desire their respects.

---

1 Hazlitt's *Discourses for the use of families, on the advantages of a free enquiry, and on the study of the scriptures* (London, 1790) were published by Joseph Johnson. The volume was prefaced by a list of 160 subscribers, including Lindsey, who subscribed for six copies.

2 Possibly Lindsey referred here to George Dyer's *Inquiry into the nature of subscription* (see Letter 382, n. 4), for which he had been soliciting subscriptions earlier in the year. Alternatively, he might have had in mind George Walker's *Sermons on various subjects*, published in London in two volumes by Joseph Johnson in 1790; prefaced to volume I is a list of 472 subscribers, including Theophilus and Hannah Lindsey.

3 John Hazlitt (1767–1837), the eldest son of William Hazlitt and his wife Grace, née Loftus (1746–1837), became a successful portrait painter and miniaturist, having been a pupil of Sir Joshua Reynolds. It is also possible, however, that Lindsey referred to John Hazlitt's younger brother William, the celebrated writer, who also enjoyed a career as a painter before devoting himself to literature.

392. To HENRY TOULMIN   5 SEPTEMBER 1789

Text: 'Original letters from the late Rev. Theophilus Lindsey to
                      the late Rev. Harry Toulmin', *CR*, NS, XI (1844), 76–8;
                      TUHS, XV, 4 (Oct. 1974), 142–3.
Addressed: To the Rev. Mr. Toulmin, Chowbent, near Wigan, Lancashire

London, September 5, 1789.

DEAR SIR,

It is a long time since our correspondence was interrupted. I hope that now it will get into its regular course. My wife desires with me to be kindly named to Mrs. Toulmin, and to congratulate you most sincerely on hers and your babe's providential escape from a fatal infectious fever. It was most happy that both were in a place where no care could be wanting to promote a recovery.[1]

I am glad to hear of the threats against you, as they are all bruta fulmina,[2] and shew that the country is not in a state of indifference to the truth, and the worst of all others.[3]

I must beg you to inform me what number I have had of your Exhortation, and of Mr. Mort, and what number you have already printed by you of both.[4] I must also desire whether I am to send a parcel of tracts that I have in readiness for you, but not made up, to Mr Baldwin's,[5] or immediately to yourself, and how to be directed.

As you saw Dr. Priestley on your road, you are acquainted with his indefatigable labours. He informs me that on Tuesday next he sets off for his brother-in-law, Mr. Wilkinson's, at Castle-head, near Lancaster, to be absent about three weeks.[6] I wish that, by their means at Birmingham, we may at length have a good collection of hymns for public worship. I am glad you made some acquaintance with Mr. Bakewell. He is a valuable convert from the Church of England, and I expect will be the instrument of great good in his place. I was sorry it was out of my power to call upon him in our late route, though we passed through Burton.[7]

We have heard of your Bishop in his progress through his wide-extended diocese, and of his great zeal against the growth of Socinianism every where expressed.[8] I like him the better for it. It is a mark of his being in earnest; and its effects will be to excite attention to the doctrine, and then I persuade myself that he will promote what he wishes to suppress. Such crafty men as Bishop Hurd are for making no noise about such matters.

You will like a No. of our Commentaries just published, which I shall send you, and two other tracts, one hardly out of the press.[9] Pray tell Mr. Valentine that I hoped he would have called again as he promised, as I had many things which I wished to have talked over with him.[10] At Birmingham, among other things, you would hear mention of *Wideheath*.[11] When you see Mr. Hawkes, of Manchester, to whom I beg my respects, pray ask him of him. When he is in a settled state, at Oldham or at Manchester, I should be glad to know.[12] I shall see Dr. Disney tomorrow, and remember you duly to him.

With my wife's kind remembrance to you, I remain always most truly yours,

T. LINDSEY.

I hope you found your worthy clerk and fellow-labourer well, after your travels.[13]

---

[1]   Henry Toulmin's first wife was Ann, née Tremlett (d. 1812), whom he married in 1787. Their first surviving child, born in 1788, was Frances Toulmin. Lindsey drew reassurance from the proximity of the Toulmin family to Manchester, where medical expertise among leading dissenters, such as Thomas Percival, was available.

[2]   'Bruta fulmina et vana', i.e. 'thunderbolts that strike blindly and in vain' (Pliny the Elder).

[3]   Evidently, threats (presumably in this instance of a verbal kind) to Henry Toulmin had started before the 1790s and the attack on Chowbent chapel in 1793 (see Letter 516). He had drawn attention to himself by his support for the repeal of the Test and Corporation Acts in 1789–90, and in 1791 he, John Holland of Bolton and other dissenting ministers in the area organized a series of lectures at Wigan on unitarian doctrine, which attracted hostile comment; see *MR*, XXI (1826), 496. Hezekiah Kirkpatrick (1738–99), minister of the Park Lane dissenting chapel near Wigan, was apparently greeted frequently during the early 1790s with the words 'Up with the church and down with the Rump'; G. Fox, *The history of Park Lane chapel* (Manchester, 1897), p. 67.

[4]   See Letter 388, n. 4. The *Exhortation* is usually attributed to Joshua Toulmin, although it is probable that Henry Toulmin had some part in its composition. For John Mort, see Vol. I, Letter 338, n. 8.

[5]   Robert Baldwin, bookseller and publisher, of the Rose, 47 Paternoster Row, London.

6   John Wilkinson of Castle-head, near Lancaster. Priestley wrote to Lindsey from Castle-head on 21 Sept. 1789; Rutt, I, 31–2.

7   William Bakewell of Burton upon Trent was listed as a new member of the Unitarian Society at its annual meeting on 12 Jan. 1792; Unitarian Society minute book, p. 29. He is listed as a member of the society in 1794; *Unitarian Society ... 1794*, p. 9. He was related to the agricultural improver Robert Bakewell, whose family had extensive presbyterian connexions; see David L. Wykes, 'Robert Bakewell (1725–1795) of Dishley: farmer and livestock improver', *Agricultural History Review*, LII, 1 (2004), 38–55. Robert Bakewell was probably the 'Mr. Bakewell of Dishley, Leicestershire', who is listed as a subscriber to Walker, *Sermons on various subjects*, I, vi. William Bakewell, who joined the Unitarian Society in 1792, was possibly the William Bakewell who contributed 'Some particulars of Dr. Priestley's residence at Northumberland, America', to the *MR*, I (1806), 393–7, 504–8, 564–7 and 622–5, and who was listed (as of Melbourn, Derbyshire) as a subscriber to the unitarian fund in 1814; *MR*, IX (1814), appendix, p. 12. See also Rutt, I, 28.

8   William Cleaver, bishop of Chester 1788–1800; see Letter 390, n. 7.

9   The 'latest number' of the *Commentaries and essays published by the society for promoting the knowledge of the scriptures* was number VII, published in the summer of 1789.

10   Probably Peter Valentine (see Vol. I, Letter 338, n. 9, and *CR*, NS, X (1843), 202) or John Valentine (see n. 13, below).

11   'Wideheath' was the pseudonym of the author of 'An attempt to prove that 1 John iv. 7, is an interpolation', in Priestley's *Theological Repository*, V (1786), 194–200. In 1817, the *MR* published a list of writers in the *Theological Repository*, with their pseudonyms. It identified 'Wideheath' as John Whitehead of Glodwick, Oldham, Lancashire; *MR*, XII (1817), 527. He died in 1815, aged sixty-four. It is evident from his obituary that Whitehead was a largely self-taught layman and 'decidedly an Unitarian'; *MR*, X (1815), 188. Lindsey probably meant that during his visit to Birmingham, Toulmin would hear talk of Whitehead's work from Priestley and other dissenting ministers, possibly including William Hawkes (1731–96), who had been minister of New Meeting, Birmingham, from 1754 to 1780.

12   Mr Hawkes of Manchester was William Hawkes (1759–1820), the son of William Hawkes (n. 11, above). He was minister, successively, at Dob Lane chapel, Oldham; at Bolton; and, from 1789, 'in a settled state', until his death, at the newly opened Mosley Street chapel, Manchester. It is likely that he too, through geographical proximity, was acquainted with Whitehead.

13   Possibly by Toulmin's 'clerk and fellow-labourer' Lindsey meant Henry Toulmin's wife, Ann; see n. 1, above. Another possibility is John Valentine (d. 1822), a long-standing member of the Chowbent congregation before, during and after Toulmin's ministry; according to his obituary in *MR*, XVII (1822), 307, he 'was rarely absent from his place of worship, constantly attending twice a day, and in the evening conducting a devotional service in his own family'. See also Wright, *The story of Chowbent chapel*, pp. 53–4, where John Valentine is described as a 'venerable presbyter'.

---

393. To WILLIAM ALEXANDER   **12 SEPTEMBER 1789**

    Text: 'Letters of the Rev. Theophilus Lindsey, No. II',
                      UH, II, 45 (8 Mar. 1862), 84.

Note: This is the only section of the letter printed by the *UH*; the manuscript has apparently not survived. The ellipsis at the beginning of the second paragraph indicates that it and the first paragraph were separated by text which the *UH* omitted. Here the paragraphs are separated by a broken line.

September 12th, 1789.

The world will soon see (and continue to see each year that he lives, by the Divine blessing), that Dr. Priestley is far from retracting his Unitarian sentiments.[1] There is *some* ground for the other report. I did at first wish and endeavour to prevent the publication of his sentiments on the miraculous conception; but not from any intimation that he had already gone far enough, but because I wished such an opinion not to be published till satisfactory evidence could be produced that the beginning of Luke's gospel was spurious, or not to be admitted.[2]

----

* * * I think your prudence commendable in not dispersing any Unitarian or other

tracts till you see your way clear before you, and that they will be likely to do good. Who but must rejoice and wish success to the noble efforts of the French for their liberties?

---

1   This seems to be a specific reference to Priestley's *Defences of unitarianism*, which appeared in 1787, 1788 and 1790, as well as to his other theological publications in these years.

2   The 'other report' almost certainly concerned Priestley's controversial opinions on the miraculous conception, which Lindsey wished him to restrain, at least in public. See G. M. Ditchfield, '"The preceptor of nations": Joseph Priestley and Theophilus Lindsey', *TUHS*, XXIII, 2 (Apr. 2004), 506–9.

394. To WILLIAM TURNER OF NEWCASTLE   3 OCTOBER 1789

    Text: DWL, MS 12.44 (49).
    Printed: McLachlan, *Letters*, p. 40 (part of eighth sentence of third
                     paragraph).
    Addressed: To/The Rev^d. M^r. Turner/Newcastle upon Tyne
    Endorsed: Oct. 3. 1789
    Postmarked: OC 3 89

London. Oct. 3. 1789

Dear Sir,

    I am the more obliged to you for your favour, which Mr Gibson[1] left for me when I was in the country this week, because I believe I was a letter in your debt. But I will strive to be a better correspondent.

    The account you transmit of Mr Whitfield's spirited and proper application to the present candidates for the county of Durham, and their answer, shall be read to our committee on Monday night, and circulated, as it ought to be.[2] And I hope Dissenters throughout the kingdom will be excited to see the dispositions of the present reigning powers towards them: for assuredly Mr Burdon's voice is theirs.[3] Mr Heywood is at present at Brighthelmstone, and I shall contrive to make him acquainted with the fact.

    The letter which you inclosed goes away this evening to it's destination which you marked. The worthy man[4] stayed but four days in Town, two of them he gave us the pleasure of his company at dinner, and we were much edified and delighted with a recital of his labours and the perils undergone for the gospel's sake, and greatly admire and value his readiness and abilities. But – to return your frankness and confidence, nevertheless he is not a person whom I would wish to have my collegue in this place, if [I] had one to seek. No one could speak more handsomely and respectfully of another than he did of yourself, without any drawback whatsoever. And indeed your behaviour was very generous. Of the immediate cause of the difference I studiously avoided to say any thing, and therefore nothing was named. But I was sorry to hear what was said of Mr Prowitt, not of his heart or conduct, but of his talents in all respects for carrying on public worship, prayer as well as preaching. Not that I gave credit to what I heard, as upon mention being made of some young man, I thought I saw that prejudice might operate, and perhaps the setting too high rate upon a regular, academical education. You will believe, that I would not on any account that Mr Prowitt whom I highly value, should know this, as it has not diminished my esteem for him.[5] Of one thing I persuade myself, that if you see any defect in his public performances, which may be corrected, you will in the kindest manner apprize him of it, and lend him any books that may be of service; and if you think there are any books that he may want, and which it would be particularly useful for him to have by him, I will contrive to send them. I should have sent him a parcell of tracts which I promised, but have been prevented by being in the country, but it shall certainly go by next Friday's waggon, if all be well, and therein I shall inclose a few things for you, and particularly the letter to the B^p. of Norwich, which is keen indeed, but not more so than the man merits.[6] I woud only now mention, as irony is often obscure for want of knowing circumstances alluded to, that the quotation at the end Mancipiis locuples eget aeris Cappadocum rex[7] refers to his Lordship having a great suit [*sic*] of needy domestics and dependants but not much to feed them with, as he has been such a bad manager and kept so good a table, tho' I believe not guilty of personal excesses, that the revenues of his Bishopric were put to nurse for a few years to redeem him.[8]

Of the author of that, and the Examination of Mr Harrison, I can only say that I believe they come both from the same hand, and one that you never heard of, which will give you pleasure, that there are such *unknown* friends to truth: yet not unknown thro fear, but proper caution.[9] I mentiond to you[r] worthy father a secret, which you I am persuaded will not divulge, and wch probably he might forget to name to you: and it is, that there is a design of a new translation of the Bible, and some persons have been engaged.[10] Names will be kept as secret as possible. Your worthy father promised me something he had formerly attempted on the epistle to the Ephesians, about which I shall in a short time write to him.[11] MSS and Comunications are to go through my hands. Have you any collection relating to such a business? Or could you procure any. Perfection not to be looked for – but if tolerably amended and aiming towards it, at first, it may come nearer the next time; and nearer the next. The great thing is to break the Ice and make the attempt. I guess one person, as proper to be consulted, will immediately occur to you, as to me. But if we meet in our ideas, that person's Temper &c &c was thought an insuperable bar to any free and friendly communications.[12] I have said so much to no man whatsoever upon the subject, in black and white, but I have no doubt that *tutis auribus committo.*[13]

I shall be most glad to see Mr Holland's.[14] I like every thing that bears that name, and of course shoud not like,[15] to whom as also to yourself my wife desires to send her best wishes. Mr Lee is at the sea side, somewhere near Hartlepoole, where his daughter is bathing to strengthen her constitution.[16] The Disneys are all of them very well. I rather dissuaded Mr Holmes from printing such a book of Comon Prayer, as you describe, unless he was encouraged by the prospect of a congregation, and by the expence being defrayed.[17] I hope your father was well when you last heard from him. I am always, Dear Sir Your much obliged and affectionate servant

     T. Lindsey.

---

1   Thomas Gibson (1759–1832), banker, treasurer of the Literary and Philosophical Society of Newcastle upon Tyne and a member of Turner's Hanover Square congregation. Lindsey met him in London again in 1796; see Letter 644.

2   On 31 Oct. 1789, the *Newcastle Courant* published a letter from 'No Freeholder of the County of Durham', strongly advocating the repeal of the Test and Corporation Acts. Probably Whitfield's 'application' been part of a previous controversy; see *Extracts from books and other small pieces,* pp. 6–10. There followed a controversy over this issue in the *Newcastle Courant* for the remainder of the year. That newspaper also printed, throughout the summer and autumn of 1789, letters to the freeholders of Durham from the three candidates for the parliamentary representation of the county, Rowland Burdon, Sir John Eden and Sir Ralph Milbanke (see n. 3, below), soliciting their support. I have not identified Mr Whitfield, but *The general election poll for knights of the shire; to represent in parliament the county palatine of Durham ...* (Newcastle upon Tyne, 1790) lists nine freeholders

of that name. 'Our committee' was either the committee of the SPKS or of the club of dissenting ministers which Lindsey attended during this period.

3   Rowland Burdon (?1757–1838), of Castle Eden, Durham, was a banker in Newcastle upon Tyne. A supporter of Pitt's administration, he was MP for the county of Durham from 1790 to 1806. At the general election of 1790, he was returned at the top of the poll for Durham, defeating two opposition whigs, Sir Ralph Milbanke (1747–1825), who was elected in second place, and Sir John Eden (1740–1812). In 1791, he was recorded as hostile to the repeal of the Test Act as it applied to Scotland; G. M. Ditchfield, 'Scotland and the Test Act, 1791: new parliamentary lists', *BIHR*, LVI (1983), 80. There is a detailed account of his career in the house of commons in Thorne, *Hist. parl.*, III, 314–18. For his bankruptcy in 1803, see Letter 749.

4   Probably this 'worthy man' was Edward Prowitt; see Letter 395.

5   Edward Prowitt was educated at the baptist college, Bristol, where his tutor was the celebrated baptist minister and controversialist Caleb Evans (1737–91); see William Turner, *A short tribute to the memory of the Rev. Edward Prowitt* (Newcastle, 1802), p. 2. For indications that deficiencies in Prowitt's conduct of public worship continued, see Harbottle, *William Turner*, p. 33.

6   For Garnham's *Letter to the Right Rev. Lewis, lord bishop of Norwich*, see Letter 390, n. 13.

7   For this quotation, see Garnham, *Letter*, p. 17, n. ‡ (the penultimate page of the work). It may be translated as 'The king of the Cappadocians, rich in slaves, wants for money'; Horace, *Epistles*, I, 6; I owe this reference to Mr David Powell.

8   For Lewis Bagot, bishop of Norwich from 1783 until June 1790, when he was succeeded by George Horne, see Letter 390, n. 13. As usual, Lindsey was receptive to unfavourable stories about high churchmen such as Bagot.

9   Lindsey referred here to Robert Edward Garnham.

10   For this project for a new translation of the Bible, see Letter 390, nn. 9 and 10.

11   William Turner of Wakefield contributed several articles to the *Theological Repository* with the pseudonyms 'Vigilius', 'Eusebius' and 'Erastus'; see *MR*, XII (1817), 527, 602, for this identification of Turner. Possibly Lindsey had in mind a long essay by 'Vigilius', entitled 'Various passages of the New Testament illustrated by Transposition', *Theological Repository*, I (1769), 45–99. In this essay (pp. 59–60), Turner included a brief section on Ephesians iv. 16. Perhaps Lindsey hoped that he would expand it; it seems that he did not.

12   Probably Gilbert Wakefield.

13   'I commit to safe ears'.

14   This appears to be a reference to a private letter, rather than a publication, perhaps of John Holland, minister of Bank Street chapel, Bolton, for whom see Letter 447, n. 10.

15   Lindsey evidently omitted, inadvertently, several words (perhaps on the lines of 'to neglect him') at this point.

16   John Lee's daughter and only child was Mary Tabitha Lee (1777–1851).

17   Edward Holmes (d. 1799) succeeded John Noble (see Vol. I, Letter 62) as headmaster of Scorton School, Yorkshire, in 1767 and held that office until 1799. Lindsey when vicar of Catterick had been his neighbour. Holmes published, in co-operation with Anthony Temple, *The Book of Common Prayer of the Church of England, reformed upon unitarian principles: together with the psalter or psalms of David* (Newcastle, 1790). An undergraduate at Magdalene College, Cambridge (BA 1762, MA 1766), he served as assistant master at Harrow before his move to Scorton. His obituary (*Gent. Mag.*, LXIX, ii (1799), 720–1) stated that he 'became a decided Unitarian' as a result of reading Lindsey's publications.

395. To WILLIAM TURNER OF NEWCASTLE   17 OCTOBER 1789

Text: DWL, MS 12.44 (50).
Addressed: For/The Rev^d. Mr Turner/Newcastle
Endorsed: Oct. 17. 1789
Postmarked: Postmark missing.

Saturday forenoon.
Octr. 17. 1789

Dear Sir,

Mr Gibson has been so obliging as to call upon me again.[1] I like his mien and manner so much though he stayed not more than one minute, that I am sorry it was not in my power to see more of him. As he has left me his address and is to leave town as he tells me to morrow, and I am very busy to day, I can only tell You, that I hope you rec[d] my last:[2] that the parcell is at last set out for Newcastle to M[r] Prowitt, that of the few put up for you, I sh[d] be obliged to you, if it be proper and in your way, to make M[r] Richardson of Alnwick[3] a present of The Vindiciae[4] and Examination of Robinson,[5] merely as a token of respect, and of the honour I bear so worthy a character. Of the few other little things I send M[r] Prowitt, I shall desire him, as he will be most disposed, to let you take what you please.

I am glad D[r] Priestley found M[rs] Priestley much better on his return out of the North.

You will be pleased with their Proceedings and Resolutions at Birmingham, and I hope all Dissenters thro' the kingdom will follow the example.[6]

I trouble M[r] Gibson with a small tract just publishd, sent to me anonymously – reported to be the composition of a young Dissenting Minister – surely very clever – [7]

With *our* best wishes for you and M[rs] Turner and your little family I remain always Dear Sir, most truly yours

T. Lindsey

---

1 For Thomas Gibson, see Letter 394, n. 1.
2 Letter 394.
3 Robert Richardson, attorney at law, of Alnwick, Northumberland, and a friend of William Turner, became a member of the Unitarian Society in 1792; see Letter 491, n. 3.
4 I.e. Lindsey's *Vindiciae*, published in 1788.
5 I.e. Lindsey's *Examination of Robinson*, published in 1785.
6 Possibly Lindsey referred here to resolutions for a 'Plan of Union' put forward by the committee of dissenters in Birmingham as part of their campaign for the repeal of the Test and Corporation Acts. The resolutions advocated the construction of a national pressure group, consisting of county and town meetings, which should elect delegates to provincial meetings, which should in turn forward delegates to a national meeting. See *Extracts from books and other small pieces*, pp. 13–14.
7 Probably this tract was a contribution to the debate over the repeal of the Test and Corporation Acts. One possibility is the anonymous *A letter to the bishops on the application of the protestant dissenters to parliament, for a repeal of the Corporation and Test Acts* (London, 1789), which was in fact written by Joshua Toulmin. Another is *Facts submitted to the consideration of the friends to civil and religious liberty, but more particularly addressed to the protestant dissenters of England and Wales; containing Bishop Horsley's extraordinary letter to the clergy of his diocese; and the substance of Mr Fox's speech on the repeal of the Test Laws* (London, 1789). Each was published by Joseph Johnson. For Horsley's 'extraordinary letter', see Letter 398, n. 6.

---

396. To JOSHUA TOULMIN   23 OCTOBER 1789

Text: Belsham, *Memoirs*, p. 204; McLachlan, *Letters*, p. 40 (second and third sentences).

Note: According to Belsham, this letter (of which the manuscript seems not to have survived) was written to 'a friend', without further identification of the recipient. However, the reference to the recipient's son and to that son's presence in Manchester with Priestley (see n. 2, below) indicates that the recipient was Joshua Toulmin, whose son Henry was at that time minister of the unitarian congregation at Chowbent. Belsham printed only the extract which is reproduced here. McLachlan did not identify the recipient and mis-dated the letter as '1790'.

I find that your son's account[1] of the Unitarian street-preachers is true, and that he was with Dr. Priestley at Manchester when he saw them.[2] It will be very desirable to have their numbers increased. We want much to have the common people applied to, as enough has been done, and is continually doing, for the learned and the higher ranks.

---

1   This 'account' presumably came to Lindsey in a (non-surviving) letter from Henry Toulmin.
2   In his letter to Lindsey of 8 Oct. 1789, Priestley described his meeting at Manchester with 'two Unitarian street-preachers, men of good sense and great zeal, who had read hardly any thing besides the Bible; nothing of mine or yours'. He added a few details about their work, noted that he had presented them with five guineas and revealed that 'young Mr. Toulmin' had been with him; Rutt, I, 33–4.

397. To HENRY TOULMIN   27 OCTOBER 1789

Text: 'Original letters from the late Rev. Theophilus Lindsey to
                  the late Rev. Harry Toulmin', *CR*, NS, XI (1844), 78–9;
                  TUHS, XV, 4 (Oct. 1974), 143–4.
Addressed: To the Rev. Mr. Toulmin, Chowbent, near Wigan, Lancashire.
                  Post-paid (6d)

London, October 27, 1789.

DEAR SIR,

You will wonder that you have not heard from me lately. I shall not, however, stay to tell you how I have been hindered, as I hope it will not happen again. I hasten to tell you that I have this moment received your packet of the date of October 17, which made a journey through London to Staindrop[1] before it arrived, and that I shall read your intended Preface for your very valuable and useful tract[2] this evening, and endeavour to send it to your father to-morrow, not having leisure at present, as I have some more letters to write, and am then obliged to go to our Quarterly dinner, and to attend a committee in the evening afterwards.[3] You say you shall have a demand for 300 of the Exhortation; I desire to be put down for 300 more.[4] Mr. Johnson some time since told me he had not one copy remaining; so that I think you want not encouragement to make this new edition. Your parcel came safe, containing six dozen of Catechisms, and three of Exhortations.[5] I am much in your debt on this score before. But we must settle all by and by.

I have inquired for this year past at Rivingtons, and set others to inquire, about Bell's tract on the Lord's Supper, and it is not to be had.[6] I suspect that it is not reprinted because heretics commend and buy it up. If upon further inquiry it is not to be had, we have some thoughts of reprinting it, not to sell, but to distribute, which can give no just offence to the author.

Mr. Frend's second Address also is out of print, but I shall put Mr. Johnson upon getting another edition. I shall, however, take an early opportunity of sending you some of the Appeals, &c.[7]

I thank you for mentioning that Mr. Cooper has printed his Arguments for Unitarianism separately, as the tract must be useful.[8] If I cannot have some of Johnson, I shall desire you to send me a couple of dozen at the bookseller's price. You may expect a few lines again very soon. With *our* respects and best wishes for Mrs. Toulmin, yourself and the little one,[9]

I remain always most truly yours,
    T. LINDSEY.

---

1   Staindrop, in County Durham, was the residence of John Lee.
2   Lindsey referred here to the second edition of Toulmin's *Exhortation*; see Letter 388, n. 4. This

second edition was published in Taunton in 1789 and had a new preface, which may be found at pp. iii–v.

3   Lindsey probably referred here to the quarterly club of dissenters which he attended during the late 1770s and the 1780s; see Vol. I, Letters 149 and 294; see also Letter 430.
4   For Toulmin's *Exhortation*, see Letters 388, n. 4, and 392, n. 4.
5   I.e. the 'Catechism of young Mr Toulmin'; see Letter 381, n. 5.
6   This work was William Bell's *An attempt to ascertain and illustrate the authority and design of the institution of Christ commonly called the communion and the Lord's supper* (London, 1780). Although J. F. and C. Rivington did not publish this work, they were among the publishers of the second, slightly enlarged, edition which appeared in 1781, and it was to the second edition that Lindsey referred in this letter. Bell (1731–1816) was a prebendary of Westminster and had been chaplain to Princess Amelia, the aunt of George III. Writing from a latitudinarian perspective, he described the Lord's supper as 'nothing more than a religious commemoration' (*Attempt*, 2nd edn, p. 36) and cited with approval Benjamin Hoadly's *Plain account of the Lord's supper*. His arguments were subsequently criticized by the high churchman Lewis Bagot, and Bell re-asserted them in a further edition of the *Attempt* in 1790. Probably Lindsey knew of (and possibly was consulted about) Bell's translation for publication by Joseph Johnson of the manuscript of Pierre François Le Courayer's *A declaration of my last sentiments on the different doctrines of religion* (London, 1787). Bell's translation was prefaced by a biographical account of Le Courayer, Lindsey's friend at the time of his connexion with the duchess of Somerset. Le Courayer had died in 1776.
7   For Frend's 'Second Address', see Letter 383, n. 5. By 'Appeals', Lindsey probably meant Frend's *Appendix to thoughts on subscription*; see Letters 384, n. 1 and 388, n. 9.
8   The final section of Thomas Cooper's *Tracts ethical, theological and political. Vol. I* (Warrington, 1789, only one volume published), pp. 465–526, was entitled 'A summary of unitarian arguments'. It was published separately with the title *Objections to the doctrine of the Trinity, as advanced in the service and articles of the Church of England: or a summary of unitarian arguments* (Manchester, 1788). Although the date of publication on the title page is 1788, the preface is dated 'Manchester – 1789'.
9   See Letter 392, n. 1.

398. To WILLIAM FREND   14 NOVEMBER 1789

Text: CUL, Add. MS 7886 (Frend papers), no. 149.
Addressed: To/Mr W. Frend/at Mr R. Frend's/Canterbury[1]
Endorsed: Lindsey
Postmarked: NO 14 89

London nov^r. 14. 1789

Dear Sir,

Heaven be praised that we have gotten you safe again to our isle. You will hardly believe how much many known and unknown to you have been concerned lest you should have suffered for want of health, or amidst the perils and dangers now on our continent.[2] I am obliged to you for y^r brief strictures on the state of things there. The revolution in France is a wonderful work of providence in our days, and we trust it will prosper and go on, and be the speedy means of putting an end to tyranny every where. I have sent Mrs Priestley her son's letter and the Doctor your testimony of him, as I happend luckily to be sending to him.[3] He will feel himself much obliged to you. He has been and is labouring as usual. Near two of the three volumes of his Ecclesiastical History are printed off.[4] I have seen his letters to the insolent and disingenous [*sic*] B^p of St David's, tho perhaps I have mentioned this, very masterly, and which will be published with letters to other opponents, the beginning of January, under the title of Defences of Unitarianism for the year 1789.[5] The said Bishop has written a letter to his clergy which Dr Kippis read at a public meeting of Dissenters, a fortnight ago, in which his Lordship dissuades them from voting at the next election for Mr Phillips the present member, because he received the thanks of the Dissenters for voting for the repeal of the Corporation and Test Acts, to the overthrowing of our ecclesiastical constitution.[6] The B^p of Salisbury, I am told, in print,[7] and Churchmen in general are as eager to prevent this repeal as in Sacheverels days; and the Dissenters are resolved to pursue their just and righteous demand. The letter to the B^p of Norwich will give you pleasure,[8] as a just rebuke of a dealer in pious frauds, and as it may turn peoples thoughts toward a new translation of the Bible. I have sent some copies of this and of your own Account,[9] which last I believe has done much good, as it has been much circulated. Along with it were sent a few Tracts, which I have always by me to give away, and are always at your service. By the way, your Second Address is out of print and the press must be set to work.[10] If you do not make any long abode in the metropolis, I trust we shall see you for a few days when you depart from Canterbury, as we shall be in your way to Cambridge, whither I apprehend you turn your face, and I trust it will [be] for good, wherever you go.

Concerning a certain work in hand, about which you have not been idle,[11] I am persuaded, however diverted by ten thousand other things, we shall talk when we meet; or otherwise I shall send any communications I may have to make, to you. Dr Disney and his are all well. He shall have y^r letter to him to morrow.[12] Mr Lambert was lately here for a few days, much better, and almost intirely well. *We* coud not help having some solicitude on no letters being received from you. A certain business was imparted to him, and mention made of the parties engaged. And I trust he will give aid, tho' he had not spirits to tye himself to any part.[13] Though free inquiry and the doctrine of the true worship of God, its consequence, does not thrive in the South, particularly under the baleful shade of a Metropolitan cathedral,[14] I can assure [*sic*] it is making its spread pretty rapidly in the West and North, and by the means using will I hope in no short time pervade the land – And the more as potentates rise up against it, the B^p of Chester, Cleaver, happily[?] charging thro' his wide diocese against Socinianism &c &c.[15] But I have not time to add a word more, but my wifes kind respects and that I am always your affectionate friend and servant
    T. Lindsey.

1   'Mr R. Frend', of Canterbury, was Richard Frend, the brother of William Frend. The *Poll of the electors for members of parliament to represent the city of Canterbury* in the general election of 1796 (Canterbury, 1796), p. 20, records his name as a wine merchant of Longport in the city. Perhaps not surprisingly, in the light of his family connexion to William Frend, he voted for the two opposition candidates, John Baker and Samuel Sawbridge. Their father, George Frend (d. 1789) was a wine merchant, as well as an alderman, and twice mayor, of Canterbury.

2   The 'perils and dangers' on the continent in the autumn of 1789, which explain Lindsey's relief at Frend's safe return, included the forcible conveyance of Louis XVI and his family from Versailles to Paris in Oct.; the breakdown of order in much of rural France; and the revolt in the Austrian Netherlands against Joseph II.

3   Priestley sent his second son William to Frankfurt, with a view to settling him with a German family of Frend's acquaintance there, as part of his education. Frend duly met William Priestley at Frankfurt in the autumn of 1789. On 18 Nov. 1789, Priestley wrote to Lindsey 'It was very fortunate that Mr Friend [*sic*] met my son at Frankfort. His account of him is very grateful to his parents. I hope he will behave so as to gain friends.' See DWL, MS 12.13, fo. 107; Rutt, I, 42–3, printed only the first sentence of this quotation. See also Knight, *William Frend*, pp. 74–5, 79. It is clear that Lindsey had forwarded Frend's favourable report of him to Priestley; I have not found the letter from William Priestley which Lindsey said he had sent to his mother.

4   For Priestley's *General history of the Christian church to the fall of the western empire*, see Letter 382, n. 6. Although Priestley's intention had been to publish it in three volumes, the final version appeared in two volumes, published by Joseph Johnson, in 1790.

5   Priestley's *Defences of unitarianism for the years 1788 & 1789* (Birmingham and London, 1790)
    included (pp. 1–74) ten letters to Horsley, as well as replies to other critics.
6   John George Phillips (1761–1816) was MP for Carmarthen from 1784 to 1803, apart from a brief
    interruption in 1796. In Mar. 1787 and May 1789, in response to requests from local dissenters, he
    voted in the house of commons for the repeal of the Test and Corporation Acts. Samuel Horsley,
    whose diocese of St David's included the borough of Carmarthen, responded by distributing a circular
    to his diocesan clergy, urging them to vote for Phillips's likely opponent, Sir William Mansel (1739–
    1804), in the forthcoming general election. In the event, Phillips was returned for Carmarthen without
    a contest in the general election of 1790. See G. M. Ditchfield, 'The parliamentary struggle over the
    repeal of the Test and Corporation Acts, 1787–1790', *EHR*, LXXXIX (1974), 574–5.
7   The bishop of Salisbury from 1782 until his translation to Durham in 1791 was Shute Barrington
    (1734–1826). It is clear that Lindsey had not read the publication of Barrington to which hearsay
    had apparently drawn his attention. In 1789, Barrington did not publish a work specifically opposing
    the repeal of the Test and Corporation Acts. Possibly Lindsey had in mind the bishop's *Letter to the
    clergy of Sarum. To which are added, directions relating to orders, institutions, and licences* (Salis-
    bury, 1789). This work did not refer to the Test Laws, although it praised the work of the Proclama-
    tion Society (pp. 4–5) and defended the church's property rights, particularly over tithe collection
    (pp. 21–3).
8   For Garnham's *Letter* to the bishop of Norwich, see Letter 390, n. 13.
9   Frend's 'own Account', was probably his *Account of some late proceedings of the 'Society for
    Promoting Christian Knowledge'*; see Letter 388, n. 2.
10 See Letter 383, n. 5.
11 This is a reference to Frend's participation in the projected new translation of the Bible; see Brooks,
    'Priestley's plan', 91–5. Frend was to undertake the translation of the historical books of the Old
    Testament (Joshua, Judges, 1 and 2 Samuel, 1 and 2 Kings).
12 This letter from Frend to Disney does not survive among the letters to Disney at DWL or in Frend's
    papers (CUL, Add. MS 7886).
13 The 'certain business' was the projected new translation of the Bible. James Lambert, professor of
    Greek at Cambridge from 1771 to 1780 and bursar of Trinity College from 1789, although approached
    as a possible contributor, did not participate in the translation.
14 Canterbury Cathedral.
15 See Letter 390, n. 7.

399. To WILLIAM TURNER OF NEWCASTLE   8 DECEMBER 1789

Text: DWL, MS 12.44 (51).
Addressed: Address missing.
Endorsed: Dec. 8. 1789
Postmarked: Postmark missing.

                                                    London. Decr. 8. 1789

Dear Sir,
    Tho' I have not acknowleged your last obliging letter, it has not been wholly
unnoticed. For it was in consequence of seeing it that Mr Heywood wrote, and it
was your humble servant that communicated to him the B^p of St Davids curious
letter to his clergy concerning the Borough of Caermarthen.[1] And I have been happy
in seeing by his means how you have gone in the North and particularly your own
useful and seasonable efforts in the cause. If you had sent me that sheet you printed
in the Newcastle paper by the post,[2] I should have been obliged to you, as postage
is by no means an article we mind, and I should not have been curious ab^t a frank
in writing to you, if I had not wished to convey to you two copies of the enclosed,
which was one of the first exertions the worthy writer was called to make on his
return from the Continent to his native city.[3] But some thing sh^d be mentioned to
take off the rudeness of the attack, which some may otherwise be apt to term it.
Before he went abroad he had been carrying on a little skirmish upon the subject

in the Canterbury News-paper, and it was upon being refused the same channel of conveyance, that he took this method of signifying his sentiments.[4] He is now in Town, and going in a few days to reside and study at Cambridge, in which I hope he will not be interrupted. But some suspect that the Dons there who seek to be on the rising list in the church, will be likely to disturb and turn him out of his fellowship.[5]

As you liked the Letter to B^p. Bagot, I hope to be able soon to send you a letter to another Bishop, most curious, useful and such as you will no less be pleased with, as I hear it will be out of the press in a week or ten days.[6]

Your friendship and testimony to Mr Prowitt, do him great credit and have given me intire satisfaction relating to that worthy man, and I hope he will now go on happily in his situation. I wish you would tell him when you see him, that I propose to write and thank him for his last: but I am dilatory that way, or rather, one is so much interrupted that one can hardly find time here to do the most necessary things.[7]

Dr Priestley has printed his letters to B^p. Horseley, and is going on with his other Opponents, to be ready by the beginning of the year.[8]

They are also laudably busy in the press at Birmingham in printing tracts to promote the present intended reassertion of Dissenters' civil rights, which it w^d seem the church is more than ever determined to oppose.[9] I believe it will be for the benefit of truth and free inquiry that they shoud go on to oppose unto the end.

There is nothing yet done, except in Dr Disney's loose papers, toward the printing of Ad^n Blackburne's life and works. But I believe there are some thoughts of setting about it soon in earnest.[10]

We are much pleased to hear that your cousin is every way so agreeably married.[11] When we passed a few hours at Wakefield this year, we could not help taking notice of her and liked her much. If you should write soon, or when you write to Wakefield, I wish you would make our best respects to your worthy father, and tell him I should be obliged to him, if not too much trouble, could he look out for and send me, what he had formerly done on the Epistle to the Ephesians, of which he made me some promise.[12]

My wife has lately for some weeks been a martyr to a pain in her face: but is somewhat better within these few days. She desires to join with me in respects to Mrs Turner and yourself with good wishes for your little folks, and I remain always, Dear Sir, very truly and affectionately Yours,

   T. Lindsey

---

1 See Letter 398, n. 6. Heywood's letter to Lindsey appears not to have survived.

2 I have not located this item by Turner.

3 I.e. William Frend (Canterbury was his 'native city'). Frend's first works after his return from his continental tour included a third edition of his *Second address to the members of the Church of England, and to protestant trinitarians in general* (London, 1789) and the second edition of his *Thoughts on subscription to religious tests* (London, 1789). The title pages of both works indicated that they were for sale by booksellers in Cambridge and Canterbury.

4 This 'little skirmish' took the form of a public controversy between Frend and George Townsend (1755–1837), independent minister of the Ebenezer congregation, Ramsgate. In 1788 Frend published *An address to the inhabitants of Canterbury and its neighbourhood: exhorting them to turn from the false worship of three persons, to the ... one true God* (St Ives, 1788); his arguments were similar to those he deployed in his *Address to the inhabitants of Cambridge* (see Letter 383, n. 5). Townsend replied with *A testimony for truth, in a brief vindication of the divinity of Christ, and a Trinity in unity, denied in the Rev. Mr. Frend's address to the citizens of Canterbury* (Canterbury, 1788). Early the following year, he went further with *A word of caution and advice against the Socinian poison of William Frend* (Canterbury, 1789). In a letter to the *Kentish Gazette*, 15–19 May 1789, Frend challenged Townsend to produce scriptural evidence in favour of the worship of Christ as God. Townsend

responded with *The brief rejoinder; in a letter to Mr. W. Frend* [on his letter in the *Kentish Gazette* of the 15–19 May] ... *with a postscript to the inhabitants of Canterbury* (Canterbury, 1789). Frend then departed for his continental tour and the dispute fizzled out.

5   Frend had been deprived of his tutorship, but not his fellowship, of Jesus College, Cambridge, in Sept. 1788. He retained his fellowship even after his banishment from the university following his publication of *Peace and union recommended to the associated bodies of republicans and anti-republicans* in St Ives in 1793.

6   Possibly this work was Robert Edward Garnham's anonymously published *A letter to the Right Rev. Dr William Cleaver, lord bishop of Chester*; see Letter 390, n. 7. The publisher was Joseph Johnson. For Garnham's *Letter* to Lewis Bagot, bishop of Norwich, see Letter 390, n. 13.

7   Edward Prowitt's 'situation' was the office of minister to a chapel of unitarian baptists at Pandon Bank, Newcastle upon Tyne. His letter to Lindsey seems not to have survived.

8   Priestley's *Letters to Dr Horsley* were published in three parts in Birmingham in 1783, 1784 and 1786. His replies to his other opponents to which Lindsey referred included his *Defences of unitarianism, for the years 1788 & 1789* (see Letter 398, n. 5) and his *Letters to the Rev. Edward Burn, of St. Mary's chapel, Birmingham, in answer to his, on the infallibility of the apostolic testimony concerning the person of Christ* (Birmingham, 1790). He also published *Familiar letters ... to the inhabitants of Birmingham*; see Letter 407.

9   Lindsey referred here to *Extracts from books, and other small pieces*. According to the title page it was 'printed by order of the committee of the seven congregations of Protestant dissenters, in Birmingham'.

10 The works of Francis Blackburne were published in seven volumes in Cambridge by Benjamin Flower in 1804–5. The first volume included a memoir of the author by his eldest son, also named Francis Blackburne.

11 Possibly Lindsey referred here to the marriage of Mary Willets to the surgeon Peter Holland (1766–1855) of Knutsford, Cheshire. For the links between the Holland, Turner and Willets families, see *Familiae min. gen.*, I, 175–9.

12 See Letter 394, n. 11.

400. To WILLIAM FREND   2 JANUARY 1790

Text: CUL, Add. MS 7886 (Frend papers), no. 150.
Addressed: Address missing.
Postmarked: Postmark missing.

London. Jan. 2. 1790

Dear Sir,

I am glad of an opportunity of telling you, that your friends are all well in Town, and woud be very glad to hear that you are got safe into your nest in Jesus college. The inclosed would have been with you four days sooner, but I was disappointed in a cover for it. You will see that I intended you no reverence, but the worthy member to whom I sent it, would rectify what he thought a mistake.[1]

I hope it brings you the best news from the other side the water. The quiet and stability of the proceedings at Paris is said to be very offensive here.[2] The Laureat doubtless speaks not barely[3] his own mind, tho' there are some political fears of others in declaring themselves openly.[4]

You see how well the Dissenters go on. The resolutions at Nottingham would particularly please you.[5] I hope some liberal ministers of the established church will dare to step forth openly in their cause. In the west, and in Lancashire, particularly from some knowlege of the fact, the freest inquiry is going on, and of course the doctrine of the Divine Unity spreading much.

We hope Mr Tyrwhitt is happy in the enjoyment of his usual health, and that you found Mr Hammond perfectly recruited, and able to face the winter when it comes.

Dr Disney and all in Sloane[6] were perfectly well yesterday. On Monday he sets out to visit his worthy mother for a fortnight at Lincoln.[7]

With my wifes kind respects I remain always sincerely and affectionately à vous
    T. Lindsey.

Mr Belsham came in as I was sealing my letter and desires kind remembrances. What an excellent creature is he, and of what use likely to be in his station! He has been already in not a few, and will be in many more to a great extent, an instrument of drawing the Dissenters from theological systems to the study of the scriptures only[?]. He hopes, with me, that you will take to your black coat as usual.[8]

---

1   'The inclosed' was probably a pamphlet or sermon. The 'worthy member' was a member of parliament, perhaps John Lee or James Martin, who used his franking privileges on Lindsey's behalf. Perhaps Lindsey had addressed the letter to 'Rev. Mr Frend', as he did in Letter 384 and other letters, but the 'worthy member', thinking incorrectly that Frend possessed a doctoral degree, altered 'M^r' to D^r'.

2   In the winter of 1789–90 the National Assembly was devising a new constitution for France, including the division of the country into eighty-three departments and the first steps towards the secularization of the Gallican church. The 'quiet and stability' did not last.

3   Lindsey's hand is not quite clear at this point; possibly he wrote 'basely', rather than 'barely'.

4   The poet laureate from 1785 until his death on 21 May 1790 was Thomas Warton (1728–90), a fellow of Trinity College, Oxford. At the beginning of 1790 an 'Ode for the New Year' was published, with his name, in several London newspapers; see, for example, the *English Chronicle or Universal Evening Post*, 31 Dec. 1789 – 2 Jan. 1790, and the *London Chronicle* of the same dates. It took the form of a paean of praise to George III and English prosperity, as contrasted with the 'all-delusive Liberty' of revolutionary France. While apparently not doubting Warton's authorship, Lindsey seems to have suspected that the ode did not represent the laureate's real opinions, and the *London Chronicle* of 31 Dec. – 2 Jan. 1790 described it as 'highly sarcastic on Government'. However, it was not Warton's work. On 2 Jan. 1790 the *St James's Chronicle* declared that the association of his name with the ode was 'a gross imposition upon the publick'. Warton himself removed all doubt when he told the Shakespeare scholar Edmond Malone on 3 Jan. 1790 that 'I appear in the Papers, not only as an Esquire, but as the author of a New Year's Ode which I never wrote'; *The correspondence of Thomas Warton*, ed. David Fairer (Athens, GA, and London, 1995), p. 650.

5   On 9 Dec. 1789, a meeting at Nottingham of deputies from dissenting congregations in Nottinghamshire, Derbyshire and 'a small adjoining Part of Yorkshire' passed a series of resolutions in favour of the repeal of the Test and Corporation Acts. One of the resolutions invited the support of members of the Church of England. Another resolution recommended a further meeting, at Derby or Leicester, as part of a 'union' of dissenters in a wider campaign. The meeting was chaired by George Walker. See *Extracts from books, and other small pieces*, pp. 11–13. For the Leicester meeting, see Letter 403, n. 8.

6   I.e. Sloane Street, Knightsbridge, where Disney and his family lived.

7   John Disney's mother was Frances, the youngest daughter of George Cartwright of Ossington. See Vol. I, Letter 373, n. 5.

8   A 'black coat' was a humorous, or satirical, term for a clergyman.

401. To WILLIAM HAZLITT SENIOR   2 JANUARY 1790

    Text: 'The Hazlitt papers', *CR*, NS, V (1838), 510.
    Addressed: To the Revd. Mr. Hazlitt, Wem, Shropshire

London, Jan. 2, 1790.
DEAR SIR,

I have at length met with Mr. Johnson; and he desires me to acquaint you, that the expense of printing 250 copies will be defrayed by the sale of 150, and leave some small matter for the author; but he does not undertake for his indemnification if he prints a greater number of copies, as sermons of known heretic Socinians, and their works in general, are soon mere old drugs that never get off.[1] – I have been informed that Mr. Rowe is chosen sole minister of the Unitarian congregation at Shrewsbury, and I am glad of it, as he is young, exceedingly well-disposed, studious, and zealous to promote the truth, and moreover, as the salary is not more than sufficient for one person. I heartily wish that the congregation may increase so as to find sufficient work and support for two ministers.[2]

I congratulate you on the *great* times we live in. The French Revolution is astonishing; and I trust they will soon lay the lasting foundation of a constitution, which other nations will make their model. And the Brabanters will be free, if it be not their own fault by differing among themselves.[3]

The Dissenters seem now every where to be in earnest in their firm resolutions not to cease their petitions till justice be done them and their long withheld civil rights restored. The abolition of penal laws in religion will then follow of course; but it seems quite right and well-judged to keep to the point with which they began.

I have not heard lately from our common friend Mr. Wiche,[4] but it is much my own fault, in not having written to him: but it is a fault difficult to mend in this town, unless necessity impel. I am glad to hear that you enjoy your health in your retired corner. My wife has not been so well of late, but is now better; and I hope this frosty air of a day or two will continue, and make both country and town more healthy. Dr. Disney and his are very well, and he and my wife desire their respects.

I am always very sincerely yours,

    T. LINDSEY.

P.S. I shall certainly be a subscriber for half a dozen copies, but cannot undertake to procure many besides.[5]

---

1   This is a reference to Hazlitt's *Discourses for the use of families*: see Letter 391, n. 1.

2   The High Street congregation, Shrewsbury, did indeed support two ministers for much of the later eighteenth century. On his nomination as minister in 1787, John Rowe was the fifth successive assistant minister to Joseph Fownes, the senior minister of the chapel from 1748 until his death in 1789. Rowe himself was the sole minister from 1789 to 1793 and from 1795 to 1798, but between 1793 and 1795 Arthur Aikin was his assistant. Born in Apr. 1764, Rowe was aged twenty-five in Jan. 1790.

3   In 1789, a revolt in the Austrian Netherlands, following resistance to Austrian rule led by the estates of Brabant, led to the deposition of the Habsburg emperor Joseph II and the declaration of a republic (Dec. 1789), followed by the proclamation (10 Jan. 1790) of an 'Act of Union' of the Belgian united provinces.

4   John Wiche was minister to a general baptist congregation at Rose Yard, Maidstone, from 1746 until his death in 1794. Hazlitt had been minister to the unitarian congregation at Earle Street, Maidstone, from 1770 to 1780.

5   The (unpaginated) list of 160 subscribers to Hazlitt's *Discourses* included Lindsey's name as a subscriber for six copies.

402. To RUSSELL SCOTT   **4 JANUARY 1790**

Text:	Scott Coll.
Printed:	McLachlan, 'Lindsey to Scott', 117, where the letter is mis-dated 5 Jan. 1789 (fourth, tenth, eleventh and twelfth sentences of first paragraph).
Addressed:	To/The Rev^d. Russell Scott/Portsmouth
Endorsed:	Jan^ry 5th. 89 [in pencil: Test and Corporation Acts]
Postmarked:	JA 4 90

Note: Lindsey's letter was written on the reverse of a printed circular, which is reproduced here immediately before the text of the letter.

LIBRARY, RED-CROSS-STREET, Dec. 22, 1789.

AT a numerous and respectable Meeting of the General Body of the PROTESTANT DISSENTING MINISTERS in and about the Cities of London and Westminster, convened for the Purpose of expressing our Concurrence with our Brethren in the Country, in their Resolutions on the Subjects of the CORPORATION AND TEST ACTS.

THE REV. SAMUEL PALMER IN THE CHAIR.

RESOLVED I. *Nem. Con.* THAT Protestant Dissenters are entitled, equally with their fellow Subjects, to the complete Possession of civil and religious Liberty.

RESOLVED II. *Nem. Con.* THAT they have been uniformly distinguished by a zealous Attachment to the Principles of our happy Constitution, as defined at the Revolution; and by a steady and unshaken Loyalty to the House of Brunswick, at the most dangerous and critical Periods.

RESOLVED III. *Nem. Con.* THAT the Exclusion of them, by the CORPORATION and TEST ACTS, from Offices of Trust and Honour, in which they might prove of Benefit to the State, or enjoy the Immunities of faithful Citizens, is disgraceful to the Justice of the Nation, the Generosity of Britons, and the liberal Spirit of the Times.

RESOLVED IV. *Nem. Con.* THAT those Acts are not only oppressive in their civil Tendency, but by enforcing the Prostitution of a solemn religious Ordinance, expose our Christian Faith to the Derision of the Profligate, and the Objections of Unbelievers.

RESOLVED V. *Nem. Con.* THAT we, therefore, view with Pleasure the temperate and manly Efforts of our Brethren in different Parts of the Kingdom, to obtain the Repeal of those dishonourable and pernicious Statutes; and are ready, vigorously to concur with them, in every wise and practical Measure for bringing about so desirable an End.

RESOLVED VI. with one dissentient Voice, THAT we cannot but add, that we hope the Time is near at Hand, when all penal Laws for the Direction of Men's Consciences shall be repealed.

RESOLVED VII. *Nem. Con.* THAT these Resolutions be signed by the Chairman, and that Copies of them be sent for Insertion to two of the Daily, and to two of the Evening Papers.[1]

RESOLVED VIII. *Nem. Con.* THAT the Thanks of this Body be given to the Chairman, for his candid and proper Behaviour on the present Occasion.

SAMUEL PALMER, Chairman.[2]

London. Jan. 4. 1790

Dear Sir,

Excuse the sending of this paper, if before received. I doubt not however but you are mindful of the subject in your part of the world. And I hope that you will consider at the approaching election, to whom you give your votes to represent and act for you for seven years to come; and I canot but wish it may be for Ld J. Russell and Sr J. Clarke, on whom certain dependance may be had.³ And I trust the dissenting Interest will go this way. Yesterday I saw a letter from Yorkshire, wch mentiond that there had been a meeting of Dissenters at Wakefield, when three delegates had been chosen to be sent to London to act with the Comittee there.⁴ I should be glad to know how you go on in your parts, and soon, for I long to know how [you] go on in all respects. In no long time I hope [to] send you a book of which I am anonymous editor, and with it shall come some tracts to disperse.⁵ Pray put down in your next, where the Portsmouth coach or waggon puts up. You will see on the cover of the Analytical Review, what Dr Priestley has been doing.⁶ We expect his Defences &c for 1789 in a Weeks time.⁷ His sermon on Novr 5. is much liked.⁸ Though not in the powerful thundering eloquence of Dr Price, with whom I am sure, you have been charmed, and will think it no bad sign to see him abused for it in the ministerial and tory papers, by churchmen and courtiers.⁹ Into what *great times* at home, but infinitely more abroad is your lot fallen, I have no doubt but you labour and will labour to cooperate with these openings of Divine Providence. My wife often asks if I have heard from you, and sends her kind regards and wishes of all good for many years to come. We were above measure hurt by Mr Jellico's unfortunate connection.¹⁰ I hope the worthy family of the Carters¹¹ are all well, and did not suffer much by it.

I am always most truly Yours
        T. Lindsey.

I hope your excellent Sister and Mr Taylor are well, and trust they are not idle inhabitants of this system. The lady certainly not, if with any sphere to work in.

---

1   These resolutions were indeed carried at a meeting of the General Body of Dissenting Ministers on 22 Dec. 1789, with Samuel Palmer in the chair, and with Lindsey himself present; DWL, MS 38.106, pp. 299–301. They were duly published in the *Gazetteer and New Daily Advertiser*, 24 Dec. 1789 and in the *St James's Chronicle*, 26 Dec. 1789; and in the *Whitehall Evening Post*, 24 Dec. 1789.

2   Samuel Palmer (1741–1813), independent minister of a dissenting congregation at St Thomas's Square, Hackney, and a leading protagonist of dissenting causes. He was the editor of *The nonconformist's memorial* (1775); see Vol. I, Letters 85, n. 1 and 88, n. 1.

3   At the general election of June 1790 in the county of Hampshire, the two opposition candidates, Lord John Russell (1766–1839) and Jervoise Clerke Jervoise (?1733–1808) were defeated by the two ministerial candidates, Sir William Heathcote (1746–1819) and William John Chute (1757–1824). Russell and Clerke Jervoise were known to be sympathetic to the repeal of the Test and Corporation Acts, which no doubt explains Lindsey's endorsement of them. Although Russell Scott does not feature in the pollbook for the election in Hampshire in 1790, a leading member of his congregation, Sir John Carter (1741–1808), voted for Russell and Clerke Jervoise; *The poll for the election of two knights of the shire for the county of Southampton ... August, 1790* (Romsey, ?1790), p. 71. Sir John Carter also chaired a pro-repeal meeting of delegates from the dissenting congregations of Hampshire, held at Southampton on 23 Dec. 1789; *General Evening Post*, 5–7 Jan. 1790.

4   The allusion to the meeting at Wakefield raises the possibility that the 'letter from Yorkshire' was a non-surviving letter from William Turner of Wakefield to Lindsey. Possibly it was a letter from a Yorkshire correspondent received by a London friend of Lindsey, which Lindsey had seen; perhaps the letter was from a member of the Milnes family, since the meeting was chaired by Pemberton Milnes. The 'Meeting of protestant dissenters and other gentlemen of the West Riding of the County of Yorkshire' to which Lindsey referred took place at Wakefield on 30 Dec. 1789. It resolved to

pursue the question of repeal of the Test and Corporation Acts and nominated delegates to the London 'repeal committee'. The resolutions of the meeting were published in the *General Evening Post*, 14–16 Jan. 1790, and in the *Public Advertiser*, 20 Jan. 1790. The meeting also resolved to invite the co-operation of sympathetic parish clergy. This last resolution produced a hostile response, signed by fifteen anglican clergymen, and published at Leeds on 15 Jan. 1790. A group of five dissenting ministers in Leeds, led by William Wood, minister of the Mill Hill chapel and the secretary of the West Riding dissenters, replied in a further statement, published at Leeds on 29 Jan. 1790, reasserting the objectives of the repeal campaign and denying that its success would harm the established church. The last two statements were published as a two-page broadsheet, with the title *At a meeting of protestant dissenters, etc* (Leeds, 1790).

5   This work was Hopton Haynes, *The scripture account of the attributes and worship of God*; see Letter 406, n. 16.

6   Lindsey referred here to the *Analytical Review*, IV (Aug. 1789), p. 512. This was the final page of this number. It reported, under 'Literary intelligence', that Priestley had made 'great progress' with his *General history of the Christian church to the fall of the western empire* and that he was beginning to print a new edition of 'all his publications on the subject of Air'.

7   See Letter 398, n. 5.

8   This work was Priestley's *The conduct to be observed by dissenters in order to procure the repeal of the Corporation and Test Acts, recommended in a sermon preached before the congregations of the Old and New Meetings at Birmingham, November 5, 1789* (Birmingham, 1789). Lindsey was drawing a comparison with Price's famous *Discourse on the love of our country*, preached on 4 Nov. 1789.

9   The *English Chronicle or Universal Evening Post*, 17–19 Nov. 1789, contained a sardonic verse attack on Price and the Revolution Society. The society had moved a vote of thanks for his sermon of 4 Nov. The *Public Advertiser*, 20 Nov. 1789, noted that the French 'comfort themselves' with the expectation that, thanks to Price and the Revolution Society, 'the Clergy and Nobles will be brought as low' in Britain as in France. On the other hand, the *Public Advertiser*, 4 Jan. 1790, defended Price's sermon as 'spoken by a man who defies venality, and glories in undisguised truths', and dismissed its critics as 'hireling scribblers'.

10 Lindsey probably referred here to the financial losses suffered by Adam Jellicoe, first clerk in the office of paymaster to the treasurer of the navy, who died on 31 Aug. 1789; *Gent. Mag.*, LIX, ii (1789), 864. Richard Price believed that Jellicoe's death had been hastened by these financial losses, which resulted from an unwise investment. *Price corr.*, II, xvi, 130, III, 257; 'Richard Price's journal for the period 25 March 1787 to 6 February 1791', deciphered by Beryl Thomas, with an introduction and notes by D. O. Thomas, *National Library of Wales Journal*, XXI (1979–80), 391. Jellicoe's family were members of Scott's congregation at Portsmouth. For Lindsey's acquaintance with him, see Vol. I, Letter 372, n. 1.

11 The Carter family, notably John Carter (1715–94) and his son Sir John Carter (see Letter 402, n. 3), were members of Scott's High Street, Portsmouth, congregation. The family's background, like that of Scott's congregation, was Presbyterian, but they adopted unitarian opinions in the later eighteenth century. See V. Bonham-Carter, *In a liberal tradition. A social biography, 1700–1950* (London, 1960), pp. 6–22.

---

403. To WILLIAM FREND   14 JANUARY 1790

Text: CUL, Add. MS 7886 (Frend papers), no. 152.
Addressed: To/Mr Wm. Frend/fellow of Jesus college/Cambridge
Postmarked: JA 14 90

Dear Sir,

I expect you will receive the parcell of tracts before this reaches you, and am glad that it will be in your way to dispose of them. I cd not help throwing in some copies of young Mr Toulmin's Exhortation, the new edition, which you will like; and I have more at your service, when you call for them.[1]

It happened that Mr Belsham was with me, when I recd your first letter, and as we had often talked of you and wished to hear you was well, you will believe that the information I could give him, woud make him very happy. On reading him that part of it relating to the association of another person into our little society, he seemed to think that there was some good ground for the reasons which had caused him originally not to be applied to.[2] There will be time enough however to do any thing of the kind hereafter, at our meeting in April, when D[r] P. comes to Town, if it shall be then deemed proper.

I am much rejoiced at what you are doing w[h] respect to the N.T. particularly the gospels. Another person is too much occupied, and otherwise unable, to pretend to any thing more than a general inspection.[3] And all assistance that you and others can give with respect to the historical parts of the N.T. will be wanted. It were to be wished, that D[r] Symonds would publish on the Epistles as he has done on the gospels, before other people come out with their work.[4]

M[r] B.[5] as well as ourselves, was much affected, with that part of your letter, which mentions your late worthy Fathers dispositions towards You.[6] And I must not forget that he desird his kind remembrances in which my wife desires to be mentioned

Thanks for the account from M[r] Edwards,[7] which I shall communicate to D[r] Priestley, who will also be solicitous to know how it fares with you, and I shall be able to gratify him. He has been very much occupied in these proceedings at Birmingham, tho he has kept out of sight, and tho' invited, did not go to the Grand Meeting yesterday at Leicester, where he sends me word the Duke of Grafton your Chancellor was expected to take the chair, as some had sent an invitation to him. But whether it woud really take place he could not say. Otherwise M[r] Russell of Birmingham, a very proper person was expected to be in the chair.[8]

This renewal of their application from the Dissenters, will be of infinite service to them and to the nation by disseminating a knowlege of their true principles, of which the body were in general most ignorant, and by uniting so cordially and universally, a thing never known before.

I must now acknowlege your second letter.[9] As soon as I rec[d]. it, I sent the letter to the World by M[r] Dodson's servant, desiring it might be returned to Boswell court, if not inserted, which I thought proper to do, that it might not be lost.[10] It has rained all the day and we have had people with us or I sh[d] have gone to inquire ab[t] it. If I had not been going out when it came, I sh[d] have transcribed it and sent it to some other paper at the same time.

I hope D[r] Disneys pious visit to his worthy aged parent, will do him good and rid him of a rheumatic complaint, which the harass he has lately been under has brought upon him.[11] I do not expect him in Town 'till the next week.

Remember that I have a copy or two of D[r] Priestleys history of early opinions from him to be disposed of when you know of any worthy subject to whom they would be useful. I shall have a book of w[ch] I am anonymous Editor to send you soon.[12] But for the negligence of the Printer, it w[d] have been out sooner.[13] I remain with all esteem, D[r] Sir most truly Yours

T. Lindsey

London. Jan[y]. 14. 1790.

---

1   See Letters 388, n. 4, and 392, n. 4. A second edition, 'with some additions and corrections', of *An exhortation to all Christian people to refrain from trinitarian worship* was published in Taunton in 1789. In common with the first edition, it was credited to Joshua Toulmin, and the latter's wife, Jane Toulmin, is named on the title page as the publisher. The work was sold in London by Joseph Johnson.

2   Possibly by 'our little society' Lindsey referred to the semi-moribund SPKS, but it is more likely that
    he meant the small group which was working on the projected new translation of the Bible. Probably
    'another person' who might have been invited to participate was Gilbert Wakefield (see Letter 409,
    n. 6). 'Our little society' would hardly have signified Essex Street chapel by 1790, and the Unitarian
    Society was not founded until Feb. 1791.

3   This was probably James Lambert; see Letter 398.

4   See Letter 385, n. 1. John Symonds published his *Observations upon the expediency of revising
    the present English version of the epistles in the New Testament. To which is prefixed, a short reply
    to some passages in a pamphlet, intitled, 'An apology for the liturgy and Church of England'* in
    Cambridge in 1794.

5   Thomas Belsham.

6   Frend's father was George Frend of Canterbury, who died on 12 Dec. 1789; *Kentish Gazette*, 18–22
    Dec. 1789; see Letter 398, n. 1. His will, dated 9 Feb. 1788 and proved on 6 Oct. 1790, named
    William Frend's brother Richard Frend (see Letter 398, n. 1) as his principal legatee and sole exec-
    utor, and contained no reference to William Frend; Canterbury Cathedral Archives, Canterbury arch-
    deaconry court, PRC 17/102, fos. 43r–43v. His 'dispositions' to William Frend were evidently made
    before his death.

7   For Thomas Edwards (*c.* 1759–1842), of Jesus College, Cambridge, and vicar of Histon, near
    Cambridge, see Vol. I, Letter 375.

8   The 'proceedings at Birmingham' formed part of the dissenters' campaign for the repeal of the Test
    and Corporation Acts in 1789–90. For the meeting of 'Deputies of protestant dissenters of the Three
    Denominations within the Midland District' at Leicester on 13 Jan. 1790, see *Aris's Birmingham
    Gazette*, 18 Jan. 1790, and John Money, *Experience and identity. Birmingham and the west midlands
    1760–1800* (Manchester, 1977), pp. 221–3. This meeting published a series of resolutions denouncing
    all penal religious legislation and nominated delegates to a 'national meeting'. Grafton was not
    present; Russell chaired the meeting and was appointed secretary and treasurer of a committee to
    correspond with other regional organizations of dissenters. Russell had chaired an earlier pro-repeal
    meeting at Birmingham on 26 Dec. 1789; see *General Evening Post*, 21–3 Jan. 1790, and Tony Rail,
    'William Russell (1740–1818)', *TUHS*, XXI, 4 (Apr. 1998), 289.

9   This letter, in common with Frend's other letters to Lindsey, seems not to have survived.

10 Michael Dodson lived at 8 Boswell Court, Carey Street. I have not found the letter from William
    Frend.

11 Disney's 'aged parent' was his mother, who lived at Swinderby, Lincolnshire.

12 See Letter 406, n. 16.

13 Joseph Johnson employed several printers at different times, including printers in Birmingham such
    as Thomas Pearson for the publication of many of Priestley's pre-1791 works. On the title page of
    Priestley's *An inquiry into the knowledge of the antient Hebrews, concerning a future state* (London,
    1801), Johnson's printer is named as D. Levi, Green Street, Mile End New Town.

404. To WILLIAM TURNER OF NEWCASTLE   15 JANUARY 1790

Text: DWL, MS 12.44 (52).
Addressed: For/The Rev^d. Mr Turner/Newcastle/upon Tyne
Endorsed: Jan. 15. 1790
Postmarked: Postmark missing.

London. Jany. 15 1790

Dear Sir,

I have not been able sooner to procure a frank, or should have transmitted to you
my New year's Gift, which I now send to go towards the expences of the Building
of the Unitarian chapel, and beg you will give it to Mr Robson with my respects
and best wishes for the prosperity of the congregation that shall assemble within
its walls.[1]

I have tryed as much as I could to procure some other contributions, wishing to
have sent them at the same time with my own, but have not been able to succeed.

To you in all respects this new Society is indebted for your exertions for them, more than to any other, and your unwearied disinterested friendship and assistance to them and to M[r] Prowitt cannot be enough acknowleged.

I have heard of you at Wakefield, I wonder how you can be able to go through so much.[2] But the cause inspires and you are young and active.

We expect D[r] Priestleys Defences of Unitarianism for 1788, 1789, in a few days, and I shall charge myself with sending it you with some copies of another piece, as soon as it appears, by the coach.[3] Be so good to tell M[r] Robson, that I had intended a larger present, but shall not be wanting another year to send my mite.

Your friend M[r] Heywood goes to the Sessions in Lancashire on Monday.[4] How much the cause of the Dissenters and of truth and liberty is indebted to his indefatigable exertions, every way, I need not tell You.

I have time to add no more at present but our joint respects to M[rs] Turner with my wifes to yourself and our good wishes for your little one, and due respects to y[r] Father when you write – I remain always Your much obliged and faithful servant
     T. Lindsey.

---

1   The ship and keel builder William Robson (d. 1824) was a leading figure among the unitarian baptists in Newcastle and took a prominent part in the construction of their chapel at Pandon Bank in 1789; Lindsey evidently sent a contribution towards the building. The congregation appointed Edward Prowitt as its minister. However, in 1797, lack of numbers obliged the Pandon Bank congregation to merge with that of Hanover Square, where Prowitt became William Turner's assistant. After 1811, Robson himself left Hanover Square and joined a smaller group of unitarians at Surgeons Hall, Newcastle. See Vol. I, Letter 358, n. 3; Harbottle, *William Turner*, pp. 32–3, 45; and E. Mackenzie, *A descriptive and historical account of the town and county of Newcastle upon Tyne, including the borough of Gateshead* (Newcastle, 1827), pp. 378–9. On his death aged eighty in Feb. 1824, the *MR*, XIX (1824), 114, stated that he was 'a Unitarian Christian of the baptist denomination' and praised his contribution to public education.
2   Lindsey was impressed by the energy of William Turner of Newcastle, whose father he had visited at Wakefield during his summer excursion in 1789; see Letter 399. Born on 20 Sept. 1761, Turner was aged twenty-eight in Jan. 1790.
3   See Letter 398, n. 5.
4   Presumably Lindsey meant the next Monday, which was 18 Jan. 1790. Heywood practised on the northern circuit, of which Lancashire was part. He and Turner had both been students, although not contemporaries, at Warrington Academy.

405. To RUSSELL SCOTT   7 FEBRUARY 1790

Text: Scott Coll.
Addressed: For/The Rev[d]. Russell Scott/at D[r] Hawes's N[r]. 8./
               Bury-Street/S[t] Mary Axe
Endorsed: Feb[ry]. 8th. – 90 [in pencil]: Read
Postmarked: Postmark missing.

Sunday. feb. 7. 1790.

Dear Sir,

I was glad to see your handwriting, and to learn that want of health had not made you silent. When your letter came, most of my tracts were disposed of, and it did not appear that the dispersion w[d] be of much service with you – therefore I did not send any.

But my wife and I shall be most glad to see you, and shall expect you, on Wednesday morning the 10th. instant to breakfast with us at half an hour past nine, which is mentioned, that you may not hurry yourself too much. Should you not be able to come that day, you will let us know and appoint your own, and any but Saturday.[1]

I reserve a 1000 things till we meet
Always most truly Y[rs]
T. Lindsey.

_____

[1]   The following Saturday was 13 Feb. 1790.

406. To WILLIAM TAYLEUR   10 FEBRUARY 1790

Text: JRUL, Lindsey Letters, vol. II, nos. 29–30.
Printed: McLachlan, *Letters*, p. 36 (most of thirteenth paragraph;
                   fourteenth paragraph); p. 38 (most of seventh paragraph).
Addressed: Address missing.
Postmarked: Postmark missing.

Wednesday. Feb. 10. 1790
Dear Sir,

Before I saw M[r] Wood's obliging note at my return home this evening I had procured the cover that conveys this to you, which I only mention to shew that I had some little compunction at not having written to you of so long a time and had intentions of amendment.[1] All I have to allege in my behalf is that I have weekly at least had the same intentions, but been prevented putting them in execution by more business of various sorts than has generally fallen to my share, and by imagining I had nothing of any consequence to communicate.

I must not however omit to acquaint you, that though I have not attended to any thing on the subject of the future state revealed in the gospel, but those passages in it which you sent me, and not to them with all the leisure due to them, I am apprehensive that notions taken up from theory and philosophy and our benevolent wishes must give way to what is expressly revealed concerning the severity of the divine government hereafter, and the number of those who shall finally be saved. But I hope some time hence to be able to consider the whole more maturely and say more to you upon the subject, which is every way an awful one.[2]

But what times, my most esteemed friend, are we fallen into? I do not however think so ill of them as to agree with those who say the nation, or rather the members of the estabilished church are not more liberal than in the days of Sacheverel, in matters of religion. I believe it with respect [to] what are called the Tory-Gentry in general, and your Oxonian clergy in particular: but I trust this will be found to be only a partial bigotry that rages so much in certain districts, and will not have any permanent effect, and that the members of the church in the middle rank of life, who are the most respectable will be found to have better principles.

We may have farther reason also to think that the present will be only a temporary insanity, when we consider the aversion of one man[3] towards the Dissenters in general, and how many find or hope to find their interest in falling in with such a disposition. In this list the zealous B[p] Horsely distinguishes himself at this time, in his Review of the Test Laws, and in his Apology for the Ch. of E. in reply to Hints to the New Association &c ascribed to the Duke of Grafton.[4] Tho' they be anonymous, no one can doubt a moment of these pieces being his productions. And he proves, in his way, that no alteration can be made in the liturgy and service of the Ch. of E. which woud not be for the worse, and compliments M[r] Pitt, and encourages him to go in his successful efforts to save the church from the dangers that threaten it in the proposed repeal of The Test Acts.[5]

The Vindication of the Ch. of E. is by B[p]. Porteous, tho' studiously seeming to conceal himself; and yet not quite in earnest in that, as those that know him are satisfied from his conclusion, and they have no doubt but he will take care the queen be made to understand who is the author. He is a man that has had a character of some sense. But this pitiful piece has not the least signature of that kind upon it.[6] I reckon it worth your seeing as a sample of An Episcopal Defence in the present day of the liturgy of the Church.

It is reported, that the supposed Author of Hints &c has kept back a third edition of that Tract, which has been very much called for, with a view in a supplement to take notice of any thing he deemed worthy of an answer produced against him by these heroes, who have been said some time to be at work.[7] White, the Bookseller in Fleetstreet, told me that he believed he coud have sold 4 or 500, if there had been any, soon after D[r] Price's Sermon was printed.[8]

The Defences of Unitarianism for 1788, 1789, are admired here excedingly [sic] by all that I know who have seen them, and highly deserve it. But of his Sermon on Nov[r]. 5. friend and foe speak most favourably.[9] And indeed I know not the man save himself, who could at once, at one sitting, with so much ease and perspicuity, put together so much excellent sense upon the subject.

I have formerly mentioned to you M[r] Porter, a pupil of M[r] Belsham's from Daventry, lately settle[d] minister to a congregation at Plymouth.[10] That congregation are desirous of having an Unitarian liturgy, and there is a prospect of estabilishing a congrega-[tion] at Dock, could money be raised for the building of a chapel. But the letter will apprize you of every thing. Knowing your continual outgoing upon some late and present occasions, besides others wholly unknown, I am almost ashamed of putting such a plan before you: but a small matter would be of service. And I must tell You, that I have already collected myself £160, tho' I do not apprehend I shall be able to go much farther.

As you will be glad to have all the information of their design before you, I shall transcribe a paragraph of a letter I rec[d] two days since, in answer to my earnest intreaties, that M[r] P. would not introduce a liturgy unless the congregation was very unanimous ab[t] it, and he was sure the thing woud not diminish the number of his hearers.[11]

"With respect to the Liturgy, the congregation is perfectly unanimous in wishing it to be introduced, and so far woud it be from diminishing the number of our hearers, that we are all of opinion it woud considerably increase it. I should be much obliged to you with the other tracts to send the Salisbury Liturgy which you mention, together with the additional half-sheet, which was printed at Shrewsbury.[12]

"The Manchester Liturgy I have lately procured, but it will not suit our purpose; as we wish, on several accounts, to have our's as much like the Church-liturgy as possible.[13] Should we compile one for our own use, and indeed we think it would be the cheapest way, as I suppose we might be sure at least of disposing of 400 copies in our own neighbourhood, it is our intention to have *your* 3 services, with some few alterations, the forms for the administration of Baptism, and the burial of the Dead, together with a form of our own for the administration of the Lords supper, including however the first part of your's. As however we are not in a very great hurry, I hope to hear farther from you and M[r] Belsham &c"[14]

As I know not one person, of whose judgment I have equal opinion as of your own, on this subject, but not on this only, I should be glad to be favoured with any hints that occur to you, which I woud transmit to Mr Porter.

You may be assured I encouraged him to leave out the Apostles' creed. Indeed I shall not be satisfied, till we have expunged it here, tho' my sentiments are not alterd with respect to the miraculous conception. But the more one reads and thinks, the very thing itself, creed, becomes odious.

I must inform you also, that Mr Belsham agreed with me in advising him that the frequent change of posture was not perhaps a thing to be objected, to prevent that universal languor which obtains in all Dissenting places of worship.[15]

I shall be much obliged to you for your additions to our service, and I will take care to convey them to Plymouth.

I inclose our Treasurers receit [*sic*] for your annual Subscription. I hope in no long time, the Society will be more productive of original pieces. In a few days I hope to send you and Mr Rowe copies of Mr Hayness work, of w^h I am Editor.[16] I do not like the Print, but Johnson was afraid of incurring too much expence, as such commodities are not at all bought by those who wish well to the cause, and who waste without scruple their money every day in the most frivolous things.

I had intended to have thanked the worthy Mr Wood for his favour,[17] but really have not time, and must beg you for the present to do it for me, and also to acquaint him, that I have sent the Copy of your Letter to your Members, which I like much to the Gazetteer, a paper which I take in, and to w^h I sometime contribute little matters.[18] I sent at the same time the Letters of the Dissenting Ministers from Leeds to the Resolutions of the Churchmen at Wakefield, if they will admit it.[19] One is glad to see the Articles in that Paper to day, relating to Manchester.[20]

I hope Mr Rowe and his lady are well. We beg to be properly rememberd to them. My wife desires her most due respects to yourself. Tho' often attacked w^h her nervous painful complaint, she is able daily to go about, endeavouring to do some good. You will forgive this hasty ill written scrawl, which yet however I think more legible than Mr Porter's. When you have no further occasion for Mr Porter's letter, please to send it to Dr Priestley.[21] With earnest desires for your health and life prolonged, if it please heaven,

I remain ever Y^r most truly obliged and affectionate T. Lindsey.

1   The date of Lindsey's previous surviving letter to Tayleur was 29 Jan. 1789 (Letter 381). Writing to Lindsey on 11 May 1790 (JRUL, C2¹³) Tayleur acknowledged Lindsey's 'long, friendly & interesting letter of the 10th of Feby last' (i.e. Letter 406). Isaac Wood's 'obliging note' seems not to have survived.

2   In his letter to Lindsey of 18 Sept. 1788 (JRUL, C2¹³), Tayleur discussed the question of eternal punishment for the wicked, and Priestley's doubts as to its likelihood. Lindsey gave his initial response to Tayleur's comments in his letter to him of 7 Oct. 1788 (Vol. I, Letter 377).

3   The 'aversion of one man' towards dissenters was a reference to George III, as was the allusion to 'temporary insanity'.

4   The full title of this work was *An apology for the liturgy and clergy of the Church of England: in answer to a pamphlet, entitled Hints, &c. Submitted to the serious attention of the clergy, nobility and gentry, newly associated: by a layman. In a letter to the author, by a clergyman* (London, 1790).

5   While denying any disparagement of the extension of human learning, the author of the *Apology* (n. 4, above) upheld the fundamental Christian truths of the liturgy and denounced 'the absurdity of a progressive religion' (pp. 68, 63). For the praise for Pitt (and Lord North) for their defence of the Test and Corporation Acts in the parliamentary debate of 28 Mar. 1787, see pp. 79–80. For Horsley's probable authorship of the *Apology*, possibly in collaboration with Samuel Hallifax, bishop of Gloucester, see Mather, *High church prophet*, p. 84.

6   This work was *A vindication of the doctrines and liturgy of the Church of England; in answer to a*

pamphlet entitled, 'Hints to the new association', and other late publications of a similar tendency. In a letter from a gentleman in the country to a friend in town (London, 1790). The attribution of this work to Beilby Porteus (1731–1809), bishop of London from 1787 until his death, cannot be confirmed. Lindsey believed that Porteus was seeking royal favour and preferment; Porteus dedicated to George III his *Sermons on several subjects* (London, 1783; 6th edn, 1789) and on 23 Apr. 1789 at St Paul's Cathedral he preached the sermon at the service of thanksgiving for George III's recovery.

7   For the four editions of Grafton's *Hints*, see Letter 384, n. 3.

8   Benjamin White was the co-publisher, with John Debrett, of the second and third editions of Grafton's *Hints*. White (*c.* 1725–94) was owner of the publisher B. White and son, with premises at Horace's Head, Fleet Street. His elder brother was the Rev. Gilbert White (1720–93), author of the well-known *Natural history and antiquities of Selborne* (London, 1789). Benjamin White was suggesting to Lindsey that the aftermath of Price's celebrated *Discourse on the love of our country* could have boosted the sale of Grafton's *Hints* by 400 or 500.

9   For this sermon, see Letter 402, n. 8.

10 Thomas Porter, a pupil of Belsham at Daventry, was minister to the dissenting congregation at Treville Street, Plymouth, from 1789 to 1794, when he emigrated to America. Although associated with the Plymouth Dock chapel opened at Devenport in 1791, it seems that he was not its minister.

11 This letter from Thomas Porter to Lindsey seems not to have survived.

12 The 'Salisbury Liturgy', was a unitarian liturgy entitled *Forms of prayer .... collected, and a liturgy selected from the Book of Common Prayer* (Salisbury, 1774); there is a copy in the library of HMCO. For the 'Additional half-sheet which was printed at Shrewsbury', see Letter 408, n. 2.

13 The 'Manchester Liturgy' was entitled *Forms of prayer, for the use of a congregation of protestant dissenters, in Manchester* (Birmingham, 1789). It was prepared for the congregation which met in Mosley Street, founded in 1789; the minister was William Hawkes (see Letter 392, n. 12). This 'Liturgy' contained four forms of prayer, of which, according to the preface (p. iii), two were derived 'with little variation' from the Book of Common Prayer as revised by Samuel Clarke, and the other two from the 'Liverpool Liturgy', meaning the form of prayer used by the short-lived (1763–76) unitarian experiment known as the Octagon chapel in Liverpool. Probably these latter two forms of service rendered it unsuitable for Porter's purposes at Plymouth, although Porter did use some elements of the Liverpool and Manchester liturgies (see n. 14, below).

14 Porter's liturgy was published, with the title *A liturgy compiled from the Book of Common Prayer reformed, according to the plan of ... Samuel Clarke; together with a collection of psalms, &c* (Plymouth, 1791). On the title page of the BL copy is the handwritten note 'Compiled by the Rev^d. Mr Porter of Plymouth'. The 'advertisement' prefaced to this volume stated that the liturgy was derived from Lindsey's Book of Common Prayer and that the hymn 'for celebrating the divine perfections, in the second service' was taken from the 'Liverpool Liturgy' (see n. 13, above). It also stated that the prayer in the third service, 'to be said by the Minister and the People alternately', was the work of Joseph Fownes, minister of the High Street chapel, Shrewsbury; and that 'some few things' had been taken from the Salisbury liturgy and from 'the Forms of Prayer lately printed at Manchester' (see n. 13, above). According to W. J. Odgers, *A brief history of the Plymouth unitarian congregation* (London, 1850), p. 27, Porter's liturgy continued to be used in the first half of the nineteenth century 'whenever a fifth Sunday occurs in the month'.

15 Kneeling and standing, as well as sitting.

16 Hopton Haynes (*c.* 1667–1749), wrote *The scripture account of the attributes and worship of God: and of the character and offices of Jesus Christ*, which was published posthumously in 1750 with the pseudonym 'A candid enquirer after truth'. In 1790, Lindsey produced for Joseph Johnson a second edition of this work, with a brief 'preface to the reader' (pp. v–viii) and a longer preface (pp. ix–xxiv) giving an account of Haynes's life and writing. It was one of the books adopted by the Unitarian Society at its first meeting on 9 Feb. 1791; Unitarian Society minute book, p. 7. The work was re-issued in a third edition in 1797 as vol. XI in the series of tracts published by the Unitarian Society. To this latter edition Lindsey added a further one-page preface (p. xxiii) above the signature 'T. L.'. He explained that the idea for the re-publication in 1790, and much of its cost, came from 'a person of high rank, distinguished by an eminent love of truth, and generous concern to promote a just critical knowledge of the sacred writings, and who is also ever ready to encourage learned and worthy men, and to serve the cause of virtue and true religion, by those ample means which Divine Providence hath put in his power'. Lindsey almost certainly referred here to the duke of Grafton. Haynes was employed for most of his life in positions of increasing seniority at the Royal Mint, where he served as assay-master from 1723. At the Mint, he was a colleague and friend of Sir Isaac Newton. The receipt was for a subscription to the SPKS; the treasurer was Michael Dodson.

17 This was presumably Wood's 'obliging note'; see n. 1, above.

¹⁸ Tayleur's letter to his MPs (for Shrewsbury, or for the county of Shropshire) cannot positively be identified. A strong candidate, however, is the letter from 'A Moderate churchman', published in the *Gazetteer and New Daily Advertiser*, 13 Feb. 1790. It defended the dissenters, advocated the repeal of the Test Laws and expressed anxiety about the behaviour at Warwick of some of the Church of England's vehement supporters. Although it did not give the location of the writer, nor did it mention any MPs, the letter undoubtedly reflected Tayleur's opinions.

¹⁹ This letter, signed by five dissenting ministers in Leeds, was published in *The Diary, or Woodfall's Register* on 3 Feb. 1790, and in the *General Evening Post*, 11–13 Feb. 1790.

²⁰ The *Gazetteer and New Daily Advertiser*, 11 Feb. 1790, printed two separate protests from dissenters in Manchester. Both complained about the conduct of an anglican-inspired public meeting in the town, chaired by the boroughreeve, which carried a series of resolutions against the repeal of the Test and Corporation Acts. The complaint was that the meeting had been called solely for a partisan purpose and that the resolutions had been pushed through in an irregular manner. For the background to these events, see G. M. Ditchfield, 'The campaign in Lancashire and Cheshire for the repeal of the Test and Corporation Acts, 1787–1790', *Transactions of the Historic Society of Lancashire and Cheshire*, 126 (1977), 123–4. Lindsey probably began this unusually long letter on 10 Feb. 1790 and completed it on 11 Feb; this would explain his reference to these two items as in the *Gazetteer* of 'to day'.

²¹ This letter from Thomas Porter seems not to have survived. In his reply, dated 11 May 1790, to this letter of Lindsey, Tayleur made no mention of it (JRUL, C2¹³), and Priestley did not refer to it in his letters of this period to Lindsey in DWL, MS 12.12. Of course, Tayleur could have forwarded it to Priestley without its being mentioned by either of them.

407. To WILLIAM FREND   18 MARCH 1790

Text: CUL, Add. MS 7886 (Frend papers), no. 153.
Addressed: Address missing.
Postmarked: Postmark missing.

London. March. 18. 1790

Dear Sir,

During our late application to Parliament and since, I could as soon fly as sit down to write to Cambridge or any where. I was not however unmindful of paying the 5 guineas to Dʳ Disney, who said that so far from not being sufficient, he believed he shoud be one or two shillings in your debt. And three doz of hymns were delivered to good Mʳ Hammond.¹ Also I shall not fail to send down a parcell soon to the latter for his use and that of our unitarian brother, the minister of the chapel.²

The Dissenters are not at all disheartened by the insolent and injurious usuage [*sic*] they met with from the house.³ This morning I met a principal one among them, who said that W.P. had deceived him once, but never shoud do it again: That he did think he had some principle, but he was persuaded that he had none at all. I apprehend this is the growing opinion of the Dissenters who certainly contributed mainly to bring him in: and how has he rewarded them?⁴ We are told that there is to be an opposition in the university.⁵ I fear there can be none made to the reigning minister with any success: and particularly that You have no great character that stands up against him.

As probably Dʳ Priestley's Familiar Letters may not have reached you, I have got a couple of franks for them, and shall transmit to you in the same way what are to follow.⁶ Nothing could be more infamous and vile than Burkes standing up to abuse him and the cause, from a garbling of a recent work of Dʳ Priestleys done for the purpose: A man with whom he professed to live upon terms of friendship.⁷ But it is thought Mʳ Burke wants to change his old Masters and I must own I wish they woud change him this approaching new Parliament, and add one to the Tories with whom he has *to me* always ranked.

It was a pleasure to hear from Mr Garnham, that you was so well and so busy, when he lately passed by you. I reckon upon him and you as our principal dependance: tho' D^r P ____ y will never be wanting in what he undertakes: Nor Mr Belsham, though he is glad to have a little more respite.[8] We expect Dr Priestley in Town, after the first Sunday in April – but if not, most assuredly after the second: when I hope it may be convenient for you some part of the three weeks of his abode, to be in the great city also.[9] I dont hear any thing certain when Dr Geddes's first vol. will be out.[10] I am glad to hear that Mr Wakefield is about to publish a Translation of the New Testament. I am persuaded it will be the most improved version that is extant. I should not be surprized if he also publish a translation of the Old, as soon as some other persons who are about it; though not of the dronish[?] kind. If I might judge from his writings, tho' it is by no means a certain way of judging, there are few with whom he woud chuse to draw in a work of that kind.[11] However I declare I have no objections to any overtures of that kind, which you or others may approve. I am sure he is and has shewn himself a scholar, and an ingenious, well-principled, bold and ardent lover of truth and the gospel; and I honour him particularly for some of his late exertions. My wife and I thought Mr Lambert did not look well when he called upon us just before he went away. Mr Hammond seemed better and in better spirits.

I met Disney to day in my walks. They are all well. His eldest boy quite recruited.[12] We shall be glad to hear that Mr Tyrwhitt is *on foot* again. We know no business the gout has with him. Mrs Jebb was pretty well yesterday. But lately she was confined for 3 weeks to her chamber with a fever, and only my wife and female friends saw her. With my wife's constant respects, I remain always, Dear Sir, truly and affectionately Yours

    T. Lindsey

P.S. I sh^d be glad, for a friend's sake, to know, if there be any likelihood of an election at the University.[13]

---

1 Lindsey did not explain which collection of hymns he dispatched in such quantity to John Hammond at Fenstanton. For much of the eighteenth century dissenting worship relied heavily on the hymns of Isaac Watts, and in 1784, John Disney edited a collection of Watts's *Divine songs attempted in easy language for the use of children*; see Vol. I, Letter 353, n. 4. However, in the later 1780s several dissenting ministers with unitarian sympathies published hymn books, initially for their own congregations. They included Newcome Cappe's *A selection of psalms for social worship* (York, 1786); George Walker's *A collection of psalms and hymns for public worship* (Nottingham, 1788); and William Hawkes and Joseph Priestley's *Psalms and hymns for use of the New Meeting, Birmingham* (Birmingham, 1790). Lindsey could have referred to any of these collections; see Alan Ruston, 'Unitarian hymnbooks 1795–1914', *TUHS*, XXV, 1 (Apr. 2011), 17–34. I am grateful to Mr Ruston for allowing me to consult this article before publication. The longer-term context of the unitarian hymn book is explored in Alan Ruston, 'James Martineau and the evolution of unitarian hymnody', in *Dissenting praise. Religious dissent and the hymn in England and Wales*, ed. Isabel Rivers and David Wykes (Oxford, 2011), pp. 173–96.

2 'Our unitarian brother' was possibly George Dyer, who lived at Swavesey, near Cambridge, between 1786 and 1792, and spent much time in the household of John Hammond. Dyer himself recorded that he worked on his *Inquiry into the nature of subscription* while at Fenstanton, and that he was there at the time of the death of Robert Robinson on 8 June 1790; see Ernest A. Payne, 'The baptist connexions of George Dyer', *Baptist Quarterly*, NS, X (1940–41), 263–67. The chapel to which Lindsey referred was possibly a private chapel in Hammond's house, where it seems that Dyer officiated for a short time between c.1786 and 1792, when he moved to London. Dyer also taught at a small school at Grantchester, near Cambridge; for the possibility that he might become a baptist minister, see Payne, 'Baptist connections of Dyer', 260–7. See also Vol. I, Letter 376, nn. 5 and 6. A unitarian chapel was built at Swavesey in 1831.

3 This is a reference to the defeat in the house of commons, by 294 votes to 105, of the motion for the repeal of the Test and Corporation Acts on 2–3 Mar. 1790.

4   I have not identified this individual, although numerous dissenters who possessed the franchise voted
    for Pitt's candidates at the general election of 1784, in the belief that Pitt, rather than Fox, who was
    politically tainted through his participation in the coalition with Lord North the previous year, was
    the more likely parliamentary, and possibly religious, reformer.
5   At the general election of June 1790, Pitt was returned at the top of the poll at Cambridge University,
    which he had represented in the commons since 1784. The other successful candidate was George
    Henry Fitzroy (1760–1844), earl of Euston, eldest son of the 3rd duke of Grafton. The opposition
    candidate, Lawrence Dundas, was easily defeated. There was no further electoral challenge to Pitt at
    Cambridge University, and he remained one of the university's MPs until his death in 1806.
6   This work was Priestley's *Familiar letters ... to the inhabitants of Birmingham*. Spencer Madan
    (1758–1836) was rector of St Philip's, Birmingham, from 1787 to 1809 and subsequently held livings
    in Staffordshire and Somerset. He became chancellor of the diocese of Peterborough in 1794; his
    father of the same name was bishop of Bristol (from 1792 to 1794) and of Peterborough (1794–1813).
    For Burn, see Letter 412, n. 2; Priestley re-published his *Letters to the Rev. Edward Burn* (see Letter
    399, n. 8) as part (pp. 201–50) of his *Familiar letters ... to the inhabitants of Birmingham*.
7   In his speech denouncing the motion for the repeal of the Test and Corporation Acts on 2–3 Mar.
    1790, Burke quoted from the preface to Priestley's *Letters to the Rev. Edward Burn*, in particular
    Priestley's references to gunpowder (pp. ix, x) and his statement 'I have always been an avowed
    enemy of all civil establishments of Christianity' (p. xv). Although Burke quoted selectively from this
    work, he did not do so in a garbled way. For the relevant section of Burke's speech, see Cobbett, *Parl.
    hist.*, XXVIII, 438–40. For Burke's previous acquaintance with Priestley, see F. P. Lock, *Edmund
    Burke. Volume I: 1730–1784* (Oxford, 1998), p. 519; and *The correspondence of Edmund Burke.
    Volume V, July 1782 – June 1789*, ed. H. Furber and P. J. Marshall (Cambridge, 1965), pp. 53–4.
8   Garnham and Frend were indeed, together with Lindsey, among Priestley's most diligent collabora-
    tors in the project for the new translation of the Bible; see Brooks, 'Priestley's plan', 99–100. In
    his *Letter to the Right Rev. Lewis, lord bishop of Norwich*, pp. 18–19, Garnham defended the new
    translation. Thomas Belsham, although playing a relatively minor part in the project, was the leading
    editor of the unitarian new translation published in 1808.
9   For Priestley's visit to London, and his sermons at Essex Street chapel, see Letter 410. Letter 411
    makes clear that he met with Frend during this visit.
10 The first volume of Alexander Geddes's *The Holy Bible, or the books accounted sacred by Jews
    and Christians; otherwise called the books of the old and new covenants: faithfully translated from
    corrected texts of the originals* was published in London in 1792. The second volume followed in
    1797, and a third volume, consisting of commentary and entitled *Critical remarks on the Hebrew
    scriptures: corresponding with a new translation of the Bible. Volume I. Containing remarks on
    the Pentateuch*, was published in London in 1800. Geddes died on 26 Feb. 1802 and his unfin-
    ished researches, edited by John Disney and the catholic lawyer and apologist Charles Butler, were
    published by Joseph Johnson with the title *A new translation of the Book of Psalms, from the original
    Hebrew; with various readings and notes ... by Alexander Geddes* (London, 1807).
11 Gilbert Wakefield's three-volume *Translation of the New Testament* was published in London in
    1791.
12 Disney's eldest son was John Disney (1779–1857), lawyer, classical scholar and benefactor of
    Cambridge University, where he endowed a professorship of archaeology in 1851.
13 See n. 5, above.

408. To JOHN ROWE   31 MARCH 1790

   Text: JRUL, Lindsey Letters, vol. II, no. 31.
   Addressed: To/The Rev^d. Mr Rowe/Shrewsbury
   Postmarked: MR 31 90

Dear Sir,

   It is not very civil to say that I am not able to fill a long letter, or should have
directed myself to our common excellent friend instead of yourself. My errand is
to beg that you will be at the trouble to send the additional sheet of prayer in your
Shrewsbury-liturgy by the post addressed to the Rev^d. Mr Porter, Plymouth, who is
rather in waiting for it, to have a sight of it, before a liturgy which he is compiling

for their use at that place is finished.[1] I am afraid I made some mistake in a letter which I wrote some time since to M[r] Tayleur, in which I intended to have made the same request to You by him.[2]

Be so good to tell him, that I have been much busied and also have not been very well of late, or he would have heard from me again. Sunday last I did not officiate, but am now much better, tho' I am going into the country to morrow for a week to recruit, and the more as D[r] Disney does the duty always on Good Friday and the first Sunday in the month.[3]

I hope you are not discouraged at Shrewsbury by this raging of High-Church. Pray tell our friend, that I think he will like the New Preface to the Hints &c by the D. of G ___ and also the defence of that work against the Vindication of the Church &c and the Apology, intitled Considerations on the Expediency of Revising the Liturgy &c – This last without doubt, tho anonymous by the B[p] of Landaff – as the Vindicator is B[p] Porteus – and the Apologist B[p] Horsley, with that late poor creature B[p]. Halifax.[4]

We hope M[rs]. Rowe and your little one are well and that Shrewsbury intirely agrees with you all; and we beg our particular due respects may be presented to M[r] Tayleur with comp[ts] to M[r] Wood, and with my wife's to yourself I remain

Always most truly Yours

T. Lindsey.

London. Mar. 31. 1790.

P.S. I shoud take it as a favour to have a line from you in a week or ten days, when I shall assuredly be returned, to know the state of our friends health, and how you do all.

---

1   See Letter 406.
2   See Lindsey's letter to Tayleur of 10 Feb. 1790 (Letter 406), where he quoted Porter's request for the 'half-sheet, which was printed at Shrewsbury' as a supplement to the Salisbury liturgy. By his 'mistake', Lindsey seems to have meant that he omitted to ask Tayleur, or through him Rowe, to forward this additional sheet to Porter. Tayleur had forwarded copies of the form of prayer which he had printed at Shrewsbury, modelled on that of Samuel Clarke and Lindsey himself, to Lindsey in 1780; see Vol. I, Letter 227.
3   31 Mar. 1790 was a Wednesday; 'Sunday last' was 28 Mar. 1790; Good Friday in 1790 fell on 2 Apr. Lindsey's visit to 'the country' was probably a week-long sojourn with Sophia and Frances Chambers at Morden.
4   In the 'new preface' to the fourth edition of his *Hints* (see Letter 384, n. 3), Grafton replied briefly to his critics, particularly the author of the *Apology*, and urged '*High-Churchmen*' to have 'less of Toleration in their Language, and more of it in their Conduct'. The other works to which Lindsey referred were Richard Watson's *Considerations on the expediency of revising the liturgy and articles of the Church of England ... by a consistent protestant* (London, 1790); *A vindication of the doctrines and liturgy of the Church of England*, for which see Letter 406, n. 6; and *Apology for the liturgy and clergy of the Church of England*. For the probable authorship of the *Apology*, see Letter 406, n. 5. Samuel Hallifax, bishop of St Asaph, had died on 4 Mar. 1790.

409. To WILLIAM FREND   **22 APRIL 1790**

Text: CUL, Add. MS 7886 (Frend papers), no. 154.
Addressed: To/The Rev^d. W. Frend/fellow of Jesus college/Cambridge
Postmarked: AP 22 [year illegible]

London. April. 22. 1790.

Dear Sir,

You would not have been so long without seeing my handwriting, had I been resident here all the while. The truth is, I have not been perfectly well, and have been out of Town part of the time – but am now grown stout again, and shall rejoice, with my wife to see you as will all our comon friends. One thing I must say, that you woud have rec^d a letter to day, if I had not been agreeably surprised with your letter and the copies of Mr Dyer from Fetter lane last night.[1] For I wanted to tell you that Dr Priestley had been a week with us, and that as he preached the last Sunday he would also the next for me, and we should be glad of your company for the day.[2] But as you have laid out your time otherwise, I trust nothing will prevent our seeing you to breakfast at nine o' clock on Wednesday morning,[3] when we shall get him to give you the meeting and we will all go together to the Old Jewry to hear Mr Belsham, and so to the annual dinner.[4] If you could do it conveniently, I should be glad if you coud bring with you a list of the subscriptions which I procured for Mr Dyer. The book in its present form would not be sold by Cadell for less than six shillings.[5]

Dr Priestley was with us when I got your letter, and you will believe I did not refuse him the satisfaction of hearing as much as he could of you. He was particularly pleased with your method in the execution of our plan as most adapted to get at the true words and meaning of the writer. I heard some time since by a friend of Mr Wakefields proposals, and was very glad through him to contribute towards the work, which cannot but be useful particularly to our plan.[6] I may mention by the way, that had he been originally applied to, he would not have been a coadjutor, chusing rather to act by himself. They are all very well in Sloan Street, and I shall take care the D^r has his own copy of Mr Dyer.[7] M^r and Mrs Dodson are both well also, and will be most glad to hear of your coming. Of Mr Tyrwhitts perfect recovery we are rejoiced to hear. He is useful, highly so in his present *high* station (for many notice and look up at him) and will always be so: but I trust he will be induced to come forth and shew himself to the world more at large to edify the present and future generation.[8] Pray remember us with all respect to him. I called with Dr Priestley to day upon Mrs Jebb, who thought that she appeared much altered and enfeebled since the last year that he saw [her]. I presume you have seen the Doctor's familiar Letters. He is going on with them – but thinks one or two more will contain all that is necessary for him to say at present.[9]

I shall be glad to talk more with you about y^r Unitarian Minister at Fen Stanton, and thank you for all you have done ab^t him.[10] Every one I know here, is elated by Our late repulse and the triumphs of the X^ch.[11] As D^r P and I were walking the Streets to day, we met B^p Horsley in the lightest[?] purple coat (with a [word illegible] cassock) I ever beheld, wch c^d not but attract notice.[12] Pray remember me to Mr Hammond, to to [*sic*] whom I do not intend to remain long indebted for a letter.

With my wife's best respects I remain ever most truly Yours

T. Lindsey

---

1   Lindsey had presumably received a letter from Frend, together with copies of Dyer's *Inquiry*, via the White Horse, Fetter Lane, London. This was the inn from which a diligence (a public stage

coach) set out for Cambridge every morning at eight; see *Universal British directory* (1793), p. 535, under 'London carriers list'). It was also an arrival point in London for coaches and waggons from Cambridge. See Letter 416.

2   The 'last' Sunday was 18 Apr. and the 'next' Sunday was 25 Apr. 1790.

3   Wednesday 28 Apr. 1790.

4   This is a reference to the annual meeting, and annual dinner, of the supporters of Hackney College on 25 Apr. 1790; for Belsham's sermon on the occasion, see Letter 410, n.5.

5   This is almost certainly a reference to Dyer's *Inquiry into the nature of subscription*. The second edition (1792) was published by Joseph Johnson, not Thomas Cadell; it cost 6s 6d. A favourable review of the work, by William Enfield, appeared in the *Monthly Review*, NS, X (1793), 76–82.

6   'Our plan' was the project for the new translation of the Bible. Although admiring Gilbert Wakefield's translation, Priestley and Lindsey were determined to proceed independently of it and regarded him as too eccentric to be enrolled as a contributor. The third volume of Wakefield's *Translation of the New Testament* included (pp. xxiii–xxxii) a list of subscribers. Lindsey was not among them, although several of his friends, including Thomas Belsham, John Disney and William Tayleur were. Lindsey's contribution probably took the form of scholarly advice.

7   Presumably Dyer's *Inquiry*; see n. 5, above.

8   By 1790, Robert Tyrwhitt (1735–1817) held no official position in Cambridge University, and had resigned his fellowship of Jesus College in 1777. However, he was much respected in the university through his scholarly reputation and for his financial generosity to Jesus College after the death of his brother Thomas Tyrwhitt in 1786 had provided him with a substantial inheritance. See A. Gray and F. Brittain, *A history of Jesus College, Cambridge* (London, 1960), pp. 122–3, 146.

9   For Priestley's *Familiar letters ... to the inhabitants of Birmingham*, see Letter 407, n. 6.

10 Possibly this is a reference to George Dyer, who, Lindsey and others believed, might become a general baptist or unitarian minister at Fenstanton; see Letter 407, n. 2. Frend, in common with John Hammond, had supported Dyer, helping to obtain subscribers for the latter's *Inquiry into the nature of subscription*.

11 This refers to the defeat of the motion for the repeal of the Test and Corporation Acts on 2–3 Mar. 1790.

12 Horsley was recorded as present in the house of lords on 20, 21 and 22 Apr. 1790; *LJ*, XXXVIII, 596, 599, 602. Lindsey's report of his and Priestley's encounter with him in London on 22 Apr. rings true.

410. To WILLIAM ALEXANDER   1 MAY 1790

   Text: 'Letters of the Rev. Theophilus Lindsey. No. I',
                    UH, II, 40 (1 Feb. 1862), 44.

Note: This is the only section of the letter printed by the *UH*; the manuscript seems not to have survived. The words in square brackets are those of the editor of the letter (probably Alexander Gordon, who edited several of Lindsey's letters to Tayleur for *Christian Life*, II (1877)). The ellipsis at the start of the letter indicates that the section quoted was not the beginning of the letter.

London, May 1st, 1790.

* * * I intend to trouble Mr. Giles[1] with a small pacquet of books to you, in which there will be one or two for his own acceptance, particularly one of my own manufacture, which will be published next week, under the title of a "Second Address to the Students of Oxford and Cambridge," &c,[2] which I shall rejoice if it may be found of that use to sincere inquiring Christians, which the writer certainly intended; and I am not a little encouraged that Dr. Priestley, who alone has seen it, has that opinion of it. He has been now near three weeks in town; the two last Sundays he preached for me.[3] The next [he preaches] for good Dr. Price, at Hackney.[4] Mr. Frend has also been in town with us. Greater happiness I cannot desire in another state than to live, and converse, and act together with such persons, especially Dr. Priestley, with whom I have been so long and intimately connected. I do not know but I may defer the sending my parcel to Mr. Giles a few days, if necessary, that I

may send him and you Mr. Belsham's sermon, which was preached on Wednesday, at the annual meeting of the governors and friends of the Academical Institution, at the New College, Hackney. I cannot say that I ever heard a discourse that affected or edified me more; and he promised he would get it printed with all expedition.[5]

---

[1] Thomas Giles of Woodbridge, Suffolk, is listed as a member of the Unitarian Society in 1791 and 1794; *Unitarian Society ... 1791*, p. 10; *Unitarian Society ... 1794*, p. 10. Probably he was the Thomas Giles, 'gentleman', of Woodbridge, Suffolk, whose will was proved on 21 Dec. 1848; TNA: PRO PROB 11/2084, fos. 329v–330v. As a further clue as to his unitarian sympathies, the *MR*, XVII (1822), 376, carried a short obituary notice: 'June 12, at Sibton, in Suffolk, deeply lamented, Thomas, youngest son of Mr. Thomas Giles, of Woodbridge, after a long-protracted illness, borne with exemplary patience and cheerful resignation.'

[2] Lindsey's *Second address* was published in May 1790.

[3] Sunday 18 and 25 Apr. 1790.

[4] Priestley preached for Price at the Gravel Pit meeting, Hackney, on the morning of Sunday 2 May 1790; his sermon was not published.

[5] The title of Belsham's sermon, when published, was *The importance of truth, and the duty of making an open profession of it: represented in a discourse, delivered on Wednesday the 28th of April, 1790, at the meeting-house in the Old Jewry, London; to the supporters of the New College at Hackney* (London, 1790).

411. To WILLIAM TURNER OF NEWCASTLE   4 MAY 1790

Text: DWL, MS 12.44 (53).
Printed: McLachlan, *Letters*, pp. 13–14 (second paragraph); p. 38 (second sentence of fourth paragraph); pp. 38–9 (fifth paragraph).
Addressed: Address missing.
Endorsed: May. 4. 1790
Postmarked: Postmark missing.

London. May. 4. 1790

Dear Sir,

I am to acknowlege two very kind letters of yours, one to myself, the other to my wife. I rejoice that you are so well recovered; I should have said, We. I hope you will be preserved long to exceed the age of your worthy father;[1] and to be more useful in the world: which is saying a great deal, but not without some grounds for it.

With respect to the regimen of your diet for the future, I would proscribe the use of tea intirely, having found benefit myself by leaving it off, and many younger persons than you being deliverd from many ugly sensations by refraining from it which they knew not how to account for.

Many thanks for your information from Ayr, and particularly for any acc^t of the truly worthy Dr Dalrymple. But after a silence of more than a year I have rec^d a letter from him (our correspondence being of betwixt one and two years standing) in which he tells me of his colleague being driven at last to make such acknowlegements and recantation, as I fear will in the end disturb his peace more than if he had let the affair go to the General Assembly.[2] There is now of course an end of publishing what your kindness for him dictated. But I hope no one will think hardly of him, but with that pity that he deserves; and not be the less ready to assist him or his family: As to the little history of his situation, [one line crossed out and illegible] I desire you will not think that you have any thing to do with the payment of such a trifling matter.[3]

We have this day had Dr Priestley among us three weeks, and have been most happy in seeing him very often you will believe, so that we shall feel some regret at parting. Two Sundays he preached for me as usual, the last for Dr Price at Hackney; And Mr Frend, who has been some time in town, preached for Mr Morgan in the afternoon, without notes as is his custom, and upon a text as Dr Priestley tells me, chosen only half an hour before he went into the pulpit; and spoke without hesitation much plain sense upon the subject.[4]

On Wednesday last we heard Mr Belsham deliver the annual Sermon before the Governors and friends of our New College. I have seldom been equally pleased and edified, and am glad that you will have an opportunity of seeing the sermon as it is to be printed. You will form some conjecture about it, when I tell you, that in more passages than one, D^r P ____ Mr Frend and myself, who sat together in the gallery of the old Jewry, could not refrain from taking out our handkerchiefs, and were particularly pleased to observe several of the youths of the college in the gallery opposite to us, equally moved.[5]

I am sorry my wife is gone out and has not left [sic] that I can find your letter and scheme of Association – so that I cannot give you my sentiments particularly upon what I so much in general like, but there will be another opportunity soon of doing it.[6] I would also wish D^r P ____ y to see it.

The Second Address to the Students of Oxford and Cambridge is at last printed, and will be made up this week, when I shall take an early opportunity of send[ing] you a few copies for yourself and a few friends. Dr P. for whom I got a copy some days past, that I might cancell any part that was wrong, encourages me much by speaking favourably of it. You may depend upon receiving with it some copies of Mr Belsham's Sermon, and I shall rather keep back my parcell a day or two, than not let that make a part.

I am forced to conclude abruptly

W^h all good wishes from *us* to you both

always most truly Yours

[No signature][7]

---

1   William Turner of Wakefield was aged seventy-five in May 1790 and lived to be seventy-nine. William Turner of Newcastle exceeded Lindsey's hopes by reaching the age of ninety-eight.

2   William Dalrymple (1723–1814) was minister of the first charge at Ayr from 1756 to 1814 and had been moderator of the general assembly of the Church of Scotland in 1781. I have not been able to locate his correspondence with Lindsey. William M'Gill became Dalrymple's colleague, and served as minister of the second charge at Ayr from 1761 until his death in 1807. In 1763 M'Gill married Dalrymple's niece, Elizabeth Dunlop (d. 1785).

3   Possibly the 'little history' of M'Gill's case was the thirty-seven-page pamphlet *Dr M'Gill vindicated from the charge of heresy, and the erroneous assertions of his adversaries briefly refuted, by references to the word of God and the Confession of Faith ... by a friend of truth* (Edinburgh, ?1789).

4   Since 1787, George Cadogan Morgan had served at the Gravel Pit meeting, Hackney, as assistant minister to Richard Price, during the decline of the latter's health. Morgan was the afternoon preacher and Frend preached for him on the afternoon of Sunday 2 May, the day on which Priestley had preached there in the morning.

5   For Belsham's sermon to the supporters of Hackney College, see Letter 410, n. 5.

6   Possibly this 'scheme of association' was the body of deputies from the protestant dissenters of Northumberland and Durham, formed to seek repeal of the Test and Corporation Acts; Turner was its secretary; see Harbottle, *William Turner*, p. 37.

7   It was most unusual for Lindsey to omit his signature to a letter. No doubt the omission was the result of the abruptness with which he was obliged to conclude this particular letter.

412. To WILLIAM TAYLEUR   7 MAY 1790

Text: JRUL, Lindsey Letters, vol. II, no. 32.
Printed: McLachlan, *Letters*, pp. 135–6 (most of third paragraph).
Addressed: To/William Tayleur Esqr/Shrewsbury/Shropshire
Endorsed: 7th May – 90
Postmarked: MA 7 90

London. may. 7. 1790.

Dear Sir,

Last night our good Doctor left us, and his brother in law Mr Wilkinson[1] having taken the whole of the coach for himself, he would travel at the more ease, and we doubt not before this time is safe in his own habitation. We feel a great void at the parting, having had the satisfaction of seeing him very often: but it is fitting that he should return to his proper station and business, having taken a large and nearer view of the present situation of things, and laid in variety of materials which will be useful to him. He never left London in such perfect health, nor in better spirits. A few days since he received a long, but very weak reply of Mr Burn to him, in a series of Letters.[2] But as it woud expose him to give a formal address to such an author, he intends only to take slight notice of him in his next Letters to the people of Birmingham.[3]

The wednesday before last we were above measure pleased with the annual Sermon by Mr Belsham before the Governors &c of the New College; and I am glad you will partake of the pleasure as he is transcribing it from his notes to print it. Dr Priestley, Mr Frend and myself, who sat together in the gallery of the Old Jewry, could not hear some passages in it with dry eyes, and I was much delighted in observing several of the pupils in the opposite gallery equally affected, and I think young Mr Harries was one of them.[4] I frequently inquire about him, though I do not see him, and have the best character of him always from the different tutors.

Mr Morgan, Dr Price's nephew, having resigned his place as classical tutor, Mr Wakefield of Nottingham has been thought of and recommended to succeed him.[5] There were some objections at first on account of his temper as being haughty and contemptuous, and ill to live with, chiefly drawn I believe from the cast of his writing. But I believe that accounts of him from different persons that know him have removed this difficulty. And no one can doubt of his being a person, who in many respects, will fill the place with great credit. His answer of B^p Horsley just published is a very tart one. At the close of it are his proposals for a translation of the New Testament, which I hope meet with encouragement, as it cannot be doubted but it will be a very great improvement of our present translation, from his known abilities, and from his long having had the matter in hand.[6] I remember that when once I asked the late B^p Law to indulge me with a sight of the alterations he had made in his english N.T. he told me that he had lent it to Mr Wakefield.[7]

As to another plan of a translation of the Bible, upon a meeting of the principal persons concerned lately in Town, it was found that it was going on a little, tho' much had not been done: But resolutions of more vigorous application were made, and it was hoped that in the compass of one year, each might have his part done and ready to be reviewed.[8] I don't hear that Dr Geddes is coming out with his promised first volume.[9]

The Dissenting Committee in London have not yet agreed upon the form of their Address or appeal to the Nation on their late ill treatment and rejection of their petition. M* Walker, who had been applied to at first, and leaving town without having done any thing, it fell into other hands. The delay is of little consequence, if it be properly executed at last. And M* Walker, we hear now, will publish his own sentiments upon the matter, which may answer a good end, as he will be more particular and argumentative, than it might be proper to be in an Address from the Body of Dissenters.[10]

M* Frend brought to Town with him some copies of M* Dyer's book on Subscriptions.[11] Your copy very generously subscribed for, which I have rec'd, shall be forwarded to you very soon, along with the Second Address to the Students of the two universities. M* Dyer has much good stuff in him, which you will like, as well as like the author for it. When you have received them, I shall be happy to hear from M* Rowe that you continue tolerably well as usual. My wife desires her most due and kind respects, and I remain always, Dear Sir

Your truly obliged and faithful affectionate servant

T. Lindsey.

---

1   This was almost certainly John Wilkinson (1728–1808) who supported Priestley financially during his later career, rather than his younger brother and fellow-ironmaster William Wilkinson (1744–1808).

2   Edward Burn published *Letters to the Rev. Dr. Priestley, on the infallibility of the apostolic testimony, concerning the person of Christ* (Birmingham, 1790). Burn (1762–1837), was educated at the countess of Huntingdon's college at Trevecca, and graduated BA at Oxford (St Edmund Hall) in 1790 (MA 1791). He became curate and lecturer at St Mary's chapel, Birmingham, in 1785 and continued in those capacities until his death.

3   In fact Priestley replied at considerable length to Burn in his *Familiar letters ... to the inhabitants of Birmingham* (see Letter 407, n. 6). Burn responded with *Letters to the Rev. Dr. Priestley, in vindication of those already addressed to him, on the infallibility of the apostolic testimony, concerning the person of Christ* (Birmingham, 1790).

4   'Young Mr Harries' was Thomas Harries (1774–1848), the eldest son of Lindsey's friend Edward Harries of Shropshire. His admission as a lay student at Hackney College was recorded in the college committee minutes on 21 Sept. 1789; DWL, MS 38.14, p. 121. On 1 Apr. 1793, he was admitted as a fellow-commoner at St John's College, Cambridge, but did not graduate. See *Alumn. Cantab.*, II, vol. III, 251, where his school is recorded as 'Hackney', and *Admissions to the College of St John the Evangelist, Part IV*, ed. Sir Robert Forsyth Scott (Cambridge, 1931), p. 291. He was subsequently a JP, deputy lieutenant and (in 1802) high sheriff of Shropshire.

5   On 2 Apr. 1790, the governors of Hackney College received the resignation of George Cadogan Morgan as classical tutor; on 25 May they received a report from Andrew Kippis that Gilbert Wakefield had accepted the invitation to succeed Morgan, on condition that he could also teach four students privately in his own house. The governors agreed to this condition (subsequently increasing the maximum to six private pupils) and appointed Wakefield as classical tutor with effect from the start of the new session in Sept. 1790. See DWL, MS 38.14 (Hackney College minutes 1785–91), pp. 133–8.

6   This work was Gilbert Wakefield's *An address to the Right Reverend Dr Samuel Horsley, bishop of St David's, on the subject of an apology for the liturgy and clergy of the Church of England* (Birmingham, 1790). Appended to it was a one-page summary of Wakefield's proposals for a new three-volume translation of the New Testament, which was published towards the end of 1791. Horsley's *Apology* was a reply to the duke of Grafton's *Hints*.

7   Lindsey evidently referred to manuscript alterations in Edmund Law's copy of the English New Testament.

8   This proposal for a new translation of the Bible was the 'plan' mentioned in Lindsey's letter to Frend of 22 Apr. 1790 (Letter 409).

9   The first volume of Geddes's biblical translation was published in 1792; see Letter 407, n. 10.

10 The 'repeal committee' set up by the protestant dissenting deputies in London commissioned the publication of *To the people of England: an address from the committee of protestant dissenters appointed to conduct the application to parliament for the repeal of the Test Laws*. It is printed in *Committees for repeal*, pp. 59–61, and was published in several London newspapers, including *The

World, 18 May 1790, the *St James's Chronicle*, 20 May 1790, and the *Public Advertiser*, 26 May 1790. George Walker's separately published work was *The dissenters' plea: or the appeal of the dissenters to the justice, the honour and the religion of the kingdom, against the Test Laws. Published at the request of the committee of the protestant dissenters of the midland district* (Birmingham, 1790).

11 For this work of Dyer, see Letter 382, n. 4.

413. To WILLIAM TAYLEUR   15 MAY 1790

    Text: JRUL, Lindsey Letters, vol. II, no. 33.
    Addressed: Address missing.
    Postmarked: Postmark missing.

London. may. 15. 1790.
Dear Sir,

By the misapprehension of the friend I employed to procure me a frank for you in dating it two days earlier than I had marked, I shall not be able to fill my page so well as I had intended.

It was a singular satisfaction to see your hand-writing, and that in such firm strokes as encourage to form the best prognotics [*sic*] of the writer's health.[1] I will not repeat my wishes upon this theme, but will add, that you will be pleased that my own health and strength have been improving much for these ten days past. I thank heaven that I had no other fear but of being laid aside as useless.

On tuesday last it was agreed in a College-committee, that a letter should be written to signify to M[r] Wakefield the terms proposed for any one who should fill the place of classical Tutor, and the person who was to mention it to him, was to write back his sentiments.[2] Many apprehensions were expressed about his temper: but M[r] Walker of Nottingham assured many, that he was very different in writing and in the commerce of life; and D[r] Enfield and D[r] Aikin have sent letters to several members of the committee, bearing the same good testimony.[3]

I trust, that all concerned in the Work you mention will use all diligence. For one of them I can answer, the anonymous author of the last Numb – of our Commentaries &c, which I believe you will have received by this time.[4]

I am concerned my parcell is not yet gone, but it will certainly be despatched this next week.

I inclose two letters, which you will be so good as to return at your full convenience.[5] You will doubtless have heard before of D[r] M[c]Gill's unfortunate recantation. He is greatly to be pitied, as his mind was enfeebled by his circumstances, and I fear he had no friend to support him. Had he only suffered the matter to have gone to General Assembly, he woud probably have been delivered without any such scandalous requisition.[6]

M[r] Millar, mentioned in the other letter is still in Town, and deserving highly the character there given of him, and we like him exceedingly for the little we have seen of him.[7]

I have no doubt but M[r] Rowe will know from Mr Clarke[8] every thing relating to Mr Williams whom that gentleman supports in so handsome a manner. But I was much edified with hearing M[r] Belsham the other day read a letter from M[r] Williams, with an account of his proceeding with his congregation. What may we not expect from young persons, indued with so much true zeal, and with minds so enlightened![9]

I am not lightly affected with what you observe on another subject near the end of your letter, and shall assuredly weigh it well, as it is of importance.[10] Believe me always with all esteem your most truly obliged and affectionate servant

    T. Lindsey.

1   Tayleur's letter to Lindsey, dated 11 May 1790, may be found in JRUL, C2[13]. Lindsey endorsed it with the words 'Answ^d. may. 15. 1790. sauf le sujet dernierem^t homme'.

2   For the terms of Wakefield's appointment as classical tutor at Hackney College, as set out at the committee meeting on 11 May 1790 ('Tuesday last'), see Letter 412, n. 5.

3   George Walker had been on friendly terms with Wakefield during their time at Nottingham in the 1780s, when Walker was minister of the High Pavement chapel and Wakefield had taken pupils in that town; the two of them formed a literary club. William Enfield had been a tutor and rector at Warrington Academy during Wakefield's period of service as a tutor there between 1779 and 1783. At Warrington, Wakefield made close friendships with several members of the Aikin family and his daughter Anne (d. 1821) subsequently married Charles Rochemont Aikin (1775–1847), the son of the physician Dr John Aikin (1747–1822).

4   In his letter of 11 May 1790 (see n. 1, above), Tayleur expressed the hope that those engaged on the new translation of the Bible would apply themselves diligently to the project. In reply, Lindsey referred to the lengthy essay entitled 'A summary view of the prophecies relating to antichrist, contained in the writings of Daniel, Paul, Peter, Jude and John' by 'Synergus' and dated 1 Jan. 1790, which was the only item in *Commentaries and essays*, VIII. 'Synergus' was Lindsey himself.

5   These two letters to Lindsey (probably those from Turner mentioned by Lindsey in the first paragraph of Letter 411) which he enclosed with this letter to Tayleur, appear not to have survived.

6   William M'Gill, minister of the second charge at Ayr, faced allegations of heterodoxy, following the publication of his *A practical essay on the death of Christ in two parts* (Edinburgh, 1786), levelled by the synod of Glasgow and Ayr. The synod referred the matter to the presbytery of Ayr, which concluded that M'Gill's work contained unorthodox doctrine, in its questioning of the divinity of Christ, its rejection of the doctrine of the atonement and its admiration for the Socinianism of Priestley. M'Gill also called for the abolition of compulsory subscription in the Church of Scotland to the confession of faith. The case dragged on through the winter of 1789–90, until on 14 Apr. 1790 the synod of Glasgow and Ayr persuaded M'Gill to issue a statement reaffirming his orthodoxy on these doctrinal questions and expressing regret for any offence caused by his publications. Lindsey, who, predictably, had much sympathy for M'Gill's theology, equally predictably deplored this 'recantation'. The circumstances which Lindsey believed had 'enfeebled' M'Gill included the death of his wife (Elizabeth, née Dunlop, the niece of William Dalrymple) in 1785 and his financial indebtedness. Lindsey was also convinced that M'Gill should have allowed his case to come before the annual meeting of the general assembly of the Church of Scotland in May 1790, where Lindsey thought that he might have a good chance of exoneration, without the need for a 'recantation'. For the background to this case, see A. McNair, *Scots theology in the eighteenth century* (London, 1928), ch. VI, and Martin Fitzpatrick, 'Varieties of candour: English and Scottish style', *E & D*, VII (1988), 35–56. For further developments over the charges against M'Gill, see Letters 444, n. 9, 454, n. 7, and 457, n. 6.

7   This was Robert Millar of Dundee, who, in his letter to Lindsey of 4 Dec. 1790, thanked Lindsey and his wife for their 'kind attention' during his visit to London earlier in the year; DWL, MS 12.46 (77).

8   Probably Richard Hall Clarke; his sister Mary married John Rowe in 1788.

9   John Williams (1768–1835), educated at Carmarthen, Hoxton and Daventry academies, was minister to a dissenting congregation at the Bridwell chapel, Uffculme, Devon, from 1789 to 1794. Born on 30 Jan. 1768, he was aged twenty-two in May 1790. He is listed as 'the Rev. John Williams, Bridwell, near Collumpton' as a member of the Western Unitarian Society in 1792; *Society of Unitarian Christians, Established in the West of England* (?Exeter, 1792), p. 8. From 1794 to 1804 he was minister at Norton chapel, Derbyshire; see Letters 549, n. 8, and 583, n. 5.

10 Towards the end of his letter of 11 May 1790 Tayleur deplored the view, expounded by Priestley, 'that *all men* will finally attain to eternal life' and describd it as 'a *modern* corruption of Xtianity'.

414. To RUSSELL SCOTT   27 MAY 1790

Text: Scott Coll.
Addressed: For/The Rev^d. M^r. Scott
Endorsed: June 3^d. 90
Postmarked: Postmark missing.

London. May. 27. 1790

Dear Sir,

The *Second Address* was not ready to be sent to meet you when you came to town, upon the important and I persuade myself most happy errand, or that, together with our heartiest congratulations should have been conveyed at the time. Ever since I have been waiting day after day for the publication of Mr Belsham's sermon[1] that you might receive both together, but that being still delayed thro' some unforeseen interruptions, I am determined to wait no longer. Accept therefore the sincere wishes of Mrs Lindsey and myself, and we beg you will make them acceptable to Mrs Scott for your mutual felicity for many, many years to come, and that your union may every year more and more contribute to your own moral improvement, and to the present and future good of others to a wide extent.[2]

We have been upon the whole very well since you saw us, and I am so much recruited that I hope to be able to go on as usual, and be of some little use to others, a circumstance and privilege for which we can none of us ever be sufficiently thankful.

You will see the Dissenters' Address to the People of England in the Newspapers, and I think will like it much.[3] Mr Walker of Nottingham takes the matter up on a larger scale, and is printing the Appeal to the People of England, which will be published either with his own name, or in that of the Midland District-Dissenters.[4] The Churchmen suppose the Dissenters to be dead, but I hope they will be convinced of the contrary, not merely by words in their Appeals and Addresses but by continued active exertions, till their grievances are redressed.

I send two copies of the Second Address, and sh^d be glad if you think proper to present one to Mr Watson of Chichester.[5] I would have sent Dr Priestley's next N^o. of Familiar Letters; but it is not yet printed, and I suppose it will be ten days at least or a fortnight before it is ready, as it has been judged right that he should obviate a calumny on *Theodosius*, which has been much credited in and about Birmingham as well as in London.[6] You will also see it noticed by him in the next Gentleman's magazine, if Mr Nicholls inserts the letter I carried him upon the subject.[7]

We are going the next week into the country in Surrey ab^t 10 miles from London, and shall be generally there with some other of our friends in the middle of each week, during the summer, unless we make any long excursion, which we are not yet determined about.

Although I may have been more tardy in compt^s on the pres^t occasion,[8] I am persuaded you will not think us the less sincere, but I hope will let me know how you do as soon as conven^t after you receive this – I remain always, Dear Sir, most truly Yours

T. Lindsey.

---

1   See Letter 410, n. 5.
2   Russell Scott married Sophia Hawes in London on 4 May 1790.
3   For this *Address*, see Letter 412, n. 10.

4   For Walker's *Appeal*, see Letter 412, n. 10. It was published with his own name and with the endorse-
    ment of the protestant dissenters of the midland district.
5   For Thomas Watson of Chichester, see Letter 388, n. 12.
6   For the 'Theodosius calumny', see below, n. 7. Priestley's *Familiar letters ... to the inhabitants
    of Birmingham* (see Letter 407, n. 6) consisted of thirty-two open letters, in five separate parts,
    published between 4 Mar. and 7 June 1790. In Letter XXI, which was one of the six letters which
    made up Part V, dated 7 June 1790, he defended himself against the allegations of 'Theodosius'.
    It may be consulted conveniently in the collected volume of Priestley's *Familiar letters ... to the
    inhabitants of Birmingham*, pp. 173–84, and Priestley added to his defence in the preface (pp. ix–xiii)
    to this volume.
7   The *Gent. Mag.* for May 1790 (vol. LX) included, as its first item (pp. 383–4), a letter from 'W. C.'
    which quoted from a pamphlet entitled *Theodosius: or a solemn admonition to protestant dissenters,
    on the proposed repeal of the Test and Corporation Acts* (London, 1790). The author of the pamphlet
    was Philip Withers (*c.* 1755–90), formerly of Trinity College and Queens' College (where he was a
    fellow-commoner), Cambridge, who was subsequently a pamphleteer and controversialist who died
    in Newgate, where he had been imprisoned following his conviction for libel. There is a brief obituary
    of Withers in *Gent. Mag.*, LX, ii (1790), 674, and a summary of his career in Daniel Lysons, *The
    environs of London: being an historical account of the towns, villages, and hamlets, within twelve
    miles of that capital* (4 vols., London, 1792–6), II, 142–4. Withers claimed (pp. 5–13) to have been
    present in Sept. 1789 during the final hours of Silas Deane (1737–89), an American envoy to France
    in 1776. He quoted Deane as disavowing Christianity and naming Priestley as his inspiration for
    doing so. Convinced that the pamphlet was the work of his enemies, Priestley denied that he had ever
    discussed religion with Deane and solicited from Dr Edward Bancroft (1744–1821), chemist, and for
    a time secretary to Deane, a letter refuting in detail the claims of 'Theodosius'. He asked Lindsey
    to convey this letter to John Nichols, the proprietor and effective editor of the *Gent. Mag.* Lindsey
    was already well acquainted with Nichols (see Vol. I, Letters 211–16) and immediately did so, and
    the *Gent. Mag.* published Bancroft's letter, and a covering note from Priestley, immediately after the
    'Theodosius' item (pp. 384–6). See Rutt, I, 63–5.
8   I.e. on the occasion of Scott's marriage.

415. To WILLIAM ALEXANDER   29 MAY 1790

   Text: 'Letters of the Rev. Theophilus Lindsey. No. I',
                      UH, II, 40 (1 Feb. 1862), 45.

Note: This is the only section of the letter printed by the *UH*; the manuscript seems not to have survived.
The ellipsis at the start of the letter indicates that the section quoted was not the beginning of the letter.

London, May 29th, 1790.

* * * I hope your apprehensions may be ungrounded that you shall lose many of
your present scholars for not teaching them the Church Catechism.[1] We shall talk
the matter over when we see you. There is, however, no remedy, as I do not wonder
that you cannot be the instrument of giving such idolatrous instruction to children.

---

1   William Alexander had taught in his small school at Yoxford, Suffolk, since June 1789; see Letter
    386, n. 1. He returned to Woodbridge, the town of his birth, in 1794.

416. To WILLIAM FREND   31 MAY 1790

   Text: CUL, Add. MS 7886 (Frend papers), no. 155.
   Addressed: To/Mr Frend/fellow of Jesus College/Cambridge
   Postmarked: MA 31 90

                                                    London may. 31. 1790

Dear Sir
    I ought to have thanked you sooner for your welcome letter, and for introducing
me to Mr Curteis whom I very much like for the little I had the opportunity of seeing

of him, of a mind much enlightened, and singular good sense. Would there were more farmers of such a description![1]

I am glad that you have a society formed, however small, that is so perfectly unitarian. I hope it will soon increase till it become a worshipping one, and by its rational and scriptural simplicity shame thousands of their still continuing in the polytheism of the country.[2] We have the best accounts from the north and west of free inquiry and the doctrine of the Divine unity spreading themselves, and being likely to go on from the means that are used. And if M[r] Wakefield settles in the South and is the Classical tutor at the New College, of which I am told there [is] little doubt, we shall have a firm phalanx in that important station, combined with those who are already there.[3]

I hope you have rec[d] the books I sent from the White horse Fetter lane.[4] I had no more by me at the time, either of Haynes or the Second Address, or should have put them into the parcell.[5] I have no absolute confidence in the Translation given of the beginning of John's gospel, and shall be most glad to see another made out, which may satisfy the common Christian that Jesus Christ is not the logos; or, if he be the logos, that he is not God.[6] Something of this kind seems to be needful to be done, as this is the leading passage that weighs with learned and unlearned to believe Jesus Christ to be a great preexistent being, God, or one next to him.

You will see in the Gentlemans magazine some Vindication of D[r] Priestley from Theodosius's calumny, if Nicholls has put in a letter which I carried him.[7]

But there will be a fuller Vindication in his 5th Numb. of familiar Letter [sic], which we expect the latter end of this next week, and which I hope to send you as soon as it arrives.[8] D[r] Heberden, and one or two other very great names in the literary world told our friend that it was absolutely necessary for him publicly to refute the calumny, or he w[d] have never thought about it. We trust that all goes on and will go on prosperously in the National Assembly, now that the formidable difficulty has been gotten over, and one man not allowed to be arbiter of peace or war.[9] You will see the Address to the People of England from the London Comitte in the News Papers: but it ought to have come forth with more dignity, and I trust will not be left there.[10]

My wife is always your admirer tho she takes great liberties with you as she does with those she likes, and is glad you got safe and well to your journeys end and sends you her best respects. I am always, with great esteem, Dear Sir, most truly your's

T. Lindsey.

---

[1] William Curtis (d. 1829) was an assistant and amanuensis to Robert Robinson of St Andrew's Street baptist church, Cambridge, and manager of Robinson's farm at nearby Chesterton. In 1786, he married Robinson's daughter Ellen. Not surprisingly, he was a subscriber to Robert Robinson's *History of baptism* and *Ecclesiastical researches* (Cambridge, 1792). After Robinson's death, he withdrew from membership of St Andrew's Street church and subsequently became an innkeeper in Cambridge. See *Church book: St Andrew's Street baptist church, Cambridge, 1720–1832*, introduction by L. Addicott (London: Baptist Historical Society, 1991), pp. xiv, 137.

[2] Frend's small Unitarian Society in Cambridge met on Sunday evenings; see Letter 430.

[3] See Letter 412, n. 5.

[4] For the White Horse inn, Fetter Lane, see Letter 409, n. 1.

[5] For Lindsey's edition of Haynes, *The scripture account of the attributes and worship of God*, see Letter 406, n. 16.

[6] In 'Section V' of his *Second address*, Lindsey presented a critique of the translation of John i. 1–14 in the 1611 English Bible and set out his own translation of those verses. In seeking to deny that the logos, or the creative word, represented Christ, he translated the first three verses of John i. as 'In

the beginning was Wisdom, and Wisdom was with God, and God was Wisdom. The same was in the beginning with God. All things were made by it, and without it was nothing made' (pp. 34–5). Lindsey presented the same translation of these verses in *List of the false readings*, p. 40.

7 For the controversy over the 'Theodosius' letter, see Letter 414, n. 7.

8 The fifth part of Priestley's *Familiar letters ... to the inhabitants of Birmingham*, with its author's refutation of 'Theodosius', was published on 7 June 1790; see Letter 414, n. 6.

9 In May 1790, the National Assembly, guided by Mirabeau, proposed that Louis XVI be given the authority to initiate proposals for war and peace, but subject to a committee of six which had the power to approve and revise treaties. The Assembly also renounced wars of conquest. The 'formidable difficulty' to which Lindsey referred was Louis XVI himself.

10 For this address, see Letter 412, n.10.

417. To WILLIAM FREND   9 JUNE 1790

Text: CUL, Add. MS 7886 (Frend papers), no. 151.
Addressed: [In Hannah Lindsey's hand] To/Mr. William Frend/Fellow of Jesus College/Cambridge
Postmarked: JU 14 [or 12?] 90

London. Jun. 9. 1790

Dear Sir,

I am altogether in the country, except the Saturday Sunday and Monday or you woud probably have heard from me again. I must first apprize you, that I have three guineas for you, which Mr Turner's Son of Abingdon desired I would pay you on Mr Dyer's account; I suppose for books received.[1]

On Saturday I recd an acct from Dr Priestley of Mr Robinson's sudden removal from this passing state.[2] You would know all the particulars from Mr Curteis.[3] I hope, or rather I doubt not that he has left his public testimony to the Divine unity, in his work on Baptism, the last sheet of which Dr P. mentiond that he was correcting.[4]

As you will certainly see Mr Garnham at your approaching election, I must beg the favour of you to tell him, that I had not time to thank him for his very acceptable letter on Saturday which I met when I came to Town, or would have done it; and you will be so good as to tell him, that I will send him a parcell of the General View &c and will in the mean time remind Dr P of its being not to be met with; so that he need not brand him with his virgula critica.[5]

We have a good hope that Mr Wakefield will answer all expectations at our New-College, and raise its credit: but now the affair is over, I may tell You, that You was the person first thought of by the Tutors; and by many others, if you had been so disengaged from the University that such an offer could have been made you: for I woud say it to you only, there was not a man who did not express an *affection* for you, and say that they could like to live with you.[6]

You will be particularly pleased with the Scotch Assembly having so nobly interferd in asserting their rights, which will come so well in aid of our next application for the repeal of the Test Acts.[7] I hope a quantity of the Proceedings of the London Committee &c have been sent to you to be dispersed.[8]

Dr Disney and Sloane Street were all well yesterday – Mr Dodson to day desired his respects – I am forced to break off and with my wifes best regards, to conclude myself always most truly Yours

T. Lindsey.

---

1 Daniel Turner (1710–98), MA, was a baptist minister at Reading from 1741 to 1748 and at Abingdon, Berkshire, from 1748 until his death; he was an admired hymn writer and the author of several

published sermons. His MA was conferred by the baptist college (subsequently Brown University), Providence, Rhode Island. See *PDM*, VI (1799), 41. He is listed as a subscriber for six copies of Robinson's *History of baptism*. For his praise for George Dyer in 1782, see Ernest A. Payne, 'The baptist connections of George Dyer: a further note', *Baptist Quarterly*, XI (1944), 237–8. The son to whom Lindsey referred was Daniel Turner junior (d. 1795), who had been a pupil of Richard Price during the 1750s and was subsequently chief clerk of the 3 per cent reduced annuity office in the Bank of England; *PDM*, VI (1799), 41–2; *Royal kalendar ... for the year 1791*, p. 226; *Gent. Mag.*, LXV, ii (1795), 622.

2   Robert Robinson died on 9 June 1790. The previous Saturday, when Lindsey said he heard this news, was 8 June 1790, the day before he began this letter. Priestley's letter to Lindsey informing him of Robinson's death is dated 11 June 1790; DWL, MS 12.12, fos. 150–1, partly printed in Rutt, I, 67–9. Lindsey presumably began this letter before he heard of Robinson's death. The postmark of the letter is not quite clear, but is apparently either 12 or 14 June 1790.

3   For William Curtis, see Letter 416, n. 1.

4   Robinson's *History of baptism* was put to the press by its author, but published after his death. Lindsey was included in the (unpaginated) list of subscribers.

5   For the third edition of Priestley's *General view*, see Letter 388, n. 3. Garnham's letter to Lindsey seems not to have survived. For Lindsey's previous use of the expression 'virgula critica' (the critical rod), see Vol. I, Letter 100. The 'approaching election' was that at Cambridge University (see Letter 407, n. 5). Predictably, Frend and Garnham both voted for Lord Euston and Lawrence Dundas and withheld their votes from William Pitt, the other candidate; see *The poll for the election of two representatives in parliament for the University of Cambridge, on Thursday, June 17, 1790* (Cambridge, n.d., ?1790), pp. 15, 26.

6   The minutes of the committee of Hackney College (DWL, MS 38.14) do not mention Frend in this connexion, and the committee's wish that Frend might become a tutor at the college was evidently expressed informally. In the event he was never employed by the college.

7   On 27 May 1790, the general assembly of the Church of Scotland, meeting in Edinburgh, passed four resolutions in favour of the repeal of the Test Act as it applied to Scotland, and set up a committee to pursue the question. This move was reported briefly in several London newspapers on 1 June 1790, for example the *General Evening Post* and the *St James's Chronicle*. For the background, see G. M. Ditchfield, 'The Scottish campaign against the Test Act, 1790–1791', *HJ*, 23 (1980), 37–61.

8   For these proceedings of the 'repeal committee' of the protestant dissenting deputies in London, see Letter 412, n. 10.

418. To WILLIAM FREND   14 JULY 1790

Text: CUL, Add. MS 7886 (Frend papers), nos. 156–7.
Addressed: For/M[r] Frend/fellow of Jesus college/Cambridge
Postmarked: Postmark missing.

July. 14. 1790
London.

Dear Sir,

I blush to look at the date of your last long welcome letter, but the truth is that for five weeks past till now, we have been altogether in the country, Sundays excepted, where I am allowed to do nothing but ride out and amuse myself, and though I am refreshed and seem made stronger by it, and am advised to continue in the same train, it seems too much propter vitam vivendi perdere causas.[1] It is a singular satisfaction to learn that M[r] Tyrwhitt is so well, and I rejoice that you with your most happy temper of mind and in all youthful vigour are to reside so near him. I expect, with the divine blessing, that myself and many will profit by the fruits of such society.[2] Pray mention to him, that I am this very day sending to Bath three dozen of his Two Discourses to a young man, formerly pupil of M[r] Belsham's, very lately settled there, as dissenting minister, who I believe, will be an instrument of great good in the place, by a wisdom above his years, and a zeal and ardour of an apostle.[3] And having furnished him with a few copies before he has desired more, as he found them peculiarly useful. I may mention, as you will like to hear it, that he has a brother, a surgeon near him at Bristol, utroque pollens apolline,[4] who is as apostolic a character, and bears testimony to the truth and does great good in his way.[5] I pay no comp[ts] to our common most respected friend in this story about his small tract, and only wish he may be disposed to give us other things out of his storehouse; at the same time acknowleging with great satisfaction that I look upon him as in his proper place of doing very extensive good, was he never to publish any thing.[6]

I rec[d]. yesterday a letter from young M[r] Toulmin, minister of a dissenting unitarian congregation at Chowbent near Wigan, Lancashire, one of the largest and most enlightened; who acquaints me that twelve ministers, himself one, in that neighbourhood, had agreed to undertake the publication of a new periodical work of the religious kind, and fixed upon their plan. "Every number, of which there is to be one monthly, is to have a practical address suited to common readers. Essays are to be introduced as often as may be, on truth of christianity, and on the principal doctrines of the gospel; and the work is to be rendered as interesting as possible, by mean of historical and biographical pieces["].[7]

This is mentioned because you will rejoice to hear of the design; but not for that merely, but to beg your assistance now and then, and I can readily transmit any thing to M[r] Toulmin, who is a most excellent young man in all respects, with a young wife, a valuable helpmate, who has just brought him a second daughter,[8] and who is also going to receive 3 of M[r] Cooper of Manchesters children boarders and for education into his house, with others, I suppose:[9] for the poor pittance comparatively which dissenting congregations in the country with the best dispositions, can afford their ministers, is but a slender support for a growing family in these days. I beg then that you give or procure me any aids towards this new undertaking, made very necessary by the multitude of gospel-magazines &c &c &c, which fall into the hands of the common people.

I am concerned on many accounts that M[r] Robinson is taken away from us, when he promised to be more and more useful as a minister of the gospel, and his life was so desireable for his large family.[10] From letters that D[r] Priestley has rec[d]. from strangers inquiring about him, and from other information, he was exceeding respected, loved and esteemed by very many in different parts, which I am persuaded he greatly deserved. The testimonies given by D[r] Priestley, M[r] Toulmin, and D[r] Rees (whose funeral sermon I suppose will be printed) will sufficiently declare that he was and had been for some time past a strict unitarian, and will counteract what he himself had preached and printed in favour of the popular estabilished system.[11]

Mr Kentish had told me of your unitarian society, and of your obligingness in admitting him into it.[12] He also is another eléve [sic] of Mr Belsham, and is to be the minister of our unitarian chapel, actually building at Plymouth-dock, under the auspices of another fellow-pupil, most highly valued by me, who has been settled the dissenting minister at Plymouth Town about two years, and is now actually going to print an unitarian liturgy, chiefly from our's, at the desire, and for the use of the congregation.[13] I think I told you, that I had made some collections for the chapel at Plymouth Dock, but if you know any disposed to spare money for such purposes, it would be very acceptable.

Your lecture, when D[r] Rees was an auditor, was most candidly conducted.[14] I think I told you of a friend of mine who wished to slit out S[t] Johns preface with a pair of scissors.[15] M[r] Hamilton however, an acquaintance of D[r] Jebb's, D[r] Priestleys and whom I sometimes see, removes at once every difficulty by maintaining that all the writings of the new Testament are spurious and adulterated, and very improperly called the Word of God.[16] There seems to me at present however unsurmountable objections to the interpretation of Philologus Christianus.[17]

At coming out of the country, I meet with a parcell from the worthy Mr Dyer, and a letter with which I am charmed more than I can tell you, bespeaking a character of native simplicity and goodness and great ingenuity.[18] I wish you woud be so good as to thank him for it, till I am able to do it myself. I have taken care of his parcell to Mrs Jebb. I am unwilling to delay this parcell wch I find left here for you a day longer, and I a[m] going as soon as this is finished to make rea[dy] for celebrating the Anniversary of the Revolution at the Crown and Anchor.[19] I send Mr Toulmins Sermon for your acceptance as you may not have seen it, and a copy of Mr Belsham, which you can dispose [of] if you have it already.[20] Dr Disney and his family are making holiday in Gloucestershire &c. I was to have met Mr Belsham at Birmingham the latter end of the next week, but fancy it will not be now till the end of the month. My wife sends you her best respects. We beg to be remembered with all due regards to Mr Tyrwhitt, and I am always most truly Yours

T. Lindsey

P.S. I had only ½ a dozen copies of the enclosed to dispose of. Your message to D^r P ___ concerning his Son at Frankfurt was not neglected.[21] Pray can you tell me where Mr Porson is to be found, whom I want to thank for the present of masterly book [sic].[22] I am told that Dr Edwards has openly declared himself in his last sermon, to have a better opinion of Jove than of Jehovah.[23]

---

1   '[And] To lose, for the sake of life, the reasons for life'; Juvenal, *Satires*, VIII, 83. I owe this reference to Mr David Powell.

2   Although Robert Tyrwhitt had resigned his fellowship of Jesus College in 1777, he continued to reside in the college. Although Frend had been deprived of his college tutorship in Sept. 1788, he remained a fellow of Jesus College until his marriage in 1808.

3   For Tyrwhitt's *Two discourses*, see Vol. I, Letter 346, n. 12. The 'young man' to whom Lindsey sent them was David Jardine (d. 1797), a former pupil of Belsham at the Daventry Academy, who was minister to the dissenting chapel at Frog Lane, Bath, from 1789 until the chapel moved to new premises at Trim Street in 1796, and from then until his death on 10 Mar. 1797.

4   'Mighty in Apollo; i.e. mighty in (or respected for) both the arts for which Apollo is famous, prophecy and healing.' I am grateful to Mr David Powell for advice on this point.

5   This brother of David Jardine was Lewis Jones Jardine, of Queen Square, Bristol, listed as a surgeon in *Universal British directory* (1791), II, 130; and see *Sermons, by the late Rev. David Jardine, of Bath* (2 vols., Bristol, 1798), I (unpaginated memoir of David Jardine by John Prior Estlin). In 1794 he emigrated to America; see Letters 583 and 589.

6   Robert Tyrwhitt.

7   This 'new periodical work' was *The Christian Miscellany; Or, Religious and Moral Magazine.* The twelve ministers included Henry Toulmin, John Holland (1766–1826) and Frank Sayers (1763–1817). It was published in London by Benjamin Kingsbury and Caleb Stower.

8   For Henry Toulmin and his (first) wife, see Letter 392, n. 1. Their second surviving child was a daughter, Lucinda Jane Toulmin, born on 3 July 1790.

9   Thomas Cooper, then of Manchester and a prominent member of the Literary and Philosophical Society of that town, and his wife Alice, née Greenwood, had five children.

10   Robert Robinson and his wife Ellen, née Payne (1733–1808) had twelve children, of whom at least one predeceased Robinson.

11   These works were Priestley, *Reflections on death. A sermon, on occasion of the death of the Rev. Robert Robinson of Cambridge, delivered at the New Meeting in Birmingham, June 13, 1790. And published at the request of those who heard it, and of Mr Robinson's family* (Birmingham, 1790); Joshua Toulmin, *Christian vigilance considered in a sermon, preached at the baptist chapel, in Taunton, on the Lord's day, after the sudden removal of ... Robert Robinson* (London, 1790); and

Abraham Rees, *The doctrine of Christ, the only effectual remedy against the fear of death: and the union of good men in the future world: in two sermons, preached at Cambridge, on ... June the 27th, 1790, on occasion of the death of the late Rev. Robert Robinson* (London, 1790). Each of them claimed that Robinson adopted unitarian opinions in later life.

12 For Frend's Unitarian Society at Cambridge, which met on Sunday evenings, see Letters 416 and 430. In the summer of 1790, John Kentish was a student at Hackney College, with relatively convenient opportunities to visit Frend at Cambridge.

13 John Kentish had been a pupil of Thomas Belsham at Daventry between 1784 and 1788; he was a student at Hackney College between 1788 and 1790, and Belsham was resident tutor there from 1789. In the autumn of 1790 Kentish became the first minister of the unitarian chapel at Plymouth Dock. For Thomas Porter and the Plymouth liturgy, see Letter 406.

14 Probably this was a lecture which Frend gave in London during the summer of 1790. The presence in the audience of Abraham Rees, minister at the Old Jewry chapel from 1783 to 1825, supports this possibility, and Frend spent much time in London in 1790; see Knight, *William Frend*, ch. 6. Although Frend did not publish the lecture, one may speculate that its subject was either political reform (see Letter 421, n. 5) or the new translation of the Bible.

15 Probably this friend was Robert Edward Garnham, who wrote to William Frend on 31 May 1790 that he had 'no absolute confidence in the Translation given of the beginning of John's gospel' and that he would be 'most glad to see another made out', quoted in Brooks, 'Priestley's plan', 90.

16 James Edward Hamilton, *Strictures upon primitive Christianity, by the Rev. Dr. Knowles, preben-dary of Ely; as also upon the theological and polemical writings of the Rt. Rev. the lord bishop of St. David's, the Rev. Dr. Priestley, and the late Rev. Mr. Badcock. Part the first* (London, 1790). The second part of this work was published in 1792; both parts were published by Joseph Johnson. Hamilton described Lindsey (p. 266n) as a 'humanist' writer, an expression which Lindsey came to dislike (see Letter 667). Thomas Knowles (1723–1802) was a prebendary of Ely from 1779 until his death; his work was entitled *Primitive Christianity; or testimonies from the writers of the first four centuries; to prove that Jesus Christ was worshipped as God from the beginning of the Christian church* (London, 1789). It also provoked a reply from Capel Lofft, *Observations on the first part of Dr Knowles's testimonies from the writers of the first four centuries, in a letter to a friend* (Bury St Edmunds, 1789).

17 Lindsey probably referred here to the essay entitled 'A new interpretation of John i. 1', by 'Philologus Christianus', *Theological Repository*, V (1786), 385–95. According to a letter from the unitarian minister William Hincks (1794–1871) in *MR*, XIV (1819), 532–3, 'Philologus Christianus' was Michael Dodson. The purpose of the letter from Hincks was to supplement the list of pseudonyms, together with the revelation of their true identities, from the *Theological Repository* in *MR*, XII (1817), 526–7. For a further reference to 'Philologus Christianus', see Letter 644, n. 9.

18 Dyer's letter to Lindsey seems not to have survived.

19 The Revolution Society held its commemoration of the anniversary of the French Revolution at the Crown and Anchor tavern, in the Strand, on 14 July 1790. The society's minute book states the bare fact that the meeting took place, with no account of the proceedings; BL, Add. MS 64814, fo. 33. The *Public Advertiser*, 16 July 1790, published a lengthy account of the meeting, with a list of the toasts drunk; it stated that 'upwards of 600 gentlemen' were present. There is a lively account of the meeting in the diary of Samuel Pipe-Wolferstan, 14 July 1790; Staffordshire RO, D1527/15. William Godwin noted in his diary the presence, among others, of Lindsey, Price and Alexander Geddes; Bodl., Abinger collection, reel 12.

20 For Toulmin's sermon, see n. 11, above. For Belsham's sermon, see Letter 410, n. 5.

21 Following his visit to Paris in the early days of the French Revolution, William Priestley resided with a family at Frankfurt before returning to Birmingham later in 1790.

22 This book was almost certainly Richard Porson's *Letters to Mr. Archdeacon Travis, in answer to his defence of the three heavenly witnesses, 1 John v. 7*, a work which argued that this key trinitarian text was a subsequent, fraudulent, interpolation. See Letter 385, n. 3. In London, Porson lived in rooms at Essex Court in the Temple.

23 Thomas Edwards, in *The predictions of the apostles concerning the end of the world. A sermon preached before the University of Cambridge, on Sunday, May 23, 1790* (Bury, 1790), pp. 2–3, compared the 'inspired language' of Jove favourably with that of Jehovah.

419. To WILLIAM FREND   **19 JULY 1790**

Text: CUL, Add. MS 7886 (Frend papers), no. 158.
Addressed: To/The Rev^d. W. Frend/fellow of Jesus college/Cambridge
Postmarked: 19 90 [postmark otherwise illegible]

London. July. 19. 1790.

Dear Sir,

Since my last to you, I have heard it reported from those who I think ought not to deal in such matters, that your friend, whose address I inquired after that I might thank him for his book which I much prize and approve, was an unbeliever and an immoral man.[1] My notion is that a man is far from being an unbeliever, who rejects a great deal of what the world believes, and which w^d make him pass for an unbeliever with many. Nor I do I [*sic*] reckon him to deserve the name of immoral, who is not so correct in many things as I should wish him. But the epithets were used without any reserve. If it be not too delicate or an impertinent question, I would thank you for two lines upon it, as it may be of some use for me to urge something on the favourable side. Whatever is said however shall remain with me.

I congratulate you upon the most glorious and grandest and I hope happiest event in human things on Wednesday last at Paris[2] –

I have time to add nothing *more*

ever Your's
T.L.

---

1 This was Richard Porson; see Letter 418.
2 'Wednesday last' was 14 July 1790, the first anniversary of the fall of the Bastille. At the Fête de la Fédération in the Champs de Mars, Louis XVI swore allegiance to the new French constitution.

420. To JOSEPH BRETLAND   **26 JULY 1790**

Text: Rutt, II, 75–6 n. ¶, 88 n. *.

Note: Rutt, citing 'MS copy, by Rev. B. Mardon',[1] printed only the sections of the letter which are presented here. Rutt did not indicate which section preceded the other, or whether the two passages were continuous, in the original manuscript. Here it is assumed that the passages appeared in the order in which Rutt presented them, and that they were not continuous; they are accordingly separated by a broken line.

London, July 26, 1790.

I am very happy the Second Address was well approved, in any degree, by such judges as you. I wish Unitarians could come to any solid and satisfactory faith about the interpretation and rendering of the preface to St. John's gospel, and upon such grounds as might approve themselves to common readers, who will continue to think that he is speaking of Christ as God, if nothing level to their capacities is laid before them to the contrary.

I hope that you, who are so qualified, and who are in the prime of life, and have leisure, will lend your assistance to Mr. Toulmin, jun., and his colleagues, in their new undertaking,[2] which might be highly useful in counteracting a farrago of things in your Christian magazines, and by degrees eradicate the seeds of superstition out of the minds of the common people.

---

¹ Benjamin Mardon (1792–1866) was a unitarian minister at St Vincent Street, Glasgow, from 1817 to
   1825; at Earl Street, Maidstone, from 1825 to 1868; and at Upper High Street, Sidmouth, from 1854
   to 1863.
² The was the *Christian Miscellany*, intended to be a monthly periodical; it ran for only one year in
   1792. Born in Apr. 1766, Henry Toulmin was aged twenty-four in July 1790; born in May 1742,
   Bretland was aged forty-eight. The 'Christian magazines' which Lindsey had in mind included such
   orthodox and evangelical publications as the *Arminian Magazine*.

421. To WILLIAM FREND   26 JULY 1790

Text: CUL, Add. MS 7886 (Frend papers), no. 159.
Addressed: To/The Rev^d. Wm Frend/fellow of Jesus college/Cambridge
Postmarked: JY 27 90

> London. July. 26.
> 1790. Monday night
> 10 o'clock

Dear Sir,

I put my date so particularly, to account for saying so little in return for your kind and obliging letter.¹

Your confidence shall not be misused. I am inclined to think well of and to esteem _____ notwithstanding the circumstances mentioned. Any thing wrong for his own sake, I trust he will correct, that he may be that great and estimable character, to which his rare abilities will carry him. If it be true, which I have heard, that out of just scruples he will resign present emoluments and future expectations, and turn out into the wide world, depending only on his own abilities and exertions for support, it is making a great sacrifice, and most praiseworthy.² I have not been negligent in calling as you directed; but finding no one within, I left a letter to be delivered.³

To morrow morning we set out for Birmingham, but shall not arrive till the Wednesday evening. To tell you the fact, it was for D^r P ___ y, that I made the inquiry to which the above relates, as from him I had the account, and to him I shall read your letter. He will be glad to know that you will speak a few words to Mr Burgess, but he will ask also concerning the Pentateuch and following histories, and I shall tell him how you have buckled to the Work for the Summer.⁴ But perhaps you have written to him.

I forgot to mention, that Mr Cooper of Manchester lately asked me about a plan that you and Mr Hobhouse had projected: and young Mr Toulmin told me that it was for the dispersion of religious tracts, but I answer^d that I believed he was mistaken, as if it were so, I shoud have heard of it.⁵

I must beg you to tell Mr Dyer, that at our return, which will be in about a fortnight, I hope to be able to thank him for his letter.⁶ From B _____ m D^r P and I go to see the venerable Mr Tayleur at Shrewsbury, who had the courage to open a church in his own house and officiate to some like minded friends, till the dissenting minister was prevailed upon to adopt our liturgy. And he being lately dead,⁷ the congregation flourishes much under a young man, one of the Rowe's of Devon, a good name, approved and patronized by him.⁸

If there be aught I can do for you in our excursion, a letter will find me at D[r] P's.
If not, you shall hear from me soon after our return.

My wife desires kind respects.

I am always with sincere esteem

truly yours

T. Lindsey.

---

1   This letter, in common with other letters from Frend to Lindsey, seems not to have survived.
2   This is almost certainly a reference to Richard Porson, who had been a fellow of Trinity College, Cambridge, since 1785. His fellowship lapsed in 1792 because, in defiance of the college statutes, he declined to be ordained to holy orders. Although he was elected to the regius professorship of Greek at Cambridge in 1792, he spent most of his time in London, virtually as an independent scholar. This, clearly, was the outcome for which Lindsey had hoped; his allusion to something 'wrong', however, might indicate that he was aware of Porson's reputation for heavy drinking.
3   Lindsey had left his letter for Porson at the latter's London lodging at Essex Court in the Temple. The letter itself appears not to have survived.
4   This refers to the new translation of the Bible. 'Mr Burgess' was possibly the classical scholar Thomas Burgess (1756–1837), formerly of Corpus Christi College, Oxford, and from 1785 to 1791 examining chaplain to Shute Barrington, bishop of Salisbury. He was subsequently a prebendary of Durham and from 1803 to 1825 bishop of St David's. Although very much later, while at St David's, he wrote vehemently against unitarians, in 1789, he published an anti-slavery work, which perhaps made him acceptable to liberal dissenters as a potential contributor to the new translation. Letter 428 shows that whether or not Frend made an approach to Burgess, nothing came of the idea of involving him with the project. Frend's 'work for the summer' included the translation of the history books of the Old Testament for the new project and Priestley evidently hoped that he would undertake (or find another competent translator for) the Pentateuch. For Burgess's cautious interest in biblical translation, see Joris Van Eijnatten, 'The Burgess generation: Dutch academic theologians and religious knowledge, 1760–1840', in *Bishop Burgess and his world. Culture, religion and society in Britain, Europe and North America in the eighteenth and nineteenth centuries*, ed. Nigel Yates (Cardiff, 2007), pp. 69–70.
5   In 1790, Frend was in communication with John Hobhouse (1712–87) of Bristol, the father of Benjamin Hobhouse, with a view to the creation in the English provinces of societies on the lines of the Society for Constitutional Information in order to promote reform by the dissemination of tracts. Thomas Cooper of Manchester hoped to establish such societies in Lancashire and Cheshire, and Henry Toulmin, minister at Chowbent, Lancashire, also showed interest in the idea. Little of a practical kind came of these proposals. See Knight, *William Frend*, pp. 91–2.
6   See Letter 418, n. 18.
7   Joseph Fownes, minister of the High Street chapel, Shrewsbury, who died on 7 Nov. 1789.
8   John Rowe, who was 'patronised' (i.e. encouraged) by William Tayleur.

---

422. To RUSSELL SCOTT   14 AUGUST 1790

Text: Scott Coll.
Addressed: To/The Rev[d]. Russell Scott/Portsmouth
Endorsed: Augu[t]. 15th. – 90 [in pencil]: Read
Postmarked: AU 14 90

London. aug. 14. 1790.

Dear Sir,

It has given me a good deal of concern that I have not of so long a space heard from you. Although by unavoidable delay I came in the rear of those who congratulated you on the change of your condition, yet neither my wife nor myself would give place to any one in the sincerity of our good wishes for you and M[rs] Scott. For a long time I imagined that both the letter and the parcell that I sent to you had miscarried, but the inquiries I made at the Angel satisfy me that nothing of this kind had happened.[1]

After you left us, and indeed to the present hour, I have been chiefly employed in attending to health in consequence of the rude interruption given to it in the spring. Since the beginning of the Summer we have been altogether in the country about 12 miles from London except at the end of each week. We have made two journeys to friends at a distance, and are only within these few days returned from a fortnight's visit to Shrewsbury and Birmingham. Mr Belsham was with us part of our time at the latter place. Mrs Priestley for whom we were very apprehensive on going down, seems likely to overcome the effects of her spitting blood, and to live I trust for many years to come.[2] Mr Tayleur at 78 is better than when we saw him at 77,[3] and is very happy in Mr Row[e], who takes great pains many ways, but I fear that this and the duty twice a day may be too much for him whose constitution is but feeble.[4]

Dr Priestley is reprinting his Familiar Letters, corrected and improved, they being all sold off, and a continued demand for them.[5]

I had intended a longer letter but a gent. and his lady just come out of the North,[6] call for me, so that I can only desire you to send me if it be but two lines to say how you and your lady are, and to present and accept our kind regards and best wishes -

always yours most truly

TH Lindsey.[7]

---

1   See Letter 414. The Angel, behind St Clement's church, in the Strand, was one of the inns from which the Portsmouth and Chichester mail coach departed.

2   Mary Priestley died at Northumberland, Pennsylvania, on 17 Sept. 1796

3   This is a reference to Lindsey's visit to Tayleur at Shrewsbury in 1789; see Letter 391. Tayleur was born in 1712.

4   Rowe, despite his apparent feebleness, lived to the age of sixty-eight.

5   Priestley published a second edition of his *Familiar letters ... to the inhabitants of Birmingham*, with additions and corrections, in Birmingham in the summer of 1790.

6   Disappointingly, Lindsey did not identify his visitors from the north; one possibility is John Lee and his wife Mary.

7   Although the letter and signature are in Lindsey's hand, his wife apparently added her initial 'H' to Lindsey's 'T'.

423. To WILLIAM ALEXANDER   15 AUGUST 1790

Text: 'Letters of the Rev. Theophilus Lindsey. No. I',
                    UH, II, 40 (1 Feb. 1862), p. 45.

Note: This is the only section of the letter printed by the *UH*; the manuscript has apparently not survived. The ellipsis at the start of the letter indicates that the section quoted was not the beginning of the original letter. The ellipsis within the first paragraph indicates that part of the text of that paragraph has been omitted.

London, Aug. 15th, 1790.

* * * It is a great pleasure to learn from your letter, which worthy Mr. Giles[1] has delivered to me, that you have been pleasingly disappointed at Yoxford with respect to the sentiments of the people concerning you, and the diminution of your school. Most happy would it be, if in time, by your wise and virtuous demeanour and conversation among them, they may be brought to see that your conduct, though singular, is right and to be approved; and that the Church Catechism contains many things very contrary to the Scriptures, and therefore very unfitting to be taught to children. We know not what may be done by a prudent perseverance in that which is right. * * My hope is that you will soon have scholars that are older under your care, and that will yield you more profit, as well as satisfaction for your labours with

them. In the meantime, very meritorious are your labours, however low in the estimate of many the objects of them: the poorest of those whose minds you endeavour to instruct and season with early good principles being no less esteemed in the eye of our common Creator than those of the highest worldly rank; and some of them may be called out to act useful and important parts in the present state.

We have been lately upwards of a fortnight with friends at a distance, chiefly at Shrewsbury and Birmingham. At the former place, there is a Unitarian congregation that makes use of our liturgy, introduced by a very respectable person, who quitted the Established Church;[2] and at Birmingham there is a noble harvest of virtuous and enlightened youth of both sexes every year, by Dr. Priestley's labours in private on Sundays, besides his instructions to the congregation at large.[3] I gave him some copies of the "Practical Instructions for Young Children", as they are, indeed, for the greater part his own; and I shall send you down fifty by Mr. Giles, and more shall be at your service whenever you want them, as I have procured 1,000 to be printed and given away.[4]

---

[1] For Thomas Giles, see Letter 410, n. 1. Alexander's letter to Lindsey seems not to have survived.

[2] This 'respectable person' was William Tayleur. It is likely that in the manuscript, Lindsey spelt 'Established' as 'Estabilished', according to his usual practice.

[3] For Priestley's Sunday school at the New Meeting, Birmingham, see Emily Bushrod, 'The history of unitarianism in Birmingham from the middle of the eighteenth century to 1893', MA dissertation, University of Birmingham, 1954, pp. 22–4.

[4] Possibly this work was *Practical instructions for children* (Aberdeen, 1785), a work which, as noted by COPAC, has been attributed to Andrew Skene, minister of the Church of Scotland at Banff. For a further note on Skene, and his possible authorship of this work, see Letter 495. On 9 Feb. 1791, on the recommendation of Lindsey, Disney and Dodson, the Unitarian Society agreed to adopt *Practical instructions for youth* as one of the society's publications, and resolved that 3,000 copies be printed for sale at 4*d* each; Unitarian Society minute book, p. 18. A work entitled *Practical instructions for youth*, a short (thirty-six page) pamphlet in the form of a catechism, was published in London in 1796, though with no indication that it appeared under the auspices of the Unitarian Society. No work entitled *Practical instructions for children*, 'young' or otherwise, or *Practical instructions for youth*, was included in the thirteen volumes of collected works reprinted by the Unitarian Society between 1791 and 1802.

---

424. To WILLIAM FREND   25 AUGUST 1790

Text: CUL, Add. MS 7886 (Frend papers), no. 160.
Addressed: Address missing.
Postmarked: Postmark missing.

London. Aug. 25.[1]

Dear Sir,

Your little paquett was deliverd very punctually and I gave D[r] Disney his yesterday morning. You may depend upon my doing every thing in my power to to [*sic*] promote the Subscription to the work of so worthy confessor as M[r] Dyer,[2] though much cannot be done at present, when our people are mostly in the country, and their pastors getting out of the smoke of this town as much as they can. D[r] Disney is this week at M[r] Brand Holliss in Essex,[3] and we are very much in the week days at a friends near Epsom in Surrey.[4] I shall always be happy to receive your commands and beg you will reckon me with high esteem most truly Your's

　　　　T. Lindsey

---

[1] Lindsey did not give the year of this letter. It is located in the Frend papers at CUL among the letters

of 1790, and the reference to the subscription for Dyer's work suggests strongly that it is in the right place there.

2   This work was George Dyer's *Inquiry into the nature of subscription*; see Letter 382, n. 4. Lindsey was seeking subscriptions for the second edition, published by Joseph Johnson in 1792.

3   Brand Hollis's estate was The Hyde, Ingatestone, Essex; he inherited it from Thomas Hollis in 1774 and bequeathed it to John Disney on his death in 1804.

4   Probably Lindsey referred here to Sophia and Frances Chambers of Morden, adjacent to Epsom, where he frequently spent his weekdays during the summer.

425. To WILLIAM FREND   13 SEPTEMBER 1790

Text: CUL, Add. MS 7886 (Frend papers), no. 161.
Addressed: To/The Rev. Wᵐ Frend/fellow of Jesus college/Cambridge
Postmarked: 13 90 [postmark otherwise illegible]

London. sept. 13. 1790.

Dear Sir,

Had not Dʳ Priestley engaged to say something to you himself, in consequence of the letter I recᵈ from you a little before we left him, some parts of which I read to him, I should I believe assuredly have written to you myself much sooner.[1] Since that we have been little at home except part of one of the weeks that Mʳ Dyer was in Town. On Saturday last we returned from Tunbridge wells, where I had spent a fortnight with some friends, and tho' I did not find any benefit from the waters and therefore drank them very little, the air of the place, the walks, and daily rides about it, have refreshed and revived me much. I was only sorry there was not a modern Whiston[2] to have catechized the company a little, and disturbed them in their patient acquiescence in things as they are, not from a full approbation of them, but from a fear of becoming unsettled, as I found in some ladies that I conversed with.

We attended Mʳ Hampson's meeting, a serious man with good natural abilities, particularly improved of late by reading Dʳ Priestley's works: formerly and originally one of Mʳ Wesley's preachers, and now in some little connection with, though in no subjection to him.[3] There is another Baptist preacher, Mʳ Joseph Haynes, who is most liberal and an Unitarian, but has not more than 20 that are his hearers. He is 66 years old as he told me, but lively and with all his faculties about him, and does great good among his poor neighbours in doctoring them, preventing law suits &c. I am to send him some books to disperse. He lives at Tunbridge-Wells.[4] Mʳ Hampson's direction is Southborough near Tunbridge Wells. I went over to Tunbridge Town, to visit Mʳ Austin, a clergiman of fortune, who some years since resigned a living out of conscientious scruples; but he and his lady and daughters are gone to Southampton.[5] I never saw him but there have been some messages past between us, and books sent. I thought you wᵈ. like to know so much of your countrymen.[6]

I am glad to find by a letter of Mʳˢ Reynolds s to my wife, that Mʳ Reynolds has called upon you at Jesus though he did not see you, and that he has bought Mʳ Robinson's book on the widows account.[7] Mʳ Dyer would tell you that he had the three guineas which I advertised you of my having recᵈ from Mʳ Turner of Abingdon.[8] But the Exeter-Subscription-money amounting to betwixt 2 & 3 pounds I still have in my hands to pay to you.[9] I was sorry to be out of Town when Mʳ Dyer last called. His conversation is most pleasing, and you continually see what a good creature he is, and also ingenious and enlightened. But I am apprehensive he is not at present disposed to settle with any congregation, especially at a great distance from his present connections.[10]

I have just rec^d a letter from Mr Freeman, minister of the unitarian church at Boston in N. England, of a noble spirit and excellent understanding.[11] He expresses astonishment and concern at the late behaviour of the british legislature in refusing the repeal of the Test-laws, and at the bigotry of the clergy of the estabilishm^t. But well observes that our oppressions keep alive our zeal, and occasion many excellent writings in defence of the equal liberties of mankind; whilst the unbounded liberty they enjoy has almost extinguished zeal in many among them but not in all; and as a proof of this last mentions that a large impression of Extracts from Emlyns Humble Enquiry had been lately published and sold in Boston.[12] The editors, a sett of gentlemen, who opposed the religious adoration of Christ, but who were in general, Arians. To oppose them a clergiman has undertaken the defence of the doctrine of the Trinity, and is now preaching a course of Sermons upon it: but has not reconverted any.[13] This is all in Order.

I forgot to mention that Mr Benson, the clergiman at Tunbridge wells, generally liked, has not given equal satisfaction this season, by preaching often against Dissenters, and Arians and Socinians.[14] At lady Hunti

We have been lately alarmed at the reports of the National Assembly, that they are in danger of soon coming to nothing.[15] But I trust they will be able to support themselves, and that their work will remain.

Dr Priestley perhaps has told you, that he is now on an excursion into the North, to visit his old congregation at Leeds, and thence to Scarborough, where he was to meet Mr Russell, who was there when we were at Birmingham.[16] All friends here are well. Mr Dodson, but just now going into the country, having been delayed by business.

I am always with sincere esteem,
      Dear Sir, most truly Yours
         T. Lindsey.

Pray remember us to Mr Hammond. I shall pay my respects to him when we become settled.

---

1   Frend's letter to Lindsey seems not to have survived.

2   William Whiston (1667–1752) became Lucasian professor of mathematics at Cambridge in succession to Sir Isaac Newton in 1703. As a result of his eccentricity and his Arian opinions, he was deprived of his professorship in 1710, and he devoted the remainder of his life to theological speculation. His best-known work was *Primitive Christianity revived* (5 vols., London, 1711–12). In 1747, he joined the baptists. Lindsey and other unitarians regarded him as a heroic pioneer of liberal theology.

3   For John Hampson (1732–95), see Vol. I, Letter 375, n. 3.

4   This is a reference to Joseph Haynes, or Haines, minister to the general baptist society at Mount Ephraim, Tunbridge Wells. The society ceased to exist after his death in 1813. See *The church book of Tunbridge Wells*, ed. Leonard J. Maguire (London, 1998), pp. 17, 116, 117, 121, where it is recorded that Haines was admitted a member of the society in 1752, and subsequently became its minister. Joseph Haynes of Tunbridge Wells is mentioned in the Thompson list of 1773 as one of the dissenting ministers who petitioned in favour of reform of the system of subscription to the doctrinal articles of the Church of England as a condition for ministerial registration. See 'A view of English nonconformity in 1773', *Transactions of the Congregational Historical Society*, V, 4 (Jan. 1912), 222.

5   For Henry Austen, see Vol. I, Letter 376, n. 9, together with Letters 447, n. 1 and 451, n. 5. Austen married Mary Hooker at Tonbridge on 4 Aug. 1763. Their two daughters were Elizabeth Matilda Austen, born in 1766, and Harriet Lennard Austen, born in 1769. The former married John Butler Harrison of Southampton; hence, probably, the visit to that town.

6   This is a reference to Frend's Kentish connexions (his family came from Canterbury).

7   Mary Catherine, née Kerrich (d. 1824), who married Richard Reynolds of Little Paxton in 1770. I

have not been able to locate her letter to Hannah Lindsey, although it was not the only communication between them (see Letter 706, n. 17). Richard Reynolds had purchased one of Robert Robinson's books, probably his *History of baptism* (see Letter 417, n. 4), in order to help provide for his widow.

8   For Daniel Turner of Abingdon, see Letter 417, n. 1.

9   Probably Lindsey referred here to subscriptions in Exeter for the second edition of Dyer's *Inquiry*.

10   Dyer never settled as a minister with a congregation. His 'present connections' were at Fenstanton, near Cambridge.

11   This letter from James Freeman of Boston to Lindsey is not among his letters at DWL or the Historical Society of Pennsylvania; nor is it included in the letters from Freeman printed in Belsham, *Memoirs*, pp. 153–64.

12   This work was Thomas Emlyn's *Extracts from an humble inquiry into the scripture account of Jesus Christ* (Boston, MA, 1790, and sold by Samuel Hall at Cornhill, London). A previous edition had appeared in Boston in 1756. Emlyn's original work, first published (probably in London) in 1702, from which this edition was excerpted, was entitled *An humble inquiry into the scripture account of Jesus Christ*. Its argument was Socinian. For a further reference to Emlyn (1663–1741), see Letter 700, n. 14.

13   See n. 11, above. The clergyman to whom Freeman referred was Jedidiah Morse (1761–1826), who from 1789 was the minister of the First Congregational church at Charlestown, Massachusetts. As Conrad Wright puts it, 'He began his ministry by preaching a series of Thursday lectures in defence of the divinity of Christ. This was an obvious slap at the liberals, and particularly at James Freeman, the Socinian'; *The beginnings of unitarianism in America* (Boston, Archon Books reprint, 1976; first published 1955), p. 271.

14   Martin Benson (1761–1833) was vicar of the church of King Charles the Martyr at Tunbridge Wells from 1786 to 1829. A high church sympathizer, he was the author of several published sermons.

15   Lindsey referred here to the problems of the National Assembly, which included the tumultuous aftermath of the revolt by the military garrison at Nancy in Aug. 1790, and the siege of the Assembly by hostile Parisian crowds early the following month. At the same time, the resignation of Necker as director-general of finance heightened financial anxiety in France. These events were reported in detail in the London press; see, for example, *Public Advertiser*, 11 Sept. 1790.

16   Priestley's 'excursion' in Sept. and early Oct. 1790 included visits to Buxton and Leeds; Rutt, I, 81–7. For Lindsey's visit to Birmingham and Shrewsbury, see Letters 422–3.

426. To WILLIAM TAYLEUR   20 SEPTEMBER 1790

Text: JRUL, Lindsey Letters, vol. II, no. 34.
Printed: McLachlan, *Letters*, pp. 39–40 (second and third sentences of
                   second paragraph); p. 100 (part of first sentence of second
                   paragraph); p. 136 (second sentence of fourth paragraph).
Addressed: To/William Tayleur Esqr/Shrewsbury
Endorsed: 20th Septr 1790
Postmarked: SE 20 90

London. sept. 20. 1790.

Dear Sir,

I should not have been contented with my silence towards you since the cordial reception I met with at Shrewsbury, if I had not desired Dr Priestley to communicate some accounts I had received from different parts and thereby shewn at the least that such a friend was not out of my thoughts.

I was grieved that during the ten days we were at Tunbridge wells, there was no opportunity of conversing freely on religious subjects but with two dissenting ministers of the place; a Mr Hampson, who was formerly in Mr Wesley's connection, but resisting some of his arbitrary decrees, and being unacceptable withdrew himself, and is now a free inquirer and nearly a perfect unitarian in chains which he cannot well shake off: And a baptist minister, Mr Joseph Haynes, originally of some trade, but now in years and enjoying a tolerable competency, preacher to a congregation consisting seldom of more than 20 or 30. He is wholly self-taught, has some smattering of learning, with a good deal of acuteness and readiness, and I fancy must acquit himself very well to the capacities of his general hearers, and would also suit others, had he not a habit of miscalling certain words, which is not likely to be cured.[1] I could not be one of his hearers, as I attended M[r] Hampson, and did not at the time know that he officiated: but if I live to go there again, I shall be one of his congregation.[2] He engaged very chearfully to distribute any tracts that were sent him. The fashion at the place is to be very orthodox and go to church; and the minister has adapted himself this season to the vogue of the times, or the lessons of his superiors in preaching against dissenters, and sometimes giving hard names to Arians and Socinians. His name is Benson, a young man said to be of good abilities, and who with what is collected for him at the Wells, and other preferment, some I think in London, has not less than £600 a year.[3]

If you have not them already, you will be much gratified with M[r] Mannings Three Discourses at the Norfolk Assizes.[4] Such free and liberal sentiments have very rarely been uttered upon such occasions. But in exemplifying, and descending to some particular explanations in the notes, he has spoken most unreservedly indeed, and like a man who has thought for himself and is not afraid of declaring it. In some things I cannot go along with him; particularly in his supposition that John's gospel is chiefly the work of his editor's.[5] But he deserves to be perused, and it appears throughout, that he has a serious belief of and concern for the purity of the gospel and to bring men to piety and virtue. He was an acquaintance of D[r] Jebb's, who used often to talk of him, and exhort him to come forth with his sentiments. They are printed for Robinson, in Pater noster row.[6]

At the opening of the session at the New college on Thursday last there was a good number of new students, and M[r] Belsham delivered an excellent charge to them on their whole conduct and especially a strict conformity to the rules of the Society.[7] M[r] Wakefield was with his fellow-tutors, and I apprehend convinced them that his manners are social and agreeable and that he is severe and formidable only with his pen in his hand. My wife presents her best respects. We hope this fine autumn is not too cold for you, but that you are able to enjoy it exspatiating [*sic*] on your beautiful terrace. We desire our due remembrances to M[r] Rowe and M[r] Wood. I remain always with a most perfect esteem, Your ever obliged and faithful

      T. Lindsey.

---

1 For Joseph Haines, see Letter 425, n. 4. *The church book of Tunbridge Wells*, ed. Maguire, does not record the trade which Haines had practised before becoming a minister.

2 There is no evidence from his later letters that Lindsey visited Tunbridge Wells again, or that he attended Haines's congregation. However, he heard reports from Tunbridge Wells at various times and in Apr. 1794 met the methodist minister of that town, John Hampson, in London (Letter 568).

3 Martin Benson's other preferment was that of rector of St Dunstan-in-the-East, London, which he held from 1789 to 1791. He was also rector of Orgaswick, Kent, from 1788 to 1791, and subsequently rector of Merstham, Surrey, from 1791 until his death in 1833.

4 William Manning, *Three sermons, preached at the Norfolk assizes in the spring and summer 1788, and in the spring 1789, on the necessity of government, and the usefulness of magistrates, and of civil and religious liberty. Illustrated with notes* (London, 1790). Manning (d. 1810) was rector of Brome from 1760 to 1810 and rector and patron of Diss from 1778 to 1810.

5 For Manning's claim that the gospel of St John was the work of editors and not primarily of the apostle himself, see the notes to his *Three sermons*, pp.126–35.

6 The firm of G. G. J. and J. Robinson of Paternoster Row was indeed the publisher.

7 'Thursday last' was 16 Sept. 1790. On 6 Sept. the committee of Hackney College resolved to ask Belsham to undertake this charge; DWL, MS 38.24, p. 140.

427. To WILLIAM TAYLEUR   5 OCTOBER 1790

Text: Royal Soc., Priestley Memorial Volume, p. 30.
Printed: Rutt, I, 83–4 (third paragraph, which is a quotation from
                   Priestley's letter to Lindsey, 22 Sept. 1790; in quoting
                   Priestley's letter, Lindsey omitted two separate sentences).
Addressed: To/William Tayleur Esqr/Shrewsbury
Endorsed: 5th Oct^r – 90
Postmarked: OC 5 90

London. Oct. 5. 1790.

Dear Sir,

I beg you will give my best thanks to Mr Rowe for his very welcome letter on many accounts, which I shall take an opportunity to acknowlege, though at present I direct myself to you.[1]

As you are solicitous about Dr Priestley, I cannot do better than transcribe an anecdote from his last letter but one, that will give you much pleasure, premising only that this last was the 4th sunday of his absence with Mrs Priestley on a Tour into Yorkshire, and that to morrow he sets out from Leeds to Birmingham

"We have found our excursion exceedingly pleasant far beyond my expectation, especially at Buxton where I made some agreeable acquaintance, and where I found some exercise even as a *preacher*. We arrived on Saturday evening, and the next day after dinner, the company at the White Hart desired me to give them a Sermon, which I did; and many persons from the other houses, tho' the notice was short, attended. In the course of the following week, when it was understood that I meant to stay another sunday, I had a deputation by General Stratton[2] and a Mr Sligo from Leith,[3] from the company at the Crescent, where were several of the Nobility and the Provost of the university of Dublin,[4] to give them a Sermon. I desired them to name their own time, and the[y] appointed the morning after the Prayers, which they said I had no occasion to attend, as there was a room adjoining to the Assembly room where the service was. Having no sermon that I thought quite proper for so mixed an audience, I composed one on *the resurrection of Christ*. There was a large audience, and I was never heard with a more fixed attention. Dr Burgh,[5] Mr Grattan,[6] and many persons of note were there, who if I may judge by their language and circumstances were much impressed. A young man of a pleasing countenance and manner, but whose name I do not know, was very particular in his acknowlegements, and said he sh^d consider the opportunity he had heard of hearing me on that subject, as the happiest circumstance in his life. An elderly clergiman was particularly attentive, and published his approbation to all that were near him. The officiating clergiman however and many others were much offended at my being requested to preach, but many the most prejudiced, I am told, expressed themselves afterwards much in my favour. On the whole, I thought it a happy opportunity, as some wavering believers were present, whose faith, I have reason to think I confirmed."

He then goes on to add much of very marked respect paid him all the time he staid, by Provost Hutchinson, and their conversations together, in which they harmonized much – and that the Arch^{bp's} Lady, (of Canterbury, I believe,[7]) and some others refused to attend.

Such events as these will contribute to remove prejudices agst Dissenters, and particularly against our friend, and may induce some to look into his most valuable writings. The choice of his subject, particularly in the manner I learn he treated it, was most happy, as many from Silas Deane's story and other things, woud continue to think him an Unbeliever.[8] One of equal zeal and less wisdom would have held forth on the church's idolatry and superstitions. He has promised me a sight of his Sermon.

I was much surprized, as were some others who know him, that the Author of *Considerations*, &c spoke out so very liberally and boldly: but it is not expected that he will proceed any farther, unless as the author of Hints, the D. of G. may draw him, with whom he is very strongly connected.[9] I think I sent you Mr Rogers's Sermon, preached this year at a Visitation at Ipswich on christian worship. He was fellow of Trinity coll. Cambridge, and I do not know whether he was not a pupil of D^r now B^p Watson's.[10] He goes our whole length, is uneasy in his situation, but satisfied himself for the present. He was at our place on Sunday, and I saw him afterwards for the first time, and was greatly pleased with his character. He left with me a Sermon on the Church of Christ &c most admirable and suited to the times, and most free, which is soon to be printed; but whether with or without his name is not yet determined.[11] He is lately become known to the D. of G.[12]

I congratulate you on the success attending Mr Rowe's labours, and I am obliged to him for the mention of such a respectable addition to your congregation. To you the prospect must be most pleasing, and I hope Shrewsbury will long possess such a pastor. Two other letters I have lately received of the kind you have returned, will come to you viâ Birmingham after our friends return, with some printed acc^{ts} of a curious sort. I sometimes reproach myself for the φιλαυτια[13] that but too much appears in sending such letters, but there is no possibility of transcribing them, and I judge from my self, that it is pleasing to you to see the whole. We are glad your late cold is better, and that you are able to go your rounds as usual. May heaven preserve your health, say we. My wife desires her due respects. We beg to [be] remembered kindly to Mr Rowe and Mr Wood. I remain always your most truly obliged and faithful affectionate Servt

T. Lindsey

---

1   Rowe's letter to Lindsey seems not to have survived. In his letter to Lindsey of 14 Oct. 1790 (JRUL, C2^{13}), Tayleur acknowledged this letter from Lindsey, adding that 'it gave uncommon pleasure to Mr Rowe, Mr Wood, & myself'.

2   Probably John Stratton, from 1787 major-general of artillery, subsequently lieutenant-general and promoted to general in May 1802; *Gent. Mag.*, LXXII, ii (1802), 679.

3   Lindsey originally wrote 'Lowth', then, without crossing that word out, wrote 'Leith' immediately above it. Rutt, I, 83, gives 'Leith'. In his preface to *The evidence of the resurrection of Jesus considered, in a discourse first delivered in the assembly-room, at Buxton, on Sunday, September 19, 1790. To which is added, an address to the Jews* (Birmingham, 1791), Priestley described this occasion at Buxton and referred (p. vii) to Mr Sligo as 'a gentleman of fortune in Scotland'. Possibly he was John Sligo, a director of the Edinburgh chamber of commerce and manufactures and of the Leith banking company; *The British almanac, and Glasgow register for 1801* (Edinburgh, ?1800), pp. 78, 90.

4   The provost of Trinity College, Dublin, from 1774 to 1794 was John Hely-Hutchinson (1724–94), who was also MP for Cork in the Irish parliament from 1760 to 1790. He was a regular visitor to the spa at Buxton and died there on 4 Sept. 1794.

5   This was almost certainly William Burgh, who, under the pseudonym 'A Layman', had published a critique of Lindsey's *Apology* in 1774; see Vol. I, Letters 132 and 169. In 1788, he was awarded the degree of DCL by Oxford University, in recognition of his defences of the doctrine of the Trinity. He was MP for the borough of Athy, county Kildare, in the Irish parliament, from 1769 to 1776.

6   Henry Grattan (1746–1820), MP for Charlemont borough in the Irish parliament from 1775 to 1790 and for Dublin city from 1790 to 1797. The leader of the 'patriot' party, he was a supporter of Fox, of moderate reform and catholic relief; he became 'The acknowledged champion of enlightened Ireland', as P. J. Jupp puts in his entry on Grattan in Thorne, *Hist. parl.*, IV, 76.

7   The archbishop of Canterbury in 1789 was John Moore; his second wife, whom he had married in 1770, was Catherine (1742–1818), the daughter of Sir Robert Eden (d. 1755) and the sister of William Eden (1744–1814), from 1789 Baron Auckland.

8   For the story that Silas Deane had attributed his abandonment of Christianity to Priestley, see Letter 414, n. 7.

9   The author of the *Considerations* was Richard Watson, bishop of Llandaff; see Letter 408, n. 4. Grafton, the chancellor of the university, admired Watson and shared his liberal theology; see *Autobiography and political correspondence of Augustus Henry,3rd duke of Grafton*, ed. Sir William R. Anson (London, 1898), p. 325. According to his own account, Watson and Grafton considered the possibility of introducing a bill in the house of lords for liturgical reform, including the removal of the Athanasian creed. However, the French Revolution, 'and the general abhorrence of all innovation, which its atrocities excited', led them to postpone, then to abandon, the idea. See *Anecdotes of the life of Richard Watson, bishop of Llandaff; written by himself* (2nd edn, 2 vols., London, 1818), I, 390–2.

10 George Rogers (d. 1835) was a fellow of Trinity College, Cambridge (where he had graduated BA in 1764), from 1767. Trinity was also the college of Richard Watson, bishop of Llandaff, where he was a fellow from 1760 and tutor from 1767 to 1771. From 1784 until his death, Rogers was rector of Sproughton, Suffolk, to which Lindsey referred, was *The place, object, and nature of Christian worship considered ... preached at the archdeacon's visitation April 23, 1790* (Ipswich, 1790). The archdeacon of Suffolk from 1781 to 1818 was John Strachey DD.

11 Rogers identified himself with theological and political radicalism in Suffolk, although he did not resign from the established church. He was a friend of Edward Evanson. His sermon on the church of Christ was included in Rogers, *Five Sermons, on the following subjects, viz. the true nature of the Christian church, and the impossibility of its being in danger. The scripture idea of heresy. Mysteries made plain. The scripture doctrine of atonement. The place, object, and manner of Christian worship. By George Rogers, M.A. rector of Sproughton, in Suffolk, and late fellow of Trinity College, Cambridge* (Ipswich, 1792; reprinted London, 1793). He was a member of the Unitarian Society from 1791.

12 The duke of Grafton.

13 Self-love, self-regard, egotism (cf. Cicero, *Epistle to Atticus*, 13.13.1); Lindsey also used this expression in Letter 498. I am grateful to Mr David Powell for the translation and the reference.

---

428. To WILLIAM FREND   **2 NOVEMBER 1790**

Text: CUL, Add. MS 7886 (Frend papers), no. 162.
Addressed: To/M^r. W. Frend./At the Post-Office/Canterbury
Postmarked: NO 2 90

London. Novr. 2. 1790.

Dear Sir,

I have been a full fortnight in Town, and should have told you of it, had I not been afraid of disturbing your studies without bringing any compensation. I shall attend to what you remark in one part of your letter.[1] I heard lately that Mr Porson was on a visit to Dr Parr at his living near Warwick, and both together had been to dine with Dr Priestley, who lives not more than 12 miles off.[2] D^r P ____ y some time since wished to have some tract from you on the necessarian doctrine, which you had recommended as a proper Appendix to Collins on the subject whom he was republishing, and had nearly printed off, and intended to write to you for it. I hope you have sent it.[3]

I am glad that you continue your unitarian society. Twenty or 30 are no contemptible church. Mr Kentish, a promising young man, was highly pleased and edified in attending you.[4] I hope Mr Dyer is well, and goes on tolerably. I have a small matter of his for him, as I told you; and would add a small matter to it when I see you, or when you intimate to whom I may transmit it. Should you happen to know any thing about Mrs Essex's distribution of her property, I should be happy to know that Mr Hammond has received that handsome share which on many accounts was due to him.[5]

You give a good account of the late Mr Robinson's society. I have little doubt of his successor becoming perfectly liberally, especially if Mr Curtis be, as I presume he is, a member of the society.[6] For the very little that I saw of him, I liked him exceedingly. I have been told by one of your university, who wished me not to mention him as to the fact, tho' he had no doubt of it; that D^r E ____[7] makes great havoc of the faith of your young men of fortune, and of others. I rejoice however that M^r T,[8] yourself and a very few others are on the spot; and are a counter-authority when you say nothing; although I have no doubt of your always offering a word where it may be seasonable.

It is a curious accusation which Mr Burke formally and with all seriousness brings against the projectors of the French revolution, of a design to overthrow the christian religion. His grand proof of it is, their curtailing of the hierarchy and appropriation of the vast surplus of the revenue of the church to civil purposes. His declamation on this topic, his assertions from his own imagination, of a similar design in our revolution society and its abettors at home, his pathetic paintings of the horrors of such an event and declarations that the english will never endure it &c &c will tend to inflame and excite the zeal of churchmen, and set us at a greater distance from Reformation.[9] I am afraid it may cool the earnestness and stop the efforts of some who but now were very forward. But let me not make bad omens. Nous verrons.

For the rest, this doughty Tory hero's book is a very pitiful performance. With all his self-boasting, and pretensions to knowlege in general, and knowlege of men, knowlege of books: he knows not the first principles of a just government; he is wholly ignorant of what true religion and the gospel is, and requires. His book, like all his speeches of late, some bright[?] things, overwhelmed with verbiage and a desultory imagination, and little sound sense upon any subjects. In some parts he is quite frantic, and talks just like one that had the strait waiscoat [sic] upon him – especially when certain ideas come across him. A friend of mine, a person of the first rank in good sense and in the world, said at the time, that if the Riots in 1780 had continued three days longer, Burke would have gone out of his senses.[10] I think his imagination has been scared with those ideas[?] ever since, so that he does not possess himself at all when bordering upon some things.

I do not know how I have come to write so much to you on this book, wch is only just this very day come out. I was very far from intending when I began. You will judge when somebody lends it you. For it is not worth laying out 5 Shillings upon it; and I shall be sorry if Mr T.[11] approves of such an author.

I am sorry not to accede to any thing you propose: but I cannot subscribe to the author you mention; because I am told he was once a Dissenter; but turned out to be a Churchman: and that now he seeks to recomend himself to his betters by beating upon Hobbes's skull-cap[?], by writing against Dr Priestley.[12]

They are all well in Sloane-Street.[13] M^r and Mrs Dodson very well – returned from Wiltshire but a few days. I shall make your *souvenirs* to them, to day. Yesterday was so rainy, there was no stirring out.

We are all at uncertainties, whether peace or war.[14] If the latter, calamity will probably come and awaken us to our duty. With my wife's best respects

I remain ever most faithfully and truly, Yours
　　　　T. Lindsey.

Son of God, has various significations. Very frequently is synonymous with the Messiah, in our Saviour's language, and that of his apostles. I sh^d thank you much for the intimation if it can be done briefly, of the meaning of the phrase which may be learned from the epistle to the Hebrews. I think you have done well in relinquishing Burgess, for the reasons you give.[15] ADieu.

1   Frend's letter to Lindsey appears not to have survived.
2   Writing to Belsham on 17 Oct. 1790, Priestley noted that he would be dining 'next Thursday' with Samuel Parr, perpetual curate of Hatton, Warwickshire, and with Richard Porson; Rutt, I, 90. 'Thursday next' was 21 Oct. 1790.
3   Priestley issued his edition of Anthony Collins, *A philosophical inquiry concerning human liberty, republished with a preface by Joseph Priestley* in Birmingham in 1790. There was no appendix to this work and Frend did not produce the tract on the necessarian doctrine for which Priestley had evidently hoped; see Rutt, I, 82, and Letter 429. Collins (1676–1729), freethinker and admirer of Locke, had first published his *Philosophical inquiry* in 1717.
4   See Letter 418, n. 13.
5   In 1785, John Hammond married Millicent (d. Jan. 1787), the only daughter of James Essex (*c.* 1722–84), the celebrated Cambridge architect, and his wife Elizabeth (née Thurlborne). Elizabeth Essex, the mother-in-law of John Hammond, died on 29 Sept. 1790; see *Gent. Mag.*, LX, i (1790), 957. Her will, dated 15 Feb., and proved on 8 Oct., 1790, may be found at TNA: PRO PROB 11/1196, fos. 324r–325r. It made no mention of Hammond.
6   Robert Robinson's successor at the St Andrew's Street baptist church, Cambridge, was Robert Hall (1764–1831), who served as minister there, at first on a temporary basis, from 1790 until 1806 and became one of the most eminent baptist preachers of the early nineteenth century. Although politically liberal, he was strongly critical of unitarians and published a hostile review of Belsham's *Memoirs* of Lindsey; see *The works of Robert Hall* (6 vols., London, 1831–2), IV, 188–225. The review was first published in the *Eclectic Review*, NS, II (Aug. 1814), 113–32. For William Curtis, see Letter 416, n. 1.
7   Probably Dr Thomas Edwards.
8   Robert Tyrwhitt.
9   Edmund Burke's *Reflections on the revolution in France and on the proceedings in certain societies in London relative to that event. In a letter intended to have been sent to a gentleman in Paris* was published on 1 Nov. 1790. Although Lindsey in this letter said that the book came out on 2 Nov. 1790, the actual date of publication was 1 Nov. It did indeed cost 5*s*.
10 As a sympathizer with the Catholic Relief Act of 1778, and as someone suspected of being a covert catholic, Burke was a potential target for the Gordon rioters in June 1780.
11 Presumably Robert Tyrwhitt; see n. 8, above.
12 Probably this work was Nehemiah Nisbett's *Observations upon the miraculous conception of our saviour: with a particular view to the exceptions of Dr Priestley on the subject. With an advertisement upon Dr. Edwards's objections to the testimony of Christ and his apostles* (Canterbury, 1790); see Letter 429. Nisbett (d. 1812) was perpetual curate of Ash, Kent. No list of subscribers was included in the book, although Nisbett requested (p. 115) that those 'who are inclined to encourage this undertaking' should leave their names at the booksellers named on the title page; one of those booksellers was Joseph Johnson. John Pope replied to Nisbett with a defence of Priestley entitled *Observations on the miraculous conception and the testimonies of Ignatius and Justin Martyr on that subject: in a series of letters to the Rev. Mr Nisbett* (London, 1792); see Letter 501, n. 5. For Thomas Edwards's work on the apostolic testimony, see Letter 418, n. 23.
13 I.e. John Disney and his family.
14 At the end of Oct. 1790, Britain signed a convention with Spain which removed the prospect of an Anglo-Spanish war over Nootka Sound (Vancouver Island), but this development did not become public knowledge until well into Nov. 1790.
15 For a possible identification of Burgess, see Letter 421, n. 4. It is clear that by Nov. 1790 Frend had abandoned hope of recruiting Burgess as a contributor to the new translation of the Bible, but the non-survival of his letter to Lindsey (see n. 1, above) means that historians, disappointingly, do not have access to his reasons for 'relinquishing Burgess'. Perhaps he thought Burgess too orthodox a churchman for his purposes; for a thorough analysis of Burgess's orthodoxy, see Peter Nockles, 'Recreating the history of the Church of England: Bishop Burgess, the Oxford Movement and nineteenth-century reconstructions of protestant and anglican identity', in *Bishop Burgess and his world*,

ed. Yates, pp. 233–89. There are no letters between Frend and Burgess in CUL, Add. MS 7886 (Frend papers).

429. To WILLIAM FREND   10 NOVEMBER 1790

Text: CUL, Add. MS 7886 (Frend papers), no. 163.
Addressed: To/M^r. W. Frend/at the Post Office/Canterbury
Postmarked: NO 10 90

London. Novr. 10. 1790.

Dear Sir,

I do not think that either you or Dr Priestley are so afraid of being called atheists so as to hinder you from doing what you believe may be useful, and it may probably be the lot of you both as it has been already of one of you to be dubbed with that character again and again: but in the present case I will acquit you intirely of holding forth this hobgoblin in terrorem to satisfy him about not sending the tract you mention.[1] I really think that you have made it out to be more prudent and proper for him to republish Collins by himself, and I have no doubt of its so appearing to the Doctor from your representation which I shall make known to him.[2]

I most truly rejoice that the friend to whom I am writing has been saved out of the vortex of infidelity, where he might have plunged deeper and deeper and drawn many after him: whereas I trust now it will be in his power, I have no doubt of it, to keep many from it.[3] The evil is unquestionably owing to the forbidding exhibitions of the gospel by the orthodox of almost all churches and sects, added to the greater inquisitiveness and discernment of the times we live in.

As we are however on the most solid grounds persuaded that the gospel is from God, it's declarations cannot but be fulfilled, and it will prevail. Mr Burke, who has no more knowlege than a horse of what it really is, imagines that it can only subsist and be supported by the splendour of riches and great secular power: in which however he has many on his side; and you have scarce an idea of the triumphant air with which many of the two learned professions[4] as well as the church speak of the service that he has done to religion by his book.

Dr Priestley is pressed much to print his Sermon on the Resurrection, preached at Buxton this summer. I have just had a sight of it, and think it most important, with some new and valuable remarks. But I hope he will enlarge it a little, before he prints it, and take in some other objections than those he considered in preaching. He has been advised by Mr Belsham, in a preface to it, to consider Dr Edwards's two discourses, and I have accordingly sent them, and hope and believe he will do it, though perhaps not immediately, as some friends have cut out some other work for him, which may occupy him a month or two, if he accede to their proposal.[5] I have however written to him not to let the preparation for a certain Translation being ready in the next spring, hinder him from attending to any present demands; because it seems to me, that it will be judged proper to delay it still another year: for probably within that space, Mr Wakefields N.T. will be out, which it may be of great use and benefit to see.[6]

Dr Geddes also has just published one Tome of his work as he calls it, containing Genesis, Exodus, and a part of Leviticus, and promises a Second Tome about Christmas, and a third at Easter.[7] This I apprehend will carry him thro' your department and you will be glad to see it.

I had some compunctions after what I had written to you, for declining the subscribing to Mr Nisbet's work, and therefore beg you will add my name to Your own and that of our other friends.[8] One ought to be tender in ascribing sinister motives to others: though of a certain R.R. Dr Priestley's great Opponent, a very able and candid layman, upon reading his works, and particularly his Review of the case of the Dissenters, sticks not to pronounce him a great R.[9]

I have orders from Dr Priestley and Mr Belsham to send you a joint publication of theirs just come out – a Sermon and Charge this summer at Warwick at the ordination of a Minister.[10] I think you will be pleased with it. If you wish to see it, tell me how I am to send it.

Thanks for your kind notice of my inquiries ab^t Mrs Essex, and the pleasing account of our friends situation at St Ives.[11] With my wife's respects,

I remain ever most truly Yours

           T. Lindsey.

---

1   Possibly this tract was *Theodosius*, by Philip Withers (see Letter 414, n. 7), which had accused Priestley of persuading Silas Deane to abandon Christianity. See also Rutt, I, 58, 61, 77.

2   See Letter 428, n. 3; Frend, in his (non-surviving) letter to Lindsey, had evidently explained why he had not provided the material for an appendix to Priestley's edition of Collins's *Philosophical inquiry concerning human liberty*. See Priestley's letters to Frend of 12 Sept. and 2 Nov. 1790; Rutt I, 82, 94.

3   This friend was William Frend himself; this sentence and the first paragraph of this letter amount to a rare hint of ironical facetiousness on Lindsey's part.

4   Law and medicine.

5   Priestley's *Evidence of the resurrection of Jesus considered* was published in Birmingham in 1791. The two discourses of Thomas Edwards were *The predictions of the apostles concerning the end of the world* (see Letter 418, n. 23); and *The Jewish and the heathen rejection of the Christian miracles: a sermon* [on 1 Thessalonians, v. 21] (Cambridge, 1790). In the preface to *The evidence of the resurrection* Priestley did not, as Belsham had suggested, deal directly with Edwards's work or mention him by name, although he refuted (p. vi) allegations that his sermon gave offence to several of the listeners. Priestley's 'other work' was possibly his *Letters to the Right Honourable Edmund Burke, occasioned by his Reflections on the revolution in France*, which he wrote in the two months after the publication (1 Nov. 1790) of Burke's *Reflections* and which were published in Birmingham in Feb. 1791.

6   Gilbert Wakefield published his *Translation of the New Testament* in three volumes in 1791.

7   For the publication of Geddes's biblical translation, see Letter 407, n. 10. Lindsey was anxious lest Geddes's work compete with that of Wakefield. Geddes's *Dr Geddes's general answer to the queries, councils, and criticisms that have been communicated to him since the publication of his proposals for printing a new translation of the Bible* (London, 1790) contained (pp. 29–32) a list of subscribers, among them Lindsey, Disney, Priestley and Price.

8   For Nehemiah Nisbett, see Letter 428, n. 12.

9   Priestley's 'great Opponent' was Samuel Horsley, bishop of St David's. Possibly the 'very able and candid layman' was Samuel Heywood, whose book *The right of protestant dissenters to a compleat toleration asserted* (London, 1787) was published with the pseudonym 'A Layman'. Heywood continued his attack on Horsley in *High church politics: being a seasonable appeal to the friends of the British constitution, against the practices and principles of high churchmen* (London, 1792).

10   This work was *A view of revealed religion; a sermon, preached at the ordination of the Rev. William Field of Warwick, July 12, 1790. By Joseph Priestley ...With a charge, delivered at the same time by the Rev. Thomas Belsham* (Birmingham, 1790). Belsham's 'Charge' may be found at pp. 46–68. See Rutt, I, 73; William Field (1768–1851) was minister to the unitarian congregation at Warwick from 1789 to 1843.

11   For Elizabeth Essex, see Letter 428, n. 5. The friend at St Ives was John Hammond, whose Fenstanton estate was some two miles from that town.

430. To WILLIAM TAYLEUR   10 NOVEMBER 1790

Text: JRUL, Lindsey Letters, vol. III, no. 29.
Printed: McLachlan, 'More letters', 372 (final sentence of second
                 paragraph and most of third paragraph, with errors); 372–3
                 (most of fourth paragraph); 367 (first, fourth and fifth
                 sentences of seventh paragraph).
Addressed: To/William Tayleur Esqr/Shrewsbury
Endorsed: 10th Novr 1790
Postmarked: Postmark illegible.

London. Novr. 10. 1790.

Dear Sir,

Your very acceptable letter deserved a speedier acknowlegement.[1] I am glad however that I can answer it, with a certain prospect of peace being continued, for a time at least, I trust for a very long one. This state of things will deprive Government of one plausible excuse for not engaging in the work of reformation, the fear of kindling a flame in the nation unseasonably.

Not a few take upon them to averr that Burke's book will indispose our Governors and governed, to any reformation in matters of religion for half a century. They must be very weak persons, and incapable judges, who can give out such an idea of it. Supposing indeed, there be a great majority of Tories in the nation, and in the administration, I can easily conceive they may be so affected with the work. But to those of any discernment, what he advances must appear mere declamation for the most part. He possesses no one good principle of civil or religious liberty. And of the real gospel of Christ, and what it is that makes a true christian, he has not the least idea.

Several answers are preparing: a short notice from Dr Towers:[2] by the American, Mr Payne, author of Comon Sense &c:[3] but as he is the most inveterate declared unbeliever I ever conversed with, he will give no proper answer to any but political matters; from Mrs Macaulay also.[4] If the thing struck our friend at B _____ m, and he w^d sit down to it in earnest, he w^d do it effectually. Dr Price does not seem to me, as if he would make any reply to it. And if he does it will not be of a long time.[5]

As Lord Stanhope had taken his name away from our Revolution-Society, and another person had declined the office of Chairman,[6] the chair was very properly filled on Thursday last, Novr. 4. by Dr Price, and he graced it well, by the Toasts proposed, and songs new and old introduced, of good note, exciting to liberty and virtue. All was going on very well, till betwixt 8 and 9, Mr John Horn Tooke interrupted the festivity and harmony, by a motion to exclude all Lords and titles from the Society. This would have brought much censure on the society, particularly at present, as if a new Revolution was our aim. After much altercation pour and contre, it was withdrawn. I was sorry that Mr Cooper of Manchester[7] in particular, and some other worthy and able supported Mr Tooke. This last named gentleman possesses great powers, to win upon a popular and mixed assembly, having wit and humour at command to soothe and win upon them. Setting out with a compliment to Dr Price, he naturally diverted to Mr Burkes composition, and stiled it, *the tears of the priesthood for the loss of their pudding*. This took prodigiously.[8] The excuse made for Mr Beaufoy, who never absented himself on the day before, was, that he had not made up his mind about the french revolution.[9]

At our quarterly dinner at the Paul's head Tavern, Cateaton-Street,[10] the week before last, I sat next to a french gentleman, minister of the first dissenting church in Bourdeaux, his congregation consisting of six thousand persons: a sincere christian on rational just grounds, of an excellent understanding well cultivated. I found he had prejudices against Dr Priestley, as not only a Deist but Atheistically inclined. You will believe I easily convinced him of his error. He is no trinitarian, if not disposed to Socinianism. But I found they never meddle with what he called *les dogmes* in their sermons, doctrinal points. He was very glad to receive some books of Dr Priestleys and others, as well as another french minister somewhat younger who was along with him, and I persuade myself they will read them. Θ He has promised to write to me when he gets back to Bourdeaux, returning by the way of Holland. They came over to promote their new Revolution, for which they were most ardent, and had no doubt, *malgré les Burkes et les Calonnes*,[11] as they said, of its standing fast.

Θ The names of these two french ministers, were S. Blachon, G. Dommengel, as I find them written by themselves on a card. May. 28. 1796.[12]

I dare say Mr Toulmin of Chowbent has written to Mr Rowe about the projected periodical work of himself and some ministers in that neighbourhood. The Plan is very good, as exhibited in an account of it, which has been handed to me to print, and which will soon be sent to Mr Rowe. And it will be most highly useful, if it be but well executed, and get into circulation.[13] I thought till now, that the business had been laid aside, thro' defect of hands and materials. But if it can but once get well on foot, I have a good hope it will excite many to contribute to it, and the more opulent to buy it to give away.

Yesterday I made up a pacquet for Priestley and inclosed in it his sermon, lately preached at Buxton on the Resurrection, which had been sent me but two days before: but he was in haste to have it returned. I think it very valuable: the direct evidence for that most important fact, admirably introduced, and well put together. Two or three of the most popular and strongest objections confuted, with much *new* as well as curious and important remark. The same marks of originality in some of the inferences. When he has enlarged it a little by considering in the same way some other objections to this fact, it will be of great service to the truth and deserve to be made public. But tho' he is much pressed to do it imediately, I have for very cogent reasons dissuaded him from it.[14]

In the parcell sent to him were three letters, to be transmitted to you after his perusal. I have ordered them purely because you desired it, and also because slight as they are, I sh^d like to have such things comunicated to me.[15] To day has brought a pleasing letter from M^r. Kentish from Plymouth upon his being left there alone on Mr Porters setting out for the South. You will like what he says of the latter, and his own character which he undesignedly draws, and I shall send it.[16] I have a great opinion of these two young men. Mr Rowe will rejoice in such missionaries being got into the West. I beg you will tell him with my respects, that I should thank him for his letter myself, but that at present I look upon writing to you in some measure the same as to him. *We* desire also to be kindly remembred to Mr Wood, whom we look upon as a *confrere* in our unitarian church and expect great services from him for many years to come. My wife always desires her particular most due respects to yourself, and I am ever your most truly obliged and faithful affectionate servant.

    T. Lindsey.

Mr Frend still keeps up his little unitarian society at Cambridge on Sunday evenings. Infidelity certainly spreads there, even among some who are clad in sable.

Dr Edwards, whose two sermons printed within the present year, you have probably seen, both in the University pulpit, is unquestionable an absolute Academic in his faith; and conversing much with young noblemen and fellow commoners, must infect them.[17] I am afraid I shall tire you with my prattle. You must excuse bad writing, and bad every thing in it. We shall rejoice if you do but continue yourself as usual. ADieu.

We are charmed with Dr Priestley's View of Revealed Religion in print; which we had heard him once deliver here and you will be no less pleased with Mr Belsham's charge, the occasion considered, than with his Sermon on the Importance of Truth.[18]

1   This is a reference to Tayleur's letter to Lindsey of 14 Oct. 1790 (JRUL, C2^{13}).

2   Joseph Towers, *Thoughts on the commencement of a new parliament. With an appendix, containing remarks on the letter of the Right Hon. Edmund Burke, on the revolution in France* (London, 1790). Towers (1737–99) was morning preacher at Stoke Newington Green.

3   Paine's *Common sense* was published in Jan. 1776; the first part of his *Rights of man; being an answer to Mr. Burke's attack on the French Revolution* was published on 16 Mar. 1791.

4   Catharine Macaulay, *Observations on the Reflections of the Right Hon. Edmund Burke, on the Revolution in France* (London, 1790). The publisher was Charles Dilly.

5   Price made a brief reply to Burke in the fourth edition of his *Discourse on the love of our country* (London, 1790), pp. vi–xi.

6   According to the minute book of the Revolution Society, Earl Stanhope withdrew from the society and 'obliterated' his name from the list of members on 11 Aug. 1790; BL, Add. MS 64814, fo. 58v. The Revolution Society minute book offers no indication as to the identity of the other member who declined the chairmanship.

7   Thomas Cooper had been a member of the Revolution Society since Apr. 1790; BL, Add. MS 64814, fo. 62v.

8   The account of this meeting in the minute book of the Revolution Society states that Horne Tooke, in attacking Burke for his 'abuse' of Price, proposed the toast 'Should Mr Burke be impeached for his Libel on the Constitution, may his Trial last as long as that of Mr Hastings.' No mention was made of Tooke's motion to excluded titled persons from membership of the society; BL, Add. MS 64814, fos. 38–41, quoted here at fo. 40r. The report of the meeting in the *Public Advertiser*, 6 Nov. 1790, noted briefly Tooke's denunciation of peerages. See also Christina and David Bewley, *Gentleman radical. A life of John Horne Tooke 1736–1812* (London and New York, 1998), pp. 96–7. The authors note Lindsey's presence at this meeting and, with excessive generosity, credit him with a doctorate.

9   Henry Beaufoy 'withdrew' his membership of the Revolution Society on 6 Nov. 1792; BL, Add. MS 64814, fo. 52r.

10   Possibly this is a reference to the quarterly club of dissenters to which Lindsey belonged; see Letter 397, n. 3. Possibly it was the same club as that described in the notebook of Joseph Towers (Bodl., MS Eng. Misc. e. 334). The club's rules, set out at the beginning of the notebook, are dated 22 Mar. 1791, although the date of its foundation might have been earlier than that. Lindsey, Disney and Dodson were among the members. I owe this reference to Dr John Seed.

11   Charles Alexandre de Calonne (1734–1802) was the controller-general of finance in France from 1783 until his dismissal, at the behest of the assembly of notables, in 1787. He went into exile in Britain and from 1789 associated himself with the royal and aristocratic émigrés and the counter-revolution. During the mid-1780s a 'patriot' opposition in the United Provinces had mounted a successful resistance to the House of Orange and the stadtholder William V (1748–1806), and had established temporary control of some of the principal cities. However, Prussian intervention, supported by Britain, restored the authority of the stadtholder in 1787.

12   Regrettably unidentified (but see Letter 449, n. 8). This letter was probably among those to Tayleur which were returned to him on the latter's death in 1796; see Letter 632.

13   This new periodical was the *Christian Miscellany*, of which Henry Toulmin was a leading promoter. See Letters 418, n. 7, and 447, n. 10.

14   For Priestley's sermon at Buxton, see Letter 429, n. 5. With his letter to Lindsey of 2 Nov. 1790, Priestley had enclosed a manuscript copy; Rutt, I, 95. In his letter to Lindsey of 23 Dec. 1790, Priestley reported that he had made a small number of minor changes at Lindsey's suggestion; Rutt, I, 97.

15   In his reply to this letter, Tayleur told Lindsey that Priestley had sent to him his *View of revealed religion* and Belsham's *Charge*, which was appended to it (see Letter 429, n. 10) before they were

published. He added that Priestley had written a letter to him which predicted 'I am *sure* you [Tayleur] will like Mr Belshams Charge.' Tayleur also referred to letters from James Freeman of Boston and David Jardine of Bath which Lindsey had sent to him via Priestley and which he undertook to return to Lindsey; JRUL, C2¹³, Tayleur to Lindsey, 25 Nov. 1790.

16 John Kentish's letter to Lindsey seems not to have survived.
17 For Edwards's two sermons, see Letter 429, n. 5.
18 See Letter 429, n. 10; the occasion was the ordination of William Field at Warwick. For Belsham's sermon on the importance of truth, see Letter 410, n. 5.

431. To WILLIAM ALEXANDER   23 NOVEMBER 1790

Text: 'Letters of the Rev. Theophilus Lindsey. No. II',
                   UH, II, 45 (8 Mar. 1862), 84.

Note: This is the only section of the letter printed by the *UH*; the manuscript has apparently not survived.

November 23, 1790.

I am sorry that you are still entangled with perplexities in your own mind, and meet with discouragements from without.[1] The former may sometimes be owing to too great scrupulosity and refinement, though springing from a good cause; the latter cannot always be avoided by conscientious minds. I think you might, without any detriment to your own integrity, and am glad that you do, teach the creed called the Apostles', as your teaching it does not imply your belief of all the articles in it; and you may pass over some of the articles in the way you mention to me, without dwelling upon them, and freely expound others. For instance, that descending into hell, should be descending into the grave, or the place of the dead, for that is the meaning of the word made use of by the first composers of the creed, and is the interpretation given by the most judicious expositors of the Established Church.

To me it seems owing to a debility of mind that you make yourself uneasy by a suspicion that you act upon sinister worldly motives, when I have no doubt, and you ought to be so persuaded yourself, that your principal, leading motive is to be useful in your generation. With respect to the taking of oaths, though I hope there will be no call upon you for that purpose, I believe you to mistake entirely the meaning of the sacred writings; and that neither Jesus nor the Apostle James had any of those scruples about the matter which haunt you; but I cannot engage with you in writing on the subject.[2] Should you any time hence come to town we may talk it over again.[3]

1 For Lindsey's response to Alexander's anxieties as to the way in which he should teach religious matters in the small school which he ran at Yoxford, and his disappointment at the disapproval which he aroused, see Letters 389, 415 and 423.
2 In the absence of Alexander's letter to Lindsey, it is difficult to be precise about his 'scruples', but they probably concerned the subscription to a general statement of belief in the scriptures which had been required of dissenting ministers and schoolteachers since the dissenters' relief act of 1779. At the time of the passage of the act, some dissenters had objected to any such declaration. Possibly Alexander was 'haunted' by the passage in Matthew v. 33–7 in which Christ urged his disciples 'swear not at all … Let your communication be, Yea, yea; Nay, nay: for whatsoever is more than these cometh of evil.' The apostle James (d. 44), the first apostle to suffer martyrdom, was present at the transfiguration of Christ and at the agony of Gethsemane. Christ described him and his brother John as 'sons of thunder' (Mark iii. 17).
3 Evidently Lindsey and Alexander had met in London on at least one previous occasion.

432. To WILLIAM TAYLEUR   24 DECEMBER 1790

Text: JRUL, Lindsey Letters, vol. II, no. 35.
Addressed: To/William Tayleur Esqr./Shrewsbury/Single sheet
Endorsed: 24th Decr 1790
Postmarked: DE [illegible] 90

Dear Sir,

There has been so much noise and writing about Mr Orator Burke and his book, that I have had nothing else of a public kind to have talked [of], and have been besides much occupied of late with a troublesome affair which is now passed over,[1] or I should have sooner had the pleasure of writing to you again. My present motive the Plan on the other page will bespeak.[2] It originated with Mr Belsham, and he and Dr Disney have drawn up the plan, Mr Dodson and myself the Revisers.

We expect the greatest things from it. That very soon unitarians of learning and fortune will favour the plan and give in their names, and these names being published every year will shew our strength and encourage other[s] in succession to give in their names, when it will appear to the confusion of orthodoxy how strong and prevalent is the party of free inquiry. Some more clause[s] are to be added. One that there be correspondence set on foot and kept open with friends in every great town and large district in the kingdom. Ireland and Scotland also by and by may come in. I shall write to Mr Kirwan on the subject. Our first Article will have an addition after virtue, by printing, purchasing and dispersing books.[3] These two alterations were suggested from Birmingham.[4] I have no doubt of your kind concurrence; nor of Mr Rowe's giving us his name at first: and indeed, as I am indebted to him in the epistolary way, I sh^d have addressed myself now to him, had I not been apprehensive, that tho' I have said single sheet, my pacquett would be charged double.[5] And I sh^d take it as a favour if he would give me a line which I may receive before Thursday next, as our first public meeting is to be on the last day of the present year.[6]

I presume you may have heard that Mr Wakefield has sent in to the Comittee his purpose of resigning his office of Classical Tutor at the end of the Session. He assigns no reasons: but these are said to be, his disappointm^t in the salary from the office, and in private pupils the Duke of Grafton and B^p of Llandaff declin[in]g to send their sons, it is said, on acc^t of his being a Tutor of a Dissenting College. I believe some efforts will be used to induce him to continue: but some that have conversed with him, seem to think, that he will not be likely to change his purpose.[7]

It is to be lamented that by our buildings and the expence of them, the college is so very much in debt. We were in hope that Mr Hollis of Ormond Street who died about ten days since had left us a large sum, but I fear there is nothing at all. To Dr Price, Dr Kippis, myself, Dr Disney and Dr Towers, he has bequeathed fifty pounds each; and I believe divided his fortune pretty equally among his many relations.[8] He was a person of singular benevolence and a true friend to liberty.

You have not seen Dr Priestley's Letters to Burke probably, but will very soon. I think them most admirable, and such as in the end must greatly serve the cause of religious and civil liberty, and by no other powder explosion but the force of truth bring on the downfall of our hierarchical powers.[9]

We hope you have been well as usual, this fine open season in general, which we have hitherto had. My wife desires to present her due respects. And we would trouble you w^h our best comp^ts to Mr Rowe and Mr Wood. I hope to write again in no long time. I am always with peculiar respect and esteem,

Dear Sir, your most truly obliged and faithful Servant

T. Lindsey.

London. Decr. 24. 1790.

---

1   Possibly this 'troublesome affair' was a dispute between John Disney and William Blackburne; see Letter 434, n. 2.

2   The 'other page' is missing. The 'Plan' was that for the Unitarian Society, inaugurated early in 1791.

3   The title finally agreed on was 'the Unitarian Society for Promoting Christian Knowledge, and the Practice of Virtue, by Distributing Books'.

4   I.e. by Priestley.

5   The rates of postage for single and double letters in England are set out in the *Universal British directory* (1791), I, 36–7. Although the 1*d* postal rate still applied to letters posted in London and Westminster to addresses within those areas, the basic charge for a single letter 'to any place not exceeding one stage, from one post office to another', was 2*d*. For the background, see Frank Staff, *The Penny Post 1680–1918* (London, 1964), pp. 66–70.

6   'Thursday next' was 30 Dec. 1790, and the meeting to which Lindsey referred was due to take place the following day. The plans for the new society were taken further at the dinner meeting on 7 Jan. 1791, to which Lindsey referred in Letter 433.

7   At its meeting on 10 Dec. 1790 the committee of Hackney College noted a communication from Wakefield signifying his intention of resigning the classical tutorship; DWL, MS 38.14, p. 141. For Wakefield's complaint about the inadequacy of his salary, see *Memoirs of the life of Gilbert Wakefield ... written by himself* (London, 1792), pp. 369–70. On 18 Nov. 1788, the committee of the college ruled that tutors' salaries should be increased or reduced according to the numbers of students. On 4 June 1789, it resolved that from the start of the forthcoming session, the principal tutors should be paid 120 guineas, and assistant tutors fifty guineas, annually; DWL, MS 38.14, pp. 100, 115. Probably Wakefield was paid approximately £120 or slightly more in the session 1790 to 1791. On 13 Jan. 1791 the committee appointed a sub-committee to discuss with him the terms on which he might withdraw his resignation. On 15 Feb., the sub-committee reported that he had withdrawn his resignation. At its meeting on 6 Mar., however, the college committee noted a further letter of resignation from Wakefield, complaining that his aspirations for educational improvements at the college had been disappointed. This time, the committee accepted his resignation with effect from the end of the session in the summer of 1791. DWL, MS 38.14, pp. 143–51. Wakefield expanded upon his critique of the college's education methods in his *Memoirs*, published in 1792; see Letter 503, n. 8.

8   Timothy Hollis died on 14 Dec. 1790. His will may be found in TNA: PRO PROB 11/1199, fos. 42v–52v; it was proved on 24 Dec. 1790, the date of this letter of Lindsey. He did indeed bequeath £50 each to Lindsey, Disney, Price, Kippis and Joseph Towers. His 'many relations', including his nephew John Hollis (see Letter 631, n. 8), are identified in his will.

9   This work was Priestley's *Letters to the Right Honourable Edmund Burke, occasioned by his Reflections on the revolution in France*. Lindsey's reference to 'powder' was an allusion to Priestley's famous claim that he and other enlightened persons were 'laying gunpowder, grain by grain, under the old building of error and superstition, which a single spark may hereafter inflame, so as to produce an instantaneous explosion'; *The importance and extent of free enquiry in matters of religion* (Birmingham, 1785), pp. 40–1.

---

433. To WILLIAM FREND   30 DECEMBER 1790

Text: CUL, Add. MS 7886 (Frend papers), no. 164.
Addressed: To/The Rev^d. W. Frend/fellow of Jesus college/Cambridge
Postmarked: DE 30 90

London. Decr. 30. 1790

Dear Sir,

I was very unlucky to be from home when Mr Dyer called and left his pacquett and your obliging letter; which however I should have prevented by writing to you, if Dr Priestley['s] letters has[1] been out or any thing worth communication had presented itself.[2] The former however will be in Town to morrow and a copy being ordered for you, I shall call on Mr Johnson to day and consult if it cannot be sent you among the monthly publications, by which means it will come with least trouble.

If public and private accounts may be credited the storm is thickening now more than ever to burst upon the new Government in France; but I trust that divine providence will continue to protect and support it. Insurrections in different parts of the kingdom: the king refusing his consent to the change of ecclesiastical property.[3] The emperor[4] having already a great force, and in six weeks time will have an army of upwards of a hundred thousand men in Flanders. The King of Sardinia, and Spain also declared to be ready to cooperate.[5] This comes from an Officer lately in the Belgic army; who says that it is believed the catholics in general, and the officers and a great part of the Soldiery will repair to the Standard in favour of the French king, which the emperor is to erect.[6]

I thank you for naming so truly worthy a character as Mr Donaldson, who has so early in life made such a sacrifice to principle; to whom if I can render any service in the way of his profession I will do it.[7] But must tell You that very lately I had occasion to use what little interest I have with one or two attornies, to engage giving a little business now and then to two young special pleaders, one of our own congregation, the other recomended by a very particular friend.[8]

On friday we are to dine at the King's head in the Poultry, and make the first opening and settlement of our new Unitarian Society.[9] I have no doubt of it producing beneficial effects in favour of free inquiry into the Scripture beyond the expectation of almost any of us. Such a phalanx of unitarians, whose names it will exhibit in a few years, will give such countenance to their cause, as will make it ever[10] creditable.

Mr Tayleur of Shrewsbury wrote to me yesterday, that as an annual subscription for the probably short term of his life, w^d amount to very little, he shall therefore soon remit to me 50 Guineas instead of it.[11]

My wife desires her kind comp^{ts} and to join in wishes of good to you of the pres^t and of all seasons, and that I would tell you that She hoped you woud not forget poor Gifford with is [*sic*] former generous patron, upon a proper occasion.[12]

If you see Mr Curtis, I beg you will tell him that I shall do all in my power to promote the Subscription to Mr Robinson's remains: but I have been once or twice actually refused where I did not expect it.[13]

I am with sincere esteem most truly Yours
    T. Lindsey.

---

1   Lindsey probably intended to write 'had', rather than 'has'.
2   Frend's 'obliging letter' seems not to have survived. The published letters of Priestley to which Lindsey referred were probably his *Letters to the Rev. Edward Burn, of St Mary's chapel, Birmingham, in answer to his, on the infallibility of the apostolic testimony* (Birmingham, 1790).
3   In Aug. 1790, Louis XVI had reluctantly consented to the civil constitution of the clergy, which provided for the election of bishops and priests and for them to be salaried by, and subordinate to, the state. At the same time, he viewed with dismay the expropriation of the property of the Gallican church and the insistence by the National (Constituent) Assembly in Nov. 1790 that all clergy take an oath of loyalty to the new constitution. Lindsey had probably read numerous references in the London press to 'insurrections' in France. For example, the *Public Advertiser*, 27 Dec. 1790, quoted at length from a letter from Paris which claimed that 'aristocratic' uprisings in Metz and Lyons were in progress. The *Morning Chronicle*, 27 Dec. 1790, described a violent outbreak at Perpignan.
4   Leopold II (1747–92), Holy Roman Emperor 1790–2.
5   Victor Amadeus (1726–96), king of Sardinia 1773–96; Charles IV (1748–1819), king of Spain 1788–1808.

6   In Nov. and early Dec. 1790, an imperial army commanded by General Bender temporarily re-established Habsburg control of the Austrian Netherlands from the republican rebels, encountering relatively little opposition. Reports as to the Belgic army and its officers circulated quite widely in the British press; see, for example, *Public Advertiser*, 22 Dec. 1790, *General Evening Post*, 23–5 Dec. 1790.

7   This is a reference to Francis Donaldson, who was admitted to Trinity College, Cambridge, at the age of twenty in 1783 and who migrated to Jesus – Frend's college – in 1786. He graduated BA in 1788, was admitted to the Middle Temple in 1781 and called to the bar in 1803. See *Alumn. Cantab.*, II, vol. II, 317, and *Register of admissions to the Honourable Society of the Middle Temple. Vol. I. Fifteenth century to 1781* (London, 1949), p. 391. He is listed as 'Esq.', of 3 Elm Co., Temple, as a special pleader in *Universal British directory* (1791), I, p. 368, in *Browne's general law list for the year 1792* (London, 1792), p. 47, and similarly in *Browne's general law list* for 1794 and for 1795. Frend had evidently recommended him to Lindsey and asked Lindsey to find work for him. Perhaps his 'sacrifice to principle' arose from support given to Frend during his disputes with the university authorities in Cambridge.

8   Probably the two attorneys were Samuel Heywood and John Lee. There is a list of seventy-four special pleaders in the *Universal British directory* (1791), I, 368–9 (see n. 7, above). From that list, the two young special pleaders to whom Lindsey referred were, possibly, John Pemberton Heywood (1756–1835) and George Nathaniel Best. Heywood (1756–1835) belonged to Lindsey's congregation; he was a member of the Heywood family of Liverpool and a relative of Samuel Heywood. He was called to the bar in 1780, and subsequently practised at Wakefield, Yorkshire; *Alumn. Cantab.*, II, vol. V, 354; and *Familiae min. gen.*, I, 66. Best was the youngest son of Elizabeth Rayner's friend Ann Wilmot (see Letter 698, n. 10); possibly he was recommended by Elizabeth Rayner; he was subsequently an executor of her will. Another special pleader (and attorney) was Lindsey's friend Michael Dodson, who was born in 1732 and hardly a 'young' special pleader in 1790 or 1791. Perhaps he was one of the two attorneys to whom Lindsey referred.

9   This dinner, at the King's Head in the Poultry on Friday 7 Jan. 1791, is not recorded in the Unitarian Society minute book, where the first entry is that for 9 Feb. 1791.

10 In Lindsey's handwriting this word looks like 'even', although 'ever' is a more likely reading.

11 Tayleur's letter, setting out this benefaction in lieu of an annual subscription and evidently written in Dec. 1790, is not among his letters to Lindsey in JRUL, C2¹³. In the event, Tayleur gave 100 guineas as his 'composition' (Unitarian Society minute book, p. 6) and lived until 6 May 1796.

12 For James Gifford the elder (1739–1813), see Vol. I, Letters 320 and 324. By his 'former generous patron', Lindsey probably meant Philip Yorke (1720–90), 2nd earl of Hardwicke, who had died on 16 May 1790.

13 Robert Robinson's *Ecclesiastical researches*, a compilation of the author's historical works on the churches of Europe, edited by Frend and George Dyer, was published in Cambridge in 1792. William Curtis (see Letter 416, n. 1) assisted with the publication; *Church book: St Andrew's Street baptist church*, p. 137 n. 70. In Robinson's *History of baptism* (see Letter 417, n. 4), p. ii, it was stated that Robinson's family intended to consult his friends as to the appropriateness of publishing these manuscripts. Lindsey was a subscriber to *Ecclesiastical researches* (two copies) and *The history of baptism* (one copy).

434. To WILLIAM TAYLEUR   22 JANUARY 1791

Text: JRUL, Lindsey Letters, vol. II, no. 36.
Addressed: For/William Tayleur Esqʳ/Shrewsbury
Endorsed: 22ᵈ Janʸ 1791
Postmarked: Postmark missing.

London. Janʸ. 22. 1791.

Dear Sir,

I am revived as always by the sight of your handwriting, but particularly so in this most relaxing unseasonable weather as some call it, when they complain of their whole nervous system being unstrung, but I am thankful with you that I have seldom been better.¹ We have indeed been much agitated and made very uneasy for the space of between two or three months last past by the vindictive and very blameable behaviour of D^r. D. towards D^r. Bl ___ the particulars whereof there is no entering into by letter; but it was such that I thought it my duty to patronize Dr B. to save him from being wholly oppressed.[2] The affair is now over, and all well: [there follows a sentence of approximately twenty words, which is heavily crossed out and illegible]. I should not however have mentioned this circumstance to you, if I had not apprehended you might perchance hear of it, and be disturbed by being ignorant of the issue.

It is a satisfaction to me that you rejoice as much as I do at Mr Jardine's continuing at Bath. I do not know whether I mentioned to you, that he had pulled at one string and tried a principal person of his congregation with respect to the introduction of a Liturgy, and found it would not do. And I think it will be best, and I shall tell him so not to push this matter for the present: for I was astonished this week at hearing a very principal dissenter, a serious christian, and liberal in very many respects, declaring that in case of a liturgy taking place, there would most probably be a new congregation formed to go on in the old way, and that he sh^d attend the service of the latter. A young gentleman, a dissenter, from the north, with his new married lady and child arrived at Bath this week; and I have written to him, that as I was persuaded he was not a worshiper of the God Trinity, or of three Persons, but of the Parent of the universe alone, I made no question of his frequenting the meeting, and at the same time told him of Mr Jardine and hoped he would not be offended at the vile hole they met in, for so it seems it is; for that they were going to build a new chapel.[3]

Dr Priestley tells me, that a Mr Aubery of Stand near Manchester, has been recommended to them to succeed Mr Blythe; but I have written to Dr Priestley by the suggestion of a friend that knows Mr A. that he is by no means fit to be his collegue: and if he be the same person whom I remember at Dr Williamss library, and who cannot be unknown to Mr Rowe, tho' he may be and I believe is a blameless character, he is wholly unfit to be placed in such a conspicuous situation as the New Chapel at Birmingham.[4]

Your taking our intended unitarian Book Society under your protection in so generous [a] way, gave us great spirits when I first related it, and gives us credit with all to whom we name it. I shall inform you of all that passes at our meeting on Feb. 9; and then you will transmit your bounty, as is most convenient.[5] I think our Society for promoting the knowlege of the Scriptures will be suspended for the present at least. I wish you would consider of the matter, and recomend some book to be adopted by us. But let it be openly unitarian. I hint this, because one person dropd something as if it might be better not at first to adopt any of Dr Priestleys writings for fear of discouraging some persons from uniting with us.[6] This however was not said when I was present, or I sh^d have spoken my mind freely about it. I intend to propose Mr Toulmin's Memoirs of Biddle, for one of our Books.[7]

I thank you for acquainting me with and shall not forget worthy Mr Harries's name, which I shall be glad of the honour of putting down as one of our members, as I have a very sincere respect for him and for his excellent character, in the midst of the many difficulties with which he has to struggle.[8]

Having the opportunity by means of the frank w^h I procured for Mr Wood, to inclose two letters, which I think you will be glad to see, I send them, being persuaded you will pass over some things in them. I do not recollect I ever sent you Mr Chidlaw's.[9] If not, you will be delighted in being brought acquainted with Mr Small.[10] I have been put upon looking out the letter, as I have sent Mr Chidlaw the plan and rules of our new Unitarian society. Mr Baynham appears to be an excellent creature; and is most probably known to Mr Rowe.[11]

I hear from Cambridge, that Dr Mainwaring, Divinity professor of Cambridge, who was of my year at St Johns, had signified a design of proposing a grace in the Senate at Cambridge to thank Burke; but found it w^d not do. Mainwaring is an eléve [*sic*] of B^p. Hurd's, and devoted to him and to the Poet Mr Mason, who was also of my year, and is gone off from his better principles, thro' the influence I apprehend of the same bishop; and took an active part in Yorkshire against the repeal of the Test-Laws.[12]

I wish you be able to read my scrawl. My wife sends her due and sincere respects. She is frequently still a martyr to a pain in her face: but nevertheless upon ye whole is far better than formerly, and thank heaven we go on chearfully. I am always your most truly obliged and faithful affectionate servant

T. Lindsey.

---

1   This letter of Tayleur, presumably written in Dec. 1790 or Jan. 1791, is not among his letters to Lindsey in JRUL, C2^{13}.

2   Lindsey appeared to refer here to a dispute between John Disney and Dr William Blackburne, in which his own sympathies were with the latter. Possibly the dispute concerned an inheritance; Disney's mother, Frances, née Cartwright, died at her house in Lincoln on 5 Jan. 1791, aged eighty-one; *Gent. Mag.*, LXI, i (1791), 92; Disney's wife was Jane, the sister of William Blackburne.

3   For David Jardine, see Letter 418, n. 3. For Hannah Lindsey's visit to Bath in 1781, and her attend-ance at Frog Lane chapel (when the minister was Jardine's predecessor Edward Armstrong), see Vol. I, Letter 238; presumably her report was part of the basis for Lindsey's description of the Frog Lane building as a 'vile hole'. Jardine's attempt to introduce a liturgy to his chapel was frustrated by the objections of a section of his congregation which insisted on the traditional dissenting practice of extempore worship. See the first three pages of H. D. Wiard, *Some notes on unitarianism in Bath* (Bath, n.d., unpaginated). Possibly the young dissenter from the north was Henry Toulmin, minister at Chowbent, Lancashire. He was aged twenty-four in Jan. 1791; he and his wife Ann, née Tremlett, were married in Sept. 1787; they had three children by Jan. 1791.

4   Educated at the Hoxton Academy, Richard Aubrey (1760–1836) was minister at Dob Lane chapel, Failsworth, from 1786 to 1797, at Stand chapel, Lancashire, from 1787 to 1797, at Barton Street, Gloucester, from 1797 to 1814 and at High Street, Swansea, from 1814 to 1836. Samuel Blyth (1718–96) was minister at New Meeting, Birmingham, from 1747 to 1791, and Priestley's co-minister there from 1780. It is not clear why Lindsey did not want Aubrey to succeed Blythe; in the event he did not, and Blythe was succeeded by John Edwards (1768–1808); see Letter 608, n. 7.

5   For this initial meeting of the Unitarian Society, on 9 Feb. 1791, see Letter 437.

6   Lindsey did not identify the person who privately expressed anxiety as to the society adopting any work of Priestley, but he was presumably one of the earliest founders of the society and probably one of the nineteen ministers and laymen who attended the society's inaugural meeting on 9 Feb. 1791; Unitarian Society minute book, p. 1. Significantly, this objection was expressed before the Birmingham riots of July 1791 and was probably motivated by anxiety that the society would suffer by association with Priestley's doctrinal opinions, rather than by fear of mob hostility. A possible speculation as to the identity of the objector might suggest the name of Samuel Shore III (1738–1828), who was present at the meeting on 9 Feb. 1791 and shortly afterwards was critical of the Socinian assertions of the Unitarian Society's preamble; see Letter 461. Despite the objection, the society resolved to adopt several of Priestley's works, including his *Appeal to the serious and candid*, at its meeting on 9 Feb. 1791; Unitarian Society minute book, p. 7.

7   Joshua Toulmin's *A review of the life and writings of the Rev. John Biddle, M.A.*, first published in London in 1789, was indeed adopted by the Unitarian Society on 9 Feb. 1791; Unitarian Society minute book, p. 8.

8   Edward Harries became a founder member of the Unitarian Society in 1791. His difficulties included his inability to attract more than a few persons to the unitarian worship which he conducted in his own house at Ascott, Shropshire, and the 'inward complaint, from which he at times suffered much' and to which he finally succumbed in 1812. See the obituary of Harries in *MR*, VII (1812), 118–20.

9   Possibly John Chidlaw (1727–1800), dissenting minister to the Crook Street congregation, Chester,

from 1765 to 1798; he had previously served that congregation as assistant minister. According to *Historical sketches of nonconformity in the County Palatine of Chester. By various ministers and laymen in the country*, ed. William Urwick (London and Manchester, 1864), p. 37, Chidlaw 'became a Socinian', and several members of his congregation seceded in protest and founded an independent chapel at Queen Street, Chester.

10 A 'Mr. Small, Holywell, Flintshire' is listed as a member of the Unitarian Society in 1791. At its monthly meeting on 10 Mar. 1791, the committee of the Unitarian Society recorded the receipt of 'A letter from M^r. Small'. It recommending the printing 'on a single leaf, a judicious selection of texts, or passages of Scripture, respecting the duty of free & full inquiry, to be prefixed to the books approved & circulated by this society'; Unitarian Society minute book, p. 10. This suggestion was not adopted in practice. Lindsey's letters to Chidlaw and to Small appear not to have survived.

11 Probably this is a reference to Henry Baynham of South Molton, Devon, who is noted in the Thompson list as one of the ministers who petitioned for reform of the system of subscription for dissenting ministers; see 'A view of English nonconformity in 1773', 214. He became minister to a dissenting congregation at Totnes, *c*. 1773, and seems to have served there until the mid-1790s; his successor, William Chaplain, became minister in 1795. There is no evidence in the published list of members or in the society's minute book that Baynham became a member of the Unitarian Society. John Rowe probably knew him through his own family connexions with Devon. See also Letter 584.

12 John Mainwaring (1724–1807) was admitted to St John's College, Cambridge, on 5 June 1742, one year after Lindsey: he was a fellow of the college from 1748 to 1788 (Lindsey was a fellow from 1747 to 1755). He was Lady Margaret professor of divinity from 1788 until his death. For his friendship with Hurd, at that time a fellow of Emmanuel College, see *The early letters of Bishop Richard Hurd 1739–1762*, ed. Sarah Brewer (Church of England Record Society, 3, 1995), especially pp. 212–14, 219, 250, 389. The University of Cambridge Grace Book (CUL, Grace Book, V (1772–99)) does not record a grace, or motion, in favour of Burke from Mainwaring or from anyone else. On 13 June 1792, however, the university senate issued an address of support to George III after the royal proclamation against sedition, the previous month; Grace Book V, pp. 272–3, with the king's reply. William Mason was admitted to St John's College, Cambridge, in 1743 (two years after Lindsey) and had been a canon of York since 1762 and precentor since 1763. In 1790, he took part in moves among the Church of England clergy in Yorkshire against the repeal of the Test and Corporation Acts.

435. To WILLIAM TAYLEUR   3 FEBRUARY 1791

Text: JRUL, Lindsey Letters, vol. II, no. 37.
Printed: Ditchfield, 'Unitarianism after the French Revolution', 40–1.
Addressed: Address missing.
Endorsed: Feby. 3^d – 91
Postmarked: Postmark missing.

London. Feb. 3. 1791

Dear Sir,

I hope you have received my acknowlegements for your last kind and most welcome letter on many accounts.

As there is nothing determined concerning the continuance of our Society for promoting the knowlege of the Scriptures, and its members I believe will not be called upon this year to pay their subscription (though you have always paid your's without being called upon) it will be sufficient at present to send your generous donation to this our new Society by itself; and I submit it to you, whether, if it be equally convenient to yourself, it might not be as well to let me have it to produce on the 9th. instant, when our Society is to be embodied, and when it will be desireable to have some money put into our Treasurer's hands, and when it is expected several other subscriptions will be paid in.[1]

There is another thing of which I must apprize you, which is, that on Mr Belsham's proposal with whom alone the thing originated, it has been agreed out of respect to you, to beg that you will name some Unitarian Book which you desire and would recommend to be adopted by the Society. I beg therefore that you will take it into your thoughts, and propose some authors work of this character, which you approve.[2]

What do you think of D[r] Priestley's history of the Christian Church?[3] Or do you know any other to recommend in a lesser form? I wish you however for various reasons to name some one, that may be decisively unitarian, because some among us, which I perhaps may have intimated, are somewhat backward about our directly avowing ourselves by certain publications with obnoxious names, lest we should give too much offence at first, and any tract or book espoused by you will be accepted. What you say on this subject, you will be so good to put in half a sheet of paper by itself.[4]

Since I wrote so far, M[r] Belsham has been with me, and desires if you have no objection, that you would recomend M[r] Haynes's book of which I was lately the editor to the Society to be adopted by them. He thinks it will be of great service as being expressly declaratory of our views to promote the divine unity.[5]

I am sorry I have not time left to fill my pages, which I fully proposed, when I sat down to write, having several things you would be glad to hear of, but they must be left to another opportunity after I next hear from you. In the mean while my wife desires her due respects and I am always, Dear Sir,

Your most truly obliged and faithful servant
    T. Lindsey

---

1 For Lindsey's detailed account of this meeting, see Letter 437.

2 The book which Tayleur proposed to the Unitarian Society was *Representation of the nature of true religion*; Unitarian Society minute book, p. 8 (9 Feb. 1791). It was reprinted in *Tracts printed and published by the Unitarian Society for Promoting Christian Knowledge and the Practice of Virtue*, vol. VI (1793). There were several editions in the eighteenth century, some of them with the title *A lady's religion*; see Letter 448, n. 4. On 14 Apr. 1791, the minute book (p. 15) recorded the thanks of the society to Tayleur for his present of 500 copies of this work, and for his gift of 100 guineas (p. 6).

3 Priestley's *A general history of the Christian church to the fall of the western empire* was published in Birmingham and sold by Joseph Johnson in London.

4 It is clear that Tayleur complied with this request, in the form of the 'short letter' to which Lindsey referred in Letter 437. Unfortunately, that 'short letter' does not survive among his letters to Lindsey in JRUL, C2[13].

5 For Lindsey's edition of Haynes, see Letter 406, n. 16. Tayleur evidently raised no objection, since on 9 Feb. 1791, the Unitarian Society agreed to the adoption of this work as one of its titles, on the recommendation of Dodson, Disney and Belsham; Unitarian Society minute book, p. 7.

---

436. To WILLIAM TAYLEUR   3 FEBRUARY 1791

Text: JRUL, Lindsey Letters, vol. II, no. 38.
Printed: McLachlan, *Letters*, p. 13 (second paragraph).
Addressed: Address missing.
Endorsed: [There are extensive notes, in the form of a draft letter, by Tayleur, on the whole of the fourth side, and the top of the second and third sides, of the letter; see n. 4, below.]
Postmarked: Postmark missing.

Note: This letter from Lindsey to Tayleur, like Letter 435, is dated 3 February 1791. The confidential tone of Letter 436 suggests that it was written after Letter 435, which made no mention of Lindsey's interview with James Martin MP.

Dear Sir,

You will easily perceive that this letter, by it's purport is intended only for yourself, at least at present.

One morning this week I breakfasted in Downing Street, Westminster, with Mr James Martin, M.P. for Tewkesbury, at his desire.[1]

After breakfast, when the other company was withdrawn, he began to mention that he had a particular concern in which he was desirous of having my advice and assistance. For some space of time, when in the country, he had quitted the worship of the estabilished church, and had prayers and a Sermon in his own house.[2] But he thought it incumbent on him, to let it be known, that if any were of the same sentiments with himself and had objections to a Trinitarian worship, his doors were open to them at such times.

He wished to draw up and print a short little piece, that might express this design in the plainest and most inoffensive manner and with all proper tenderness and respect for the minister of the parish, with whom he was and wished to be upon the best terms.[3]

And it occurred to him (and I believe your example at Shrewsbury first suggested the thought) that Mr Tayleur perhaps had taken some such method and composed some address of the kind, when he first separated from the church. He therefore wished me with his most respectful comp^ts. to intimate to you, as he knew that I sometimes wrote to Shrewsbury, that he should take it as a great favour if you had done any thing of the sort, to impart it to him, and no other use would be made of it, than what would be intirely agreeable to You.

You will believe that I was glad to hear of a purpose of this kind, as if it was to become pretty general, it would soon either put the church upon reforming itself, or put others on doing it for them, and polytheism and idolatry would no longer defile our land.

Now, my excellent friend, if you should have any manuscript of the sort, or suchlike, by you, I can have no doubt of your readiness to lend it on such an occasion.[4]

But if you should have nothing that would serve the purpose, I wish, that at your full leisure, a fortnight, three weeks or a month hence you would send me a letter such as I might produce before this worthy person, and such as might suggest any proper ideas, or tend to encourage him in his design.[5]

P.S. I do not know any thing that should hinder your communicating this matter to our worthy friends who meet at your house, tho' without naming names, as it will give them singular pleasure.[6]

       T.L.

London. Feb. 3. 1791

N.B. This frank was given me with a view to my writing to you. I need not perhaps add, that Mr M. belongs to our chapel, and also Dr Kippis's,[7] and is a most worthy upright character in all respects.

---

1   James Martin was MP for Tewkesbury from 1776 to 1807. His London residence was in Downing Street; *Boyle's new fashionable court and country guide; and town visiting directory for 1796* (London, 1796), p. 86. He lived next door to the prime minister, William Pitt; see Iain S. Black's article on the Martin family, *ODNB*, XXXVI, 917. In *Holden's triennial directory, 1802, 1803 & 1804* (3rd edn, London, ?1804: unpaginated), his address was 10 George Street, Westminster. The premises of his family bank were in Lombard Street. Martin is listed as a member of the Unitarian Society in 1791 and in 1794; *Unitarian Society ... 1791*, p. 12; *Unitarian Society ... 1794*, p. 12.

He also subscribed to a number of unitarian publications, including those of Gilbert Wakefield and William Enfield.

2   James Martin's country house was at Overbury, Worcestershire.

3   Martin's parish was that of St Faith, Overbury; inside the church, there is a wall memorial to him as one 'universally admired for his Political Integrity and his Love of Civil and Religious Liberty'. The incumbent of the parish from Dec. 1788 to May 1796 was George Shelton (d. 1812), a graduate of Oxford University (Worcester College).

4   Tayleur drafted a reply on the reverse of this letter from Lindsey, in which he expressed approval of Martin's initiative but regretted that he had 'no tract of the sort he mentions'. However, he added a brief summary of his own practice of holding non-trinitarian services in his own house, and subsequently his success in persuading the minister of the High Street chapel, Shrewsbury, to adopt unitarian worship.

5   Tayleur did indeed provide this letter for Martin's benefit, and Lindsey delivered it to Martin in person on 28 Feb. 1791; see Letter 441. Although the letter itself does not survive in JRUL, C2[13], his comments written on this letter from Lindsey (see n. 4, above) probably amount to a draft of it.

6   These 'worthy friends' included John Rowe, Edward Harries and Isaac Wood.

7   The congregation of Andrew Kippis met at Princes Street, Westminster.

437. To WILLIAM TAYLEUR   9 FEBRUARY 1791

Text: JRUL, Lindsey Letters, vol. II, no. 39.
Addressed: Address missing.
Postmarked: Postmark missing.

London. Wednesday night. Feb. 9. 1791.

Dear Sir,

This has been truly a day of triumph and joy, and chiefly furnished by you. I cannot describe to you the surprize and silent satisfaction with which your short letter was heard, w[ch] mentioned your most generous benefaction to our new society; and an impression of the same kind was continued when I read what came from you through M[r] Wood relating to the small tract, to which I could not refrain from giving my testimony and heartiest approbation, and your offer of a donation of 500 copies.[1] We chose D[r] Disney with M[r] Belsham as a coadjutor for our secretary and he will transmit to you the acknowlegements of our new Society for your signal encouragement to it. The names of those that were present and of the members then announced will soon be printed at the end of our plan and rules a little alter'd, with a short preamble, which M[r] Belsham is to draw up.[2] But no account now, or at any time, will be publishd of the sums subscribed. I shall immediately dispatch it to you, when printed. I reckond it no small honour to be your confidential messenger and reporter upon the occasion. Haynes was approved nem. con.[3] and a set of various other tracts proposed, some few by D[r] Disney, the rest by M[r] Belsham and myself were proposed to be adopted by the society. I wish we had more of the practical kind. But they will come I trust in time.

You will not be surprised, when I tell you, that by more channels than one I have heard already, that our new society has given alarm to the orthodox churchmen.

I presented to M[r] Dodson, nephew to the late judge Foster, a learned and most worthy zealous christian, who was chosen our treasurer and chairman for the day, near forty names of subscribers from different parts of the country as well as the metropolis. One, anonymous, who called himself a well-wisher to the plan, gave me ten guineas: Another, a subscriber of ten guineas.[4] You will be pleased with what relates to this latter, after the account given of him in M[r] Chidlaw's letter, lately returned to me by M[r] Wood, and therefore as I have procured a frank, I inclose the two letters which I have received from him, which will shew what spirit he is of, and will give you pleasure.[5]

You would hardly credit the accounts I have had, from some liberal christians, of objections to our calling ourselves an unitarian society, as if it was making ourselves of a party in religion; but the objection I persuade myself, has more frequently originated in a secret apprehension, perhaps unknown to themselves, of appearing in print as unitarians. This timidity however I trust will wear away in time, and particularly I persuade myself, by the increasing number of members of our new Society.

In canvassing about this business I have been peculiarly happy in being brought to the knowlege and history of a most eminent christian confessor of our own times, and who has favoured me with a pretty large account of himself on condition of mentioning it only to one or two friends, and one of those whom I had always in my thoughts was yourself. It will fill a cover itself, and therefore I shall take another opportunity of transmitting it to you, and that will be at the latest, at the beginning of the next week, when I have procured a frank.[6]

The more one inquires the more it appears that divine truth is making its way in this country of our's. I may not omit to mention, that one of the names I gave in, was "Mr Peter Valentine in the name of the congregation of Dissenters at Chowbent.["][7] And it was suggested that the like perhaps woud be done by other congregations.[8] I shall not look to hear from or of you, till you have recd my next letter, when I shall be glad to know, by the return of the post, that it has arrived safe.[9] I beg leave through you to thank Mr Wood for his last favour. Mr Harries and Mr Rowes names, following your's graced my list;[10] I beg to be respectfully remembered to them and Mr Wood in which my wife joins, and with her most due respects to yourself, I remain always Dear Sir, Your most truly obliged and faithful servant
                    T. Lindsey.

---

[1]   This 'small tract' was *Representation of the nature of true religion*; see Letter 435, n. 2, and Letter 438. Tayleur's 'short letter' seems not to have survived; see Letter 435, n. 4.

[2]   The preamble to the Unitarian Society's rules may be found in *Unitarian Society for Promoting Christian Knowledge and the Practice of Virtue* (London, 1791), a fourteen-page pamphlet, pp. 1–3. The title page was simply headed 'Unitarian Society'.

[3]   See Letter 406, n. 16.

[4]   Neither Lindsey not the Unitarian Society minute book identified these anonymous (or pseudonymous) subscriptions. The entry in the minute book (pp. 4–6) for the meeting of 9 Feb. 1791 listed seventy-four members but did not detail the amount which they paid. The admission fee for the society was one guinea and the annual subscription was a minimum of one guinea. A payment of ten guineas secured life membership.

[5]   For a possible identification of Chidlaw, see Letter 434, n. 9. The two letters from him to Lindsey seem not to have survived.

[6]   This 'most eminent Christian confessor' was James Martin, MP. It is evident from Letter 440 that Lindsey did indeed send Martin's letter to Tayleur. It is also evident (Letter 441) that Tayleur responded to it with a letter of his own to Martin, but that, at least by the beginning of Jan. 1792, Martin had not at that time followed it up; see the postscript to Letter 482.

[7]   Peter Valentine and the dissenting congregation at Chowbent are indeed listed among the first members of the Unitarian Society in 1791; *Unitarian Society ... 1791*, p. 13.

[8]   Four other subscriptions, apart from that of Chowbent (n. 2, above) to the Unitarian Society in 1791 were in the names of congregations; see the printed list of 155 members annexed to the rules and preamble of the society (n. 2, above).

[9]   Lindsey's next surviving letter to Tayleur was dated 23 Feb. 1791 (Letter 440); in it, Lindsey thanked Tayleur for his 'long' (and evidently prompt) letter in response to his request for a reply by return of post. Unfortunately, this letter of Tayleur is not in JRUL, C2[13].

438. To WILLIAM FREND   **14 FEBRUARY 1791**

Text: CUL, Add. MS 7886 (Frend papers), no. 165.
Addressed: To/The Rev[d]. W. Frend/fellow of Jesus college/Cambridge
Postmarked: FE 14 91

London. Feb. 14. 1791

Dear Sir,

I presume that D[r] Disney may have written to you, and told you of our respectable commencem[t] of the New Society on Wednesday, in the gentlemen present, the names of members produced and particularly in the excellent M[r] Tayleur of Shrewsburys letter which I produced, received the day before, in which he sent, instead of the fifty promised, which I believe I mentioned to you,[1] one hundred guineas as his composition for ten years, and one for his admission fee.[2]

He also, as I had requested of him something of the kind, sent a small practical tract, which he had printed for dispersion several years since, being a letter to a lady written about the beginning of the present century, and added that if it was thought worthy to be adopted, he should be glad to present our new society with 500 which he had by him. I liked the tract much on a cursory perusal, and believe we shall receive it, and follow the method which you pointed out in your letter, respecting such gifts, and which I read as from you to the society.[3]

My [*sic*] Tyrwhitt's emendation of christian for religious knowlege, was very proper, as we are already called a Society of Deists.[4] But it seems to me that Unitarian and Unity would not be so well so near each other in the title which you mention and incline to as his; viz. "The Unitarian Society for promoting christian knowlege on the principle of the Unity of God." However I have no idea of differing either from him or you, if we were a quarter of an hour together. And I would say <u>to you</u>; that all the mootings about any points you were witness to here; that all goes on most amicably and will I trust so continue, in this matter; and other movements also made by us, for peace sake and for the gospel's, in another.[5]

Yours and M[r] Hammonds present will be most thankfully received: but as we are likely to be a rich society, sh[d] you deprive yourselves of the means of promoting the truth, by so large a donation to such a body.[6]

I read to the company also your idea about correspondents,[7] and it will be attended to at our next meeting: though I hope to engage M[r] Kirwan of Dublin to be a *member*.[8] A worthy person present added, that he hoped we should have not only correspondents but members in America, and also upon the Continent of Europe, where our language is very wide spread. So you perceive we already see big expectations.

I hope M[r] Wakefield will be prevailed with to continue among us, for a few years at least. Fr[om] the short conversation I had with him, and from his whole manner of going on, seldom have I found any one whom I liked equally. I believe him not only exceeding able but most conscientious to fulfill this or any trust in which he engages, and that he would not continue in any where he could not be useful.

We were much grieved that M[r] Dyer could not bring himself to engage with M[r] Estlyn at Bristol, where he might have been so extremely serviceable by his good taste as well as excellent principles. If there be any way of his becoming settled any where, we sh^d be glad to contribute our mite to it.[9] I beg you will make mine and my wife's respects acceptable to Mr Tyrwhitt, whom none hold in higher esteem; and with the lady's to yourself, I remain always very truly Yours

T. Lindsey.

---

1   See Letter 437.

2   This was probably Tayleur's 'short letter' mentioned by Lindsey in Letter 437. For Tayleur's gift of 100 guineas, see Unitarian Society minute book, p. 6. If Disney wrote to Frend on the lines suggested by Lindsey, his letter seems not to have survived. It is not one of the three surviving letters from Disney to Frend in CUL, Add. MS 7886, nor is it among the few letters of Disney or Frend at DWL. The previous Wednesday was 9 Feb. 1791.

3   This tract was *Representation of the nature of true religion*; see Letter 435, n. 2. It was indeed adopted by the Unitarian Society.

4   Robert Tyrwhitt's suggestion indicates the sensitivity of unitarians to any accusation of deism levelled against them.

5   The title of the society finally decided upon was 'The Unitarian Society for Promoting Christian Knowledge, and the Practice of Virtue, by Distributing Books'. For all Lindsey's friendly tone, the following month he became involved in a dispute with Tyrwhitt, Frend and other Cambridge sympathizers over the society's doctrinal position; see, in particular, Letters 443, 444, 446 and 458. Frend's letter, to which Lindsey referred in this paragraph, seems not to have survived.

6   Frend and John Hammond were both listed as members of the Unitarian Society in 1791; *Unitarian Society ... 1791*, p. 10.

7   I.e. corresponding members, outside Britain.

8   There is no evidence from the published lists of members of the Unitarian Society or from the society's minute book that Richard Kirwan ever became a member, although it is clear that he was in general a sympathizer with its objectives.

9   John Prior Estlin was assistant minister to Thomas Wright (d. 1797) at the Lewin's Mead chapel, Bristol, from 1771 to 1797, and senior minister there from 1797 to 1817. Dyer did not settle as a minister with a congregation at Bristol or anywhere else; see Letter 425, n. 10.

---

439. To RUSSELL SCOTT   22 FEBRUARY 1791

Text: Scott Coll.
Printed: McLachlan, 'Lindsey to Scott', 117 (short quotation from the first paragraph; most of eighth and ninth paragraphs).
Addressed: Address missing.
Postmarked: Postmark missing.

London. Feb. 22. 1791

Dear Sir,

I hope that you and Mrs Scott arrived safe and well from the great city at your own home, and so continue, yourself in particular: for you I believe were the much greater invalid.

Since your departure we have had a new Unitarian Society instituted for distributing books, which perhaps I might mention to you as it was I believe in agitation when you were in Town.

The first meeting and commencement of it was on Wednesday the ninth inst. when there was a very respectable appearance of gentlemen favourers of it, and the names of many absent produced, desiring to become members. I not only gave in your name, but also your admission fee and subscription, one guinea each, with my own and many others, to the tune of betwixt 30 and 40 at the same time; and instead of a book or two which I intended to have sent you, I must beg you to accept this trifle.[1]

But you will soon see our plan reprinted, with the names then produced, and since come in annexed, and also a short preamble to the whole, by M[r] Belsham, which I think you will much approve. Our Secretary, D[r]. Disney, will send you this of course, and I suppose you will have it in a few days: but if he does not, I shall take care to transmit it.

Since you left Town, little is talked of in the literary way, but M[r] Burke and his Answerers: tho' of late the subject has been changed for the Bill for the Relief of the Catholics, a motion for which is to be made this day.[2]

They have no doubt of obtaining a full relief and to be considered intirely as good subjects, if the Protestant Dissenters did not stand in their way: But at all events they expect, tho' not perhaps all at once to be put upon the same footing as they are.

Since you went away D[r] Kippis gave notice to the Trustees of the college that he should resign his office. It was believed that this was done by him upon some just umbrage taken at some things said concerning him. But I trust he will retract his resolution, as there has been a motion unanimously agreed to to desire him to continue, and the young men his pupils have also sent him a very handsome letter, desiring his continuance among them: and to day M[r] Rogers, M[r] Jeffries and M[r] Dodson were to wait upon him on the occasion, and I have no doubt of his acceding to their proposal.[3] I mention this as you may like to know what has passed, and contradict any wrong rumours about it. Otherwise it may be as well not to mention it.

I must not omit to mention to you, that the excellent M[r] Tayleur of Shrewsbury when first I acquainted him with our New Unitarian Society, sent me word that he should send us 50 Guineas for his composition as at his age, 78, he could not expect long to be an annual Subscriber.

But the day before our meeting he sent me a draft for 100 Guineas his composition and one his admission fee; and moreover made the Society an offer of 500 of a small practical Tract, which he had got printed several years before to disperse. He sent me one copy, and it is a very valuable little piece.[4]

Perhaps M[r] Carter[5] or some others of your congregation may favour us with their names when they have seen our plan.

My wife desires to join in kind comp[ts] to M[rs] Scott and yourself and I am always most truly Yours

      T. Lindsey.

M[r] Taylor and your worthy sister I hope are well. D[r] Kippis undertook to make our friends at Chichester acquainted with the plan of our new society, or I sh[d] have taken the liberty to write thither.[6]

---

1 By 'this trifle', perhaps Lindsey referred in a tone of affected modesty to one of his own publications – possibly *A list of false readings of the scriptures, and the mistranslations of the English Bible, which contribute to support the great errors concerning Jesus Christ* (London, 1790), a work of fewer than 100 pages.

2 In fact it was on 21 Feb. 1791, not 22 Feb., that John Mitford, MP for Bere Alston, introduced a motion in the house of commons for leave to bring in a catholic relief bill. His motion was referred to a committee of the whole house for 1 Mar.; Cobbett, *Parl. hist.*, XXVIII, 1262–9. For a survey of Burke's 'Answerers' in 1790 and early 1791, see F. P. Lock, *Edmund Burke. Volume II: 1784–1797* (Oxford, 2006), pp. 332–50.

3 At the committee of Hackney College on 1 Feb. 1791 a letter from Kippis, signifying his intention to resign his office of tutor in *belles-lettres* at the end of the academic session, was read. On 15 Feb., the committee delegated its chairman Thomas Rogers, together with Thomas Brand Hollis and Michael Dodson, to meet Kippis and urge him to withdraw his resignation. On 22 Feb., they reported that Kippis had expressed his 'warm attachment' to the college and had agreed to remain a tutor for 'some time longer'. See DWL, MS 38.14, pp. 147, 148–9. On 22 Feb. the minute book simply

noted Kippis's change of mind with gratitude and did not identify those of its members who were asked to convey this gratitude to Kippis in person. Thomas Rogers (1735–93), banker and briefly MP for Coventry in 1780–1 before being unseated on petition, was a member of the committee for the establishment of Hackney College in 1785–6. He was the father of the poet Samuel Rogers. Edward Jeffries, also one of the first committee members of the college, was chairman of the protestant dissenting deputies from 1785 to 1802 and treasurer of St Thomas's Hospital. He was a member of the Unitarian Society from 1791; see his obituary, *MR*, IX (1814), 246–7.

4   This 'small practical tract' was *Representation of the nature of true religion*; see Letter 435, n. 2.
5   This was John Carter (1715–94) of Wimering, a prominent citizen of Portsmouth, of which he was seven times mayor. He was the father of Sir John Carter (1741–1808) and the grandfather of John Carter (1788–1838), MP for Portsmouth from 1816 to 1838. The Carter family were members of Scott's congregation at High Street, Portsmouth; see Bonham-Carter, *In a liberal tradition*, pp. 15–21. Scott was a member of the Unitarian Society from its inception; John Carter and 'Mr. W. P.'. of Portsmouth were both listed as members in 1794; *Unitarian Society ... 1791*, p. 13, and *Unitarian Society ... 1794*, pp. 10, 13. 'Mr W. P.' was almost certainly William Joseph Porter of the victualling office, who was also a member of Scott's congregation; see Letter 602, n. 1.
6   Three members of the Unitarian Society in 1791 were from Chichester, namely the physicians John Bayly and Thomas Sanden, and the dissenting minister Thomas Watson, minister to the Baffins Lane congregation in that city. See Letter 388, n. 12, and *Unitarian Society ... 1791*, pp. 9, 13, 14.

440. To WILLIAM TAYLEUR   23 FEBRUARY 1791

Text: JRUL, Lindsey Letters, vol. II, no. 40.
Printed: McLachlan, *Letters*, p. 131 (fourth sentence of fifth
                   paragraph).
Addressed: To/William Tayleur Esq[r]/Shrewsbury
Endorsed: Feb[y]. 23[d] – 91
Postmarked: FE 23 91

London. Feb. 23. 1791.
Dear Sir,

Many thanks for your kind long letter, and the satisfaction given me in knowing that the M.S. sent was received safe. Of it's acceptableness to you I could have no doubt, and one or two of your remarks I shall mention to the worthy writer, as he knows it was to be comunicated to you, and they will give him pleasure.[1]

After your writing so long a letter it is unreasonable to solicit any thing farther of the sort, but I should take it as a favour at your leisure to furnish me with something that I may say to M[r] Martin from you on the subject I wrote about from him;[2] but still I say at your leisure, and if there be any thing that requires the pen much, M[r] Rowe will be ready to undertaken that.

I am glad that without committing you in any respect, or doing any thing but barely mention your's, D[r] Priestleys and the names of several other friends as concurring in opinion with myself against saying any thing in the title-page, of our books being printed by the unitarian society, it hath been given up; so that now, and with the addition of a short preamble drawn up by M[r] Belsham, I trust there will be nothing but what you will approve, though I have not seen it since the alterations were made.[3] But you will see it soon, as D[r] Disney, by a note yesterday, acquaints me that he had ordered 25 copies to be sent to you, and different quantities to other persons to distribute where they may be of use. Our treasurer tells me that the sum received in his hands is £360 odd pounds, and the number of names about fourscore.[4]

I do not know whether you have heard any thing of the invitation given to D[r] Priestley to preach the Anniversary sermon of our New College this year. His reasons against accepting it sent up to me at first were so cogent, taking in at the same time the particular manner in which he signified he shoud treat the subject, that I was convinced by them and wished him to decline it. He has however hesitated since, and has even composed and sent up the sermon, which I have now in my Bureau. If he should not preach it, I shall desire it may be sent to you to peruse. But I shall be able to tell you of his decision in my next.[5] His spirits of late have been but low, on acc[t] of his disappointment from M[rs] Priestleys eldest brother, in the estabilishm[t]. of his two elder sons.[6] But he is much recruited within these ten days, since somewhat promising has turned out for the eldest at Manchester, and the second is at present in M[r] Russells Counting house, to fit him for any thing that may fall out.[7]

You would be delighted with M[r] Fox's speech on Monday upon the motion for relieving the Catholics.[8] The minister I am told appeared much hurt by it, and shewed some not very good passions in his countenance. But these circumstances must pave the way for equal universal toleration in religious matters. M[r] Paine's book against M[r] Burke has some fine thing[s] upon the subject as ever I read, and which must affect every mind: but the book is so intirely republican, tho' full of most excellent matter, and contains such reflections on the Brunswick princes, that M[r] Johnson, for whom it is printed, is advised not to sell it.[9] I shall send soon a long letter I have rec[d] from M[r] W. Christie of Montrose.[10] His sermons are now reprinted on better paper, and likely to be useful: I think I mentiond to you their being recomended to be adopted by our Society. At the conclusion of them, there is a page or two addressed to Unitarians continuing to attend Trinitarian worship, that deserves to be printed and circulated.[11] Farewel, my excellent Friend. My wife desires her ever due and kind respects. We both beg our respectful comp[ts] to M[r] Rowe and M[r] Wood, and I wish the former to know that as I am troubling you so often with my rescripts, I on that acc[t] only do not write to him. I am ever, Dear Sir,
    Your most truly obliged and faithful servant.
            T. Lindsey.

1   For Tayleur's (non-surviving) letter, see Letter 437, n. 9. The manuscript in question was James Martin's letter to Lindsey, which Lindsey had forwarded to Tayleur; see Letter 437, n.6.
2   See Letter 436.
3   See Letter 437, n. 2.
4   The treasurer of the Unitarian Society from its foundation in 1791 until his death in 1799 was Michael Dodson. The Unitarian Society minute book (pp. 4–6, 11–12) listed seventy-four members on 9 Feb. and a further forty-four on 14 Apr. 1791. The number of members listed in *Unitarian Society... 1791*, pp. 9–14, was 155, of whom 143 were named individuals. *Unitarian Society ... 1794*, pp. 9–15, listed 168 members, of whom 154 were named individuals.
5   Priestley did preach this sermon; see Letter 445, n. 10.
6   Mary Priestley's eldest brother was the ironmaster John Wilkinson. In 1790, Priestley hoped that Wilkinson might employ his second son William at Birmingham, but, probably because of William's temperamental unsuitability for such work, nothing came of this possibility. Nor did Wilkinson employ Priestley's eldest son Joseph; see n. 7, below.
7   From Feb. 1791, Priestley's eldest son, Joseph junior, was briefly employed as a clerk by a merchant named Ashworth, in Manchester. His second son, William, was articled to William Russell in Birmingham for a short time; Schofield, *Enlightened Joseph Priestley*, pp. 317–18.
8   On Monday 21 Feb. 1791, Fox appealed to the principle of universal toleration when speaking in the house of commons in support of John Mitford's motion for leave to introduce a catholic relief bill; Cobbett, *Parl. hist.*, XXVIII, 1267–9.
9   The first part of Thomas Paine, *Rights of man: being an answer to Mr. Burke's attack on the French Revolution*, was published by J. S. Jordan in London on 16 Mar. 1791. Joseph Johnson had prepared it for publication on 21 Feb. 1791, but, fearing prosecution, withdrew it. A few copies of Johnson's version actually appeared, however, and it was in that version (pp. 124–5) that Lindsey read the

reference to the Brunswick princes. Referring to the use by Britain of German soldiers in the War of American Independence, Paine wrote 'God help that country … be it England or elsewhere, whose liberties are to be protected by German principles of Government, and Princes of Brunswick.' This statement appeared (pp. 131–2) in the third edition of J. S. Jordan's published version of *Rights of man*, and in some (though not all) of Jordan's subsequent editions in 1791.

10   William Christie's long letter to Lindsey seems not to have survived.

11   Christie's *Discourses on the divine unity* were indeed adopted by the Unitarian Society at its meeting on 14 Apr. 1791 and 200 copies were purchased; Unitarian Society minute book, p. 14. Christie's warning to unitarians to avoid attendance at trinitarian worship may be found in his *Discourses*, pp. 269–81.

441. To WILLIAM TAYLEUR   1 MARCH 1791

Text: JRUL, Lindsey Letters, vol. II, no. 41.
Printed: McLachlan, *Letters*, p. 66 (most of second paragraph).
Addressed: Address missing.
Postmarked: Postmark missing.

London. March. 1. 1791.

Dear Sir,

I can only say of the letter which I received on Saturday, than that I do not know in what other way or terms it could have been better couched to produce its effect.[1] The civil, proper things said to M^r _____ ,[2] and the encouragement given, and then the short but well told narrative of your own case, and the serious satisfaction expressed on the retrospect of it. It affected us very greatly, and will I trust the person for whom it was written, and at whose house I delivered it yesterday morning, but did not see him till this, when I called again for some covers which I had left to be franked, and one for you among the rest. He expressed himself highly obliged to you, and edified with the example, said he ought to have thanked you immediately himself, but as he concluded from the cover I had left with him for to day, that I was writing to You, he desired I would do it for him on the most respectful terms. And here ends effort, which I trust will be for good, and for which I cannot but greatly thank you as it was done at my desire. Forgive my saying, that a better letter, every way, you could not have written at 30.

On Friday last the deputies for the Dissenters in England and Wales, resident in London, held a meeting, in which they came to a resolution to address the Catholics now petitioning Parliam^t that altho they themselves had been disappointed, they most cordially wished them success in their present application, and should truly rejoice in their obtaining.[3] This resolution was communicated to the Catholics by their Chairman, and produced an answer which I saw to day from their body assembled, thanking the Dissenters for their kindness to them, and for their very seasonable encouragement – implying as if they had rather expected opposition from that quarter.[4] So far I am sure, you will say, all is well: and it cannot be doubted that the Catholics and their friends will in their turn assist the Dissenters in their next application to the legislature. It is expected that there will be a good debate in the house upon the subject to day. Several of my friends are gone down to hear it. Some say, that the Minister will try [to] put a stop to the business, foreseeing that it will involve him in difficulties respecting the Dissenters. We shall soon see however what he does.[5] And do what he will, truth will get the better of him.

Having such a convenient opportunity I transmit another letter since received from [word or words omitted] – which I am sure will give pleasure, tho' I was somewhat surprized and concerned that the attendance in any way on the worship – could be endured.[6] I shall hope that in time by some free conversation this may be dropt, as rather wanting to compleat what has been done. The long character given to the brother in law is in answer to something said by me when M[r] H. brought me the first manuscript. This Gentleman did not sit down, but in standing and asking various questions, amidst the highest comendations of M[r]. A's heart, benevolence, great sprightliness, he mentiond how much at other times all these amiable qualities were obscured by hypocondriac affections, which prevented mixing with or seeing any company.[7]

I dare say you have received the copies of the new impression of our plan &c with the list of names annexed.[8] I am not certain that I told you, that D[r]. Price subscribed ten guineas for his composition, which does him great credit, as we rather go farther than he approves.[9] But a man of greater simplicity or of a better heart lives not.

You have had trouble enough in writing lately. I propose to write again soon. With my wifes kind respects, I remain always Your most truly obliged and faithful affectionate servant

    T. Lindsey.

Our best comp[ls] to M[r] Rowe, and M[r] Wood, and M[r] Harries, when you see him.

---

1   The previous Saturday was 26 Feb. 1791. For a draft of Tayleur's letter to Lindsey, with its account of his initiative in starting unitarian worship in his own house, see Letter 436. Tayleur's letter itself does not survive.

2   James Martin, MP, whose London house was in Downing Street (see Letter 436, n. 1), and from whom Lindsey collected franked covers for his letters.

3   'Friday last' was 25 Feb. 1791. There is no record of a meeting of the protestant dissenting deputies on this date. The deputies' committee met on 21 Jan., 8 Mar. and 21 May 1791, with no reference to the catholic bill; London Metropolitan Archives, MS 3083/2, pp. 504–8 (deputies' meetings). On 1 Mar., William Smith, speaking in the house of commons, declared that 'the relief proposed to be given to Roman Catholicks, was to none more agreeable than to the dissenters'; *World*, 2 Mar. 1791. The chairman of the dissenting deputies from 1785 to 1801 was Edward Jeffries (see Letter 439, n. 3).

4   This answer from the catholic committee to the protestant dissenting deputies is not mentioned in the minutes of the catholic committee for 26 Feb. and 1 Mar. 1791; BL, Add. MS 7961, fos. 176–9. However, the *Whitehall Evening Post*, 3–5 Mar. 1791, published 'the case of the English Catholic dissenters' for relief.

5   On 1 Mar. 1791, the house of commons went into a committee of the whole house and agreed without a division to John Mitford's motion for the introduction of a catholic relief bill; Cobbett, *Parl. hist.*, XXVIII, 1364–76. Fox moved an amendment to add the words 'and others' to the 'persons called protesting Catholic dissenters' for whom the bill was intended, but withdrew it when Pitt, far from trying to 'put a stop to the business', supported the motion and advocated the repeal of intolerant statutes either by that or by a subsequent bill.

6   Lindsey omitted the name of the writer of this letter; the letter itself has (apparently) not survived.

7   Mr A. was probably Henry Austen; see Vol. I, Letter 376, n. 9; also Letter 447, n. 1. In Letter 447, Lindsey described his 'hypochondria' and unease as to attendance at church worship. 'Mr H.' was probably John Hampson of Tunbridge Wells; see Vol. I, Letter 375, n. 3, and Letters 425–6. Although not brothers-in-law, Austen and Hampson were related by marriage; see Irene Collins, *Jane Austen and the clergy* (London, 1993), p. 7.

8   This is a reference to the preamble, rules and list of members of the Unitarian Society; see Letter 437, n. 2.

9   Although an Arian, Price joined the Unitarian Society on its foundation in 1791; he was listed as a member on 14 Apr. (Unitarian Society minute book, p. 12, where no mention is made of his composition). However, he died on 19 Apr. of that year and it is at least open to question as to whether he would have remained a member after the bitter disputes over the preamble to the society's rules.

442. To WILLIAM FREND   12 MARCH 1791

Text: CUL, Add. MS 7886 (Frend papers), no. 166.
Addressed: To/The Rev^d. W. Frend/fellow of Jesus college/Cambridge
Endorsed: Wednesday/Mr Donovan[1]
Postmarked: MR 12 91

London. March. 12. 1791

Dear Sir

I was much obliged to you for your long, friendly letter,[2] relating to our new Society, which I have not time to acknowlege as I ought. The principal part of it however, which related to your wishes for our reconsidering and making some alteration in the preamble of our plan and rules in what relates to the character of Christ, I read to Mr Dodson, Mr Belsham, Dr Disney and Mr Garnham, on Thursday after the Society was up, and they all shewed themselves dissatisfied with the things advanced concerning our Saviour's character and his office of Mediator in particular, as being without any grounds from Scripture:[3]

and they no less disapproved the conclusion you would build on them.

The calling Jesus the most distinguished of the prophets seemed to them only a different expression of his being the Messiah.

And they wondered how any objection could be made to his being called the creature and messenger of God; when his own constant language of God being his Father, and of his being sent by the Father, evidently implied the one and the other.

And as to the term Vicegerent, it was only intended in the strongest manner to condemn the idea of Jesus being in any sort or degree an object of religious worship.

It was mentioned also, that it was not our view to induce men of very discordant opinions to join us, for that our preface would have been very differently worded if that had been the case; but those who held the divine unity and proper humanity of Christ; or who had no objection to rank themselves with such.

It was hoped however that though they could not see cause to adopt and admit the proposed alterations, we should still have the countenance and assistance of such a friend.

This appeared to me as far as I recollect the sense of our friends upon the occasion.

Have you seen the Heads of the Bill now in the Commons house for the relief of Protesting Catholic Dissenters.

I have a curious *fact*, which may be depended upon, to tell you relating to it.

Among the Conditions and Restrictions at the end of it, is this article

<u>Proviso</u>, That the Act shall not extend to Persons writing against the Trinity.[4]

What business have Catholics with this? They are known Trinitarians, and never to be supposed to write against it.

The truth is, this article did not come from the Catholics themselves, but was imposed upon them as necessary to make their bill pass. This I hope you will hear to be expatiated upon by some of the members in the house of Commons on Thursday next in the second reading of the bill.[5]

How curious and cunning to bring in thus by a side wind a confirmation by Parliament of An Act made a century past, and known to be of so shocking a nature that they dare not act upon it?[6] I hope it will get out properly authenticated and be long ecchoed like thunder in the ears of its contrivers and fabricators.

I have not time to add one word more but my wife's respects and that I ever am with true esteem most sincerely yours T. Lindsey

1   Possibly Richard Donovan (d. 1816), who was admitted to St John's College, Cambridge (Lindsey's former college) on 4 Oct. 1790. On 26 July 1790, he was admitted to Gray's Inn, but as a fellow-commoner from 14 Oct. 1790, he probably retained an association with the college and with Cambridge during the early 1790s, and Lindsey might have requested him to convey this letter to Frend. I am grateful to Dr Frances Willmoth, archivist, Jesus College, Cambridge, for advice on this point. See *Alumn. Cantab.*, II, vol. II, 319–20, and *The register of admissions to Gray's Inn, 1521–1889*, ed. Joseph Foster (2 parts, London, 1889), II, 395.

2   Lindsey referred to this 'very curious' letter from Frend (which seems not to have survived) in his letter to Tayleur of 12 Mar. 1791 (Letter 443).

3   The previous Thursday was 10 Mar. 1791. The Unitarian Society minute book (p. 7) has a brief record of the monthly committee meeting, at the King's Head tavern in the Poultry, on that date. It made no mention of Frend's objections to the society's preamble, and Lindsey's letter indicates that the discussion and rejection of these objections took place informally after the meeting.

4   For the draft of the catholic relief bill, with its clause excluding from its benefits persons who denied the doctrine of the Trinity, see G. M. Ditchfield, 'Anti-trinitarianism and toleration in late eighteenth-century British politics: the unitarian petition of 1792', *JEH*, XLII, 1 (1991), 54–5. The clause was removed from the final version of the bill.

5   On 'Thursday next', 17 Mar. 1791, the house of commons was counted out and the catholic bill was not discussed. The bill was read a second time and committed on 21 Mar 1791; *CJ*, XLVI, 295, 333.

6   The Toleration Act of 1689 (1 William & Mary, c. 18) specifically excluded from its benefits catholics and those who denied the doctrine of the Trinity. The Blasphemy Act of 1698 (9 & 10 William III, c. 32) prescribed severe penalties (deprivation of eligibility for public office on a first conviction; disqualification from all legal rights and imprisonment for three years on a second conviction) for denial of the doctrine of the Trinity.

443. To WILLIAM TAYLEUR   12 MARCH 1791

Text: JRUL, Lindsey Letters, vol. II, no. 42.
Printed: McLachlan, *Letters*, pp. 66–7 (fifth to eleventh paragraphs).
Addressed: Address missing.
Postmarked: Postmark missing.

London March. 12. 1791

Dear Sir,

I have delayed longer than intended to apprize you of the arrival of your present of the 500 little Tracts for our New Society.

We had a meeting on Thursday, when some few more names of members were given in, and some previous measures adopted with respect to the priority of Tracts. Some members also mentioned objections being made, tho' not by themselves at our declaring ourselves so strictly unitarian in our preamble to our Plan. And I had a very curious letter from M[r] Frend at Cambridge, objecting to our stiling Christ, the most distinguished of the prophets; a creature and messenger of God, and not his Vicegerent.[1] I conceive the objections to have taken their rise principally from M[r] Tyrwhitt, who, as long ago D[r] Jebb told me, had some very singular notions of something like an atonement that Christ wrought by his perfect obedience &c &c. But it was agreed that no alteration was to be made in our Preface.

You will be pleased to see how things go on at Plymouth, and therefore I send the inclosed.[2]

But I must mention a very extraordinary fact, which deserves to be known, and which I have just been transmitting to Birmingham.[3]

You may perhaps have seen the printed Heads of the Bill now pending in the Comons House for the Relief of Protesting Catholic Dissenters. Among the Conditions and Restrictions, near the close of it, is the following article.

Proviso, that the Act shall not extend to persons writing against the Trinity.

Now what have Catholics to do with such a clause? They are known Trinitarians. They cannot be otherwise.

The truth is, This article did not come from the Catholics themselves, but was imposed upon them. This they told a member of Parliament, upon his questioning them concerning it.

It was thought however that such a strange thing, which had caused surprize in some, might have been dropped when the Bill was first read on Thursday last. But the same Member of Parliament took particular notice of it being repeated by the Speaker in reading it.[4]

I have this from the first authority, and was desired to make the fact known among my friends.

It certainly will not be forgotten at the 2ᵈ reading in the house of Commons; nor, I can also say, when it comes to the upper house. But what low cunning thus to lug in by a side wind, a second confirmation, at a hundred years distance, by Parlament [*sic*], of an Act so shocking that the times will not suffer the most forward orthodoxy to put in execution, merely to hang it up in *terrorem*, against those who <u>write</u> against the Trinity?

I trust to be able to write again soon. We have a pleasure in thinking that this weather agrees with you, as I thank heaven, it does with us. My wife sends her kind respects. We desire also to be rememberd to Mʳ Rowe and Mʳ Wood. And I am always, Dear Sir, Your most truly obliged and faithful servant

      T. Lindsey.

---

1   See Letter 442, n. 2; Letter 442 is Lindsey's reply to this letter from Frend.

2   Lindsey referred here to the preparation for the new unitarian chapel at Plymouth Dock, which was opened on 27 Apr. 1791. Possibly 'the inclosed' was a copy of the liturgy compiled by Thomas Porter (see Letter 406).

3   Lindsey's letter to Priestley on the catholic relief bill has not survived, but Priestley's reply to it, dated 14 Mar. 1791, is printed in Rutt, I, 106.

4   See Letter 442, n. 4. The speaker of the house of commons was Henry Addington. On 10 Mar. 1791 ('Thursday last') in the house of commons, the catholic relief bill was read a first time without debate and it was ordered that the bill be printed; *CJ*, XLVI, 295. It is not quite clear which MP 'took particular notice' of the trinitarian clause. However, on 1 Apr. 1791, during the debate on the committee stage of the bill, Fox objected to this clause, and John Mitford, the sponsor of the bill, replied that it 'was preserved, because it was found in the act of toleration [of 1689], and he intended to have left it out, for the sake of avoiding discussion'; Cobbett, *Parl. hist.*, XXIX, 114–15.

444. To WILLIAM TAYLEUR   22 MARCH 1791

  Text: JRUL, Lindsey Letters, vol. II, no. 43.
  Printed: McLachlan, *Letters*, p. 67 (second paragraph).
  Addressed: Address missing.
  Postmarked: Postmark missing.

                      London. March. 22. 1791
Dear Sir,

In my last,[1] when I acknowleged the receit of your present of the 500 little tracts to our new Society, I forgot to mention that if you had one or two dozen more to spare I should be much obliged to you for them, as I could dispose of them very usefully.

The restriction about the Trinity which I then mentioned as foisted onto the Bill for the relief of the Catholics is said to have been put in by the Chancellor,[2] and to make their toleration correspond with that of the Protestant Dissenters: but I hope no such excuse will pass. I have been told that Ld Stanhope intends to notice it in the upper house. I had before been told that another Lord would speak his mind upon it. I wish the former would consult and act in concert with his brethren. Else he may do harm, where he intends good, and prevent or defeat the exertions of others in the cause.[3]

Who is this able Dissenting country Attorney who does understand the cause and defend it well in his Letter to Mr Burke? The variety of curious facts he mentions ought to be generally known, and Dissenters in particular should study him to be acquainted with their own principles and situation.[4]

I omitted in my last to mention, that at the meeting of our unitarian Society the second Thursday in this month, we received several additional names of members, and settled some matters about the mode of printing books. Some objections were mentioned by one or two of the members present, not as their own, but as coming from another person, that we should have expressed ourselves in the preamble to our plan in more general terms, &c but these were overruled by it being generally agreed, that we did not intend to be more comprehensive, nor to draw in persons to unite with us who did not hold the proper humanity of Christ, or at least had no objections to be classed with those of that sentiment. But all were surprized at a letter I had received from Mr Frend to be communicated to the society, somewhat to the same purpose as the above objections, but containing some very singular sentiments of the efficacy of X$^{t's}$ obedience as Mediator for the remission of sins, and concluded with wishing that we might expunge out of our preface the words "the most distinguished of the prophets; the creature and messenger of God", and "not his vicegerent".[5] It was however here also agreed to make no alteration.

In a long letter lately come from Mr W. Christie of Montrose, he writes: "You inquire of the state of things in these parts, I am sorry I can give you no very flattering idea of it. In the south of Scotland D^r McGills submission has afforded no little triumph to the orthodox, and will contribute no doubt to prevent the spread of rational religion in that quarter.[6] Dr Erskine, one of the ministers of Edinburgh, has lately published a Vol 12mo. mostly translated from German writers; in which Unitarians, and particularly Dr Priestley are treated with ridicule and disrespect, and disingenuously classed with Deists. As the Doctor is popular, this book will increase the prejudices of readers of a certain class. Several small pieces also in favour of the Trinity have been late published at Edinburgh".[7]

He then goes on to add, that their congregation at Montrose had been much hurt by one or two of them lately turning Deists, but that he hoped good in the end w^d accrue from it, as it had put him on a course of sermons to guard against such errors, which had been of service.[8]

But since this letter from Montrose, I have had a letter from Mr Palmer at Dundee with an account of a far better appearance in that Town and neighbourhood. He also added the inclosed, which I send to you; and which has led me to write to Dr Dalrymple D^r McGill's collegue, and to another person, to be farther informed concerning the facts and the state of D^r McGill's mind, and what was done formerly ab^t a year ago in Lanar[k]shire before his yielding to his adversaries, and what may be done now to save him from doing any thing, thro dejection and fear, against the sense of his own mind. And when I hear any thing more of the matter, you shall be acquainted with it.[9]

We have been much alarmed this last week for the excellent Dr Price. The beginning of it, monday-morning I went to Hackney to see him, having heard that he was much recovered from a fever that had confined him for some time, when I found a surgeon and physician with him. He had neglected himself in a complaint he is subject to, a retention of urine, and the parts were so inflamed, that it was a long time before he could obtain any relief, and still only obtains it by means of an instrument: but I trust he will recover, though it will be slowly.

I have reason to be thankful on all accounts, and particularly that I am so much better in health now than I was about this time last year. Dr Price was 68 completed the 4th of the present month, which I shall be the first of July if I live to see it, so that there is very little difference between us.[10] You are singularly happy that at a much later period you retain such vigour of faculties and usefulness, and tolerable health. May they all continue till the lamp burns out of itself! My wife joins in this pious wish and sends her due respects. I am always Dear Sir

Your most truly obliged and faithful servant

T. Lindsey

We beg to be respectfully remembred to Mr Rowe and Mr Wood.

---

1   Letter 443.

2   Lindsey probably referred here to Lord Thurlow, the lord chancellor, rather than to Pitt, who was chancellor of the exchequer as well as first lord of the treasury.

3   By the time that the catholic relief bill was debated in the house of lords, the 'trinity clause' had been removed from it. Stanhope spoke strongly in favour of the bill during its second reading on 31 May 1791, as did the duke of Leeds and the marquis of Lansdowne, the latter observing 'he had always supported upon the same grounds, the protestant dissenters, and the repeal of the Test Act, as a matter of right to them'; Cobbett, *Parl. hist.*, XXIX, 681–2. The bill, with amendments, was carried in the lords without a division and received the royal assent on 7 June 1791 as 31 Geo. III, c. 32.

4   This work was *A letter to the Right Hon. Edmund Burke, Esq., from a dissenting country attorney; in defence of his civil profession, and religious dissent* (Birmingham, 1791).The Cambridge University Library catalogue attributes this work to 'W. Nash'. A William Nash appears in an unpaginated section of *Browne's general law list for the year 1790* (London, 1790) under Royston, Hertfordshire. 'Mr Nash, Attorney at Law' Royston, Cambridgeshire, is listed as a member of the Unitarian Society in 1791 and 1794; in 1813, he is listed as a member of the society as 'Wm. Nash, Esq. Attorney at Law, Royston, Cambridgeshire'. See *Unitarian Society ... 1791*, p. 12; *Unitarian Society ... 1794*, p. 12; *Unitarian Society ... 1813*, p. 16. It is reasonable to speculate that the 'dissenting country attorney' was William Nash, although Lindsey himself did not make this suggestion in any surviving letter. I am indebted to Professor Wilf Prest for advice on this point.

5   This is a quotation from the preamble to the Unitarian Society's rules and membership (see Letter 437, n. 2), p. 2.

6   For the developments in M'Gill's case, see n. 9, below.

7   Christie's letter to Lindsey seems not to have survived. Christie referred to John Erskine's edition of *Sketches and hints of church history and theological controversy. Chiefly translated or abridged from modern foreign writers. Volume I* (Edinburgh, 1790). In the preface, Erskine criticized Priestley's *History of the corruptions of Christianity* and claimed (p. vi) that, because Priestley rejected the scriptural account of the divinity of Christ, his work was tantamount to deism. A second volume of this work was published in Edinburgh in 1797. Erskine (1721–1803), who held the degree of DD from Glasgow University (1766), was minister of the collegiate, or second charge, of Old Greyfriars, Edinburgh. The 'other small pieces on the Trinity lately published in Edinburgh' included Robert Chalmers, *A sermon preached at the opening of the General Associate synod, at Edinburgh, April 29, 1789* (Edinburgh, 1790); Chalmers, presbyterian minister at Haddington, referred (p. 23) to the 'daring effrontery' of those who attacked the doctrine of the Trinity.

8   Lindsey referred here to William Christie, *An essay on ecclesiastical establishments in religion: shewing their hurtful tendency; and that they cannot be defended, either on principles of reason or scripture. To which are annexed, two discourses. By a protestant dissenter* (Montrose, 1791). The work was dedicated to Thomas Fyshe Palmer. In the first of these discourses, Christie attacked priestcraft and defended revealed religion, by implication in refutation of deist critiques of it. He did not publish the sermons specifically directed against deists.

9   This letter from Thomas Fyshe Palmer to Lindsey is not in DWL or HMCO and seems not to have
    survived. The 'inclosed' is also missing; evidently it contained further information about the case of
    William M'Gill. The events in Lanarkshire the previous year, to which Lindsey referred, concerned
    the accusations of heterodoxy made against M'Gill in the synod of Glasgow and Ayr; see Letter 413,
    n. 6. William Dalrymple was minister of the first charge at Ayr from 1756 until his death in 1814.
10 Lindsey regarded his date of birth as 20 June 1723 (old style) and after the change of calendar in
    1752 considered his birthday to be 1 July (new style). Price's birth is usually stated to have been 23
    Feb. 1723 (old style); see, for example, *Price corr.*, I, xxix. However, Priestley in the 'short sketch'
    of Price's life which he appended to his *Discourse on occasion of the death of Dr. Price, delivered
    at Hackney, on Sunday, May 1, 1791. Also a short sketch of the life of Dr Price, with an account of
    his publications* (London, 1791), p. 37, gave the date of Price's birth as 22 Feb. 1723. If correct, this
    might explain why Lindsey (and presumably Price himself) thought that Price's sixty-eighth birthday
    fell on 4 Mar. 1791 (new style).

445. To RUSSELL SCOTT   24 MARCH 1791

Text:	Scott Coll.
Printed:	McLachlan, 'Lindsey to Scott', 117 (short quotations from second and third paragraphs; first sentence of fourth paragraph; tenth paragraph).
Addressed:	Address missing.
Postmarked:	Postmark missing.

March 24 1791

Dear Sir,

I was greatly relieved by your letter,[1] as was also my wife. For as neither you nor your lady had been in health to boast of, we were alarmed sometimes for one and sometimes for the other. One rule, not a medical one but worth many of them, I would prescribe, which is to avoid anxiety, as much as possible, than which nothing more undermines health & produces chronical complaints; and to be easy and chearful in doing what one is persuaded to be right and our duty, and not to mind consequences, which belong not to us.

It gives me singular satisfaction that our new Society has your approbation, and that you do not blame me for introducing you into it. I wish you would write to your friends at Chichester to send up their names before our general meeting in April, that they may grace our list, which will then be reprinted, with several additional respectable names which have gone through my hands.[2] You will do well not to urge those who have any reluctance, tho' the objections that you mention to have been made, have very little weight in them. I have no doubt but the Society will go on to increase, though we wish to make as good an appearance as we can at first, because it will help to draw out the more timid.

You will probably have heard of the excellent Dr Prices illness – a suppression of urine coming upon him ab^t 10 days since, when he was barely recovered of a bad fever; and for which he has scarce ever, but once or twice since obtained relief, but by the catheter. I trust heaven will preserve his valuable[3] for the public, and for the comfort of many: but he is thought to be in great danger.[4] The day he was first taken ill I had gone to visit him, hearing his fever was past, and unfortunately found the Surgeon and physician at his house.

The case of your brother in law is greatly to be lamented, particularly in hindring that great usefulness which he might have been of to others, had he not given way to vain scruples and scepticism of which there is no end. And in the mean time your worthy sister is highly to be pitied.[5]

The bill for the relief of the Catholic Dissenters is expected to be discussed to day in the house of Commons. You woud be exceedingly pleased with what Mr Fox has twice said upon it.[6] To day it is said he will speak of one of the singular restrictions of their bill; viz.

That this Act is not to extend to any person writing against the Trinity.[7]

What have catholic Dissenters to do with such a Clause, who are all Trinitarian.

The fact is, it did not come from them, but was imposed upon, and brought in to operate in terrorem, and to add a fresh confirmation at a hundred years distance, of the horrid Act of the 9th and 10th of W^m & Mary, which no one dares to put in execution and all pretend to disclaim as illiberal.[8]

I hear too that it will not be suffered to pass unnoticed in the upper house.

I was told yesterday, that 700 of the third edition of Mr Paine's answer to Burke are already sold. It is indeed an admirable work, and Burke a very child in his hands. We are also exceedingly pleased with the letter of a Dissenting County Attorney to him, a real character, and most worthy man; which every Dissenter ought to read, to know his own principles, and also what churchmen are.[9]

If I have omitted noticing any thing in your letter, you must excuse me, as some how or other it has been lost in a confusion of papers, and I have never looked into it since the postman first brought it. My wife joins in kind regards for Mrs Scott and yourself, and I am always very sincerely Yours

T. Lindsey

Dr Priestley will be in Town ab^t the middle of April to stay as usual. He preaches our Anniversary sermon for the college.[10]

London. March. 24
1791.

---

1   Scott's letter to Lindsey seems not to have survived; at the end of this letter to Scott, Lindsey apologized for having lost it 'in a confusion of papers'.

2   This meeting of the Unitarian Society took place at the King's Head tavern in the Poultry on 14 Apr. 1791; Unitarian Society minute book, pp. 11–15. The enrolment of Scott's three friends at Chichester as members was recorded in the minute book (pp. 11–12) on that day; for their names, see Letter 439, n. 6. Scott himself was listed as a member of the society in its first published list of names; *Unitarian Society ... 1791*, p. 11.

3   Word omitted, evidently 'life'.

4   Price died on 19 Apr. 1791.

5   Mary Scott's husband, John Taylor, abandoned unitarianism in the early 1790s and became a quaker; Scott, *Family biography*, pp. 68–73. For the adverse effect on their marriage, see H. McLachlan, *Essays and addresses* (Manchester, 1950), pp. 81ff. Mary Taylor died on 4 June 1793.

6   There was no debate in the commons on the catholic relief bill on 24 Mar. 1791; the next debate on the subject took place on 1 Apr. The two speeches of Fox on the catholic relief bill to which Lindsey referred were probably those of 21 Feb. and 1 Mar. 1791; Cobbett, *Parl. hist.*, XXVIII, 1267–9, 1365–9.

7   See Letter 442, n. 4.

8   The Blasphemy Act of 1698 was an Act of William III (9 and 10 William III, c. 32), not William and Mary; Queen Mary died in 1694. In subsequent letters, Lindsey referred to it in its correct form.

9   See Letter 444, n. 4.

10   This sermon was published as *The proper objects of education in the present state of the world: represented in a discourse delivered on Wednesday, April 27, 1791, at the meeting-house in the Old Jewry, London, to the supporters of the New College at Hackney* (London, 1791). It was preached to commemorate the college's fifth anniversary. See Letter 440 for Priestley's earlier reluctance to give this discourse.

446. To THOMAS BELSHAM   26 MARCH 1791

Text: DWL, MS 12.57 (2).
Printed: Rutt, II, 114 n. § (part of the fifth paragraph, with omissions:
                'I have considered … paid to Christ')
Addressed: To/The Rev^d. Mr Belsham/New College/Hackney
Postmarked: Postmark missing.

Note: Lindsey did not give the year of this letter, although the context of the debates over the preamble
to the unitarian society's rules makes clear that the year was 1791. The year was added in brackets by
another hand immediately beneath the day, month and date, which are in Lindsey's hand. The absence of
a postmark probably indicates that Lindsey arranged for the letter to be delivered to Belsham by hand,
as indicated in the final paragraph.

Saturday. march. 26.
(1791)

Dear Sir,

Where many are concerned and some do not heartily accord, it is hard to represent
any thing in such a way as shall not be cavil'd at.

It has been alleged, that in the Preamble to the plan of our Unitarian society, we
appear not quite certain ourselves of the truth of Christianity:

that we labour for words to express ourselves by repeating the same again and
again in our two first paragraphs, besides making use of violent and railing language
afterwards.

I do not know whether it be worth the while to attend to these things. But if it
be of any consequence, you will judge whether your excellent sentiments might be
varied in their dress in some such way as I have put them in the inclosed.[1]

I have considered again and again the language objected to by Mr Frend, *viz. is
the creature and messenger of God*, and do not see how we can relinquish it. And I
must own *not his Vicegerent* seems to have a particular propriety in it as opposed to
the worship which Socinus paid to Christ: though I shall not stand out alone against
any alterations or concessions you and others may agree to make, if consistent with
our fixed principle.[2]

The *intemperate* language objected to you was so good as to say that you would
try to vary it a little, tho' I hope so as not to lose its force –

And as I have heard our speaking of trying the *grand* experiment as a mountebank
phrase, perhaps it may not be amiss to leave it out and say simply; *to try the
experiment.*[3]

Pag. 3. Quere. As there is *excite* the attention in the first page – if it were here,
draw the attention.[4]

I expect to have an opportunity to send this by some hand to morrow. With my
wifes best respects I remain always your much obliged and faithful affectionate
servant

        T. Lindsey.

---

1   The 'inclosed', clearly, was a draft of the Unitarian Society's preamble, with amendments in Lind-
    sey's hand. It appears not to have survived.
2   In the Unitarian Society's preamble the expression settled upon was that Christ was 'the creature and
    messenger of God, and not his equal, nor his vicegerent'; *Unitarian Society … 1791*, p. 2. Frend had
    declared in his *Thoughts on subscription to religious tests* (St Ives, 1788), p. 26n, that he 'professes
    himself to be a unitarian, distinguished from the Arians, by denying the pre-existence of Christ; and
    from the Socinians, by denying the propriety of addressing prayers to any but the one true God. The
    time it is hoped is not far distant when men will cease to be called by the names of Athanasius, Arius,
    or Socinus.'

3   'Try the experiment' was the expression which appeared in *Unitarian Society ... 1791*, p. 2.

4   In *Unitarian Society ... 1791*, p. 1, the relevant phraseology was 'exciting the attention of men to the genuine doctrines of revelation'; on p. 3, the expression settled upon was 'naturally attract the attention of others, and produce that freedom of enquiry, that liberal discussion, and that fearless profession of principles embraced after due examination, which can be formidable to nothing but error and vice, and which must eventually be subservient to the cause of truth and virtue, and to the best interests of mankind'.

447. To WILLIAM TAYLEUR   2 APRIL 1791

Text: JRUL, Lindsey Letters, vol. II, no. 44.
Printed: McLachlan, *Letters*, pp. 99–100 (fifth and sixth paragraphs).
Addressed: Address missing.
Postmarked: Postmark missing.

London. April. 2. 1791

Dear Sir,

I hope you continue to enjoy tolerable health, as we do, heaven be praised for it. I wish I coud say any thing like this of good Dr Price: but I fear his continuance will not be long among us. The latter end of the last and the begining of this week he was better, but his disorder has returned with unpromising symptoms, and there has another surgeon been called in, who inclines to think the source of the complaint may be the stone, and not ulcerations in the bladder as was supposed. But this to be particularly examined into to day. If there be any better hopes of his recovery, I will write again very soon.

Who should call upon me here not many days ago but Mr Austen from Tunbridge? Unluckily I was not within, but he left a note where he was, and I waited on him the next morning as he could not undertake to walk again to us from the city, where he took up his abode at a friend's. He is a good figure and the manners of a gentleman, aspect rather severe, but soon unbent to discover, the warm heart and good affections underneath. Hypochondriac, you soon perceive; always as he says, with a kind of stupor in his head: of real, or supposed (wch in his case are the same) debility in his feet, (tho' an apparent firm tread) so that he said he c^d not have walked to our house had he not supported himself by the arm of a gentleman all the way. We soon became acquainted, and particularly as he was only about three years below my standing, and of Queens college, Cambridge, where we had many comon acquaintance. He is not to be touched directly about frequenting the Church-service, but I think he will be brought himself to see its wrongness.[1]

On the demise of their late vicar, a candid, liberal man,[2] the famous M^r or Dr Vicessimus Knox, Mast^r of their free school, tho he had never once offer^d to assist the infirm vicar, put himself forward to serve the sequestration: and in his first sermon, from *why art thou so heavy* o my soul, &c[3] he first descanted with so much rhetoric on the loss of a promising infant, as to set all the women in tears, who were mothers: next on the loss of a friend, with the same pathos described: then at once he turned himself to the doctrine of the Trinity, deplored the defection of many from it, to the loss of their own souls, and great danger of infecting others, and so to the end, plainly aiming at Mr A. who was present. The next sunday the Preacher sang the same song again, but Mr A. suspecting it, was not present, but was told of it by his family and friends; and particularly that with a short preface, that he was assurd the congregation in general would be glad to hear it repeated again, he concluded his discourse with the four invocations in the litany.[4] It was thought Mr K. wanted to have had the vicarage, but was disappointed.[5] And he is said now, to be often preaching in London, and always vehemently orthodox. His school, which some years since consisted of 70 or 80 boarders, is now reduced to seven or eight; which is not to be regretted. He is so utterly disliked by the gentlemen of the county, who at first favoured him, that he will rather contribute among them to bring the doctrine of the Trinity into discredit.[6]

I hope that now Mr A. has once been in Town, tho business compelled him, he will make the attempt again; and I have promised, that if we sh^d have a call to Tunbridge wells this year, we shall certainly wait upon him.[7]

You will see in Mr John Wesley's funeral sermon, if that be a true sample, that the doctrine of the foundery is become much more liberal and rational than it was wont to be, tho still retaining some of their peculiarities. But the concluding part, which contains an account of their old father as they call him, for some days before he went out of the world, is far more unscriptural and enthusiastic: but it seems to have [been] put upon the pious old man, by the zealous and devout women that were around him.[8]

Dr Priestley may have told you that we expect a free and unprejudiced account of him from one who was formerly in connection with him as a preacher, but now left[?] the estabilished church; a Mr Hampson.[9]

Having received the inclosed from Mr Toulmin of Chowbent I send it to shew the zeal and attention of him, and his fellow minister of Bolton, J.H. John Holland. The good temper shewn by both cannot be sufficiently commended.[10]

The week after next we expect Dr Priestley; this he is at Manchester, where he is to preach to morrow, according to his last letter to me.[11]

My wife sends her due respects, and I am always, Dear Sir, Your most truly obliged and faithful servant

    T. Lindsey.

---

1 Born in 1726, Henry Austen was three years younger than Lindsey. A former pupil of Tonbridge school, Kent, he was admitted to Queens' College, Cambridge, in 1743 and obtained his BA in 1747. He took his MA from Clare College in 1750, was a fellow of Clare from 1748 to 1760, and became rector of West Wickham, Kent, in 1761.

2 The 'late vicar' of St Peter and St Paul's church, Tonbridge, was Henry Harpur, a product of St John's College, Cambridge, who, having served since 1756, died in Oct. 1790. His successor as vicar was not Vicesimus Knox (1752–1821), but John Rawstorn Papillon (d. 1837) who held this vicarage from 1791 to 1803 and was rector of Chawton from 1802 to 1836. Like Henry Austen, Papillon was a former undergraduate at Queens' College, Cambridge. He was subsequently a fellow of the college and in later life was much associated with Jane Austen's circle at Chawton.

3 Psalm xlii. 5, 'Why art thou cast down, o my soul'; rendered as 'Why art thou so heavy, o my soul' in a motet of Orlando Gibbons. Knox included this sermon in his collected *Sermons, chiefly intended to promote faith, hope and charity* (London, 1792); it is Sermon II, entitled 'Hope in God', and may be found at pp. 22–48. After the references to the loss of a child and of a friend, Knox denounced, without naming anyone, the 'enlightened despiser of the Holy Trinity, who dares to strip our Saviour of all share of the divine nature, and to blaspheme the Holy Ghost, his sanctifier, and to cast Jesus, his redeemer, from the throne of heaven (p. 38).

4 The four invocations in the Church of England litany were those to God the father, God the son, God the holy ghost and the Trinity.

5 See n. 2, above. During his headmastership of Tonbridge school, Knox was also curate of the chapelry of Shipbourne, Kent, and vicar of Hadlow, Kent. He also held livings in Essex.

6 Knox was headmaster of Tonbridge school from 1778 to 1812, in succession to his father. He was succeeded by his own son, Thomas Knox, who held this office from 1812 until his death in 1843.

7 There is no evidence that Lindsey re-visited Tunbridge Wells later in 1791.

8 John Whitehead, *A discourse delivered at the new chapel in the city-road, on the ninth of March 1791, at the funeral of the late Rev. Mr. John Wesley* (London, 1791). The description of Wesley's last days

may be found at pp. 58–70. Whitehead (?1740–1804), at various times a methodist lay preacher, schoolmaster and physician, published a two-volume *Life of the Rev. John Wesley ... with the life of the Rev. Charles Wesley ... The whole forming a history of methodism, in which the principles and economy of the methodists are unfolded* (London, 1793–6). This work provoked much controversy among methodists, partly because of its critique of Wesley's 'superstition' and partly through its claim that some of Wesley's most prominent followers had exploited their founding father's supposed senility to arrogate power to themselves. The foundry chapel, at Moorfields, London, so called because its origin was in a former royal cannon foundry purchased by Wesley in 1739, after his break with the Moravians, became an important centre of early methodism. The site is close to what became Wesley's chapel in the City Road.

9   The work was John Hampson, *Memoirs of the late Rev. John Wesley, A.M. With a review of his life and writing, and a history of methodism, from it's commencement in 1729, to the present time* (3 vols., Sunderland, 1791). Hampson (1760–1819) was brought up as a methodist, left the movement, graduated at Oxford University (BA 1791, MA 1792), conformed to the established church and served as rector of Holy Trinity church, Sunderland, from 1795 to 1819. He was the son of John Hampson of Tunbridge Wells, with whom Lindsey was acquainted; see Vol. I, Letter 375; also Letters 425–6.

10   Probably the 'inclosed' was a copy of the short-lived *Christian Miscellany*; see Letters 418, n. 7 and 420, n. 2. J. H. was John Holland, minister of Bank Street chapel, Bolton, from 1789 to 1820.

11   For Priestley's visit to Manchester in Apr. 1791, where he preached for William Hawkes at Mosley Street chapel, see Rutt, I, 108–10. See also G. M. Ditchfield, 'The early history of Manchester College', *Transactions of the Historic Society of Lancashire and Cheshire*, CXXIII (1971), 83–4.

448. To WILLIAM TAYLEUR   9 APRIL 1791

Text: JRUL, Lindsey Letters, vol. II, no. 45.
Printed: McLachlan, *Letters*, p. 67 (seventh paragraph, where the letter is mis-dated 7 April 1791); p. 131 (all but last sentence of fourth paragraph).
Addressed: Address missing.
Postmarked: Postmark missing.

London. April. 9. 1791

Dear Sir,

I take a small sheet, that I may not too much croud my cover, and foreseeing that it will contain all I have to say.

Your sanction, and that of Mr Harries and Mr Rowe of the sufficient comprehensiveness of the Preamble of our unitarian Society, comes very seasonably to give encouragement if there should be any farther question raised about it, and I thank you for it.[1] We propose to desire Dr Priestley to take the chair at the meeting, and then I doubt not of all going on well.

After the meeting is over, I shall be glad, as you most surely have a claim, to acquaint you with all the particulars which I think you w^d wish to know relating to it and the members.

I am as much an idolater of Mr Paine's book as you are, and trust our nation will profit by it: but think it w^d have been more read if some things toward the latter end had been omitted.[2] It still continues to sell rapidly.

It reminds me of Mr Day's life, by the fine pen of Mr Keir, just come out, which by all means you must see. How edifying the example itself and the reflexions of the biographer, in religious as well as civil respects! And yet the latter is cautious of saying that his friend was a christian, or had any respect to a future state: although he mentions his reading prayers on a Sunday and the moral parts of the gospel to his family and neighbours.[3]

I have not yet been able to procure Warner's edition of A Lady's religion, but hope soon to have it by means of a friend.[4]

How much to be honoured and esteemed by all is Mr Fox! Upon the Catholic Dissenters Bill last night, among other excellent things, he declared his intention of bring[ing] in a bill on better and more extensive principles for the relief of Protestant as well as Catholic Dissenters; if the ministry w^d not undertake it.[5]

The times certainly require and countenance such an undertaking. Mr Wardrop's letter w^h I inclose, shews what an evil spirit is still stirring in Scotland.[6] I put in also Mr Palmers letter to me, that you may know as much as I do of the worthy man, except some things in his praise a year ago to me by Dr Dalrymple of Ayr.[7]

As I am not certain that I sent you a short letter relating to D^r McGill, which I got printed at the time of his last persecution and intended to have had circulated for his benefit, but was prevented by his unfortunate concessions to his adversaries, I inclose a copy. It was written to me by a valuable person, Mr Turner, Dissenting Minister at Newcastle upon Tyne.[8]

I think I shewed you one letter from good Mr Moore, when I had the pleasure of seeing You at Shrewsbury, upon his removal from a congregation of fiery Calvinists to his present quiet abode. You will not be displeased with this. The friend he alludes to was not Mr Dodson, our Treasurer, who is not wont to do such things.[9]

Two days since the account of Dr Price was that there was some hope: I am fearful for him, on acc^t of his extreme debility; but shall send you what I learn of him to day, before I seal my letter. My wife desires her respects and congratulates you on our fine mild weather. Our best comp^ts wait upon Mr Rowe and Mr Wood and I am always your most truly obliged and faithful affectionate servant

T. Lindsey

P.S. Dr Price was something better at 10 o'clock last night, as his nephew[10] acquaints.

Pray look on the outside of the cover, which will yield some amusement.[11]

1   The letter (presumably from Tayleur) to Lindsey conveying this 'sanction' seems not to have survived.

2   Although no letters from Tayleur to Lindsey from 1791 survive in JRUL, C2^13, Tayleur's approbation of Paine's *Rights of man*, part I, was not surprising. One of the 'things towards the latter end' of which Lindsey disapproved was Paine's comment on the Brunswick princes (see Letter 440, n. 9).

3   James Keir's *An account of the life and writings of Thomas Day, Esq.*, was published in London by John Stockdale in 1791. For Day's cautiously expressed Christianity, see p. 121; for his scepticism, see pp. 108–9; for his philanthropic activities in his Surrey neighbourhood, see pp. 134–5. Day (1748–89), a political pamphleteer and member of the Lunar Society of Birmingham, was married to Esther Milnes, in whose matrimonial prospects Lindsey had taken an interest in 1776; see Vol. I, Letter 160.

4   *A lady's religion. In a letter to the Honourable my Lady Howard* was first published in London, without an author's name, in 1697, with a second edition in 1704. In 1748, a third edition appeared in London, entitled *A lady's religion. In two letters to the Honourable Lady Howard. By a divine of the Church of England*. The preface to the 1748 edition appeared with the initials of the editor, F. W., i.e. Ferdinando Warner (1703–68), at that time rector of St Michael and Holy Trinity, Queenhithe, London, and subsequently a prolific author on religious topics. The version which was re-published in 1793 with the title *A representation of true religion* in *Tracts printed and published by the Unitarian Society*, vol. VI (see Letter 435, n. 2) was based on Warner's edition of 1748.

5   On 8 Apr. 1791 ('last night') during the debate on the report stage of the catholic relief bill, Fox complained that the bill did not go far enough and stated that, if no other MP did so, he would bring in 'a better and more extensive one'; Cobbett, *Parl. hist.*, XXIX, 118–19.

6   James Wardrop of Glasgow is listed as a member of the Unitarian Society in 1791. On 14 May 1801 the monthly committee meeting of the Unitarian Society noted that his name had been 'withdrawn from the catalogue of members'; Unitarian Society minute book, p. 74. There is no evidence of the survival of his letter to Lindsey, whose reference to 'an Evil spirit' still stirring in Scotland probably

reflects a concern over the prosecution of William M'Gill; see Letters 413, n. 6, 444, n. 9 and 454, n. 7.

7   This letter from Palmer to Lindsey, like that to which Lindsey referred in Letter 444 – assuming that it was a different letter – seems not to have survived. William Dalrymple evidently expressed this praise for Palmer in a (regrettably non-surviving) letter to Lindsey.

8   Possibly this was a non-surviving manuscript letter from William Turner of Newcastle to Lindsey, who probably arranged for it to be printed by Joseph Johnson in London, although I have not located a copy. It is likely that a source for this letter was *Dr M'Gill vindicated from the charge of heresy, and the erroneous assertions of his adversaries briefly refuted ... by a friend to truth* (Edinburgh, n.d.).

9   This was Henry Moore (1732–1802), a former pupil of Philip Doddridge at Northampton and of Caleb Ashworth at Daventry; minister at Modbury, Devon, from 1757 to 1788 and at Liskeard, Cornwall, from 1788 until his death in 1802. He is listed as a member of the Unitarian Society in 1791 (minute book, p. 12; *Unitarian Society ... 1791*, p. 12). His 'present quiet abode' was Liskeard; the 'fiery Calvinists' had been part of his congregation at Modbury. He was to have been a contributor to Priestley's proposed translation of the Bible between 1788 and 1791; see Brooks, 'Priestley's plan', 92 (where he is wrongly named as John Moore); he contributed to the series of *Commentaries and essays* published by the SPKS; and was a noted hymn-writer. Moore's letter to Lindsey seems not to have survived, so the friend to whom he alluded remains unidentified.

10   Probably George Cadogan Morgan of the Gravel Pit meeting, Hackney.

11   The cover, disappointingly, has not survived.

449. To WILLIAM TAYLEUR   14 APRIL 1791

Text: JRUL, Lindsey Letters, vol. III, no. 30.
Printed: McLachlan, 'More letters', 370–1 (fifth and seventh
                 paragraphs; first part of first sentence of eighth paragraph).
Addressed: To/William Tayleur Esqr./Shrewsbury
Postmarked: AP 15 91

London
Thursday night
April. 14. 1791

Dear Sir,

I returned from our society about 8 o' clock, leaving a great part of the company behind me adjourning into another room to take tea and coffee, and finding some company at home, it is somewhat late before I can take pen in hand, but I am resolved to say a few words, as I am engaged to call on Dr Priestley early to morrow morning to attend the Examinations at the college.

Our first business to day at the King's head was to chuse a Chairman, which Dr Priestley obligingly complied with at last on being much pressed into the Office.[1]

We then took account of the New Members whose names had been given in since our former meeting: and that being settled, we began to ballot for the different books that has [*sic*] been before proposed to the society, some to be purchased, some reprinted, and what number of copies of each. Last of all your obliging present of 500 copies of the tract you sent was balloted for, and I need not say, that it was universally approved and accepted, and the thanks of the Society I [word illegible] I was desired to present to you for it.[2]

We were very nearly unanimous in approving our preamble with some few small alterations that had been made in it, and the two paragraphs in your letter relating to it which I read contributed not a little to bring us to this disposition.[3]

But what will give you singular pleasure, after this business was over, a proposal was made, which had been before concerted by D^r P ___ y, Mr S. Heywood and one or two more of us; that whereas by certain Acts of Parliament we were liable to heavy penalties for pursuing the objects of the Society, the Chairman with two other persons sh^d wait upon Mr Fox who had always been a true friend to the Rights of private judgment &c to desire he would at the time he judged proper move the Commons house to have the 9. 10. of William and any other Acts repealed to which we were obnoxious.

This was unanimously approved; and in consequence of it, as soon as the Catholic Dissenters bill has been through both houses, Mr Fox is to be applied to.[4]

Nothing could be more fortunate than to have a Society of persons formed who were particularly aggrieved by the laws in question, and who might with such propriety apply for a remedy, when it would not have been easy to have brought the Dissenters in general to unite in such an application.

There were near 60 persons who dined together to day, wth some few gentlemen who favoured our cause brought in by some Members, Mr Rous, author of that very clever reply to Burke,[5] Sir Geo. Stanton,[6] Mr Perry,[7] Mr Porson two foreigners.[8] Every thing went on with great hilarity and decorum: the toast[s] were well chosen, and I believe will be printed.[9] We had with us two M.P. Mr Martin, and Mr W. Smith.

As soon as our Preamble, Rules, and New list of names are printed, they will be sent, but I shall most probably write again before.

It is thought the minister will not dare to engage in a war, with so large a minority against him.[10] The king is said to be very low-spirited and nervous. The Doctor and Surgeons are now agreed that the excellent Dr Price cannot now continue many days: a kind of atrophy come on, that nothing nourishes him. I congratulate you on this fine mild season. My wife desires to add her due respects, and I am always your most truly obliged and affectionate servant

T. Lindsey.

---

1   The Unitarian Society minute book, p. 11, and the report of the meeting in the *Morning Chronicle*, 15 Apr. 1791, confirm that Priestley was indeed in the chair at the meeting on 14 Apr. 1791.

2   Forty-four new members were listed at the meeting on 14 Apr. 1791; a series of books to be adopted by the society was approved; the tract sent by Tayleur was *Representation of the nature of true religion*; Unitarian Society minute book, pp. 11–15. The *Morning Chronicle,* 15 Apr. 1791, reported that the meeting was attended, *inter alia*, by 'A number of the most distinguished gentlemen in the metropolis, of Unitarian principles'.

3   The entry in the Unitarian Society minute book for the meeting on 14 Apr. 1791 (pp. 11–15) made no mention of any discussion over the preamble or of Tayleur's letter. It simply noted (p. 12) a resolution that a new impression of the rules, the revised circular letter, and a new list of members be printed 'forthwith'. This letter from Tayleur to Lindsey is not in JRUL, C2¹³.

4   This resolution may be found in the Unitarian Society minute book, p. 14. For the society's leadership in the promotion of this petition, see Ditchfield, 'Unitarian petition', 46–52.

5   George Rous, *Thoughts on government: occasioned by Mr Burke's reflections, &c. In a letter to a friend* (London, 1790). The book reached a fourth edition in 1791. Rous (1744–1802) was the chairman of the meeting at the Crown and Anchor on 14 July 1791; see *Morning Chronicle*, 15 July 1791. He was also the author of *A letter to the Right Honourable Edmund Burke, in reply to his appeal from the new to the old whigs* (London, 1791).

6   Possibly Sir George Staunton (1737–1801), diplomat, physician and adviser to colonial governors; he served as secretary to Lord Macartney when the latter was governor of Madras in the 1780s; was created a baronet in 1785; and provided important information about India to Edmund Burke.

7   Probably James Perry (1756–1821), joint proprietor of the *Morning Chronicle* and a supporter of the Foxite whigs. In 1793, he was prosecuted (and acquitted) on a charge of seditious libel.

8   No surviving report of the meeting identifies the two foreigners. Possible candidates are the two French protestant ministers named by Lindsey in Letter 430.

9   A list of these toasts was published in the *Morning Chronicle*, 15 Apr. 1791. According to the Unitarian Society minute book (p. 16), fifty members and friends of the society attended the dinner on 14 Apr.

10 On 12 Apr. 1791, in the house of commons, an opposition motion moved by Charles Grey and critical of the ministry's belligerent approach to Russia over the Turkish fortress of Ochakov was defeated by 253 votes to 173. Three days later, a further opposition motion criticizing the ministry's proposals for supplies in support of the necessary armaments was defeated by 254 votes to 162; Cobbett, *Parl. hist.*, XXIX, 164–217, 217–49. The size of the minority vote was considerably higher than usual, and indicated that there was considerable unease over Pitt's policy towards Russia.

450. To WILLIAM FREND   23 APRIL 1791

Text: CUL, Add. MS 7886 (Frend papers), no. 167.
Addressed: To/The Rev^d. W^m. Frend/fellow of Jesus college/Cambridge.
Endorsed: [A few mathematical calculations]
Postmarked: AP 23 91

London April. 23. 1791.

Dear Sir,

I had intended to have written several days since Dr Priestley came among us, but have not found time for it. I presume you may have heard something of our proceedings at our General Meeting the day after his arrival, and perhaps have seen in the papers the account of some matters that passed after dinner.[1] The business of balloting for books &c went readily on without any interruption but that of some of our members to caution us not to outgo our finances at our first setting out. And no exception was made to the preface to our plan save to one or two epithets we had used, which we agreed to soften though we could not intirely give up as was desired. But we hope that an explanation of the design of our society by one of our members, you will easily conjecture who, which will be printed and distributed, will take off all objections of the kind.[2]

It was but two days ago that I had the opportunity of seeing Mr Dodson and Dr Priestley together, and talking with them of the Translation, and the state it was in. D^r P _____ y has brought up the Psalms, Proverbs and Ecclesiastes, and says that what he has done has cost him more labour than any other work he had been engaged in. He is to go on to Ezekiel and Daniel, and Mr Dodson undertakes Jeremiah and the Minor prophets, and has made progress in the latter: but they do not expect to be in readiness to go to the Press before the next spring.[3]

They were rejoiced to see that you were in such forwardness and good heart as your last letter bespoke, and hope you will go on with the same alacrity. And I trust all will be in such forwardness so as to have time to look over each others work before any part be handed to the press.[4]

I mentiond to Dr Priestley your invitation to take Cambridge in his way to Birmingham. And he desired I would tell you with his kind respects that it is absolutely impossible, as he is engaged in Town every day till it is of necessity for him to set out for home, which is to be, May 5. Besides his anniversary sermon on wednesday next, he has found new work cut out for him, being pressed and having consented to preach the excellent Dr Price's funeral sermon, which will be the sunday following; to morrow being his duty for me, when he gives us the 2^d part of his Sermon on the resurrection, originally preached at Buxton, which will be printed, as will the two other sermons of course, and all do great good.[5]

I must not omit to mention a resolution passed at our General Meeting, to apply to Mr Fox to move for a repeal of those Acts which particularly aggrieve our society, especially that of 9 and 10 W^m. but to leave it to his discretion to chuse the proper time. And he is to be waited upon for this purpose to day.[6] What with the expenses of the Spanish armament, the preparations for and threatenings of a Russian war, tho' the Minister it is thought has been driven off from this last;[7] the free discourse on religious impositions in the house of Commons occasioned by the Catholic Bill; M[r] Burke's obstinate churchism, his extreme favour with the king, the stirrings in Kent and Sussex ab[t] tithes particularly of hops;[8] those at Manchester which you will see in the papers[9] &c &c &c matters seem in a vast ferment, and working towards something I believe for the good of our nation and of the world. A friend of mine is so persuaded of it, that he wants the bustle to begin soon now that he is not old and able to bear his part in it.[10]

Believe me always, with my wifes respects
            most sincerely Yours
                  T. Lindsey.

I have forgot to add that no ones labours are beyond those of M[r] Garnham.[11] How far M[r] Belsham has gone with Job, we are to learn in a day or two when we are to meet him.[12]

---

1   See Letter 449.

2   The member of the Unitarian Society who was asked to undertake this explanation was Thomas Belsham; minute book, p. 15. It served as a draft of the published preamble to the *Unitarian Society ... 1791*.

3   For the projected new translation of the Bible, see Letter 390, nn. 9 and 10. For this division of labour between Priestley and Dodson, see Brooks, 'Priestley's plan', 91–2. The project was brought to an end by the destruction of most of Priestley's manuscripts in the Birmingham riots of July 1791, although it played some part in his *Notes on all the books of scripture, for the use of the pulpit and private families* (4 vols., Northumberland, 1803–4).

4   Frend's contribution to the new translation of the Bible was to be the historical books of the Old Testament; see Brooks, 'Priestley's plan', 91. The plan was that the contributors would review and comment critically on each other's work, as Garnham did in his letters to Frend, CUL, Add. MS 7886, nos. 80 and 82–3, 28 Mar. 1790 and n.d. (?1790). The letter from Frend to Lindsey, reporting good progress, seems not to have survived.

5   For Priestley's discourse on the death of Price, see Letter 452, n. 2; for his sermon at the anniversary of Hackney College, see Letter 445, n. 10; for his sermon on the resurrection, preached at Buxton in Sept. 1790, see Letter 429, n. 5.

6   This resolution was duly recorded in the Unitarian Society minute book, p. 15.

7   War with Spain had been avoided in Oct. 1790; see Letter 428, n. 14; for the possibility of war with Russia over Ochakov, see Letter 449, n. 10.

8   When, speaking in the house of commons on the corn importation and exportation bill on 4 Apr. 1791, Charles James Fox denounced tithes as oppressive and their collection as 'harsh and injurious', he was probably responding to the 'stirrings' to which Lindsey referred. See *St James's Chronicle*, 2–5 Apr. 1791. The tithing of relatively 'new' crops, particularly hops, had been controversial in the diocese of Canterbury from the late seventeenth century; see Jeremy Gregory, *Restoration, Reformation and reform, 1660–1828. Archbishops of Canterbury and their diocese* (Oxford, 2000), pp. 150–1. The background to this question is analysed in Eric J. Evans, *The contentious tithe: the tithe problem and English agriculture 1750–1850* (London, 1976).

9   The 'stirrings' at Manchester included a conflict between local high church anglicans and whigs over the town's hospital board and a series of clashes between the boroughreeve Thomas Walker and the barrister and Tory lawyer William Roberts. Walker was publicly attacked as a supporter of the French Revolution. See John Bohstedt, *Riots and community politics in England and Wales, 1790–1810* (Cambridge, MA, 1983), pp. 106–7. For examples of 'stirrings' in Manchester over moves for the repeal of the Test and Corporation Acts, see Letter 406, n. 20.

10   Lindsey did not name this friend; obvious possibilities include William Turner of Newcastle and John Rowe.

11   In 1790 and early in 1791, Garnham was 'labouring' at the epistle of St Paul to the Hebrews as part of his section of the new translation of the Bible; CUL, Add. MS 7886, nos. 82–3, Garnham to Frend, n.d., ?1790.

12 Belsham was indeed working on the book of Job for the new translation of the Bible; see Rutt, I, 73.

451. To WILLIAM TAYLEUR   27 APRIL 1791

Text:	JRUL, Lindsey Letters, vol. II, no. 46.
Printed:	McLachlan, *Letters*, p. 126 (most of sixth paragraph).
Addressed:	[In Hannah Lindsey's hand] To/William Tayleur Esqʳ./ Shrewsbury
Endorsed:	27ᵗʰ Ap – 91
Postmarked:	AP 27 91

London. april. 27 1791.

Dear Sir,

Since Dʳ Priestley came to Town, I have not, and believe I shall not have the leisure I wish to write to you. It will be a pleasure to you however to hear that he is in the most compleat health I have seen at any time. The two sundays which he has been with us, he has preached to the largest audiences that were ever seen in our chapel, especially the last sunday.[1] I need not say how most important both discourses were, being those preached at Buxton, and I am persuaded will be of great use to many when printed which they are soon to be, as many and some unbelievers in particular were much impressed with them.[2]

Since my last I attended the examinations at the college. Dʳ Priestley as well as myself were above measure pleased with all the lectures and the pupils, especially those under Mʳ Belshams care, and when able I never shall miss attendance for the future. Young Mʳ Harries acquitted himself remarkably well, and there is not any one of better character in all respects in the college.[3]

As I am writing in the midst of company, your obliging present is brought from Mʳ. Longman's, for which I thank You.[4]

I must also beg the favour of you to send me Mʳ Austen's letter with an accᵗ of his quitting, directed for me under Cover to –

John Lee Esqʳ. Lincolns Inn fields, London as I want to shew it to Dʳ Priestley having the writers permission.[5] He returns to Birmingham the latter end of the next week, and is engaged every day, as wᵈ be the case was he to stay ever so long.

Yesterday we attended the funeral of the excellent Dʳ Price.[6] Dʳ Kippis spoke over the grave, which I could not well hear: but the scene itself was most instructive.[7] He was in much torture two days before he died but perfectly sensible to the last. I reckon it a great privilege and felicity that he died in the midst of his usefulness, before great infirmity came on. His private & public virtues considered, I do not think Dissenters had ever his equal.

I write this as I am going to the Old Jewry to hear Dʳ Priestley, and afterwards to dine at the college.

My wife desires her due respects to you, and we desire to be rememberd with all regards to Mʳ Rowe and Mʳ Wood. Excuse this υστερον προτερον,[8] I shall hope soon to write again, and remain always,

Dear Sir, Your most truly obliged and faithful affectionate servant

T. Lindsey.

---

1 Sunday 17 and 24 Apr. 1791.

2 In referring to 'both discourses', Lindsey probably meant that Priestley's *The evidence of the resurrection of Jesus considered* had been preached in two parts at Essex Street chapel as well as at

Buxton. Moreover, in his *Address to the Jews*, Priestley cited the resurrection (pp. xviii–xix) 'as the most important fact in the gospel history' and proof that Jesus was a true prophet.

3   For 'Young Mr Harries' (i.e. Thomas Harries) at Hackney College, see Letter 412, n. 4.

4   Possibly this 'obliging present' from Tayeur, via Thomas Longman in Piccadilly, was the batch of 500 copies of *A representation of true religion*; see Letter 435, n. 2.

5   Henry Austen's resignation of the rectory of West Wickham, Kent, was formally accepted by the bishop of Rochester (John Thomas) on 18 Dec. 1783; Centre for Kentish Studies, ref. DRb/Ar1/18 (Rochester Bishop's Register). Disappointingly, I have not located Austen's letter which contained the account of his resignation.

6   Richard Price's funeral, and interment in Bunhill Fields burial ground, took place on 26 Apr. 1791. According to the *Morning Chronicle*, 27 Apr. 1791, those present, in addition to Lindsey, Priestley, Kippis and Joseph Towers, included the duke of Portland and Earl Stanhope.

7   Andrew Kippis published this sermon as *An address, delivered at the interment of the late Rev. Dr. Richard Price* (London, 1791).

8   'Making the latter thing the former', i.e. putting the last thing first. I am indebted to Mr David Powell for advice as to this quotation.

452. To WILLIAM TAYLEUR   7 MAY 1791

Text: JRUL, Lindsey Letters, vol. II, no. 47.
Printed: McLachlan, *Letters*, p. 68 (sixth paragraph); pp. 115–16
                    (third paragraph).
Addressed: To/William Tayleur Esqr/Shrewsbury
Endorsed: 7th May – 91
Postmarked: MA 7 91

-------------- Heaven be thanked, my most worthy friend, that your life has been so much prolonged beyond the age of man. May the days that shall be added be still days of usefulness, as you wish to Dr Priestley, and of no painful suffering. Feeble as the body is and has been, I reckon you peculiarly happy that the mind is so vigorous and retains its powers. I know but one like you; but he, tho' liberal in some degree, has lost his openness to conviction and stopt short.[1]

It will be a great satisfaction to you to know that Dr Priestley left us yester-evening at 5 in perfect health, and we trust has been some hours safely arrived at home. He acknowleges that at no period of his life was he ever better. And his fatigues of all sorts here called for all his strength. An hour before he set out he corrected the last proof of his College-anniversary sermon and of that for the excellent Dr Price: and as they will both be out by the middle of next week, I shall inquire of Mr Longman if he has any parcell soon for Eddowes, and desire him to inclose a copy of each for you.[2] His important Discourses on Christ's resurrection he prints at Birmingham.[3]

Two anecdotes concerning the former Sermon at the Old Jewry, you will be pleased with. A great number of ministers of the Independants as well as the ch. of E. were present. One of the former, when the whole was over, said to one that stood next him: *Well, it must be said he fears neither God nor man*. Another, on the idolatry of Jesus Christ being named as one of the present great corruptions of Christianity, said to some about him; *he ought to be sent to Newgate for that*.[4]

Yesterday a merchant in the city read us an account he had received from Holland, that the Poles had at last exerted themselves, and with the connivance and aid of their present excellent King, Poniatowsky, were in a way to gain their freedom, and from the basest vassals upon earth the greatest part of them likely to emerge into a liberty equal to that of the French. It will be most happy, if any thing approaching to this take place.[5]

You will see in the debates of last night that M[r] Burke is endeavouring all he can to keep all the word[6] in such civil and religious fetters as he thinks good for them. Many wish that he had been allowed to speak his whole mind, so that there might have been an intire separation of such an high-church declaimer from better men.[7]

The other day I met D[r] Somerville, one of the Ministers from Scotland to carry on their application to Parliament for relief from the Test laws.[8] He does not think they shall succeed, but expects their cause will be well argued and supported. One thing however I was glad to hear, because the contrary had been reported, that they will not recede from their purpose, nor accept of any other religious test in lieu of the present, nor of any religious test at all.

I trust that I shall now find leisure to write sometimes. My wife desires her best respects to you, and we beg our due comp[ts] to M[r] Rowe and M[r] Wood. I remain always with highest esteem, Dear Sir,

Your truly obliged and faithful servant

T. Lindsey.

London. May. 7. 1791.

---

[1]   Possibly Lindsey referred here to his Cambridge contemporary and friend William Mason of York.

[2]   For Priestley's Hackney College anniversary sermon at Old Jewry, see Letter 445, n. 10. His *Discourse on occasion of the death of Dr. Price* was published in London in 1791. Lindsey proposed to send these works to Tayleur via Joshua Eddowes, printer and bookseller in Shrewsbury.

[3]   See Letters 429, n. 5, and 451, n. 2.

[4]   Although the *Public Advertiser*, 7 May 1791, reported Priestley's sermon, and although it was advertised for sale in the *London Chronicle*, 10 May 1791, and in the *St James's Chronicle*, 10–12 May 1791, it has not proved possible to identify these ministers. There are no clues in Priestley's letters, published and unpublished, or in William Morgan, *Memoirs of the life of the Rev. Richard Price, DD, FRS* (London, 1815).

[5]   The short-lived Polish constitution of May 1791 reflected enlightenment thought and admiration for the forms of government in Britain and America. In addition to a dynastic, as distinct from the previous elective, monarchy, it prescribed a separation of the powers, the rule of law and toleration for the non-catholic minorities. These reforms were brought to an end by Russian military intervention, followed by the extinction of the Polish state in the second and third partitions in 1793 and 1795. Stanislaw Poniatowsky (1732–98) was king of Poland from 1764 until his enforced abdication in 1795. Lindsey did not identify the 'merchant in the city', but possibilities include Samuel Vaughan or a member of his family (see Letter 468); and Christopher Chambers (see Letters 684, n. 2, and 741, n. 3).

[6]   Lindsey undoubtedly intended to write 'world'.

[7]   'Last night' was 6 May 1791, the date of the famous quarrel between Burke and Fox over the French Revolution during the commons' debate over the committee stage of the Quebec bill. The debate was fully reported in the London press, including Lindsey's preferred newspaper, the *Morning Chronicle*, 7 May 1791.

[8]   Thomas Somerville (1741–1830) was minister of the Church of Scotland at Jedburgh. For his unsuccessful efforts to free Scottish presbyterians from the stipulations of the Test Act, see Ditchfield, 'Scottish campaign'.

453. *To RUSSELL SCOTT   **12 MAY 1791**

Text:	Scott Coll.
Addressed:	[In the hand of John Lee, MP] London twelfth May 1791/
	Rev^d. Russell Scott/Portsmouth/JfreeLee
	[In Hannah Lindsey's hand] Revd Russel/Scot/Portsmouth/
	May 13th 1791
Endorsed:	[In pencil] Read
Postmarked:	MA 12 91

May the twelfth, this frank being written for, & the whole publication being above weight, the other half will be sent to morrow in another cover, and a few lines by M^r. L: who has really so much business that his friends who know his kind intentions will wait readily for their accomplishment.[1]

I hope both Y^rself & M^rs. Scot are in better health & spirits than was the case some time ago, for this & all other good things you have the best wishes of y^r oblig'd

HL

Essex House

---

1   'The other half' was Priestley's anniversary sermon at Hackney (see Letter 445, n. 10). As Letter 454 shows, Lindsey also had to send it in two parts to William Turner of Newcastle.

454. To WILLIAM TURNER OF NEWCASTLE   **12 MAY 1791**

Text:	LPN, MS ('Two letters from Theophilus Lindsey to William Turner of Newcastle (12 May 1791 and 22 November 1798')).
Printed:	Rutt, I, 72 n. § (first sentence of fifth paragraph) and 107 n. * (most of last sentence of fifth paragraph).
Addressed:	[In Lee's hand] London twelfth May 1791/Revd Mr Turner/ Newcastle on Tyne/JfreeLee
Postmarked:	FREE MA 12 91 MA 12 91

London. May. 12 1791

Dear Sir,

Under this cover comes to you one part of D^r P ___ ys sermon on the anniversary of our college, and to day, if I can procure another, or to morrow will come a second part. I was in hope that by cutting the leaves one frank might have done, but have been mistaken. It was greatly liked by many, but disliked by some others on hearing it: but the last without cause; and it is most seasonable for the times and will do good. And having the conveniency, I wished you to see it as soon as possible.

You will be pleased to hear that the franker of my letter is nearly as well as he used to be, some little remains of hypochondriasm excepted.[1] He tell me, that on Friday, against Mr Burke and his book; and on Tuesday, in pleading for the exemption of the Scotch from the Test Laws, Mr Fox deliverd two of the finest speeches ever uttered, a defence of the rights of man, civil and religious.[2] And though they had no present success, their effect cannot be lost.[3]

The unitarian chapel at Plymouth Dock has been opend with great acceptation to a very crouded audience by Mr Toulmin of Taunton, and there is prospect of a large congregation being soon formed there.[4] The two young men, Mr Porter, dissenting minister at Plymouth, who had a chief head[5] in building the chapel, and his friend

Mr Kentish, who is to officiate in it, are very extraordinary characters for zeal and industry and great knowlege at their years accompanied with the best principles of every kind.

I should be glad if you w^d remember me kindly to Mr Prowitt, and tell him [I] should be glad of a few lines from him at his [?convenience] to know how their unitarian chapel goes on.^{6}

I have had a few lines from Mr Wardrop of Gla[sgow] who tells me that the second storm, which threatened good D^r McGill is happily blown over.^{7} Dr Priestley left town on friday last.^{8} We none of us never remember him in equal good health. He is printing at Birmingham his sermons on the resurrection of Jesus; which are most invaluable, and much improved.^{9} Mr Christie's answer to Mr Burke, the first part, is one of the noblest confutations of that Orator's abusive misrepresentation of the French Revolution.^{10}

We hope that Mrs Turner and your little family are well, and with our kind regards and good wishes for all, I remain always your often obliged and affectionate
                                    T. Lindsey

1   John Lee.

2   'Friday last' was 6 May 1791. Fox's speech on Tuesday 10 May in favour of the repeal of the Test Act as it applied to Scotland was reported in the *Morning Chronicle*, 11 May 1791, and other newspapers. The most detailed account of the debate may be found in Debrett, *Parl. reg.*, XXIX, 357–78; Fox's speech at 370–8.

3   The motion for the repeal of the Test Act as it applied to Scotland was defeated in the house of commons by 149 votes to 62.

4   The Plymouth Dock chapel was opened on 27 Apr. 1791 with a sermon preached by Joshua Toulmin, which was published with the title *Paul's defence before Felix, considered and applied in a sermon, preached April 27th, 1791, at the opening of the new chapel, in George-Street, Plymouth-Dock* (Taunton, 1791). There is a short review of this sermon in *Gent. Mag.*, LXI, ii (1791), 740–1. *Pace* Evans, *Vestiges*, p. 69, and R. K. Webb's article on John Kentish, *ODNB*, XXXI, 335, Lindsey did not preach this inaugural sermon, nor was he present at the opening of the Plymouth Dock chapel, although he had helped to inspire its liturgy.

5   Possibly Lindsey wrote 'lead', rather than 'head'.

6   The manuscript is very slightly torn at this point.

7   For James Wardrop of Glasgow, a member of the Unitarian Society, see Letter 448, n. 6. His letter to Lindsey seems not to have survived. The 'Second storm' refers to attempts within the Church of Scotland to revive the prosecution of William M'Gill after his 'recantation' in Apr. 1790; see Letter 413, n. 6. His case was finally dismissed by the general assembly on 28 May 1791; see Letter 457, n. 6, and McNair, *Scots theology in the eighteenth century*, p. 103.

8   6 May 1791.

9   See Letters 429, n. 5, and 451, n.2.

10 Thomas Christie's attack on Burke was published as *Letters on the revolution in France and the new constitution* (London, 1791). This was the 'first' and only part of the work.

455. To RUSSELL SCOTT   **13 MAY 1791**

Text:	Scott Coll.
Addressed:	[In the hand of John Lee, MP] London thirteenth May 1791/
	Rev[d] Russell Scott/Portsmouth/JfreeLee
	[In Hannah Lindsey's hand] Rev[d]
	Russel/Scot/Portsmouth/May 13th 1791
Endorsed:	[In pencil] Read
Postmarked:	MA 13 91

London. May. 13. 1791.

Dear Sir,

If my wife promised I sh[d] write a long letter to day, it was more than I find myself able to perform, having been out, and broke in upon by one friend or other, till it is time my letter should be finished. I will only say then, that we beg your acceptance of this discourse,[1] as a token that you are not forgotten by us, and a hint that we sh[d] be glad at your leisure to know that you and M[rs] Scott are both well as we truly wish you.

You w[d] be pleased in reading the speeches of M[r] Fox in the Morning chronicle of this day week, and of Tuesday last, in defence of civil liberty against M[r] Burke, and of religion,[2] in pleading for the exemption of Scotch men from the Test Law.[3] M[r] Lee, who is come to Town, very well, says that they were the finest that were ever uttered. It is generally wished, that Burk [*sic*] may separate himself from men with whom he has no principles in common.[4] D[r] P___ ys Sermons on the resurrection of Jesus, are now printing at Birmingham, which were preached to great crowds and with the greatest applause at our chapel.[5] How may a pamphlet or any thing of that kind be occasionally sent to you? M[r] Christie's book against M[r] Burke is greatly worth the purchase of those who have money to spare and purchase such books. He was upon the spot at the time and tells facts. He is now at Paris.[6] I was in hope this Sermon w[d] have been contained in one frank, and then I should have also sent you the funeral Sermon on D[r] Price.[7]

You w[d] see this song perhaps in the Morning chronicle. I send it because by an able hand, you know, but I am not allowed to name.[8] By the efforts that are making, but which sh[d] be continued, I hope a wanton Russian war will be prevented.[9] I do not recollect any thing capital come, or coming out in the theological way.

My wife sends you her antient regards and joins in comp[ts] and all good wishes to M[rs] Scott.

I remain always most truly Yours T. Lindsey.

---

1 See Letter 453; the 'discourse' was Priestley's sermon on the anniversary of Hackney College, of which Hannah Lindsey had sent the first half to Scott the previous day.

2 Possibly Lindsey wrote 'religions', rather than 'religion'; his handwriting is not quite clear.

3 'This day week' was Friday 6 May 1791; see Letter 454, n. 2. Fox's speech in reply to Burke featured at length in the report of the debate in the *Morning Chronicle*, 7 May 1791. 'Tuesday last' was 10 May 1791, the date of the commons' debate on the motion for the repeal of the Test Act as it applied to Scotland.

4 Burke's separation from the whig opposition, although not yet formalized, was accentuated by his altercation with Fox on 6 May 1791.

5 For Priestley's discourses on the resurrection, see Letters 429, n. 5, and 451, n. 2.

6 See Letter 454, n. 10. Thomas Christie paid several visits to Paris between 1790 and 1792, including a sojourn of six months early in 1790.

7 See n. 1, above. Lindsey referred also to Priestley's funeral sermon for Richard Price (see Letter 452, n. 2).

8   By 'this song', Lindsey possibly meant a versified parody, highly sardonic in tone, published in the *Morning Chronicle*, 13 May 1791, of a speech by Pitt advocating war against Russia. I have not been able to identify the author, although Lindsey claimed to know who it was. An obvious candidate is Anna Letitia Barbauld, but this item is not included in *The poems of Anna Letitia Barbauld*, ed. William McCarthy and Elizabeth Kraft (Athens, GA, and London, 1994).

9   See Letter 449, n. 10; war between Britain and Russia was indeed avoided, as Pitt's ministry backed down from its earlier anti-Russian threats.

456. To WILLIAM TAYLEUR   21 MAY 1791

Text: JRUL, Lindsey Letters, vol. II, no. 48.
Printed: McLachlan, *Letters*, p. 68 (most of fifth paragraph); p. 88 (eighth paragraph); p. 116 (most of second paragraph).
Addressed: Address missing.
Endorsed: 21 May – 91
Postmarked: Postmark missing.

London. May. 21. 1791.

Dear Sir,

I hope you recᵈ. Dʳ Priestleys two Sermons somewhat sooner for Mʳ Johnson's sending them to Mʳ Longman as soon as printed to be conveyed to Mʳ Eddowes for you.

Concerning the very valuable New College=sermon, you will not wonder it is spoken against, but would hardly expect that there should have been any thought of calling the preacher to account for it.[1] Such thoughts however have been entertained, and only a week ago two of the first rank in the law expressed themselves in that way towards Dʳ P. to a friend of his not much inferior to themselves, who however upon talking with and cross-examining them, found that neither of them had read the Sermon themselves, but spoke by hearsay merely, and only in general terms without coming to any thing specific.[2]

But on tuesday last it was apprehended there was discovery made where the grievance lay, when upon a cause that had some relation to the Trinity coming before Lord Kenyon, he dwelt very particularly on writers disturbing by [*sic*] people by putting it into their heads that they were guilty of idolatry, and seemed as if he himself had been disturbed by it. And my Informant had no doubt of his alluding to what Dʳ P- speaks of the idolatrous worship of Jesus Christ being one of the corruptions of christianity that was left untouched at the reformation. Lord K. was one of the complainants above intimated.[3]

I received yesterday a long letter from Glasgow, which mentions that Dʳ MᶜGill was "once more going before the Assembly, (I will give you my correspondent's own words) "to which the Presbytery by dint of Eldership refer the cause simpliciter, instead of putting an end to it, as was universally expected and certainly intended by both parties here. I cannot join my good friend Dʳ Dalrymple in his grief, who sends me word of and laments it. Let Dʳ MᶜGill console himself in the idea of the Good which from his sufferings will result to his fellow citizens".[4]

I hope then that we shall hear something important from that quarter, both respecting the decisions in Dʳ MᶜGill's case, and also the very rude treatment which the Scotch deputies met with from the Minister and House of Commons in the rejection of their petition for a repeal of the Test-Law.

Mr Russell is come from Birmingham to Town since Dʳ Priestley left it, on a variety of business of a public kind. He has also been not a little engaged in attending to the affairs of our New college at Hackney, which are in a most indifferent way, owing to our over-building ourselves, and to want of proper inspection over the persons employed therein; great reform also needed in the expenses of the house &c &c by which our debt is greatly increased.[5] I trust that such a change will be made by the endeavours using, that we may be able to go on without yearly running in debt. The studiousness and discipline of the place, thanks to M[r] Belsham principally, is not only unimpeachable but comendable.

If I can procure a frank I intend to inclose a letter very lately come from Boston from M[r] Freeman, which you will read with great satisfaction. My principal joy from it, was in the news it brought of the reestabilishment of his health, which at one time we despaired of.[6]

It is not easy to describe the panic fears that are entertained by many at the West end of the Town of Dissenters, Unitarians, favourers of the french revolution, as if the like was to be brought about in the same way, and that particularly the meeting to celebrate the anniversary of the french Revolution, the 14th of august,[7] is the time assigned for the commencement of it, and a confederation at home. Those who invent these things I suppose have their views in to serve their own purposes, but they often contribute to raise the ferment they w[d] pretend to allay. I am glad however that the conductors of this annual celebration will not be wanting to use every precaution against disturbance of every kind.

We are a little afraid for you in these cold northwesterly blasts that have been so rife of late, only that we rely upon your old experience and habit of keeping quiet and sheltered at such seasons. My wife presents her most hearty respects and I am always

Dear Sir, your most truly obliged and faithful

T. Lindsey.

P.S. Our best compt[s] with your good leave to M[r] Rowe and M[r] Wood. Pray let the inclosed or any other letter I may have sent be conveyed at y[r] leisure to D[r] Priestley, who will put them in the parcells he is often sending.

---

1   These condemnations of Priestley's Hackney anniversary sermon were presumably made in conversation. One published attack upon it was by Samuel Turner, *A letter to Joseph Priestley ... on his discourse delivered on Wednesday, April 27, 1791, to the supporters of the New College at Hackney* (London, 1791), although it did not demand that Priestley be 'called to account' for it. A brief review stated that it 'contains some simple truths, below Dr. P.'s notice'; *Gent. Mag.*, LXI, ii (1791), 653.

2   As the third paragraph of this letter reveals, one of these two 'of the first rank in the law' was Lloyd Kenyon (1732–1802), from 1788 Baron Kenyon and from 1788 to 1802 the chief justice of the court of king's bench. Probably the friend of Priestley, 'not much inferior to themselves', was John Lee, a king's counsel, former solicitor-general and attorney-general, who was at that time in London (see Letter 455).

3   'Tuesday last' was 17 May 1791. A list of cases before the court of king's bench on that day and the days immediately preceding may be found in TNA: KB 168/35 (Hilary term, 31st Geo 3d), but it is not clear to which case Lindsey referred. According to *The Times*, Wednesday 18 May 1791, on the previous day 'Lord Kenyon sat at ten o'clock, but no business of any consequence but to the suitors occurred.'

4   For the developments in M'Gill's case, see Letters 413, n. 6, and 454, n. 7. The writer of this letter was probably James Wardrop; see Letter 448, n. 6. William Dalrymple was a sympathizer with M'Gill, whose wife Elizabeth, née Dunlop (d. 1785), was his niece.

5   William Russell was listed as one of the 'annual governors and subscribers' of Hackney College in 1786; he subscribed ten guineas; DWL, MS 12.90 (1). However, there is no evidence from the minute book (DWL, MS 38.14) that he attended committee meetings. On 2 June 1791, Priestley wrote to Lindsey that he feared that Russell's attempt to serve the college would be 'ineffectual, the manager

[*sic*] having no sufficient interest to see that the new regulation be put in execution ... I fear *they* are jealous of his interference' (DWL, MS 12.12, fos. 214–15).

6   Although several letters from James Freeman to Lindsey survive for the later 1780s and for the years 1792 to 1796, this one is not among Freeman's letters at DWL or at the Historical Society of Pennsylvania; nor is it among the letters from Freeman printed in Belsham, *Memoirs*, pp. 153–64. Its apparent non-survival might be the result of Lindsey's having sent it to Tayleur. Unfortunately, no letters from Tayleur to Lindsey from 1791 survive in JRUL, C2[13] and it is not possible to ascertain whether or not Tayleur acknowledged its receipt.

7   Lindsey presumably meant 14 July, the anniversary of the destruction of the Bastille in 1789.

457. To WILLIAM TAYLEUR   7 JUNE 1791

Text: JRUL, Lindsey Letters, vol. II, no. 49.
Printed: McLachlan, *Letters*, pp. 31–2 (all but first sentence of third paragraph); pp. 68–9 (sixth and seventh paragraphs).
Addressed: To/William Tayleur Esq[r]/Shrewsbury
Endorsed: 7th June – 91
Postmarked: JU 7 91

London June. 7. 1791

Dear Sir,

I trust that this fine summer-weather often sees you on your beautiful terrace and sometime expatiating on your walks by old Severn's side. My wife and I have great reason to be thankful for the share of health we enjoy in it. The week before last we passed at Halsted place near Sennoak with our friends M[r] and M[rs] Sargent at their Son's house, to whom they have resigned it of a year or two: rather a charitable visit, as the two former are quite invalids, the first with spirits quite sunk and deprest, but seemed somewhat better whilst we were with them and since as we have been informed.[1]

Before I went, there were several meetings on the state of our New College, respecting it's debts and expensive and improvident management, and to find a remedy, without which we must be bankrupts. M[r] Russell from Birmingham was in Town and took an active part in the affair and I am glad he is returned again, that he may see it finished.[2] It cannot be enough lamented, that the Seminary should flourish in the best discipline, and in the sobriety, studiousness and improvement of the youth, and yet be in danger of coming to nothing by imprudent management, in having overbuilt ourselves, and for want of a frugal plan of provision for the house. I think we should send for your M[r] Wood, to profit by his skill in your House of Industry.[3]

Our people are now beginning to disperse themselves to their country-abodes, Parliament being breaking up, tho' the uncomon length of the Law-term will keep us some of that body till towards the end of July.[4] Our chapel however is always filled in the forenoons with foreigners, if our own members are absent. But it is far from being so in the afternoons in any part of the year for several years past. And such is our solitude, that had I no collegue, I should be tempted to drop the afternoon service intirely, with this declaration and reserve to be resumed if a competent number of the congregation would engage themselves to attend. We have the comfort, if there be any comfort in that, that there are the same empty walls at the Old Jewry, Prince's Street &c; but I cannot say that there is much satisfaction in it.

A new correspondent of mine, of Glasgow, a gentleman of easy fortunes, formerly a merchant,[5] sent me yesterday two or 3 copies of An Account of D[r] M[c]Gill's affair before the General Assembly, who have dismissed this second Prosecution 93 against 7. Though it is an Account that was hawked about in the Streets, he tells me, and indeed it appears to be genuine, and drawn up with a good design, and likely to do good.[6] If my wife succeeds in procuring me a frank to day, it shall come along with my letter: if not, in a day or two.

But it will gratify you to see what was done or rather what was not done at the same time in the said General Assembly, relating to their late application to our Parliament for relief from the Test Laws. And I shall transcribe the part of the letter, which I also received yesterday from Mr Palmer.[7]

"I am returned from my expedition to Edinburgh ------ . The matter of the Test Act was compromised between the heads of the two parties. The ministerial party intended a vote of censure on the Committee who had applied to Parliament for not presenting the Petition according to their instructions. These were to chuse the *earliest* and the *properest* time. And that could never they maintained be the properest time, when they previously knew they should meet with a refusal, and which they knew to be offensive to government. The popular party on the other hand intended to move a vote of thanks to the Committee for their proper conduct. The heads met together previously the night before, and had very high debates. They were mutually the Moderator[8] tells me afraid of each other. The ministerial party not without fears of a defeat, but still more of a discussion, when the minds of men were so agitated. For it is now the Moderator thinks in the power of the popular leaders by the least exertion to raise a tumult equal to any in Charles the First's days. The popular party were not without fears of a defeat if it came to a vote, they agreed therefore if the ministerial party would withdraw their vote of censure, they would that of thanks. Only one person a lawyer spoke. He said it was the most extraordinary occurrence in the annals of history for government to refuse the prayer of a whole nation. But he was always averse to its being presented, from a conviction that it was needless, he being of opinion and he was supported by the best authorities in the kingdom, that the Test laws have no operation on Scottish men members of the Kirk-estabilishment.[9]

The moment he had done, a creature of Dundas moved the next question.[10] The popular party think they have gained a triumph, the question being still open, and will most assuredly come on the next Assembly. The ministerial party endeavour to sooth them by douceurs. They have given the Clergy an exemption from the late house-tax, and are promising them an augmentation of stipend.[11] But this will not quiet the lay-members nor the ruffled minds of the kingdom. And you may be assured that the Test-Act must very shortly within a year or two be repealed, if it be not already virtually so by the nullity of effect on presbyterians. A trial in the King's bench would bring this to a decision at once".[12]

What Mr Palmer mentions of the popular partys fears of being outvoted in the Assembly, was from the craft which the Ministerial party had used in procuring ruling Elders to be chosen to their purpose, who have votes in the Assembly. Another year it will be endeavoured to prevent this trick.[12]

I have a present from Mr Toulmin of his Sermon on the opening of the Chapel at Plymouth Dock to send you.[14] They go on nobly there. Mr Kentish in a letter a few days since, mentions ninety seats taken.[15] I must take my leave at present with my wife's hearty respects, and our joint rememberances to Mr Rowe and Mr Wood. I remain always Dear Sir, your most truly obliged and affectionate T. Lindsey.

P.S. Mr Harries and Mr Rowe's paymts to the Unitarian Book Society are received.

1   John Sargent, of Halstead Place, Kent, was aged seventy-six in 1791 and died on 20 Sept. of that year; his wife Rosamund Sargent, née Chambers, was aged sixty-nine in 1791 and died the following year. Their son John Sargent (1750–1831) was MP for Seaford from 1790 to 1793, for Queenborough, Kent, from 1794 to 1802 and for Bodmin from 1802 to 1806.

2   See Letter 456, n. 5.

3   Isaac Wood was a leading light in the foundation of the Shrewsbury workhouse and author of *Some account of the Shrewsbury house of industry, its establishment and regulations; with hints to those who may have similar institutions in view* (Shrewsbury, 1791). A second edition followed in 1791, a third in 1792, a fourth in 1795 and a fifth, much enlarged, in 1800.

4   The parliamentary session ended on 10 June 1791. Of the law terms, the Easter term began on 11 May and ended on 6 June 1791; the Trinity term began on 24 June and ended on 13 July 1791; *Royal kalendar ... for the year 1791*, p. 27.

5   This was probably James Wardrop of Glasgow, see Letter 448, n. 6.

6   There is a copy of this 'Full and particular Account of the Proceedings of the General Assembly, relative to the Prosecution of Doctor M'GILL for HERESY' in DWL, (L). 5601.I.7. It is dated Edinburgh, 28 May 1791, and takes the form of a single sheet. It summarized the debate over the complaint against M'Gill (see Letters 413 and 444) and recorded the vote to dismiss the case by ninety-three to seven, as Lindsey noted. It concluded with the words 'We may yet see the gospel professed in its native purity and simplicity, when no man shall be persecuted, for preferring the pure Word of God to the standards of any church', words which no doubt explain Lindsey's conclusion that this 'Account' was 'likely to do good'. See also *Gent. Mag.*, LXI, i (1791), 576–7.

7   This letter from Palmer to Lindsey does not survive in DWL or HMCO.

8   The moderator of the general assembly of the Church of Scotland in 1791 was Robert Small (1732–1808), minister at Dundee. He held the degree of DD from the University of St Andrews. In 1800, he was admonished by the general assembly for allegedly not requiring subscription to the confession of faith in the appointment of elders, a matter of much interest to Lindsey; see Letters 690, 692, 696, 698 and 699.

9   Probably this lawyer to whom Palmer referred was Robert Mackintosh; see *Scots Magazine*, LIII (1791), 302.

10   The 'creature of Dundas' who moved 'the next question' on 26 May 1791 (a legal case concerning the parish of Ancrum) was George Hill (1750–1819), the professor of divinity and from 1791 the principal of St Andrew's; see *Scots Magazine*, LIII (1791), 302. Hill, who had been the moderator of the general assembly in 1789, managed the ecclesiastical affairs of Scotland on behalf of the Dundas interest; see Donald P. McCallum's entry for Hill, *ODNB*, XXVII, 132–3. As a mark of the favour with which he was regarded in governmental circles, in 1791, Hill was made one of the king's chaplains for Scotland. 'Dundas' signified Henry Dundas, MP for Edinburgh and from June 1791 to July 1794 home secretary, and his nephew Robert Dundas (1758–1819), MP for Edinburghshire and lord advocate.

11   On 28 May 1791, the general assembly heard a report that the clergy of the Church of Scotland were to be exempted from the new house and widow duty of 10 per cent of the existing taxes. On 21 May, a new committee for the 'general augmentation of stipends was appointed, and made optimistic reports as to progress; *Scots Magazine*, LIII (1791), 303, 301.

12   The sacramental provisions of the Test Act were not repealed until 1828.

13   Lindsey (and Palmer) referred here to the ways in which the ruling 'Moderate' party in the Church of Scotland used various management techniques to secure the election from congregations to the general assembly of elders sympathetic to its own interests. Although strongly opposed to lay patronage, the opposition 'popular' party used similar techniques in the election of elders. See Ian D. L. Clark, 'From protest to reaction: the moderate regime in the Church of Scotland, 1752–1805', in *Scotland in the age of improvement. Essays in Scottish history in the eighteenth century*, ed. N. T. Phillipson and R. Mitchison (Edinburgh, 1970), pp. 203–4, 214.

14   For Toulmin's sermon and the opening of the Plymouth Dock chapel, see Letter 454, n. 4.

15   This letter from John Kentish to Lindsey seems not to have survived.

458. To WILLIAM TAYLEUR   **18 JUNE 1791**

Text: JRUL, Lindsey Letters, vol. III, no. 31.
Printed: Mclachlan, 'More letters', 368 (short extracts from the first
                 three sentences of third paragraph).
Addressed: To/William Tayleur Esqr./Shrewsbury
Endorsed: 18th June – 91
Postmarked: JU 18 91

London. June. 18. 1791

Dear Sir,

I wish I could inform you that matters relating to the college at Hackney were settled, and put into a good and permanent train. I can only say, that they are endeavouring that something may be done before the end of the session.[1]

We expected, as his nephew Mr Morgan declined on thinking himself not respectfully used in the intended mode of election by ballot, that Mr Belsham would have been chosen unanimously successor to Dr Price in the Meeting. But he has many opposers. I wished for his election principally as it would be likely to attach him to the college. No tutor do I know of equal talents and abilities for his office. The congregation have agreed to suspend their determination till the beginning of October; which may perhaps operate in his favour.[2]

You will have very great pleasure in hearing that Unitarian Worship is going to be instituted in Dunkirk. Some merchants and others, many of the of [*sic*] church of England, disapproving trinitarians, have agreed to adopt a liturgy after Dr Clarke's, either ours, or one of those that have been composed and printed since. And they have chosen for their Minister, Mr Worsley, son of Mr Worsley, schoolmaster in Hertford, who had his education in part at Daventry under Mr Belsham, but afterwards went to Aberdeen and took a degree there.[3] He was thence recommended to the Scotch church at Rotterdam, but declined on acc^t of the subscription required.[4] What may not we expect from Unitarian congregations settled in different parts of France, and christian religion held forth in that country as a rational thing? Superstition and Atheism must soon give way.[5]

I was pleased to read to day in the papers the manly resolution and decree of the national assembly with respect to the Prince of Condé, who has been long hovering upon their frontiers and threat[e]ning them with invasion, aided by the aristocrats and malecontents at home as they expected. This shews they are in spirits and will damp their enemies.[6] And I trust they will soon get the better of their extreme difficulties with respect to Money. Some of our friends, english Aristocrats say that a national bankruptcy must unavoidably come on in France. I trust they will be found false prophets in that respect as in many others.

Dr Disney and Mr Dodson have been to visit Mr Frend &c at Cambridge this week, where Mr Dodson, who had never before been there was much pleased. But they have brought with them the repeated objections of Mr F. joined by Mr Tyrwhitt and Mr Lambert to the *Preamble* of the Plan of our Unitarian Society, with which Mr D. was more moved than he ought to be, and wished them to be considered by us. Mr Belsham and I have told him, that they are quite inadmissible, but that we w^d consult others. I have not the alterations or w^d send them. And even sh^d these be accepted, Mr Tyrwhitt thinks he shall be obliged to withdraw his name, as he has some peculiar opinions of Christ and something like an atonement made by him, tho he did not put his sentiments in writing as Mr Dodson desired him.[7]

A friend said yesterday, that some of them have not fully come out of Babylon, or they would have had no objection, among other things to the term *idolatrous*, as we used it: for Mr L. who is Bursar of the college, and Mr F. who is fellow may sometimes perhaps find it decorous to attend the Church Service.[8]

But to say no more, what a handle would it give to our adversaries to appear so variable in our sentiments, and to speak mildly and timidly, for their alterations greatly diminish the force of our expressions, after having declared ourselves with such zeal? And our friends also would be discouraged. I have ventured to say, that neither you nor Dr Priestley would approve of any alterations.

Mr Kenrick of Exeter has just now called upon me with a letter from Mr Bretland.[9] I never saw him before. Seldom any one more agreable in his appearance, but still more in his mind and whole congregation. I took his call most kindly, and am only sorry I could see so little of him. He leaves town on monday and talks of taking Birmingham and Shrewsbury in his way.

We had fully set our thoughts on seeing you this year for a day or two, but are agreed it will be impracticable, as we must go to visit my wife's mother at Richmond, although our first visit was thence to You.[10] I hope to have a line to know how the late cold weather has affected you. Thank heaven we are very well. My wife sends due respects. We beg to be properly remembered to Mr Rowe and Mr Wood. Always y^r most truly obliged and affectionate T. Lindsey

1   The session at Hackney College ended on 30 June 1791; see Letter 459.

2   George Cadogan Morgan did not succeed his uncle Richard Price, to whom he had been assistant minister, as minister to the Gravel Pit meeting, Hackney. Price's successor, elected by the congregation on 6 Nov. 1791, was Joseph Priestley.

3   Isaac Worsley (1768–1836) was the son of John Worsley (d. 1807) and the grandson of another John Worsley (d. 1767), who, in succession, conducted a school in Hertford. Israel Worsley was indeed a pupil of Belsham at the Daventry Academy in the late 1780s. In Mar. 1790, he was recorded as attending fourth-year classes in Arts at Marischal College, Aberdeen, although it is not certain whether or not he graduated. I owe this information to June Ellner, Special Libraries and Archives, King's College, University of Aberdeen.

4   For the Scottish church at Rotterdam, founded in 1643, see *Fasti Ecclesiae Scoticanae*, VII, 549–53. The subscription in question was the Confession of Faith of the Church of Scotland.

5   From Dec. 1790 to 1793, Israel Worsley served as minister in Dunkirk to a congregation of British merchants, at their request, using a prayer book modelled on that of Lindsey. After a brief imprisonment on his return to France in 1802 and 1803, he was minister, successively, to dissenting congregations at Lincoln and at Plymouth, before a final sojourn in France in the early 1830s, when he opened a unitarian chapel in Paris. There is a note on the English church at Dunkirk in Benjamin Flower, *The French constitution; with remarks on some of its principal articles; in which their importance in a political, moral and religious point of view is illustrated; and the necessity of a reformation in church and state in Great Britain, enforced* (London, 1792), pp. 416–18. Lindsey quoted it in his *Conversations on Christian idolatry*, pp. 166–8, n. (b).

6   On 18 June 1791, several London newspapers, including the *Morning Chronicle* and the *Gazetteer and New Daily Advertiser*, reported that the National Assembly had issued a decree in the form of an ultimatum to Louis Joseph, prince de Condé (1736–1818), a prince of the blood. It stated that unless he returned to France or departed from the French border and gave an undertaking not to threaten the new constitution, he would be proclaimed a rebel, deprived of all rights of succession to the crown and would forfeit his property. Initially based at Coblenz, Condé and his army of émigrés subsequently entered service, at various times, with Austria, Britain and Russia.

7   Robert Tyrwhitt's objections to the Socinian principles of the Unitarian Society led him to resign his membership; see Letter 459, n. 2.

8   James Lambert was bursar of Trinity College, Cambridge, from 1789 to 1799; Frend was a fellow of Jesus College from 1781 until his marriage in 1808. For Lindsey's own admission that he had remained too long in 'Babylon', see Vol. I, Letter 252.

9   Timothy Kenrick was minister to the George's meeting, Exeter, from 1784 until his death. The letter

from Joseph Bretland which he brought with him was presumably addressed to Lindsey; it seems not
to have survived.

10 For Lindsey's visit to Richmond in Aug. 1791, see Letters 470 and 471.

459. To WILLIAM TAYLEUR   27 JUNE 1791

Text: JRUL, Lindsey Letters, vol. II, no. 50.
Printed: McLachlan, *Letters*, p. 16 (first section of third paragraph);
                  p. 88 (second section of third paragraph); p. 116 (last three
                  sentences of second paragraph).
Addressed: To/William Tayleur Esqr/Shrewsbury
Endorsed: 27th June – 91
Postmarked: JU 27 91

London. June. 27. 1791

Dear Sir,

You were kind as usual to let me hear from you immediately on the subject of
the properest alterations in our preamble, and your labour has not been lost, though
I was sorry you should be put to write in any hurry.[1] Backed by your's and D^r
Priestley's authority, for I had received a similar letter from him, and supported by
good arguments I have resisted the making the alterations in the preamble which our
gentlemen who had been at Cambridge urged from various pleas and particularly
not to disgust such learned men and real unitarians, who might even withdraw
themselves from us. But I said we were ready to take all such consequences,
however sorry for them. And it was intimated that probably Mr Lambert as well as
Mr Tyrwhitt might take back his name, and also mentioned that the Mr Manning
who published the last year those free discourses before the High Sheriff for Norfolk
woud be prevented giving his name.[2] But well may a Gentleman not like to have the
least intimation of a church or doctrine being idolatrous, of which he is a member
and visible professor. We are told also of one or two other gentlemen intending to
retire on the same account, in which they do well to follow their own judgments.

I trust that this proper summer weather will recruit the health and spirits that
have been affected by the late most unusual and unseasonable cold. As to defect of
memory, I feel it more than you though some years younger: On Friday next if I
live so long, I shall be 68 compleat.[3] But I have all cause to be thankful for every
thing, and particularly that I am so much stronger in body and mind than I was about
a year ago; though I never shall recover the shock I then had.[4] Your kind desire of
seeing me affects me not a little, and will put us upon trying what may be done
on our return out of the north. If I can accomplish it, my wife proposes to prevent
your being too much incumbred [*sic*], which you nor can nor ought to bear, that she
will remain at Birmingham, and Dr Priestley and I pass forward and stay a day or
two with you at Shrewsbury. But there will be opportunity to talk of these matters
another time. We propose setting out for the north, if nothing unforeseen happen,
the last week in July.[5]

July – this reminds of the 14th. when the anniversary of the french revolution
is proposed to be celebrated at the Crown and Anchor near us, where I was the
last year, and intended this[6] – altho' on Saturday there was a rumour that all was
over with the Revolutionists as the king, queen and royal family had escaped – but
yesterday an account that they were retaken, and hopes that the Revolution would
still maintain it's ground, as I trust it will.[7]

You will be pleased to learn that I am writing to day to Edinburgh to Mr Houlbrooke, who has most obligingly upon hearing from Mr Palmer that I wished to see it, sent me a copy of the Resolutions of the General Assembly of the Ch. of Scotland, 1790, respecting the Test Act, and the Memorial of the Committee appointed by the Assembly, with some account of their Petition to Parliam^t.[8] I take the first opportunity of thanking him for the favour and for a large account of the present state of that country particularly of its Ecclesiastics and ecclesiastical affairs. It was no small addition to hear that your grandsons were well and in all respects what he wished 'em.[9]

Mr Belsham, who was much rejoiced at the letter you wrote ab^t the Preamble,[10] tells me that he hopes there is now some prospect of things being put into a good train with respect to the management of the college. It would be an utter shame that it sh^d fail in this respect when the students are altogether comendable, very few of those now there going off and fresh pupils heard of. The sessions end on Thursday[11] – as there is no examination for particular reasons, I shall not attend the Orations, being engaged to be in the country. Mr Belsham intends to visit Birmingham and the West, after the 14th of July. My wife desires her most due and kind respects to yourself, and to join in compt^s to Mr Rowe and Mr Wood. I shall keep my letter open to the last, if these sh^d be any thing more to add as I expect a friend who deals in good intelligence to call upon me.[12] I am ever Dear Sir, with the utmost esteem your most truly obliged and faithful affectionate serv^t

T. Lindsey.

P.S. I congratulate you and every friend of humanity on the capture of the French King. I hope the national assembly will act with their usual wisdom and humanity, and it may contribute to estabilish the New Government.[13]

---

1 This letter from Tayleur to Lindsey, strongly critical of the proposed modifications to the preamble to the Unitarian Society's rules, does not survive among Tayleur's letters in JRUL, C2^{13}. Its purport, however, is evident in the references to it made by Lindsey in his letter to Belsham of 11 July 1791 (Letter 460).

2 Priestley's letter to Lindsey supporting his resistance to the alterations in the preamble does not survive in DWL, MS 12.13 and is not printed in Rutt. It was probably with reference to this letter that Priestley wrote to Lindsey on 29 June 1791 'I hope the Preamble will now stand. It would be better to omit it entirely, than alter it any more'; Rutt, I, 114. At the meeting of the Unitarian Society on 14 July 1791, it was recorded that James Lambert and Robert Tyrwhitt had withdrawn from the society; Unitarian Society minute book, p. 20. William Manning is not listed as a member of the Unitarian Society in 1791 or in 1794 and there is no evidence from the society's minute book that he became a member. For his 'free discourses', published in 1790; see Letter 426.

3 Lindsey did indeed reach the age of sixty-eight on 1 July 1791. It would appear that Tayleur in his (non-surviving) letter to Lindsey (see n. 1, above) had lamented his 'defect of memory'; he was eleven years older than Lindsey.

4 For the improvement of his health, Lindsey had spent much of June and early July 1790 in the country; see Letters 417 and 418.

5 Lindsey did not visit Tayleur at Shrewsbury in 1791; see Letters 469 and 472.

6 For this meeting of the Revolution Society, see Letter 461.

7 The flight of Louis XVI and Marie Antoinette from Paris to Varennes took place on 20–1 June 1791; see n. 13, below.

8 The 'Memorial of the committee of the general assembly of the Church of Scotland, concerning the Test Act' was compiled in Nov. 1790 and may be found in the Scottish Record Office, 1/5/124, pp. 1–4 ('Minutes of the proceedings of the committee of the general assembly on the subject of the Test Act'). See Ditchfield, 'Scottish campaign', 42–6. A Thomas Houlbrooke was a pupil of Dugald Stewart in ethics at Edinburgh University in 1790; I owe this information to Rona Morrison of the Centre for Research Collections, Edinburgh University Library. Possibly Theophilus Houlbrooke was

a relative; the reason for his residence in Edinburgh in the early 1790s might have been a wish to accompany him there. Houlbrooke's letter to Lindsey from Edinburgh seems not to have survived.

9 Tayleur had three grandsons, the children of his only child William Tayleur (1741–1813) and his wife Martha (d. 1775), née Bowen. The grandsons to whom Lindsey referred were John Tayleur (1772–1856), who matriculated in medicine at Edinburgh University in 1790, and William Tayleur (1774–1836), who submitted a thesis 'De Pneumonia' in 1795 and who probably also matriculated in medicine at Edinburgh University in or about 1790. As with n. 8, above, I owe this information to Rona Morrison. The third grandson was Charles Tayleur (1774–1854), subsequently of Liverpool, who is listed as a subscriber to William Enfield, *Sermons on practical subjects* (3 vols., London, 1798), I, xl. See also Letter 490, n. 7.

10 See n. 1, above.

11 Thursday 30 June 1791.

12 Possibly this friend 'who deals in good intelligence' was Samuel Shore; see Letter 461, n. 8. Other possibilities are Samuel Heywood and John Lee.

13 The first reports in the British press of the capture of Louis XVI and his family appeared on 27 June 1791; see, for example, the *Morning Chronicle* and the *Public Advertiser* of that date. On 14 Sept., Louis XVI accepted the new French constitution; on 1 Oct., the National (Constituent) Assembly was replaced by the Legislative Assembly.

460. To THOMAS BELSHAM   **11 JULY 1791**

  Text: Williams, pp. 438–40.

Note: The manuscript of this letter appears not to have survived. The double inverted commas are reproduced as they appear in the printed text.

"*Essex House, July* 11, 1791.

"DEAR SIR,

"As I cannot be at the meeting of our Unitarian Society on Thursday,[1] I judge it proper to acquaint you, that since our conversation with Dr. Disney and Mr. Dodson, the former has written to Dr. Priestley, signifying to him, that *he and Mr. Dodson still wish to have the preamble of our plan altered, upon the principle of greater comprehension, and to accommodate some very valuable Unitarians at Cambridge*; but Dr. Priestley has written back to him, that he by no means approves the design.[2]

"I apprehend, that notwithstanding this opposition to any alteration, endeavours may still be used to carry it, and perhaps at the meeting on Thursday. You, who first proposed to me the formation of this Society, are conscious that this principle of greater comprehension was *the very thing* that we wished not to hold forth, as being likely in the event to hurt the design, and therefore we can by no means think of altering our preamble from any view of this kind.

"I think I read to you out of the venerable Mr. Tayleur's letter, his sentiments in reply to my letter upon the subject; but I transcribe them that you may repeat them if necessary.

"'You might very well say, that neither I nor Dr. Priestley would consent to the alteration proposed by the gentlemen at Cambridge. For my own part, if the whole Society could possibly be so inconsistent as to approve of the alterations, I should think that, instead of being the most respectable society in Europe, (which I trust they will ere long be,) they would be the most contemptible.'[3]

"Indeed there is great force in this reflection. Our Preamble is gone forth, and we are now to make such changes in it as would amount to a concession that we had taken the matter up too highly in alleging that there was any idolatry in the Christian church in our own country, and mistaken in saying, *that rational Christians have hitherto been too cautious of publicly acknowledging their principles, and that this disgraceful timidity hath been prejudicial to the progress of truth and virtue.* Is it a time to dissemble such facts as these, out of compliment to any one?

"I have not room nor time to transcribe Dr. Priestley's letter to me on the occasion, but he expresses himself more strongly than Mr. Tayleur, and particularly with respect to any gentlemen withdrawing their names and subscriptions on account of not complying with the proposed alterations; and he dwells more particularly on our not expunging the term *idolatrous*; – that such a demand is totally inadmissible.[4] Mr. Russell is entirely of his mind.

"I am always, with the truest respect, most sincerely yours,
"T. LINDSEY."

---

[1] The following Thursday was 14 July, the second anniversary of the fall of the Bastille, when Lindsey attended the commemoration of the French Revolution at the Crown and Anchor tavern; see Letter 461. Accordingly, he was not present at the meeting of the Unitarian Society committee at the King's Head in the Poultry, on that day; Unitarian Society minute book, p. 19.

[2] This exchange of letters between Disney and Priestley seems not to have survived.

[3] See Letter 459, n. 1.

[4] For Priestley's letter to Lindsey on this subject, see Letter 459, n. 2.

461. To WILLIAM TAYLEUR   15 JULY 1791

Text:	JRUL, Lindsey Letters, vol. II, no. 51.
Printed:	McLachlan, *Letters*, p. 16 (most of first sentence of seventh paragraph).
Addressed:	Address missing.
Postmarked:	Postmark missing.

London. July. 15. 1791

Dear Sir,

I am happy to be able to give you so pleasing an account of two events of yesterday, in which you are much interested.

The affair of the alteration of our preamble was I hope finally decided that it shall remain as it is. Dr D. & Mr D.[1] I was pretty sure would relent upon receiving a letter from Dr Priestley sent to me open, which I transmitted to him[2] by the penny post on monday morning,[3] and which was firm as a rock against the term idolatrous in particular being omitted.[4] So that Dr Disney said nothing yesterday at the meeting about the preamble, and only mentioned Mr Tyrwhitt and Lambert withdrawing their names from the society on account of the alterations they and Mr Frend had proposed not being admitted, and made a motion also for Mr Tyrwhitt's subscription money of £30 being restored to him, which was done accordingly.[5] He also, Dr Disney mentiond his own resignation of the Secretaryship, in wch there was nothing unexpected, as it is an office of trouble, and he first took it with the view of quitting it, but the doing it at that time, as Mr Belsham observed to me, had something particular in it.[6]

Upon this Mr Shore asked if there was not something else to be considered at the meeting, the alteration of the preamble, particularly with respect to the term idolatrous, to which he and others had objections. This was opposed by Mr Belsham, Mr Rowe also, whom I had desired to be present spoke very firmly particularly in mentioning your name. But what chiefly carried the point, was a most admirable letter upon it, which Belsham had rec^d the day before from Dr Priestley, and which the Doctor introduced by mentioning a letter he had just had from Dr Disney and

Mr Dodson, wishing his concurrence, for the sake of accomodating some valuable Unitarians at Cambridge, although themselves perfectly approving the Preamble as it stood.[7]

One argument among many others used by him, and of great force, was that the charge of idolatry brought by individuals, would be but little regarded: but a standing declaration of such a sentiment in a whole society of men, would not fail to have great effect.

I had been the day before discussing the matter with Mr Shore, but could not say, that I made any impression, and I presume also that he will withdraw his name, which I said any gentleman surely would act laudably in doing, who could not approve of what we laid down.[8]

I cannot describe to you how much I am relieved by this disagreeable business being thus happily over, in which Dr D. has behaved with much art to carry his point, for Mr Belsham and I had no doubt that he had acquiesced in tho' not approved of our arguments in not making the alterations proposed to accomodate the Cambridge-men – when behold afterward he wrote to Dr Priestley that they still persisted in their desire to carry their point, and were sorry they could not have him with them.[9] But farewel to it now for ever.

The other event of yesterday, was, our Commemoration of the French Revolution, where every thing passed in the way that every friend to the meeting could desire. About 500 in the room we dined in; i.e. Mr Belsham, Mr Rowe, any [sic] your humble servant, for we contrived to sit near together. About 200 in an adjoining room. The toasts I inclose. But you will see a very good brief account of the whole affair in the Morning chronicle, which has been this year the best daily paper.[10] Mr Rowe had designed to write himself, but telling him I had a frank and asking him if he wishd to inclose any thing, he wished me to say, that he sh^d decline writing till another opportunity. He is perfectly well, and was quite charmed with the regular easy proceedings of such a large company eating in one room together. I inclose another paper, which was distributed in the streets, but I coud only get the copy I send which some one snatched at as I was laying hold of it. It came from a wellwisher.[11]

My wife desires her sincere respects: and I now send you our route for our northern journey &c. We leave town the 27th of this month, take a friend or two in our way to Richmond. After our abode there we shall return by another route, where we have some friends to call upon, by Birmingham: there I shall leave my wife, whose kind wishes I shall carry to you, and Dr Priestley and I proceed to Shrewsbury.[12]

Excuse more than usual hurry. Believe me always Dear Sir your most truly obliged and affectionate

　　　　　　T. Lindsey.

P.S. I purposely avoided being at the meeting of the Unitarian Society at the King's head, Poultry to avoid anything Disagreeable – but I had written to Mr Belsham ab^t it, and desired some other friends to be there.[13]

1　John Disney and Michael Dodson.
2　This letter from Priestley to Lindsey, and forwarded by the latter to Disney, appears not to have survived.
3　The previous Monday was 11 July 1791.
4　This was probably the letter from Priestley to which Lindsey referred in Letter 459.

5   These proceedings were recorded in the Unitarian Society minute book, pp. 19–21 (meeting of 14 July 1791).

6   At the meeting on 14 July 1791, Disney signified his intention to resign as secretary; Unitarian Society minute book, p. 21. His successor, appointed in 1792, was Thomas Jervis. On 9 June 1791, perhaps in anticipation (and disapproval) of Disney's resignation, the monthly committee meeting resolved that the person nominated as secretary should upon entering office 'give security for his fidelity in the execution of the same, in the penal sum of two hundred pounds'; Unitarian Society minute book, p. 17

7   I have not located this letter from Priestley to Belsham.

8   This is a reference to Samuel Shore III (1738–1828), formerly of Norton Hall, Derbyshire, who resided at Clapham for much of the 1780s and early 1790s and was thus in a position to attend meetings of the Unitarian Society. The society's minute book (p. 19) reveals that he was present at the meeting on 14 July 1791. He did not withdraw from the society.

9   This, presumably, was Disney's letter to Priestley to which Lindsey referred in Letter 460.

10 The minute book of the Revolution Society (BL, Add. MS 64814) has no record of this commemorative meeting at the Crown and Anchor tavern on 14 July 1791. Reports of the meeting appeared in the *Morning Chronicle*, 15 July 1791, and in the *Public Advertiser*, 15 July 1791.

11 This was presumably a handbill or broadsheet which, regrettably, has not survived.

12 Writing to Tayleur on 4 Aug. 1791 (Letter 469), Lindsey explained that the joint visit to Shrewsbury planned by Priestley and himself could not take place because of the Birmingham riots, and that he would find it 'melancholy' to undertake the visit alone.

13 This letter of Lindsey to Belsham is Letter 460.

462. To WILLIAM TAYLEUR   16 JULY 1791

Text: JRUL, Lindsey Letters, vol. III, no. 32.
Printed: McLachlan, 'More Letters', 376 (third paragraph).
Addressed: To/William Tayleur Esqr/Shrewsbury
Endorsed: 16th July – 91
Postmarked: JY 16 91

London. July. 16. 1791

Dear Sir,

Mr Rowe having just called upon us, and finding by him, that he does not write this post, I thought it woud not be amiss to mention to you though you might have heard it from the first hand, but not being certain of it, that Dr Priestley himself and his family have escaped out of this great calamity, in which the Old and New Meeting house, and his own house and those of some of his friends have been burned, by a mob pretended to be excited against them for their their [*sic*] celebrating the anniversary of the French Revolution, but most assuredly prompted by the High-church-party, on acc^t of their triumphs over them in argument, in the affair of the repeal of the Test laws.[1]

We are deeply concerned that our friend is the victim in such a cause, but are persuaded that it will have a contrary effect to what his enemies intended.

But in the mean while we, who have been wanderers without a home, have some feeling of what he and Mrs Priestley must experience, thus strip^d of every thing.

The greatest calamity however is the loss of his Manuscripts, which can not be repaired. In his letter to me, he intimates as if he could hardly ever live in Birmingham again.[2] I trust however his adversaries will not have such a triumph and thus gain their end, though unquestionably the security of his most valuable life is first of all things to be attended to and secured. For that seems most peculiarly his station.

Mr Belsham tells me his brother at Bedford heard Dr Prettyman their Bishop deliver his charge.[3] It consisted

1. of advice to the clergy concerning their tithes.
2. informed them that Government was peculiarly friendly to them.
3. mentioned the indulgence granted to R Catholics; but lest offence sh^d be taken at it, added a long string of what had not been granted to them.

The whole of what remained was a libel against the dissenters, reprobating in very strong terms their late attempt to procure a repeal of the test laws.[4]

With this brand the good Bishop travels round one of the largest dioceses in the kingdom, by no means certainly a messenger of peace, which his divine master woud have his disciples to preach.

Mr Rowe continues remarkably well – is much hurt by these Birmingham proceedings, but we are none of us discouraged – but the contrary I trust. My wife desires kind and respectful remembrances – I am ever Dear Sir your truly obliged and affectionate servant

T. Lindsey.

---

1   During the four days (14–18 July 1791) of rioting in the Birmingham area, the New Meeting (where Priestley was minister) and the Old Meeting in the town itself were destroyed; so were a baptist chapel at King's Heath and the unitarian chapel at Kingswood; see Wykes, ' "Spirit of persecutors"', 18–19. The parliamentary motion for the repeal of the Test and Corporation Acts had been defeated by 294 votes to 105 on 2–3 Mar. 1790.

2   This letter from Priestley to Lindsey, dated 15 July 1791, is printed in Rutt, I, 123–4. Priestley did not reside in, or even visit, Birmingham again after the riots.

3   Belsham's brother at Bedford was the historian William Belsham. George Pretyman (1750–1827), from 1803 Pretyman-Tomline, was bishop of Lincoln from 1787 to 1820 and of Winchester from 1820 until his death. His significance lay in his close political relationship with Pitt the Younger, to whom he served as secretary and ecclesiastical advisor; see G. M. Ditchfield, 'Sir George Pretyman-Tomline: ecclesiastical politician and theological polemicist', in *Religious identities in Britain, 1660–1832*, ed. William Gibson and Robert G. Ingram (Aldershot and Burlington, VT, 2005), pp. 277–98.

4   Pretyman's charge, delivered in several districts of his large diocese as part of his triennial visitation in 1791, was not published. The 'indulgence' to catholics is a reference to the Catholic Relief Act of 1791; Pretyman himself was one of the most strongly anti-catholic of the anglican bishops.

---

463. To RUSSELL SCOTT   **19 JULY 1791**

Text: Scott Coll.
Printed: McLachlan, 'Lindsey to Scott', 117–18 (second paragraph; first two sentences of third paragraph).
Addressed: To/The Rev^d. Russell Scott/Portsmouth
Endorsed: July 20th. – 91 [in pencil] Read
Postmarked: JY 19 91

London. July. 19. 1791

Dear Sir

I had not time to write two words yesterday, and not much more at leisure to day.

Dr Priestley came to our house yesterday morning betwixt 6 and 7, in good health, tho much wearied in having had little rest for several nights, and in those spirits which will never leave him.[1]

The continuation of the riots at Birmingham which might have been easily suppressed at first had those whom it became to exert themselves, taken proper care, make our friends destination at present uncertain: but I hope the design of his enemies will not succede in dragging him away from Birmingham. He left his family and friends well, tho' many deprived of their habitations[2] – I can add no more at present but our kind regards to yourself and M[rs] Scott, and that I am always most truly yours

T. Lindsey

1   Priestley narrowly escaped the Birmingham rioters who attacked his house at Fair Hill. Helped by Russell and Samuel Ryland, he then travelled to London via Heath (near Dudley), Kidderminster and Worcester.
2   Among the friends of Priestley who suffered the destruction of their houses in the Birmingham riots were William Russell, the chairman of Priestley's New Meeting congregation; John Ryland; William Hutton; and John Taylor.

464. To WILLIAM TAYLEUR   19 JULY 1791

Text: Royal Soc., Priestley Memorial Volume, p. 45.
Addressed: To/William Tayleur Esq[r]/Shrewsbury
Postmarked: JY 19 [year missing]

London. July. 19. 1791

Dear Sir,

It will be a satisfaction to you to be informed that D[r] Priestley arrived at our house betwixt 6 and 7 yesterday morning, having gone thro much fatigue to reach Worcester by the time the mail set out, which brought him to Town. Thank heaven he is in good spirits and undismayed by his calamities and dangers.

Not long after, M[r] Russell called upon us, having just come up with his daughters, and with a view to inform administration of the proceedings at Birmingham, which were calculated not to stop the evil, and to let them know what was the nature of their Meeting on the 14th and what was done at it, and that the riots have proceeded from very different causes; and also to concert measures for bringing to justice the authors and abettors, if to be found.[1]

Probably as you see most of the papers, at your Coffee-house,[2] *The Times* is one of them. If so, you will easily account for the horrible opinions entertained by the Great and Little of D[r] Priestley and his friends at Birmingham.[3]

You will see in the morning chronicle for to morrow a letter from our friend to the inhabitants of Birmingham, calculated, if any reasoning can effect it, to allay their heats, but at all events, must have a good effect upon the Public. There will be a thousand printed to be disposed of to friends; And as this will be followed by other Numbers, it will in time grow into a size to be sold.[4]

We are informed by letters, that the military were arrived, and all things quiet: but we have other alarming reports to the contrary, which keep our friend in uneasy suspence [*sic*] for his family, particularly M[rs] Finch who is near her time;[5] though there are no accounts of any personal injury being offered to any one, which is a consolation to him.

M[r] Rowe is to call here to morrow forenoon and let me know whether he goes to Shrewsbury this week. I am sorry to send you such a meagre epistle. D[r] Priestley and my wife charge me with their kind respects to you, and I remain always Dear Sir, Your most truly obliged and faithful servant

T. Lindsey.

1   This is a reference to the dinner held at the Birmingham hotel on 14 July 1791 by admirers of the

French Revolution to celebrate the second anniversary of the storming of the Bastille. Priestley himself did not attend this dinner. William Russell and his two (as yet unmarried) daughters Martha (1766–1807) and Mary (1768–1839) arrived in London on 18 July 1791, after escaping from the Birmingham rioters. Russell himself immediately established contact with Pitt to present the case of the victims of the riots, and used his authority as a magistrate to pursue the rioters. See Jeyes, *The Russells of Birmingham*, p. 37. Russell also published a letter in the *Gent. Mag.*, LXI, ii (1791) 599–600, dated 20 July 1791, responding to the attack on Priestley in *The Times* of the previous day (see Letter 467, n. 3) and asserting that the proceedings at the Birmingham dinner had been models of loyalty to the British constitution.

2   Possibly Lindsey referred to the Coffee House Shut, which adjoined the music hall in the centre of Shrewsbury; it had 'in its roof an old tie-beam with date 1577', H. E. Forrest, *The old houses of Shrewsbury. Their history and associations* (4th ed.n, Shrewsbury, 1935), p. 17. A 'Shut' in its Shrewsbury connotation signified an alley open at both ends.

3   For the hostility to Priestley in *The Times* in the aftermath of the Birmingham riots, see Letter 467, n. 3.

4   Priestley's letter to the inhabitants of Birmingham was published in the *Morning Chronicle*, 20 July 1791. He later expanded it into *Appeal to the public*. The *Thoughts on the late riot at Birmingham* had been published anonymously in London in 1791; its tone was highly critical of Priestley, who attributed it (*Appeal*, p. 117) to a high churchman. Priestley's *An appeal to the public, on the subject of the riots in Birmingham, Part II. To which is added, a letter from W. Russell, Esq. to the author* was published by Joseph Johnson in London in Nov. 1792.

5   Priestley's daughter Sarah, the husband of William Finch, gave birth to her third child, and second son, John Finch, on 17 Sept. 1791. He died after 1820. See Toulmin, 'Descendants of Priestley', 14.

465. To WILLIAM TAYLEUR   20 JULY 1791

Text: Royal Soc., Priestley Memorial Volume, p. 45.
Addressed: [In John Lee's hand] London twentieth July 1791/William
                  Tayleur Esqr/Shrewsbury/JfreeLee
Postmarked: JY 20 91

Note: Lindsey himself did not date this letter; the date is indicated by the address and postmark. Below the letter, on the same page, is, in John Lee's hand, a frank to Priestley, addressed 'London eighteenth July 1791/D^r. Priestley/Heath/near Dudley/Warwickshire/JfreeLee'. According to a manuscript note in the Priestley Memorial Volume, p. 45, possibly by the compiler of the volume, the unitarian minister James Yates (1789–1871), 'the frank was first intended for Priestley, but afterwards changed'.

Dear Sir

I have only time to acquaint you that all your friends here are well, Dr Priestley in particular and Mr Rowe also included, and that I inclose 2 Copies of a paper wch Dr Priestley printed this morning in the Morning Chronicle, which you will be glad to see.[1]

Mr Russell has been with Administration today, and finds them really alarmed, and desirous to do every thing in this riotous business at Birmingham, to stop it and punish the authors, tho' he expressed himself far from desiring undue severity.[2]

Dr Priestley, Mr Russell, joins [*sic*] us in their respects to you. I am always Your most truly obliged

          T. Lindsey

1   See Letter 464, n.4.
2   For the immediate response of Pitt's ministry to the Birmingham riots, see R.B. Rose, 'The Priestley riots of 1791', *Past and Present*, XVIII (Nov. 1960), 77–8, and Ehrman, *The Younger Pitt. The reluctant transition*, pp. 131–3.

466. *To RUSSELL SCOTT   21 JULY 1791

Text: Scott Coll.
Addressed: [In the hand of John Lee, MP] London twenty first July 1791/
                 Revd Mr Russel Scott/Portsmouth/JfreeLee
Endorsed: [In pencil] Read
Postmarked: JY 21 91

D^r. Sir

M^r. L: has not a moments time to write[;]¹ the inclosed you will like to see & comunicate the violence & prejudice gone forth against the Dissenters is astonishing: Time & better information alone can cure it.² D^r. P: continues very well & is supported by that hand alone who knows the hearts of all the children of men. With best wishes for Y^rself & M^rs. Scot I am always y^r sincere f^d

                                                             HL

---

1   In the haste of the moment, Hannah Lindsey evidently omitted to include a semi-colon at this point.
2   Possibly the 'inclosed' was Priestley's letter published in the *Morning Chronicle*, 20 July 1791; see
     Letter 464, n. 4.

467. To SAMUEL SHORE III   23 JULY 1791

Text: DWL, MS 12.57 (3) (copy).
Addressed: [At top of first page] Saml. Shore Esq/Meersbrook

Note: This letter is a copy of an original manuscript which seems not to have survived.

                                                  London July 23. 1791
Dear Sir

We hope that you will all have had a safe & pleasant journey to Meersbrook, before this reaches you, & have found the family at Norton Hall in good health[.]

M^r. Russell left town last night about 6 O'Clock, with his daughters, whom he intended to leave at Worcester, & to proceed thence to Birmingham. We are under some apprehensions for his safety, but trust that a good providence will preserve him. All agree that his presence is necessary, if he can come with any security.

I asked him, when he was going, what I should signify to you, when he wished me to say,

That everything was getting into a state of regularity at Birmingham &, likewise, that things were in a good train in town.

That such measures as were judged proper, had been taken with respect to the Counsel employed here, and that he hoped the Government had given some assurance of their being in earnest, by their immediately sending down M^r. Chamberlain the Solicitor of the Treasury;¹ and he desired me to add, with his compliments, that if, at any time, you wish for any further information, upon writing to him, he shall be glad to tender it you.

The ministerial papers still continue their abuse. The Attorney General² is much blamed for not prosecuting ex officio, the Times, for asserting that one of the toasts at Birmingham was destruction to Church & the King's Head on a charger. But, perhaps, he waits for orders from his superiors.³

I think you will be pleased with the following remarks, which I have this morning received from a person of some note, a churchman, but a friend to the dissenters.

"What a hand-bill from magistrates, Lord Aylesford at the head of them! Calling incendiaries, *friends*, speaking of them, yourselves & the *other* friends *of the* Church. – As you love the King & his laws? No statement of their crime: no mention of the consequences to which the laws rendered them liable. In short, *almost* implying that, though actuated by a good motive, they had carried it too far."[4]

Unluckily, I lost the note I had taken of the person by whom the Morning Chronicle was to be sent you, but I have spoken to the person from whom we have ours, whose name is at the end of it Mr Westley, N°. 201 opposite to S^t. Clements Church, Strand, to send it regularly to you till further orders.[5]

My wife joins in respects to yourself, & your lady, & Mr Flower,[6] & we beg to be remembered at Norton Hall, & I am always, Your most truly obliged & faithful Servant

    T. Lindsey

P.S. M^r. Russell was advised immediately to set about rebuilding the meeting-house, without loss of a day, & D^r. Priestley thinks of going down this next week, & preaching the 31st instant, perhaps in the riding-house if they cannot be admitted at the Wesley-Methodists Chapel, if M^r. Russell sends word that he may come without danger.[7]

---

1   The solicitor to the treasury from 1775 to 1795 was William Chamberlayne (d. 1799) of Coley Park, Reading. From 1795 until his death, he was a commissioner of public accounts. His son of the same name was MP for Christchurch from 1800 to 1802 and for Southampton from 1818 until his death in 1829.

2   The attorney-general from 1788 to 1793 was Sir Archibald Macdonald; see Vol. I, Letter 140, n. 13.

3   In a lengthy report on the Birmingham riots, *Times*, 19 July 1791, claimed that one of the toasts at the dinner at the Birmingham hotel on 14 July was 'Destruction to the present government and the King's Head upon a Charger!'. On 21 July, the *Times* printed Priestley's letter 'To the inhabitants of Birmingham' and acknowledged that some of its earlier reports about the 'inflammatory' proceedings of Priestley and his friends were unfounded.

4   Possibly this churchman was Samuel Parr, whose sympathy with the victims of the Priestley riots is evident in his *Letter from Irenopolis to the inhabitants of Eleutheropolis* (Birmingham, 1792). Heneage Finch (1751–1812), 4th earl of Aylesford, was captain of the yeomen of the guard from 1783 to 1804 and a former lord of the bedchamber. For the *rôle* of the magistrates and the alleged handbill, see Rose, 'Priestley riots', pp. 80–2, and Wykes, '"A finished monster"', pp. 55, 66 n. 50.

5   Robert Hall Westley, bookseller and stationer, operated from 201 the Strand from 1790 to 1799; and his family continued the business at 159 the Strand from 1800 to 1829. He printed the *Morning Chronicle* in 1790–1. Hannah Lindsey referred to 'Westley our newsman' when writing to her half-brother Francis Blackburne of Brignall, 13 Aug. 1803; CUL, Add. MS. 7886 (Frend papers), no. 140.

6   This is a reference to Samuel Shore III's father-in-law Freeman Flower of Clapham, Surrey, whose daughter Lydia he married (as his second wife) in 1788.

7   Russell returned to Birmingham at the end of July 1791 to assess the damage to his house at Showell Green, to Priestley's house, and to the New Meeting House; see Jeyes, *The Russells of Birmingham*, pp. 37–8. In fact the Wesleyan methodists refused to allow the use of their chapel and the combined Old and New Meetings in Birmingham met at the Carr's Lane independent chapel during the first three months after the riots. They were then able to obtain a three-year lease of the amphitheatre in Livery Street. I owe this information to Wykes, '"A finished monster"', pp. 55–6. New Meeting was rebuild, and re-opened, with a sermon preached by Thomas Belsham, in 1802.

468. To WILLIAM TAYLEUR   **30 JULY 1791**

> **Text:**   JRUL, Lindsey Letters, vol. II, nos. 52–3.
> **Addressed:**   [In John Lee's hand] London thirtieth July 1791/Wᵐ. Tayleur
>   Esqr/Shrewsbury
> **Endorsed:**   J free Lee
> **Postmarked:**   FREE 30 JY 91 [also postmarked JY 30 91]

Note: There is no evidence that Lindsey dated this letter; the address and postmark are the only indications of the date.

Dear Sir,

I hope Mʳ Rowe is safe arrived at Shrewsbury, and found his own family well, and yourself in your wonted tolerable good way for one that is so much past the age of man.

Dʳ Priestley continues very well in health, and in spirits also, in which he is ever to be admired and worthy of imitation. Only yesterday he was more affected than I have seen him, by some information, that several of the principal of his congregation, are not in haste to have their meeting rebuilt, or shew any proper zeal for him who has done them so much benefit and honour in th[e] character of pastor. But he wants to know something explicit and decisive upon this point.

As we find that we are not of much imediate use to Dʳ Priestley, and he will probably not be much in Town, but with some friends in the neighbourhood, his letters always to be directed to him, to Mʳ Vaughan, Mincing lane,[1] or Mʳ Johnson's bookseller Sᵗ Pauls Churchyard, we have therefore fixed upon friday next[2] to set out to see my wife's mother in Yorkshire, who expects us, tho we shᵈ have delayed or put off intirely the journey, had any essential service for our friend required our stay in Town.

We have heard nothing of the State of the Examinations carrying on at Birmingham only that many are backward thro fear or worse motives to give their evidence against[3]

My wife presents her due respects, and we desire our best comptˢ to Mʳ Rowe and Mʳ Wood.

I will endeavour to write again before our journey takes place – I am ever Dear Sir

Your truly obliged and faithful servant

T. Lindsey

P.S. Dʳ Priestley had to day receive[d] a most pleasing Address from the Ministers and people of the Three Denominations of Dissenters in Yarmouth, extremely well couched[?], which will do good by being made public, and will I hope be printed.[4]

I make a little postscript to my letter to mention a circumstance or two relating to Mʳ Frend and Mʳ Dyer, which I would wish to be mentiond only to yourself.

These worthy men, both of them, disapprove the two christian ordinances of Baptism and the Lords supper.

Three weeks ago Mʳ Dyer was to preach at the Dissenting congregation in Bedford. Mʳ Frend and a most worthy zealous Unitarian living now near Cambridge, formerly of it, accompanied him.[5] They contrived before Service, to put in the Mayor's pew in the church at Bedford, and in some others, Mʳ Tyrwhitt's little pieces, lately publishd, and one or two of Dʳ Priestley's: and after Service gave away at the doors the same little tracts.[6]

Mʳ Hammond, who is a widower, and lives with his wife's mother, at Fennystanton, on the high road betwixt Cambridge and Huntingdon, whilst the African slave affair was depending in the house, threw into coaches and postchaises, and gave to Travellers on the road, little pamphlets favouring the abolition of that shocking traffick.[7]

One is glad to know such anecdotes of remarkable persons, and therefore I send them you.

1   Samuel Vaughan (1720–1802), West India merchant, was in partnership with his second son William Vaughan (1752–1830) at 1 Dunster Court, Mincing Lane; *Universal British directory* (1793), p. 318. William Vaughan was a former student of Warrington Academy and from 1786, a governor of Hackney College. He was also a subscriber to the sermons of Paul Henry Maty in 1788 (see Vol. I, Letter 353).

2   'Friday next' was 5 Aug. 1791, the date of Lindsey's departure for Yorkshire; see Letter 469.

3   Lindsey left this sentence unfinished.

4   This address, dated 29 July 1791, is printed in Rutt, I, 126, and in Priestley's *Appeal to the public*, appendix, pp. 172–3.

5   Possibly the congregation to which Lindsey referred and to which Dyer was to preach was Bunyan Meeting, Bedford, where in 1791 there was an interregnum between the ministry of Joshua Symonds (who died on 23 Nov. 1788) and that of Samuel Hillyard (d. 1839), who was ordained as minister in June 1792. During this interval, several potential candidates for the ministry preached at the Bunyan Meeting. See H. G. Tibbutt, *Bunyan Meeting Bedford 1650–1950* (Bedford, 1950), pp. 40–2. Dyer himself had several baptist connexions; see Letter 407, n. 2. The 'worthy zealous unitarian living now near Cambridge' who accompanied Dyer and Frend was John Hammond of Fenstanton; he had been a fellow of Queens' College and lecturer at Holy Trinity church, Cambridge. The mayor of Bedford in 1791 was Thomas Small; the holder of this office probably had his own pew in John Bunyan's chapel.

6   For Robert Tyrwhitt's 'little pieces', see Vol. I, Letter 346, n. 12. In view of the extensive hostility to Priestley in the immediate aftermath of the Birmingham riots, it is probable that those of his works given away by Frend and Hammond at Bedford included his various *Familiar letters … to the inhabitants of Birmingham*, published in 1790, and his *Letters to the Rev. Edward Burn*, published in the same year.

7   For John Hammond's wife, Millicent, née Essex, see Letter 428, n. 5. She died in 1787 and in fact her mother (Hammond's mother-in-law) had died on 29 Sept. 1790. The debate on the slave trade to which Lindsey referred took place in the house of commons on 18–19 Apr. 1791, when Wilberforce's motion for abolition was defeated by 163 votes to 88; see Cobbett, *Parl. hist.*, XXIX, 250–359.

469. To WILLIAM TAYLEUR   4 AUGUST 1791

Text: Royal Soc., Priestley Memorial Volume, p. 53.
Addressed: To/William Tayleur Esq[r]./Shrewsbury
Endorsed: 4th Aug[t] – 91
Postmarked: AU 4 91

London. Aug. 4. 1791

Dear Sir,

We hope you continue well, and not discouraged by the violent intolerant spirit, that has gone abroad, or rather been drawn forth, when we had some hope that even the seeds of it did not exist.

Thank heaven we are well, D[r] Priestley in particular, and by no means dejected, but the contrary, tho' he is so great a sufferer, and feels this the more almost every hour as he wants to resume his usual exertions for the good of mankind; but at present the thread is broken, tho' I trust it will not be long.

You will be pleased to learn that he received yesterday an Address from the principal persons of his congregation, very proper and christian, regretting his great losses and their own in being deprived of his labours, to make them good men, good christians, and *good subjects* &c &c. signed by Mr Russell at the unanimous desire of the congregation.[1]

I was rejoiced at this, because there was a report that a spirit of great timidity had seized many, so as to make them reluctant to avow their principles.

They say nothing of the time of his return among them. And he thinks now, and all agree, that it would be improper to make his appearance till the Assizes are over.[2]

Mr R.[3] in a letter to him yesterday, mentioned that he had just committed another of the unhappy inferior actors, and another letter said that some fresh evidence had appeard against the magistrates as encouragers of the mischief. The great thing to be wished is, that it may be brought home to them, that they may be punished. And this will be the most likely to quell the outragious [*sic*] spirit in their instruments, the mob.

I do not know whether I mentioned to you how very pleasing an Address Dr Priestley had received from Great Yarmouth, signed by the Ministers and People of the Three Denominations of Dissenters in that Town.[4]

It were to be wished, that the example might be followed in other places, as it would intimidate the enemies and encourage the friends of liberal Dissenters, and shew that they are not afraid of their good cause, though it exposes its votaries to such vile outragious use.

As Mr Burke's book has contributed in some [measure?] to kindle the present flame, he seems resolved to let it go out[?]. For his appeal from [the] New to the Old Whigs, is calculated with the g[reatest] malignity to depress the party he has hitherto acted with and encourage the high tory.[5] I have not looked much into it – but it sells fast – Our college at Hackney he stiles the Arsenal of sedition, as I am told by a friend, who remarked that he sh^d not wonder if it were some time or other set on fire.[6]

We are sorry to be obliged to begin our northern journey so soon as tomorrow, tho' we sh^d have seen our friend more rarely, as he will be only now and then in Town, while he stays in these parts; and tho' he does not decline going about, he does not show himself much in public places, to avoid parade and any thing like Dr Sacheverel's, wch his enemies w^d. be glad to lay hold of, and who have accordingly already exhibited in one of to days papers, preaching his doctrines at Bristol.[7] He desires to join my wife and me in respects to yourself and remembrances to Mr Rowe and Mr Wood.

As at present I cannot pay you a visit along with him, and w^d rather be melancholy to do it alone, for the present it must be laid aside. He however does not despair himself even this year of seeing you. There will soon be a good song in the papers.[8] Farewell. May health and good spirits be your portion, and then nothing will be wanting. Ever your most truly obliged and affectionate

T. Lindsey.

---

1   This address, dated 2 Aug. 1791, is printed in Rutt, I, 133–4, and in Priestley's *Appeal to the public*, appendix, pp. 153–4.

2   This is a reference to the assizes at Worcester, where the trials of the Birmingham rioters were taking place; see Letter 471.

3   See Priestley's letters to Russell, 29 July, 5, 8 Aug. 1791; Rutt, I, 124–6, 136–8.

4   See Letter 468, n. 4.

5   The manuscript is slightly torn at this point. Burke's *An appeal from the new to the old whigs, in consequence of some late discussions in parliament, relative to the reflections on the French Revolution* was first published in London on 3 Aug. 1791.

6   Lindsey's (unidentified) friend was correct. In his *Appeal* (n. 5, above), Burke denounced 'rights

of man' theorists, associated them with John Ball (d. 1381), the leader of the peasants' revolt and predicted (p. 133) that they would be supplied with propaganda 'from the new arsenal at Hackney'.

7   The *Public Advertiser*, Thursday 4 Aug. 1791, quoted 'a letter from Bristol' which stated that 'the most serious apprehensions were yesterday entertained of popular commotions, in consequence of a report in general acceptation, that Doctor Priestly [*sic*] was to preach in the New Meeting House on Sunday'. It added that the corporation of Bristol, in a large degree 'composed of Dissenters', having invited 'this Political Divine', would protect him from 'popular outrage', but also that the populace, 'blinded by prejudice, consider him as a mischievous fanatic'. In 1710, the high church anglican clergyman Henry Sacheverell was impeached before the house of lords on charges, *inter alia*, of preaching the doctrine of non-resistance and impugning the revolution of 1688–9. Although found guilty, his sentence (the burning of his sermons and a three-year ban from preaching) was so light as to amount to a propaganda victory for him and his supporters. Later in that year, he undertook triumphal tours through Oxford, the west country, parts of North Wales and much of the west midlands, where he was received with acclamation. See Geoffrey Holmes, *The trial of Dr Sacheverell* (London, 1973), pp. 239–48.

8   By 'A good song in the papers', Lindsey almost certainly meant an item in defence of Priestley, probably published in the sympathetic *Morning Chronicle*. Perhaps he had in mind Anna Letitia Barbauld's poem 'to Dr Priestley', although it did not appear in the *Morning Chronicle* until 8 Jan, 1793. See Letter 624, n. 10.

470. To SAMUEL SHORE III   14 AUGUST 1791

Text: DWL, MS 12.57 (4) (copy).
Addressed: [At the foot of the letter] To Samuel Shore Esq Meersbrook/
                 near Sheffield

Note: This letter takes the form of a one-sheet copy, of which the original manuscript seems not to have survived. The copy is in the same hand as that of Letters 467 and 471 and was probably made at the same time; it is dated 'vii.8.30'. It was presumably made for J. T. Rutt, to whom it is addressed, although there is no covering letter.

Dear Sir

On the first page I send the transcript of the letter I promised, yesterday, & leave the other side blank, if, perchance you should think proper to send it to any whom it may excite to follow the example.[1]

It would be truly noble, if any of the Church of England would publicly protest in a body against the proceedings at Birmingham, & the cry of the Church being in danger, which some of their brethren have sounded forth, previous to those outrages, in their sermons. If I see M[r]. Wyvill, before we leave Richmond, which we probably may, I shall mention this to him. A circumstance of this kind, & government taking up the cause & admitting Dissenters to the common rights of other subjects, would soon be the means of bringing the nation to a better temper. But this, I fear, is a vain hope; & therefore must resolutely take up & maintain their own cause.

Having taken so long a journey to see my wife's mother, we shall stay some time with her, as such things are not to be undertaken every year. If I learn anything by letters from town, I shall trouble you again. But, at all events, as soon as we can fix, when our departure from this house may take place, & we can expect to pay our visit at Norton-Hall, I shall write to your Son.[2] And, in the mean time, should our call there be inconvenient, from their being obliged to be absent or many other unforeseen accidents, I hope that either he or yourself will do me the favour to acquaint me. We beg our due respects to them, & your lady[3] & all your family, & I remain, always, dear Sir, Your most truly obliged & faithful servant

T. Lindsey.

P.S. Having occasion to write to Leeds to M[r]. Wood, I have sent him a copy, & said that such a public act & testimony would come with peculiar propriety & weight from that town.[4]

To Samuel Shore Esq Meersbrook/near Sheffield

---

1   The transcript to which Lindsey referred in this letter seems not to have survived.
2   The recipient of this letter was Samuel Shore III (1738–1828) of Meersbrook; his son was Samuel Shore IV (1761–1836), of Norton Hall. For Lindsey's visit to Norton, see Letter 474.
3   Samuel Shore's second wife, whom he married in 1788, was Lydia, daughter of Freeman Flower of Clapham. See Letter 467, n. 6.
4   Lindsey's letter to William Wood, minister of Mill Hill chapel, Leeds, seems not to have survived. Probably Lindsey sent him, as well as Shore, a copy of a letter of support for Priestley, suggesting that similar support from Priestley's former congregation would have a favourable effect upon public attitudes towards unitarians. A letter of support to Priestley from the Mill Hill congregation, dated 24 Aug. 1791, duly appeared in the *Morning Chronicle*, 14 Sept. 1791. It is printed in Rutt, I, 141–2.

471. To SAMUEL SHORE III   16 AUGUST 1791

    Text: DWL, MS 12.57 (5); copy at MS 12.57 (6).
    Addressed: To/Samuel Shore Esq[r]/Meersbrooke/near/Sheffield
    Postmarked: RICHMOND Y. [date of postmark missing]

Note: This letter is a copy; the original manuscript seems not to have survived. The copy is in the same hand as that of Letters 467 and 470. It is addressed to Rutt, for whom it was presumably made, although there is no covering letter. It is dated 'vii.8.30'.

Richmond. aug. 16. 1791

Dear Sir,

As I engaged to write again, if I had any thing to send, which you might probably not be informed of from other sources or not so exactly, I shall transcribe what came yesterday.

The state of things at B ＿＿ m is really frightful. D[r] P. cannot come there with safety of a long time, if ever. Had he ventured to come and preach, there was a scheme formed to have defeated him, and to have attacked and overpowered the soldiers, had he been protected by them. The Church people in general have agreed to have no dealings with the Dissenters.

The trials at Worcester are over, and of four rioters, three of the most notorious are acquitted, contrary to the opinion of the judge, and all the council that attended; and only one condemned, and he so insignificant, that M[r] Russell said he should recommend him to mercy.[1]

This being the case at Worcester, one may guess what will be done at Warwick, where prejudices run so much higher.[2]

The Birmingham Newspapers are full of the most inflammatory things, and handbills of the same kind are in continual circulation.[3] There are two printed answers to D[r] Priestley's letter, one a pamphlet, full of the most virulent invectives.[4] Many of the Dissenters begin to think of quitting the town, some to go to America.

It is to be hoped, that in time there may be other Walpoles, and Pelhams in power who will shew themselves favourable to Dissenters, and that Government may at length be wise enough to allow their just rights and to afford equal protection to all citizens who demean themselves peaceably, whatever be their religious persuasions. In the mean time let us not be discouraged. With our *best* respects to your lady and yourself, and due rememberances to all our friends with you and at Norton-hall, I remain ever Your most truly obliged and faithful servant

T. Lindsey.

---

1   At the summer assizes of 1791, five rioters were tried at Worcester and twelve at Warwick. Eight of the twelve at Warwick were acquitted. Altogether, four rioters were convicted; one of them was reprieved. Two rioters were executed at Warwick in Sept. 1791. See Rose, 'Priestley riots', 82, and Wykes, '"A finished monster"', pp. 52–3. William Russell acted in his capacity as a justice of the peace in Worcestershire.

2   This is a reference to the claims for damages made by Priestley and other victims of the Birmingham riots, which were heard before the Warwick assizes in Apr. 1792; see Letter 493, n. 7.

3   The Birmingham newspapers were *Aris's Birmingham Gazette* and *Swinney's Birmingham and Stafford Chronicle*. For the 'handbills' and the anti-dissenter feeling which they aroused, see Money, *Experience and identity*, pp. 227ff and Wykes, '"A finished monster"', pp. 49–52.

4   This is a reference to Priestley's letter to the inhabitants of Birmingham, in the *Morning Chronicle*, 20 July 1791; see Letter 464, n. 5. The first of the two replies to which Lindsey referred was a letter from 'Observator' in the *Public Advertiser*, 1 Aug. 1791. The second was an anonymous pamphlet entitled *A letter to the Reverend Joseph Priestley, LL.D, F.R.S., occasioned by his late address to the inhabitants of Birmingham* (Birmingham, 1791). It was advertised as to be published 'this day' in *The World*, 11 Aug. 1791.

472. To WILLIAM TAYLEUR   12 SEPTEMBER 1791

Text: JRUL, Lindsey Letters, vol. II, no. 54.
Printed: McLachlan, *Letters*, pp. 116–17 (first sentence of first
                   paragraph; first four sentences of second paragraph);
                   pp. 118–19 (last sentence of third paragraph; fourth
                   paragraph).
Addressed: To/William Tayleur Esqr./Shrewsbury
Endorsed: 12 Sept^r – 91
Postmarked: SE 12 91

London. Septr. 12. 1791

Dear Sir,

We are at length returned out of the north not without many regrets that we could not make Shrewsbury in our way, as was originally intended, and formerly accomplished. But if we all live, nothing I trust will prevent seeing you another year.[1]

It was a great pleasure to find Dr Priestley well and chearful as ever in the midst of all the vile calumnies daily contrived against him added to the outrages of his enemies and their abetters throughout the kingdom. But such aggressors never forgive. On thursday last when we came to Town and first saw him, he had rec^d. letters from one or two friends, that encouraged him to come to Birmingham, just to shew himself for one day, and go to see his daughter, and thence to proceed as he intends to Mr Wilkinson's at Castlehead near Lancaster.[2] But the next day a letter came from his son William representing the state of the Town in a more favourable view, tho' I would hope magnified by filial apprehensions; he does not now however purpose to pass through Birmingham, but to go another way to Mr Finch's, pay a visit perhaps to Mr Galton at Barr, and thence to proceed to Castlehead.[3] I mention these things as I am persuaded you are ever anxious to know the whole of what relates to one in whom you are so much interested above others and so much love and have given such proofs of it. If he does not go back to Birmingham, which I fear he will not be able to do with safety to his person, tho' I shall be infinitely concerned if it so happen, his only place then will be the metropolis or its neighbourhood, and nothing more honourable or suitable than to fill the place of his friend Dr Price.[4] Nothing however is yet determined upon. But he thinks he shall be able to see his way in six weeks time: for so long he imagines it will be till he returns hither again. And last night when we parted from him, he thought he should leave London this evening. But I shall tell you more certainly as I shall see him before I seal my letter: for his visits being ended to friends in the neighbourhood of the Town, and almost all in it being absent, we have the satisfaction of his company the whole day; which I need not say to you, is pleasant as well as edifying.

We were glad last night to hear from Dr Kippis, who lately passed thro Kidderminster with Dr Rees, that Mr Bott, the clergyman of the Town shews such an excellent example in his behaviour towards Dissenters, and in publicly and openly condemning the spirit of the Birm rioters.[5] But we were more surprized the day before to learn from the father of Mr Field of Warwick, that the B^p of the Diocese, upon what occasion I know not, had written to the clergy of the Town, commending their zeal, but telling them it was wrong directed, and ordering them to make the matter up with the Dissenters. Which has accordingly been done. The Dissenters and Mr Field invited to dine with the corporation in the Town hall and thus all quiet.[6] And I think it must induce some to inquire and to think better of the former and their cause. What might not the R.Rs do towards allaying all heats and animosities in the present moment. But alas! some of them have been the chief fomenters of them. We have had a very bad account of the behaviour of the Church-people towards the Dissenters at Stourbridge, and particularly towards Mr Carpenter:[7] but you are more in the ways of knowing what passes there than we.

On our journey, we perceived great ignorance of and indifference ab^t what had passed at Birm. Mr Wyvill, who holds the whole in abhorrence, and is a firm well-wisher to the french revolution, told me that he was ashamed of many of the Yorkshire Gents – whom he had just seen at their Music-meeting, who upon his mentioning the horrid transactions, with great levity, asked, if Dr Priestley had not given provocation.[8]

My wife begs her kind respects to you; and we desire to be properly ~~to~~ rememberd to Mr Rowe and Mr Wood. As the Doctor is going away, we shall be in the country as usual, for a few weeks, the middle part of each. I am always, with a most affectionate esteem,

Dear Sir Your most truly obliged and faithful servant

T. Lindsey

---

1   Lindsey and Tayleur never met again.
2   'Thursday last' was 8 Sept. 1791. Several letters to Priestley from Birmingham, encouraging him to return, are reproduced as appendices to his *Appeal to the public*. See, for example, the address from the New Meeting congregation, dated 2 Aug. 1791 and signed by William Russell, and the addresses from the young people of the congregation, *Appeal to the public*, pp. 153–5, 157–60, 162–5.
3   I have not located this letter from William Priestley. Mr Galton was Samuel Galton junior (1753–1832) of Great Barr, near Birmingham, a scion of a prominent and wealthy quaker industrial family, a former student of Warrington Academy and a member of the Lunar Society of Birmingham. He was for many years a financial supporter of Priestley's scientific research. His eldest child Mary Anne (1778–1856) achieved fame as the author Mrs Schimmelpenninck. Priestley's daughter Sarah and her husband William Finch lived at Heath Forge, near Dudley; Castlehead, Lancashire, was the residence of Priestley's brother-in-law John Wilkinson.
4   Price had been minister at the Gravel Pit meeting house, Hackney.

5   George Butt (d. 1795) was vicar of Kidderminster from 1787 to 1795. He was the author of *Sermons*
     (2 vols., Kidderminster, 1791). Priestley and Samuel Parr, as well as Richard Hurd, and George
     Pretyman, bishop of Lincoln, were among the subscribers.
6   The father of William Field (1768–1851), dissenting minister at the High Street chapel, Warwick,
     was John Field (1719–96), a medical practitioner in London. Warwick was part of the diocese of
     Worcester, where the bishop from 1781 to 1808 was Richard Hurd. For the background to his inter-
     vention, see P. Styles, 'The corporation of Warwick, 1660–1835', *Transactions & Proceedings of
     Birmingham Archaeological Society for the year 1935*, LIX (1938), 98–101, and *Derby Mercury*, 5,
     12 Oct. 1791.
7   Benjamin Carpenter (1752–1816), a former student of the Daventry Academy, was minister to the
     presbyterian congregation at High Street, Stourbridge, from 1778 to 1795 and from 1807 to 1816.
     Although there was no riot at Stourbridge in the aftermath of the Birmingham disorders, Priestley
     claimed that hostility towards dissenters there included boycotts of shops owned by dissenters and the
     successful obstruction of a plan for a dissenting meeting house, supported by Carpenter, at the nearby
     Lye-waste; *Appeal to the public on the subject of the riots in Birmingham. Part II*, pp. 197–205. The
     same impression emerges from James Scott's MS 'History of Cradley', pp. 55–63. Scott (1768–1827)
     was minister to the dissenting congregation at Cradley from 1789 to 1827 and also to a congregation
     at Stourbridge from 1807 to 1827. His manuscript history is in the custody of Higgs and Sons and
     Harward and Evers, solicitors, Stourbridge, and I am grateful to them for permission to consult it.
     For further background, see Wykes, '"Spirit of persecutors"', 21–2.
8   No doubt Wyvill communicated his sense of shame to Lindsey in person during the latter's visit to
     Yorkshire in Aug. 1791.

473. To WILLIAM TAYLEUR   19 SEPTEMBER 1791

Text: JRUL, Lindsey Letters, vol. III, no. 33.
Printed: McLachlan, 'More letters', 376 (second to sixth sentences,
                   inclusive, of fourth paragraph).
Addressed: To/William Tayleur Esqr/Shrewsbury
Endorsed: 19 Sept^r – 91
Postmarked: SE 19 91

London. sept^r. 19. 1791

Dear Sir,

I do not know that I have at any time seen Dr Priestley in better, or more equable
good spirits, than these three last days that he has been with us. I fear the enemy
will succeed and triumph in having driven him away from Birmingham, for there
is no abatement but the contrary of the vile malignity entertained against him by
the mob, and this continually fed by the vilest calumnies, which no one contradicts.

Mr Belsham was with us yesterday, and mentiond that the matter had been made
up at Warwick betwixt the church people and dissenters by overtures from the
former of their mistake, but that there had been no dinner together in the Town-
hall; and added, that B^p. Hurd was the person that interfered, but this I cannot well
account for, unless Warwick be in Worcester diocese.[1]

One present observed, that B^p. Hurd, than whom no one is more violent against
Dissenters, and Dr P. in particular, woud not have interposed but to save the church
from the infamy of persisting in their bad conduct.

Dr P. desires his respects and thanks for the very kind terms in which you mention
him. He has accounts sent him of two thousand vol^s. of his library being saved,
though in what intireness as to the setts and condition he cannot tell. A good number
also of the volumes of his MS exposition of the N.T. are preserved.[2] Memoirs of
his life.[3] A register of experiments. His library consisted of 3300 and odd. If his
losses must be left to a Warwickshire-Jury to decide upon the value of them, it is to

be apprehended, that even less justice will be done to him than to any of the other sufferers.[4]

M[r] B. says, there was not any riot at Stourbridge, but that they were under some apprehensions, and that the people of the place had lately shewn themselves particularly hostile and intolerant towards the Dissenters.[5]

Yesterday I saw a person just come from Paris, and who had passed a year in a merchants house and to learn the language. One circumstance you will be pleased with, that a few months ago, he was at the openning [sic] of a chapel of the Protestants, where people of the best fashion, and others in crouds attended, when the Preacher took for his text – *the night is far spent, the day is at hand*,[6] and by a nervous affecting narrative of the sufferings they had endured for their religion, particularly since the revocation of the Edict of Nantes,[7] and a representation of the liberty and free enjoyment of the public worship of God which they had now in prospect, moved the whole audience in such a manner that there was not a dry eye in the place.[8]

The committee of protestant Dissenting lay-men and ministers of the three denominations for the West Riding of the county of York, have printed a noble Address to the People of England, together with their Letter to D[r] Priestley. It is ordered to be published in the General Evening Post, and in some Morning-papers.[9] Watson Scatcherd, who signs it, is a gentleman of character, at the Bar, very worthy, but orthodox, and not the worse for that. I hope all the orthodox will unite in such remonstrances.[10]

With my wifes kindest respects, I remain ever Dear Sir, Your most truly obliged and faithful affectionate servant

T. Lindsey

Due remembrances to M[r] Rowe and M[r] Wood.

---

[1] For these events and their background, see Letter 472.

[2] Priestley estimated that approximately 2,000 volumes (some two-thirds of the total) were salvaged from the riots, although many of them were damaged. Most of the volumes of his manuscript exposition of the New Testament (although apparently not the drafts of the proposed new translation of it) survived. See Wykes, 'Priestley at Hackney', pp. 517–18.

[3] Priestley's 'Memoirs of his life' did indeed survive the Birmingham riots and formed the basis of Rutt's *Life and correspondence* of Priestley. A separate edition, with the title *Autobiography of Joseph Priestley*, ed. Jack Lindsay, was published in Bath in 1970.

[4] See n. 2, above. For Priestley's claim for compensation and the outcome of his claim, see Letter 493, n. 7.

[5] See Letter 472, n. 7.

[6] Romans xiii. 12.

[7] The Edict of Nantes (1598) had granted limited civil and religious liberties to Huguenots. Its revocation by Louis XIV in 1685 led to a substantial exodus of Huguenots from France.

[8] Probably the English person who had returned from France was the political writer Thomas Christie, or a member of the family of John Hurford Stone; another possibility is the lawyer Felix Vaughan; see Knight, *William Frend*, pp. 94–7, and Letters 480, n. 8, and 679, n. 7. Possibly the protestant chapel opened in Paris to which Lindsey referred was that of the (recently vacant) church of the Théatins; see Nigel Aston, *Religion and revolution in France 1780–1804* (Basingstoke, 2000), pp. 245–6.

[9] The address to the people of England, and the letter of sympathy and support to Priestley, issued by the quarterly meeting of the protestant dissenters of the West Riding of Yorkshire at Wakefield on 1 Sept. 1791, were printed in the *General Evening Post*, 17–20 Sept. 1791. They also appeared in several morning newspapers, including the *Morning Chronicle*, 19 Sept. 1791.

[10] This address was indeed signed by Watson Scatcherd (d. 1817), the chairman of the Wakefield meeting (n. 9, above) and a successful attorney on the northern circuit.

474. To SAMUEL SHORE III   **26 SEPTEMBER 1791**

Text: DWL, MS 12.57 (7).
Addressed: To/Samuel Shore Esqr/Meersbrook/near/Sheffield [the last
                  three lines of the address are crossed out in another hand, and
                  'at Mr Wrights/Millhill/Leeds'[1] substituted]
Postmarked: SE 26 91 [although crossed out, the postmark is nonetheless
                  legible]

London. sept^r. 26. 1791

Dear Sir,

Having sent a few lines of acknowlegement to your worthy and highly esteemed son for our kind reception at Norton Hall, and my wife having written to Mrs S. Shore,[2] I have not been in haste to return our thanks to yourself and Mrs Shore, partly through our absence from town unless at the end of the week, but more, as nothing very important occurred to communicate.

At the end of each week, Dr Priestley has been with us and passed the sunday, though he did not preach; but yesterday I learned that he was gone to Missenden, Bucks, a house lately taken by Mr Vaughan the elder for his family, where the D^r is to stay till the end of the next week.[3]

You will like to be informed, that the D^r. has taken a house at Clapton, next door to Mr G. Morgan's, and not far from the college,[4] and as Mrs Finch is brought to bed, and doing well,[5] I believe that Mrs Priestley will soon join her husband at Mr Vaughans, in order to look over the house he has taken, and prepare it for their living in it.

This I said, you would like to know, because it is decisive against the Doctors returning to Birm. to settle; which I apprehend it would by no means be safe for him to do. A gentleman who came thence only on friday,[6] told me that the same malignant intolerant spirit subsists, and in general no one is at all sorry for the outrages committed, or expresses any concern about them. And this spirit was observed to be renewed with more vigour, after the return of Mr Brooks, the Under-sheriff from Town;[7] against whom there were some very strong suspicions, and more than suspicions, of his having given countenance to the late riots;[8] I have heard that there were some affidavit's concerning his behaviour sent up to the Minister: but he came back quite triumphant, having had a most gracious reception both from Mr Pitt and Mr Dundas.[9]

There is no public news stirring of any kind. None that I meet with, doubt of the stability of the New French Constitution. The reports of the combination of the Emperor and other powers against the French to attack them, is a mere chimera to fill the papers.[10]

At Paris, there has been for some time, a protestant congregation, very numerous, attended by many of rank and fortune. A gentleman, who was present at the opening of it some months ago, told me that the preacher, who is a man of eminence, chose for his text, *the night is far spent*; *the day is at hand*: when he recapitulated the sufferings of protestants, especially since the revocation of the Edict of Nantes, and expatiated upon their present prospect, in so affecting a manner, that there was not a dry eye throughout the whole audience.[11] The protestants, I think, have purchased a church, belonging to some convent, near the Louvre. Protestant churches are also opened at Rouen, and in other places.[12] And if the ill-treatment and abasement of protestants continues here, as it probably will, many will remove, and some actually now have thoughts of removing to a country, where their lives and properties will be protected.

My wife desires to join in respects to you and your lady and Mr Flower[13] with all kind remembrances at Norton hall, and I am always,

Dear Sir, Your most truly obliged and faithful servant

T. Lindsey.

I think I never observed the west end of the town to be so empty. Scarce any but hackney-coaches to be seen moving about.

[1] Possibly Joseph Wright of Mill Hill, Leeds, listed as a merchant in *Holden's triennial directory, 1808* (2 vols., London, 1808), II, 177; one might conjecture that he was the Mr Wright of Leeds who is listed as a subscriber to Walker, *Sermons on various subjects*, I, xviii.

[2] Mrs S. Shore was Lydia, née Flower, the second wife of Samuel Shore III of Norton Hall, to whom this letter was addressed. I have not been able to locate Hannah Lindsey's letter to her. Shore's 'worthy and esteemed son' (and Lydia Shore's step-son) was Samuel Shore IV (1761–1836), of Norton Hall.

[3] 'Mr Vaughan the elder' was Samuel Vaughan, merchant, of London, the father of Benjamin, John and William Vaughan; see Letter 468, n. 1.

[4] For Priestley's move to Clapham, and his house in close proximity to the Gravel Pit meeting, Hackney, and to Price's nephew George Cadogan Morgan, see Wykes, 'Priestley at Hackney'. For the exact location of Priestley's house, on Lower Clapton road, see M. Gray, 'Joseph Priestley in Hackney', *E & D*, II (1983), 107–10.

[5] See Letter 464, n. 5.

[6] Friday 23 Sept. 1791.

[7] John Brooke (1755–1802) was the under sheriff of the county of Warwickshire. He was subsequently a leading figure in the local church and king club and the Association for the Protection of Liberty and Property against Republicans and Levellers.

[8] Lindsey at first wrote 'outrages', then over-wrote 'riots'.

[9] For John Brooke, see n. 7, above. George III, while deploring the riots, wrote: 'I cannot but feel better pleased that Priestley is the sufferer for the doctrines he and his party have instilled'; *The later correspondence of George III* (5 vols., Cambridge, 1966–70), I, 551. But Lindsey exaggerated in suggesting that the magistrates of Birmingham were well received by the ministry; in fact Henry Dundas, in his capacity of home secretary, wrote to them urging them greater activity against the rioters; Rose, 'Priestley riots', 82.

[10] On 27 Aug. 1791, the Holy Roman Emperor Leopold II and Frederick William II of Prussia issued the Declaration of Pillnitz, whereby they expressed a willingness to intervene in France to safeguard the position of Louis XVI, but made it clear that they would do so only if other rulers, including George III and his government, would join them. Throughout Sept. 1791, the London newspapers claimed repeatedly that talk of intervention was merely hot air issuing from émigrés led by the comte d'Artois, the future King Charles X. The *Morning Chronicle*'s prognosis of 19 Sept. 1791 was typical: 'Notwithstanding the constant revival of the reports of an external attack upon France, nothing can be more certain than that no bodies of troops are collecting or in motion on the Continent at all calculated for such an enterprise'. See also the *Whitehall Evening Post*, 22–4 Sept. 1791, and the *London Chronicle* of the same date. Louis XVI accepted the new French constitution on 14 Sept. 1791. For Lindsey's reference in 1778 to Leopold II (1747–92), emperor from 1790 until his death on 1 Mar. 1792, and formerly the 'enlightened' grand duke of Tuscany, see Vol. I, Letter 187, n. 8.

[11] See Letter 473.

[12] See Aston, *Religion and revolution in France*, pp. 245–50. The leading protestant minister in Rouen was Pierre Mordant (1754–1813), pastor of the reformed church in Rouen from 1792 to 1813. For Lindsey's optimism as to the prospects for the growth of religious freedom for protestants in France, see his *Conversations on Christian idolatry*, pp. 165–9.

[13] See Letter 467, n. 6.

475. To WILLIAM TAYLEUR   15 OCTOBER 1791

Text: JRUL, Lindsey Letters, vol. II, no. 56.
Printed: McLachlan, *Letters*, p. 38 (sixth sentence of first paragraph);
                   p. 117 (second and most of third sentences of fourth
                   paragraph; first and part of second sentence of fifth paragraph;
                   first and third sentences of sixth paragraphs); p. 137 (third
                   paragraph).
Addressed: To/William Tayleur Esqre/Shrewsbury
Endorsed: 15th Octr 91
Postmarked: OC 15 91

London. Oct. 15. 1791

Dear Sir,

It is rather a long time, I think, since I had the pleasure of writing to you, and it has not been wholly my own fault.[1] Till this day sennight, that we came away for good, we were altogether in the country the greater part of the week. But this is not all. I met with an accident, upon Epsom downs from my horse, which might have been fatal: but I thank God, I am now nearly, but not altogether recovered. It did not however once prevent my doing the duty of the chapel, tho' it made it uneasy to sit down and write much. The Sunday before last was most painful: but I went through the whole, both parts of the day, tho' it was the communion and Dr Priestley present: it shd be added also that he had come without a sermon.[2] Dr and Mrs Disney have been a fortnight at Bath, chiefly for a bilious complaint of the latter; but the Doctor also both bathes and drinks the water, having a sort of gouty habit, for which it is recomended.

And so much for the history of my silence. I have rejoiced however to hear of your continuing in your usual state of health, and hope that the fresh instance of your beneficence to our new college will excite others and all in their several departments to those exertions which will be necessary to preserve and make it flourish.[3] On the part of the tutors and pupils, every thing I am satisfied goes on very well. And I hear a good report of the new Tutor Mr Pope.[4]

Mr Wakefield, whom he succeeds, has not done himself much credit by his Tract on Social and Public Worship.[5] It shews how prejudice may blind the judgment; and though perhaps intended for that purpose it furnishes no very solid apology for his not attending public worship. But I would not wish him to hear this from me; as he is one of the last men with whom I would desire to have a controversy if I could avoid it. His translation of the N.T. was to have been delivered this week: but his bookseller told me a few days ago, that he had not yet received some of the sheets.[6]

Though I have not yet named him, Dr Priestley has never been out of my thoughts since I began my letter. He was very well yesterday, and I expect him today, as also to preach for me to morrow, which he also did the sunday before: but the day was so exceeding rainy we had a very thin audience.[7] He has had a return of his bilious complaint, which has reduced him a little: otherwise he is very well and chearful; but very busy in fitting up his laboratory and the house he has taken at lower Clapton, which is a continuation of Hackney and not far from the college. Mrs Priestley is also with him, and doing her part towards the house and it's furniture.[8]

This day week he sent an answer to a very affecting address from his people with a very many signatures, pressing his return among them, and promising him security and liberty: the latter I fear more than they could answer for. With much reluctance he sent a negative, but signified, that when the temporary place of their own, which they were preparing was ready, he w[d] come down and officiate among them for a few weeks till X[mas] by which time he hoped they might be settled with a successor, and he w[d] resign his pastoral office.[9] What the congregation have signified to him [in] return, I know not yet, nor did he yesterday. In the mean time, it grieves me beyond measure that he sh[d] be so driven from his most hon[bl] and useful station, and likewise for the precedent it furnishes for the like feats when an excellent pastor at any future time becomes troublesome.

Many at Hackney are endeavouring to procure his being elected in D[r] Price's room; and a majority are for him: but two thirds by a former agreem[t] are to decide. He would not however wish to be named or to be chosen, if there be great clamour and opposition: which I trust is not likely.[10] If this sh[d] not take place, it is proposed by several friends to erect an Unitarian chapel, wherein he will officiate with a liturgy; to which a great majority are disposed.

After yourself, we hope M[r] Rowe his lady and family are well, and M[r] Wood: and that you go on in your unitarian chapel, without seceders, and without fear of disturbance, which latter we heard you had been in part threatened with. My wife desires to join in respects to yourself and in due comp[ts] to our friends, and I am always Dear Sir, Your most truly obliged and faithful affect[e] servant

T. Lindsey.

There are many things worth reading in the Second Vol. of Essays philosophical historical and literary, printed for Dilly, with[t] name, but M[r] Belshams brother the author.[11]

---

1 Lindsey's previous (surviving) letter to Tayleur was that of 19 Sept. 1791 (Letter 473).

2 15 Oct. 1791 was a Saturday; the 'Sunday before last' was 2 Oct. 1791.

3 This benefaction from Tayleur to Hackney College is not recorded in the college committee minute book (DWL, MS 38.14), which in any case is blank after Sept. 1791. At the time of the college's foundation in 1786, he became a 'governor for life' and was a benefactor to the extent of £200. For another gift from Tayleur to the college, in 1794, see Letter 575.

4 John Pope succeeded Gilbert Wakefield as classical tutor at Hackney College in 1791. He held that office until 1793, when he became minister to a unitarian congregation at Blackley, Manchester, which he served until his death on 28 Oct. 1802.

5 Gilbert Wakefield's *An enquiry into the expediency and propriety of public or social worship* was published in London in 1791.

6 Wakefield's *A translation of the New Testament* was published in three volumes in London in 1791. His bookseller and publisher was John Deighton (1748–1828), who established a reputation in Cambridge between 1778 and 1785, and operated from premises at 274 High Holborn between 1786 and 1791, and at 325 High Holborn between 1792 and 1794. He returned to Cambridge in 1794, took over the firm of Merrill (see Vol. I, Letter 360, n. 5) and became one of the city's most successful booksellers; see the article by Jonathan R. Topham, *ODNB*, XV, 695–6.

7 The previous Sunday, when Priestley preached at Essex Street chapel, was 9 Oct. 1791.

8 See Wykes, 'Priestley at Hackney', 513–27.

9 The address to Priestley from the New Meeting congregation, Birmingham, dated 22 Sept. 1791, requesting him to resume his office as minister, and Priestley's reply, dated 8 Oct. 1791, reluctantly declining the request, are printed in Rutt, I, 159–60 and 164–6.

10 For Priestley's election as minister at the Gravel Pit meeting, Hackney, see Letter 478.

11 William Belsham published his one-volume *Essays, philosophical, historical and literary* in London in 1789, without his name. An extended, two-volume edition was published in Dublin in 1790 and 1791, and it was to the second volume of this edition that Lindsey referred. Two further volumes were published in Dublin later in 1791, again without Belsham's name.

476. To WILLIAM ALEXANDER   15 OCTOBER 1791

Text: 'Letters of the Rev. Theophilus Lindsey. No. II',
              UH, II, 45 (8 Mar. 1862), 84.

Note: This is the only section of the letter printed by the *UH*; the manuscript has apparently not survived. The ellipsis at the end of the first paragraph suggests that it and the second paragraph were separated by text which the *UH* omitted. Here the two paragraphs are separated by a broken line.

October 15th, 1791.

Your letter[1] gave me much satisfaction in your just remarks on the shocking effects of the spirit of bigotry at Birmingham, and the probability of truth being a gainer at present and in future, by its being known that Dr. Priestley has been the victim of that evil spirit, whose invincible arguments for the unity of God are his great offence. He is very well, and with his wonted cheerfulness, which has never forsaken him. Sunday last, he preached for me for the first time since he has been expelled by fire and destruction out of his own place of worship, and he does me that favour to-morrow again.[2] He has at last, though very reluctantly and much to the concern of his late beloved people, given up the thought of continuing the pastoral office among them, as the exercise of it would not, probably, be consistent with his personal safety and liberty; such is the temper of his many adversaries still and so hostile to him. Some imagine he may be chosen pastor in the room of his most excellent friend Dr. Price; but there is nothing certain about his successor.[3] Dr. Priestley has, however, taken a house at Lower Clapton, which is a sort of continuation of Hackney, and I should apprehend that if he be not appointed to the Gravel Pit Meeting, as it is called, it is probable that his many friends at Hackney and its neighbourhood will build a Unitarian chapel expressly for him to officiate in. Nothing, however, is yet decided. So much to satisfy your inquiries after this illustrious sufferer for the truth. ***

Mr. Lion is surely a most worthy creature, and if the rest of his life be according to his light and abilities, will rise to the greater honour in another world for his depressed station in this.[4] It will be fortunate, if the engagement to undertake the care of the ten poor children this worthy man educates at his own expense, does not embroil you with the clergyman of the parish, and with the more orthodox of the parishioners in consequence, but I promise myself you will do all in your power, with a good conscience, to keep matters quiet, and the more so as your usefulness in the village and neighbourhood seems to be increasing.[5]

---

1   Alexander's letter to Lindsey seems not to have survived.
2   See Letter 475, n. 7. 'Tomorrow' was Sunday 16 Oct. 1791.
3   See Letter 478. Priestley did indeed succeed Price at the Gravel Pit meeting, Hackney, where he served from 1791 to 1794; his own successor at the New Meeting, Birmingham, was David Jones, who served the congregation from 1792 to 1795. John Edwards, who had been appointed as Priestley's assistant in succession to Samuel Blyth in Apr. 1791, remained as minister at New Meeting until 1802. See Wykes, '"A finished monster"', pp. 55–6, 66.
4   I have not made a positive identification of Mr Lion. However, Lindsey implies that he was a relatively young man, known, and living close to, William Alexander, and probably a dissenter. On this basis, one might conjecture that Mr Lion was either Henry Lion of Huntingfield, who was born on 18 June and baptized on 20 June 1769, or James Lion of Heveningham, who was born on 1 Dec. 1770 and baptized on 4 Jan. 1771. Their dates of birth are consistent with Lindsey's comment. Both were baptized by John Walker (1719–1805), a former pupil of Doddridge at Northampton, and minister of the independent congregation of Walpole, Suffolk, from 1767 to 1805; TNA: RG4/1862, fos. 3, 5. Huntingfield and Heveningham are within six miles of Yoxford, where Alexander lived.

477. To WILLIAM TAYLEUR   19 OCTOBER 1791

Text: JRUL, Lindsey Letters, vol. II, no. 57.
Printed: McLachlan, *Letters*, pp. 117–18 (part of fourth sentence of fourth paragraph; fifth paragraph).
Addressed: To/William Tayleur Esqr/Shrewsbury
Endorsed: 19th Oct^r – 91
Postmarked: OC 19 91

London. Octr. 19. 1791

Dear Sir,

Somebody is always devising liberal things. May heaven which gives the disposition still prolong the life in tolerable ease and comfort! D^r and Mrs Priestley dine with us to day, to go on in the afternoon to visit Mrs Rayner, who is another constant deviser of liberal things. I shall then communicate the contents of your generous letter to him, and write to you again perhaps to morrow, or the day following: but having half an hour's vacancy for our house is seldom empty, I thought I would tell you of the arrival of your letter.[1] I wished also to acquaint you that I had at that instant finished a letter to Dr Disney at Bath, in reply to one, which had communicated to me the first notice of the intended chapel at Newark, and his desire to promote it, and wishes for my assistance.[2] And I had wrote him back, that I was sorry my hands were so much tyed at present by engagements to help them still farther at Plymouth Dock, where the arrears of their building &c tho' in nothing extravagant, were still considerable, and I had promised Mr Jardine my assistance for their new chapel: but that ten guineas sh^d be at his service, and I hoped they wou'd begin and go on with their intended chapel and trust a good providence for friends, as great good must result from it. But no mention was made to me, that he himself had been thought of as the Minister.[3]

I shall most truly be glad to do all I can to forward the business. Newark is so very conspicuous a place, upon the great North road, that an Unitarian chapel there must attract continual notice.

You may depend upon learning from me as soon as any thing is decided relating to Dr Price's successor. I am daily inquisitive about it, and receive various accounts, the last not so favourable, but nothing can be known till the trial is made.

We saw D^r. Priestley yesterday, when he appeared quite stout. Mr Rous's letter, among other excellent things, is a noble defence of Dr Priestley, and Dissenters, and contains some manly bold strictures on Birm. riots and the management about them.[4] On second thoughts I shall keep my letter open, till Dr P. comes, and give you his reply to y^r kindness to day: for why sh^d you pay postage for 2 letters, who calculate so well how to lay out every mite. Dr P. is just come in, and desires me to say, that he knows not how to express himself for this late instance of your most generous kindness to him after all the preceding, but will write himself soon: and in the mean time, as you in such a way[5] it, he will thank you to send your bounty to him by a draft to me, or in any other manner you shall judge proper.[6]

He has a letter to day from Mr Russell, signifying to him, that himself and the congregation have upon farther deliberation on his proposal of coming amongst them for a few weeks decided, that it will be better for him not to come at all, lest the Savages sh^d be let loose upon him, the words used.[7] But he is to receive a letter in form from the congregation. By his acc^t. the intolerant spirit grows worse and worse in that town. Alas! no wonder, when it has been so fed.

Heaven be praised that you are well, and your congregation quiet.[8] I still persuade myself, being always disposed to hope, that good will come from these great evils, and that soon, and that we shall live to see it. With my wifes most due respects to you

I remain always, Dear Sir, Your most truly obliged and faithful affectionate servant

T. Lindsey.

---

1   This letter from Tayleur to Lindsey is not among Tayleur's letters in JRUL, C2^{13}.
2   This proposal for a unitarian chapel at Newark was not realized, although it is possible that Disney envisaged some kind of private unitarian worship among his own family and other sympathizers; *Unitarian Society … 1794*, p. 21, listed as a member of the society John Huddlestone of Newark, whose subscription was conveyed by Disney. The first record of a unitarian chapel at Newark was that in King's Road, founded in 1862; see Evans, *Vestiges*, p. 180. I am grateful to the Rev. Andrew Hill for advice on this point.
3   See n. 2, above. Disney did not leave Essex Street chapel, where he remained until his retirement in 1805, to become the minister at Newark or anywhere else. I have not located this exchange of letters between him and Lindsey. For David Jardine, see Letter 418, n. 3; for the chapel at Plymouth Dock, see Letter 454.
4   George Rous published his defence of Priestley in the form of an open letter which appeared as an appendix to David Jones's *Stricture on a pamphlet, entitled, thoughts on the late riot at Birmingham. By a Welsh freeholder* (London, 1791), pp. 26–9. For the *Thoughts on the late riot at Birmingham*, see Letter 464, n. 4. For Rous, see Letter 449, n. 5.
5   Word missing: probably 'suggest'.
6   This latest example of Tayleur's generosity to Priestley is not mentioned in a surviving letter from Priestley to Lindsey; and no letters from Tayleur to Lindsey survive from 1791 in JRUL, C2^{13}. On 29 June 1791, Priestley had written to Lindsey: 'While Mr. Tayleur lives, at least let us never neglect to see him annually. His time, and indeed ours, cannot be long. Let us often meet, and encourage one another'; Rutt, I, 114. Barely two weeks later, the Birmingham riots rendered impossible these hoped-for meetings with Tayleur.
7   This letter from William Russell to Priestley appears not to have survived. Priestley's letters to Russell, dated 29 Sept. and 3 Oct. 1791 (Rutt, I, 161–3) indicate that he still thought of returning to Birmingham. He signified the same intention, albeit on a temporary basis, in his letter to the New Meeting congregation of 8 Oct. 1791; Rutt, I, 164–6. Possibly Priestley's letter to his congregation of 28 Oct. 1791, in which he acknowledged the impossibility even of a brief visit to Birmingham, was a reply to the letter from Russell to which Lindsey referred; Rutt, I, 169–70.
8   The unitarian congregation in the High Street chapel, Shrewsbury.

478. To WILLIAM TAYLEUR   6 NOVEMBER 1791

Text: JRUL, Lindsey Letters, vol. II, no. 58.
Printed: McLachlan, *Letters*, p. 89 (third paragraph, where the letter is
                  mis-dated 8 Nov. 1791); p. 118 (first paragraph and latter
                  section of second paragraph).
Addressed: To/William Tayleur Esqr./Shrewsbury
Endorsed: 6th Nov^r – 91
Postmarked: NO 7 91

Sunday night. 9 o'clock
Novr. 6. 1791

Dear Sir

You will wonder at the date of my letter; but being to set out early in the morning to see a friend who has been ill, ten miles off,[1] in order to return early in the evening the same day, I was desirous thus to take the very first opportunity of acquainting you that Dr Priestley has this day been declared by a great majority, 51 to 19, successor to Dr Price at the Gravel pits meeting, and I sit down to write to you the moment the D^r and his eldest son who is come to see him from Manchester leave us, having passed the day with us.[2]

I cannot but look upon this as the most honourable situation for him as a Dissenting Minister after having been driven away from his own, and likely to be extremely useful to many, & particularly to our New College which you foster with such kind and unceasing care. To name one circumstance only; the students will every week hear his admirable exposition of the N.T. from which they will every way learn so much, and which he will unquestionably resume there.[3] This event fills us with the more joy, as there was much underhand opposition made to his election from some ministerial persons.[4]

You would see in the Morning Chronicle how well every thing went on at the London Tavern on the 4th. of November. Much of it was owing to our worthy Chairman, Mr Walker of Manchester, who with an ample commanding figure has a nobler spirit to fill and animate it; and to the music being happily intermixed with the toasts, with some excellent songs; and the famous french revolution tune, *ça ira*, seemed to inspire the whole company with a portion of their spirit. It is very simple, with no variety, yet chearing in a high degree. I thought I could observe several absent that used to be constant attendants, whom I suspected to keep away lest the court sh^d suspect they had any connection with the thing called a revolution a hundred years ago. The room however was very full, tho' not so crouded as the two last years.[5]

I am not certain whether I told you that Dr Priestleys appeal to the Public will probably be in Town in less than three weeks. He has lately added a Preface which I like greatly. I think I told you how much I admired the short Dedication to the people of England: so much, that I only wished it had been longer.[6]

I hope this cold day, has not hurt you, as it is dry. With my wife's sincere respects, I remain ever Your most truly obliged and faithful servant

T. Lindsey.

[1] This friend was Rosamund Sargent, who was staying with her Chambers relatives at Morden; see Letter 479.

[2] This ballot took place on 6 Nov. 1791 and Priestley was elected minister of the Gravel Pit meeting, Hackney, in succession to Price, by more than the necessary two-thirds majority. For the background,

see Wykes, 'Priestley at Hackney', 513–17. For Priestley's eldest son, Joseph junior, at this time, see Letter 440, n. 7.

3   Although Priestley published the chemical lectures which he delivered at Hackney College in 1791 and 1792, he did not publish his lectures on the New Testament.

4   Priestley served at the Gravel Pit meeting, Hackney, from 1791 until his emigration to America in Apr. 1794. Much of the opposition to his appointment sprang from a fear that he would attract notoriety and possibly violence to the congregation; see Rutt, I, 161–4, and Wykes, 'Priestley at Hackney', 516–17. There was also an undercurrent of suspicion of his Socinian opinions; a significant section of the congregation would have preferred another Arian as Price's successor.

5   The *Morning Chronicle*, 5 Nov. 1791, reported in detail the meeting of the Revolution Society at the London Tavern the previous day. It listed the toasts given, noted that Thomas Walker of Manchester was the chairman of the meeting and stated that 250 persons were present. The minute book of the Revolution Society estimated that 'near 300 Friends to Freedom' attended, but did not list the toasts; BL, Add. MS 64814, fos. 48r–50v.

6   Priestley's *Appeal to the public* was published in Birmingham in 1791. The dedication 'to the people of England', dated 1 Nov. 1791, advocated reform as an antidote to revolution and Priestley insisted that he was 'a friend to the general principles of our constitution'. He signed himself 'Your injured Countryman' (pp. xiv–xv).

479. To SAMUEL SHORE III   7 NOVEMBER 1791

Text: DWL, MS 12.57 (8).
Addressed: To/Samuel Shore Esqr/Meersbrook/near/Sheffield
Postmarked: NO 7 91

London. Novr. 7. 1791.

Dear Sir,

You will be somewhat surprised to see my handwriting so soon again, but I persuade myself that you will not scruple the postage of a letter extraordinary, which carries you the news of Dr Priestley being yesterday chosen successor to Dr Price at the Meeting at Hackney. He had a letter from one of his voters last night when he was with us, with an account of it. It was first agreed, that two gentlemen of the two parties should be chosen, to compare the lists together, and by their report the matter was to be decided. Their report was, that there were full two thirds for Dr Priestley: but an old Gentlewoman desiring there might be a ballot, it was acquiesced in, and the number were 51 for and 19 against: Upon which he was declared to be elected.[1]

No situation equally honourable in the kingdom for a Dissenting Minister, than to be a successor to Dr Price in such circumstances. It will also sound particularly well abroad at this time. It will also be useful to many in a high degree. The youth of our New College will hear weekly his most valuable exposition of the N.T. a good part of which he has recovered, and which he will certainly resume. And thirteen years hence I trust your grandson Sydney will be of the number.[2]

You will excuse the breaking off so abruptly, but we are setting out this morning at the hour of eight to see Mrs Sargent at Mordon and are to return in the evening. You know perhaps she has lately lost Mr S.[3]

My wife desires to join in due respects to your lady and at Norton-Hall, and I remain always your most truly obliged and faithful servant

T. Lindsey.

1   See Letter 478.
2   Sydney Shore (1790–1827), born on 14 Apr. 1790, was the son of Samuel Shore IV (1761–1836) of Norton Hall and his wife Harriet (née Foye), and the grandson of Samuel Shore III (1738–1828). As Hackney College closed in 1796, he was educated at Manchester College, York, which was founded at Manchester in the same year (1786) as Hackney.

3   The former MP John Sargent, of Halstead Place, Kent, died on 20 Sept. 1791. His widow, Rosamund
    Sargent, who died in 1792, was the sister of Sophia and Frances Chambers of Morden. See Letter
    457, n. 1.

480. To WILLIAM TAYLEUR   3 DECEMBER 1791

Text: JRUL, Lindsey Letters, vol. III, no. 34.
Printed: McLachlan, 'More letters', 376 (first two sentences of second
                  paragraph; 362 (third paragraph, mis-dated to 19 Sept. 1791,
                  and with errors of transcription); 373 (fourth paragraph, with
                  errors of transcription).
Addressed: To/William Tayleur Esq[r]/Shrewsbury
Endorsed: 3[d] Dec[r] – 1791
Postmarked: DE 3 91

London. Dec[r]. 3. 1791.

Dear Sir,

I write by the return of the post, tho Saturday in general is a very busy day, because I think it will give you pleasure to learn that your letter is received by me, and also to hear that the party you wrote about has consented to suspend, and not to send out any thing but what may be agreeable to the friends, of whom I formerly spoke, and from one of whom I have received the account.[1]

M[r] Russell has lately been in Town, and seems to think that M[r] P.[2] is disposed to let every thing be done to indemnify the sufferers at Birmingham. But M[r] Dundas, who is more immediately concerned in those affairs, has shewn himself so hostile, that many give very little credit to the Minister's promises.[3] At all events I fear our friends losses will not be made up by any thing that the justice of the country will afford him.

It was a very good plan to commit to the flames the letter I sent, and I dare say I need not desire that the same way may be taken with respect to any confidential letters I may have formerly sent. One cannot be too cautious, when living, in this respect, as one knows not who will come after us.[4]

I presume you must have heard the particulars of the late little rebellion at your own school, Westminster. It seems, the Rights of Man has been the favourite book, and they have thoroughly imbibed the spirit of it.[5] In consequence of this, fagging has been intirely banished, as aristocratical. On what immediate occasion it happened, I know not, but the boys all joined in singing the famous tune *ça ira*, before the Masters, who were at last obliged to submit, by the intervention of the Mediators, at which I am told Dr Vincent expressed himself not well pleased.[6]

There has been somewhat of an attempt of the same kind at the Charterhouse school: but it was carried against the Democrates.[7]

I am much concerned at the account of a friend lately come from Paris, who has also been in the provinces.[8] The Emigrants are 70,000 strong in Germany. They have 300 of the late national Assembly with them. Calonne[9] has been in Spain, and has actually procured for them 40 millions of livres, a million and half sterling, transmitted to them by way of Holland: and they are supported by Russia, Sweden, the Emperor as far as he can, Prussia, England as far as it dares. The weakness of the princes and the trigues and quarrels among the nobles and generals may perhaps impede the business but it wears a formidable aspect.[10] Add to this, the national Assembly with no proportion of able men, and without any great leading characters.

I send you what I hear, and still hope providence will support the cause of liberty and the rights of men.

I have time only to add my wifes respects, and that I remain always Dear Sir Your most truly obliged and affectionate

T. Lindsey.

Pray how does good D[r] Jane? and where is he?[11]

---

1   The non-survival in JRUL, C2[13] of any letters from Tayleur to Lindsey between Nov. 1790 and Apr. 1792 renders difficult the identification of the 'party' to whom Tayleur had written, or the subject of his letter. Possibilities include the debate over the preamble to the Unitarian Society's rules and the opposition to Priestley's appointment as minister to the Gravel Pit meeting, Hackney.

2   William Pitt.

3   Henry Dundas was home secretary from June 1791 to July 1794.

4   There is no clue as to which letter from Lindsey Tayleur burned; it was presumably a letter written by Lindsey himself, rather than a letter to Lindsey from someone else which Lindsey had forwarded to Tayleur, although this cannot now be verified. One can only speculate ruefully as to the numbers of other letters of Lindsey which might have been lost in this way.

5   Paine's *Rights of man*, part I.

6   For this outbreak of disorder at Westminster school, apparently occasioned by a fight between two boys in Dean's Yard, but perhaps influenced also by fashionable Painite ideas, see *Public Advertiser*, 26 and 29 Nov. 1791, and John D. Carleton, *Westminster school. A history* (London, rev. edn, 1965), pp. 39–40. William Vincent (1739–1815) was headmaster of Westminster school from 1788 to 1801 and rector of All Hallows-the-Great, London, from 1788 to 1803. A former chaplain to George III, he was dean of Westminster from 1802 until his death.

7   There is a comment on an outbreak of disorder at the Charterhouse in 1792, apparently provoked by 'libellous notices about the imposition of certain charges' and a demonstration against the house-keeper, which was 'settled without undue fuss', in Anthony Quick, *Charterhouse. A history of the school* (London, 1990), p. 39. See also *Public Advertiser*, 21 July 1792. If Lindsey had detected an earlier incident of this type at the Charterhouse in the latter months of 1791, it seems to have been settled with even less 'fuss'.

8   Possibly this was the friend to whom Lindsey referred in Letter 473; for a possible identification, see Letter 473, n. 8.

9   For Charles Alexandre, vicomte de Calonne, see Letter 430, n. 11. In the autumn of 1791, he sought support for the émigré cause against the French revolutionary regime from Sweden, Spain and Russia. From Spain, he received only expressions of good will. Between Dec. 1792 and July 1793 he was actually in Spain, under the pseudonym Baron de Ringler, hoping for Spanish military intervention on behalf of the émigrés. In July 1793, he left Spain for the Bourbon kingdom of Naples. See Robert Lacour-Gayet, *Calonne. Financier, reformateur. Contre-revolutionnaire 1734–1802* (Paris, 1963), pp. 378, 436–43.

10 See n. 9, above. The émigrés had established a camp at Coblenz, where they were indeed preparing an army on the borders of France. They were encouraged by the denunciations of the French regime made by the emperor Leopold II, and hoped for assistance from Russia and Sweden. For the background, see T. C. W. Blanning, *The origin of the French revolutionary wars* (London, 1986), ch. 4.

11 Possibly Joseph Jane (1716–95), with whom Tayleur seems to have been acquainted; see Vol. I, Letter 345, n. 2.

481. To RUSSELL SCOTT   **31 DECEMBER 1791**

Text: Scott Coll.
Printed: McLachlan, 'Lindsey to Scott', 118 (second and third
                 sentences of first paragraph).
Addressed: To/The Rev^d. Russell Scott/Portsmouth
Postmarked: Postmark missing.

London. December. 31. 1791

Dear Sir,

I have been rather in expectation of a few lines to say how you were at home, and how things went on around you. And it was by the mere accident of meeting a worthy person of your congregation in Johnson's shop, that I learned that Mrs Scott had made some addition to your family.[1] We hope that she and the little one are well, and the good father also; and as this will salute you on the beginning of the year, we desire to present the stranger with the inclosed £10 bill for a New Years gift, with earnest wishes that it may live and be useful in the world and become a comfort to its parents half a century hence, if it so please Divine Providence. As soon as you conveniently can, you will take the trouble to let me know how you all do, and that this comes to hand.

I inclose a few copies of the plan of the Christian Miscellany, which Mr Kingsbury, recomended by Mr Belsham has undertaken to conduct as Editor, and I heartily wish he may succeed in it. And as the price is so easy, I hope there will not be wanting encouragement for him to make the experiment he proposes.[2] But there must be many and able hands engaged in such a work to make it answer expectation, and I hope they will come forth if it can once get on a good footing.

Dr Priestley has publishd his first sermon at Hackney, and that intended to have been preached at Birmingham, but delivered here for him by Mr Cotes.[3] His Appeal to the Public on the Riots at Birmingham will not be out before the latter end of January.[4] There is a little piece just printed by Mr Johnson, Timothy Sobersides – to Jonathan Blast, price 6^d is very well drawn up, and likely to do good among those for whom it is calculated. I may tell you, but do not mention it so as to have it get into the News-papers, that it is by Mr Keir, the great chymist, intimate with Dr Priestley, and author of the life of Mr Day.[5]

I hope your sister is well. I am sorry to withdraw without filling my pages as I had intended – but I have literally had [a] gentleman who has called in on business so long, that I have only time to unite *our* kind respects to Mrs Scott, and with my wife's to yourself to say that I am always Dear Sir most truly Yours

T. Lindsey.

---

1   Scott's first child, a son (Russell Scott) was born on 27 Oct. 1791, but died on 24 May 1797; see Letter 658, n. 1, and Scott, *Family biography*, table IV. Possibly the 'worthy' member of Scott's congregation whom Lindsey met in Johnson's shop was a member of the Carter family (see Letters 402 and 439); or William Joseph Porter (see Letter 602, n. 1); or Richard Godman Temple (see Letter 522, n. 3).

2   For the *Christian Miscellany*, see Letter 418, n. 7, and 420, n. 2. Mr Kingsbury was probably Benjamin Kingsbury, a former pupil of Belsham at the Daventry Academy, and minister at High Street chapel, Warwick, from 1786 to 1789 and at Evesham from 1790 to 1791, when he retired from the ministry.

3   For these two sermons of Priestley, see Letter 482, n. 1. In the preface (pp. iii–v) to the *Discourse* intended to have been preached at Birmingham, Priestley explained that because of popular hostility to him, he felt unable to preach at, or even visit, that town. His colleague Samuel Blyth offered to deliver it in Priestley's name, but was unable to do so because of his age (born on 31 Jan. 1718,

he was aged almost seventy-four in Dec. 1791, when the sermon was due to be preached). John Coates (d. 1836), assistant minister to Radcliffe Scholefield at the Old Meeting, Birmingham, delivered the sermon instead. Priestley's preface was dated 12 Dec. 1791. Coates, a pupil at Warrington Academy from 1779 to 1780 and subsequently at Hoxton, was assistant minister at the Old Meeting, Birmingham from 1785 to 1801; and was minister to the congregation at St Thomas's, Southwark, from 1802 to 1813. He was also a member of the Presbyterian board, a trustee of Dr Williams's Library (from 1804 to 1821) and Dr Williams's librarian at Red Cross Street from 1821 to 1834. See the obituary of Coates in *CR*, NS, III (1836), 514.

4   See Letter 478, n. 6. Priestley's *Appeal to the public* was advertised as 'this day is published' in the *Morning Chronicle*, 24 Jan. 1792, although newspapers frequently made this statement about newly published books on different dates.

5   This work was the pseudonymous *A letter from Timothy Sobersides, extinguisher-maker at Wolverhampton, to Jonathan Blast, bellows-maker at Birmingham* (London, 1792). The publisher was Joseph Johnson. The work is attributed by modern scholars to James Keir (1735–1820), chemist, industrialist and whig; see the entry for Keir by Barbara M. D. Smith, *ODNB*, XXXI, 51. For what was probably another reference by Lindsey to this work, see Letter 491, n. 7. Keir's *An account of the life and writings of Thomas Day* was published in London in 1791; see Letter 448.

482. To WILLIAM TAYLEUR   5 JANUARY 1792

Text: JRUL, Lindsey Letters, vol. II, no. 59.
Printed: McLachlan, *Letters*, p. 101 (most of third paragraph).
Addressed: To/William Tayleur Esqr/Shrewsbury
Endorsed: 5th Jany 1792
Postmarked: JA 5 92

London. Jan. 5. 1792.

Dear Sir,

So many days of the new year would not have passed without carrying mine and my wife's most cordial respects and wishes of every good to yourself and the continuance of the same usefulness to others, a high and happy privilege, which we trust you will still enjoy for years to come: if I had not been wholly engaged in visits and the avocations of the season. The beginning of the week Dr Priestley was with us, and I am to meet him to day to dine at a common friend's. In better health, or a more pleasing flow of spirits I never beheld him, and he says, that his situation becomes more and more acceptable to him. Mrs Priestley indeed busies herself in the house in her labours and exertions to make it neat and convenient. His library and conveniences for his philosophical apparatus and experiments are particularly suitable and agreeable. I dare say you have had sent you his two sermons, and probably Dr Disney's.[1] The Laymans Pamphlet has been out two days; I doubt not you will get it soon; but I wish you could circulate it, as I think it will be of service to have it dispersed – The title is – High-Church-Politics: Being a seasonable Appeal to the Friends of the British Constitution, against the Practices and Principles of High Churchmen, as exemplified in the late Opposition to the repeal of the Test laws, and in the riots at Birmingham. – for Johnson.[2]

I think in my last I mentioned our new arrangements in the college at Hackney.[3] We shall now I trust go on without fear of total bankruptcy. Mr Jones's loss at the college, as tutor and lecturer, would be more felt than it will, now that Dr Priestley has generously offerd to give some lectures to the young men in chymistry and experimental philosophy.[4] I rejoice that Mr Jones, who is now at Birm. a candidate to succeed Dr Priestley there, is so well approved.[5] He is indeed in all respects, in theology, in philosophy, in zeal for the truth, one of our most promising subjects.

They are going on remarkably well at Plymouth, and at the Dock.[6] Only M[r] Porter has a little Draw-back of illness through overplying the machine, but is now better.[7] In Suffolk also, particularly about Woodbridge, Yoxford &c there are several excellent persons, of great piety, and sober but active zeal, who have been lately enlightened with respect to the Divine unity. One of them in a letter yesterday tells me he had just read their Bishops charge (Horn) and pities him for his narrowness of mind. I have not yet seen this charge, but shall now get it.[8]

There are great divisions among M[r] J. Wesley's followers. A large party, under D[r] Coke, have written to D[r] Whitehead, to insist on their seeing the life of M[r] Wesley, which D[r] W. is compiling by desire of the Trustees, one of em, D[r] C. himself, with the liberty of making such alterations as they shall judge proper. This not being granted, they are about to compile a life of their leader themselves.[9] I was yesterday informed by a judicious person, who had been that morning with D[r] Whitehead, and conversed with him on the subject, that his life of Wesley will be well conducted, not too flattering, abounding with many curious particulars from letters, MSS. &c, particularly two little excellent MS. Vol. of Meditations by Old M[rs] Wesley, the mother of them all.[10] The Arminian Magazine, w[ch] is carried on for the great sum it brings in, is full of nauseous accounts of *experiences* &c.[11]

We hope that M[r] Rowe and his family and M[r] Wood are well, and beg to be properly and kindly remembered to them. I remain, always, writing or silent, ever

Dear Sir, Your most truly obliged and affectionate servant

T. Lindsey.

I have been twice with M[r] M. to whom you wrote the letter some time since: but nothing has transpired with regard to its effects.[12]

---

1   Priestley's two sermons were *A particular attention to the instruction of the young recommended, in a discourse, delivered at the Gravel-Pit meeting, in Hackney, December 4, 1791, on entering on the office of pastor to the congregation of protestant dissenters, assembling in that place* (London, 1791), and *The duty of forgiveness of injuries: a discourse intended to be delivered soon after the riots in Birmingham* (Birmingham, 1791). Disney's work was *A defence of public or social worship. A sermon preached in the unitarian chapel, in Essex Street, on Sunday, December 4, 1791* (London, 1792).

2   This work was Samuel Heywood's *High church politics*; Lindsey set out the full title correctly. It appeared without Heywood's name, although his authorship was no secret. Joseph Johnson was indeed the publisher.

3   Lindsey's previous surviving letter to Tayleur, dated 3 Dec. 1791 (Letter 480), did not mention the new arrangements at Hackney College, although its predecessor (Letter 478) made brief reference to Priestley's theological lectures there. Possibly Lindsey had described them in a non-surviving letter to Tayleur (perhaps that which Tayleur burned; see Letter 480). These new arrangements included the assumption of the responsibility for the domestic management of the college by Belsham's unmarried sister Ann, a function which she had discharged at Daventry. Belsham himself took responsibility for discipline, and Priestley gave his lectures without charge. See Williams, pp. 442–4. Belsham wryly noted: 'Had the college set out [i.e. from its foundation] upon this prudent plan, it might have subsisted in spite of its enemies'; Williams, p. 444.

4   Priestley published these lectures as *Heads of lectures on a course of experimental philosophy, particularly including chemistry, delivered at the New College in Hackney* (London, 1794). The volume was dedicated to the Hackney students. Another edition was published in Dublin in 1794.

5   David Jones, a former senior student at Hackney College, served as a tutor in experimental science there from 1789 to 1792. He did indeed succeed Priestley as minister (alongside John Edwards) at the New Meeting, Birmingham; see Letter 476, n. 3.

6   The unitarian chapel at Plymouth Dock was opened on 27 Apr. 1791; see Letter 454, n. 4.

7   Thomas Porter was minister to the dissenting congregation at Treville Street, Plymouth, from 1789 to 1794. Perhaps his over-exertion was partly occasioned by his work on the unitarian liturgy adopted by his congregation; see Letter 406.

8   Probably the writer of this (apparently non-surviving) letter was William Alexander of Yoxford or
    Edward Evanson, who at that time resided at Great Blakenham, near Ipswich. George Horne was
    bishop of Norwich from June 1790 until his death on 17 Jan. 1792. His *Charge intended to have been
    delivered to the clergy of Norwich, at the primary visitation* was published in London in Norwich
    in 1791; in a brief 'advertisement', Horne explained that ill-health prevented him from visiting his
    diocesan clergy and delivering the *Charge* in person. In the *Charge* he deplored (pp. 8–9) what he
    saw as a decline of belief, which he attributed to 'an abuse of abstract reasoning', in the doctrine of
    the Trinity.

9   Thomas Coke (1747–1814), one of John Wesley's closest advisors, was superintendent, and subse-
    quently a bishop, of the methodist church in post-independence America. On Wesley's death, he
    returned rapidly to Britain. He and other methodist preachers disagreed with John Whitehead's
    proposals for his *Life* of John Wesley (see Letter 447, n. 8), partly because of a dispute over the use
    of the financial proceedings of its sale. They also resented Whitehead's insistence on retaining exclu-
    sive possession of Wesley's papers until the completion of his work, whereas Wesley had bequeathed
    them to Coke and to the methodist preacher Henry Moore (1751–1844) as well as to Whitehead. As
    a result, Coke and Moore published their own biography, entitled *The life of the Rev. John Wesley,
    A.M., including an account of the great revival of religion, in Europe and America, of which he was
    the first and chief instrument* (London, 1792). It appeared one year before the publication of the first
    volume of Whitehead's *Life* of Wesley.

10 Susanna Wesley (1669–1742), née Annesley, was indeed the mother of Charles and John Wesley and
    a formative influence over their lives. For Whitehead's use of her 'Meditiations', see his *Life* of John
    Wesley, I, 38–42, 380.

11 The *Arminian Magazine, Consisting of Extracts, and Original Translations on Universal Redemp-
    tion*, was founded by John Wesley in 1778, mainly to counteract the arguments of Calvinistic method-
    ists. It ran until 1797 and was edited by Wesley himself until 1791.

12 Tayleur had written to James Martin MP, encouraging him to embrace unitarianism publicly; see
    Letter 437, n. 6, and 440, n. 1.

483. To SAMUEL SHORE   7 JANUARY 1792

    Text: NYRO, ZFW 7/2/72/2, Wyvill of Constable Burton MSS.

    Printed: Ditchfield, 'Lindsey–Wyvill correspondence', 162 (second and
                      third sentences of first paragraph; whole of third paragraph).

    Addressed: To/Samuel Shore Esq[r]/Meersbrook/near/Sheffield

    Endorsed: From M[r] Lindsey inclosing a Letter from M[r] W. Morgan
                      Jan. 7. 1792 respecting an invitation to D[r] Price to go over to
                      America to assist y[e] promotion [of] the Revolution[1]

    Postmarked: JA 7 92

London. 7. Jan[y]. 1792

Dear Sir,

    You will perceive by the date on the opposite page, that it was not in my power
to return the answer to M[r] Wyvill sooner, and having no time to procure a frank you
will excuse it being sent without one.[2] I have sent to M[r] Johnson to send you High
Church Politics &c.[3] It is a book that sh[d] be in the hands of every Dissenter and
liberal person in England. The french, I see, are not discouraged by this duplicity of
the Emperor. They are only afraid we are playing the same game, and subsidizing
in the same cause, *pour la surete des couronnes*, as the emperor expresses himself.[4]

    I am well assured by those competent to know, that our Cabinet have had several
meetings on the Catholic demands in Ireland, and that they are much disturbed by
them.[5] The Irish nation will certainly never cooperate in an open attempt against
the present french government: Nor will the english, not even the tories, when they
are pinched by one tax more, which they are sure to be. There is to be a meeting of
the Country-Delegates on Wednesday.[6] They all wish that you were in Town: but I

yesterday learned from Mrs Crompton,[7] that you are not expected at[?] Clapham till the parliament meets.[8]

I am glad to inform you, that the B^p of Landaff – Watson's charge to his clergy, in 1791, is printing. You may have heard of its boldness, in declaring[?] an approbation of the Fr. Revolution, of the repeal of the Test-laws, and the Reformation of the Liturgy.[9] These movements must do good.

My wife has been poorly, but is much better. *We* hope you and yours are all well – and desires [*sic*] due respects to your lady, with my wifes to yourself, and proper remembrances at Norton Hall and else where. The day before yesterday Mrs Blackburne presented her husband with another little girl.[10]

I remain always Dear Sir, your most truly obliged and faithful affectionate servant
T: Lindsey.

Dr Priestley is very well, and in spirits. His Appeal comes out, as I think I mentioned, at the end of the month.[11]

---

1   This letter from William Morgan to Lindsey, 7 Jan. 1792, may be found in NYRO, ZFW 7/2/72/3. In it, Morgan responded to Wyvill's questions by explaining that Richard Price, his uncle, had been invited to the United States in 1780 to provide financial advice, rather than to assist in drawing up the constitution. He added that although Price did not write a specific work on public provision for the clergy, in his *Observations on the importance of the American Revolution* (London, 1784), he denounced church establishments in general and expressed opposition to all but voluntary payments to the clergy.

2   I.e. the date of Morgan's letter (see n. 1, above), which Lindsey had obtained in response to queries from Wyvill.

3   For Samuel Heywood's *High church politics*, see Letter 429, n. 9.

4   See *Morning Chronicle*, 2, 4, and 6 Jan. 1792. Following the declaration of Pillnitz on 27 Aug., the emperor Leopold II issued a declaration in Dec. 1791 insisting on the restoration of all the feudal rights of the German princes in Alsace and Lorraine. In Paris, the Girondin party, enjoying a temporary ascendancy, rejected the emperor's demands and urged war against Austria. In 1791 and 1792, Britain maintained a policy of neutrality and Lindsey exaggerated the sympathy of Pitt's ministry with the Austrian position.

5   For these cabinet meetings and catholic demands for a relief bill in the winter of 1791–2, see Ehrman, *The Younger Pitt. The reluctant transition*, pp. 219–24.

6   The following Wednesday was 11 Jan. 1792. There is no record of this 'meeting of country delegates' in the Unitarian Society minute book or in the minutes of the protestant dissenting deputies, London Metropolitan Archives, 3083/3. However, for what was evidently a meeting of these delegates in June 1792, see Letter 501, n. 1.

7   Probably Sarah, née Fox, the wife of Samuel Crompton (1750–1810) of Wood End, Thirsk, Yorkshire,who was a supporter of Wyvill's moves for reform. See Wyvill, *Political papers*, VI, 1. She was probably the Mrs Crompton of Clapham listed as a subscriber to William Enfield's *Sermons on practical subjects*, I, xxxi. See also Letter 765.

8   Samuel Shore III had a residence at Clapham, as did William Smith, MP. He was one of the 'country delegates' to the committee for the repeal of the Test and Corporation Acts in 1790; *Committees for repeal*, p. 65. The new session of parliament opened on 31 Jan. 1792.

9   Richard Watson's *A charge delivered to the clergy of the diocese of Llandaff, June, 1791* was published in London in 1792. Watson gave qualified support to the French Revolution, rejoicing at 'the emancipation of the French nation from the tyranny of regal despotism', and applauding the suppression of the monasteries. He advocated full civil equality for dissenters as conducive to public harmony, and argued that the Church of England should be open to reform; *Charge*, pp. 6, 9, 14–15, 19–22.

10   Hannah, née Wilson, the wife of Dr William Blackburne, gave birth to Elizabeth Rachel Blackburne, the elder of their two daughters, on 5 Jan. 1792. Her baptism, on 4 Feb. 1792, is recorded at DWL.

11   See Letter 478, n. 6. Priestley's *Appeal to the public*, Part I, although with a publication date on the title page of 1791, and with a dedication dated 1 Nov. 1791, actually appeared at the end of Jan. 1792.

484. To RUSSELL SCOTT   **4 FEBRUARY 1792**

> **Text:**   Scott Coll.
> **Addressed:**   To/The Rev^d. M^r. Russell Scott/Portsmouth
> **Endorsed:**   Feby. 5th. – 92 [in pencil] Read
> **Postmarked:** FE 4 92

London Feb. 4. 1792.

Dear Sir,

I have just received your letter, inclosing 3 guineas, to pay our Treasurer, Mr Carters, yours, and Mr Porters annual Subscriptions to the unitarian society.[1] Yours I had already paid, and shall take the first opportunity of paying the others. But if you chuse I should be repaid your's, it shall be so.

I shall take care to deliver yours and Mr Carters, letters of appointment to Mr Johnson; but he can send you no books, till you send your nominations of such as you w^d chuse to the amount of your Subscription. There is an ambiguity in the Secretarys letter, which has misled you and many others.[2]

I write by the first[3] post, that I may be in time for your friend who is coming to town the beginning of the approaching week.[4] By him you may send to Mr Johnson for your books. And I beg he may call at our house, as I have a little parcell, *at this moment made up*, standing by me, for you – containing Dr Priestleys 2 Sermons – his appeal on the riots,[5] and another book, highly to be prized, High-church Politics; or a seasonable appeal &c.[6]

We are glad that Mrs Scott and your little man[7] are well – Our best comp^ts attend her with my wifes to yourself and every good wish for you all.

I have not time, or could easily procure a frank. Let me hear from you when you are at leisure, and have gotten the parcell, and I shal [*sic*] write more at length. I wish the Christian Miscellany may answer[8] – in haste but always most truly Yours

> T. Lindsey.

---

1 John Carter of Wimmering, near Portsmouth, and William Joseph Porter were both listed as members of the Unitarian Society in 1791. The subscription was one guinea per person. Scott's letter to Lindsey seems not to have survived.

2 I have not found a copy of this circular letter from the secretary (John Disney) of the Unitarian Society. Perhaps understandably, this matter is not mentioned in the society's minute book.

3 Lindsey originally wrote 'return of', then over-wrote 'first'.

4 For a possible identification of this friend of Scott, see Letter 481, n. 1.

5 For Priestley's two sermons, see Letter 482, n. 1. For his *Appeal to the public*, see Letter 483, n, 11.

6 See Letter 482, n. 2.

7 Scott's son Russell Scott, born on 27 Oct. 1791.

8 For the *Christian Miscellany*, see Letters 418, n. 7 and 481, n. 2.

485. To WILLIAM TAYLEUR   **15 FEBRUARY 1792**

Text: JRUL, Lindsey Letters, vol. II, no. 60.
Printed: McLachlan, *Letters*, p. 70 (third and most of fourth
              paragraphs); p. 132 (sixth, seventh and eighth paragraphs).
Addressed: Address missing.
Postmarked: Postmark missing.

London. Feb. 15. 1792.

Dear Sir,

Looking in at Mr Johnson's yesterday, and finding him distressed how to send the Society books to yourself, Mr Harries and Mr Rowe, I undertook to convey the inclosed, that you may each send your respective nominations to the amount of y^r subscriptions, and he will immediately expedite the books. There is an ambiguity in our circular letter, which has misled almost all the members, and will deserve to be amended the next year.[1]

I have been much occupied, and partly without any novelties worth the comunication, or you would have been troubled with a line from me as usual. I trust that the mild season has agreed with you as it has with me. My wife has sufferd much with her old pain in her face, but is now better. Dr Priestley is very well, but rather thin, which my wife attributes to some little touches of his old bilious complaint; but he will not allow that any thing is the matter with him. He has been disturbed however, as we all are an[d] have been, by the rather unhandsome opposition given to Mr Belsham from Dr Rees in being chosen collegue with Dr Priestley at the Meeting at Hackney. We still hope however that Mr Belsham may be chosen. I shall then have no doubt of every thing going on well especially what relates to the New College.[2]

To morrow there is to be a general meeting of the members of our Unitarian Society to consider of a petition to Parliament for the repeal of the Laws against Antitrinitarians. Mr Dodson, Dr Priestley and another person were last Thursday appointed to draw up a Petition to be offered to the Meeting, and the former of them has drawn up a very proper one. Whether it is to be presented or no this session, is undetermined. Mr Fox has very obligingly offerd his service, which however we do not mention but to friends, and advised this mode of application.[3]

There is a printed paper which Dr Priestley had seen, from some high-churchman, inviting all that wish well to the estabilishm^t to unite against the efforts that are making against it, by Socinians, Republicans, Deists &c: he says it shews that the writer and all concerned in it are under great alarms; I expect him to call here to day with it.[4]

Dr Disney has just now published a very seasonable and spirited rebuke to Dr Vicesimus Knox for some reflections on Unitarians very lately published by him.[5] I think I formerly gave you a character of the gentleman from Mr Austen. He is certainly an aspirant after preferment.[6]

A gentleman a few days ago arrived from the neighbourhood of Sheffield, says that there is a society of 2000 in that town, well behaved men, most of em of the lower sort of workmen, who have regular meetings to discuss various subject[s] particularly that of government. They had all of them read and approved Mr Paine's Rights of man half a year ago, which we heard of when in the North – but they are now printing a cheap copy to disperse.[7]

Mr Paines second Volume, which I have just had a sight of, will fall in with and promote their speculations: and indeed in time must promote no small change in the minds of men, and in time on all the governments on the earth, where such plain striking truths will probably be dispersed and adopted.[8]

Mr Barlow's Advice to the privileged orders &c is a book of the same class and by an able hand.[9] Such just ideas of government make one look forward with satisfaction to this earth of ours when they will probably be realized every where, and wars be no more.

My wife presents you with her best respects. We desire to be duly remembered to your Gentlemen, and I am always

Dear Sir, Your most truly obliged and affectionate servant

T. Lindsey.

---

1   See Letter 484, n. 2.

2   See Letter 487. In Feb. 1792, Thomas Belsham's nomination as co-minister with Joseph Priestley at the Gravel Pit meeting, Hackney, was vetoed by the congregation. According to Belsham himself, his election was lost by one vote, after '*** very unexpectedly opposed'; Williams, p. 445. '***' was almost certainly Abraham Rees, minister of the Old Jewry congregation. According to H. McLachlan, 'The old Hackney College, 1786–1796', *TUHS*, III, 3 (Oct. 1925), 202, a 'coolness' developed between Belsham and Rees as a result. Another possible opponent of Belsham was William Basnett, subsequently of Bath; see Letters 487 and 701. The objections to Belsham arose from his Socinian theology; having, with some reservations, accepted Priestley as successor to Richard Price (see Letter 478), many members of the congregation were not prepared to accept another Socinian as co-minister.

3   'Last Thursday' was 9 Feb. 1792. The meeting of the Unitarian Society on that date resolved that a special general meeting be summoned at the King's Head tavern on Thursday 16 Feb. to consider a petition to parliament for the repeal of laws against anti-trinitarians; Dodson, as a lawyer, was deputed to draw up the petition. At the same time, the meeting resolved that the minutes arising from the petition should be recorded 'separately and distinctly, this being an object not properly cognizable by the Unitarian Society' (Unitarian Society minute book, pp. 30–1). No separate minutes from the preparation and presentation of the petition have apparently survived and, accordingly, Lindsey's letters are the principal sources for the background to the petition.

4   Priestley replied to allegations of this kind in *An appeal to the public*, and in particular (pp. 56–7) sought to dismiss suggestions that 'Unitarians, heretofore more generally called Socinians', were any more dangerous to the civil government than were any other religious groups.

5   This work was John Disney's *Letters to the Rev. Vicesimus Knox, DD, occasioned by his reflections on unitarian Christians in his 'Advertisement' prefixed to a volume of his sermons, lately published* (London, 1792). In the 'advertisement' to *Sermons chiefly intended to promote faith, hope, and charity* (London, 1792), p. vii, Knox accused unitarians of 'zealously lowering our Saviour in the opinion of his followers'.

6   See Letter 447.

7   This was the Sheffield Society for Constitutional Information, founded in the final months of 1791; see J. Stevenson, *Artisans and democrats. Sheffield in the French Revolution, 1789–1797* (Sheffield, 1989), pp. 15–21.

8   The second part of Paine's *Rights of man* was published on 17 Feb. 1792.

9   The American-born Joel Barlow (1754–1812) was an entrepreneur, poet and radical. His *Advice to the privileged orders in the several states of Europe, resulting from the necessity and propriety of a general revolution in the principle of government. Part I*, was published by Joseph Johnson in London on 4 Feb. 1792. The second part was published in Paris in 1793.

486. To RUSSELL SCOTT   **21 FEBRUARY 1792**

Text:	Scott Coll.
Printed:	McLachlan, 'Lindsey to Scott', 118 (most of second paragraph; brief mis-quotations from eighth paragraph).
Addressed:	To/The Rev^d. Russell Scott/Portsmouth/Post paid
Endorsed:	Feb^ry. 22^d. – 92 [in pencil] "Rights of man" Petition to Parliament
Postmarked:	FE 21 92

London. Feb. 21. 1792

Dear Sir,

Nobody having called from you, and the little pacquet being ready, my wife finding that Mr Johnson was sending a parcell of the Societys books to you got him to inclose it, so that we hope it is received. However on Sunday your Portsmouth friend very obligingly spoke to me, and inquired if I had any thing to send, and is to call here before he goes away.[1]

This 2^d Vol. of Rights of man, excells the former. It is indeed a wonderful production for originality of thought, for the most plain and powerful reasoning, and for a sublime simplicity, and eloquence at times far surpassing Mr Burkes bombast.

But I must now come to the business, in which I am deputed to desire you to take a part.

There have lately been several meetings here of Dissenters, principally unitarians, concerning an application to Parliament, for relief from the penal laws which affect antitrinitarians: whether to apply this session, and if so, in what mode, by petition or motion. And it has been determined not to lose the present session, if possible, and to go to the house by a Petition.

The petition has been drawn up by a deputation of three, of which Mr Dodson and Dr Priestley were[2] – but the former undertook it and after some revision made and[?] I think it will be found well drawn up. For it is such as Calvinists and Churchmen can have no scruple to sign, but the contrary, who wish well to religious liberty and free inquiry into the scriptures.

A copy of it this day is sent to you, and you are requested to procure as many names to it, and as speedily as you conveniently can. For the session will be so short, that we must make all possible haste to secure a day before the members are retiring into the country.[3]

Dr Priestley has undertaken Leeds, Manchester, Bristol, Shrewsbury &c – Mr Jervis the West with Chichester.[4]

I need not desire you to take all possible care the Petition be not dirtied or creased, and particularly that no copy be taken of it, because it would be very prejudicial to us to have it get into print before presented. You will let me know what the carriage [is], as it has been agreed that the gentlemen who take the trouble in the country shall not be saddled with that addition expence, and that makes me pay the postage of my letter. I may mention to you, but will only be named to friends, that Mr Fox has been consulted, and advised this method of application, and also engaged to present the Petition and give us his assistance – Some think it may have success in the commons, as Lord North declared that the Toleration if incompleat ought to be rendered compleat, when he was arguing against the repeal of the Test Laws.[5]

I have got a bad cold, and write in haste, so that you will excuse my scrawl, if you can read it. We hope Mrs Scott and your little one are well: to her we both desire to be kindly remembered, and with my wifes sincere regards for yourself I remain always Dear Sir most truly Yours

T. Lindsey.

Be so good to let me know when you receive the parcell. It is now one o'clock, and perhaps the coach to Portsmouth may not set out till to morrow morning. I mention this to prevent uneasiness. But you will be so good as to make inquiry.

---

1   For possible identifications of Scott's Portsmouth friend, see Letter 481, n. 1.
2   Lindsey evidently omitted the word 'two' at this point.
3   The session (the second of the parliament of 1790 to 1796) lasted from 31 Jan. to 15 June 1792.
4   This was probably John Jervis (1752–1820), dissenting minister at Lympstone, Devon, from 1773 until his death, rather than his elder brother Thomas Jervis, at that time minister to the presbyterian congregation at St Thomas Street, Southwark.
5   Although he spoke against the repeal of the Test Act in the commons' debate of 28 Mar. 1787, North added his opinion that 'if any actual point remained behind to render the toleration granted to Dissenters still more complete, it ought to be brought forward'; Cobbett, *Parl. hist.*, XXVI, 818. The speech was widely reported in the London press.

487. To WILLIAM TAYLEUR   27 FEBRUARY 1792

Text: JRUL, Lindsey Letters, vol. II, no. 61.
Printed: McLachlan, *Letters*, p. 70 (first sentence of first paragraph; most of fourth paragraph).
Addressed: To/William Tayleur Esq[r]/Shrewsbury
Endorsed: 27th Feb[y] – 92
Postmarked: FE 27 92

London. Feb. 27. 1792.

Dear Sir,

Our friend undertook to send you the petition, otherwise I should have done it. Ever since, I have been disturbed with a troublesome cold and feverett,[1] which has not however hindred attendance on the chapel, tho' it has confined me within the doors till to day. In my walks in the city I met D[r] Priestley, who having mentiond that you wish to have early notice of what passed yesterday at Hackney, I shall transcribe the acc[t] he sent me last night.

"Sorry I am, exceedingly sorry to inform you, that M[r] Belsham is *not* elected my collegue. The votes for him were 41, and against him 22, or rather 21, one of the latter being disputed. The students voted, and it is said for him. No other proposal was made, and no term fixed for any future meeting. Several who had been neuter the last time, and even voted *for* M[r] Belsham, now voted against him, especially M[r] Basnett. To what this tends I do not see."[2]

So the D[r] wrote last night. To day he told me, that D[r] Rees advised the students to vote this time. It was unfortunate he had not thought of doing it before. My chief apprehensions are for the college; lest this affair should put an end to the good way that we hoped things were in.

I am glad you are exerting yourselves to procure a good number of signatures at Shrewsbury.[3] Various things seem to have concurred to prevent any great thing being done here with respect to obtaining a great number of hands. At least at present I see no efforts that were to be expected. To day in the street when I met D[r] Kippis, he told me he had not seen the Petition, whereas I should have hoped it would have been laid in the Vestry at his meeting to be signed yesterday, as it was at ours.[4] We had about thirty names, and I sh[d] hope shall have about thirty or forty more.

I am sorry to take my leave so abruptly – but some company prevent going on.

You shall have a line again before the end of the week. I am glad D[r] Priestley gives such a good acc[t] of your health.[5] With my wifes kind respects, I remain ever y[r] most truly obliged and affectionate

T. Lindsey.

1   A slight fever.
2   For these events, see Letter 485, n. 2. I have not located the letter from Priestley to Lindsey of 26 Feb. 1792; no letters from Priestley to Lindsey from the year 1792 appear to survive. Possibly Mr Basnett was William Basnett, subsequently of Bath and formerly a member of Essex Street chapel (see Letter 701) and a member of the Unitarian Society; *Unitarian Society ... 1794*, p. 9.
3   I.e. signatures to the unitarian petition.
4   Kippis was minister of the presbyterian chapel at Princes Street, Westminster.
5   Priestley had evidently visited Tayleur at Shrewsbury in Jan. or Feb. 1792. In his letter to Lindsey of 26 Apr. 1792 (JRUL, C2[13]), the first of his letters which survives after Nov. 1790, Tayleur did not mention this visit either, although he noted that Priestley had written to him from Warwick at the time of his claim for compensation.

488. To JOHN ROWE   6 MARCH 1792

Text: JRUL, Lindsey Letters, vol. III, no. 35.
Addressed: To/The Rev[d]. J. Rowe/Shrewsbury.
Printed: McLachlan, 'More letters', 371 (first two paragraphs and first part of first sentence of third paragraph, with errors); 377 (fifth and sixth sentences of fourth paragraph).
Endorsed: John
Postmarked: MR 6 92

London. March. 6. 1792

Dear Sir,

Your pacquet with the Petition came yesterday most opportunely, so that I had an opportunity of taking it with me to the Committee for settling our application to Parliament.[1] The thursday before,[2] we had received so very few names, and returns of Petitions out of the country, that some who were averse to our going to Parliament this year were for putting it off, and stated that without a thousand signatures at least it was not to be thought of. Very happily M[r] Toulmin, who had labourd most diligently sent me a list of 288.[3] Good M[r] Wiche no less than 86 from Maidstone; M[r] Scott 38 from Portsmouth. 93 from Birmingham. 70 from Yarmouth – 74 from M[r] Hammond Fenstanton – 49 from You – 70 our chapel list.

I am here interrupted by D[r] Priestley and M[r] Heywood – whom with M[r] Brand Hollis our chairman yesterday, we deputed to wait upon M[r] Fox to day with our Petition – and we have been packing[4] and adding several from the country which are come in, so that it will now go to the house, consisting of betwixt 1400 and 1500; as proper for aught I conceive as if it had been 14000. I must not forget to add that as many again as at the first are returned from Birmingham. I was sorry to hear D[r] Priestley say, that whilst D[r] Barnes of Manchester was very hearty for the thing, whilst M[r] Hawkes declined to sign it: so much it is said had he been intimidated since the outrages at Birmingham.[5] M[r] Wood, with a good number of names from Leeds, sends word that some Dissenters declined giving their names, thinking the application woud succeed, and that it would prevent any future success in the repeal of the Test Laws. Several churchmen in Leeds gave their signatures – The mayor and some Aldermen.[6]

M[r] Wiche from Maidstone acquaints me that many churchmen gave him their names, and some Trinitarians who declared that they did it as being against persecution on any religious account. I thought that you and our excellent friend would be glad to know all these little particulars, which I put down in haste. M[r] Frend from Cambridge, sent a number of reasons why he and M[r] Tyrwhitt and Lambert could not sign the Petition – and at the same time desired that his name might be drawn from the list of our unitarian society, on account of some things said of Christ, which he cannot agree to – the same with M[r] Tyrwhitt and which I formerly sent to Shrewsbury. I must not forget that D[r] Priestley before he went off to wait upon M[r] Fox desired I would remember him properly to you and M[r] Tayleur. The last named I wish you woud tell, with mine and my wife's respects, that I beg pardon for my last shabby letter,[7] but will write again e'er long: and that some of D[r] Priestley's congregation still think they shall be able to bring in M[r] Belsham. Others doubt it. The affair will have unpleasing and bad consequences, sh[d] he be intirely rejected. Pray also add, that distant proposals have been talked of as to be made to D[r] Priestley to have an *Arian* Pastor of his own choosing, which I think is not using him well.

With great pleasure do I read the account of y[r] good brother in laws noble christian spirit.[8] From such exertions, the greatest good, the good we wish, must and will in time arise. – With regard to our unitarian society, all that you have to do, is to send to M[r] Johnson a list of the books you wish to have to the amount of your respective subscriptions. But you will do well to send soon. I am going to purchase M[r] Wakefield's 2[d] Ed. on Prayer, w[ch] he has printed before the first sold off, to answer some of his opponents. The ablest, D[r] Priestley says, is the Dissenting Minister, Wilson or Watson of Stockport, to whom D[r] Priestley thinks there is a reply in M[r] W's second edition.[9] I am under the same apprehensions with you ab[t] the fate of the X[n] Miscellany, and lament it.[10]

My wife joins in respects to you and your Lady and in very sincere joy at the restoration of the whole family.[11] And I am always with a most sincere esteem and very truly Yours

> T. Lindsey

---

1   The minutes of this committee were kept separately from those of the Unitarian Society itself, and have apparently not survived; see Letter 485, n. 3.

2   The previous Thursday was 1 Mar. 1792.

3   This refers to Joshua Toulmin of Taunton (to whom Lindsey referred as Mr as well as Dr) rather than Henry Toulmin of Chowbent.

4   It is possible that Lindsey wrote 'parting' rather than 'packing'; his handwriting is not quite clear. However, 'packing' seems to fit the context more appropriately, as Lindsey was preparing the various copies of the petitions for delivery to Fox.

5   For this intimidation of Hawkes, see G. M. Ditchfield, 'Public and parliamentary support for the unitarian petition of 1792', *E & D*, XII (1993), 41.

6   The mayor of Leeds in 1791–2 was the merchant Wade Browne (d. 1821); R. G. Wilson, *Gentlemen merchants. The merchant community in Leeds 1700–1830* (Manchester, 1971), pp. 241–2. For the merchant elite who provided many of the aldermen of Leeds, and the evidence of dissenting sympathies amongst them, see ch. 8 of this work.

7   Lindsey referred here to his letter to Tayleur of 27 Feb. 1792 (Letter 487), in which he had apologized for its abrupt ending.

8   Rowe's brother-in-law was Richard Hall Clarke (d. 1822), one of the founders, and the first treasurer, of the Western Unitarian Society.

9   Wakefield responded to his critics in *A general reply to the arguments against the enquiry into public worship* (London, 1792). James Wilson (1754–1829) was the author of *A defence of public or social worship; in a letter, addressed to Gilbert Wakefield. In answer to the latter's "Enquiry"* (Stockport, 1792). Wilson was minster of the High Street chapel, Stockport, from 1785 to 1792; *Historical sketches of nonconformity in the County Palatine of Chester*, ed. Urwick, p. 299. From Dec. 1792 to May 1794, he was minister in the Church of Scotland at Mid-Calder and from 1794 until his death, he was minister at Falkirk; he held the degrees of MA (Glasgow, 1781) and DD (Edinburgh, 1802); *Fasti Ecclesiae Scoticanae*, I, 207. Wakefield's reply to Wilson may be found in his *A general reply*, at pp. 17–18.

10 The *Christian Miscellany* ceased publication after Aug. 1792.

11 This probably refers to the restoration of Rowe's family to good health, although the absence of letters from Tayleur between Nov. 1790 and May 1792 in JRUL, C2[13] renders this a conjecture.

489. To RUSSELL SCOTT   9 MARCH 1792

Text:	Scott Coll.
Addressed:	[In James Martin's hand] London, *Ninth March* 1792/Rev: Russell Scot/Portsmouth/~~J Martin~~. [in Lindsey's hand, opposite address] Rev[d]. Russell Scott/Portsmouth/March. 9
Endorsed:	[In pencil] Read
Postmarked:	MR 9 92

London. March. 9. 1792

Dear Sir,

You will see in the morning chronicle to day, how well your and the efforts of other friends have succeeded, in giving M[r] Fox an opportunity at some future day to engage the attention of the house to his proposal for the repeal of all penal laws in religion, and if that cannot be effected, at least to procure relief from those which immediately threaten antitrinitarians.[1] A remarkable readiness has shewn itself to come forward in several parts of the country, not only among unitarians but even churchmen to give their concurrence, and if another application be wanted another year, some of the London Ministers are of opinion, that fifty thousand signatures might be procure[d].[2] Some dissenters refused to sign our petition, lest it should be granted, and the repeal of the test laws on that account prevented, at least taking place so soon.

I inclose the only publication that has hitherto appeared upon the question.[3] M[r] Wilson, dissenting minister at Stockport in Cheshire, has publis[he]d a very able reply to M[r] Wakefield's objections to Social worship.[4] I will endeavour to s[end][5] it You. M[r] W. has published another edition with some sort of answer: but it really does him no credit.[6]

My wife joins in kind regards to your lady and with hers to yourself I remain alway

Dear Sir, very truly Yours

T. Lindsey

1   The *Morning Chronicle*, 9 Mar. 1792, reported that on the previous day, Fox had announced in the house of commons his receipt of the unitarian petition, with 1,600 signatures, and his intention of introducing a motion on the subject 'before much time elapsed'. Fox added his own preference for more radical action, leading to the abolition of 'all penal religious laws'. See *CJ*, XLVII, 522–3.

2   Lindsey referred here to the unitarian sympathizers among the General Body of Dissenting Ministers in London, although the minutes of the General Body for 1791 and 1792 do not mention the petition; DWL, MS 38.106, pp. 305–13.

3   Lindsey probably referred here to Benjamin Hobhouse's *Treatise on heresy*; see Letter 490, n. 10.

4   See Letter 488, n. 9.
5   The manuscript is slightly torn at this point.
6   See Letter 488, n. 9.

490. To WILLIAM TAYLEUR   26 MARCH 1792

Text: JRUL, Lindsey Letters, vol. II, no. 62.
Printed: McLachlan, *Letters*, pp. 70–1 (all but last two sentences of
                    second paragraph); p. 137 (fifth and eighth sentences of first
                    paragraph).
Addressed: To/William Tayleur Esqr/Shrewsbury
Endorsed: 26th March – 92
Postmarked: MR 26 92

London. March. 26. 1792

Dear Sir,

I reckon it high time that I should write to one, whom I often think and talk of. The other day also Mr Martin asked how you did, which I was pleased with, as it shewed that he thought of you too. You have a claim to every information in the first place about the college. I find it more calumniated in different companies in this Town than you can have any idea of, for shameful irregularities, &c; But I am happy to inform you, from most particular inquiry and certain knowlege, that the behaviour of the young men, is universally not only unblameable, but commendable. You will have heard I presume by the way of young Mr Harris,[1] that Mr Wakefields tract on prayer has rather made some disturbance among them with respect to their attendance on the public devotions of the house: but I trust this will pass away; as several of them have withdrawn from the association, and I hope a publication of Dr Priestley, in the press, will bring them all back.[2] In this publication he takes notice of what appears to him wrongly advanced by Mr Wakefield on the subject of social worship; and at the same time makes a reply to Mr Evanson, who has fallen upon him in a very angry, contemptuous and unjustifiable manner at any time, but at this particularly wrong when it bears the appear[ance] of joining the common enemy to sink him.[3] But he will emerge only the more illustrious and formidable with truth and good temper on his side. Mr Wakefield will unavoidably be much offended, as Dr Priestley esteemed it a duty to speak a few things in vindication of his friend Dr Price, whom that gentleman has treated very unhandsomely.[4] You will see the work soon, being not long, and nearly printed off: but it is a little delayed by his going down to Warwick, to which place he set out yesterday evening at 5 after drinking a dish of coffee with us.[5] He was very unwilling to go, but it was thought necessary for him to be upon the spot, if he should be wanted. Upon the whole he is very well; though he has been much harassed lately by this and other things. You will perhaps have heard, that the election of a Co-pastor with him is put off for three months: but it is believed, and Dr Priestley believes that the choice of Mr Belsham at the last will thereby be the better ascertained: and then I trust all will go on well, the college and every thing else.[6]

It is still thought by not a few that our Petition to the Commons house will succeede. Dr Heberden told me the other day, that he had been pressing upon the subject, a member of some note, bred at Oxford, proving to him, that instead of hurting such a step would be a security to the church; and his friend replied to him, that he had not heard any thing be against it, and that he believd, if Mr Pitt did not directly oppose, it would pass. I was much pleased the other day with a sight of the signatures of your two grandsons to the copy of the petition I had sent to Mr Houlbrooke, and hope that all their future acts will be in support of truth and liberty, and that the world may be the better for their living in it.[7] I have rec^d now 400 names from different quarters to be added to the 1600 with which Mr Fox first announced it.[8] We do not find any day yet fixed for bringing the business on, and it is imagined it will not be till the return of the lawyers from the circuit.[9] A treatise on Heresy, as cognizeable by the Spiritual courts, will nobly come in aid of it. If it has not come in your way, you will be highly delighted with it – It is printed for Cadell; anonymous, but probably you may know it is by Mr Hobhouse, a magistrate in Wiltshire, formerly at the Bar, able and worthy, one who has intirely separated from the estabilished church.[10]

There is also another larger and noble work, which will do great good: I cannot give you the exact title as Dr P. took away with him a copy I had just bought, but It is Remark[s] on the French Constitution &c &c &c by Benjamin Flower. He is a dissenter, among the Independants – formerly in business.[11] I sh^d think that what he and Mr Hobhouse remark in particular, concerning the necessity of a reform in spirituals in our country, must contribute to accelerate.

I have space only to add, that my wife sends her due respects and is tolerably well. I am just got out of a cold that has harassed me for near six weeks, cætera lietus.[12] It will be a pleasure to hear you continue in your good train. We desire to be remembered to Mr Rowe and Mr Wood – hope the former his lady and family are got quite well. I remain always your most truly obliged and faithful affectionate

T. Lindsey

1   This is probably a reference to Thomas Harries (see Letter 412, n. 4), a student at Hackney College, who had communicated with his father Edward Harries in Shropshire, and, through him, to Tayleur in Shrewsbury.

2   For Wakefield's work on social worship, see Letter 475, n. 5. The 'association' seems to have been a group of students at Hackney College who had been pupils of Wakefield and who sympathized with his radical opinions, and especially with his critique of public worship, in a manner which threatened college discipline. See McLachlan, 'The old Hackney College, 1786–1796', 201–2, and *Memoirs of the life of Gilbert Wakefield ... written by himself*, pp. 374–8.

3   This work was Priestley, *Letters to a young man, occasioned by Mr Wakefield's essay on public worship; to which is added, a reply to Mr Evanson's objections to the observance of the Lord's Day* (London, 1792). Evanson set out his sometimes sardonic critique of Priestley in his *Arguments against and for the sabbatical observance of Sunday, by a cessation from all labour, contained in the letters of sundry writers in the Theological Repository, with an additional letter to the Reverend Dr Priestley, in continuation of the same subject* (Ipswich, 1792), pp. 121–75. He repeated the arguments against Sunday observance which he had previously deployed (with the pseudonym 'Eubulus') in the *Theological Repository*, V (1786), 342–55, VI (1788), 352–66.

4   In the 'advertisement' to his *Enquiry into the expediency of public worship* (new edn, 'with considerable alterations' (London, 1792), pp. iii–iv, Wakefield conceded that Price was 'in the main, a very virtuous and amiable man' and 'proficient in various parts of learning', but added that he was 'exceedingly illiterate, like the majority of the Dissenting ministers ... in the branch most essential to theology; and with all his zeal for civil freedom, no true friend of religious liberty'. He also criticized Price for having opposed his nomination to the classical tutorship at Hackney College. For an example of Priestley's reply, see Letter 501, n. 4.

5   Priestley's claim for compensation for damages after the Birmingham riots was heard at Warwick assizes in Apr. 1792; see Letter 493, n. 7.

6   Belsham was not chosen as Priestley's co-minister at the Gravel Pit meeting, Hackney; see Letter 485, n. 2. Michael Maurice served as Priestley's assistant minister there from 1792 to 1794; see Letter 501, n. 3.

7   Lindsey probably referred here to Tayleur's two eldest grandsons, John and William Tayleur; see

Letter 459, n. 9. Theophilus Houlbrooke obtained the signatures in Edinburgh to the unitarian petition. Apparently no manuscript copy of the petition, with signatures, has survived. Possibly it was
incinerated in the fire which destroyed the houses of parliament in 1834.

8   See Letter 489, n. 1.

9   The Lent circuit of the judges took place between 1 and 29 Mar. 1792; see *Gent. Mag.*, LXII, i (1792),
180. The house of commons debate on the unitarian petition took place on 11 May 1792.

10   This work was Benjamin Hobhouse, *A treatise on heresy, as cognizable by the spiritual courts. And
an examination of the statute 9th and 10th of William IIId. c. 32* (London, 1792). Hobhouse was
called to the bar from the Middle Temple in 1781 and practised briefly on the western circuit in the
early 1780s. He was a justice of the peace in Wiltshire, and in 1798, accepted a commission in the
Bradford (Wiltshire) volunteers.

11   For the full title of Benjamin Flower's work on the French constitution, see Letter 458, n. 5. Between
1785 and 1791, Flower worked as the European agent for the Devonshire woollen manufacturing
company of Smale and Dennys. He had previously worked briefly for his father's stationary business
in London, and (unsuccessfully) as a tea-dealer. See *Politics, religion and romance. The letters of
Benjamin and Eliza Flower*, edited and transcribed by Timothy D. Whelan (Aberystwyth, 2008), pp.
xiv, xvii–xviii, xx–xxi. From 1791, Flower concentrated exclusively on his career as a writer and
(from 1793) as the editor of the *Cambridge Intelligencer*.

12   Cætera lætus, 'happy in everything else', the final two words of Horace, *Epistles*, book 1, epistle 10,
line 50. I owe this reference to Mr David Powell.

491. To WILLIAM TURNER OF NEWCASTLE   26 MARCH 1792

Text: DWL, MS 24.86 (4)
Addressed: Address missing.
Postmarked: Postmark missing.

London. March. 26. 1792

Dear Sir,

I know no one who on all occasions of public good has greater energies than
yourself. Your copy of the Petition, so amply attested, did not indeed arrive in time,
not through your fault, to be included when M[r] Fox introduced it to the house, but
the signatures with others since arrived, to the amount of upwards of 400 will be
given to him before his motion, for which there is no day yet fixed, nor will be it is
thought till after the circuit and the Easter adjournment.[1]

Many think that we shall obtain what we ask for. Some are even afraid of it,
imagining with certain that you met with, that success will be an obstacle to the
abolition of all penal laws whatsoever, and therefore declined the giving in of their
names; in which list I may mention a person you know, the worthy M[r] Shore.[2]

I shall be attentive to M[r] Richardsons being added to the list of our unitarian
Society. His name does us great credit. And when it is next printed, M[r] A. Doeg's
place of abode shall be rectified.[3]

I shall be obliged to you to take an opportunity of intimating to M[r] Prowitt that
I shall most gladly desire his acceptance of the remittance I make to him for the
present year: but that after that I hope he will be able to do very well without it.[4]
And I have more pressing demands for what we can spare to promote the unitarian
cause in places where assistance is more needed and of more use than as I can learn
it is in your town.

I am sorry to tell you, that it is said the Petition for the abolition of the Slave trade
will be laid over to another,[5] and so on afterwards the next year: the ministers people
opposing, though he himself strenuous for it. I do think it, in a merely political view,
they should decide something one way or other: for suspense may have dreadful
effects.[6]

As my frank will contain it I inclose a small publication that has come out in aid of our Petition.[7] But there is a much nobler one, which I hope will be read by many, and will serve the whole cause of religious liberty, *viz*; A treatise on Heresy, as cognizeable in the Spiritual courts &c &c by a Barrister at law – who last year wrote for the repeal of the Test Laws, under the title of M.A. of the university of Oxford: M[r] Hobhouse, a magistrate in Wiltshire, not very far from Bath, who some years since openly separated from the ch. of England, and attends Dissenting worship.[8]

There is also a most excellent work to the same end, but for political as well as religious reformation – Remarks I think on the French revolution &c &c &c &c &c by Benjamin Flower, a gentleman of easy fortunes, formerly in trade, resident in the city, and of the independent persuasion: but nothing narrow even of that kind in this publication. D[r] Priestley drank coffee with [us?][9] yesterday afternoon in his way to the coach that was to carry him to the Warwick Assizes, and carried off my copy with him, a large work, upwards of 500 pages, or I could have been more particular about it. I shall be glad when this Assize business is over as the D[r] has been much harassed by preparations for it. He goes down with reluctance, but the Attorneys say, he *may* be called for. But he does not intend to go to Birmingham, but meets his friends and M[r] and M[rs] Finch at Warwick.[10]

I may not omit to mention to you, that this journey will retard a few days a little publication of the Doctors respecting M[r] Wakefield. The tract on prayer of the latter has had such effect upon some of the more serious of his former pupils, who had a reverence for him, which he well deserved, that our friend has been advised by many to publish something to counteract it;[11] and also at the same time to say something in defence of good D[r] Price, whom M[r] Wakefield has aspersed and sought to lower and degrade very unhandsomely and I think unjustly, in the entrance of the second edition of his Tract on prayer.[12] I need not desire you w[d] not mention that you heard any thing of this kind of M[r] W. from me, so that he may hear it, as he is one with whom I w[d] not willingly commit myself; though I think that D[r] Disney in his sermon, and others have approached him with too much awe, so as to increase that high-conceit of himself which is his bane, and for which there is really no such mighty foundation.[13]

My wife joins in comp[ts] to M[rs] Turner and every good wish for your family and I am always very sincerely Yours

T. Lindsey.

I have heard nothing from y[r] worthy Father of his copy of the petition.

1   For the Lent circuit, see Letter 490, n. 9. The house of commons adjourned from 5 to 17 Apr. 1792; *CJ*, XLVII, 697. Good Friday in 1792 fell on 6 Apr. and Easter Sunday on 8 Apr.

2   This was Samuel Shore III; see Letter 461, n. 8.

3   Robert Richardson, attorney at law, of Alnwick, Northumberland, was listed as a new member of the Unitarian Society at its monthly committee meeting on 10 May 1792; Unitarian Society minute book, p. 36. 'Mr A. Doeg, in the name of a society, in and near Manchester', is listed as a member of the Unitarian Society in its first published list; *Unitarian Society ... 1791*, p. 10. In the list appended to *Unitarian Society ... 1794*, p. 10, he was named, correctly, as 'Mr A. Doeg, in the name of a society near Newcastle upon Tyne.' Alexander Doeg of North Shore, Newcastle, was a member of the Literary and Philosophical Society of Newcastle; see *Third Year's Report of the Literary and Philosophical Society of Newcastle upon Tyne* (Newcastle, 1796), p. 9. He and his wife Lily were also members of the Hanover Square chapel, where Turner baptized their children; see Tyne and Wear Archives, Hanover Square baptismal record (TNA: PRO/RG4/1777), fos. 41v, 44r, 47v and 53r. Possibly he was the Alexander Doag, ship-builder, who is listed under 'traders' of Newcastle upon Tyne in *Universal British dictionary*, IV, 33.

4   There is no indication in the Unitarian Society minute book that Edward Prowett ever formally

enrolled as a member of the society, although Lindsey provided him with unitarian literature on an informal basis.

5   Lindsey omitted a word – probably 'day' – at this point.

6   After the house of commons voted for the gradual abolition of the British slave trade on 3 Apr. 1792, the matter was repeatedly delayed by demands for the hearing of evidence and by procedural objections. The hearings were then postponed until the next parliamentary session and subsequently lapsed as the impact of the French Revolution and the outbreak of war dominated public debate. See Roger Anstey, *The Atlantic slave trade and British abolition 1760–1810* (London, 1975), pp. 275–6, and Letter 493, n. 4. Pitt as an individual MP favoured abolition but the opposition to it was too strong for him to make abolition government policy.

7   Possibly Lindsey had in mind *A letter from Timothy Sobersides, extinguisher-maker, at Wolver-hampton, to Jonathan Blast, bellows-maker at Birmingham*; see Letter 481, n. 5. It was a work of twenty-seven pages, published by Joseph Johnson and reviewed favourably in the *Monthly Review*, NS, VII (1792), 460. The author urged complete complete freedom of religious worship, including denial of the doctrine of the Trinity. Another possibility was *Thoughts on the riots at Birmingham. By a Welsh freeholder* [i.e. David Jones] (Bath, 1791, a tract of twenty-eight pages published in late 1791.

8   For Benjamin Hobhouse's *Treatise on heresy*, see Letter 490, n. 10. The other work by Hobhouse to which Lindsey referred was *An address to the public, in which an answer is given to the principal objections urged in the house of commons, by the Right Hon. Frederick Lord North ... and the Right Hon. William Pitt, against the repeal of the Test Laws; and the consequences of an injudicious concession on the part of the advocates for the claim of the protestant dissenters stated. With occasional remarks. By a Master of Arts of the University of Oxford* (Bath, 1790). Lindsey post-dated its publication by one year. Hobhouse's country seat was Cottles House, Wiltshire; he was indeed MA of Oxford University (Brasenose College).

9   The manuscript is very slightly torn at this point; possibly Lindsey wrote 'me'.

10 See Letter 493, n. 7. Priestley's daughter Sarah and her husband William Finch lived at Heath Forge, Dudley. Priestley, understandably reluctant to return to Birmingham, met them at Warwick. According to the *St James's Chronicle*, 5–7 Apr. 1792, Priestley was not present in court but remained at the house of a friend opposite the building. According to the *Public Advertiser*, 7 Apr. 1792, quoting 'a letter from Warwick', Priestley preached twice on Sunday 1 Apr. at the High Street chapel, Warwick, where the minister was William Field.

11 Possibly this is a reference to the 'association' of students at Hackney College; see Letter 490.

12 See Letter 490, n. 4.

13 This is a reference to Disney's *A defence of public or social worship*; see Letter 482, n. 1.

492. To WILLIAM TAYLEUR   11 APRIL 1792

Text: JRUL, vol. II, no. 63.
Addressed: To/William Tayleur Esqʳ/Shrewsbury
Endorsed: 11ᵗʰ April – 92
Postmarked: AP 11 92

London. April. 11. 1792.

Dear Sir,

Mʳ Longman informing me that he was sending a parcell to Mʳ Eddowes I have desired him to inclose a small one for you, which contains six copies of *Conversations on christian idolatry in the year 1791*. two for your own obliging acceptance, and the others for Mʳ Rowe, Mʳ Wood, Mʳ Harries and Mʳ Hazlitt, which Mʳ Rowe will be so good as to take the trouble of sending. I shall be very happy if the tract pleases You. It struck me as a thing that was seasonable, when some very liberal men had left our unitarian society, on account of the term idolatrous being used in our preamble to the list of our members, and others were talking of taking away their names.

As to the form of it, I thought that in the way of conversation more free things might be said with less offence than when more directly put. And perhaps I could censure the church of England with more propriety than many others.[1]

We expected D[r] Priestley on Sunday[2] to have been with us as he presumed he sh[d] not be able to reach Hackney early enough for the morning service; but yesterday I rec[d] a letter that he had stayed at Warwick, but sh[d] call on us in his way home. But as we did not see him, I fancy he had not time. Probably he will call to day. If before I have occasion to send my letter away, I shall tell you how he does. As I mentioned your solicitude about him he may probably have sent a few lines from Warwick.[3]

I am glad to find that M[r] Flower's book on the French Revolution &c &c goes off a little, but hope it will have much more vent when known, as it is so admirably calculated to promote the desired reformation both in the state and in the church; the latter very particularly.[4]

I am just returned from walking out and find Miss Ryland D[r] Priestley's intended daughter left by the D[r] and M[r] Priestley who are by and by to call upon her again.[5] The D[r] came to Hackney late last night is very well and in good spirits. The sufferers at *Birm* have had so much less than their just claims granted, that they have some thoughts of applying to Government for indemnification.[6]

D[r] P ___ y is just come in and is extraordinary well. I have only time to add my wifes and the D[rs] respects and I [*sic*] that I am always your most truly obliged and affectionate servant

T. Lindsey.

[At the end of the letter is the following note in Tayleur's hand]: who, being persuaded, that as the gospel was preach'd, it must be level to the capacities of the poor; did in consequence of this persuasion apply himself closely to the reading of the N.T. many years, till by this means he attain'd to such a conviction of the great but simple truths reveal'd by Christ as determin'd him, by the help of a few friends, to institute a Church in his own House. &c. This is the Fact – all what you say beyond this, tho' I doubt not your sincerity is in reality owing to the unperceived partiality of a Friend.[7]

---

1   Lindsey's *Conversations on Christian idolatry* took the form of a series of imaginary, or semi-imaginary, discussions, over five separate days, between a group of friends, one of whom, 'Volusian', begins by objecting strongly to notions of the humanity of Christ and to condemnations of the worship of Christ as 'idolatrous'. After listening to the arguments of his friends and making a detailed study of the Bible, he changes his opinions completely, accepts the unitarian position on both points and concludes by enquiring as to where he might be able to attend unitarian worship. The friends also called for reform of the Church of England's liturgy in a unitarian direction. The immediate relevance to the controversy over the preamble to the rules of the Unitarian Society was unmistakable, and Lindsey made it explicit in Letter 499.

2   11 Apr. 1792 was a Wednesday; the previous Sunday was 8 Apr. 1792.

3   Among Tayleur's letters to Lindsey in JRUL, C2[13] is a draft of a letter from Tayleur to Priestley, dated 'May 1792'. It is evidently a reply to a non-surviving letter from Priestley, perhaps the letter from Warwick to which Lindsey referred. In this draft, Tayleur thanked Priestley for gifts of his recent works and added 'I have receiv'd every thing that you have publish'd since the riots, & particularly your answer to M[r] W ___ d' (i.e. Gilbert Wakefield; see Letter 490, n. 3).

4   For the full title of Benjamin Flower's work on the French constitution, see Letter 458, n. 5.

5   Joseph Priestley junior married Elizabeth Ryland (1769–1816), the elder daughter of Samuel Ryland of Birmingham, on 11 Apr. 1792; she became Priestley's daughter-in-law.

6   See Letter 493, n. 7.

7   In his *Conversations on Christian idolatry*, pp. 155–6, Lindsey referred to 'an excellent person, of fine parts', who organized worship based on Samuel Clarke's reformed liturgy in his own house. That person subsequently 'prevailed to have this reformed service of the church adopted by a considerable, and very liberal, congregation of Dissenters in the place, now become a flourishing, professed society

of Unitarian christians'. The allusion to Tayleur and the High Street congregation at Shrewsbury would have been evident to the *cognoscenti*. In his brief annotation to this letter, Tayleur wrote of himself in the third person. See Letter 498, n. 2.

493. To WILLIAM FREND   13 APRIL 1792

Text: CUL, Add. MS 7886 (Frend papers), no. 168.
Addressed: For/The Rev^d. W. Frend
Postmarked: Postmark missing.

London. April. 13. 1792

Dear Sir,

I had intended to have let alone acknowleging your letter till I coud do it in person, but Mr Dyer calling a few days since and mentioning that you did not yet think of coming to town of a fortnight at least, and not willing to delay so long the conveying to you and one or two of our comon friends a little piece I have lately printed, but not yet published, I resolved a short note shoud accompany it.[1] I am sorry to give you the extraordinary trouble with Mr Gifford, but it may lie till a convenient opportunity offers.[2]

I had really given over thinking of Mr Wyvill's comission, as I had signified to him, that my friend at Cambridge could give me no satisfactory information about it, which I concluded from your silence. We are daily expecting his work, and think it will cooperate with other efforts that are making to bring about a parliamentary reform.[3]

Mrs Reynolds acquainted my wife with your being at Paxton and traversing the country in so good a cause, and which we now hope will succeed much sooner than Mr Dundas intended.[4] And the good effects of the application we also hope will not end here, but will point out to the nation what may be done in other cases by a whole or the greater part of [two words crossed out] petitioning at any future time.

The B^p of Landaff I am to told [*sic*] is gone to his planting in the north, where however I trust he takes some care to sow the good seed of the word of truth, or I should not think so well of him as I am disposed to do.[5] I have been informed however that he is to come back if the Petition of the Antitrinitarians passes the Commons-house, which is by some persons expected, Dr Heberden in particular tells me that he sees no reason why it should not, and I know he has had not unfavourable answers from one or two Tory members, if the *Premier* does not declare against it.[6] We live in times in which stranger things may come to pass.

Dr Priestley is come back safe from the Warwick-Assizes. Indeed he never met with any insult but from one low person of Warwick. And I think he is better for the excursion, though the Jury have not sent him home with heavy pockets.[7] There is however a talk of the sufferers in general applying to Government for indemnification, as the Judges, who both behaved very handsomely were not all satisfied with the verdicts given.[8]

I am glad you think with me that much good is to be expected from the Methodists in future, as much has already been done by them in bringing thousands off from vice, and to some sense of God and another world.

I hope you will be quite recruited and stout before you venture into this dusty hot town with its easterly breezes of this season, which are already set [in?]. My wife sends her best wishes and respects

I am always very sincerely Yours

T. Lindsey.

Copies for yourself

\--------- Mr Tyrwhitt

Mr Lambert

Mr Gifford

---

1 This work was Lindsey's *Conversations on Christian idolatry*. Lindsey sent copies for Frend and the three Cambridge sympathizers listed below his signature to this letter.

2 James Gifford the elder (see Vol. I, Letter 320, n. 9, and Letter 433, n. 12) lived at Girton, near Cambridge, from 1788 until his death in 1813.

3 Probably Wyvill had 'commissioned' Lindsey to seek information from Frend, perhaps in connexion with his forthcoming work, *Defence of Price*, which was published in London in the spring of 1792.

4 On 3 Apr. 1792, the house of commons voted for the gradual abolition of the British slave trade. Henry Dundas took the lead in persuading the house to vote for gradual, rather than immediate, abolition and on 27 Apr., the commons nominated 1 Jan. 1796 as the date for complete abolition. However, this aspiration was overtaken by the war with France and was not implemented.

5 Richard Watson had acquired a substantial estate at Calgarth, near Troutbeck, on the shore of Lake Windermere, where he devoted himself to agriculture, and built a new mansion at Calgarth Park. He was much criticized for a consequent lack of attention to his Llandaff diocese. See Timothy Brain, 'Richard Watson: Westmorland "statesman"?', *Transactions of the Cumberland & Westmorland Antiquarian & Archaeological Society*, XCIV (1994), 171–200.

6 Pitt did declare against the unitarian petition in the commons' debate on 11 May 1792 and the petition was duly rejected.

7 Priestley's claim for damages arising from the destruction of his house, furniture, books, manuscripts and scientific equipment amounted to £4,083 10s 3d. On 5 Apr. 1792, the jury at Warwick assizes awarded him £2,996 10s, and he did not receive this compensation (albeit with the addition of interest of £101 10s 6d) until 1793. It has been estimated that the total cost of the destruction of the property of the victims of the riots was approximately £50,000. A total of £26,961 2s 3d was paid in compensation; Schofield, *Enlightened Joseph Priestley*, p. 298. The compensation was financed by an additional local rate upon the hundred of Hemlingford, Warwickshire, which had to obtain a private act of parliament (33 George III c. 39) to sanction this rate and permit the hundred to borrow necessary funds. There is a detailed summary of Priestley's claim in R. E. W. and Francis R. Maddison, 'Joseph Priestley and the Birmingham riots', *Notes and Records of the Royal Society of London*, XII (1956), 104–6.

8 The two judges in Priestley's case for compensation were Sir James Eyre (1734–99), from 1787, the chief baron of the court of exchequer, who also presided over the trials of Thomas Hardy and John Horne Tooke in 1794; and the Welsh-born Sir Richard Penryn (1723–1803), a baron of the exchequer from 1776 to 1799. Evidently, it had been intended that another judge of the exchequer, Sir Alexander Thompson, was to be one of the two judges in Priestley's case, but he was prevented by indisposition from serving in this capacity; *Public Advertiser*, 7 Apr. 1792.

494. To CHRISTOPHER WYVILL   19 APRIL 1792

Text: NYRO, ZFW 7/2/72/3, Wyvill of Constable Burton MSS.
Printed: Wyvill, *Political papers*, V, 10–12 (with a few errors);
                 McLachlan, *Letters*, p. 139 (short quotation from first
                 paragraph); p. 140 (part of third paragraph; fourth and fifth
                 paragraphs).
Addressed: To/The Rev[d]. Christopher Wyvill/Burton near Bedale/
                 Yorkshire
Endorsed: From the Rev[d] M[r] Lindsey April 19th 1792
Postmarked: AP 19 92

London. April. 19. 1792

Dear Sir,

I take an early opportunity of thanking you for a noble pamphlet indeed, worthy of one of England's Reformers, and which I trust will excite a zeal for the same wise temperate and steady reform of our whole constitution, for which you plead – with such invincible force of argument, though the reformers who may now stand forth may not precisely adopt for instance the particular plan of amending the system of parliamentary representation proposed to the Commons house in 1785, to which I dare say you do not wish to confine them.[1]

A treatise so choice and full with respect to its matter, and in which every expression is so accurate, just and well weighed, with such well drawn portraits presenting themselves in proper time and place, must have cost the writer great labour: but it has been well bestowed.

Never had the good D[r] Price, but never had the Dissenters in general an equal defender; and I trust that in time your book will contribute to reason and to shame the churchmen out of their ignorance and bad spirit of intolerance towards them.

M[r] Burke will be found from what others but very much from the just light in which you have exhibited him, to have raised his head, as a mere political sophist for a while, only to sink down for ever in greater infamy; and the strong painting of another higher character and enemy of all reformation is such as must strike every eye.

I assure you I like the defence so much, and think it so calculated to be useful, that I have bought a dozen to disperse.

A few days before yours arrived I had printed a tract on a subject, which certainly was intended and I hope will come in aid of some part of the meliorating plan you propose.[2] As soon as I can learn how to convey it, it shall come to you at Burton for your acceptance.

My wife desires to join in respects to yourself and M[rs] Wyvill and wishes of health to you and your amiable children whom we saw, but hope that divine providence will give you more pledges of its favour, and that you and your lady will live together to see them all fixed in good principles and happily settled in the world.[3]

I remain always, Dear Sir, Your obliged and affectionate servant

T. Lindsey.

P.S. Excuse me saying, that I have often wondered a little at a friend's continuing to belong to a certain estabilishment: but I now see the hand of good and of providence in it.[4]

---

[1]   This pamphlet was Wyvill's *Defence of Price*. A second edition appeared later in 1792. One of the publishers advertised on the title page was Joseph Johnson. On 18 Apr. 1785, the house of commons

had rejected Pitt's motion for moderate parliamentary reform, involving the disenfranchisement of thirty-six small boroughs and the transfer of their seats to the English counties, which Wyvill had helped to inspire.

2   This tract was Lindsey's *Conversations on Christian idolatry*, which advocated liturgical reform of the Church of England of the type approved by Wyvill; see Letter 492, n. 1.

3   Wyvill's second wife Sarah, née Codling; their children in Apr. 1792 included their daughter Elizabeth-Anne (b. 1789) and son Marmaduke (b. 1791).

4   Wyvill was the (absentee) rector of Black Notley, Essex, from 1763 to 1806.

495. To THOMAS SIMONS   4 MAY 1792

Text: JRUL, Unitarian College Collection, Lindsey to T. S[imons], 4 May 1792. There is also a typescript copy in DWL, MS 12.56 (37).

Addressed: To/Mr Simons/N°. 15 Henrietta Street/Cavendish-Square

Endorsed: Revd Mr Lindsay's [*sic*] Letters

Postmark: Postmark missing.

Dear Sir,

Many things have prevented an earlier acknowlegement of your obliging favour.

I cannot tell you how much I honour that benevolent zeal that leads you to bestow so much time and labour for that most numerous part of our species, who would otherwise be lost to society, and to every thing that is good. I most ardently wish that the plan was universally adopted.[1]

It seems to me that it would be very wrong to make any scruple of concurring in so good a work on account of the books put into the childrens hands not being in some respects such as we should prefer. We must bear with such things till time enables to rectify them.

There is a little tract drawn up some years ago by a gentleman in Scotland, which I recomended to our Unitarian Society among their books to be dispersed, which to me seems an excellent sample of instruction for young persons.[2] Something of that kind some years hence may perhaps make it's way into Parish-industry-schools. I have taken the liberty to send you a copy.

Go on and prosper in your endeavours to serve mankind. In no way could you be more usefully employed. I am very glad that any thing I have published has been found serviceable to the cause of truth, especially among my friends.[3]

I am always, Sir, very sincerely Yours
                T. Lindsey
May. 4. 1792.
        Essex Street.

---

1   The *Universal British directory* (1791), V, in its list of the livery of London, p. 124, included: 'Simons, Thomas, Henrietta-Street, Caven. Sq. Vintners'. Henrietta Street, Cavendish Square, was in the parish of St Marylebone. Thomas Simons was the author of a pamphlet entitled *A letter to every housekeeper in London, on behalf of parochial industry schools, for every child who has no other opportunity of receiving any instruction in the several duties of life. From a citizen of the world* [i.e. Thomas Simons] (London, 1792: 2nd edn, enlarged, ?1792). I owe this reference, and the identification of Simons as the author, to Dr Joanna Innes. Simons claimed that the types of schools which he advocated would supplement the *rôle* of charity schools by teaching skills which would make for employability and would inculcate Christian morality. It is clear from Lindsey's letter that Simons had sent Lindsey a copy of this work.

2   On 9 Feb. 1791, on the recommendation of Lindsey, Disney and Dodson, the Unitarian Society

agreed to adopt *Practical instructions for youth* as one of the society's publications, and resolved that 3,000 copies be printed at 4*d* each; Unitarian Society minute book, p. 18; see Letter 423, n. 4. Lindsey believed this tract to have been *Practical instructions for children*, which, as noted by COPAC, has sometimes been attributed to Andrew Skene (*c.* 1728–92), a graduate in medicine from Aberdeen, and Church of Scotland minister at Banff (Presbytery of Fordyce) from 1762 until his death (at Bath) on 2 Dec. 1792. Some members of Skene's congregation seceded and formed a separate congregational church after allegedly objecting to Skene's Socinian preaching; *Fasti Ecclesiae Scoticanae*, VI, 277. For a note on Skene's family, see *Memorials of the family of Skene of Skene*, ed. William Forbes Skene (Aberdeen, 1887), p. 150.

3   Possibly Simons had written to Lindsey to express approval of one of the latter's publications; if so, the letter seems not to have survived.

496. To WILLIAM TURNER OF NEWCASTLE   4 MAY 1792

Text:	DWL, MS 12.44 (54).
Printed:	McLachlan, *Letters*, p. 71 (first two paragraphs); p. 93 (third and fourth paragraphs).
Addressed:	Address missing.
Endorsed:	May. 4. 1792
Postmarked:	Postmark missing.

London. May. 4. 1792.

Dear Sir,

I assured myself without all question that I should have been able with this cover to convey to you an account of the fate of our present application to Parliament, which you who have taken so much pains in to support with names, had some claim to be acquainted with, but M*r* Pitt, by putting the affair off till this day, has defeated my purpose.[1]

Report will have it, that the Minister postponed it to consult the Cabinet and the Bishops, and with a view to let our petition be granted, as a sop to Cerberus, to quiet all other grumblings. Others say the B*ps* and a Great Personage[2] will never consent to such a slur being put upon the doctrine of the trinity as to take off all penalties for writing and speaking against it. We shall soon see however what comes to pass.

It will [cause] some surprize perhaps to you tho' not so to us, to see that in the debates in the Lords house yesterday, one of the Royal Dukes declared himself to be against the abolition of the trade of dealing in human flesh. It is said, unless they sh*d* think better of it, that both the Pr of Wales, D. of York, and of Gloucester also will give their votes against it. To say nothing more of it, such conduct in them is certainly impolitic at this juncture.[3]

You see what an interdict the Minister put [on] all attempts to reform our body Politic, the other day. He must know best what he has to do. But this has been thought inconsiderate in him, because it is acting so directly in the face of his own self on the setting out on his political career. Some will have it, that it was to conciliate matters with a great personage, who has taken amiss his going so far in reprobating the Slave trade.[4]

I dare say you have been attentive to your old tutors late publications, though I am inclined to think sorry for the cast of some of them, not much to his credit.[5] D*r* Priestley called here yesterday, and mentioned having seen the greatest part of M*rs* Barbauld's address, or whatever it is named, to M*r* Wakefield, and spoke in the highest terms of it. I should otherwise however have rather questiond her writing to very general approbation on the subject of prayer, unless it be treated differently from what she published some years ago, on devotional Taste, which seemed to me liable to many objections.[6]

M[r] Johnson promised to send you a copy of a late publication from me, and also for M[r] Prowitt and M[r] Robson, and Mr Richardson of Alnwick: if there sh[d] be another copy, which I desired, I sh[d] be obliged to you to desire the gentlemans acceptance of, who has a congregation somewhere in the neighbourhood of Newcastle, and some years since called upon me in Town.[7]

M[r] Richardson's admission into our Unitarian Society is not forgotten.[8]

My wife joins in kind regards and good wishes for yourself and M[rs] Turner and your little family – and I am always Dear Sir very sincerely Yours
    T. Lindsey.

---

[1] For the postponement of the commons' debate on the unitarian petition from 4 to 11 May 1792, see Letter 498, n. 12.

[2] George III.

[3] For the duke of Clarence's opposition to the abolition of the slave trade, see Letter 497, n. 5. George III's sons George, prince of Wales, and Frederick, duke of York, and the king's brother William, duke of Gloucester, did not openly oppose abolition in the house of lords.

[4] On Monday 30 Apr. 1792, in the Commons' debate on Charles Grey's notice of a motion relative to parliamentary reform, Pitt praised the constitution as 'a monument to human wisdom' and denounced those reformers who aspired to the 'overthrow of the whole system of our present government'. Although he opposed reform in the current circumstances, however, he did not rule it out for all time. See Cobbett, *Parl. hist.*, XXIX, 1302–12. The speech was widely reported in the London press. In 1782, 1783 and 1785, Pitt had introduced in the house of commons's proposals for parliamentary reform.

[5] William Turner had been a pupil at Warrington Academy between 1777 and 1781, where Gilbert Wakefield was the classical tutor from the summer of 1779 to 1783.

[6] Anna Laetitia Barbauld's *Remarks on Mr. Gilbert Wakefield's enquiry into the expediency of public or social worship* was published in London in 1792. This was the work to which Lindsey alluded when referring to 'her writing … on the subject of prayer'. Barbauld's *Devotional pieces, compiled from the Psalms and the Book of Job; to which are prefixed, thoughts on the devotional taste, on sects, and on establishments* was published in London in 1775.

[7] This publication was Lindsey's *Conversations on Christian idolatry*. For William Robson, see Letter 404, n. 1.

[8] For Robert Richardson of Alnwick, see Letter 491, n. 3.

497. To CHRISTOPHER WYVILL   4 MAY 1792

Text: NYRO, ZFW 7/2/71/9, Wyvill of Constable Burton MSS.
Printed: Wyvill, *Political papers*, V, 14–15 (with errors and omissions);
                 McLachlan, *Letters*, p. 140 (part of third sentence of second
                 paragraph; third paragraph; first sentence of fourth paragraph).
Addressed: To/The Rev[d]. Christopher Wyvill/Burton Hall, near Bedale./
                 Yorkshire
Endorsed: From the Rev[d] M[r] Lindsey May 4th 1792
Postmarked: MA 4 92

London. May. 4. 1792.

Dear Sir,

Two days since I promised M[r] Shore I sh[d] write to you and engaged to say for him that he also would soon give you a few lines.

I am not able to say any thing of the faults found with your Defence,[1] for I have mixed with none but those who greatly approve, and they have not been a few. I would name M[r] Lee[2] among the first; though the mode of reform of the representation proposed he does not think you yourself woud now commend: but enters not much into that subject. Only I must say, that I do not think that you have advanced any thing against Mr Burke *in particular*, but he agrees with you in it. And that gentleman I believe has sunk much in his reputation with all but the very high Aristocrats indeed.

I am in hope that you will add your name to the New Association for the Reform of Parliament, of which the two Mr Shores are members, although the Minister has exerted his utmost efforts to check it in its very bud: and unquestionably will succeed with all the timid and interested.[3]

It is thought however, that to qualify such a reprobation of reform, and to quiet the murmurs a little, Mr Fox will be permitted to day to carry his motion for the repeal of the Penal statutes of 9th and 10th of W. iii and 1st of W. iii. as affecting Antitrinitarians. Mr Shore is afraid of this, and would rather things remained as they are till all Penal laws whatsoever in religion are abolished, a ground which Mr Fox will set out upon, though glad to carry a part of his demand, if he cannot succeed for the whole.[4]

You will be surprized perhaps to see in yesterdays acc^t of the house of Lords the Duke of Clarence declaring together with Ld Stormont and the Chancellor, against the abolition of the Slave-trade.[5] But a great personage[6] has been said all along not to approve the business. It is said all the other Royal Dukes will appear against it. In which however, sh^d it be so, I should deem them not merely impolitic, but infatuated with respect to their own interests.

I called at Mr Duncombe's yesterday; but he is not yet returnd since the recess, and I dare say has been much concerned at M^rs [word illegible] death, as I know there was always a great affection between them; as well as taken up since with her affairs.[7]

Whether Mr Morgan and his brother have written their sentiments to you I know not, but I have heard the elder declare himself most highly satisfied with the honour and credit you have done his uncle as well as the Dissenters, and the support given to their cause.[8]

If M^r. Johnson, the bookseller, is not negligent, my small matter is travelling towards you.[9] I have a good hope, that you will approve the temper, if not the subject and train of argument.

My wife joins in respectful compt^s to you and Mrs Wyvill with all wishes of good for your fine family. Mr Shore never ceases comending your son, and I wonder not he was struck with his look [?] as we were: but it is a great deal for him, who has such a very fine grandson of his own.[10] I am always, Dear Sir, your obliged and faithful servant

			T. Lindsey

P.S. We shall be most happy at all times to pay our respects at Burton Hall.

1	I.e. Wyvill's *Defence of Price.*

2	John Lee.

3	Probably this 'new association' was the Sheffield Constitutional Society; see NYRO, ZFW 7/2/71/14, Samuel Shore to Wyvill, 11 May 1792; see also Letter 485, n. 7. It is also possible that Lindsey referred to the Society of the Friends of the People, formed by members of the parliamentary whig opposition on 11 Apr. 1792.

4	Lindsey referred here to the Blasphemy Act of 1698 (9 and 10 William III, c. 32) and the clause of the Toleration Act of 1689 (1 William and Mary, c. 18) which excluded unitarians from its provisions. The commons' debate on the unitarian petition, introduced by Fox, took place on 11 May 1792, not on 4 May as Lindsey had expected.

5   William, duke of Clarence (1765–1837), from 1830 to 1837 King William IV, was the third son of
     George III. He spoke in the house of lords against the abolition of the slave trade on 3 and 8 May
     1792; Cobbett, *Parl. Hist.*, XXIX, 1349–50, 1351–2. For his consistent opposition to abolition until
     its enactment in 1806 and 1807, see Anstey, *Atlantic slave trade*, pp. 305–6, 315, 330–2, 370, 373,
     378, where Professor Anstey suggests (p. 315) that Clarence's naval service in the Caribbean led
     him to attach particular importance to the West Indies. William Murray, 7th Baron Stormont in the
     Scottish peerage (and from Mar. 1793 2nd earl of Mansfield) spoke against abolition on 3 and 8 May
     1792, raising procedural objections; Cobbett, *Parl. Hist.*, XXIX, 1349, 1352. For Lindsey's earlier
     references to him, see Vol. I, Letters 21, 262 and 293. Edward Thurlow, 1st Baron Thurlow, spoke
     against abolition on 8 May 1792; Cobbett, *Parl. Hist.*, XXIX, 1354–5. He had been lord chancellor
     in Pitt's ministry since 1783, but was dismissed by the prime minister in June 1792.
6   George III.
7   Lindsey's hand is uncharacteristically obscure at this point. The surname of the person to whom he
     referred seems to have begun with the letter C, but is otherwise illegible. Henry Duncombe was MP
     for Yorkshire from 1780 to 1796. On 21 May 1792, Lindsey's friend William Mason of York wrote to
     Christopher Wyvill that Duncombe 'was much affected by two late losses, & that particularly of our
     mutual friend Mr Weddel' (William Weddell (1736–92), MP for Malton, who died on 30 Apr. 1792);
     NYRO, ZFW 7/2/71/16. Probably the other late loss was that of the lady to whom Lindsey referred.
8   William Morgan and his younger brother George Cadogan Morgan were nephews of Richard Price.
9   This 'small matter' was Lindsey's *Conversations on Christian idolatry*; Wyvill acknowledged its
     receipt in his letter to Lindsey of 28 May 1792; *Wyvill papers*, V, 15–17.
10   The eldest son of Christopher Wyvill and his second wife Sarah, née Codling, was Marmaduke
     Wyvill (1791–1872), born on 14 Feb. 1791. In 1813, he married Rachel Milnes, the daughter of
     Richard Slater Milnes, MP, of Fryston, Yorkshire, and was himself MP for York from 1820 to 1830.
     There were no children of Wyvill's first marriage. For Samuel Shore's grandson Sydney, see Letter
     479, n. 2.

498. To WILLIAM TAYLEUR   5 MAY 1792

Text: JRUL, Lindsey Letters, vol. II, no. 64.
Printed: McLachlan, *Letters*, pp. 71–2 (first two sentences of fourth
                 paragraph); p. 72 (seventh paragraph); p. 93 (first two
                 sentences of fifth paragraph).
Addressed: To William Tayleur Esqr/Shrewsbury
Endorsed: 5th May – 92 [in pencil]: D of Clarence agt Slave Trade
                 Abolition
Postmarked: MA 5 92

London May 5. 1792.
Dear Sir,

If I had not been persuaded that I should have been almost laid under an intire
interdict with respect to even any proper intimation concerning the person intended
p. 155.[1] I should have consulted beforehand concerning the propriety of what I had
to say. As it is past however, I hope you will excuse it on account of the good effect
that may follow from curiosity being excited thereby, which has already happened
in more instances than one. That you approve the treatise in other respects is a great
satisfaction to me;[2] which I have also received from the very particular manner in
which Baron Maseres has entered into its commendation and expressed his hope
that it may put an end to the Polytheism of the public national worship.[3] You will
forgive the φιλαυτια[4] of mentioning this circumstance; but I know it will give you
pleasure as he is a serious christian and a good judge. I had been accustomed to
present him with my publications, as he was one of those who at my first coming to
Town, subscribed £20 towards our first temporary place of worship.[5] And he replied
that he had bought it and read it twice over, before the present came.[6]

I saw Dr Priestley yesterday. His health remarkably good. He is preaching a course of excellent sermons in defense of the Mosaic Dispensation. My wife went with Mrs Rayner on Sunday morning last to hear him.[7]

I am told that there is an intention among some principal Dissenters to promote a subscription to indemnify him intirely for his pecuniary losses from the rioters. You will not mention it as from me, as I woud not spread about such a thing, till in the way of being carried into effect. But I shall apprize you as soon as I hear of any thing done.[8]

I have seen no paper nor any person to give an account how our Petition fared in the house under our noble leader who presented and patronized it. But it was believed the Minister would accede to the repeal of the two obnoxious statutes to pacify the murmurs which his Monday's speech and declaration against all reform of Parliament had excited.[9] His edict may keep back and discourage some; but I am told it will excite and animate others, in no small numbers.

You would be surprized perhaps at the Duke of Clarence joining Lord Stormont and the Chancellor in declaring himself against the abolition of the trade in human flesh. But they say even the other royal Dukes will appear against it. The reason you will be at no loss to conjecture. The whole business however appears to be impolitic, as it will give no favourable impressions of the humanity of the parties.[10]

I was much disturbed yesterday at the account of so many as four thousand french being cut off, by the treachery of some of their people and the Austrians.[11] But now the sword is unsheathed, may heaven favour them, as their views are I am persuaded for liberty and universal peace.

I find from the morning paper, that Mr Fox put off the bringing in of our petition till the next Friday, being too much indisposed to attend the house.[12] I hope the vast n^{rs} that have twice waited many hours to secure a place for the purpose, and been disappointed, will not be wearied out.

I have a frank for this very day for Mr Houlbrooke at Edinburgh – but find by a letter from Mr Palmer, that he has left the place. I had sent him a little parcell, containing a few copies of "Conversations &c" for himself & one or two more friends. I write this post to desire Mr Palmer to take the parcell under his care – [13]

My wife desires her best respects. I am happy to see your long welcome epistle; whence we augure not amiss concerning the writer.[14] Thank heaven we have cause to be thankful for health as well as other blessings. I remain always, Dear Sir, Your most truly obliged and affectionate servant

        T. Lindsey

---

1   For Lindsey's compliment to Tayleur, see *Conversations on Christian idolatry*, pp. 155–6, and Letter 492, n. 7.

2   In his letter to Lindsey of 26 Apr. 1792 (JRUL, C2^{13}), Tayleur acknowledged receipt of Lindsey's letter of 11 Apr. 1792 (Letter 492) and expressed himself 'very well pleased' with the argument of the *Conversations on Christian idolatry* that worship to any person other than God the father was idolatrous. He added the modest disclaimer appended to Letter 492, to the effect that Lindsey's praise for him was the result of 'the unperceiv'd partiality of a Friend'.

3   Francis Maseres was cursitor baron of the exchequer from 1773 until his death.

4   Self-love, self-regard, egotism; Lindsey used this expression in Letter 427. As before, I am indebted to Mr David Powell for advice as to this quotation.

5   Although Maseres does not feature on any surviving list of subscribers to Essex Street chapel and is not listed as a member of the SPKS or Unitarian Society, he was a subscriber to several unitarian publications, including Disney's edition of the works of John Jebb in 1787. Lindsey presented several of his books to him; see, for example, Letter 701, n. 10.

6   Maseres's letter to Lindsey seems not to have survived.

7   The previous Sunday was 29 Apr. 1792, when Priestley preached at the Gravel Pit meeting, Hackney. His series of sermons evolved into *Discourses relating to the evidences of revealed religion. Vol. I.*

8   HMCO, MS Priestley 2/i, has two lists of subscribers to funds to compensate Priestley after his losses in the Birmingham riots. The first (fo. 7), in a letter from James West to Messrs Lewis and Hayward of Norwich and dated 4 June 1792, lists eighteen subscribers whose contributions amounted to £462.5.0. They included Samuel Shore senior (£50), William Smith (£50) and Michael Dodson (£25). The second list (fo. 15) was inserted in a letter from Philip Martineau of Norwich to Priestley, 30 June 1792, and names twenty-eight contributors, plus one anonymous donor, who between them subscribed a total of £232. The contributors named in the second list were almost all drawn from East Anglia; no contributor appears on both lists.

9   See Letter 496, n. 4.

10 See Letter 497, n. 5.

11 France declared war on Austria on 20 Apr. 1792. On 4 May the *Evening Mail* in London reported that a French attack on Tournai in the Austrian Netherlands had ended in defeat and rout; further reports of French losses and Austrian successes appeared in the *Gazetteer and New Daily Advertiser* and in the *General Evening Post* on 5 May.

12 The *Morning Chronicle*, 5 May 1792, reported that because of Fox's illness, his motion on the penal religious statutes would be postponed from 4 to 11 May. The debate itself took place on the latter day.

13 For Theophilus Houlbrooke's residence in Edinburgh in the early 1790s, see Letter 459, n. 8. After his departure from Edinburgh he became tutor to the sons of William Rathbone at Liverpool; see Letter 500, n. 1. Lindsey had sent to him copies of *Conversations on Christian idolatry*. The letter from Palmer to Lindsey seems not to have survived.

14 For this epistle, see n. 2, above.

499. To TIMOTHY KENRICK   29 MAY 1792

Text:	The Sharpe papers, UCL Library Services, Special Collections (Kenrick papers), 178/35.
Printed:	'The Kenrick letters', *TUHS*, IV, 1 (Oct. 1927), 75–7 (with minor errors).
Addressed:	Address missing.
Endorsed:	Mr Lindsey on Preamble and Idolatry
Postmarked:	Postmark missing.

Dear Sir,

As soon as I received your parcel, about a week since, with the contents of which I was highly pleased, I sent the Letter and a copy of the Rules of your Society to our Secretary, and I communicated them to Mr Dodson, Dr Priestley, Dr Disney; Mr Belsham had several of the copies, and I shall be happy in sending them to some friends at a distance, as I shall rejoice at your having many subscribers, but still more at the like Societies being erected in different parts of the kingdom by your example, which I trust will be the case.[1] Mr Frend is in Town, and I see him often, but did not make any communications to him, as the preamble of your rules holds forth the same, or it may be, more obnoxious language concerning Christ to them, than our's, although he is equally believed to be a human being, which caused him, Mr Tyrwhitt and Mr Lambert, all three of the University of Cambridge to withdraw their names from our Society, tho' I believe only the last objected to the term idolatrous.[2] Quisque suos patimur manes.[3] We have all of us some unaccountable particularities; and few more liberal men than these any where to be found. But I thought proper to mention this circumstance that you might be apprized of the objection made by some. We could not accede to make any change in our preamble after some thousands had been circulated, and on no account to leave out the term idolatrous, though many others took umbrage at it, and during the late debate in the house, wished it had not been inserted.

And to tell you the truth, it was this noise and objection to the use of the word idolatrous, that put me upon drawing up the Conversations that were sent, and which I am glad you did not disapprove. A friend of mine told me that Sr John Scot, the Solicitor General said in the house on the day of our Petition, that even M^r L ___ one of the most moderate of these unitarians did not hesitate to call all the members of the church idolaters.[4] I have had a letter however from one person of rank in the profession, still in the church, who declares his approbation of what I have advanced both matter and manner, and thinks that in half a century the church may become unitarian.[5] But so much, if not too much – for this.

Some of our common friends here had prepared me for the account of the pusillanimous behaviour of M^r B ____ d, or I shoud have been more surprized at it.[6] But he and others should be told, that notwithstanding Mr Burke's ravings against unitarians, the doctrine itself was creditable in the house of Commons ----

I am here interrupted by a friend, who desires to carry me to see Dr Priestley at Clapton, and as I am unwilling to miss the opportunity, I am sure you will excuse the abrupt taking leave, which I engage to make atonement for another time – but must first desire to be put down as a Subscriber to y^r Society of five guineas, and beg you will acquaint me where I may[7] my five guineas and a half.[8]

I trust you will never mind franks to me, as I sh^d not defer on that acc^t writing to you. With mine and my wifes best wishes for your continuance in health & usefulness, I remain very sincerely always Yours

T. Lindsey

May. 29. 1792.

London

---

1 *Society of Unitarian Christians, Established in the West of England*; the rules of the society are set out on pp. 3–7. The names of thirty-one members (including Lindsey, a life member) are listed on p. 8. Timothy Kenrick was nominated as the secretary to the society. It was usually known, and is referred to in this volume, as the Western Unitarian Society.

2 The preamble to the Western Unitarian Society's rules (p. 2) stated: 'While we thus declare our belief in the strict unity of God, and cannot but regard every practice as idolatrous which attributes any of the prerogatives of the Deity to another, a conclusion in which we think ourselves warranted by the language of scripture, we would not be understood to assert that we think such practices are attended with the same immoral consequences as the idolatry which prevailed in the ancient heathen world.' This phraseology differed in form, but not in substance, from that of the preamble to the Unitarian Society's rules in 1791.

3 'We bear each his own spirit', a quotation from Virgil's Aeneid, book 6, line 743. A freer translation, in the context of Lindsey's letter, might be 'we all have our infirmities', or perhaps 'each of us has his own character'. I owe these suggestions and this reference to Mr David Powell.

4 John Scott (1751–1838), MP for Weobley from 1783 to 1796, and for Boroughbridge from 1796 to 1799, was solicitor-general from 1788 to 1793 and attorney-general from 1793 to 1799. As Baron Eldon (and from 1821 1st earl of Eldon) he served as lord chancellor from 1801 to 1806 and from 1807 to 1827. There is no indication in any published reports of the debate on the unitarian petition on 11 May 1792 that Scott spoke in the debate; perhaps his alleged remarks were made informally, in the vicinity of the commons' chamber, on that day. 'M^r L ____' was presumable Lindsey; a more remote possibility is James Lambert of Cambridge.

5 In the light of his allusion to Scott (n. 4, above) immediately before this reference to a 'person of rank in the profession, still in the church', it is likely that Lindsey had in mind an eminent member of the legal profession. A possibility is Benjamin Hobhouse, although in Letter 490 Lindsey noted that Hobhouse had entirely abandoned the church and attended dissenting worship. Another possibility is Francis Maseres, cursitor baron of the exchequer. The letter to Lindsey from this person 'of rank' seems not to have survived.

6 'M^r B ____ d' was presumably Joseph Bretland, the minister of the Mint meeting, Exeter. Lindsey evidently thought that he had been insufficiently zealous, perhaps in canvassing support for the unitarian petition. By Burke's 'ravings', Lindsey meant his strong attack on the petition in the house of commons on 11 May 1792.

7 Word missing, probably 'send'.

8 See n. 2, above, for Lindsey's life membership of the Western Unitarian Society. The cost of life membership was five guineas; the cost of admission was half a guinea.

500. To WILLIAM RATHBONE   4 JUNE 1792

Text:	University of Liverpool, University Library: Rathbone papers, RP XXI.11.12 (3)
Addressed:	Address missing.
Endorsed:	Theoph. Lindsey/ 4 June 1792
Postmarked:	Postmark missing.

London. June. 4. 1792.

Dear Sir,

It has lain much upon my mind that I did not immediately thank you for your most friendly letter, which accompanied the Edinburgh Petition you conveyed to me from Mr Houlbrooke.[1] Seldom have I rec^d more satisfaction than in being told that any thing I had written had been of service to an upright inquiring mind like yours, and this I mentioned at the time to my worthy friend above named. As some small mite of acknowlegement, I had also desired Mr Johnson to send you a publication lately printed;[2] but I cannot rest satisfied without telling you, that I think myself happy and honoured in counting you in the number of my friends.

The state of things on this globe of ours is much agitated and eventful, almost beyond any former period; but I believe you concur with me in the wish and hope that truth and liberty and virtue and real happiness will in the conflict prevail beyond what has hitherto been seen, although there will always remain a mixture of the contrary to exercise and exalt human characters, and fit them for still happier scenes and a more purified state of virtue and benevolence hereafter.

As I see you are become a member of our Unitarian Society, I inclose a copy of the Rules of a similar society lately instituted, which you will be pleased with.[3]

I remain, with sincere respect,

Your much obliged

T. Lindsey.

1 Possibly the 'Edinburgh petition' was a petition from Edinburgh which formed part of the unitarian petition to parliament in Feb.–Apr. 1792. Theophilus Houlbrooke, of Market Drayton, Shropshire, spent some time in Edinburgh in the early 1790s before becoming tutor to William Rathbone's sons and residing for that purpose at Rathbone's house at Green Bank, Liverpool.

2 This publication was probably Lindsey's *Conversations on Christian idolatry*. Rathbone's letter to Lindsey seems not to have survived, although a copy of a letter from him to Lindsey, dated 17 Apr. 1804, may be found in the Rathbone papers, University of Liverpool, University Library, RP II.1.168, p. 189.

3 William 'Rathwell' (clearly an error for Rathbone) of Liverpool was named as a new member of the Unitarian Society at its meeting on 10 May 1792; Unitarian Society minute book, p. 36. He was listed as a member in *Unitarian Society ... 1794*, p. 14. The 'similar society lately instituted' was the Western Unitarian Society.

501. To WILLIAM TAYLEUR   **6 JUNE 1792**

Text: JRUL, Lindsey Letters, vol. II, no. 65.
Printed: McLachlan, *Letters*, pp. 40–1 (short quotations, with
                   transcriptional errors, from fourth and fifth paragraphs,
                   concerning Thomas Evans); p. 72 (part of seventh, and whole
                   of eighth sentence, of first paragraph).
Addressed: Address missing.
Postmarked: Postmark missing.

London. June. 6. 1792

Dear Sir,

I dont know how it is that I have debard myself of the satisfaction of conversing with you for rather a longer interval than usual at this season. It certainly has not been for want of being reminded of such a friend by thinking and talking of him, but rather I believe by a greater multiplicity of engagements and business of one sort or other. I naturally begin with hopes that your health is as it has been and as we most ardently wish it. You will be pleased to hear, that my wife, who desires to be most respectfully remembred, has been lately in her best plight, and myself, I thank heaven, well as usual, though I have for some time found I cannot exert myself as I have been wont. But such things are natural and to be expected. Before you I naturally slide in the next place into the mention of Dr Priestley, or rather he ought to have come imediately after yourself. He eat his morsel with us yesterday, after we had met together on a public call to consider what steps were to be taken in consequence of our late petition to Parliament; and we expected him to day, as he was to be in town again on business; but as we have not seen him, I suppose he was kept at home. The result of our meeting was a series of resolutions concerning returning thanks to Mr Fox principally, and to the other gentlemen, who so nobly supported our cause; and to signify to our brethren and friends that we should by no means give up but pursue it the next session, though nothing was determined particularly in what mode this was to be done, but another meeting appointed on that day fortnight to settle it.[1]

I should truly rejoice, and I think Dr Priestley would be happier and better estabilished if Mr Belsham could but be chosen his collegue. You probably have heard, that the little arian party of the congregation were gratified in having the worthy Mr Barbauld to preach as a candidate: but his voice and manner did not please, and it is said he will not be the person.[2] I am told also that Mr Morice of Yarmouth was applied to, but refused to come and preach for the purpose of interfering in the least degree as a competitor with Mr Belsham.[3] I have spoken my sentiments and wish much that the majority would take courage and chuse the person they approve. Two preachers brought in in such a way has not a good appearance, and would hardly answer the design of instruction and edification, I sh^d think.

I say nothing of Mr Wakefield's publications. I wished at the time, that our friend had refrained from every thing personal with respect to one so irritable.[4] I have seen none of Mr Popes publications; but this last, should it be ever so learned and in many things exposing Mr Wakefield's pretences to superior classical knowledge as unfounded, he will have the address to engage the public ear, and turn the bulk of readers against Mr Pope.[5] If after all, our new college shoud not flourish at present, it will not be for want of very singular encouragement from you. I reckon much on the support it has, and I hope will continue to have from Dr Priestley: although this cannot be expected nor must be suffered to be always gratis.[6]

I do not recollect that I told you of an application sent to us at the annual dinner of our unitarian society by Dr Williams, minister at Sydenham,[7] in behalf of a self taught unitarian in Wales, who had instructed many in the village he lived in, and brought them on so much, that after meeting for some time in a room and it not being sufficient to hold their numbers, they were desirous and solicited assistance towards building them a place to assemble in.[8]

Nothing was done however at our Society meeting; and after some time, not being able to procure any knowlege of the facts and state of the case, I wrote to Mr Thos. Evans myself, which produced the inclosed letter from him. How much I was stuck and delighted with it, I need not say from one so educated, or rather without any education, and so young.[9] I have written to him, that I shall endeavour to serve him, and have desired to know what sum they have calculated they still want for their building added to their own resources within themselves, and in the neighbourhood. I have already procured something, and if your benevolent outgoings have not exceeded your funds, I dare say you will give us a small matter. I should be glad to have the letter returned as soon as you have satisfied yourself with it.[10] And as Mr Martin is going into the country, sh^d none of your own members be at hand; if you direct your outward cover *To John Lee Esq. Lincolns Inn fields, London,* we shall have it safe – as he is much an invalid a little hypochondriac, and my wife sees him most days, I often. I trust that Mr Rowe and his lady and Mr Wood are perfectly.[11] The former I hear intends to visit the West this summer and I heartily wish him a good journey and every thing prosperous. His worthy brother in law is the great strength of our cause in those parts.[12] I say nothing of political matters, tho' they at present [are] of a magnitude and importance to affect one. I wish the French Revolutionists were more united. I read no less than four Parisian Newspapers of the date only of Saturday last, to day. Lord Lauderdale's Protest on our late Proclamation, deserves to be circulated and in every ones hands, to prevent the mischief that may arise from such an alarm given to the country.[13] We hear Birmingham is going to follow the example of the City common council in Addressing and it will be well, if it does not go round the county.[14] I remain Dear Sir ever y^r faithful & affectionate

                              T. Lindsey

1   There is no record in the Unitarian Society minute book of any meeting on 5 June 1792. The meeting on that day to which Lindsey referred was probably a gathering of those involved in the organization of the unitarian petition; see Letter 485, n. 3. After that gathering, a resolution of thanks to Christopher Wyvill was carried; see NYRO, ZFW 7/2/72/18, Michael Dodson to Wyvill, 6 June 1792. Dodson was described in this resolution as 'Chairman of a General Meeting of the Deputies and Delegates from the protestant Dissenters of England and Wales appointed to obtain the Repeal of the Test Laws'. Wyvill's appreciative reply, dated 16 June 1792, may be found in NYRO, ZFW 7/2/72/10.

2   Rochemont Barbauld and Anna Laetitia Barbauld, having supervised a school at Palgrave, Suffolk, between 1774 and 1786, resided at Hampstead from 1787, where they took pupils. Rochemont Barbauld did not become minister at Hackney.

3   Michael Maurice (1766–1855), minister of the Old Meeting, Great Yarmouth from 1787 to 1792, became assistant minister to Priestley at the Gravel Pit meeting, Hackney, in 1792, after the congregation's rejection of Belsham as Priestley's assistant. He served there until 1794, and thereafter undertook a series of independent ministries and worked as a schoolmaster. From 1801 to 1812, he was minister at Normanstone, Lowestoft, and subsequently at Frenchay, near Bristol, and at Sidmouth. See David Young, *F.D. Maurice and unitarianism* (Oxford, 1992), ch. 3.

4   In his *Letters to a young man* (see Letter 490, n. 3), Priestley accused Wakefield of 'virulent and unprovoked censures of Dr Price' (p. v) and of indulging in 'a strain of invective surely not becoming any extraordinary measure of the spirit of Christianity' (p viii).

5   The work of John Pope to which Lindsey referred was *Divine worship, founded in nature and supported by scripture authority. An essay. Remarks on Mr. Wakefield's arguments against public worship, etc* (London, 1792). For Wakefield's sardonic response to it, see his *General reply* (Letter 488, n. 9), pp. 35–7. Pope (1745–1802) was minister at Blackley, Lancashire, from 1767 to 1791 and from 1793 until his death on 28 Oct. 1802. He was tutor in belles-lettres and classical literature at Hackney College from 1791 to 1793. Before his *Divine worship*, he had published *The religious improvement of awful events. A sermon preached at Blackley, Sept. 21, 1777, on occasion of an earthquake which happened the preceding lord's day* (Warrington, 1777) and *Observations on the miraculous conception and the testimonies of Ignatius and Justin Martyr on that subject: in a series of letters to the Rev. Mr. Nisbett; occasioned by his appeal to the public, and his observations on Dr. Priestley* (London, 1792). The advertisement to this latter work was dated 14 Jan. 1792.

6   At Hackney College between 1791 and 1794, Priestley lectured on experimental philosophy, on 'history and general policy', and on theology; see Rutt, I, 120, and Schofield, *Enlightened Joseph Priestley*, pp. 304–8. He published his scientific lectures as *Heads of lectures on a course of experimental philosophy*. He offered these lectures without charge and many, and possibly all, of them were indeed delivered *gratis*.

7   John Williams (1727–98) was minister at Sydenham, Kent, from 1767 to 1795 and served as curator of Dr Williams's Library from 1777 to 1782. Apparently 'At some point in his career he received the degree of LL.D' in recognition of his biblical scholarship'; see the entry for Williams by Diana K. Jones in *ODNB*, LIX, 237. He was a contributor to the *Theological Repository*, III (1771). He probably knew Thomas Evans (n. 8, below) and his family through his Carmarthen connexions; Williams had been trained for the dissenting ministry at the Cambrian Academy, Carmarthen.

8   This 'self-taught unitarian in Wales' was Thomas Evans. At its quarterly meeting on 11 Oct. 1792, the Unitarian Society resolved to send a gift of five guineas to Evans as a contribution to the costs he had incurred in printing unitarian tracts in Welsh; Unitarian Society minute book, p. 38.

9   Born on 20 June 1764, Thomas Evans was two weeks short of his twenty-eighth birthday at this time of this letter.

10 This letter from Thomas Evans to Lindsey, and Lindsey's reply, seem not to have survived.

11 Lindsey omitted a word – probably 'well' – at this point.

12 Rowe's brother-in-law, the 'great strength of our cause' in the west, was Richard Hall Clarke, the treasurer and a leading founder of the Western Unitarian Society.

13 On 21 May 1792, George III, with the full support of Pitt's ministry, issued a royal proclamation against seditious meetings and publications. It was debated in the house of lords on 31 May 1792; Debrett, *Parl. reg.*, XXXIII, 457–93. For Lauderdale's protest against the lords' address in support of the proclamation, see *LJ*, XXXIX, 456–7, and Debrett, *Parl. reg.*, XXXIII, 489–93; it was reported in several London newspapers, for example the *Morning Chronicle*, 4 June 1792. James Maitland (1759–1839), from 1789, 8th earl of Lauderdale, was a Scottish representative peer from 1790 to 1796 and a sympathizer with the Foxite opposition. During the 1790s, he went through a 'Jacobin' phase and called himself 'Citizen Maitland'. Created Baron Lauderdale in the British peerage in 1806, he adopted a more conventional political approach and became a noted writer on political economy.

14 On 1 June 1792, the common council of the city of London presented an address at St James's in support of the royal proclamation against sedition; *London Chronicle*, 2–5 June 1792. By 'county' Lindsey presumably meant similar address from the county of Warwickshire.

502. To WILLIAM ALEXANDER   7 JUNE 1792

Text: 'Letters of the Rev. Theophilus Lindsey. No. III', *UH*, II, 64
                   (19 July 1862), 248.

Note: This is the only section of the letter printed by the *UH*; the manuscript seems not to have survived. The ellipsis at the beginning of the section printed by the *UH* indicates that this was not the beginning of the letter itself. The ellipsis at the end of the second paragraph suggests that it and the third paragraph were separated by text which the *UH* omitted. Here the second and third paragraphs are separated by a broken line.

London, June 7, 1792.

* * * I have a good hope that by going on in that straight upright road in which you have always walked, attending to your proper duty, doing injury to no man by word or deed, but ready to serve every one to your ability, you will overcome the unreasonable prejudices taken up against you, and continue in your laborious and useful employment in your present situation.[1] Should it prove otherwise, I trust that Providence will some way or other point out a station in which you may be able as much or more to benefit others and provide a decent competence for yourself.

I am very glad that the tracts sent are found to contain useful and seasonable truths. When an opportunity next presents, I shall take care to send you Mrs. Barbauld's Remarks on Mr. Wakefield,[2] which contain everything you can wish to see upon the subject, and I hope will close the controversy. * * *

I am sorry to hear unpleasing accounts from Paris, and that the party of the Jacobins are for carrying matters to extremes. But I trust they will see what makes for the good of their country and stability of their new constitution; and by their unanimity be able to overcome the united efforts of despotism against them.[3] And I hope it will be seen in the peaceful demeanour of our own countrymen, in their several meetings and publications, that they aim not to overturn, but to restore and confirm our excellent constitution of government, in the way Mr. Wyvill well describes, though not precisely according to his ideas;[4] and thereby show that there was no just ground for the late proclamation, and the alarm it seems calculated to spread.[5]

---

[1]   William Alexander's 'present situation' was that of a schoolmaster at Yoxford, Suffolk.
[2]   For Anna Laetitia Barbauld's reply to Gilbert Wakefield, see Letter 496, n. 6.
[3]   Louis XVI had accepted the new French constitution, with its severely limited monarchy, on 14 Sept. 1791. The Jacobin Club in Paris, though still in a minority, pressed for a republic. By the 'united efforts of despotism', Lindsey referred to the resistance within France to the new constitution, notably from the court, and the threats, encouraged by the émigré princes, to invade France posed by Prussia and Austria.
[4]   This is a reference to Wyvill's *Defence of Price*.
[5]   For the royal proclamation of 21 May 1792, see Letter 501, n. 13.

503. To WILLIAM TURNER OF NEWCASTLE   14 JUNE 1792

Text: DWL, MS 12.44 (55).
Printed: McLachlan, *Letters*, pp. 119–20 (second and third paragraphs; most of fourth paragraph); pp. 137–8 (fifth paragraph).
Addressed: To/The Rev^d. Mr Turner/Newcastle upon Tyne
Endorsed: Lond°. June. 14. 1792
Postmarked: Postmark missing.

London. June. 14. 1792

Dear Sir,

As I am going to call on our friend in Lincolns Inn fields,[1] and expect to get a frank from him, I make the less scruple in sending you a mere howd'you letter, and begin with saying that I hope you rec^d my last, and also that the parcell arrived safe.[2]

In these times of ferment, I hope all is quiet with you, and will so continue. It gave me satisfaction to learn that the Dissenters at Birmingham had determined to have no meeting on the 14ʰ of July, and had publicly signified this in the Birmingham paper, before Irenopolis's letter to Eleutheropolis came out, in which the author by various arguments exhorts them to refrain from their public dinner upon the occasion, and is none other than the celebrated Dʳ Parr, who has lately said so many things so well, for liberty civil and religious, in behalf of the French Revolutionists and of Dʳ Priestley in his Sequel &c or controversy with the Birmingham Rector.³

I am sorry however to learn by a letter from Exeter this post that they have had, (i.e. the dissenters) some very unexpected disturbances there.⁴ A merchant of no esteem in that city, thought proper to send cards of invitation to celebrate the kings birthday June. 4, and mentioned his purpose of having a bonfire in the evening to burn the works of Paine, Priestley and Mʳ Kenrick's excellent sermon there on the last 5ᵗʰ. Novʳ. by the hands of the comon Scavanger.⁵ This was accordingly done after reading some part of his Majesty's late Proclamation. Much prudence and caution was used by the Dissenters, who have never given them any offence, or there might have ensued great mischief, as the mob collected upon the occasion muttered many menaces against them. The mayor has *advised* the booksellers to remove every thing that may give offence from their windows, in consequence of which all political books and political prints have disappeared, and nothing particularly of the above-named authors to be seen.⁶ And the Clergy of the Cathedral and in the neighbourhood have taken to preaching up the doctrine of the Trinity, and Athanasius's creed is resumed again in places where it had been omitted for many years past.

Dʳ Priestley is very well, and very happy in his situation, and in pursuing his experiments: but was made very uneasy yesterday by the account of his second son's naturalization in France, which he read for the first time in the morning chronicle of yesterday. He is a bold impetuous young man, tho' with no bad qualities: he went to France to be in a mercantile house; but I should not be surprized to hear that he followed the camp.⁷ The whole of this circumstance will however furnish Mʳ Burke and the public prints with ample materials against the Doctor and all dissenters, particularly Unitarians.

The whole of the disagreable affair betwixt Mʳ Wakefield and the opponents he has raised, I wish we cᵈ. bury in silence. I am persuaded he is a worthy upright character. And I think they are wrong who deny him the praise of an ingenious classical scholar, and an easy agreeable writer. But certainly the man of sense or good reasoner has not appeared in this controversy which he has begun on public social worship. The new college will certainly suffer from what he is [sic] said of it and its tutors at the end of the Memoirs of his life.⁸

I desire you will let me know what extraordinary expence you was at in circulating our petition, that I may mention it. My wife desires to join compts to Mʳˢ Turner and good wishes for your young folks, and I am always

very sincerely Yours

T. Lindsey.

I did not receive any names from your good father, nor have heard from him lately. Mʳˢ R. Milnes was at our chapel on Sunday, and is on the return to Wakefield.⁹ Young Mʳ Shore and his lady set out a fortnight ago – His father &c leave Clapham in abᵗ ten days.¹⁰

---

1   John Lee.

2   Lindsey's previous surviving letter to William Turner of Newcastle was that of 4 May 1792 (Letter

496); the parcel was probably that which contained the publications Lindsey had requested Joseph Johnson to send to Newcastle.

3   Samuel Parr's *A letter from Irenopolis* was published in Birmingham in 1791. Parr was also the author of *A sequel to the printed paper lately circulated in Warwickshire by the Rev. Charles Curtis, brother of Alderman Curtis, a Birmingham rector, &c* (London, 1792). For the decision of dissenters at Birmingham, following Parr's advice, not to hold celebrations on 14 July 1792, see Wykes, '"Spirit of persecutors"', 24. The Birmingham newspaper was *Aris's Birmingham Gazette*. Charles Curtis (d. 1829) was rector of St Martin's, Birmingham, from 1781 to 1829 and of Solihull, 1789–1829. His brother was William Curtis (1752–1829), an alderman of the City of London from 1785 until his death (and lord mayor from 1795 to 1796) and one of the four MPs for the City from 1790 to 1818.

4   This was probably a (non-surviving) letter to Lindsey from Timothy Kenrick.

5   This latter work was Timothy Kenrick's *The spirit of persecutors exemplified; and the conduct to be observed towards their descendants. A sermon, delivered at George's meeting-house, Exeter, November 5th, 1791. To which are prefixed, some observations upon the causes of the late riots at Birmingham* (Exeter, 1792).

6   George III's fifty-fourth birthday was 4 June (new style) 1792. On 2 June 1792, the mayor, aldermen and common council of Exeter sent a loyal address to George III, thanking him for the royal procla-mation of 21 May; *London Gazette*, 5–9 June 1792. The mayor of Exeter in 1792 was John Pinhey, who had been sheriff of the city in 1790. On 9 June 1792 the *Morning Herald* reported: 'It is mentioned as a *remarkable event*, at Exeter, that when the Political Works of PAINE and PRIESTLEY were thrown, by the common hangman, upon the pile to be publicly burnt at that place, they were found to be of so *combustible* a kind, that the whole *burst into a blaze* the moment they were depos-ited.'

7   The *Morning Chronicle* of 13 June 1792 reported that Priestley's second son William (1771–c. 1835) had been granted naturalization as a French citizen by the legislative assembly in Paris. The resolu-tion granting the French citizenship heaped lavish praise upon Priestley himself.

8   At the end of his *Memoirs of the life of Gilbert Wakefield ... written by himself*, the author devoted more than forty pages (pp. 336–81) to his experience as classical tutor at Hackney College. He was critical of the college's teaching of Hebrew, of its lack of an 'elegant' classical education, and of its lay supporters. He complained of the high cost of the building and its proximity to the temptations of London, and alleged that Richard Price had neglected him. He predicted the 'speedy dissolution' (p. 367) of the college unless it could be reformed.

9   Mrs R. Milnes was Esther Milnes (d. 1799), the widow of Robert Milnes of Wakefield (1719–71); see Vol. I, Letter 160, n. 12.

10   'Young Mr Shore' was Samuel Shore IV (1761–1836), the son of Lindsey's friend Samuel Shore III (1738–1828). His wife, whom he married in 1788, was Harrriet, née Foye (1761–1826). For Samuel Shore III and Clapham, see Letter 461, n. 8.

504. To TIMOTHY KENRICK   16 JUNE 1792

Text: The Sharpe papers, UCL Library Services, Special Collections (Kenrick papers), 178/34.

Printed: 'The Kenrick letters', *TUHS*, IV, 1 (Oct. 1927), 77–9 (with very minor errors).

Addressed: Address missing.

Endorsed: M^r. Lindsey June 16–92 outrages at Exeter

Postmarked: Postmark missing.

London June. 16. 1792

Dear Sir,

I am much vexed to hear of the shameful doings at your city on the kings birthday.[1] I was in hope there was a more liberal spirit in the place, and I should think that if your Bishop had been in vigour, the known discountenance, which I presume he woud have given to such proceedings would have prevented them. But he has been declining in intellect, as Dr Heberden told me lately, for some time, and now in his health, so that he is expected not to hold out long, and I was told the other day that about the court they have given him a successor, not Dr Horsley who had been talked of, but Dr Buller Dean of Canterbury, and who is to hold the Bishopric with his deanery.[2]

Still I will hope it was not the general temper of the church people, but only of some principal persons stird up by one boutefeu. I rejoice however that you were unmolested; and henceforth I think you need not fear, as I trust this bad spirit will evaporate from the odium that will attend it and the impolitic acts of those who excite it, raising alarms and jealousies where all would be quiet but for themselves. This wild indiscretion of Dr Priestley's second son in putting himself forward in such a way to be naturalized in France, opens the mouths of many persons against the father, who, I can say, is much concerned for it; and who was far from authorizing his son to use such language.[3] But it was natural for foreigners to dwell on the excellence and superior worth of a character to which mean jealousy and envy and party-spirit makes his countrymen quite insensible.

I have not seen him or Mr Belsham since I was favoured with yours or sh^d have told them the name of the Bankers to whom any subscriptions to your unitarian Society might be paid.[4] They were apprized however some days since of what had happend at Exeter, tho' not acquainted with the particular circumstances, at least did not mention them to me.

Having the opportunity of a frank I have inclosed a little tract just come out, the begining I hope of a long series of others of the same stile and excellence, which cannot fail of being of the greatest service, if they may be but universally read. Such writings will tend to make them not only good citizens, but good in every relation of life. The writer, whoever he be, is not a common person.[5]

I have been confined by a cold a day or two but my wife has paid my subscription to Messrs Downe &c in Bartholomew lane.[6] I hope, tho' I have no reason to expect any long life, to see more societies of the kind rise, and that the day is not very distant when your townsmen will be ashamed of their unworthy opposition to you. At all times it is a pleasure to hear from you, for I am with great esteem most truly Yours

T. Lindsey.

---

1 For these events at Exeter, see Letter 503, n. 6.

2 John Ross, bishop of Exeter since 1778, died on 14 Aug. 1792, aged seventy-three, barely two months after Lindsey wrote this letter. His successor was indeed William Buller, who remained bishop of Exeter until his death in Dec. 1796. Buller relinquished the deanery of Canterbury (which he had held since succeeding George Horne in 1790) upon his elevation to Exeter. Samuel Horsley was bishop of St David's from 1788 until his translation to Rochester in 1793.

3 See Letter 503.

4 See n. 6, below.

5 Possibly this 'little tract' was *Thoughts on the necessity and means of a reform of the Church of England. By a friend to religion and his country* (London, 1792). The publisher was Joseph Johnson, and the tract was reviewed favourably in the *Monthly Review*, NS, VIII (1792), 474–5. Another possibility is the tract to which Lindsey referred in Letter 506.

6 This was Lindsey's subscription to the Western Unitarian Society (see Letter 499), of which Timothy Kenrick was secretary. The bankers to whom Lindsey referred were Downe, Thornton and Free, 1 Bartholomew Lane, London.

505. To WILLIAM TAYLEUR   **25 JUNE 1792**

Text: Royal Soc., Priestley Memorial Volume, p. 53.
Addressed: To/William Tayleur Esqʳ/Shrewsbury
Endorsed: June 25 – 92
Postmarked: JU 25 92

London. June. 25. 1792

Dear Sir,

In my last page I have made an extract out of Mʳ Evans's letter, which I received on Saturday, of all that he says, relative to the expence of building their chapel, and to his translations and publications in Welsh for the present. I must tell you that I have already collected twenty pounds for him, and shall not be negligent as occasion serves in procuring somewhat more. As you kindly propose to give him something at present, you will be so good as to let me know what you can conveniently spare for so good a creature's purposes and designs, and I shall transmit it. I should have procured a frank and inclosed his letter, if I had not had some occasion for it at present; but I shall contrive to give you a sight of it, as it will give you pleasure.

I have not seen Dʳ Priestley since the beginning of the last week; but have heard of his having been since in Town; and that he is well.

Mʳ Wakefield has appeared again in his controversy, and in his own way. His Tract is intitled, "*A General Reply to the arguments against the Enquiry into Public Worship*["]: By Gilbert Wakefield, B.A. late fellow of Jesus College Cambridge, the Author of that Enquiry. He musters up all his antagonists in order, and assails them one by one. Dʳ Disney and Mʳ Simpson are alone his favourites. His treatment of Dʳ Priestley is, if possible, more insolent and contemptuous than before.[1] But in the end, he must hurt himself more than others by such publications. A controversy more useless never was stir'd up; and it was my advice from the first that no one shᵈ take any notice of the author of it.

I have lately heard out of Suffolk, where Mʳ Evanson lives, near Ipswich, that his work upon the Canon of Scripture is nearly ready to go to the press. You know that he was formerly of opinion, that Luke's gospel alone was genuine. We shall see on what grounds he argues.[2] This is a controversy that must be of service in the end; although at first and in its progress it may disturb some persons. From inquiry and discussion of such nice but important questions, truth must in the end come out with greater clearness.

I shall add no more at present but my wife's cordial respects and that I am always Dear Sir, Your most truly obliged and faithful affectionate servant

T. Lindsey.

Our due remembrances to your two gentlemen, our friends.[3]

[On the opposite page, i.e. the third side of the double sheet]:

from Mʳ Evans's letter – dated Penpistyll near Brechfa[4]
June. 20. 1792

----- "After calculating how much expence will go to build the Chappel according to the plan we wish, we are in want of about 46 pounds at least besides what we know that we can procure in the neighbourhood: but if you, Dear Sir, can procure much less than this, it will be received very thankfully, and we shall build the Chappel according to what we can get.

"*An Appeal to the Professors of christianity* is in the press, and will be published in the course of a fortnight.[5] Some friends have promised to lend me the money towards paying for the publication, being £4. 17s for 500, untill such time as the pamphlet shall be sold. Should you and your friends therefore be disposed to encourage the publication of Unitarian Tracts in Welsh, I beg you would withhold your kindness for that, untill such time as I shall publish D[r] Priestley's Familiar Illustration, which I intend soon to attempt.[6] But I shall be glad to be assured whether I can expect any assistance for publishing the Illustration in a short time, this being the season of the year in which I can best afford time for the Translation. My first Sermon is ready for the Press: but the other tracts are not correct enough without rewriting them, if they are to be printed."[7]

1   This work was Wakefield's *A general reply*. His reply to Disney's *A defence of public or social worship. A sermon preached* may be found at pp. 11–14. His reply to John Simpson's *Christian arguments for social and public worship. A sermon preached before an annual assembly of protestant dissenting ministers at the chapel in Lewin's Mead, Bristol, on Friday the 13th of April, 1792* (Bath, 1792) may be found at pp. 29–30; his reply to Priestley's *Letters to a young man* may be found at pp. 26–9. Wakefield had also attacked Priestley in his *Short strictures on the Rev. Doctor Priestley's letters to a young man, concerning Mr. Wakefield's treatise on public worship: by the author of that treatise* (London, 1792); preface dated 15 Apr. 1792). Mr Simpson was probably John Simpson (1746–1812), educated at Warrington Academy (where he was a pupil of Priestley) and Glasgow University, and minister to dissenting congregations at High Pavement chapel, Nottingham (from 1772 to 1777), and Walthamstow (1777 to 1779). He relinquished his ministry in 1779 and in 1791 retired to Bath, where he published a series of theological works; see also Letter 701.
2   Edward Evanson's *The dissonance of the four generally received evangelists, and the evidence of their respective authenticity examined* was published in Ipswich in 1792.
3   Probably Edward Harries and Isaac Wood.
4   The original manuscript of Thomas Evans's letter to Lindsey appears not to have survived.
5   Priestley's *Appeal to the serious and candid* was first published in Leeds in 1770, with further editions in 1771, 1772, 1775, 1783, 1784, 1788, 1791 and 1792. The Welsh translation by Thomas Evans was published at Carmarthen in 1792, with a second edition at Merthyr Tydfil in 1812.
6   Priestley's *Familiar illustration of certain passages of scripture* was first published in Leeds in 1770, with further editions in 1772, 1785 and 1794. Evans published a Welsh translation of this work at Carmarthen in 1792.
7   Evans's 'first sermon' – and the first unitarian sermon published in Welsh – was *Amddifyniad o bennadwriaeth y Tad* (Carmarthen, 1792). One of his other tracts was a translation of the trial of Edward Elwall, entitled *The triumph of truth*, with a preface by Priestley (for the full title, see Vol. I, Letter 365, n. 3), which was published by Evans in Carmarthen in 1793. See Geraint H. Jenkins, '"A very horrid affair": sedition and unitarianism in the age of revolutions', in *From medieval to modern Wales. Historical essays in honour of Kenneth O. Morgan and Ralph A. Griffiths*, ed. R. R. Davies and Geraint H. Jenkins (Cardiff, 2004), pp. 182–3.

506. To RUSSELL SCOTT   26 JUNE 1792

    Text: Scott Coll.
    Printed: McLachlan, 'Lindsey to Scott', 118 (third and fourth sentences of second paragraph).
    Addressed: [In the hand of John Lee MP] London twenty sixth June 1792/ Rev[d] Russell Scott/Portsmouth/JfreeLee [in Lindsey's hand, opposite address] Rev[d]. Russell Scott/Portsmouth
    Postmarked: JU 26 92

Dear Sir,
    Having been assured that a small parcel some time since came safe to your hands, from an obliging letter in acknowlegement of a copy of The Conversations

&c received from Mr Porter,[1] I have been ever since waiting for a line from yourself to tell us how you and Mrs Scott and your little one do. I assure you we cannot help being interested for one we esteem so much, and therefore must beg you will relieve us by a short line the first convenient opportunity.

Many things of moment have passed since I heard from you, both of a public and more private nature, and many are still passing. I trust in the event that every thing will even at present turn out what in our estimate will be favourable to liberty and virtue; in the final issue it will undoubtedly be so. The session ends on Thursday at the New College.[2] Never I believe have a number of young men no less than 40 been more studious and regular; but many events and particularly what has happened with respect to Mr Wakefield and the things he has thrown out, will it is feared hurt the Seminary in future.[3] And unquestionably the situation so near this metropolis, is and ever will be adverse to good discipline.

We shall soon be going into the country to visit some old friends as usual in the middle of each week, but shall not take any long journey this year, but shall probably be altogether absent during the month of [Au]gust[4] as our chapel is then to undergo some repair and be shut up for 4 or 5 weeks. Dr Priestley is very well and comfortably settled at Hackney; his house most comodious in all respects, and particularly for his experiments, in which he is most assiduous. Dr Kippis is at Camberwell with Mrs Kippis, but comes to Town frequently as he is wanted. D^r & Mrs Disney are going into the north the latter end of the next month, where we were the last year, to visit my wifes and Mrs Disney's mother. The inclosed is intended to be followed with a series to the same purpose, and may do great good, if carried on with equal ability, moderation and good sense and universally read. Who is the author I have not been able to learn.[5]

My wife desires to join in every kind regard for yourself, Mrs Scott and your little one and I am always Dear Sir most truly Yours

T. Lindsey

London. June. 26. 1792

Pray make my comp^ts to Mr Porter and thanks for his letter.

---

1   Lindsey referred here to his *Conversations on Christian idolatry*. William Joseph Porter's letter to Lindsey seems not to have survived.
2   The following Thursday was 28 June 1792.
3   Lindsey referred here to Wakefield's attack upon social worship (see Letter 475, n. 5) and to his criticisms of Hackney College in his *Memoirs*; see Letter 503, n. 8.
4   The first two letters of the word 'August' are partly overlaid by the seal.
5   Possibly this work was *The Patriot; Or, Political, Moral and Philosophical Repository, Volume I*, which advocated moderate reform. Lindsey implied that it was the first of a series; clearly by June 1792, he cannot have referred to the first number of the *Christian Miscellany*. See also Letter 504, n. 5.

507. To RUSSELL SCOTT   25 OCTOBER 1792

Text:	Scott Coll.
Printed:	McLachlan, 'Lindsey to Scott', 118 (short quotation from first paragraph, concerning the baptism of Scott's son; third and fourth sentences of fifth paragraph; first sentence of sixth paragraph; first three sentences of final paragraph of postscript).
Addressed:	To/The Rev^d. Mr Russell Scott/Portsmouth
Endorsed:	Oct. 26th – 92
Postmarked:	OC 25 92

London. Oct. 25. 1792

Dear Sir,

If any one had told me that your long letter of July last had been unacknowleged, except yourself, I certainly sh^d not have believed them.[1] I really had persuaded myself that it was so because I fully intended it, and beg your pardon for a neglect unintentional, when I am always happy in shew[ing] my sincere regards. But I suppose, that continued absence from Town the whole summer, except at the end of each week may have caused this oversight. You shall not however have cause of future complaint of the kind when I am able to handle a pen.

One thing more I will add upon the subject, that I presumed on having written to you by mentioning to Mr Watson when he called upon me, which I took very kindly, that I expected to be called upon to baptize your little boy: which You may be assured I shall at any time be glad to do, and have been all along this month of October expecting to hear from You on the subject, though glad it was otherwise, as this is the very first week that we have taken up our abode for the winter: but now I shall be on the spot and always at your service.[2]

Now to y^r last epistle as the first is out of date.

You will have pleasure in being informed, that my wife and I have been all the summer and are returned out of the country very well, heaven be praised, and it will be a satisfaction to have the same tidings of you and Mrs Scott and your little boy.

Dr Priestley was with us on Monday, very well. He then told me, that he had just sent his reply to Mr Burn to the Press.[3] I apprehend that there are no better lectures read in any University than at this time in our New College, by Dr Priestley tuesdays & saturdays, on natural philosophy and history; and by Mr Belsham in his department of Ethics, Metaphysics, the evidences of X^ty &c. Dr Rees, the old Tutors lectures you are well acquainted with.[4] And better discipline cannot be observed, as far as lies in the power of Mr Belsham, the resident Tutor; And the Students were never so happy as since the care of the Commons has been in Miss Belshams hands and She & her brother always dine with them.[5]

It was owing to some men's mean opposition and interference, that Mr Belsham was not chosen Afternoon Preacher at the Gravel pits. Be this said with^t any disparagement to Mr Morice, of whom I have heard a very good character every way.[6] I have forgot to mention, that Mr Pope is said to intend to quit the college at X^mas, and retire into Lancashire to the situation he was before in, as more eligible.[7]

We hope that the French are in the way to have a good and durable settlement. A friend who has just left me, observes that if the despots had succeeded, it would not have been safe even in England in favour of liberty: but now the case is altered.[8] We shall have pleasure in talking over these matters and I hope the progress of their success when you come to Town. It is thought, that notwithstanding all that has been said and printed on the subject, those concerned in the Regium Donum, will find means to elude the business, and the public be left unsatisfied. I find great silence upon it.[9]

There is a tract on the Persecution of Christians by Jews, heathens, and christians, the author A. Robinson, now in the north, some few years since an independent minister in Town. I like it & shall be glad to put it into your hands.[10] I know nothing else on Ecclesiastical subjects. Mr Paine's Address to the Addressers &c is too coarse in some parts. You will say he might have introduced better the chapter from Samuel.[11] But there are some republican propositions that will be very grating to many.

I write this in great haste after a walk in the park and not to lose the return of the post. We join in every kind regard for Mrs Scott, yourself and your little boy. And I am always, Dear Sir, most truly Yours

T. Lindsey.

P.S. I believe Mr Mallet built the place of worship you mention intirely on speculation[n]: certainly with no well grounded expectation of its being occupied by Dr J.[?] It is however ready for any Unitarian Minister who can raise a congregation.[12]

Dr Priestleys lectures on the Sundays to young persons are greatly attended and likely to be of Sovereign use. I do not think that the congregation properly relish or understand his excellence.[13] But I may be mistaken. Pray when you see Mr Watson, do us the favour to present our congratulations.[14]

1   Scott's 'long letter' to Lindsey, July 1792, appears not to have survived.

2   Scott's 'little boy' was his first son, Russell, born on 27 Oct. 1791. According to Scott, *Family biography*, p. 96, Lindsey baptized him at the house of his maternal grandfather, Dr William Hawes at 8, Spital Square, London. Hannah Lindsey indicated to Catharine Cappe in a letter of 14 June 1801 that the baptism took place in 1792. See Cappe, *Memoirs*, p. 316. The boy died in 1797, but on 9 June 1801 Lindsey baptized Scott's second son (also named Russell), who was born on 3 Feb. 1801. See Scott, *Family biography*, p. 96, and Cappe, *Memoirs*, p. 316. The Hawes residence was close to Spital chapel, Norton-Folgate, where Lindsey had been morning preacher in the late 1740s. According to Hannah Lindsey, in June 1801 'He looked at his old chapel going now to ruin, all the old inhabitants dead or beggared, the silk trade being ruined'; Cappe, *Memoirs*, p. 316. Mr Watson was probably Thomas Watson, the minister of the dissenting congregation at Baffins Lane, Chichester; see Letter 388, n. 12.

3   Edward Burn published *A reply to the Reverend Dr. Priestley's appeal to the public, on the subject of the late riots at Birmingham, in vindication of the clergy, and other respectable inhabitants of the town* (Birmingham, 1792). Amongst other allegations, Burn claimed (p. 102) that 'Unitarianism, in the person of Dr. Priestley, has for some time been inviting the *aids* of persecution, and of persecution from the *clergy*.' Priestley replied at length to this and other charges in his *Appeal to the public. Part II*. The preface was dated 1 Jan. 1793 and the work appeared in that month. For Priestley's previous controversy with Burn over the doctrine of the Trinity, see Letters 399, 407 and 412.

4   Scott had been a student, successively, at the Daventry, Homerton and Hoxton academies. At Hoxton during the early 1780s, his teachers included the resident tutor Abraham Rees and the classical tutor Andrew Kippis.

5   For these new arrangements at Hackney College, see Letter 482. In 1792, Thomas Belsham had two unmarried sisters, namely Elizabeth (1743–1819), who married Timothy Kenrick in 1794 and thereafter lived at Exeter; and Ann (d. 1824), who never married. Ann Belsham took over the domestic arrangements at Hackney College. See Ann Belsham's will, TNA: PRO PROB 11/1689, folio number not available at TNA.

6   See Letter 501, n. 3.

7   For John Pope, see Letter 501, n. 5.

8   After its setback at Valmy on 20 Sept. 1792, the Prussian army evacuated Verdun (14 Oct.) and Longwy (22 Oct.).

9   In Aug. 1792, a controversy over the *regium donum*, a modest charity established by George I in 1722

for the support of impoverished dissenting ministers and their widows, broke out in the newspaper press, with allegations that acceptance of this money from the crown contradicted the voluntary principle and compromised dissenters by bringing them under government influence. The trustees of the fund encountered particular criticism that their distribution of the fund was insufficiently open to public scrutiny. The *regium donum* became even more unacceptable to many dissenters in the later 1790s when John Martin, a pro-ministerial baptist minister, became the sole distributor of the fund. Among the trustees known personally to Lindsey were Andrew Kippis, Abraham Rees, Thomas Morgan and Hugh Worthington. See K. R. M. Short, 'The English Regium Donum', *EHR*, LXXXIV (1969), 64–8. For Richard Price's strong disapproval of the fund, see *Price corr.*, II, 179, n. 3.

10 Anthony Robinson, *A short history of the persecution of Christians by Jews, heathens and Christians. To which are added an account of the present state of religion in the United States of America and some observations on civil establishments of religion* (Carlisle, 1793). Robinson (1762–1827) was briefly preacher to the general baptist chapel at Worship Street, London, during the late 1780s. He then removed to the region of his birth, Cumberland, and financed the building of a chapel at Wigton, where he sometimes preached. In 1796, he returned to London, achieved considerable wealth as a sugar refiner, and belonged to the radical literary circles of Henry Crabb Robinson (no relation) and William Hazlitt.

11 Thomas Paine's *Letter addressed to the addressers on the late proclamation* was published in London in 1792. It included (p. 10) a quotation from I Samuel, ch. viii, which set out Samuel's objections to the proposal that the Jews should be ruled by a king. Paine introduced the quotation by describing Samuel, with mock disapproval, 'as mad as any Man-of-Rights-Man now-a-days'. For George III's proclamation of 21 May 1792, see Letter 501, n. 13. The 'addressers' were those institutions, including local corporations, which had sent addresses of thanks to the crown for the proclamation.

12 In the absence of Scott's letter, it is difficult to be certain as to the place of worship to which he had referred. Probably it was a chapel in the west country; possibly the philanthropic 'Mr Mallet' was the lawyer Philip Mallet; see *MR*, VII (1812), 258. I have not identified 'Dr J[?]'. But see Letter 612, n. 6.

13 For these Sunday lectures to the young people of the Gravel Pit meeting, which Priestley did not publish separately, see Rutt, I, 118, and Wykes, 'Priestley at Hackney', 520–1.

14 Lindsey wished to congratulate Thomas Watson of Chichester on his marriage to Margaret Webster, the daughter of the London merchant George Webster, on 8 Oct. 1792; see *Familiae min. gen.*, I, 188.

---

508. To JOHN ROWE   1 DECEMBER 1792

Text: JRUL, Lindsey Letters, vol. II, no. 66.
Addressed: To/The Rev^d. John Rowe/Shrewsbury
Postmarked: DE 1 92

London. Decr. 1. 1792

Dear Sir,

My wife desires I would begin my letter with our hearty congratulations to yourself and your lady on the good state of herself and the little stranger that has lately made it's appearance, who, we hope, will add to the comfort of both the parents and fill a useful station in the theatre on which she is produced.[1]

We next beg our due respects to our common excellent friend upon the hill, whose handwriting though we do not see as usual we are glad he is in such health and vigour in other respects.[2] For my own part I thank him much for his very judicious advice and directions comunicated by You, and shall profit by them. And as you are so good as not to think much of the trouble, I should take it as a favour, if you would transcribe and send by the post the alterations which Mr Buller has made in our Litany by writing some of the Petitions.[3]

You will be so good as to tell Mr Tayleur that I always intended, as I told Dr Disney, to pay what attention I coud to his alterations, but as a very judicious member of our congregation observes, he appears in several instances to have not been sufficiently attentive to that simplicity and devotional spirit which marks the original.[4]

It is with great difficulty that I have been able to write so far. For as I was taking up my pen, D[r] P ___ y called to take his lot with us at our dinner, and is but just gone home.

He is very well – desired to be remembered to M[r] Tayleur and yourself. His 2[d] Part of the Appeal on the Riots &c will be out in a fortnights time. You will be delighted w[h] the whole, particularly the preface and appendix.[5] I am always, with sincere esteem, Dear Sir most truly Yours

T. Lindsey.

This day M[r] Jones, D[r] P's successor, sends me his sermon, just printed. It is every way masterly.[6] It is the composition of a man of genius, availing himself of all the lights of these enlightened times.

M[r] Martin was with us this morning. He is very well, and will also be one among the not a few glorious lights, of whom Dissenters have to boast in these days.[7]

---

1   This is a reference to Eliza Clarke Rowe, the daughter of John and Mary Rowe, who was born on 25 Nov. 1792 and died in 1839; see TNA: RG4/1818, fo. 23, and *CR*, VI (1839), 830.

2   This is a reference to William Tayleur and his estate at Rodington House, Shropshire, about six miles from Shrewsbury. The Tayleur family's town house was No. 4, Belmont, Shrewsbury, which was in an elevated position overlooking the river Severn. See Forrest, *The old houses of Shrewsbury*, p. 45.

3   For William Buller of Wiltshire, see Vol. I, Letter 354, n. 7. Lindsey here used the word 'petitions' in the sense of prayers or supplications. For the 'Salisbury liturgy', see Letter 406, n. 12.

4   Since the late 1770s, Lindsey and Tayleur had been in correspondence over the latter's proposals for amendments to the liturgy of Essex Street chapel; see Vol. I, Letters 227, 294, 298 and 304. The fourth edition of Lindsey's *Book of Common Prayer reformed according to the plan of the late Samuel Clarke* was nearing completion in Dec. 1792; see Letter 514, n. 10. Although Lindsey did not identify the 'very judicious' member of the congregation, obvious possibilities are Michael Dodson, Samuel Heywood and Elizabeth Rayner.

5   Priestley's *Appeal to the public. Part II* included a preface (pp. iii–xxi) which referred to his controversy with Edward Burn, defended the Unitarian Society against allegations that it was politically motivated, and deplored the ignorance and superstition of mobs in manufacturing districts. It expressed gratitude to Samuel Parr, William Russell and Samuel Whitbread MP for their support for the victims of the Birmingham riots. The appendix (pp. 145–205) contained nineteen separate items of evidence, some of them drawn from the newspaper press, of attitudes for and against the dissenters, including 'an account of the high church spirit which has long prevailed at Stourbridge' (see Letter 472, n. 7).

6   This sermon was David Jones's *The nature and duties of the office of a minister of religion; also, the impiety, injustice, and absurdity of persecution, considered in a discourse delivered before the congregations of the New and Old Meetings* (Birmingham, 1792).

7   This is probably a reference to James Martin MP, who had advocated dissenting causes in the house of commons.

---

509. To JOSEPH CHADWICK   5 DECEMBER 1792

    Text: DWL, MS 12.80, opp. p. 196.
    Addressed: Address missing.
    Endorsed: from the Rev[d]. Theop. Lindsey to the Rev[d]. J. Chadwick
                     [in pencil: 'for Edw[d] M. Martin']
    Postmarked: Postmark missing.

Note: MS 12.80 is a folio-size volume into which are pasted the pages of Rutt, I. The manuscript of this letter is affixed to a blank page opposite p. 196. At the top of the blank page are the words 'Autograph Letter of the Rev[d]. Theophilus Lindsey, Addressed to the Rev[d]. Joseph Chadwick of Oundle. Presented by M[r]. Edward Martin, Birmingham'.[1]

London. Decr. 5. 1792.

Dear Sir,

I am very sorry that I so totally forgot to send you the Apology, and thank you for reminding me of it.[2] As to the Second Vol. of Commentaries I could not have promised it, because no such book ever existed, but some few tracts for a second volume were printed, one of wch was Mr Dodsons notes on a part of Isaiah, which he has now superseded by printing the whole: but I will endeavour to send the Numbers.[3] And both shall come in my next parcell.

I should think that miraculous facts are as capable of being supported by human testimony as any other facts, and it must be a very singular scepticism that does not allow this.

As my history of Taunton is lent out, I really do not know what *appendix* of Mr Toulmins you woud wish your name to be put to as a Subscriber, and sh^d be glad for you to explain yourself.[4]

I do not wonder that persons that have been wont to look upon our Saviour as above the condition as a creature shd be hurt at first by Mr Elwalls language which you quote: but he himself held it his chief honour and happiness that he always did the will of his heavenly Father: and was thus but what he was bound to do, his duty. I have no doubt of its being language which he would now use concerning himself.[5]

Farmer Truman is not yet publish^d by our Society, nor any price set upon it. When it is, I shall acquaint you and hope not to forget.[6] As I corrected the press, I procured a few copies for myself to dispose of to a few friends, and am glad a copy was not unacceptable to Mrs Chadwick, to whom you will give mine and my wifes best wishes.[7]

Who Mr A. Robinson is I know not; only that he was a Baptist minister a few years ago in London, tho' not that I know well any congregation; and left London and went into the North on some fortune coming to him.[8]

I think I have taken some notice of most of the particulars which You asked ab^t in your letter.[9] And I shoud have prolonged mine at present, which makes such a diminutive figure before yours, had I not been unavoidably called off to some business, and the cover will not let me delay sending it to another day.

As I expect D^r P _____ y's Second Appeal to the Public on the riots at B _____ m will be out in ab^t 10 days,[10] I hope not to be hinderd sending a small parcell, and sh^d be glad always to commit what I have for you to Mr Ash[11] to convey to Oundle, if you will only give me his direction –

I remain always, Dear Sir very sincerely Yours

T. Lindsey.

---

1   Probably Edward Martin of Edgbaston, who died at the age of ninety-three on 27 Jan. 1866; *The Inquirer*, 1231 (3 Feb. 1866), p. 77. I owe this reference to Mr Alan Ruston.

2   Lindsey presumably referred here to one of the editions of his own *Apology*.

3   For Michael Dodson's two translations of sections of Isaiah, see Vol. I, Letters 286, n. 6, 288, n. 20, and 313, n. 9. They were printed, respectively, in the first and third numbers of the *Commentaries and essays*. The first five numbers of the *Commentaries and essays* were subsequently bound into a single volume, without a date; it may be found in DWL, 1036. M.19. Numbers six to ten were also later bound into one volume, which also was undated (DWL, 1036. M.20). The items which made up the second volume had not been bound together at the time of this letter of Lindsey.

4   Joshua Toulmin's *History of the town of Taunton, in the county of Somerset* was published in Taunton in 1791 and sold in London by Joseph Johnson. Lindsey was included in the prefatory list of subscribers; Chadwick was not. There was no appendix to Toulmin's book, although a brief list of 'addenda' may be found at pp. 191–2.

5   For Edward Elwall, see Vol. I, Letters 199, n. 14, and 365, n. 3. It is not clear which passage from his
    work Chadwick had quoted. In *A true testimony for God and for his sacred law. Being a plain, honest,
    defence of the first Commandment of God. Against all the trinitarians under heaven* (Wolverhampton,
    1724), Elwall denied that Christ was supreme God and asserted: 'Now if any Man should say, that
    God the Father is not greater than Christ the Son, he makes him a Lyar' (p. 15).

6   At its opening meeting, on 9 Feb. 1791, the Unitarian Society decided to adopt in its catalogue *Advice
    from Farmer Trueman to his daughter Mary*; Unitarian Society minute book, p. 8. The work was first
    published in Edinburgh in 1789 (see Letter 381); the Unitarian Society's edition was duly published
    in London in 1792.

7   The marriage of Rev. Joseph Chadwick to Mary Kerbey at Wellington, Somerset, on 13 Apr. 1780, is
    recorded in the parish registers of St John, Wellington; transcript consulted via genuki.org.uk. Joseph
    Chadwick was assistant minister to a dissenting congregation at Wellington from 1778 to 1781, and
    minister from 1781 to 1785.

8   For Anthony Robinson, see Letter 507, n. 10.

9   Chadwick's letter to Lindsey appears not to have survived, a particularly unfortunate loss, since it
    was apparently quite a long (and perhaps an informative) one.

10 For Priestley's *An appeal to the public. Part II*, see Letters 472, n. 7.

11 Possibly William Ash, bookseller, of 15 Little Tower-hill, London; see *Universal British directory*
    (1793), p. 56.

510. To WILLIAM ALEXANDER   11 DECEMBER 1792

Text: 'Letters of the Rev. Theophilus Lindsey. No. III',
                        UH, II, 64 (19 July 1862), 248.

Note: This is the only section of the letter printed by the *UH*; the manuscript has apparently not survived.
The ellipsis at the start of the section printed by the *UH* indicates that this was not the beginning of the
letter.

London, Dec. 11, 1792.

* * * We in London do not really know any grounds whatsoever for the alarms and
preparations for danger which have been and are making; but presume that when
the Parliament meets that there will be some discoveries made.[1] The only thing
many are alarmed at is a war, in which we are to join our allies upon the continent
against the French. But it is hoped and believed that when Mr. Pitt comes seriously
to the point, he will not be for it, as it would defeat all his plans.[2] One is concerned
to hear that the French are not in the way soon to come to a good settlement. Some
that were engaged in the massacres at the beginning of September, Robespierre and
others are said to keep up too much sway, so as to silence and overawe numbers of
able and worthier men in the National Convention.[3] Still, however, we hope for the
best; that they may be governed by principles of justice and humanity, and adhering
to their original constitution, may become a blessing to all other nations as well as
their own.

1   The government ordered the embodiment of the militia during the first week of Dec. 1792, amid
    ministerial anxiety (not shared by Pitt himself) of a national uprising stimulated by French agitators.
    The tension was increased by deteriorating relations between Britain and France, and by the prospect
    of a French invasion of the United Provinces. By the time of the opening of the new session of parlia-
    ment on 13 Dec. 1792, the immediate sense of crisis had passed. See J. Mori, 'Responses to revolu-
    tion: the November crisis of 1792', *Historical Research*, LXIX (1996), 284–305, and C. Emsley, 'The
    London "insurrection" of December 1792: fact, fiction or fantasy?', *Journal of British Studies*, XVII
    (1977–8), 74–81.

2   France declared war on Britain and the Dutch on 1 Feb. 1793.

3   During the first week of Sept. 1792, as the prospect of foreign invasion threatened the revolution,
    approximately 1,400 people, mainly prisoners and suspected 'traitors', were massacred in Paris,

under the aegis of the city's revolutionary commune. On 21 Sept. 1792, the National Convention, soon to be dominated by Maximilien François Marie Isidore de Robespierre (1758–94), replaced the Legislative Assembly as the government of France.

511. To WILLIAM ALEXANDER   1 JANUARY 1793

Text: 'Letters of the Rev. Theophilus Lindsey. No. III',
                 UH, II, 64 (19 July 1862), 248–9.

Note: This is the only section of the letter printed by the *UH*; the manuscript seems not to have survived. The ellipsis at the start of the section printed by the *UH* indicates that this was not the beginning of the letter.

London, Jan. 1. 1793.

* * As you promised, it would be right for you of your own accord to go to the justices, and say that you came as you wished to explain what you had said of Paine's works which seemed to give such offence, and which Mr. Davey, in his great haste, did not give you an opportunity of doing, as you wished, at the time.[1] I do not know one man that approves of Mr. Paine's works throughout, as your words seem to have conveyed to the justice, or that approves many things in him as at all fit for this country. Your opinions I really do not know. But I presume you will say, that though you like many things in Mr. Paine, you are, as you say in your letter,[2] far from being disaffected to the present Government, or from wishing any change in our constitution of King, Lords and Commons, as fixed at the Revolution.

If you be asked whether you have a license to keep school, it will be proper to reply, with all respect, that you do not come to tell anything concerning yourself, but to hear and answer any charges made against you; not surely to give information, but to answer any informations brought against you. But you may add, if necessary, that if the charge be against you for not having a license, you apprehend, with all respect, that it is a matter which belongs not to the jurisdiction of the justices of the peace, but to that of the spiritual court; and you may refer them to the case of Dr. Doddridge, who was fined by the spiritual court, but liberated by King George II.[3] It is believed that they cannot lay a fine upon you for not having a license; but if they do, and prosecute you for teaching a school without a license, the committee for the Dissenters in London are wont to defray the expense of such suits, and I have no doubt of their readiness to support such innocent and deserving characters as you are.[4] You may refuse to give answers to any questions put to you, nor can such refusal be construed into a contempt of the court, if made with modesty and civility, in which respect you will never be wanting. If you are told you are brought before the justice for circulating seditious writings, of which from your own account you are wholly innocent, you are advised not to answer any questions relating to such matters, but so far as may tend to clear your character from any *false* reports that have been spread concerning you. And you will take especial care of all you say, as you may depend upon every word being taken down, and from the hostile dispositions discovered towards you, all the use that is possible, you may depend upon it, will be made of it against you. This is the more necessary for you to attend to, as your innocence makes you unsuspecting, and you do not dislike talking.

It is by the Act of 19 George III. that Dissenting schoolmasters, making the declaration that they believe the Bible to contain the word of God, are dispensed with from taking out a license.[5] You will remember that unless your house is licensed, it is against the Conventicle Act to have worship in it for more than three persons besides your own family.[6] As I am writing this, the friend whom I consulted about your case and situation sends me the following, which corrects one circumstance above mentioned: – "I find, on looking into the books, that magistrates have cognizance of the offence of keeping schools without license, and that it is not confined to the spiritual courts".[7] But the charge must be made against you, and whether the proof lies on you or them makes no difference as to your conduct before the magistrates; for, at all events, you may insist upon their proving it before you are committed. To avoid which, however, you should be provided with bail. The oaths and declarations must be made at the sessions, and your making them after the prosecution is begun will not operate to stop it.

I should be glad to know if your letter to me was sent with some wax only put upon it without a seal. If otherwise it would seem that it had been opened.[8] I most heartily wish you well out of this most troublesome affair. I have before advised you, with your simplicity and vehemence of expression against what you esteem wrong, to be cautious what you say and what you write, especially in these times. I trust all will be quiet soon.[9]

---

1 Possibly Eleajar Davy, esquire, who served as one of the justices assigned to the Beccles and to the Ipswich quarter sessions between 1790 and 1793; Ipswich RO, B105/2/49, quarter sessions order book, 1790–94; FAA/2/54 archdeaconry of Suffolk, general court book, 1787–97. I am grateful to Suffolk RO for advice on this point. Other possibilities are David E. Davy and E. Davy, both esquire, who are listed under 'gentry' for Yoxford in the *Universal British directory* (1791), IV, 980.

2 Alexander's letter to Lindsey appears not to have survived.

3 In 1733, the chancellor of the diocese of Lincoln, George Reynolds, initiated a prosecution against Philip Doddridge for conducting his academy at Northampton without an episcopal licence, in the absence of which he was not protected by the Toleration Act of 1689. Doddridge received support from the protestant dissenting deputies in London, and from sympathetic whig politicians; hence on 31 Jan. 1734 he could write confidently to his wife 'I am just come from Westminster Hall, where our Cause was gained without any Opposition worth Naming. The Judges order'd a prohibition to be issued which secures me from all further Trouble'; *Calendar of the correspondence of Philip Doddridge DD (1702–1751)*, ed. G. F. Nuttall (London: Historical Manuscripts Commission, 1979), p. 70. For the story that the prosecution was halted on the personal instructions of George II, see *The works of the Rev. P. Doddridge, DD* (10 vols., Leeds, 1802), I, 148–9 ('the life of Dr Doddridge', by Job Orton). George Reynolds was the son of Richard Reynolds, bishop of Lincoln from 1723 to 1744 (see Vol. I, p. xxv) and the father of Lindsey's 'chum' at St John's College, Cambridge, Richard Reynolds, who was subsequently the squire of Little Paxton, a close friend of Lindsey who visited him there several times, and a provider of succour to unitarians in the region of Cambridge.

4 Alexander's problem does not feature in the minutes of the protestant dissenting deputies. However, at a special meeting of the deputies' committee on 9 July 1793, a letter was noted from the baptist minister James Hinton of Oxford, complaining that a house near Oxford was due to be registered as a dissenting meeting house at the local quarter sessions, where he anticipated opposition to the registration. The committee advised Hinton that the Toleration Act of 1689 specified that for the purposes of such registration, 'a simple application to the Bishops Court, Archdeacons Court or General Quarter Sessions' was all that was necessary, and that the quarter sessions was not the only body to which application could be made. Hinton's case bore some resemblance to that of Alexander.

5 19 Geo. III, c. 44 ('An Act for the Relief of Protestant Dissenting Ministers'), 1779.

6 The 'Act to Prevent and Suppress Seditious Conventicles' of 1670 (22 Charles II, c. 1) forbade attendance at dissenting worship in any dwelling where five or more persons, in addition to those of the household, were present; in a dwelling where there was no family, the offending number was five or more persons. The Act prescribed fines of 5*s* for a first offence and of 10*s* for subsequent offences. For preaching in any such dwelling, however, the penalty was a fine of £20 for a first offence and £20 for subsequent offences. It is not quite clear why Lindsey referred (at least in the printed text of this letter; the manuscript appears not to have survived) to the relevant number of persons as three. The Conventicle Act and the Five Mile Act of 1665 were repealed in 1812.

7 This friend, presumably a lawyer, was probably Samuel Heywood or Benjamin Hobhouse; John Lee,

to whom Lindsey had turned for legal advice in the early days of Essex Street chapel, was in declining health and died in Aug. 1793. Under the Conventicle Act, a prosecution could proceed through the quarter sessions or the ecclesiastical courts.

8 See n. 2, above. For Lindsey's concern that his letters were being opened by the authorities, see Letter 514. For the interception of letters in this period, see K. L. Ellis, *The Post Office in the eighteenth century. A study in administrative history* (Oxford, 1958), ch. 6, especially pp. 69–73.

9 I have not found evidence at Suffolk RO (see n. 1, above) that a prosecution of William Alexander was formally undertaken in the ecclesiastical courts or quarter sessions. It seems clear, however, that on at least one occasion he was threatened with prosecution, and that this threat understandably caused him much distress.

512. To WILLIAM ALEXANDER   7 FEBRUARY 1793

Text: 'Letters of the Rev. Theophilus Lindsey. No. IV',
                 UH, II, 71 (6 Sept. 1862), 304.

Note: This is the only section of the letter printed by the *UH*; the manuscript seems not to have survived. The ellipsis at the start of the section printed by the *UH* indicates that this was not the beginning of the original letter. The ellipsis within the second paragraph indicates that text from that paragraph was omitted by the *UH*.

London, February 7, 1793.

* * As there are such heats and animosities about political matters I need not advise you not to say anything about such subjects; and particularly because if you should only say you wish well to the liberties of the French, you would by many be accused of approving the late shocking putting to death of their king, and of wishing for a republic like theirs to be established in England, than which nothing is more to be deprecated and abhorred.[1]

It is thought that matters are now so far gone that a war with the French is unavoidable. I have not a friend, great or small, that does not lament it and dread the consequences every way. * * Dr. Priestley has lately printed some letters to the French nation on the subject of religion, which is in a very desolate state among them.[2]

1 Louis XVI was executed in Paris on 21 Jan. 1793.

2 This work was Priestley's *Letters to the philosophers and politicians of France on the subject of religion* (London, 1793).

513. To CHRISTOPHER WYVILL   7 FEBRUARY 1793

Text: NYRO, ZFW 7/2/80/2, Wyvill of Constable Burton MSS.

Printed: Ditchfield, 'Lindsey–Wyvill correspondence', 163 (sixth paragraph).

Addressed: To/The Rev[d]./Christopher Wyvill/Burton Hall/Bedale/ Yorkshire

Endorsed: From the Rev[d] M[r] Lindsey March 7th 1793

Postmarked: MR 7 93

Note: There is a problem of dating with this letter. Lindsey dated it 7 February 1793, but the postmark and Wyvill's endorsement both give 7 March of that year. Perhaps Lindsey wrote 'Feb. 7' in mistake for 'March 7'; possibly Lindsey delayed posting the letter until 7 March. For the purposes of this edition Lindsey's date is given.

London. Feb. 7. 1793

Dear Sir,

A more honourable post cannot be than that of Watchman for the Public, who sees the danger approaching, and gives warning of it, and this post has been nobly filled by the author of the Defence of Dr Price and of the Reformers of England, and of the recent letter to Mr Pitt, for which last I tender you my heartiest thanks.[1]

Although intended, it has not come forth early enough to prevent a war that may turn out most fatal, but it may contribute to shorten it and so prevent the greater ruin.

It is hoped that an Address to the minister so fair and open and free, and yet so friendly and respectful may have its effect upon every mind that is not so warped as to present the most powerful arguments having access to it.

Such I am much afraid is my old friend and college cotemporary Mason, who happened to call on me yesterday just after I had got it, and gave me no encouragement to say much of its argument by the slight way in which he spoke of all Reformers in the lump. Indeed the best apology that can be made for him, and a just one it is, that he has not paid that attention to such subjects, which ought to have been done by one that pronounces so decidedly upon them.[2]

Mr Shore however who had called on me just before, with a mind of a very different stamp, was overjoyed to hear of so seasonable a publication, and soon went to Johnson's, to procure some copies. He was but two days before come out of the North by way of Dudley in Warwickshire, where he had passed a fortnight with a near relation.[3]

Your pamphlet will contribute to revive the spirits of worthy men, many of whom are quite drooping from the Starchamber times into which we seem to have been cast in six months time. No one hardly dares think, but certainly not to speak, much less to publish his thoughts freely on subjects the most important: So that the liberty of the Press seems to be lost all at once. What grieves me most, is that our nation turns out so base and supine, and void of energy and principle, that the greater part like the present state of things, if they can but indulge themselves. A Reform of Parliament, and nothing else seems likely to set all things right, and revive lost principles.

My wife desires to join in respectful compliments to yourself and Mrs Wyvill with every good wish for your amiable family, and I remain always, Dear Sir, Your much obliged and faithful servant

T. Lindsey.

---

[1] For Wyvill's *Defence of Price*, see Letter 494, n.1; His *Letter to the Right Hon. William Pitt, by the Rev. Christopher Wyvill, late chairman of the committee of association of the county of York* was published in York in 1793, with a second edition later in the same year.

[2] William Mason was admitted to St John's College, Cambridge, in July 1742, one year after Lindsey, and graduated BA one year after Lindsey. He received his MA in 1749, by which time he had moved to Pembroke College, of which he was a fellow from 1749 to 1759. Lindsey was a fellow of St John's from 1747 to 1755. See Letters 434 and 737.

[3] This was Samuel Shore III, who had a residence at Clapham. His 'near relation' to whom Lindsey referred was probably Priestley's son-in-law William Finch of Heath Forge, Dudley, who was the nephew of Shore's first cousin John Finch (d. 1791), ironmonger and banker, of Wolverhampton Street, Dudley. See G. M. Ditchfield, 'Two unpublished letters of Theophilus Lindsey', *TUHS*, XX, 2 (Apr. 1992), 138. See also Letter 529 for Lindsey's identification of Shore's family relationship with William Finch.

514. To WILLIAM TAYLEUR   **8 FEBRUARY 1793**

Text:	JRUL, Lindsey Letters, vol. II, no. 67.
Printed:	McLachlan, *Letters*, pp. 10–11 (first paragraph, with errors of transcription); pp. 109–10 (fourth paragraph); pp. 120–1 (second paragraph; first sentence of third paragraph; most of sixth paragraph).
Addressed:	To/William Tayleur Esqʳ/Shrewsbury
Endorsed:	Febʸ 8ᵗʰ – 93
Postmarked:	FE 8 93

London. Febʸ. 8. 1793

Dear Sir,

I should have written to you again since my last, but that nothing very particular hath presented itself, and I had no great heart to it on being told from various parts that the letters of Dissenters particularly Unitarians were very comonly inspected at the Post-Office. Not that this was a circumstance that gave me any apprehensions on account of any thing I might say to any one, but it is not pleasing to be the subject of impertinent curiosity and remarks.[1]

I was sorry to hear that a portion of the same spirit had shewn itself at Shrewsbury which had broken out at other places, and that Mʳ Rowe was in some danger from the threats of the populace. I will however hope that his own most worthy character and your venerable name and high estimation will be his protection in that town, till the storm is over.[2]

It is a great satisfaction that every thing is quiet in this respect throughout this monstrous city and it's environs; and although dissenters are aspersed and detested as much as in the latter end of Queen Anne's reign, no outward violence is offered or seems meditated against them or their places of worship. Yesterday a friend sent me a long extract from Lord Chedworth's charge to the Grand Jury at the Quarter-Sessions at Ipswich, which contains seasonable and candid observations on the bad intolerant spirit against Dissenters as do him great honour, and will I hope do good in that most bigotted county.[3] In which a schoolmaster, with whom we have some children, a very valuable character, has been put to much trouble and expence, on very false surmises of his favouring Paine's works and being an enemy to the constitution of his country.[4]

You have probably heard of the most illiberal and unhandsome treatment which Mʳ Evanson has experienced in the neighbourhood of Ipswich, on account of both his last publications, particularly the Dissonance.[5] They have struck his name from some of their book-societies, and several of the clergy and gentry refuse any comunication with him.[6] This shews that it is the old tory orthodox spirit, and not any political consideration that is prevalent through the kingdom, and which displayed itself at Birmingham.

About a fortnight since there was sent me by the author, "A Letter vindicating the Dissenters from the charge of Disloyalty in reply to the Revᵈ Wᵐ L. Fancourt, curate of the Parish of Wellingborough, Northamptonshire, by Robert Jacomb. Bristol – 1793.["][7] Mʳ Jacomb went from Salter's Hall to be minister at Wellingborough, but I presume from the date of his pamphlet may have left it on the death of his wife. It is a very short piece, but written with a spirit, and the assertion of such principles as do the writer great honour at this time, when some are shy of avowing their sentiments.[8]

I presume you are not unacquainted with the design of a migration to America entertained by several dissenting families in Lancashire whose situation has been rendered very uneasy to them of late and is not likely to men[d]. I am concerned that those who might every way be serviceable to their country by staying in it feel themselves thus constrained to leave it. Mʳ Toulmin of Taunton expressed great anxieties on the prospect of parting with his son. I shall be glad if it may be some consolation what I told him, that Dʳ Priestley has reconciled himself to his eldest son's crossing the Atlantic, and that who knows but that he and the Doctor years hence may find if not an asylum, yet very peculiar satisfaction and joy in visiting their sons, and beholding their increase and happiness and great usefulness.[9]

Our Liturgy has been printed some time, and is waiting only for the Psalm-tunes. I shall beg your acceptance of a copy, when finished.[10] I will not think of troubling you to write: but Mʳ Rowe perhaps at his leisure will give us the pleasure of knowing that you are well, and that you are all safe. My wife sends you her sincere and hearty respects. Our kind remembrances attend Mʳ and Mʳˢ Rowe and their little family and Mʳ Wood: and I am always, Dear Sir, Your most truly obliged and affectionate servant

     T. Lindsey.

Dʳ Priestley was here two days ago, in perfect health and spirits, rather grown plump. Bᵖ. Horsley, I am told, strove to point him out to public execration in his 30ᵗʰ Jan. sermon.[11]

---

1   See Letter 511, n. 8.

2   Probably Lindsey had heard of this trouble through private communications from provincial dissenters. From his next surviving letter to Rowe (15 Apr. 1793; Letter 521), it appears that the latter thought of emigrating.

3   John Howe (1754–1804), 4th Baron Chedworth, a sympathizer with reform and an admirer of Fox, was chairman of the general quarter sessions for the county of Suffolk. In that capacity, he delivered a charge to the grand jury of the county at Ipswich on 18 Jan. 1793. While defending the existing constitution, he claimed that threats to its safety had been exaggerated and deplored displays of prejudice against dissenters and burnings of effigies of Paine. His *Charge* was published in Ipswich shortly thereafter and may be found in *Charges to the grand jury 1689–1803*, ed. Georges Lamoine (Camden fourth series, vol. 43, London, 1992), pp. 485–98. Probably the friend who sent the extract from Chedworth's *Charge* was Edward Evanson or William Alexander, who both resided in Suffolk at this time.

4   This schoolmaster was almost certainly William Alexander; see Letter 511.

5   Evanson's two most recent publications were his *Dissonance* (see Letter 505, n. 2) and his *Arguments against and for the sabbatical observance of Sunday*.

6   Since 1789, Evanson had resided at Great Blakenham, near Ipswich.

7   William John Lowfield Fancourt (1765–1840) had published a short (eight-page) leaflet, dated Wellingborough, 3 Dec. 1792, which began with the words 'Britons and fellow-countrymen', denounced 'Republicans and Levellers' and urged support for loyal associations. A graduate of Cambridge (Clare College; BA 1789, MA 1800, DD 1823), he was curate of Bletsoe, near Bedford, from 1789 (the year of his ordination) and curate of Melchbourne, near Higham Ferrers, a short distance from Wellingborough. He was subsequently headmaster of St Saviour's grammar school, Southwark, from 1793 to 1823, and vicar of St Mary's, Leicester. See *Alumn. Cantab.*, II, vol. II, 456.

8   Robert Jacomb's work was *A letter vindicating dissenters from the charge of disloyalty, in reply to the Rev. Wm. L. Fancourt, curate of the parish church of Wellingborough, Northamptonshire* (Bristol, 1793). Jacomb (*c.* 1768–1832), was assistant minister at Salters' Hall from 1782 to 1786; minister at Wellingborough from 1786 to 1793; at Great Meeting, Leicester, from 1793 to 1803; and at Cheese Lane, Wellingborough, from 1812 to 1826. He married Sarah, née Danvers, in, or possibly shortly before, 1789; *Gent. Mag.*, LIX, i (1789), 87. She died at Wellingborough on 10 June 1791.

9   Henry Toulmin left Bristol in May 1793 and arrived at Norfolk, Virginia, in July. Priestley's eldest son Joseph departed for America with his brothers in Aug. 1793 and arrived in Oct.

10   This is a reference to the 4th edn of *The Book of Common Prayer reformed*. Its 'advertisement', dated Jan. 1793, was Lindsey's work.

11 Samuel Horsley, *A sermon, preached before the lords spiritual and temporal, in the Abbey church of St. Peter, Westminster, on Wednesday, January 30, 1793: being the anniversary of the martyrdom of King Charles the First. With an appendix, concerning the political principles of Calvin* (London, 1793), did not mention Priestley or Socinianism by name, although it excoriated 'republican divines' and 'atheism' (p. 12) and 'modern levellers' (p. 20) in its well-known denunciation of the execution of Louis XVI.

515. To RUSSELL SCOTT   9 MARCH 1793

Text: Scott Coll.
Printed: McLachlan, 'Lindsey to Scott', 118 (very short quotation
                    from second paragraph).
Addressed: [In the hand of James Martin] Westm^r. Ninth ~~Apl~~ March 1793/
                    Rev: Russel Scot/Portsmouth/~~J.Martin~~ [in Hannah Lindsey's
                    hand, opposite address] Saturday March/9th 1793/Revd Russel/
                    Scot,/Portsmouth
Postmarked: FREE MR 9 93

Dear Sir,

I shall be glad to hear that you and Mrs Scott and your little man are well as we wish you, and that you received a parcell which Mr Redman[1] told me was duly sent to you at your desire at the end of the month.

Having a frank by means of a friend, I am glad to give you an early sight of the inclosed,[2] which I am sure will give you pleasure, as it has a tendency to peace, tho' comes too late to prevent war, and also shews that there are worthy men, who watch over the dangerous encroachments made on our liberties, and are bold and honest to give warning of them; even amongst the friends of the Minister.

Dr Priestley was very well yesterday. You will soon see in the Morning Chronicle a letter of his to Mr Burke, very properly calling upon him to verify some assertions which he has made concerning him in a late speech.[3]

My wife desires to join in kind remembrances to you and Mrs Scott and I remain always most truly Yours

T. Lindsey

London. March. 9. 1793

1   Possibly George Redmayne, printer, of Creed Lane, Ludgate Hill, London; see *Universal British directory* (1793), p. 265.
2   Possibly the enclosed was Wyvill's *Letter to the Right Hon. William Pitt*; Wyvill had been on friendly terms with Pitt. See Letter 513, where Lindsey described Wyvill as the 'Watchman for the Public'.
3   This letter from Priestley, dated 7 Mar. 1793, appeared in the *Morning Chronicle* of 9 Mar. 1793. In it, he replied to Burke's speech in the house of commons on 4 Mar. 1793, during the debate on Richard Brinsley Sheridan's motion for a committee to investigate allegedly seditious practices. Burke had claimed that Priestley had been granted honorary citizenship of France because of his declared hostility to the British constitution; Cobbett, *Parl. Hist.*, XXX, 552. Priestley denied this charge and also denied that he had expressed support for the Jacobins. He reprinted the letter in his *Sermon preached at the Gravel Pit meeting, in Hackney, April 19th, 1793, being the day appointed for a general fast* (London, 1793), pp. xiii–xvi.

516. To RUSSELL SCOTT   **26 MARCH 1793**

Text: Scott Coll.
Printed: Scott, *Family biography*, pp. 85–6 (second and third
              paragraphs; fifth and sixth sentences of fifth paragraph);
              'Chowbent chapel and its ministers' (no author named), in
              'Record section', *TUHS*, IX, 1 (Oct. 1947), 36 (fourth and
              fifth sentences of fourth paragraph); McLachlan, 'Lindsey to
              Scott', 118–19 (second to seventh sentences of first paragraph;
              second and third sentences of second paragraph, with errors
              of transcription; whole of third paragraph; first four sentences
              of fourth paragraph; third and fourth sentences of fifth
              paragraph).
Addressed: Address missing.
Postmarked: Postmark missing.

London. March. 26. 1793

Dear Sir,

I could not sooner obtain a satisfactory account of such things as your friend might wish to know of M[r] Morgan's terms, or should have written to you. The whole of the pay for education is one hundred pounds a year. Nothing for entrance. The pupils, at choice to wash for themselves, or to pay five guineas a year for it. For this they are taught the Classics, greek and latin, a course of history, mathematics, chymistry, and other branches of natural philosophy. The pupils are treated remarkably well, and retain great affection and esteem for M[r] M. when they quit him. Large as this sum is, I am told, that things are so dear, that M[r] Morgan has not been a gainer, and that he has some thoughts of removing to the distance of about ten miles from London. This account I had from one of the pupils. If you should be desirous to learn any more particulars. I shall inquire of M[r] Morgan himself, or his brother in Chatham Square.[1]

I am not acquainted with any other Tutor, in the neighbourhood of London or at a distance, whom I can recommend. M[r] Morgan has laid aside the clerical character and he and his family attend D[r] Priestley at the Gravel Pits I am told that he ~~has~~ excells in discovering the genius of boys and in making hard things easy to them, and carrying them quickly forwards in whatever he teaches them. And he has all his uncle's principles, civil and religious.[2]

Both my wife and I are greatly concerned at the very infirm state of your health, owing to that radical gouty indisposition, which seems to have been born with you. And we really think that you would do well to look out, if there be any thing which You can do in the way of business, or in which M[rs] Scott may be able to bear a part, and to embrace it. Any thing of this kind, mercantile or any other, I am very far from thinking incompatible with the duty of a teacher of the gospel, or to disqualify for it. And with regard to Sermons, I think you should not be nice about giving your own compositions, but transcribe with little alteration, unless perhaps of the text, from Jortin, Secker, Pyle, Duchall &c &c with now and then some little addition and not much, which would be particularly applicable to your congregation, and make it sufficiently your own.[3]

With respect to dissenting ministers I do not think matters likely to mend in this country, but the contrary. Through fears of the world, or of being singular, or now to recommend themselves to the reigning powers their rich members will desert them, as they have begun to do in some places already, through the influence of the court and the fear of losing their places under it. And they will be more and more scouted and ill-treated by Churchmen. On the Sunday before last, the 17ᵗʰ. at Chowbent, Mʳ H. Toulmin tells me, that in the midst of Service, a recruiting party, (who with their attendants had been parading at 11 and 12 o'clock on the Saturday night, with torches, and huzzaing and knocking at the houses of Dissenters) passed by the chapel with drums and fifes, and shoutings when opposite to it, crying down with the rump, so as to hinder him from going on till they had done; and after service, a party of the rabble waited to lay hold on him to put a cockade in his hat, as they had forced many of the congregation, but being apprized of their design, he escaped out by another door. And Mʳ Chandler of Gloucester[4] told me on Sunday that he had heard thence from Mʳ Tremlett, that there was an information lodged against Mʳ H. Toulmin for something said in conversation.[5] Such are the times we seem dropᵗ into within a year, but which unfortunately seem as if they would last.

I thank you much for your accᵗ how things are going on with You. I send you four copies of Dʳ Priestleys letter to Mʳ Burke for his calumnies and uncivil treatment in one of his speeches in the house.[6] I am told, that Dʳ Rees, who was mentiond by Burke at the same time, has written a proper letter to him, which he procured to be inserted in The Times; The editor insisted on a guinea & half, but at last took a guinea for inserting it.[7] But I am sorry to tell You, that at a meeting lately and dinner together of Dʳ Rees's congregation, the following toast was negatived "Dʳ Priestleys health, and to the memory of Dʳ Price."[8] We rejoice that Mʳˢ Scott and your little boy are got well and yourself better. Accept our kind regards to yourselves & best wishes for him. I remain always very truly Yours

T. Lindsey.

---

1   After the death of his uncle Richard Price in 1791, George Cadogan Morgan founded his own school at Southgate, Middlesex, where he taught until his death on 17 Nov. 1798. His (elder) brother, William Morgan, was from 1775 the chief actuary of the Equitable Assurance Society; the society's offices were situated at Chatham Place, near Blackfriars Bridge.

2   George Cadogan Morgan had served as a dissenting minister at the Octagon chapel, Norwich, and at Great Yarmouth, and between 1787 and 1791 gave informal assistance to Richard Price at the Gravel Pit meeting, Hackney. After 1791, he ceased to serve in any formal ministerial capacity.

3   John Jortin (1698–1770), latitudinarian clergyman, theologian and historian; John Disney published a memoir of him in 1792. His *Sermons on different subjects* were published in seven volumes in London in 1771–2. Thomas Secker (1693–1768), archbishop of Canterbury from 1758 to 1768, was a *bête-noir* of Francis Blackburne; many of his sermons were in print by the 1790s; perhaps Lindsey had in mind his *Fourteen sermons preached on several occasions* (London, 1771). Thomas Pyle (1674–1756), was a latitudinarian admirer of Benjamin Hoadly and developed Arian views on the Trinity; he was a prebendary of Salisbury from 1726 to 1756 and perpetual curate of South Lynn, Norfolk, from 1718 to 1754. His *Sixty sermons on plain and practical subjects* (2 vols., Norwich, 1773), were published by his son Philip Pyle, with further editions in 1776 and 1785. James Duchall (d. 1761) was a non-subscribing presbyterian minister, successively, at Cambridge, Antrim and Dublin; a three-volume edition of his sermons was published in London between 1762 and 1764. According to Alexander Gordon, he possessed 'the most considerable mind among the Irish non-subscribers' (*DNB*, VI, 86).

4   Richard Chandler (d. 1810), wool-stapler, of Gloucester, to whom Lindsey possibly referred in 1783; see Vol. I, Letter 270, n. 13. He was a prominent member of the association of dissenters in Gloucester who participated in the move for the repeal of the Test and Corporation Acts in 1789 and 1790; see *Committees for repeal*, p. 37; and obituary of Chandler in *MR*, V (1810), 408.

5   Mr Tremlett was probably John Tremlett (d. 1836), minister to the unitarian congregation at Barton Street, Gloucester, from 1784 to 1795, who was known to Richard Chandler (n. 4, above). He was subsequently minister at Palgrave (Suffolk) and at Hapton (Norfolk); see Letter 619, n. 7. For the background to the attack on Harry Toulmin at Chowbent, and on other dissenters in that region, see Alan Booth, 'Popular loyalism and public violence in the north-west of England, 1790–1800', *Social*

History, VIII (1983), 295–313. Such was the hostility to Toulmin that it is not surprising that the
reporting of incriminating intelligence against him was evidently made at this time.

6   See Letter 515, n. 3.

7   *Times*, 5 Mar. 1793, quoted Burke as referring to Abraham Rees and Joseph Towers, as well as to
     Priestley, as sympathetic towards the French Revolution in his Commons' speech of 4 Mar (see Letter
     515, n. 3). Rees's letter, dated Hackney, 9 Mar. 1793, was published in the *Times*, 14 Mar. 1793. In
     it, Rees accused Burke of misrepresentation, denied any connexion with the French revolutionary
     regime and asserted the fidelity of dissenters to the British constitution, citing their loyalty during the
     Jacobite rebellions of 1715 and 1745.

8   Rees was minister to the Old Jewry congregation, London, from 1783 until his death in 1825. Unsur-
     prisingly, there is no record of this 'negatived' toast in the surviving records of the Old Jewry chapel;
     TNA: RG4/4349 and RG4/4408, nor in the sections on the Old Jewry congregation in Walter Wilson,
     Dissenting churches of London (4 vols., London, 1808–14), II, 302–400, III, 354–7. On 6 Mar. 1793,
     The World complained that, in the whig club, 'they never at any of their public dinners, *once drank
     the King's health*', that the omission of this toast was deliberate and that many of the toasts actually
     drunk 'were the reverse of either loyalty or constitutional attachment'. Perhaps reports of this nature
     acted as a deterrent effect upon the toasting of persons deemed lacking in 'loyalty or constitutional
     attachment'.

517. To WILLIAM TAYLEUR   30 MARCH 1793

Text:	JRUL, Lindsey Letters, vol. II, no. 68.
Printed:	McLachlan, *Letters*, p. 42 (last part of third sentence of fourth paragraph, where 'vice' is rendered as 'dice').
Addressed:	[In Duncombe's hand] March thirtieth/London/1793/Wm Tayleur/Shrewsbury
Endorsed:	Free H Duncombe[1]
Postmarked:	Free MR 30 93

Note: Lindsey did not date this letter, and there is no salutation or valediction. The address and postmark
are the only indications of the date. Possibly the first and last pages of the letter are missing; the surviving
text has the appearance of a postscript, and there is a larger than usual gap between the paragraphs.

[Date added in pencil] March 30 1793

Dr Priestley was very well yesterday, and in good Spirits. Mrs Priestley better
with respect to the return of her complaint of spitting blood. In which I do not find
any danger is apprehended.

My wife was with Mrs Benyon yesterday, whom She mu[ch li]kes[2] as a character
most amiable.[3] She had been much affected with what had happened at Liverpoole
– but was very well, in perfect health.[4]

The inclosed are sent, as I thought you would like to[5] what is passing, tho' one
you have read in the Morning Chronicle.[6]

Saturday 4 o'clock. The day tempted me to walk out after I had finished my
letter. During my absence, Dr Priestley left the inclosed for you from Mr Belsham.[7]
It comes in consequence of a conversation I had with M^r. B. yesterday, who was
apprehensive from some things which an unknown gentleman lately said to him
about young Mr Harries, that his worthy father was not apprized of the reasons why
the young man was desired not to come any more to the college – no vice, but such a
habit of driving hackney coaches that he was continually on the box.[8] He was afraid
Mr Harries the father might not have received his letters, and therefore desired I w^d
inclose this to you to deliver safe to his own hands.[9] Excuse this scrawl.

1   Henry Duncombe was MP for Yorkshire from 1780 to 1796.
2   The manuscript is partly overlaid by the seal at this point.
3   Elizabeth Benyon (née Mason), of Shrewsbury, married Samuel Yate Benyon on 26 Oct. 1789. She
    died in 1802; see Letter 742, nn. 1 and 2.
4   It is not clear as to the happening(s) in Liverpool which had 'much affected' Elizabeth Benyon. One
    might speculate that they concerned a personal matter, or evidence of local opposition to the abolition
    of the slave trade.
5   Word missing, probably 'know'.
6   Possibly one of the enclosures was Priestley's letter to Burke, published in the *Morning Chronicle*,
    9 Mar. 1793; Lindsey sent a copy to William Alexander on 15 Apr. See Letter 519.
7   The 'inclosed' was evidently a private communication (or report) from Belsham to Tayleur concerning
    the conduct of Thomas Harries (n. 8, below), the son of his Shropshire friend Edward Harries. It
    appears not to have survived.
8   This is a reference to Thomas Harries (see Letter 412, n. 4). The college committee minutes do not
    survive for the post-1791 period, and there is no official record of the young man's alleged misde-
    meanours; 'On the box' refers to the box situated under the driver's seat on a hackney coach. On 1
    Apr. 1793 Harries was admitted to St John's College, Cambridge.
9   'Mr Harries the father' was Edward Harries of Shropshire.

518. To TIMOTHY KENRICK   6 APRIL 1793

Text: The Sharpe papers, UCL Library Services, Special Collections
                   (Kenrick papers), 178/37.
Printed: 'The Kenrick letters', *TUHS*, IV, 2 (Oct. 1928), 180–2 (minor
                   variations).
Addressed: To/The Revd. Mr Kenrick/Exeter
Postmarked: AP 6 93

London. April. 6. 1793

Dear Sir,

I am much concerned for you and the difficulties of your present situation; which must be the more felt as coming upon a mind so much hurt by a late event and by the extreme narrowness and ill usage of some from whom better might have been expected, and who I am told still continue the same dispositions towards You.[1] Does not it however merit some little consideration, whether these particular circumstances may not prevent your making that fair and equal estimate of the part you are to act in the present emergency?[2]

Without any false humility I really do not think myself equal to the task of advising you upon it, but as You desire it, will tell You my thoughts frankly.

And you will excuse my beginning with saying; that you seem to me so much decided already, that I do not think I can furnish any argument to dissuade you from the intention of declining to take any part in the approaching Fast-Service, however much I wish it.[3]

It is not a new or peculiar case. The late American war was as much and as justly disapproved as the present, and the objections were equally forcible against fasting and praying for the success of it from year to year, to which the people of this country were invited by their rulers; and yet dissenting ministers and people met together on the day appointed to edify one another in the way they judged proper.[4]

No one can judge for another; but as far as I can enter into your case, I think I could officiate at your meeting, and acquit myself therein to my own mind, without doing any thing contrary to integrity, or that could justly be reckoned mean, trimming, or accomodating to the times. I would in the begining of my discourse tell my hearers; that however persons might differ with respect to political questions, and the justness of those counsels and measures, whereby our country was brought into its present most dangerous condition: there could be no difference or di[s]agreement among christians as we were, that War was a most heavy calamity, one of the scourges of divine Providence, with which nations were visited for their sins: And that therefore it was a call upon every one, and a fit season for me to remind them to consider their ways, wherein they may have offended the Alm. Governor of the world, and to amend, to avert the impending calamity or break the stroke of it.

Of the authority that called the nation together that day, persons w^d form different judgments. One set of X^{tns}. disallowed it. But I thought it became one, as they chose to assemble together, to join them, and to lay before them such things as appeared to me seasonable and useful. Should you see the matter in this light, I think no one, who knows your motives, can justly arraign your conduct; and you will thereby secure the good opinion of your people, who will perceive, that you do not give up your own sentiments and dislike of the war by officiating on the day, but only take the opportunity afforded of meeting them, to call them to what is incontestably their duty upon the occasion.

I say nothing to the case you put as a similar one, because it does not appear such and misleads you. But whatever be your final determination, I hope it will tend to your own intire satisfaction.[5]

I thank you much for reminding me of the half-guinea, my admission-fee, which I had intirely forgotten; and for putting me in a way to pay it, by means of your annual Subscription to our Society, which I shall take the first opportunity of giving to Mr Dodson.[6] Dr Priestley and Mr Belsham were both very well the other day when I saw them, and I shall not forget your comp^{ts} to them. If I had been sure of meeting them soon, I sh^d have put your letter into their hands to have answerd it, and as it is shall let them see it the first opportunity. I do not find that Dr P. has any scruples about officiating on the day. I cannot help adding in the end, that I hope nothing will happen to prevent your continuing to bear your testimony in your present station of most extensive usefulness. With great esteem I am ever, Dear Sir, most sincerely Yours

T. Lindsey

---

1   A letter from Timothy Kenrick to Lindsey has apparently not survived. The 'late event' referred to the controversy over the day appointed for the forthcoming general fast, namely Friday 19 Apr. 1793, and the pressure on all clergy to use the occasion to pray for British victory. Kenrick refused to take part in any such proceeding and drew much hostile publicity to himself as a result. A section of his congregation at the George meeting, Exeter, objected to his stance on this issue and provoked him, on 28 Apr., into offering his resignation as minister. See A. Brockett, *Nonconformity in Exeter 1650–1875* (Manchester, 1962), pp. 142–5.

2   The 'present emergency' was the outbreak of war between Britain and France on 1 Feb. 1793 and its consequences for unitarians who opposed British participation in the war.

3   Priestley preached a fast sermon on this particular fast day and published it as *A sermon preached at the Gravel Pit meeting, in Hackney, April 19th, 1793*.

4   For Lindsey's disapproval of official fast days during the American war, see Vol. I, Letter 198; for the background, see Henry P. Ippel, 'British sermons and the American Revolution', *Journal of Religious History*, XII (1982–83), 191–205.

5   Kenrick's 'final determination', in early May 1793, was to adhere to his decision not to preach on the fast day, and, in response to the pleas of a general meeting of his congregation, to withdraw his threat to resign as minister; Brockett, *Nonconformity in Exeter*, p. 145; 'The Kenrick letters', *TUHS*, IV, 3 (Oct. 1929), 295–99.

6   Michael Dodson was treasurer of the Unitarian Society; Lindsey became a member of the Western Unitarian Society on its foundation in 1792. See Letter 499 and 'The Kenrick letters', *TUHS*, IV, 1 (Oct. 1927), 78 n. 2.

519. To WILLIAM ALEXANDER   13 APRIL 1793

Text: 'Letters of the Rev. Theophilus Lindsey. No. IV',
                UH, II, 71 (6 Sept. 1862), 304.

Note: This is the only section of this letter printed by the *UH*; the manuscript seems not to have survived. The ellipsis at the beginning of the extract printed by the *UH* indicates that this was not the beginning of the original letter. The ellipsis within the first paragraph indicates that text from that paragraph has been omitted. The ellipsis at the end of the second paragraph indicates that the third paragraph did not immediately follow the second in the original letter and accordingly the second and third paragraphs are separated here by a broken line. The words in square brackets are those of the editor of the letter for the *UH*.

London, April 13, 1793.

* * With respect to the "Dissonance", &c. [Evanson's], it is the opinion of some of my most able and judicious friends, that although there are in it several things deserving attention, and the whole is written with a most serious design, yet the far greater part is hasty and too peremptory decision with respect to the criticisms on particular passages of the gospel, as well as the exclusion of whole books of the evangelists and of the epistles from the canon of Scripture.[1]* * I should rejoice in it; and I wish I knew any able and dispassionate hand that would undertake to answer Mr. Evanson's arguments. But I hear of none. Politics or attacks on Dissenters is the better road to preferment.

We sat down thirty yesterday at the annual meeting and dinner of the Unitarian Society.[2] * *

Alas! all is now afloat again in France, and no way, I fear, for this country to peace and a settlement but through seas of blood.[3] I enclose a letter of Dr. Priestley's to Mr. Burke, printed a few week's[4] since in the *Morning Chronicle*, which you will be glad to have by you, if you should have seen it already.[5]

---

1   For Evanson's *The dissonance of the four generally revealed evangelists*, and the controversy which it provoked, see G. M. Ditchfield, 'Varieties of heterodoxy: the career of Edward Evanson (1731–1805)', in *Religion, politics and dissent, 1660–1832. Essays in honour of James E. Bradley*, ed. Robert D. Cornwall and William Gibson (Farnham and Burlington, VT, 2010), pp. 111–26.
2   According to the Unitarian Society minute book (p. 41), twenty-nine members of the society dined at the King's Head tavern on Thursday 11 Apr. 1793. Although Lindsey, writing on 13 Apr., stated that the dinner took place 'yesterday' (i.e. 12 Apr.), Thursday was the regular meeting day for the society and either the *UH* mis-dated this letter as 13 and not 12 Apr. 1793, or Lindsey himself did so.
3   The spring of 1793 in France saw the development of the 'Terror' and the ascendancy of Marat (assassinated 13 July 1793).
4   The *UH* gives 'week's', not 'weeks'.
5   See Letter 515, n. 3.

520. To MARY HAYS   15 APRIL 1793

Text: DWL, MS 24.93 (1).
Printed: *The correspondence of Mary Hays (1799–1843), British
                   novelist*, ed. Marilyn L. Brooks (Mellen Critical Editions
                   and Translations, vol. 13, Lewiston, 2004), p. 280; *The idea
                   of being free. A Mary Hays reader*, ed. Gina Luria Walker
                   (Toronto, 2006), pp. 190–1.
Addressed: Address missing
Endorsed: April 15/1793
Postmarked: Postmark missing.

Note: This letter has no addressee, but the identification of Mary Hays as the recipient is possible through her authorship of the *Letters and Essays*, which she published in 1793 and of which she evidently presented Lindsey with a copy. She had used the pseudonym 'Eusebia' in her *Cursory remarks* in reply to Gilbert Wakefield.

Essex Street, Strand
April. 15. 1793

Madam,

I should be glad to know any way in which I could make a return for the valuable present of your book; for which you would have received my thanks much earlier, had I been acquainted with your address.[1]

Eusebia had led me to think highly of the author:[2] but many things in the Letters and Essays have raised my ideas much higher, in which are such traces of just thoughts and well-digested reading on a variety of subjects, and of a lively correct imagination.[3]

The scarecrow doctrine of Necessity you have known how to strip of its horrid form, and to familiarize and make it easy, and I think to vindicate it's truth, to those that will read and make use of their understandings.[4]

In short I like both your metaphysics and divinity: but most of all, what appears in every page, the enlightened mind, turned to virtue and to God, and ardent to inspire others with the same sentiments and engage in the same pursuits,

Madam, always Your much obliged servant,

T. Lindsey.

---

[1] The address page of Lindsey's letter has not survived. In 1793, Mary Hays resided with her mother and younger sister at 5 Gainsford Street, Horselydown, Southwark.

[2] This work was *Cursory remarks on an enquiry into the expediency and propriety of public worship: inscribed to Gilbert Wakefield, B.A., late fellow of Jesus-College, Cambridge. By Eusebia* (i.e. Mary Hays) (London, 1791; 2nd edn, 1792). The copy of the second edition in Dr Williams's Library has Lindsey's signature and was a gift to him from Mary Hays. I am grateful to Gina Luria Walker for advice on this point.

[3] Mary Hays, *Letters and essays, moral and miscellaneous* was published in the spring of 1793, with a dedication to John Disney.

[4] The 'Doctrine of necessity', as developed by Priestley, building on the work of David Hartley, asserted that man was 'wholly material', rather than a union of matter and spirit, and that, accordingly, a mechanistic interpretation of human thinking and actions followed.

521. To JOHN ROWE   **15 APRIL 1793**

Text: JRUL, Lindsey Letters, vol. II, no. 69.
Printed: McLachlan, *Letters*, p. 89 (fifth paragraph).
Addressed: For/The Rev^d. J. Rowe
Postmarked: Postmark illegible.

London. April. 15. 1793.

Dear Sir,

Your obliging letter ought to have been sooner acknowleged. We were much rejoiced to receive such a pleasing account of our venerable friend,[1] and hope his valuable life will still be prolonged with satisfaction to himself, and for the sake of us all, and for the truth's sake. Your remark that God will support his own cause is a source of consolation in the most unpromising seasons. I firmly believe it, and that is now going on most remarkably, and will appear so to have been hereafter. Only we are apt to be too hasty, and to calculate wrong. Our clocks go too fast for God's dial, a saying of good Mr Henry's, which Mr Belsham quoted the other day, with which I was much gratified.[2]

I wish well to America; but I cannot endure the thought of such worthies as Mr Clarke, and yourself having any thoughts of migrating thither. It is enough that we are to lose such a worthy creature as H. Toulmin: if indeed we are to lose him: for his removal will depend upon his finding the country to answer where they intend to settle.[3]

I am correcting Mr Rogers's sermons for our unitarian Society;[4] and also Dr Lardner on the Logos, the latter by whom proposed I know not, but I do not dislike though I should have postponed it.[5]

I approve much our having a book of Devotions; and only wish you would prepare that which you mention, which I remember many years ago to have seen and to have liked much.[6] Perhaps some few, from some other collections might be added. And I make no doubt of procuring it's adoption. At present I have a new Edition of Mr Mort's life, with some improvements, to be proposed.[7] Such books are sought for and do much good.

Every thing seems again afloat in France, and I fear a sea of bloodshed and misery to be waded through, before they can come to any good settlement. I trust, that in the result, divine providence will secure to them their liberties, of which too many among them have shewn themselves unworthy.

I have time to add no more but mine and my wifes respects to yourself and Mrs Rowe with every wish of good to your little family, and with sincere esteem I am always your affectionate servant

T. Lindsey

---

1   William Tayleur.
2   'We are apt to set our clock before God's dial, and then to quarrel because they do not agree; but the Lord is a God of judgment, and it is fit we should wait for him.' This is a quotation from Matthew Henry's *An exposition of the Old and New Testament* (4th ed., 5 vols., London, 1737–38), III, *sub* Jeremiah, ch. XXVII; this work is unpaginated. Matthew Henry (1662–1714), a leading presbyterian minister, served congregations at Chester, and, towards the end of his life, at Mare Street, Hackney. His *Exposition of the Old and New Testament* was first published in 1707–12.
3   Henry Toulmin emigrated to America in May 1793 and settled in Kentucky, and (much later) in Alabama. Richard Hall Clarke (d. 1822) of Bridwell, near Cullompton, was a member (and treasurer) of the Western Unitarian Society, and brother-in-law to John Rowe. He did not emigrate.
4   At its quarterly meeting on 12 Apr. 1792 the Unitarian Society resolved that *Five sermons* should be adopted into the society's catalogue. On 8 Feb. 1798, the society resolved that 750 copies of it be

printed; Unitarian Society minute book, p. 63, and a further edition was duly published in London in 1798. A new edition appeared in London in 1832. The heterodox credentials of this work were evident in the dedication to Frederick Augustus Hervey, 4th earl of Bristol, and bishop of Derry from 1768 to 1803.

5   At the first meeting of the Unitarian Society on 9 Feb. 1791, two works of Lardner were proposed for adoption by the society, on the recommendation of Dodson, Disney and Lindsey. They were his *Letter, written in the year 1730, concerning the question whether the Logos supplied the place of a human soul in the person of Jesus Christ*, and his *Two schemes of a trinity considered, and the divine unity asserted; in four discourses upon Philippians II. 5–11*. Both works were formally adopted for the society's catalogue on 14 Apr. 1791, and 1,000 copies of each were to be printed; Unitarian Society minute book, pp. 7, 13. Both works were published in London in 1793, although without the imprint of the Unitarian Society.

6   By 'our', Lindsey probably referred to the Unitarian Society. For Tayleur's suggestions for a 'book of devotions' and liturgical innovations, see Vol. I, Letter 227.

7   For Henry Toulmin's short biography of John Mort, first published in 1789, see Vol. I, Letter 338, n. 8. The second edition, 'corrected and improved', was published in London in 1793. At the monthly committee meeting on 9 May 1793, the Unitarian Society, on Lindsey's motion, resolved to include this work in its catalogue and that 2,000 copies be printed by the society; Unitarian Society minute book, p. 42.

522. To RUSSELL SCOTT   17 APRIL 1793

Text: Scott Coll.
Addressed: [?In Henry Ducombe's hand] April seventeenth/London/1793/ Revd Mr Scott/Portsmouth/Free H/Duncombe [in Lindsey's hand, opposite address] April. 17./Rev^d. Mr Scott./Portsmouth
Postmarked: FREE AP 17 93

London. April. 17. 1793.

Dear Sir,

It will give us pleasure to hear that you are better, and Mrs Scott and your little one as we truly wish them. The inclosed has been published only a day or two, and being desirous you sh^d see it at this time rather than later I have procured a frank to convey it.[1]

Last Sunday I preached a Sermon on prayer, chiefly with a view to a new edition of our Liturgy to be first used on Sunday next, in which some considerable alterations have been made.[2] I hope soon to send you a copy and two or three for my good friends at Chichester, as a mark of respect; and sh^d. be glad, if Mr Temple be in your neighbourhood, to let me know, as we have not lately, nay for ~~may~~ many months seen any thing of him.[3] In some haste, but always with great truth I am Yours T. Lindsey.

My wife joins in all kind regards.

---

1   Lindsey did not identify the enclosure, which was evidently a very recent publication; perhaps it was Mary Hays's *Letters and essays*; see Letter 520.

2   This sermon was published as *On prayer; and forms of prayer, their defects, and remedy; a sermon, preached at the chapel in Essex Street, Strand, on Sunday, April XIV, MDCCXCIII* (London, 1793). The previous Sunday was indeed 14 Apr. 1793. Lindsey used this sermon to provide a short summary of what he thought were deficiencies in existing forms of public prayer, before outlining the history of reformed versions of the Book of Common Prayer on the model of that of Samuel Clarke, including improvements in the three previous editions of the Essex Street chapel liturgy published between 1774 and 1785. He then drew attention to the fourth edition, 'just now finished for use', of his *Book of Common Prayer revised* (see Letter 514, n. 10) and justified (pp. xiii–xv) the changes which it introduced, notably the omission of the apostles' creed and the substitution at the beginning of the litany of the one invocation for the previous three. He used exactly the same phraseology in the 'advertisement' to the fourth edition of the *Book of Common Prayer revised*, pp. xiii–xv.

3   'Mr Temple' was almost certainly Richard Godman Temple, who was baptized at the High Street
     chapel, Portsmouth, on 27 Apr. 1752. His burial, when he was noted as 'Esq.', was registered at the
     Trim Street chapel, Bath, on 23 Sept. 1830. See TNA: RG4/405, fo. 71r, RG4/2348, fo. 4r; and Vol.
     I, Letter 366, n. 1. It is clear from Lindsey's letters that during the 1790s, Temple spent much time
     in London and visited Portsmouth regularly. He was probably the 'Richard G. Temple' of Mortlake,
     Surrey, who was a member of the Unitarian Society in 1791 and 1794; *Unitarian Society ... 1791*, p.
     13, and *Unitarian Society ... 1794*, p. 14. He was also a subscriber of £100 to Hackney College in
     1786; DWL, MS 12.90 (1). There is a short account of him in Joseph Hunter's 'Biographical notices',
     BL, Add. MS 36527, fo. 87, where Hunter assessed his wealth at £500,000 and described him as
     'overbearing and insolent' in later life. For Lindsey's unitarian friends at Chichester, see Letter 388,
     n. 12.

523. *To RUSSELL SCOTT   1 MAY 1793

Text:	Scott Coll.
Printed:	G. M. Ditchfield, *George III. An essay in monarchy* (Basingstoke, 2002), p. 158 (lines 22–30 of the poem).
Addressed:	Address missing.
Endorsed:	[Opposite the text of the letter, in Hannah Lindsey's hand] Revd Russel Scot [?in Scott's hand] May – 93 – [immediately after the poem, in Hannah Lindsey's hand] For R.S. [i.e. Russell Scott]

Note: With this letter is a poem, in Hannah Lindsey's hand, entitled 'On the first Fast by Royal Proclamation'. It is reproduced here immediately after the letter. Also with this letter, and not reproduced here,
is a copy of the same poem in a different hand, together with a note which states 'The verses on the
"Fast by Proclamation" were amongst the papers of the Rev Russell Scott, brought after his death from
Portsmouth. They are in the hand-writing of Mrs Lindsey, wife of the Rev Theophilus Lindsey, & were
accompanied by a letter from her dated May 1st. 1793.'

                                                                           May 1st – 93
Dr Sir,

M^r. Lindsey not having time to write desires me to beg the favor of you to send
the little pieces as directed.[1] We know not where Mr Temple is, if in y^r neighborhood
be so good as send it, if not that & the one not directed you may dispose of as you
please.[2] The other things are for y^rself, if you have not seen them, they are specimens
of what is going: But I am not certain that some of them have not been sent before.
However it only marks our bad memories & unwillingness to forget you.

We hope you will be able to send us a better account of y^r health when you
write next, & also that Mrs Scot & y^r little man are well. M^r. Lindsey keeps up
wonderfully, and so did I, till this vile cold & cough attacked me three weeks ago,
I hope it cannot remain with violence for three months, as has be [*sic*] the case of
many. Some people begin to be sick of the consequences of War, who yet wish it to
go on from hatred to the French. If one did not know in whose supreme direction
all things are, the prospect before us would be dark indeed. D^r P's Fast Sermon is
printing & several others:[3] He is in good health, & has not the sleepless nights that
our prime Minister is now said to have. With joint best wishes for you & Y^rs I am
y^r sincere f^d HL

On the first Fast by Royal Proclamation[4]

Is this the far fam'd spot of Earth
That gave immortal Milton birth?
Is this the soil where Hampden bled

And Hampden's tyrant lost his head?
Is this the insulated ground
For men of virtuous souls renowned,
Of men who felt as men should feel
And nobly grasped the avenging steel
Of men who rous'd in nature's sacred cause,
Bar'd the red arm of war & spurn'd the oppressor's laws.
Yes, Patriot, yes, behold the land
Once press'd by many a sturdy band
Of men, who shewed the world that Kings
Opposed to men are puny things.
Yes, view that Britain now combined
With the worst foes of human kind:
Behold her sons with savage ire,
Eager to quench fair freedom's fire
And mark her lordly sovereign's care,
Who spreads wide wasting war
And whets the sword with prayer.
Shall I because this tiny thing
Whom fate not merit made a King,
Has dared in slav'rys cause once more
To drench the earth with British gore,
Shall I implore the God of peace,
To grant that slaughter may increase
No, from my soul the war I execrate,
And would not join the prayer
T'avoid the felon's fate.
If o'er a Murderer's back you fling
The purple robe that decks a King,
Or dizen out a band of thieves
In Mitres, crosiers, or lawn sleeves
You'll find, disguise them as you will
That villains will be villains still.
So Britons, whilst your warriors die
In the curst cause of tyranny,
How e're you fast, pray, whine or groan
T'is all a useless farce
Guilt marks you for her own.[5]

---

1   These 'little pieces' were probably single sermons, including Priestley's fast sermon of 19 Apr. 1793
    (see Letter 518, n. 3) and Lindsey's own sermon on prayer (see Letter 522, n. 2).
2   Probably Richard Godman Temple; see Letter 522, n. 3.
3   For Priestley's fast sermon of 1793, see Letter 518, n. 3.
4   The date of the fast day was 19 Apr. 1793.
5   I have not been able to identify the author of this poem; possibly it was the work of Russell Scott
    himself. Hannah Lindsey might also have been the author or co-author; the poem certainly is expres-
    sive of her opinions.

524. To WILLIAM ALEXANDER   6 MAY 1793

Text: 'Letters of the Rev. Theophilus Lindsey. No. IV',
                        UH, II, 71 (6 Sept. 1862), 304.

Note: This is the only section of this letter printed by the *UH*; the manuscript appears not to have survived. The ellipsis at the beginning of the extract printed by the *UH* indicates that this was not the beginning of the original letter.

London, May 6, 1793.

* * I think I told you of the very arbitrary proceedings against Mr. Frend, by the Master and Fellows of Jesus College, for his pamphlet, which really contains nothing but a general censure of all sects and churches by which all might profit, and for which the author ought to have been thanked, instead of being condemned to withdraw himself from the college for a certain time.[1] The University at large, not content with this punishment, are prosecuting him in the Vice-Chancellor's Court, on the same account; but I trust his enemies will not be able to compass their ends in depriving him of his degrees and of his fellowship in consequence, and forcing him out of the University.[2] I am told some persons of great consequence in the University have signified to the prosecutors their dislike of such a fresh attack, and that they ought to have been satisfied with what he had suffered from his college, which it is hoped may give a check to them.[3]

The calamities of war being already so grievously felt through the nation, and certain to increase, will, it is hoped, induce the ministry to put a stop to it. And it is expected that there will soon be a motion made for the purpose in the House of Commons, which will be powerfully supported.[4] I do most heartily wish it, for the sake of humanity and the public good, and also on account of numberless individuals, many of them friends and acquaintances, who are already, but must be greater sufferers if the war goes on.

---

1   William Frend's pamphlet was entitled *Peace and union recommended to the associated bodies of republicans and anti-republicans*.

2   The prosecution of Frend before the vice-chancellor's court in Cambridge opened formally on 3 May 1793. On that day, the charges against Frend arising from *Peace and union* were read, and Frend requested a postponement in order to prepare his defence. The proceedings were then adjourned for one week, until 10 May. See Frend's *An account of the proceedings in the University of Cambridge, against William Frend, M.A., fellow of Jesus College, Cambridge, for publishing a pamphlet, intitled Peace and Union, &c. Containing the proceedings in Jesus College, the trial in the vice-chancellor's court, and in the court of delegates. Published by the defendant* (Cambridge, published by Benjamin Flower, 1793), pp. 1–14. For the subsequent progress of the trial, see Letters 526 and 529. The vice-chancellor of Cambridge University in 1793 was Isaac Milner (1750–1820), president of Queens' College from 1788 until his death and Lucasian professor of mathematics from 1798. A distinguished natural philosopher and a leading evangelical, he regarded the conviction of Frend as a defeat for Jacobinism within the university.

3   The persons of great consequence in Cambridge University whose political and religious opinions led them to disapprove of the sentence against Frend included the duke of Grafton, the university's chancellor, and John Hey (1734–1815), Norrisian professor of divinity and a noted latitudinarian. They also included, more remotely, Richard Watson, bishop of Llandaff and regius professor of divinity, although he paid a deputy, Thomas Kipling, to perform the duties of the latter office. In 1788 Jesus College had deprived Frend of his tutorship, following his attack on compulsory subscription to religious tests; see Vol. I, Letter 373.

4   On 17 June 1793, Charles James Fox moved in the house of commons a motion for the re-establishment of peace with France. It was defeated by 187 votes to 47; Cobbett, *Parl. hist.*, XXX, 994–1024.

525. To THE TRUSTEES OF ESSEX STREET CHAPEL   ?MAY 1793

Text: Belsham, *Memoirs*, p. 226.

Note: Belsham printed only the extracts of the letter which are presented here, and described it as 'a circular letter to the Trustees', of whom there were twelve in May 1793. According to Belsham, the letter was written 'in the beginning of the summer' (i.e. of 1793); 'A Lawyer', 'Deeds', 264, presumably having seen the original manuscript, gave the date as May 1793. The words in square brackets are Belsham's.

Dear Sir, – I beg leave to address you in the capacity of a Trustee for the chapel in Essex Street, and to inform you of my intention of resigning my office of minister of it.

My advanced age and growing infirmities have for some time intimated to me the rightness and necessity of this step; but as I was enabled to perform the service, I thought it my duty to accomplish two points previous to my retiring from my station.

[The points to which the writer alludes, were a renewal of the Trust, and a complete repair of the whole premises, which had been done in the best manner possible.[1] Having stated these circumstances for the information of the Trustees, Mr. Lindsey adds:] I have fixed the middle of July next for the time of my resignation; and I am happy in having a candidate as a successor in my colleague Dr. Disney, whose zeal for the principle upon which the society was founded, and whose abilities, assiduity, and acceptableness to you and the congregation, in the discharge of his duty, have been for a long time ascertained.[2]

---

[1] The trust was renewed, with three new trustees to replace those who had died since the original trust of 1783, in Dec. 1793; see 'A Lawyer', 'Deeds', 264. The surviving evidence in the Essex Hall archives does not deal with these repairs.

[2] For the appreciative reply of the trustees, see Belsham, *Memoirs*, pp. 226–7. Belsham did not give the date of the trustees' letter, but a date in May 1793 may safely be assumed. Lindsey was due to preach his farewell sermon on Sunday 14 July 1793; see Letter 534, n. 1.

526. To JOHN ROWE   7 MAY 1793

Text: JRUL, Lindsey Letters, vol. II, no. 70.
Printed: McLachlan, *Letters*, p. 129 (last three sentences of third
                  paragraph).
Addressed: To/The Rev^d. John Rowe/Shrewsbury
Postmarked: MA 7 93

London. May. 7 1793.

Dear Sir,

It is a pleasure to hear of our common venerable friend being so tolerably well and free from pain at his great age,[1] which I conclude from your saying nothing to the contrary; and though I have had now for near twenty years singular satisfaction and benefit from his valuable correspondence, I should be most unreasonable to desire it being continued by him when it cannot be done without difficulty; and my wife and I beg you to present our due respects to him, with our congratulations to the traveller on having proceeded so far on his journey, with such honour to himself and singular usefulness to others, in what respects their present and future happiness.

I do not believe I should have thanked you quite so soon for your letter, had not I heard last night that the worthy Mr Kenrick has resigned his ministerial office at

Exeter, on account of some untoward opposition he had met with, and I wished to suggest to you as early as possible, whether it might not be agreeable to yourself and acceptable to your congregation to have a collegue of such a character, so respectable and agreeable, as I believe him to be on report, and as he appeared to me 5 or 6 Years ago, from a single hour's conversation with him, and tho' he has some fortune, £60 a year may be a desireable addition to one who has a family. I know I shall be excused by you for having mentioned such a circumstance.[2]

The rain prevents to day, or I should have called at Mr Longman's myself to know when his next parcell goes to Mr Eddowes, that I might send a little one to Mr Tayleur; but I hope to be there to morrow; and engage to take care in future that any thing of Dr P.'s be sent properly to Shrewsbury. The Doctor was very well on Saturday, but was under some concern about his second Son who was settled at Nantes, not having heard of or from him for two or three months. But I am told to day, that he had a letter yesterday, which had come round about by Switzerland, which mentioned that he was very well, and was the next day to set sail in an American ship for Philadelphia.[3] I add nothing, having no time or space for it, on this painful subject of migration. You will be glad to be informed that the shameful renewal of the attack of^4 Mr Frend by the University, after his being tried and sentenced to rustication in his own college, is likely to come to nothing. On friday last Mr Frend was convened before the Vicechancellor's court, and behaved with great courage and coolness, and good sense. But the business was put off till friday next, by his objecting to the Jurisdiction of the court in his case.[5]

I am glad that you and our friend are so much satisfied with Farmer Truman.[6] It was with some difficulty that I prevailed to have it printed. I have already dispersed a hundred copies. But at our next meeting I must remonstrate against it being called an Unitarian tract, and a title page to that effect put upon it. This was done at a meeting when I was not present. I sh^d have been against it as wrong in itself; but besides this, a relation of Mr Jonas Hanway, I am told is much displeased, as she says and very truly, that he was no unitarian.[7] Certainly then such a title is very objectionable, and sh^d be given only to tracts that are upon the question itself, not to those of a practical kind.[8]

Give me leave at last to say, that though concerned for the occasion of your declining the whole duty of your place I am not surprised at and rejoice in the honourable testimony the Society bears to one who has hitherto filled it with such credit and benefit to many.[9] We hope Mrs Rowe and your little family [are well][10], and with *our* best comp^{ts} to her, and my wife's to yourself, I am always, Dear Sir, Your affectionate friend and servant

T. Lindsey.

1   William Tayleur reached the age of eighty-one in May 1793.
2   On 28 Apr. 1793, Kenrick offered to resign as minister of the George meeting, Exeter, following a division in his congregation over his refusal to preach on the fast day; early the following month, he withdrew his resignation; see Letter 518. He did not move to Shrewsbury. He and his first wife Mary, née Waymouth (d. 1793), had five surviving children; and he and his second wife, Elizabeth, née Belsham, had no children. Although Kenrick himself lived on a relatively small stipend at Exeter, his father John Kenrick possessed considerable landed wealth in Denbighshire.
3   Priestley's second son William, who was already a French citizen, returned to France in 1793 with a view to securing employment through the influence of his father's admirers in the Friends of the Constitution at Nantes. When this failed, William Priestley travelled to America and arrived at Philadelphia in the summer of 1793.
4   Lindsey probably intended to write 'upon', rather than 'of'.

⁵ See Letter 524. 'Friday next' was 10 May 1793, when the vice-chancellor's court resumed its prosecution of Frend. On that day, witnesses were called, testifying that Frend had published, and distributed copies of, *Peace and union*; Frend was able to cross-examine these witnesses. See Frend, *An
  account of the proceedings in the University of Cambridge, against William Frend, M.A., Fellow of
  Jesus College, Cambridge, for publishing a pamphlet, intitled Peace and union, &c* (Cambridge,
  1793), pp. 14–80. The trial was then adjourned until 17 May. For the outcome, see Letter 529, n. 3.
⁶ Hanway, *Advice from Farmer Trueman to his daughter Mary*.
⁷ For *Advice from Farmer Trueman to his daughter Mary*, adapted from the work of Jonas Hanway,
  see Letter 509, n. 6. Lindsey did not identify Hanway's female relative; possibly he referred to one of
  the daughters of Hanway's sister Mary Altham; see James Stephen Taylor, *Jonas Hanway. Founder of
  the Marine Society. Charity and policy in eighteenth-century Britain* (London and Berkeley, 1985), p.
  131. This matter is not mentioned in the minutes of the Unitarian Society in 1793. A new edition of
  the *Advice* was published in 1796, without the imprint of the Unitarian Society, although it was listed
  in the printed 'Catalogue of books distributed by the Unitarian Society' in 1796; there is a copy of
  this catalogue in DWL, MS 12.46 (9). Lindsey meant that to label any work of Hanway as 'unitarian'
  was 'objectionable'.
⁸ See n. 7, above.
⁹ Finding his task of sole minister at the High Street chapel, Shrewsbury, to be arduous, Rowe had a
  co-minister (Arthur Aikin) between Sept. 1793 and July 1795.
¹⁰ Lindsey inadvertently omitted the words 'are well'; his previous letters indicate that these were the
  words he intended to write.

527. To WILLIAM TAYLEUR   10 MAY 1793

Text: JRUL, Lindsey Letters, vol. II, no. 71.
Printed: McLachlan, *Letters*, p. 37 (last sentence of first paragraph).
Addressed: [In Hannah Lindsey's hand] William Tayleur Esqʳ
Endorsed: 10ᵗʰ May – 94 [*sic*]
Postmarked: Postmark missing.

London. May. 10. 1793.
Dear Sir,

Mʳ Longman acquainting me that he has a parcell for Mʳ Eddowes to morrow,
and that he could send any thing in it, I take the opportunity of conveying from Dʳ
Priestley his two last Publications:¹ a sermon also of Mʳ Walker's of which my wife
begs your acceptance, as she likes it much and thinks it will be agreeable to you.²
In perusing it you will wonder how it could give any persons such mighty offence.³
I beg you also to accept a copy of the last edition of our Liturgy. Mʳ Johnson is
ashamed, but too late, of having printed it on so poor a paper. Many things are left
in, which my successor will alter probably in a future edition, but which I judged
right to leave untouched; especially the k. and royal family engrossing so much
particular attention and space.⁴

Dʳ Priestley's eldest son, that was settled at Manchester has been with us to
day with the Doctor. He, his wife and infant child, and his youngest brother, are
going together to America, to look after a settlement there, the latter end of July.⁵
I think I took notice to Mʳ Rowe, that the Doctor had a letter from his second son
William, and that he had set out from Nantes in Brittany in an American vessel for
Philadelphia. Thus our friend will have three of his sons in America.⁶

I had intended a longer epistle for you; but as my messenger waits, and I have
a few lines to convey in yours to Mʳ Harries, and Mʳ Wood,⁷ I take my leave at
present, and with my wifes most kind respects, remain always Dear Sir, Your most
truly obliged and faithful affectionate servant

T. Lindsey.

1   Priestley's 'two last publications' were his *Letters to the philosophers and politicians of France* (see Letter 512, n. 2) and his 1793 fast sermon (see Letter 518, n. 3). On 1 May, Lindsey had noted that the latter was 'printing' (Letter 523); it appeared a few days later.
2   This work of George Walker was *Christian fortitude: a sermon, preached at Salter's-Hall, on Sunday, March 24th, 1793* (London, 1793).
3   Walker's sermon (n. 2, above) so annoyed some of his listeners at Salter's Hall that a small number of the audience walked out; see *Monthly Review*, NS, XII (1794), 236, which praised the sermon, adding 'we can find nothing in it which could at all vindicate or excuse such behaviour'. It was reprinted in Walker's *Sermons on various subjects* (4 vols., 1808), with an advertisement expressing regret and incredulity at the walk-out; this advertisement did not appear in the edition published in 1793.
4   The prayers for the king and for the royal family were retained in the fourth edition of *The Book of Common Prayer reformed* and in the fifth edition, published in 1805.
5   From 1791, Joseph Priestley junior had been employed as a clerk to a merchant in Manchester. His (first) wife was Elizabeth, née Ryland (1769–1816), and their first child, born at Manchester on 23 Mar. 1793, was Joseph Rayner Priestley (d. 1863). His youngest brother was Henry Priestley (see n. 6, below).
6   See Letter 526. Priestley's three sons were Joseph Junior, William and Henry.
7   The enclosures for Edward Harries and for Isaac Wood seem not to have survived.

528. To 'A FRIEND'   13 JUNE 1793

Text: Belsham, *Memoirs*, pp. 231–2 n. *.

Note: The manuscript of this letter seems not to have survived. The only available text is that printed by Belsham, who did not identify the 'friend' to whom the letter was written, although he did give the date as 13 June 1793. One may conclude, however, that the 'friend' was not William Turner of Newcastle, who was described by Belsham as 'another friend' when quoting from Lindsey's letter to him of 9 Sept. 1793 (*Memoirs*, p. 232 n. *) immediately after this letter. For that letter to Turner in full, see Letter 536.

I ought not to keep secret any longer from you what was known to one or two friends a year ago, and lately been signified to the Trustees of the chapel, that I intend very soon to resign my office of minister of it. On the first of July I enter into my seventieth year;[1] and though I have cause of all thankfulness for the health and strength I enjoy, being able tolerably to go through the duty, yet I find infirmities coming, and have had some nervous spasms, particularly in my head, that have long satisfied me that it is right to retire with a good grace. I have recommended my worthy colleague, and he will certainly be chosen to succeed me. But we shall continue to live on in our present situation. For the whole premises being purchased, and the chapel, &c., built by money collected by me from various friends, with not less than five hundred pounds of our own, and the accommodations, &c., being much owing to my wife's attention, skill, and daily superintendence, when I gave up the fee of the whole, which was vested in me, and made choice of the Trustees in the trust-deed, which perpetuates the premises for the proper uses, they settled the house rent-free to my wife for her life.[2]

1   Lindsey entered his seventy-first year on 1 July (new style) 1793.
2   For Lindsey's subscription of £500 towards the construction of the Essex Street chapel, see Vol. I, appendix I; for the settlement of the dwelling-house upon Lindsey and his wife, see 'A Lawyer', 'Deeds', 262.

529. To JOHN LEE   **22 JUNE 1793**

Text: William L. Clements Library, University of Michigan,
                 Ann Arbor: Lee papers, Box 2, item 35.
Printed: G. M. Ditchfield, 'Two unpublished letters of Theophilus
                 Lindsey', *TUHS*, XX, 2 (Apr. 1992), 139–40.
Addressed: Address missing.
Postmarked: Postmark missing

June 22. 1793

Dear Sir,

I have to thank you for the receipt of your generous annual subscription to our chapel yesterday, remitted to me in a Bank note by your lady, to whom I beg my best acknowledgements for her trouble and obliging letter. From the first, you have been alike generous towards myself, and in your benefactions towards the purchase and building the chapel and our habitation, of all which I hope I am duly sensible. But I can never sufficiently acknowledge the friendship which you have been ever ready to shew me upon all occasions, and the happiness which I have enjoyed from year to year in seeing and being with you, a happiness, which as I believe, I have intimated before, I shall hope to enjoy with you and many of our common friends in another state, which I do not apprehend will be so very different from this, as it is commonly imagined. But if it might please the Almighty to bless the means used to relieve your painful cough, which I earnestly pray, I trust you will still live on with some comfort, and that I shall be so happy as to see it.[1]

Sunday last the Duke and Duchess of Grafton with one of the young ladies were at our chapel.[2] It will give you pleasure to hear that the Duke has been more frequently with us this year than usual, when he has been in town and particularly I have observed during Mr Frend's tryal at Cambridge, which I think does him credit.[3]

If you had been able to have come to Town this year, you would have had little satisfaction with the public scene of things that has been carrying on, though you would have unavoidably mixed in it. Mr Fox has borne a noble testimony against the beginning and continuance of the war in which we are unhappily engaged; but no one can now see the end of it, or of the miseries in which it will involve us. Great is the distress for want of money among those that are the most opulent, but also do not know to what wants they may be reduced. And the distresses of the midling and inferior classes are daily increasing; especially in the neighbourhood of manufacturing places. You would see in the papers some accounts of the nailers at and near Dudley.[4] Mr Finch, Mr Shore's relation, found himself obliged to pack up what valuables he had and take an account of what he could not remove, and leave the place.[5] For their violence is still chiefly directed against Dissenters.

Dr Priestley is very well, but in some anxiety about his daughter and son in law, who lives [*sic*] within 6 miles of Dudley: though Mrs Priestley who is with them tells him there is nothing to be apprehended. He has just now been here, and desires to be most kindly remembered. I must tell you also, that Lord G. Cavendish[6] has called at the door, since I sat down to write, and our maid-servant most foolishly told him I was gone out, without coming in to inquire. I suppose he is going into the Country, and is in by way of taking leave.

My wife desires to join in kind respects and good wishes for yourself and Mrs Lee and your amiable daughter.[7]

I remain always, Dear Sir,

Your most truly obliged and faithful affectionate servant,

   T. Lindsey

1 John Lee died on 5 Aug. 1793.

2 'Sunday last' was 16 June 1793. The duchess of Grafton was Elizabeth (1745–1822), daughter of Sir Richard Wrottesley, dean of Worcester. She was the second wife of Augustus Henry, 3rd duke of Grafton; they were married in 1769. 'One of the young ladies' was presumably one of their eight daughters.

3 After the proceedings on 10 May 1793 (see Letter 526), Frend's trial at Cambridge continued on 17, 24, 28 and 30 May 1793; on the latter date, Frend was pronounced guilty and, following his refusal to retract his opinions, sentenced to banishment from the university. See Frend, *An account of the proceedings in the University of Cambridge, against William Frend, M.A.*, pp. 80–187, and Knight, *William Frend*, chs. 10 and 11.

4 Lindsey had probably read newspaper reports, such as that in the *General Evening Post*, 18–20 June 1793, of rioting by nailers and colliers, for higher wages, at Dudley, Worcestershire.

5 William Finch, of Heath Forge, near Dudley, who had married Priestley's daughter Sarah in 1786; see Letter 513, n. 3.

6 Either Lord George Augustus Cavendish (*c.* 1727–94), MP for Derbyshire, or his nephew Lord George Augustus Henry Cavendish (1754–1834), MP for Derby. Both were supporters of the whig opposition.

7 Lee's wife was Mary (d. 1813), née Hutchinson; his daughter and only child was Mary Tabitha Lee (1777–1851).

530. *To RUSSELL SCOTT   1 JULY 1793

Text: Scott Coll.

Printed: McLachlan, 'Lindsey to Scott', 119 (short quotation from first paragraph; part of first sentence of fourth paragraph, concerning Lindsey's retirement; most of first sentence of fifth paragraph; third sentence of sixth paragraph; postscript).

Addressed: To/The Rev^d. Russel Scot./Portsmouth

Endorsed: July 2^d. – 93

Portsmouth: JY 1 93

                    July 1st. 1793

Dear Sir,

M^r. Lindsey is so much occupied at this time that he has deputed me to write and tell you how sincerely we sympathize with you on the loss of your worthy sister: Happily for her she feels no more, and those she has left behind are under the care of a good providence, who knows what is best for them, and for us all.[1]

We hope that M^rs. Scots coming to see her Sister will satisfy her mind so much that it will be a means of securing her from the accident wch. harrass of mind alone might have occasioned, & prevent the lasting regret she might have felt, if she had not been gratified in seeing her sister;[2] & as we trust she is arrived safe & with her Father & Mother,[3] that you will also feel a little comforted and look to happier days to come; and we are sure that you look to and submit to the hand that afflicts, as well as give us our joys, which is only the road to something purely & durably joyous.

What you have heard respecting M^r. Lindsey is true, and what of D^r. Disney without any foundation that we know of: I rather think that he is near the attainment of the point & object of his ambition, to be the leader of this Congregation: One fortnight more will we hope put him into possession of that hon^{ble} & important Station, & that it will be his earnest desire & endeavour to be useful in it.[4]

The age of threescore & ten, and growing infirmities have for sometime determined him (tho' unknown to others) to take this right & necessary step, of which he gave notice to the Trustees near six weeks ago that he s^d. resign about the middle of July,[5] and we intend to set out for the North to see my good old Mother of fourscore, directly after our business here is finished: You will [have] received at the end of the Month by Mr Johnson a discourse which M^r. Lindsey will publish on the occasion, wch. will convey many particulars of his own reasons told by himself, & wch. I therefore need not enter into before.[6] You will easily believe that he is, & will be sincerely regretted by many of his old friends & first hearers, who know & value his excellent character and unremitted labours for their good, tho' they cannot but admire and approve a conduct so consonant with that of his whole life: And he is happy in leaving a successor so very acceptable to the Congregation by his abilities & zeal for the principle of the divine Unity.

If it please God to give M^r. Lindsey tolerable health, he will continue to be useful in various ways, & as he is able: The stress work he has had for many years, has worn him down so much accompanied by a tender, & scrupulous mind that he was not longer able to continue it; & nothing but principle & zeal could have kept him up so long. I shall be much more at ease about him when the whole is finished, & hope a journey without the anxiety he has always had to return, will recruit him a good deal. I have not been an idle person in the preparatory steps to this change of station, having had the whole expensive repair of the whole premises upon my hand,[7] & to get executed in the best manner possible, to put them in a good state into the possession of the Trustees: We shall continue to live in the house, and do all we can to promote the cause.

We should be happy to hear a better account of you & M^{rs}. Scot before we set out, a letter that shall arrive here by the 16th will reach us in time. We shall not probably return before the end of Sept^r., as we have many friends to see on our return, and cannot travel as expeditiously as formerly, nor repeat such long journies, as we have given up one source of support in the income of the Chapel.[8] Adieu, be of good courage these are times of difficulty & trial public & private. D^r. Priestley is a pattern of fortitude under great private anxieties for his family who are all going to leave him for America, & his only daughters husband (with four children) are now as much the subject of popular odium with other Dissenters at Dudley, as he & his friends were at Birmingham.[9] Under all things the Governor of the world is sufficient to protect & support those who trust in him. With our kind regards & best wishes for you & yours, I am

Dr Sir Y^{rs} sincerely

HL

P.S.

M^r. Morgan takes but ten, or twelve pupils, has not more than half the number at present, and has them of different ages, but none very young.[10]

---

1   Russell Scott's sister, the poet Mary Taylor, died at Bristol on 5 June 1793.

2   Presumably Lindsey referred here to Russell Scott's wife Sophia; Mary Taylor was her sister-in-law.

3   Sophia Scott's father and mother were Dr William Hawes and his wife Sarah, née Fox (1740–1815), of 8 Spital Square, Bishopsgate Street, London.

4   John Disney succeeded Lindsey as minister of Essex Street chapel in July 1793. It is not clear what Scott might have heard about Disney. However, Hannah Lindsey's comment that she 'rather' (signi-

fying a contrast to what Scott had heard) thought that Disney was 'near the attainment of the point & object of his ambition' suggests that Scott had encountered rumours to the effect that Disney was reluctant to become the sole minister of the Essex Street chapel.

5 Letter 525.
6 For Lindsey's 'farewell sermon', see Letter 531, n. 2.
7 See Letter 525, n. 1.
8 In Letters 528 and 536 Lindsey described some of the ways in which he and his wife intended to support themselves financially after his retirement. It was possible, accordingly, for them to undertake several long journeys in and after 1793, beginning with their visit to Richmond, Yorkshire, in Aug. –Sept. 1793. In 1800, moreover, Lindsey received a substantial legacy from the will of Elizabeth Rayner.
9 For the departure of Priestley's three sons for America, see Letter 514, n. 9. His only daughter, married to William Finch, lived at Heath Forge, near Dudley.
10 For George Cadogan Morgan and his school, see Letter 516, n. 1.

531. To WILLIAM TAYLEUR   8 JULY 1793

Text: JRUL, Lindsey Letters, vol. II, no. 72.
Addressed: To/William Tayleur Esqr/Shrewsbury
Endorsed: July 8th – 93
Postmarked: JY 8 93

London. July. 8. 1793.

Dear Sir,

My time has been very much filled up of late by a variety of business and engagements, or my acknowlegements would have been sooner offered for your last kind testimony of regard and friendship, which was such a satisfaction to me, though I had no doubt of it, and did me so much honour with your fellow-trustees.[1]

The necessary arrangements are made and all preparatives for making my resignation in form this day week and for Dr Disney's election by 8 of the Trustees the same day. The sunday morning before I shall take my final leave of the pulpit, and endeavour to say something proper, though nothing by way of taking leave, which my own nerves would not bear, and all my old friends and many others of the congregation, say that they should keep away that day, was there to be any thing of the kind. I have therefore prepared and nearly printed off a discourse, addressed to the congregation, which indeed I had at first thoughts of delivering to them, in which I have endeavoured to impress them with a sense of the importance of the principle which distinguishes us from other christian churches, and of the strict obligations which it lays upon us to holiness of life; and shall take care that some copies of it be sent with the earliest to Shrewsbury.[2]

Though I have been remarkably well this spring, and full as ~~well~~ able to go through the duty as for some years past, I have great satisfaction in my retiring from it, as proper for me on many accounts, and for the credit of the cause, which I shall be happy to serve so long as I live; and as I leave the society flourishing and a successor in vigour of life, firm in our principle, and acceptable to the people.

Dr Priestley was with us on Saturday,[2] and we look for him to day. He is very well in health, heaven be praised, and though retaining his even chearful mind, yet with unavoidable anxieties at intervals, considering the times, his own state in them, and that of all the branches of his family.

Mr Corrie, who is I believe now at Shrewsbury, and a great favourite of mine, will tell you all particulars concerning the D^r. and his family; concerning the new arrangements with regard to the college at Hackney, and the part Mr Belsham has undertaken, and wch he, Mr Corrie, takes, to which he is, though so young, very equal.[3] In short, he and a few more, several of them known to you, are the young men of the rising generation, whom I reckon upon, as under divine providence, likely to be instruments of extensive good, wherever they are placed.

At the latter end of the next week we take our biennial course into the North to visit my wife's mother, and having many other calls by the way at the habitations of different friends, shall be absent about six weeks, more or less. It would be quite out of our route, or we sh^d have been most happy to have paid our respects to you for one day. My wife begs to tender her most due respects, and I remain always Dear Sir, with high esteem, Your most truly obliged, and faithful affectionate servant

T. Lindsey.

We beg to be duly remembered to M^r and Mrs Rowe and Mr Wood – &c

---

1   Tayleur remained a trustee of Essex Street chapel until his death in 1796; probably Lindsey referred here to the letter from the trustees in response to his resignation (see Letter 525, n. 2), rather than to a non-surviving letter from Tayleur.

2   Although Lindsey conducted his final service at Essex Street chapel on 14 July 1793, he did not deliver his planned farewell sermon, but published it separately with the title *A discourse addressed to the congregation at the chapel in Essex Street, Strand, on resigning the pastoral office among them* (London, 1793). In the 'advertisement' to this discourse, he explained that he had at first intended to deliver it from the pulpit, but decided not to do so because he was 'too tenderly impressed with taking leave of so many indulgent friends to be capable of personally addressing them with any tolerable degree of vigour'.

3   6 July 1793.

4   John Corrie (1769–1839) was a pupil of Belsham at Daventry between 1783 and 1787, and a student at Hackney College between 1787 and 1790. On the completion of his studies at Hackney he became an assistant tutor at the college, and in 1793 succeeded John Pope as classical tutor; see Williams, p. 444. For his subsequent career, see Letter 575, n. 2.

532. To JOSHUA TOULMIN   8 JULY 1793

Text: Belsham, *Memoirs*, p. 227 n. *.

Note: Belsham gave the date of this letter as 8 July 1783, which is clearly a printing error; the reference to the immediate prospect of Lindsey's resignation of his ministry at Essex Street chapel means that the year could only have been 1793. 8 July 1793 was a Monday; Lindsey was due to preach the following Sunday. This is the only section of the letter printed by Belsham; the manuscript seems not to have survived.

I take my final leave of the pulpit in this chapel on Sunday next,[1] in the morning, and shall endeavour to say something suitable, though without any hint of bidding farewell, which my own nerves would not bear; and many kind friends of those who are not yet gone into the country say, that they must keep away from the chapel if I do anything of this kind.

---

1   14 July 1793.

533. *To SOPHIA SCOTT   **17 JULY 1793**

Text:	Scott Coll.
Printed:	McLachlan, 'Lindsey to Scott', 119 (first sentence of third paragraph).
Addressed:	To/M^rs. Scot/at D^r. Hawes's/Spital Square
Endorsed:	July 7th – 93
Postmarked:	Postmark missing.

July 17th
Essex House

Dear Madam,

By a letter yesterday we are happy to hear a better account of your spirits & health and of M^r. Scots also.[1]

He desires a direction may be sent to you where M^r. Morgan lives to whom one of his friends wants to write: His direction is Mr George Morgan Clapton near Hackney.[2]

We send with this a small parcel for M^r. Scot, wch you will send when convenient being only a few of Mr Lindsey's last discourse upon quiting [*sic*] his Office of Pastor of this Congregation for himself & any of his particular friends at Portsmouth.[3] We are just setting out for the North to see my good old Mother & to recruit after much anxious business, & to be better able to perform any other work Almighty God appoints. With best wishes for you & y^rs I am y^r sincere f^d HLindsey

---

1   Scott's letter to Lindsey seems not to have survived. Sophia Scott (née Hawes) was the wife of Russell Scott.

2   George Cadogan Morgan retained an address at Clapton, only a few doors from that of Priestley, after founding his school at Southgate, Middlesex. He was still paying rates at Clapton in 1793; see Gray, 'Joseph Priestley in Hackney', 109.

3   See Letter 531, n. 2.

534. To WILLIAM TAYLEUR   **18 JULY 1793**

Text:	JRUL, Lindsey Letters, vol. II, no. 73.
Printed:	McLachlan, *Letters*, pp. 129–30 (fifth, sixth and seventh sentences of second paragraph).
Addressed:	To/William Tayleur Esqr/Shrewsbury
Endorsed:	July 18th – 93
Postmarked:	JY 19 93

London. July. 18. 1793

Dear Sir,

My wife having packed a few copies of the Discourses I have addressed to the congregation &c for your obliging acceptance and of a few of my friends about you, I am sure you will excuse the trouble given in directing them to You.

You will have pleasure in hearing that Sunday passed off very well. Though I have seldom preached on a hotter day, and the audience for the time of the year was large, and my sermon not short, I never preached with more ease to myself.[1] Some desired to have it printed, but whatever I may do hereafter I declined it for the present. The next day I made my resignation, and Dr Disney's appointment was signed, and every thing ended in the most harmonious way.[2] We have been busied the whole of this week in various ways, and shall be to the end of it, Saturday, when we set out for my friend's Mr Reynolds of Paxton, to pass some days there in our way into the North. Perhaps as it is not far from Cambridge, we may see Mr Frend. He has had a call for a second edition of his Tract for which he has been persecuted, Peace and Union, and has printed 1500; his own account of the Proceeding against him is in the press, and will make a good sized Volume. I observe his adversaries have been before him in publishing their account of the business.[3]

Dr Priestley went on Monday on a visit to Mr Russell, at Wotton Hall near Gloucester, to enjoy a little fresh air and conversation with an old friend.[4] Hard is his lot, which forbids him this intercourse with many: but it has been the fate of the eminently good in all times.

We often talk with great satisfaction of looking in upon you for half a day, so as not to disturb too much: but it is not to be thought of for this year. We set out to morrow morning early on our visit to my wifes mother, who is 80 compleat, and tolerably well. Our proposed pleasure is much damped by recent accounts of Mr Lee's health, at Staindrop, on the other side of the Tees, within a few hours ride: one from whose pleasant conversation you always rose up pleased and satisfied with much that you wished to remember more than of any one I ever conversed with: and so says always Dr Priestley.[5]

Sometime in the month of September we look to be on our return to the South; and one of my first businesses shall be to make inquiries after you. Yesterday Mr Porter, who is on a visit to his friends in the South, from Plymouth was here. I observed with pleasure that the ardour of his mind to promote the truth increases with the opposition it meets with. His last answer to Dr Hawker, does him great credit, and I learn from Mr Kentish that it has been particularly serviceable in that town and neighbourhood.[6]

We have for this fortnight enjoyed Summer which had not visited us before of some years, and we hope it will cherish and revive you as it does us. My wife charges me with her most sincere respects to you. And we desire to be duly and kindly remembered to M^r and Mrs Rowe, with all your Gentlemen, the newcomer in particular, Mr Corrie[7] – With all esteem and respect, I remain, Dear Sir, Your ever truly obliged and faithful servant

T. Lindsey.

---

1   See Letter 531, n. 2.

2   The previous Sunday was 14 July 1793; Lindsey formally resigned as minister on 15 July and on the same day Disney was formally appointed to succeed him; see 'A Lawyer', 'Deeds', 264.

3   Frend published the second edition of *Peace and union* in Cambridge in 1793. His *Account of the proceedings in the University of Cambridge, against William Frend* was also published in Cambridge in 1793; the printer of both works was Benjamin Flower. The case of Frend's opponents was published as the *Trial of William Frend, MA ... in the vice-chancellor's court. For writing and publishing a pamphlet, intitled Peace and union ... by John Beverley, MA* (Cambridge, 1793). John Beverley (1743–1827) was esquire bedell of the university from 1770 to 1827, and the proctor of the vice-chancellor's court.

4   This is a reference to Wotton Hall, Gloucester, which was the home of the Russell family during the early 1790s. On 24 July 1793, during a visit to William Russell, Priestley wrote to Lindsey from 'Wooton'; Rutt, I, 203–4.

5   John Lee died at Staindrop on 5 Aug. 1793.

6   Thomas Porter was the author of *A defence of unitarianism, intended as an answer to Dr Hawker's sermons, on the divinity of Christ* (Plymouth, 1793). Robert Hawker's *Sermons on the divinity of Christ* were published in one volume in London in 1792; in recognition of this work he was awarded the degree of DD by Edinburgh University. He replied to Porter in *The evidences of a plenary inspiration: a letter to Mr. Thomas Porter, in reply to his defence of unitarianism* (Plymouth, 1793). Porter

retaliated with *A letter to Dr. Hawker, on his pretended reply to Mr. Porter's defence of unitarianism, by the author of that defence* (Plymouth, 1793); this was Porter's 'last answer to Dr Hawker', to which Lindsey referred. Hawker (1753–1827), a staunch Calvinist evangelical, was vicar of Charles, Plymouth, from 1784 until his death.

7   For John Corrie, see Letter 531, n. 4. Although he visited Shrewsbury, he did not become a minister there.

535. To WILLIAM TAYLEUR   5 AUGUST 1793

Text: JRUL, Lindsey Letters, vol. II, no. 74.
Printed: McLachlan, *Letters*, p. 130 (most of second paragraph; third paragraph).
Addressed: To/William Tayleur Esqr/Shrewsbury
Endorsed: 5th Aug^t – 93
Postmarked: Postmark missing.

Richmond. Yorkshire Aug. 5. 1793.

Dear Sir,

We arrived here at our journeys end, at my wife's mother's on saturday,[1] having left London the Saturday fortnight preceding.

At my old College-Chum's, Mr Reynolds of Paxton in Huntingdonshire, Mr Frend from Cambridge met us, and passed most of the time with us. He seemed at first harassed with what he had gone through and not in such good spirits, in part owing to a bilious habit, but he was quite cheered and recruited before he left us. To all his other valuable parts and virtues, there is[2] added an open chearful disposition, which renders his company very agreeable. He has not yet determined what steps next to take. But will have time to deliberate and consult his friends before the October term commences. He is at present busy in printing his account of the Proceedings against him.[3] When that is finished, he makes an excursion into Kent, his own county, to visit his friends and refresh himself.

The court of delegates to whom he appealed, confirmed the Vicechancellor's sentence. Some doubt of the Courts in Westminster Hall interfering, on an appeal to them, as they may allege the affair to be an Act of Discipline in the exercise of which the University ought not to be interrupted.[4]

Of all the Provincial Papers, there is scarce any so bad as the Cambridge One; hostile to every good principle, civil and religious. It has long been thought of to set on foot another; but never undertaken till just now, when the Saturday I was at Mr Reynoldss, the first number came out, under the title of the Cambridge Intelligencer. It is conducted by Mr Benjamin Flower, Printer; who has lately settled at Cambridge for the purpose.[5] I have no doubt of your having read his large Octavo Vol. on *The French Constitution*, with Remarks &c with high approbation.[6] This bespeaks his qualifications for such a work. But I must add concerning him, from some little knowlege; that I do not know a christian of a more enlarged mind or of more excellent dispositions. And though he is not rich, I am persuaded, that he would not traduce any one, or falsify any fact to gain the greatest riches. The paper will be sent to any part of England, for 16s a year, or 4s a quarter. I take it in. It is sent to me here. Some few of my friends have been induced by me to have it sent them, and like it much. You will encourage a good work and a most worthy man by ordering it, and if there be not particular objection I wish you would do it, and also recommend it to Mr Holbrooke, who will be glad to see also what is going on at Cambridge.[7] His address is to Mr Benjamin Flower, Printer, Bridge Street, Cambridge.

We have the happiness of finding my wifes mother very tolerably well in all respects in her eighty first year. But feel a great drawback upon the satisfaction proposed in our journey, by my excellent & highly valued friend, Mr Lee, being in such a state as not likely to last long, and not able to see us. Of all the men I ever knew, without one exception, his conversation was the most easy, pleasant, and instructive, and ever most friendly and benevolent. Dr Priestley who has known him longer will be hurt by his loss.[8]

This reminds me of mentioning, that I have here met a letter from the Doctor, which gives a most pleasing account of his reception at Glocester, whither he went the week we left London – that on the Sunday the Mayor and his Son came to hear him preach – and came afterwards to see him, at Mr Chandlers in Glocester, and at Mr Russells house near that city.[9] Mr Pitt also the member of Parliament invited him to dine with him whenever congenial.[10] I trust this is some little symptom of the tide turning in favour of our most valued and persecuted friend. I should take it as a favour to receive a few lines from Mr Rowe at this place, where we shall be stationary a while to tell us how You do, and also himself his lady and all our friends with You. Should you chuse it, I w^d write to Mr Flower to send You the Cambridge Intelligencer.

W^h. my wifes due & hearty respects, Dear Sir, Your ever obliged, T. Lindsey.

1   The previous Saturday was 3 Aug. 1793.
2   Lindsey at first wrote 'has', over-wrote it and wrote 'is'.
3   For the full title of this work, see Letter 524, n. 2.
4   For Frend's unsuccessful appeal to the court of delegates against his sentence of banishment from Cambridge, see Frend, *An account of the proceedings in the University of Cambridge, against William Frend, M.A.*, pp. 191–248.
5   The first number of the *Cambridge Intelligencer*, published by Benjamin Flower, appeared on 20 July 1793. It was a weekly newspaper, published on Saturdays, and ran until 1803. The Cambridge newspaper to which Lindsey referred in such derogatory terms was the *Cambridge Chronicle*, to which the *Intelligencer* became a radical rival.
6   For the full title of Benjamin Flower's work on the French constitution, see Letter 458, n. 5.
7   Theophilus Houlbrooke had been an undergraduate at St John's College, Cambridge, in the 1760s.
8   John Lee died at Staindrop, on the day on which Lindsey wrote this letter, 5 Aug. 1793. Priestley's friendship with Lee dated from the late 1760s, when Priestley was minister of Mill Hill chapel, Leeds.
9   For Richard Chandler, see Letter 516, n. 4. The mayor of Gloucester in 1793 was Thomas Mee; there is not much surviving evidence about his family. Russell's house was Wotton Hall (see Letter 534, n. 4).
10   John Pitt (*c.* 1727–1805), of Palace Yard, Gloucester, was MP for Gloucester from 1789 to 1805, and usually supported the ministry of his namesake.

536. To WILLIAM TURNER OF NEWCASTLE   9 SEPTEMBER 1793

Text:	DWL, MS 12.44 (56).
Printed:	Belsham, *Memoirs*, p. 232 n. * (most of second paragraph); McLachlan, *Letters*, p. 15 (part of second sentence of eleventh paragraph); pp. 89–90 (seventh paragraph); p. 94 (fifth paragraph).
Addressed:	To/The Rev^d. Mr Turner/Newcastle/upon Tyne
Endorsed:	Sep^t: 9: 1793
Postmarked:	RICHMOND [date of postmark illegible]

Note: Belsham identified the recipient of this letter as 'another friend'. The evidence of the manuscript establishes beyond doubt that the recipient was William Turner of Newcastle.

Richmond. Sept[r]. 9. 1793

Dear Sir,

I am happy in receiving your kind letter sent to Essex Street by M[r] Rankin,[1] before we leave the north, and thank you for the kind expressions contained in it. It is a boon and mercy for which we can never be enough thankful, if we have been made instruments of good to our fellow creatures in any degree.

I shall still however be glad to receive any communications from you, and hope to be more punctual in attending to them, as we shall continue to live in the house in Essex-Street. For the Trustees of the Chapel would not appoint a Successor but under the limitation of my enjoying the house &c for life, as was appointed in the original Trust-Deed for my wife, if I had died the minister and she had survived me. This was thought reasonable, as by collections from our friends, with no small sum of our own, we had purchased, built and furnished the Premisses.[2]

I find by a letter from D[r] Priestley, that his answer to M[r] Evanson's Dissonance &c is printed off; which I am persuaded will be an useful work, and hope it will be acceptable and meet with a large vent, and the shocking prejudices against the worthy author be diminished by seeing him not discouraged by the treatment he has received, from standing forth in the comon cause of all christians, churchmen as well as others.[3]

We may expect much also from a reply to this work by M[r] Martin, who succeded M[r] Morris at Yarmouth in Norfolk about a year ago, a very young man, M[r] Belsham's pupil, but very ingenious and laborious. The Manuscript is finished, and I am told will be put to the Press immediately.[4]

Many judicious persons and some of no small note in this neighbourhood, highly disapprove the adjudication against M[r] Muir. It would have been illegal and not to be borne in England, as his offence could not be construed into any thing more than a breach of the peace; and it is hoped the same law and equity may reach beyond the Tweed.[5]

Our old acquaintance has certainly been indiscreet, as he owns in a letter which I received lately from him: but I hope his benevolent upright views will plead and influence in his favour.[6]

One is grieved that the war is likely to continue, as: it will prevent the nation from cooling and returning to a better temper in laying the unavoidable evils and burdens that must result from it at the door of Dissenters of all sorts, instead of attending to the true cause of all our miseries.

We came into the north some days before the exit but too lately to see our wise and most valuable friend at Staindrop,[7] who was much concerned at the present train of public affairs. To us his [friends], who had the pleasure of being frequently with him, his loss can never be repaired. It was a satisfaction to us a fortnight ago, on a visit to M[rs] Lee, to find her and her amiable daughter yielding to all those consolations which the gospel suggests in situations like theirs. The short character of the deceased, put into the Morning Chronicle at the time, was from his old friend D[r] Priestley.[8] I hear that he bears well [MS torn] [s]eparation from his sons, who are [MS torn – c. 3 words missing] gone to America: but am [MS torn – c.2 words missing] [M[rs]] Priestley appears rather [MS torn – c.3 words missing] is not at first to be wondered at.[9]

I [?should] be much beholden to you for [the] patriot baker's defence of himself, when it comes out.[10]

I must not forget to tell you, that our common friends, the most worthy family of the Shores, have contributed much to our happiness since we came into the north. From Richmond we paid them a visit of 8 days at Coatham by the sea side, where I had an opportunity of riding on the sands and ab^t. ye country every day, as they had no less than 13 horses with them, and was much refreshed by it.[11] They have also been to see this beautiful place. And to morrow we call upon them at Harrogate in our way into the south: but as we have other calls to make, it is likely to be the end of the month before we arrive at our own house.

My wife joins in all kind regards for yourself and Mrs Turner and good wishes for your little folks, especially the present invalid.[12] Mr Shore mention^d the state of your good father:[13] but that he was easy and happy. I am always

Dear Sir, your obliged and affectionate serv^t

T. Lindsey.

1   Probably Lindsey referred here to the sugar refiner Robert Rankin of Newcastle, a member of Turner's Hanover Square congregation; see Harbottle, *William Turner*, pp. 46, 95, 125. His daughter Elizabeth married Thomas Martineau; they were the parents of James and Harriet Martineau. It is also possible Lindsey referred to one of Robert Rankin's two sons, John Cole Rankin (b. 1768) or Robert Rankin (b. 1769); see Tyne and Wear Archives, Hanover Square baptismal record (TNA: PRO/RG4/1777), fo. 36v. Both sons were members of the Literary and Philosophical Society of Newcastle from its foundation in 1793.

2   See Letter 528 and Vol. I, appendix I.

3   This work was Priestley's *Letters to a young man, Part II. Occasioned by Mr Evanson's treatise on the dissonance of the four generally-received evangelists* (London, 1793).

4   Thomas Martin succeeded Michael Maurice as co-minister (with John Matthew Beynon) of the Middlegate Street congregation, Yarmouth, in 1792 and remained there in that capacity until 1797. According to Evans, *Vestiges*, pp. 87, 261, he was at the same time minister of Filby chapel, Norfolk, where, as at Yarmouth, his predecessor was Michael Maurice. He was almost certainly the Thomas Martin, who entered Hackney College as a student in Sept. 1787, where he was Belsham's pupil and served as college librarian; see DWL, MS 38.14, fo. 29, and Birm. MS 281, fo. 123. He was listed as 'Hackney Student N° 1', the beneficiary of £3 from the Lady Hewley fund in 1790, 1791 and 1792; NYRO, ZTP VIII/4 (account book 1761–1809). I have not been able to trace a reply by him to Evanson's *Dissonance*. For a further note on Martin, see Letter 663, n. 6.

5   Thomas Muir was arrested on his return to Scotland (via Ireland) from France, in July 1793. His trial before the Scottish high court of justiciary took place at Edinburgh on 30–1 Aug., when he was convicted of sedition and sentenced to transportation for fourteen years. Lindsey and others believed that under the greater flexibility of the English law of sedition, Muir's 'offence' of circulating reformist literature, including the *Rights of man*, would have led to his acquittal, or to a relatively mild sentence for seditious libel. See Christina Bewley, *Muir of Huntershill. A Scottish patriot's adventures around the world* (Oxford, 1981), pp. 82–4.

6   Probably 'our old acquaintance' was Thomas Fyshe Palmer, whom Turner knew, since Palmer had briefly taken charge of a Unitarian Society at Newcastle upon Tyne in 1789 and had preached there during visits from Dundee; see *MR*, VI (1811), 136. This letter from Palmer to Lindsey, presumably written from Edinburgh where he was bailed prior to his trial, when began on 12 Sept. 1793, seems not to have survived.

7   John Lee.

8   This short obituary of Lee was published, without Priestley's name, in the *Morning Chronicle*, 10 Aug. 1793. It concluded by stating that Lee was 'among the first supporters of Mr. Lindsey's chapel in Essex-street'.

9   The manuscript is slightly torn at this point.

10 This work was a nineteen-page pamphlet, price 6*d*, entitled *An account of the trial of Alexander Whyte, baker, for a false, malicious, and seditious libel; of which charge he was honourably acquitted, at the quarter sessions, held for the town and county of Newcastle upon Tyne, on Wednesday, July 17, 1793. Published by the defendant, for the benefit of his family; who have suffered much during his long confinement* (Newcastle, n.d., ?1793). Whyte complained that he had been arrested on a charge that he had published a paper containing seditious material. He denied the charge, but since he was unable to find the necessary sureties, he was imprisoned for five months, until freed on his acquittal in 17 July 1793. He claimed (p. 19) that his family and his trade had been ruined by his imprisonment.

Whyte's trial is noticed briefly in Mackenzie, *A descriptive and historical account of the town and county of Newcastle upon Tyne*, p. 83.

11 Coatham, near Redcar, on the north Yorkshire coast, was a seaside resort, regularly frequented by the Shore family of Norton Hall.

12 Lindsey did not identify 'the present invalid'; possibly he or she was one of the children of Turner and his first wife Mary (née Holland). By Sept. 1793 they had four sons and a daughter.

13 William Turner of Wakefield.

537. To WILLIAM ALEXANDER　　　　　　　　21 OCTOBER 1793

Text:　　　　　'Letters of the Rev. Theophilus Lindsey. No. IV',
　　　　　　　　UH, II, 71 (6 Sept. 1862), 304.

Note: This is the only section of this letter printed by the *UH*; the manuscript seems not to have survived. The ellipsis at the beginning of the section of the letter printed by the *UH* indicates that this was not the beginning of the original letter.

London, Oct. 21, 1793

* * At the expiration of our long tour we were highly gratified in finding Dr. Priestley in the most perfect health, and with that tranquillity of mind which belongs only to such virtue and benevolence as mark his character, and is a sure test of heaven's favourable regards. As I am now a little more at liberty, we spent one Sunday with him since our return, when I was much edified by a discourse on "He that hath this hope in him purifieth himself, even as he is pure".[1] The papers have sent, and are continually sending him to America, whilst he is pursuing his studies and philosophical pursuits as if there was no such country. But now that his sons have all been almost forced to seek another country, what he may do hereafter, if they should be happily settled, no one may say.[2]

1 'And every man that hath this hope in him purifieth himself, even as he is pure' (I John iii. 3). This was the text of 'Discourse I, The importance of religion to enlarge the mind of man' in Priestley's *Discourses relating to the evidences of revealed religion. Vol. I.*

2 William Priestley arrived at Philadelphia in the summer of 1793; Joseph junior and Henry Priestley left England for America in Aug. 1793 and arrived at New York the following month.

538. To ROBERT MILLAR　　　　　　　　16 NOVEMBER 1793

Text:　　　　　DWL, MS 12.46 (1).
Printed:　　　Graham, 'Unhappy country', 127–8 (first four paragraphs and the postscript).
Addressed:　To/M^r. R. Miller [*sic*],/merchant/Dundee/North Britain
Endorsed:　[Not in Lindsey's hand] London Novr. 16. 93/T Lindsey/About M^r. Palmer. north B
Postmarked: No 16 93

Essex-Street-Strand.
London. Novr. 16
1793

Dear Sir,

About three weeks since, or not quite so much I received a very friendly and affecting letter from our most valuable suffering friend Mr Palmer, in consequence of which I wrote to him, and sent him a few books which he wished for to alleviate his solitude, and a letter, in which I mention that myself and I was persuaded that others would be glad to send any pecuniary helps if wanted.[1]

To this I have rec^d no answer; but yesterday I had a letter from a friend in the country, acquainting me that he had heard that there were orders for our friend to be ready to depart the country at a moment's warning.[2]

If this be so, you cannot fail to know it, and I will beg the favour of you to convey to him twenty pounds which is sent him for his kind acceptance by two of his friends, and the sum shall be repaid you immediately on your giving me notice of it, either by the post, in a Bank Post Bill, or to any correspondent of yours in London.[3]

I confess that I have some hope my friend's information is premature, as I was lately told that not only Mr Palmers but Mr Muirs sentence would be mitigated, as over-proportioned to their respective offences.[4]

I am a letter in your debt, my much-esteemed friend, which came to me whilst [we] were in the North, and I have never been intirely settled in London, till this very week that I am writing, or I should have acknowleged it.[5] You mentioned your intention of visiting Perth, which I hope you was able to accomplish, and should be glad to know the situation in which you found every thing[.]

I am sure you will excuse this trouble and my constrained brevity at present: in my next I shall write more at length. My wife did not reap so much benefit for health from our northern journey as myself. We hope, with our joint respects that Mrs Miller and yourself are well as we wish You.[6] I remain always Your obliged friend & servant

T. Lindsey.

P.S. Since writing the foregoing, the post is come in, and has brought me a letter from Mr Palmer himself, about a matter relating to his fellowship.[7] I find with concern that he had not rec^d the books I sent him by Johnson – wch I shall go to inquire after. But I must beg the favour of you at all events to transmit to him the twenty pounds by a safe hand, and to let me know at the same time, that there may be no delay in returning the money to You.

---

1   This letter from Palmer to Lindsey, written, it must be presumed, from the Perth Tolbooth, where he was detained before being transferred to the hulks in the Thames, seems not to have survived.

2   Possibly this friend in the country was William Turner of Newcastle, who was acquainted with Palmer following the latter's brief period as a unitarian minister at Newcastle in 1789. Palmer and Muir were taken by ship from the Leith roads to the hulks in the Thames on 22 Nov. 1793.

3   Although Lindsey did not identify these two generous friends (probably in London) of Palmer, possibilities include Joseph Johnson, Samuel Heywood and Lindsey himself. Perhaps Lindsey solicited small contributions from his own friends. Bank post bills, introduced in 1728, served as post-dated cheques (usually payable after seven days) and were designed to thwart highway robbery of the mail coaches, since they could not be cashed as easily as bank notes.

4   On 31 Aug. 1793, Muir was sentenced to fourteen years' transportation. In Sept. 1793, Palmer was sentenced to seven years' transportation. The sentences were not mitigated.

5   This letter from Millar to Lindsey is not among Millar's papers at DWL and appears not to have survived.

6   In 1790, Millar married Jean Scott (1743–1801), the daughter of Daniel Scott (d. 1773), minister of Auchterhouse, near Dundee; see *The Christian Pioneer*, NS, VII (1841), 377, and *Fasti Ecclesiæ Scoticanæ*, V, 310. On 27 Nov. 1789 Thomas Fyshe Palmer wrote to congratulate Millar on this forthcoming marriage to Jean Scott, adding 'I do confess I did not think you capable of it'; DWL, MS 12.46 (91).

7   Palmer was a fellow of Queens' College, Cambridge, from 1771 until Jan. 1794, when he was expelled from the college after his conviction for sedition. Palmer's letter to Lindsey seems not to have survived.

539. To WILLIAM TAYLEUR   **2 DECEMBER 1793**

Text:	JRUL, Lindsey Letters, vol. II, no. 75.
Printed:	McLachlan, *Letters*, p. 90 (last five sentences of second paragraph); p. 94 (first four sentences of second paragraph).
Addressed:	To/William Tayleur Esqr/Shrewsbury
Endorsed:	Dec^r – 2^d – 93
Postmarked:	DE 2 93

London. Decr. 2. 1793

Dear Sir,

I beg you will tell Mr Rowe, with my best respects to him and his lady, that his last favour which I rec^d ab^t 10 days since was most acceptable in bringing us the good news of yourself and of the animal machine being in a more comfortable frame than it had been for some time past, which I hope will continue and carry you through the approaching winter, which some people prophesy will be very severe, notwithstanding the contrary appearances so far onwards to it. I was also much gratified, as were several of our common friends, with his testimony to Mr Aikin's good qualities and promising ministerial abilities, and his account and character of the person who is to succeed Mr Bretland at the Mint.[1] There is a good prospect of the cause of truth being well supported in the west, if only a proper person can be found for the chapel at Plymouth Dock: for I fear, as Mr Kentish's mother is dead, that his father will the more insist upon his coming to reside with him at St Albans.[2] Unfortunately, it is not only a person with good dispositions, principles and talents that is wanted, but he must also be one that can afford to live upon little, as the chapel by no means supplies[3] a sufficiency at present to maintain a minister.

This day week I had a letter from Perth, dated November 20. from one that belonged to Mr Palmer,[4] that he had that morning been carried away from the prison, at four o clock, without previous notice or time to prepare any thing, by a party [of] dragoons in a Post-chaise, to be put into a Cutter in Leith-road; all this alarm, as if he were a dangerous person, and there was fear of his [being] rescued in the day-time. What has since become of him, I have been inquiring, but have heard nothing. He had expected his sentence to be mitigated.[5] This does not look like it. Some late adjudications in our courts, particularly that of Mr Winterbottom, have shocked many indifferent persons as most enormously severe.[6] There is no doubt of the Lawyers veering about and changing their tone and measures against such sort of offenders, if there was but a prospect of Mr Fox coming into power, who would certainly bring better principles with [him] and require them to be acted upon: But the day at present is distant. I presume you know, that there has lately been a sort of negociation of the Minister with the D. of Portland (as Mr Pitt must doubtless be tired of the war and wish others to take the load from his shoulders[)]: three Cabinet Ministers and patronage without end was offered, and without reserve, only Mr Fox was to be excluded, for that the king could not bear him. It did not go on however, as the Duke did not chuse to submit to this last condition. But as he and others of the Whig Lords are much under Mr Burkes direction, one can be surprized at nothing. They must have strange principles or a strange itch after places, not to stand aloof from a junction with the present men in power.[7]

We wonder that Dr Symondss second Part is not yet published, as all but the preface was printed, to my knowlege, six weeks ago.[8] I had great pleasure however in learning about a week since, from Faulder of Bond Street, Archdⁿ Paley's bookseller and printer, that ten sheets have been already struck off, and the remainder in great readiness, of another work, on the evidences of Christianity, a sort of sequel to his Horae Paulinae.[9] I hope it will please the divine Providence that there may be such a firm rational conviction in many of the truth[s] of divine revelation, and the Scriptures be so well understood, loved, valued and attended to, that shoud the day of tryal come, we may not fall into that forlorn, desolate, unprincipled State in which the French now unhappily are. If you have Whiston's Essay on the Revelation of St John, Ed. 2^d. 1744, I wish you would read a remark of Sr Isaac Newtons, introduced by him, p. 321.[10] I shewed it to Dr Priestley the other day, who was much taken with it, as very applicable to the times we live in. If you have not the book, and Mr Rowe will be so good as to tell me, it will be not trouble to me to transcribe the passage as it is really curious. Dr P. was very well on Thursday. had heard that the Pegou that carried his two sons &c was arrived safe in port.[11] My wife presents you with her kind respects. We hope that Mr Wood is well. I remain always, Dear Sir, Your truly obliged & faithful affectionate servant

          T. Lindsey.

---

1   Arthur Aikin was briefly assistant minister to John Rowe at Shrewsbury between 1793 and 1795. The successor to Joseph Bretland at the Mint meeting, Exeter, was Theophilus Edwards (1750–1833), who served there from 1794 to 1810.

2   The mother of John Kentish, Hannah, née Vanderplank, died at Bath in 1793. Kentish was born in 1768 at St Albans, where his father, also named John Kentish, ran a drapery business; his family also had brewing and landowning connexions. In the event, the younger John Kentish did not move back to St Albans and remained at Plymouth, where he was minister at the newly opened Dock chapel.

3   Lindsey originally wrote 'affords', but over-wrote 'supplies'.

4   Probably Robert Millar, a member of Palmer's congregation at Perth, was the writer of this letter. It seems not to have survived.

5   Palmer's sentence, indeed, was not mitigated.

6   The baptist minister William Winterbotham (1763–1829) was tried on a change of sedition at Exeter assizes on 25–6 July 1793, after making observations sympathetic to the French revolution in his preaching. He was convicted and on 27 Nov. 1793 sentenced to imprisonment for two years and a fine of £200. He spent most of his imprisonment in Newgate.

7   In late Nov. and early Dec. 1792, the divisions in the whig opposition became more pronounced, as the aristocratic leadership, notably the duke of Portland and Earl Fitzwilliam, took alarm at the French decision to open the river Scheldt and to offer assistance to all oppressed people. They gave some support to the proclamation for the embodiment of the militia on 1 Dec. and to the Aliens bill. Fox and his friends, by contrast, strongly opposed both measures. Pitt sought to exploit these divisions and in Jan. 1793 persuaded the party's legal authority Lord Loughborough to accept the office of lord chancellor. Although Portland's followers did not join Pitt's ministry in a formal coalition until July 1794, they were beginning to move in that direction by the end of 1792. See David Wilkinson, *The duke of Portland. Politics and party in the age of George III* (Basingstoke, 2003), pp. 91–9.

8   Probably this was Symonds, *Observations upon the expediency of revising the present English version of the epistles in the New Testament*, which was published in Cambridge early in 1794. For the first part of this work, see Letter 385, n. 1. The work to which Symonds replied was *Apology for the liturgy and clergy of the Church of England*, of which Samuel Horsley was probably the author or co-author (possibly in collaboration with Samuel Hallifax, bishop of St Asaph until his death in 1790). This *Apology* was itself a reply to the duke of Grafton's *Hints* (see Letter 384). For the background to Horsley's likely involvement, see Mather, *High church prophet*, p. 84.

9   William Paley's *A view of the evidences of Christianity in three parts* was published in London by Robert Faulder, of 42 New Bond Street, in 1794, with a second edition in the same year. His *Horæ Paulinæ, or the truth of the scripture history of St Paul evinced, by a comparison of the epistles which bear his name with the Acts of the Apostles, and with one another* was published in London, also by Robert Faulder, in 1790.

10   The relevant passage is 'Sir *Isaac Newton* had a very sagacious Conjecture, which he told Dr. *Clarke*, from whom I received it, that the overbearing Tyranny and persecuting Power of the Anti-Christian Party, which hath so long corrupted Christianity, and enslaved the Christian World, must be put a Stop

to, and broken to Pieces by the prevalence of Infidelity, for some time, before primitive Christianity could be restored; which seems to be the very Means that is now working in *Europe*, for the same good End of Providence.' As Lindsey noted, the source is William Whiston, *An essay on the Revelation of St. John, so far as concerns the past and present times* (2nd edn, London, 1744), p. 321.

11   The *Pegu* was indeed the ship which carried Joseph junior and Henry Priestley to America.

540. To JOSHUA TOULMIN   14 DECEMBER 1793

Text: Belsham, *Memoirs*, p. 233 n. *.

Note: The manuscript of this letter seems not to have survived; the only section of it which has survived is that printed by Belsham.

Mr. Muir and Mr. Palmer are on board the hulks with the felons, and many of my friends have been to see them. I also hear from Mr. Palmer, and have sent him some books.[1] Neither of them, I believe, is in want of anything, the place considered. But the situation is, upon the whole, horrible. Mr. Palmer, however, is most cheerful in the midst of it, and Mr. Muir not otherwise.

1   See Letter 538.

541. To JOSEPH CHADWICK   17 DECEMBER 1793

Text: DWL, MS 12.80, opp. p. 208.
Addressed: To/The Rev^d. Mr Chadwick/Oundle/Northamptonshire
Endorsed: [MS annotation] 'This is a genuine *autograph* of the late
                  excellent Mr L. whose character deserves to be held in the
                  highest regard' [followed by a brief eulogy of Lindsey];
                  alongside this annotation is the MS comment 'This Note is in
                  the Handwriting of Mr Chadwick'
Postmarked: DE 19 [postmark otherwise illegible]

London. Decr. 17. 1793
Dear Sir
I have at length put up for your obliging acceptance a few Tracts, which I hope will reach you in due time. They were booked at the Bear and Ragged Staff Smithfield on friday to go by the Oundle Waggon, which was to set out from thence the next day.[1]
I am almost afraid to ask after Mrs Chadwick's heath: but it will give us pleasure to hear it is not worse, as that may give hope that in time she may grow better.[2] My wife is far from well with her painful complaint, chiefly in her face. But as she is able to go about, and some days better, she says she has no right to complain.
They are continually sending Dr Priestley to AMERICA in the reports current about him. Yet he continues quietly in the midst of his philosophical pursuits and pastoral labours. But sh^d his three sons who are all now safely arrived in America gain good settlements, and there be an opening for him, wch I doubt not might easily be found, it will be natural for him to look thither.
I rec^d not many days since a letter from young Mr Toulmin, dated Winchester in Virginia, Oct. 28. He had not passed thro Philadelphia to avoid the infectious fever. But had met with many friends, and in one place in particular was much pressed, and tempted with a handsome salary to settle among them as an instructor of Youth.

But he could listen to nothing, till he had visited Kentucky, which had above all places been recommended to him, and which he was engaged to see and examine, on account of his Lancashire friends, who had in some measure deputed him to spy out the promised land for them, and advise them in what part of it they might settle with advantage and comfort.[3]

You see in the public newspapers the present state of things, and of our country and of other countries. But no where could you find it so faithfully and justly exhibited as in the Cambridge Intelligencer, if any in your neighbourhood takes in that admirable paper. The printer and chief conductor of it, is that excellent person, M[r] Benjamin Flower, whose private character and known writings are above all praise. Since my parcell was sent to you, there is a very valuable pamphlet come out w[ch] I could wish you to see, and if you could point out to me where the person is who sends down the monthly things to Oundle, I would take care that he should have this before the end of the month to send at the same time to you.[4]

It is to be hoped that as the present war has not yet promoted any of the ends proposed by it, but the contrary, viz. the antimonarchical power in France, which grows stronger and stronger the more it is opposed, that it will be an admonition to the Allied powers to withdraw and cease their attacks, and leave that people to settle their government for themselves. I shall hope for a few lines, tho' I have not much deserved them, when the parcell reaches you. With mine and my wifes kind regards and every wish of good for M[rs] Chadwick and yourself, I remain always, Dear Sir

very truly Yours,

T. Lindsey.

---

1   Lindsey probably referred to the Bear and Staff, Smithfield, which is listed as the starting point for the Oundle waggon (which departed each Saturday at 1.00 in the afternoon) in the *Universal British directory* (1791), I, 583.

2   For Mary Chadwick, see Letter 509, n. 7.

3   I have not located Henry Toulmin's letter to Lindsey from Winchester, Virginia. The commonwealth of Kentucky, having seceded from Virginia, was admitted to the union as the fifteenth state in 1792. For Toulmin's settlement, and public service, in Kentucky, see Letter 656, n. 2.

4   Lindsey did not identify this pamphlet, but a possibility is Wyvill's *A state of the representation of the people of England on the principles of Mr Pitt in 1785* (York, 1793); see Letter 545, n. 1.

542. To JOSHUA TOULMIN   10 JANUARY 1794

Text: Belsham, *Memoirs*, pp. 233 n. *, 241.

Note: The manuscript of this letter seems not to have survived. Belsham printed two extracts from it and they are presented here in the order in which he presented them, although it is not clear whether or not that was the order in the original manuscript. Belsham did not make it clear whether or not the two extracts were continuous in the manuscript; here the extracts are separated by a broken line.

Since I last wrote, opinions have varied about the destiny of Mr. Palmer and Mr. Muir, as the Scotch judges have, upon revisal, adhered to the sentences pronounced upon them.[1] Mr Palmer's health and spirits are most cheerful; Mr. Muir far from well in health since the cold weather set in; both of them supported by their integrity and future hopes. Some friends who visited the hulks on Wednesday had a commission from some others to offer a purse to Mr. Palmer and Mr. Muir. The former declined taking anything, but Mr. Muir thankfully accepted it.[2]

We have seen Dr. Priestley very frequently of late, as also Mrs Priestley, and they are both very well. If his sons do well in America, I have no doubt of his following them, but do not apprehend that he will remove thither at any time but upon some opening or prospect of being provided for, so as to be useful in his own way as a teacher of philosophy. He is now preaching at Hackney a course of lectures on the Evidences of the Mosaic and Christian Revelations, which he intends afterwards to print;[3] and which, from what I have seen of the former, will be most useful and highly seasonable at a period when many in this country, and the greater part upon the continent, count all revealed religion as a fable, which might be well intended at first, but has proved most destructive to the morals and happiness of mankind.

1   See Letter 538, n. 4. For the possibility that the sentences of Muir and Palmer might be remitted, see Bewley, *Muir of Huntershill*, pp. 87–8.
2   Belsham added (*Memoirs*, p. 233 n. *) 'Mr Palmer afterwards saw reason to alter his mind, and accepted the proffered kindness of his friends.'
3   They were published as *Discourses relating to the evidences of revealed religion. Vol. I.* This was a second edition of the edition cited in Letter 537, n. 1.

543. To JOSHUA TOULMIN   post-10 JANUARY 1794

    Text: Belsham, *Memoirs*, p. 233 n. *.

Note: Belsham printed only the section of this letter which is reproduced here. He did not explicitly state that Joshua Toulmin was the recipient, but the two previous extracts from Lindsey's letters from which Belsham quoted in *Memoirs*, p. 233 n.* were both addressed to Toulmin, and Belsham stated that this letter was addressed to 'his friend', implying that Toulmin was that friend. Belsham did not give a date for the letter except to note that it was 'subsequent' to that of 10 January 1794 (Letter 542). The words in square brackets are Belsham's.

[In a subsequent letter, Mr. Lindsey informs his friend that the amount of the contribution was between five and six hundred pounds, and that it was vested in the hands of a committee of seven for the benefit of Messrs. Palmer, Muir, Skirving, and even Margarot,] who, as a joint sufferer, was not to be overlooked, though his general character was not so high as the others.[1]

1   Belsham added (*Memoirs*, p. 233 n. *) 'How true this observation of Mr. Lindsey's was, and how justly this person was entitled to participate in the bounty of Mr. Palmer's friends, those who were witnesses to his conduct to that gentleman on board the transport in the passage to South Wales [*sic*] could properly appreciate.' Lindsey was presumably a member of this 'committee of seven', to which he made no other recorded reference. Belsham did not print the section of Lindsey's subsequent letter which quoted a sum of between £500 and £600; possibly it was part of Lindsey's letters to Joshua Toulmin of 8 Feb. 1794 (Letter 550), or 20 Feb. 1794 (Letter 551) or 8 Mar. 1794 (Letter 552). For Margarot's reputation, see Bewley, *Muir of Huntershill*, p. 106.

544. To ROBERT MILLAR   **13 JANUARY 1794**

Text: DWL, MS 12.46 (2).
Printed: Graham, 'Unhappy country', 129–30 (first paragraph; most of
              second paragraph; sixth and ninth paragraphs).
Addressed: Address missing.
Postmarked: Postmark missing.

London. Jany. 13. 1794
Dear Sir,

I thank you for your friendly welcome epistle, which came in it's due time a few days ago, and to morrow I expect by a friend to communicate its contents to Mr Palmer. In the morning chronicle of the 11th. inst. it was said, that the king in council had signed the warrants for his and Mr Muir's transportation to Botany Bay: but I am told, and wish it may be so, that it does not follow that they will be immediately sent away, and in delay there is hope.[1]

Three days since a particular friend[2] paid a visit to both the Prisoners. Mr Palmer is ever chearful, his health firm. Mr Muir was ill in bed in a cold and fever, but would get up to see his visitors. His mind is always calm and firm, tho the bodily case will not allow him to shew such spirits. Money was pressed upon Mr Palmer, but he declined taking any, saying that he had sufficient at present. But Mr Muir accepted what was offerd. These private particulars will not go beyond the circle of your family and friends.

One is much concerned that your wise and candid endeavours to bring about an union with your brethren of the Arian persuasion have not succeeded. But you have done your duty, and I am glad to see that, as you ought, you console yourself with this, and wait in patience for a happier turn of things, come it or not in your time. I do not see how you could have acted in a more christian manner.

I rejoice that you keep up your own religious Society, and trust that no ill health or any sinister accident will prevent your progress, and that your old pastor,[3] if banished, at his return, will be made happy by seeing it. Should he contrary to expectation go at last to Botany Bay, we may not doubt of God's sending him, and that he will be an instrument of much good to that country, both he and Mr Muir, for by all report this last named worthy master[?], whose address to the Jury fills one with admiration of his virtue and integrity, is actuated by a true religious principle, and regards to a future immortal life, brought to light by Jesus Christ.[4]

That infidelity increases among you is no matter of surprize. Your great and rich and many of the learned are said to lean that way, and not a few openly to declare it. But it is the natural consequence of their prejudices, and early secular habits, and total want of proper inquiry.

Dr Priestley is now preaching to his congregation at Hackney a series of Discourses on the evidences for the Mosaic and Christian Revelations. I have seen many of them in M.S. and he intends to print them imediately, and I shall take care you have a copy.[5]

But in the mean time, till You receive these discourses of his, which are admirable, I should be glad to send you a few [of] our Unitarian Society Tracts, and especially Dr Hartley *Of the Truth of the Christian Religion*, which I have recomended to be adopted by the Society, and am now correcting the press for it. In less than a month's time it will be ready and you will do me a favour by accepting some copies to disperse. I do not know a Tract, of the size, or indeed of any size, which holds forth such a mass of evidence for the genuineness of the Scriptures of the Old and New Testament and for the truth of the facts, natural and miraculous contained in them. It is of such weight, that I should think no fair mind can resist it.[6] I shoud be glad when I next hear from you to be acquainted by what conveyance a parcell may be conveyed to you in the safest and cheapest way.

Your account and amiable character of your partner and fellow traveller in this life and towards a better affects much both myself and my wife, and we wish you increasing comforts on the journey from the glorious prospects at the end of it, and desire to be kindly remembered to her as well as yourself.[7]

But I must not forget to tell You, that a few days past Mr Palmer sent a verbal message to me by a friend, desiring I woud give my approbation to the printing of the Address of your congregation to him. To this I consented as I had that very day rec'd your last letter, and I apprehend it will soon make its appearance in the morning chronicle. I am persuaded it will do no discredit but the contrary to your *religious* Society, as there is nothing political in it, and it may be of service to Mr Palmer and soften the minds of his adversaries towards him, to read the character of a truly christian pastor which is given him by those who had no idea of its being made public.[8]

I shall be glad at y^r leisure to have a few lines by the conveyance specified in my last,[9] and now the members are coming to town, at this most interesting period, I shall easily find signatures to convey my letters to You.[10] With prayers for your success in the gospel, I remain ever Dear Sir, most truly Y^rs   T. Lindsey

---

1 'On Wednesday [i.e. 8 Jan.] the King in Council signed an order for the transportation of Messrs. Muir and Palmer, to Botany Bay, for the terms specified in their respective sentences', *Morning Chronicle*, 11 Jan. 1794.

2 Probably Thomas Belsham or John Disney. There are lists of visitors to Muir when the latter was in Newgate prison between 16 Jan. and Feb. 1794 in TNA: TS 11/954.

3 Thomas Palmer.

4 Lindsey might have consulted Muir's address to the jury in the published account of his trial. The title was *The trial of Thomas Muir, Esq., younger, of Huntershill: before the high court of justiciary, upon Friday and Saturday the 30th and 31st days of August 1793, on a charge of sedition* (Edinburgh, 1793, with several subsequent editions in Edinburgh and London, and an edition in New York in 1794). For Muir's address to the jury, see pp. 73–131. Muir's trial, together with his address, was reported in several London newspapers, including the *Morning Chronicle* and the *Gazetteer and New Daily Advertiser*, on 4 Sept. 1793. See also *State trials*, XXIII, 117–238. For the background, see Bewley, *Muir of Huntershill*, ch. 6, with quotations from Muir's address, pp. 77–9.

5 Priestley's *Discourses relating to the evidences of revealed religion. Vol. I*, with a dedication to Thomas Belsham, were published by Joseph Johnson in London in 1794.

6 At the monthly meeting of the Unitarian Society on 14 Feb. 1793, it was resolved that 'the chapter of Dr Hartley's Observations on man, which treats of the truth of the Christian religion' be received into the society's catalogue and 1,000 copies be printed; Unitarian Society minute book, p. 41. See Letter 547, n. 2.

7 Millar's 'partner and fellow traveller in this life' was his wife, Jean, née Scott; see Letter 538, n. 6.

8 This address was published in the *Morning Chronicle*, 13 Jan. 1794; see Letter 548, n. 2.

9 The method of conveyance specified in Lindsey's previous surviving letter, namely that of 16 Nov. 1793 (Letter 538), was the post, or via any correspondent of Millar in London.

10 The new session of parliament opened on 21 Jan. 1794.

545. To CHRISTOPHER WYVILL　　　　　16 JANUARY 1794

Text:　　　　NYRO, ZFW 7/2/85/8, Wyvill of Constable Burton MSS.
Printed:　　Ditchfield, 'Lindsey–Wyvill correspondence', 163
　　　　　　　(first paragraph).
Addressed:　To/The Revd Christopher Wyvill/Burton Hall/near Bedale/
　　　　　　　Yorkshire
Endorsed:　From the Revd Mr Lindsey Jan. 16. 1794
Postmarked: JA 16 94

London. Jany. 16. 1794

Dear Sir,

It is high time for me to return thanks for your well-weighed and noble attempt to serve I may add save the public at this important juncture. In the opinion of far abler judges than myself, your plan comes out very greatly improved, and fitted quietly to work the desired effectual Reform in the popular Representation, slowly but surely, in putting an end to the venal Burghs, and in easy and most practicable regulations to prevent tumult and delay as well as expence in elections. It is so very feasible, that it might be adopted to day, or to morrow, or at any moment, without just offence or disturbance.[1]

The exhibition also made of Mr A. Young in the appendix, is calculated to make his patrons blush, and apprize others of the profligacy of his political principles.[2]

This however had been done as it were to your hand in a very valuable pamphlet just at the time that yours appeared, which I rejoice to find much read, though had it been contrived to be less bulky, it would have had a much more diffusive circulation; I need not perhaps say that the Title of it is "Peace and Reform against War and Corruption."[3]

I have not been inattentive to the circulation of another valuable piece, which I need not name.[4]

Most happy will it be, if these various efforts have their effect on the nation and our Governors. Never perhaps was a more interesting period than the approaching session of Parliament that we are entering upon. If the War *must* be carried on another year as a very eminent merchant told me yesterday, as being his own opinion, and the determination of the Ministry, I fear the consequences. There was a report that the D. of Portland was to make a motion for a general Pacification, but to day I am told quite the contrary.[5] In short one can trust no reports, but must wait the event which now will soon come.

We hope you take care of your health, particularly in cloathing well. You cannot take too much care both for your family's sake and the Public's. Our joint respects wait upon Mrs Wyvill and yourself, with all good wishes of all seasons and of many many years to come for yourselves and your amiable little flock.

I am always with great esteem,
　　　　　Your much obliged faithful servant
　　　　　　　T. Lindsey.

1　This was Wyvill's *A state of the representation of the people of England on the principles of Mr Pitt in 1785* (York, 1793). A second and a third edition appeared in 1794.

2　In *A state of the representation*, Wyvill took issue with the pamphlet *The example of France a warning to Britain* (Bury St Edmunds, 1793) by the agricultural commentator Arthur Young. He accused Young of taking an alarmist view of the French Revolution, of misrepresenting Wyvill's opinion, and of denying that the house of commons should represent the will of the people; *State of the representation*, pp. 17, 23, 45. In the 'appendix', pp. 51–5, Wyvill provided a series of quotations from Young's *The example of France* in order to hold up to public scrutiny the views which he was attacking.

3   This work was Daniel Stuart, *Peace and reform, against war and corruption. In answer to a pamphlet. Written by Arthur Young, Esq. entitled, 'The example of France. A warning to Britain'* (London, 1794). There was a second edition in 1794 and a fourth edition in 1795. Stuart (1766–1846) was the printer, and from 1795 the owner, of the *Morning Post*. He was deputy secretary to the Society of the Friends of the People, a meeting of which on 15 Mar. 1794 voted its thanks to him for this pamphlet.
4   Possibly this other 'valuable piece' was Priestley's *Discourses*; see Letter 544, n. 5.
5   Portland did not make any such motion in the house of lords; he and many of his party were in the process of moving closer towards Pitt's ministry. The *Morning Chronicle* of 16 Jan. 1794, the date on which Lindsey wrote this letter, carried a hint that moves for peace were unlikely to be forthcoming.

546. To WILLIAM ALEXANDER   20 JANUARY 1794

>   **Text:**   'Letters of the Rev. Theophilus Lindsey. No. V', *UH*, II, 73
>   (20 Sept.1862), 320.

Note: This is the only section of this letter printed by the *UH*; the manuscript seems not to have survived. The ellipsis at the beginning of the extract printed by the *UH* indicates that this was not the beginning of the original letter. The ellipsis at the end of the first paragraph indicates that the second paragraph did not immediately follow the first in the original letter. Accordingly, the two paragraphs are presented here separated by a broken line.

London, Jan. 20, 1794.

* * Dr. Priestley's letter, &c., which animadverts on the "Dissonance", is a solid confutation of what the author has advanced against three of the Gospels, though the writer has not attended to every minute objection.[1] You will in a short time receive a letter from the secretary of our society[2] to make choice of your allotment of books for the present year. To one of the books I would point your choice, which I am now correcting in the press, and recommended its adoption, "Hartley on the Truth of the Christian Religion", which, in the shortest compass, contains a mass of evidence for the genuineness of the books of the Old and New Testament, and also the truth of the facts contained in them, which no fair, unprejudiced man can resist.[3] Had Mr. Evanson considered many things alleged by this great author in a general way, I think he would have hesitated in many of his assertions, and I think this work will contribute not a little to quiet your mind. * *

I have taken in the *Cambridge Intelligencer*[*4] ever since it came out. The editor is the worthiest of men, and together with the best and earliest intelligence, gives the most useful and seasonable instruction. It is calculated to oppose the calumnies and misrepresentations which are industriously held forth by the greater part of newspapers. I wish to make you and other worthy friends about you a present of it; but as it would mark you too much to have it sent to you, I should be glad to know if you have any friend in your village to whom it might be directed, or whether, if the worthy Mr. Toms gives me leave to send it to him, he could conveniently convey it to you after perusal.[5] The period in which we live is so interesting and big with important events, that it must not only give satisfaction but be of moral use to every thinking mind to be acquainted with them.

1   This work was Priestley's *Letters to a young man, Part II*. See Letter 536, n. 3.
2   Although Thomas Jervis resigned as secretary at the monthly meeting of the Unitarian Society on 9 Jan. 1794, he seems to have continued in that capacity for several months thereafter, and it was to

him that Lindsey referred in this letter. On 14 Jan. 1796, John Kentish was formally appointed as secretary; Unitarian Society minute book, pp. 46, 56.

3   See Letter 544, n. 6.

4   The *UH* has the following note marked * at this point: 'Edited by Mr. Benjamin Flower, by whom, as Mr. W.J. Fox says, "it was raised to a rank and vested with an influence to which scarcely any other provincial journal has ever attained".' William Johnson Fox (1786–1864), unitarian minister and editor of the *MR* from 1827 to 1836, wrote these words in his *Public principle essential to the excellence of private character: a sermon on occasion of the death of Mr. B. Flower* (London, 1829), p. 11. The *Cambridge Intelligencer* first came out on 20 July 1793.

5   Samuel Say Toms (d. 1834) was a former pupil at the Daventry Academy and minister to a dissenting congregation at Framlingham, Suffolk, from 1773 until his retirement in 1829. He had befriended William Alexander when the latter opened his school at Yoxford in 1789; see the obituary of Toms, to which Alexander contributed, in *CR*, NS, I (1834), 816–20.

547. To RUSSELL SCOTT   24 JANUARY 1794

Text: Scott Coll.
Printed: McLachlan, 'Lindsey to Scott', 119 (first two sentences of fifth paragraph).
Addressed: Address missing.
Endorsed: [In pencil] Jan 24ᵗʰ 1794
Postmarked: Postmark missing.

Dear Sir,

I was careful to fulfill your commission in disposing of the two guineas you sent for Mʳ Carter and another person, whose name will be properly put in the new list of subscribers which is printing.[1]

The reason of delaying in the dispersion of this list and the allotments to the members has been our waiting for the finishing of a tract in the press, which is one of our new adopted books, Dʳ Hartley on the truth of yᵉ Xᵗ Religion.[2]

I shall be glad to send You Mʳ Jones's the Farewel Epistles of the Welsh Freeholder to Bᵖ Horsley on his circular letter,[3] when opportunity offers and also Dʳ Symonds Second Part, in the preface of which he chastises that and another prelate, not a little severely, though without naming them.[4]

I am sorry you were prevented writing more at length by so anxious a pain as the tooth ach, and when you write again like to have a better account of You all. I am forced to be shorter than I intended, because my frank is for to day, and I was out last night till a late hour, when I had intended to have written.

You will be sorry with us, that war is decreed. But a member told me last night, that never did he observe so heartless a vote given to any measure; and he was sure many woud have said otherwise had they been their own Masters. Very few *hear hims* for the Minister, though Mʳ Burke and others endeavoured to lead the way.[5]

My wife has been very ill since I last wrote, and sufferd extremely – but is now somewhat better and goes out. I thank God, I remain wonderfully well. Our kind regards attend Mʳˢ Scott and yourself and best wishes for you and your young folks. Ever most truly Yours

                    T. Lindsey

1   This is a reference to the subscription of John Carter, Esq., of Wimering, near Portsmouth, to the Unitarian Society. His name duly appeared in the list of subscribers to the society appended to *Unitarian Society ... 1794*, p. 10. The minimum annual subscription to the society was one guinea.

2   See Letter 544, n. 6. *Of the truth of the Christian religion. From 'Observations on man', &x. Part II.*

    By David Hartley, MA was published in London in early 1794 (although with a 1793 date of publication). It bore no publisher's name and no mention of the Unitarian Society. However, it is one of the three works which comprise *Tracts. Printed and published by the Unitarian Society for Promoting Christian Knowledge and the Practice of Virtue*, vol. VIII (London, 1793).

3   David Jones, *The Welsh freeholder's farewell epistles to the Right Rev. Samuel Lord Bishop ... of Rochester; in which the unitarian dissenters, and the dissenters in general, are vindicated from charges advanced against them in his lordship's circular letter, on the case of the emigrant French clergy* (London, 1794).

4   The preface to John Symonds, *Observations upon the expediency of revising the present English version of the epistles in the New Testament*, responded in detail (pp. i-xxxii) to the *Apology for the liturgy and clergy of the Church of England*, which was possibly the work of Samuel Horsley and Samuel Hallifax (see Letter 539 n. 8). Symonds noted that the *Apology* was 'considered by many as the joint production of two prelates' and deplored its 'coarse and illiberal' tone (p. ii).

5   The debate in the house of commons to which Lindsey referred was that on 21 Jan. 1794 on the address of thanks for the king's speech. An opposition amendment to the address, moved by Fox and urging peace with France at the earliest and most prudential opportunity, was defeated by 277 votes to 59, and the motion for the address was then carried without a division; see *St James's Chronicle*, 21–3 Jan. 1794, and Cobbett, *Parl. hist.*, XXX, 1088–287. The opposition-supporting *Morning Chronicle*, 24 Jan. 1794, reported that 'On no occasion since the two or three last days of the ministry of Lord NORTH, in the year 1782, did we see a majority so cheerless and disconsolate as on Tuesday last [21 Jan. 1794]. Ministers stood on the defensive, and all the multitude around them hung their heads in sadness and dismay.'

548. To ROBERT MILLAR   27 JANUARY 1794

Text:	DWL, MS 12.46 (3).
Printed:	Graham, 'Unhappy country', 130 (most of first two paragraphs).
Addressed:	[In Whitmore's hand] London, January, twenty seventh,/1794/ M^r R: Millar, Merchant,/Dundee/Free Thos:/ Whitmore[1]
Endorsed:	London 27 Jany. 1794./T. Lindsey/Mr Palmer & Muir/and political affairs
Postmarked:	JA 27 94

London. Jany. 27. 1794.

Dear Sir,

    Having an opportunity of a frank by a friend calling at our house, I am glad to give you a sight of Your Address to Mr Palmer as printed in the morning Chronicle, which reflects much credit and honour on both parties.[2] You woud receive a few hasty lines from me inclosed in a frank[3] which I had procured to convey a letter from Mr Palmer to one of your town. I wish I was able to send you any certain good news of the mitigation of the sentence against both Mr Muir and Mr Palmer. For the present we can only be in a state of hope. In the mean while, all that see the former, speak of his health as being very infirm, and inclined to be consumptive.[4]

    It has been a great satisfaction to hear from several members of the house of commons, that although on tuesday night last in the debate on the kings speech, there was so very large a majority with the minister and for the war, yet they never saw so heartless a majority, and the speech of the minister met with very [few] applauses of *hear him, hear him*, though some of his partisans, Mr Burke in particular, used all the art they could to promote them.[5]

    I must not forget to inform you, not to address any more letters to me under Mr Sargent's signature Mincing Lane, London; as he has just now taken a place, and his seat become vacated, and it is not certain he will be chosen again.[6]

To day, for the first time, this winter, we have snow and rather severe weather, whereas hitherto it has been very mild. My wife joins in all kind wishes to yourself and Mrs Millar, with Your's most truly

T. Lindsey.

1 Thomas Whitmore, MP, who provided the frank.
2 This address to Palmer, at the Stanislaus hulk, Woolwich, and dated Dundee, 12 Dec. 1793, was signed by Robert Millar, David Hughs and David Ramsay, 'in the name of the unitarian congregation here'. It was published in the *Morning Chronicle*, 13 Jan. 1794.
3 Lindsey wrote 'frank' over the words 'letter to'.
4 On board the hulks, Muir suffered from fevers, rheumatism and (possibly) consumption; Bewley, *Muir of Huntershill*, p. 96.
5 See Letter 547. The previous Tuesday was 21 Jan. 1794.
6 In Nov. 1793, John Sargent (1750–1831) vacated his seat at Seaford, where he had been one of the MPs since 1790, on being appointed clerk to the ordnance by the duke of Richmond. He returned to the house of commons as MP for the ordnance borough of Queenborough in Feb. 1794. The premises of his firm, Sargent, Chambers and Co., merchants, were situated at 38 Mincing Lane, London.

549. To WILLIAM TAYLEUR   8 FEBRUARY 1794

Text: JRUL, Lindsey Letters, vol. II, no. 76.
Addressed: To/William Tayleur Esqr/Shrewsbury
Endorsed: February 8th – 94
Postmarked: FE 10 94

London. Feb. 8. 1794.

Dear Sir,

You will have pleasure in hearing that my wife's health and spirits are considerably improved, which, under a good providence we attribute in part to the remarkably fine season. We earnestly wish it may have had the same happy effect upon you, my friend, to relieve, for one cannot expect wholly to have removed, those various and sometimes painful infirmities, which are the common attendants on life in its decline, especially when protracted to such a period as yours. Dr Heberden, of whose happy old age I have sometimes spoken begins now to feel his eye-sight fail, and another cotemporary friend of his is nearly deprived of that blessing, in which however I trust you do not feel any great decay. The greatest privilege however of life, long or short, is to have been enabled to turn our faculties to the service of God and our fellow-creatures to the last. And this is your consolation in a degree above many.

Mr Rowe asks me of the Gentleman who some time since wished me to put some questions to You with a view to the having unitarian worship in his house. To this I have to say, that he has not yet thrown open his door in the country to others, but is always the priest of his own family every day, both by some short moral printed instruction as well as prayer. But as there will soon be a change in his family by an unitarian minister being taken into it to be tutor to his sons, I shall hope that then his former good purposes may be put in execution.[1]

Mr Russell, from his new situation in the neighbourhood of Gloucester, with his daughters, are at present upon a visit to Dr Priestley; but I do not understand that Mr R. has now any thoughts of America.[2] Dr P. is however gradually making preparations, which with him must be a work of time, as he must provide himself with an infinite number of things for a philosophical apparatus which he cannot expect to meet with on the other side the Atlantic. And I have no doubt of his high usefulness there, both as a teacher of true religion, and a philosopher. I was much struck two posts ago, with the conclusion of a letter I had from his successor, Mr Jones at Birmingham; that there is hardly a man who distinguished himself in the riots there and against Dr P. whom some mischance has not befallen.[3] Two have laid violent hands on themselves, several have become bankrupts and sent to jail, Mr Careles, the magistrate, among the last committed to Warwick jail for debt and likely to continue there.[4] I hear that Dr Parr says upon the occasion, that the only mistake is that he should have [been] put on the other, the felon side.[5]

I met the other day the brother of the Mr Stone who is at Paris, and who lived at Hackney, and was pleased to hear that he and Miss Williams, the author of the letters are employed in a periodical publication there for their own benefit under the sanction of the present powers. We were all afraid for her, as she had been taken up with other english, and had in her letters spoken most freely of Robespierre and Danton by name.[6]

In the present awful eventful times, which we have lived to see, many wise and good are persuaded that Providence is therein bringing about its greatest purposes for the virtue and happiness of mankind, in the furtherance of the gospel, however prostrate it may for the present appear. Of this Dr Priestley will speak largely and particularly in his intended sermon on the fast-day, which I have had the perusal of, and which you will also have the pleasure of perusing as it is to be printed.[7]

I expect soon to hear from Mr Shore's and to be able to tell Mr Rowe who inquires about it, how Mr Williams takes with that worthy family.[8] Well I have no doubt. With mine and my wifes kind regards to M^r & Mrs Rowe, I beg you will tell him not to write till he hears from me, as I shall write soon.[9] My wife charges me with her most due and cordial respects to you. We beg to be remembered to Mr Wood, and I remain always Dear Sir, Your truly obliged and affectionate

T. Lindsey.

---

[1] This gentleman was probably James Martin MP; see Letter 436. It is not clear whether or not he employed a unitarian minister as tutor to his sons, or, if he did, who that minister was. Martin's will (TNA: PRO PROB 11/1508, fos. 295v–296v) gives no clue. Presumably Rowe had written to Lindsey on this subject.

[2] William Russell and his family left Birmingham after the Priestley riots and settled in Gloucestershire. On 13 Aug. 1794, they embarked from Falmouth with the intention of embarking for America. Their adventurous journey included capture by a French warship and internment in France, and they did not reach America until a year later.

[3] David Jones had succeeded Priestley as minister of the New Meeting at Birmingham in Oct. 1792; his letter to Lindsey seems not to have survived.

[4] Joseph Carles (1740–96), of Handsworth, was a Warwickshire magistrate at the time of the Birmingham riots. I have not been able to confirm the story about his arrest for debt, or to locate his will. There is a family history, namely T. A. C. Attwood, *Pedigree of the family of Carless or Carles* (London, 1916).

[5] Such a remark, if accurately recorded, would have been characteristic of Parr, whose disapproval of the conduct of the local authorities at the time of the Birmingham riots was well known.

[6] This was William Stone, soon to be arrested on a charge of treason; see Letter 574, n. 3. His brother was John Hurford Stone, at that time in Paris with his lover, Helen Maria Williams. In Paris, John Hurford Stone and Williams set up a publishing house, the Imprimerie Anglaise, and printed several works in support of the revolutionary regime. Williams's 'Letters from France' were published in eight volumes between 1790 and 1796. Since they were British subjects when France was at war with Britain, Williams and several members of her family were imprisoned for six weeks in Paris in Oct.–Nov. 1793. Lindsey had been a subscriber to her poems in 1786; see Vol. I, Letter 328, n. 9.

[7] This work was Priestley's *Present state of Europe*. A second and a third edition appeared later in 1794.

[8] John Williams was minister at Norton from 1794 to 1804.

9   The date of Lindsey's next surviving letter to Rowe was 13 Sept. 1794 (Letter 583); no doubt several
    letters from Lindsey to Rowe in the intervening period have not survived.

550. To JOSHUA TOULMIN   **8 FEBRUARY 1794**
   Text: Belsham, *Memoirs*, pp. 237, 241–2.

Note: The manuscript of this letter seems not to have survived. Belsham printed two extracts from what
he described as a letter from Lindsey to Joshua Toulmin dated 8 Feb. 1794 and it is an editorial assumption that they came from the same letter. The two extracts are presented here in the order in which they
appeared in Belsham, although it is not clear whether or not that was the order in the original manuscript.
The two extracts might or might not have been continuous; here they are separated by a broken line.

I have not read Mr. Winterbotham's trial, but lawyers, and others whom I have seen,
declare that there never was a more iniquitous verdict.[1]

I return your son's[2] two letters, which I like much, as everything which comes from
him. They show a good mind, sensible, active, and ever attentive to the proper business of his journeyings. At Dr. Priestley's request, I let him take them home with
him a day or two since to show to Mrs Priestley, as they are every day more and
more interested in what relates to America; and I now believe, in the course of not
many months, will both of them remove thither. This full decision I have come to
the knowledge of since I last wrote, though I have for some time suspected it. It
will cut off a great source of the highest satisfaction to me, amongst many others.
But I hope it will be for his greater good and contentment upon the whole, as his
family have gone before him; and I have for some time thought that his chief business was done here, and we were no longer worthy of him, and that he may be of
eminent service to that other country, retaining still in great vigour his powers of
body and mind; and there can be no doubt of the intimate friend of Franklin's being
there well received.[3]

1   Winterbotham's trial was reported in *State trials*, XXII, 823–76; for the verdict and sentence against
    him, see Letter 539, n. 6. There was also a separately published account, with the title *The trial of
    Wm. Winterbotham, assistant preacher at How's Lane meeting, Plymouth* (London, 1794, with a
    second and a third edition in the same year).
2   Henry Toulmin arrived at Norfolk, Virginia, in July 1793. He then settled in Lexington, Kentucky,
    where he served as president of the Transylvania seminary from 1794 to 1796.
3   For Priestley's friendship with Franklin, see Robert E. Schofield, *The enlightenment of Joseph
    Priestley. A study of his life and work from 1733 to 1773* (University Park, PA, 1997), pp. 140–3,
    151, 163, 234–5. In 1767, Franklin had recommended to the Royal Society that Priestley be awarded
    its Copley medal. Unfortunately for Priestley, Franklin died in 1790, four years before Priestley's
    emigration to America.

551. To JOSHUA TOULMIN   **20 FEBRUARY 1794**
   Text: Belsham, *Memoirs*, pp. 235 n. *, 242–3.

Note: The manuscript of this letter seems not to have survived. Belsham printed two extracts from what
he described as a letter from Lindsey to Joshua Toulmin dated 20 Feb. 1794, and it is an editorial assumption that they belonged to the same letter. The two extracts are presented here in the order in which they
appeared in Belsham, although it is not clear whether or not that was the order in the original manuscript.
The two extracts might or might not have been continuous; here they are separated by a broken line.

The sentence against Mr. Muir and Mr. Palmer is so unjust, that I can hardly persuade myself still that it will be executed, at least till their case has undergone the intended parliamentary discussion.[1] My friends say this is hoping against hope. At present they are at Portsmouth, and it is said are to remain there a fortnight.

The Doctor has received letters which are very encouraging. The family of V ____ here, who have two sons (that were both the Doctor's pupils) in America, one well settled in Philadelphia, the other in Kennebec, but who is part of the year at Boston, all advise and rather press him to go, though greatly grieved to lose him hence.[2] As to the Doctor, his purpose is certainly fixed to leave England towards April, and he is making preparations for the purpose.[3]

---

[1] For the sentences against Muir and Palmer, see Letter 538, n. 4. The 'parliamentary discussion' took place on 24 Feb. 1794; see Letter 557, n. 2.

[2] Lindsey referred here to the family of Vaughan, two members of which had emigrated to America. John Vaughan (1756–1841) was a student at the Warrington Academy which he entered in 1772; by 1794, he was a merchant in Philadelphia. His younger brother was Charles Vaughan (1759–1839), who entered Warrington Academy in 1775, and by 1794 had settled in Kennebeck, at that time part of British North America (Nova Scotia), but which subsequently became part of the state of Maine. They were both sons of Samuel Vaughan (1720–1802) and younger brothers of Benjamin and William Vaughan, who had both been Priestley's pupils at Warrington. Although John and Charles Vaughan were students at Warrington after Priestley had ceased to be a tutor there, it is possible that they received private tuition from him elsewhere. See 'Historical account of students educated in the Warrington Academy', in William Turner, *The Warrington Academy*, ed. G. A. Carter (Warrington, 1957), pp. 61, 68, 80, and Graham, *Revolutionary in exile*, pp. 4–6, 22–4.

[3] Priestley departed for America on 8 Apr. 1794.

552. To JOSHUA TOULMIN   **8 MARCH 1794**

   Text: Belsham, *Memoirs*, pp. 235 n. *, 243.

Note: The manuscript of this letter seems not to have survived. Belsham printed two extracts from what he described as a letter from Lindsey to Joshua Toulmin dated 8 March 1794, and it is an editorial assumption that they belonged to the same letter. The two extracts are presented here in the order in which they appeared in Belsham, although it is not clear whether or not that was the order in the original manuscript. The two extracts might or might not have been continuous; here they are separated by a broken line.

I hear that Mr. Palmer was not quite so well at Portsmouth on board the ship, and that their fare and accommodations were not such as were expected. However, some of my friends still flatter me with hope that Government will not take such a bold step as to send these men away whilst the legality of their sentence is questioned, and its discussion pending in the national legislature.[1]

You will be pleased to know that our friend, though we cannot think of losing him without deep concern, has taken places for himself, Mrs Priestley, and two servants, in the Sansom,[2] which is to be ready to sail the latter end of this or the very beginning of next month. Happily, the other persons, all of them emigrants, who are going in the same ship, are known to him or his friends.

---

[1] See Letter 557, n. 2.

[2] See Letter 563, n. 3.

553. To TIMOTHY KENRICK   13 MARCH 1794

Text:	The Sharpe papers, UCL Library Services, Special Collections (Kenrick papers), 178/45.
Printed:	'The Kenrick letters', *TUHS*, IV, 3 (Oct. 1929), 300–1 (minor errors).
Addressed:	Address missing.
Endorsed:	[In pencil] Theophilus Lindsey/to Rev. T. Kenrick/1793–94/ Fast day for War
Postmarked:	Postmark missing.

London. March. 13. 1794.

Dear Sir,

I ought to have acknowleged your letter sooner, because I could have told you the Society had unanimously agreed to your Proposal of printing a cheap edition of Dr Priestley's Institutes; but the avocations and the events of the times often put necessary business out of one's thoughts.[1]

I am just returned from a meeting of our Unitarian Society, where were several of your friends, particularly Dr Priestley and Mr Belsham,[2] the former much hurried with his affairs as you will believe, but perfectly well, save that he has for two days past been disturbed with the return of a spitting of blood which Mrs Priestley had some years ago, but which her Doctors assure him, is of no consequence. We cannot help seeing him with some concern, as we are so soon to lose him, but he is under the leading of divine providence, and not his own, for greater good to that New World I have no doubt: for assuredly his own desire would be to remain here; and share the fate of his country which he has endeavoured to benefit in the most essential manner all his life-time, whatever it be; but his three sons in America, absolutely wanting a guide and help, draw him thither.

Having procured a frank, and not willing it sh^d. go empty, I inclose a Sermon of a member of our unitarian Society, which you would of course see in a fortnight or three weeks time, for it has this day been proposed and agreed to by our Society to print it with some few additions of the author's, and to send a copy gratis to every member of the Society with their allotment of books, for the present year, which on various accounts comes forth so much later than usual. There will be a large number struck off, so that your Sister society may have them if desired.[3]

I wish I could give a brighter prospect of things than seemed to be clouding over our country than when you wrote about a month ago.[4] But the continuance of the war and a settled disposition against all reform whatsoever, seem to threaten us with serious evils.

I have really time to add no more at present but my wifes best respects and good wishes for all your little folks, and that I am with a sincere respect, very truly Yours

T. Lindsey.

---

1   At its monthly committee meeting on 13 Feb. 1794, the Unitarian Society resolved, on Kenrick's recommendation, seconded by Lindsey, that Priestley's *Institutes of natural and revealed religion* be printed in two volumes duodecimo for the use of the society; Unitarian Society minute book, p. 47.

2   Belsham's presence, but not that of Priestley, was recorded at the Unitarian Society monthly committee meeting on 13 Mar. 1794; Unitarian Society minute book, p. 47. The meeting resolved to call an extraordinary general meeting for 18 Mar. in order to present an address of appreciation to Priestley on the eve of his departure for America; see Letter 555.

3   This work was Robert Garnham's *A sermon preached in the chapel of Trinity College, Cambridge, on Thursday, December XIX, M.DCC.XCIII. The day appointed for the commemoration of the benefac-*

tors to that society (London, 1794); Unitarian Society minute book, p. 47. The 'sister society' was
the Western Unitarian Society.
4   Timothy Kenrick's letter to Lindsey 'about a month ago' seems not to have survived.

554. To WILLIAM ALEXANDER   15 MARCH 1794

    Text: 'Letters of the Rev. Theophilus Lindsey. No. V', *UH*, II, 73
                        (20 Sept. 1862), 320.

Note: This is the only section of the letter printed by the *UH*; the manuscript appears not to have survived.

London, March 15, 1794.

The enclosed ten pound note comes to you from your kind benefactor,*[1] who,
I hope, will still continue to befriend you for many years to come. And yet I think
it meet to tell you that there is something uncertain as to its continuance, as the
times are strange and very precarious, and he may find it right for him to leave this
country.

This reminds me of a subject in which you and so many are interested, the near
approach of Dr. Priestley's departure; and you will be pleased to hear that he is very
well, but much harassed with preparations, and various fatigues attendant on it, and
on quitting so many friends.[2]

—————————

1   The *UH*, II, 73 (20 Sept. 1862), p. 320, has the following note marked * at this point: 'This benefactor, who had sent the same sum several years, appears to have been Dr. Priestley.' Yet, as Lindsey
made clear to Alexander in this letter, Priestley's departure was settled, not simply under consideration. Perhaps Lindsey wished to issue a veiled warning to Alexander that the benefaction was unlikely
to be continued, while concealing Priestley's identity as the benefactor. Or possibly the benefactor
was someone else, perhaps Joshua Toulmin.
2   Priestley departed for America on 8 Apr. 1794.

555. LINDSEY AND THE UNITARIAN SOCIETY TO JOSEPH
PRIESTLEY, 18 MARCH 1794

    Text: Rutt, I, 212–15; DWL, Unitarian Society minute book,
                        pp. 48–50.

Note: The version of this address presented here is that printed by Rutt, who stated that he drew upon an
autograph copy, which apparently does not survive, written by Thomas Belsham. However, Rutt (I, 212
n. §) noted that several passages in Belsham's manuscript version were omitted from the version actually
adopted by the society for presentation to Priestley. Rutt added 'I shall here preserve the passages omitted
on its adoption by the Society' and gave the omitted sections in footnotes; here they are introduced into
the text of the letter and their presence in the text is indicated by square brackets. There is a manuscript
copy of the letter, without the passages added by Rutt, in the Unitarian Society minute book for 18 Mar.
1794, when an 'extraordinary meeting' resolved that it should be presented to the recipient as he prepared
to depart for America. The minute book (p. 50) recorded thanks to Belsham for the preparation of the
address. However, Rutt also noted (p. 215 n. †) that the letter was signed by Lindsey, who was indeed
in the chair at the meeting on 18 Mar. 1794. Possibly it was composed jointly by Lindsey and Belsham;
at the very least it is unlikely that Belsham did not consult Lindsey about its composition. It therefore
merits inclusion in the corpus of Lindsey's letters.

London, March 18, 1794.

REV. AND DEAR SIR,

Your friends, the members of the Unitarian Society, address you upon the
present interesting occasion, to express the regret with which they are penetrated,

at your approaching departure from this country, and their warmest wishes for your happiness in the place of your future destination.

So little as you have at any time interfered in national politics, it is but too obvious that the outrageous violence which you have experienced, and the atrocious calumnies which have been circulated with such unexampled industry to injure your character, and to render your residence in your native country unpleasant, and even unsafe, are entirely owing to that manly spirit with which you have avowed and defended what you *firmly* believed to be the pure and rational doctrines of the gospel, and to that truly Christian zeal with which you have entered your protest against those prevailing errors by which the religion of Jesus has been corrupted and debased [and against those antichristian hierarchies and civil establishments of religion by which these corruptions have been in all ages supported, the cause of truth oppressed, and the meek and benevolent religion of the gospel converted into an engine of sacerdotal tyranny and political oppression].

But you, Sir, have instructed us, both by your doctrine and example, to refer events to a higher cause, and while we regard with pity the conduct of men who, under the cover of religious zeal, are gratifying their own perverse passions, we also view them as instruments, under the direction of a superior Power, for the accomplishment of purposes the most distant from their own intentions, and we bow with humble acquiescence to the all-wise, disposing will of Heaven. The history of the Christian church from its first origin, through the revolutions of successive ages, has taught us this lesson, that it is the order of Providence that religious truth should be promulgated and confirmed by the sufferings of its most enlightened and most zealous advocates. In this part of the world you, Sir, have kindled a resplendent light, which no length of time, nor violence of opposition, will be able to extinguish; and you have been honoured as the instrument of diffusing religious knowledge beyond almost any individual in later ages. We anticipate, therefore, with pleasing hope, the extensive success of your future labours in America. Favoured as we have been with your rising and your meridian lustre, we ought not to envy our brethren in the Western continent the benefit of your evening ray.

Hitherto, Sir, you have been our pattern in every meritorious exertion in the investigation of religious truth, in every thing open and courageous in the profession of it; and when you are removed to a distant region, we trust that you will occasionally hear that your illustrious example has not been so long exhibited before us in vain. We shall think it our duty upon every proper occasion, and at all hazards, to avow our attachment to the genuine truths of the Christian religion; [and, fearless of all personal consequences, to persist in our public protest against popular and long-established errors]; and if in the discharge of this duty we should be exposed even to severer persecutions than those which you have encountered, [though it does not become us to boast of untried fortitude], we hope that our conduct will not disgrace the honourable cause in which we suffer. [We view with awful expectation the progress of those events which, by accelerating the overthrow of antichristian establishments of religion, are preparing the way for the universal acceptance of rational and pure Christianity, and for its establishment, where alone it ought to be established, in the hearts of men].

We, Sir, rejoice with you in the assurance of the ultimate triumph of the kingdom of God and of Christ, and of the universal dominion of truth and virtue, of order, liberty and peace. And though we deplore the probable distresses of the intervening period, we are happy in the persuasion that Infinite Wisdom will direct and controul the storm, [that no truly virtuous person shall be finally a sufferer], and that all the intermediate calamities will be as an evanescent point in comparison with that glorious and happy state of things of which they are the necessary means, and to which they ultimately tend.

In the meantime, we shall regard it as our indispensable duty to prepare ourselves and others for these interesting events, not only by the zealous propagation of what we judge to be important truth, by every fair and honourable method, [and especially by the distribution of religious books, which is the proper object of our association[1]], but likewise by exemplifying in our whole conduct the tendency of the principles of the Christian religion, when properly understood, to form the human mind to that strength and elevation of character in which the true dignity of our nature consists, and by which we may most effectually put to shame the calumnies of malignity, the prejudices of ignorance, and the scoffs of infidelity.

That your voyage may be prosperous, that your future lot may be happy beyond the most sanguine expectations of your warmest friends, and that your sphere of usefulness may be widely extended and prolonged to the most distant period of human exertion, is the ardent wish and fervent prayer of, Rev. and dear Sir, your affectionate friends, [and brethren in the profession of faith in the proper unity of God, and the proper humanity of our common Master, Jesus Christ], the members of the Unitarian Society. [T. Lindsey, Chairman].

---

1   The full title of the society was 'The Unitarian Society for Promoting Christian Knowledge and the Practice of Virtue by the Distribution of Books'.

556. To WILLIAM ALEXANDER   21 MARCH 1794

Text: 'Letters of the Rev. Theophilus Lindsey. No. V', *UH*, II, 73
               (20 Sept. 1862), 320.

Note: This is the only section of the letter printed by the *UH*; the manuscript has apparently not survived. The ellipsis at the start of the section printed by the *UH* indicates that this was not the beginning of the letter.

London, March 21, 1794.

* * Dr. Priestley continues very well, but was much distressed the last week by Mrs. Priestley's spitting of blood in large quantities for two or three days. She had something of the kind about three years ago. But she is now better, though low with it; and her doctors say that the sea, and particularly sea-sickness, would be salutary to her, rather than the contrary. I presume they will not sail before the end of this or the beginning of the next month. He still continues preaching to great crowds at Hackney. I think I told you all his late discourses will be printed.[1328] If he has many enemies, his friends are many also, and their prayers will be heard for his safety and usefulness.

---

1   This is a reference to Priestley's *Discourses relating to the evidences of revealed religion, Vol. I*. A second volume, entitled *Discourses relating to the evidences of revealed religion* was published in Philadelphia in 1796.

557. To WILLIAM TURNER OF NEWCASTLE   24 MARCH 1794

Text: DWL, MS 12.44 (57).
Printed: McLachlan, *Letters*, pp. 95–6 (second paragraph; parts of first
                 and last sentences of third paragraph); pp. 121–2 (first four
                 sentences of fourth paragraph); Graham, 'Unhappy country',
                 131–2 (second, third and fourth paragraphs, and the first
                 sentence of the fifth paragraph).
Addressed: Address missing.
Endorsed: Mar. 24. 1794
Postmarked: Postmark missing.

London. March. 24. 1794

Dear Sir,

Presuming that Mr Carr has given you all satisfaction concerning the receit of your pacquett sent to Mr Martin, and hoping that you may have recived an answer to your letter from Mr Palmer himself, I say no more on that subject, but would only add that I have seldom found any whose principles and good sense I more approved than Mr Carr's from the short conversation I had with him.[1]

Within the last fortnight I have received two letters from our friend on board the Surprize off Portsmouth. The first, when he complained of not being quite well in health, but worse in spirits on account of the most injudicious hasty reflexion thrown out against him by Mr Whitbread Senior in the house of Commons. But he would be consoled for this by the vindication of his character in the house some days after, in this and all respects, by Mr Sherridan, Mr Whitbread jun^r and others.[2]

The other letter is dated monday last the 17th, in which he mentions his having a confirmed dysentery brought on by the wet and dampness of his situation night and day, desiring me to mention his case to Dr Blackburne whom he had formerly consulted and ask his advice. His letter was answerd by myself and Dr Blackburne the next day, but we have heard no more, only that he continued ill.[3] I forgot to add that in his letter, he said, that he was permitted to be in the cabin by day, and was to sleep that night in a dry place. I trust it will please the divine providence to spare him, as he is likely to be an instrument of great good in that country and goes with the most ardent dispositions to be useful in every way in his power.

You will be glad to hear that Dr Priestley keeps up his spirits and enjoys intire health in the midst of his great fatigue and harassings, attending the preparations for leaving the country. These however are now finished. They have evacuated their house. All his things, and Mrs Priestley's, no less than 19 large bales are packed, and ready to be carried to the ship. They are in lodgings at Clapton (as they have sent away some of their beds) till every thing is sent off, and will then be at Mr Vaughans in Dunster Court, Mincing Lane, Fenchurch Street. Mrs Finch is with them, but returns to her own home a day or two before they sail, which probably will be the beginning of April.[4]

You will have seen his Fast Sermon advertised.[5] The course of Lectures, which he has been lately preaching, on the evidence for the Mosaic and Christian Institutions is printed as preached and will be ready to be published as soon as he leaves the country: a precious legacy, well becoming him, after so many other benefits to it. There will be prefixd to it his correspondence with Mr Gibbon, which though short is curious, and make a very proper ornament of the work.[6] Mr Gibbon, if you have seen it, opposed the publication, which however Dr Priestley did not give up, tho' he never produced it. But now Mr G. is gone off the stage, there can be no breach of honour in letting the public see it.[7]

I am happy to be able to inform you that my wife is much better, and I hope will in time grow stronger, tho' never likely to be so well as she has been. She desires to join in kind rememberances to Mrs Turner and yourself with all good wishes for your young family. It affords a satisfaction however melancholy that your good father is not unhappy in the ruin of his noble mental powers, so faithfully improved and used by him for the good of others agreeable to the will of the Great Donor, and which will therefore one day be restored to him with every advantage.[8] I remain always Dear Sir, most truly Your's

T. Lindsey

1 Probably Thomas William Carr, one of Turner's pupils at Newcastle from 1789, and subsequently the solicitor of the excise; see Harbottle, *William Turner*, p. 49, and *Royal kalendar ... for the year 1829*, p. 245.

2 On 24 Feb. 1794, in a debate on Thomas Palmer's petition against his sentence, Samuel Whitbread senior (1720–96), who was MP for Bedford from 1768 to 1774 and from 1775 to 1790, and for Steyning from 1792 and 1796, expressed sympathy with Palmer and acquitted him of malevolent intentions against the government. However, he declared Palmer to be 'somewhat deranged in his intellects' and certifiably insane; Cobbett, *Parl. Hist*, XXX, 1455–6). On 10 Mar. 1794, in the debate on William Adam's motion concerning the trials of Palmer and Muir, Samuel Whitbread junior (1764–1815), MP for Bedford from 1790 to 1815, repudiated his father's allegation as to Palmer's insanity, while Richard Brinsley Sheridan and Charles James Fox defended Palmer and Muir; Cobbett, *Parl. hist.*, XXX, 1559–60, 1554–9, 1562–72. Each of these debates was reported in the London press; probably Lindsey read the reports, respectively, in the *Morning Chronicle*, 25 Feb. and 11 Mar. 1794. Possibly the 'insanity' allegation was the result of a misunderstanding over claims that Palmer's brother James Fish (or Fyshe) Palmer was insane; see *Alumn. Cantab.*, II, vol. V, 14.

3 I have not located these letters from Palmer, or the replies from Lindsey and William Blackburne. The only surviving letters from Palmer to Lindsey were written from Botany Bay, and are dated 5 May and 16 Sept. 1796; they may be consulted at HMCO, Shepherd MS, vol. X, nos. 11 and 12.

4 For the Vaughan family premises at Dunster Court, Mincing Lane, See Letter 468, n. 1. The head of the firm was Samuel Vaughan; Lindsey referred here either to him or to his second son William Vaughan (1752–1850). J. T. Rutt noted that his last meeting with Priestley before the latter's embarkation was at the house of William Vaughan; Rutt, I, 225; see also Letter 551, n. 2. Mrs Finch's home was in Dudley, Warwickshire.

5 See Letter 549, n. 7.

6 Priestley's *Discourses on the evidences of revealed religion. Vol. I. Delivered at Hackney in 1793, 1794* (London, 1794), pp. 412–20, included Priestley's exchange of letters with Gibbon in Dec. 1782. It began with Priestley's note presenting Gibbon with a copy of the *History of the corruptions of Christianity* and was followed by three letters from Gibbon to Priestley and three replies. The outcome was that Gibbon declined entering a public controversy with Priestley. See Letter 385, n. 5.

7 Edward Gibbon died on 16 Jan. 1794.

8 William Turner of Wakefield died on 28 Aug. 1794.

558. **To RUSSELL SCOTT   **25 MARCH 1794**

Text: Scott Coll.
Addressed: Address missing.
Endorsed: To Rev. Russell Scott/Portsmouth
Postmarked: Postmark missing.

Note: The first three paragraphs of this letter are in Lindsey's hand; the remainder of the letter is in Hannah Lindsey's hand.

[In Hannah Lindsey's hand] March 25ᵗʰ. 1794

Dear Sir,

We hope you had a safe and pleasant journey and found all well at the end of it.

I had yesterday a letter from Mʳ Palmer in return to one I had sent him, in which he speaks favourably of his health, which I hope soon will be restored, but it will be a great satisfaction to have it confirmed by you.[1]

Through an accident that happened to the letter I had sent him being torn to pieces, he had not given particular attention and therefore made no reply to the inquiries I had made about the disposal of his money which I had sent to me for him out of Scotland, and also what to do with his books which remained in that country: if I receive no directions from him, I shall certainly lodge both with his brother at Bedford, but should be glad, whatever be the case, to know his mind about them.[2]

[From this point, the rest of the letter is in Hannah Lindsey's hand]

If there is yet access to the Ship, wᶜʰ. Mʳ. Palmer believes there will be, as he desired to hear again from Dʳ. Blackburne, perhaps you could by Mʳ. Ellis[3] get to know if Mʳ. P. would have the money paid to himself, in which case be so good as pay it directly, and Mʳ. Lindsey will send you the bill to repay you, as soon as we know, you have paid it. Mʳ. L: is gone out, but expects the Post will bring a letter from you, as you promised to write on Monday[4] at the farthest, and under that persuasion a frank was procured.

2 o'clock and no letter from you, wᶜʰ. makes me conclude, either that you are unwell, or that the chanel [*sic*] of communication is stopped. Under the apprehension that it is so, we forbear to inclose any farther medical advice wᶜʰ. Mʳ. P. desired: He must be left to the Providence & will of God to live or die. We have just heard from a letter written to a friend in town by Mʳ Bogue,[5] (that tho' Dʳ Waller[6] incouraged his patient to hope everything & order him the gradual, but free use of wine to keep him up, & said he wᵈ soon be well as Mʳ. P. relates in his own letter) that the Dʳ. thinks him in great danger. This has sunk our hopes a good deal, & induces me to mention these particulars in hopes that you may be able to tell us a true story, from Dʳ. Waller one way or other. As Mʳ. L: may not return in time for the post I dispatch this, wishing to hear of yʳ own health & safe arrival, which with every other good wish for yʳself Mʳˢ Scot & family, I am Dʳ Sir Yʳˢ sincerely

HL

I have no doubt but you will remember my injunctions about the parcel I gave you, as it was an effort of friendship to yʳself, of wᶜʰ. you will take no notice.[7]

---

1 I have not found these letters between Lindsey and Palmer; see Letter 557, n. 3.

2 In his will, originally dated 22 Nov. 1793, Palmer named three brothers, namely Jeremy, John and Edward Palmer; TNA: PROB 11/1403, fos. 424v–425r. Probably the brother whom Lindsey had in mind was Jeremy Fyshe Palmer of Bedford (d. 1798); see Letter 678, n. 7.

3 James Ellis of Dundee accompanied Palmer to New South Wales as protégé and servant. Possibly Palmer, who had helped to educate Ellis at Dundee, also regarded him as an adopted son; he bequeathed most of his estate to Ellis. It seems that Ellis and his father of the same name were cotton-

spinners; the former is so described in Palmer's will, TNA: PRO PROB 11/1403, fos. 424v-425v. Immediately before his meeting with Palmer, the younger Ellis had a post as a clerk in Paisley; see *Dundee celebrities of the nineteenth century: being a series of biographies of distinguished or noted persons connected by birth, residence, official appointment or otherwise with the town of Dundee; and who have died during the present century*, comp. W. Norrie (Dundee, 1873), p. 12. Although little is known about Ellis biographically, it is clear that he was a loyal friend to Palmer during his transportation and exile.

4   The date of this letter, 25 Mar. 1794, was a Tuesday; presumably Hannah Lindsey meant Monday 17 or 24 Mar. 1794.

5   Probably David Bogue (1750–1825), independent minister at Gosport, Hampshire, and a leading teacher in the Gosport Academy for Independent Ministers. He is best known for the *History of dissenters from the revolution in 1688 to the year 1808* (4 vols., London, 1808–12), which he wrote in collaboration with James Bennett (1774–1862). I have not been able to identify 'friend in town', who might have been a friend of Bogue or Lindsey (or both).

6   Thomas Waller, MD, who is listed as a physician among the 'principal inhabitants' of Portsea, Hampshire, in *Universal British directory* (1791), IV, 203. He was a witness to the codicil which Palmer made to his will on 1 Apr. 1794, on board the *Surprise*; TNA: PRO PROB 11/1403, fo. 425. Perhaps he was the Dr Waller who was a member of the Southern Unitarian Society in 1803; see list of members appended to Thomas Belsham, *The study of the scriptures recommended in a discourse. Delivered at Newport, in the Isle of Wight, July 13, 1803 before the Society of Unitarian Christians established in the south of England* (London, 1803), p. 35.

7   Lindsey regularly sent parcels of books and periodicals to Scott. His 'injunctions' as to this particular parcel were probably expressed in a non-surviving letter to Scott; possibly it contained a gift of money. In his letter of 4 Apr. 1794 (Letter 561), he promised Scott a further parcel.

559. To RUSSELL SCOTT   28 MARCH 1794

Text: Scott Coll.
Addressed: To/The Revd Russell Scott/Portsmouth
Postmarked: Postmark missing.

London. March. 28 1794

Dear Sir,

I thank you for your obliging letter, and for all your care about Mr Palmer. I am sorry however that by a mistake the frank I now use was dated a day later than it was desired, as by that means the Bank-Post Bill comes to you a day later. But it is of less consequence, as my wife tells me, that in finishing my last imperfect scrawl, she had begged of You to advance the money for the inclosed Bill, if necessary; and as Mr Palmer wished to receive it, I make no doubt of your indulgence in this matter.[1] I wrote to him yesterday, under Mr Gilmour's care,[2] to acquaint him again with the particulars I had sent before concerning the letter from Dundee, the money that was returned to him, his books still left behind in that country &c &c. I must trouble you to let me know of the receit of the inclosed, and at the same time I hope to have the account of his recovery confirmed so as to be in no danger of a relapse.[3] For we are not at all easy about our friend, especially as you had not had an opportunity of seeing Dr Waller and asking his opinion of him.[4] As soon as I received yours on wednesday,[5] I went to several places to learn if there was any foundation for the intelligence of a physician being sent down by Government to examine into the state of his health, and his ability to go through the voyage, but could hear nothing of it.[6]

Every little circumstance relating to our suffering friend, and the state of his companions, will be very grateful to us. I am afraid that there has not been so much virtue and disinterestedness in the distribution of the *public* goods, by which he was principally to be benefited, as his friends were great contributors to the common stock that was to provide them. But this suspicion is mentioned to you only, that you may direct your inquiries that way, as much as you can, if opportunity presents.

I beg you will assure him of mine and my wifes affectionate regards and earnest prayers for him.

Mr Perkins and his son at the college breakfasted with us yesterday, and asked much after you.[7] Mr Toulmin from Taunton called upon us yesterday and we are to see him to day. Dr Priestley is to be ready to sail on monday next, but it is thought it will not be needful for him to go down to Gravesend till the wednesday. At the desire of his congregation he gives them a farewel Sermon on Sunday next.[8] You shall have his course of Sermons as soon as they come out.[9]

We had great satisfaction in your good intelligence about Mrs Scott and your young folks. Our kind regards attend the former with every wish of good for the last. I am always, with affectionate esteem most truly Yours

T. Lindsey.

---

1   See Letter 558.
2   For Nathaniel Gilmore of Gosport, see Letter 563, n. 6.
3   The letter to Lindsey from Dundee was probably sent by Robert Millar.
4   For a possible identification of Dr Waller, see Letter 558, n. 6.
5   Scott's letter to Lindsey seems not to have survived. The previous Wednesday was 26 Mar. 1794.
6   Palmer did not identify, in his *Narrative* or elsewhere, any physician 'sent down by Government' to investigate the state of his health. However, one of the witnesses to the codicil which Palmer made to his will on board the *Surprise* on 1 Apr. 1794 was the surgeon James Monson; TNA: PRO PROB 11/1403, fo. 425. It is not clear, however, whether or not he was the physician in question – if, indeed, one was dispatched for this purpose.
7   The son was probably Richard Perkins, 'of the College, Hackney', who was proposed for member-ship of the Unitarian Society on 12 June 1794 and elected a member on 11 Dec. 1794, by which time it was noted that he was 'late of the college, Hackney'; unitarian minute book, pp. 52, 53. He entered the college in Sept. 1789, recommended by John Prior Estlin of Bristol; see DWL, MS 38.14, p. 90, and Birm. MS 281, fo. 124. His family originated from the west country; his father was of Shepton Mallet, Somerset. See Letters 580 and 581.
8   This work was Priestley's *The uses of Christianity, especially in difficult times; a sermon delivered at the Gravel-Pit meeting in Hackney, March 30, 1794, being the author's farewell discourse to his congregation* (London, 1794).
9   These sermons of Priestley were published with the title *Discourses relating to the evidences of revealed religion. Vol. I.*

560. To WILLIAM TAYLEUR   30 MARCH 1794

Text: JRUL, Lindsey Letters, vol. III, no. 36.
Printed: McLachlan, 'More letters', 376 (first four sentences of second
                 paragraph); 375 (seventh sentence of second paragraph); 377
                 (final three sentences of third paragraph and short extract from
                 fourth sentence); 376 (short extracts from fourth paragraph).
Addressed: [In Hannah Lindsey's hand] To/William Tayleur Esqr./
                 Shrewsbury
Endorsed: 30th of March 1794
Postmarked: MR 31 94

March. 30. London
Sunday Even

Dear Sir,

For this fortnight past I have [been] continually meditating to write, but have been always occupied, happily so, in something relating to Dr Priestley, or in being with him. You would be pleased to see his health and spirits amidst his perpetual harass; but he visibly feels regret at times, especially on the thought of leaving such friends as him, to whom I am writing, whom he has invariably esteemed and honoured from the first hour he has known. He looks forward however to a future assembly in still happier scenes, there to meet again those whom he loved and honoured here. And let us look thither.

I am told by a friend,[1] who heard him this morning at Hackney, that his place was as crouded as on the foregoing sunday, when several hundreds stood without the doors. It was a farewel discourse to his congregation which he had not intended to make, as his Fast-Sermon was something of the kind. But the principal persons of the meeting would not be contented with that, and I can hardly describe by what snatches and in how short a time he drew it up. My friend tells me he liked it prodigiously. We shall have it printed, together with the series of Discourses he has lately preached. I am glad you had the dates of his correspondence with Mr Gibbon, which will very properly be prefixed, and be esteemed a curiosity.[2] I had a copy in his own hand, which I furnished him with, but without any marks of the time. It will be a seasonable publication, considering the increased tendency in our own country and every where to reject revelation, and even the very existence of an intelligent author of nature. Mr Godwin on Political Justice is said to have produced this last extreme in many, in some whom I personally know, though with no intimacy.[3] And to my certain knowlege, Mr Godwin, and his friend, foster-father and patron of the sect, Mr Holcroft, author of *Anna S^t. Ives*, &c; strenuously labour to make proselytes.[4] Dr Priestley, the other day, was promised by a friend a copy of a paper, in which Mr G. undertook by several arguments to shew that the belief of the being of a God was as incredible and absurd as that of the creed of St Athanasius.[5]

Mr Evanson has been exerting himself with all his might to get his defence of ye Dissonance ready before the Doctor sails. It came to Town yesterday, but he will not have leisure to read it. The title, "A Letter to Dr Priestley's young man; with a Postscript["].[6] Any thing more contemptuous, more scurrilous, more cavilling I never looked into; for I have not been able to read it. Some it may please, but can do the writer no credit. If his former work, and reprobation of three of our gospels with several of St Paul's and all the Catholic epistles was a triumph to unbelievers, and actually made many: this has a manifest tendency to increase their number, by the manner of it.[7] Nay a friend of mine, will have this to be his design. But such a censure is most uncandid and false. The author of the *Rights of man*, M[r] Payne, has lately turned his pen this way, and published a flaming pamphlet against revelation. Some few copies have found their way across the channel, and I am promised a sight of one. The few times that I was in company with him, he commonly took occasion [to] shoot his bolt against the Bible.[8]

On friday afternoon my wife and I went with the Doctor to visit their ship which lay a little off the Tower, and we were highly delighted with its great conveniences, so as almost to tempt to take the journey. The next day, Saturday, it fell down the river, to stop a day at Deptford and then proceed to Gravesend, where our friends and the passengers are all to embark, some day this week, wednesday or thursday, most probably. We sometimes flatter ourselves that he may come back, not to stay, but to fetch M[rs] Finch (who is now with them) if she do not soon follow.[9] He has within a few days received some agreable letters from his sons, from whom he had not heard of a long time.

We have been quite revived by M[r] Rowe's account of your health being improved. May Providence still spare and preserve you in some comfort to be useful.

I must not omitt to tell You that I was highly pleased with the examination of the Students at Hackney a week ago. 22 more promising youths no seminary can furnish. I was particularly charmed with a pleasing character, M[r] Mason, of your town I think. He answerd well, and is I find very studious.[10]

My wife sends her kind respects. I remain always, Dear Sir, Your truly obliged and faithful affectionate servant

T. Lindsey.

I have heard frequently from M[r] Palmer, since he was on board the Surprize off Portsmouth. He has been dangerously ill of a dysentery, but is better. I hope to hear to morrow, he is quite recoverd. How is[11]

---

1   This friend of Lindsey was probably a minister, perhaps Thomas Belsham or Jeremiah Joyce.

2   See Letter 557, n. 6.

3   Probably one of those whom Lindsey had in mind was Joseph Fawcett; see Letter 604. Lindsey met Godwin on several occasions during the later 1780s and early 1790s, sometimes at the house of Timothy Hollis or of Thomas Brand Hollis; see Bodl., Abinger collection, reel 12, William Godwin journals, 6 Feb., 4 Nov. 1789, 13 July, 12 Oct., 30 Nov. 1790, 11 June 1792.

4   Thomas Holcroft's epistolary novel *Anna St. Ives*, with its expressions of sympathy with the French Revolution, was published in seven volumes in London in 1792.

5   Godwin did not share Priestley's materialism, and it appears that some kind of brief disagreement, and personal offence, took place between them in 1791. However, Godwin retained considerable respect for Priestley and other rational dissenters and in Mar. 1794, immediately before Priestley's departure for America, Godwin sought an interview with Priestley to discuss the latter's orally expressed criticisms of (and praise for) Godwin's *Enquiry concerning political justice* (London, 1793). See Martin Fitzpatrick, 'William Godwin and the rational dissenters', *Price–Priestley Newsletter*, III (1979), 4–28, especially pp. 10–15. Although the story recounted by Lindsey cannot be dismissed, it is not entirely consistent with Godwin's respect for Priestley.

6   This work was Evanson's *A letter to Dr. Priestley's young man; with a postscript concerning the Rev. D. Simpson's essay, &c, in answer to Evanson's Dissonance and Volney's Ruins* (Ipswich, 1794). David Simpson had published *An essay on the authenticity of the New Testament: designed as an answer to Evanson's Dissonance and Volney's Ruins* (Macclesfield, 1793); Evanson replied to it in the 'postscript' (pp. 111–20) of his *Letter to Dr Priestley's young man*. For Lindsey's previous acquaintance with Simpson (1745–99) at Catterick, see Vol. I, p. xlvii; see also Mark Smith's entry for Simpson in *ODNB*, L, 683–4. At the time of his riposte to Evanson, Simpson, a determined evangelical, was minister at Christ Church, Macclesfield. The French philosopher Constantin François Chasseboeuf, comte de Volney (1757–1820) was the author of *Les ruines, ou méditation sur les révolutions des empires* (Geneva, 1791).

7   In his *Dissonance*, Evanson rejected the authenticity of the gospels of Matthew, Mark and John, and
    some parts of Luke, together with Paul's epistles to the Romans, Philippians, Philemon and Hebrews.
    He claimed that much of their text could only have been written later than in biblical times, and that
    they contained fraudulent interpolations. The 'catholic', or general, epistles are those books in the
    New Testament (namely the two epistles of Peter, the three epistles of John, together with that of
    James and that of Jude) which are addressed to early Christians in general. They are to be distin-
    guished from the epistles of St Paul, which are addressed to an individual (Timothy) or to specific
    groups of Christians.
8   For an earlier indication that Lindsey had met and conversed with Paine, see Letter 430.
9   Priestley's daughter Sarah Finch did not emigrate.
10 'A week ago' to the day was Sunday 23 Mar. 1794. James Mason (1779–1827) of Shrewsbury was
    a lay student at the college during the early 1790s. A supporter of Charles James Fox, he became a
    playwright and political author. See the article by G. Le G. Norgate (revised by H. C. G. Matthew)
    in *ODNB*, XXXVII, 177.
11 Lindsey did not complete this sentence.

561. To RUSSELL SCOTT   4 APRIL 1794

Text: Scott Coll.
Printed: McLachlan, 'Lindsey to Scott', 120 (part of second sentence
                 of third paragraph).
Addressed: To/The Rev^d. Russell Scott/Portsmouth [in Hannah Lindsey's
                 hand] Post Paid
Endorsed: April 4th. 1794
Postmarked: POST PAID AP 3 94

London. April. 4. 1794.

Dear Sir,

I thank you for your letter, though the delay had made us a little anxious both
with respect to Mr Palmers health and your receit of the Bank Post Bill.[1] But we
are satisfied with your assurance of his health being restored, though it would have
added much to have had the pleasing news confirmed by Dr Waller's personal word
to yourself, but still more by your own ocular testimony.[2]

I send this by the return of the post, that it may reach you before saturday,[3] when
you purpose carrying the money to Mr Palmer yourself, should an opportunity not
be afforded to put it into Mr J. Ellis's hands.

Should you see our dear friend yourself, more endeared to us by his grievous
persecution and sufferings so nobly and chearfully endured, you will be so good as
to learn every particular you can relating to his health, his situation and prospects
aboard the ship with respect to ease, and conveniences, and the stores provided for
him with others, but in which he was principally to be considered. And if you do
not go to Spithead yourself, you will make every inquiry from James Ellis, to whom
my wife and I beg to be most kindly remembered, and we should be glad to know
at your leisure in what capacity Mr Ellis goes, and every thing about so worthy a
creature.[4] And I wish you w^d mention to him to remind Mr Palmer of informing me
what I am to [do] about his books &c in wch. I [?would be][5] useful to him.

Dr Priestley is here at this moment desires to be kindly remembered to you,
and that you woud say for him as well as us, every thing tender and friendly to M^r
Palmer. Mr Wainwright[6] also who is just come in, and Mr Russell of Birmingham
desire to be named to him.

I am sorry I am hindered from adding a word more. You may expect a parcell

from me in a few days. Our kind regards to Mrs Russell[7] – with my wife's to yourself
–

I remain always most truly Yours
T. Lindsey

---

1 Scott's letter to Lindsey seems not to have survived. For this bank post bill for Palmer, see Letters 558 and 559; for a note on bank post bills, see Letter 538, n. 3.
2 For a possible identification of Dr Waller, see Letter 558, n. 6.
3 Presumably Lindsey meant Saturday 12 Apr. rather than 5 Apr. 1794.
4 For James Ellis, see Letter 558, n. 3.
5 Lindsey seems to have omitted two words – probably 'would be' – at this point.
6 Probably Robert Wainewright (d. 1841) of Gray's Inn, Esq., who became a trustee of Essex Street chapel in 1803; see 'A Lawyer', 'Deeds', 265. He is listed as one of the sworn clerks in the six clerks office, Chancery Lane, in *Browne's general law list for the year 1794* (London, 1794), p. 188, and in *Browne's general law list for the year 1800* (London, 1800), p. 100. For his involvement in fund-raising for Priestley's last two major works, see Letter 739, n. 3. For a reference to his family, see CUL, Add. MS 7886 (Frend papers), no. 141, Hannah Lindsey to William Frend, 17 Sept. 1803. Possibly he was the Robert Wainewright who was an executor of Hannah Lindsey's will; TNA: PRO PROB 11/ 1529, fo. 235r.
7 Lindsey presumably meant Sophia (i.e. Mrs Russell) Scott; he referred to her as 'Mrs Russell' on another occasion (see Letter 633, n. 1).

562. To RUSSELL SCOTT   8 APRIL 1794

Text: Scott Coll.
Addressed: Address missing.
Postmarked: Postmark missing.

Note: The date at the beginning of this letter is not in Lindsey's hand.

April 8th 1794

Dear Sir,

I am sure I should have received a few lines from you, if opportunity had served.

I am sorry to observe an article in the morning Chronicle of to day, that all[?] communication of friends is stoppd with Messrs Muir, Palmer, &c.[1]

You will perhaps however find a way to convey they [*sic*] inclosed, which I leave opened to tell you all our news of Dr Priestley, but which you will be so good to put a wafer in before you send it. I do this because I have not time to write at length myself.

When you write back, which I wish may be as early as you can, tell me how you and your's are, how Mr Palmer goes on; and also how I may best send You a copy of Dr P. Sermons[2] on the Mosaic & X^t Institutions, which has been printed a few days, and his farewel Sermon, which is not from the Press.[3]

Mr Hawes, after taking the trouble before found me at last at home, when I endorsed the former Post Bill, and told him that I had a frank going for you, if they wanted to send a letter.[4]

Mine and my wifes kind regards to Mrs Scott and yourself – I remain ever
Dear Sir most truly Yours
T. Lindsey
April 8.
London

[There follow six lines of shorthand in Russell Scott's hand. On the opposite page is a transcription of the shorthand in a different hand. The transcript and note are reproduced here]

Shorthand note by Russell Scott

D^r. Priestley left Mr Lindsey Monday morning March the 7th. for Gravesend,[5] and went on board at the Hope Tuesday morning. Mr Russell has some [blank: one word missing] of acres of land not far from a district which there is a design of purchasing by Dr Priestley and many of his friends, lying between Philadelphia and the Federal State, and where M^r. Russell intends to make further purchase.[6] It will be a spot occupied by Unitarians –

---

1   The *Morning Chronicle*, 8 Apr. 1794, quoted 'a letter from Portsmouth' to this effect.
2   Lindsey at first wrote 'Lectures', then crossed it out and over-wrote 'Sermons'.
3   Priestley's sermons 'on the Mosaic & X^t Institutions' were published as *Discourses relating to the evidences of revealed religion. Vol. I*; see Letter 542, n.3. For his 'farewell sermon', see Letter 559, n. 8.
4   Possibly Lindsey referred here to Scott's father-in-law Dr William Hawes, although he would normally have used the title 'Dr'. Perhaps he meant one of Scott's brothers-in-law, Thomas (d. 1849), Benjamin (1770–1860) or William (1775–1855) Hawes. Another possibility is the brother of Dr William Hawes and uncle of Sophia Scott, Benjamin Hawes (d. 1822), starch-maker, of Thames Street, London.
5   7 Mar. 1794 was a Friday; the correct date was Monday 7 Apr. 1794.
6   William Russell had planned that he and his family should settle near to Priestley's home at Northumberland, Pennsylvania, and establish a small unitarian community there. Russell's agent had purchased land in that area before Russell himself visited Priestley at Northumberland in 1795, but Russell and his family took such a dislike to the area that they settled instead at Middletown, Connecticut. See Rutt, I, 317, 320, and Jeyes, *The Russells of Birmingham*, pp. 257ff.

---

563. To RUSSELL SCOTT   10 APRIL 1794

Text: Scott Coll.
Addressed: [In James Martin's hand] Rev: Russell Scott/Portsmouth
Endorsed: Westm^r. *Tenth Ap^l*. 1794. J. Martin [in Hannah Lindsey's hand, opposite address] April 10th 1794/Rev^d. Russel Scot/ Portsmouth
Postmarked: FREE AP 10 94

London. April. 10. 1794

Dear Sir,

I have this morning receivd a letter from Dr Priestley dated yesterday at 8 o'clock in the morning off Deal, in which is the following paragraph.

"Our captain has just informed us, that if he fall in with the fleet of Merchantmen at Portsmouth, he will join them for the sake of the convoy."[1]

In consequence of this notice I have written to him the inclosed, and intreat you by means of your friends, to be so good as to make all inquiry about[?] and procure it to be safely conveyed to him.

The ship he sails in, is the Sansom, Capt Sm[ith][2] bound for New York.[3] Any expence which it m[ay] cost, I shall desire to defray, it being enough to give You so much trouble. Should you not be able to convey it to him, or hear that the ship is passed by and has not touched there, I must beg you to inclosed [*sic*] it to me under cover To *James Martin Esqr. Downing-Street, Westminster*.[4]

And our friend Mr P.[5] who we trust is well and beg comp^{ts} to him, will be glad to know that D^r & Mrs P. are so far well, and have sufferd a little but not much from the sickness.

I have some expectation that this may cross a letter from you on its road to me, as I am in no small concern about M[r] Palmer, to whom I have lately sent a small parcell of books directed to M[r] Nathanael Gilmore, Gosport,[6] for him, and should be glad to know other particulars about him, which I have mentioned to You. I beg you will never mind the postage of a double letter to me.[7]

If you can convey the inclosed to D[r] Priestley, pray if necessary put it under another cover and re-direct it to him.

My wife joins in all kind regards for yourself M[rs] Scott and your little folks – I remain most sincerely Yours

T. Lindsey

[1] This letter from Priestley to Lindsey, dated Deal, 9 Apr. 1794, and including the passage quoted by Lindsey, is printed in Rutt, I, 230.

[2] The manuscript is very slightly torn at this point.

[3] This is a reference to Captain Smith of the *Sansom*, which arrived off Deal, from New York, on 16 Feb. 1794, before its return voyage to New York with Priestley; see *Public Advertiser or Political and Literary Diary*, 18 Feb. 1794. The ship's name was not the *Samson*, as stated in L. Kieft, *The Priestley house* (Northumberland, 2006), p. 7.

[4] Lindsey's letter to Priestley, to be conveyed by Scott, has not survived.

[5] Thomas Fyshe Palmer.

[6] Nathaniel Gilmore of Gosport is recorded as a freeholder voter in the county of Hampshire at the general election of 1790; see *The poll for the election of two knights*, p. 53. Perhaps Lindsey did not know that he voted for the two successful ministerial candidates, Sir William Heathcote and William John Chute, and not (as Lindsey had advised Russell Scott in Letter 402) for the two opposition candidates, Lord John Russell and Jervoise Clerke Jervoise. Gilmore also voted for the two Pittite candidates in the general election of 1806; *The poll for the election of two knights, for the county of Southampton ... 1806* (Winchester, ?1806), p. 92.

[7] For these postal costs, see Letter 432, n. 5.

## 564. To WILLIAM TAYLEUR										10 APRIL 1794

Text: JRUL, Lindsey Letters, vol. III, no. 37.
Printed: McLachlan, 'More letters', 376 (fourth, fifth and sixth sentences of first paragraph); 368 (sixth paragraph); 373–4 (most of seventh paragraph).
Addressed: To/William Tayleur Esq[r]./Shrewsbury
Endorsed: 10th of April 1794
Postmarked: 94 [postmark otherwise illegible]

London. April. 10
Thursday evening

Dear Sir,

Learning from M[r] Howe,[1] who I saw a few hours since at our Unitarian Society dinner, that he had written lately and should not write again of some days, I thought it would give you pleasure to know that I had this day received a letter from our beloved and honoured friend, dated Wednesday morn ½ past 8 off Deal, in which he mentions their good voyage so far. Most of the passengers had been very sick, above all their servant maid, who promises to be most useful; M[rs] P. and the Doctor did not escape though better than most of them. But at the hour he wrote they seemed to be all pretty well, and ready for their breakfast. The Cabin passengers only nine and promise to to [*sic*] be sufficiently agreeable, tho almost all unknown to each other. A M[r] Lyon in particular a most worthy sensible person, an excellent farmer of some fortune.[2] The Captain had just told them, that if he fall in with the fleet of

Merchantmen at Portsmouth, he should join them for the sake of the convoy.[3] To that place therefore I have sent him a long letter to day, under cover to a friend, inclosing some papers &c that had been received since he went away, particularly the Address of the united Society of Irishmen in Dublin to him, which is very affectionate and clever, and in a fine strain: we think from some internal marks that it has been drawn up by Mr Kirwan. It has been inserted by some person in one of the daily papers, but has not yet made it's appearance in the Morn. Chronicle.[4]

You may depend upon knowing from time to time what I hear of him on his voyage or receive from him, and he has promised to send me a letter if they stop any time at Portsmouth.

I was told to day at our dinner by a friend that they had seen M[r] Moffat, the Edinburgh lawyer,[5] M[r] Muir's intimate, just come from Portsmouth, that he and his fellow-sufferers are exposed to uncommon indignities and hardships, in one particular way from the soldiers who bring 5 or 6 women of the town at the time into their small cabin, and cannot be prevented. This and several of their other grievances will be at an end, when once they get out to sea.

This arrest and trial of Danton at Paris seems to be a most serious affair, and by some expected to overset Robespierre and the present ruling powers.[6] Others apprehend it to be a necessary step which will strengthen them, especially by enlarging their ground[?], in making a full liberty of worship not only easy, but creditable in the eye of the laws, which it is not at present. In the mean while our consolation is that every event is under the same direction and tending to the best ends of virtue and final happiness.

I hear that M[r] Belsham is to print his first sermon preached Sunday last, "I am not ashamed of the gospel of Christ". And M[r] Toulmin has been desired to print two discourses preached on the two last Sundays for D[r] Disney.[7]

I am glad to hear that M[r] Aikin takes so well to Shrewsbury, and gives such good satisfaction to your congregation.

I cannot help congratulating you on M[r] Walker's escape from men who hunted after his ruin with such unrelenting cruelty and villany.[8] For the good of the world, I hope that those who bribed Dunn, will be detected.[9] M[r] Shore was at Lancaster to attend the trial, M[r] Walker having married his sister, a most excellent amiable lady of singular fortitude.[10] Farewel, my excellent friend! My wife presents her kind respects. I remain ever your truly obliged and affectionate

T. Lindsey.

---

[1] Lindsey at first wrote 'Howe' (possibly Thomas Howe (1788–1820), minister of the 'respectable society' of unitarians at Bridport from 1788 to 1820). In the manuscript, however, the H of Howe is over-written in pencil with the letter R – probably to indicate John Rowe of Shrewsbury. Since this is a letter to Tayleur, Rowe is the more likely reading.

[2] In his letter to Lindsey of 9 Apr. 1794, Priestley identified Mr Lyon as 'an excellent farmer' who would be 'a valuable associate' for him and William Russell in their proposed purchase of land in Pennsylvania; Rutt, I, 230. 'Wednesday' was 9 Apr. 1794.

[3] For this letter from Priestley to Lindsey, see Rutt, I, 230.

[4] This 'Address of the Society of United Irishmen' to Priestley, dated Dublin, 28 Mar. 1794, was published as a separate (four-page) document; it is printed in Rutt, I, 218–22. I have not found a version in the London press. Lindsey's 'long letter' to Priestley has not survived.

[5] William Moffat, a friend of Muir and a lawyer in Edinburgh, attended Muir during his imprisonment in England prior to his transportation. Shortly after Muir's trial, he too was arrested in Scotland, but not charged with any offence; Bewley, *Muir of Huntershill*, p. 94.

[6] The trial of Danton took place on 2–4 Apr. 1794 and he was executed on 5 Apr. Robespierre was overthrown on 27 July 1794 and executed the following day.

⁷   Thomas Belsham, *Dishonest shame the primary source of the corruptions of the Christian doctrine.
     A sermon, preached at the Gravel Pit meeting, in Hackney, April 6, 1794* (London, 1794); the text
     is from Romans i. 16. Joshua Toulmin, *The immutability of God, and the trials of Christ's ministry;
     represented in two sermons, preached at Essex chapel in the Strand, March 30, and April 6, 1794*
     (London, 1794).

⁸   Thomas Walker (1749–1817), cotton merchant and prominent reformer in Manchester, was a leading
     member of the Manchester Revolution Society and co-founder of the *Manchester Herald*. In 1791,
     he became a member of the Unitarian Society; Unitarian Society minute book, p. 23. He incurred
     much hostility for his radical opinions and in Dec. 1792 his house was attacked by a loyalist mob. In
     1793, he was charged with seeking to overthrow the government and wishing for the king's death;
     see n. 9, below.

⁹   Walker and nine of his friends were tried at Lancaster assizes on 2 Apr. 1794. His defence was led by
     Thomas Erskine and he was acquitted on both the charges against him. The principal witness against
     Walker was an Irish weaver, Thomas Dunn (d. 1798), who had been loosely associated with reform
     societies in Manchester. At the trial, Dunn's evidence was shown to be perjured and he was sentenced
     to the pillory and two years' imprisonment. See Frida Knight, *The strange case of Thomas Walker.
     Ten years in the life of a Manchester radical* (London, 1957), chs. XII–XVI; and *State trials*, XXIII,
     1055–166.

¹⁰ Thomas Walker married in 1775 Hannah Shore (d. 1821), the sister of Lindsey's friend Samuel Shore
     III (1738–1828).

565. To RUSSELL SCOTT   14 APRIL 1794

Text: Scott Coll.
Addressed: Address missing.
Postmarked: Postmark missing.

London. April. 14 1794

Dear Sir

I thank you much for your long and most satisfactory letter which I received on Saturday, and particularly for your kind attention about the letter to Dʳ Priestley, that if possible it may not miss falling into his hands, if the ship should touch at your port.¹

Some things before I had heard which tended to lessen the respect I otherwise had entertained for Mʳ _____ :² but the facts you mention shew what poor creatures and how inconsistent the most promising characters may turn out, when filled with conceit of their own importance, and no due guard kept over their selfish passions. What concerns me especially in such cases, is that worthier men must thereby suffer so essentially and be deprived of those few comforts designed for them and so much needed in the wretched situation.

For what is past I apprehend, there can be no remedy, but a friend, Mʳ Joyce yesterday told me that he should use every endeavour in his power that things should be impartially adjusted in future, and intends to set out on Thursday even for Portsmouth, and see you on the friday, &c. I desired him expressly, neither in Town nor any where else to mention mine or any names, but only to state and inquire into the facts with which I had acquainted him.³

I hope Mʳ Palmer has received the money from Scotland which I remitted to him, though he does not take notice of it in the letter which I last received from him; which I wish he would do, that I may have it to shew, if the person in Scotland who sent it me, or any of his own relatives should inquire after it.⁴

Pray mention this to Mʳ J. Ellis, and at the same time acquaint him that about a fortnight ago I had the following inquiry after him in a postscript to a letter which I received from Dundee.

"The friends of J. Ellis here are anxious to learn about him. Do you hear that he is to be allowed to accompany Mr Palmer? I will thank you for any hints concerning him."[5]

We are much concerned at the report of J. Ellis having been put to so great expence in providing for Mr Palmer. If Mr Palmer lives, he will amply make it up to him; but as he has many rich relations, and I apprehend some property, in justice to Mr Ellis he will by some writing secure an ample compensation to him.[6]

On Saturday agreably to y^r direction, my wife sent a little parcell for you to Dr Hawes's N° 8 Spital Square, containing Dr Priestley's volume of lectures, and farewel Sermon.

I was not at the meeting of the Unitarian Society on Thursday last, though at the dinner after, where there was a respectable number. I do not find that any summons have been sent out to the members to send for their allotment of books, but apprehend it will not be very soon.[7]

We are truly grieved, that you still suffer so much from your dispiriting complaint, but apprehend it may be owing to too great exertions – therefore beg you will take care and spare yourself – and particularly not to expose yourself in going out to visit Mr Palmer or any body.[8]

I have time to add no more at present. You will be likely to hear from me again probably by Mr Joyce on Thursday.

Our kind regards to Mrs Scott with my wife's to yourself, not forgetting your young family.

Dear --- always most truly Yours
T. Lindsey.

P.S.

I have barely time to tell you that I have rec^d a letter from Dr P. at Falmouth,[9] so that there is no expectation of your seeing him, and you will have no trouble on that account which you so readily and kindly undertook.

I have left my letter to Mr Palmer unsealed, as it says more than I can add now, having been from home all morning and finding my letters at my return.[10] And you will as I mention hear from me again on Thursday.[11]

ADieu.

You will put a wafer in the letter inclosed.

Pray put Dr Priestleys letter in a cover directed to to [sic] me, and inclose it in a cover to

James Martin Esqr. Downing Street
Westminster.

---

1   The previous Saturday was 12 Apr. 1794. Although Scott's 'long and satisfactory' letter seems not to have survived, it is almost certainly the letter from which Lindsey quoted in his letter to Robert Millar of 17 Apr. 1794 (Letter 566).

2   This was Maurice Margarot (1745–1815), whom Palmer disliked; Bewley, *Muir of Huntershill*, pp. 106, 110.

3   'Thursday even' was 17 Apr. 1794.

4   I have not located this letter from Palmer to Lindsey. However, at HMCO there is a copy of a letter from Palmer to an unnamed recipient, written on board the *Surprise* and dated 23 Apr. 1794. It described the recipient as 'one of my best friends & benefactors' and thanked him or her for recent numbers of the *Cambridge Intelligencer*, 'a paper I hold in the highest estimation'; HMCO, Shepherd MSS, vol. X, no. 11. Probably the money from Scotland which Lindsey had remitted to Palmer had been gathered by members of the unitarian congregation in Dundee and forwarded to Lindsey by Robert Millar.

5 Lindsey almost certainly quoted here from a non-surviving letter from Robert Millar of Dundee, who was acquainted with James Ellis and his family. Ellis was indeed allowed to accompany Palmer to Botany Bay.

6 Palmer's family possessed considerable landed property in Bedfordshire, Berkshire and Wiltshire. Thomas Palmer himself ultimately made James Ellis his principal legatee.

7 'Thursday last' was 10 Apr. 1794, the day of the 'general quarterly meeting' of the Unitarian Society. Lindsey, indeed, was not present. The brief record of the meeting in the society's minute book (p. 51) made no mention of a summons to members to claim their allocation of books. It added, without giving names, that thirty-one members attended the dinner after the meeting.

8 Scott's 'dispiriting complaint' was gout; see Letter 574. Scott visited Palmer on board ship in Portsmouth harbour on several occasions.

9 See Rutt, I, 230–1.

10 Lindsey's letter to Palmer appears not to have survived.

11 The following Thursday was 17 Apr. 1794, the date of Lindsey's next (surviving) letter to Scott (Letter 567).

566. To ROBERT MILLAR   17 APRIL 1794

Text: DWL, MS 12.46 (4).
Printed: Graham, 'Unhappy country', 132–4 (first six paragraphs).
Addressed: Address missing.
Postmarked: Postmark missing.

London. April. 17. 1794.

Dear Sir,

A more than ordinary accumulation of business, and a reluctance to lose any moments I could spend with D[r] Priestley, from the time I received your last letter till he left us, has prevented my writing again, and particularly answering your inquiry about James Ellis, but which however I did not wholly neglect, for I took an early opportunity of mentioning it to Mr Palmer in my letter to him, and hope M[r] Ellis's friends have had satisfactory accounts of him.[1] I may not omit however to add here as I am on the subject, that in several letters rec[d] within these ten days from Portsmouth, one of them yesterday, James Ellis who is every day with my friend[2] when on land is continually named with those comendations due to him for his attachment to M[r] Palmer and many valuable qualities; and I shall transcribe a paragraph out of M[r] Palmer's last letter to me, which I rec[d] on tuesday,[3] which will give pleasure to all his and M[r] Ellis's friends.

"Providence, says he, has sent a young man of the name of Boston, one of general science and formerly belonging to the medical faculty. It was he who ran by night, and informed D[r] Priestley that his house would be burned. His whole time is spent among the sick and in supplying the deficiencies of the government doctor. His labours are very successful. It is for him I want the books &c. He is going out Settler, and our greatest comfort arises from the hope of living together. His experience in agriculture will be of infinite use to James Ellis, and his knowlege of the arts to all the colony."[4]

You see from this, that people of character are not discouraged from going voluntarily even to Botany bay, and to settle in the country. The grand objection is the distance, a six months voyage.

I will transcribe also for your satisfaction and that of others of M[r] Palmer, and M[r] Ellis's friends another paragraph of a letter from my friend at Portsmouth.

"I understand, that forty pounds each, has been been [*sic*] paid to the Capt. out of the common stock subscribed by the friends of liberty, for Mess[rs]. Palmer, Muir,

Skirving, Ellis and Margarot, in order that they might have a proper supply of fresh provisions &c instead of the comon salt food given to the convicts. For this the Capt. allows them every day every day [*sic*] either roast or boiled beef, roast or boiled mutton &c &c. a pint of port wine each after dinner, with some bottled porter, and a proper proportion of these after supper. The provisions are good, and they have plenty of live-stock for the voyage."[5]

How much we feel D[r] Priestley's separation, in this house, where we comonly were happy in seeing him once or twice a week or oftner, is not to be described, for with all his other powers, he excelled eminently in the private virtues of a friend and chearful, social converse. I have had two letters from him since he left us, the last in Falmouth road,[6] and hope I shall hear no more till he gets to New York, unless a letter come by a ship they meet with by the way. We trust that the Divine Providence leads him for greater good beyond the Atlantic, now he has finished all that seemed to be designed and laid out for him here. And I am glad to observe already, and others report to me the same, that peoples minds begin to be greatly softened and changed towards him, and some who were otherwise before disposed, to say, why should he have gone away: nobody would have hurt him. M[r] Johnson also notes a greater demand for his works.

I have never acknowledged an obliging letter I rec[d] from M[r] Duncan of your town, with a remittance of money which he had taken the trouble to collect for our friend, by the sale of his goods &c; unless in a short line, which I desired you to deliver to him.[7] I must beg you to send the inclosed which contains my acknowlegements more at length.[8]

It was a satisfaction to me and my wife to learn from your last, that M[rs] Millar and yourself were in good health. My wife is in her best plight; and desires to join in kind regards and wishes for you both, and that we may all live so here as to be approved by our maker, and meet together in the heavenly kingdom; wherever it be, hereafter. It was a sentiment of D[r] Priestleys, and not of him alone, that it might be perhaps in this present beautiful world; which certainly would be a paradise, if man was but what he ought to be, and all were christians indeed.

Pray, at your full leisure, let me know how your church goes on, now that you have lost your pastor.[9] I remain always with much esteem
          affectionately Yours
          T. Lindsey.

---

1 I have not been able to trace this letter from Lindsey to Palmer.

2 Russell Scott.

3 The previous Tuesday was 15 Apr. 1794.

4 I have not located this letter from Palmer to Lindsey (but see Letter 565, n. 4). John Boston (d. 1804), a sympathizer with Priestley and admirer of Paine, voluntarily accompanied Palmer, Skirving and Margarot to New South Wales, where he settled and set up as a merchant and farmer, and where his radical opinions led him into a series of clashes with the authorities. His claim that he forewarned Priestley of the riots at Birmingham in July 1791 cannot be verified, although Lindsey and several of his contemporaries evidently believed it.

5 This letter was almost certainly the 'long and most satisfactory' letter from Russell Scott to Lindsey which the latter acknowledged in Letter 565.

6 For Priestley's two letters to Lindsey, 9 and 11 Apr. 1794, see Rutt, I, 230–1.

7 This is the first of several references which Lindsey made to a Mr Duncan of Dundee. This is a fairly common name and identification is not easy, especially as there was no Church of Scotland clergyman of that name in Dundee at this time. Four men named Duncan are listed in the *Dundee register 1783*, ed. Ada Pellow (Dundee, 2003), p. 8. One might conjecture that the Mr Duncan who

wrote a (non-surviving) letter to Lindsey was James Duncan junior, a member of the speculative society; *Dundee register*, p. 8. For the collection of money for Palmer, see Letter 565, n. 4.

8   The 'inclosed' seems not to have survived.

9   Palmer had been the minister to the unitarian congregation at Dundee.

567. To RUSSELL SCOTT   17 APRIL 1794

Text: Scott Coll.
Printed: McLachlan, 'Lindsey to Scott', 120, where the letter is
                 mis-dated 10 Apr. 1794 (most of first paragraph; first sentence
                 of fourth paragraph).
Addressed: [In Hannah Lindsey's hand] Revd Russel Scot/Portsmouth
Postmarked: Postmark missing.

London. april. 17. 1794

Dear Sir,

Yesterday forenoon, on receiving your letter I immediately went to St Pauls Churchyard, and got from Mr Johnson, Evanson, Christie's Sermons, ½ doz. of the new French Constitution, a Bible the largest print he had in 8vo. to which I added a copy of Daniels Septuagint of my own, much valued by me, because John Biddel supported himself in prison by correcting the Press for Daniel – with two copies of Lardners logos, and Hartley on the X^t Religion and six copies of Mr Palmer's Letter to Inglis:[1]

These were all packed up for Mr Palmer and on the outside directed for you, and in a note I desired you to take the trouble and be at the expence of conveying them to Mr Palmer: and I trust he will receive them in time, before they sail.

This parcell went by [the] Portsmouth Coach, from the Angel Inn, behind St Clements, and our Servant saw it booked, and they promised to take all care of it.[2]

I also here inclose a Bank Bill for £10. the gift of a friend of ours to Mr Palmer,[3] and which I think it advisable to send to you, that you may get it turned into cash and safely conveyed to him, as I imagine a bank note would be of no use at Botany bay. Perhaps you may be able to see James Ellis or some friend who is going to Spithead, and along with it I beg you to let this short letter be conveyed to him.

With respect to the Septuagint, Graber,[4] which Mr Dyer sent, and for which I have paid him, if you have not a copy already, I would beg your acceptance of it: otherwise you may send it up directed for me at Mr Johnson's, as it does not suit Mr Palmer.

If only three lines, I should be glad to hear from you by the return of the post, to know that the inclosed arrives safe, and also how the wind stands and whether our friend will certainly sail on Saturday.[5]

With our joint kind remembrances to Mrs Scott and yourself I remain Dear Sir Your much obliged

          T. Lindsey

Mr Toulmin is here to breakfast with us. He proposes leaving town to morrow. I think I told you several of the congregation have desired him to print two sermons preached in our chapel, and have engaged he shall be at no expence about it.[6]

---

1   It is not clear to which of Edward Evanson's works Lindsey referred; a possibility is the second edition of his *Letter to the Right Reverend Richard Hurd, DD, Lord Bishop of Worcester, wherein the importance of the prohecies of the New Testament and the nature of the grand apostacy predicted in them are particularly and impartially considered* (London, 1792). For William Christie's *Discourses*

on the divine unity, see Vol. I, Letter 287, n. 12. For Benjamin Flower's work on the French constitution, see Letter 458, n. 5. While imprisoned for his anti-trinitarian opinions in 1652, John Biddle
(1616–62) corrected the proofs of the edition of the Greek Septuagint prepared for publication by the
printer Roger Daniel, and it was published in 1653. Nathaniel Lardner's *Letter written in the year
1730, concerning the question, whether the Logos supplied the place of an human soul in the person
of Jesus Christ* (first published in London in 1759) was re-issued in 1793 (by the Unitarian Society);
for 'Hartley on the Christian religion', see Letter 544, n. 6. 'Palmer's letter to Inglis' was Thomas
Fyshe Palmer's *An attempt to refute a sermon on the godhead of Jesus Christ and to restore the long
lost truth of the first commandment* (Edinburgh, 1792). Palmer was replying to Henry David Inglis,
Sermon, proving, from the word of God, the all-important doctrine of the godhead of Jesus Christ
(Edinburgh, 1792). Inglis (1757–1806) was an attorney and a pastor at the baptist meeting house in
Edinburgh. Palmer's *Attempt* took the form of a series of letters addressed to Inglis. He dedicated it
to the unitarian congregations of Edinburgh, Dundee, Forfar, Arbroath, Montrose and Newburgh.

2   For the Angel Inn, the point of departure for the Portsmouth mail coach, see Letter 422. The rate
books (poor rate, watch rate, paving rate) of the parish of St Clement Danes, where Essex Street was
situated, may be consulted at the City of Westminster Archive Centre. However, they do not reveal
the names of servants.

3   McLachlan, 'Lindsey to Scott', 128 n. 20, speculates that the donor was Grafton. Another possibility
is William Tayleur, who gave £10 to William Winterbotham (see Letter 575).

4   The German-born biblical scholar Johannes Ernst Grabe (1666–1711), who settled at Oxford in the
late 1690s, edited a series of volumes incorporating most of the Septuagint in four volumes published
in Oxford between 1707 and 1720; the last two volumes to appear (vols. II and III) were published
after his death.

5   Saturday 19 Apr. 1794. Palmer and his fellow-prisoners finally sailed for Australia on 2 May 1794.

6   For Toulmin's two sermons preached at Essex Street chapel in Mar. and Apr. 1794, see Letter 564,
n. 7.

568. To WILLIAM TAYLEUR   19 APRIL 1794

Text: JRUL, Lindsey Letters, vol. III, no. 38.
Printed: McLachlan, 'More letters', 376–7 (very short extracts from
                  first, second and seventh paragraphs); 373 (first five sentences
                  of eleventh paragraph); 374 (the 'p.s'.).
Addressed: To/William Tayleur Esqr/Shrewsbury
Endorsed: 19th April 1794
Postmarked: AP 19 94

London. Apr. 19. 1794

Dear Sir,

As I am persuaded that few things will give you greater pleasure, than to hear
of Dr Priestleys welfare and happiness in his voyage as well as in his settlement
afterwards, I shall send an extract from his last letter to me, dated friday evening –
april. 11. off Falmouth.

After describing their having met with a strong gale, which had made him and
Mrs Priestley, with others very sick, but that they soon recruited when it grew more
calm, and mentioning their peculiar felicity, that they had gotten farther in *three
days*, than the Captain told them, he got in *three weeks and five days*, his last voyage;

"We begin, says he, to be acquainted with all our Cabin – and many of the
Steerage-passengers, and like them very well. They are all well behaved, and good
company. The only woman cabin passenger is come from France, knows our friends
there, and seems well acquainted with the Politics of the country.

On the whole I think we shall pass our time pretty well during the voyage"

What follows you will be so good to let be for yourself alone.

"I have much time for reading, and shall be able to write. I am meditating a discourse on the *causes of infidelity*, led to it by reflection on that of the person we talked of the last time but one that [we] were together,[1] and of other intelligent men.

" I think I shall nearly read over my Greek Testament, before I get to New York; and I think I read it with more satisfaction than ever. Unbelievers, I am confident, do not read it, except with a predisposition to cavil".[2]

M[r] Rowe took his breakfast with us this morning, where he met M[r] Hampson, the Minister at Tunbridge wells, formerly of the late M[r] John Wesleys connection, whom you may have heard D[r] P. or myself speak of. He says the methodists are growing more and more liberal, in religious matters, and also in political, and that the late decision of the Chancellor with respect to the investment of the property of their places of worship in the hands of their Trustees, and not of their ministers will promote this good end.[3]

Having rec[d] this week a letter from M[r] Palmer, on board the Surprize, at Spithead, I shall add a short extract. Upon my having said to him in my letter, that if on his return from his seven years exile at Botany-bay, this country should not be such as he could safely live in, America, where he would find D[r] Priestley, would be open; he begins

"I hear of the promised land with rapture, and nothing could be so much my heart's wish as to live and to die there. Indeed it will be necessary as in my present ruined circumstances, I should not be able to live in England". N.B. The Master of Queens' college Camb. his old enemy has deprived him of his fellowship on acc[t] of the sentence against him,[4] and he has lost no small part of his fortune by lending it to worthy unfortunate men in Scotland. But to proceed with his letter

"Providence has sent a young man of the name of Boston, one of general science and formerly belonging to the faculty. He was one of those at Birmingham who ran by night, and informed D[r] Priestley that his house would be burned. His whole time is spent among the sick, and in supplying the deficiencies of the government-doctor. His labours are very successful. It is for him I want M[r] Christie's Unitarian Discourses &c for which he is well prepared by having attended D[r] Priestley. We are sworn brothers. He is going out Settler, and our greatest comfort arises from the hope of our being together. His experience in agriculture will be of infinite use to James Ellis, and his knowlege of the arts to all the colony".[5]

My wife sends most kind respects. I remain your ever obliged & affectionate
T. Lindsey.

M[r] Rowe hopes you have rec[d] D[r] Priestley sermons and Discourses, a present from the author; and desires me to add that the Society-books will soon be ready to be delivered.[6]

P.S. Robespierre was massacred yesterday, upon the Exchange. To day he has released the Son of Capet, and declared for the Monarchy.[7]

---

1   Lindsey omitted the name of this person: it was Thomas Cooper; see DWL, MS 12.12, fos. 232–3 and Rutt, I, 231.
2   For this letter of Priestley to Lindsey, 11 Apr. 1794, see Rutt, I, 230–1.
3   For John Hampson of Tunbridge Wells, see Vol. I, Letter 375, n. 3, and for Lindsey's visit to him in 1790, see Letter 425. In 1784, John Wesley's 'deed of declaration', registered in the court of chancery, had vested legal control of his connexion in a group of 100 preachers whom he had carefully selected. He was anxious to prevent any encouragement of heterodoxy by lay trustees, as had happened among numerous English presbyterian congregations in the eighteenth century. See Michael R. Watts, *The dissenters. Volume II. The expansion of evangelical nonconformity* (Oxford, 1995), pp. 30–1.
4   See Letter 538, n. 7. The president of Queens' College, Cambridge, from 1788 until his death in 1820 was Isaac Milner.

5 For John Boston, see Letter 566.

6 These publications were Priestley's *Discourses on revealed religion*, and *Present state of Europe*, together with his farewell discourse (see Letter 565, n. 7). By the 'Society-books' Lindsey meant the books published that year (1794) by the Unitarian Society; see *Unitarian Society ... 1794*, unpaginated list of the society's publications, following the rules and list of members. David Hartley's *Of the truth of the Christian religion* (see Letter 544, n. 6) was one of them.

7 Lindsey's source for this bizarre story is unclear. The *Morning Chronicle*, 16 Apr. 1794, reported allegations in the national convention that the Girondin Jacques Guillaume Thouret (1746–94) and others in the Luxembourg prison had planned to break out and to release 'Capet' (i.e. the son of Louis XVI, known to French royalists as Louis XVII). They would then 'put him into the arms of Danton, who was to present to the people their new Despot'. Danton was executed on 5 Apr. 1794 and Thouret on 22 Apr.

569. To RUSSELL SCOTT   22 APRIL 1794

Text: Scott Coll.
Addressed: Address missing.
Postmarked: Postmark missing.

London. Apr. 22. 1794

Dear Sir,

It was not in my power to write yesterday to thank you for all your attentions to make the most worthy sufferers Palmer and Skirving comfortable and happy.

We are rejoiced also to hear of Mr Gurneys being with you at so fortunate a moment, and his exerting himself so successfully for Messrs. Palmer, Skirving and Ellis.[1] We shall be happy to see him whenever he calls, and to learn further particulars of the D. of Grafton &c, as Mr Palmer had time only to write a short letter and mention the Dukes letter.[2]

By your acc^t., James Ellis's going to Botany bay is likely to be of substantial benefit and comfort to his friend to a much greater extent than was thought of. I persuade myself that providence will bless [this] disinterested design of accompanying Mr Palmer to himself and to many others. We hope Mr Shields has taken his face as well as of the other gentleman, as one would be glad to have and to preserve it.[3]

We are glad that Mr Palmer will be provided with a Bible at last, as also that the good creature Skirving has gotten what he likes. I hope you have brought back the Septuagint Mr Dyer sent, which was not wanted, and will keep it; if it may be of any service as I payed for it.[4] Mr Dyer brought me the inclosed for Mr Palmer, but I am apprehensive the Surprize will have sailed before this arrives. Mr Palmer expresses himself highly delighted with my wife's spectacles: but he will feel still greater comfort and security for his eyesight in the addition of glasses that the last parcell conveyed, to him, and which we were glad had come safe to You.[5]

When you next write, we shall be happy to know all the particulars of Messrs Palmer, Ellis, Skirving &c till they sail away out of sight especially if the Capt. had received full instructions concerning the most friendly treatment of Mr Ellis as a free Settler.

Our earnest prayers for them go along with them, that they may be happy and instruments of the greatest good to others. If you shoud see or have an opportunity of writing to Mr Palmer after you have received this, you will tell him I did not write, as I was assured here that no letter would reach him, and I had nothing to add more than in my last. My wife joins in kind rememberances to Mrs Scott and yourself – and I remain ever most truly

Yours T. Lindsey

I expect very soon to have Mr Paley's new work to convey to you.[6]

---

1   John Gurney (1768–1845) married Maria Hawes, the sister of Scott's wife, in 1797. A lawyer and subsequently a judge, he was called to the bar at the Inner Temple on 3 May 1793. In 1794, he participated in the defence of Daniel Isaac Eaton, Thomas Hardy and John Horne Tooke. Having established a rewarding practice on the home circuit, and a reputation for effective forensic performances, in 1832, he was appointed a baron of the exchequer and knighted. According to the article by J. A. Hamilton, revised by C. Pease-Watkin, in *ODNB*, XXIV, 285–6, Gurney was a dissenter in his youth, but attended anglican worship in his later years. Because of his sympathy with radicals under threat of prosecution in the 1790s and because of his family connexions with Scott, Lindsey had several communications with him.

2   I have not located these letters between Palmer and Grafton. For a possible gift from Grafton to Palmer, see Letter 567, n. 3.

3   Mr Shields was probably the artist Richard Shields, a friend of the Barbaulds at Hampstead; see Bewley, *Muir of Huntershill*, pp. 12, 97, 151. I have not located his portrait of Palmer.

4   Probably this was Grabe's edition of the Septuagint; see Letter 567, n. 4.

5   On 15 Sept. 1795, Palmer wrote to Lindsey, from New South Wales, 'Mrs Lindsey will accept of my best regard; her spectacles often recall her to my mind'; Belsham, *Memoirs*, p. 362.

6   This was William Paley's *A view of the evidences of Christianity in three parts. Part I. Of the direct historical evidence of Christianity ... Part II. Of the auxiliary evidences ... Part III. A brief consideration of some popular objections*. It was published in London in 1794. There was a sixth edition in 1797 and numerous further editions thereafter.

---

570. To RUSSELL SCOTT   25 APRIL 1794

Text: Scott Coll.
Addressed: To/The Rev^d. Russell Scott/Portsmouth
Postmarked: Postmark missing.

London. April. 25. 1794.

Dear Sir,

I am very sorry that Mr Ellis is still neglected above.[1] It will be well if it be not owing to some evill leaven working against him, through evil reports, for his honest principles. I shall however endeavour this very day to speak to the D. of Grafton about him, carrying this letter under a cover for him to Frank: and if I learn any thing from him, or he can do any thing for him, will write it to you on the inside of the cover.

Mr Gurney brought back the books and did us the favour to call and give a full account of all matters, and particularly of your intercourse with a great person, which I apprehend was unsuccessful in the issue.[2]

It is but too plain, quam male patrissat,[3] and it would seem to have been a commission much against the grain. I must ever however honour you for the kind exertions you have made for J^s Ellis and Messrs Palmer and Skirving in particular, who must without further assistance have gone away wretchedly unprovided. And as Mr Gurney intimates, now is the time for their friends to settle the means of such annual provisions as they will want, being sent to them.

I do not write to Mr Palmer, as it would be merely a repetition of a last farewell: but having gotten a copy of Mr Paleys work, just out,[4] which I am persuaded will be useful and gratifying and yield him comfort, my wife engages to put up a copy and send it to you by the Coach this evening, that if possible he may received [*sic*] it before they sail away. But if he be out of reach, you will be so good as to accept it, as I intended you a copy very soon.

Yesterday I buried Mr West in Bunhill=fields. It had been his desire by writing, that either Dr Priestley or myself shoud do him that sad office. Had life been spared and faculties, he might have continued a useful public man, and servicable to his family. I am glad however they are very sufficiently provided for.[5] Mrs West was buried but six weeks before him.[6] A few years back, where could you have found so fine a couple, so likely for life.

I am sending a parcell to Dr Priestley in a ship that is going to New York, and which may arrive there soon after him, and I trust will find him and his as we all wish him. I have no doubt of his being honourable received in that State as well as any other in that continent.

My wife joins in kind regards for Mrs Scott, yourself and little folks with Yours ever

T. Lindsey

P.S. I was sorry Mr Gurney had the trouble of bringing back Graber.[7] I presume you had it, or hope you w^d have kept it. Pray send 3 lines to Mr Palmer, if not gone, with my reasons for not writing.

---

1   Since James Ellis proposed to travel with Palmer to Australia as a free settler and not as a convict, Palmer proposed that he should be conveyed there at public expense. However, Patrick Campbell, the captain of the *Surprise* transport, refused this request and insisted that Palmer should pay Ellis's fare. Appeals to the the ministry in London were unavailing. See Bewley, *Muir of Huntershill*, pp. 109–10, and TNA: HO 42/29, fos. 298r–299v (Campbell to the secretary of state's office, Whitehall, 17 Mar. 1794).

2   For John Gurney, see Letter 569, n. 1. Lindsey often referred to George III as a 'great person'. This seems to be a reference to a petition made by Scott for clemency for Palmer and his associates, although I have not located it in the relevant home office files, TNA: HO 42/28–9.

3   How poorly (or how little) he resembles his father. I am obliged to Mr David Powell for advice on this expression. Possibly this is a veiled reference to George III and his father, Frederick, prince of Wales (1707–44), or to Pitt the younger and his father William Pitt the elder (1708–78).

4   See Letter 569, n. 6.

5   James West was indeed buried in Bunhill Fields on 24 Apr. 1794; TNA: RG4/3987, fo. 124 (Register of burials at Bunhill Fields burial ground). He was a benefactor of Essex Street chapel and (in 1783) a member of the SPKS; see Vol. I, Letter 282, n. 33, and Appendix I, p. 568.

6   The wife of James West does not appear in the Bunhill Fields burial register (n. 5, above), and I have not been able to trace her date and place of burial in the RG4 records. Disappointingly, the will of James West (TNA: PRO PROB11/1246, fos. 78r–81r) refers to his 'dear wife' without stating her first name(s).

7   See Letter 567, n. 4.

---

571. To RUSSELL SCOTT   1 MAY 1794

Text: Scott Coll.
Addressed: [In Hannah Lindsey's hand] Revd Russel Scot/Portsmouth
Postmarked: Postmark missing.

London. May. 1. 1794.

Dear Sir,

I must in the first place inform you, that unfortunately your letter inclosing mine to Dr Priestley, did not come to me regularly till some days after it arrived in Downing-street, on wch account a letter you inclosed, which I sent imediately by the penny post, would be received later than it ought to have been.[1]

In the next; I did not answer your letter of the 27th. which came to me the next day, as the D. of Grafton had set out that morning for Northamptonshire, not to return till the end of the week, and I had no knowlege whatsoever of L^d. Euston nor means of making application to him.[2]

For the same cause also, though your second letter came yesterday, I deferred writing till this day, as I had already procured a frank for the purpose. You did well however to remind me of Mr Johnson's monthly parcell, though my parcell for you had been sent to him before I received your letter, and I hope he will send it without fail. I spoke to him myself yesterday about it, and my wife called in the evening, and it is well she did so, as Mr Johnson was ill, and not able to attend to any thing, and she took the parcell out of a heap of others, and gave it to the shopman[3] to see to it's going, so that I hope after all you will have it.

I reckon it very unfortunate that James Ellis's business was not settled sooner with the Captain, and fear that nothing further can be done in it here, before the ship sails.[4] But though the wind that has brought back and still keeps it in port, will I fear bring nothing favourable to J. Ellis's affair, it has been very fortunate that it has afforded an opportunity of laying in a cargo of so necessary an article as fresh water, the defect of which must have been owing to a very blameable neglect somewhere.

From the first of your visiting Mr Palmer before you came up to London, and since your return, my wife and I have particularly remarked your compassionate regards for him and his fellow-sufferers, and unwearied endeavours to relieve their sufferings, and to serve them by every means in your power. And it has been principally owing to your endeavours, and Mr Gurneys having been fortunately with you at the time, that M^{rss} Palmer, Skirving and J^s Ellis have been so comfortably provided with all necessaries, and if in any thing the last has fallen short, it has not been owing to any want of the most earnest zeal in you to procure it for him, to the last moment. And as you have been at a great deal of extra expence in boats, paying of carriage &c &c at our desire we beg you will accept this small bill of £5 only to round off matters a little, and to testify our own acknowlegements of your benevolent exertions.

You may depend on my telling Dr Priestley that you follow him with every wish of happiness and usefulness to him and his family. We trust he is now sailing away with a fair wind, but do not expect to hear of him of some time unless by accident of their meeting with a vessel bound to England. You will be so good as to let me know by two lines of the arrival of this letter, and I hope of the parcell at the same time, about which we have been not a little anxious.

No less than two extraordinary Gazettes, with intelligence of success from the D. of Yorke [*sic*] were cried about the Streets yesterday, with the firing of the Park and Tower Guns: Some are so wicked as to say this was done to influence the debates last night on the Prussian Subsidy.[5] I have however not heard what passed, nor seen any account of our victories.[6] We beg both to be kindly remembered to Mrs Scott, my wife to yourself. I remain always with sincere esteem very truly Yours

T. Lindsey

[In Hannah Lindsey's hand]

Pray did you ever get D^r P's three last publications wch went to D^r. Hawes's directed to be sent to you by Mr Gurney, who however was then gone.[7]

---

1   Neither Scott's letter to Lindsey, nor Lindsey's to Priestley with which it was enclosed (evidently sent via James Martin MP in Downing Street), has survived.

2   Similarly, Scott's letter to Lindsey of 27 Apr. 1794 has not survived. Grafton had departed from
    London to his country retreat at Wakefield Lodge, Northamptonshire. George Henry Fitzroy (1760–
    1844), earl of Euston, was the eldest son of the 3rd duke of Grafton. He was MP for Cambridge
    University from 1784 until he succeeded his father as 4th duke of Grafton in 1811.

3   I have not been able to identify Joseph Johnson's 'shopman', from the biographies of Johnson by
    Gerald P. Tyson or by Helen Braithwaite; from Johnson's will; or from the letterbook containing his
    business correspondence, which only covers the years from 1795 to 1809; Humanities and Social
    Sciences Library, New York Public Library.

4   Possibly Lindsey referred here to James Ellis's business as a cotton spinner in Dundee.

5   On 1 May 1794, the *Morning Chronicle* quoted two *London Gazettes Extraordinary*, both dated 30
    Apr., with messages from Frederick, duke of York, announcing a victory of the British and Austrian
    forces in the region of Le Cateau, in the campaign against the French in the Netherlands. This was
    the battle of Troisvilles on 26 Apr., and it followed allied victories at Château Cambrésis (17 Apr.)
    and Villers-en-Cauchies (24 Apr.). On 1 May 1794 the *London Chronicle* reported that guns in the
    'park' (probably Green Park) and the Tower were fired 'yesterday' (i.e. 30 Apr.) to celebrate these
    victories. On 30 Apr. 1794, the house of commons and the house of lords both debated the subsidy
    treaty with Prussia and the convention with the Dutch. In the commons' committee, Fox's amendment
    to reduce the British subsidy to Prussia from £2.5 million to £1.5 million was defeated by 134 votes
    to 33, and the two treaties were approved. In the lords, the treaties were approved by 99 votes to 6;
    Cobbett, *Parl. hist.*, XXXIII, 437–52, 452–67. Lindsey's use of the word 'wicked' in this context was
    presumably ironical.

6   For these victories, see n. 5, above. The British campaign in the Netherlands ended in defeat and
    withdrawal in 1794–5.

7   For these three publications of Priestley, see Letter 568, n. 6.

572. To ROBERT MILLAR   **2 MAY 1794**

Text: DWL, MS 12.46 (5).
Printed: Graham, 'Unhappy country', 135 (most of first paragraph;
                 parts of sixth and seventh paragraphs, with minor errors of
                 transcription).
Addressed: Address missing.
Endorsed: Lond⁰ 2ᵈ May 1794/Mr Lindsey/Various
Postmarked: Postmark missing.

London. May. 2. 1794

Dear Sir,

Many engagements of different kinds have hindred me from acknowleging
earlier your long and friendly letter; several of them some way or other relating
to our friend Mᵣ Palmer or his companions, that they might not sail away without
every convenience that could be procured for them. A common friend, a minister
at Portsmouth,[1] followed him with a small parcell and letter, in a boat, no less that
14 miles and was happy soon to find the Surprize amidst so many other ships on
Saturday afternoon last, and after staying two hours, took a final farewel as he
thought, but the wind changing the whole fleet was forced to put back and has not
yet sailed. Mᵣ. P. is perfectly recovered. Mᵣ J. Ellis had not been so well, but was also
quite recruited; and all longed to get out to sea, that they might get rid of some great
nusances [*sic*] in port, by women being suffered to come on board to the soldiers &c
and that they might be less confined and enjoy more air and exercise.

I do not wonder that you have been considerably affected by the seemingly
unfriendly neglect which you describe, but which I am inclined to think was not
really so, and he[2] must have written but the letters never have reached You. This
I am rather inclined to believe, as for a long space no notice was taken of many
letters I sent him although I found afterwards that he had written punctually, but

the letters had been suppressed or lost. For assuredly your long friendship, intimate connection, constant kind attention towards him especially after his imprisonment and the thought that on you would so much devolve, at his departure, the care of your little church at Dundee, these circumstance[s] all together would compell him to write. At all events however I am pleased to see your disposition towards him to be still the same as if your correspondence had been ever so frequent, and your value for his many excellent qualities undiminished.

I do not wonder you are so much taken with many most serious things in Dr Priestleys Fast-Sermon. One thing I hesitate about, the speedy, and personal appearance of Christ: but it was an idea with which he was much impressed.[3] You may depend upon my sending You the copies of it which you desire, with my own farewel discourse and some other little things which I have purely to give away, and I shall not fail to mention how you may indemnify me. And I shall desire our bookseller Mr Johnson to inquire out the first Dundee ship that comes to You.

Your large account of your society and your zeal and labours to keep it up, in the midst of so many difficulties, give me the greatest satisfaction. May the Almighty strengthen and support you in so necessary and important a service; and also dispose and qualify your collegues to fill their useful parts in the work. I wish you could point out any books that I could send, which might be of use to You.

It will give you pleasure to learn that Mr Belsham who is the principal and resident tutor and Divinity teacher in our college at Hackney, and who at Dr Priestleys recomendation was chosen to suceed [*sic*] him as pastor and morning preacher to the congregation, is likely to fill that station with singular benefit, as he continues the same methods wch D^r P adopted, and has betwixt 30 and 40 catechumens in his highest class every sunday of young persons from 17 or 18 to 30, some of them married who come from different parts.

We seem to be driven on by a strange fatality to make ourselves principals in a war with which we have properly nothing to do, especially now the proposed object is changed from what it was at first to the settling of the interior government of the french and restoring the monarchy instead of leaving them to their own choice.[4]

I had intended a longer letter but cannot accomplish it in time. I inclose two copies of an address to Dr Priestley which came since he left us. It has been reprinted here, with the little addition that you see at the end.[5] My wife desires to join in kind rememberances to Mrs Millar.[6] You are a high favourite, as she honours you exceeding for your mild and gentle manners and prudent active zeal at the same time. I remain with high esteem most truly Yours

T. Lindsey

1   Russell Scott.

2   Thomas Fyshe Palmer.

3   This was Priestley's *Present state of Europe*; for the millenarian expectations to which Lindsey referred, see pp. 27–31.

4   Lindsey believed that British objectives in the war had changed from self-defence to an aspiration to co-operate with French royalists with a view to effecting the restoration of the Bourbons. The powerful counter-revolutionary rising in the Vendée had been defeated only with difficulty at the end of 1793 and further royalist risings were anticipated.

5   Probably this was the address of the United Irishmen to Priestley; see Letter 564, n. 4. By 'the little addition that you see at the end', Lindsey probably meant the fourth and last page of this document, which took the form of a letter of support, dated 28 Mar. 1794, to Palmer, Muir, Skirving, Margarot and Gerrald.

6   Robert Millar's wife, whom he married in 1790, was Jean, née Scott; she died in 1801.

573. To ?JOSHUA TOULMIN   3 MAY 1794

Text: Belsham, *Memoirs*, p. 235 n. *.

Note: The manuscript of this letter seems not to have survived. Belsham identified Toulmin as the recipient by noting that the letter was addressed to the 'same friend' as those of 20 Feb. (Letter 551) and
8 Mar. 1794 (Letter 552). Belsham printed two separate extracts from this letter in the same footnote,
although he did not state explicitly that the two extracts came from the same letter; that they did is an
editorial assumption, based on the arrangement of Belsham's footnote (*Memoirs*, p. 235 n. *) and on the
references to Russell Scott which are common to both extracts. It is also an editorial assumption that the
two passages were not continuous in that same letter. Hence the extracts are presented here in the order
in which they appeared in Belsham's *Memoirs* and are separated by a broken line. The words in square
brackets are Belsham's; the context was the transportation of Muir and Palmer.

[In a letter to the same friend, dated May 3, 1794, Mr. Lindsey states, that they had
then actually set sail, and taken leave of their native country, never, alas! to return
again.] A letter from Mr. Scott this day[1] mentions the whole fleet being at length out
of sight yesterday morning, with a very fair wind down the channel; and whatever
some intend, I trust a good Providence carries some to Botany Bay for most important purposes of human virtue and happiness.

Mr Scott cannot enough be commended for his exertions to serve those worthy
martyrs, and to see them accommodated with everything needful.

1   I have not located this letter from Russell Scott to Lindsey, and presumably it has not survived.

574. To RUSSELL SCOTT   6 MAY 1794

Text: Scott Coll.
Printed: Scott, *Family biography*, pp. 87–8 (first, second and ninth
                  paragraphs); McLachlan, 'Lindsey to Scott', 120 (part of first
                  two sentences of fifth paragraph, concerning William Stone).
Addressed: To/The Rev^d. Russell Scott/Portsmouth
Endorsed: May 6./94
Postmarked: Postmark missing.

London. May. 6. 1794

Dear Sir,
    I should not have written to day, as I have so little time left for it, if I had not
got a bit[?] of a frank for you, which however will suit the dimensions of my letter.
    There are a few characters, who by their benevolent dispositions and upright
manly, generous conduct compell ones affectionate regards and esteem the more
you see and know them, and these have always been mine and my wife's feelings
towards yourself, so that you are not to wonder that we are at any time desirous of
expressing our regards.
    What we are most solicitous for at present is the state of your health, which the
gouty habit of your inheritance makes so tender and precarious, and which you
must watch over, and take all the care you can of not overplying the machine, till it
becomes stronger, which I trust it will in time.
    M^essrs Palmer, Skirving and Ellis will have cause always to remember your kind
and successful efforts for them, and I hope the latter, as it was a case of necessity,
would so make up matters with Capt. Campbell as not to have him hostile to him
during the voyage or after it.[1]

The two Mr Belshams are just gone out with my wife to the Exhibition,[2] which interval I I [*sic*] seize to write a few lines: they had been speaking of the seizure of Mr Wm Stone by a king's messenger a few days since. You know his brother is naturalized at Paris, and he may have been indiscreet in writing to him tho' far from any treasonable intentions or as some surmize, may have sent him money, of which the english have lately been in the greatest want at Paris.[3] In all times, but in these especially where peoples minds are so agitated and in such extremes, too much caution cannot be used to do nothing liable to misinterpretation.

You will have seen Mr T. Paynes Age of Reason &c advertised – and also his creed, an extract from it, in the morning chronicle, if that paper has fallen in your way.[4] The creed will lead to think better of the work than it will be found to deserve. His objections to Revelation are not taken from itself, but the corruptions of it, and shew his exceeding great ignorance of the subject; for I cannot think it dissimulation, as some call it.

Mr Toulmin preached two sermons at our chapel, which he was desired to print, but a gentleman observing, that it would only be desiring him to put himself to a certain expence for an uncertain return, the hint was taken, and the printing defrayed, chiefly by Mr Brand Hollis. I shall take an opportunity of sending them, as they are very good, and as it happens seasonable.[5]

If you should wish to have any more of our society's books, I mean any particular ones to give away, I beg you to let me know, and I shall take care that they be sent, and hope in future not to be unmindful of the latter end of the month affording so easy and cheap a conveyance of transmitting any thing to you.

My wife is just come back from the Exhibition, but the crowd and stifling so great that without much difficulty she coud not move along. Dr Priestleys picture by Artaud she does not like at all. It seems that by Opie is not in the exhibition.[6]

My wife unites with me in kind regards and every good wish for Mrs Scott and your little folks and I remain always most truly yours

T. Lindsey.

---

1   Captain Patrick Campbell, the commander of the *Surprise* transport, which conveyed Palmer, Muir and other reformers to Botany Bay, was, according to Palmer's *Narrative*, a sadist who persecuted his prisoners. Palmer, admittedly not a witness biased in Campbell's favour, asserted that he 'had been for near 30 years in that traffic of human misery the slave trade' and that, having failed in several commercial enterprises, he regarded the command of the *Surprise* as a desperate attempt to restore his fortunes. See DWL, MS 12.46 (101), Palmer to 'My Dear Friend' (probably Robert Millar), Sydney, New South Wales, 25 Oct. 1795.

2   The exhibition which Thomas Belsham attended with his brother William was the annual exhibition at the Royal Academy; see below, n. 6.

3   William Stone was arrested on 3 May 1794 and subjected to examination at the secretary of state's offices on 8 May. See *Morning Chronicle*, 10 May 1794, and Cobbett, *Parl. hist.*, XXXI, 519, for the debate on the suspension of the Habeas Corpus Act on 16 May, in which Sheridan raised Stone's case and asserted his innocence. Stone was detained in Newgate until his trial on a charge of high treason on 28 and 29 Jan. 1796. The charge against him was based on letters to him from his brother John Hurford Stone (1763–1818) in Paris, which contained incriminating and potentially subversive material. On 29 Jan. 1796 he was acquitted; see *State trials*, XXV, 1155–438. John Hurford Stone, however, was unable to return to Britain because of his quasi-conspiratorial activities and remained in France for the rest of his life. William Stone was listed as a governor and benefactor of Hackney College in 1786; DWL, MS 12.90 (1).

4   The publication of the first part of Paine's *Age of reason* was announced in the *Oracle and Public Advertiser*, 20 Mar. 1794 and in *The World*, 20 Mar. 1794. Predicting that 'few of our readers will have the opportunity of seeing the work itself', the *Morning Chronicle* of 5 May 1794 published a short summary of its main contentions with the heading 'Mr. Paine's creed'.

5   See Letter 564, n. 7.
6   The report of the exhibition of the Royal Academy in the *Morning Chronicle*, 29 Apr. 1794, listed many of the portraits on view, including the 1794 portrait of Priestley by William Artaud (1763–1823), which is now held by Dr Williams's Library and is reproduced on the dust jacket of *Joseph Priestley. Scientist, philosopher and theologian*, ed. Isabel Rivers and David L. Wykes (Oxford, 2008). In 1795, an engraving from this painting was made by Thomas Holloway. The report in the *Morning Chronicle* did not list the oil painting of Priestley by John Opie, undertaken in 1781, which is held by Harris Manchester College, Oxford.

575. To WILLIAM TAYLEUR   17 MAY 1794

Text: JRUL, Lindsey Letters, vol. II, no. 77.
Addressed: To/William Tayleur Esqr/Shrewsbury
Endorsed: ~~19th~~ 17th May 94 ~~Mr Rowe has a Letter from/Mr Lindsey dated 15th June~~
Postmarked: MA 17 94

London. May. 17. 1794

Dear Sir,

I have to inform you, that I have this morning received Mr Rowe's letter inclosing a bill from you of £110, £100 your generous gift to Hackney college, and £10 for Mr Winterbotham, that worthy sufferer under a most unjust condemnation.[1] Both the sums I shall take care to deliver according to your direction. The college, of which you have been from the first so noble a patron, never at any time deserved it more, in the abilities and exertions of the Tutors, their attention to the morals and conduct of the Students, and the happy success of their labours in the improvements of all under their care. I am sorry that Mr Corrie's health and the too great fatigue of his place, has put him upon resigning his post of classical tutor, and shall be glad if we can find one fit to replace him in all respects.[2]

I cannot but rejoice on your account and on that of very many others, that it pleases the Divine Providence to lengthen your life so much beyond the ordinary limit (without any great pain I trust to yourself) to enable you to serve it's best purposes, and particularly to support by the weight of your example, and influence as well as your constant kindness, the cause of truth, and those engaged in it. For besides the credit and benefit which our college derives from you, I cannot but attribute to the same cause, that Mr Rowe found things at your chapel on his return in so much better a train than he expected. I beg, that with mine and my wife's respects to him and his lady, You will do me the favour to thank him for his obliging letter and for telling me that he found his young folks quite recovered.

We are all in perfect astonishment at this sudden measure of suspending the Habeas Corpus Act. Your old college friend Mr W. Ellis I see is chosen one of the secret committee, and it is observed that it is mostly composed of the New Converts as they are called.[3] The Morning Chronicle is just now only delivered. I observe that Mr Martin bears his honest and firm testimony against the necessity and adoption of so strange a measure.[4]

Mr Shore is this moment come in, and made very happy by my mention of your generosity to the college. He is also full of amazement at the measure, that such a power should be voted, and without any limitation to its duration. He was glad however to see two of the *New Converts* vote against it – L^d GAH Cavendish and Mr Pelham, Knight of the shire for Lincoln.[5] We cannot help rejoicing now almost for the first time that Dr Priestley has left the country as the prejudices were so great against him, that right or wrong he might have been implicated in the present accusations.

I beg your pardon for dwelling so much on politicall matters, but those of the day are so extraordinary, that one can hardly think and few talk of any others. It is a consolation for those that wish for and seek the virtue and happiness of the world, that the great Ruler of it directs every thing to promote this end however the means are at times harsh and to us unpromising. My wife charges me with her kind and respectful regards. We hope Mr Wood and his brother[6] and Mr Harris[7] are well and desire to be remembered to them. I remain ever Dear Sir, Your truly obliged and faithful affectionate servant

T. Lindsey.

---

1   Rowe's letter to Lindsey is not in JRUL, C2^{13}. Since the Hackney College minute book does not cover the years after 1791, no formal record of this gift of £100 from Tayleur to the college survives. It was characteristic of his financial generosity to rational dissenting enterprises, as was his gift to the imprisoned William Winterbotham (see Letter 539, n. 6). For another of Tayleur's contributions to Hackney College, see Letter 475, n. 3.

2   For John Corrie, see Letter 531, n. 4. He became an assistant tutor at Hackney in 1790, and succeeded John Pope as classical tutor in 1793. He resigned his tutorship in 1794 and became minister to a unitarian congregation at Bromsgrove, where he served for a short period from 1795. He also served as minister at Old Meeting, Birmingham from 1817 to 1819. He was not replaced as classical tutor at Hackney, although, as Lindsey subsequently noted (see Letter 625), Belsham deputized for him in the immediate aftermath of his departure.

3   The Habeas Corpus Act was suspended until 1 Feb. 1795 by act of parliament (34 Geo. III, c. 54), which received the royal assent on 23 May 1794; *LJ*, XL, 207. The debate in the house of commons of 16 May 1794 was widely reported in the newspaper press and may be found in Cobbett, *Parl. hist.*, XXXI, 497–526. Welbore Ellis (1713–1802), MP for Petersfield, had been Tayleur's contemporary at Westminster school and Christ Church Oxford; for Lindsey's earlier reference to him, see Vol. I, Letter 286. On 14 May 1794, he was nominated to the commons' secret committee, to which allegedly seditious papers were to be submitted; *CJ*, XLIX, 594. By 'New Converts', Lindsey meant the supporters of the duke of Portland who were in the process of joining Pitt's ministry. Ellis, a former supporter of Lord North, associated himself with Portland's following. After representing several constituencies, he was MP for Petersfield from 1791 until Aug. 1794, when he was created Baron Mendip.

4   The *Morning Chronicle*, 17 May 1794, reported the speech of James Martin against the suspension of the Habeas Corpus Act in the debate of 16 May, and his presence in the minority of forty-one MPs who voted against the motion to take the suspension bill into consideration.

5   Lord George Augustus Henry Cavendish (1754–1834) was MP for Derby from 1780 to 1796 and for Derbyshire from 1797 until 1831, when he was created earl of Burlington. Charles Anderson Pelham (1749–1823) was MP for Lincolnshire from 1774 until 13 Aug. 1794, when he was created Baron Yarborough.

6   In his will, dated Aug. 1800 and proved on 13 June 1801, Isaac Wood identified two brothers, namely Richard Wood, merchant, of Liverpool, and William Wood, whose occupation and location were not specified; TNA: PRO PROB 11/1359, fos. 398r–400r. It is not clear to which (if, indeed, either) brother Lindsey referred.

7   Edward Harries.

576. To WILLIAM TAYLEUR   **29 MAY 1794**

Text:	JRUL, Lindsey Letters, vol. II, no. 78.
Printed:	McLachlan, *Letters*, pp. 132–3 (fourth paragraph).
Addressed:	To/William Tayleur Esqr./Shrewsbury
Endorsed:	[In Tayleur's hand] 29th of May 94 Mr Rowe had a letter from Mr Lindsey dated 15th June[1]
Postmarked:	MA 30 94

London. May. 29. 1794.

Dear Sir,

Two days ago, at a meeting of the Committee on the affairs of our college at Hackney, Mr Towgood in the chair, present Mr Shore, Dr Kippis, Dr Rees, Mr Thompson, Mr Morgan &c I had the agreeable province assigned me of presenting you with sincere acknowlegements for your noble support of the seminary from the first of it's institution, and for your last generous and most seasonable benefaction of one hundred pounds paid by me into the Treasurers hands, with the farther expression of our hope and persuasion that your continued and honourable patronage will do us credit abroad and excite others to think well of and assist us.[2] Mr Belsham gave in a very pleasing statement of the diligence and improvements of the students, and two days were appointed for their examination and delivering public orations. But we were much concerned at a letter sent to the Chairman by Mr Corrie to signify his intention of quitting his place of classical tutor.[3] After the reading of it some gentlemen were appointed to converse with him on the subject, and inquire into the reasons of his resignation, for he assigned none in his letter, and to try if he might not be prevailed with to continue in his office, at least a year or two longer. I have heard him speak of his want of health and spirits and the too great fatigues of his situation. One person hinted, that he might have a view to change his condition in life.[4] But all bore testimony to his worth.[5]

I was sorry to hear more than one of our number speak so far from well of the moral character and honesty of Wm Stone, now in Newgate, and who was one of our committee, whom I had taken to be a better sort of man.[6]

Yesterday I was told by a respectable friend and one of the Society of the Friends of the people, that at their appointed meeting on Saturday, they will come forth with dignity and shew by their declaration which has been drawn up by an able hand, that they are not dejected or intimidated by the late extraordinary tendencies to arbitrary power, and obstinate refusal of all reformation in the body politic; but are resolved to persevere intrepidly till it be accomplished, though they do not think it proper at the present moment to bring forward any thing particular relating to it.[7]

Mr Rowe will have told you of Mr Tho. Paine's book, called, The age of reason; &c pointed against all divine revelation. He seems to speak the sentiments of Robespierre and the present leaders in France. And it is a noble foundation which they have laid on the divine unity and on a perfect liberty in religious matters. On this basis the gospel in time will be preached in its native simplicity and firmly estabilished in such a way as it never yet has been. To which Thomas Paine leads the way without intending it by exciting free inquiry. I wish Mr Wakefield had taken more time in his answer to him, and been less abusive in some places, though he is candid in others.[8]

It is said Parliament will be up by the birth-day; and some say we are to have a new Parliament, from which the ministry expect to keep out not a few of the present small number of their opponents, and so to have the whole business of the nation to themselves and their party without any perceivable opposition.[9]

I beg you will give our best respects to M[r] and M[rs] Rowe, and say for me that I hope he will at his leisure let me know how yourself are and all our friends at Shrewsbury. My wife presents you with her kind & most respectful regards and I remain always your ever truly obliged and affectionate servant

T. Lindsey.

P.S. A few days since there was a report said to come from Bristol, that the Sansom had been spoken with far out at sea, D[r] Priestley said all well; which gave us great joy: but M[r] Sansom, who lives in London, says it cannot be so, for that otherwise he sh[d] certainly have known it.[10] We persuade ourselves however that he is now safe on Terra firma.[11] It is said we shall give up the forts, and not have a war with America.[12]

---

[1] Lindsey's letter to Rowe, dated 15 June 1794, has not survived; for Lindsey's hope that Rowe had received it, see Letter 581, n. 5.

[2] Mr Thompson was Isaac Thompson, of St Mary Hill, London, a governor and benefactor of Hackney College, who gave £50 to the college at its foundation; DWL, MS 12.90 (1). On 2 Feb. 1790, the college committee appointed him to the committee of accounts; DWL, MS 38.14, p. 128. At the opening of the college, two treasurers were appointed, namely Matthew Towgood (see Vol. I, Letter 373, n. 3) and Michael Dodson, who were authorized to act in conjunction with the chairman, Thomas Rogers; Birm. MS 281, fo. 123. The minutes of the Hackney College committee refer at various times to a treasurer, without naming him, and to the treasurers in the plural, again without naming anyone. The minutes also refer to a 'committee of treasury'; see DWL, MS 38.14, pp. 55, 71, 84, 89, 104.

[3] Following the death of Thomas Rogers on 1 June 1793 (*Gent. Mag.*, LXIII, ii (1793), 671), the chairman of the Hackney College committee was William Smith MP. For Corrie's resignation as classical tutor, see Letter 575, n. 2.

[4] John Corrie 'changed his condition in life' on his marriage in 1796; see Letter 640, n. 6.

[5] These matters are unrecorded in the minute book of the Hackney College committee (DWL, MS 38.14), which only covers the period 1785 to 15 Sept. 1791.

[6] See Letter 574, n. 3.

[7] On Saturday 31 May 1794, a general meeting at the Freemason's tavern, London, of the Association of Friends of the People published a declaration to the effect that it would hold no further public meetings in the immediate future. Recognizing the level of popular discontent, and lamenting that the association 'found no credit with his Majesty's Ministers', the declaration condemned the government's repressive measures and reasserted the association's belief in parliamentary reform; see *Morning Chronicle*, 2 June 1794. The meeting had been advertised in advance; see, for example, *Morning Chronicle*, 14 May 1794, and *Morning Post*, 28 May 1794. In Jan. 1795, the association suspended all its activities and thereafter faded away.

[8] Gilbert Wakefield, *An examination of the age of reason, or an investigation of true and fabulous theology, by Thomas Paine* (London, 1794). Subsequently, Wakefield published *A reply to Thomas Paine's second part of the age of reason* (London, 1795).

[9] I.e. 4 June, the birthday of George III. The parliamentary session ended on 11 July 1794. The dissolution of parliament and the consequent general election did not take place until the summer of 1796.

[10] Lindsey did not identify, or make any other references to, Mr Sansom. A possibility is Philip Sansom, the chairman of the committee of America merchants in London; see *Whitehall Evening Post*, 15–17 July 1794. Possibly, too, he was the owner, or co-owner, of the ship of the same name.

[11] Priestley landed at New York on 4 June 1794.

[12] In the spring of 1794, the United States dispatched John Jay (1745–1829) to negotiate with Britain over points of contention which remained unresolved after the War of American Independence. Jay was the first chief justice of the United States (from 1790 to 1795) and governor of New York (from 1795 to 1801). His diplomatic reputation had been established in 1783, when he served as one of the American peace commissioners in Paris. The agreement which he negotiated with Britain, known as the Jay treaty, averted the prospect of war between Britain and America; as one of its provisions Britain agreed to relinquish six forts on American territory. The treaty was signed on 19 Nov. 1794, but strong objections in America, based on claims that Jay had conceded too much to Britain, meant that Congress did not ratify the treaty until Aug. 1795.

577. To RUSSELL SCOTT   **2 JUNE 1794**

> **Text:**   Scott Coll.
> **Printed:**   McLachlan, 'Lindsey to Scott', 120 (first sentence of fourth
>   paragraph; sixth paragraph).
> **Addressed:**   Address missing.
> **Postmarked:** Postmark missing.

London. June. 2. 1794

Dear Sir,

I have not much to say, but having the opportunity of a frank I am desirous to make use of it to inquire how your health is, as it was not very strong when you last gave account of yourself, and we are afraid your benevolent exertions for our friends, and for one in particular[1] may have hurt you.

There was nothing newly come out to send at the end of this month but M[r] Wakefields answer to T. Paine Age of reason, which I thought you would be glad to see, and pleased with some things in it, though you may wish the writer had taken more time, and not hurt his very laudable candour in some parts by a harshness bordering upon abuse in others.[2]

The public prints inform you of the politics and events both at home and abroad, which I wish to become less interesting, and peace and quiet to return.

There is a tract 3/6 titled Antipolemus; or the plea of reason, religion and humanity against war: which contains many good remarks that woud please you much, upon the subject, and I should be glad to send it if you could point out the way before the end of this month.[3] I did not see it before to day, or it should have come at the end of the last.

It is expected, I am told, that the Minister will come forth with some strong measure after the discussion of the Second report of the Secret Committee on Tuesday next.[4] After that it is said the Parliament will rise, but not be dissolved as has been reported.[5]

I hear M[r] W[m] Stone, who is in Newgate not well spoken of for his dishonesty in his mercantile transactions, it turning out, as reported, that he has defrauded and taken in several persons, and will not be able to live in England when he comes out of prison.[6]

We hope our comon friend, whom we had the pleasure of seeing when you was in town continues well,[7] and also M[rs] Scott and your young folks. I remain always, Dear Sir, with much esteem, affectionately yours

                                    T. Lindsey

My wife desires to join in kind remembrances to M[rs] Scott

You will acquaint me when you want any more of the Societys books than your own quota, and what, and I shall be glad to supply You.

---

1   Thomas Palmer.
2   For Wakefield's reply to Paine's *Age of reason*, see Letter 576, n. 8.
3   *Antipolemus: or the plea of reason, religion, and humanity against war. A fragment. Translated from Erasmus and addressed to aggressors* (London, 1794). Its price was indeed 3s 6d. The author was Vicesimus Knox. For Lindsey's previous disapproval of Knox's vehement trinitarian orthodoxy, see Letter 447.
4   For this secret committee, see Letter 575, n. 3. 'Tuesday next' was 3 June 1794.
5   See Letter 576, n. 9.
6   See Letter 574, n. 3. William Stone and his family were coal merchants. On his release from prison after his acquittal, he joined his brother John Hurford Stone in Paris.
7   Possibly this member of Scott's Portsmouth congregation who had been in London was Richard

Godman Temple (see Letter 522, n. 3) or William Joseph Porter (see Letter 602, n. 1). Another possibility is a member of the Carter family (see Letters, 402 n. 11, and 439).

578. To WILLIAM TURNER OF NEWCASTLE 10 JUNE 1794

Text: DWL, MS 12.44 (58).
Printed: Belsham, *Memoirs*, p. 255 n. * (third paragraph); Graham, 'Unhappy country', 135–6 (third paragraph).
Addressed: Address missing.
Endorsed: June. 10. 1794
Postmarked: Postmark missing.

London. June. 10 1794

Dear Sir,

I was very much pleased with Young M[r] Robson, and I am persuaded, shoud have been more so, had circumstances allowed a more particular knowlege and acquaintance with his many valuable qualities.[1]

Had it been in his way to have apprized me of his departure from London and not taken me unprovided, I should certainly have acknowleged your letter by the hand that brought it, which on some accounts might have been more desireable.[2]

Nothing has been known of or from D[r] Priestley since his being off Falmouth between seven and eight weeks since: but under the protection of a good providence, we persuade ourselves that he has ere this touched the American shores.[3] And such have been the changes since, that some of his best friends, who sought to detain him here, are now glad at his departure. For the prejudices against Dissenters, especially the more liberal sort, as enemies to their country because they are against the present war, are so violent, and would have been so much heightened against him, that it might have made his life unpleasant, though I hope not insecure.

I am afraid your triumph with respect to the resistance of the North Riding of Yorkshire to Bene[v]olences on the present occasion will be shortlived. For it is reported that Ministers have wished the matter to be reconsidered. And a Meeting of the Whole Riding has been called for to morrow, when it is to be canvassed over again, and it is believed the measure of Subscription will then be carried with a high hand.[4]

If you have seen M[r] Wakefields reply to M[r] Paynes Age of reason, &c; you would wish I think that he had taken more time and thought, and had been uniformly candid towards his opponent. But though no one is more pleasing and agreeable company, whenever he takes pen in hand, he has no controul over himself in censuring unmercifully those he dislikes. There is first come out to day, a trimming reply, as I am told to his spirit of Christianity, dedicated to M[r] Windham of Norfolk, M[r] Burke's disciple.[5]

M[r]. Archd[n] Paleys excellent and seasonable work may have reached you before it came to us. He shews the value and importance of D[r] Lardners labours to those that come after him, and which he is not backward to own. I am glad to learn that the first impression is nearly sold off, which is a great deal to say in these times, when the side of the question he treats is not much in fashion, and many are seriously engaged on other important civil and political concerns.[6]

We hope M[r] Robson has arrived safe and with his health improved. My wife joins in all kind wishes for Mrs Turner, yourself and your little family, and I remain always very sincerely Yours

      T. Lindsey.

What a noble testimony is borne by Mr Miln in his Discourse on the rise and fatal effects of war, on the last Fast-day? Who is this worthy man, that comes forth with so much piety, good sense and boldness. As the discourse is printed at Carlisle, you cannot but be acquainted with him.[7]

I beg you will remember that postage is no matter of consideration with us, and that I only use franks because they fall in my way. Mr R. Milnes left town the middle of last week, a real patriot he.[8]

1   Possibly 'Young Mr Robson' was Caleb, the son of William Robson of Newcastle (for whom see Letters 404 and 496, and Harbottle, *William Turner*, pp. 32–3, 45) and his wife Margaret. He was born on 23 Dec. 1773 and baptized at Hanover Square chapel by Turner's predecessor but one, Samuel Lowthian; Tyne and Wear Archives, Hanover Square baptismal record (TNA: PRO/RG4/1777), fo. 24r. Hence Caleb Robson was aged twenty at the time of this letter.

2   This letter from William Turner of Newcastle to Lindsey seems not to have survived.

3   Priestley landed at New York on 4 June 1794.

4   Despite the disapproval of Wyvill, Turner and other reformers, a meeting of the nobility, gentry, clergy and freeholders of the north riding of Yorkshire at Northallerton on 12 June 1794 resolved to raise subscriptions to raise troops for external and internal defence. Fifty-four subscribers, headed by the lord lieutenant, Earl Fauconberg, pledged a total of £3,035. 15. 0. The resolutions and subscribers are set out in a two-page printed document headed 'North-riding of Yorkshire'; copy in NYRO, ZFW 7/2/87/20.

5   This reply was *Vindiciae Britannicae ... being strictures on a late pamphlet by Gilbert Wakefield ... intituled 'The spirit of Christianity compared with the spirit of the times in Great Britain.' By an under graduate* (London, 1794). It was indeed dedicated to William Windham, who, though formerly a supporter of the parliamentary opposition, became secretary at war in July 1794 as the Portland whigs joined in coalition with Pitt's ministry. The author was William Penn (1776–1845), who was admitted as an undergraduate at St John's College, Cambridge, in Apr. 1795; he was the great-grandson of William Penn (1644–1718), the founder of Pennsylvania. He subsequently wrote for the *Anti-Jacobin* and the *Gentleman's Magazine*, before spending much of his later life in debtors' prisons. See the entry for his father, Richard Penn (c. 1734–1811) by Charlotte Fell-Smith, revised by Troy O. Bickham, in *ODNB*, XLIII, 533.

6   For Paley's *View of the evidences of Christianity*, see Letter 569, n. 6. He made extensive use of Nath-aniel Lardner's *The credibility of the gospel history*, his *Collection of ancient Jewish and heathen testimonies to the truth of the Christian religion* and his posthumously published *Historie of the heretics of the first two centuries*. Paley's explicit acknowledgments of Lardner's work may be found in his *View of the evidences*, I, 218 n. * and 320 n. *.

7   Robert Miln (d. 1800), a graduate of Aberdeen, was minister to the dissenting congregation at Fisher Street, Carlisle, from 1755 to 1800. His work *The rise and fatal effects of war: a discourse* [on Jeremiah. iv. 19] *delivered on March 28, 1794; being the day appointed for a general fast* was published in Carlisle in 1794 and sold by Joseph Johnson in London. It drew upon biblical texts to denounce warfare in general, deplored Britain's participation in war against revolutionary France and criticized the consequent high taxation and curtailment of civil liberties. See Letter 580, n. 8.

8   Richard Slater Milnes, MP for York, 1784–1802, had won Lindsey's approval by voting against the suspension of Habeas Corpus on 16 and 17 May 1794 and by voting against the war on 30 May.

579. To WILLIAM ALEXANDER   10 JUNE 1794

    Text: 'Letters of the Rev. Theophilus Lindsey. No. V', *UH*, II, 73
                    (20 Sept. 1862), 320.

Note: This is the only section of the letter printed by the UH; the manuscript seems not to have survived. The ellipsis at the start of the section printed by the UH indicates that this was not the beginning of the original letter.

London, June 10, 1794.

* * No accounts whatsoever have been received of or from Dr. Priestley since the letter I had from him off Falmouth, seven weeks since on Saturday last.[1] We have no doubt, however, under Divine Providence, of his being safely landed on the American shore; and such have been the changes since he went that many of his friends who were grieved at his going away, and wished to detaim[2] him here, do even rejoice at his departure.

---

1 Lindsey referred here to Priestley's letter from Falmouth of 11 Apr. 1794; see Letters 565 and 568. 'Saturday last' was 7 June 1794; the Saturday seven weeks previously was 19 Apr. 1794.

2 I.e. 'detain'; this is a misprint in the *UH*.

580. To RUSSELL SCOTT   30 JUNE 1794

Text: Scott Coll.
Printed: Scott, *Family biography*, p. 88 (first, tenth, eleventh
                  paragraphs, and last two sentences of thirteenth paragraph);
                  McLachlan, 'Lindsey to Scott', 120 (fourth paragraph; first
                  sentence of sixth paragraph; seventh, eighth and eleventh
                  paragraphs).
Addressed: To/The Rev[d]. Russell Scott/Portsmouth
Postmarked: Postmark illegible.

London. June. 30 1794.

Dear Sir,

We are relieved by having some little account of you at last; though it is not so good as we could have wished: but we hope the proposed expedition to the west will recruit both father and daughter, and rejoice that the good mother needs it not immediately, though the change and air must be of benefit.[1]

On Saturday as soon as your letter came, my wife packed up and sent to M[r] Johnsons for you, to go with the Monthlies to day:[2]

4 Conversations on X[n]. Idolatry.[3] 4 Hartley.[4]

2 Seddon.[5] 4 Rogers.[6] List of false readings. the only copy I happened to have by me.[7] Miln's fast Sermon. an old Minister at Carlisle. annually relieved by D[r] Kippis out of the Dissenters' fund. But this sermon, having given umbrage, he has been forced to suppress – so y[t] it is not to be bought, and you will shew it to friends.[8]

M[r] Belsham's sermon you will be pleased with. It is very free. And there are not many congregations so well disposed as to be pleased with a Minister delivering himself in so unreserved a way.[9]

Antipolemus – by M[r] Knox contains good things. A worthy person is so much pleased with it, that he has made me a present of half a score copies to give away.[10]

I was very much satisfied with the Orations on Thursday at our college, being the last day of the session.[11] Two latin orations by M[r] Bruen,[12] and M[r] Pardo,[13] both worthy of great commendation. An english one by M[r] Rogers, son of the late and brother of the present Banker: full of good sense; and well, but rather too hastily delivered.[14] M[r] Reed from Bristol, an english oration – highly extolled, but spoken with such rapidity, that few could keep pace with him.[15]

M[r] Perkins, a worthy son of a worthy father, near Shepton-Mallet. In english, in comendation of Hartley's philosophy, very well done: but his principal subject a defence of Materialism. Dr Priestley woud have heard it with pleasure and approbation. And it was delivered like a scholar and philosopher.[16]

Mr Fletcher from Bristol. An excellent Sermon on that Subject – John – xiv Peace I leave with you &c.[17] and this gospel declaration and character justified, notwithstanding the miseries, wars, and discords among X^{ts} followers, for near 18 centuries. It was extremely well delivered.[18]

In about ten days or a fortnight, we propose setting out for Cheltenham to try the effect of those waters for my wife, whether they will give relief in her old bilious complaint, so as to prevent or palliate those extreme sufferings she has gone through for many years, particularly the last autumn.

No direct accounts, nor indeed any accounts have been rec^d, nor it is said, could yet be received of Dr Priestleys arrival in America. In about ten days or a fortnight, it may be looked for.

You will hear, if you have not already heard of many migrations out of the west among Dissenters. Some who have already suffered or are threatened, and others willing to get out of the storm, which they think to be coming.

I hope M^r and Mrs Watson of Chichester[19] are recovered, and all our friend[s] there well, particularly one worthy person much esteemed, whom we had the pleasure of seeing in town at the same time with you.[20]

How long we shall be absent, we cannot tell. I suppose you will procure as long a furlow as you can.[21] Our kind regards and every good wish attend the travellers, and I remain always,

Dear Sir, affectionately Yours

T. Lindsey.

---

1   The daughter of Russell and Sophia Scott was Sophia Russell Scott (1793–1832); she was born on 11 Sept. 1793; TNA: RG4/564, fo. 30v (register of baptisms, High Street chapel, Portsmouth). In 1824, she married her cousin John Edward Taylor (1791–1844), the first proprietor of the *Manchester Guardian*.

2   Lindsey referred here to the *Monthly Review, Analytical Review, Monthly Magazine* and the *Critical Review*.

3   This work was Lindsey's *Conversations on Christian idolatry*.

4   For this edition of Hartley's *Of the truth of the Christian religion*, see Letters 544, n. 6, and 547, n. 2.

5   This work was probably *Discourses on the person of Christ, on the holy spirit, and on self-deception; by the late Rev. John Seddon, minister of a dissenting society in Manchester. With an account of the author, by E, Harrison* (Warrington, 1793). On 10 Oct. 1793, the Unitarian Society agreed to Lindsey's proposal that Seddon's *Discourses* be received into the society's catalogue, and that 200 copies be purchased for distribution to members; Unitarian Society minute book, p. 44. Seddon (*c.* 1717–69) was a pupil of Caleb Rotheram at the Kendal Academy and held the degree of MA from Glasgow University. From 1739 until his death, he was minister at Cross Street chapel, Manchester, and in later life he adopted Socinian opinions. He should be distinguished from the better-known John Seddon, the rector of Warrington Academy (see Vol. I, Letter 168, n. 2); possibly they were distant cousins.

6   For George Rogers, *Five sermons*, see Letters 427, n. 11, 521, n. 4.

7   This work was Lindsey's *List of the false readings*.

8   For Robert Miln of Carlisle and his fast sermon, see Letter 578, n. 8. According to a brief notice of his death in *Gent. Mag.*, LXX, ii (1800), 699, he had reached 'a very advanced age'. From 1783 to 1795 inclusive, Miln received an annual grant of £5 from the Presbyterian fund; Kippis was a manager of the fund and it was he who nominated Miln for the grant in 1790, 1791, 1792, 1794 and 1795. See DWL, Presbyterian fund minutes, vol. VII, pp. 253, 281, 300, 326, 356, 381, 400, 422, 439, 456, 478, 495, 511. I am grateful to Dr David Wykes for allowing me to consult these minutes via CD-ROM.

9   For this sermon of Belsham, see Letter 564, n. 7.

10 See Letter 577, n. 3. The Unitarian Society minute book gives no clue as to the identity of the 'worthy person'. A possibility is the duke of Grafton, who spoke against the war in the house of lords on 30 May 1794; Cobbett, *Parl. hist.*, XXXI, 675–8. Knox's *Antipolemus* would have appealed to him.

11 20 June 1794 was a Monday; the previous Thursday was 26 June 1794.

12 This student's surname was Brewin, and he was admitted as a lay student on 6 Oct. 1789; DWL, MS 38.14, p. 140. He evidently came from Yorkshire; Birm. MS 281, fo. 125. There is no record of his first name(s).

13 Robert Pardoe of Worcestershire was admitted as a lay student in Sept. 1791; DWL, MS 38.14, p. 159. He was subsequently a lawyer, and a major in the Worcestershire militia.

14 Henry Rogers (d. 1832) entered the college in Sept. 1790; he was the youngest son of Thomas Rogers (1735–93), banker, and the chairman of the Hackney College committee. The 'present Banker' was his brother Samuel Rogers (1763–1855), better known as a poet and salon host; Henry Rogers gradually took over Samuel's banking responsibilities, as the latter devoted himself to literature. See P. W. Clayden, *Rogers and his contemporaries* (2 vols., London, 1889), II, 82.

15 Samuel Read of Bristol was a lay student who entered the college in 1791; DWL, MS 38.14, p. 159; Birm. MS 281, fo. 125. See also Letter 610, n. 8.

16 For a possible identification of Perkins and his son Richard, see Letter 559, n. 7.

17 John xiv. 27.

18 For John Fletcher of Bristol, see Letter 581, n. 4.

19 For Thomas Watson of Chichester, see Letter 388, n. 12; for his marriage to Margaret, née Webster, see Letter 507, n. 14. His wife predeceased him. Of their two sons, one was named Thomas Sanden Watson, in honour of Dr Thomas Sanden of Chichester (see Letter 388, n. 12), and the other was named Andrew Kippis Watson, in honour of Andrew Kippis, minister to the dissenting congregation at Princes Street, Westminster. See TNA: PRO PROB 11/1870, fos. 439r–440v (will of Thomas Watson).

20 See Letter 577, n. 7.

21 This is a reference to Scott's projected visit to the west country, which Lindsey mentioned at the start of this letter. His expedition probably included Milborne Port and Wrington, Somerset, where he had been minister in the 1780s.

581. To WILLIAM TAYLEUR   30 JUNE 1794

Text: JRUL, Lindsey Letters, vol. III, no. 39.
Addressed: To/William Tayleur Esqr./Shrewsbury
Endorsed: June 30th – 94
Postmarked: JU 30 94

London. June. 30. 1794

Dear Sir,

On Thursday last I attended the delivery of the orations &c at our college at Hackney, and could not find an earlier opportunity to give some account of what passed on the day, or should have done it to one who has from the first shewn himself most truly interested for the prosperity of that seminary in every thing virtuous, laudable and truly pious, and who has so substantially contributed to its existence and support. I could not be present at the examination of the students two days before by reason of an unavoidable engagement, otherwise I doubt not of my having had a good account to give you of them all, and particularly of Mr Mason whom I did not see on the Thursday.[1]

Mr Rogers, son of the late & brother of the present Mr Rogers, the bankers, began with an english oration, full of good sense, well composed, and delivered so as to shew that he himself was impressed with it; but rather in too much haste.[2] Next followed a latin oration, by Mr Bruen, very sensible and connected – not so perfect in its latinity, as you would have exhibited at Christ-church in your day, but which you would have comended.

A young man also, a Mr Pardo, from Bewdley, gave us a latin oration, in pure language and ingenious, and exceedingly well delivered.

A Mr Reed from Bristol, next gave an english oration, ab imâ philosophiâ

Hartleianâ deprompta,[3] on Luxury and its effects on Society, but spoken with such uncommon rapidity that no common ear or apprehension could keep pace with him, so that I was prompted to have called out to him not to make so much haste and envy us the hearing of so many excellent remarks: but I am glad I did it not: for I was told it would have utterly disconcerted him: he being extremely modest and of too great sensibility. He is spoken of however by all, and particularly by Mr Belsham, as a genius of the first rate.

Mr Perkins next ascended the rostrum; and after a well drawn up general account of Dr Hartley's system, entered upon a formal defence of the doctrine of Materialism. Our friend, now I doubt not safe on the american shore, was all along in my thoughts, and I am persuaded would have listened with pleasure and approbation. The reasoning throughout was close, and concise but perspicuous. The orator felt the force of his arguments, and made you feel it, by a most judicious, well toned emphasis and elocution, and his moral inferences were short, and becoming a philosopher.

Mr Fletcher of Birmingham closed the whole by an excellent discourse on John – Peace I leave with you, my peace I give unto you &c &c. His design to justify the gospel as a doctrine of peace and harmony and happiness notwithstanding the rude exhibition of 18 centuries so much the contrary. His principal argument – that we are not to judge of the whole plan what has hitherto appeared; that one day with God is as a thousand years, and a thousand years as one day; that the gospel is but in its infancy at present, and will appear so hereafter, when thousands of thousands of years of most perfect felicity procured by it shall be fulfilled, and when 1800 years will be looked back upon only as its dawn. The discourse was extremely well composed and delivered with pathos and affection, at which I particularly rejoice, as this very promising young person, is going to supply the place of our Dock chapel at Plymouth, vacated by Mr Kentish being chosen minister at Plymouth town, in Mr Porter's place, who driven by the times, is going to America.[4]

And so much for these matters: the short recital of which I thought would give you the pleasure I felt at the rehearsal. Pray tell Mr Rowe, that I hope he rec^d my last.[5] In about ten days we think of going to Cheltenham for my wife to try those waters, if they will save her from the pain she underwent the last year from her old ailing complaint.[6] She desires most kind respects to you. We beg also to be kindly remembered to M^r & Mrs Rowe, Mr Wood, Mr Aikin, &c. With all esteem I remain, ever, Dear Sir, Your truly obliged and affectionate Servt

T. Lindsey.

1 Thursday 26 June 1794. For identification of the Hackney students mentioned in this letter, see Letter 580. Mr Mason was probably James Mason of Shrewsbury (see Letter 560, n. 10).
2 For Henry Rogers, the son of Thomas Rogers (1735–93), see Letter 580, n. 14.
3 'Drawn from the very depths of [David] Hartley's philosophy'.
4 Thomas Porter emigrated to America in the summer of 1794 and was succeeded as minister at Treville Street, Plymouth, by John Kentish, who served there from 1794 to 1795. John Fletcher, a student at Daventry who moved to Hackney in 1790, was nominated to be minister at Plymouth Dock in 1794. However, he died soon after he completed his studies and never took up the appointment.
5 The date of Lindsey's previous surviving letter to Rowe was 7 May 1793 (Letter 526). Probably Lindsey's 'last' letter to Rowe was the non-surviving letter of 15 June 1794, to which Tayleur referred in his endorsement of Letter 576.
6 Lindsey wrote to Tayleur from Cheltenham on 1 Aug. 1794 (Letter 582).

582. To WILLIAM TAYLEUR   1 AUGUST 1794

Text: JRUL, Lindsey Letters, vol. III, no. 40.
Printed: McLachlan, 'More letters', 369 (brief extracts from last four
                sentences of third paragraph).
Addressed: To/William Tayleur Esqr./Shrewsbury
Endorsed: 1st of August – ~~95~~ 94
Postmarked: CHELTENHAM [date of postmark illegible]

Cheltenham. Aug. 1. 1794

Dear Sir,

Having received a letter since we came to this place, from my friend and old correspondent, Mr Freeman of Boston, N.E, and as you used to like his communications, I thought some account of this would be agreeable, and therefore promised to send it.

After mentioning much at large the benefit which had been received by the dispersion of the different tracts, which I make a point of sending him two or three times a year, whenever I have opportunity.

"They have sown the seeds of truth, says he, particularly in the minds of our younger clergymen. At this season of the year, (June 5) when our ministers from all parts of the State, assemble at Boston; I have an opportunity of distributing them, particularly Your Examin. of Robinson, Vindiciae Priestleianae, Conversations on X^{tn} idolatry, and Haynes,[1] which are read with great avidity. In former letters I have given you an account of the progress of unitarianism and liberal sentiments along with it, in the eastern part of the State.[2] At present it seems to be making rapid strides in the southern part.

"The counties of Plymouth, Barnstable, and Bristol, were the first part of New England settled by the English, and till the year 1692, when they were annexed to Massachusetts, constituted a distinct province. These first settlers were a religious and industrious people, of more candid minds, and less disposed to persecution than the settlers of Massachusetts. Though the country is barren, yet it has become one of the most populous districts of the United States. The inhabitants are enlightened and virtuous. Crimes are unknown, and there has not been a capital execution for upwards of sixty years. Such characters are valuable acquisitions to the cause of truth. It must give you pleasure therefore to learn, that two ministers, one in the county of Plymouth, and the other in the county of Barnstable, have lately come forwards, and openly opposed the doctrine of the Trinity.[3] Their preaching has made a deep impression, and converts have been multiplied. In Barnstable county in particular, there is a very large body of unitarians. Several ministers of that county have prevailed upon their people to use Enfield's forms of Prayer in their families.[4] A very numerous edition has been printed, with additions from Dr Priestley and B^p. Hoadly, to be read in churches, when the ministers are occasionally absent". (N.B. I like this idea hugely, and so will You.[5]) "I forward a copy for your acceptance, and, (at the request of General Freeman of Sandwich,[6] one of the editors of the book,) another for Dr Enfield, which you will have the goodness to convey to him. The same persons, who have adopted Enfield's prayers, intend soon to reprint Christie's Discourses,[7] to which no doubt there will be large subscriptions.["][8]

He then goes on to speak of Mr H. Toulmin, from whom he had frequently heard, he had not seen him, and of what a blessing such an enlightened active person would be in that new country; where he would be so much wanted. Of the new settlement upon the branches of the Susquehanna by our friends from England, I am pleased to hear him speak so very favourably, from his own knowlege; that they will find there a pleasant climate, and a fertile soil; as they will lay the foundations of a purer christianity, which may in time lead the Pennsylvanians to reject the doctrines of Athanasius and Calvin.

My wife sends her kindest respects, and hopes with me, that this fine summer weather will contribute to invigorate you. Dean Tucker is here at the spaw [*sic*] in his 82ᵈ year, complaining, but very vigorous.[9] I wish you was as stout in body. He is civil and we chat together as in former days. But on church and state matters no one touches.

On monday we depart to visit a widow lady for a week or ten days, a friend of my wife's, near Ross.[10] After that we are to pass a few days at Mʳ Martin's, by invitation;[11] and if Mʳ Rowe will be so good as to send under his cover two lines, to say you have received these two epistles,[12] and that you are tolerably well, and also his self, lady, and family, I shall thank him for that and his former favour when we get back to London.

I remain always, Dear Sir, Your most truly obliged and faithful affectionate servᵗ

T. Lindsey.

P.S. I am sorry Mʳ Toulmin is in such continual hot water from the violent spirit against him & Dissenters in that town; They are now threat[e]ning him for dissuading, by the mothers desire, a young man from enlisting in the army. They will not rest, till they have forced him to America.[13]

---

1   Lindsey added the words 'particularly ... Haynes' to the quotation from Freeman's letter. For the full titles of these works, see the list of abbreviations to Vols. I and II. For Lindsey's edition of Hopton Haynes, *The scripture account of the attributes and worship of God*, see Letter 406, n. 16.

2   Freeman had described these developments in his letters to Lindsey of 21 May 1792 and 25 June 1792 and, at greater length, in that of 16 June 1793; see, respectively, Belsham, *Memoirs*, p. 160, DWL, MS 12.57 (35) and MS 12.57 (36).

3   I have not been able to make positive identifications of the two anti-trinitarian ministers to whom Freeman referred. However, there are some interesting suggestions in Bower's excellent *Priestley and English unitarianism in America*, pp. 57–62, which provides information about some of Freeman's unitarian friends.

4   This work was probably William Enfield's *Prayers for the use of families* (London, 1770). A second edition, with additions, was published at Warrington in 1777 and a third edition, enlarged, was published at Warrington in 1785. A fourth edition appeared in Birmingham in 1793, and in 1794, a further edition was published in Boston, Massachusetts, with the words 'containing prayers for congregations, when destitute of a minister' added to the original title.

5   Lindsey inserted the words in rounded brackets into the quotation from Freeman's letter and referred to Tayleur's introduction of unitarian worship in his own household.

6   Probably this was Nathaniel Freeman (1741–1827), of Sandwich, Massachusetts, a medical practitioner, a brigadier-general in the Massachusetts militia during the War of American Independence, a judge and a member of the Massachusetts congress. I owe this information to Professor J. D. Bowers.

7   For William Christie's *Discourses on the divine unity*, see Vol. I, Letter 287, n. 12.

8   This letter from James Freeman to Lindsey may be found in DWL, MS 12.57 (37). An extract from it, commenting on Lindsey's retirement from his ministry and praising his efforts on behalf of unitarianism, is printed in Belsham, *Memoirs*, p. 162.

9   Josiah Tucker, dean of Gloucester from 1758 until his death in 1799, was born in Dec. 1713 and was aged eighty at the time of this letter. Lindsey's acquaintance with him probably dated from the 1750s; see Vol. I, Letter 92, n. 8.

10   This friend was Eliza Maria Clifford of Perrystone, Herefordshire; see Letters 588 and 741.

11   James Martin, MP for Tewkesbury; his family residence was at Overbury, Worcestershire.

12   By 'these two epistles', Lindsey probably meant his own letter to Tayleur and the extracts from Freeman's letter which it quoted.

13   Joshua Toulmin, unlike his son Henry, did not emigrate to America. For the hostility to him in

Taunton, see David L. Wykes, 'Joshua Toulmin (1740–1815) of Taunton: baptist minister, historian and religious radical', *Baptist Quarterly*, XXXIX, 5 (Jan. 2002), 234–7.

583. To JOHN ROWE   13 SEPTEMBER 1794

Text: JRUL, Lindsey Letters, vol. II, no. 79.
Printed: McLachlan, *Letters*, p. 8 (second paragraph).
Addressed: To/The Rev^d. John Rowe/Shrewsbury
Postmarked: SE 13 94

London. Septr. 13. 1794.

Dear Sir,

I am just returned from our friends in Surrey, where I think I told you we commonly pass from Monday evening till Saturday morn at this time of the year, and am much affected with your letter: for though you have frequently with kindness given warning of it, I have not allowed myself to look upon the loss of one of the most excellent of men so near as you with too much cause I fear now speak of it, and especially as you encouraged me to write, I was drawn on to think I should still go on so to converse with and consult him as I was wont upon all emergencies.[1] A period however must come to all human things. Whenever it comes, may it please the Almighty to grant his faithful servant his dismission in the way he earnestly desires, and if we are to survive may he not leave to us in vain such a finished example of wisdom and virtue and the truest christian fortitude!

To your request concerning the correspondence which you urge in so friendly a way, I would say that I do not think I should have any objection, or rather I have none to it's remaining with you on condition of being never made public. Only I could wish to look over them, when perhaps I might render your happiness compleat by intrusting with you on the same terms with our friends letters, most if not all of which I have preserved, and they invaluable.[2]

I am much hurt by the latter part of your letter. On Mr Porter's first writing and mentioning to me the design of his removal to America in company with Mr Jardine the surgeon, I apprized him of what I had heard of his friend's sentiments, tending even towards Atheism, and received by the first post a warm vindication of M^r J, as I understood it. The letter I preserved, but cannot immediately recurr to it. When I saw Mr P. in town, he talked of laying himself out to be a teacher of divine truth, wherever he was, though without wearing a black coat and professing to devote himself to the work. And in my last letter to him, I particularly cautioned him to make a point of daily private prayer to the divine being, lest otherwise the habit and all sense of the relation to such a being be lost, and practical if not real atheism be the consequence, which I think I mentioned to have been the unhappy case of more than one of my acquaintance.[3] I still should be sorry to think Mr P. such a Deceiver in his letters and conversation with me, as your representations if they be true, must make him. And therefore wish you would at your leisure sift out the facts which may be only in a loose and general manner reported to you: but I beg this may be done without mentioning my name, or even throwing out any suspicions.

I observe in your letter, that Mr Jenkins, says nothing of atheism, but that they were both avowed infidels.[4] And you are a judge whether he woud not give that title to a Socinian.

I have a singular pleasure in hearing that Mr Williams is so happily settled at

Norton, and beg you will tell him how much I rejoice in it, and that I hope in time to have a personal acquaintance with one I so much esteem.[5]

We both rejoice in Mrs Rowe's intire recovery and beg your acceptance of our most kind respects, and desire the same may be tenderd to our common friend – I am ever most sincerely Yours

T. Lindsey.

P.S. I should be glad to find a letter from you on Saturday next, to know how our friend does, and whether you would advise me to write to him as usual.[6]

---

1   It is evident that Lindsey had received a (non-surviving) letter from Rowe, informing him that Tayleur was seriously ill and within days of death.

2   Tayleur survived until 6 May 1796, when Rowe did indeed return Lindsey's letters to him; see Letter 637 and McLachlan, *Letters*, pp. 8–9. Of Tayleur's letters to Lindsey, fifty-two survive in JRUL, C2^{13} but it is unlikely that they constitute more than half of the total number written by Tayleur to Lindsey.

3   Lindsey's letters to Thomas Porter of Plymouth seem not to have survived. For 'Mr Jardine the surgeon', i.e. Lewis Jones Jardine of Bristol, the brother of David Jardine of Bath, see Letter 418, n. 5.

4   Writing to Lindsey on 5 Nov. 1794, Thomas Jenkins, presbyterian minister at Whitchurch, Shropshire, from 1783 to 1815, reported that Thomas Porter and Dr Lewis Jones Jardine, whom he had met at Chester, immediately before their departure for America, were 'both very great infidels'; DWL, MS 12.57 (42). Evidently he had conveyed the same information by letter to Rowe.

5   John Williams (1768–1835) was minister to the Norton congregation from 1794 to 1804; see C. J. Street, 'The old nonconformity at Norton, Derbyshire. Part II. – The story of a vanished chapel', *TUHS*, I, 2 (May 1918), 135–39. For his earlier career, see Letter 413, n. 9.

6   'Our friend' was William Tayleur; 'Saturday next' was 20 Sept. 1794.

---

584. To WILLIAM TAYLEUR   29 SEPTEMBER 1794

Text: JRUL, Lindsey Letters, vol. III, no. 41.
Printed: McLachlan, 'More letters', 374 (short extracts from first two paragraphs; seventh paragraph).
Addressed: To/William Tayleur Esqr/Shrewsbury
Endorsed: 29th Sept^r – 94
Postmarked: SE 29 94

London. Septr. 29. 1794.

Dear Sir,

It is a satisfaction to you and to me, who have both passed the age of man in the Psalmist's computation,[1] to have lived so long as to have a sight of a new æra taking place in the christian world, in which all interference of the civil power in things sacred, all constraint on conscience will be removed, and the gospel have its free course to stand and spread by its own force.

This is what is expected to take place in France, when the present violent state of things is over, and the principles of their proposed Government will be allowed to operate.

It will be well, if the other nations of Europe take warning in time, and by a reformation of their great sin in invading God's authority, prevent that severer discipline which in all probability will otherwise be exercised over them, to prevent their opposing his moral government, and drawing his creatures from their innocence and integrity by the snares and allurements or the terrors of this world.

I am persuaded, from what I have learned concerning it, that you will have great satisfaction in Mrs Wollstonecrafts work, if it be not too troublesome to you to attend to it, and as it is so much historical, I hope it will not.[2]

You see it advertised in the Morning Chronicle of Saturday Sep^t. 27.[3] That first volume will be out the latter end of this week, and will soon be followed by two other volumes, one of which is already printed off. She writes the history of things of which she has been in a great part witness; having for the greater part of the last year been in Paris, and trembled under Robespierre. As she is said to be married in France to Imlay the American, and was with him there in the month of August last when I saw a letter from her, one may wonder she does not inscribe her work by that name, unless she thinks she shall be better known and the work have larger encouragement and sale by her old name.[4]

I must beg the favour of you to acquaint Mr Rowe, that I received his letter the latter end of the last week, and had intended to have thanked him by you for it, but could not find the time.[5] I believe he knows the very worthy Mr Baynham of Totness, who called upon me, and I liked him in person and present, as I had in several letters and communications I had had with him.[6] He told me that Mr Porter of Plymouth had called on him when he left the country, but left him not so satisfied with his conversation as formerly.[7]

A person who is much concerned for an acquaintance in the tower, of whose innocence he has the fullest persuasion, expresses himself full of concern, on hearing that all the prisoners are to be included in one indictment for high treason, and that it will be very long and complicate. This was used in the case of the rioters, tried in the year 1780 in the Borough by Lord Loughborough.[8]

It will be a pleasure to me to learn by my friend Mr Rowe, that these two or three fine cool days which we have had, have contributed to brace and invigorate the feeble machine. My wife desires to join in kind respects and all good wishes. I remain ever, Dear Sir your truly obliged and faithful servant

T. Lindsey.

---

1 I.e. to the age of seventy: cf. Psalm xc. 10.

2 Lindsey referred here to volume I of Mary Wollstonecraft's *An historical and moral view of the origins and progress of the French Revolution; and the effect it has produced in Europe* (London, 1794). It was published by Joseph Johnson.

3 The *Morning Chronicle*, 27 Sept. 1794, advertised that Mary Wollstonecraft's book would be published 'in a few days'.

4 Mary Wollstonecraft lived in France from Dec. 1792 until Apr. 1795, and was in Paris at the time of the execution of Louis XVI in Jan. 1793. Gilbert Imlay (1754–1828), an American-born land speculator, author and former soldier, was a sympathizer with the French Revolution. He and Wollstonecraft became lovers in France in 1793; she gave birth to his child, Fanny Imlay, in May 1794. They were never legally married and their liaison ended shortly after Wollstonecraft's return to England in 1795. See *Collected letters of Mary Wollstonecraft*, ed. Ralph M. Wardle (Ithaca and London, 1979), pp. 225–83. It would have been interesting to know which of her letters Lindsey had seen.

5 Rowe's (non-surviving) letter to Lindsey was probably a reply to Lindsey's letter to him of 13 Sept. 1794 (Letter 583).

6 For Henry Baynham of Totnes, see Letter 434, n. 11. Lindsey's correspondence with him seems not to have survived.

7 Thomas Porter emigrated to America in 1794.

8 Jeremiah Joyce was arrested on 14 May 1794. From 19 May to 24 Oct. 1794, he was detained in the Tower of London, before being taken to Newgate to await his trial. For the indictment, see Issitt, *Jeremiah Joyce*, pp. 50–4. Alexander Wedderburn (1733–1805), Baron Loughborough, was lord chief justice of common pleas from June 1780 until 1793 and lord chancellor from 1793 to 1801. In the former capacity he had presided over the trials of many of the Gordon rioters in 1780.

585. To WILLIAM ALEXANDER   20 OCTOBER 1794

Text: 'Letters of the Rev. Theophilus Lindsey. No. V', *UH*, II, 73
                    (20 Sept. 1862), 320.

Note: This is the only section of the letter printed by the *UH*; the manuscript seems not to have survived. The ellipsis at the start of the section printed by the *UH* indicates that this was not the beginning of the original letter.

London, Oct. 20, 1794.

* * As Mr. Martin[1] has acquainted you with what I wrote to him concerning Dr. Priestley, I will only add that I have heard nothing since of his settlement, but only a letter from Northumberland upon the Susquehana, whither he had gone to avoid the heats in Philadelphia, and to view the situation which his sons had recommended to him as being near the new purchase, to a great amount in which they and many others are concerned.[2] One thing I must mention to prevent your being too much alarmed should you see it in the public prints; that although the most worthy Mr. Russell, Dr. Priestley's friend and fellow-sufferer, has been captured with his family, in their way to Boston, in New England, he is probably by this time liberated out of the prison in Brest, into which he had been thrown. We are only anxious about his health and that of his amiable daughters and sons. The capture has been adjudged illegal in France, as it was an American vessel. Upon what pretence he was taken we have not yet learned.[3] I hope the cloud that hangs over our own and other countries will disperse, and liberty and peace be enjoyed over the globe.

---

1   Probably this was Thomas Martin of Great Yarmouth and Filby; see Letter 536, n. 4.
2   For the abortive 'new purchase', see Letter 587, n. 7. The letter from Priestley was probably that written to Belsham, from Northumberland, dated 27 Aug. 1794; Rutt, I, 270–3.
3   William Russell and his family left Falmouth, on an American ship, the *Mary*, on 13 Aug. 1794 with the intention of emigration to America. However, five days later their ship was apprehended by a French frigate, the *Proserpine*, and the whole family was taken prisoner; France and Britain were at war at this time. They were held on board ship in Brest harbour from Sept. to 30 Dec. 1794 when, still prisoners, they were taken to Paris. With Russell were his two daughters, Martha (1766–1807) and Mary (1768–1839) and his son Thomas Pougher Russell (1775–1851). See Jeyes, *The Russells of Birmingham*, chs. 6 and 7.

586. To JOSHUA TOULMIN   8 NOVEMBER 1794

Text: Belsham, *Memoirs*, p. 236 n. *.

Note: The manuscript of this letter seems not to have survived. Belsham printed only the extract which is presented here.

Serious apprehensions are entertained by Mr. Palmer and Mr. Skirving's friends – I am concerned to mention it – that they have been engaged in some mutinous intention of rising and seizing the ship on their parting from the grand fleet, and going off to America; I wish there may be no truth in this report.[1]

---

1   For this allegation, see Letter 588, n. 10. The ship to which Lindsey referred was the *Surprise* transport, which conveyed Palmer, Muir and Skirving to New South Wales. By the 'grand fleet', Lindsey meant the vessels which escorted the *Surprise*, namely the frigate *Suffolk* and the corvette *Swift*.

587. To WILLIAM TURNER OF NEWCASTLE   9 NOVEMBER 1794

Text: LPN, MS 59 (p).

Printed: Belsham, *Memoirs*, p. 255 n. * (second, third and fourth paragraphs, with minor errors and the omission from the third paragraph of the references to Priestley's son and to Thomas Cooper); Nicholson and McLachlan, 160–2 (entire letter, with very minor errors).

Addressed: To/The Revd Mr Turner/Newcastle upon/Tyne

Endorsed: [By Belsham] Nov: 10: 1794 [followed by two lines of shorthand]

Postmarked: NO 10 94 PAID

London Novr. 9. 1794

Dear Sir,

I rec^d your letter, which Mr Rogerson left in Essex Street, this last week, in the country.[1] And this is the first week of our being settled at our own home. I hope he will be induced to take the trouble to call again, when I shall be glad to see one whom you commend. Mr Carr[2] is of worth and sense much above the common rate.

I rejoice to hear that you have so fair an opportunity of bearing testimony to such injured worth in exile from our unworthy country[3] and of recording that intimate friendship, and union of studies and pursuits which subsisted between that excellent person and your most worthy father. To have any place in the niche with two such eminent characters is a real honour.[4] No satisfaction do I know beyond that of recollecting the hours past and benefit received in friendly communications with both. For some years, particularly when I resigned Catterick;[5] there was no step of importance which I took without consulting both, and the sketch of the Apology soon after published, they were so good as to take the trouble of meeting and passing a day with me at an Inn in Knaresborough, when I read it to them.[6] [There follow three or four words heavily crossed out and illegible].

I have been made happy by several letters received from Dr Priestley since his arrival in America. In his last, and the last as far as I learn, which has come from him, he mentions a very important matter, the large Purchase of lands on the Susquehanna, in which his son with Mr Cooper of Manchester and others, had embarked, was *all over*: they had been deceived by the proprietors, and by evidence that did not turn out satisfactory; and thus after much delay, and some expense, many will be much disappointed, several worthy persons of my knowlege, who had engaged for shares and are gone to America.[7]

In the same letter he says, he had an invitation from New York, to read lectures philosophical, and to open an unitarian congregation: but had declined on account of the distance from the place where his sons would be likely to settle. I am grieved at it; because New York was the place for him, the english American Metropolis, the inhabitants most cultivated, of most easy access from Europe, &c. &c. This concern however was a little abated, by the subsequent paragraph of his letter, relating that the chymical professor of the college in Philadelphia was believed to be on his deathbed, and that Dr Rush[8] had told him that he believed he would be invited to succed [*sic*] him. This, he adds, will oblige him to four or five months residence in Philadelphia, and as there is a certain prospect of being able to estabilish an unitarian congregation in the place, he shall not hesitate to accept the offer. This letter was dated from Northumberland, Septr. 14.[9]

Mr Serj^t. Heywood was very well yesterday, and as I told him I was about to write to you, desired he might be particularly remembered. He was to go to day in his Serj^{ts} coif to dine with the new Lord Mayor, a good whig, when Mr Fox is invited, as well as the Minister. The judges and Serjeants it seems attend of course.[10]

We say that Mr Erskines speech at Hardy's trial deserves to be imprinted on every British heart.[11]

My wife desires to present you with her best wishes as well as Mrs Turner and your little folks.

I am always, Dear Sir, very cordially Yours

T. Lindsey.

---

1 Turner's letter to Lindsey seems not to have survived. Nicholson and McLachlan, p. 162, speculate that 'Mr Rogerson' was a son of Richard Rogerson (d. 1760), the minister of Hanover Square chapel, Newcastle upon Tyne, from 1733 to 1760.

2 This was probably Turner's pupil Thomas William Carr; see Letter 557, n. 1.

3 Joseph Priestley.

4 This is a reference to William Wood's sermon preached on 7 Sept. 1794 upon the death of William Turner of Wakefield; it was accompanied by a memoir of its subject. Turner had evidently informed Lindsey of it in his (non-surviving) letter. He subsequently provided Lindsey with a copy; see Letter 594, n. 1, where the full bibliographical details of Wood's sermon are set out.

5 I.e. in Nov. 1773.

6 For references to Lindsey's meetings with William Turner of Wakefield at Knaresborough in 1773, see Vol. I, Letters 98 and 102.

7 There are four surviving letters from Priestley to Lindsey between the former's arrival in America and Sept. 1794, dated 15 June, 24 June, 5 July and 14 Sept 1794. All four are in DWL, MS 12.13 and are partly printed in Rutt, I, 255–9, 263–6, 268–70, 273–5. In his letter of 14 Sept., Priestley wrote that 'the settlement that my son and Mr. Cooper were projecting' was 'all over'; Rutt, I, 274. He described the disappointment in more detail in a passage omitted by Rutt from this letter. Joseph Priestley junior and Thomas Cooper had hoped to form a company to purchase large tracts of land in the Susquehanna region to form the basis of a settlement for emigrants from Britain.

8 Benjamin Rush (1746–1813), medical practitioner at Philadelphia, became the first professor of the institutes of medicine at the University of Pennsylvania in 1792. The chemistry professor at the university on his deathbed was John Carson (1752–94), who was appointed to the chair in 1794 and who died on 26 Oct. of that year. A graduate of the college of Philadelphia, he held the degree of MD from the University of Edinburgh and was a physician at the Philadelphia dispensary. He was a fellow of the APS.

9 For this letter, see Rutt, I, 273–5.

10 The lord mayor of London from Nov. 1794 to Nov. 1795 was Thomas Skinner; the occasion to which Lindsey referred was his installation at the Guildhall on Saturday 8 Nov. 1794, when he was sworn in to his new office. Skinner's whig credentials were evident in his dinner invitation to Fox, Grey and Sheridan on 10 Nov; *Morning Chronicle*, 10 Nov. 1794, and in the endorsement of that newspaper, which predicted on 12 Nov. that he 'will never be made the tool of office, nor the dupe of faction'. Heywood was entitled to wear the coif (white cap) of a serjeant-at-law.

11 *Mr Erskine's speech in defence of Mr. Hardy, on a trial for high treason, 1st November, 1794* was published in Dublin in 1794. It also appeared in *The trials at large of Thomas Hardy and others; for high treason, which began on Saturday, October 25, 1794. At the Old Bailey* (Nottingham, 1794), pp. 159–95. The latter work was published by, among others, Daniel Holt (see Letter 663). The speech was also widely reported in the London press.

588. To RUSSELL SCOTT   **27 NOVEMBER 1794**

Text: Scott Coll.
Printed: McLachlan, 'Lindsey to Scott', 120–1 (very short summaries
                 of third and seventh paragraphs).
Addressed: To/The Revd Russell Scott/Portsmouth
Postmarked: Postmark missing.

London. Novr. 27 1794

Dear Sir,

We have been not quite three weeks resident in Essex Street, since the beginning of the summer when we went to Cheltenham; but from the middle of September to that time were with some friends a few miles from Epsom,[1] coming to town on the Saturdays and returning on the mondays. I blame myself for not writing to make my inquiries after you sooner, but think you are not wholly without blame in not hazarding a few lines to Essex-Street. We hope yourself Mrs Scott, and your young folks are well, but we are not without some anxieties about your own health, which has always, but especially of late been very imperfect.

You will be glad to be informed, that my wife has been upon the whole much better for our Summer excursion, and the Cheltenham waters, though not greatly relieved upon the spot, and we passed the time very agreeably at that place, and at Mrs Clyffords at Perrystone near Ross in Herefordshire, a friend of my wifes,[2] and at Overbury in Worcestershire, the mansion and pleasant hospitable abode of the worthy friend whose signature conveys this to you,[3] and who is a little indignant at being dragd from it a month sooner than necessary, the farther prorogation of Parliament meeting him and his family when advanced towards town as far as Oxford.[4]

I live in hope that some occasion may bring you to town when I shall have great pleasure in communicating to you the intelligence from our worthy and excellent friend Dr Priestley, his reception, views of things, prospects &c which I have pretty regularly received from him since his arrival in America at New York the 4th. of June. At present I shall only acquaint you with some principal things in his last letter, dated Septr. 14. at Northumberland a beautiful little town, with about 500 inhabitants, but likely to increase, situated upon a branch of the Susquehanna, and near Sunbury, another town of the same size, and like situation. At this town of Northumberland, Mrs Priestley, with other english families are desirous to settle, and as a sort of country house, it may be a healthy situation for Dr Priestley to retire to, if it be near the place of his son's settlement; but he is made for cultivated society, and not to live among a few new settlers; and this I believe will soon be his lot. For in this his last letter, he mentions that he had received an invitation to begin a course of lectures, and to open an unitarian chapel in New York; but says, that he had declined the offer, on account of the distance from the place where his sons would probably settle.[5] I could wish he had decided otherwise, as New York is the properest place of all others for him, and where he is likely to be most usefull, and should have been grievd at his giving it up, if in the same letter he had not added; that he had received an account that the chymical Professor of the college at Philadelphia, was in a bad state of health beyond recovery, and that Dr Rush had signified to him, that he believed he would be incited to suceed him. And this offer he expresses himself disposed to accept, especially as he had before this a view of estabilishing an unitarian congregation there in which he had reasons to believe there would be no difficulty. And since this there has been no letter received from him.[6]

In the same letter he relates, that the intended purchase on the Susquehanna, to a large amount, in which his son, Mr Cooper of Manchester, Mr Russell, and many other emigrants to America had embarked, was all over. On a nearer view, happily before the bargain was too far gone, they found that they had been deceived by the proprietors, and the evidence that had appeared satisfactory turned out otherwise, so that instead of purchasing, a great part of it was not worth accepting. This has been a great disappointment.[7]

But about ten days after my letter from the D^r. an acquaintance in London had a letter from Mrs Davy, (late of Crediton)[9] from Philadelphia, telling him that he was setting out with Dr Priestleys son toward Northumberland, and with a design to examine some other situations, of less extent, where it might be convenient to make a settlement.

I have thus given you a hasty sketch of what you will be glad to know concerning America, and Dr P. and his family.

I must now desire that after an account of yourself and family, you will favour me with any thing that can be depended upon relating to this ugly report of our friends Mr Palmer and Skirvin[g] in particular, being concerned in a mutiny on board the Surprize, to run off with the ship to America, on their parting with the grand fleet. I am persuaded, that Mr Palmer was utterly incapable of engaging in any thing base, or cruel or dishonourable, which such a wanton unprovoked attempt as is described, would be, unless by vile treatment or any other way he had lost his right mind.[10]

I say nothing of the late acquittals, which have given so much sober joy and satisfaction, and which do such great honour to the justice of our country; and which decisions are likely to influence in the future trials on the same indictment.[11]

The unfortunate war in which we are engaged is in a way to cure many of the fatal infatuation [sic] they were possessed with about it. There is a report, and I hope well founded, that though we are making vast preparations for continuing the war, the Ministry are desirous of peace, if they did but know how to bring it about. Mr Jay would be a very proper person, if he be gone on this errand to Paris, to feel the pulse of the convention about it.[12]

I do not know a book of any account that is lately come out. Theological objects Mr Johnson says it would be fruitless at this time to strive to call mens attention to them. Nor has he any new work of that kind in hand, or has heard of any.

On[e] thing I find I have forgotten to speak of; the capture of the vessel of an American, in which Mr Russell and his family were carried into Brest harbour, and detaind. It is a dark business, a manueuvre [sic] of the Captain to serve his own purposes. By the intervention however of the American ambassador here, who was Mr Russell's acquaintance, with Mr Jay, and the cooperation of the American ambassador at Paris and all the Americans of note there, there is no doubt of his having been delivered; and we trust they would be able to sail so as to be about this time arrived at Boston, the intended place of their landing at first.[13] But we are not easy in there being no letters from himself or his family to apprize us of these particulars, which we wish to be assured of.

My wife joins with me in respects to Mrs Scott and yourself, with all kind wishes for your little family. We beg also to be kindly remembered to the worthy Mr Porter, and shoud be glad to know that he and his are well when you write.

Mr Kentish from Plymouth has been here preaching as Candidate to suceed M^r

Maurice as Afternoon Preacher at the Gravel Pits. The day of election is Sunday; and it is thought he will be chosen without opposition.[14] I am concerned that by his and M[r] Porters removal the chapel at Plymouth Dock will want a Minister. Plymouth itself will be more easily supplied.[15] Do you know a young minister, an unitarian, whose circumstances would allow him to undertake the charge of that little flock.

ADieu. Dear Sir I am always cordially Yours

T. Lindsey.

---

[1] Probably Sophia and Frances Chambers at Morden.

[2] Eliza Maria Clifford, or Clyfford (née Lewis), was the widow of William Morgan Clifford (d. 1789), barrister at law and recorder of Monmouth, of Perrystone, Herefordshire. She died in 1815. See also Letter 741.

[3] At this point there is a subsequent manuscript annotation to the letter which states that it was 'franked by James Martin', i.e. James Martin, MP for Tewkesbury, whose residence was at Overbury, Worcestershire. He was the 'worthy friend'. Martin's signature, confirming the frank, is missing.

[4] On 2 Oct. 1794, the house of commons was prorogued until 4 Nov., when it was further prorogued until 25 Nov., the date upon which Martin had expected it to meet. On 25 Nov., there was a further prorogation until 30 Dec. 1794; *CJ*, XLIX, 745.

[5] In a passage omitted by Rutt from Priestley's letter to Lindsey of 14 Sept. 1794, Priestley wrote that he had recommended Mr Porter (Thomas Porter, formerly minister to the Treville Street congregation, Plymouth) to give this course of lectures; DWL, MS 12.13.

[6] This section of Priestley's letter to Lindsey of 14 Sept. 1794 (see n. 5, above) is printed in Rutt, I, 273–5.

[7] See Letter 587, n. 7.

[8] Lindsey first wrote 'D[r]', then made the alteration to 'M[r]'. He had used the expression 'D[r]' earlier in the same sentence and perhaps it was particularly fresh in his mind.

[9] Lindsey's correspondent William Davy, of Crediton, Devon, before his emigration to America; his first surviving letter to Lindsey is Letter 656. Lindsey did not identify the acquaintance in London to whom Davy had written in 1794.

[10] According to Palmer, on 31 May 1794, Patrick Campbell, the captain of the *Surprise*, declared that he had uncovered a plot among the soldiers on board to seize the ship, murder the senior officers and escape with the ship to France and then to America. Campbell accused Palmer and Skirving of fomenting this 'mutiny' and subjected them to close confinement in appalling conditions below deck. Only with their arrival in New South Wales in Oct. 1794 did their conditions improve. Palmer denied any involvement in any such 'mutiny'; see Palmer, *Narrative*, pp. 20–56. For Lindsey's source of information about this story, see Letters 590 and 595.

[11] Jeremiah Joyce (see Letter 584, n. 8) was released on 1 Dec. after the attorney-general announced that he would proceed no further with the prosecution. Thomas Hardy, arrested on 12 May 1794, was acquitted on a charge of high treason 5 Nov. 1794. John Horne Tooke was acquitted on a similar charge on 22 Nov. 1794. John Thelwall's acquittal on a charge of high treason followed on 5 Dec. 1795.

[12] Rumours that peace negotiations were about to start appeared frequently in the London press during the latter part of Nov. 1794; see, for example, *Morning Chronicle*, 25 Nov. 1794, and *Morning Post and Fashionable World*, 25 Nov. 1794. John Jay (see Letter 576, n. 12) arrived in Britain in June 1794 as a special envoy from the American government; he remained in Britain until Apr. 1795. He did not go to Paris on this occasion, although he had been a member of the American delegation in Paris in 1782–83, when conducting negotiations with France at the end of the War of American Independence.

[13] See Letter 585, n. 3. Russell and his family were not released from their (relatively mild) confinement in Paris until June 1795. Later in that month they left Le Havre, on board the *Nancy* for New York, where they arrived on 23 July. The United States minister to Britain between 1791 and 1796 was Thomas Pinckney (1750–1828), who also served as envoy extraordinary to Spain in 1794–5; he was a vice-presidential candidate in 1796. The United States ambassador in Paris from 1792 to 1794 was Gouveneur Morris (1752–1816); he was elected to the United States senate in 1800. Morris's successor from 1794 to 1796 was James Monroe (1758–1831), subsequently the fifth president of the United States. In 1795, Monroe appointed as consul general in Paris Fulwar Skipwith (1765– 1839), who had previously served with the American delegation in France. The Russell family were acquainted with Skipwith during their stay in Paris. The American ship captured by the *Proserpine*

(on 29 Aug. 1795) was the *Ivor* (Captain Gooderich). See Jeyes, *The Russells of Birmingham*, pp. 74, 122, 139.

14 Michael Maurice (1767–1855), a former student at Hoxton Academy and Hackney College, was assistant minister at Old Meeting, Great Yarmouth, from 1787 to 1792, and assistant minister at the Gravel Pit meeting, Hackney, from 1792 to 1794. For Maurice, see *Christian Reformer*, 1855, pp. 407–17, and Young, *F. D. Maurice and unitarianism*, pp. 62–82. John Kentish was not chosen as Maurice's successor at Hackney; that successor was Thomas Belsham, who served as minister there from 1794 until he succeeded Disney as minister at Essex Street chapel in 1805. By 'Sunday', Lindsey meant 30 Nov. 1794.

15 John Kentish was the first minister of the newly opened Plymouth Dock chapel in 1791; his successor in 1794 was James Holt (1756–1830), who served the congregation from that year until 1799.

589. To WILLIAM TAYLEUR   8 DECEMBER 1794

Text: JRUL, Lindsey Letters, vol. II, no. 80.
Printed: McLachlan, *Letters*, p. 90 (last three sentences of ninth paragraph).
Addressed: To/William Tayleur Esqr/Shrewsbury
Endorsed: 8th Dec^r. – 94
Postmarked: DE 8 94

London. Decr. 8 1794.

Dear Sir,

I do not commend myself for it, but since I have heard that you have been considerably improved in health, I have been more negligent in writing to you[1] or to Mr Rowe, which I consider in some respects as the same; and I will beg leave, in the entry, before I go any farther to thank him for his mention of your Society having adopted the Salisbury Liturgy with a general consent, which I have heard well spoken of, though I have never seen it, and hope it will contribute to confirm in you and to spread around you the knowlege and worship of the one true God, and holy and virtuous practice.[2] Mr Aikin did not surprize me by relating that You generously proposed to bestow books upon those to whom it might not be so convenient to purchase new ones.[3]

I do not know whether I ought to mention to you, who have been so noble towards our Unitarian Book-Society, a sort of distress into which we have inadvertently drawn ourselves.

Last summer, at the request of some worthy absent members, it was agreed to reprint, for which we had the author and the bookseller's leave, a new and cheap edition of Dr Priestleys Institutes, in two small volumes, and no less than 1500 copies were ordered to be struck off. But at our last meeting, when the bills were brought in, all were in astonishment at the expence, no less than ninety pounds for the mere article of Paper, and £175 – paper and printing together. I have no doubt of the impression going off in time to members, but it will be a long time, and in the mean while our finances are much abridged and we are obliged to suspend the reprinting of one or two tracts that were much wanted. I shall acquaint you what measures are taken about it at our quarterly meeting which will be on thursday next.[4]

I presume that Mr Aikin may have sent you, Mr Joyce's Sermon, printed while he was in prison, with an Appendix.[5]

The Sermon is a valuable discourse, which does credit to his christian principles and dispositions and also to his understanding, and the matter in the Appendix, relating himself and Bonney, is curious.[6] Already I find the publication has done good. For some persons before very unfriendly to the late State-prisoners, begin to say, that they are glad to find they are not all such wicked ruffians as they thought them, and that it is not to be wondered that Lord Stanhope had such a good opinion of M[r]. Joyce.

Yesterday I had the following paragraph in a letter from Plymouth. "This morning M[r] Tingecombe[7] rec[d]. a letter from M[r] Porter, dated Philadelphia, Oct[r]. 16.

"It is not long, only mentions in general his, Jardine's and Coopers arrival in health, with the civilities and attention paid them; their design to go into the neighbouring country – does not name D[r] Priestley[".]"[8]

I, and others, are surprized to receive no farther intelligence from the Doctor by these Philadelphia ships. But we attribute it to his being at their country recess in Northumberland, which is quite out of the way for writing to or hearing from his friends. I am not a little anxious to receive his next letter, which I expect will give some farther information about the chymical Professorship of Philadelphia, and his removal thither.[9]

I beg you will tell M[r] Rowe, with our best comp[ts] to him and M[rs] Rowe, that I most heartily congratulate him and our country on the noble honest verdicts of the three Juries who have acquitted our friend Joyce whose principles we knew, and the other State-prisoners, of any conspiracy against the King and Constitution.[10] It seems already to have quieted the minds of the people, and my friends tell me, they see, or think they see fewer spies about than usual. I am afraid nothing can be more black than the prospect of our affairs upon the continent. England's sun, I fear is certainly set for ever. And it may be, will be better for the world, as we would not walk in it's light nor suffer others.

My wife sends most due respects. Do not forget us to M[r] Wood and his brother[11] and M[r] Harries. I am always y[r] truly obliged & affectionate

T. Lindsey.

---

1   Lindsey wrote 'your' and crossed out the 'r'.
2   For the Salisbury liturgy, and Tayleur's additions to it for use at Shrewsbury, see Letters 406, n. 12 and 408, n. 2.
3   I have not been able to locate Arthur Aikin's letter to Lindsey.
4   On 13 Feb. 1794, the monthly committee of the Unitarian Society resolved, on the motion of Timothy Kenrick of Exeter, supported by Lindsey, that a two-volume duodecimo edition of Priestley's *Institutes of natural and revealed religion* be printed for the use of the society. The quarterly meeting on 10 Apr. 1794 decreed that 1,500 copies be printed; Unitarian Society minute book, pp. 47, 51. The minutes of the 'last [monthly] meeting' on 13 Nov. 1794 made no mention of Priestley's *Institutes* or of a financial deficit, although the monthly committee meeting on 'Thursday next' (11 Dec. 1794) expressed concern about uncollected subscriptions to the society; Unitarian Society minute book, p. 53. On 12 Mar. 1795, the monthly committee meeting decided that members be allowed to purchase Priestley's *Institutes*, 'lately printed by the society', for 3*s* 6*d* per set, in boards; Unitarian Society minute book, p. 54.
5   This work was *A sermon preached on Sunday, February the 23d, 1794. By Jeremiah Joyce. Twenty-three weeks a close prisoner in the Tower of London. To which is added an appendix, containing an account of the author's arrest for 'treasonable practices'; his examination before His Majesty's most honourable privy council; his commitment to the Tower, and subsequent treatment* (London, 1794).
6   The 'Appendix' to Joyce's *Sermon* included accounts of the examinations before the privy council of Joyce himself (pp. 36–9) and of the attorney John Augustus Bonney (pp. 39–41). Bonney (1763–1813) was acquitted and released at the same time as Joyce, on 1 Dec. 1794.
7   Probably John Tingecombe (1771–1848), educated under Belsham's tuition at Daventry and Hackney, and minister at Kingswood from 1792 to 1795 and at Plymouth Dock (Devenport), 'as layman', to 1798. He was minister at Treville Street, Plymouth, from 1798 to 1806, and subsequently served dissenting congregations at Newport (Isle of Wight), Bridgwater and Frenchay. See his obituary in

CR, NS, IV (1848), 703, and Evans, *Vestiges*, p. 69. Possibly he was the 'John Tingecombe Esq., of Plymouth', a subscriber to Gilbert Wakefield's translation of the New Testament (1791).

8   It is not clear who wrote this (apparently non-surviving) letter to Lindsey from Plymouth; possibly the writer was a member of John Tingecombe's family or congregation (see n. 7, above). Thomas Porter emigrated to America earlier in 1794, as did Thomas Cooper and the surgeon Lewis Jardine.

9   Writing to Lindsey on 12 Nov. 1794, Priestley reported that after the death of John Carson (see Letter 587, n. 8), he had been formally invited to succeed him as professor of chemistry at the University of Pennsylvania at Philadelphia. Although at first inclined to accept, he told Lindsey that the prospect of spending four months of the year at Philadelphia caused him to decline the offer. He also believed that he could more effectively promote the cause of unitarianism at Northumberland, where he hoped to establish a college; Rutt, I, 280–1. He repeated this news in his letter to Belsham of 14 Dec. 1794; Rutt, I, 282–3. In late Nov. and early Dec. 1794, the London press reported the arrival of several ships from Philadelphia; on 4 Dec., the *Morning Post and Fashionable World* announced that the *Holland*, from Philadelphia, had reached Dartmouth.

10   See Letter 588, n. 11.

11   See Letter 575, n. 6.

590. To ROBERT MILLAR   9 DECEMBER 1794

Text: DWL, MS 12.46 (6).
Printed: Graham, 'Unhappy country', 136–9 (entire letter, except for the first two sentences of the sixth paragraph).
Addressed: Address missing.
Postmarked: Postmark missing.

London. Decr. 9. 1794.

Dear Sir,

Though I have nothing whatsoever to comunicate directly to clear up the late calumny, for so I will call it, of our dear and valuable friend, yet as I have received a letter from one I no less value, who lives at Portsmouth and was very intimate with and serviceable both to him and James Ellis whilst the Surprize lay off that Port, which gave me some satisfaction with respect to the improbability of what is laid to his charge, I shall transcribe for you what relates to the subject. N.B. The writer had been many months from Portsmouth and had but just heard of our return to London.[1]

"What an infamous account was lately given in one of the public papers[2] concerning our worthy friend Palmer and the honest-hearted Skirving? Whoever drew it up discovered the greatest ignorance of both their characters. For in my opinion, independant of the horrid imputation of having murdered their captain, they would be the two last men to excite or promote any insurrection or tumult on board that *floating hell* which imprisoned them. The whole story appears to me to outrage credulity itself; for the Suffolk, a 74 gun ship and their convoy is said to have been in company. In such a situation therefore even madmen would not have made the attempt to gain possession of the helm. Had not the Suffolk been said to be in company, I should have been inclined from the circumstances of the report to credit the existence of a riot and even the attempt to get the command of the ship, but I could not then even think Palmer or Skirving implicated in it."[3]

It will be curious, if, as some think, the whole turn out to be a fiction fabricated here, not long before the late trials, to increase the alarm and prejudices of the nation against the prisoners, who were associates and intimate some of them with Muir and Palmer.[4]

I congratulate you on the late verdicts of the three honest juries, who have acquitted the State prisoners, and vindicated them from the imputation of a conspiracy against the king and to overturn the constitution.[5] The names of Erskine and Gibbs will be for ever to be honoured in the annals of our country for the assistance given to them in their defence, and particularly the former, for his intrepidity in asserting the rights of Britons, and not scrupling sometimes to go out of his way to impress it the more strongly.[6] An abstract of the several trials is said to be preparing as brief as may be consistent with losing nothing of importance, and to be of as easy purchase as possible, and not less than fifty thousand copies are to be thrown off.[7] You will be pleased to hear that these decisions of the juries appear already to have quieted the minds of many in this great city, and to have taken off that air of suspicion and ferociousness with which they have been observed lately to have looked upon one another.

The accounts of officers and others whom we have seen within these few days arrived from the British army, all confirm the indisposition of the Dutch towards our troops and towards this country. Two thirds of them are supposed to favour the French, and should they in the issue make peace with and join them, the Stadtholder would be no more, and we in England have every thing to dread from their union.[8]

I should be glad to know if there be at any time any of your Dundee acquaintance who may be returning from London, and could convey in their pockets a small pamphlet, or any such trifle. I was sorry that nothing presented itself at the time, when Miss Scott was here.[9] There is just come out a Sermon, by Mr Joyce, one of the late State prisoners, printed while he was in Newgate, with an Appendix, which is one of those fugitive pieces I should be glad you coud see at the time, without much trouble. We know him well and esteem him, and so would you from this specimen of himself. We have taken ¼ of a 100 to circulate. It is calculated to do much moral good, at the same time that it gratifies the curiosity of the reader respecting the Writer.[10]

Whilst a man does not himself give into any sinful compliances, it seems to me that it would not be the part of wisdom to set up for too violent a reformer and thereby hurt the cause he is desirous to promote. This appears to me to be applicable to some circumstances intimated in your own situation. The *fisher of men*[11] must watch the tides and the winds and adapt himself to them, to insure success.

No accounts are come from Dr Priestley by these last Philadelphia-ships, which we attribute to his continuance at Northumberland. I saw a letter that came by one of them which takes no notice of the Doctor being there at the time.[12] We beg our joint kind respects to Mrs Millar and Miss Scott, not forgetting the Master of the house, and to Mr Duncan when you see him.[13] So alarmed are not a few at our present situation that they fear the French may pay us a visit: but may heaven avert the evil, and reform us that we may not feel such a scourge. Always with a most real esteem Yours

T. Lindsey.

x this alludes to the shocking scenes continually exhibited by the soldiers and men and women convicts on board.[14]

---

1   This 'calumny' against Palmer concerned the alleged mutiny on board the *Surprise*; see Letter 588, n. 10. Lindsey referred to, and quoted from, a seemingly non-surviving letter from Russell Scott, who had been away from Portsmouth for his trip to the west country; see Letter 580.

2   For this alleged mutiny on board the *Surprise*, see Letter 588, n. 10. In the last week of Oct. 1794, several London newspapers reported that Palmer, Skirving and the ship's chief mate had instigated the mutiny and that, after its suppression, Palmer and Skirving has been placed in irons; *Whitehall Evening Post*, 23–5 Oct. 1794, the *General Evening Post* of the same dates and *Lloyd's Evening Post*,

22–4 Oct. 1794. The *London Chronicle*, 30 Oct.–1 Nov. 1794, quoted from 'a letter to a Gentleman in Edinburgh' to the effect that Palmer and others had plotted a mutiny, and the *Whitehall Evening Post*, 1–4 Nov. 1794, quoted from 'a Letter from an Officer on board the *Queen* outward-bound East-Indiaman, to a Gentleman in Glasgow' to the same effect. On Saturday 25 Nov. 1794, however, several newspapers cast doubt on the story; see, for example, *Courier and Evening Gazette* of that date.

3   The frigate *Suffolk* was one of the vessels escorting the *Surprise* on the first stage of its journey. Immediately after his discovery of the alleged mutiny, Campbell reported the affair to the captain of the *Suffolk* and transferred to it his chief mate, with whom he had quarrelled violently; Palmer, *Narrative*, p. 23.

4   For the suppression of radicalism in Scotland immediately after the trials of Muir and Palmer, see Bob Harris, *The Scottish people and the French Revolution* (London, 2008), ch. IV.

5   See Letter 588, n. 11.

6   Lindsey referred here to the six-hour speech of Thomas Erskine in *The trial at large of Thomas Hardy, for high treason* (London, 1794), pp. 108–43. The attorney Erskine (1750–1823), MP for Portsmouth from 1783 to 1784, was created Baron Erskine in 1806 and was lord chancellor during the ministry of all the talents in 1806–7. Vicary Gibbs (1751–1820) was junior counsel to Erskine at the trials of John Horne Tooke and Thomas Hardy and played an important part in their acquittals. He had previously defended (unsuccessfully) William Winterbotham in 1793. A supporter of opposition in the 1790s, he joined Pitt's ministry as solicitor-general in 1805, held thereafter a series of senior legal appointments and was MP, successively, for Totnes, Great Bedwin and Cambridge University.

7   Possibly Lindsey referred here to *Bell's reports of the state trials for high treason* (London, 1794), which reported the trials of Thomas Hardy, John Horne Tooke, Jeremiah Joyce and others. According to McLachlan, 'Lindsey to Scott', 128 n. 22, Lindsey collected the published volumes of the *State trials*. The collected edition of the *State trials*, edited by W. Cobbett, T. B. Howell and T. J. Howell, was published in London between 1809 and 1828.

8   Between Nov. 1794 and Jan. 1795, the Dutch republic was invaded and overrun by the French revolutionary armies, with some support from the anti-Orange Dutch patriots, leading to the birth of the pro-French Batavian republic. The stadtholder of the Dutch republic from 1751 to 1795 was William V (1748–1806) of Orange. He was overthrown by the French revolutionary armies and went into exile in England.

9   The sister of Millar's first wife, Jean Scott.

10 See Letter 589, n. 5.

11 Matthew iv. 19; Mark 1. 17.

12 See Letter 589, n. 9.

13 For a possible identification of Mr Duncan, see Letter 566, n. 7.

14 This last sentence is a footnote, in Lindsey's hand, to the quotation from Scott's letter.

591. To WILLIAM TAYLEUR   10 DECEMBER 1794

Text: JRUL, Lindsey Letters, vol. II, no. 81.
Addressed: To/William Tayleur Esqr/Shrewsbury
Endorsed: 10th Dec^r – 94
Postmarked: DE 10 94

London. Decr. 10. 1794.

Dear Sir,

Though I wrote so lately, I must not let the post go out to day without writing again to inform you, that I this morning had sent me the extract of a letter from Philadelphia dated Novr. 5, sent by a gentleman to his brother in London, and acquainting him, "that there had been a meeting at the college of the State of Pennsylvania, on the vacancy of the professorship of Chymistry, and that they had been unanimous in an invitation to Dr Priestley to fill the chair; and that a letter was immediately sent to him at Northumberland to acquaint him with it.["]^1

I have also this moment that I am writing another letter from Mr Belsham^2 informing me that he had just received a letter from Philadelphia containing the same good news, with this addition, that the emolument of the professorship was 300 guineas per ann. I wish this latter article may not be magnified, but hope one may conclude from it, that the income of the place is very handsome.

I have literally time to add no more but my wifes kind respects, and that I remain ever your truly obliged and affectionate servant

T. Lindsey.

---

1   Possibly the gentleman who wrote from Philadelphia to his brother in London was John Vaughan (1756–1841), who had settled at Philadelphia in the early 1780s. The fourth son of Samuel Vaughan, his brothers in London were Benjamin and William Vaughan, both of whom were known personally to Lindsey. From 1791, John Vaughan was the treasurer of the APS. For this invitation to Priestley, see Letter 589, n. 9.
2   Belsham's letter to Lindsey seems not to have survived.

592. To ?JOSHUA TOULMIN   15 DECEMBER 1794

Text: Belsham, *Memoirs*, p. 236 n. *.

Note: Belsham did not positively identify Toulmin as the recipient of this letter, but presented it as 'a succeeding letter' immediately after that to Toulmin of 8 Nov. 1794 (Letter 586); he probably assumed that the reader would understand that Toulmin was the recipient. The manuscript of this letter seems not to have survived. Belsham printed only the extract which is presented here. The words in square brackets are Belsham's. The context was the trials of Muir, Palmer and Skirving.

[In a succeeding letter, dated December 15, Mr. Lindsey expresses his conviction that these worthy men were wrongfully accused.] There is reason to believe that there have been disturbances on board the Surprise, and that Messrs. Palmer and Skirving have been very injuriously accused, as principally concerned in fomenting of them.[1]

---

1   For this alleged mutiny, see Letters 588, 590 and 595.

593. To RUSSELL SCOTT   16 DECEMBER 1794

Text: Scott Coll.
Printed: McLachlan, 'Lindsey to Scott', 121 (third and fourth
                   paragraphs; most of fifth paragraph).
Addressed: Address missing.
Postmarked: Postmark missing.

London. Decr. 16. 1794

Dear Sir,

I was very happy that my last crossed yours on the road, as it would furnish a reply to your kind inquiries about us, as your's relieved us from our anxieties about you and Mrs Scott and your family at present.

To the chapter I gave you about Dr Priestley,[1] I have to add; that there is good ground to believe he is at this time chymical professor at the college in Philadelphia since he had told me he should accept the place if offered to him, and there are letters which assure us of the vacancy, and that he would be invited to fill it, and that message was preparing to be sent to him at Northumberland to apprize him of his honourable and unanimous election. No letters can yet be received from him about it, and it has been unlucky for his friends in England that his absence at

Northumberland has prevented his availing himself of the opportunity of writing to them by several ships which have lately come from Philadelphia.[2]

In many ways it is a felicity, and we have reason to be thankful, that the late State prisoners have been acquitted, being found by an honest impartial jury innocent of the charge of conspiring the death of the king or the subversion of the Constitution.[3] I tremble for the consequences of the reverse, or if any blood had been shed on this occasion. And I know many persons, excellent characters, of rank and fortune, who would have construed their condemnation into a condemnation of the cause of Reform for ever, and on such an alternative had determined to leave the kingdom.

The printing of the trials in Numbers, which is intended, will be of infinite service, in disseminating the knowlege of their free constitution of government, and of their rights to all throughout the kingdom and must animate them to preserve them.[4] Much does the kingdom owe to Erskine and Gibbs.[5] The former I hear is greatly censured by the court for two things; the mention of his being told that he was to lose his place in a great Persons service if he defended Thomas Payne, and accordingly losing it; and saying that there would be a future rehearing of the adjudication of Muir and Palmer, when most probably their sentence would be reversed.[6]

When an opportunity next presents I shall send a copy of Mr Joyce's Sermon and Appendix. We are much pleased with it, as indicating a serious good mind, and christian principles, and good natural abilities and the Appendix is curious.[7] Upon his return to Ld Stanhope's family at Chevening he was received with great exultation by all but the Minister of the parish and the village was illuminated.[8] I am glad to find his little publication softens peoples prejudices, several whom we know and hear of upon reading it, owning that they had been mistaken about these State prisoners and that they were far from being all such wicked ruffians as had been represented.

I do not learn that there is any thing coming forth on theological subjects, and it may be as well to have such discussions suspended for a while, as they would not be attended to at the present moment that politics and the state of the nation engross every one's thoughts. I have read a few pages in Mr Belsham's Memoirs of Geo. III. and was very much delighted with the free spirit with which he sets out, and with which I doubt not of his work being conducted throughout. At the end of a long note, in which he quotes B^p Horsley's language concerning dissenters, and the treatment they meet with, he makes the fine apostrophe, "Rest, rest, immortal spirits of Locke, Hoadly, Somers![9] Seek not to know by what improvements on your exploded principles the house of Brunswic now governs the empire of Britain."[10]

A letter came very lately to a political Society near us, from Margarot, one of whom we know[11] encouraging them to pursue the great work of a reform of Parliament: in it the writer said there had been some little bustle in the Surprize, that the blame had been laid upon Palmer and Skirving, which occasioned a stricter guard to be set over them, but that it woud soon be set to rights, as they were within two months of arriving at their destination: but nothing of chains or crimes. I thought I would name this circumstance, as it serves to set against other things. I long much to have the mystery cleared up.[12]

We desire to be kindly remembered to Mrs Scott, who is recovered we hope from her indisposition, and are glad your boys are well. With my wifes sincere respects to yourself I remain always Dear Sir, cordially Yours

T. Lindsey.

1   See Letter 588.
2   Priestley declined the offer of the professorship of chemistry, much to Lindsey's regret.
3   For these acquittals, see Letter 588, n. 11.
4   See Letter 590, n. 7.
5   See Letter 590, n. 6.
6   Though not directly involved in the defence of Thomas Muir, Erskine strongly sympathized with his
     case. In 1792, Erskine undertook to defend Thomas Paine when the latter was summoned to face a
     charge of seditious libel. Paine departed for France in Sept. 1792 before the trial could take place.
     Erskine in consequence was dismissed as attorney-general to the prince of Wales.
7   See Letter 589, n. 5.
8   Jeremiah Joyce was released from Newgate prison on 1 Dec. 1794; there is a vivid description of
     this celebration in *Gent. Mag.*, LXV, i (1795), 73. The rector of the parish of Chevening from 1774
     until his death in 1803 was Samuel Preston.
9   John Somers, baron Somers (1651–1716), lord chancellor, 1697–1700, and a leading member of the
     whig junto of the 1690s. His libertarian reputation owed much to his part in the successful defence
     of the seven bishops in 1688.
10   This quotation is from William Belsham, *Memoirs of the reign of George III. To the session of parlia-
     ment ending in 1793* (4 vols., London, 1795), I, 24 n. *.
11   I.e. Lindsey and his circle knew Maurice Margarot (n. 12, below) by reputation.
12   The 'political Society near us' was the London Corresponding Society, which met in a variety of
     locations in London, some of them quite close to Essex Street. Maurice Margarot was its chairman in
     1792–3. See *Selections from the papers of the London Corresponding Society 1792–1799*, ed. Mary
     Thale (Cambridge, 1983), pp. viii, ix. In 1793, the society reprinted an extract from Frend's *Peace
     and Union*. The 'mystery' was the alleged mutiny on board the *Surprise*.

594. To WILLIAM TURNER OF NEWCASTLE   7 JANUARY 1795

Text: LPN, MS 59(q).
Printed: Nicholson and McLachlan, 162 (short quotation – 'your
                  excellent Father and his writings' – from first sentence of first
                  paragraph; most of third paragraph; first sentence of fourth
                  paragraph).
Addressed: Address missing.
Postmarked: Postmark missing.

London. Jany. 7. 1795

Dear Sir,

Highly am I indebted to you for Mr Wood's valuable sermon and the short but
most satisfactory memoirs relating to your excellent Father and his writings, drawn
up by no ordinary hand. From these documents the reader will form some idea of
his most amiable benevolent character, of his singular piety and eminent usefulness
in his honourable profession of a christian minister and teacher, and may perceive
some traits of that genuine modesty and humility which was his great ornament,
though it prevented his great worth and knowlege from being so widely displayed
as they otherwise would have been; and which particularly appears by his scarce
ever having produced any thing from his large stores before the public, but what
necessity, friendship or some special occasion drew from him. My obligations to
him were very peculiar in many seasons as well as that which is specified, where so
much honour is done me by recording them, and uniting my name with his.[1]

I could and should say more to you, but being tied down to write to day and
unexpectedly more engaged than usual, must desist.

But not before I acquaint you that I have rec^d a letter from Dr Priestley dated
Northumberland, Novr. 12. in which he acquaints me that the place of chemical

professor in the college at Philadelphia had been offered to him, and to my great concern and surprize, that he had hesitated about and should decline it.[2]

But I have still hope that it will be accepted. For M[r] Jay here has said to more than one of my friends, that the Electors had it under consideration to annex a salary of £500 sterling to the office for D[r] Priestley. Now the Doctor mentions nothing of this kind, which makes me still to think, that they will not lose such a subject as him to fill the vacancy, but will come forward in the honourable way M[r] Jay intimates, and our friend will change his mind.[3]

His next letter will clear up the matter and I shall not forget to acquaint you early with it.[4]

M[r] Rogerson has called on us once or twice, and done us the pleasure to take a breakfast with us. He appears a modest, sensible, studious youth, and I dare say will avoid every thing wrong and improve himself in this great city.[5]

My wife desires to join in kind respects to M[rs] Turner and yourself, and in all good wishes for many years to come for yourselves and your young folks. I remain always

Dear Sir, Your much obliged and affectionate servant

T. Lindsey.

---

[1] William Wood, *A sermon, preached, Sept. 7, 1794, on occasion of the death of the Rev. William Turner; more than thirty years minister of the congregation of protestant dissenters in Westgate, Wakefield ... To which are added, memoirs of Mr. Turner's life and writings*, was published in Newcastle upon Tyne in 1794. Turner had died on 28 Aug. 1794. Wood referred to Turner's friends, including (p. 55) 'the excellent Mr Lindsey', stating that Lindsey and Turner first met in 1768, when Lindsey was vicar of Catterick. The season 'which is specified' was probably the time of Lindsey's resignation of the vicarage of Catterick in 1773.

[2] For this letter, see Rutt, I, 279–81, with the reference the chemistry professorship at p. 280. Priestley gave as his reason for declining it the necessity of spending four months of the year at Philadelphia, away from his home in Northumberland. He also hoped to found a unitarian college at Northumberland.

[3] For the background to this affair, see Schofield, *Enlightened Joseph Priestley*, p. 351 nn. 15–17. For John Jay, who at this time was in London to negotiate a treaty with the British government, see Letter 576, n. 12. During his visit, he met socially many of the leading figures in British politics, including William Wilberforce, Lord Loughborough, Jeremy Bentham and Thomas Pinckney (see Letter 588, n. 13), the American minister in London, who had intervened in William Russell's case. It is not clear to which of Lindsey's friends Jay had spoken; a possibility is William Smith, MP. See Walter Stahr, *John Jay. Founding father* (New York and London, 2005), pp. 330–4. Despite the enhancement of the remuneration, Priestley finally declined the professorship.

[4] See Letter 589, n. 9. In his letter to Belsham of 14 Dec. 1794, Priestley reaffirmed his decision to decline the professorship; Rutt, I, 282–3. His next surviving letter to Lindsey, dated 20 Dec. 1794, did not directly mention the professorship, but repeated his hope for a unitarian college at Northumberland; DWL, MS 12.13, partly printed in Rutt, I, 283–5.

[5] For a possible identification of Rogerson, see Letter 587, n. 1.

595. To JOHN ROWE   **23 JANUARY 1795**

Text: JRUL, Lindsey Letters, vol. II, no. 82.
Printed: McLachlan, *Letters*, p. 91 (part of third, and whole of fourth,
             sentences of fourth paragraph); p. 96 (most of third paragraph,
             with errors of transcription).
Addressed: To/The Rev^d. Mr Rowe/Shrewsbury
Postmarked: JA 23 95

London. Jany. 23. 1795

Dear Sir,

I sent a few lines to our excellent friend soon after the receit of the letter you favoured me with last, which conveyed the account of the sad accident and of his providential escape from all immediate harm from it.[1] We have not however been without our fears for him, especially since this most severe season has set in, which still continues; and therefore I should take it as a favour to have a line at your leisure, to say how he does, and also how you and Mrs Rowe bear up in this very cold weather. For ourselves, as there have been few days in which we have not been able to walk out for two or three hours, it has agreed much both with my wife and myself.

I think my last letter to Mr Tayleur mentioned the surprise and concern I was under, on hearing that Mr Russell was still confined at Brest, when we made no doubt of his being liberated and even arrived at Boston. But we hope that the fresh efforts that are using will at length succeed. And I have been glad to learn since, that although confined, he is well treated, and as easy as possible under it. But still it is a sore disappointment to receive no letter or account from himself.[2]

A few days ago, Mr Joyce was in Town from Chevening, and told us one morning that he called, that he had that day seen a letter from Margarot to a friend in London; which mentioned, what I was sorry to hear, that there had actually been a mutiny on board the Surprize, and that the ringleaders to whose names he does not tell, were in irons, adding that Messrs Palmer and Skirving, were under some slight confinement for being privy to the intent, and that all of them were to undergo a trial, when the[y] arrived at Botany bay.[3]

If You have seen the memoirs of the reign of Geo. iii, I am sure you have been highly gratified and instructed by them, thought there may be some few things, in which he is not so accurate. Neither this nor his former work will make the readers in love with the reigning family.[4] And they will lament, and with reason, that so presumptuous a young man as Mr Pitt was ever placed at the helm in this country, which he has now by his want of wisdom brought to the very brink of ruin. The fascination however for him still seems to continue, and may go on till he has compleated our fate. Holcrofts letter to Mr Windham, breathes a benevolent spirit, and is full of excellent sent[iments], and must mortify the man beyond measure, if his pride will suffer him to read it. I am told it sells, and shall endeavour to promote the sale, as it appears that it is by his publications that the worthy author supports himself and family and an aged parent. Such virtuous exertions, where, as I am told, Deity is not owned, bespeak a very extraordinary character and turn of mind; which however I have not doubt might be easily developed did one know all the circumstances of it, and his unhappy error accounted for.[5] My wife joins in respects to Mrs Rowe and yourself and in good wishes for your little family, We beg you will say every thing kind and respectful for us to our most valuable friend, and hope you will be able soon to tell us good news about him. Pray remember us to Mr Wood, Mr Aikin &c. I remain always very cordially Yours

T. Lindsey

---

1 I have not found in the *Shrewsbury Chronicle* or elsewhere a record of this 'accident' to Tayleur. Lindsey's previous surviving letter to him, dated 10 Dec. 1794 (Letter 591), did not mention it; its immediate predecessor, dated 8 Dec. 1794 (Letter 589) referred to Tayleur's improved health. Either Letter 591 constituted the 'few lines' or a short note from Lindsey to Tayleur from this period has not survived.

2 For the confinement of William Russell and his family at Brest and subsequently at Paris, see Letter 588, n. 13.

3 See Letter 588, n. 10. According to Palmer, Maurice Margarot took Captain Campbell's side in the alleged mutiny on board the *Surprise*, and, since he became the 'determined foe' of Palmer and Skirving, could not be regarded as a reliable witness. Palmer also alleged that Margarot thwarted his attempts to secure witness statements denying the existence of any mutiny. In the event, there was no trial of the alleged mutineers at Botany Bay; see Palmer, *Narrative*, pp. 33, 57.

4 For William Belsham's *Memoirs of the reign of George III. To ... 1793*, see Letter 593, n. 10. His 'former work' was *Memoirs of the kings of Great Britain of the house of Brunswic-Lunenburg* (2 vols., London, 1793).

5 This work was Thomas Holcroft's *Letter to the Right Honourable William Windham, on the intemperance and dangerous tendency of his public conduct* (London, 1795). William Windham was MP for Norwich from 1784 to 1802, and secretary at war from 1794 to 1801. By 'Deity is not owned', Lindsey referred to Holcroft's rejection of revealed religion. Holcroft's father (also Thomas Holcroft), a shoemaker, died in 1797; Holcroft supported his parents financially during the 1790s. With his third wife, Dinah Robinson (d. 1790), he had several children, including the future author Fanny Margaretta Holcroft (1785–1844). Holcroft made a living as a writer, as a journalist, dramatist, novelist and political commentator. See the entry for Holcroft by Gary Kelly, *ODNB*, XXVII, 598–603.

---

596. To WILLIAM ALEXANDER   26 JANUARY 1795

Text: 'Letters of the Rev. Theophilus Lindsey. No. VI', *UH*, II, 74 (27 Sept. 1862), 330.

Note: This is the only section of this letter printed by the *UH*; the manuscript seems not to have survived. The ellipsis at the start of the extract printed by the *UH* indicates that this was not the beginning of the original letter.

London, Jan. 26th, 1795.

* * My last letter from Dr. Priestley was dated Northumberland, Nov. 12. In this he mentions that he had a few days before received an invitation from Philadelphia to the chemical professorship in the college, vacant by death, but after that much deliberation he had declined it, as he found himself happy, and thought he might be useful, though on a smaller scale in his present situation.[1] I am, however, in some hope that he may still change his mind with respect to the professorship, if, as is here given out by Mr. Jay, the State of Pensylvania [*sic*] had it under consideration to annex £500 sterling for an annual salary to him as professor.[2] This, I think, would overcome many of his objections. Four months' residence is all that the professorship requires, and he may still live the rest of the year in Northumberland, and be near his family. I therefore wait anxiously for his next letter, to know the full issue of this matter. In the meantime, he says, and I hear it from other quarters, that his arrival and fixing in America, his character, and his writings (of which Mr. Johnson has sent a large quantity) inquired after in all parts and bought up, have already been of service in bringing many off from superstition and scepticism. He has also published some small pieces which have been well received, particularly an answer

to Paine's "Age of Reason", which has been much sought after, as Mr. Paine's tract had been very industriously circulated before.

---

1   See Rutt, I, 279–81, and Letter 594.
2   See Letter 594, n 3. The professorship of chemistry at the University of Pennsylvania had been vacated by the death of John Carson, who died on 26 Oct. 1794.

597. To RUSSELL SCOTT   5 FEBRUARY 1795

Text: Scott Coll.
Addressed: Address missing.
Postmarked: Postmark missing.

London. feb. 5. 1795.

Dear Sir,

Far from being tired, I have read with much satisfaction your long letter,[1] in which you have increased my esteem, if it could be, for you, in respect of your truly christian and prudent conduct as a minister of the gospel in these times, and have convinced me that those who heard you and took offence at what you delivered, must have come either full of fear and terror and alarm, or with prejudices against you as a political character and with a design to criminate and condemn you. A disposition this last against which the most perfect unblameableness and innocence can be no security. Of this general spirit of alarm the worthy St John Carter[2] must have partaken very largely, or he would not have undertaken to speak to you, though in real friendship, upon the subject, but would have rather set himself to quiet the suspicions and jealousies of those who blamed you, and have told them how much they misunderstood you, and desired them to attend more impartially to your discourses in future, and if at the same[3] he had given you intimation by which you might have avoided terms otherwise innocent, but by very ignorant, and irritated minds, liable to be misconstrued, all might have been composed and gone on well.[4]

And I do most heartily wish that by this or some such method these prejudices and disquiets might be laid asleep, and the artful designs of the adversary be defeated. For assuredly there are those who make it their business, for some private, political, interested ends to blow up these flames, though you may not have any certain knowlege of them or of their operations.

You are the best judge of what is proper upon the occasion. But I would wish you to consult with sincere and judicious friends, whether by drawing up and after its being shewn to and approved by them, preaching a sermon by way of apology and defence of yourself, you might not remove the prejudices of the greater part, and reinstate yourself in their favour and esteem.[5] So far from there being any thing mean or degrading in such an effort, it is in itself right and highly becoming a christian.

I canot but wish you the more to pursue this line of conciliation, because of the difficulty of the present times in general. I have heard Messrs Porter and Kentish speak of the reserve and nicety in the persons with whom they associated themselves, to which they were constrained, such as I declare to you I thought even too much. And liberal situations, where there is any tolerable competency of provision for the support of a family, you know are very hard to be procured, and become daily more so by the growing number of candidates for them.

You will turn these things over in your thoughts, and consult with friends. Any services in our power, you may depend upon. Only I should be glad to know as soon as you can, what letter I am to write to Mr Kentish, as the purport of my letter to him was to suspend any decisions, till he heard from me again. A few days before he had sent me word, that upon young Mr Rennel's refusal, another person had been recommended whom he was about to write to.[6] I did not mention, nor bind myself to mention any names to him. I apprehend that the loss of the family of the Tingecombes woud hurt the income of the congregation very sensibly.[7]

I think that the preaching of a Sermon to your people, which you might afterwards print, if called for, might be more attended to, and would not be liable to [be] slighted and suppressed as a letter to them; being of such notoriety, and more proper for a person in a Public station as you are. But of these matters, you with your friends on the spot will be able to form the proper judgment and determination.

Mr Taylor, whom you inquire after, is a young man, who 3 years since finished his studies at the college at Hackney, having I imagine begun them under Dr Kippis and Dr Rees, as he is favourite with the former and often preaches for him, is said to be a worthy character and good preacher. I think his father is of Dr Kippis's congregation.[8] Dr Blackburne, who belongs to it, commends his preaching much.[9] D^r. K. intended to have recomended him to Mr Shore's at Norton near Sheffield, but the young man declines it on account of the great distance from London.[10]

Our joint kind respects to Mrs Scott and my wifes to yourself. We sympathise with her – but hope you will emerge out of this little storm and see better days. Evermost sincerely Yours T. Lindsey.

---

1   Unfortunately, Scott's 'long letter' to Lindsey appears not to have survived.

2   For Sir John Carter (d. 1808) of Portsmouth, see Letter 402, n. 3. His son John Carter (1788–1838), educated at the dissenting academy at Cheshunt, and MP for Portsmouth from 1816 until his death, added the name Bonham before that of Carter.

3   Lindsey evidently omitted a word – probably 'time' – at this point.

4   There is hardly any surviving evidence, apart from Lindsey's letters, as to these divisions within the High Street, Portsmouth, congregation. As one would expect, there is no hint of them in the chapel registers: TNA: RG4/564. Probably Scott's Socinianism was too much for some of the chapel's members.

5   It seems likely that Scott did indeed preach such a sermon, as Lindsey suggested, but that he did not publish it.

6   Possibly this was Thomas Reynell (d. 1830), a former pupil of Thomas Belsham at Daventry, and dissenting minister at Crediton from 1791 to 1797. According to his obituary in *CR*, XVII (1831), 43–4, he was in his sixty-third year when he died, indicating that he was born *c.* 1767–8; he would thus have been twenty-seven or twenty-eight at the time of this letter, when Lindsey referred to him as 'young'.

7   The family of Tingecombe remained members of the Plymouth Dock congregation, where John Kentish was minister. For John Tingecombe, see Letter 589, n. 7. Lindsey wrote this final sentence of the paragraph in the margin, at right angles to the rest of the paragraph.

8   James Tayler (1765–1831) was a student at Hackney College from 1788 to 1792; he was minister at Walthamstow from 1794 to 1796; at St Thomas's, Southwark, from 1796 to 1802; and at High Pavement chapel, Nottingham, from 1802 to 1831. He was the father of John James Tayler (1797–1869), professor of ecclesiastical history and (from 1853 to 1869) principal of Manchester College. In the late 1790s, James Tayler was a member of, and sometimes preached at, Kippis's chapel at Princes's Street, Westminster. See DWL (to be catalogued), vestry minute book of Princes Street chapel, fos. 34, 37. The absence of any entries in the minute book for the period between Oct. 1753 and Oct. 1795 renders it impossible to determine whether Tayler's father was a member of this congregation.

9   I.e. William Blackburne.

10   On James Tayler's declining the office of minister at Norton, John Williams accepted it; see Letter 583.

598. To ROBERT MILLAR   7 FEBRUARY 1795

Text: DWL, MS 12.46 (7).
Printed: Graham, 'Unhappy country', 139–40 (second and third
                   paragraphs, parts of fourth, seventh and eighth paragraphs).
Addressed: Address missing.
Postmarked: Postmark missing.

London. Feb. 7. 1795

Dear Sir,

Your letter came to me yesterday very fortunately to apprize you of it, before I sent off one to you under a cover which I had procured a few days since.[1]

My principal errand in writing is to inform you, that at last an authentic account is arrived, in a letter from James Ellis, of the whole affair, of which Mr Palmer and Mr Skirving have been accused, and have undergone much hardship and oppression. And it turns out to be intirely a false accusation, too much listened to by the Captain of the Surprize,[2] coming from a worthless fellow, who had been much befriended by Mr Palmer, of a mutinous intention in those two gentlemen, without any foundation whatsoever. The letter concerning it, which I heard read, was written by a passenger in the ship who went over on some business of Government, and sent to Mr Joyce, (whose late publication I inclose as the frank will hold it[3]) in the inside of which were a few words from James Ellis to Mr Joyce, acquainting him, that he himself had sent an account of what had happened to Mr Gurney in Essex court in the Temple, and desiring that a copy of what he had sent might be communicated to some persons whom he names, and particularly he says, (I took down his words) *to my Father, James Ellis, Staymaker, Dundee, and tell him I never had better health in my life.*[4]

It was dated – Rio de Janeiro. July. 28. 1794. Perhaps it might be a consolation to his father[5] to mention this circumstance, if Mr Joyce have not at yet apprized him of it.

Let me now thank you for your letter which was very acceptable in bringing so favourable an account of the health of you and your household in the late very trying severity of the weather, which still continues though with less rigour. It is a great satisfaction to see, in the midst of many other sad scenes and events, that the public and private charitable exertions of this metropolis have been and are so widely and judiciously applied, that few I hope if any have suffered much for want of the necessaries of life. But no exertions can call back again to life those thousands who have perished or who are destined to perish in this fatal War, which it [is] absolutely determined by Administration is to be carried on through another campaign, when as an eminent merchant who is an old friend, and I am sorry to say it, much for the war,[6] tells me, that both we and the french must then seek for peace, and lay down our arms through mere inability to carry on the war any longer. I tell him, that his calculations may be just with respect to ourselves, but can by no means be depended upon respecting the French. Alas! humanity, christianity, all moral considerations and regard to the God and governor of the world, are laid aside. And I reply to some of my friends, that I wish they who accuse the French of being Atheists, were less liable to the imputation.

I had long ago lamented over the loss sustained by his family, friends and the public, by the sudden removal of so excellent a character as the late Mr Provost Christie.[7] With such fair and just prospects before them as they had a few years ago they seem to have been peculiarly unfortunate. But I hope it will be reserved for the most worthy and ingenious Mr T. Christie who is settled in this town, to repair in some measure these misfortunes.[8]

I wish I had it in my power to recomend to you at Dundee such an enlightened minister and with such truly apostolic zeal, as you describe and long for. I am sorry to observe to you, that the turn of too many, who of late, have quitted the church of E. for scruples of conscience on account of its unscriptural subscriptions and Service, has been such as to make it appear as if one motive with them had been to be more at liberty to mix with the world and follow its diversions and amusements.[9]

Dr Priestley in more than one of his letters, has expressed an earnest desire, that I could send him over a few such characters as you call out for at Dundee.[10] One or two, from whom I expected better things, have of late with their black coats thrown off all regards to the gospel and to Divine Revelation in general, so as to traduce it and try to disparage it in the eyes of other[s].[11] Mr Archd^n. Paley, on the evidences of X^{ty}, which I have recomended to some who were in danger from such company, has been of real service.[12]

I think my last told you of Dr Priestleys having declined the offer made him of the chemical[13] professorship in the college of Philadelphia, and of the hopes I entertained that it woud still be made worth his acceptance.[14] His answer to Paynes Age of Reason, and some other lesser publications, wch he mentions to have sent have never come. If I have it in my power, and there are sufficient copies, you shall see them, when they do arrive. He is that apostolic man, who is so much wanted: of whom we in this country have shewn ourselves unworthy. As you have opportunity of seeing all the papers, I say nothing of public affairs. Your ladies[15] and yourself will be glad to hear that my wife and I have rather enjoyed better health than usual in this frosty season. Our kind wishes and respects attend You all. I hope Mr Duncan[16] is well, and beg to be rememberd to him. I remain with a cordial esteem Yours

T. Lindsey

---

1   This letter from Millar to Lindsey has not survived. However, Millar's reply to Lindsey's letter of 7 Feb. 1795 may be found in DWL, MS 46 (79). In it, Millar referred to the relief among his Dundee friends at the news that the alleged 'mutiny' on board the *Surprise* was a fabrication.

2   For this alleged mutiny, see Letter 588, n. 10. The 'worthless fellow' was the convict John Grant; see Letter 599, n. 5, and Bewley, *Muir of Huntershill*, p. 110.

3   See Letter 589, n. 5.

4   James Ellis's letter to John Gurney seems not to have survived. In his reply to this letter (see n. 1, above), Millar asked Lindsey to request from John Gurney any further information from James Ellis. The latter's father, of the same name, was an acquaintance of Millar at Dundee.

5   Presumably this refers to the father of James Ellis.

6   Disappointingly, Lindsey did not name this merchant. One might speculate that he was one of Lindsey's London friends from the 1770s who had shared Lindsey's disapproval of the American war.

7   Alexander Christie, the father of Thomas Christie and the brother of William Christie, was born *c.* 1721 and died on 29 Dec. 1794. A merchant and bank agent for the British linen company, he was provost of Montrose on several occasions between 1765 and 1780, and a member of the unitarian congregation at Montrose founded by William Christie.

8   After spending much time in Paris in the early 1790s, Thomas Christie returned to London and worked as a partner of the carpet manufacturer Moore & Co in Finsbury Square. He remained in London until 1796, when he travelled to Surinam on behalf of this company, and died there in that year.

9   See n. 11, below.

10   Writing to Lindsey on 24 June 1794, Priestley expressed the wish that he and Belsham would 'look out for proper persons to establish in New York and Philadelphia' and to supply his projected unitarian college; Rutt, I, 266. See also Rutt, I, 269, 270.

11 Lindsey probably had in mind Joseph Fawcett, and possibly Edward Evanson.
12 See Letter 569, n. 6.
13 Lindsey at first wrote 'chymical', then replaced the 'y' with an 'e'.
14 The date of Lindsey's previous surviving letter to Millar was 9 Dec. 1794 (Letter 590).
15 Lindsey probably referred here to Millar's wife, Jean, née Scott, and her female relatives.
16 For a possible identification of Mr Duncan of Dundee, see Letter 566, n. 7.

599. To RUSSELL SCOTT   16 FEBRUARY 1795

Text: Scott Coll.
Printed: McLachlan, 'Lindsey to Scott', 121 (most of second
                   paragraph).
Addressed: To/The Rev^d. Russell Scott/Portsmouth
Postmarked: Postmark missing.

London. feb. 16. 1795

Dear Sir,

Your letter of the 8th. was most welcome to us.¹ We hope the settlement of matters will be permanent, or at least endure till the impending storm is over, when, if it be necessary to make a change, a man may see better his way before him. I took care to write imediately to Messrs Kentish and Toulmin, of whom I had made inquiry respectively, relating to Plymouth and Warminster, to thank them for the trouble given them, for I had a letter from each, and to acquaint them that the difficulties were removed, and that my friend would not now be under any necessity of seeking another situation. But I forbore the mentioning any names of place and person, and thought it prudent to do it.²

The day after I received yours, Mr Gurney very kindly sent me a letter he had rec^d from Ja^s. Ellis, with another from Mr Muir.³ The latter prudently, in all probability, took no notice of what had passed respecting Mr Palmer. The [*sic*]⁴ was very particular respecting the whole affair. And though I believe, that Mr Palmer's insisting so much with the captain on his keeping his word with James Ellis, and probably his very free speeches of him and to him, on that subject, may have irritated a proud despot to revenge himself upon him, and may in part have produced the hardships he has endured, and still endures; yet notwithstanding, I cannot but incline to the opinion that the business originated on this side the water, and that, to exculpate themselves, intimations were here given to do every thing to excite, exasperate, and thereby to criminate worthy innocent men, to justify their condemnation of them. And your suspicion and mention of the name of Grant confirms me in it.⁵ But you will still be able [to] form a better judgment of the whole case, as Mr Gurney, in the note that came with the letters, told me that he had sent you a copy of them. I called at his chambers in Essex court the next day, to return the letters, and to thank him for the sight of them, but had not the good fortune to meet with him.⁶

When you have occasion to write to him, but I would by no means wish you to do it on purpose, be so good to mention, by the way, that I expressed myself to you as much obliged to him for his attentions.⁷

Had I not procured this frank, last week, under a presumption of hearing from you again, I should not perhaps have written, but rather have waited for your letter. But dont hurry yourself in writing. We are now quite satisfied, that there are no other quarters to seek at present. I shall keep open my letter to see if any thing comes before the post goes out. Our kind respects await Mrs Scott and yourself, with our best wishes for your young folks. I am always Dear Sir, most truly Yours

T. Lindsey.

Young Mr Tremlett, that was at Oxford, but was there disgusted against the church, is chosen minister of Warminster in Mr Andrews' stead, who went to America in the summer.[8] Mr J. Jones is said to be one of the candidates for Plymouth: he that was tutor at the college at Swansea.[9] Mr Toulmin tells me that he recommended Mr Awbrey.[10] Mr Rennell, I think I told you, had declined the offer.[11]

1   Scott's letter to Lindsey of 8 Feb. 1795 seems not to have survived. Evidently, Lindsey investigated the possibility of Scott's moving to be minister, or co-minister, at Warminster or Plymouth if the internal divisions at the High Street congregation, Portsmouth, were not resolved.

2   This allusion concerns the discords within Scott's congregation (see Letter 597) and to the possibility of Scott's moving elsewhere.

3   I have not located these letters from James Ellis and Thomas Muir to John Gurney.

4   Lindsey probably omitted the word 'former' (signifying James Ellis) at this point.

5   For the Scottish-born, former law student, John Grant, who was sentenced to transportation for forgery and accompanied Palmer and Muir to Botany Bay, see Bewley, *Muir of Huntershill*, pp. 92–3, 95, 110. He incurred the intense dislike of his fellow-prisoners, who regarded him as an *agent provocateur* and believed that he was the instigator of the allegations that they had planned a mutiny on board the *Surprise*. This was the view of Palmer, expressed in his *Narrative*, where he described Grant (p. 13) as 'a Highland attorney … a convict for forgery', who had been sheriff depute of Inverness.

6   John Gurney's chambers were situated at 5 Essex Court, Middle Temple; see *Browne's general law list for the year 1794*, p. 32, under 'List of Counsel'.

7   Although Scott was related to John Gurney and probably wrote to him as Lindsey suggested, I have not located their correspondence.

8   Thomas Tremlett matriculated at St Alban Hall, Oxford, on 13 Dec. 1793, at the age of twenty-six but, according to the Surman index, he 'withdrew, unable to subscribe'. He was minister at Old Meeting, Warminster, from 1795 to 1800, where he was 'the first minister who preached to the congregation doctrines commonly called Unitarian'; H. M. Gunn, *The history of nonconformity in Warminster* (new edn, Warminster, 2003), p. 45. He then left the ministry and became a commercial traveller and accountant in London; *Alumn. Oxon.*, IV, 1436. His predecessor at Warminster, between 1782 and 1794, was Nathanael Andrews, who departed to America in the latter year and resided at Baltimore, where he died in 1826. See Murch, *A history of the presbyterian and general baptist churches in the west of England*, pp. 91–2.

9   This was John Jones (*c*. 1766–1827), originally of Carmarthenshire, who was assistant tutor at the presbyterian college, Swansea, in the early 1790s. Adopting unitarian opinions, he was minister at Treville Street, Plymouth, from 1795 to 1798, when he moved to Halifax, established a school and was briefly minister at the Northgate End chapel. From 1804, he lived in London, took pupils as a classical tutor, married the daughter of Abraham Rees and served as a trustee of Dr Williams's Trust. In 1818, he was awarded the degree of DD by the University of Aberdeen. See the entry for Jones by Anne Pimlott Baker, in *ODNB*, XXX, 550–1.

10   Possibly Richard Aubrey (see Letter 434, n. 4), at this time minister at Stand chapel, Lancashire; he did not become minister at Plymouth.

11   For a possible identification of Thomas Reynell, see Letter 597, n. 6.

600. To WILLIAM ALEXANDER   3 MARCH 1795

Text: 'Letters of the Rev. Theophilus Lindsey. No. VI', *UH*, II, 74 (27 Sept. 1862), 330.

Note: This is the only section of this letter printed by the *UH*; the manuscript seems not to have survived. The ellipsis at the start of the extract printed by the *UH* indicates that this was not the beginning of the original letter.

London, March 3rd, 1795.

* * In times like the present, all that good men can do is to attend cheerfully to the discharge of their own duty in the station assigned them, and to rely upon the Divine wisdom that all events are tending to bring about the best proposes of virtue, and human happiness, present and future.

It is hard to say whether there be more of folly or vanity in the present atheistical system that goes about. I know something of its original promoters, and must do them the justice to say that, though one cannot look upon their neglect and exclusion of Deity without horror, they themselves are far from being wicked men, or entertaining bad designs.[1] But be in no fear about the spread of their doctrine. Common sense, in these enlightened times, reclaims too much against it to prevent its ever becoming general, and indeed in all times. Such sentiments, as you well observe, do but serve to enhance the value of Revelation.[2]

There are letters from Dr. Priestley, which are lately arrived, dated the middle of December, which give the best accounts of the health of himself and his family, and his being happy, and likely to remain in his present situation at Northumberland.[3] I could not but wish he had suffered himself to be drawn from it, and had accepted the chemical professorship at the college in Philadelphia.

1   Lindsey referred in particular to William Godwin and Thomas Holcroft.
2   The letter to Lindsey in which Alexander expressed this opinion seems not to have survived.
3   Lindsey referred here to a letter from Priestley to Belsham, dated 14 Dec. 1794, and one from Priestley to Lindsey, dated 20 Dec. 1794; see Rutt, I, 282–5.

601. To WILLIAM TAYLEUR   10 MARCH 1795

Text: JRUL, Lindsey Letters, vol. III, no. 42.
Addressed: To/William Tayleur Esq[r]/Shrewsbury
Endorsed: 10th March 1795
Postmarked: MR 10 [postmark otherwise illegible]

London. March. 10. 1795

Dear Sir,

I trust that by the blessing of heaven you continue tolerably well under the late variations of the weather, and on the return of this pleasant mild season. Indeed I sometimes learn by the way of good D[r] Aikin[1] how you go on, which makes me more easy about you. M[r] Belsham having received a letter not long ago from our friend D[r] Priestley, who had written one to me at the same time which has never arrived, you will be glad to know that it brings the confirmation of his good health and that of his family, and also tho' not so agreeable, of his resolution continuing unmoved respecting the refusal of the chair of chemical Professor in the college at Philadelphia, yet intimating that this was not wholly owing to himself.[2] But since this, M[r] Belsham has had a letter from M[r] Kenrick of Exeter, which tells him, that they had just heard there from the Eddowess at Philadelphia,[3] that D[r] Priestley, on the renewed offer of the chemical professorship, had agreed to accept it.[4] This good news we hope will be found true. And we think, that one inducement to it may have been M[rs] Priestleys finding the winter at Northumberland more desolate and uncomfortable than expected, which may render the passing of the four winter months in Philadelphia more agreeable, for that is the whole space of time which the functions of the professorship alone will require of the Doctor, if he undertakes it. In short, we earnestly wish him to be stationed upon a wider theatre for him to be seen and to act in than Northumberland as it is at present, and must be for years to come, and shall rejoice in any thing that draws him forth into the world.

Notwithstanding some discouraging accounts that have been sent over, there have been and are continual migrations to America from the port of London. Five american vessels, to my knowlege have been filled with different parties of our countrymen; two of them setting out this week; one carrying a minister of Kent with his family and friends amounting to upwards of twenty persons; for whose accomodation he took the whole steerage, that they might be more comfortable together, and as he also told me, that they might worship God unmolested, when disposed to it.[5] These all flie the country, as in the *Laudean* times.

I do not suppose that you have attended much to our prophets, Mr Brothers, and his interpreter, Mr Halhed.[6] Whatever the former be, he wants not shrewdness and acuteness, as I am assured from a capable friend, who has sifted and conversed with him, and is persuaded he is under some unknown direction, what or of whom, he takes not upon him to say. At first I took Halhed to be a Banterer, and who meant among other things to burlesque revelation and the Bible: which his known character and history of the Gentoos seemed to lead to.[7] But I have intirely changed my mind, from the testimony of his intimate friends, and am persuaded that his brain is touched *quoad hoc*,[8] and that he is a very enthusiast. In the mean while these prophecies and declarations from heaven concerning kings and potentates and their approaching fate have a vast effect on people great and small and prepare em to look for the events foretold, as necessary and of divine appointment.

But my paper forbids my adding any thing more at present, save my wife's most kind respects and our due remembrances to all friends, M^{rs} and Mr Rowe in particular, the latter of whom I wish to be made sensible, that I reckon my writing to you in part of acknowlegem^t of his favours to me. What mighty providential causes my dear friend, are in operation! You and I shall not live to see the glorious issue. But under his almighty direction, it must be for the best.

I am ever faithfully and affectionately Yours

T. Lindsey.

Those are fine prophetic lines in the hymn of last year, which I transcribe [On address page]:

Make bare thine arm, great king of kings!
Thine arm alone salvation brings,
That wonder-working arm, which broke
From Israel's neck th' egyptian yoke

Burst every dungeon, every chain;
Give injur'd slaves their rights again;
Let truth prevail, let discord cease;
Speak! ---- and the world shall smile in peace.[10]

1 John Aikin (1747–1822), physician, whose degree of MD was awarded by the University of Leiden, was the father of Arthur Aikin, assistant minister to John Rowe at the High Street chapel, Shrewsbury, from 1793 to 1795.

2 Possibly this was Priestley's letter to Belsham of 14 Dec. 1794; see Letter 600, n. 3.

3 The printer Ralph Eddowes (d. 1814), originally of Chester and a former student at Warrington Academy, emigrated with his family to America in 1794; his wife was Sarah, née Kenrick, the sister of Timothy Kenrick of Exeter. See W. Byng Kenrick, *Chronicles of a nonconformist family. The*

Kenricks of Wynne Hall, Exeter and Birmingham (Birmingham, 1932), pp. 96–100; Bowers, *Priestley and English unitarianism in America*, pp. 86, 108–14.

4   This was incorrect.

5   This minister who from Kent who emigrated to America in early Mar. 1795 was probably John Austen, of the general baptist congregation at Bessels Green, near Sevenoaks, together with his kins-folk, the Colgate family. This was the best known of several general baptist emigrations to America in the 1790s. I am grateful to Andrew Hill for advice on this point.

6   Richard Brothers (1757–1824), former seaman and subsequently millenarian prophet, published *A revealed knowledge of the prophecies and times* (2 vols., London, 1794). Nathaniel Brassey Halhed (1751–1830), MP for Lymington from 1791 to 1796, was a strong supporter of Brothers and published *Testimony of the authenticity of the prophecies of Richard Brothers* (London, 1795).

7   Halhed, an eminent Sanskrit scholar, had served in India under Warren Hastings, and with the latter's encouragement published *A code of Gentoo laws* (London, 1776).

8   'With respect to this'; or, 'as far as this (is concerned)'.

9   The word which Lindsey omitted at this point was almost certainly 'Wood', i.e. Isaac Wood.

10 Lindsey wrote these lines on the address page of the letter. They form the last two verses of a 'hymn' which was published anonymously in the *Cambridge Intelligencer*, 15 Mar. 1794.

602. To RUSSELL SCOTT   14 MARCH 1795

Text: Scott Coll.
Printed: McLachlan, 'Lindsey to Scott', p. 121 (brief quotation from fourth paragraph).
Addressed: To/The Rev^d. Russell Scott/Portsmouth
Postmarked: Postmark illegible.

London. march. 14. 1795.

Dear Sir,

We were apprehensive that you had some return of your old complaint; as has really turned out; but are glad from your own and M^r. Ps[1] account that you were better. Him I met in the streets coming towards our house, but prevented him, as I was going from it; but he has promised to let us see him, but could not name any day or hour, as we wished, he is so much engaged. Your developement and (to use another french term,) the denouement of a certain affair gives us much satisfaction.[2] We are pleased you have so judicious and true a friend.[3] I am happy that I never mentioned it to any one; and now, as you (and I think properly) desire it. I never shall, as I can easily put off one person, whom I had consulted and said I would name place and person when I saw him.[4]

I do not wonder you are anxious to come at the knowlege of Mr Skirvings account of what passed on board the Surprize, and thank you for your solicitude also to make me acquainted with it, and for setting me right in one particular, which I had understood differently from the other two narratives, the behaviour of the Capt.[5]

I have had a very agreeable letter this very day from Dr Priestley, dated Decr. 20. Northumberland.[6]

We had been in an agreeable reverie concerning him for some days, by a letter from the Eddowess who migrated last summer, said to be received at Exeter;[7] that on a renewed offer of the chemical professorship made to him, he had accepted it. But alas! he says nothing of this himself. He is however happy, making himself as useful as he can in his confined situation, and in the way to be more so by his publications, which he has in hand. He is also making provision for his sons, as farmers, which they all resolve to become. None of his American publications are come to me or I should have contrived you to have seen them, or to have had them if possible. He is projecting an addition to his Vol. of Letters to Unbelievers – which will be on the subject of Prophecy.[8]

His Successor M[r] D. Jones, at Birmingham, has just publish[d] a Sermon preached on the last Fast day, for w[ch] they would have stoned the D[r], but it seems to be generally well taken.[9] I suppose however the times may be somewhat alterd since. I shall hope also to send one of Williamss.[10]

Bishop Hurd has at length sent for his life of Warburton, which he had resolved sh[d] be posthumous.[11] The Biographer, is, what I always took him for, a much greater and more intolerant High Churchman than his hero, and a far worse-temperd man.

He suppresses the praises justly due to eminent Dissenters, who exposed and confuted some of the nostrums of B[p] Warburton, about Julians returning the temple of Jerusalem, about the pagan mysteries, &c &c and gives no mercy to one class, whose good faith and honesty he calls in question, and speaks of Socinian Impieties.[12] But he treats B[p] Lowth in particular in so degrading a way, that he will be likely to be called to account for it by some Oxford;[13] or rather by D[r] Parr, who had the B[p] of London for his patron.[14]

I wish I could send any political good new: but none such can come unless it be of peace, and that we seem [to] put away from us.

We hope your next will bring a confirmation of your own and of M[rs] Scotts intire recovery. You were very obliging not to forget me to M[r] Gurney, for whom as well as for his whole family I have a great respect, for their characters sake. Of an aunt of his, my wife has a very high opinion, tho wholly unknown to her, as she often[?] converses[?] with and buys some trifles of her.[15]

The lady joins in kind regards to M[rs] Scott and yourself with all good wishes for your little folks. I am always, Dear Sir, cordially Yours

T. Lindsey.

---

1   This was almost certainly William Joseph Porter (1764–1815). He was the son of Thomas Porter (1734–86), dissenting minister, successively, at Bury Street, St Mary Axe, Great Meeting, Hinckley, and at King's Head Lane, Northampton. After naval service in the Caribbean during the War of American Independence, he was clerk of the cheque at Portsmouth and served in the victualling office at Deptford, until his retirement in 1809. See *Royal calendar ... for the year 1798*, p. 139. He was a member of the High Street chapel, Portsmouth, where Russell Scott baptized his son Henry Gibson Porter on 15 Mar. 1789; TNA: RG4/564, fo. 22r. He was probably the 'Mr W. P., Portsmouth' who was listed as a member of the Unitarian Society in 1794; *Unitarian Society ... 1794*, p. 13. In his later years he lived at Leigh Street, Brunswick Square, and according to his obituary in *MR*, X (1815), 253–4, he 'was known to, and highly respected by the venerable Lindsey'. His dissenting credentials were confirmed by his burial in Bunhill Fields (8 Apr. 1815); TNA: RG4/3993, fo. 99r.

2   This 'certain affair', and its resolution, was probably the discord in Scott's congregation to which Lindsey referred in Letter 597.

3   Scott's 'judicious and true friend' was probably Sir John Carter of William Joseph Porter.

4   It is clear that Lindsey had sought the advice of a friend in London – almost certainly a dissenting minister – in very general terms about Scott's problems (n. 2, above), without naming Scott or the location of his chapel. Having heard from Scott that the difficulty had been overcome (or at least mitigated), he longer needed to 'name place and person'. The 'one person' whom Lindsey consulted was possibly Thomas Belsham, who had experience of divisions within a congregation when his proposed nomination as Priestley's co-minister at the Gravel Pit meeting, Hackney, was rejected in 1792. Other possibilities include Andrew Kippis of the Princes Street meeting, Westminster, and Thomas Jervis, of St Thomas's meeting, Southwark.

5   In the early months of 1795, several letters from the exiles in Botany Bay reached England; one from Muir, written from Rio de Janiero, where the *Surprise* had called on its journey to Australia, was published in the *Cambridge Intelligencer*, 7 Feb. 1795. See Issitt, *Jeremiah Joyce*, pp. 107–8 and Bewley, *Muir of Huntershill*, pp. 116–18.

6   This letter from Priestley to Lindsey is indeed dated 20 Dec. 1794, and may be found in DWL, MS 12.13. The letter is printed, with some omissions, in Rutt, I, 283–5.

7   See Letter 601, n. 3.

8   Priestley included a chapter entitled 'of prophecy' in three separate works, each published in 1795. They were *An answer to Mr. Paine's Age of reason, being a continuation of letters to the philosophers and politicians of France on the subject of religion, and of the letters to a philosophical unbeliever. With a preface by Theophilus Lindsey, A.M.* (London, 1795), pp. 89–96; *Letters to a philosophical unbeliever. Part III. Containing an answer to Mr Paine's Age of reason* (2nd edn, Philadelphia, 1795), pp. 75–82; and *A continuation of the letters to the philosophers and politicians of France, on the subject of religion; and of the letters to a philosophical unbeliever; in answer to Mr Paine's Age of reason* (Northumberland, 1795), pp. 66–9. In each case, the chapter was chapter VI.

9   This sermon was David Jones, *Reasons for peace, stated in a discourse, delivered in the Union chapel, Birmingham, on Wednesday, February 25, 1795, being the day appointed for a general fast* (Birmingham, 1795).

10 This sermon was John Williams, *War the stumbling block of a Christian; or, the absurdity of defending religion by the sword. A sermon on the public fast, February 25, 1795* (London, 1795). For Williams's opposition to the war, see Colin Haydon, *John Henry Williams (1747–1829) 'Political clergyman'. War, the French Revolution and the Church of England* (Woodbridge, 2007), ch. 5. Williams was vicar of Wellesbourne, Warwickshire, from 1779 to 1829.

11 Richard Hurd's *A discourse by way of general preface to the quarto edition of Bishop Warburton's works, containing some account of the life, writings, and character of the author* was published in London in 1794. William Warburton died in 1779.

12 In his *Discourse* (n. 11, above), Hurd referred to Warburton's 'anxiety to guard the public from being bewildered and misled either by a Popish or Socinian comment' (p. 97); to 'Socinian impieties' (p. 112); and to the 'immoderate presumption' and 'ill faith' which Warburton imputed to Socinians (p. 119). He did not mention Priestley by name. Julian, the Roman emperor from 361 to 363, restored the pagan temples which had been suppressed under his Christian predecessors. He tried and failed to bring about the rebuilding of the Temple of Jerusalem.

13 Lindsey omitted a word – probably 'writer' – at this point.

14 In his *Discourse*, p. 94, Hurd alluded to Lowth's criticisms of the new edition of Warburton's *Divine legation of Moses demonstrated* of 1765 and compared Lowth's intellectual qualities unfavourably with those of Warburton. For the background to this controversy, see B. W. Young, *Religion and enlightenment in eighteenth-century England. Theological debate from Locke to Burke* (Oxford, 1998), pp. 199–205. Lowth was bishop of London from 1777 to 1787, and in that capacity had in 1783 conferred upon Samuel Parr a prebend of St Paul's Cathedral.

15 Lindsey's handwriting is not quite clear at this point. Nor is it clear as to which aunt of John Gurney he referred; Gurney himself married Maria (d. 1849) Scott, the sister of Russell Scott.

603. To JAMES FREEMAN   23 MARCH 1795

Text: Historical Society of Pennsylvania, Gratz MSS, Case 10, Box 32.

Addressed: To/The Rev^d. M^r. Freeman/Boston/New England

Endorsed: Rev. Theophilus Lindsey/London. Mar: 23. 1795

London. March. 23. 1795

Dear Sir,

Never did I receive a more acceptable favour from you than your letter of June 5. 1794, containing such expressions of your friendship, and of your own state of health which were most welcome to me, and also a description of the progress of free inquiry and divine truth in the southern part of Massachusetts, where I trust it is taking deep root, and will in time spread to the middle and southern states of America, which are at present overwhelmed with ignorance and superstition.[1] I hope your correspondence with Mr Toulmin at Lexington in Kentucky,[2] as it will be useful to him. He has every thing to recomend him in that important situation, wisdom, learning, knowlege of the scriptures, the virtues and zeal of an apostle.

But there are fears for his health, that the climate will be too hot for him and his family to abide in it.

His and Dr Priestleys accounts of of [*sic*] the state of religious improvement about them are very low, but the worst circumstance is the prevalence of scepticism and infidelity mention[ed] by the latter, which may prevent the good seed being sown, but which will not deter or discourage him from his endeavours to do it, which he has already begun, in some little publications, particularly in his Answer to Paine's Age of Reason,[3] and will exert himself I am persuaded in the good cause so long as life is given. I am concerned at his having declined the offer of the chemical professorship at Philadelphia, as it is so much fitter a sphere for him to act in than Northumberland, and furnishing opportunities of being more extensively useful. But there is a letter very lately come from his eldest son who was at Philadelphia on the seventh of February, and mentions, that the place of Professor was not yet filled up, the electors seeming still to wait for his fathers acceptance of it, which I ardently wish may be the case.[4]

It is well for him, that he left this unworthy country, most unworthy of him, at the time he did; for such was the malice of his enemies, that they would have tried and perhaps succeeded to involve him in the accusations of sedition, for which so many were taken up and tried, but most happily delivered by an honest english jury.[5] And the same violent high-church intolerant prejudices still subsist in Churchmen and in the upper ranks amongst us, so that I can assure you, they think it is an affront, and would not bear to have Dr Priestley named and commended in their presence.

What will be the issue of things amongst us, is, I fear but too obvious and certain; that it must be calamity and ruin, bent as the nation and its rulers are upon this wanton fatal war against the french; who are now in possession of Holland, and at our door, and may pay us a visit to morrow.[6] That they will land and attack us on our coasts is a very general expectation and apprehension. We are also, at this moment, committed with Ireland by such strange measures on our part, about the emancipation of the Catholics and repeal of the penal laws, that there is some danger of that country being sever'd from England, if the french should find means to land a large body of troops among them.[7]

I must now observe, that I entertain some fears lest you have not received my acknowlegements of your letter and presents by Mr Coolidge,[8] and also a parcell of book [*sic*] and tracts which I had sent to you before; which were to have come along with Mr Russell and his family, who were unfortunately captured and carried into Brest the latter end of September last; the vessel however was allowed to go on, in which were Dr Edwards and his family,[9] and I hoped my parcell would have reached you. From Mr Russell I have never heard, but about 5 weeks since he was liberated with honour by the national convention, and all his losses made up, with a house allowed and all his expences borne, whilst he chose to stay at Paris. He is said however to have gone thence to Hamburgh, and was soon to set sail for America, but for what part I know not.[10] Dr Priestley writes to me, that he expected him at Northumberland, where there was a house provided for him.[11]

To compensate for this disappointment, which has debard me of the high pleasure and satisfaction of hearing from you, and of putting into your hand some tracts to disperse which you give some hope of being likely to be of use, and which you oblige me by accepting and taking the trouble of in that view, I here send another box, which my friend Mr W. Vaughan[12] takes the care of and answers for their coming safe to you, the danger of the winds and seas accepted. Any little thing that may not be already in your own library, you will do me the favour to put in it. If you sh^d have rec^d the former parcell, and have Paley's Evidences &c already, you will know how to dispose of the copy of that invaluable work which I now send.[13] I think you will like the neatness of the edition of Dr Priestley's Institutes, especially as being more portable than two bulky 8vo volumes.[14]

As the times and the events are awful and interesting to us as christians as any perhaps that have ever happened at any period of our religion, we have published continually new and old interpretations and applications of the Prophetic Scriptures without end: but there are none that I can recommend. Mr Winthrops tract for which I thank you, is very ingenious, but does not throw much of the light we want upon a book which I cannot but consider as of divine authority, after all that has been said for and against it.[15]

I shall have singular satisfaction in knowing that this letter and the contents of the box in which it is, reach your hands as I shall then have no doubt of hearing from you at your convenience, that you and Mrs Freeman,[16] by the blessing of heaven, enjoy your wonted health, and that your State the Massachusetts, in this season of very general falling off from the belief of the gospel, becomes more confirmed in it on the grounds of farther research into it.

Should Mr Coolidge pass through the Metropolis at any time that we are in it, I hope he will do us the favour to renew his call in Essex Street.

My wife desires to unite her respects with mine to Mrs Freeman and yourself, with wishes of all good to you both. I remain with a constant esteem, Dear Sir,

Your much obliged friend and faithful servant

T. Lindsey.

I rejoice to hear that your university last year bestowed the degree of D.D. on Mr Toulmin, who will do credit to their appointment. Not long before the excellent Dr Price, was taken away from the evil to come I fear upon this country, he was to send a paper of recomendation of Mr Toulmin signed by him, Dr Priestley and myself. But we were not certain that he had an opportunity of transmitting it.[17]

---

1 This letter may be found in DWL, MS 12.57 (37); see Letter 582, n. 8.
2 Lindsey seems to have omitted, inadvertently, two words – perhaps 'will continue' – at this point.
3 For Priestley's reply to Paine, edited by Lindsey, see Letter 602, n. 8.
4 Priestley's letter of 20 Dec. 1794 (see Letter 602, n. 6) bears the following annotation in Lindsey's hand; 'Jos. Priestley's letter to Mr Johnson, dated Feb. 7. 1795. Philadelphia was come thither to try to raise collections for [one word overlaid by the binding] college. His father wish^d in the mean time to give a course of chymical lectures at Philadelphia. The college had not *taken up* his father's letter of refusal of the Professorship – but kept it open till the next year. If his father succeeds in a college & settling at Philadelphia, he himself shall then take a farm and settle there. No cordiality among the English. Many of em Aristocrats.' 'Jos. Priestley' was Priestley's eldest son Joseph junior; Mr Johnson was Joseph Johnson the publisher. Lindsey's annotation concluded, barely legibly, with the words 'If his father has a college at N ___ d Mr Palmer[?] to come to him. Infidelity almost universal[?] among them[?] that think and [word illegible].'
5 For these acquittals, see Letter 588, n. 11.
6 In the autumn of 1794, a French army overran the United Provinces, which were often referred to in England as Holland, the wealthiest of the Dutch provinces. In May 1795, the Dutch were obliged to abolish their stadtholderate, and the Batavian republic was established as a pro-French regime. The French control of the Dutch coast increased the possibility of a French invasion of Britain.
7 In Nov. 1794, the ministry of Pitt, now in coalition with the followers of the duke of Portland, appointed William, Earl Fitzwilliam (1748–1833) as lord lieutenant of Ireland, with a view to conciliating opinion in that country and rendering it less vulnerable to a French invasion. Fitzwilliam arrived in Dublin at the beginning of Jan. 1795 and immediately dismissed some of the leading members of the protestant ascendancy from their positions of power and replaced them with his own whig

friends. He also expressed sympathy with a measure of catholic relief to be introduced in the Irish parliament by Henry Grattan. He proceeded too rapidly and too far for the purposes of the ministry in London, and he was controversially recalled, leaving Ireland on 25 Mar 1795, two days after the date of Lindsey's letter to Freeman. See E. A. Smith, *Whig principles and party politics. Earl Fitzwilliam and the whig party 1748–1833* (Manchester, 1975), ch. 7.

8   Possibly Joseph Coolidge (1747–1821), a prosperous silversmith, jeweller and investor in real estate in Boston, Massachusetts, who became one of the city's wealthiest citizens. An engraving of his house, with its imposing classical façade, may be found on the website of the New York Public Library digital collection: http://digitalgallery.nypl.org/nypldigital/id?54244.

9   Dr Edwards, his wife and a Miss Clarkson, 'who passed as his niece', accompanied William Russell and his family on board the *Mary* on what they hoped would be their voyage to America in Aug. 1794; Jeyes, *The Russells of Birmingham*, p. 62. After the detention of Russell's family in France (see Letter 585, n. 3), Edwards and his family were allowed to proceed; Edwards himself was evidently a 'particular friend' of James Monroe, the American minister in Paris, and future president; Jeyes, *The Russells of Birmingham*, p. 70.

10   William Russell and his family left Paris from Le Havre on 25 June 1795 and sailed for America in early July. They arrived at New York in late Aug. They did not call at Hamburg *en route*, although Russell did visit Hamburg, where he had commercial interests, during his return to Europe in 1801.

11   William Russell joined Priestley at Northumberland in the autumn of 1795 but, disliking the location and the climate, settled instead at Middletown, Connecticut.

12   Probably William Vaughan (1752–1850), the younger brother of Benjamin Vaughan. A pupil of Priestley at Warrington Academy, he was a director of the Royal Exchange assurance corporation and a leading promoter of the London docks; in later life he was a governor of the New England corporation.

13   For Paley's *Evidences of Christianity*, see Letter 569, n. 6.

14   Lindsey referred here to the third edition of Priestley's *Institutes of natural and revealed religion* (2 vols., London, 1794), printed in duodecimo form for the Unitarian Society (see Letter 553, n. 1). The only octavo edition of Priestley's *Institutes* was the second edition, published in two volumes in Birmingham in 1782.

15   Probably Lindsey referred here to James Winthrop's *An attempt to translate the prophetic part of the apocalypse of Saint John into familiar language* (Boston, MA, 1794). Winthrop, who was designated 'Esq' on the title page of his works, was also the author of *A systematic arrangement of several scripture prophecies relating to antichrist; with their application to the course of history* (Boston, 1795).

16   Martha, formerly Clarke (d. 1841), who married James Freeman in 1783.

17   See *Price corr.*, III, 321–2, 336.

604. To RUSSELL SCOTT   30 APRIL 1795

Text: Scott Coll.
Printed: McLachlan, 'Lindsey to Scott', 121–2 (part of first sentence of
                 first paragraph; first two sentences of third paragraph; most of
                 fifth paragraph).
Addressed: Address missing.
Postmarked: Postmark missing.

London April. 30. 1795.

Dear Sir,

I am ashamed I have not sooner acknowleged your long kind letter, and your great trouble in giving me all the information I could possibly have with respect to our friends, by this time I hope, safely landed in Botany Bay; for which I am much indebted to you, and which has gratified many friends as well as myself.[1] Of this I shall say no more at present.

Many things have prevented my writing, particularly the printer's delay in dispatching D[r] Priestley's Answer to Paine, which I was desirous to send you, to which I have prefixed a short preface in vindication of my friend's much injured name.[2] I am in hope of three copies being ready to be sent to you to morrow together with the monthlies, one for yourself, the others for M[r] Porter,[3] and M[r] Watson of Chichester, when you see him: but if they be not ready you may depend upon them soon, as I should be glad to have your judgment of both.

We have lately had a disagreeable affair in the college at Hackney. Two young, very young,[4] neither more than 19, have been induced to become unbelievers, perhaps to go a little farther, through the freedom of the times, and as I am told by becoming acquainted with M[r] Godwin & M[r] Holcroft. This has made a great disturbance, and one of the young men has retired from the college, and I suppose so will the other.[5] Some have[?] endeavoured to bring discredit on the college from the circumstance, but I hope it will not answer. I thought it right however to mention to you a circumstance of so peculiar a kind, lest it might be misrepresented. It was reported about 6 weeks since, that M[r] Fawcett, on retiring from Walthamstow, and given up not only Revelation, but even the belief of a God.[6] I was very glad to hear this last absurdity strenuously contradicted by a person of his acquaintance, tho' it is certain that M[r] Godwin is very earnest to bring persons over to the Atheistical doctrine, and has pointed his whole artillery against M[r] Fawcett, but quite in vain and to no effect, as I am told.[7]

I have about a fortnight ago received two letters at once from D[r] Priestley, one dated the beginning the other the latter end of the month of February, of which last I have thought it proper to give some little account at the Conclusion of my Preface.[8]

His whole letter,[9] of which that is an extract, is altogether agreable, the most so of any that I have received from him. He is well and happy, is already very useful as a preacher in a small church in a house[?] and is in the way to be more so, to a much larger society. His eldest son is in a way to be estabilished in partnership with some gentlemen at Philadelphia. His second son, William, is with M[r] Wells, to learn farming, the Gentleman that went about a year and half since from Bromsgrove with his family,[10] and is become happily settled upon a farm in the New State of Vermont,[11] where is also the priest on the Sundays, and the farmer and labourer in the Week days. With him D[r] Priestleys son William is at present. So that I hope and he says, that all his sons are in the way to obtain a comfortable competence by the means of their own industry, and he does not wish that they should have it without. I am glad to learn from his letters, that as M[r] Cooper of Manchester is near him, he sees him some times, as I hope it will be of use to recall that Gentleman, once so firm an unitarian and Xtian from an intire rejection of Revelation, which he declared to be his sentiment when in England, not quite a year since, some few weeks before he embarked for America. As he has something fickle in his sentiments of revelation, and has changed already several times, I hope under D[r] Priestleys good auspices he will at length come round to the belief of the mission of Christ, upon such evidence as will not be shaken.[12]

Miss Russell a few weeks since favoured my wife with a very long letter, in which she mentioned M[r][s] Huddys great loss in M[r] Huddy.[13] Her letter was long, and very instructive and entertaining.[14] My wife had a commission to send her drugs, and many other things for their voyage to America which was to take place soon, and which she has accordingly executed.

We were in expectation of a Peace with France, when within a few days, we have been told that our Minister will crush the whole business for a time, by the success his negociations and assistance with money and arms to the people of La Vendée, and the vast number of Emigrants we have sent over, will enable the Inhabitants to make a powerful stand against the convention, and perhaps to restore a moderate royalty and the Nobility, which are the points Charette is said to have insisted upon.[15]

I have not time [to] look over what I have written. Respects from us both to M[rs] Scott and yourself, and all good wishes attend you and your family. I hope soon to write a few lines – when the pamphlet or two comes to you. In the mean time and always I remain, Dear Sir, ever most truly yours

T. Lindsey.

---

1   Scott's 'long, kind letter' to Lindsey seems not to have survived. Palmer arrived at Port Jackson, nine miles to the north of Botany Bay and the site of present-day Sydney, on 25 Oct. 1794.

2   Lindsey's preface to Priestley's *Answer to Mr Paine's Age of reason* may be found on pp. xi–xxxvii of this work.

3   William Joseph Porter (see Letter 602, n. 1). For the 'monthlies', see Letter 580, n. 2.

4   Lindsey inadvertently omitted a word – probably 'men' or 'students' – at this point.

5   The minutes of the Hackney College do not cover this period. A list of the students, divinity and lay, compiled by Stephen Burley, is available via the website of the Centre for Dissenting Studies. However, it is not possible to identify with certainty the two young men to whom Lindsey referred. The college's declining years are discussed briefly in McLachlan, 'The old Hackney College', 201–5.

6   Joseph Fawcett (*c.* 1758–1804) resigned as morning preacher at Marsh Street presbyterian chapel, Walthamstow (where he had served since 1780), in 1787. From 1785, he was the Sunday evening lecturer at the Old Jewry meeting house in London; in 1795, he retired from this lectureship and took up farming in Hertfordshire. In the 1790s, he published several anti-war poems.

7   For William Godwin's friendship with Fawcett, whom he regarded as one of his intellectual mentors, see Peter H. Marshall, *William Godwin* (New Haven and London, 1984), pp. 46–7, 85. Although highly unorthodox, Fawcett was no atheist.

8   In his preface to Priestley's *Answer to Mr Paine's Age of reason*, Lindsey quoted from three of Priestley's letters addressed to him from America. He printed brief extracts from Priestley's letters from New York, 6 and 15 June 1794 (p. xxxv); and a longer extract from Priestley's letter from Northumberland, 22 Feb. 1795 (pp. xxxvi–xxxvii). These letters are printed in Rutt, I, respectively, at pp. 244–6, 255–9 and 295–6.

9   This refers to Priestley's letter to Lindsey of 22 Feb. 1795; Rutt, I, 295–6.

10 William Wells (d. 1827) was minister to a dissenting congregation at Bromsgrove, Worcestershire, from 1770 to *c.* 1790; in 1793, he emigrated to North America with his wife and four sons and four daughters, and ministered to a church at Brattleborough, Vermont, where he resided for the remainder of his life. See his obituary in *MR*, NS, II (1828), 272. There is an account of Wells by Samuel Kenrick in his letter to James Wodrow, 28 Aug. 1793, DWL, MS 24.157 (182).

11 Vermont was admitted to the United States as the fourteenth state in 1791.

12 Thomas Cooper had lived in the Manchester area between 1785, where he had been a prominent member of the Literary and Philosophical Society and the Manchester Constitutional Society, and 1794, when he emigrated to America. He and his family lived near to Priestley in Pennsylvania and they were frequently in each other's company; for Priestley's concern at his abandonment of revealed religion, see Letter 613, n. 7.

13 Miss Russell was probably Martha (1766–1807), the eldest daughter of William Russell; see Letter 645, n. 14. Mr and Mrs Huddy were among the fellow-passengers of the Russells on board the *Mary*, the ship on which they departed from Falmouth on 13 Aug. 1794 with the intention of proceeding to America. David Huddy, of Pen-y-fai, was educated for the baptist ministry at the Bristol Baptist college between 1788 and 1791. Hoping to emigrate to America with William Russell and his family, he was captured by a French ship and shared the Russells' confinement at Brest. According to G. F. Nuttall, 'Welsh students at Bristol baptist college, 1720–1797', *Transactions of the Honourable Society of Cymmrodorion* (1978), 178, 193, Huddy returned to Britain, 'abandoned the ministry and became a farmer at Nottage' (178). I have not been able to confirm the date of the death of his wife.

14 I have not located this letter from Miss (probably Martha) Russell to Hannah Lindsey; it is not among the small group of Huddy papers in the Scott Coll.

15 The counter-revolution in the Vendée, beginning in 1793, was crushed by the revolutionary regime in 1793–4. For the British government's plan to land an émigré army on the Quiberon peninsula in the expectation of exploiting the continuing discontent in the Vendée, see Ehrman, *The Younger Pitt. The reluctant transition*, pp. 568–9, 572–3. François de Charette (1763–96), a French aristocrat, was one of the leaders of the unsuccessful revolt in the Vendée against the French Revolution in 1793–5.

The national convention was the effective governing body in France from 21 Sept. 1792, when it replaced the legislative assembly, to 26 Oct. 1795.

605. To WILLIAM TAYLEUR   2 MAY 1795

Text: 'Unpublished letters of Theophilus Lindsey', *CL*, III, no. 101 (20 Apr. 1878), 193; McLachlan, *Letters*, p. 91 (all but last sentence of fourth paragraph); p. 133 (first sentence of second paragraph).

Note: The editor (probably Alexander Gordon) stated (p. 193) that he printed the entire text of this letter; the manuscript seems not to have survived. He also stated that Lindsey did not date the letter, but that Tayleur endorsed it 1 May 1795, and then corrected it to 2 May, a date, according to the editor, confirmed by the postmark.

DEAR SIR AND MOST ESTEEMED FRIEND, –

I have been for some time self-condemned for not having sooner renewed the tender of my sincere affectionate regards (with those of my wife) to one for whom we constantly feel them, but though you have been often in our thoughts, I have as usual delayed to tell you so, through one hindrance or another.

It becomes me however, now the main hindrance is removed, to acquaint you that for these last three weeks all the spare moments I could get have been spent in re-printing by Mr. Johnson's means, Dr. Priestley's Answer to Mr. Paine's Age of Reason, and in preparing a Preface for it in vindication of our friend's name, which I shall be happy if you approve.[1] Through some delays of the printer the piece has not been ready till to-day, but yesterday Mr. Johnson received orders from me to send four copies to you, one of which I beg you will accept, and present the others to Mr. Rowe, Mr. Aitkin [*sic*] and Mr. Wood, with mine and my wife's compliments and hopes that they are all well. To Mr. Rowe I have been longer indebted in the epistolary way than I ought to have been, but rely on his usual goodness to excuse it.

I have taken but very little notice of Bishop Hurd's unhandsome language, though he does not directly name him, against Dr. Priestley and Socinians, in his lately published life of Bp Warburton, but did not think it right wholly to omit it.[2] I own I had no very high opinion of Hurd before, but this publication has sunk him very low, and shews him brimfull of ecclesiastic high-church pride and intolerance, with no small dash of spleen and ill-temper, for which I remember him noted at Cambridge.[3]

If we may believe the ministerial prints and the conversation of those who would be thought to be in the secret of affairs, the national convention has never been so near its fall as at present, by the prodigious force which the Royalist party have in la Vendée, especially by the vast increase that has been given to it by us within these last two months, by the emigrants we have sent over with some troops of our own, and quantities of ammunition and stores.[4] A priest of my acquaintance received a letter last week from a town in Poitou near the coast, from an officer of family and fortune who had landed but three weeks before from hence in company with other emigrants, telling him that he was very happily settled with his tenants all about, and that he would answer for it, that he might come over safely.[5] I am, however, afraid that all our tampering, as hitherto, will only serve to keep up a most bloody war, which, without our interference, might never have begun, certainly would have much sooner ended, as at present we are the principals and the prime agents in it. And the blessing of peace to the world is by our means withheld. Our great comfort, and sufficient comfort it is, that divine providence, by its present severe dispensations and *shaking of the nations* beyond example of all former times, is hastening the fulfilment of it's greatest purposes for the success of the gospel and the virtue and happiness of the world.

I have heard within this fortnight twice, or rather received two letters from Dr. Priestley at the same time of different dates, the beginning and the latter end of february. The last was the most pleasing that I had received, as it bespoke him quite happy, and in the way to be useful.[6] I shall not be more particular, as I thought it proper to transcribe at the conclusion of my Preface, a part of this last and one or two passages out of his former letters.[7] I expect soon to receive a letter from him for you.[8] What cause have we to rejoice that he is in the way to become such a shining useful luminary in that hemisphere. I trust this fine weather will revive you and enable [you] to continue your wonted walks on your very beautiful terrace, more beautiful because it overlooks the haunts of men as well as nature's fairest form, at this season of the year especially. With my wife's due respects, I remain, Dear Sir, Your ever truly obliged and faithful affectionate servant, T. LINDSEY.

1   See Letter 604, n. 2.
2   For Hurd's attack upon Socinians in his 'life' of Warburton, see Letter 602, n. 12. Lindsey's response to these criticisms may be found in his 'preface' to Priestley's *Answer to Mr Paine's Age of reason*, pp. xxi–xxiii.
3   Hurd was three years older than Lindsey. He was an undergraduate at Emmanuel College, Cambridge, graduating BA in 1739. From 1742 until 1756 he was a fellow of the college. Lindsey was an undergraduate at St John's from 1741 until 1745 and a fellow of the college from 1747 until 1755.
4   See Letter 604, n. 15.
5   The authoritative work on this subject is Dominic Aidan Bellenger, *The French exiled clergy in the British Isles after 1789. An historical introduction and working list* (Bath, 1986), which lists 6,680 French émigré priests, including (p. 128) eighteen from the diocese of Poitiers. However, in this instance, a positive identification is not possible from the very sparse information provided by Lindsey.
6   Probably these were letters of Priestley to Lindsey, 10 and 22 Feb. 1795; Rutt, I, 293–5 and 295–6.
7   See Letter 604, n. 8.
8   In his letter to Lindsey of 12 July 1795, Priestley expressed an intention of writing to Tayleur, although he had previously concluded from Lindsey's account of Tayleur's health 'that it was too late to write to him at all'; Rutt, I, 310. If Priestley did in fact write this letter it seems not to have survived.

606. To RUSSELL SCOTT   23 MAY 1795

Text: Scott Coll.
Printed: McLachlan, 'Lindsey to Scott', 122 (most of fourth paragraph; first sentence of fifth paragraph).
Addressed: To/The Rev^d. Russell Scott/Portsmouth
Endorsed: May 24th. – 95
Postmarked: Postmark missing.

St Pauls Churchyard.
May. 23. 1795

Dear Sir,

The moment I received yours I hastend hither, when I found to my great concern a parcell tied up for you, which was kept till an opportunity presented of sending it, through mistake, when I had desired it to be immediately forwarded.[1]

I inclose the letter I have written for M[r] Palmer, begging you to seal it up and send it with a copy of D[r] Priestley's Answer to M[r] Paine, and wish you to read my letter to him, as it will save me the trouble of writing over again for you some few of the things it contains.[2]

In the preface, in a note, there is a hint given concerning the great efforts used by M[r] Godwin & M[r] Holcroft and some of their disciples.[3] I am sorry to hear of their being so much attended. But M[r] Thelwall carries on the propagation of the same doctrines in his lectures, and thereby does great harm to the minds of many of his hearers, by effacing from them every moral principles [*sic*], and brings unworthy discredit on the cause in which he and the *acquitted felons*[4] were supposed only to be engaged, the reformation of our Representative body.[5]

I presume you have correspondents who acquaint You with the state of things and your old friends and connections here. But lest you shoud be ignorant, I would barely mention, that M[r] Lewis of Carter lane, has just given up the ministry, Sunday last preaching his farewel sermon, and being to embark with some partner in the Wine-trade.[6] I have not heard that he give[s] up X[ty], but the contrary. Its enemies however will suspect it. M[r] Wellbeloved, who happens to be here from York preaches at Carter lane to morrow as a Candidate to succeed him, of which I hope there is little doubt, as he is most deserving, and I have every way the highest opinion of him, from what I saw of him when at the college, when we visited York two years ago, and now upon his coming to London with his wife & child merely to see her friends.[7]

M[r] David Jones, D[r] P's successor at Birmingham, is about to give up the clerical character, and turn himself to the study of the law.[8] M[r] Fawcett is I hope unjustly reported to have gone into all M[r] Godwins nostrums. I suppose he has resigned on acc[t] of his rejection of Revelation.[9] Although I have no authority to say even that upon any certain knowlege of his motives. Amongst young persons in Town, intended for the learned professions, and the younger mercantile sort at their ease, the rejection of Christianity is said to be most rife, in the great city, at Birmingham, Norwich: perhaps at other places: but I name those only, where I have some assurance of it being the fact. Most extraordinary this effect at a time when its evidence was perhaps never more clearly and fully made out. Providence has I doubt not great designs to serve by this extraordinary effect. In the mean time it will not diminish our convictions of it's truth, or slacken our endeavours to promote it. I have desired M[r] Johnson to add one or two more copys of the Doctors Answer,[10] which you will be so good as to dispose of where you think best. As you say nothing, we hope yourself, M[rs] Scott, and y[r] little folks are after their best sort, which is mine and my wifes constant wish. I am always Dear Sir, on many accounts your much obliged and affectionate friend & servant

T. Lindsey.

---

1   Lindsey evidently wrote this letter from Joseph Johnson's premises at 72 St Paul's Churchyard.

2   Lindsey's letter to Palmer, sent via Russell Scott, seems not to have survived.

3   Lindsey made this point, without naming any individual, in his preface to Priestley's *Answer to Mr Paine's Age of reason*, p. xv n. *.

4   Lindsey's use of this expression with respect to Joyce was heavily ironical. On 30 Dec. 1794, the secretary at war, William Windham, had referred in the house of commons to 'acquitted felons' with respect to Thomas Hardy and other acquitted reformers; see Cobbett, *Parl. hist.*, XXXI, 1028–9 and Issitt, *Jeremiah Joyce*, p. 59.

5   John Thelwall, *Political lectures (No. I). On the moral tendency of a system of spies and informers, and the conduct to be observed by the friends of liberty during the continuance of such a system* was

published in London in 1794. In Feb. 1796, Thelwall published his *Prospectus of a course of lectures, to be delivered every Monday, Wednesday and Friday, during the ensuing Lent. In strict conformity with the restrictions of Mr. Pitt's Convention Act* (London, 1796). A second edition, with a postscript, followed later in 1796.

6 George Lewis was afternoon preacher at Carter Lane, London, from 1785 to 1796, when he resigned from the ministry and became a merchant, evidently in the wine trade. See Vol. I, Letter 309, n. 7, and *MR*, XVII (1822), 198. 'Sunday last' was 17 May 1795. Lewis is listed as a trustee of Dr Williams's Trust from 1791 to 1823; Walter D. Jeremy, *The Presbyterian fund and Dr Daniel Williams's Trust: with biographical notes of the trustees* (London and Edinburgh, 1885), p. 175.

7 Charles Wellbeloved did not succeed Lewis at Carter Lane. That successor was George Watson (d. 1817), who served as assistant minister there from 1797 to 1799. The senior minister from 1778 to 1811 was Thomas Tayler (1735–1831), a former pupil of Philip Doddridge at Northampton. Wellbeloved became assistant minister to Newcome Cappe at St Saviourgate, York, in Jan. 1792. The college to which Lindsey referred was Hackney, where Wellbeloved had been a student between 1787 and 1792. Lindsey and his wife made a prolonged excursion to Yorkshire in Aug.–Sept. 1793 (see Letters 535 and 536) and evidently visited Wellbeloved at York at that time. It is likely that they also met Wellbeloved's wife Ann, née Kinder, whom he had married on 1 July 1793.

8 David Jones was admitted to Lincoln's Inn on 1 May 1795; *The records of the honorable society of Lincoln's Inn. Vol. I. Admissions from 1420 to 1799* (Lincoln's Inn, 1896), p. 554. He was called to the bar in 1800 and practised in the court of chancery and on the Oxford and South Wales circuit. He died in 1816.

9 For Joseph Fawcett, his resignation, and his friendship with William Godwin, see Letter 604, nn. 6 and 7.

10 This work was Priestley's *Answer to Mr Paine's Age of reason.*

607. To WILLIAM TAYLEUR   25 MAY 1795

Text: JRUL, Lindsey Letters, vol. II, no. 83.
Printed: McLachlan, *Letters*, pp. 48–9 (first two sentences of third
                   paragraph).
Addressed: To/William Tayleur Esqr/Shrewsbury
Endorsed: May 25 – 95
Postmarked: MA 25 95

London. May. 25. 1795

Dear Sir,

It will give us great pleasure to find that this favourable entrance of warm summer weather is favourable to you. We have both of us reason to be thankful that we have so well passed over the winter, and are in such tolerable health at present.

I think I mentioned to You a book lately come out, "The Secret History of a Private Man["], by Francis Wollaston, LL.B. F.R.S. printed only to be given away; with one copy of which I have been favoured.[1]

You remember, that when we applied in a Petition from the Feathers Tavern to Parliament for the removal of Subscription &c; this gentleman was at the head of another set of Petitioners who thought it more proper to apply through the Bishops for the same end, when he published An *Address to the Clergy* upon the occasion.[2] It appears that he was very sincere in the matter, but not some others of his coadjutors, now upon the bench, who made their court to their Superiors by the part they acted.[3] He then gives an account of two pamphlets published by him, which did him great credit, particularly the last "Queries relating to the Book of Common Prayer with proposed Amendments".[4] But being disappointed and discouraged in his attempts – he says the *Times* afterwards became such as to dissuade any [foot of page torn: approximately six words missing] but concludes this head,[5] with some remarkable words, which You will be glad to read, and I shall transcribe at length.

"He trusts, with *most full and assured confidence*, that <u>true christianity</u> will in the end prevail over all opposition. But he knows that man must wait, till the Almighty Ruler of us all, judges that men are properly disposed to receive it. When that shall be, is yet in the womb of time: perhaps not many generations distant. For he has lived to *see the beginnings of a very great change working in the world*. A few years more, may calm the *blaspheming and ferocious spirit* of the first movers; who are most clearly mere instruments, in the hand of the God whom they deny, for purging mankind of their errors, and forwarding the wise designs of his providence. Then will all parties be brought to a more firm acknowlegement of the truth, and succeeding generations will see *Good* spring up, out of the present accumulation of *Evil*. Prophecies seem to point that way".[6]

There is a great deal of seriousness and justice in this remark.

I wish the Author shewed less eagerness to wash himself clean of the imputation of Socinianism; because some will ascribe it to too earnest a desire to recomend himself to the present powers [page torn: possibly the missing words are 'for a seat'] upon the bench. I shall however give [line missing: foot of page torn: possibly the missing words are 'my full attention to the'] subject.

"A book was sent him, by which it was said, that Mr W. was reclaimed from Socinianism. Had that been so, Mr W. would readily have acknowleged it. But the truth is, no one was ever farther from the *leading characteristic of Socinianism*, than he has been in every part of his life. For, though a large set, nine folio volumes, of the Fratres Poloni, were given him by one of that persuasion; he must confess that he never could think of wading through them.[7] He was always willing to hear and consider what any one could say on either side of any question; and thereupon most inclined to look into such authors who were of an opinion contrary to his own: but the little that he has dipped into any of those writers, did not so far make him hesitate, as to think it necessary to waste his time in diving deeper. What he has heard in conversation, or read in the writings of Priestley (whose parts and learning he admires, but whose injudicious vehemence he laments) and of Lindsey (whose conscientious conduct he reveres) he thought sufficient, to give him an insight into the main force of what can be urged on that side: but far short were they, of bringing him to accede to that opinion; or in any degree to lean to that way".[8]

I am afraid the length of these extracts may tire you, my good friend, but Mr Rowe may be glad to see them. M^r. W. goes on to declare himself of the B^p. of Clogher, Clayton's opinion of Christ being a high angel, and the holy Ghost an inferior one.[9] But no more of this.

Would I could send you word that the world was restored to Peace. But alas! our Governors seem to drive it farther and farther from us. My wife sends her kind respects. We desire to be rememberd to M^r & Mrs Rowe, Messrs Wood, Aikin, &c. I remain ever Dear Sir, Your truly obliged and affectionate servant

T. Lindsey

Since the account I gave of Dr Priestley, a letter is come from him, dated March 22, Northumberland a large [foot of page torn: approximately three words missing] Subscription has been raised in Philadelphia for [last line of page missing][10] means by the *leading characteristic* of Socinianism.[11]

---

[1]   Francis Wollaston (1731–1815), rector of Chiselhurst from 1769 until his death, published privately in London in 1795 an autobiography entitled *The secret history of a private man*, an account of his career as a latitudinarian clergyman. It focused particularly upon his support in the early 1770s for the abolition of clerical subscription to the thirty-nine articles; hence Lindsey's interest in the book.

2   This work was Wollaston's *An address to the clergy of the Church of England in particular, and to all Christians in general. Humbly proposing an application ... for ... relief in the matter of subscription* (London, 1772, with a second edition the following year).

3   These coadjutors included Beilby Porteus (1731–1809), subsequently bishop, successively, of Chester and of London; James Yorke (1730–1808), subsequently bishop, successively, of St David's, Gloucester and Ely; and Thomas Percy (1729–1811), from 1782, bishop of Dromore.

4   These two pamphlets by Wollaston were *Considerations on the state of subscription to the articles and liturgy of the Church of England, towards the close of the year 1773 ... by a consistent protestant* (London, 1774) and *Queries relating to the Book of Common Prayer ... with proposed amendments* (London, 1774). Although his name was not attached to either, Wollaston's authorship of both was no secret.

5   'Head': i.e. heading or section.

6   This passage, apart from some minor alterations of punctuation and italicization, is an exact transcription from Wollaston's *Secret history of a private man*, pp. 33–4.

7   Fratres Poloni (brothers of Poland) was the name adopted by anti-trinitarians in sixteenth-century Poland, after the Conference of Piotrków (1565). By the 'nine volumes', Wollaston referred to the *Bibliotheca Fratrum Polonorum,* an eight-volume edition of their principal theological works, including those of Faustus Socinus, published in Amsterdam between 1665 and 1668. A ninth volume was added to this edition in 1692. See E. M. Wilbur, *A history of unitarianism. Socinianism and its antecedents* (Boston, MA, 1945), pp. 569–70, and the same author's *A history of unitarianism. In Transylvania, England and America* (Boston, MA, 1952), pp. 46–8.

8   This passage, apart from a few small omissions, is an exact transcription from Wollaston's *Secret history of a private man*, pp. 35–7.

9   Wollaston made this observation, without mentioning Richard Clayton, bishop of Clogher from 1745 to 1758, in *Secret history of a private man*, pp. 56–59. For Clayton, see Vol. I, Letters 15, n. 3, and 145, n. 6.

10 This probably refers to Priestley's letter to Belsham, dated Northumberland, 22 Mar. 1795; Rutt, I, 296–7.

11 Lindsey added these words on the address page; they relate, evidently, to the quotation from Wollaston in the seventh paragraph of this letter.

608. To RUSSELL SCOTT   21 JUNE 1795

Text: Scott Coll.
Printed: McLachlan, 'Lindsey to Scott', 122 (part of first sentence
                   of first paragraph; part of first and last sentences of third
                   paragraph).
Addressed: To/The Rev^d. Russell Scott/Portsmouth
Postmarked: Postmark missing.

London. June. 21. 1795.

Dear Sir,

When I received a short but acceptable letter from you on Saturday the 23^d. of may, acquainting me with Mr Gerald's approaching departure for Botany Bay, and the opportunity afforded thereby of sending a letter or small parcell to Mr Palmer, but recomending the parcell to be sent by sunday evening's mail, for that otherwise it would be too late.[1] I immediately went to Mr Johnson's in St Pauls Churchyard, and there wrote a letter to Mr Palmer, inclosed in a short one to you, and paid Mr Johnson for the carriage, who solemnly promised the small parcell should go by the mail that (Saturday) evening, so that I reckoned upon it being with you a day before the time you had fixed; and Mr Johnson has often since assured me that it did go at the time.[2] I have however to rue, that I did not carry it myself to the mail, as I fear, from not having heard of it, that it never reached you; unless indeed you have been ill. For either event, but particularly the last I should be much grieved, and should be glad to be relieved from anxiety by a few lines which may reach me by friday next the 26th, as early on y[e] Saturday morning we set out on our biennial visit into the north to see my wife's mother, and shall be absent some time from home.

You will have heard, during this interval, of some extraordinary changes and occurrences with respect to young dissenting Ministers, following M[r] Fawcett of Walthamstow's steps; M[r] Lewis resigning Carter lane and engaging in a partnership with a wine merchant;[3] M[r] D. Jones of Birmingham, quitting his office of teacher and entering himself at Lincolns Inn to study the law;[4] reports of M[r] Jardine of Bath being dissatisfied and withdrawing himself from the chapel, but this last I find is not true.[5] It is however but too much so, that M[r] A. Aikin at Shrewsbury will soon give up his ministerial office and christianity along with it. This last you will not name *from me*; but it came to me from one you know, to whom he made no secret of it, nor even of his scruples with regard to the divine existence.[6] You will think it a sample of his judgment, that he told the same person, that he never saw so poor a thing in his life as D[r] Priestleys answer to M[r] Paine, that it had neither argument nor sense in it.

I really cannot help thinking, with respect to some who are gone to America and others who stay behind so suddenly shaking off all belief not only of Xtianity but even of deity, that besides infinite self-conceit, it is owing to something awry, some wrong twist in their minds and composition, and I am told that something of the sort, in some of them, may be traced to run in the blood, and in their families. M[r] Edwards, Jones's colleague, is chosen sole pastor.[7] M[r] Lewis's place is not to be filled up of some time.[8] What they will do at Shrewsbury I know not, but I learn that the young mans way of preaching of late has made great disturbance.[9] And in the mean time, the common adversary triumphs in the proof as they imagine of Socinianism leading the way to atheism.

We hope M[rs] Scott, yourself and your little folks are well, as we ardently wish you to be. My wife has been far otherwise of late, but I hope, she will be patched up tolerably before we set out on our long journey, which is now so near, and that this, by the divine blessing, will contribute to restore and confirm her health. As soon as we return you shall hear from me: and at the same time that you say something to my inquiries above, pray let us know what becomes of you this summer. With mine and my wife's united affectionate regards, I remain Dear Sir, always most truly Yours

T. Lindsey.

---

1   Scott's letter to Lindsey, which the latter received on 23 May 1795, seems not to have survived. Joseph Gerrald (1763–96), a radical writer and speaker, was, together with Maurice Margarot (1745–1815), a delegate from the London Corresponding Society to the British Convention at Edinburgh in 1793. He was arrested on a charge of sedition in Dec. 1793 and subsequently sentenced to fourteen years' transportation to Australia. He left England in the convict ship 'Sovereign' in May 1795 and arrived in Sydney in Nov. 1795.

2   Neither Lindsey's letter to Palmer nor his 'short letter' to Scott seems to have survived.

3   See Letter 606, n. 6.

4   See Letter 606, n. 8.

5   Lindsey was correct; David Jardine remained the minister to the Trim Street congregation at Bath from 1789 until his death on 10 Mar. 1797.

6   Arthur Aikin at Shrewsbury was assistant minister at the High Street chapel, Shrewsbury, from Sept. 1793 until June 1795. He then pursued a successful career as a geologist, mineralogist and author. It is likely that Rowe was Lindsey's informant; Scott and Rowe had been fellow-students at Hoxton Academy.

7   John Edwards (1768–1808), a former student at Hoxton and Daventry, was appointed assistant minister to Priestley at New Meeting, Birmingham, after the resignation of Samuel Blyth in Apr.

1791. He was sole minister there, in succession to David Jones, from 1795 to 1802. He had been minister at the Gateacre chapel, Lancashire, from 1787 to 1791, and subsequently served congregations in Middlesex, Newport (Isle of Wight) and Crediton.

8   See Letter 606, n. 7.

9   This is a reference to Arthur Aikin; see Letter 609.

609. To JOHN ROWE   26 JUNE 1795

Text: JRUL, Lindsey Letters, vol. II, no. 84.
Printed: McLachlan, *Letters*, p. 122 (postscript).
Addressed: Address missing.
Endorsed: [In pencil] [To Rev J. Rowe]
Postmarked: Postmark missing.

Note: Lindsey wrote letters to Rowe (Letter 609) and to Tayleur (Letter 610) and dated both 26 June 1795. In the second paragraph of the letter to Tayleur, he referred to a letter which he had written to Rowe 'yesterday' (25 June 1795); probably he wrote the letter on 25 June and dated it the following day. Moreover, in the third paragraph of his letter to Rowe, Lindsey noted that he was in the process of sending to Tayleur an account of the orations at Hackney College. It is therefore an editorial assumption that Lindsey wrote the letter to Rowe before he wrote that to Tayleur, and accordingly they are presented here in that order.

London. June. 26. 1795

Dear Sir,

With kind respects to Mrs Rowe and yourself, my wife and I desire to assure you both of the sincere part we take in the afflictions of your family, particularly in the loss of so lovely and promising a boy, who might have been the joy and comfort of his parents, and the staff of your old age, if that period is destined for you.[1] But it seemed otherwise to infinite wisdom, all whose works are in perfect goodness: and happily you are disposed there to look up for your consolation.

The unhappy turn of Mr A. must I am persuaded have lain very heavy upon your spirits, and I am glad that a way has been opened to you to retire for a while from the scenes in which you have suffered so much by his consenting to officiate.[2] With what consistency he can continue to do it, is his own affair to judge. It seems to me, that in his, and Hazlitt's conduct, there seems to be not only a ground of infinite self-conceit, but something that bespeaks an unsound state of mind, not guided by any rational principles.[3]

The Students of the college acquitted themselves with great credit, in their orations, all of them. I send Mr Tayleur a general account, which you will probably see.[4] Mr Morgan, who comes out of the west, where you are now, by his delivery and manner of handling his subject, promised to do credit to the ministry, for which I learn he is designed.[5]

The general character and behaviour of the students, and laudable proficiency of all, makes the continuance of such a seminary greatly to be wished for, and I am glad that it was the determination of the Committee, not to be discouraged by the bad state of its finances at present.

I have given direction to Mr Morgan to send yours and Mr Tayleur's catalogues to you at Crediton, but intimated that one woud do for you both, as you can signify to Mr Johnson, that both your allotments are put together.[6]

I have a good hope, that by your own prudent conduct the breach lately made in your congregation will be repaired, and the cause of truth, through the divine blessing, be the more promoted by what has happened.

We were with some friends in the country, part of the last week, but passed an anxious[7] not merely on account of the weather, which was altogether rainy and cold, but from a very violent attack of the bilious kind, in which my wife suffered much and was in some danger for two days together, but is happily now much better, though still very weak. But for this, we should have yesterday set out on our northern journey to visit her mother, but delay it to the end of the week. Till the end of July we shall be – *at Mrs Blackburne's, Richmond, Yorkshire.* After that we cannot now tell exactly which way our route will be. There or any where else I should rejoice to be of any use to you. We hope that change of air, gentle exercise, and the salt water, if necessary will be of service to you and your lady, and little folks.

I remain always affectionately Yours

T. Lindsey.

Nothing of Dr Priestley since his letter of march 22. mentioning the Subscription raised for the building of a college at Northumberland on his account: only that accounts are come, of the state, upon application to them, having granted ground to build it on and five thousand acres to go to it's support.[8]

[1]   Neither the records of the High Street chapel, Shrewsbury, TNA: RG4/1818, nor the transcript of those records at Shropshire Archives contains an entry for the death of a son of John and Mary Rowe in 1795. In the introduction to the transcript, pp. vi and vii, however, is a note to the effect that John and Mary Rowe had eight children, of whom five died in infancy.

[2]   As the fifth paragraph of this letter indicates, Rowe was at this time residing temporarily at Crediton, close to the place of his birth and where he still had family connexions.

[3]   Lindsey referred here to Arthur Aikin's abandonment of the ministry and of Christianity. William Hazlitt senior was minister to a dissenting congregation at Wem, Shropshire, from 1787 to 1813. Lindsey, while admiring his intellectual abilities, regarded him as rather headstrong.

[4]   This account may be found in Letter 610.

[5]   See Letter 610, n. 6.

[6]   This refers to the copy of the catalogues of the Unitarian Society's publications which had been sent to Rowe for his and Tayleur's choice of books. Thomas Morgan (1752–1821) served as the secretary of the Unitarian Society from Jan. 1794 to Jan. 1796 (although he announced his resignation in Dec. 1794, he appears to have continued in the office until Jan 1796). He was minister of the Great Alie Street congregation, London, from 1771, a trustee of Dr Williams's Trust from 1783 to 1809 and librarian of Dr Williams's Library from 1804 until his death. In 1796, he was succeeded as secretary of the Unitarian Society by John Kentish. See Unitarian Society minute book, pp. 46, 53, 57.

[7]   Word missing, probably 'time'.

[8]   Probably Lindsey referred here to Priestley's letter to Belsham, dated 22 Mar. 1795, Rutt, I, 296–7. For Priestley's abortive project in 1794 to 1797 for a unitarian college at Northumberland, see Graham, *Revolutionary in exile*, pp. 77–8, 82–3, 99–100.

610. To WILLIAM TAYLEUR   26 JUNE 1795

Text: JRUL, Lindsey Letters, vol. II, no. 85.
Addressed: To/William Tayleur Esqr/Shrewsbury
Endorsed: [?Not by Tayleur] June 26 95
Postmarked: JU 26 95

London. June. 26. 1795.

Dear Sir, and my much honoured friend;

I have had a very singular satisfaction, since I last wrote, in the report of one or two friends who have seen you, and have told me the pleasure they had in observing how well the bodily machine wore as also the mind that informed it, and that they thought you were full as well as two years before.[1] May heaven still continue its goodness, and preserve you as hitherto, comfortable in yourself, and useful to others, in filling the station appointed and employing the talents lent by Divine Providence.

I have been much concerned that the very worthy Mr Rowe has lately been made to drink so deeply of the cup of affliction, but a mind so early nurtured in piety and goodness will soon be reconciled to the appointments of the heavenly father, which are all for good, though we cannot always and at once see it: and I trust that the change of the scene and climate for a short season, will contribute to restore his and Mrs Rowe's health, which has been impaired by the troubles they have gone through. Yesterday I wrote to him in reply to a kind letter I had received ten days ago, and told him I hoped to find leisure to give you some account of things in our college at Hackney at the termination of session on monday last.[2]

I never saw the hall of assembly so full of ladies and gentlemen, and had great pleasure in it, as they would be both entertained and edified, by the fare they met with, and I thought I perceived it in their countenances. A very amiable youth, your townsman, Mr Mason had just begun his oration when I entered with a lady I brought along with me,[3] and was much applauded for his delivery as for the spirited, improving manner of handling his subject, the benefits arising from that pity and fellow feeling for others which makes a part of our frame.[4] The next speaker was a young man, whose name was Fenton, out of the north, who, not in a manner so graceful as his predecessor, but with an enlightened spirit and strong sense, dilated on the evils and wickedness of war, especially of that in which we have been and are now fatally engaged.[5]

Mr Morgan, son of the late worthy Mr Morgan of Collumpton, designed for the ministry, shewd himself well qualified for it, by his grace and excellent delivery of a discourse concerning the best methods of education of youth, in which he condemned the wasting of so many years upon the classic authors in the dead languages, to the intire neglect of all moral and religious knowlege and attainments, and censured very pointedly the reading of novels, which so much hurt the tender mind, and with which I thought I saw not a few inwardly reproved, of the fair who attended.[6]

The next orator, a Mr Skey, shewed himself a genius, of a still higher form and improvements, in a dissertation on the limits of sensation and perception, which he ingeniously extended to the vegetable tribe, and spoke highly and feelingly of the benevolence of the Deity therein.[7]

The next was a Mr Read from Bristol, of very superior powers indeed, upon the connexion of knowlege and virtue, which older scholar[s] could not listen to without being made wiser and better; the only fault that it was rather too rapidly deliverd; but his modesty is as remarkable as the eminence of his abilities.[8]

The whole was well closed by Mr Rogers, son of the late Mr Rogers, the banker, Dr Price's friend, in an oration to prove that the knowlege of a future state is only to be attained by divine revelation. His reasoning was just throughout, and some new ideas in it.[9]

And now, my excellent friend, what a calamity would it be, that a seminary for the education of youth the only one in the kingdom, that is truly liberal and unshackled, should fall to nothing, through the debts most improvidently contracted, by a series of negligence and by overbuilding themselves. The whole matter was seriously debated at a meeting of all the Subscribers after the Orations were over; at one time I thought we must give up, but at last determined that we were to live; and earnestly do I wish such as Institution may live for ever, being calculated to promote the best good of man.[10]

I think I sent you word, that we were going into the north this year, to pay a biennial visit of piety most due to my wife's excellent mother. We should have set out on Wednesday last but for a severe attack her daughter has had within these ten days of what the Doctors call the cholera morbus, but is happily now so far recruited that we leave town in a few days.[11]

At our return, I hope to hear from Mr Rowe, that you continue tolerably as usual. She[12] desires kind and respectful rememberances to yourself. I remain always, Dear Sir, faithfully and affectionately Yours

T. Lindsey.

I beg our sincere respects may be made acceptable to Mr Wood and all our friends in & about Shrewsbury.

---

1 These friends, who had seen Tayleur at Shrewsbury, and reported to Lindsey on his good health, probably included John Rowe, Edward Harries and the Hackney student James Mason whose oratorical efforts Lindsey described in this letter.

2 Letter 609.

3 Disappointingly, Lindsey did not identify the lady who accompanied him to these orations at Hackney College. A strong possibility, however, is Elizabeth Rayner, who in her will (dated 28 Apr. 1795) bequeathed a legacy to the college in 3 per cent Bank of England annuities. On the college's dissolution the following year, she added a codicil, transferring this legacy to the trustees of Essex Street chapel; TNA: PRO PROB 11/1345, fos. 264r–273v.

4 This was James Mason of Shrewsbury; see Letter 560, n. 10.

5 No student named Fenton is to be found in the Hackney College committee minutes (DWL, MS 38.14), which do not survive after 15 Sept. 1791; possibly a student of that name was admitted to the college after that date. Similarly, the name Fenton does not appear in Birm. MS 281, fos. 123–5.

6 The younger Morgan is not recorded as a student at Hackney College, either in the college minutes (DWL, MS 38.14) or in Birm. MS 281. Possibly he was the Thomas Morgan of Bristol, who is listed as a member of the Western Unitarian Society in 1802; see the list of members appended to Theophilus Browne, *The necessity of a new version of the sacred writings. A discourse delivered at Bath, July 7, 1802, before the Society of Unitarian Christians, Established in the West of England* (Warminster, 1802), p. 35; he does not seem to have become a dissenting minister. His father was Samuel Morgan (1731–94), a product of the Carmarthen Academy and minister to dissenting congregations at Dulverton, Somerset, from 1753 to 1754, and at Cullompton, Devon, from 1754 until his death on 15 Sept. 1794.

7 Probably Joseph Skey (1773–1866), of Bewdley, Worcestershire, a lay student who attended the college in the early and mid -1790s. He was subsequently a licentiate of the Royal College of Physicians and physician to the royal forces; see DWL, MS 24.157 (188), I, and Birm. MS 281, fo. 124.

8 Samuel Read (or Reid) of Bristol; see Letter 580, n. 15.

9 For Henry Rogers, see Letter 580, n. 14.

10 The minutes of the Hackney College committee do not survive for the period after Sept. 1791. As early as 1793, there was public discussion of the possibility that financial pressures might force the college to move from London, or to close; see *Gent. Mag.*, LXIII, i (1793), 334, 397. In May 1793, the dissenting minister and biblical scholar Edward Harwood (1729–94) published a letter which criticized the committee for launching the college on such an extravagant basis, so 'inconsistent with the plainness and simplicity of the dissenters'; *Gent. Mag.*, LXIII, i (1793), 409. For the declining years of the college, including efforts by sub-committees to reduce expenditure, see H. McLachlan, 'The old Hackney College 1786–1796', 198–205.

11 Lindsey referred to his return from this northern journey in Letter 612.

12 Hannah Lindsey.

611. To WILLIAM ALEXANDER   27 JUNE 1795

Text: 'Letters of the Rev. Theophilus Lindsey. No. VI', *UH*, II, 74
                      (27 Sept. 1862), 330.

Note: The ellipsis at the beginning of the extract printed by the *UH* indicates that this was not the beginning of the original letter. The further ellipsis at the end of the first paragraph indicates that the second
paragraph did not immediately follow the first in the original letter. Accordingly, the two paragraphs are
presented here separated by a broken line. The words in square brackets are those of the *UH*.

London, June 27th, 1795.
* * I have to add that there has been a large sum subscribed to build a college at
Northumberland Town, on his [Dr. Priestley's] account; and also that upon application to the State to grant them ground to build it upon, they have done this, with
an additional grant of five thousand acres of land to go to the future support of
the college. Several English, some of whom I know, have been induced on these
accounts, and for the excellence of the climate, to go to settle at Northumberland;
so there is likely to be quite an English colony.[1] * *

Great are the trials of many we know in these hard times, and likely to be greater.
It is a great and present felicity, which we should endeavour to possess, to see the
hand of God in everything for good; which is really so whether we can see it or no.

[1]   The English settlers expected at Northumberland included Thomas Cooper and William Russell.

612. To WILLIAM TAYLEUR   16 SEPTEMBER 1795

Text: JRUL, Lindsey Letters, vol. II, no. 86.
Printed: McLachlan, *Letters*, p. 39 (short quotation from first three
                      sentences of third paragraph, with errors of transcription).
Addressed: To/William Tayleur Esqr/Shrewsbury
Endorsed: Septr. 16 – 95
Postmarked: SE 18 95

Dear Sir, and my much hon^d. friend,[1]
Mordon. Surrey. Septr. 16. 1795.
    We have never hitherto been settled at our own home, since we came off our long
journey into the north, or most assuredly I should have paid my respects to you. I
hope you have had an agreeable summer for health, and then every thing else would
be agreable and well with a mind like your's. When Mr Rowe returns to Shrewsbury,
which will be I trust with the recovered health and spirits of himself and his lady, I
shall expect a few lines to say how you and they do. I have heard of him however
in the interim, that he was so far recruited as to be able to compose and deliver a
very excellent, suitable christian discourse to his brethren assembled at Exeter.[2]
    It will give you pleasure to be informed, that my wife's health, which was
uncomonly feeble and precarious when we left London, was imediately improved
by the change of air and exercise, and has proceeded gradually amending through
our whole excursion, that I scarce remember the time she has been in better health,
or more disposed and able to employ her active talents for the good of others. It was
no small accession to our own happiness, not only to find the chief object of our
visit, a most valuable character, my wife's mother, in health and capable of enjoying

the satisfaction of having her family about, but also to see many other friends and relations whom we visited, well and happy, and without one sinister accident in a tour of 600 miles at least: for all which we ought to be duly thankful.

Dr Disney not being come back out of the north whither he followed us, when we returned, we went on the Sunday to Hackney to hear Mr Belsham. I have always been edified and instructed under him; never more than at this time. He substitutes, as Dr Priestley did, a short exposition of a portion of the Scripture for the reading of a chapter, which takes him about ten or 12 minutes, more or less, as it happens. He has gone thro' St Pauls epistles to the Thessalonians. He is now in the midst of that to the Hebrews. And from the brief sketch of his manner of handling it, and the portion which he dilated upon, relating to Melchizedek &c, a difficult part in which, at the same time apologizing for him, he shewed how much the apostle was mistaken in the argument before him, and in his mode of reasoning, such as threw great light and must give general satisfaction to all his hearers, which are always numerous.[3] I know not any thing that woud be more useful, than his particular exposition of this epistle; and so I told him. Had he time for it, I believe he would not be unwilling to print this and some other things.[4]

During our travels, I rec^d from London several letters that had come from Dr Priestley.[5] He mentions also the having written to you. In all mine he speaks very chearfully of the good progress making in providing a good settlement for himself, and also for a seminary at Northumberland, of which he is to be Principal, for which a large subscription has been made at Philadelphia, and an endowment of six thousand acres of land bestowed by the State of Pennsylvania.[6] He is also reprinting an enlarged Edition of his *Observations on the causes of Infidelity*,[7] and will soon be in readiness to put into the press two additional Vols of Ecclesiastical history: but with the particulars of his studies, and also of his philosophical experiments, for he is going on with them, I presume he has acquainted you, and therefore I say the less.[8]

I say nothing of this most wretched war, in which a presumptuous minister keeps us, who will be chronicled in wisdom for want of wisdom, and for being the cause of the ruin of England's greatness.

My wife desires her kind respects, and every good wish. I remain, Dear Sir, ever your most obliged and faithful affectionate servant

T. Lindsey.

We beg due and respectful remembrances to Mr Rowe &c when they arrive, and to Mr Wood and Harries, and all friends.

You will be glad to hear, that notwithstanding the shameful calumnies and undue prejudices against the college at Hackney, on account of a late affair, there will be nine or ten new students admitted at the opening of the session this week, to supply the place of those who go off.[9]

---

1   Unusually, Lindsey in this letter wrote the salutation above his current location.
2   Rowe's sermon preached at Exeter was not published. Lindsey's informant as to its quality was probably Timothy Kenrick.
3   Hebrews, vii.
4   Belsham did not publish this sermon.
5   These letters of Priestley to Lindsey were those of 17 May 1795 (Rutt, I, 302–3), 17 June 1795 (Rutt, I, 305–6); and 12 July 1795 (Rutt, I, 310–12). In his letter to Lindsey of 12 July 1795, Priestley expressed his intention of writing to Tayleur; Rutt I (ii), 310. In his letter to Lindsey of 9 Nov. 1795, he stated that he had done so; DWL, MS 12.13 (passage omitted in Rutt, I, 319–21).
6   For this project for a college, and the possibility of an endowment in land to support it, see Schofield,

Enlightened Joseph Priestley, pp. 330–1, 339. After the failure of the project in 1795, there was a brief attempt to revive the idea in 1799, with help from the state of Pennsylvania.

7   For this work, see Letter 613, n. 8.

8   The first two volumes of Priestley's *General history of the Christian church* were published in Birmingham in 1790; he completed the work with four further volumes, published in Northumberlandvin 1802–3. His *Experiments and observations relating to the analysis of atmospherical air; also farther experiments relating to the generation of air from water ... to which are added, considerations on the doctrine of phlogiston* was published in Philadelphia and London, 1796.

9   See Letter 604, n. 5. The surviving evidence does not permit the identification of the new Hackney College students of 1795.

613. To JOHN ROWE   26 OCTOBER 1795

Text: JRUL, Lindsey Letters, vol. II, no. 87.
Printed: McLachlan, *Letters*, p. 133 (seventh paragraph, with errors of transcription).
Addressed: To/The Rev^d. John Rowe/Shrewsbury
Postmarked: OC 26 95

London. Octr. 26. 1795.

Dear Sir,

I had fully proposed to have thanked you for your welcome letter, at the end of the last week,[1] when we returned to Town: but was prevented. We are however now at length come to fix in town altogether, and I employ my first leisure in acquainting you, that the recovery of your health with that of your family, and still more your return to the congregation has been a real cordial to me; I only fear the duty may be too much for you.

It is a great pleasure also to hear that you found our common excellent friend so much himself after so long an absence. Of this to me no better proof can be given than his generous effort and provision for the worthy person you mention; of whose worth and character I have heard, but shall be desirous to hear more, as I should be also to know him, should I ever come into your parts, or any thing happen to send him here.[2]

Since my last to Shrewsbury, I have rec^d. two letters from Dr Priestley, one that had been missing, dated June. 12. 1795; the other Aug. 12. 1795, the latest that has come from him.[3]

His own health continues very good, as also of his [so]ns[4] and of the family of the eldest; but M^rs [Priestley has][5] had thrice a return of the spitting of blood, of the same kind that had alarmed them before she left England, but was become very well when his letter came away. "I was never more fully employed, (says he, in his last letter that I may give you some of his own words) especially about my *Church History*, in which I am now writing the history of the War with the Albigenses. I hope to make it a useful work, but it is very laborious. The only thing that I repent of here is my undertaking to build a house, not foreseeing the difficulty or expence of it; but the price of every thing is advanced full one third since I began."[6]

He tells me, that Mr Cooper of Manchester, who went over in the same vessel with Messrs Porter and Jardine, is an avowed unbeliever, and is writing some thing against the gospel; which shews an extraordinary zeal in a convert just gone to settle in the country to provide for a family carried over with him.[7]

At last he has sent me his Observations on the Increase of Infidelity, written with a very serious spirit, not likely as he says to be read by unbelievers, but which may confirm others in the truth which they have embraced. It is not so animated as he would have drawn it up had he been surrounded with friends likeminded with himself, but is calculated to be of great use, and therefore I shall give it this week to Mr Johnson to reprint.[8]

Mr Paine's second part of his Age of Reason is come out. I have not read it but expect, that, like the former part, it will make [foot of page torn: two or three words missing] reject revelation intirely, who took up the belief of it from others without enquiry into the grounds of its evidence for themselves.[9]

It is a candid wish worthy of you, and I hope will be verified, that Arthur Aikin may reverse his late very hasty decision and more firmly embrace the truth of the gospel. He called upon my wife a week ago when I was out, who rallied him a good deal upon his precipitancy, and told him the astonishment as well as concern that it had caused to his good friends at York, of which we heard much when we were there.[10] All which he took in very good part.

We do not learn who is to come into the place of the worthy Dr Kippis. Our wishes are for Dr Toulmin of Taunton, who in many respects resembles D^r K, but is an Unitarian with more decision. I wish some one of authority and weight in the congregation would take him up. Be so good not to intimate I have mentioned him lest it should be to his prejudice.[11] Mr Manning from Exeter, who it seems is a Trustee of Dr Harris's will, preached his funeral Sermon to day.[12] Dr Rees's for Dr Kippis will soon make it's appearance from the press.[13]

We cannot be thankful enough for the blessing of health which we both enjoy: we trust it is still continued to you. I honour Mr Harries for his readiness to serve your place in your absence, and beg to be respectfully remembered to him.[14] I trust he has that comfort from both his sons, which his character and care intitles him to. My wife joins me in respects to Mrs Rowe and yourself, and we beg you will name us with all affectionate respect to the venerable friend, whom providence still kindly lends to us, for an example to all, and a singular benefit to many. You will take your own time about the letters. Sorry I am that you should have suffered by negligence or roguery in conveyance by the coach. I am always affectionately Yours

T. Lindsey.

---

1   Rowe's letter to Lindsey seems not to have survived.

2   'Our common excellent friend' was William Tayleur. Possibly the 'worthy person' whom Tayleur had helped was Thomas Jenkins of Whitchurch, Shropshire; see Letter 583, n. 4.

3   There is no letter from Priestley to Lindsey of 12 June 1795 in DWL, MS 12.13 or in Rutt. Possibly Lindsey referred to Priestley's letter to him of 12 July 1795, which is in DWL, MS 12.13 and is partly printed in Rutt, I, 310–12; it referred to Priestley's good health and that of his sons. Priestley's letter to Lindsey of 17 Aug. 1795 is in DWL, MS 12.13 and is partly printed in Rutt, I, 314–15; in it, Priestley did indeed mention his wife's 'spitting blood'.

4   The manuscript is slightly torn at this point.

5   The foot of this page of the manuscript is slightly torn at this point.

6   This is a part-quotation from Priestley's letter to Lindsey of 12 Aug 1795; see n. 3, above.

7   In his letter to Lindsey, 12 Aug. 1795, Priestley wrote 'Mr Cooper is an avowed unbeliever, and is now writing something against X^{ty}, to assist him in which I lend him books. However, from what drops from him occasionally, I have no great apprehension from any thing that he may produce. I shall be expected to answer it'; DWL, MS 12.13 (passage omitted in Rutt, I, 314–15).

8   Priestley's *Observations relating to the causes of the general prevalence of infidelity* was first published as an appendage to his *Letters addressed to the philosophers and politicians of France, on the subject of religion* (Philadelphia, 1794). In the latter months of 1795, Lindsey was in the process of arranging for an enlarged version of the *Observations* to be reprinted separately in London by Joseph Johnson; it was published in 1796. For a criticism of this latter version, see Letter 645, n. 9.

9   Thomas Paine's *The age of reason. Part the second. Being an investigation of true and fabulous*

theology was first published (in French and English) in Paris in the autumn of 1795. An edition in London, published by H. D. Symonds, appeared shortly thereafter. The introductory note addressed 'to the reader' in Gilbert Wakefield's *A reply to Thomas Paine's second part of the age of reason* was dated Hackney, 26 Oct. 1795, indicating that part two of *The age of reason* was available in England by that date, and probably several weeks earlier.

10   Arthur Aikin's friends at York included Charles Wellbeloved, and Newcome and Catharine Cappe.

11   Andrew Kippis died on 8 Oct. 1795. His successor as minister to the Princes Street, Westminster, congregation was Thomas Jervis, who served there from 1796 to 1808.

12   James Manning, *A sermon, occasioned by the death of the Rev. Rice Harris, DD. ... October 25, 1795* (London, 1795). For Rice Harris, who died on 10 Oct. 1795, see Vol. I, Letter 318, n. 7, and *Gent. Mag.*, LXV, ii (1795), 884. Harris (1731–95) was minister at Hanover Street, Long Acre, London, from 1768 until his death on 10 Oct. 1795. Manning (1754–1831) was minister at George's meeting, Exeter, from 1776 to 1831, succeeding his former tutor at the Exeter Academy, Micaiah Towgood (1700–92) as sole minister in 1782. He was indeed an executor of Harris's will, and a beneficiary of £100 under that will; TNA: PRO PROB 11/1267, fos. 247r–248r.

13   Abraham Rees, *A sermon preached at the meeting house in Prince's-Street, Westminster, on the eighteenth of October, 1795, upon occasion of the much lamented death of the Rev. Andrew Kippis, DD* (London, 1795).

14   Edward Harries was an ordained clergyman of the Church of England who had resigned his parish living in 1782 and associated thereafter with the unitarians of Shrewsbury.

614. To RUSSELL SCOTT   31 OCTOBER 1795

Text: Scott Coll.
Printed: McLachlan, 'Lindsey to Scott', 122 (short quotations from second and fourth paragraphs).
Addressed: To/The Rev^d. Russell Scott [added, in Lindsey's hand]
                  Mr Johnson is desired to inclose this letter in the copy of
                  Mr Paine's Second Part, which he sends to Mr Scott
Endorsed: Novr. 1st. – 95
Postmarked: Postmark missing.

Dear Sir,

It is very long since I had the pleasure of hearing from you, and of your health and welfare and that of your family.

I write this in haste that it may go in a copy of Paine's 2^d Part, a most illiberal attack, full of the grossest ignorance and mistakes, but to which it will not be easy to give a reply that will not be too grave and dull to be read.[1]

Mr Temple[2] told me at the chapel on Sunday, on my inquiring after you, that you were not in Portsmouth when he was there.

We have lately had letters from Dr Priestley, who is very well, as also his sons: but Mrs P. has lately had a return of the spitting of blood which alarmed them so much before she went abroad.[3] He has sent me, Observations on the Increase of Infidelity, which I have given to Mr Johnson to reprint, and shall take care you have a copy as soon as it comes out of the press.[4]

This is the first week of our being settled in Town, having sojourned with our friends in Surrey four days in each week since we came out of the North.

Happily my wife's health has been much benefited, and still continues. We shall rejoice to have the like good account of your own and of that of your family.

In haste but always very sincerely and affectionately Yours

                              T. Lindsey

My wife desires to join in kind respects. Pray remember me to M[r] Porter. We hope he is able to keep the gout at a distance, and that all his family are well.
Oct. 31

1   For part two of Paine's *Age of reason*, see Letter 613, n. 9.

2   This was almost certainly Richard Godman Temple (see Letter 522, n. 3).

3   Priestley referred to this symptom of his wife in his letter to Lindsey of 12 Aug. 1795, DWL, MS 12.13 (passage omitted in Rutt, I, 314–15).

4   In his letter of 12 Aug. 1795 (n. 3, above, passage omitted by Rutt) Priestley informed Lindsey that he had sent these copies to him.

615. To RUSSELL SCOTT   4 DECEMBER 1795

Text: Scott Coll.
Addressed: To/The Rev[d]. Russell Scott/Portsmouth [added, in Lindsey's hand] W[th]. D[r] Rees's Sermon[1]
Endorsed: Dec[r]. 4th. – 95
Postmarked: Postmark missing.

Dear Sir,

I am glad, We are glad to hear that you are at length tolerably well after your having suffered so long.

Our friend[2] tells me there is a ship going soon to Botany Bay, I shall probably trouble you with a letter, but should be glad in the mean time, if you coud tell me what, or whether any thing has been sent or is sending to M[r] Palmer.

No successor appointed to D[r] Kippis[3] – nor D[r] Harris[4] – nor to M[r] G. Lewis the afternoon preacher at Carter lane.[5]

I write this in haste expecting our friend[6] to return every moment – who cannot stay. We are well upon the whole – heaven all[?] be praised – wish you and yours intirely so. Our kindest regards to you both, and Your's.

T.L.

Tuesday forenoon.[7]

1   For Rees's sermon, see Letter 613, n. 13.

2   This friend was almost certainly Richard Godman Temple.

3   See Letter 613, n. 11.

4   See Letter 613, n. 12. No successor to Rice Harris as minister to the dissenting congregation at Hanover Street, Long Acre, London, was immediately appointed. Robert Winter (1762–1833) served as minister there from 1796 to 1803, when he was succeeded by Nathaniel Philips (see Letter 619, n. 7). See Jeremy, *The Presbyterian fund and Dr Williams's Trust*, p. 5.

5   For George Lewis, see Letter 606, n. 6.

6   Richard Godman Temple; see n. 2, above.

7   4 Dec. 1795 was a Friday; the previous Tuesday was 1 Dec. The postmark indicates that the letter was posted on Friday 4 Dec.

616. To CHRISTOPHER WYVILL   **7 DECEMBER 1795**

Text: NYRO, ZFW 7/2/95/27, Wyvill of Constable Burton MSS.
Printed: Ditchfield, 'Lindsey–Wyvill correspondence', 163 (second and sixth paragraphs).
Addressed: To/The Rev^d. Christopher Wvyill/Burton Hall/Bedale/ Yorkshire
Endorsed: From Revd T. Lindsey Dec. 7. 1795
Postmarked: DE 7 95

London. Decr. 7. 1795

Dear Sir,

It is high time I should thank you for your letter to me and the noble seasonable address to the Yorkshire Freeholders which accompanied it, and also for your bold and spirited exertions at the meeting, which will have their effect by and by, though they did not succeed so much as was desireable at the time, through want of proper support from those who ought to have been present, and through your being outjockeyed by Mr Wilberforce and his ministerial adherents.[1]

Your efforts however I believe will not be lost at present. You will find that our liberties, which the daring minister, once a reformer, has presumed to wrest from us all at once, by surprise, in these two shocking and still pending bills,[2] will not yet be given up.

His Convention bill is yet to enter the Lords' house, and will there meet with a most powerful opposition from Lord Thurlow,[3] as being a manifest violation of the Constitution, and the same friend high in Rank who mentions this, tells me also that Lord Moira will oppose it as a most flagrant attack on the freedom and birthright of englishmen.[4]

It is also said, that the bill, as it has passed thro' the Commons, upon a nearer inspection into its provisions which attention to its horrid principle only prevented observing during its passing, so shocking and exceptionable, that on that account only it must come back to the Commons. I beg pardon for this interlining, but hope you will understand me.[5]

Through inability likewise to procure resources to carry on the wasteful war, it is reckoned that the Minister must have recourse to peace, as the only way to continue in his power, which he wants not acuteness to see that he woud otherwise be unable to preserve. This is what we are told Mr Wilberforce held out to the county of York, and coming from such a confidant of the Minister, was thought to make an impression on them, and dispose them to side with him.[6]

And as endeavours, I trust, will be used through the nation, in a quiet legal way, to keep up the sense of the loss of their liberties by these two bills when they shall take place; the people will thereby be awakened out of that ignorance which has possessed them, and be excited in every constitutional way to assert their freedom and become more worthy of it.

I write before the morning papers come out, so that I know nothing of what was done by the friends of the people on Saturday, but was told by one of them that their resolutions would be found equal to the momentous occasion.[7] If the members of the corresponding society had adopted any principles not compatible with our present constitution, it is said they were confined only to a few; that a parliamentary reform was their main object, and those who were for universal suffrage may be brought to believe that the vote of every householder in elections of their representatives may be a better means of securing the object they wish.[8]

Mr B. Hollis came up to Town on friday to attend the meeting of the friends of the people and has just now stopd at our door in his way out, but could tell us nothing of the meeting as he could not stay till the business was begun. He seems indeed past taking any active part in any measure, though his health upon the whole is better than it was sometime since. I shall be happy to hear at your leisure that you have not suffered by your fatigues and that Mrs Wyvill[9] and your lovely family continue well. Our united respects attend the former with my wifes to yourself and our best wishes for you all. I remain always, with a true esteem, Dear Sir, Your much obliged and faithful affectionate servant,

T. Lindsey.

1 Wyvill's 'Address to the worthy freeholders of Yorkshire', dated 27 Nov. 1795, is printed in Wyvill, *Political papers*, V, xxx–xxxi. The York meeting took place on 1 Dec. 1795; its reform resolutions are printed in *ibid.*, V, xxxiv–xxxvii. For Wyvill's 'being outjockeyed' by Wilberforce, see n. 6, below.

2 Following the attack on George III's carriage on 29 Oct. 1795, as he drove to the opening of parliament, the Treasonable Practices Act (36 George III, c. 7) and the Seditious Meetings Act (36 George III, c. 8) were introduced into the house of commons in Nov. 1795 and received the royal assent by commission on 18 Dec. 1795.

3 Thurlow had been dismissed by Pitt from the lord chancellorship in June 1792 and had thereafter been a critic of Pitt's ministry in the house of lords. He spoke against the Treasonable Practices bill in the house of lords on 11 Nov. 1795; Cobbett, *Parl. hist.*, XXXII, 255–6. He spoke against the Seditious Meetings bill on 9 Dec. 1795 and voted against its third reading on 14 Dec; Cobbett, *Parl. hist.*, XXXII, 540–4, 554. He argued that existing laws were sufficient for the purposes of maintaining order and the safety of the king and constitution and that the new laws were unnecessary and badly formulated.

4 Francis Rawdon-Hastings (1754–1826), 2nd earl of Moira in the Irish peerage and Baron Rawdon in the British peerage, and from 1817, marquess of Hastings. He was the son of John Rawdon, Baron Rawdon (from 1762, 1st earl of Moira), who had been Lindsey's correspondent in the 1750s and early 1760s. The identity of Lindsey's aristocratic informant remains a matter for speculation. One possibility is the duke of Grafton; another is Lindsey's former pupil Hugh Percy, formerly Smithson (1742–1817), 2nd duke of Northumberland; for whose disapproval of Pitt's ministry in the later 1790s, see Letter 634.

5 Lindsey's interlining in this paragraph, though written in a cramped manner, is entirely legible.

6 Wyvill complained that during the county meeting at the Guildhall at York on 1 Dec. 1795, Wilberforce, who was one of the two MPs for the county, associated himself with 'a considerable number of persons' who were not freeholders of the county and therefore not entitled to vote. He suggested to Wilberforce that, to avoid disorder, he and his associates should withdraw and leave the meeting in the hands of those who had summoned it. Although at first reluctant to do so, Wilberforce and those who supported him eventually withdrew to the Castle at York. Wyvill suspected that they did so only because of '*their fear* to meet a fair and free discussion of their questions', or, more practically, because they wished to show that any criticism of the government made, at Wyvill's instigation, by the meeting, lacked numerical support and could not be taken as representative of the county's opinion. See Wyvill's letter to Wilberforce, 3 Dec. 1795, Wyvill, *Political papers*, V, 308–11. In the event, the pro-government meeting at the Castle was more numerous than that of Wyvill and his followers at the Guildhall and the motion which it passed, expressing confidence in Pitt's ministry and approbation of the two acts of Dec. 1795 (n. 2, above), amounted to a considerable propaganda victory for the government. See Dinwiddy, *Wyvill and reform*, pp. 9–10.

7 A meeting of the Friends of the People was held at Freemasons' tavern in London on Saturday 5 Dec. 1795. It issued an 'address to the people', condemning the high level of taxation and national debt, defending the Bill of Rights as 'our buckler and defence', deploring the introduction of the two acts (see n. 2, above) and advocating parliamentary reform; *Morning Chronicle*, 7 Dec. 1795.

8 The London Corresponding Society held a large public meeting at Marylebone Fields on 7 Dec. 1795 (the date of this letter of Lindsey) and drew up a remonstrance to the king in protest against the two acts (n. 2, above). William Frend was one of the speakers; see *Morning Chronicle*, 9 Dec. 1795. For the background, and the society's programme for social and political reform, see A. Goodwin, *The

friends of liberty. The English democratic movement in the age of the French Revolution (London, 1979), ch. 10.

9   Sarah, *née* Codling, Wyvill's second wife.

617. To WILLIAM TAYLEUR   14 DECEMBER 1795

Text: JRUL, Lindsey Letters, vol. II, no. 88.
Printed: McLachlan, *Letters*, p. 122 (short quotations from second
                   paragraph).
Addressed: To/William Tayleur Esqʳ./Shrewsbury
Endorsed: Decʳ 14ᵗʰ – 95
Postmarked: DE 14 95

London. Decʳ. 14. 1795.

Dear Sir,

I have really been prevented writing to you by the various business of writing and sending papers and tracts to different parts, which has been created by these two bills, which are still depending, but will soon pass. I was glad to hear that the king does not intend to go to the house himself to give his fiat to them, lest any disturbance should arise, but to do it by proxy. In political matters I have always studiously avoided to take any part, but in this sudden unexpected attempt to deprive us of our most valuable rights, one could not be indifferent while any thing could be done to defeat it.[1]

You will be gratified in hearing that my wife has seen a long letter from Miss Russell to Mʳˢ. Finch, Dʳ Priestley's daughter, dated from the Dʳ's house at Northumberland, the beginning of October, with a most pleasing description of the health of him and all his family, their places of abode, way of living, employments and designs, which almost transports one to them, and shews how happy they all are.[2] The Doctor looks remarkably well in his own looks, partly gray, and a little bald, has his different occupations and studies in his laboratory and among his books as at Fair Hill. Mʳ Russell, having taken a house at Philadelphia, Dʳ Priestley is to be with them two months in the winter.[3] And the Russell family propose to pass the summer months at Northumberland. No mention is made of any of the outrages against Mʳ Jay's treaty with England, which some of the public papers have mentioned, particularly the President Washingtons person having been in danger, so that I trust it is all a false report.[4] I hope you will now soon receive Dʳ Priestleys "Observations on the increase of Infidelity", as Mʳ Johnson has had directions to send it.[5] It will certainly do good. But I fear it will not stop the very general bent to Infidelity, which perhaps may be by Providence intended to be a scourge to this nation as it has been to a neighbouring one, and become the means of planting the pure religion of the gospel in the end.

It will give you concern to be informed, that our college at Hackney, to which you have been such a signal and generous benefactor, must now at last be broken up, and the premises disposed of, on account of the debts incurred and the clamours of the creditors. Mʳ Belsham has done every thing that was in his power by economy in his department, but the evil was done before he came. There were some at a meeting of the Committee this last week, who pleaded for the doors being shut up after Christmas at the middle of the session, and the pupils dismissed. But this would have been great injustice to the students and their friends who had made their engagements for one year's education at least; and to the Tutors no less, to turn them adrift at once, &c &c. With some difficulty this motion was over-ruled, and it was resolved, that the Premisses should continue to be occupied for the use of the Institution to the end of the session, the beginning of July.[6] Thus by sad unaccountable mismanagement of great sums from a generous Public, favourable to liberal principles, have the fairest prospects of a lasting Seminary for the education of Youth among Dissenters been blasted.

We beg to be remembered most kindly to M^r and Mrs Rowe, and I wish you would tell him, that we begin to be apprehensive that Dr Toulmin will have no chance of succeeding Dr Kippis, an event earnestly desired, and as far as our interference could go, promoted by us, by my wife especially. At first the objections were to his being a Baptist. Now it is said the congregation is Arian, and a professed Unitarian cannot be admitted. But D^r. Kippis was unquestionably a Socinian, though it might not be know[n] to many of his congregation. How noble was that conduct of the late Dr Fleming, who in a sett[7] Discourse acquainted his congregation with such a change in his opinions, and did not lose one of his flock by the declaration![8]

May you, my excellent friend, still be preserved in life, with some comfort to yourself and with the blessed disposition and ability to do good to others!

My wife presents her kind respects. I am always, Dear Sir, Your obliged and faithful affectionate servant

T. Lindsey.

---

[1] For these two measures, see Letter 616, n. 2. As Lindsey noted, George III gave the royal assent to them by commission, not in person, on 18 Dec. 1795; *LJ*, XL, 570.

[2] I have not found this letter from Miss (probably Martha) Russell to Priestley's daughter Sarah Finch.

[3] Although Russell did not settle at Northumberland, he and his family paid several visits to Priestley there; see Jeyes, *The Russells of Birmingham*, pp. 169, 197–200, 207.

[4] For the violent campaign against the Jay treaty, and the personal vituperation of Washington, which included the threat of impeachment, see Todd Estes, *The Jay treaty debate, public opinion, and the evolution of early American political culture* (Amherst and Boston, MA, 2006), pp. 96–111. Priestley wrote to Lindsey on 12 Aug. 1795 'Mr. Jay's treaty is almost universally condemned, so that many think the President will not ratify it'; Rutt, I, 315. Its principal critics were Jefferson and the anti-Federalists, and the treaty was not ratified until Aug. 1795, and only after the removal of a clause relating to American trade with the British West Indies.

[5] This enlarged version of Priestley's *Observations on the increase of infidelity* was published in Northumberland, Pennsylvania, and reprinted for Joseph Johnson in London, in 1796. See Letter 613, n. 8.

[6] The Hackney College committee minutes do not survive for the years after 1791. Although the college session was due to end at the beginning of July 1796, it actually ended in June of that year, and the college and grounds were advertised for sale on 23 June 1796; see the *Morning Chronicle* and the *Daily Advertiser* of that date.

[7] Possibly Lindsey wrote 'self' rather than 'sett', although 'sett' is the more likely reading.

[8] Caleb Fleming (1698–1779) was minister of the presbyterian congregation at Bartholomew Close, London, from 1740 to 1753. During the latter part of his ministry there, he moved from an Arian to a Socinian theological position and, according to his friend Sylas Neville, proclaimed his change of opinion in 'a sermon from the first 14 verses of the 1st chapter of John'; *The diary of Sylas Neville 1767–1788*, ed. B. Cozens-Hardy, p. 33. See also William Turner, *Lives of eminent unitarians; with a notice of dissenting academies* (2 vols., London, 1840–3), II, 291. Neville and Turner insisted that Fleming did not alienate any of his hearers by this declaration, although the Bartholomew Close meeting closed shortly thereafter. Fleming then served as minister to the Independent chapel at Pinners Hall, Old Broad Street, London, from 1753 until 1777. There, too, he made no secret of his Socinian convictions; Turner, *Eminent unitarians*, pp. 291–2.

618. To ROBERT MILLAR   **19 DECEMBER 1795**

Text:	DWL, MS 12.46 (8).
Printed:	Graham, 'Unhappy country', 140–2 (two sentences from second paragraph ('Dr Priestleys Observations … vilified'); third, fourth and fifth paragraphs).
Addressed:	To/Mr Robt Millar/Merchant/Dundee
Postmark:	Postmark missing.

London. Decr. 19. 1795

Dear Sir,

In expectation of a frank, for which I have waited some days to convey a few lines to you, I sit down to acknowlege the receit of a very acceptable letter and of a bill for £5 inclosed in it.[1]

I am vexed to find that the parcell of books was such a long time in it's voyage to Dundee. I hope you will put me in a way to send the next by a speedier passage. The tracts at any time sent for your kind acceptance are only such things as we are in the habit of dispersing, and are happy when we have reason to believe they fall into hands that will turn them to good account and make the use of them we wish. But as your generous mind is not satisfied with being thus on the receiving hand altogether, you shall in general be obeyed, and the money you have sent shall be expended for you as far as we are able to judge in such a way as you would like. You shall have a large assortment of the little tracts recommended by my wife and which you so much approve, together with a few others that are come out since from the same mint.[2] I think my wife told you that some very valuable characters, and many learned and ingenious, were engaged in the labour of this undertaking to set forth small tracts for the edification of their Xtian brethren who might not have leisure or capacity for longer works, and without mixing doctrinal points, keeping chiefly to what is practical. They have not always observed the rule, but you will have sent by us such of em only as we ourselves chuse to circulate: although if curiosity sh^d prompt to see all they publish, a copy of each of those which we do not circulate shall be sent, and they will be of very little cost. Indeed twenty shillings will furnish, we think, an ample store of these little publications for you at once: so that I must beg you to let me know any thing that you would wish to have sent which may be of greater amount, either for your own use, or for that of others. Dr Priestleys Observations on the Increase of Infidelity, which I have very lately reprinted here I shall certainly desire you to receive from the Editor.[3] I have sent him Mr Paine's second part of the Age of reason, but it is written in such a manner, with such gross and unlearned ignorance of the subject, and with such a series of virulent abuse, that it will not be easy to make a reply to it: tho' I expect our friend will be desirous of vindicating, prophets, apostles, and writers so unworthily vilified. I shall send this second part of the Age of Reason, as you desire, and along with it Mr Wakefields answer, which is too much in Mr Paines own way, but M^r W's ardent mind was provoked by the shameful attack on the friends he loved and esteemed, and could not resist the impulse of retaliating on the aggressor.[4]

What a ferment has this unhappy country of ours been in since the begining of Novr. when your letter was written, and the two fatal bills were brought in, which two days since were passed into laws, and had the royal assent by comission.[5] The Duke of Leeds[6] and L^d. Thurlow[7] are said to have tried each their influence with a great personage[8] to stop them in time, but could not succeed; though they urged that the bills were notoriously not so much for his safety, as that of his ministers.

The die however is now cast, and what will be the issue no one can tell. There certainly was a much greater opposition to the bills whilst they were pending, than the ministry expected, or others thought of, considering the suddenness of the measure and the unexampled rapidity with which it was hurried thro' the two houses.

Some bold measure also for the public at this momentous juncture is expected from the Whig-Club, which meets to day, by extraordinary appointment, to deliberate what is to be done, especially if their own meeting should be found to be within the restraint of these new laws.[9] Good, even of the best kind, virtue and the knowlege and spread of divine truth and the gospel, I have no doubt will in the end be produced by these commotions in our own and in all the countries around us. In the mean time, may we all be directed to act the right part and fill our places so as to approve ourselves to the Sovereign master who appointed them for us. You woud be pleased with M[r] Fox's reflections more than once on the injurious banishm[t] of our friends to Botany Bay.[10] I hope soon to have an opportunity of sending M[r] James Ellis's letter, to a friend at Portsmouth.[11]

I cannot remember the like period, when my wife and I have enjoyed a greater share of health, than from the time that she had been a few weeks in Yorkshire to the present hour. We hope we may conclude the same of M[rs] Millar and yourself, and her sister.[12] I had a letter from and wrote to M[r] W. Christie on his embarking for Virginia.[13] I hope you have good accounts of that most worthy man. I am always, Dear Sir, affectionately Yours

T. Lindsey

P.S. Your account of the deficiency of your harvest was very acceptable to several intelligent friends, who are glad to know *facts*, in such cases.[14] Many are not without fears of great distress on that account, if the war go on; and they see nothing to persuade the contrary.

---

1   This letter from Millar to Lindsey, with the accompanying bill, seems not to have survived.

2   It is not clear which tracts Hannah Lindsey recommended, although it can be assumed that they were items from the Unitarian Society's portfolio. It is also an interesting example of the initiatives which she took in collaborating with her husband in the promotion of unitarianism.

3   See Letter 613, n. 8. Lindsey was the editor of the London reprint of Priestley's *Observations on the increase of infidelity*, and of several London reprints of American editions of Priestley's later works.

4   In his *Reply to Thomas Paine's second part of the age of reason*, Wakefield wrote (p. vi) 'I am not acquainted with such a compound of vanity and ignorance as Thomas Paine, in the records of literary history.'

5   See Letter 616, n. 2.

6   Francis Godolphin Osborne (1751–99), marquess of Carmarthen and from 1789, 5th duke of Leeds, was foreign secretary from 1783 to 1791.

7   See Letter 616, n. 3.

8   George III.

9   An 'extraordinary general meeting' of the whig club of England meeting was held on 19 Dec. 1795, at the Crown and Anchor tavern in the Strand. There were speeches by the chairman of the meeting, Thomas Erskine, and by Fox and the duke of Bedford. The meeting resolved to form an association to seek the repeal of the Seditious Meetings and Treasonable Practices Acts, and to appoint a committee charged with organizing a form of association to that end. There is a detailed account of the proceedings in the *Morning Chronicle*, 20 Dec. 1795.

10   Fox made these comments, with particular reference to Palmer and Muir, in the house of commons on 30 Nov. 1795, when opposing the motion for the house to resolve itself into a committee of the whole house on the Treasonable Practices bill on 30 Nov. 1795; Cobbett, *Parl. hist.*, XXXII, 499.

11 The friend at Portsmouth was Russell Scott. Lindsey sent James Ellis's letter to him. Ellis's letter itself (presumably to Lindsey) appears not to have survived.

12 See Letter 590, n. 10.

13 William Christie (1750–1823) and his family emigrated to America in Aug. 1795. He and his family lived at first at Philadelphia, then moved to Winchester (Virginia), to Northumberland (where he lived from 1801 to 1806), and thereafter lived in Pennsylvania and New Jersey. Letters from Lindsey to Christie seem not to have survived; however, there is a letter from Christie to Lindsey, dated Glasgow, 12 Dec. 1794, in DWL, MS 24.86 (12).

14 For the high prices of grain in Dundee and the adjacent areas, following the poor harvest of 1795, see Christopher A. Whatley, 'Roots of 1790s radicalism: reviewing the economic and social background', in *Scotland in the age of the French Revolution*, ed. Bob Harris (Edinburgh, 2005), pp. 35–6. It has been noted that although there were food riots in the Dundee area in 1795 and 1796, there were no prosecutions of inhabitants of Dundee before the Edinburgh high court between Jan. 1792 and Feb. 1796; see David G. Barrie, 'Urban order in Georgian Dundee c. 1770–1820', in *Dundee. Renaissance to Enlightenment*, ed. Charles McKean, Bob Harris and Christopher Whatley (Dundee, 2009), p. 228.

619. To WILLIAM TAYLEUR   27 DECEMBER 1795

Text: JRUL, Lindsey Letters, vol. II, no. 89.
Addressed: To/William Tayleur Esqr/Shrewsbury
Endorsed: Decr 27 – 1795
Postmarked: Postmark missing.

London. Decr. 27. 1795.

Dear Sir,

I cannot say how much we are gratified by Mr Wood taking the trouble to call upon us and acquaint us with so many things that we were desirous to know, of the state of your own health, of your worthy minister and his family, and of the church of your happy planting and which has been lately so much rent by the hasty unconcocted speculations of an ingenuous but overweening young man, who in the very short space of a very few months, could overleap the bounds of christianity and approach the confines of atheism. His escape from such depths of error, will depend upon the society he falls into and the encouragement he finds in it.[1] Some, though not all the causes of the unbelief of the day, I think Dr Priestley well develops in his Observations &c. which I hope you have before this rec^d. from Mr Johnson by way of Mr Eddowes.[2] In all the letters of this our most excellent friend, as in all his writings, this turn and temper of the times to reject all divine revelation, gives him deep concern, and calls forth all his energies to counteract it. A great part of a letter which Mr Belsham received from him a few days since is filled with it, and particularly with wonder at so many young men among liberal dissenters, turning their backs either on christianity or the ministry.[3] Ambition, and love of ease and of the world, I hope I am not uncandid in imagining that I perceive to be the motives with the greater part of whom I have had any knowlege. If objections of a serious nature to the gospel have weighed with them and produced so great a change, nothing would be more useful than to lay these open before the public. And this I have mentioned to more than one person. "I am labouring at my *Church history*, says our friend, in this last account of himself, and before winter be over, expect to have brought the outline of it to the Reformation. I have already brought it to the conclusion of the Council of Constance.[4] At present I am very busy with some experiments, which promise well. They seem to be almost decisive against the most essential principle of the French system".[5]

I do not know whether I mentioned in my last, that Mrs Vaughan had rec^d a letter lately from Mrs Priestley, recounting that she had been ill of a dangerous intermittent fever, and that her youngest son, Henry was not recovered from an attack of the same. But Dr Priestleys lette[r], dated, Octr. 27, the last that has come from Northumberland, taking no notice of either the one or the other, we presume the disease has not been of any great consequence and is quite over.[6]

I should be glad for Mr Rowe to know, that Mr Wellbeloved is expected from York this week in his way to Diss in Suffolk, as a Candidate for the school and congregation there, filled by Mr Barbauld who was succeeded by Dr Phillips who now quits it at Lady Day; a place where both prospered so far as to acquire each a handsome fortune of some thousand pounds, in which I hope Mr Wellbeloved will be equally successful, as he has a growing family, and neither of his predecessors any children.[7] I wish it the more, because Mr Wellbeloved has a soul above all thoughts of gain for his chief object, with a zeal for the truth most enlightened, which disposes him to go out of the common road, and labour in season and out of season to benefit mankind. His friend Arthur Aikin would not long continue in his present *egarements*[8] as the french say, if he were to consort altogether with him.

My wife presents her most kind respects. We desire to be particularly remembered to M^r and Mrs Rowe, with all good wishes for them and their family. I remain ever, Dear Sir Your truly obliged and affectionate servant

T. Lindsey.

---

1   This refers to Arthur Aikin.

2   This is a reference to Joshua Eddowes, printer and bookseller at Shrewsbury. For Priestley's *Observations on infidelity*, see Letter 613, n. 8.

3   This was probably Priestley's letter to Thomas Belsham of 30 Aug. 1795, which deplored the 'lukewarmness' of those who had abandoned the prospect of becoming 'a public preacher of Unitarian Christianity'; Rutt, I, 316.

4   For Priestley's discussion of the Council of Constance (1414–18) see his *General history of the Christian church from the fall of the western empire*, II, 472–88.

5   These are almost exact quotations from Priestley's letter to Belsham, dated Nothumberland, 27 Oct. 1795; DWL, MS 24.86 (2).

6   This was Priestley's letter to Belsham of 27 Oct. 1795; see n. 5, above. Henry Priestley died on 11 Dec. 1795; see Letter 623. I have not located this letter of Mary Priestley. Possibly 'Mrs Vaughan' was Sarah, née Manning (d. 1835), the wife of Benjamin Vaughan, who remained in London after her husband's flight to France in 1794 when facing the prospect of interrogation by the privy council as a result of his association with William Stone (see Letter 574, n. 3).

7   Rochemont Barbauld was minister at Palgrave, where he and his wife Anna Laetitia Barbauld also ran a school, from 1774 to 1786. He was succeeded there in both capacities by Nathaniel Philips (1757–1842), a former student of Hoxton Academy, who held the degree of DD from Edinburgh University. In 1796, Phillips succeeded James Tayler as minister to a dissenting congregation at Walthamstow, Essex, and served there until 1801. He was succeeded at Palgrave not by Charles Wellbeloved but by John Tremlett (d. 1836), previously assistant minister to the Barton Street congregation, Gloucester, who served as minister at Palgrave from 1796 to 1802, and at Hapton, Norfolk, from 1802 to 1836.

8   I.e. 'égarements', mental aberrations.

620. To WILLIAM ALEXANDER   29 DECEMBER 1795

Text: 'Letters of the Rev. Theophilus Lindsey. No. VI', *UH*, II, 74
                   (27 Sept. 1862), 330.

Note: This is the only section of this letter printed by the *UH*; the manuscript seems not to have survived. The ellipsis at the beginning of the extract indicates that this was not the beginning of the original letter. The words in square brackets are those of the editor of the letters for the *UH*.

London, Dec. 29th, 1795.

* * This work of Dr. Priestley's [*"Observations on the Causes of Infidelity"*] will, I think, tend in part to account for that too common rejection of Christianity by those who are called rational believers, which gives you so much disturbance, and cannot but be a subject of real concern to all that love the truth, believing the virtue and final happiness of mankind connected with it. The number of those who have of late shown themselves unbelievers among rational Dissenters, I apprehend to be much magnified. As far as I know anything of them, they are all young men, who had not given themselves time to consider the subject in reprobation of which they so hastily decided. In some of them I observe much fickleness, with no small spice of ambition and love of the world. To such minds the office of a teacher of the gospel in these times must be peculiarly irksome; and its being discarded by such can be no discredit to it, however it may be a stumbling-block to some weak persons. I should suspect that the young man you mention as having lately turned away from the gospel, never saw it in its true light, as a divine plan to bring mankind to perfection in virtue and happiness for ever.[1] With such views of it, he never could have suffered himself to ridicule the Scriptures that treat of it.

---

[1]   The non-survival of Alexander's letter means that the 'young man' whom he had mentioned cannot be identified. Of the young men to whom Lindsey referred, one was probably Arthur Aiken; others probably included some of Wakefield's former pupils at Hackney and the associates of William Godwin, who was himself educated at Hoxton Academy but had become an unbeliever by the 1790s; he was aged thirty-nine in Dec. 1795.

621. To RUSSELL SCOTT   30 DECEMBER 1795

Text: Scott Coll.
Printed: McLachlan, 'Lindsey to Scott', 122 (short quotations from sixth paragraph).
Addressed: To/The Rev^d. Russell Scott/Portsmouth
Endorsed: Jan^{ry}. 1st – 96
Postmarked: Postmark illegible.

London. Decr. 30. 1795.

Dear Sir,

I have waited till the end of the month to thank you for your very welcome letter[1] at the same time that I beg your acceptance of Dr Priestley's Observations &c, and through you I would beg to present the other copy to Mr Porter, as a mark of the sincere esteem I have for him, and wch. encreases the more I see of him.

Our transatlantic friend has I think well accounted for the present rejection of Xtianity in some instances.[2] I am not quite so candid as you with respect to some you hint at who have turned their back on X^{ty} and the ministry at the same time, within our own knowlege. Unperceived by themselves I think I see a secret love of ease and of the world, with ambitious views in others, making a strong part of the character, and quite incompatible with the humble teacher of the gospel among despised dissenters.

One of a very different caste is to breakfast with us to morrow morning, Mr Wellbeloved, one of those who left the Academy at Hummerton and went with several others to Daventry.[3] He has been about two years at York, an Assistant to Mr Cappe, at York, for whom he does the whole duty. I know a little of him after he came to Hackney with Mr Belsham, and saw him much this summer when we were ten days at York. In zeal to promote true piety and virtue, in improved talents, and indefatigable industry and labours he ranks very high. He is coming to Town, in his way to Diss or Palgrave in Suffolk, where Mr Barbauld was minister and had a school, and was succeeded by Dr Phillips, and this last being chosen at Walthhamptow [*sic*] in Mr Fawcitt's place, Mr Wellbeloved is going to offer himself a candidate, as he has no certainty at York, has a young wife and growing family and her friends are anxious for their not being at a distance of 200 miles from them.[4] I wish he may succeed as I am persuaded he will fill his station usefully as a Minister and Schoolmaster. Both of those who have been there before are said to have amassed some thousands of pounds in a very short time. I wish M^r W, if he succeeds, may have as much of that saving knowlege as he ought to have.[5]

I am now to thank you for your kind care and attention in respect of Mr Palmer, to whom you have said and done for me every thing that I could wish and you had in your power. And I depend upon your acquainting me as early as you can with the time of the next Transports sailing, when I shall call upon Mr Gurney and concert what I can best transmit to him, at the same time that I shall write at large to him.

I hear that Mr Jardine had actually given notice of his quitting Bath, upon the obstinate perseverance of a few in the congregation, not to open the new chapel; but that this proposal of his to resign has worked the desired effect, and the cause of difference will be removed. Mr Hobhouse is his great friend, and is one of the persons who is most desirous of keeping him.[6]

On Sunday last,[7] after morning service, there was a meeting of the congregation belonging to Prince's street to consider of a successor to Dr Kippis. Mr Jervis, Mr Manning of Exeter, and Dr Toulmin of Taunton were the persons named. The last appeared to be excluded on account of his being an Antipædobaptist; which seems narrow and unreasonable, as he w^d be able easily to find those who would perform that ceremony. Nothing however was determined with respect to any of the Candidates, as many of the members, who were persons of some consequence, were absent in the country. Of the two others, Mr Jervis would surely have my vote, if I was a party to be consulted.[8] Mrs Kippis is tolerably well, but so infirm, that it is thought she will not last very long. A sister that came out of Lincolnshire to see her since the Doctor's death, died soon after her return of a rupture of a blood vessell.[9] I am told that they cannot reckon upon the income of Prince's Street as more than £120 a year, though the Doctor made of it £170 or £180. I thought it had been more advantageous. But it seems the numbers have of late diminished much, altho' some continued their subscription to the Doctor after they ceased to be his hearers.

A letter from Dr Priestley this last week gave us particular satisfaction on acc^t of his taking no notice of a dangerous intermittent fever which Mrs Priestley and his youngest son had been ill of, which satisfies us that it had been exaggerated in an account of it which had come over in a private letter. For the rest, he himself continues remarkably, and happy in being continually employed; in his philosophical pursuits, which promise well, as he says; and in his theological, having brought down his ecclesiastical history, fairly written out, to the council of Constance; and looking to fill up the outline of it to the era of the Reformation, in the course of the winter.[10]

We beg both of us to be remembred most kindly to Mrs Scott, my wife to yourself, with all good wishes for you both and your lovely children, who deservedly make up so much of your happiness. You will be so good as to say with our respects to Mr Porter, that we are particularly sorry for the cause that has prevented his coming to town, and debard us of the pleasure of seeing him.[11] Were it not for the uncertainty of any thing coming from Mr Johnson's shop, when it might reach you, my wife, to whose good managem^t I owe everything would have sent a small inclosure in this packet, merely to shew our good will and to round off some corners at the end of the year; but will take the opportunity when the members come back to Town;[12] till which time I will not trouble you to give any notice of the arrival of this. I inclose a letter from his father to James Ellis, which you will be kind to send to him by the next transport.[13] It came to me, from a merchant of Dundee, whom I know by person a little, and frequently hear from. Though a layman, he has the courage, with one or two men, but he principally, to officiate every sunday and keep up Mr Palmers congregation.[14] They want much a constant minister, who could devote himself more to the work, but cannot afford to engage one.

Believe me affectionately Yours

T. Lindsey.

1   Scott's letter to Lindsey seems not to have survived.

2   This work was Priestley's *Answer to Mr Paine's Age of reason*; it was reprinted in 1796. Priestley's explanations for 'the present rejection of Christianity in some instances' included a discontinuation of reading the scriptures (partly as a result of natural religion) and the contempt for religion generated by popery. He added that unbelievers, following Hume, dismissed miracles without properly studying the historical evidence; and he also cited the ascription of the rise of Christianity to 'priestcraft' and the imposition of superstition upon a credulous people (this was a hit against Gibbon).

3   Charles Wellbeloved was a student at the Homerton Academy from 1785 to 1787, when he moved to Hackney College (he did not transfer to the Daventry Academy, although his friend David Jardine, subsequently minister at Bath, did). Wellbeloved became assistant minister to Newcome Cappe at St Saviourgate chapel, York, in Jan. 1792.

4   For Nathaniel Philips, see Letter 619, n. 7. For Joseph Fawcett and his resignation, see Letter 604, n. 6.

5   Wellbeloved did not become minister at Diss or Palgrave and remained at York until his death in 1858. The two 'predecessors' at Palgrave to whom Lindsey referred were Benjamin Davis (d. 1784), who served there from 1769 to 1774, and Rochemont Barbauld (see Letter 619, n. 7).

6   David Jardine remained minister at Bath until his death in 1797; see Letter 608, n. 5. Possibly the 'new chapel' was that to which Lindsey referred in his letter to Scott in Letter 507. Benjamin Hobhouse was a regular attender at dissenting worship in this period.

7   I.e. Sunday 27 Dec. 1795.

8   The successor to Kippis as minister of the Princes Street, Westminster, congregation was Thomas Jervis.

9   Elizabeth Kippis, née Bott, died on 17 Nov. 1796; *Gent. Mag.*, LXVI, ii (1796), 971. Her sister was Esther Bott of Kirton, Lincolnshire, and she is named as a beneficiary in the will of Elizabeth Kippis, TNA: PRO PROB 11/1281, fos. 274r–276r.

10   This letter from Priestley to Lindsey, dated 9 Nov. 1795, may be found in DWL, MS 12.13, and is partly quoted in Rutt, I, 319–21. As Lindsey noted, the letter made no mention of the illnesses of Priestley's wife and son.

11   The records of the High Street chapel, Portsmouth (TNA: RG4/564), do not reveal what had prevented William Joseph Porter from coming to town. Possibly the cause was a professional rather than a family commitment.

12   The parliamentary session had begun on 29 Oct. 1795; both houses adjourned from 24 Dec. 1795 until 2 Feb. 1796.

13   This letter to James Ellis from his father of the same name seems not to have survived.

14   The merchant who kept up Palmer's congregation at Dundee was Robert Millar.

622. To CHRISTOPHER WYVILL   4 JANUARY 1796

Text: NYRO, ZFW 7/2/95/38, Wyvill of Constable Burton MSS.
Printed: Ditchfield, 'Lindsey–Wyvill correspondence', 172 (fifth
                paragraph).
Addressed: [In Hannah Lindsey's hand] To/The Rev^d. Christopher Wyville
                /Burton-Hall/near Bedale/Yorkshire
Postmarked: JA 4 96

London. Jany. 4. 1796.

Dear Sir,

I was highly gratified with your kind comunication ten days ago, duplicates of which I received on Saturday and have disposed of them as you desired.[1] Dr Blackburne desired me to return his thanks and to tell you that he had borrowed a copy of a friend before and had read it to many, who wanted to see the Advertisement, and how you delivered yourself at York. The spirit and firmness which you shewed in the Advertisement, and in your second speech to the Meeting, would shame and discourage your unworthy calumniators and defeat their purposes by being published and dispersed, and I rejoice to hear they have already had this effect in part.[2]

A Gentleman called upon us a few days ago, who was in York at the time, and had the curiosity to go into the Castle Yard, where he said there was a great deal of oratory which he expected, and not a little false colouring and groundless vaunting which he did not expect, and shall never think well of Mr Wilberforce again.[3]

I am glad you do not give up a good cause. The person abovenamed is very much of your sentiments concerning it, and is persuaded it has of late and will gain ground. So that I trust it was substantial comfort that you administred at Copgrove and that our friend, vir prisca fide, was revived by it.[4] Saturday which brought me your letter with his passport brought one from the D. of N ___ nd at Bath, who is already a cripple from the gout, which began its attack at 8 years old; in which the first words are; "Many thanks for Mr Wyvill's publication relating to the honourable part he has lately taken, and which I approve very much. It is his lot, as of many before him, bene facere male audire.[5] He has merited much from his country, and has seen what was preparing for us by his old friend the minister,[6] sooner than it was discovered by other people. I rejoice much that the opposers of these bills mean not to let things rest here, but to pledge themselves solemnly to the Public, that they will use every legal and constitutional method to procure their repeal. To this measure they shall certainly have my approbation and concurrence."[7] I thought you would like to see all he said upon the subject.

I do not understand that Lord Stanhope has got this last little justificatory piece, as one who came from Chevening yesterday told us he thinks he should have known it, as he shewed him the Address to the Freeholders which you had sent him.[8] In about ten days or a fortnight his Lordship will present to the king, an Address for peace, signed by twenty thousand freeholders.[9]

Good Dr Heberden had an ugly accident sunday week in St James's chapel.[10] As he was entring in his foot catched upon the carpet, which threw him down with such violence, that he dislocated his thigh bone. It was with difficulty set by two surgeons, and he is said to be doing well; but at 85 such accidents can never wholly be recovered from.[11] Not many weeks ago when he called upon us, he walked down our steps upright like a stripling without taking hold of the rails. It falls to the lot of few to be so useful and to do so much good as he has done. Fewer still have the happy disposition.

We rejoice that you are all in so good a way, and your amiable lady in particular in the happy groupe; to whom with yourself, my wife desires to join in sending due respects and wishes of health and every thing good for you all for many long years to come. I remain always, Dear Sir, Your much obliged and faithful servant

T. Lindsey.

By a letter from Dr Priestley, dated the 10th of November, received a few days since, and quite happy, employed in his experiments, which as he says, promise well, and in compiling a continuation of his ecclesiastical history; two volumes more of it will soon be put to the Press at Northumberland Town.[12]

1   Wyvill sent to Lindsey and others copies of a printed two-sheet document entitled *The address of the Rev. Christopher Wyvill to the worthy freeholders of Yorkshire, dated November 27th, 1795, with his speeches at York on the 1st of December 1795, &c annexed, submitted by Mr Wyvill to the consideration of the public* (York, Dec. 1795). The Saturday to which Lindsey referred was 2 Jan. 1796.

2   Wyvill's two speeches at the York meeting on 1 Dec. 1795, denouncing the Seditious Meetings and Treasonable Practices Acts, may be found on p. 2 of Wyvill's *Address*.

3   For Wilberforce's part in the York meeting of 1 Dec. 1795, see Letter 616, n. 6. Probably the gentleman who informed Lindsey about these events was Thomas Duncombe; see n. 4, below, and Letter 634.

4   Copgrove, near Knaresborough, Yorkshire, was the residence of Henry Duncombe, MP for Yorkshire from 1780 to 1796. He did not seek re-election at the general election of 1796, on grounds of health, although his friend Wyvill urged him to offer himself for the county again. 'Vir prisca fide' may be translated as 'a man of antique faith (or trustworthiness)'; antique in this sense signifies 'belonging to the good old days'. I am grateful to Mr David Powell for advice on this point.

5   To do good [and] to hear ill; or, more idiomatically, to do good and yet to be ill-spoken of. I am grateful to Mr David Powell for advice on this point.

6   William Pitt, with whom Wyvill had been on friendly terms, and whose previous reforming measures he had supported.

7   This letter to Lindsey from his former pupil Hugh Percy, formerly Lord Warkworth and from 1786 2nd duke of Northumberland, seems not to have survived. Although rarely attending the house of lords, Northumberland was a critic of Pitt's ministry and supported Wyvill's reforming efforts.

8   Possibly this 'last little justificatory piece' which Stanhope had not received was *The correspondence of the Rev. C. Wyvill with the Right Honourable William Pitt. Part I*, a work published in Newcastle in 1796 and sold in London by Joseph Johnson. For *The address of the Rev. Christopher Wyvill to the worthy freeholders of Yorkshire*, see n. 1, above. The messenger from Chevening was probably Jeremiah Joyce.

9   This address for peace and for the repeal of the Seditious Meetings and Treasonable Practices Acts was approved at a meeting of the county of Kent, held at Maidstone on 5 Dec. 1795. The address itself and the series of associated resolutions were printed in the *Morning Chronicle*, 8 Dec. 1795. According to this report the meeting was 'by far the most numerous and respectable ever known in that county'. Lindsey probably learnt more about the meeting from Jeremiah Joyce, who was present and spoke in favour of the address. See also Aubrey Newman, *The Stanhopes of Chevening. A family biography* (London, 1969), p. 160. Stanhope duly presented the address in Jan. 1796.

10 William Heberden the elder was a regular worshipper at the Chapel Royal, St James's. Although in 1761 he had declined George III's offer of appointment as physician to Queen Charlotte, he retained many connexions with the royal family and his son William Heberden the younger (1767–1845) was appointed physician in ordinary to Queen Charlotte in 1795.

11 Born on 13 Aug. 1710, Heberden was indeed aged eighty-five at the time of this letter.

12 Possibly Lindsey referred here to Priestley's letter to him, dated Northumberland, 9 Nov. 1795, and printed in Rutt, I, 319–21, in which Priestley wrote that with his books and instruments around him, he was happy in his employment, and that he was making good progress with his 'Church History'. On 10 Nov. 1795, Priestley wrote to William Russell at Boston, but it is unlikely that Lindsey had seen that letter by 4 Jan. 1796; Rutt, I, 321–2.

623. To RUSSELL SCOTT   **8 JANUARY 1796**

Text: Scott Coll.
Addressed: To/The Rev^d. Russell Scott/Portsmouth
Postmarked: Postmark missing.

Note: Lindsey did not give the year of this letter. However, the year was clearly 1796. 8 Jan. 1796 was a Friday and Lindsey referred in the second paragraph of the letter to three years of war; for Britain, the war began officially on 1 Feb. 1793.

London. friday night Jany. 8.

Dear Sir,

I am sorry any thing like a preface or mention beforehand was made of the trifle that comes herein inclosed. You will accept it merely as a subscription which we should be happy to make if we were of your audience, or as my wife bid[s] me say, to round off some hard corners in these dear times.[1]

We hope better will come soon, and that you will enjoy sounder health in them, as in the Telegraph to day, there is an account from Paris, certain, that the French and Austrians have agreed to a cessation of arms, which though but for a short time may be a prelude to a total one.[2] And I could not help noting yesterday when I was in the city, that some merchants of rather intimate connection with the minister, and who have always espoused him, changed the language they have used for three years past, and directly asserted, that we must now have peace, and that if not immediately, it would take place in 3 or 4 months without fail.

It may be, the Emperor, perceiving that we cannot hold out long to support him at such vast expence and fearing a reverse, may be willing to suspend a little and try what terms may be likely to be offered.[3] Certainly in London, the number of those who are displeased with the war, and particularly with the prodigious sums lavished on the Austrians increases every day, and with it their dislike to the Minister.

You received I hope a letter from me with the Monthlies from Mr Johnson.[4] In it I am not certain I mentioned a letter just rec^d from Dr Priestley, containing an account of Mrs P. having been overtaken with a bad intermittent fever, which had hung long upon her, but he himself had escaped it, and continued in the most perfect health. These particulars, and his happiness in the pursuit of his studies, in making experiments with some success, and in the continuation of his Ecclesiastical History, of which he has two more volumes transcribed for the press, were the substance of his comunications.[5] I am glad his Answer to Paine has sold off here, of which there were first printed 750 if not a thousand; and we are going to the Press again, which I am sure Mr Johnson would not engage in, was he not pretty sure of a sale.[6] And I think this looks not unfavourable to the cause of Xtianity, that a work should find purchasers, which *alone* confutes most of the modern arguments for Infidelity, and particularly those of the greater part of the modern Seceders from it, of whom I have any knowlege; and this amidst the vast prejudices against the author, which are still kept up with unrelenting violence. I was advised to insert more at length, in *my* Preface, the passages applauded by the British Critic, in the Review of the vile attack on the Doctor: but on farther consideration, I determined not to soil the page with such shocking abuse, and the rather, as the ignorance and prejudices of the greater part are so inveterate, that they would pay more regard to it than to any vindication of him that was offered.[7]

We hope you and you[r] lady and little family have all begun the new year in tolerable health, and will all live long and be happy and useful – our kind respects attend yourselves and am always Dear Sir, affectionately Yours

T. Lindsey

<hr>

1   Perhaps this was a small gift of money.
2   On 5 Jan. 1796, the *Tomahawk or Censor General* described *The Telegraph* as 'the most shameless of all the Opposition papers' and rejected as an exaggeration its report of an Austrian defeat on the Rhine, with its implication that the Austrians must soon sue for peace with France. I have not found the specific *Telegraph* report of 8 Jan. 1796 to which Lindsey referred. France and Austria did not conclude a peace until the Treaty of Campo Formio in Oct. 1797.
3   The Holy Roman Emperor was Francis II (1768–1835), the last holder (1792–1806) of that title.
4   This was Lindsey's letter to Scott of 30 Dec. 1795 (Letter 621). For the 'monthlies', see Letter 580, n. 2.
5   This probably refers to Priestley's letter to Lindsey of 6 Dec. 1795, partly printed in Rutt, I, 322–5; it referred to Mary Priestley's recovery from 'a long illness' and reported that Priestley himself was in tolerable health.
6   For this work, see Letter 621, n. 2.
7   The 'vile attack' on Priestley, to which Lindsey referred, was the anonymous *Observations on the emigration of Dr Joseph Priestley, and on the several addresses delivered to him on his arrival at New York* (Philadelphia, reprinted London, 1794). Among other allegations, the pamphlet accused Priestley of hypocrisy for denouncing the Birmingham rioters yet applauding the storming of the Bastille. It was favourably reviewed by the high church and loyalist *British Critic*, IV (Nov. 1794), 498–503. In his preface to Priestley's *Answer to Paine*, Lindsey indeed refrained from responding to the *British Critic*'s attack on Priestley.

624. To WILLIAM TAYLEUR   7 MARCH 1796

Text: JRUL, Lindsey Letters, vol. II, no. 90.
Printed: McLachlan, *Letters*, p. 134 (first sentence of fifth paragraph).
Addressed: [In Hannah Lindsey's hand] To/William Tayleur Esqʳ./ Shrewsbury
Endorsed: March 7ᵗʰ – 96
Postmarked: MR 7 96

London. March. 7. 1796.

Dear Sir,

I have refrained from writing a week or two in the hope of receiving a letter from Dʳ Priestley himself, that I might be able to inform you what effect the unexpected loss of his beloved youngest son had upon him, and was likely to have upon his present situation and pursuits, on all which accounts we are anxious about him: but nothing is yet come from that quarter to London, except the very short note from Philadelphia, which related the melancholy event, and that it was owing to taking cold after a fever.[1]

I have however within these ten days had a very agreeable letter from Mʳ H. Toulmin, from Lexington in Kentucky, which has relieved us much with respect to him and his family, by the assurance that the heat of that climate the last summer, was far from being oppressive and unwholesome as the preceding year, so that he entertains a good hope that they shall have no reason to object to it on that score. And though he meets with opposition to his endeavours to serve the colony from the ignorance, bigotry and jealousy of individuals, particularly as being an englishman, there are those who see his very superior talents and merits and the meekness of wisdom, tho' firmness at the same time, with which he conducts himself, that I have no doubted [*sic*] of his being supported, and turning out an eminent blessing to that state, even in civil, as well as moral and religious views.[2]

You will be pleased with the following extract of his letter, where he is mentioning that there was some little uncertainty, whether he might not quit his situation, and go to live upon and cultivate some new land, which he, and his "good friend ["], as he calls him, "old Col[l]. Hart, an unitarian had lately purchased from the state at a very cheap rate.[3]

"But wherever I may be, says he, or however I may be otherwise engaged, I feel no disposition to turn my back on the office of a christian preacher. Indeed, every day seems to shew me, that it is my duty to bear the best testimony I can to religion in general, and particularly to rational views of religion. Scepticism seems to have its day: but I trust it will turn out to be nothing more than the dawn of that day, which will introduce pure christianity in the place of that superstition and mysticism, which hath caused a long dark night in the moral hemisphere". After this he proceeds to mention the judicious and rational methods of instruction and information which he was pursuing, and which must in time have a happy effect.[4]

The other day I called upon a friend of the B[p]. of Llandaffs, who told me [he] had been perusing some of the Sheets of his answer to Paine's second part, and spoke in the highest terms of it. It seems it is drawn up in the form of letters, and in the same small size as his answer to Gibbon.[5] From the author himself, and from the character given me of the work by a person to whose judgment I deferr much,[6] I flatter myself, that it will be of use in these days of cavil against Divine revelation.

We shall hope to be favoured with a few lines from M[r] Rowe to inform us how you bear this change to winter, and how he himself and his lady and family are. But I beg you will tell him, that I do not expect or desire this from him, till I shall acknowlege his last letter, which, if all be well, I shall do in three or four days.[7] My wife sends her kind respects to yourself, and desires with me to be kindly rememberd to the friends above-named and to M[r] Wood. We shall be glad, if this new monthly Magazine may in time contribute to put down the Gentlemans which has had such a long and wide reign, and has of late especially contributed to poison the principles of the nation, and asperse all good men.[8] *Cosmogunia* is it seems, M[rs] Barbauld's, and very ingenious.[9] I honour her most particularly for contriving to bear testimony to D[r]. Priestley's eminent and injured worth.[10]

May the Almighty continue to preserve you, my friend, in tolerable ease and comfort, and in usefulness to your fellow creatures. I am always, Dear Sir, Your much obliged and faithful affectionate servant T. Lindsey

1   This is a reference to the death of Henry Priestley on 11 Dec. 1795. For Priestley's letter to Lindsey informing him of the death, dated Northumberland, 17 Dec. 1795, see Rutt, I, 327–9. I have not located the 'very short note from Philadelphia'.

2   This letter from Henry Toulmin to Lindsey seems not to have survived.

3   'Old Col[l] Hart' was Thomas Hart (1730–1808), originally of Virginia, who served as a colonel in the sixth North Carolina regiment during the War of American Independence, and moved to Kentucky in 1794 where he established himself as a landowner, entrepreneur and leading citizen. His daughter Lucretia married the future secretary of state and presidential candidate Henry Clay.

4   In fact Henry Toulmin soon abandoned his ministerial career, became secretary of state for Kentucky and subsequently a judge in the Mississippi territory and a member of the Alabama legislature.

5   This work was Richard Watson's *Apology for the Bible*. For Watson's *An apology for Christianity, in a series of letters addressed to Edward Gibbon, Esq.* (Cambridge, 1776), see Vol. I, Letters 163–5. There is no clue in *Anecdotes of the life of Richard Watson* as to the identity of the friend of the bishop who discussed the book with Lindsey; a possibility is the duke of Grafton.

6 Lindsey did not identify the person upon whose judgment he placed so high a valuation. Obvious
   possibilities include Thomas Belsham, Samuel Shore III and Joshua Toulmin.
7 Lindsey did so on 9 Mar. 1796 (Letter 625).
8 This is a reference to the *MM*, which began publication in 1796; see Letter 640, n. 5. The *Gent. Mag.*
   began publication in Jan. 1731.
9 Lindsey referred here to the short essay entitled 'Dialogue between Madam Cosmogunia, and a
   philosophical enquirer of the 18th century', published in the *MM*, I (Feb. 1796), 19–22. The author
   was indeed Mrs Barbauld; see William McCarthy, *Anna Letitia Barbauld. Voice of the Enlightenment* (Baltimore, 2008), p. 373. Originally written in 1793, the essay is reproduced in *The works
   of Anna Laetitia Barbauld . With a memoir by Lucy Aikin* (2 vols., London, 1825), II, 277–87. The
   'philosophical enquirer' represents Barbauld's opinions.
10 Lindsey referred here to Barbauld's poem 'To Dr Priestley', which sympathized with Priestley after
   the Birmingham riots. It was first published in the *Morning Chronicle* on 8 Jan. 1793, without the
   author's name. See *The poems of Anna Letitia Barbauld*, ed. McCarthy and Kraft, p. 125, 292–3.
   Lindsey reprinted the poem in his preface to Priestley's *An Answer to Mr Paine's Age of reason*, pp.
   xxiv–xv, adding that Milton would have been proud to have written it.

625. To JOHN ROWE   9 MARCH 1796

Text: JRUL, Lindsey Letters, vol. II, no. 91.
Addressed: To/The Revd John Rowe/Shrewsbury
Postmarked: MR 9 96

London. March. 9. 1796

Dear Sir

A few days since I paid my respects to our venerable friend. I did not mention to
him, but presume you have heard of one or two late defections at the college, which
seem to be a consequence of the spirit of scepticism already raised, and of young
men taking upon them to decide on a most important and complicated subject,
without the proper dispositions and before they were competent to form a definitive
judgment concerning it. The debt incurred and the clamours of creditors for their
money, had some time ago brought forward a determination to sell the premises
and break up the seminary at the end of the present session, and this unhappy affair
leaves not one advocate, as I could observe, for it's continuance. At a late meeting of
the committee for taking into consideration Mr Corry's letter signifying the necessity
of resigning his office of classical tutor at Lady day, it was proposed by one or two
to dissolve the society at that time; but this was overruled, and Mr Belsham engaged
to supply his place together with his own to the end of june.[1]

One is shocked at the profaneness no less than the effrontery of the young person,
you hint at, who could be bent upon inserting in a public paper such an indecent
argument against the Being of a God.[2] I guess, it was from that, or a congenial
quarter, that a manuscript was lately offered to a Bookseller to print, ~~in confutation~~
in confutation of Dr Priestleys weak and foolish reasoning, as it was stiled, in his
Observations on the increase of Infidelity. But the offer was refused. I have it from
a party concerned: yet as these things are points of honour in the trade, it will
remain with yourself. We shall see if it gets out under any other protection.[3] It
struck others as well as you, that the Monthly Magazine might have such a bias:
I should hope it would not, as it is likely on the whole to be well conducted. But
I trust that you – especially, who are young, will have your eye upon it, and warn
the public, should any such insidious aim shew itself. I heartily wish that the B^p of
Llandaff may answer the expectations that many have formed of his fully confuting
Mr Paines second part in this work of his that is I am told already nearly printed, will

be worked off on Saturday next, and be ready for sale some part of the following week. Some small portions of it I heard read yesterday, and if all be of the same complexion it will be a valuable book, consisting of near 400 pages, but of the duodecimo size.[4]

To morrow, if all be well, I shall leave a little parcel at Mr Longman's myself, for Mr Tayleur, to be sent in Mr Eddowes' next parcel, which will contain half a dozen copies of a little minikin tract, which I lately received from Mr Freeman of Boston, and pleased me so much, as likely to be seasonable and useful that I have reprinted it.[5] Mr Tayleur, yourself and Mr Wood will do me the favour to accept a copy, and the others will be disposed as you shall think best. When you have seen it, I shall be glad of a few lines to know that you are all well, and particularly, of the state of our excellent friend.

We are happy to have from York such desireable information of Mr Wellbeloved's well-doing. He has taken a larger house at the outskirts of the city, with a garden and field adjoining, and has thirteen day-pupils, at fifteen pounds each, which is much easier for Mrs Wellby[6] than to have the trouble of boarding them.[7] He is particularly suited for that place, which abounds with many young persons, attorneys' clerks &c &c who have the cast of your ---- but yet more modest I would hope. He has a well tempered zeal and fortitude, with an enlightened and strong mind, but with humility and deep piety, two most important requisites in every great and good character, which I fear have not been so cultivated as they ought to have been elsewhere.

I am glad to observe that you keep up your spirits in the midst of the present unfavourable appearances to virtue and true religion, under a persuasion that they and every thing else, are under the best direction, and tending to the good we wish and desire, though we cannot see it.

Be so good as to renew our respects to Mr Tayleur, and tell him that he shall certainly have a few lines from me, as soon as I hear, or any letter comes from Dr Priestley, to tell us how they are after their great loss.[8]

My wife desires to join in all kind regards for Mrs Rowe and yourself and wishes for your little family. I remain always Dear Sir most truly Yours

T. Lindsey.

---

[1] Although the minutes of the Hackney College committee do not survive for the post-1791 period, it is clear that the 'unhappy affair' to which Lindsey referred amounted to allegations of irreligion and radicalism at the college, together with the over-ambitious expenditure which led to the college's financial collapse and closure in 1796. For John Corrie's resignation as classical tutor in 1794, see Letter 575, n. 2. The college's decline, including the 'defections', is recorded, in rather discreet terms, in Williams, pp. 456–75.

[2] Possibly this young person was Arthur Aikin, although neither Lindsey (nor, it seems, Rowe) mentioned his name directly.

[3] It did not 'get out under any other protection' in book or pamphlet form, although Volney published a brief tract entitled *Volney's answer to Doctor Priestley, on his pamphlet, entitled Observations on the increase of infidelity* (Philadelphia, 1797).

[4] This duodecimo edition of Watson's *Apology for the Bible* consisted of 389 pages and cost 4s.

[5] This 'minikin' tract was *Answer to the question*. The author was John Clarke (1755–98), minister of the first church in Boston, Massachusetts, and it was first published in Boston in 1795. According to its title page, the edition printed for Lindsey by Joseph Johnson was the 'sixth' edition and the year of publication was 1797. The work carried (pp. iii–iv) a short advertisement with Lindsey's name. Another edition, described on the title page as 'A new edition' was published by Johnson, also in 1797; it carried the same introduction but with Lindsey's initials, not his name set out in full as in the 'sixth' edition.

[6] Ann, née Kinder (d. 1823), who married Charles Wellbeloved on 1 July 1793.

[7] Wellbeloved began a small school at York in 1794; for his earliest day pupils, paying £15 per annum

each, see David Wykes, 'Wellbeloved, Charles', *ODNB*, LVII, 998–9. In 1796, he moved to a larger house at the end of Gilligate, York, in order to accommodate boarders. In 1799, he bought a house at 38 Monkgate and expanded his school considerably. See Kenrick, *Memoir of Wellbeloved*, pp. 46–7.

8   The 'great loss' was the death of Priestley's youngest son Henry on 11 Dec. 1795.

626. To WILLIAM ALEXANDER   23 MARCH 1796

Text: 'Letters of the Rev. Theophilus Lindsey. No. VI', *UH*, II, 74
                      (27 Sept. 1862), 330.

Note: This is the only section of this letter printed by the *UH*; the manuscript seems not to have survived. The ellipsis at the beginning of the extract printed by the *UH* indicates that this was not the beginning of the original letter. The words in square brackets are those of the editor of the letter for the *UH*.

London, March 23rd, 1796.

* * It has indeed been a most heavy affliction to Dr. Priestley to lose a beloved son [his youngest] of such hopes in all respects; but I have had the happiness of receiving a letter from him within these few days which shows, what could not be doubted, that the tender parents bear their great loss with that piety and resignation which becomes them; and also, what we were rather apprehensive of, that their health is not likely to suffer essentially from it. They had before been engaged to pass some part of the present winter in Philadelphia with Mr. Russell and his family, which would be of great relief to their minds.[1]

1   Probably this refers to Priestley's letter to Lindsey of 6 Dec. 1795, in which he expressed the intention of meeting Russell and his family in Philadelphia; Rutt, I, 325. He told Lindsey in his letter from Philadelphia of 15 Feb. 1796 that he was Russell's guest there; Rutt, I, 332–3.

627. To JOHN ROWE   6 APRIL 1796

Text: JRUL, Lindsey Letters, vol. II, no. 92.
Printed: McLachlan, *Letters*, pp. 122–3 (postscript).
Addressed: To/The Rev^d. J. Rowe/Shrewsbury.
Postmarked: AP 6 96

London. April. 6. 1796.

Dear Sir,

I should have anticipated your last letter most assuredly,[1] for I was under some uneasiness on not hearing from you, if I had not been prevented writing or doing any thing for near ten days by a sort of epidemical cold and fever that has gone about. I was more apprehensive I own of your own indisposition and that of your family, than of any material change in our excellent friend,[2] whom as a kind providence had lent us so long, I was led to hope the blessing would be continued. But we are all in the best hands, and nothing will happen but what is best for him and for all of us. And I trust he will have the great privilege of preserving the tolerable use of his faculties, and of enjoying to the last that sense of the divine presence and goodness which has been his neverfailing comfort and support, and enabled him to be singularly useful in his generation beyond the period comonly allotted to mortals.

I do not write to him, unless you encourage it. I think I sent either him or yourself some account of a letter I had received from Dr Priestley on the event of the death of his youngest son, and of his and Mrs Priestleys christian demeanor and fortitude. But

I am somewhat dubious about it as you take no note whatsoever of it, and therefore shall transcribe a paragraph or two, which shew the state of his mind

"Having had little or no apprehension of danger till near the time, the shock was very great, and being the first event of the kind, I am affected more than I thought I should have been, though I have unspeakable consolation in believing that nothing can befall us without the appointment of the best of Beings, and that we shall meet our departed children and friends in a better state. He is hardly ever out of my thoughts, but much more with respect to another state than this".[3] After which he goes on to mention his freedom from vice, and those good dispositions, which persuade him, that at so early an age as 18, he has the foundation of something in his character on which a good superstructure will be raised hereafter.[4] He was preparing to pass some time with Mr Russell and his family in Philadelphia during the winter. No letters however have been received from him since this to me.

The letters to Mr T. have not yet been sent to me.[5] It will not require any long time for me to cast my eye over them, when they do come, when I shall return them with those which I promised you. I congratulate you on B^p. Watson's Apology, a most seasonable and valuable work, exceedingly decried already by the partisans of Paine, which is no small testimony to its merit. If there be a few things, which one would wish to have been suppressed, or differently put, these may make the book more generally read. non ego paucis offendar- ubi plura nitent.[6] It is already come to a 2^d Edition.[7] I have circulated several copies, where I knew they were wanted, to save some well meaning but indolent characters, from being turned away from Xtianity.

As to the little American tract, which I have printed, Johnson has never set any price on nor advertised it.[8] I rejoice it is approved by you and all our common friends, as it is by some few here to whom I have given it, who think it calculated for present use. You will oblige me by the acceptance of a few more copies, after which we will see farther about it. As to our Unitarian Society, we are in no feather to print any new things: having just struck off a large edition of Farmer Truman, and nothing yet done with regard to Haynes.[9]

As you say nothing, we conclude that yourself, Mrs Rowe and family are in good health. I cannot say it for my wife, though her painful sufferings hinder her not from going about and serving others. We beg you will name us with all affection, esteem and respect to our excellent friend. I desire no other happiness hereafter than to be with him and others like him. And I promise myself that I shall enjoy that happiness. With all due and kind regards from us both to yourself and Mrs Rowe I remain, Dear Sir, affectionately Yours

T. Lindsey.

We beg to be respectfully remembered to all our common friends.

P.S. I have opened my letter to inform you, that I have just now heard, that Dr Priestley possessed himself so much as to speak over his son's grave, which affected and astonished exceedingly all the people, a great number, who were assembled, out of respect, on the occasion, having never been accustomed to any thing of the kind.[10]

---

1 Rowe's letter to Lindsey seems not to have survived.

2 William Tayleur.

3 This is a quotation, with a few omissions, from Priestley's letter to Lindsey of 17 Dec. 1795; DWL, MS 12.13. Rutt, I, 328, reproduces the passage accurately.

4 This sentence summarizes the section of Priestley's letter to Lindsey of 17 Dec. 1795, which immediately follows the quotation identified in n. 3, above.

5   Some, at least, of Lindsey's letters to William Tayleur were returned to him in 1796: McLachlan, *Letters*, pp. 8–9.

6   'I shall not be offended by a few [blemishes] where many things shine.' This is an adaptation from Horace's *Ars Poetica*, lines 351–3 and these lines are quoted in Henry Fielding's *Tom Jones* (London, 1749), book XI, ch. 1. I owe these references to Mr David Powell.

7   The second edition of Watson's *Apology for the Bible* was published in London in Mar. 1796. Attacks upon Watson's book included Allan Macleod, *The bishop of Landaff's 'Apology for the Bible' examined* (London, 1796); the pseudonymous *Thomas Paine vindicated. Being a short letter to the bishop of Landaff's reply to Thomas Paine's Age of reason. By a deist* (London, 1796); and 'A citizen of New York', *Strictures on Bishop Watson's 'Apology for the Bible'* (New York, 1796). This latter work has been attributed to Joel Barlow, for whom see Letter 485, n. 9.

8   This 'little American tract' was John Clarke's *Answer to the question* which Lindsey edited and which Johnson reprinted; see Letters 625, 630 and 645. The price of the various editions in which it appeared was usually 3*d* or 4*d*.

9   For the Unitarian Society's edition of *Advice from Farmer Trueman to his daughter Mary*, see Letter 509, n. 6. A new edition was published in London (without the imprint of the Unitarian Society) in 1796. For Lindsey's edition of Hopton Haynes, *The scripture account of the attributes and worship of God*, see Letter 406, n. 16. A further edition was published by the Unitarian Society in 1815.

10 For Priestley's preaching at the funeral of his son Henry, see *MR*, I (1806), 396. Lindsey had almost certainly heard this news from a letter written by Priestley to one of his friends, rather than to himself.

628. To CHRISTOPHER WYVILL   7 APRIL 1796

Text: NYRO, ZFW 7/2/104/1, Wyvill of Constable Burton MSS.
Addressed: To/The Rev^d. Christopher Wyvill/Burton Hall/Bedale/ Yorkshire
Endorsed: From the Revd Mr Lindsey May 7th. 1796
Postmarked: Postmark illegible.

London. April. 7. 1796

Dear Sir,

The expectation which had been raised merely on casting my eyes slightly on your pamphlet, has been since most fully gratified, and I think the *Case* contains many things of immediate importance to be suggested to the public, and the whole of the publication exhibits a most full justification of yourself in considering M^r P __ 's communication as a trust for the public and not a matter of private confidential correspondence.[1] One impression which was made on my mind by more than one perusal was that you had spoken too highly of your correspondent; but perhaps it may be as well to err on that side.[2]

I write this on coming from M^r. Johnson's, where I have been to inquire whether the copies by the waggon were arrived, which I am sorry to say they were not, betwixt one and two, but hope they may to morrow, if not to day. However on talking the matter over with Mr Johnson, I have settled it for him to have it advertised without fail in the Morning Chronicle on Monday next, as he has about fifty to answer the immediate demand, and we may presume on the others arrival by the waggon on monday or tuesday at the farthest.[3]

Such is the indifference of many about what is most momentous to them, such the sway and influence of the Minister, and the fears of Alarmists who continue to multiply, against whoever or whatever opposes his plans as thereby furnishing arms to the enemy they dread, that I have my apprehensions that this valuable and most seasonable publication will not have the vent that is to be wished or might be expected. But I hope it will be otherwise.

S^t. Pauls Church yard – 5 o'clock.

I have brought my letter here to seal it in the hope of being able to tell you of the parcell being arrived – but find it is not. I shall add no more at present, but that I shall write again when it arrives, and that I am always, Dear Sir

Your much obliged and faithful servant

T. Lindsey.

---

1   'The case of the Rev. C. Wyvill respecting the Right Honourable William Pitt, and his paper, intituled "Heads of a bill or bills for amending the representation"', may be found, as 'Paper XX', in Wyvill's *The correspondence of the Rev. C. Wyvill with the Right Hon. W. Pitt. Part I*, pp. 50–92. It was dated Burton Hall, 6 Apr. 1796. A second edition of this *Correspondence* was published in Newcastle later in 1796. Part II of the *Correspondence*, a very much shorter work, appeared Newcastle in 1797.

2   In his published correspondence with Pitt (n. 1, above), Wyvill, while critical of Pitt's abandonment of parliamentary reform, praised Pitt's reform proposals, made 'in the purer period of his Administration' (p. 91), of 1783 and 1785.

3   Lindsey referred here to extra copies of *The correspondence of the Rev. C. Wyvill with the Right Hon. W. Pitt, Part I* (n. 1, above). Monday next was 11 Apr. 1796. In fact this work was not advertised in the *Morning Chronicle* until 9, 10, 16 and 19 May 1796; it was also advertised in the *General Evening Post* and in the *St James's Chronicle and British Evening Post*, both on 14 May 1796. Perhaps Joseph Johnson, the co-publisher of the work, lived up to his reputation (in Lindsey's eyes) for procrastination.

629. To WILLIAM TAYLEUR   18 APRIL 1796

Text: JRUL, Lindsey Letters, vol. II, no. 93.
Addressed: To/William Tayleur Esqr/Shrewsbury
Endorsed: April 18th – 96
Postmarked: AP [postmark otherwise illegible]

London. April. 18. 1796

Dear Sir,

Mr Rowe's last letter was a very reviving cordial to us in bringing the good tidings of your physician's prescription having been effectual to your relief by the blessing of the sovereign physician, without whose appointment nothing whatsoever happens. And the heavenly boon and respite will I trust be still comfortable to yourself and useful to others.

I was much affected the other day, in calling on Dr Heberden and seeing him for the first time after his fall and dislocation of his thigh bone about three months since, to observe him so much brought down by it, from being able to walk strong and upright to be reduced to sit in a chair and be carried by others, and his strength much broken, which however I ascribe in part to the loss of a most promising son of 22, of a decline, in the same interval. He edified me greatly by his wise and pious remarks on the change of his situation in a short time, on the many comforts he had enjoyed through a very long life, and the many that still remained; his happiness in looking forward to those scenes in futurity which the gospel opened to us, and what enemies those philosophers were to their fellow-creatures who with thoughtless gaiety endeavourd to rob them of such prospects; and at parting desired to be kindly remembered to Dr Priestley, and to add that he knew how to sympathize with him for the loss of a beloved child, just coming into life and usefulness. He told me that in a few days he should be in his 87th year.[1]

I hope soon to receive another letter from Dr Priestley, the last being written not many days after the death of his son, and to inform you of his welfare and proceedings at Philadelphia, where he was to spend the winter months with M^r

Russells family, and to preach to many that were desirous to be his hearers, and wished him to come to settle among them. It is not I trust presumptuous to say, that his removal to America, far from being sought by himself, was intended by divine providence for the furtherance of the gospel; an end, which it hath in no small degree already answered, by the efforts he himself has made, by the transporting of his writings into that country, and the curiosity excited about him and them. And if his life be prolonged to the extent of that of his ancestors and which his temperance encourages to hope, he may still be of unknown benefit in the way of the gospel, to planted it deep in that new world, and so as never to be rooted up.

I have sent to him, and to other parts of America, copies of B^p Watsons reply and letters to Mr Paine, which will do great good, although they are not every thing that one would have expected from him. It is however no small recomendation of his work that unbelievers rail at it and the author.[2]

There is something very excellent and truly pious in Mr Cappe of York's "Discourses on the providence and government of God["]; lately published by Mr Johnson, especially in some of them towards the conclusion. It is only a small 3/6 volume.[3]

I must beg the favour of you to tell Mr Rowe that I shall write to him bye and bye. He will be glad as well as you to know that a relation of Dr Disney's has left him £200 a year for life, tho' it comes charged with the care of three sons, one of wch is nearly of age; and Dr D. will well earn it.[4]

My wife desires her kind respects, and to join with me in due rememberances to M^r and Mrs Rowe, Mr Wood, and our other friends. I am ever, Dear Sir, Your most truly obliged and affectionate
                         T. Lindsey.

---

1   William Heberden the elder was born on 13 Aug. 1710. Lindsey presumably visited him at his house in Pall Mall. The 'promising son' was Charles Heberden, who, after a distinguished career at St John's College, Cambridge, had entered Lincoln's Inn in 1793. He died on 25 Jan. 1796, aged twenty-three; *Alumn. Cantab.*, II, vol. III, p. 319. He was Heberden's sixth son, and his third son with his second wife, Mary, née Wollaston (1729–1813).

2   For Watson's *Apology for the Bible* and for Painite attacks upon it, see Letter 627, n. 7.

3   This work was Newcome Cappe, *Discourses on the providence and government of God* (London, 1795). The publisher was indeed Joseph Johnson. According to the review of this work in the *Monthly Review*, NS, XXI (1796), 136, the price was 4*s*.

4   This relative was Disney's cousin Henry Woolhouse Disney Roebuck, of Ingress Park, Kent, whose will was proved on 7 Apr. 1796; TNA: PRO PROB 11/1274, fos. 150r–151v. Disney was appointed one of the executors and indeed received an annuity of £200. Although the will named the three sons, it did not specify any guardianship *rôle* for Disney.

630. *To RUSSELL SCOTT   29 APRIL 1796

Text:	Scott Coll.
Printed:	McLachlan, 'Lindsey to Scott', 122 (second sentence of third paragraph).
Addressed:	[In Hannah Lindsey's hand] To/The Rev^d. Russell Scott/ Portsmouth
Endorsed:	May 1st. 96.
Postmarked:	Postmark missing.

Note: Hannah Lindsey dated this letter 29 Apr. 1796 (a Friday); Scott endorsed it 1 May 1796 (a Sunday). In the absence of the postmark, it seems probable that Hannah Lindsey wrote the letter on 29 Apr.; it is accordingly included here under that date.

Dear Sir,

We are really very uneasy at not having heard from you of so long a time, nor even of you since M^r. Porter left town.

We are afraid that you have suffered more than usual in your gouty headachs, as this has been an uncomon Spring for excess in all the sad tribe of gouty & nervous complaints: I have had an accumulation of nervous misery from a long diseased Stomach, but have been growing something better for the last fortnight by the use of Bark & Hemlock: M^r. Lindsey (thank God) has been very well as to health, wch. is in a great measure owing to the absence of anything wch. require too much attention, or confinement to the study: even writing letters are not so easy to him as formerly, except upon pressing occasions: He has therefore desired me to write a few lines of inquiry along with a few little things of wch. he desires y^r acceptance. The Bishops Apology is very good upon the whole;[1] the little American piece M^r. L: has reprinted as it is short, forcible, & animated, & may catch the attention of some readers, who w^d not look into a larger work.[2] The other publication of Sharman's M^r. L: thinks you had, but not being sure, & there being many baptists in y^r neighborhood to whom it may apply, two copies are sent for you at a proper opportunity to throw in their way:[3] The Unitarian Society books are nearly ready for dispersion, & y^r Subscription is paid to give you the choice, instead of M^r. L: sending such as you might want. As I know not whether his Manuscripts were at all useful or acceptable to you, I have not sent any more, but as I have told M^r. L: that I had sent some, to induce him not to destroy what in trusty hands might be useful, you may mention Y^r. wishes for more, if you feel any benefit from having before you some assistance in y^r own labors for the Pulpit.[4]

We have lately had a very satisfactory & pleasant account of D^r. Priestleys health, & state of mind under the new trial of the loss of his Son, so excellent and promising a young man of 16 is rarely found:[5] But the feelings of a parent, were united & moderated by the true Christian & Philosopher in the Father. He is now at Philadelphia with M^r. Russell, & delivering weekly in M^r. Winchesters Pulpit a new set of discourses on the Evidences for Revelation, to a numerous, & very attentive audience most of the Members of Congress attend:[6] And the President[7] behaves in a most friendly & distinguished manner to him: He thinks a permanent Unitarian worshiping [*sic*] Society might be formed, if there was any proper person to conduct it in his absence. Some good however will arise from what he is doing, and more will follow no doubt by some means or other.

Pray let us hear from you very soon, & tell us of M^{rs}. Scott, the children, and also of M^r. Porter. We had once a thought of coming to Portsmouth for a week, & perhaps may be able, if my Mothers advanced age & weak state does not oblige us to go North.[8]

M^r. Lindsey joins in best & kindest wishes for you & yours with D^r. Sir y^r sincere f^d

HLindsey
April 29th. 1796

---

1   This is a reference to Watson's *Apology for the Bible*.
2   The 'little American piece' was John Clarke's *Answer to the question*; see Letter 625, n. 5.
3   Probably Hannah Lindsey referred here to two anti-trinitarian works by Edward Sharman. These works were *A letter on the doctrine of the Trinity; addressed to the Baptist Society at Guilsborough, Northamptonshire* (London, 1795), and *A second letter on the doctrine of the Trinity: addressed to the Baptist Society at Guilsborough, Northamptonshire* (Market Harborough, 1796). The first 'letter'

is signed (p. 74) Edward Sharman, Cottesbrook, Northamptonshire, July 24, 1795. Sharman is listed as the particular baptist minister of Moulton, Northamptonshire, in *The baptist annual register, for 1790, 1791, 1792, and part of 1793* (London, ?1793), p. 10, and *The Carey centenary. Account of the services: with a sketch of the history of the baptist church at Moulton* (Northampton, 1886), pp. 33–4. In 1799, Sharman published *A caution against trinitarianism: or, an inquiry whether those who now follow the example of the ancient fathers, by invoking God's servant the messiah as supreme deity, are the only true worshippers of the one almighty God revealed in the Bible; or do not deserve the name of idolaters: in five letters addressed to the Reverend Mr. Davis, Wigton, Leicestershire, containing some remarks upon his late publication, stiled 'A caution against Socinianism, &C'. By a Northamptonshire farmer* (Market Harborough, 1799). The 'Northamptonshire farmer' was probably Sharman himself. Henry Davis (d. 1815) a former student at Daventry, was minister to dissenting congregations at St Neots, Huntingdonshire, from 1766 to 1772, and at Wigston Magna (also known as Great Wigston), Leicestershire, from 1772 to 1815. I am grateful to the Rev. Dr Roger Hayden and to Dr David Wykes for information about Sharman and Davis; and see Letter 707, n. 9. *A caution against Socinianism* was also the title of a discourse preached and published by the high churchman George Berkeley, a prebendary of Canterbury Cathedral, in 1787.

4   For the possibility that Theophilus and Hannah Lindsey might present Scott with further manuscripts of Lindsey's sermons, see Letters 633 and 645.
5   This is a reference to Priestley's letter to Lindsey from Philadelphia, dated 15 Feb. 1796; Rutt, I, 332–4. Henry Priestley died on 11 Dec. 1795, aged eighteen.
6   Elhanan Winchester (1751–97) was the founder of the first universalist church in Philadelphia, where he was minister. He had met Priestley, Price and other leading dissenters during an extended visit to England between 1787 and 1794. One of the members of Congress who heard Priestley preach was the committed unitarian George Thatcher (1754–1824), lawyer, member for the Maine district of Massachusetts, and a Federalist sympathizer.
7   George Washington.
8   Lindsey was obliged to abandon his plan to visit Portsmouth when the illness of his wife's mother necessitated an expedition to Richmond, Yorkshire, instead; see Letter 638.

631. To JOHN ROWE   2 MAY 1796

Text: JRUL, Lindsey Letters, vol. III, no. 43.
Printed: McLachlan, 'More letters', 377 (first sentence of second
                    paragraph).
Addressed: To/The Rev^d. Mr Rowe/Shrewsbury
Postmarked: MA 2 96

London. May. 2. 1796.

Dear Sir,

Having been one whole day in the country, and wholly engaged on another, the latter part of the week, since your letter came, I delayed my acknowlegements of it, and now am distressed what to say from my having been told yesterday by M^rs. Wolley[1] and Lady Markham,[2] who hear sometimes from Mr Holbrooke,[3] that one of the most excellent of men and who lived in the world only to do good in it, was no more. In some such way I was glad to hear such strangers as it were express themselves. But as they might represent only what [was] most likely to happen, and which your last favour gave me sorrowful reason to expect, when you had not long before raised a hope of somewhat longer continuance; if the change should not have taken place, and it would give no disturbance, I should be glad if you could thank him for his parting rememberance, and say that I reckon myself happy in having enjoyed his friendship from which I have derived comfort and many advantages, and that I can propose to myself nothing more desireable in the world to which he is going, than to live in the company of the wise and good like him, which I have always sought here.[4]

I think I told him of Dr Priestleys pleasing reception by the President Washington when he went with Mr Russell to visit him the day of the D^{rs} arrival at Philadelphia; and of his numerous and respectable audience, when he preached, the sunday after; among whom was a large number of the members of the Congress. This was in the middle of February. Mr Belsham has had a letter since, dated March 5. in which he relates his still continuing to preach with equal acceptance, and that there was a desire in many to have his sermons printed.[5] This I shall be glad of, as he had composed them deliberately beforehand for the occasion, and as they are upon the Evidences of the gospel, but different he says, from those he preached on leaving England, and such as he remarks would well bind up with them. And this indeed the subjects themselves, which he has named to me, indicate.[6]

I am glad of such an accession to your congregation: but the chasm now taking place will not easily be filled. The father of the lady used to come sometimes formerly to our chapel: especially when D^r P ____ y preached for me. But he apprehended that he had doubts about the system of revelation.[7]

I am much concerned a very worthy person, who was of our congregation has been induced to publish his reasons for ceasing to be a Believer, with his name. Not that his reasons are formidable, but because I think he will by such a step diminish his own happiness. I wished him to wait, and review his work before he published it; or at least, not to add his name: but in vain. It's title: "Sober and serious reasons for Scepticism, as it concerns revealed religion. In a letter to a Friend. By John Hollis Esqr.["]8

My wife desires to join in respects to Mrs Rowe and yourself and in all good wishes for you and your family. I am always, Dear Sir, most truly Your's

T. Lindsey.

---

1   Possibly Mrs Wolley was Mary, née Edwards, who married George Wolley at Clunbury, Shropshire, in 1762; see *The registers of Clunbury, Shropshire, 1574–1812*, transcribed by W. G. Clark Maxwell (Parish Register Society, XXXVII, London, 1901), 134.

2   Sarah, née Clive (1737–1828), was the widow of Sir James John Markham (1698–79), 4th baronet, whom she married in 1755. She was a younger sister of Robert Clive (1725–74), from 1762, Baron Clive of Plassey in the Irish peerage. The Clive family residence was Styche Hall, near Market Drayton, Shropshire.

3   Theophilus Houlbrooke.

4   William Tayleur died on 6 May 1796; *Shrewsbury Chronicle*, 13 May 1796. It is clear that Rowe's letter to Lindsey, which seems not to have survived, informed him of Tayleur's nearness to death.

5   See Rutt, I, 334–6.

6   Priestley's sermons delivered in the church of the universalists at Philadelphia in the spring of 1796, which were attended by numerous members of Congress, were published as *Discourses relating to the evidences of revealed religion*, and reprinted in London by Joseph Johnson. They were dedicated to John Adams. Priestley set out the subjects of the discourses in his letter to Lindsey of 12 Feb. 1796; Rutt, I, 331–2.

7   Possibly this addition to Rowe's congregation at Shrewsbury was Mary Wolley (see n. 1, above). Her father, who – one might conjecture – attended Essex Street chapel was Richard Edwards; see *The registers of Clunbury, Shropshire, 1574–1812*, 110, which records her baptism at Clunbury on 8 Oct. 1837. The father of Lady Markham, Richard Clive, died in Apr. 1771, three years before the opening of Essex Street chapel.

8   John Hollis's book, which was indeed entitled *Sober and serious reasons for scepticism, as it concerns revealed religion. In a letter to a friend*, was published in London by Joseph Johnson in 1796. He was a nephew of Timothy Hollis (see Letter 432, n. 8) and a distant cousin of Thomas Hollis. Shortly after his death in Nov. 1824, a complimentary obituary appeared in *MR*, XX (1825), 55.

632. To JOHN ROWE   **10 MAY 1796**

> **Text:**   JRUL, Lindsey Letters, vol. II, no. 94.
> **Addressed:**   To/The Rev^d. Mr Rowe/Shrewsbury
> **Endorsed:**   Three lines of shorthand notes
> **Postmarked:** MA 10 96

London. may. 10. 1796

Dear Sir,

After the preparation given by the report of Lady Markham concerning our excellent friend, your account of his having taken leave of all human things was not unexpected.[1] Who that knew him but must ardently say, may my last end be like his! But the circumstances of it which you describe were also desireable. To have been confined, and shut out from the society he loved for so short a space, and the scene to close at last so quietly and without pain. I hope with you that we shall all be led by this lesson to quicken our tardy pace, and finish our work and follow him, where I trust there can be no doubt that virtuous friends, connexions and acquaintances, will meet and rejoice together over all the trials and difficulties of the present state.

If our friendship, as you kindly intimate, afforded him some pleasure and satisfaction in his declining years, I can truly say that I reaped from it continual comfort and support and benefit during a course of many years after quitting Catterick and settling in London.

This well appears by a record of the intercourse I had with him during that period, in the letters I sent to him, which your brother no longer ago than Saturday last safely conveyed to me by my worthy neighbour Mr Joyce, but whom I should have been glad to have seen himself.[2] These I shall carefully return to you, and along with them those of our friends[3] to me, which I have preserved, and of which I think very few will be found wanting.

I would add that I would by no means limit you with respect to any use you may make of them, should you be disposed at any time yourself to publish any memorials of so excellent a person; but I could wish that they might not go out of your hands into those of any other person.

I am highly gratified to find a small account which I put into the Papers at the time of my most intimate friend Dr Chambers and one of the many excellent ones on earth; of which I had not kept a copy.[4]

I promise myself and am happy in the thought, that one for whom I have such a sincere affectionate esteem as yourself will be kind enough to supply the loss I have had in two such friends,[5] and favour me with writing sometimes, which I shall not be negligent in acknowlege [*sic*].

We hope in your next, which will be at your full leisure, for you must now be much occupied, to be informed of the good health of Mrs Rowe and your family. I remain Dear Sir most truly Yours

T. Lindsey.

Lady M ____ and Mrs Wolley[6] mention that Mr Houlbrook suffers much from the gout. I hope however in general that he enjoys the blessing of health; and shoud be obliged to you to give my respects to him.

---

[1] See Letter 631, n. 2. Lady Markham, with her Shropshire connexions, was well placed to acquire news of Tayleur's declining health.

[2] Probably Lawrence Rowe (d. 1823) of Brentford, the brother of John Rowe; see Murch, *A history of the presbyterian and general baptist churches in the west of England*, p. 134. Lindsey's neighbour

was Joshua Joyce (d. 1816), tallow and wax chandler, of 48 Essex Street, and a witness to Lindsey's will, rather than his brother Jeremiah Joyce. For Joshua Joyce, see Jeremiah Joyce's obituary of him in *MR*, XI (1816), 244.

3   Lindsey wrote 'friends', but clearly meant 'friend's'.

4   For Lindsey's obituary of William Chambers, published in the *General Evening Post*, and the *Gent. Mag.*, in 1777, see Vol. I, Letter 175. Lindsey had sent a copy to Tayleur; see Vol. I, Letter 176. Now Rowe returned it to Lindsey. For a note on Lindsey's use of the expression 'Excellent ones on earth', see Vol. I, Letter 46, n. 6.

5   Those friends were Tayleur and Priestley.

6   For identifications of Lady Markham and Mrs Wolley, see Letter 631, nn. 1 and 2. After his resignation of the rectory of Stockton-on-Teme in 1784, Houlbrooke resided in Edinburgh, and subsequently served as tutor to the son of William Rathbone of Liverpool. But he retained his connexions with Shropshire and preached the funeral sermon for William Tayleur on 15 May 1796, five days after the date of this letter (Letter 636, n. 6).

633. To RUSSELL SCOTT   16 MAY 1796

Text: Scott Coll.
Printed: McLachlan, 'Lindsey to Scott', 122 (brief quotation from seventh paragraph).
Addressed: Address missing.
Postmarked: Postmark missing.

London. May. 16. 1796

Dear Sir,

I am afraid I was more remiss in writing to you than I ought to have been, though I have this excuse to offer, that having certainly intended and some how or other been hindered at the time, through forgetfulness I presumed I had done it and rather expected a letter from you.

It is with a very sincere concern that we learn that you have been so severely handled in various ways, yourself for so long a space, and also your family, but it has been happy that Mrs Russell[1] kept up so well all the while to take care of you all, though we are sorry she is but indifferent of late, but hope that will pass, and that the summer weather which we may expect after these rains will do much for you. I hope some means or other will be found out to give you more vigour and to fortify you against these continual attacks.

I hope you will no more suffer yourself to be depressed (which of itself must bring on or add to your bodily indisposition) by anxious thoughts at not being able to pursue your studies and render yourself so widely useful in your profession and station as you could have wished. Far more good is done in the world by patience under sufferings, by always standing up for principles of virtue and integrity, and the constant light of a worthy example, than by compositions ever so accurate and valuable; which are not always so much attended to as they ought to be, from the pulpit or the press. As to any more supplies of that commodity, for which my wife has dealt with you, she bids me say that she has more of it ready which shall be sent you, and I would add that you may look on it as your own and do with it what you please, so that my name may no ways be mentioned.[2]

I shall get a friend to make inquiry about these ships of which you very obligingly advertise me as being soon to leave the Downs and come to Portsmouth, and of what is intended to be done for our friends at Botany Bay, particularly Mr Palmer; that we may throw in our mite: but shall nevertheless be desirous to learn from you, when these ships actually do arrive with you and how long they may stay. In the mean while I shall perhaps advertise you the first of an unhappy change in the condition of Mess.rs Muir, Palmer, Ellis &c so much the reverse of what their former letters to us gave ground to expect. It is contained in the inclosed, which for obvious reasons has been abridged, and would be properly in its present form confined to friends, lest a wrong use should be made of it.[3] Soon after writing of it, tis to be hoped that Governor Hunter[4] would arrive, and give a check to the military tyranny of the officers; and some think, that as there was no other resort or remedy, it would have been more prudent far for M.r Ellis and M.r Boston to have submitted to the monopoly.[5]

The letter came no longer ago than wednesday in the last week to D.r Disney, being addressed equally to my wife and me and to him.[6]

There is another letter come from D.r Priestley dated March 5. posterior to that of which my wife gave you an account[7] – in which he mentions that he had preached three more of his discourses to still larger audiences, made up of still a greater number of the members of the congress; that he had been pressed to print them, eleven in number, which he sh.d do before he left Philadelphia; that they w.d sort and bind up with the Volume he printed before he left England, being different though with the same view and object, the evidences of Xtianity. He has promised to preach every year for two or three months during the sitting of congress.[8]

Nothing could be more honourable to him and useful to that great continent, than this transaction. His shewing himself to and becoming connected with and approved by the chiefs of the country, will most effectually defeat the vile calumnies sent hence and spread there against him as a violent religionist, forcing his own opinions upon every one, and at the same time a turbulent political character, from both which imputations no one can be more free. And at the same time his eminence as a philosopher must conciliate respect to him, and make em think it an honour to have such a man among them.

You will be glad to know that B.p Watson's Apology is printing by him at a cheap price for sale. Although it is not every thing one could wish it will do great good, and prevent the lower classes from being hurt by Paines bold assertions. I shall endeavour to send you a few of them, and of the American tract.[9]

M.r John Hollis's scepticism w.h regard to Reveald [*sic*] Religion, in which he declares himself an unbeliever is a weak performance, yet written without petulance, and under a serious frame of mind. I dissuaded [him] from publishing at all, at least not for a year, or without his name, because I thought it woud bring neither credit nor comfort. But he was bent upon it. It is very short[10]

I have not time to add any more at present but *our* kind respects and good wishes for you both and for your little folks. I am always,

Dear Sir, very sincerely and affectionately Yours

T. Lindsey.

---

1   Lindsey referred here to Sophia Russell (née Hawes), the wife of Russell Scott; for his previous reference to her by this designation, see Letter 561, n. 7.

2   This appears to be a reference to Lindsey's manuscript sermons, some of which he had forwarded to Scott; see Letter 630.

3   Probably the 'inclosed' was a copy of Palmer's letter to John Disney, dated Sydney, New South Wales, 13 June 1795. It was published by J. T. Rutt in *MR*, XII (1817), 262–4, with a note that it was received on 4 May 1796. Disney arranged for a small number of copies to be printed and sent to sympathetic friends; one copy, with a covering note from Disney to Wyvill dated 9 May 1796, may be found in NYRO, ZFW 7/2/101/4. In his letter, Palmer wrote that he had entrusted his 'character', i.e. the manuscript of his *Narrative*, to John White (d. 1832), the surgeon-general of New South

Wales, for conveyance to Britain. Rutt added that this and other documents reached him safely and that they were edited by Jeremiah Joyce to form Palmer's *Narrative*, which was published in 1797, although some copies appear to have been available in Dec. 1796. See Michael T. Davis, '"A register of vexations and persecutions": some letters of Thomas Fyshe Palmer from Botany Bay during the 1790s', *E & D*, XXIII (2004–7), 154 n. 29.

4   John Hunter (1737–1821), a naval officer by profession, was governor of New South Wales, where he arrived on 7 Sept. 1795, until his recall in 1800. In 1801, he was listed as an honorary member of the Literary and Philosophical Society of Newcastle; see *Rules of the Literary and Philosophical Society of Newcastle upon Tyne: to which are annexed, a catalogue of the books, and a list of the members* (Newcastle, 1801), p. 45.

5   In his letter to Disney of 13 June 1795 (n. 3, above), Palmer reported that he, James Ellis and John Boston formed a trading company at Botany Bay, but complained that this enterprise was seriously handicapped by the monopoly of produce imposed by officers of the New South Wales corps. See Davis, '"A register of vexations and persecutions"', 154–7.

6   16 May 1796 was a Monday; the Wednesday of the previous week was 11 May. For this letter from Palmer to Disney, see n. 4, above.

7   See Letter 630.

8   This letter from Priestley, written to Thomas Belsham, was dated 5 Mar. 1796; see Rutt, I, 334–6. For Priestley's sermons in Philadelphia, see Letter 631, n. 6. He delivered a further series of sermons in Philadelphia in the spring of 1797; they were published as *Discourses relating to the evidences of revealed religion. Vol. 2.*

9   At least eight abbreviated editions of Watson's *Apology for the Bible*, some costing as little as 8*d*, were published in 1796. For the 'American tract', see Letter 625, n. 5.

10   For John Hollis's book, see Letter 631, n. 8. It consisted of thirty-seven pages of text, plus a one-page 'advertisement'. Contrary to Lindsey's advice, it was published with John Hollis named as the author.

634. To CHRISTOPHER WYVILL   23 MAY 1796

Text: NYRO, ZFW 7/2/104/14, Wyvill of Constable Burton MSS.
Printed: Ditchfield, 'Lindsey–Wyvill correspondence', 164 (fourth
                 paragraph); 165 (sixth paragraph).
Addressed: To/The Rev^d. Christopher Wyvill/Burton Hall/Bedale/
                 Yorkshire
Endorsed: From the Rev. Mr Lindsey May 23. 1796
Postmarked: MA 23 96

London. May. 23. 1796

Dear Sir,

I am sorry I have not had the occasion I have been waiting for to write to you, that I might inform you of the reception The Correspondence had met with from some whose opinion you would be desirous to know.[1]

Mr Duncombe, your late member, I could never get a sight of, after it came to Town, though I more than once knockd at his door,[2] so busied or engaged was he at home or abroad, which I presume prevented his calling in Essex-Street, which he has seldom failed on leaving Town. By the way, it has surprized many, as unaccountable, that he should in his advertisement in which he takes leave of the county, pronounce his last collegue equal in parts and integrity to his former, Sir Geo. Savile.[3]

Mr Montague[4] left town before I could reach him, and Ld John Cavendish earlier than he. The former is too much attached to his friends, L^d. Fitzwilliam and the Duke of Portland, to bring in a fair verdict on a publication so unfavourable to their conduct. The D. of Grafton told me that he thought you justifiable in the publication intended, and the reasons good; but he did not find some he conversed with of that sentiment. Mr Wilberforce I was told condemned it much. It is reported that M^r

Duncombe's nephew is to be brought in for your county in conjunction with and under the wing of Mr Wilberforce.[5] One circumstance however I will mention to you relating to the county, wch fell from Mr Shore in private conversation, and which in my opinion does him honour; that he woud have voted neither for Duncombe nor Wilberforce had they stood again, so little was he satisfied wth their general conduct and constant countenance given to the minister.[6]

Such has been the early vigilance and exertions used by Mr Horne Took and his friends, that the latter stick not to say that he will be chosen for Westminster, and pretend to be offended with Mr Fox for refusing to join Took or coming into his measures for excluding a court candidate from succeeding. Candid and dispassionate men I believe will approve Mr Fox's conduct, and address to the freeholders of Westminster; and should he not be rechosen, I shall think it among the many bad omens belonging to our country at this time.[7]

I do not find that the Correspondence has any degree of that vent which might have been expected. One cause undoubtedly was, that it came too late. Parliament, it was then known, would be dissolved in ten days; and the minds of all were made up with respect to the demerits of the minister, and were more indifferent than they would have been before, about facts which shewed his degeneracy and double conduct in a still stronger light. A time may come however, on the new parliament being returned, when they will perhaps more than ever attend to such just representations in which the public are so much interested. And then I shall recommend to your bookseller to advertise.[8]

I apprehend you know that Mr James Milnes has bought a moiety of the borough of Shaftesbury, for thirteen thous^d pounds, said to be very cheap if he has not bought a contest with it. For Paul Benwell,[9] the purchaser of the other part is extremely indignant he cannot bring in his friend Boyd, and on that account as I am well informed, has behaved so imperiously and exasperated the voters so much, as will in the issue make it easy for Mr Milnes to come in himself, but not to bring in his friend Dawson, as he himself proposed, and for that end has taken him down with him. I cannot say this traffic is very seemly for a religious dissenter to engage in, and at such a time in particular.[10]

We hope soon to hear the best news of all others, that your Lady is well in the straw[11] and yourself and fine amiable family are in health as we wish you. In these hopes my wife desires to join. For the rest we must be content to acquiesce in what cannot be avoided. I have forgotten to say that I have again attempted in vain to meet with S^r. Robt Hildyard,[12] and believe I shall give it up, as he is so outlying and distant. "Addi[ti]onal Facts, [word illegible] by Mr Morgan is well spoken of, and is well worth every gentlemans seeing who has a stake in his country.[13]

I am ever, Dear [Sir] Your much obliged
          T. Lindsey.

P.S. Since the writing of the above I receive a letter from the D. of N ___ nd, in which he says he is much obliged by the present of your pamphlet, which contains much most seasonable remark if any one woud mind it, and wonders that any man should take upon him to say that you were precluded publishing the heads of Mr Pitt's bill of Reform, as he cannot see any possible grounds on wch any one should think it wrong. I give you his words.[14] He adds that he is sorry for Mr Duncombe's resignation, but is comforted by the probability of there being a contest and the hyp ____ l W.[15] being thrown out.

1 For Wyvill's publication of his correspondence with Pitt, see Letter 628, n. 1.
2 Henry Duncombe's London address was 113 Pall Mall; *Directory to the nobility, gentry, and families of distinction in London, Westminster, &c* (London, 1793), p. 17.
3 Henry Duncombe was MP for Yorkshire from 1780 to 1796. His advertisement, 'to the freeholders of the county of York', in which he announced his decision not to seek re-election, was dated Pall Mall, 7 May 1796, and appeared in the *Morning Chronicle* on 14 May 1796. Immediately afterwards, several London newspapers reported his decision; see, for example, *Lloyd's Evening Post*, 13–16 May 1796, *Oracle and Public Advertiser*, 16 May 1796. Duncombe's advertisement did not refer to Sir George Savile, one of the MPs for the county from 1759 to 1783, by name but did express Duncombe's appreciation of 'the happiness I enjoyed in being united with my late and present Colleagues, with whom I have ever lived in intimacy and friendship'.
4 Probably Frederick Montagu (1733–1800), a supporter of Rockingham's party and, from 1768 to 1790, MP for Higham Ferrers, Northamptonshire, a Fitzwilliam borough.
5 Charles Duncombe (1764–1841), the nephew of Henry Duncombe, sought unsuccessfully to succeed his uncle as MP for Yorkshire in 1796, and placed advertisements in several London newspapers to solicit support; see the *Sun*, 17 May 1796, *Oracle and Public Advertiser*, 18 May 1796. He never achieved his ambition to become MP for Yorkshire, although he was MP for Shaftesbury from 1790 to 1796 and for Aldborough from 1796 to 1806.
6 Samuel Shore III did not have the opportunity of withholding his votes from Duncombe and Wilberforce, since at the general election of 1796 in Yorkshire, Duncombe was not a candidate and Wilberforce and Henry Lascelles (1767–1841), a supporter of Pitt, were returned without a poll; see below, n. 15.
7 At Westminster in the general election of 1796, Fox was top of the poll with 5,160 votes and Sir Alan Gardner, with 4,814 votes, was also elected. John Horne Tooke was in third place with 2,819 votes; Thorne, *Hist. parl.*, II, 267. Fox's speeches at the Westminster election of 1796 were published in *The Westminster election, in the year 1796. Being an accurate state of the poll each day: also a complete collection of the addresses and speeches (from the hustings in Covent Garden) of the Right Hon. Charles James Fox, Vice Admiral Sir Alan Gardner, Bart, and John Horne Tooke, Esq. The whole carefully collected* (London, 1796).
8 The parliament elected in 1790 was dissolved on 20 May 1796; the first session of the new parliament began on 27 Sept. 1796. *The correspondence of the Rev. C. Wyvill with the Right Honourable William Pitt. Part I* was published in Newcastle by S. Hodgson; the booksellers' names on the title page were Joseph Johnson in London and J. Todd in York.
9 I.e. Paul Benfield (1741–1810), MP for Cricklade 1780–4, Malmesbury 1790–2 and Shaftesbury 1793–1802, borough-monger and nabob.
10 Walter Boyd (1753–1837) was Benfield's banking partner. He and Benfield were elected for Shaftesbury in 1796 and Boyd was its MP from that year until 1802. He was MP for Lymington from 1823 to 1830. William Dawson was the business partner of James Milnes; he and Milnes were defeated by Benfield and Boyd at Shaftesbury in the general election of 1796.
11 William, son of Christopher Wyvill and his wife Sarah, was born on 11 May and baptized on 13 June 1796; NYRO, PR/FIN 1/3 (Finghall parish register).
12 Sir Robert Hildyard (1743–1814), 4th baronet; he succeeded his father as 4th baronet in 1781 and was high sheriff of Yorkshire in 1783. He was the owner of Sedbury Hall, near Richmond, and possessed estates at Winestead and at Patrington, near Hull; probably it was to the latter estate that Lindsey referred as 'outlying and distant'.
13 William Morgan, *Additional facts, addressed to the serious attention of the people of Great Britain, respecting the expences of the war, and the state of the national debt* (London, 1796). The work reached a fourth edition before the end of the year. Morgan, a nephew of Richard Price, was chief actuary to the Equitable Assurance Society.
14 I have not found this letter from the duke of Northumberland to Lindsey. The pamphlet to which Northumberland referred was Wyvill's published correspondence between himself and Pitt; see n. 8, above, and Letter 628, n. 1. In addition to this (apparently non-surviving) letter to Lindsey, Northumberland wrote several letters to Wyvill in the later 1790s expressing strong disapproval of Pitt's ministry and support for Wyvill's reforming endeavours: see, for example, NYRO, ZFW 7/2/110/26, 34, Northumberland to Wyvill, 29 May and 3 June 1797.
15 I.e. the 'hypocritical' Wilberforce, who was in fact returned as one of the two MPs for Yorkshire at the general election of 1796, together with Henry Lascelles, who replaced Henry Duncombe.

635. To ROBERT MILLAR   **30 MAY 1796**

Text:	DWL, MS 12.46 (9).
Printed:	Graham, 'Unhappy country', 142 (latter part of second paragraph; third paragraph).
Addressed:	To/Mr Robert Millar,/Merchant/Dundee./single sheet
Endorsed:	[In Lindsey's hand, on address page] M^r. Robert Millar/ Merchant/Dundee. June. 1
Postmarked:	MA 30 96

Note: This letter was written upon the reverse sheets of a double sheet, printed, entitled 'A CATALOGUE of BOOKS distributed by the UNITARIAN SOCIETY, for Promoting Christian Knowlege [*sic*] and the Practice of Virtue, which are sold at the Price annexed to each Article, to Subscribers and Non-Subscribers without Distinction, by J. Johnson, No. 72, St. Paul's Church-Yard'. The catalogue is dated '*London, April*, 1796'.

London. May 30. 1796.

Dear Sir,

I here send you a catalogue of y^e. Society's books, out of which You will chuse such a number as amounts to a guinea, and let me know our choice in a letter to me, and I will procure the books for you from Mr Johnson, and send them with the other things. If at the same time you could mention any ship which you know to be coming to Dundee, and the Master's name, I will send them by that ship.

I was in hope of procuring a Frank to convey this to you together with a letter to Mr Duncan, and for that purpose called upon a noble Lord but did not find him at home.[1] I must beg the favour of you to mention this my design to Mr Duncan, and tell him that I have sent the letter he inclosed to me to Mr Palmer's brother according to his direction, which I take to be very right, but that I would not have him on any account send Mr Palmer's books to me, as I can have no right to dispose of them, nor could know where to put them;[2] I hope he will have the proper directions for this end from Mr J.F. Palmer of Bedford: and please to add that I shall take an opportunity of thanking Mr Duncan for his letter.[3] In the Cambridge Intelligencer of Saturday last, may 28, you have a short letter of Mr Jeremiah Joyce's, introducing a letter which he rec^d only 3 weeks since, from Sydney Cove. dated Novr. 9. 1794 and signed Muir, Fyshe Palmer, Skirving, in vindication of themselves for having no more to do with Mr Margarot.[4] Mr Joyce [?also[5]] says he shall speedily publish a narrative he has received of the charges against Mr Palmer and Skirving, with an acc^t of their cruel unjust sufferings [word illegible] them during their voyage on board the Transport. We have had an account that a ship will sail to Botany Bay in a short time: but are anxious to hear of Governor Hunter's arrival there and of the state of our friends.[6]

I never remember a time when the aspect of things relating to the public created so much apprehension in all good men; and the more as they see no remedy.

My wife continues upon the whole tolerably well, and we hope that yourself, M^{rs}. Millar, and are [*sic*][7] sister are so. We expect now to be in the country, commonly, a part of every week. When you write, be so good as to mention whether there be any book &c you woud wish me to purchase to send along with your parcell which I hope will at length find its way to you; I mean, to purchase with your own money in my hands. Our joint respects attend you all. I remain always, Dear Sir, your much obliged servant

T. Lindsey.

P.S. Pray are any accounts rec^d from Mr William Christie since he went to America.[8]

1   Probably the 'noble lord' was the duke of Grafton, whose London residence was 45 Clarges Street, Piccadilly.

2   See n. 3, below. For a possible identification of Mr Duncan of Dundee, see Letter 566, n. 7.

3   Probably the brother of Thomas Fyshe Palmer to whom Lindsey referred was either Jeremy Fyshe Palmer (d. 1798) of Bedford (see Letter 678, n. 7), or John Fyshe Palmer, MD, 'who for many years practised at Peterborough', and whose death aged seventy-three in Bedfordshire was recorded in *Gent. Mag.*, LXXXIV (1814), 609.

4   On Saturday 28 May 1796, the *Cambridge Intelligencer* published a letter from Jeremiah Joyce, dated Chevening, 22 May 1796, forwarding and requesting the publication of a letter from Muir, Palmer and Skirving, from Sydney-Cove and dated 9 Nov. 1794. This letter, which the *Intelligencer* printed immediately after that of Joyce, condemned the behaviour of Maurice Margarot and his collusion with the captain of the *Surprise*, Patrick Campbell. It repudiated the allegations that the prisoners had conspired to murder the ship's crew, seize the vessel and make their escape. It concluded by stating that Margarot should not presume to associate his name with those of Muir, Palmer and Skirving.

5   The manuscript is slightly torn at this point.

6   For John Hunter, who arrived in New South Wales on 7 Sept. 1795, see Letter 633. In his letter to the *Cambridge Intelligencer* of 28 May 1796 (see n. 4, above), Joyce revealed that he had recently received a 'narrative' of the voyage of the *Surprise* which would expose the inhuman treatment inflicted upon Muir, Palmer and Skirving. He promised that it would 'speedily' be published. This work was Palmer's *Narrative* and it appeared, with a preface by Joyce, in 1797.

7   Lindsey evidently intended to write 'her'.

8   William Christie and his family arrived at New York in Oct. 1795 and moved to Philadelphia in Dec. of that year. By May 1796, he had moved to Winchester, Virginia, where for a time he taught French at the Winchester Academy. See Willard C. Frank, Jr, '"I shall never be intimidated". Harry Toulmin and William Christie in Virginia 1793–1801', *TUHS*, XIX, 1 (Apr. 1987), 31.

636. To JOHN ROWE   10 JUNE 1796

Text: JRUL, Lindsey Letters, vol. III, no. 44.
Printed: McLachlan, 'More letters', 377 (short extracts from parts of fourth and fifth sentences of sixth paragraph).
Addressed: To/The Revᵈ. J. Rowe/Shrewsbury
Postmarked: JU 10 96

London. June 10. 1796

Dear Sir,

I must first acquaint you that your letter with the £10 Bill came safe yesterday forenoon, and soon after, in my way to the monthly meeting of our Unitarian Society, I called at Newgate and spent all the time I could spare with Mʳ Winterbotham, with whose character and conversation I am more and more pleased and edified each time that I see him, and this last was the third time in the compass of a few months. In the midst of many trials peculiar to his situation his faith in the gospel revelation on the best rational grounds is daily strengthened, and his moral and virtuous habits likewise. My wife coud not help shedding tears on my opening your letter, and reading to her the accᵗ of this last benefaction of one of the most excellent men to persecuted worth, which he chiefly sought out, and particularly the sufferers for righteousness. Mʳ Winterbotham was also suitably affected with such a token from such a friend, and desired his thanks to your [*sic*] for remembering him so soon.[1]

I no sooner read to the Committee of the society your inquiry and mentioned the state of the case with respect to our deceased friend's annual allotment of books, when it was immediately agreed that you had a most strict claim to it as usual, and I was desired to signify to you to send your nomination to Mʳ Johnson as you have been wont to do. It is proper however to advertise you, that through a blameable neglect somewhere, two of our most useful Articles, Representation of true religion, and Practical Instructions, are out of print.[2]

Sir Richard Hill's conduct in your present election, and Mr Wilberforce's in many respects but particularly in encouraging this cruel, wicked and unchristian war, do not give much credit to the morality of the Methodists, when their chieftains can act such a part. I thank you for your account of the manner in which the election has been carried on, for it is useful to know facts.[3] I am highly pleased with the noble principles of Mr Fox, which he shews in his speeches every day at the Hustings in Covent-Garden, and particularly with his generous behaviour to Mr Horne Took, the first day and all along.[4]

I cannot describe how much I am gratified with your account of our friend's Grandsons, and attestation to the promising worthy characters of all of them. I trust he will in some measure live in them, and they will be all pious and useful characters, though in different degrees.[5]

My wife and I both wished, that although it would have been a most painful task, it had fallen to You to preach at our friend's interment. It was a favourable moment lost by not touching upon what was most prominent and distinguished among the excellencies of his character, and what the very place of assembly as well as the occasion must have induced every one to expect.[6]

I am not disappointed tho' concerned at what you mention of the late addition to your congregation.[7] But I trust that you, my friend, will not easily be discouraged from going on to bear your testimony to the truth of God, however indifferent many may at present appear about it. Wait only a little, and the times themselves will make them serious, and then they will listen to You. Had our friend been with us, he woud have been delighted as you will be with the joyful repeted accounts I have of the good already done by Dr Priestleys discourses at Philadelphia, where a large proportion of the members of Congress and all the principal Officers of State are his constant and most attentive hearers. They have desired him to print them, and also to be themselves at the expence of it, and he dedicates them to Mr Adams, the Vice President, his old acquaintance and correspondent, who has been most punctual in his attendance. His stay will be twelve weeks at Philadelphia, as he had composed 12 discourses for the occasion.[8] How evident is it, may we not humbly say, that God sent him hither for the greatest good, whilst the evil dispositions of his countrymen were the immediate instrument? My wife desires to join in kind respects, and wishes for every thing happy in Mrs Rowe's confinement.[9] We beg to be rememberd to Mr Wood in particular and Mr Harries.

I am always, Dear Sir, affectionately Yours
                                              T. Lindsey.

---

1   This was a gift from William Tayleur to the imprisoned William Winterbotham.
2   For the titles of these two books, which were adopted by the Unitarian Society at its opening meeting on 9 Feb. 1791, see Letters 435, n. 2, and 423, n. 4. The minute book for the monthly committee meeting on 9 June 1796, with Lindsey in the chair, simply recorded (p. 58) that no business was transacted. On 8 Dec. 1796, the society resolved (minute book, p. 59) that both these two works should be reprinted; see Letter 670.
3   Sir Richard Hill (1773–1808), an evangelical supporter of Wilberforce, was MP for Shropshire from 1780 to 1806. At the general election of 1796, his younger brother John Hill (1740–1824), who had been MP for Shrewsbury since 1784, was defeated in that constituency as a result of the intervention of his kinsman William Hill (1773–1842), who was MP for Shrewsbury from 1796 to 1812. Sir Richard Hill exerted himself strongly but unavailingly on his brother's behalf. See Thorne, *Hist. parl.*, II, 336–8, IV, 198–9, 201.

⁴ See Letter 634, n. 7.
⁵ For William Tayleur's grandsons, see Letters 459, n. 9, and 490, n. 7. They are not mentioned
   in Tayleur's will, which, after legacies to the minister of the High Street chapel, Shrewsbury, to
   the Salop infirmary and to his servants, bequeathed his remaining estate to his only child, William
   Tayleur (1741–1813), subsequently of Buntingsdale Hall, near Market Drayton.
⁶ Tayleur's funeral sermon was preached by Theophilus Houlbrooke and published as *A sermon, occasioned by the death of William Tayleur, Esq., delivered at a meeting of unitarian dissenters in Shrewsbury upon the fifteenth day of May, 1796* (Liverpool, 1796).
⁷ For a possible identification of this 'late addition' to Rowe's congregation, see Letter 631, n. 7.
⁸ Priestley described these developments in his letter to Lindsey of 8 Apr. 1796, DWL, MS 12.13,
   partly printed in Rutt, I, 336–7. John Adams was indeed the dedicatee of Priestley's *Discourses
   relating to the evidences of revealed religion.*
⁹ Possibly this refers to William Tayleur Rowe, the son of John and Mary Rowe, born on 22 Jan. 1796
   and baptized on the following 20 July; TNA: RG4/1818, fo. 26.

637. To JOHN ROWE   29 JUNE 1796

Text: JRUL, Lindsey Letters, vol. II, no. 95
Printed: McLachlan, *Letters*, p. 9 (most of first and third paragraphs).
Addressed: To/The Revᵈ John Rowe/Shrewsbury
Postmarked: JU 29 96

London. June. 29. 1796

Dear Sir,

Tho' the Post-hour will not allow me to say much, I must inform you that I have
this afternoon sent a box directed for you to the only Shrewsbury Waggon, the
Castle and Falcon, Aldersgate, which sets out to morrow morning, Thursday, and
will arrive, I trust safe, in six days.¹ It contains the Letters you sent me, and added
to them, all I had preserved of my late excellent friend's, some of which however I
think are missing, but not many. In particular I cannot account for there being none
of his in the year 1787.²

They are however a most valuable treasure, and I am peculiarly happy in putting
them into the hands of one who loved him and knows how to value them.³

In perusing them You will not wonder that without attending to and waiting
for formal returns of letter for letter I was happy in taking every opportunity of
pouring out my mind and conversing with a friend of such wisdom, and candour
and goodness and of so exact a judgment, cultivated with such general knowlege,
as well as of the world he lived in.

When the box is delivered to you, which I have no doubt of it being very safely,
I shall be glad to know and hope that by that time you will be able to inform us
that all is well with Mʳ⁽ˢ⁾ Rowe, and she has presented you with another pledge of
heaven's love to you both.⁴

My wife desires to join in this earnest prayer for you, and for all good besides to
You and Your's. I am always Dear Sir affectionately Yours

T. Lindsey.

We hope Mʳ Tayleurs housekeeper is well after her fatigues in his illness, and
loss of such a friend. We entertain no doubt of her being handsomely provided for.⁵

¹ The Castle and Falcon, Aldersgate, is listed as the starting point for the Shrewsbury waggon in 'A
   guide to stage coaches, etc', in *A London directory* (London, 1795), p. 70; the waggon was scheduled
   to depart on Thursday mornings at 9.00 and on Saturday afternoons at 4.00.
² This concerns the return to Lindsey of his letters to Tayleur, and his return of those letters to Rowe:

See McLachlan, *Letters*, pp. 8–9. In fact four letters from Tayleur to Lindsey from 1787 survive and may be consulted at JRUL, C2[13]. See Appendix I, 'Letters to Lindsey'.

3   John Rowe.

4   See Letter 636, n. 9.

5   Tayleur did not identify his housekeeper in his will (TNA: PRO PROB 11/1281, fos. 1r–2r), although he bequeathed to all of his servants four guineas for each year of their service. Probably he made a separate provision for his housekeeper before his death, as was the case with most of his benefactions. His will is a relatively short document; for all his generosity to Lindsey and other unitarian causes, the only unitarian-related legacy in his will was one to the minister or ministers of the High Street chapel, Shrewsbury. That his housekeeper was indeed well provided for is evident from Letter 643.

638. To RUSSELL SCOTT   1 JULY 1796

Text: Scott Coll.
Addressed: To/The Rev[d]. Russell Scott/Portsmouth
Endorsed: July 2[d]. 1796
Postmarked: JY 3[?] 1796

Dear Sir,

I thank you for your kind attention to my comission, and sh[d] have done it sooner but that we have been in the country.

At our return last night, my wife had a letter from her brother at Richmond with such an account of her feeble and uncertain,[1] which, tho she may still linger on, makes it necessary for her to go immediately to her, especially as she wishes it. We therefore set out this afternoon.

I am afraid our visit to our friends to Portsmouth must now be put off to another year.[2] I hope in the mean time you will not be wanting in using every method to estabilish your health.

I have time only to add our kind respects to M[rs] Scott and best wishes for your young folks –

in haste but always most truly Yours,

                                                         T. Lindsey.

        July. 1. 1796
                London.

---

1   Lindsey omitted a word, probably 'condition', at this point. His wife's half-brother was Francis Blackburne, vicar of Brignall.

2   See Letter 630. Lindsey did not go to Portsmouth in the 1790s and his personal acquaintance with Scott was confined to the latter's visits to London.

639. To THOMAS BELSHAM   26 JULY 1796

Text: DWL, MS 12.57 (9).
Addressed: To/The Rev[d]. T. Belsham,/at M[rs] Richards's/Crescent/
                Birmingham[1]
Endorsed: [By Belsham] M[r] Lindsey July 26: 1796
Postmarked: Postmark illegible.

                                          Richmond. July 26. 1796

Dear Sir,

I thank you for your letter, partly from Bedford and partly from town, which was the more agreeable as it contained such a pleasing account of your brother as well as your sister and yourself.[2] We do not despair of looking in upon him for part of a day, if, on our return, our friends at Paxton[3] should be at home to receive us for a few days. Your news of the additions and improvem[ts] of his history and intended completion of it from the Revolution is most welcome to me, as it will be for the benefit of all that come after us to receive information from his hands.[4]

In return for the communications from Philadelphia I have not much to add though I have rec[d] a letter likewise from our friend, as it was written at the same time, I presume, the beginning of may and therefore could not be very different.[5] He finds daily more reason to be satisfied with his being in Philadelphia, with the connection made there and with so many others from the different states, and with the prospect of success from his preaching and publications. The profits from the sale of the Discourses he has delivered is to be appropriated to the fitting up of a place for unitarian worship, which they have in view. The next winter however he is to have the use of the university Common Hall, which is more central than the place he preached in.[6] They had made such progress in the printing of the Discourses, that he hoped to be able to send off 25 copies in a Ship that M[r] Davy charter'd for London.[7] All his unitarian Tracts had been printed in Philadelphia.

He laments that the english emigrants were generally Unbelievers. M[r] Nicklin, M[r] Houlbrooke's nephew who had attended his lectures at Birmingham,[8] and his partner, M[r] Griffiths, a scholar of M[r] Scholefield's,[9] had not been among his hearers, and went to no place of worship. The young Humphreys, are all declared unbelievers, and avoid him as much as they can, as do all their acquaintance.[10] You will only mention these particulars where it may be proper. I have been all along persuaded myself, that what has chiefly prevailed with so many of the young men of our acquaintance and knowlege, to reject the Xtian revelation has been their impatience of the restraints it laid them under with respect to self-indulgence and the gains and commerce of the world. And as these motives will go on increasing, their recovery will be impossible.

I must not omit that the D[r]. speaks of the pleasure he had in attending the debates in Congress, particularly on the subject of the treaty with England, which was carried only by a very small majority. The members for the northern States were in general in favour of it; those from the southern, the contrary. Some of the Speakers very eminent.[11] He intends to send a copy of the debates on this ocasion, as they are to be printed.[12] – complains of no letters or parcells from England; whereas, this year 1796, I have written nine times, and almost always parcells, small or large. Some of the letters of importance.[13]

This morning a letter from Town says, that the not calling the Parliament together is a sign that peace is in agitation, as the Minister chuses to manage it quietly in his own way: which is the opinion of an M.P. who is much connected with him. And at the end of the same letter; "Pitt has made overtures of peace to the French, which have not been accepted, nor listened to. The French want to attack Portugal, if Spain will allow them to march their troops thro' their territory["].[14]

This town is at present very gay with the poor remains of the 65th Regiment returned from the West Indies. 26 Officers, and about 60 common men, sent to recruit, but hitherto prevented from sending parties into the country for want of money. This morning there was a great uproar in the streets from a vast croud of women who had assembled to prevent two soldiers from being floggd for drunkenness, and carried their purpose with the officers by their intreaties and warlike appearance, with stones and sticks. It put one in mind of the interference of the sex at Paris.[15]

I am glad you have laid your plan to make a summer excursion among your friends, which I trust will serve various good purposes which you have in view, and give fresh health and vigour to sit down and benefit others with those distinguished talents which have been given you and which you have so much improved. My wish, I own, is, that you may have leisure to perfect those thoughts on various subjects which you intend to lay before the public, and in that or any other way, we shall be happy to contribute our mite. You will be pleased in being informed, that my wife's mother continues improving in health and strength. For 12 days to come a letter will find us here. You will probably be flying about so much that it may be difficult to catch you. I hope however you will have better weather than we have had for this fortnight past, perpetual rain, and the air so chilld that a fire is not disagreable. My wife sends her kind respects. We beg to be remembered to all our friends, particularly to the worthy family of the Hunts[16] and the Mansells particularly M[rs] Bull.[17] I wish I could think of the town of Birmingham in the mass with more equanimity. I trust that M[r] Corry does well and will do good in it.[18] You will not forget us to him, nor especially to M[r] Scholefield, M[r] Hawkes,[19] M[r] Edwards,[20] M[r] Coates,[21] and any other friends; I am always Dear Sir, Yours most truly and faithfully,

T. Lindsey.

1   Probably Lydia Rickards, whose husband, a close friend of Belsham, had died in 1786; see Williams, pp. 321–3. She is listed in 1793 as a subscriber of £100 towards the rebuilding of the Old Meeting after the riots of July 1791; *Memorials of the Old Meeting House*, p. 4. Another branch of the family lived in Newington Green and Hackney; Thomas Rickards was one of the five signatories of an address to Priestley, 7 Nov. 1791, from the committee of the Gravel Pit meeting, Hackney, urging him to accept the office of pastor, in succession to Richard Price; Rutt, I, 170–1. See Carl B. Cone, 'Newington Green; a study of a dissenting community', *Catholic Historical Review*, LIV, 1 (Apr. 1968), 6–7.

2   Thomas Belsham's brother was the historian William Belsham (see n. 4, below).The sister to whom Lindsey referred was Ann Belsham (d. 1824), who, after 1794, was Thomas Belsham's only unmarried sister; she lived at his house in Grove Place, Hackney. She was the Miss Belsham who took over the domestic management of Hackney College in 1792; see Letter 507, n. 5.

3   This is a reference to the family of Richard Reynolds at Little Paxton, Huntingdonshire.

4   This work was William Belsham's *History of Great Britain, from the Revolution to the session of parliament ending A.D. 1793* (4 vols., London, 1798). A two-volume edition, entitled *History of Great Britain, from the Revolution to the accession of the house of Hanover*, was published in London in the same year.

5   This letter from Priestley to Lindsey, from Philadelphia and dated 3 May 1796, may be found in DWL, MS 12.13; it is partly printed in Rutt, I, 338–40. The 'communications from Philadelphia' which Lindsey acknowledged probably included Priestley's letters to Belsham, dated Philadelphia 5 Mar and 8 Apr. 1796; Rutt, I, 334–6, 337–8, which Belsham had forwarded to him.

6   In his letter of 3 May 1796 (n. 5, above), Priestley wrote that during the forthcoming winter he would have the use of the 'common hall' of the University of Pennsylvania for unitarian worship, a location 'generally used for the accommodation of particular congregations, when their places of worship are repairing, or for strangers'. He added that although the use of the hall was formally conditional upon subscription to a strictly Calvinist creed, this requirement was rarely enforced, and was not enforced in his case because of the popularity of his discourses; Rutt, I, 339.

7   Priestley's *Discourses relating to the evidences of revealed religion. Part I.* Mr Davy was probably Lindsey's correspondent William Davy (see Letter 656).

8   For a possible identification of Nicklin, see Vol. I., Letter 241, n. 4. A Mr Nicklin was minister to a dissenting congregation at Bloxham, but soon moved to Dudley, before giving up preaching; he died at Dudley, *c.* 1781; possibly Lindsey referred to a member of his family.

9   Radcliffe Scholefield was the minister of Old Meeting, Birmingham, from 1772 to 1799. Apart from his emigration to America, I have not been able to establish any biographical information about Mr Griffiths.

10 The 'young Humphreys' were probably members of the family of John Humphreys, one of Priestley's neighbours at Northumberland. On visiting Priestley, William Russell and his family found John Humphreys to be a professed unbeliever; Jeyes, *The Russells of Birmingham*, p. 207.

11 Priestley described this debate in his letter to Lindsey of 3 May 1796; DWL, MS 12.13, partly printed in Rutt, I, 340.

12 For the debates in Congress on the Jay treaty from 7 Mar. to 7 Apr. 1796, see *An abridgement of the debates of Congress, from 1789 to 1856* (16 vols., New York, 1857–61), I, 639–702. There followed debates as to the means by which the treaty was to be put into effect; I, 710–54. The treaty was indeed approved only by a very narrow majority.

13 These letters were almost certainly among those destroyed by Priestley at the end of his life; see Rutt, I, iv.

14 Possibly the MP was Robert Smith, who attended at Essex Street chapel and was Pitt's banker, or James Martin, Pitt's neighbour in Downing Street. For Pitt's approaches, via Denmark, to France for peace negotiations in the late summer of 1796, and the British government's anxiety about the possibility of war with Spain, see Ehrman, *The Younger Pitt. The reluctant transition*, pp. 624–35. After the general election of June 1796, the first session of the new parliament opened on 27 Sept.

15 There is no record of this incident in the *York Courant*, although that newspaper reported on 1 Aug. 1796 the appointment of James Tate, the former amanuensis to Francis Blackburne (see Vol. I, Letter 319, n. 2), to the mastership of Richmond School. Lindsey probably had in mind the march of the *poissardes* to bring Louis XVI and his family from Versailles to Paris in Oct. 1789.

16 Possibly Lindsey referred here to the Hunt family, who were members of Old Meeting, Birmingham. See *Memorials of the Old Meeting House*, memorials section (unpaginated), memorial numbers 98–100. Henry ('Harry') Hunt (d. 1797) was a chapel warden at the Old Meeting, while he and William Hunt were each subscribers of £100 towards the rebuilding of the Old Meeting after the riots of July 1791; *Memorials of the Old Meeting House*, p. 54, and unpaginated list of chapel wardens.

17 Four members of the Mansell family are named in *Memorials of the Old Meeting House* (n. 16, above), memorials section, memorial number 60. Their names were Mary Mansell (d. 1818, aged seventy-six), Ann Mansell (d. 1820, aged eighty-one), Martha Mansell (d. 1823, aged seventy-nine) and Judith Mansell (d. 1828, aged eighty-three). It is not clear whether Lindsey wrote Mrs Bull or Mrtrs (?Masters) Bull; possibly he referred to a member of the family of William Bull (1738–1814), minister of the independent chapel at Newport Pagnell, or his son Thomas; William Bull had been a pupil of Belsham's father, James Belsham, at Newport Pagnell. Another possibility is Joseph Bull (d. 1854) subsequently Bull Bristowe, a student at Manchester College in 1800 and unitarian minister at Hinckley, Ringwood (Hampshire), Topsham and Shepton Mallet.

18 John Corrie had become minister at Bromsgrove in 1795 and had married the following year; see Letter 640, n. 6.

19 Possibly William Hawkes (1731–96), minister of New Meeting, Birmingham, from 1754 to 1780; see Vol. I, Letters 244 and 269. But he had died on 5 Apr. 1796. Possibly Lindsey referred to his son of the same name, who was minister to the Mosley Street chapel, Manchester, from 1789 to 1820. But since Lindsey wrote to Belsham at Birmingham, and since the other friends to whom he sent good wishes in this letter lived in the Birmingham area, perhaps Lindsey meant the elder William Hawkes and was unaware of his death more than three months earlier. That would be explained by Lindsey's absence from London, and his main sources of news, for much of the summer of 1796.

20 For John Edwards, see Letter 608, n. 7.

21 John Coates, assistant minister to Radcliffe Schofield at Old Meeting, Birmingham; see Letter 481, n. 3.

640. To THOMAS BELSHAM   9 AUGUST 1796

Text: DWL, MS 12.57 (10).
Addressed: To/The Rev^d. Mr Belsham/at Mrs Richard's/in the Crescent/
                  Birmingham
Endorsed: [By Belsham] Mr Lindsey Aug^t: 9: 1796
Postmarked: Postmark illegible.

                                                    Richmond. Aug. 9. 1796
Dear Sir,

I thank you for a very acceptable favour, concluded the 3^d. inst. at Warrington, and hope I shall have calculated right, that this may meet you according to your direction on the 12th at Birmingham.[1]

I am sorry that there are good and virtuous young men that reject christianity and look upon it as a fable. I apprehend it must be owing to their being early warped by prejudice and not having done themselves justice in their inquiries, or to some secret undue bias to the world and dislike to the severity of the christian moral. I have always found it so and now find it.

You will receive pleasure in being informed that Mr Paine's Age of Reason, which is said to have terrified so many half-christians and some ministers and made them fear their bible was a fabulous story, does begin already to produce the best effects in making persons look into the Scriptures for themselves and find out their truth and importance and how little Mr Paine knew of them. This I have myself found to be the case in several instances, where I have had an opportunity of putting B^p. Watson's Apology into people's hands, from letters I have received, and from conversation with not a few.[2] They were christians before, but they hardly knew why.[3] They are now satisfied, and have something to say why they are so, and have a pleasure in reading the Bible which they never had before.

I have to confirm this by the best authority. A letter from my excellent friend at Dundee, who first set on foot an application to the B^p. of Ll. to reprint his Apology there, at a low price.[4] It has not been out 3 months, and so great is the demand for it, that already another edition is in the press of 2000 copies. I have not time to transcribe what he says in just comendation of the work, but he concludes from certain premisses, that great good has already arisen and may be expected to arise in consequence of Mr Paine's Age of Reason. It woud seem however from the article, *Theology*, in the *monthly magazine*, and the remarks on the B^p and Dr Priestley, that Mr Paine and Infidelity are still triumphant.[5]

You are very good in giving us an account of Mr Corrie's happy connection. We are really interested for him in his new situation and wish you woud tell him so and that we should rejoice to have it in our power to shew it.[6]

I must now tell You that I have received two days ago a parcell from London, containing two or 3 copies of Dr Priestleys separate discourse and a copy of the Volume lately preached and printed at Philadelphia.[7] The former I much approve, as I also do your reading it to your congregation at Hackney and lending it for that purpose to Mr Edwards. It was a Word in due season, and would do good. I have been able meerly to read the Dedication of the Volume to the Vice President Mr Adams, wch is like all the Doctors compositions of the kind, well adapted to the person and occasion.[8] I have also a letter dated N ____ nd. June. 12; but not written in so chearful a strain as one could have wished, but I do not wonder at it, as it is filled with complaints of receiving no letter or parcell from you or me of 3 months, the last he had being the 2^d of march at Philadelphia.[9] I am really as much disturbed at this as he is, as I had sent letters with parcels more than once a month during 1796, and several in 1795, which he never mentions having come to his hands. Under all circumstances however he contrives to be as happy as possible by being always usefully employed. He was transcribing for the press a small piece in answer to the *New Theory of Chemistry*;[10] was continually busy with his experiments, but the work on which he was chiefly employed was his Church-history, for which he desires his friends to furnish him with any materials which may serve to carry it down to the present times.[11] He had not been negligent in making enquiry about the money in the French Funds, but hitherto it had not answered.[12] He was pleased w^h his son William's ardour in applying to the business of his farm, which was something like poor Harry's but hoped it w^d have a better issue. He had got a very suitable wife, tho' without any fortune.[13] He and his wife were not at a distance to hinder their attending generally at divine service on Sundays. An english printer was just arrived at N ___ nd.[14] Mrs Priestley was pretty we[ll but][15] very much difficulted for want of a servant.

My wife has just rec^d a letter from a friend in the neighbourhood of Leeds, which says that they begin to speak another language there since the stopping of the port of Leghorn.[16] They now see the nation on the brink of a dangerous precipice, for several of them declare they are perfectly uncertain whether they themselves are not already intirely ruined.

Should you write to Mr Kentish before you see him, I would beg you to thank him much for his long letter to me and to say that I shall be happy to concurr all in my power to make young Mr Tingcombe officiating at the Chapel at Dock agreeable to him; I sh^d be still more glad, if You write to Plymouth, to say this for me to him.[17]

We carry my wife's good parent, quite recruited, to her son's at Brignal on Monday next. If you sh^d have time to write a few lines at Birmingham and any thing occur, a letter will be sure to find me, directed at the Rev^d. Mr Blackburne's at Brignal, Greta-bridge, Yorkshire till the 22^d inst. My wife joins in kind respects to Miss Belsham[18] and yourself, and desire you will not forget our sincere salutations to Mr Broadbent when you write to [him]. We sympathize with him in his great loss.[19] Be so good as to distribute our grateful remembrances to the Hunts,[20] Mansells,[21] Russells[22] &c from whom we have rec^d many civilities, and due comp^{ts} to our worthy acquaintance,[23] I am always Dear Sir, very affectionately Yours

T. Lindsey.

---

1   This letter from Thomas Belsham to Lindsey is not in DWL and seems not to have survived.
2   I.e. Watson's *Apology for the Bible*.
3   See Letter 641, where Lindsey quoted a more extended version of this observation.
4   This letter from Robert Millar to Lindsey seems not to have survived. For the Dundee edition of Watson's *Apology for the Bible*, see Letter 641, n. 1.
5   The *MM*, I (July 1796) featured a 'brief retrospect of the state of domestic literature' which included (pp. 481–3) a section headed 'Theology'. In this section, there was praise for Watson's *Apology for the Bible* and for Priestley's work on the evidences of revealed religion. But the writer also complained that other replies to Paine's *Age of reason* were relatively weak and that Paine's 'talents well suited to catch the popular ear' had gained his book much attention (p. 482). The *MM*, founded in 1796, was co-published by Joseph Johnson and Richard Phillips (1767–1840) his fellow-bookseller in St Paul's Churchyard; see Helen Braithwaite, *Romanticism, publishing and dissent. Joseph Johnson and the cause of liberty* (Basingstoke, 2003), p. 159. Phillips, the founder of the *Leicester Herald* in 1792, had been imprisoned in 1793 for selling Paine's *Rights of man* but despite his radical past, he became a leading figure in the City of London and was knighted in 1808.
6   This is a reference to John Corrie (1769–1839), a former pupil of Belsham at the Daventry Academy

and from 1795, minister to a dissenting congregation at Bromsgrove, Worcestershire. His 'happy connection' was his marriage to Mary Read at Kidderminster on 1 July 1796. The new Mrs Corrie died, aged twenty-nine, on 2 Mar. 1804; see *Gent. Mag.*, LXXIV, i (1804), 283, and *Memorials of the Old Meeting House*, memorials section (unpaginated), memorial number 155.

7 Priestley's 'separate' discourse was his *Unitarianism explained and defended*. The volume 'lately preached and printed at Philadelphia' was his *Discourses relating to the evidences of revealed religion, delivered in the Church of the Universalists at Philadelphia*.

8 Priestley's *Discourses relating to the evidences of revealed religion: delivered in the Church of the Universalists at Philadelphia* contained a dedication (pp. iii–viii) to John Adams (1735–1826), the first vice-president (1789–97) and the second president (1797–1801) of the United States. In paying compliments to Adams, Priestley also (p. viii) thanked his adopted country for the 'asylum' which it had afforded him after his departure from England.

9 Priestley made this complaint in his letter to Lindsey of 12 June 1796; Rutt, I, 346–7.

10 Lindsey probably referred here to 'An interesting letter from Dr. Priestley, concerning the principles of the New Theory of Chemistry', published in *MM*, V (1798), 159–60. For the scientific controversy which formed the background to this publication, see Schofield, *Enlightened Joseph Priestley*, pp. 355–6.

11 This is a reference to Priestley's *A general history of the Christian church*.

12 In autumn 1791, John Wilkinson gave £5,000 to Benjamin Vaughan to invest in French government bonds funds on Priestley's behalf, and between then and the autumn of 1793, Wilkinson placed a further sum of £5,000 in the French funds for Priestley. This investment did not yield a profitable return and after Priestley's emigration to America, Wilkinson in compensation allowed Priestley an annual pension of £200 from his own resources. The details may be found in W. H. Chaloner, 'Dr. Joseph Priestley, John Wilkinson and the French Revolution, 1789–1802', *Transactions of the Royal Historical Society*, 5th series, VIII (1958), 27–9.

13 William Priestley's wife was Margaret, née Foulke (1771–1857), the daughter of a Pennsylvania farmer. They were married on 3 Feb. 1796; see Toulmin, 'Descendants of Priestley', 16. After working on a farm near Boston, William Priestley returned to Northumberland, helped his brother Henry with the latter's farm and for a short time managed the whole farm after Henry Priestley's death in Dec. 1795.

14 This English printer was either Ralph Eddowes (Letter 601, n. 3) or Joseph Gales (Letter 646, n. 4).

15 The manuscript is slightly torn at this point.

16 Possibly this friend from the neighbourhood of Leeds was Joseph Bowden (see Letter 697, n. 10), Joseph Wright (see Letter 474, n. 1), a member of the Milnes family of Fryston, Yorkshire, or William Wood, minister of Mill Hill chapel. A remoter possibility is a friend of Lindsey from the late 1730s, when he had been a pupil at the free grammar school in Leeds. Reports of the French army's entry into Leghorn and the closure of the port to British vessels was reported in stages in the British press during July 1796; see, for example, *General Evening Post*, 7–9 July, 14–16 July; *Morning Chronicle*, 16, 19 July 1796.

17 For John Tingecombe and Plymouth Dock chapel, see Letter 589, n. 7. Kentish's letter to Lindsey seems not to have survived.

18 Miss Belsham is a reference to Thomas Belsham's sister Ann; see Letter 639, n. 2.

19 William Broadbent (1755–1827), a pupil of Belsham at Daventry, was minister to the dissenting congregation at Cairo Street, Warrington, from 1792 to 1822. His 'great loss' was the death of his wife Rebecca, who died in early 1796; their only surviving son, Thomas Biggin Broadbent (1793–1817) was a unitarian minister and teacher.

20 See Letter 639, n. 16.

21 See Letter 639, n. 17.

22 Possibly this refers to the family of George Russell, the younger brother of William Russell, who married, firstly, Sarah Grundy and, secondly, Martha Skey, the younger sister of James Skey (1754–1838). George Russell remained in Birmingham to look after the family's commercial interests and did not follow William Russell and his family to America or France.

23 Possibly the 'worthy acquaintance' was Lydia Rickards; see Letter 639, n. 1.

641. To ROBERT MILLAR   **11 AUGUST 1796**

Text: DWL, MS 12.46 (10).
Printed: Graham, 'Unhappy country', 143–4 (fifth paragraph, with
                 omissions).
Addressed: To/M[r] Robert Millar/Merchant/Dundee./By the North Mail
Postmarked: AU 13   RICHMOND

Richmond Yorkshire.
Aug. 11. 1796

Dear Sir,

Two days ago your friendly letter dated the latter end of june came down to me in a parcell from London with 2 copies only of your Dundee Ed. of the Apology, our servant not judging it needful to send more.[1] She does not mark when the parcell arrived, but it is high time it should be acknowleged.[2]

We set out for this place the last day of june, on a few hours warning, upon my wife's receiving a letter from her eldest brother that her mother was in immediate danger from a violent bilious attack and desired to see her. We arrived in 48 hours when happily her illness had taken a somewhat favourable return, which by my wife's nursing and care and the blessing of heaven has been so improved, that though at the age of 83 completed, we trust that a valuable parent, of very extraordinary faculties for her years, and of eminent piety, will have her life prolonged in comfort and usefulness to many for some time to come.[3] We accompany her the next week to her son's at Brignal near Greta bridge, where she has been wont to pass the summer and autumnal months. And having other relations to see and visits to make now we are in the country, and the metropolis empty, we may not return to our own home till the latter end of September.

I have great satisfaction in being able from experience to join in that approbation of B[p] Watson's Apology which you so well express and enlarge upon. We brought down with us some copies of the cheap edition, and have been most agreeably surprized in several instances to find the good effect produced in persons to whom it was given and their acquaintance to whom they lent it. "They were christians before, but they did not know why. they had nothing to say when any body asked them about it, and what the scriptures were and why they believed them. but now they are quite satisfied in their religion, and read their bibles with pleasure and hope they understand them".[4]

I wish the clergy of the established church in general may not be negligent in spreading that needful information which the circulation of this work woud produce. I am told that at a Visitation (i.e.) a clerical meeting) held her[e] ten days before we came, the Apology was spoken of very slightly by some of the leading characters, and the B[p] of Llandaff blamed even for having published it, and put objections in people's way against their religion, which they would otherwise never have heard of.[5]

Together with your letter I had one from D[r] Priestley, and a copy of his Discourses preached and printed this spring at Philadelphia. The last of these is printed and sold separately and not bound up with the others, as it contains his sentiments concerning the Divine Unity &c which he would avoid obtruding upon those to whom they might be unacceptable. The title of the Volume is Discourses *relating* to the Evidences of Revealed Religion; of the last Discourse, Unitarianism explained and defended.[6] M[r] Belsham who you know was the principal Tutor of the college at Hackney, and D[r]

Priestley's successor in the congregation there, sends me word in a letter I lately received from Birmingham; that he had read this Discourse of the Doctor's from the pulpit at Hackney the Sunday before he came away, and had lent it there to Mr Edwards, Dr Priestleys successor, who had repeted it in the Meeting there to a most crouded audience, and that the joy and delight was not to be described with which his former disciples and their families heard the words and message of their old teacher. It was a Word in season, and could not but have a happy effect in reviving and cherishing good principles. As the Doctor's Discourses were all delivered in the Church of the Universalists in Philadelphia, he very properly, at the close of this last, takes occasion to express himself very strongly on the doctrine of Universal Salvation, concluding with a fine passage from Dr Hartley upon the subject.[7] I hope your congregation would not dislike to have this discourse read to them. I have not had time to look into the other Discourses, but barely to read the Dedication to the Vice President Mr Adams, which, like all his compositions of the kind, is excellent, suited to the person and occasion.[8] The Doctor's letter was from N ____ nd,[9] june 12. containing an acc^t of his happiness in his family, (tho' the wound from the loss of his youngest favourite son is not yet healed) Mrs Priestley well and his two other sons virtuous and industrious characters – much employed in his experiments but chiefly in finishing his ecclesiastical history, intended to be carried down to the present times.[10]

I do not suppose the Narrative you inquire after is come out, as I have not heard, nor seen any thing of it in the Papers.[11] My wife had a letter this morning from a lady in the neighbourhood of London, related to and connected with members of both houses and with the ministry, who tells her; that "Two overtures have been certainly made for peace: but the French will not listen to them, except we give up our conquests, every ship we have taken, and seven millions in money. This does not agree, so we must weather out the Storm as well as we can. The Emigrants are removed from Jersey, and from the isle of Wight, through fear, that in case of an attack, they should join their countrymen, as many certainly would; but Ministry are sadly embarrassed, as the french threaten to throw us into confusion before they have done with us".[12]

I do not think the difficulties in St Pauls epistles are to [be] cleared up by a systematic comment however valuable. I sh^d take it as a favour to know particularly those you meet with in the epistle to the Romans and would endeavour to solve them. At our return to London I hope to find that you have rec^d the box of tracts which were forwarded to you when I shall have the pleasure I always feel in writing to you. My wife desires to join in due and kind respects to your ladies and yourself, and I am always, Dear Sir, your much obliged and affectionate servant

T. Lindsey.

---

1   The Dundee edition of Richard Watson's *Apology for the Bible* was printed in London, and reprinted for Edward Lesslie in Dundee, in the summer of 1796. According to the title page it was the seventh edition of that work. It consisted of 112 pages and cost 8d. Similar editions were reprinted in Glasgow, Dublin, Cork and New York.

2   The rate books for the parish of St Clement Danes do not permit the identification of this female servant; see Letter 567, n. 2.

3   I have not been able to discover the exact date of birth of Hannah Lindsey's mother. Possibly she was the Hannah Hotham, daughter of Thomas Hotham, who was baptized on 21 Mar. 1713 (old style: 1714 new style) in the parish of St Margaret's, York (Borthwick Institute for Archives, PR Y/MARG 3). If so, she would have been eighty-two, not eighty-three, 'complete' in Aug. 1796, although it is possible that Lindsey was either mistaken or calculated her age on the basis of the pre-1752 calendar.

St Margaret's was approximately one mile from the parish of St Helen's, where Hannah Hotham married her first husband, Joshua Elsworth, on 1 Jan. 1737/1738; *The parish register of St Crux, York, II, Baptisms, marriages, etc 1716–1837*, ed. Margaret E. Smith (York, 1985), p. 101. Hannah Blackburne died on 23 Aug. 1799 (see Letter 684).

4   For another example of Lindsey's use of this aphorism, see Letter 640.

5   I have not found evidence of a visitation in the archdeaconry of Richmond (which included the deanery of Richmond) between 1794 and 1799; see Cheshire Archives and Local Studies, Chester, diocese of Chester, records of visitations 1554–1846 (DEV).

6   See Letter 640, n. 7.

7   Priestley delivered his 'Discourses on the evidences of divine revelation' at the univeralist church in Philadelphia in Feb. and Mar. 1796. On 15 Feb. 1796 he wrote to Lindsey 'I have the use of Mr. Winchester's pulpit every morning'; Rutt, I, 333. For Elhanah Winchester, see Letter 630, n. 6. The quotation from David Hartley, to which Lindsey referred, may be found in Priestley's *Unitarianism explained and defended*, p. 32. The quotation itself is from Hartley's *Observations on man, his frame, his duty, and his expectations. In two parts* (2 vols., London, 1749), II, 438–9.

8   See Letter 640, n. 8.

9   I.e. Northumberland, Pennsylvania.

10 See Letter 639.

11 This is a reference to Thomas Fyshe Palmer.

12 For these unsuccessful British overtures for peace with France which began in the late summer of 1796 and continued into the autumn, see Letter 639, n. 14, and 642, n. 2. The unpopularity of the French emigrants to Britain after the revolution, and especially those émigré priests who were accused of proselytizing, had increased greatly by 1796; see Dominic Bellenger, 'The émigré clergy and the English church, 1789–1815', *JEH*, XXXIV, 3 (1983), 401ff. Probably the lady who informed Hannah Lindsey was Elizabeth Rayner of Clapham and Sunbury, whose political connexions included members of the Burrell family, including Sir Peter Burrell, from 1796 Baron Gwydir (see Letter 698, n. 5). Lindsey probably did not refer to her by name because he had not mentioned her name in any previous (surviving) letter to Millar.

642. To ROBERT MILLAR   5 OCTOBER 1796

Text: DWL, MS 12.46 (11).
Printed: Graham, 'Unhappy country', 144–6 (second, third, fifth and sixth paragraphs).
Addressed: To/Mr Robert Millar/Merchant/Dundee
Endorsed: A few figures, evidently financial calculations, are written on the address page.
Postmarked: Postmark missing.

London. Oct. 5. 1796

Dear Sir,

After a long absence we arrived here a few days since, the great purpose of our journey answerd in the perfect recovery of my wife's mother, and many other blessings recd. in seeing many friends and relations in good health, and in pursuit of the best things both for themselves and others.

I am happy to be able to inform you, that an opportunity offered soon after Mr Ellis's letter for his son was left at our house, to send it to Botany Bay; and also that accounts have come thence lately and one or two months since, that things are going on much better with our friends, and that they experience much kindness and countenance from Governor Hunter: but I do not find any letter has been received from any of them the three months that we have been in the country.[1]

I am sorry to find that Peace is not a thing at all expected at present, either among the merchants or Gentry, ministerial or antiministerial. Nor is much expected to be revealed about it when the King goes to the house to morrow.[2]

I hopy [*sic*] got my acknowlegements of the kind and welcome letter which came to me from [you] whilst in the country, containing an acc^t of the demand there was in your neighbourhood for the cheap edition of the Bishop's Apology in answer to Mr Paine. I trust this valuable work still continues in[?] request, and shoud be glad to hear that another edition of 2000 was called for. The Bishops bookseller here informs me that the sale continues very lively both of the cheap and the larger edition, and that 6000 had been sold.[3] But he complained of little being to be gained by the cheap edition and seemed to betray a little jealousy at that of Dundee going off so rapidly, which convinced me that he had no value for the work but from the money he could get by it.[4]

I have this week rec^d two letters from Dr Priestley, which gave me the more joy as they brought an account of two out of nine letters with parcells that I had sent him this year being come to his hands. N^r 5 and 6. for I number them: wch gives some hope that the others may reach him in time. He himself was quite depressed, & thought something must have happened to us in hearing nothing.[5]

I think I acquainted you with the very extraordinary attention that was paid to his Discourses this last spring, during the meeting of the congress; and the respect paid to the preacher, by a great proportion of the members of congress, and the rich and learned out of the diff^t provinces.[6] I do not wonder that the discourses were listend to so well, and approved. They form a very valuable addition to those he preached before he left England and printed, on the Evidences of christianity.[7] Some of them appear to me equal if not superior to any thing he has written. Johnson is reprinting them, and when finishd I shall acquaint you and be glad to be put in a way to convey them to You. I have now lying before me a letter from one of his hearers,[8] who with some others has joined in instituting a Society for Xtian Unitarian worship, in wch. the several members take their turning in presiding at the worship. When their n^{rs} increase, or when a proper Minister offers, they intend to adopt one. I have told them what you have done and the example you have set since Mr Palmer went away from Dundee.[9]

Mr Johnson tells me, that Mr Paine has nearly finished an answer to B^p Watson's Apology. I rejoice in it, and so will You, as good of the best kind will arise from it. I shall be desirous to have it, as soon as it comes over.[10]

I am ashamed to produce a former excuse, that I have been forced to write in ye greatest haste, my frank being confined to a day and not having been hardly ever so much engaged the whole day. My wife unites in kind respects and every good wish to yourself, Mrs Millar, and her sister – I remain always Dear Sir Your much obliged and affectionate serv^t

      T. Lindsey.

I should thank you if you could send me any intelligence of Mr Wm Christie. How he goes on in the Seminary to wch he was appointed – and his family that went over with him.[11] He is one I much honour and respect.

---

1   This letter to James Ellis from his father of the same name in Dundee appears not to have survived. For a note on Ellis's family, see Bewley, *Muir of Huntershill*, p. 184.

2   On 6 Oct. 1796, George III formally opened the first session of the new parliament after the general election of May–June 1796. The king's speech referred to efforts for peace with France, stated that an envoy would be dispatched to Paris for this purpose and insisted that meanwhile a determined war effort must be maintained; *LJ*, XLI, 14. In the debate on the address of thanks, Pitt went into further detail about the aspiration for peace; Cobbett, *Parl. hist.*, XXXIII, 1201–6. On 18 Oct. 1796, the

experienced diplomat James Harris (1746–1820), Baron Malmesbury, departed for France on behalf of the British government on what turned out to be an unsuccessful peace mission.

3 For the various editions of Watson's *Apology for the Bible*, see Letters 625, n. 4, 627, n. 7, 633, n. 9 and 641, n. 1. His regular bookseller was Robert Faulder of 42 Bond Street, who also published key works of William Paley.

4 See Letter 641, n. 1.

5 Lindsey probably referred here to Priestley's letters to him dated 28 July and 1 Aug. 1796, DWL, MS 12.13 and partly printed in Rutt, I, 347–9 and 349–50. The reference to 'N^r 5 and 6' may be found in the letter of 1 Aug. 1796. Lindsey evidently numbered his letters to Priestley, probably in a separate sequence for each calendar year; Priestley referred to the fifth and sixth letters from Lindsey to him in 1796.

6 Lindsey referred here to his letter to Millar of 11 Aug. 1796 (Letter 641).

7 For Priestley's *Discourses relating to the evidence of revealed religion. Vol. I*, preached at Hackney and published in London in 1794, see Letter 542.

8 Possibly this hearer was Ralph Eddowes; see Letter 601, n. 3. Possibly, too, the letter which Lindsey mentioned was written by Eddowes to his brother-in-law, Timothy Kenrick, whose second wife was Elizabeth, the sister of Thomas Belsham, and through that connexion came to Lindsey's attention.

9 Millar had in effect kept the unitarian congregation in Dundee in existence since Palmer's transportation.

10 On 3 Mar. 1797, Paine told Wolfe Tone in Paris that he was preparing a reply to Bishop Watson, 'in which he belabours the prelate without mercy'; quoted in A. O. Aldridge, *Man of reason. The life of Thomas Paine* (London, 1960), p. 258. In the preface to his *Agrarian justice opposed to agrarian law and to agrarian monopoly* (Paris and London, 1797), p. 3, Paine threatened that Watson 'may depend on hearing from me'. In *A letter to the honourable Thomas Erskine, on the prosecution of Thomas Williams, for publishing the age of reason* (Paris, 1797), pp. 24–5, Paine asserted that the prosecution of Williams was undertaken only after it became known that Paine would reply to Watson's *Apology for the Bible*. He claimed that since the prosecution was promoted by the clergy, and that if 'the object be to prevent an exposure of the numerous and gross errors he [Watson] has committed in his work … it is a confession that he feels the weakness of his cause, and finds himself unable to maintain it. In this case, he has given me a triumph I did not seek.'

11 For William Christie's early career in America and his work as a teacher of French at the Winchester Academy, Virginia, see Letter 635, n. 8, and *MR*, VI (1811), 198–201. He remained in Winchester until 1801 and lived in Pennsylvania from 1801 to 1806.

643. To JOHN ROWE   7 OCTOBER 1796

Text: JRUL, Lindsey Letters, vol. II, no. 96.
Printed: McLachlan, *Letters*, p. 123 (first five sentences of
                 third paragraph); p. 134 (third and fourth sentences of first
                 paragraph).
Addressed: To/The Rev^d. John Rowe/Shrewsbury
Postmarked: OC 7 96

London. Octr. 7. 1796

Dear Sir,

We returned to our own home the latter end of the last week, after a much unexpected absence of full three months, happy in the main object of our sudden journey being accomplished in the restoration of my wife's aged parent to health and comfort and some degree of usefulness, to which under providence she seems to have contributed. Nor has the rest of the time been wholly mispent, as we have had opportunities of observing the course and tendency of things and seen various friends, all of them in health, and in the pursuit of the best things both for themselves and others, which alone can yield solid comfort. I am happy to be able to inform you, from my own experience and that of others, that the circulation of the B^p of Llandaffs Apology, the cheap edition, in different parts of England, and especially in Scotland, has been of infinite service in recalling some few, and in fortifying and preserving great numbers who were in danger of rejecting the gospel, through the prevalent infidel conversation and zeal of the times increased by the publication of Mr Paines Age of Reason; I speak only of the lowest and middle ranks of life. So that a valuable and most enlightened christian friend of mine, by whose first suggestion B^p. Watson was applied to for leave to print a cheap edition of the Apology at Dundee, is fully persuaded, that Mr Paine's book has already been of great service in promoting that gospel which he seeks to destroy.[1] I myself find, that those who have heard of or read M^r. Paine's objections, and have seen the B^{ps} Apology, say, that they never before were so fully satisfied in being christians. They now understand what it is to be christians, and why they are so, and are not at a loss what to answer to those that make objection to the Bible, &c &c. I shall rejoice if you have had the good fortune to meet with any pleasing instances of this kind, in your intended excursion this last summer to the sea-side, with Mrs Rowe and your family, which she signified to me in a very kind and obliging letter, that came to London about ten days after we left it, and which I did not receive till You had probably left Shrewsbury and it might be uncertain where a letter might meet with You. At all events I hope you will be able to give us the great satisfaction of acquainting us, that the sea air and water, has been of service to the health of you all, and particularly that the little stranger thrives and does well, of whose arrival we took it most kindly in your lady to inform us as well as of her own intire recovery.[2]

We have been told that Mr Arthur Aikin has passed some days at Shrewsbury this summer. I sh^d be glad to know whether you was there at the time, and how he comported himself. It comes to me from a report, whose foundation I should be glad to call in question, that he is not only a rejecter of Divine Revelation but entertains doubts about the very being of a God, if he does not intirely discard the idea out of his system. He is so young, and has Shewn himself so fickle and rapid in giving up opinions in which he appeared to be well estabilished, that I do not expect he will long remain in his present extreme.[3] I rec^d. two letters from Dr Priestley whilst we were in the North. In one of them, written just before he left Philadelphia, after having passed three months in the city and preached his Discourses, he appears quite overjoyed at the attention wch had been paid to them, by all the first of the country and others, and at the prospect of the good effects of them, in enlightening their minds and checking the progress of infidelity.[4] And it is no more than is to be expected from them, & which you will say they are capable of, when you read them, and Johnson tells me the Vol. wch he is reprinting here, will soon be out of the Press.[5]

The Doctor's last letter is dated Aug. 6. speaks therein of his philosophical, but more of his theological labours.[6] He has already carried down his Ecclesiastical History to the Reformation, and is about to print. It will take up 4 vol^s. of the size of the two published in this country. He is collecting Materials to carry the history on from the Reformation to the present times.[7] His writings grow more and more in request in that country. But in general they[8] are universally void of all serious sense of God, desire to know his truth; which have been extinguished by ignorance, superstition, french and english principles, and the thirst of gain perhaps more than all the rest.

I was much gratified by Mrs Rowe's taking the trouble of mentioning Mr Tayleur's housekeeper being so well provided for, so as not to be in any anxiety about her worldly maintenance.[9] Dr Priestley remarks, that tho' we can none of us enjoy any more *terrace-walks*, we shall hereafter expatiate together in still better scenes.[10] I am often asked when his funeral discourse will be publishd. Pray tell me what you know of it.[11] My wife unites in cordial respects to you and M[rs] Rowe, and wishes for health and all good to you and yours. We beg to be kindly and respectfully remembered to M[r] Wood and his brother[12] and M[r] Harries. I remain always Dear Sir Your obliged friend and servant

T. Lindsey.

1   This 'enlightened christian friend' was almost certainly Robert Millar.
2   See Letter 636, n. 9.
3   In the summer of 1796, Arthur Aikin and his brother Charles Rochemont Aikin embarked on a walking tour of Shropshire and North Wales, in pursuit of their geological interests. By his 'present extremes', Lindsey meant the former's scepticism as to revealed religion, a scepticism which he did not abandon. Born on 19 May 1773, Arthur Aikin was aged twenty-three in Oct. 1796.
4   See Letter 642.
5   For these *Discourses*, see Letter 640, n. 8.
6   This refers to Priestley's letter to Lindsey of 1 (not 6) Aug. 1796; DWL, MS 12.13, partly printed in Rutt, I, 349–50. In a passage from this letter omitted by Rutt, Priestley wrote 'I am now employd in the *History of the Reformation*, and hope to continue it to the present time.'
7   This work was Priestley's *A general history of the Christian church from the fall of the western empire*. The latter section of Vol. III (1803) covered the period 'from the beginning of the Reformation in Germany' to 'the conclusion of the Council of Trent'.
8   It is safe to assume that Lindsey referred here not to Priestley's works but to Americans in general.
9   See Letter 637, n. 5.
10 Priestley referred to Tayleur's death in his letter to Lindsey of 1 Aug. 1796; Rutt, I, 349–50. The reference to 'terrace walks', however, was omitted by Rutt and may be found in the manuscript of this letter in DWL, MS 12.13.
11 For Theophilus Houlbrooke's funeral sermon for Tayleur, see Letter 636, n. 6.
12 See Letter 575, n. 6.

644. WILLIAM TURNER OF NEWCASTLE   20 OCTOBER 1796

Text: DWL, MS 12.44 (59).
Printed: McLachlan, *Letters*, p. 7 (sixth sentence of fifth paragraph); p. 123 (first two sentences of third paragraph).
Addressed: To/The Rev[d] M[r] Turner/Newcastle upon Tyne
Endorsed: [?By Thomas Belsham] Oct[r]. 20: 1796
Postmarked: Postmark missing

London. Oct. 20. 1796

Dear Sir,

I thank you for a very welcome letter, which was delivered to me by M[r] Gibson,[1] who brought a letter of recomendation in his ingenuous modest countenance and demeanor, if you had said nothing in his behalf. He and M[r] Freron did us the pleasure of taking a breakfast with us a few days after, when my wife took to both our guests as much as myself. I had some conversation with M[r] Gibson alone, when he first called, and have a good hope that he will be upon his guard against vice and bad principles, in which I trust he will be aided by his young friend M[r] Freron.[2] The latter very obligingly called upon me yesterevening to remind me of a friend of his setting out to Newcastle by whom he had told me I might convey any little parcell to You; when I gave him D[r] Priestleys Disc. at Philadelphia, the last of the sett there delivered this last spring, and published by itself; a philosophical piece of his,[3] and D[r] Toulmins late defence of Unitarians against the accusations of M[r] Fuller, of which I beg your kind acceptance.[4]

I am glad you liked the little American tract, which I hoped would do good to some, and have been rejoiced to find it much in request in the north; and in the West, where there is a cheap edition, of 4^d a piece printing.[5] Dr D. did not acquaint me with your having received a copy.

In these last 4 months I have had 4 letters from Dr Priestley, the last dated so late as August, desiring books and other things to be sent to him, whence you may conclude that the report of his coming to settle in France, wherever it was forged has no sort of foundation.[6] By his own account, and that of others, I fancy hardly ever any discourses were heard with more attention and benefit than those preached this last spring during the sitting of Congress at Philadelphia, and printed at the desire of their[7] hearers. You will not be surprized at their reception when you peruse them, and Johnson gives out that the new edition will be ready this week. The D^r. tells me had sent 25 copies of the last Disc. of which I have sent you one, and the same number of the Volume, all the first, but only one copy of the last has been delivered to me. He is wholly occupied in his theological and philosophical pursuits at Northumberland, & in composing a sett of Discourses to be preached this next spring at Philadelphia. He has finished and transcribed for the press, the continuation of his Ecclesiastical History to the time of the Reformation, and says it will take up four additional Vol^s. of the size of those two which he printed in England. He intends to carry this history downwards to the present times, and has already made a beginning.[8]

I suppose you may have seen the additional numbers of our Comentaries, lately printed, and should be glad to know your sentiments on the article relating to Mr Evanson's Dissonance.[9] If You have not got it, and will let me know, I will send it.

I am intirely of accord with you in your remarks on the present turn to infidelity and the providential ends which it is likely to answer for the present and in the result, all for good: but times of tribulation are certainly coming upon us, and very fast.

I do not wonder you are pleased with the ingenious Mr Cogan's tract. Pity tis that it had been drawn up in the easy perspicuous stile, in which Dr Priestley would have put it. As it is it must affect every mind that is not shut up against conviction: which is the case with many. And the transition from unbelief to Atheism is but too easy, and natural, as Dr P. has well remarked in these discourses of his that are coming forth.[10] I shall inquire of Johnson ab^t your Subscription. He is a worthy and most honest man, but incorrigibly neglectful, often to his own detriment. I was not in town last week at the quarterly meeting of the society, and I understand there was no business done, through want of a sufficient number, but at the meeting the next month will mention your kind offer of 30 copies of Mr Holland's Thoughts on Truth, which I am persuaded will be thankfully accepted.[11]

I beg leave to trouble you with the inclosed to Mr Garnet,[12] to whom you have been and are a true friend, and who is grateful for it. We conclude that Mrs Turner and your little family are well from your saying nothing to the contrary. My wife joins me in kind respects to you both. I am always, Dear Sir, affectionately Yours
T. Lindsey.

---

1   Thomas Gibson (1759–1832), a banker in Newcastle upon Tyne and the first treasurer of the Newcastle Literary and Philosophical Society. For Lindsey's previous meetings with him in London, see Letters 394 and 395.

2   Probably William Fearon, listed as a member of the Literary and Philosophical Society of Newcastle from its inception in 1793, where he is denominated 'Esq'. See the printed 'List of members … 1793',

p. 4, which formed part of the Society's first annual report. It is unlikely that Lindsey referred to Louis-Marie Stanislas Fréron (1754–1802), a leading French revolutionary, member of the Convention, and subsequently an opponent of Robespierre and ally of Napoleon.

3 Probably this work was Priestley's *A continuation of the letters to the philosophers and politicians of France.*

4 Joshua Toulmin, *The practical efficacy of the unitarian doctrine considered, in a series of letters to the Reverend Andrew Fuller: occasioned by his publication entitled the calvinistic and Socinian systems examined and compared as to their moral tendency* (London, 1796). For the controversy between Toulmin and the Calvinist baptist Andrew Fuller (1754–1815), see Alan P. F. Sell, 'Andrew Fuller and the Socinians', *E & D*, XIX (2000), 91–115.

5 The 'little American tract' was John Clarke's *Answer to the question.* The 'new edition' of 1797 (see Letter 625, n. 5) was priced at 4*d*, or 28*s* per hundred. Probably it was reprinted by the Western Unitarian Society; or possibly Lindsey referred to Joshua Toulmin's edition of 1797 (see Letter 645, n. 7), which was priced at 3*d* or 16*s* per hundred.

6 These four letters from Priestley to Lindsey were probably those of 3 May, 12 June, 28 July and 1 Aug. 1796. All four letters are in DWL, MS 12.13 and are partly printed in Rutt, I, respectively at 338–9, 346–7, 347–9 and 349–50.

7 Lindsey first wrote 'their', then crossed out the last two letters of the word.

8 For this letter from Priestley to Lindsey, dated 1 Aug. 1796, see Letter 643, n. 6.

9 Number IX of *Commentaries and essays* was published in Sept. 1796. It included (pp. 313–46) essay number XXIII, entitled 'A letter to the Rev. Mr Evanson, in defence of his principal object in his book intitled, The dissonance of the four generally received evangelists, and the evidence of their respective authenticity examined'. It was dated 1 June 1796 and its author was 'Philologus Christianus' (possibly Michael Dodson; see Letter 418, n. 17).

10 This work was Eliezer Cogan's *Reflections on the evidences of Christianity* (London, 1796), which defended revealed religion and miracles. For a note on Cogan, see Letter 388, n. 18.

11 The Unitarian Society minute book (p. 59) stated that there was no 'general quarterly meeting' of the society in Oct. 1796. Its record (p. 59) of the monthly committee meeting on 3 Nov. 1796 made no mention of Turner's gift of John Holland's *Thoughts on truth, on prejudice, and on sincerity* (?London, 1795). The author, the Rev. John Holland of Mobberly, Cheshire, was related to Turner on Turner's mother's side.

12 Possibly the chemist and physician Thomas Garnett (1766–1802), a popular lecturer on scientific subjects, whom Turner persuaded to give lectures in Newcastle in 1798–9. Garnett became professor of natural philosophy at Anderson's Institution in Glasgow and, from 1799, professor of natural philosophy and chemistry at the Royal Institution in London. See Harbottle, *William Turner*, p. 67.

645. To RUSSELL SCOTT 12 NOVEMBER 1796

Text: Scott Coll.
Printed: McLachlan, 'Lindsey to Scott', 122–3 (short quotations from sixth paragraph; first two sentences of seventh paragraph; sixth sentence of eighth paragraph).
Addressed: To/The Rev[d]. Russell Scott/Portsmouth
Endorsed: Nov[r]. 13th/96
Postmarked: NO 12 96

London. Nov[r]. 12. 1796

Dear Sir,

Part of the time since we came out of the North we have been in Surrey wth some friends who woud not dispense with our paying them a visit, and during the rest I have been unusually engaged, or should not have waited for a line from you, but shoud have provoked you by a letter of inquiry after you; not to mention a very troublesome cold lately which prevented seeing our valuable friend when he called upon us, w[ch] I much regret and you will be so good as to tell him;[1] and my wife also happened to be peculiarly taken up with a young lady in the house so that she c^d not leave her a minute, with wch she will acquaint him when he favours us again.[2] But too much perhaps for this.

We are most truly rejoiced to find that you are now in tolerable health, though concerned to learn that you have been far from being to boast of in that respect during the summer, by M^r P's relation.[3]

I hope that by the blessing of divine providence, which has so evidently thrown in your way the new engagement you are soon to enter upon, You will be indued with health and strength to discharge it.[4] Certainly it does you great credit, and on that account must give you pleasure, in such a singular testimony to your worth and character and talents. And they who are desirous of putting such a trust in your hands, cannot but be the more careful that you do not suffer in it, from seeing the disinterested manner in which you undertake it. I flatter myself that a little employment and attention of this kind will do you good many ways. We cannot offer to be of any service; but my wife bids me tell You, that should you want any more of those papers formerly sent she will readily accomodate you with them on the terms on which the former have been sent.[5]

With regard to the £5 You acted most rightly in not mentioning the contributor. Mr Palmer's benefit alone was intended for particular reasons, but as Skirving was his fellow-sufferer under Campbell it is desired that the trifle may be for those two only; if you could have an opportunity of applying it, or if you transmit it to M^r. Rutt.[6]

Mr Porter would probably tell you of the pleasure which we had in the country in perceiving the great use of circulating B^p Watsons apology in counteracting the endeavours industriously used to turn men against X^ty and the Bible by spreading Paine's Age of Reason, and various other books. I should be glad to know if a dozen of the Bishops tract, or a number of the American tract, or any other of those printed by our Society, would be acceptable to you, and be in your way to dispose of. Dr Toulmin has lately reprinted the little American piece at a cheap price, and I am glad to say that we have found this very seasonable, in giving christians something to say for their religion, when attacked.[7] If proper efforts be made in this way to fortify the minds of ordinary christians against the comon objections, I am persuaded that Divine revelation will be a gainer by the opposition of Mr Payne and others.

I must not forget to satisfy you with respect to an accusation brought against the editor of Dr Priestley's Cause of Infidelity, in one of the periodical prints, of suppressing some things in it. Tis true, there were a few paragraphs suppressed, and the Editor had authority for it; but woud not have done it, had he deemed it likely to get abroad. He did[8] however think it proper to take notice of the insinuation but to let it die away. The paragraphs in question related to the millennium and Christ's personal appearance on earth, which is a nostrum of the author's, advanced indeed before, but which it was thought might better be omitted. Sh^d it however come to a 2^d Edition the part will be inserted.[9]

Our college in Hackney seems now as if it had never been, no one talking of it, no thought of reviving it. Mr Belsham has taken a house in Grove Place, wch will contain 5 pupils and no more. He has already four, and has another engaged, which will be his complement.[10] You woud see the acc^t of the meeting of the Body of Dissenters of the three Denominations at Dr Williams's Library, and the *Declaration* they publishd relating to the Militia Act, and profanation of the Lords day.[11] It is expected the Declaration will be followed up by some resolutions: but that it sh^d be published alone, is matter of wonder, Dr Rees the mover, seconded by a M^r or D^r. Barber.[12]

I have had no letters from Dr Priestley since the middle of August. He was then meditating the subject of his discourses before Congress the ensuing Spring; and busy in his experiments. Mr Chandler from Gloucester called on us the other day, and mentioned that Mr Russell was coming back with his family from America.[13] The young ladies, the eldest of whom corresponds with my wife, woud be very glad of it.[14] An American ship that bro^t packets from her & Dr Priestley, was lately taken by the French as carrying English commodities. D^r P's son W^m is married to a German Farmer's daughter, a very suitable match I hear.[15] My wife joins in all kind regards to Mrs Scott and yourself and good wishes for your young folks. I remain always your affectionate & obliged

      T. Lindsey.

---

1   This 'valuable friend' of Scott and Lindsey was probably a Portsmouth connexion. Sir John Carter, William John Porter and Richard Godman Temple are obvious possibilities.

2   Regrettably, Lindsey did not identify the young lady.

3   It is an editorial assumption that Lindsey meant 'by Mr P's account', rather than a family relative of Mr P.

4   For the possibility that Scott might move to Bath as minister to the Trim Street congregation there, see Letter 653.

5   This is probably a reference to Lindsey and his wife sending to Scott some of Lindsey's manuscript sermons; 'the terms' were that Lindsey's name was not to be mentioned if Scott were to draw upon them in his own preaching. See Letters 630 and 633, n. 2.

6   This appears to be a reference to Captain Patrick Campbell of the *Surprise*.

7   This 'little American piece' was John Clarke's *Answer to the question*; Joshua Toulmin reprinted it, with a one-page advertisement in his name, dated Taunton, 11 Oct. 1796. Toulmin's edition also included Lindsey's advertisement to the edition which he reprinted in 1797; see Letter 625, n. 5. The title page of Toulmin's edition stated that it was reprinted in London and Taunton in 1797, but it was evidently in circulation well before the end of 1796. On 3 Nov. 1796, the committee of the Unitarian Society decided to purchase 250 copies of Toulmin's edition; Unitarian Society minute book, p. 59.

8   Lindsey seems to have omitted the word 'not' at this point.

9   Lindsey referred here to a review in the *Critical Review*, XVI (Mar. 1796), 307–12, of the London reprint of Priestley's *Observations on the prevalence of infidelity*; see Letter 613, n. 8. The review complained that material concerning miracles and the millennium, included in the original (American) edition, had been 'suppressed' in the edition under review, because the publishers believed Priestley's opinions on these subjects 'would either not suit the climate of England, or give a sanction to an opinion which they may think ill founded' (p. 307). It added that such omissions should have been indicated on the title page and strongly criticized the publishers and editor(s) for the omission. The omitted material was restored in the next (in effect the third) edition, for which see Letter 652, n. 2.

10   Belsham's house was in Grove Place, Hackney.

11   At an extraordinary meeting of the General Body of Protestant Dissenting Ministers in London, on 3 Nov. 1796, Abraham Rees proposed and Joseph Barber (see n. 12, below) seconded a motion expressing the hope that that the Militia bill going through parliament would not involve any profanation of the Sabbath. In particular, they were concerned lest officers would call out their men for training and exercise on Sundays. The meeting noted that the bill, after its third reading in the house of commons, had been sent to the house of lords with the omission of this 'most obnoxious clause which had occasioned this Extraordinary Meeting' but that doubts remained respecting the meaning and possible operation of other clauses; DWL, MS 38.196, p. 340. For the background, see J. R. Western, *The English militia in the eighteenth century. The story of a political issue 1660–1802* (London, 1965), pp. 219–20, 301.

12   Joseph Barber (1727–1810), minister at Founders Hall, London, from 1764 to 1797, and at Aldermanbury Postern from 1797 to 1810. He was theological tutor at Hoxton Academy from 1778 to 1791; see Wilson, *Dissenting churches*, II, 555–7. He was Mr, not Dr, Barber.

13   For Richard Chandler of Gloucester, see Letter 516, n. 4. Although William Russell contemplated a return to England in 1796, he remained in America until 1801. He then travelled in the first place to

Hamburg, where he had commercial interests, then resided in France until the end of the Napoleonic war in 1814, before finally returning to England. Chandler's knowledge of Russell's possible movements is probably explained by their Gloucestershire connexion.

14 Russell's eldest daughter was Martha (1766–1807), who married James Skey in 1798. Her letter to Hannah Lindsey appears not to have survived.

15 Priestley's second son William married Margaret Foulke (see Letter 640, n. 13) in Feb. 1796.

646. To ROBERT MILLAR   19 NOVEMBER 1796

Text: DWL, MS 12.46 (12).
Printed: Graham, 'Unhappy country', 146–8 (most of first paragraph; third and sixth paragraphs).
Addressed: Address missing.
Postmarked: Postmark missing.

London. Novr. 19. 1796.

Dear Sir,

I received great pleasure from your favour of Octr. 21. as it was fraught with the good news of your own and your lady and sisters healths, and a variety of other friendly communications, and particularly the affecting account of our friend and his sufferings under his own hand.[1] I had heard most of the things recounted at different times and more dilated upon; but there is a singular though melancholy satisfaction in his own words[2] to a friend, conveying the history of so horrid a plot against his life and reputation, without any undue passion or resentment against the vile agents employed in it. The account of this transaction, which he mentions in this letter to have been sent over by him, with a view of having it published; and also a subsequent account, sent off after the former, under the apprehension of that being lost; have both of them come safe, and that last received has been for some time in the hands of a Printer, and expected to be made public: but I am disposed to believe that the delay has been and is occasioned by the apprehension of exciting powerful enmities and adding to the load that already lies so heavy on innocent men: a danger, which you very wisely wish we should guard against, and you may depend upon my attention to it. But I shall take the liberty to keep our friends letter a little longer in my possession, as there are some persons not yet come to Town, whom I should be glad to gratify with a sight of it. And perhaps I may take the liberty to shew it to those who have in hand the publication of the case (at whatever time it may come out) if it can be of any assistance to them.[3] It must yield great satisfaction, that your efforts to help and to comfort him in such a trying hour of distress, were so seasonable as his letter describes them to have been.

I am not surprized that the state of your Society does not flourish by an increase of your stated hearers. From the loss of some of your members, the scepticism of others, and the secular minds of too many, the thinness of such an unfashionable audience is easily to be accounted for. And you have nothing to attract the multitude, particularly to teach them a new way of getting to heaven without the trouble of forsaking their sins and a strict moral practice. But the service you do to virtue and true religion, though much of it may be unknown to you, is I am persuaded, very great. The example you set, the pure worship of God which you preside over, are conspicuous things, are talked over, canvassed, and produce silent good effects, which you never hear of. If I had the happiness of being at Dundee, I am persuaded I should find out much for encouragement, which you do not see. I do however most truly honour you for persevering in the midst of many obstacles, and unpleasant circumstances.

You have a claim on account of your own efforts, and will be delighted with the account of his similar society, which I this very day, since I began my letter, have rec^d from Dr Priestley, dated Septr 11.

"I have the greatest satisfaction in the Lay-Unitarian Society I have been the means of estabilishing in Philadelphia. Mr Gales (who was a printer in Sheffield) writes me word, that the congregation increases, and all who attend have increasing satisfaction.[4] At first they allowed too many to read the Service: but now they have improved that plan. Six persons, chosen by ballot, are to direct every thing, and one of this number to administer the Lord's Supper. In our present circumstances, a society of this kind is better than with a Minister. It both prevents superstition, and is propagated without expence. It also cuts off all objections to a congregation from the improper conduct of a Minister. And my going occasionally, and preaching without salary, may have a better effect than if I had resided on the spot.["]][5]

My wife, who takes the trouble of keeping an exact statement of all money-matters, desires me to inform you, that after paying for Dr Priestley's Vol. of Discourses printed at Philadelphia, there will be one guinea and half due to you. And an opportunity presents, I hope, of sending the volume soon, as the post has brought me a letter from Mr Duncan, with a commission for some books to be sent to Dundee by Mr Johnson, which I shall urge him to dispatch as expeditiously as possible. I shall also trouble you with a few lines which I shall inclose to Mr Duncan, as I have procured a frank for monday to convey this to You.

But alas! how uncertain are human things! Another letter is brought in from Dr Priestley, written but 8 days after the former, in which he acquaints me that that very day Mrs Priestley was to be buried.[6] At the close of the other he mentioned her having had a slight feverish indisposition, but was growing better; but soon after the disorder took an unfavourable turn. She had never recovered her wonted spirits after the loss of their youngest son nine months before. You would be greatly edified with the manner in which he speaks of this sad event, and the sudden unexpected dissolution of such an intimate union and friendship of 34 years duration; supported by the sure prospect of meeting again hereafter with all we loved and valued here.[7] Happy is it for him, that he is not alone in that distant country to sustain the shock: but has his two sons, both happily married and settled near him, so near as to be part of the congregation that are his weekly hearers. With his eldest son, who has only one child, and daughter in law, a very amiable sensible character, I should imagine he will live, as he has no more idea of taking care of and providing for a family than a child.[8] The late Mrs P. was every thing to him that he could want, with a strong, well-cultivated virtuous mind, in a comely form, seemingly built for a longer duration.

I have forgotten to thank you for the intimation of a certain description of persons in your neighbourhood. Your judgment of such men and meetings I have often experienced to be true. They are always decide [*sic*] characters and unchangeable. Books put in the way of those that will read, might be of service: particularly our just named Hero's Letters to Unbelievers; which I fear is a book at present nearly, if not altogether out of print.[9] Perhaps, if you favour me with a few lines pretty soon, they may come in time for me to add any other book or pamphlet to the parcell that

is to come to Mr Martin for Dundee.[10] My wife desires her kind respects to yourself and to be recommended with me to your fair party. I am always most truly Yours
T. Lindsey.

I send you in my postscript in what way I have been wont to satisfy myself with respect to the story in John. v. 2.3.4. I wish it may do the same for you.[11]

I find I have not time, nor will my cover I fear, carry another letter; I must therefore beg you to acquaint Mr Duncan that I have rec^d his letter containing Mr Martins commission to Mr Johnson, which I have delivered to him and which he will set about executing forthwith. You will be pleased to add my kind respects to Mr Duncan, and that I fully intend to thank him myself for his not declining to write to me, tho I have been so negligent a correspondent.

1   Millar's letter to Lindsey, with the account of Palmer's sufferings, seems not to have survived. For another example of Lindsey's receipt of a report of Palmer's misfortunes, see Letter 633, n. 3.
2   I.e. Thomas Palmer's own words.
3   Lindsey had in mind Jeremiah Joyce, who took a leading part in the preparation of Palmer's *Narrative* for publication, and Benjamin Flower, who was its publisher. The *Narrative* first became available in Dec. 1796, although the title page gives 1797 as the year of publication.
4   This is indeed a quotation from Priestley's letter to Lindsey of 11 Sept. 1796; Rutt, I, 352. Joseph Gales (1761–1841) founded the radical newspaper, the *Sheffield Register* in 1787. He was a prominent supporter of the Sheffield Constitutional Society, published the first cheap edition of Paine's *Rights of man* and, from 1792 to 1794, ran the radical fortnightly periodical, *The Patriot*. His association with leading radicals, including Priestley, led Gales and his family to emigrate, in the first place to Germany, and in 1795 to America, where he established a small Unitarian Society at Philadelphia. In America he continued his career as a publisher; like Priestley, he never returned to Britain.
5   This letter may be found in Rutt, I, 352–4.
6   Priestley communicated the news of the death of his wife in his letter to Lindsey of 19 Sept. 1796; DWL, MS 12.13, partly printed in Rutt, I, 354–5. Mary Priestley died at Northumberland, Pennsylvania, on 17 Sept. 1796.
7   Priestley and Mary Wilkinson were married at Wrexham on 23 June 1762.
8   Joseph Priestley junior and his wife Elizabeth, née Ryland, had one child in 1796, namely their son Joseph Rayner Priestley, who was born on 23 Mar. 1793 and died in 1863. See Toulmin, 'Descendants of Priestley', 18.
9   See Letter 644, n. 3.
10   James Martin, bookseller of Dundee and an associate of Edward Lesslie (see Letter 641, n. 1). He was a sympathizer with the London Corresponding Society and forwarded some of its publications to Dundee; see Harris, *The Scottish people and the French Revolution*, p. 162.
11   This postscript took the form of a separate document (DWL, MS 12.46 (38)), consisting of two and a half sides, in Lindsey's hand, setting out his interpretation of John v. 2–16 (the story of the pool of Bethesda, and of Christ's healing a lame man on the Sabbath).

647. To ROBERT MILLAR   10 DECEMBER 1796

Text: DWL, MS 12.46 (13).
Addressed: To/M^r. Robert Millar/Merchant/Dundee
Postmarked: Postmark missing.

London. Decr. 10. 1796

Dear Sir,

I have been extremely mortified to find that at last your copy of Dr Priestleys last Discourses at Philadelphia did not go along with the Dundee parcell to Mr Martin.[1] Mr Johnson however promises me that it shall go soon. With respect to the state of your finances in my wife's hands, You have certainly one guinea and a half at present after Dr Priestleys Volume paid for, for she is exactness itself in that and in every thing else.

I thank you for giving me leave to retain Mr Palmer's letter, and shall make the use I ought of your confidence. It is at present in the hands of M^r. Gurney the counsellor to compare with his other narratives, which are larger, and more formally drawn up. It is expected that the Statement will soon be made public, as it has been carefully inspected, that it may carry nothing forth to the public that may hurt the author.[2] We are waiting for the issue of another business, relating to our exiled friends, with which you shall be acquainted with when it is known: but I do not look for much from it.[3]

I have not time to say all I intended with respect to some things in your letter, and to other matters, having been twice interrupted since I began by two friends whom I could not turn away, my cover confining me to the day, and having to inclose a few lines to Mr Duncan, as I engaged to do. I shall therefore only desire you to make our best regards acceptable to your two ladies and accept my wife's, till You have a few lines again from your affectionate servant[4]

T. Lindsey.

---

[1] For Priestley's *Discourses* preached at Philadephia in 1796, see Letter 631, n. 6. For James Martin of Dundee, see Letter 646, n. 10.

[2] This letter from Palmer was almost certainly either that to Disney (see Letter 633, n. 3) or that to which he referred in Letter 646. By Palmer's 'other narratives' Lindsey meant his *Narrative* ('larger, and more formally drawn up').

[3] Possibly 'another business' was an idea for a petition on behalf of Palmer and his fellow-convicts, or a parliamentary initiative in their favour, such as that of 24 Feb. 1794 (see Letter 557, n. 2). Neither idea came to anything.

[4] Lindsey's next surviving letter to Millar was that of 21 Feb. 1797 (Letter 650).

648. To JOHN ROWE   23 DECEMBER 1796

Text: Royal Soc., Priestley Memorial Volume, p. 59.
Addressed: To/The Rev^d. Mr Rowe/Shrewsbury
Postmarked: Postmark illegible.

London. Decr. 23. 1796.

Dear Sir,

I dare not look back or say any thing about the date of your letter, which has lain by me so long unacknowleged; not however without oft thinking and talking and sometimes writing of you, to common friends. The fortnight or three weeks that Mr Kenrick was at Hackney he generally called whenever he came to Town, when Shrewsbury was always mentiond and he shewed me his letter from your young man, who happened then to be in town, to which he proposed to make reply on his return to Exeter, and will I hope gratify me with a sight of the correspondence.[1] The slenderness of the foundations on which these gentlemen reject not only divine revelation but question the being of a God, and their very sudden transition to such violent extremes would not be likely to be lasting, if they did not consort and correspond with those who cherish and encourage the ferment so raised. It is however most desireable that they should come forth and publish their several objections: for that will do good, and is the only way to have them confuted: as I have found in one instance that great advantage to the truth has resulted and will result from Mr Paine's Age of Reason by the same persons and others being put upon reading B^p. Watson's answer to him, which is in general so good a confutation of him, and so solid a defence of the Bible, notwithstanding some church-narrowness which will prevent a higher class of prejudiced persons from receiving any benefit from the work. But this I believe I have told you before.[2]

I am sorry to mention that these zealous antichristians have had but too much success in proselyting [*sic*] some of the other and better sex; one or two of my own knowlege. There is also lately come forth a novel, Emma Courtenay, by Mary Hays. You may perhaps have met with this ingenious young woman, a Dissenter, as she used sometimes to come to our Chapel. I am told, for I have not read it, that this book, w[ch] I should apprehend is written for bread as well as fame, retails too much of the principles of Helvetius[3] and other french writers, as well as M[r] Godwin, all of whom she frequently quotes: the plan of it, being an unedifying ranking[4] love-story, though without any indecencies, as my wife tells me, who has read it.[5]

You would be greatly affected with D[r] Priestleys most heavy loss in M[rs] Priestley, but nine months after their being deprived of a favourite youngest son. But tho' he feels and will long feel the void w[ch] the unexpected separation has left with respect to earthly comforts, he bears the affection as might be looked for in so true a practical christian, whose views have been still, if possible more led to that other world more constantly by the change in his situation and the disappointments that has caused and continually causes with respect to present comforts. I should have written to you, but was for some time prevented doing any thing by a violent cold which lay chiefly in the head. I have had only one letter from him since the event, w[ch] was dated the very day M[rs] Priestley was buried, Sept[r]. 19.[6]

It is happy for him that his two sons are settled at Northumberland, and he can reside as he proposes in the house his good wife had been building with one of them: as otherwise he w[d] have been wholly unsettled and probably quitted the place, being above all men to seek in domestic concerns and taking care of a family: having been always wont to tell M[rs] P. that he was only her lodger, she providing every thing, and leaving him all his time for his theological and philosophical pursuits. He sent me the particular subjects which he has already drawn up a sett of Discourses upon, for his audience at Philadelphia the next spring: still on the evidences of Christianity, though more indirectly, but much originality in them upon a much beaten theme, which I dare say you have perceived in the vol. of his Discourses at Philadelphia this last spring, which M[r] Johnson has reprinted here, and which are in my estimate very valuable.[7] I now more than ever lament that you were not called to say something concerning our late excellent friend at the moment on his being taken from us when it might have been of great service in your town in particular, as well as to others at a distance: for I now begin to apprehend, that for some reason or other, perhaps diffidence, or low spirits, or I know not what, M[r] Houlbrooke may not publish his sermon.[8] M[r] Rathbone, his valuable friend at Liverpoole, is said to be the writer of some Strictures on Burke's Regicide letters, which are deservedly prized, and a second part promised, but not yet published.[9] I was highly obliged to M[r] Wood or You some time since for sending a Shrewsbury paper, containing a very serious and seasonable essay against the fashionable system.[10] D[r] P ___ ys son W[m]. I always thought of a singular disposition and somew[t] wrong-headed; and Harry might be hurt by the turn taking among the young men just before he left Hackney, or by the Society with w[ch]. he passed over to America. Is it a proper question to ask, from whom you might learn the report you mention of them?[11] This however puts me upon telling you that I have passed a full hour this day with M[r] Winterbotham, and am more and more persuaded of his worth, and of the prison having been a school of moral discipline to him, in wch also he has become a very esteemable and enlightened confirmed christian.

I shall most truly rejoice if your short satisfactory tour has been the means of restoring health and spirits, after your afflictive dispensation to yourself and Mrs Rowe. It is no small consolation that such has been the manner of the heavenly father's dealing with his most beloved and chosen servants. My wife desires to unite her kind respects with mine to you both with all wishes of good for you and yours; and we beg to be particularly and respectfully remember^d to Mr Wood, and Mr Harries. I hope the sons of the last named take good courses and that he has comfort in them.[12] I am always, Dear Sir very affectionately Yours

T. Lindsey.

I hope Mr Tayleur's late housekeeper has her health, and then[?] I trust she has principles wch will make her happy in her change of situation.[13]

1   Rowe's 'young man' was probably Arthur Aikin.
2   Lindsey had discussed Watson's reply to Paine at some length in his previous surviving letter to Rowe, dated 7 Oct. 1796 (Letter 643).
3   Claude-Adrien Helvétius (1715–71), author of *De l'esprit* (1758) and *De l'homme de ses facultés intellectuelles et de son éducation* (1772).
4   Possibly Lindsey wrote 'ranting' rather than 'ranking'.
5   Mary Hays's novel, *Memoirs of Emma Courtney*, was published in two volumes in London in Nov. 1796. The publisher was George Robinson of Paternoster Row. Her second novel, *The victim of prejudice* (2 vols., London, 1799), was published by Joseph Johnson.
6   For this letter of Priestley, see Letter 646, n. 6.
7   Lindsey referred here to the discourses which Priestley intended to preach in Philadelphia in the spring of 1797. They were published as *Discourses relating to the evidences of revealed religion. Vol. 2*. Priestley outlined the main topics of these discourses in his letter to Lindsey of 11 Sept. 1796; Rutt, I, 352. For the previous volume of these *Discourses*, reprinted in London by Joseph Johnson, see Letter 631.
8   Houlbrooke did publish this funeral sermon: see Letter 636, n. 6.
9   This work was probably the anonymously published *Strictures on Mr. Burke's two letters, addressed to a member of the present parliament. Part the first* (London, 1796). In ECCO and in COPAC it is attributed to the Liverpool unitarian, historian and art connoisseur William Roscoe (1753–1831), which might explain Lindsey's having heard that William Rathbone, also of Liverpool and a friend of Roscoe, was the author. The second part was never published, perhaps because Burke died on 9 July 1797. This work was quite different from *Strictures on Mr. Burke's two letters, addressed to a member of the present parliament on the proposals for peace with the regicide directory of France, and upon the proposal for funding the navy debt. By the author of Simkin's letters* (London, 1796). The author was Ralph Broome (d. 1805), a 'veteran opponent' of Burke, who, in his 'Simkin letters' had ridiculed his conduct of the impeachment of Warren Hastings; see Lock, *Edmund Burke. Volume II, 1784–1797*, p. 559.
10   Lindsey's allusion to this 'Shrewsbury paper' is insufficiently precise for a positive identification of it to be made. A possibility, however, is an essay in the *Shrewsbury Chronicle*, 26 Aug. 1796, reviewing Thomas Paine's *Decline and fall of the English system of finance* (London, 1796). The article, while disagreeing with Paine on several points, deplored the extravagance and debt of the British government and predicted that a continuation of such extravagance would lead to the type of bankruptcy which had befallen the old regime in France. Lindsey on this occasion perhaps referred to the 'fashionable system' in public finance rather then theology (i.e. deism); perhaps, too, the newspaper was sent to him by Isaac Wood, whose interest in such matters had been displayed by his leading *rôle* in the Shrewsbury house of industry.
11   William Priestley had become a French citizen; Henry Priestley, having been a pupil of John Prior Estlin at Bristol, came to Hackney to study the classics under the supervision of Gilbert Wakefield before emigrating to America in Aug. 1793. Rowe's letter to Lindsey containing this (presumably unfavourable) 'report' of them appears not to have survived.
12   For Thomas Harries, the elder of the two sons of Edward Harries and a former student at Hackney College, see Letter 412, n. 4. The other son of Edward Harries was Francis-Blithe Harries (1776–1848), subsequently of Benthall Hall, Shropshire.

13 See Letters 637 and 643. Presumably, Tayleur's former housekeeper had found other employment.

649. To WILLIAM ALEXANDER   27 JANUARY 1797

    Text: 'Letters of the Rev. Theophilus Lindsey. No. VII', *UH*, II, 75
                  (4 Oct. 1862), 338–9.

Note: This is the only section of this letter printed by the *UH*; the manuscript seems not to have survived. The ellipsis at the start of the extract indicates that this was not the beginning of the original letter. The ellipsis at the end of the first paragraph indicates that the second paragraph did not immediately follow the first in the original letter. Accordingly, the two paragraphs are presented here separated by a broken line.

London, Jan. 27th, 1797.

* * There can be none more worthy than my friend, your new neighbour, Mr. Evanson, who has made such noble sacrifices for truth and a good conscience that no one can doubt of his being a sincere Christian, though he entertains the prejudice you mention against all evidence for the truth of revelation but that which arises from prophecy.[1] Every day teaches us to be more candid, and to make allowance for others differing from us even in points that we hold dear, and that seem to us important. * *

It is a great pleasure to hear of your two young friends at Baltimore prospering in their trade in that country, and particularly of their retaining virtuous and religious principles, where I fear there is but little example to encourage them therein.[2] For our countrymen throughout that continent, but especially in the Southern States, are said to have lost their religious, and together with it, all moral character, and of late are fallen into the scepticism which Mr. Paine's "Age of Reason" is calculated to generate.

You would see some little accounts of Dr. Priestley lately in the Cambridge paper. The last inserted came to a person in London who had sent the doctor a book, and received it in answer.[3] The American papers have made mention of his being a candidate for chaplain to their Congress, but I cannot but question it, or that if he were put upon the list it was entirely without his seeking.[4] It was at Northumberland, the beginning of December, that my last letter from him was dated, but he was preparing to go earlier to Philadelphia, and pass the winter there, as he had not the same tie to remain at Northumberland, and to be in the way to preach the discourses he had engaged to deliver before the Congress this spring.[5]

1 In the late 1790s, Evanson moved from Great Blakenham to Great Bealings, near Woodbridge, Suffolk, very close to Alexander, who had moved from Yoxford to Woodbridge in 1794. For Evanson's later publications, see Ditchfield, 'Varieties of heterodoxy', pp. 111–16.
2 I have not been able to identify Alexander's two young friends in Baltimore.
3 On 26 Nov. 1796, the *Cambridge Intelligencer* reported the death of Priestley's wife. On 14 Jan. 1797, the same newspaper published extracts from a letter, dated Northumberland 4 Oct. 1796, from Priestley to an (unnamed) friend in London. In it, he referred to the deaths of his wife and youngest son, and commented on the advantages of life in America, noting that 'we have no church establishment and hardly any taxes'. This letter was the 'last inserted' item to which Lindsey referred. It was subsequently published in several London newspapers, including *The Star*, 14 Jan. 1797, *Bell's Weekly Messenger*, Sunday 15 Jan. 1797, and the *Whitehall Evening Post*, 19 Jan. 1797. The friend in London was George Dyer and the letter itself is printed in Rutt, I, 355–7; Priestley thanked Dyer for sending to him several recent publications.

4   For these reports of Priestley's nomination as chaplain to the house of representatives, see Letter 650, n. 13.

5   This was Priestley's letter to Lindsey, dated Northumberland, 3 Dec. 1796, DWL, MS 12.13, partly printed in Rutt, I, 362–3. Priestley's *Discourses relating to the evidences of revealed religion. Vol. 2*, delivered in the spring of 1797, were published in that city in that year. Several members of Congress attended them; see Schofield, *Enlightened Joseph Priestley*, p. 381.

650. To ROBERT MILLAR   21 FEBRUARY 1797

Text: DWL, MS 12.46 (14).
Printed: Graham, 'Unhappy country', 148–51 (entire letter, except for omission of sixth paragraph, the last two sentences of ninth paragraph, tenth paragraph, and the postscript).
Addressed: Address missing.
Postmarked: Postmark missing.

London. Feb. 21. 1797.

Dear Sir,

I begin to think it an age since I heard from you. I trust you have received the Vol. of D[r] Priestley's Sermons[1] and M[r] Palmer's Narrative of his horrid sufferings,[2] which M[r] Johnson long ago engaged to get conveyed to you. Within these 3 weeks past I have received two letters from our friend at B.B. The first rec[d], dated December, 1795; the other brought only this day by the post, though dated 3 months before the other.[3] In both he speaks of the delightfulness of the climate, and the health of all our friends, and the general plenty procured by their own industry, with some few drawbacks however to their happiness from the state of the country, which they hoped time w[d] alleviate if not intirely remove. In both letters he speaks of the probability of their being recalled to their native country, and their sentence reversed; in the last, in so sanguine a strain as to look forward to shake hands with his friends probably before his letter was received. To this hope they were led by some letters written to them, but principally from some Newspapers sent them, of what stamp I cannot conjecture, for there has been no just ground for any such information. The reason of the two letters being such a long time in arriving, was the vessel[4] that brought them going round by the East Indies Home.

As you will be pleased with a sample of the chearful happy disposition of your old Pastor in his exile, I shall transcribe a paragraph from the begining of his letter.

"I have nothing material to say but that we have received two pounds of tea and three loaves of sugar each, with the Newspapers and several pamphlets. All of us enjoy good health, as every one does in this climate. My eyes are a good deal better, w[ch]. I attribute to bathing them with Port wine.

"You cannot expect news from a desart very interesting. The wheat is now getting in (Dec[r]. 20.) in excellent weather and is very plentiful. I believe the land in general greatly to exceed in fertility European soil. Word is sent home, I hear, that there is no occasion to send out any more flour: indeed with the least management and honesty it might not only be independent but abundant in the sustenance of human life. But" &c[5]

There is a report in London, which gains credit, that M[r] Muir whose confinement was for 14 years has been enabled to make his escape by means of an American vessel that touched at the Bay. And I perceived it was given in the Cambridge Intelligencer of Saturday last.[6] Our friends look only for deliverance from the justice of their country, or after having satisfied the law, and happily one half the period of their confinement is over.

In the said Intelligencer I had a very singular satisfaction in perusing the account of the great number of Book Societies instituted only in one part of Scotland, and Dundee I observed brought up the rear.[7] One may I trust on the best grounds anticipate the vast spread of light and knowlege, natural, moral and religious, which will be derived from this source, and by a happy contagion influence not only all Scotland, but our part of the Island and all countries to imitate the example. As I am persuaded, from what may be learned of the ordinary and extraordinary providence of the heavenly Father, that knowlege of all kinds and with it virtue and happiness, will in time pervade the whole face of the earth in a manner that has never yet been seen, may this little cloud arising among you be the beginning of it. Amen. And this reminds me of desiring you with my best comp^{ts} to tell Mr Duncan that I trust no offence was taken at the gentle admonition I took the liberty to give about the too promiscuous admission of books of a certain sort into your Book-Society, especially where no antidote can go along with them, lest the ignorant and unwary be surprized and overpowered by false facts and bold dogmatical assertions without proof.[8] I was led to make the remark from observing, as I recollect, Volney's ruins, Rousseau's Confessions[9] and Varietés de la Literature[10] among the orders given by your infant Society.

I had a letter from Dr Priestley dated in December last from Northumberland, a little before his setting out to pass the winter at Philadelphia, as he had lost one that used to make his abode there pleasant and comfortable, not to return till he had preached his promised Discourses before the congress, which will not be till May.[11] Of those Discourses he has given me the subjects and heads, and they promise to be very original and most highly useful, still, as I might perhaps have intimated to you before, on the Evidences of Christianity, but more indirectly.[12] I trust and believe, that he has an appointment on that Continent from heaven for the defence and propagation of the gospel, of that pure and holy and benevolent doctrine which our great Master taught and exemplified, consisting in constant energies to promote the present and future happiness of our fellowcreatures, on the largest scale.

You woud see in the public papers, that Dr Priestley was a candidate for the Chaplainship to the Congress. I have since heard, that he was put upon the lists by a friend without his privity, and I am not certain he would not be displeased at it, tho' the minority he was in, 27 against 34, voting for so notorious an heretic, was no disparagement to him.[13]

I presume you must have seen Mr Erskine's view of the causes and consequences of the war.[14] As I know him a little and most highly esteem, it is a pleasure to see and to hear with what avidity and approbation of foe as well as friend, this pamp[h] let is read and most widely circulated. All agree that if our country is to be saved, it is only by a retrograde contrary course to that most fatal one of the present Minister which he has traced out with such admirable temper, candor and truth. As no one has had a greater hand in the measures that have brought us to this wretched pass than Mr Dundas, if it be true that that gentleman's state of health will not permit him any longer to take an active part, without the help of so able a collegue the minister will find it difficult to go on.[15] But I beg your pardon for such a dash of politics wch I sedulously avoid but Mr Erskine's wise and noble exertions draw me on to express my wishes that they may not be lost. My wife desires to unite her respects and kind wishes with mine to yrself and lady and sister, with hope that you are all well, a blessing which we have cause to be thankful for the degree in which we enjoy it.

I hope you will never suffer the want of a cheap conveyance to debar me of the satisfaction of hearing from you, when you are di[s]posed to write. I only make use of franks because they are at this season easily procured, and to give you an opportunity of disposing of the money better than its falling into the gulph which devours every thing and is never satisfied. farewel

Your much obliged and affectionate servant

T. Lindsey.

P.S. Your Subscription to the Society is paid for this year, also Dr Priestley's volume,[16] and yet you have still some shillings due.

---

[1] This refers to the previous volume of Priestley's *Discourses relating to the evidences of revealed religion* (Philadelphia, 1796), reprinted in London by Johnson.

[2] Palmer's *Narrative* was published in Cambridge by Benjamin Flower and distributed by several other booksellers, including Joseph Johnson. Flower published a second edition later in 1797.

[3] I have not located these two letters from Palmer to Lindsey. There are two letters from Palmer to Lindsey in HMCO, Shepherd MS, vol. X, nos. 11 and 12, but they are dated 5 May and 16 Sept. 1796, and it is unlikely that Lindsey would have received even the first of them by Feb. 1797.

[4] It is not quite clear whether Lindsey wrote 'vessel' or 'vessels'.

[5] This quotation renders all the more regrettable the non-survival of this letter of Palmer.

[6] In Feb. 1796, Thomas Muir escaped from Botany Bay on board an American ship, the *Otter*, which took him across the Pacific to the coast of Vancouver Island. From there he embarked upon a remarkable odyssey via central America and the Caribbean, before he ultimately arrived in France. His escape was indeed reported in the *Cambridge Intelligencer* of Saturday 18 Feb. 1797; it cited as its source a letter from Maurice Margarot, dated Port Jackson, 1 Mar. 1796, and received (presumably in London), by Thomas Hardy, the secretary of the London Corresponding Society.

[7] An article entitled 'Book clubs' in the *Cambridge Intelligencer*, 18 Feb. 1797, listed forty-one such societies 'in the most industrious parts' of Scotland'; eleven were located in the Glasgow area, and most other towns, including Dundee, were credited with one.

[8] The letter in which Lindsey gave this admonition seems not to have survived.

[9] Rousseau's *Confessions* were first published (posthumously) in 1781. For Volney, see Letter 560, n. 6. Between 1795 and 1799, he lived in America, and for part of that time stayed in Philadelphia; his work helped to inspire Priestley's *Observations on the increase of infidelity*.

[10] Probably François Artaud, *Variétés littéraires, ou recueil de pièces tant originales que traduites concernant la philosophie, la literature et les arts* (4 vols., Paris, 1768–9).

[11] This letter, dated Northumberland, 3 Dec. 1796, may be found in DWL, MS 12.13 and is partly printed in Rutt, I, 362–3. Priestley's wife had died the previous Sept.

[12] Priestley set out these subject heads in his letter to Lindsey of 3 Dec. 1796 (see n. 11, above), in a passage omitted by Rutt. He enlarged upon the version of those headings which he had sent to Lindsey in his letter of 11 Sept. 1796 (see Letter 648, n. 7).

[13] This story, with the (almost) exact voting figures quoted by Lindsey, appeared in several London newspapers, citing reports of proceedings in Congress from American sources. See *The Star*, 17 Jan. 1797, *The Sun*, 18 Jan. 1797, and *The True Briton*, 18 Jan. 1797. The attendance of numerous members of Congress at Priestley's sermons in Philadelphia in 1796 no doubt generated support for this nomination as chaplain to the house of representatives, although Priestley himself did not seek or desire the office. In 1802, he was nominated, but not elected, as chaplain to the United States senate; Bowers, *Priestley and English unitarianism in America*, pp. 97–8.

[14] Thomas Erskine's *A view of the causes and consequences of the present war with France* was published in Dublin and in London in Feb. 1797 and went through at least thirty-five editions, as well as a French translation, in the same year. In addition to his advocacy at the bar, Erskine was MP for Portsmouth from 1783 to 1784 and from 1790 to 1806; and from 1806 to 1807, he served (as 1st Baron Erskine) as lord chancellor in the short-lived ministry of all the talents. For Lindsey's admiration of his defence of Thomas Hardy and other reformers, see Letter 587.

[15] The *Morning Chronicle*, 2 Feb. 1797, reported that Dundas had suffered a 'violent indisposition'; in its issue of 4–7 Feb. 1797, the *London Chronicle* added that Dundas's ailment 'has been a violent bilious fever, which at one time had a very alarming appearance'. A few days later, several news-

papers reported his recovery; see *London Chronicle,* 9–11 Feb. 1797, and the *St James's Chronicle, or the British Evening Post* of the same date. Perhaps Lindsey was, from his own point of view, excessively optimistic.

[16] I.e. the volume of Priestley's *Discourses*; see n. 1, above.

651. To ROBERT MILLAR   3 MARCH 1797

Text: DWL, MS 12.46 (15).
Printed: Graham, 'Unhappy country', 151 (second paragraph).
Addressed: To/Mr Robt Millar/Merchant/Dundee
Endorsed: [Figures, apparently adding up to 4*s* 4*d*.]
Postmarked: Postmark missing.

London. march. 3. 1797

Dear Sir,

It was somewhat singular, that writing so seldom, our letters should cross each other in the road. I am glad of it as it gives me an opportunity of conversing with you sooner again, tho' vexed that you should not have rec^d Dr Priestleys Discourses and Mr Palmer's Narrative.[1] Upon interrogating Mr Johnson he assures me that he ordered them and his man[2] testifies that he carried them more than 6 weeks ago to a Mr Ogilvy[3] who is in the habit of sending parcells to Dundee, and who says that he did send them and presumes that by this time they must have come to hand. I shall hope then to have this confirmed by you, and if not, I will engage you Shall have them.

You talked in your last of the cloud around you being impenetrably thick. So dark a day in London, or one in which all faces were so full of consternation I never beheld, as Monday last, when it was first known that the payment of bills in cash was stopt at the Bank by a requisition of the Privy Council; requiring the Bank to do that for the doing of which the Bank might be prosecuted at common law, as the Duke of Grafton told the Secretary Ld Grenville, on the evening of the same day, in the debate upon it in the house of Lords.[4] The matter is now at issue in the house of Commons. The house has plainly lost its confidence in the Minister, as an observant member tells me; but if by places and pensions and promises and the incalculable influence he has in his power, he be able to keep his majorities, as he still appears to do, though some few have fallen off, and if he succeed in the Parliament estabilishing Paper to be a legal tender, all is over with Britain, the security of its property and liberties.[5] Some not weak or superstitious men, think that the credit of the country is utterly gone by this fatal blow given to it.

You ask after Mr Thos Christie. I had a very affectionate esteem for him, and always saw him on terms of intimacy, during the diff^t stages of his pursuits in town, first in the medical line and afterwards in the mercantile, before his passing over to France and after his return, but we did not meet much after his marriage.[6] About that time I fear his doubts about divine revelation, which had commenced before became realized, and before he left England to go to Surinam, a friend of mine, who had been such a friend of his as to advance to him several thousand pounds upon an emergency, which he honorably repaid; told me that spending an evening along with him and an acquaintance a professed sceptic, in the conversation that passed T.C. carried his scepticism considerably beyond christianity itself. You will not mention this fact but to very particular friends, as it might do harm, and can do no good. Sceptical company, vanity and too eager a desire of getting rich all at once were his bane. The same gentleman who had lent them money, assured me of his own knowlege, that if the partners could have been contented with a profit of one thousand p^{ds} per annum each, and a good probability of a gradual increase to each partner, he might have been now in England doing well and happy. It was to redress the affairs of the house & recover debts, that he was deputed to go to Surinam, where he died, through his own obstinacy at last in refusing to take the usual remedies in his case. Had he returned, there is reason to think their affairs woud have been restored, and they w^d have risen into a state of affluence again.[7] I sh^d fear this long detail might tire you, only you will like to hear the fate of our most promising friend if the particulars were unknown to You.

Could you in return favour me with any authentic particulars of the state of M^r W^m. Christie and his family in America, and their well-doing it would be a high satisfaction. They were a family worthy of a better lot than has seemed to attend them in this world. Your account of the state of your Manufacture at Dundee was very acceptable as one loves to know facts: as was also the character and conduct of M^r. T.[8] We are in daily expectation of further news concerning Dr Priestley. I beg to be rememberd to Dr Duncan.[9] My wife joins in kind wishes and respects to your ladies and yourself. I am always affectionately Yours

T. Lindsey.

---

[1] See Letter 650, nn. 1 and 2.

[2] Presumably Joseph Johnson's 'shopman'; see Letter 571, n. 3.

[3] This is possibly a reference to David Ogilvy and son, booksellers, 315 High Holborn, London; see *A London directory* (London 1798), p. 114.

[4] On Monday 27 Feb. 1797, public anxiety over a possible French invasion (and a small-scale invasion attempt in Pembrokeshire on 22 Feb.), coupled with a shortage of specie, forced Pitt's ministry to issue an order in council for a temporary suspension of payments in cash by the Bank of England. On the same day, Grafton intervened in debate in the house of lords, claiming that the suspension of cash payments was illegal; John Debrett, *The parliamentary register, or history of the proceedings and debates of the house of commons* (18 vols., London, 1797–1802), ser. 3, vol. III (48), p. 48. William Wyndham Grenville, Baron Grenville, was foreign secretary from 1791 to 1801 and leader of the ministry in the house of lords.

[5] After the suspension of cash payments by the Bank of England (n. 4, above), the Bank issued paper notes to the value of £1 and £2. Although these notes were only legal tender at the Bank of England itself, they nonetheless gave rise to charges that paper currency, with all its inflationary implications, was to become the national means of exchange. In Mar. and Apr. 1797, the house of commons debated the Bank Restriction bill, which was passed into law without a serious reduction in the ministerial majority. In the course of these debates, on 9 Mar. 1797, Sheridan compared the suspension of cash payments to the 'ruin of the French finances'; Cobbett, *Parl. hist.*, XXXIII, 55. For the background, see Ehrman, *The Younger Pitt. The consuming struggle*, pp. 5–16. Possibly Lindsey's informant was William Smith, MP, who criticized the Bank Restriction bill on 9 Mar. 1797; Cobbett, *Parl. hist.*, XXXIII, 57–8.

[6] Thomas Christie (1761–96) married Rebecca Thomson on 19 Sept. 1792.

[7] Thomas Christie died in Surinam in Oct. 1796, while seeking to collect debts owed to the London carpet manufacturer Moore and Co., of which he was a partner.

[8] Regrettably unidentified. There is a brief list of trades people whose surname began with T in the *Dundee Register*, but speculation as to which of them Millar might have referred – if indeed he referred to any of them – seems pointless.

[9] Possibly James Duncan; see Letter 566, n. 7. However, since this is Lindsey's only reference to Dr, as distinct from Mr, Duncan, perhaps he had a different person in mind. A (remote) possibility is Andrew Duncan (1773–1832), MD (1794), physician to the royal public dispensary in Edinburgh, who had studied in London in 1794 and 1795, or his father of the same name (1744–1828), also MD, and professor of medicine at Edinburgh University.

652. To WILLIAM ALEXANDER   28 APRIL 1797

Text: 'Letters of the Rev. Theophilus Lindsey. No. VII', *UH*, II, 75
               (4 Oct. 1862), 339.

Note: This is the only section of this letter printed by the *UH*; the manuscript seems not to have survived.
The ellipsis at the start of the extract printed by the *UH* indicates that this was not the beginning of the
original letter.

London, April 28th, 1797.

* * You will be glad to learn that my last accounts of Dr. Priestley, from a letter of
his dated the middle of January, were very favourable.[1] He had been come [*sic*] to
Philadelphia from Northumberland, with his son and daughter-in-law, to pass the
winter, about a fortnight, and had already preached with great acceptance, and was
likely to be so employed till he began his set of lectures which he had composed
to preach before the Congress, and which he intends to print, as he did those of the
preceding year. He has already sent to the press there a new edition of his "Observations on the increase of Infidelity", enlarged with much curious matter and remark,
which I hope we shall see here soon, and is about to print the continuation of his
"Ecclesiastical History", in four additional volumes.[2]

---

1   This letter from Priestley to Lindsey, dated Philadelphia 13 Jan. 1797, may be found in DWL, MS
    12.13 and is partly printed in Rutt, I, 369–71.
2   This work was Priestley's *Observations on the increase of infidelity. To which are added, animadver-
    sions on the writings of several modern unbelievers, and especially the ruins of M. Volney* (Phila-
    delphia, 1797). It was the third edition of the *Observations*. The first two volumes of Priestley's
    A general history of the Christian church from the fall of the western empire were published in
    Northumberland, Pennsylvania in 1802; the second two volumes were published in Northumberland
    in 1803.

653. To RUSSELL SCOTT   29 APRIL 1797

Text: Scott Coll.
Printed: McLachlan, 'Lindsey to Scott', 123 (last sentence of third
               paragraph; first two sentences of fifth paragraph).
Addressed: [In Hobhouse's hand] London April twenty nine 1797/The
               Rev^d. Russell Scott/Portsmouth/Bfree/<u>Hobhouse</u> [Opposite
               first page, in Lindsey's hand] To/The Rev^d. Russell Scott/
               Portsmouth
Endorsed: [In Lindsey's hand] Rev^d. Russell Scott/Portsmouth/April. 29
Postmarked: FREE AP 29 97

London April 29. 1797

Dear Sir,

I am extremely obliged to you for your two last comunications, which enabled
me also to oblige several friends who were much gratified with such early authentic
information.[1]

How you at Portsmouth look upon what has lately passed there respecting the
fleet, I cannot tell; but all I converse with consider it as a most serious, momentous
business, conducted with a prudence and ability that are quite astonishing, and
coming from a quarter unexpected by all, makes the greater impression.[2] If any
thing farther occurs relating to it, I shall take it as a favour to know.

Probably you will have heard from Mr Porter that my wife was ill. This is the first day she has been able to walk out of a whole month. Her complaint was one of the epidemic cold of the late unhealthy season attended with intolerable pain on one side of the head, with no outward tumour or inflammation, for which blisters were in vain applied, the cause of which was not known till found to be an abscess in the head by a discharge of matter from the ear. There was a danger at first that this organ woud be intirely destroyed, but we now hope it will not be greatly injured. For a week past she has been growing better, Yet still far from being well; but we hope that two or three days in the country this next week will contribute to it. We had not much opportunity to talk to Mr Porter, but presume he will be removed from you, for which we shall be greatly concerned on your account. From your not naming it yourself, we presume that you may not be known at Bath, and therefore have had no invitation to remove thither.[3] My wife however has learned from a friend at York, that Mr Wellbeloved, Mr Cappe's assistant there has been invited and declined it; and Dr Toulmin tells me that Mr Broadhurst who lately went from Taunton to Halifax had an offer made him, but it was not known whether he would accept it.[4] Their desire it seems is to have some ingenious young man, hoping he would help to raise a congregation and remain long with them.

I had a very agreeable letter from Dr Priestley from Philadelphia, the middle of January last, where he had come to settle with his son and daughter in law for the winter and to preach his second sett of discourses before the congress which will be printed, and will keep him at Philadelphia till the month of May.[5] But no longer ago than yesterday my wife had a letter from Miss Russell from Middletown in Connecticut, a most delightful spot and excellent neighbourhood, where they had at last settled. It was dated March. 3.[6] Mr Russell had been to visit Dr Priestley at Philadelphia the beginning of the winter, when he was in perfect health, and not only popular but even fashionable, every one pressing to be acquainted with him, and most numerously attended wherever he preached. In this list was Mr Liston, the english ambassador or envoy, who was a very liberal person and most obliging to the Doctor.[7] All this must contribute to make him and his writings known, and serve the interests of the pure gospel of Christ which he has chiefly at heart. In a new and enlarged edition of his Observations on the increase of Infidelity, amid much other curious and useful remark, he will take notice of Volney, the famous french unbeliever, who denies there was such a person as Jesus Christ, and lives at Philadelphia, and is a most zealous Proselyte-maker and not a few who adhere to him. I hope this work will e'er long find it's way to England, when I should be happy to hand it to you.[8]

Mr Wilberforce's book is what you would expect from a pious methodist, with whom he classes and attends their preachers. The scriptures continually misapplied to favour their peculiar doctrines of the original corruption of human nature &c &c; with frequent aspersions of Socinians for explaining away the true meaning of Scripture, and much feebleness of judgment throughout.[9] It has however great vogue, the first edition being very soon sold off, and will not fail to recomend the Minister to many as being the friend of such a pious man, and whom he vindicates by name in a note from the false slander of having feasted on a fast day, wch Mr W. denies from his own knowlege.[10] We hope your daughter's eyes are grown stronger and your son and his father and mother in the health we wish them.[11] My wife joins in kind respects to you both, and I remain always, Dear Sir, your obliged and affectionate

T. Lindsey.

1   Scott's two letters to Lindsey seem not to have survived.
2   The naval mutiny in protest at pay and conditions began in the Channel fleet at Portsmouth and
     Spithead in mid-Apr. 1797. It ended with relatively little violence on 15 May, after the intervention
     of Admiral Lord Howe (1726–99), who, though retired from active service, was still nominally in
     command of the Channel fleet, and who promised redress of the most serious grievances and secured
     a royal pardon for the participants. On 17 May, the Channel fleet was able to put to sea.
3   See Letter 645, n. 4.
4   Thomas Broadhurst (c. 1767–1851) was minister of the Tancred Street Presbyterian chapel, Taunton,
     from 1793 to 1795, and of Northgate End chapel, Halifax, from 1795 to 1796. From 1797 to 1809,
     he was minister to the congregation at Trim Street, Bath, in succession to David Jardine. See Vol. I,
     Letter 354, n. 21.
5   See Letter 652, n. 1.
6   This was almost certainly a letter from Martha Russell (see Letter 645, n. 14) and was probably the
     letter to which Lindsey referred in Letter 654; it seems not to have survived. For the settlement of the
     Russell family at Middletown, Connecticut, see Jeyes, *The Russells of Birmingham*, chs. XII–XVI.
7   Robert Liston (1742–1836) was British minister to the United States from 1796 to 1800, having
     previously served as envoy to Sweden and to the Ottoman empire. He held the degree of LLD from
     Edinburgh University and was knighted in 1816. Priestley referred to this meeting in his letter to
     Lindsey of 13 Jan. 1797 (see Letter 652, n. 1). In Rutt, I, 369, and in Schofield, *Enlightened Joseph
     Priestley*, p. 381, Liston's name is wrongly rendered as 'Lister'.
8   For the full title of this work, see Letter 652, n. 2. In section IV, Priestley attributed the infidelity of
     Volney and other French philosophers to 'inattention and gross ignorance' (p. 45). In particular, he
     referred to their failure to study the historical evidence for miracles in the age of the early church, and
     to the 'corruptions and abuses of christianity' which led them to explain the rise of Christianity as the
     result of the impositions of priestcraft upon the credulity of the people' (pp. 47, 73–5, 83). Priestley's
     Observations were originally prefixed to the American edition of his *Letters to the philosophers and
     politicians of France on the subject of religion*.
9   This book was William Wilberforce's *A practical view of the prevailing religious system of professed
     Christians, in the higher and middle classes in this country, contrasted with real Christianity* (London,
     1797). It was published on 12 Apr. 1797 and five editions appeared in 1797 alone. For the author's
     critique of unitarians, see pp. 474–9.
10   See Wilberforce, *Practical view*, p. 377 n. *, where he denied newspaper reports that Pitt had given
     an 'entertainment' on a fast day.
11   Scott's daughter, Sophia Russell Scott, was born on 11 Sept. 1793; for his first son, Russell Scott,
     who was born in 1791 but died in May 1797, see Letter 481.

654. To ?WILLIAM TURNER OF NEWCASTLE   1 MAY 1797

Text: DWL, to be catalogued.
Endorsed: May. 1. 1797 [There are also two annotations by Turner,
                       marked ˣ, noted in the text.]
Addressed: Address missing.
Postmarked: Postmark missing.

Note: Although the address is missing, it is clear from the text that the recipient was William Turner of
Newcastle; the reference to 'your great loss' is explained by the death of Turner's first wife, Mary (née
Holland), on 16 Jan. 1797.

                                                         London. May 1. 1797.
Dear Sir,
     I was much concerned that I did not open the pacquet which Mʳ Rankin brought
immediately, that I might have thanked him at least for his trouble and obliging
attention, but as I remember I was prevented by Dʳ Blackburne coming in at that
moment to see my wife who was very ill, and her illness continuing hindered my
calling which I had otherwise done upon Mʳ R. at his Inn to make some inquiry after
your health and apology for my seeming rudeness.[1]

My wife's disorder was an attack of the epidemic cold in the late unhealthy season in the most exquisite torture for some days on one side of the head; blisters and outward application had no effect; there was not tumour or inflammation, so that the cause was not known till a copious discharge of well concocted matter by the ear shewed it to be an abscess in the head. The discharge continued with pain for more than a week, but abated upon an inflammation shewing itself in the arm which however did not come to any thing, and the discharge as well as pain have now nearly ceased. She has been out once or twice in a carriage; and we are going into the country on tuesday for a few days to a friend's to try what the air and change will do to restore her appetite and depressed spirits. My apprehensions of what might be the event for some days brought your great loss to my recollection.[2] But the Divine goodness spared this chief amid the thousand other blessings to my declining years and strength.

It was natural for those so immediately concerned to desire to preserve the Introductory Address,[x] and kind and right in you to comply with the request. And I am glad of it and thank you for a sight of such just sentiments of the ordinance itself, and of the most affecting application in the conclusion; and by the whole of it all into whose hands it may fall, and I hope they will be many, will be instructed and deeply edified. [In Turner's hand: [x] on the baptism of Catharine Rankin, now M[rs] H. Turner. 1819.[3]]

It is also a word in due season, and likely I believe to do good to many, who may be surprized to meet it there, in your "fourth year's report" where you shew the serious cast of your own mind, in your reflections at the conclusion of it, on the early removal of two such promising subjects[x] from those present scenes, and the just and affecting view which your present of them in their connection with the life that will never end. I call this the not being ashamed of the gospel of Christ in these days. [In Turner's hand: [x] M[r]. Will[m]. Burrell & M[r]. W. J. Rayner.[4]]

I presume you may have seen M[r] Wilberforce's volume on real Xtianity contrasted with what is exhibited in the lives of it's professors, especially in high life. But I think you would be satisfied with lightly turning the leaves over as I have been. In doing which I must own I found nothing new. For having been much in my early youth with Lady Huntingdon and a hearer of the principal preachers among the Methodists, there is nothing that M[r]. W. advances on the original corruption of human nature or any other of his peculiar topics, upon which I did not only know by heart all he had to say, but all the texts of Scripture which he brings to prove it. His book however would not have half it's value with those for whom it is calculated, if he did not season it and gratify them with telling how ignorant Socinians and Unitarians are of the Scriptures, explaining them quite away, and their preaching wholly without effect upon the lives of their hearers.[5] We are however obliged to him for abstaining from all harsh and abusive epithets. If any notice should be taken of it by way of reply I hope it will be done by a liberal as well as able pen and with all good temper.[6] There is a feebleness of judgment throughout greater than I expected.

My last account from D[r] Priestley on his arrival in Philadelphia in January for the winter was most pleasing with respect to his health and the acceptableness of his labours, from the pulpit every sunday morning, numerously attended and by people of the first respect.[7] My wife has lately had a letter from a young lady dated march 3 who says, that the D[r] is not only popular but quite fashionable, every one being eager for his acquaintance and to invite him to their entertainments, as well as to frequent the places where he preaches.[8] Volney who obstinately persists in his denial of there having been such a person as Jesus Christ is at Philadelphia making converts with all his might and wishing that he could preach as well as D[r]. P. A man very noisy and most conceited. In a new Edition of his Observations on the Increase of Infidelity very much enlarged, which the D[r] tells me he had just sent to the press he takes notice of him, and also makes great use of D'Alembert's and Voltaire's correspondence.[9] One cannot but be curious to see it, as it must be valuable and important. Be so good as to acquaint worthy Mr Prowitt that I hope soon to acknowlege his letter and attend to it's contents.[10] My wife sends her kind respects. I am always, Dear Sir,

> Your most sincerely obliged
> T. Lindsey.

---

1 Probably Robert Rankin of Newcastle, or one of his sons; see Letter 536, n. 1.
2 Mary Turner, née Holland, Turner's first wife, died on 16 Jan. 1797. For Edward Prowitt's funeral address, see n. 10, below.
3 The 'Introductory Address' was Turner's *Introductory address at the baptism, or religious dedication, of Catharine Rankin, daughter of John and Catharine* (Newcastle, 1797). The 'ordinance' was the baptism service of Hanover Square chapel. Catharine Rankin, the daughter of John Cole Rankin and his wife Catharine, was born on 21 Feb. 1797 and baptized by William Turner on 12 Mar. of that year; see Tyne and Wear Archives, Hanover Square baptismal record (TNA: PRO/RG4/1777), fo. 41v. In 1819, Catharine Rankin, then aged twenty-two, married William Turner's fourth son (and fifth child) Henry Turner (1792–1822), who was subsequently minister to the High Pavement chapel, Nottingham. For a note on the Rankin family, see Letter 536, n. 1.
4 The 'fourth year's report' was the *Fourth year's report of the Literary and Philosophical Society of Newcastle upon Tyne: to which are annexed a list of the new members* (Newcastle, 1797). Turner was the joint secretary of the society. The two 'promising subjects' were William Burrell and W. J. Rayner, both members of the society who had contributed to papers presented to the society's meetings. Their deaths were lamented in the *Fourth year's report*, pp. 9–10. Neither was a relation of Mrs Elizabeth Rayner.
5 See Letter 653, n. 9.
6 For a survey of the replies to Wilberforce's *Practical view*, see John Wolffe, 'William Wilberforce's *Practical view* (1797) and its reception', in *Revival and resurgence in Christian history*, ed. Kate Cooper and Jeremy Gregory (Woodbridge, 2008), pp. 181–4. Thomas Belsham and Gilbert Wakefield were among those who replied to Wilberforce.
7 For this letter from Priestley, see Letter 652, n. 1.
8 The young lady was almost certainly Martha Russell; see Letter 653, n. 6.
9 In the third edition of his *Observations on the increase of infidelity* (Philadelphia, 1797), Priestley attacked Volney in section IX, 'Of the tendency to atheism in modern unbelievers' (pp. 125–42) and in Appendix II (pp. 168–70), where he took issue with Volney's opinions of the theology of the ancient Egyptians. His critique of Voltaire and the philosopher and mathematician Jean le Rond d'Alembert (1717–83) may be found in section VII, entitled 'Of the spirit and moral influence of infidelity, as exemplified in the correspondence between Voltaire and D'Alembert' (pp. 62–101).
10 Edward Prowitt preached the funeral address for Turner's wife Mary (see n. 2, above). It was published, with the title *A funeral address, delivered at the chapel in Hanover-Square, Newcastle upon Tyne, Jan. 22, 1797, occasioned by the death of Mrs Turner* (Newcastle, 1797). Prowitt's letter to Lindsey seems not to have survived.

655. To RUSSELL SCOTT   **17 MAY 1797**

Text:	Scott Coll.
Printed:	McLachlan, 'Lindsey to Scott', 123 (second, third and fourth sentences of first paragraph; most of second paragraph; fourth and fifth sentences of third paragraph).
Addressed:	[?In Martin's hand] Westm^r; seventeenth May/1797/Rev: Mr Scott/Portsmouth/~~Js. Martin~~ [opposite first page, in Lindsey's hand] To/The Rev^d. Russell Scott/Portsmouth
Endorsed:	[In Lindsey's hand] Rev^d. Mr Scott/Portsmouth/May. 17
Postmarked:	FREE MA 17 97

London. May 17. 1797

Dear Sir,

It is high time I shoud acknowlege your late most kind attention in writing so frequently at so critical a moment,[1] and thereby gratifying some of our valuable friends as well as ourselves and relieving our minds from the anxious uncertainty under which we shoud have been kept by the vague reports of each day and even hour sometimes. We all looked upon this affair of the fleet as of more serious concern than even the stoppage of the Bank,[2] and are thankful that the storm is so far happily blown over, and trust that there will now be wisdom and forecast to prevent its ever returning. The part which Sr John Carter took was worthy of him, in quieting the minds of men by promoting soothing and moderate measures.[3] The present report is that these are not complaints peculiar to our seamen, but are at this moment rife among the french and spaniard too; though this may be given out to palliate our own supineness and inattention which unquestionably has been the cause of this dangerous extremity to which things have been lately carried.[4]

The *extraordinary written orders* of the Duke of York read yesterday to a regiment of the Guards in the Duke's hearing, is thought to proceed from a timely attention to prevent cabals and di[s]quiet in the army, as it is not doubted that the increase of pay there promised will be extended throughout the whole.[5] I only wish that blessed peace was returned to this country and am sorry not to see any immediate token of it: although all agree it must come soon, but probably not without some sacrifices being made for it which may be very grating to us. In such a state of things it may be well that wild man, now poor Burke, is languishing at Bath, not likely ever to come thence; as, if he possessed the powers he lately had, he would probably have tried again to blow his trumpet and excite to continue the war and prevent a regicide peace.[6]

We are uneasy not to have heard from Dr Priestley since Jany. 13.[7] when he wrote to me, adding that he should write again soon and several ships have lately arrived, bringing letters from Philadelphia in the months of February and march. However one ship we know has been seized by the French, and there may have been others, by which he may have written. We really want to be refreshed and edified with some of his valuable theological publications, of which there is so great a dearth and likely to be. Mr Wakefield has indeed just now relieved us by his Letter to Mr Wilberforce on the subject of his late Publication, drawn up in a very short space of time, but written after his best manner of controversy, I should rather say, admirably well done.[8] His having known Mr Wilberforce at College gives a natural introduction to his Address to him, and he very happily avails himself of the opportunity of saying some home-truths both to him and to his friend M^r.

Pitt.[9] I will take the first opportunity of sending it you, but if in the mean time, you could look in to Mr Wilberforce's book (so weak a performance and full of such ignorance, presumption and misapplication of Scripture is not worth having) and observe particularly his manner, and how he repeats again and again *Looking unto Jesus*, you will understand the ingenuity and cleverness of Mr Wakefields remarks.[10]

A friend of mine had a letter very lately from the worthy Primate of Ireland, Dr Newcome, with a pastoral charge he has lately publishd, and the information that his new Translation of the New Testament will be published the beginning of the winter.[11] At this I rejoice, as I expect much from it, and cannot but think it does him great honour to have carried it on in the midst of the infinite business and avocations of State matters in which he is forced to take a part as well as those of his own ecclesiastical department.

We hope M^{rs}. Scott and yourself are both well, with your son and daughter, and the eyes of the latter particularly. Since the year 1782, when my wife was for some time not likely to live,[12] she has not sufferd so severely or been in such danger as from an illness wch began about six weeks ago, the cold of the season, with an intolerable pain in the head for many days, wch discovered itself at last to be an abscess in the head, by a discharge of matter at the ear. The discharge still continues a little – for these last ten days she has been able to go out, and in a mending way, tho' slowly. She desires to join in sincere regards to you both and kind wishes for your young folks. We suppose Mr Porter may have left Portsmouth. If not, pray remember us kindly to him and Mrs Porter.[13] If there be any hand or method in wch I can send you Wakefield before the end of the month, pray tell me I bespeak your liking of it. I am always Dr Sir, Y^r much obliged and affectionate
     T. Lindsey.

---

1 Scott's letters to Lindsey seem not to have survived. The 'critical moment' probably referred to the naval mutiny at Portsmouth.

2 For the Bank of England's suspension of cash payments in Feb. 1797, see Letter 651, nn. 4 and 5.

3 During the naval mutiny at Portsmouth, a group of mutineers imprisoned Admiral Sir John Colpoys (*c.* 1742–1821) and other officers on board the warship *London*. Sir John Carter, in his capacity as mayor of Portsmouth, intervened, helped to secure the release of Colpoys and assured the mutineers that the admiralty would redress their grievances. See Bonham-Carter, *In a liberal tradition*, pp. 3–6; for the background, see G. E. Manwaring and B. Dobrée, *The floating republic* (London, new impression, 1966), ch. VII.

4 On 14 May 1797, the *Observer* reported that the Spanish fleet in Cadiz was 'disheartened' by recent reverses. In its edition of 16–18 May 1797, the *London Chronicle* claimed that the French fleet was 'certainly in a very disorganized state' because of arrears of pay; immediately afterwards, the *London Packet, or New Lloyd's Evening Post*, 17–19 May 1797, quoted an account of a mutiny in the Brest fleet.

5 On 16 May 1797, the *Oracle and Public Advertiser* reported, under the heading 'ARMY EXTRAOR-DINARIES', that 'yesterday' orders from the duke of York to the assembled Coldstream Guards announced that the conditions of the troops would be made 'more comfortable than it has hitherto been'. The news was greeted by exclamations of '*God bless the duke of York*'. Other newspapers carried the same story. Frederick, duke of York (1763–1827), was made commander-in-chief of the British army in 1798.

6 Burke stayed at Bath from the end of Jan. to 24 May 1797 when he returned to his country estate at Beaconsfield, Buckinghamshire. He died there on 9 July 1797.

7 See Letter 652, n. 1.

8 This work was Gilbert Wakefield, *A letter to W. Wilberforce, Esq. on the subject of his late publication* [i.e. Wilberforce's *Practical view*] (London, 1797).

9 Three years older than Wilberforce, Wakefield was a fellow of Jesus College, Cambridge, from 1776 to 1779; Wilberforce matriculated at St John's College, Cambridge, in 1776. In his *Letter to*

W. Wilberforce, Wakefield made several criticisms of Wilberforce's association with Pitt, whom he described (p. 55) as 'that grand national imposter'.

10 In Wilberforce's *Practical view*, between pp. 332 and 342, there are six sub-headings, each entitled 'LOOKING UNTO JESUS'.

11 This work was William Newcome, *The duty of Christian subjects. A pastoral letter to the inhabitants of the diocese of Armagh* (Dublin, 1797). Newcome's *Attempt toward revising our English translation of the Greek scriptures, or the new covenant of Jesus Christ, and toward illustrating the sense by philological explanatory notes* was published in two volumes in Dublin in 1796. Newcome was archbishop of Armagh from 1795 until his death in 1800. Probably the friend who received the letter from Newcome was Thomas Belsham, who admired Newcome's work and drew upon it for *The New Testament, in an improved version, upon the basis of Archbishop Newcome's New Translation* (London, 1808).

12 See Vol. I, Letter 248.

13 Ann, née Gibson, who married William Joseph Porter on 17 Jan. 1788. For their first child, see Letter 602, n. 1.

656. To WILLIAM DAVY   1 JUNE 1797

> **Text:**   DWL, Davy letterbook, p. 62.
> **Addressed:**   To/William Davy Esqr/Philadelphia
> **Endorsed:**   T. Lindsay[*sic*]/Rec^d. Decr. 5/97

London. June. 1. 1797

Dear Sir,

Your brother has just now very obligingly taken the trouble to send me a letter from Philadelphia from Dr Priestley, for which favour I shall take an early opportunity of calling in Gould-Square to thank him.[1] Before it arrived I had made up the parcell which accompanies this letter and intended to make free to trouble you with it, for our common worthy and valuable friend Mr H. Toulmin, at Frankfort, Kentucky. My wife in directing it has left out Rev^d. and inserted what is presumed to be his present Address: should there be any thing improper in it, you will be so good as to correct it.[2] The parcell contains only the Morning Posts, and Monthly Magazines, and till You have an opportunity of transmitting them to him, I am persuaded he would have no objection to your looking into the articles of News they contain.

You will be concerned that it presents such a state of your native country, which many fear to be at the eve of unknown misery and confusion; as Ireland is nearly in a state of insurrection,[3] the mutiny and disturbances among our seamen not yet appeased, and much to be apprehended from the victorious French having no other enemy but us to encounter.[4] It is said the Ministry are exerting every effort to procure peace, and it becomes them well as their existence in power must depend upon it; and I most heartily wish they may succeed; although there is really no prospect of it at present.[5]

Believe me, Sir, Your much obliged servant

T. Lindsey.

1   This was probably Priestley's letter to Lindsey of 3 Apr. 1797, in which he referred to the ship which would carry it; Rutt, I, 374–6. The brother of William Davy to whom Lindsey referred was Thomas Davy, druggist, of 4 Gould Square, Crutched-friars, London; see *Kent's directory for the year 1799* (London, 1799), p. 55.

2   By the time of his removal to Frankfort, Kentucky, Henry Toulmin had effectively ended his career as a minister. He was the secretary of the commonwealth of Kentucky from 13 Oct. 1796 to 5 Sept. 1804. He was the second holder of that office, which was popularly referred to as that of secretary of state.

3   For the increasing disorder in Ireland following the attempted French landing in Bantry Bay in Dec.

1796, see R. B. McDowell, *Ireland in the age of imperialism and revolution, 1760–1801* (Oxford, 1979), pp. 508–15, 541–5, 569–77. The government's counter-measures in the spring and summer of 1797 included an increase in the number of prosecutions of members of the United Irishmen, the burning of the houses of suspected rebels and the deployment of troops.

4   Although the naval mutiny at Portsmouth had been settled by 15 May 1797, the more serious outbreak at the Nore began at that time. In Italy, a series of French victories over Britain's ally Austria in the spring of 1797 led to the peace preliminaries of Leoben in Aug. and to the treaty of Campo Formio, concluded on 17 Oct. 1797, whereby Austria made significant territorial concessions to the French and received compensation through the acquisition of Venice.

5   For Pitt's ministry's interest in peace negotiations with France in the summer of 1797, see Ehrman, *The Younger Pitt. The consuming struggle*, pp. 56–68. Between July and Sept., Lord Malmesbury, who had been in charge of the abortive peace negotiations of 1796 (see Letter 642, n. 2), led a mission to Lille and sought peace terms with the Directory in France. The negotiations failed, partly because of the British demand for the retention of all their colonial conquests and the *coup d'état* of 4 Sept. 1797 (18 Fructidor), after which the French negotiating team was withdrawn from Lille. Despite the intended secrecy of Malmesbury's mission, leaks to the newspaper press had appeared by mid-July 1797.

657. To SAMUEL SHORE   12 JUNE 1797

Text: DWL, MS 12.57 (11).
Addressed: To/Samuel Shore/Esqr./Meersbrook/near/Sheffield
Postmarked: JU 12 97

London. June 12. 1797

Dear Sir,

We were sensible of your kind attentions by M^r. Johnson in acquainting us that your nursery went on very well, which has made us very easy about you, as we trust you will still keep the same train.[1] Had I been to write any thing about the Public, any day since my last, I must have said, worse and worse, for such will its state turn out whilst under the direction of its present Governors who scout every idea of reform, or change of those measures which have brought the country to its present wretched condition; for though some overtures are said to have been made for a sort of change by taking in some of Mr Fox's friends and expressly excluding him, no radical reform or total exclusion of the authors of our miseries was ever intended.[2] What the intelligence of to day is with respect to the Seamen, I cannot tell, as I write this before the papers come out, and we are to set out this morning at nine for Clapham to take the opportunity of Mrs Rayner's coach to our friends at Mordon, with whom we shall stay to the end of the week, if my wife's spirits will suffer her: But it was the talk yesterday that every thing was in a way to be quietly composed at Sheerness, and that the Sandwich only stood out, and 400 of the men were for accepting the offers of Government.[3]

As we hear nothing of any meeting at York, we suppose that upon a nearer examination of the probabilities of carrying any thing against the Court, it has been judged more prudent not to engage in a contest in which you might fail.[4]

You will be glad to learn that I have had letters lately from Dr Priestley, the last of them dated April 30, in which he gives a pleasing account of his own health and acceptableness at Philadelphia, and at the same time of the opposition he finds raised agains[t] christianity, with too much success, from the ignorance of many and their being wholly intent on lucre, and from the efforts of the Opposers of Revelation, among whom he particularly names Mr Volney with others of his country.[5] The Doctor however goes on in his course of writing as well as preaching, and has sent over several of his late Publications, of which two or three copies are come for particular Persons, but his Printer has sent a large quantity for sale to M[r] Johnson, who expects them every day, and when they come, I shall order him to send copies of each of them to You.[6] His Tract on the Increase of Infidelity is much enlarged; although if I had been to advise, it would have been to print his additions separate by themselves.[7] His Vol. of Discourses is very valuable; some parts quite new, and in others, to his American Readers, very proper.[8] And two or three smaller Publications shew his great exertions in the cause of truth and the state of the country.[9] But M[r] Finch's failure and the distress in which it will involve his daughter and her large family, w[ch] he had recently been made acquainted with had affected him very deeply.[10] At first he thought of coming to England thro' France, to try if he c[d] in the latter place procure for them any of M[r] John Wilkinsons money w[ch] had been placed in their funds and settled on M[rs] Priestley,[11] but the continuance of war made him lay aside that thought, and determined him to return to Philadelphia and to his studies there: but in the mean time, I believe that much of what he receives from the Marquis of Lansdown will be made over to M[rs] Finch.[12] It is well for him that Lord Lansdown is not like the Duke of Leeds, who has so ruined his affairs by gambling, that he is scarce able to keep his doors open.[13]

If you take in the Analytical Review, you will meet with a very judicious critique on M[r] Wilberforce's book; not that I think you woud want any one to point out the weakness of his judgment, his constant misinterpretation of the sacred writings, and overweening partialities to his own and condemnation of the opinions of others.[14]

My wife desires to unite her respects with mine to yourself and M[rs] Shore[15] with all our friends at Meersbrook and Norton. Our best wishes particularly attend all your grandchildren, and I remain always Dear Sir Your truly obliged and faithful affectionate servant

T. Lindsey.

1   This is a reference to the grandchildren of Samuel Shore III (1738–1828), who were the children of Samuel Shore IV (1761–1836) of Norton Hall.

2   In the early summer of 1797, there were moves among several opposition leaders, including Francis Rawdon-Hastings (1754–1826), 2nd earl of Moira, and Richard Brinsley Sheridan, to broaden the ministry by including some of Fox's followers, although not Fox himself. They received encouragement from some backbench supporters of Pitt, and Fox gave cautious backing to the idea, but it was strongly opposed by the ministry and by George III, and came to nothing. See Ehrman, *The Younger Pitt. The consuming struggle*, pp. 42–5, and L. G. Mitchell, *Charles James Fox* (Oxford, 1992), pp. 149–50. When the future 2nd earl of Moira was a boy, Lindsey had met him at the house of his father, John, Baron Rawdon (from 1762, 1st earl of Moira), in Ireland; see Vol. I, Letters 35, n. 12, and 37, n. 18.

3   The *Sandwich* was at the centre of the Nore mutiny and was the ship on which Richard Parker (1767–97), the 'president' of the mutineers' delegates, served as a supernumerary able seaman. Under pressure from the government, and with supplies of food and water cut off, the mutineers on board the *Sandwich* began to surrender on 12 June, and the Nore mutiny as a whole ended on 16 June. The London evening papers on Saturday 10 June 1797, including the *General Evening Post* and *London Evening Post*, reported that order was gradually being restored; the *Observer* on Sunday 11 June reported the likely collapse of the mutiny on board the *Sandwich*. The 'offers' of the government included a royal pardon for all except the ringleaders; see Manwaring and Dobrée, *The floating republic*, chs. XVII and XVIII.

4   For Wyvill's unsuccessful attempts to stimulate support for a county meeting in Yorkshire in 1797, which had the support of Samuel Shore III, see Wyvill, *Political papers*, V, xlvi–xlvii, 367–8. For the unpropitious background for reformers in Yorkshire in the later 1790s, see Dinwiddy, *Wyvill and reform*, p. 10.

5   Priestley's letters to Lindsey from Philadelphia, dated 20 Feb, 3 Apr. and 30 Apr. 1797, are printed

in Rutt, I, respectively, at 371, 374–6, and 377–9. In his letter of 3 Apr. 1797, Priestley wrote that Volney 'is much looked up to by the unbelievers of this country', Rutt, I, 374.

6   Lindsey probably referred here to Thomas Dobson of Philadelphia, who, amongst several other works of Priestley, printed his *Discourses relating to the evidences of revealed religion* (1796) and his *Letters to Mr Volney, occasioned by a work of his entitled Ruins, and by his letter to the author* (Philadelphia, 1797). A less likely reference is to John Thompson, also of Philadelphia, who printed Priestley's *Unitarianism explained and defended*. Priestley's printer at Northumberland was Andrew Kennedy.

7   See Letter 652, n. 2.

8   This is a reference to Priestley's *Discourses relating to the evidences of revealed religion, delivered in Philadelphia, Vol. II* (Philadelphia, 1797).

9   The 'smaller publications' which Lindsey had in mind were Priestley's *Unitarianism explained and defended*; *The case of poor emigrants recommended, in a discourse delivered at the university hall in Philadelphia, on Sunday, February 19, 1797* (Philadelphia, 1797); and *An address to the unitarian congregation at Philadelphia; delivered on Sunday, March 5, 1797* (Philadelphia, 1797).

10 Priestley's son-in-law William Finch, ironmaster at Dudley, suffered bankruptcy in 1797. He and Priestley's daughter Sarah had six children by 1797, and seven in all; the sixth child, Lucy Finch, was born on 2 Apr. 1797; Toulmin, 'Descendants of Priestley', 13–14.

11 For these funds, see Letter 640, n. 12.

12 After Priestley relinquished his position as librarian and literary companion to Lord Shelburne (from 1784 1st marquis of Lansdowne) in 1780, he received an annuity of £150 from his former employer.

13 Francis Godolphin Osborne, known as the marquis of Carmarthen, and from 1789, 5th duke of Leeds, was foreign secretary from Dec. 1783 to 1791. He had a considerable reputation as a man about town.

14 The *Analytical Review*, XXV (Apr. 1797), 503–11, included a detailed review of Wilberforce's *Practical view*. Since the *Analytical Review* was published by Joseph Johnson, the hostile nature of the review occasioned no surprise; it concluded that the book 'will make little impression on minds not already prepossessed in favour of his [Wilberforce's] system' (p. 510).

15 Lydia (née Flower), the second wife of Samuel Shore III of Meersbrook.

658. To RUSSELL SCOTT   1 JULY 1797

Text: Scott Coll.
Printed: Scott, *Family biography*, pp. 92–3 (first and third sentences of first paragraph); McLachlan, 'Lindsey to Scott', 123 (brief reference to first paragraph; whole of third paragraph; first two sentences of fourth paragraph).
Addressed: [In Hannah Lindsey's hand] To/The Rev^d. Russell Scott/ Portsmouth
Endorsed: July 2^d./97
Postmarked: Postmark illegible.

London. July 1. 1797.

Dear Sir,

We were most truly affected on hearing from worthy Mr Porter of your late loss of a most beloved and promising son, but have felt inexpressibly more for you on reading your own most moving narrative of your tender anxieties whilst there was any hope of life and endeavours to preserve it; and in seeing the humble and kindly submission of the parents to such an awful and afflictive providence, when the delight of their eyes and for whose increasing virtue and future usefulness they had formed the most well grounded hopes, was taken away from them.[1] I can only wish that neither Mrs Scott's nor your own health may have suffered so as to hinder your enjoying the full benefit of those consolations which you have under this sorrowful event and which you so well describe, that nothing can be added to it. I cannot tell you how much I was interested in a child of such hopes and so amiable from the incidental mention you had sometimes made of him.

My wife is much gratified as well as myself by your affectionate solicitude for her recovery to her wonted strength and spirits, which our being in the country for four or five days in the week with some true friends has much promoted, and by the divine blessing will I trust, in time, compleat; for we shall in all probability make no farther excursions this year, unless my wife's mother should be so ill as to desire to see her, which we do not expect, as we have continual favourable accounts of her. So that I doubt not of our having the pleasure of seeing you more than once during the fortnight which you propose to spend in Town the latter part of the month of August.[2]

As soon as I read that part of your letter relating to Griesbach, as I had to call upon the Duke of Grafton the next morning, I determined to try if I could not procure a copy of Griesbach's N.T. which you know the Public owes to him that they can have it on such fair paper at so reasonable a price, several of the copies of which he distributes himself.[3] And I am happy to tell you that on hearing what I could say for the worth and learning of such a friend, he immediately told me he would take care that a copy should be sent to me for you. You know that this is only the first volume, containing the four gospels. The other Vol. is expected some time next year.[4] When it comes out, if I am living, I shall remind the Duke of sending it to you also.[5]

The last letter of D[r] Priestley's was dated the beginning of may, when he was leaving Philadelphia to return to Northumberland, in perfect health, but under no small concern on having just heard of the failure of M[r]. Finch, who married his daughter so excellent a character, and more resembling her father than any of his other children.[6] Had there been a peace, I have no doubt of his coming to England, on his daughter's behalf, tho not to settle there, and to see his friends. Some of his late Publications he has sent over. Of three of them I beg your acceptance, and am assured by M[r] Johnson positively that they shall come to you this day with the monthly Publications that are sent to Portsmouth.[7] You will be so good as to acquaint me at your leisure, if he should not keep his word. If the parcell be not gone, when I call on him, this letter is to be inclosed for you. We have resided in town all this week, as we shall also the next. My wife joins in all kind wishes and regards for M[rs]. Scott and yourself, and I am always Dear Sir, truly and affectionately Yours

T. Lindsey.

---

[1]   Scott's son and first child Russell died on 24 May 1797, aged five years; Scott, *Family biography*, Table IV.

[2]   See Letter 660.

[3]   John Jacob Griesbach (1745–1812) was professor of the New Testament at the University of Jena from 1775 to 1812. His new edition of the Greek New Testament was published at Halle in 1775–7. He published an enlarged second edition in two volumes, in London and Halle, of which the first appeared in 1796 and the second in 1806. Grafton met the costs of printing 700 copies of the 1796 volume; see Peter Durrant's entry for Grafton in *ODNB*, XIX, 929. Presumably Lindsey called on Grafton at the latter's London house in Clarges Street, Piccadilly. Wakefield Lodge was Grafton's country retreat in Northamptonshire.

[4]   See n. 3, above.

[5]   Lindsey was still alive, although much handicapped by ill-health, when the second volume of Griesbach's *New Testament* appeared in 1806.

[6]   Sarah Priestley married William Finch in 1786. For Finch's business failure, see Letter 657, n. 10. Possibly Lindsey referred to Priestley's letter of 30 Apr. 1797, in which he referred to his intention to leave Philadelphia for Northumberland; Rutt, I, 377–9. Perhaps the date of the postmark of this letter was early in May 1797.

7   For examples of the monthly publications which Lindsey sent to his correspondents, see Letter 580, n. 2, and Letter 656.

659. To ROBERT MILLAR   25 JULY 1797

Text: DWL, MS 12.46 (16).
Printed: Rutt, I, 380 (most of first sentence of fourth paragraph, i.e. from 'By means of ... attention to the subject').
Addressed: To/Mʳ Robᵗ. Millar/Merchant/Dundee
Postmarked: Postmark missing.

London. July 25. 1797.

Dear Sir,

I have this day had the pleasure of receiving your letter, inclosing the list of the Society's books marked with those you have made choice of for the present year, wᶜʰ I shall take all care to have sent to you, together with Mʳ Palmer's Narrative &c.[1] And having the opportunity of a Frank from a friend who is this day going into the country for the summer, all our franking acquaintance being already gone, I would not miss the conveniency of acquainting you that your favour was arrived safe and of thanking you for it, though I shall not be able to do it so much at large as I could wish, as we expect a friend to dinner and my letter must be finished before.[2]

Your pleasing account of the promising appearance of your little united society calls to mind the feeling declaration of the psalmist, "Behold, how good and how pleasant it is for brethren to dwell together in unity".[3] The sight was so fragrant and refreshing, that he was at a loss by what image to describe it.[4] Cemented as you are by the bonds of christian love and amity and mutual forbearance, far from all desire of being lords over each others faith, and willing that others should enjoy that liberty which each claims for himself. I can have no thought but that you will continue to grow and edify one another in holiness and in all virtue, to the end of your christian course. I trust that your plan will be realized, and that there will be more and more a call for a more commodious place for public worship. Whenever it is undertaken, I shall be happy to send you my mite of five pounds, for such purposes I should be sorry if we could not manage to spare it: but I have been of late so troublesome to more opulent friends in applications of this kind, and receive annual contributions from some of them for the support of unitarian ministers that I cannot engage to procure you any assistance from others.

A few days ago I recᵈ a letter from Dʳ Priestley, of so late a date as may 29. You will be pleased with the following extract from it.

"By means of Dʳ. Ross, who has been much in the East, and whom I knew in England,[5] I have now almost every book that I wanted, respecting the religion and learning of the Hindoos, and I intend to make use of them in drawing a comparison between that system, so much boasted of by Unbelievers, and that of Moses, both of nearly equal antiquity, and I think it must be so much to the advantage of revelation, as to strike all who will give attention to the subject: but in this country very few will read any thing of the kind. Occupied as you say all are about you with politics, they cannot be more so than they are here, and also about wild speculations, which have ruined many and produced such distress as was never known before. Many of the first merchants have failed &c"[6]

Dʳ Priestley is however himself happy in the enjoyment of perfect health and in the thought of being of some use by his experiments and theological studies in which he is agreably and incessantly employed. I rejoice to hear that the trade of your Town is brisker, but am glad that the prospect of peace does not tempt you into any speculations upon it: because some very intelligent merchants, tho they wish it, and think the country cannot possibly go on without peace, hold it still uncertain. A Great Personage[7] is said to set himself obstinately against it.

It is with singular satisfaction, that I can announce to you, that my wife has recoverd her vigour and spirits in a great measure, and so as to promise, by the divine blessing, that she may go on for many long years I trust and be of some use to others, without which life would yield her no comfort. We hope the sea will send back Miss Scott quite recruited to you.[8] My wife joins in respects and all wishes of good to M^rs. Millar and yourself, and I remain always with a most sincere esteem, affectionately Yours

                                    T. Lindsey.
I beg to be kindly remembered to Mr Duncan.

[1]   Millar's letter, with his selection of books from the Unitarian Society's list, seems not to have survived. Possibly Lindsey referred to the second, rather than the first, edition of Palmer's *Narrative*; each edition was published by Benjamin Flower in 1797.

[2]   Probably this frank was provided by Benjamin Hobhouse (who was first elected to the house of commons as MP for Bletchingley in 20 Feb. 1797), James Martin or William Smith.

[3]   Psalm cxxxiii. 1.

[4]   *Ibid.*, 2, 3.

[5]   See Rutt, I, 380. In the preface to his *Comparison of the institutions*, p. viii, Priestley acknowledged the help and support of Dr Andrew Ross, 'lately of Philadelphia, but now returned to his native country, Scotland'.

[6]   There is an extract from this letter of Priestley to Lindsey, dated 29 May 1797, in Rutt, I, 380–1. Rutt reproduced (p. 380) Lindsey's quotation from the letter, from 'By means of Dr Ross … attention to the subject', but omitted the rest; see DWL, MS 12.13. Lindsey himself slightly misquoted the letter: Priestley wrote 'as must strike', not 'as to strike'. In a further passage omitted by Rutt, immediately after the reference to the failure of merchants, Priestley reported the anxiety of some of his friends over the financial solvency of Benjamin Vaughan, 'who has all the money I have in this country'. But he added that he himself had no uneasiness on the subject, since Vaughan and his brother Charles 'have given me their joint bond for it, and they have promised me landed security'.

[7]   George III.

[8]   Probably this was the Miss Scott who was the sister of Millar's wife Jean. I regret that I have not identified the seaside resort which she had visited.

660. To RUSSELL SCOTT   12 AUGUST 1797

Text: Scott Coll.
Addressed: To/The Rev^d. Russell Scott/at Dr Hawes's/N°. 8./Spital Square
Endorsed: Aug^st. 12th./97
Postmarked: Postmark missing.

                                    Essex Street. Aug. 12. 5 o'clock 1797
Dear Sir,

Not expecting you to be in Town quite so early in the month, I omitted to leave a letter for you, should you call in our absence.

We are with some very old friends at Morden in Surrey[1] ab^t 11 miles from Town from Monday morn till Saturday. My wife has found great benefit from it, and therefore we are desirous she should not miss the advantage, tho' sorry that it takes away the liberty of seeing such friends as yourself.

But we are in Town from Saturday noon till Monday morning, and therefore beg you will let us have the pleasure of seeing you on Saturday afternoon, or on Sunday to dine at ½ past one o'clock or to drink tea in the afternoon – during your stay in London.[2] But if you are not engaged, to morrow Sunday, the soonest possible we shall be happy to have the pleasure of your company. Our dinner is so early, on account of the Afternoon Service.[3]

We are sending this by a person, who is to enquire of M[rs] Gurney in Holbourn,[4] where a letter may find You –

With our joint most kind regards I am always Dear Sir, Your sincere obliged friend

T. Lindsey.

---

1   Sophia and Frances Chambers.
2   12 Aug. 1797 was a Saturday. The dates to which Lindsey referred were Saturday 19, Sunday 20 and Monday 21 Aug. 1797. 'Tomorrow' was Sunday 13 Aug. 1797.
3   The afternoon service at Essex Street chapel during the 1790s began at three o'clock; Staffordshire RO, D1527/4, diary of Samuel Pipe-Wolferstan, 19 May 1793.
4   Mrs Gurney was probably the mother of John Gurney and the wife of Gurney's father, the stenographer and court reporter Joseph Gurney (1744–1815), of 123 Holborn; see *Browne's general law list for the year 1794*, p. 48. John Gurney married Russell Scott's sister-in-law Maria Hawes on 11 Dec. 1797; she was not the Mrs Gurney to whom Lindsey referred.

---

661. To CHRISTOPHER WYVILL   5 NOVEMBER 1797

Text: NYRO, ZFW 7/2/112/4, Wyvill of Constable Burton MSS.
Printed: Ditchfield, 'Lindsey–Wyvill correspondence', 164 (most of third paragraph); p. 166 (most of fifth paragraph).
Addressed: To/The Rev[d]. Christopher Wyvill/Burton Hall/near Bedale/ Yorkshire
Postmarked: NO 5 97

London. Nov[r]. 5. 1797

Dear Sir,

I am much obliged to you for your kind rememembrance from Leven Grove,[1] in your way home, after such an agreeable excursion, and for favouring me with an account of what passed of most importance among the friends You had the pleasure of meeting. The character of the One whom you so well describe is born for no mean things, and I hope he will be called to accomplish them for his country's deliverance.[2]

The plan you mention and so warmly recommend is most seasonable, and something of the sort of absolute necessity in many parts, but I am sorry to find so much needed in the North of the Tees where I had presumed they were better instructed. I shall do what I can to forward it, though it will not be so much as I could wish. I apprehend, you have communicated it to M[r] Battley s[3] and to M[r] Brand Hollis, who being in the habit of receiving comunications from you, would not like to hear of this business at second hand from me.[4] The former are in Town though I have not lately seen them; the latter is come up from the Hide[5] for a few days, but goes back into the country to stay three weeks when he returns to be settled for the winter. I write by the Post to apprize the D. of G[6] of the design. I do not find that he intends to come up to Town soon. As the Publication will issue from and is instead primarily to operate in what is a good deal i[t]s own territory, the D. of N.[7]

would take it well to be advised with and made privy to the design by some one principally concerned in it.

From Mr Wilberforce's speech at the opening of the session against Mr Fox, you see the very little part he is capable of acting, and his defect of sense and judgment, for which you have all [of] You given him too much credit, till he knows not on whose legs he stands, and thinks himself to be some great one.[8] From others as well as from him one learns their great mortification at the Secession of the Minority, particularly of Mr Fox and the Heads of it. Though highly contemned by the court, and by some of those who have always acted with them who allege that it plainly appears to be wrong already by it, having had no effect upon the public mind, I think it was a right measure, and they will do well to try it.[9]

Mr Bryan Edwards came forth unexpected by many and spoke boldly without any reserve of the Minister,[10] but it was a disappointment that more were not brought out in the occasion. We will hope it will be better in time to come. I do not think that the Review of Mr Wilberforce's practical Xtianity will appear on this side Christmas. When it does it will well show the extent of his knowlege and his degree of judgment on such subjects.[11]

Before the French had made peace with the Emperor and when it was judged unlikely to take place I was well informed that we meditated a descent upon Holland.[12] That scheme perhaps may now be altered. The conduct of y^e. French Directory in condem[n]ing some of their number and so many others to banishment without trial, has divided the friends of liberty in these parts. [Mr] B. Flower in the Cambridge Directory condemns them à l'outrance.[13] Messrs. Godwin and Holcroft it is said embrace that sentiment and have published it in Squibs in the Papers.[14] All my friends are of a contrary opinion, particularly Mr W. Belsham, whom I name as a judge in such points. I profess I had never a doubt of their being justifiable in it, as I had long known of the trains that had been laid to bring ab^t a counter-revolution, and the restoration of Monarchy, which by this vigour beyond the law they prevented burning[?].

We have the greatest pleasure in hearing that yourself, Mrs Wyvill and all your lovely family are well, and my wife unites in respects to you both and all kind wishes for them. I beg leave to repeat that it will be little in my power to be of service in the intended plan, but I shall endeavour and shall always be here at hand and ready to execute what you may have to command Your faithful affectionate serv^t

T. Lindsey.

---

1   This letter from Wyvill to Lindsey in the autumn of 1797 seems not to have survived. Leven Grove, in the north riding of Yorkshire, was the home of the family of General George Cary (d. 1792). Wyvill was frequently a guest there.

2   Probably Wyvill had referred in this letter to a relatively young politician with a longer-term prospect of high office, perhaps Charles Grey, MP for Northumberland, who was aged thirty-three in 1797.

3   Jeremiah Batley was a prominent member of the Society for Constitutional Information during the early 1780s. He came to public notice in May 1791 when he was the author of a resolution of the society which was strongly critical of Burke's attack on the French Revolution. Wyvill described him as 'one of the earliest and most judicious Advocates for a Reformation of Parliament', who 'adhered to the principles of moderate Reform'; Wyvill, *Political papers*, V, 7 n. * See E. C. Black, *The Association. British extraparliamentary political organization 1769–1793* (Cambridge, MA, 1963), pp. 189–90, 203. Batley's son John Lodge Batley was a supporter of the repeal of the Test and Corporation Acts in 1789; *Committees for repeal*, p. 40. Both Batleys were members of the Revolution Society; BL, Add. MS 64814, fos. 59v, 62r.

4   Probably this 'plan' was the proposal for the *Oeconomist; or Englishman's Magazine*. See Letter 662, n. 2.

5 The Hyde, the residence in Essex of Thomas Brand Hollis.

6 The duke of Grafton; Lindsey's letter to him seems not to have survived.

7 In 1797 and early 1798, Wyvill and the duke of Northumberland exchanged letters in support of a county meeting in Yorkshire; see Letter 634, n. 14, and NYRO, ZFW 7/2/119/1, Wyvill to Northumberland, 10 Feb. 1798; ZFW 7/2/119/3, Northumberland to Wyvill, 14 Feb. 1798.

8 The new session of parliament opened on 2 Nov. 1797. During the debate on the king's speech on that date, Wilberforce derided Charles James Fox's secession from parliament and condemned his policies; Cobbett, *Parl. hist.*, XXXIII, 898–901.

9 Fox and his followers, frustrated by years of apparently hopeless opposition, seceded from parliament from May 1797 until the session of 1801–2.

10 Bryan Edwards (1743–1800) was MP for Grampound from 1796 to 1800 and a member of the Jamaican assembly. In the debate on the king's speech on 2 Nov. 1797 he attacked Pitt's conduct of the war and lamented Fox's secession from parliament as a loss to the nation; Cobbett, *Parl. hist.*, XXXIII, 893–8.

11 This work was Thomas Belsham's *Review of Mr Wilberforce's treatise, entitled a practical view of the prevailing system of professed Christians &c. In letters to a lady*, published in 1798. It was advertised for sale ('this day is published') in the *Morning Chronicle* of 28 May 1798 and in several issues of that newspaper immediately thereafter.

12 France and the Holy Roman Emperor Francis II concluded peace by the treaty of Campo Formio on 17 Oct. 1797. Six days earlier, the British North Sea fleet commanded by Admiral Adam Duncan (1731–1804) had defeated the Dutch fleet at the battle of Camperdown. Britain launched a brief and unsuccessful military invasion of Holland in Aug.–Nov. 1799.

13 Lindsey presumably meant that Benjamin Flower had condemned the Directory in the *Cambridge Intelligencer*, rather than in the 'Cambridge Directory'. Flower did indeed condemn the Directory in the *Cambridge Intelligencer* through 1797. In the issues of 9 and 16 Nov. 1797 he denounced the *coup* of 4 Sept. 1797 whereby the Directory seized additional powers and condemned several of its opponents to transportation. On 16 Nov. the *Cambridge Intelligencer* attacked the Directory's arrest and imprisonment of a number of journalists.

14 For some of these squibs, and the replies to them in the *Anti-Jacobin*, see Marshall, *William Godwin*, pp. 211ff.

662. To CHRISTOPHER WYVILL   **9 NOVEMBER 1797**

Text: NYRO, ZFW 7/2/112/8, Wyvill of Constable Burton MSS.
Printed: Ditchfield, 'Lindsey–Wyvill correspondence', 164 (most of
                   seventh paragraph); 166 (fifth paragraph); 167 (first, second,
                   third and fourth paragraphs, and most of sixth paragraph).
Addressed: To/The Rev^d. Christopher Wyvill/Burton Hall/near/Bedale/
                   Yorkshire
Postmarked: NO 9 97

                                                      London. Novr. 9. 1797
Dear Sir,

Having much at heart the success of the business comunicated in your last, I write again so soon to acquaint you with the judgments of different friends which I have collected concerning it, and which I confess have no small weight with me.[1]

Mr Johnson observed very well that the original Promoters must first publish one or two specimens of the intended work, and then it will be seen what is intended and how to cooperate with it. It was also his remark that no Dissertations however excellent would ever be read or spread, unless accompanied by something of a different kind, tho tending to the same end, poetical or historical. He also added, that he would be ready to undertake whatever could be expected of him as a Bookseller.[2]

But some other friends of a higher class are persuaded, that nothing of the kind or name I mentioned will ever circulate to be of any effect: that it will be liable to be counteracted and defeated by counter-publications, for which there will be workmen, in great numbers, every where to be had; that essays by themselves will not be understood, nor have any effect on those you wish to be moved by them; and that if matter of entertainment were added, that alone would be attended to by them.

But it was mentioned as the most effectual way to answer the end proposed, to send 50, a 100, or more of M^r. Flower's Cambridge Intelligencer, to Publicans, Farmers and others into different parts; and to engage him, wch he w^d most gladly undertake, from time to time to insert in his paper, such essays and information as you would wish to convey, which would not fail to answer the end proposed, and would produce the effect you wish gradually, and without suspicion, and is what may be begun, and act imediately.

As to his being so vehement against the conduct of the present French Directory in banishing so many without a hearing, it is on this account the better, that it shews his perfect good principle and honesty in it; it is a conduct that recommends him to many partisans of the present government; but nothing is capable of warping him from those sentiments and right principles, which we all wish to be universal, and which he invariably and weekly circulates as far as he can through the kingdom.[3]

If you sh^d think this proposal feasible and right wch I have hastily scribbled, I wish you would mention it to Mr B.[4] A little money thus disposed of will go a great way and do much good. One paper will be read by a whole village or neighbourhood. And together with this method larger discussions of necessary points or needful information may be sent forth in pamphlets to aid a good cause.

I find the Ministers are more [and] more vexed and disturbed at the secession, which I wish was more intire, as it would not fail in our present most deplorable posture of things, every day becoming worse, to put people upon thinking of the remedy, which such secession points out so obviously.[5] I add no more but mine and my wifes respects to your lady and yourself and best wishes for all your lovely family – ever most faithfully Yours

T. Lindsey.

---

1   Wyvill's 'last' letter seems not to have survived; see Letter 661, n.1. The 'business' was almost certainly the proposal for the *Oeconomist; or Englishman's Magazine*; see n. 2, below.

2   This 'intended work' was the *Oeconomist; or Englishman's Magazine*, a duodecimo monthly periodical which began publication in Jan. 1798 and continued until the end of 1799. It contained a variety of items, including short essays ('dissertations'), anecdotes, poetry and historical items. It was printed by Margaret Angus in Newcastle and sold by booksellers in several parts of the country; Joseph Johnson, who regularly published the works of Wyvill and other moderate reformers, is listed on the title page of the first number as the bookseller who sold it in London. Its founders were Wyvill's friends Thomas Bigge of Benton, Newcastle, and James Losh, both of whom were lawyers. See Losh diary, 9, 10 and 12 Dec. 1797, where the diarist records the preparations for the first numbers. For a conjecture that the *Oeconomist* outsold other 'liberal' journals in London, where 1,000 or 1,500 copies were sent from Newcastle to Johnson, see J. E. Cookson, *The friends of peace. Anti-war liberalism in England, 1793–1815* (Cambridge, 1982), p. 95.

3   See Letter 661.

4   Probably Jeremiah Batley; see Letter 661, n. 3.

5   For the secession from parliament of Fox and his small group of followers in 1797, see Letter 661. The 'remedy' which Lindsey regarded as obvious was an end to British participation in the war.

663. To JOHN ROWE   **27 NOVEMBER 1797**

Text: JRUL, Lindsey Letters, vol. II, no. 97.
Printed: McLachlan, *Letters*, p. 20 (fourth paragraph); p. 97
                   (most of first sentence of third paragraph).
Addressed: To/The Rev[d]. John Rowe/Shrewsbury
Postmarked: NO 27 97

London. Nov[r]. 27. 1797

Dear Sir,

I hope that by this hour, you and your family are all safely reposed in Shrewsbury, and the invalids in it restored to better health. I did not neglect to communicate to M[r] Winterbotham, the first opportunity, the part of your letter so kind towards him, with which he was duly affected, and sensible of the friendship which you had all along realized to him during his long imprisonment, by substantial benefits from yourself or others.[1] He and his most worthy fellow-sufferer, M[r] Holt, the Newark printer, are this day liberated, and relieved of the burden of their fines and other expences they have incurred; *certainly*, I am told, for I do not know it, with respect to Winterbotham; and I hope it has been the case with respect to Holt. By his no small exertion in prison he has been able to keep his booksellers shop and Press on some sort of foot in Newark, and by the help of a careful wife. With what joy must he return to her and three young children, from whom he has been four years severed?[2]

Before your last came I had been so exactly apprized of the temper of the congregation at Bristol, that I was not disappointed at their disinclination to admit another teacher of so liberal a cast as yourself.[3] And I have pleasure in seeing you put on it that pious construction which we ought to do on the failure of the most desireable events respecting ourselves, which are not in our own disposal.

I have forgot to mention, that M[r] Winterbotham it is said, will soon be married to a modest but sickly young woman, whom I have sometime seen in prison with him.[4] Besides his former congregation at Plymouth, he is said to have had an invitation [to] Birmingham, and another to Norwich. I should think he would prefer the latter, as there is certainly too much of the Church and King-spirit in Birmingham for one of his sentiments to live with comfort or even security in the place.[5] This will always more or less be the case so long as it is made a matter of worldly advantage and credit to profess a particular sett of religious opinions.

M[r] Martin, that was at Yarmouth,[6] is in town, attending a course of chemical lectures, he and your M[r] Wicksted;[7] both lodging together at a place called Maze-pond in the Borough, to be near S[t] Thomas's Hospital, where the lectures are read. My wife remarks that the place of their abode is ominous, both the gentlemen being in a sad maze.

I presume you may have heard it whispered before you left the West, that M[r] Wilberforce's *Practical Christianity* &c so full of all the superstition and narrowness of the Methodists, and such vogue with Religionists, high & low, will soon meet with due discussion by an able hand. If you should not have heard M[r] Belsham named, you will not tell it from me. But I can add that I believe you will have great satisfaction in the Work, tho' I am sorry his very great engagem[ts] with pupils, lectures, &c delay its appearance.[8]

Since I heard from D[r] Priestley of the date of the last day in August,[9] there have letters come from Miss Russell intimating that her father had gone from Middleton in Connecticut, the place of their abode to visit Dr Priestley, and to try to engage his return to pass the winter with them at Middleton.[10]

My wife happily still keeps up her good health and spirits. She unites her kind respects with mine to Mrs Rowe; and with the same from her to yourself, and our good wishes for your young folks, I remain, Dear Sir

Your affectionate servant
T. Lindsey.

1 Rowe's letter to Lindsey seems not to have survived.

2 Daniel Holt (1766–99), printer and bookseller with premises in Stodman Street, Newark, was the publisher of the *Newark Herald* from 1791 to 1794. In 1793, he was imprisoned in Newgate for four years and fined £100 after selling works of Paine; he was also one of the booksellers who sold *The trial of William Winterbotham* in 1794 (see Letter 550, n. 1). He was released in Nov. 1797 but died on 31 Jan. 1799. His wife and business partner was Eliza, née Hankin, whom he married in 1789. See Alan Dorling, 'A friend of liberty: the Newark printer Daniel Holt', *The Nottinghamshire Historian*, 64 (spring/summer 2000), 9–15.

3 The unitarian congregation in Bristol to which Rowe became minister, and formally took up his appointment in May 1798, was that which met at Lewin's Mead. The 'other teacher' was John Estlin. Lindsey evidently had some doubts as to whether Rowe's nomination as minister there would be confirmed.

4 On 26 Nov. 1797, the day on which he was released from Newgate, Winterbotham married Mary Brend (d. 1833) of Plymouth. She had been a defence witness at his trial; see the article on Winterbotham by Susan J. Mills, *ODNB*, LIX, 794.

5 Winterbotham had been assistant minister to the How's Lane, Plymouth, baptist congregation from 1790. He returned there after his release and became sole minister in 1801.

6 Thomas Martin, minister at Great Yarmouth, and at Filby, from 1792 to 1797; see Letter 536, n. 4. In 1797, he resigned as minister at Yarmouth, explaining that he had undergone a 'change of opinion' and was no longer 'able to maintain the miracles of Christianity'; see *A letter to the society of protestant dissenters, at the Old Meeting, Yarmouth, from Thomas Martin, on his resignation of the office of minister among them* (London, 1797). This short work was published by Joseph Johnson and Lindsey almost certainly knew of it.

7 Possibly 'Your Mr Wickstd' was John Wicksteed (1774–1837), starch manufacturer at Shrewsbury and father of the unitarian minister Charles Wicksteed (1810–85); see P. H. Wicksteed, *Memorials of the Rev. Charles Wicksteed* (London, 1886).

8 For Belsham's reply to Wilberforce, see Letter 661, n. 11.

9 Rutt, I, 383–5, printed a letter from Priestley to Lindsey dated 27 Aug. 1797 and one from Priestley to Russell, 31 Aug. 1797.

10 Probably these letters were written by Martha Russell; see Letter 645, n. 14 and 653, n. 6. For the Russell family's life at Middletown and their visits to Priestley at Northumberland, see Jeyes, *The Russells of Birmingham*, chs. XIV–XVI.

664. To CHRISTOPHER WYVILL   13 DECEMBER 1797

Text: NYRO, ZFW 7/2/112/29, Wyvill of Constable Burton MSS.
Printed: Ditchfield, 'Lindsey–Wyvill correspondence', 167 (second paragraph); 168 (most of third paragraph, and whole of fourth and fifth paragraphs).
Addressed: To/The Rev^d. Christopher Wyvill/Burton Hall/near/Bedale/ Yorkshire
Postmarked: DE 13 97   NEWCASTLE

London. Decr. 13. 1797

Dear Sir,

I received your pacquett by Mr Yarker[1] as you would perceive by a word or two scribbled within my last letter after it was sealed, and just as I was sending it to the post; in which way also I intimated to you to let all drop which I had suggested concerning the title of Oeconomist, at which I had perhaps been overmuch alarmed.[2]

I shall not be wanting in my endeavours to procure circulation for a Paper which is calculated to do so much good, as well as to serve the best of causes at this particular moment. In a letter I receive[d] to day from the Duke of Grafton is this short paragraph relating to it. "I am glad that the Oeconomist is to start under so respectable a patronage. I shall order the Stationer, Staunton, in the Strand, to send me a dozen copies each month."[3]

A friend who has been some days at Chevening, and just returned, says that Ld Stanhope is vastly desirous of county-meetings at the present moment but adds, that to be effectual they should be general, or else not to be at all.[4] And that the apprehension of opposition only has prevented him from moving. It is however to be lamented, that the nation at large does not at this time cooperate with the city in its opposition to this most cruel, and iniquitous Assessment Bill.[5] I am just now informed, that 6 of the common council of Faringdon Without have resigned their gowns, to avoid taking an active part against the Minister to day, whose creatures they have hitherto been.[6] I wish Mr Wishart's words at the Meeting of St Martin in the Fields, yesterday, when comending Mr Fox's *temporary absence* from Parliament, may be verified, "that it had hurried an imbecile Administration to Acts of such frantic violence as had united the whole kingdom in opposition to them."[7]

I may not omit to mention, that in many places, particularly in one district which I am acquainted with,[8] it has been signified to the Minister, that the expenses of execution and seizure was in some hundreds of instances more than the property He[9] could recover, and therefore he desired to know by what method he was to get the arrears of the old taxes, before any new ones were imposed.

From this hasty account of things here You will see, that however quiet you may be in the country, there is no small ferment here about this Assessment Bill, which may impede its progress, if the Minister be wise.

My wife joins in respects to Mrs Wyvill, and with hers to yourself, and our cordial wishes for your amiable family,

I am, always, Dear Sir, Your obliged and faithful servant
                                    T. Lindsey.

---

1   Probably Luke Yarker (d. 1803, a product of Richmond School, Yorkshire, and Trinity College, Cambridge; he was rector of Finghall, Yorkshire. Another possibility is his father, John Yarker of Finghall, a neighbour of Wyvill and a supporter of his reform proposals: see, for example, NYRO, ZFW 7/2/94/3, Yarker to Wyvill, 25 Nov. 1795. Wyvill referred to 'their accustomed spirit and zeal in the Cause of Constitutional Freedom' in helping him to obtain signatures to his requisition for a Yorkshire county meeting to protest against the two acts of Dec. 1795; Wyvill, *Political papers*, V, 306 n. *. Lindsey's previous (surviving) letter to Wyvill was that of 9 Nov. 1797 (Letter 662). There is no postscript-like 'scribble' either in the letter itself or on the address page.

2   It is not clear why Lindsey had been 'alarmed' at the title of 'Oeconomist' for this new periodical. Perhaps he feared that Burke's famous lament, in his *Reflections on the revolution in France*, about the end of the 'age of chivalry', and its replacement by that of 'sophisters, economists and calculators' had brought the name of 'Oeconomist' into disrepute.

3   *The Oeconomist, or Englishman's Magazine*, was published at Newcastle upon Tyne in 1798 and 1799. Sandys Staunton (d. 1828), stationer and bookseller, worked from premises at 481 The Strand from 1796 to 1800 and at 474 The Strand from 1801 to 1811. Grafton's letter to Lindsey seems not to have survived.

4   For Stanhope's attempts to stimulate county meetings to protest against the war and to promote reform, see Newman, *The Stanhopes of Chevening*, p. 160. Lindsey's informant was probably Jeremiah Joyce.

5 Pitt's 'Act for granting to his majesty an aid and contribution for the prosecution of the war' (38 Geo.
   III, c. 16) received the royal assent on 12 Jan. 1798; *LJ*, XLI, 470. It became known as the 'triple
   assessment' because it tripled the rate of all assessed taxes except those on houses and windows,
   which were increased in slightly different proportions, with a triple increase applied to the highest
   gradations.
6 On 13 Dec. 1797, the ward of Farringdon Without voted their 'decided disapprobation' of the ministry's triple assessment; *Morning Post and Gazetteer*, 14 Dec. 1797. There is a list of the resolutions
   and an account of the debate in this ward in the *General Evening Post*, 12–14 Dec. 1797; only one
   common councillor was recorded as speaking in favour of the ministry. A list of the common councillors for Farringdon Without may be found in *Royal Kalendar ... for the year 1797*, pp. 233–4. I have
   not been able to confirm Lindsey's story of the resignations.
7 This meeting of the inhabitants of the parish of St Martin in the Fields at the Globe Tavern in The
   Strand took place on 12 Dec. 1797. Thomas Wishart, tobacconist, of 24 Coventry Street, was in the
   chair. Possibly this was the Thomas Wishart, tobacconist, of Bath, formerly of London, whose will
   was proved on 14 Apr. 1823: TNA: PRO PROB 11/1669, fos. 395r–395v. See J. A. Hone, *For the
   cause of truth. Radicalism in London, 1696–1821* (Oxford, 1982), pp. 36–7. The proceedings of the
   meeting, attended by 'near six hundred householders' of the parish, and the resolutions denouncing
   Pitt's 'triple assessment', were reported in the *Morning Chronicle*, 13 Dec. 1797; Lindsey's quotation
   from the report of Wishart's speech was accurate.
8 Lindsey probably referred to Aldersgate, Aldgate or Cornhill wards; examples of opposition in
   London to the triple assessment may be found in Hone, *For the cause of truth*, pp. 35–8.
9 Lindsey originally wrote 'they', then over-wrote 'He', presumably meaning Pitt.

665. To JOHN ROWE   14 DECEMBER 1797

Text: JRUL, Lindsey Letters, vol. II, no. 98.
Addressed: To/The Rev^d. John Rowe/Shrewsbury
Postmarked: DE 14 97

London. Decr. 14. 1797

Dear Sir,

Since I wrote to you I have had some reason to think that Mr Kentish is not
so immoveably attached to his present situation, but that he may be induced to
deliberate on changing it, upon a prospect of being more eminently useful as a
minister of the gospel and teacher of its divine truth than he can be at present.[1]

And this circumstance makes me wish that my former letter concerning him had
not been written to you, or now it is written to rectify it.[2]

I have seen your letter to Mr Belsham about a supply for Shrewsbury, but I
apprehend some delicate circumstances would prevent his comunication of it to M^r
Kentish, or recomending it to him as if he might be thought to wish his removal.[3]

As I do not know the person who would supply your place with so much
acceptance to the congregation and approbation of yourself or of our deceased
friend,[4] could he be called to life, as this gentleman, I earnestly wish you to write
directly to himself, if you shall think proper, tell him the whole state of things, for
and against, but particularly what opportunities there may be of his doing good by
instruction of the younger part &c &c; and you will add what was the true reason
if You please why you did not write to him sooner, that you had been led to think
that he was so particularly attached to his present situation as not to be prevailed
upon to quit it.

My name you will be so good as not to mention.

I am far from thinking it certain that he will be glad to make an exchange for
Shrewsbury, but I wish the trial to be made, if you think proper, by laying the
whole of the situation before him. One thing I have long known, that he has a great
preference for a liturgy.[5]

I write this in great haste, and when the post is going out.

I am just come out of the city, where they think it impossible that the Minister can pass his Assessment Bill.[6]

I am always affectionately Yours

T. Lindsey.

---

1   John Kentish's 'present situation' was that of afternoon preacher at the Gravel Pit meeting, Hackney, a position which he held from 1795 until 1803, when he became the minister at New Meeting, Birmingham.

2   Lindsey's previous surviving letter to Rowe is that of 23 Dec. 1796 (Letter 648); it did not mention Kentish and it is likely that a letter during the intervening period has not survived.

3   Rowe took up his appointment as assistant minister to John Prior Estlin at Lewin's Mead chapel, Bristol, in May 1798. His letter to Belsham seems not to have survived.

4   William Tayleur. Rowe's successor at Shrewsbury was not John Kentish but George Augustus Case (d. 1831), who served as sole minister of the High Street chapel from 1798 until his death.

5   As minister at Plymouth Dock chapel, between 1790 and 1795, Kentish had used a form of prayer book inspired by Lindsey's liturgy.

6   This was over-optimistic; see Letter 664, n. 5.

---

666. To WILLIAM ALEXANDER   **27 JANUARY 1798**

Text: 'Letters of the Rev. Theophilus Lindsey. No. VII', *UH*, II, 75 (4 Oct. 1862), 339.

Note: This is the only section of this letter printed by the *UH*; the manuscript seems not to have survived. The ellipsis at the start of the extract indicates that this was not the start of the original letter.

London, Jan. 27th, 1798.

* * I have very lately heard from Dr. Priestley (his letter dated the middle of November), in good health and busied in his studious pursuits, but wishing for peace, that he may come in safety to visit his daughter and friends in England.[1] When he does come, I shall advise him to bring with him the continuation of his "Ecclesiastical History", which he has completed and transcribed for the press, so far as the revocation of the edict of Nantes in 1686, and to commit it here to the press, where it will meet still with many purchasers.[2]

I think I told, or intended to tell you, that Mr. Belsham, of Hackney, was preparing an examination of Mr. Wilberforce's late work which has made so much noise.[3] It is now in the press, and nearly finished; when it is I shall take an early opportunity of sending you a copy. If I mistake not, it is a book with which you will be much instructed and edified, though it may give offence to those who are not disposed to relinquish old errors.

I am happy that I can say to you that hitherto my wife has enjoyed a share of health and ease to which she had not been accustomed of a long time. I have been, upon the whole, a fortunate passenger in that respect, but particularly of late, thanks to the Giver of every blessing to us and to all.

---

1   Priestley's letter to Lindsey of mid-Nov. was that of 16 Nov. 1797; see Rutt, I, 387–8. Neither in the passages quoted by Rutt nor in the letter as a whole (DWL, MS 12.13) did Priestley mention his hopes for Anglo-French peace and the possibility of returning to England to visit his daughter and friends. However, in his letter to Lindsey of 4 Nov. 1797 Priestley referred to his (dwindling) hopes for peace and to his wish to make this visit; Rutt, I, 385–7. Probably Lindsey had in mind the letter of 4 Nov. rather than that of 16 Nov. when writing to Alexander. Priestley's daughter was Sarah (Sally) Finch; he did not come to England to visit her and her friends.

2   The fourth and final volume of Priestley's *General history of the Christian church from the fall of the western empire* was divided into two periods. 'Period XIII' covered the years from the conclusion of the Council of Trent to the revocation of the Edict of Nantes; 'Period XIV' covered the years from the revocation of the Edict of Nantes to 'the present time, a.d. 1802'. But since Vol. III is divided into 'Period XXI' and 'Period XXII', it is likely that an 'X' was omitted from the number of each period in Vol. IV. Priestley gave 1685 as the date of the revocation of the Edict of Nantes and it is likely that Lindsey did the same. 1686 was probably a printing error in the *UH*, although in the absence of the manuscript one cannot be certain.

3   See Letter 661, n. 11.

667. To JOHN ROWE   13 FEBRUARY 1798

Text: JRUL, Lindsey Letters, vol. III, no. 45.
Printed: McLachlan, 'More letters', 368 (most of second paragraph and first three sentences of third paragraph); 362 (final sentence of third paragraph); 367 (fifth paragraph).
Addressed: To/The Rev^d. John Rowe/Shrewsbury
Postmarked: FE 12 98

Note: The letter is postmarked 12 Feb. 1798, although Lindsey dated it the following day.

London. Feb. 13. 1798

Dear Sir,

I should not have neglected the acknowlegement of a letter so agreeable to me as your last, and upon business too in some measure which might demand an answer, had I not been in real perplexity how to write.[1]

The first an expression of your *fear of the unfortunate Newgate-business*, was so discouraging that it prevented the putting into the Post a letter which I had actually written to Mr Wood and had shewn to Mr Joyce, and which he intirely approved, being persuaded it would be more proper to delay it, especially as it was impracticable to come to Shrewsbury and preach if it had been desired and required, and moreover as it could not be positively declared when the Candidate would be fully at liberty, though it was presumed he would, by Lord S ____ e with his family going abroad; which however is not yet absolutely fixed.[2] After this, when I was sitting down to write, a friend came in and said he had received the intelligence from Dr Aikin, who perhaps had it from his son, that Mr Broadhurst from Bath, was thought of a[s] a proper successor to You, and that the choice would certainly light upon him; I therefore determined to wait before I wrote.[3] If this rumour be true, I hope the Congregation will be accomodated to Yours and their own satisfaction as Mr Broadhursts principles, character, and abilities are so wholly unexceptionable and even highly commendable.

You cannot well conceive how mu[ch] you have raised my opinion of Mr Coleridge by your account of him. Such shining lights, so virtuous and disinterested will contribute to redeem the age we live in from being so destitute of apostolic zeal. And I shall be most curious to see his intended publication so soon as it makes it's appearance.[4] I have formerly announced to you M^r B's reply to Mr Wilberforce, tho' you had heard of it: I am sorry I cannot tell You it is yet out of the Press, but it certainly will be printed off this week; and if I mistake not will be instrumental to correct hurtful fanatical errors and to teach the pure religion of Jesus, to a degree and in a way in which it is seldom taught; and if M^r W's prejudices will permit him, I should think he might be converted from his narrow, irrational and unScriptural system. Mr Belsham, to whom I read what you said of Mr Kell of Wareham,[5] spoke very highly of him, and thought he would accept a call from Shrewsbury, if it was made to him. By the way, I cannot bear that ugly, new-coined word *Humanist*, which is growing into use concerning those who believe X^ts humanity.

In my letter to Mr Wood, I had desired him to tell his brother Capt Wood,[6] that I had not yet seen Mr Winterbotham to put into his hands the money which he had kindly transmitted to me for him, nor have I yet set my eyes upon him, as he is still travelling in different parts, and preaching also I find for the diff^t friends who took pity on and helped him in and out of prison: but Mr Stennet of Paternoster row with whom he lodged, informs me that he is expected this week.[7] Give me leave now [to] present my wifes kind respects with my own [to] your lady and yourself, with our hopes that she promises to be well and bless you with another pledge of heaven's favour.[8] May those you already possess live and do good in the world.

I do not know whether you are acquainted that Mr Wellbeloved was believed to be appointed to be Divinity Tutor at the College in Manchester in the room of D^r. Barnes.[9] I have very lately heard, that the matter is dubious, he being so much liked at York, that it is thought the Gentlemen, whose sons are his pupils, will prevail with him to stay there. If Mr Cappe, for whom he officiates altogether, who is a paralytic subject, should drop, he might be likely to succeed him, and the settled stipend is I believe the largest that belongs to any Dissenting congregation.[10]

I hope you are in the way of procuring a situation for you and your family, at Bristol, every way to your liking.[11] I am always, Dear Sir, affectionately Yours

T. Lindsey.

---

1   Rowe's letter to Lindsey seems not to have survived.

2   Lindsey tried to obtain the pastorate of a dissenting congregation for Jeremiah Joyce, and raised the possibility of his succeeding Rowe as minister of the High Street chapel, Shrewsbury. It is clear that Rowe, and possibly members of this congregation, were anxious about Joyce's political reputation; the 'Newgate business' is a reference to Joyce's imprisonment in Newgate prison in 1794; see Issitt, *Jeremiah Joyce*, p. 72. Lindsey meant that Joyce would be at liberty if his employment in Lord Stanhope's household were to cease. I have not been able to confirm that Stanhope and his family went abroad in 1798; by that year, his daughters had left home and his sons were about to do so. In early 1798, although absenting himself from the house of lords, Stanhope was engaged in his design for a steamship. See Newman, *The Stanhopes of Chevening*, pp. 174–7, 186–95. Lindsey's decision not to send the letter which he had written to Isaac Wood no doubt explains its apparent non-survival.

3   For Thomas Broadhurst, see Letter 653, n. 4; he did not succeed Rowe as minister at Shrewsbury. The son of the physician Dr John Aikin (1747–1822), who appears to have been a source for this rumour, was probably Arthur Aikin, who had been assistant minister at Shrewsbury from 1793 to 1795 and who by 1798 was well acquainted with Shropshire during his early career as a natural scientist.

4   There was a serious prospect in 1798 that Samuel Taylor Coleridge might have become a unitarian minister. In Jan. 1798, he preached for Rowe (as a candidate to be Rowe's possible successor) at the High Street chapel, Shrewsbury, as a candidate to succeed John Rowe as minister there. William Hazlitt the essayist walked ten miles from his father's house at Wem to hear him, and described the experience in 'My first acquaintance with poets'; see Hazlitt, *Selected essays*, ed. George Sampson (Cambridge, 1926), pp. 1–20. In the event, Rowe's successor at Shrewsbury was not Coleridge but George Augustus Case (Letter 665, n. 4). Lindsey evidently anticipated a religious publication, probably a sermon, from Coleridge.

5   Robert Kell (1761–1842), a former pupil of Belsham at Daventry, was minister of the Old Meeting Wareham, from 1789 to 1799, and had previously kept an academy in that town. He was minister of the High Pavement chapel, Nottingham, from 1799 to 1801 and of Old Meeting, Birmingham, from 1801 to 1821.

6   For the two brothers identified in Isaac Wood's will, see Letter 575, n. 6. Wood did not name either of them as a captain, or as the holder of any other rank. Possibly 'Captain Wood' was James Athol Wood, a captain in the royal navy from 1797; see *Royal kalendar ... for the year 1803*, p. 149.

⁷ After his release from Newgate on 26 Nov. 1797, Winterbotham continued to serve as a baptist minister at Plymouth until 1804, when he became minister to a baptist church at Shortwood, Gloucestershire. From 1808 until his death in 1829, he lived at Newmarket, Gloucestershire. 'Mr Stennet' was probably Benjamin Stennet of 60 Paternoster Row; his entry under 'profession' was 'Staffordshire Warehouse'; *A London directory* (London, 1798), p. 144.

⁸ This was Rowe's son John, born in 1798; he died in Dec. 1827, aged twenty-nine; see *CR*, NS, I (1834), 270.

⁹ George Walker, not Wellbeloved, succeeded Thomas Barnes as principal of Manchester College in 1798.

¹⁰ Newcome Cappe died on 24 Dec. 1800 and Wellbeloved was appointed to succeed him at St Saviourgate, York, in 1801. The total income which the congregation could provide for the payment of its minister was £180 per annum; of this sum, Wellbeloved had received £60 as Cappe's assistant and it may be presumed that the full amount was paid to him on his appointment as sole minister. Probably Lindsey assessed his income at so high a level because of the additional remuneration which Wellbeloved received from his pupils. See Kenrick, *Memoir of Wellbeloved*, p. 35.

¹¹ Rowe's first residence after his move to Lewin's Mead chapel, Bristol, was at Ashley Place, near that city; see Letters 685 and 707. In 1812, his address was registered as Southwell Street in the St Michael's district of Bristol; see *The Bristol poll book ... 1812* (Bristol, 1818), which also records that Rowe, predictably, voted for the (unsuccessful) whig candidate Sir Samuel Romilly (1757–1818).

668. To THOMAS EVANS   17 FEBRUARY 1798

Text: *UH*, XXXIX, 1945 (20 Sept. 1913), 531.

Note: The manuscript of this letter seems not to have survived, although mention of it is made in the printed text. The printed version is headed 'AN OLD LETTER/Copy of a letter from Rev. Theophilus Lindsey to Rev. Thomas Evans, Penpistyll, near Brechfa, later of Aberdare'.

London, February 17th, 1798.

Dear Sir, – I should have written sooner, as well as sent the books you desired, had I not been waiting for a particular book which a friend of mine had in the Press, that I might send it to you with the earliest, as it is a work I most highly esteem, and persuade myself you will be able to learn many things from it. The book, however, has been unavoidably delayed in coming out, and is not yet printed off, but certainly will be the very next week. And as soon as may be after it is delivered, I will take care to send it by the Caermarthen waggon in a parcel to you.¹

In the meantime, I have the greatest pleasure in having to communicate to you the Duke of Grafton's most kind bounty on my representing to him what I know of yourself and the state of your numerous family, when I received ten guineas from him, which I yesterday paid into the hands of Messrs. Champante and Whitrow² to be transmitted to Mr Ross, of Caermarthen, for your use.³ I should be glad if you would let me hear from you as soon as may be convenient after you receive this letter; and take the trouble at the same time to mention your family and their ages, and also your own services at your own chapel and elsewhere, as it will be most agreeable to him⁴ to hear of anything whereby the divine truth of the gospel and the virtue and final happiness of mankind is promoted. You will have a pleasure in hearing that my wife has of late enjoyed a much better state of health than has been usual with her, and I have continual cause to be thankful for that and numberless other blessings.

I shall reserve the writing more at large to you till I have the opportunity of sending my intended parcel to you, and in the meantime, with every kind wish to

Mrs Evans,[5] yourself, and your little flock, I remain, with much esteem, dear Sir, your sincere friend,

      T. LINDSEY.

    P.S. Pray remember me to the good family of Llysten, and the worthy matron at the head of it, whose health, I hope, is restored.[6]

    Lee & Hurst, bookseller, No. 32, Paternoster-row, London, a parcel to be enclosed in Mr Ross's.[7]

---

1   Probably this was Belsham's *A review of Mr Wilberforce's treatise*; see Letter 661, n. 11.
2   In the printed text at this point is the statement 'both names indistinct in the MS'.
3   Champante and Whitrow, of 1 Jewry Street, are listed as 'wholesale stationers' in *Universal British directory* (1793), p. 100. The printed text of this letter has a footnote * 'Mr John Ross was a printer and publisher at Carmarthen for many years.'
4   The duke of Grafton.
5   Evans's wife was Ann, née Davies; they had eleven children.
6   This appears to be a reference to Evan John and Hannah Evans, the parents of Thomas Evans.
7   Lee and Hurst operated their bookselling business at 32 Paternoster Row during the later 1790s. From 1799 to 1805, the firm was in the charge of Thomas Hurst. See Ian Maxted, *The London Book Trades 1775–1800. A preliminary checklist of members* (Woking, 1977), pp. 117, 136.

669. To RUSSELL SCOTT   22 FEBRUARY 1798

Text: Scott Coll.
Printed: McLachlan, 'Lindsey to Scott', 123–4 (fourth paragraph).
Addressed: [In Grafton's hand] London February twenty second 1798/ To/the Rev^d. Russell Scot/Portsmouth/Grafton [opposite first page, in Lindsey's hand] To/The Rev^d. Russell Scott/ Portsmouth
Endorsed: [In Hannah Lindsey's hand] Rev Russell Scott/Portsmouth/ Feby 22nd
Postmarked: Postmark illegible.

                                   London. Feb. 22. 1798

Dear Sir,

    When you last took leave of us in Essex Street, you promised soon to let us know how things went on and how you and your's were in Portsmouth: But from that hour till I received your Letter of the 16th inst. not one syllable had transpired about you, and I was at times anxious, but we kept on in expectation every day.[1] You will judge then of my surprize on reading your complaint of not hearing from me, but I certainly never received one word from You.

    I am glad however to know you are tolerably well and have nothing to complain of but the impoverishment which the times bring on, in which nevertheless the nations seems [*sic*] very patiently to acquiesce, and still to trust that those who led them into it, will lead them out. Most heartily do I wish that you may find another equally agreeable to take up the place of your present pupil when he quits you.[2] And we shall both be mindful of you should a proper subject present itself, under the fullest persuasion that we should conferr a benefit on the friends or parents by such a recomendation.

    Mr Porter was so good as to call once six weeks or two months since, when we were unluckily both of us from home, and from that time I have but once heard of him, that he had his time much taken up: which I apprehend is the case through all the naval offices and departments.[3]

Of Dr Priestley I have often heard and rec^d. several letters since you left us, the last dated at the end of November, when he was happily very well and very busy, in his philosophical pursuits, and with his ecclesiastical History, having nearly transcribe[d] the whole continuation to the present times, which will make 5 8vo Vol^s. equal in size to the two already published.[4] He expects Mr Russell to assist in the expence of printing, yet hesitates whether he should not send it to England: there being little or no zeal in America for any thing but getting money.

The papers will have informed you of Mr Wakefields printer, Cuthen [*sic*], being taken up for publishing his answer to the B^p. of Landaffs letter to the People of Great Britain, containing an unqualified approbation of all the present measures of the Ministry, which was not expected from him.[5] The part of M^r W's letter, which I understand has given the most offence, is where he is thought to discourage any efforts being made at the pres^t time to repell our invaders; tho' many lawyers think that it is a trifling accusation and what they will not be able, and I trust they will not make much of.[6] Perhaps some of y^r friends may have let you see the Letter. I shall send you at the latter end of the Month Mr Belsham's Letters to a Lady in reply to Mr Wilberforce's celebrated work.[7] Johnson will have it ready to sell to morrow. I persuade myself you will be much pleased with the most if not all of what it advanced; which I profess has my full approbation.

Dr Blackburne sits by as I am writing, being come to dine with us, and sends his best comp^ts. My wife joins in kind regards to Mrs Scott and yourself, with all good wishes for Miss Scott.[8] I am, always, Dear Sir, Yours most affectionately

T. Lindsey.

---

1   Scott's letter to Lindsey of 16 Feb. 1798 appears not to have survived.
2   For a possible identification of Scott's new pupil, see Letter 678, n. 2.
3   William Joseph Porter was clerk of the cheque at Portsmouth; cf. *Royal calendar ... for the year 1798*, pp. 137, 139, and was also employed in the victualling office at Deptford.
4   Priestley's letter to Lindsey of 30 Nov. 1797 is partly printed in Rutt, I, 388–9. In a passage omitted by Rutt, Priestley wrote 'I have finished, and transcribed, my *Church History*; having brought it to the present time. It will make *five volumes*, in addition to the *two* already printed. As soon as I can possibly afford it, or get any assistance, I shall put it to the press. If not, it must be left to my executor' (DWL, MS 12.13). In its final form, the second section of Priestley's *General history of the Christian church from the western empire* was published in four, not five, volumes.
5   John Cuthell (d. 1828) of Middle-row, Holborn, was one of the booksellers who sold Gilbert Wakefield's embittered *A reply to some parts of the Bishop of Llandaff's address to the people of Great Britain* (London, 1798). The work was dated Hackney, 30 Jan. 1798. Cuthell's was the only bookseller's name to appear on the title page. In Feb. 1799, he was arrested and convicted of seditious libel although, defended by Thomas Erskine, he was sentenced to a fine rather than imprisonment. Richard Watson's *An address to the people of Great Britain* was published in London in 1798; at least fourteen editions had appeared by the end of that year.
6   Wakefield's *Reply to some parts of the Bishop of Landaff's address* accused Pitt's ministry of insincerity in its peace negotiations with France (pp. 10–15) and discouraged efforts for defence in the event of a French invasion (p. 22).
7   See Letter 661, n. 11.
8   This refers to Scott's daughter Sophia Russell Scott, born on 11 Sept. 1793.

670. To RUSSELL SCOTT   27 FEBRUARY 1798

Text: Scott Coll.
Addressed: Rev^d M^r. Russell Scott/Portsmouth
Postmarked: Postmark missing.

Dear Sir,

London. Feb. 27 1798

I take the first opportunity of fulfilling my promise and sending you Mr Belsham's Review &c of Mr Wilberforce.

As far as I can judge there is hardly any other book I could put into your hands which would be more acceptable. And tho' perhaps you may altogether accord in all the sentiments of the writer at first, upon a second reading you may not find any great cause to differ. Together with it I send two little Tracts which I have caused to be reprinted for our Unitarian Society. The one as practical, the other more controversial yet not not [*sic*] unconnected with practice, and somewhat seasonable.[1] I think you will not disapprove.

I hope you will have received a letter which I wrote in acknowlegement of your last.[2] My wife desires to join in all kind regards to Mrs Scott and yourself with Yours always most truly, tho' in haste

T. Lindsey.

---

1   These two tracts were *Practical instructions for young children* and *A representation of true religion*. Lindsey had noted in June 1796 that both were out of print; see Letter 636. On 8 Dec. 1796, the Unitarian Society at its monthly committee meeting resolved that 1,000 copies of each be printed and that Lindsey be requested to superintend the printing; Unitarian Society minute book, p. 59.
2   Lindsey's previous surviving letter to Scott was that of 22 Feb. 1798 (Letter 669).

671. To WILLIAM ALEXANDER   21 MAY 1798

Text: 'Letters of the Rev. Theophilus Lindsey. No. VII', *UH*, II, 75
                  (4 Oct. 1862), 339.

Note: This is the only section of this letter printed by the *UH*; the manuscript seems not to have survived. The ellipsis at the beginning of the extract indicates that this was not the beginning of the original letter. The ellipsis towards the end of the extract indicates the omission of text and that the two passages were not continuous in the original letter. Accordingly the two passages are separated here by a broken line.

London, May 21st, 1798.

* *As you will not do anything ostentatiously to attract notice, or to give offence, I hope your having public family worship in your house, and open to your neighbours who are like-minded with yourself, under protection of the laws, will not bring any inconvenience upon you.[1] This puts me on reminding you never to deal in censuring the times we live in, or inveighing against the wickedness of many. Such things only serve to make the hearers conceited, and fancy they are better Christians than their neighbours. Nor do I think these censures just. For the world in general does not seem to me so bad as many would have it, nor our own times worse than those that have preceded.

----

* * I think you very right to avoid entering into all political matters in these times;

but in no times should any discussions of them have admittance into societies assembled for divine worship.

---

1   Alexander held 'public family worship' in his house at Woodbridge, which he had licensed as a place of worship and where he made use of Lindsey's reformed liturgy; see *MR*, NS, XIV (1858), 189.

672. WILLIAM TURNER OF NEWCASTLE   2 JULY 1798

Text:	DWL, MS 12.44 (60).
Printed:	Graham, 'Unhappy country', 152 (brief extracts from third and fourth paragraphs).
Addressed:	To The Rev^d. Mr Turner/Newcastle/upon Tyne
Endorsed:	[In pencil] July 2 1798

London July 2. 1798

Dear Sir,

I am much gratified by your kind remembrance which I found on Saturday at our return from the country,[1] where we have passed the greatest part of each week for the last month on my wife's account, who has lately been affected with a lowness of spirits and loss of appetite, which alarmed us. The last week happily she was somewhat recruited, so as I hope will enable her to undertake our biennial visit to her aged parent, who expects her much about this time. We are to follow Dr Blackburne and his amiable wife and children three, who are now at Richmond as we learn by letter to day, but he returns in a weeks time to attend his business.[2] The change of air and exercise he predicts will restore my wife if she can but bring herself to undertake the journey, and in two days time we are to set out. For myself I have cause of great thankfulness for the share of health I enjoy at my age. So much for the history of your friends, in which you are so kind as to interest yourself, and in return for the pleasing picture of yourself and little family, in which most strongly appears the power and force of those excellent christian principles in which you have been nourished, and whose effects are seen in that temper of mind you exhibit, and in the varied exertions you are continually making to serve your fellow creatures. I thank you for some of the fruits of them which you send me in your Fifth year's report of your Society, which records what is so much for the honour of it's first Secretary,[3] and in the Signatures with which you favour me, from the Oeconomist and Monthly Magazine,[4] for which notice I thank you, not to forget the Answer to the Question, Why are you a Christian? in which you have done wisely to leave out the Preface &c wch might hurt the book with some readers from the name of our excellent friend in it, as I conjecture;[5] for not more than ten days since I had a letter from a Clergiman of a Sea-port like yours, desiring he might omit that name and some other things in his edition, which he proposed to make.[6]

I barely saw worthy Mr Prowit on Sunday morning, who confirmed the account you give of your own health, but he has promised to take a breakfast with us to morrow morn, when I shall see more of him and likewise hear more of you.

Very recent relations of Dr Priestleys good looks and good spirits are come over by a gentleman who had seen him not more than six weeks ago at Northumberland.[7] I have accounts from himself of somewhat later date, that he had brought down his Church-History to the present time, and that it woud make five more volumes, of the size of the other two printed in England. But he wants a patron to undertake to print it.[8] Being the only *Unitarian* Church history, I sh^d think it would sell in England notwithstanding the violent prejudices against his name. He has already transcribed for the press, what must be both most curious and useful, "A comparison of the Institutions of Moses with those of the Hindoos and other Eastern-nations ["], wch he persuades himself would remove objections of some Unbelievers.[9] He has also other things on the Anvil.

I mentioned to your most valuable neighbour Mr Bigge, that I had hope an ingenious friend or [MS torn: one word missing] who had promised, would enable me to supply [him] with some little pieces for his public-spirited useful design; and hope he is sowing good seed that will spring up in this wretched country, where there is such an universal dearth of all sense of liberty and good principle.[10]

We desire to rejoice with you in your pleasing prospects from your young family, particularly of the two eldest.[11] May they all live to be a balm of lasting comfort to your mind, and do good in the world. My wife joins in these good wishes for them, and in sincere respects to yourself. I am always, Dear Sir, Your obliged and affectionate servant,

    T. Lindsey.

My wife called to day at Mr Dodsons of Boswell court Carey Street, who is treasurer to the Unitarian society and a most upright punctual man, who says he has not received any Subscription Money of Mr Turner's since 1793, which accounts for his having no list of books sent for the last two years.[12] For the rest the Society holds up its head tolerably well, the times considered.

---

1   This 'kind remembrance' was evidently a non-surviving letter from Turner to Lindsey.

2   Dr William Blackburne's wife was Hannah, née Wilson; they were married in 1788. Their three children were William Theophilus (named after Lindsey), Elizabeth Rachel (see Letter 483, n. 10) and Dorothea Frances, all born between 1790 and 1794. See *Familiae min. gen.*, II, 767–70.

3   This was the *Fifth year's report of the Literary and Philosophical Society of Newcastle upon Tyne: to which is annexed a list of the new members* (Newcastle, 1798). Turner had been one of the two joint secretaries of the society since its foundation in 1793 and had contributed extensively to the compilation of this report.

4   The essays in the *Oeconomist; or Englishman's Magazine* were published anonymously. Turner evidently provided Lindsey with a list of some or all of the authors. He himself contributed essays entitled 'A short sketch of the public establishment for the poor in Bavaria' in Feb. 1798 and 'Abstract of Count Rumford's essay on food' in Apr. 1798; see *The Oeconomist; or Englishman's Magazine*, I (1798), 43–7, 73–5. For Turner's authorship, see Harbottle, *William Turner*, p. 48. The American-born Benjamin Thompson (1753–1814) entered the service of the elector of Bavaria, who granted him the title of Count Rumford for his reforms, notably in the area of poor relief, of the Bavarian government. Possibly Turner also sent Lindsey a list of authors of essays in Joseph Johnson's *Monthly Magazine*, founded in 1796; or perhaps he misquoted the full title of *The Oeconomist; or Englishman's Magazine*.

5   This short work of twenty-four duodecimo pages was Clarke's *Answer to the question*. The 'advertisement' by Lindsey for the 'new' edition of 1797 (see Letter 625, n. 5) and the edition reprinted by Toulmin (see Letter 645, n. 7) included a footnote reference in praise of Priestley ('our excellent friend') and his *Answer to Mr. Paine's Age of reason*. The 'fifth' edition, reprinted in London, Taunton and Newcastle in 1797, which was edited or co-edited by Turner, did not include the advertisement. On 8 Nov. 1798, the monthly committee of the Unitarian Society resolved to print 1,000 copies of this work; Unitarian Society minute book, p. 64; when it appeared, it carried the advertisement but not the footnote.

6   Possibly this clergyman in a sea-port was John Rowe, newly arrived as minister of Lewin's Mead chapel, Bristol, who (perhaps) noted in a non-surviving letter to Lindsey that he was proposing to reprint Clarke's pamphlet for the Western Unitarian Society. It is clear that, more than four years after his emigration, Priestley's name still made some unitarian sympathizers nervous about the possibility of a backlash against them.

7   Priestley's letters to Lindsey do not provide a convincing identification of this gentleman. A possi-

bility, however, is a friend of John Vaughan of Philadelphia, who did much to publicize Priestley's work in America. See Bowers, *Joseph Priestley and English unitarianism*, pp. 52–3.

8   Priestley's attempt to find subscribers in Philadelphia to finance the publication of the later volumes of his *General history of the Christian church* was unsuccessful. However, in 1802 and 1803, Lindsey, Hannah Lindsey and Thomas Belsham took the lead in raising a subscription which met the cost of the publication of these volumes and for Priestley's *Notes on all the books of scripture*. See Letter 736, n. 5.

9   Priestley, *A comparison of the institutions*. For a note on Dupuis, see Letter 717, n. 12; Writing to Lindsey on 17 May 1798, Priestley described Dupuis's work as 'the *ne plus ultra* of infidelity'; Rutt, I, 400. The *Comparison* contained an appendix entitled 'Of the allegorizing talents of Mr. Boulanger' (pp. 365–72), in which Priestley criticized Boulanger's identification of St Peter with figures from classical history including Aeneas of Troy. The work of the philosopher Nicolas Antoine Boulanger (1722–59) which Priestley attacked was his posthumously published *Dissertation sur Saint Pierre* (Paris, 1770). A collected edition of his works was published in Paris in 1792.

10 Thomas Bigge of Benton House, Little Benton, Newcastle upon Tyne; his 'public-spirited useful design' was *The Oeconomist; or Englishman's Magazine*, of which he was co-founder and editor. For his co-operation with Wyvill, see *Wyvill Papers*, V, 156–8, 167–76, VI, 32–4.

11 Turner and his first wife Mary (d. 1797), née Holland, had four surviving sons in 1798; the two eldest were William Turner III (1788–1853), tutor at Manchester College, York, from 1809 to 1827 and minister at Northend unitarian chapel, Halifax, from 1827 to 1853; and Philip Holland Turner (1790–1811).

12 See Letter 676, where Lindsey explained that Turner's subscription had been paid in full, but had not been properly recorded by the Unitarian Society.

673. To THOMAS BELSHAM   1 AUGUST 1798

Text: DWL, MS 12.57 (12).
Addressed: To/The Rev^d. Mr Belsham/William Belsham's Esqr/Bedford
Endorsed: [In Lindsey's hand] Thanks for the acc^t. of y^r. route,
                  remembrances to y^r. brother. Am glad you accompany him to
                  Wakefield
Postmarked: RICHMOND   Y   AU 4 98

Richmond. August 1. 1798

Dear Sir,

Unfortunately for my writing to you as you desired before Saturday, we did not return from Mr Wyvill's before the Saturday, when I concluded a letter would not reach till you had set forward on your intended short tour, absolutely necessary for health and vigour considering your constant long confinement and which we advise and trust that you will be able to extend to four weeks and an absence of three sundays, relying on your people to furnish themselves with a minister for one day or to officiate some one of them himself to the rest in case of a regular supply not being to be obtained. Surely master Evans had no claim upon your bounty after having fed him so often and been so kind to him and I shall think myself bound to repay what you advanced for his immediate wants to carry him down into the west. But I cannot help thinking he must have an extraordinary front to look for more from that quarter after what had been done for him, and he will find himself disappointed in any future expectations of the kind.[1] We are glad you have at last done what we have long wished and exhorted you to, that you may be some little gainer in worldly respects, though it will still be a paltry matter, in recompense of those invaluable labours you bestow on your young men. I should be sorry to think so meanly of any one as to hesitate a moment about a compliance with your demand.

I have been surprized that in the two letters you have favoured me with, not the least conjecture was ever hinted concerning the state of M[r] Pitt. I have presumed that it was because you had nothing to be depended upon that you could write about it. I have very lately heard from a person in a line of life to have good information, that there is some grounds for what has been often thrown out of a temporary derangement having taken place, whether from the gout having affected his head, or from whatever other cause. Whatever it be, it has been endeavoured to keep it as secret as possible, and it has obliged him to be intirely secluded from society. He has been down quietly at the Speaker's in Berkshire, and since for a few days at Mr Dundas's at Wimbledon, and although somewhat better, is still in an aukward way. And one thing may be depended upon, that all the accounts of his having been at the Levée, or having any where appeared in Public, are all absolutely false.[2]

Your account of Mr Johnson's trial was very acceptable, though the issue of it was so unfavourable. It is to be lamented that his case was not set forth with all the force and distinction that was due to it. I am grieved that an English jury could be induced to bring in guilty a Publisher so circumstanced, and I own it is what makes me tremble more and more for our liberties.[3] M[r] Wakefield I fear can have nothing to expect of good in his case, though he make his innocence ever so clear and plead with a more than mortal eloquence.[4]

M[r] Shore sends me word that M[r]. and M[rs] Sam[l] Shore were to carry his grandson to M[r] Corrie's as yesterday to fix him there, and I persuade myself it will be for his great benefit and improvement. I do not know where a spirited youth, that had been so much indulged, especially in horsemanship &c could be lodged with equal security.[5] M[r] S. adds, that on Wednesday last M[r] Sitwell was married to M[rs] Stovin's daughter and came the same day to Renishaw Hall, a pleasing seat, about seven miles from Meersbrook and near Chesterfield.[6]

I learn from a lawyer of some eminence upon the northern circuit, that Ben. Flower's history of the Society for promoting persecution, which came out the Saturday before last, was read by many of them at York with much edification, and with admiration of Erskine's conduct and the striking contrast between his liberality and their bigotry.[7] In his last Intelligencer he has exhibited in their proper colours some of the chiefs of these R[t]. Rev[d]. and Laic Persecutors, B[p]. Porteus, S[r] Ric[d]. Hill, M[r] Wilberforce &c; and his account of the Principles of a very large separation from the late M[r] Wesley's Societies is well worth looking at when it falls in your way.[8]

You must not look for the Letters to a lady on M[r] Wilberforce's doctrines of christianity being read by any of the ladies of gentlemen in the clothing towns in the West riding of Yorkshire, as I am told that copies of his performance were presented at first very promiscuously among them by himself or his adherents, and have quite closed their eyes and ears against admitting any thing that can call in question his infallibility.[9] The only thing that can bring it in doubt with some of them will be M[r] Pitt's downfall, whether brought about by the hand of God or of men.

I am in hope, by means of M[r] Wyvill, who has read the said letters with the greatest approbation and is a perfect judge on the subject, to be able to procure a frank for this letter, which I shall send to you at Hackney, and may thence be forwarded and follow you free cost wherever you shall be. And as we shall be in Yorkshire till the latter end of the month, I hope you will give me an opportunity of hearing from you and acknowleging it when on your route, and telling you how it is with us, which I shall not fail to do. At present nothing can be better than we are, my wife in particular, thanks to your good wishes and prophetic augury. With her most cordial respects I remain, Dear Sir, ever your most truly obliged

T. Lindsey.

---

1 'Master Evans' was probably one of the pupils whom Belsham taught privately at Hackney after the closure of the college. It may be assumed safely that he was not related to Lindsey's correspondent Thomas Evans.

2 For Pitt's ill-health in the summer of 1798, see Ehrman, *The Younger Pitt. The consuming struggle*, pp. 81–2. The speaker of the house of commons was Henry Addington, whose estate was situated at Woodley, near Reading, Berkshire. Henry Dundas, the secretary of state for war and Pitt's closest colleague (as well as drinking companion), had a residence at Wimbledon. George III's levee days were Wednesday and Friday; *Royal kalendar … for the year 1798*, p. 95.

3 On 17 July 1798, Joseph Johnson was tried and convicted at the Guildhall on a charge of seditious libel, after co-publishing (with John Cuthell and Jeremiah Jordan) Gilbert Wakefield's *A reply to some parts of the bishop of Llandaff's address*. However, sentence was postponed until 15 Nov., when it was postponed again, and Johnson committed to the custody of the marshal of the Marshalsea prison. On 11 Feb. 1799, he was fined £50, ordered to provide sureties of £700 for his future conduct, and sentenced to six months' incarceration in the king's bench prison. He was duly released the following Aug; the conditions of his imprisonment seem to have been relatively mild. See Gerald P. Tyson, *Joseph Johnson: a liberal publisher* (Iowa City, 1979), pp. 158–70, and Braithwaite, *Romanticism, publishing and dissent*, pp. 155–69. Lindsey's regret over the conduct of the defence case reflected the decision of Johnson's counsel, Thomas Erskine, to defend Wakefield's book; since the book had already been declared a libel in Jeremiah Jordan's trial, this effectively associated Johnson with Wakefield's opinions.

4 Following the publication of his *A reply to … the bishop of Llandaff* (n. 3, above), Wakefield was arrested, granted bail and tried before Lord Kenyon in the court of king's bench on 21 Feb. 1799. He conducted his own defence, which was subsequently published as *Defence of Gilbert Wakefield on an official information from the attorney-general for a reply to the bishop of Llandaff's address to the people of Great Britain, on February 21, 1799* (London, 1799). He was convicted of seditious libel; on 18 Apr. 1799, at a further hearing before sentence, he made a speech in his defence and was committed to the king's bench prison. On 30 May 1799, he was sentenced to two years' imprisonment in Dorchester gaol and required to provided sureties to a total of £1,000 for his future good behaviour. See *State trials*, XXVII, 679–760.

5 Lindsey probably referred here to Sydney Shore (see Letter 479, n. 2), the eldest grandson of Samuel Shore III. He was born in 1790 and died in 1827. John Corrie, after his resignation as classical tutor at Hackney College, served briefly as minister at Bromsgrove and then, in Belsham's words, 'kept a select school near Birmingham' (DWL, MS 12.56, 'List of the students educated at Daventry', fo. 96), where, presumably, Sydney Shore was one of his pupils. According to Lady Stephen, 'The Shores of Sheffield and the Offleys of Norton Hall', *Transactions of the Hunter Archaeological Society*, V, i (Jan. 1938), 11, Sydney Shore was subsequently educated at Manchester College, York, as was his younger brother Offley (1797–1870).

6 On 25 July 1798 ('Wednesday last'), Sitwell Sitwell (1769–1811) of Renishaw Hall, Eckington, Derbyshire, married, as his second wife, Sarah Caroline (d. 1860),the youngest daughter of James Stovin of Whitgift Hall, Rossington, near Doncaster, Yorkshire; *Gent. Mag.*, LXVIII, ii (1798), 808. Her mother was Theodosia, née Sparrow, the second wife of James Stovin and she was the sister of Frederick Stovin (see Letters 674 and 700); *Familiae min. gen.*, IV, 1244–5. The *CR*, NS, I (1834), 501, noted the death of Theodosia, 'relict of James Stovin, Esq., late of Whitgift-hall, Yorkshire', in her ninetieth year; she died at Newbold, near Chesterfield, on 21 May 1834. Sitwell Sitwell was MP for West Looe from 1796 to 1802, and gave some support to the parliamentary opposition. He was created a baronet in 1808. Sparrow Stovin, a younger son of James and Theodosia Stovin, was very briefly (Jan. to June 1788) a student at Manchester College; see *The roll of students entered at the Manchester Academy* (Manchester, 1868), unpaginated, *sub* 1788. Probably Lindsey's acquaintance with the family arose through his friendship with Samuel Shore III. For a further note on the Stovin family, see Letter 700, n. 10.

7 Benjamin Flower's *Cambridge Intelligencer* of 21 July 1798 carried an editorial strongly criticizing the prosecution of Thomas Williams of Blackfriars, the printer of a cheap edition of Paine's *Age of reason*, by the Society for Enforcing the King's Proclamation against Immorality and Idleness (usually known as the Proclamation Society), which Flower dubbed the 'Persecution society'; see Letter 384, n. 4. Flower's editorial regretted that the celebrated defence advocate and libertarian

whig Thomas Erskine had agreed to be retained by the society to undertake this prosecution. It also published a report of a meeting of the society on 27 Feb. 1798, which resolved to reject Erskine's suggestion that the case against Williams (who was already in Newgate prison) should not be taken further, and noted that Erskine, accordingly, had indicated by letter that he declined to take any further part in the affair. Thomas Williams was tried for blasphemy in the court of king's bench on 24 June 1797 and, on conviction, was sentenced to one year's imprisonment and required to find a surety of £1,000 for his conduct for the remainder of his life; see *State trials*, XXVI, 653–720. The prosecution of Williams is discussed by Innes, 'Politics and morals', pp. 100–1.

8   The *Cambridge Intelligencer* of 28 July 1798 denounced the bishop of London (Beilby Porteus), the bishop of Llandaff (Richard Watson), William Wilberforce and Sir Richard Hill for supporting the policies of Pitt's ministry while making 'long and loud professions of their regard to liberty and Christianity'. Porteus in particular was a leading protagonist for the Proclamation Society, serving as its president from 1793. The same issue of the *Cambridge Intelligencer* also carried a letter from William Thom (1751–1811) and Alexander Kilham (1762–98), two of the leading figures of the methodist New Connexion, which broke away from the Wesleyan mainstream of methodism in 1796. The letter set out the principles of 'Methodists late in Connexion with the Rev. J. Wesley'.

9   This work was Belsham's *A review of Mr Wilberforce's treatise* (see Letter 661, n. 11). Wilberforce was one of the two MPs for the county of Yorkshire.

674. To THOMAS BELSHAM   10 SEPTEMBER 1798

Text: DWL, MS 12.57 (13).
Addressed: [In Hannah Lindsey's hand] To/The Rev^d. Thos. Belsham/
                  Grove Place/Hackney./Penny Post
Postmarked: [Two separate postmarks] Fenchurch St Unpaid [and] 4
                  o'clock SP 13 [otherwise illegible]

Richmond. Septr. 10. 1798

Dear Sir,

We left York on Saturday morning,[1] and arrived here by one o'clock, 44 miles, not a bad proof you will say of the vigour as well as diligence of the travellers. My wife indeed keeps up wonderfully, and I trust will not abate of her health and good spirits, when you see her.

No where are you in higher esteem than with those we associated with at York, and we left M^r and Mrs Wellbeloved and our hosts the Cappes charged with every thing respectful and most friendly to you. Never did we see Mr Wellbeloved equally chearful and happy. But he has his house as full of pupils as it can hold, and these and his day-scholars all make proficiency as he wishes and are well-behaved. And Mrs Wellby and his lovely family are every thing he could desire.[2] The smallness of his congregation gives one pain, as he is indeed a most edifying preacher, and greatly improved in this as in all respects. I attribute it to the prevalence of Mr Wilberforces methodism in several of the churches and the prejudices against Dissenters in general and those that are liberal in particular, and to the no small spread of the disciples of Mr Paine and Godwin.

Your account of Birmingham during your longer abode was very acceptable, as we are much interested in respect of many of its inhabitants, tho' for my part I never wish to see the place again and would go some miles out of my way to avoid it.

We and all friends at York, to whom I communicated your design, highly approved the advance in the terms for your pupils, and we persuade ourselves that your house will soon be so full, that vacancies in it will be waited for.[3] My wife above all praises the bold step as you call it, and says it will make you to be valued and in the request you ought to be.

We Shall probably leave this place on tuesday, to morrow sen'night, in our way home, but shall halt more than once, and for some days at Mr Reynolds's at Paxton, where we think we shall arrive on the Saturday and are promised the pleasure of meeting your good brother, whom they saw lately at Bedford, and settled the matter with him. If Mrs Stovin be at home as we pass thro' Doncaster, we shall see her and learn what are her intentions with respect to Frederic;[4] and if there be any thing worth communicating I shall give you a few lines from Paxton, if I do not write again before we leave Richmond.

Letters from London yesterday tell us that nothing decisive was arrived with respect to the French in Ireland. But Lady Darlington in this neighbourhood read very lately at a public meeting a letter from her Lord, who is a Capt. in the Durham Militia in Ireland, which mentioned that the French were defeated, and the greater part taken prisoners, that he himself in a few days should have a furloug to come to England, adding that as he sent his letter by Port-patrick, it would be some days before the good news could reach London so as to come down thence into the country.[5]

This town is not quite so agreeable as it was when we were last in it, as the family at Green,[6] as they call it, are gone for the benefit of the Sea-air and water, to Burlington-Bay,[7] and Mr Wyvill and his family to Hartlepoole. Dr Disney and his family we had the pleasure of seeing for part of a day at Brignall as they passed along from the Lakes to Richmond to visit the venerable parent, under whose roof we now are.[8] The Disneys left her this day week, but were to call by the way at different places, so that the D^r will not be in Town I should suppose, at the soonest, till Sunday next.[9]

I am sorry to have nothing more interesting than these naked journals for you to pay eight-pence for, but such has been the sovereign decree of William Pitt that intercourse with friends shall not be a cheap business.[10] He seems still to lie concealed behind the curtain, as we see no mention made of him, but I presume it is that he may be able to come forth with greater power and eclat.[11]

My wife joins in respects to Miss Belsham[12] and with her most kind remembrances to yourself

I am, Dear Sir, Your constantly obliged and affectionate servant
                                T. Lindsey.

---

1   The previous Saturday was 8 Sept. 1798.
2   Charles Wellbeloved and his wife Ann had seven children in all.
3   See Letter 645; after the closure of Hackney College in 1796, Belsham taught a small number of pupils at his house at Grove Place, Hackney. In 1797, he noted privately 'I have had much labour with my pupils, who engross a great deal of my time in consequence of having no assistant'; Williams, p. 482. In 1798, he felt sufficiently confident as to increase the charges for their tuition.
4   For the Stovin family, see Letters 673, n. 6, and 700, n. 10.
5   William Harry Vane (1766–1842), from 1792, 4th earl of Darlington; and from 1827, marquis, and from 1833, duke, of Cleveland; in 1787, he married Katherine Powlett (1766–1807), daughter of Harry Powlett, 6th duke of Bolton. For Lindsey's acquaintance with the Vane family of Raby Castle during the 1760s, see Vol. I, Letters 56 and 57. For the service of militia regiments in Ireland during the later 1790s, see Western, *The English militia in the eighteenth century*, pp. 225–7; for the involvement of the Durham 'fencibles', see McDowell, *Ireland in the age of imperialism and revolution*, pp. 631, 636. On 8 Sept. 1798, a small French force under General Humbert (1755–1823) was defeated at Ballinamuck, county Longford; a further French force was defeated off the Donegal coast on 12 Oct. 1798. Earlier, on 21 June 1798, the main Irish rebellion was defeated at Vinegar Hill, county Wexford.
6   Probably Lindsey referred here to the Yorke family, which had provided MPs for Richmond in the

middle years of the eighteenth century. The Yorke family residence was the mansion on the Green, Richmond. The head of the family, John Yorke (d. 1813), was a prominent local figure who presided over a salon-like atmosphere at the Green. A historian of Richmond notes that in this company 'poetry, novels, music and the theatre were topics of conversation and discussion as well as those of politics and religion … the majority opinion there was pro-whig and anti-Tory', Leslie P. Wenham, *James Tate* (Northallerton, 1991), pp. 187–8.

7 Bridlington, Yorkshire.

8 I.e. Hannah, widow of archdeacon Francis Blackburne and mother of Hannah Lindsey.

9 Sunday 16 Sept. 1798.

10 The postal rates were increased by act of parliament (37 Geo. III, c. 18) in 1797, and again in 1801 and 1805; see Staff, *The Penny Post*, pp. 71–2.

11 For the state of Pitt's health, and his temporary absence from parliament in the summer of 1798, see Ehrman, *The Younger Pitt. The Consuming Struggle*, pp. 81–2. See also Letter 673, n. 2.

12 Ann Belsham, the only unmarried sister of Thomas Belsham.

675. To JOHN ROWE   15 OCTOBER 1798

Text: Theophilus Lindsey, Letter to John Rowe, 15 Oct. 1798,
                  James Marshall and Marie-Louise Osborn Collection,
                  Beinecke Rare Book and Manuscript Library, Yale University.
Addressed: To/The Revd. John Rowe/at the Revd. Mr. Estlyn's/Bristol
Postmarked: Postmark illegible.

London. Oct. 15. 1798

Dear Sir,

After an absence of full three months, we are at last arrived in safety at our own home, and have all cause to be thankful to a good providence for many pleasant things we have enjoyed in the most delightful season I ever remember, in finding our various friends happy and comfortable, particularly my wifes venerable parent at the age of 85, and, which was the chief object of our journey, in my wife's intire recovery of her health and spirits, and being restored to her wonted strength of mind and some degree of usefulness without which last life is little desireable to her. At York we passed ten days with our friends Mr and Mrs. Cappe, most eminent Christians both, with their family, and doers of good to their power to the minds and bodies of all around them; Mr. C. unfortunately debilitated but not so much in his understanding as incapacitated for action; some very slight specimen of Mrs. C. you see in the Monthly Magazine:[1] But Mr Wellbeloved, who is Mr Cappe's assistant, is a burning and shining light, his abilities and constant improvements of them of a superior kind. I am always edified with the depth of thought and piety of his discourses, and most particularly, with his manner of administring [*sic*] the Lord's supper. Add to this, that he has the education of 16 or 18 young gentlemen, some of them of best families in the country, 4 boarded in his house; and I am persuaded he is no less eminent in this part of his charge; and withall, a most amiable, modest, unassuming creature. He was of Mr Kentishs standing at Hackney.[2]

I did not intend and ought to beg pardon for being so prolix on this one subject, but I thought it would give you pleasure to know how the gospel of Jesus is supported in one district in the North, and this worthy man has sometimes to cope both with the deist and atheist, a combat to which he is equal.

Pray what is become of Mr Coleridge, who promised such great things to You at Shrewsbury, and where is he? In our travels homeward, about 60 miles short of London, at a friend's, where we passed some days, Mr Basil Montague Mr Godwin's intimate friend, and a young acquaintance with him, dropt in to dinner as accidental visitors. The company had not conversed long together before Mr M. let us perceive that he was of Mr Godwins school, though the name of this last gentleman was not mentioned.[3] In the course of the afternoon we had a great deal, even to satiety, about the eternity of truth, and the new philosophy, but nothing of Mind, or Deity, as if that was to be wholly discarded out of the system. The table was full, and amongst many sensible people, two of very eminent and known abilities, who pushed the Respondent into many absurdities: but all passed with good humour on all sides. I began with asking ab^t Mr Coleridge; when he told me that he was gone to pursue his studies in Germany: My wife asked if he had taken his wife along with [*sic*]. Oh, no, says he; what could he do with that clog about his neck.[4] He woud then be able to think freely. It was impossible in such a state of Society as this for a man of genius to expand his faculties &c &c.

I cannot say that Mr M. spoke of his own particular intimacy with Mr Coleridge. You can inform more fully and particularly about him.

I shall be happy to be informed of the health and prosperity of your lady, yourself and family, and of your comfort and satisfaction in your ministry; and also of the health and welfare of y^r worthy collegue and his family.[5]

We are not yet fixed in town, but spend the week from monday morn to Saturday with our old friends in Surrey, and so shall continue one week after this, to the end of the present month.

Believe me, Dear Sir, ever very affectionately Yours.

T. Lindsey

Forget not our due and kind respects at home and to all we have the pleasure of knowing.

[On address page] I have mislaid your letter and cannot recollect your direction, which you will please to send when you write. Mr Estlyn[6] will excuse this trouble.

---

1   Catharine Cappe was the author of two letters in the *MM* during the first half of 1798. The first, in the Apr. number, described a female benefit society at York, of which she was a leading promoter; the second, in the May number, was an account of charity schools for girls; *MM*, V (1798), 239–41, 319–20. They were part of series of Cappe's letters to that publication and offer revealing evidence of her charitable enterprises; see Helen Plant, *Unitarian philanthropy and feminism in York, 1782–1821: the career of Catharine Cappe* (York, 2003).

2   For Wellbeloved's early years as minister of St Saviourgate, York, and for his school in the city, see Kenrick, *Memoir of Wellbeloved*, ch. III. Wellbeloved and John Kentish had indeed been contemporaries as students at Hackney College (Wellbeloved attended the college from 1787 to Jan. 1792, Kentish from 1788 to 1790).

3   Basil Montagu (1770–1851), lawyer and expert on the laws of bankruptcy, was a close friend of William Godwin in the late 1790s and, for a time, concurred with many of his radical opinions. He formed an even closer connexion with William Wordsworth and regularly played host at his London house to leading literary figures. In the 1820s and 1830s, he published a sixteen-volume edition of the works of Francis Bacon.

4   Samuel Taylor Coleridge married Sara Fricker (1770–1845) in 1794. In company with William and Dorothy Wordsworth, he travelled to Germany in Sept. 1798. His visit included a period of study at the University of Göttingen. He returned to England in July 1799.

5   John Prior Estlin (1747–1817) was the senior minister at the Lewin's Mead chapel, Bristol; Rowe had been assistant minister there since May 1798.

6   John Prior Estlin (n. 5, above).

676. To WILLIAM TURNER OF NEWCASTLE   22 NOVEMBER 1798

Text: LPN, MS ('Two letters from Theophilus Lindsey to William
                 Turner of Newcastle (12 May 1791 and 22 November 1798')).
Addressed: To/The Rev^d. Mr Turner/Newcastle/upon Tyne
Postmarked: Postmark missing.

London. Novr. 22. 1798

Dear Sir,

When we returned to Town in October and I received your letter of Aug. 16,[1] as
soon as I had the opportunity of making inquiry I found it would not be needful for
me to write to you on the principal subject of it; for that you had been duly informed
that Mr Johnson had paid the Subscriptions of yourself and your friends and allowed
it in his accounts with the Society, but by not paying or signifying it to the treasurer
it had not been entered regularly or known to him. I was also told that lists of our
books for the current year had been sent to you to make your election, tho' I think
your having paid your money and having received no books in other years ought to
have been considered, as the fault has been all along the Society's and not yours.[2]
But you may certainly depend on stricter attention in future.

So much would certainly have been noticed to you with acknowlegements for
your letter and pamphlet much sooner, had not I thought it better to wait till the
members came to town that I might save needless expence, besides that we were
almost wholly with our old friends in Surrey till November after we came out of
the north.[3]

By this delay I have also the happiness of assuring you that my wife's recovery
of her health and spirits which had been effected by our journey and abode of full
three months with our friends in different parts, appears now to be fully confirmed,
and the more as she will not fail to continue the milk-diet morning and night which
by the blessing of heaven has mainly contributed to it.

I am much gratified by the perusal of the "View of the moral and political
Epidemic["], wch does great credit to the genius and good sense of the writer: but do
not wonder that the innocent title-page shoud affright the booksellers from medding
[*sic*] with the publication of a composition still more innocent.[4] Poor Johnson's
fate will add to the apprehensions of the trade. For no man could be more free
from design to offend the laws or hurt the constitution. I am at a loss to conceive
how an honest intelligent jury of freemen could convict him.[5] I have been to visit
him you will believe since his confinement, and was rejoiced to find it so airy and
convenient, like a country-lodging near Town. We are in anxious suspence about
him till we know his sentence: the duration of his confinement and the place. For
the lawyers say, he may still be sent to Newgate.[6] I tremble for the fate of the most
worthy and undaunted Mr Wakefield more than he does for himself; though the
apprehensions of his family for him create him some distress. He appears decided
to plead his cause himself, and perhaps it is as likely to do good as any thing said
by others in his behalf; Would that I were one of his jury! His liberty should be
inviolate.[7]

For your present of a pamphlet, if I were near you, I sh^d send you a shilling one
lately published by Cadell, on Universal Redemption, by a Mr Brown of Sidney
college Camb. It is on a most favourite doctrine, with you, I question not as well as
myself. Any large variety of discussion cannot be expected in so small a compass.
But the subject is handled neatly and with simplicity, and some good criticism. The

conclusion "the final, eternal, and infinite happiness of the whole creation of God", every heart must delight in.[8]

You would be much hurt with Mr G. Morgan's death. He lay 5 weeks ill of a low putrid fever, but the latter part of the time dosed [i.e. dozed] a good deal. [He] will be an infinite loss to a most amiable wife, and 8 if not 9 children. His parts were of the first rate, and a character virtuous & irreproachable.[9]

May you be long preserved to your own family. I am glad you are happy in such a valuable relation to take off a part of your cares for them. In the year 1737 I was for half a year, to learn Arithmetic at Rosthern near Knutsford, where was at the same school, a Mr Peter Holland, somewhat older than myself, whom I liked much, and whose family did not live at any great distance. I suppose he may not be living. I think he was your mothers brother.[10]

My wife desires her kind respects and thanks for your solicitude for her, and joins in all wishes of good to your little folks. I am always, with sincere esteem, Dear Sir, Your affectionate servant

T. Lindsey.

Tho' I waited for a frank to convey this, I beg the lack of one may never prevent my hearing from You.

---

1   Turner's letter to Lindsey of 16 Aug. 1798 appears not to have survived.

2   See Letter 672.

3   For the pamphlet to which Lindsey referred, see n. 4, below. The new parliamentary session began on 20 Nov. 1798 and the presence of sympathetic MPs in London made it easier for Lindsey to obtain franks for his outward letters.

4   This work was *A view of the moral and political epidemic: which has devastated Europe for several years, and now rages with equal if not increased violence ... By a friend to the king and country* (London, 1798). Probably it was to this short pamphlet, rather than to a publication of Turner himself, that Lindsey referred in the second paragraph of this letter.

5   For Johnson's trial and imprisonment, see Letter 673, n. 3.

6   From 15 Nov. 1798 to Feb. 1799, Johnson was placed in the custody of the marshal of the Marshalsea prison; from Feb. to Aug. 1799, he was held in the king's bench prison. He was not imprisoned in Newgate.

7   For Gilbert Wakefield's case, see Letter 673, n. 4. At this time Wakefield and his wife Anne (née Watson) had seven children.

8   This work was John Browne, *An essay on universal redemption; tending to prove that the general sense of scripture favours the opinion of the final salvation of all mankind* (London, 1798). Lindsey slightly misquoted the final words of this work, which are (in capital letters) 'The final, eternal, and infinite happiness of his whole creation' (p. 42). The publishers were Cadell and Davies in the Strand, and Deighton in Cambridge. On the title page, Browne is identified as MA, 'late of Sidney Sussex college, Cambridge'. According to *Alumn. Cantab.*, II, vol. I, 415, his schools were St Hilary (Cornwall) and Hackney (Mr Rees). He was admitted to Sidney Sussex College in 1789 and graduated BA in 1794 and MA in 1797. 'Mr Rees' was presumably Abraham Rees, who was tutor in Hebrew and mathematics at Hackney College from 1786 to 1796, and John Browne was possibly the lay student identified only as 'Brown', who entered Hackney College in Sept. 1788; DWL, MS 38.14, fo. 90. He was admitted to the Middle Temple on 8 Nov. 1794; *Register of admissions to the Honourable Society of the Middle Temple*, Vol. II (London, 1949), p. 412. It appears that this work on universal redemption was John Browne's only publication.

9   George Cadogan Morgan died on 17 Nov. 1798. His widow was Anne, née Hurry, whom he had married in 1783. At the time of his death, they had eight children (seven sons and one daughter); see D. O. Thomas, 'George Cadogan Morgan (1754–1798)', *Price-Priestley Newsletter*, III (1979), 66.

10   For Peter Holland (1722–61), see Vol. I, p. xxii, and Letter 364, n. 4. Holland was indeed not living in Nov. 1798. He was the brother of William Turner's mother Mary (1725–84), née Holland.

677. *To RUSSELL SCOTT   **30 NOVEMBER 1798**

> **Text:**   Scott Coll.
> **Printed:**   McLachlan, 'Lindsey to Scott', 124 (third paragraph).
> **Addressed:**   To/The Revd Russell Scot/Portsmouth
> **Endorsed:**   Decr. 1st. 98
> **Postmarked:**   Postmark missing.

Essex S^t
Novr 30th

Dr Sir,

We cannot imagine what is become of you, unless you are about removing to Nottingham, to wch. place we heard that you are invited as Mr Walkers successor:[1] Our comon friend from Deptford[2] called more than once during our four Month absence from home: We are now setled [sic] in Winter quarters, & well.

By the blessing of God, a milk diet, & long journey into the North, has amended my stomach & relieved the wretched nervous feelings, wch. afflicted me for above four months in the Spring.

We long to hear a good account of you & yours: Mr Lindsey send[s] a new thing on an agreable subject, in a parcel from Mr Johnsons; who is in the Kings bench, a prisoner but not unhappy.[3] Adieu accept our joint kind regards & best wishes, & believe me always y^r. sincere f^d

HL

[1] George Walker was succeeded as minister of the High Pavement chapel, Nottingham, not by Russell Scott, but by Robert Kell (1761–1842), who served there from 1799 to 1801, before moving to the pastorate of Old Meeting, Birmingham. Kell was joint minister at Nottingham with William Walters, who was minister there from 1794 to 1806. Walker had departed for Manchester in 1798, in order to become divinity tutor and principal of the new dissenting academy in that town.

[2] This friend from Deptford was William Joseph Porter; see Letters 602, n. 1, and 669, n. 3.

[3] For Joseph Johnson's imprisonment, see Letter 673, n. 3. Contrary to Hannah Lindsey's apparent belief, he was in the custody of the marshal of the Marshalsea prison from 15 Nov. 1798 to 11 Feb. 1799; only on the latter date did his imprisonment in the king's bench prison begin.

678. To RUSSELL SCOTT   **14 JANUARY 1799**

> **Text:**   Scott Coll.
> **Printed:**   McLachlan, 'Lindsey to Scott', 124 (fourth paragraph; most of
>   fifth paragraph; sixth paragraph).
> **Addressed:**   To/The Rev^d. Russell Scott/Portsmouth
> **Postmarked:**   Postmark missing.

London. Jan. 14. 1799

My good friend,

It is a sincere pleasure, after so long a suspension, to see your handwriting, and to find that sorrow has not been added to sorrow, and a kind providence has preserved your beloved daughter for a comfort to her parents and to be happy and useful I trust in the world when their long day is over and their work finished.[1]

You would have heard from me, but I did not know how to frame myself to write, not being able to meet with Mr Porter, and fearing the worst. I can very readily see how intirely Your time must have been engrossed by preparatories for Mr Savery's son, and by your other constant occupations, and am heartily glad you have not suffered more, with your gouty habit from such extraordinary application.[2]

We cannot divine how our worthy Secretary M[r] Kentish[3] could make such a mistake with respect to your non-payment of your subscription, my wife having it marked down as paid by herself for 1798, and being about to pay it this week for 1799. So that you will not let this any longer prevent your sending for your allotment of books. We Shall take care to apprize the secretary of M[r] Carters death,[4] and I doubt not of being able to furnish you with a copy of D[r] Toulmin's reply to M[rs] Fuller.[6]

Have you lately heard any thing of or about M[r] Fysh: Palmer at Botany bay. I think I sent you word that I had assurance from one who had seen his own letter to his brother at Bedford, that he was in very thriving circumstances with a brewery and a farm; and by the death of that brother in October last we are told that our friend's part of his fortune will not be less than four thousand pounds.[7]

I dont know whether you remember a young Minister, M[r] Lewis, a welchman, much befriended by the late D[r] Kippis, by him recomended to be Secretary to M[r] Beaufoy, who behaved unhandsomely to him at his death – upon which event he engaged by the advice of his friends in the business of Stock-broker, and was doing very handsomely, getting at least his three or four hundred [a] year – but six weeks, tempted for present[?] again[8] to engage too far, would not stand it, but waddled out of the Alley.[9] He is now said to be on board the Manchester in the Downs bound for Philadelphia, his last letter being so dated.[10] It is presumed he will call at Portsmouth. It will be doing a good deed and saving a worthy and I would say honest man, notwithstanding this one faux pas, if you could contrive to acquaint him, if the ship touches, as is expected at Portsmouth, that far from being necessary to withdraw himself his affair will be easily made up, and he will be received by all his old friends, and by all worthy persons with the same countenance as ever. This I am desired to communicate to him. M[rs] Kippis left him very handsomely at her death, and still more in reversion on the death of her sister.[11] By his thus running away, he shews he is that honest man, his friends always took him to be.

We were by no means surprized, that they should think of you to fill up the vacancy at Nottingham; and we thought that on this account it might be eligible to You, as there was duty only once a day, and a collegue always at hand to give help when wanted, and the situation very healthy[.][12]

I hope that when M[rs] Scott makes her visit to her friends in the Spring, she will not come alone, when we shall have the greatest pleasure in going over a thousand things that in so long an interval have passed unnoticed.[13] I hope to be able to get a frank for this scrawl otherwise shall send it without, and hope you will never be withheld writing on such account. My wife unites her sincere and cordial respects with mine to *You both*, and I remain always, Dear Sir, Your obliged and affectionate servant

T. Lindsey.

---

1   This refers to Scott's daughter Sophia Russell Scott.

2   Possibly Mr Savery's son was Scott's 'new pupil'; see Letter 669, or a subsequent pupil. A Mr Savery was enrolled as a student at Manchester College between 1798 and 1799, and expelled in 1800; see G. M. Ditchfield, 'Manchester College and anti-slavery', in *Truth, Liberty, Religion. Essays celebrating two hundred years of Manchester College*, ed. Barbara Smith (Manchester College, Oxford, 1986), p. 216 n. 32.

3   Kentish was secretary to the Unitarian Society from 1796, in succession to Thomas Morgan, until succeeded in 1802 by Jeremiah Joyce.

4   This refers to the death on 7 Feb. 1794 of John Carter of Wimering, an alderman of Portsmouth and the father of Sir John Carter; see *Gent. Mag.*, LXIV, i (1794), 189. He was a member of Scott's congregation and of the Unitarian Society; Lindsey undertook to inform the society's secretary (John Kentish) of Carter's death.

5   Lindsey at first wrote 'Dr' and over-wrote 'Mr'.

6   See Letter 644, n. 4. In additions to the works mentioned there, Toulmin was the author of a further reply to Andrew Fuller, entitled *The injustice of classing unitarians with deists and atheists* (London, 1797).

7   This is almost certainly a reference to Jeremy Fyshe Palmer of Bedford, whose will (where he is described as 'gentleman') was proved on 22 Oct. 1798; TNA: PRO PROB 11/1314, fos. 85r–86r. He bequeathed to Thomas Fyshe Palmer a share (along with his brothers John and Edward and his sister Elizabeth) in landed property in Bedfordshire, Berkshire and Wiltshire; that share was worth several thouand pounds.

8   Lindsey presumably intended to write 'gain' rather than 'again'.

9   This was almost certainly John Williams Lewis (see n. 11, below), not George Lewis, formerly the minister of Carter Lane. Henry Beaufoy was MP for Great Yarmouth from 1784 until his death, and secretary to the board of control from May 1791 to July 1793. Beaufoy died on 17 May 1795; Lewis was not mentioned in his will; TNA: PRO PROB 11/1260, fos. 190r–192r. By 'The Alley', Lindsey probably meant Exchange, or 'Change' Alley , adjacent to Lombard Street and Cornhill in the City of London, which was the location of numerous coffee houses where commercial affairs were transacted; it was famously associated with the South Sea Bubble of 1720.

10   This 'last letter' of Lewis seems not to have survived.

11   Elizabeth Kippis died on 17 Nov. 1796; see Letter 621, n. 9. In her will (TNA: PRO PROB 11/1281, fos. 274r–276r) she bequeathed to John Williams Lewis all her household possessions, together with £100 and a substantial residuary bequest. She also left legacies to the Presbyterian fund and to the Princes Street congregation, Westminster, where Andrew Kippis had been minister until his death in 1795. DWL, MS OD 43 (account book of the Princes Street congregation, pp. 115, 117) names Lewis as executor of Elizabeth Kippis's will. For her sister, Esther Bott, see Letter 621, n. 9. The same source (p. 117) notes the receipt of a legacy of £30 to the presbyterian fund from the executors of Mrs E. Bott of Kirton, Lincolnshire. However, I have not located her will.

12   For the possibility that Scott might fill the vacancy at the High Pavement meeting, Nottingham, after the departure of George Walker, see Letter 677, n. 1.

13   I have not found a documentary record of Sophia Scott's visit to London in the spring of 1799; if the visit took place, she probably stayed with her parents, Dr William and Sarah Hawes in Spital Square.

679. To RUSSELL SCOTT   31 JANUARY 1799

Text: Scott Coll.
Printed: McLachlan, 'Lindsey to Scott', 124 (second paragraph; fourth sentence of third paragraph; first sentence of fifth paragraph).
Addressed: To/The Revd Russell Scott/Portsmouth
Endorsed: Feby 1st./99
Postmarked: Postmark missing.

London. Jan. 31. 1799.

Dear Sir,

It is somewhat singular that I cannot procure you a copy of Dr Toulmin's reply to Fuller, not being able to meet with my own, and moreover that there is not as I am told a copy in London.[1] I do not however give up the search, and in the mean time send you Mr Kentish,[2] and two copies of a little Tract wch I yesterday received out of Northamptonshire from that worthy minister, who we told you had been ejected from his congregation and silenced by a self-created synod of Dissenting ministers in his neighbourhood. He tells me he has drawn it up and put it in this form, to be some answer to a minister who has printed a catechism in which he has endeavoured to represent him as an enemy to Christ, for his opinions, and has dispersed it in the village where he lives and preaches occasionally in a room to a small audience who are still desirous to learn from him.[3]

By your silence about the Manchester I have no doubt of the ships not having put in at Portsmouth but gone directly down the channel to Falmouth. So that he[re] I presume is an end of poor Lewis ever appearing with any credit. I am told that what he had from M[rs] Kippis at her decease, and what will come to him on the decease of her aged sister, will be upwards of a thousand pounds.[4]

D[r] Priestleys eldest son whom we have expected for some time, is not yet arrived. The Doctor had told me he was to take his passage in the William Penn of Philadelphia, but I have learned that its destination was changed and it is gone to Batavia. And the Amiable is just come from Philadelphia, and we hear nothing of him. I think I told you that M[r] Priestley comes on the invitation of his uncle, the great Iron Master, M[r] John Wilkinson, and tis hoped that such promising overtures may be made as to induce him with his family to return and settle in England, and we trust will in the end draw the Doctor after him.[5]

I do not know of any thing in the theological way soon to make its appearance; only to day by accident I heard that M[r] John Hollis is soon to give us a second attack on the gospel. Tho he is in town, and I see him sometimes he has never named it to me. When it comes out I will take care you shall have it.[6]

I have been glad to learn lately that M[r] Wakefield had laid aside his design of making a long defence of himself when his trial comes as it would but irritate and exasperate the minds of many and intends only to be very short. I am told he has consulted with M[r] Gurney, and M[r] F. Vaughan.[7] His own mind is undaunted, but his body feeble; and his family, particularly an amiable sensible daughter and wife are much affected and distressed for him.[8]

M[r] Johnson, who never had the gout before, has for some time been afflicted with it in both his feet, but is getting better.[9]

I do not recomend it to be purchased, but if in book-societies, or circulating libraries, *Public characters of 1798*, falls in your way, you would be amused with it, and meet with some information. All are far from being equally well drawn up. The irish characters are much comended as done by no ordinary pen.[10] But perhaps I may have mentioned this before.[11]

We hope that your amiable daughter, M[rs] Scott, and yourself are in tolerable health. My wife joins in respects and every good wish for you all. I remain always Dear Sir very affectionately Yours

               T. Lindsey.

1   See Letter 678, n. 6.

2   This work was John Kentish's *Strictures upon the reply of Mr. A Fuller, to Mr. Kentish's discourse, entitled The moral tendency of the genuine Christian doctrine. By the author of that discourse* (London, 1798). Andrew Fuller had written *Socinianism indefensible, on the ground of its moral tendency: containing a reply to two late publications: the one by Dr. Toulmin, entitled The practical efficacy of the unitarian doctrine; the other by Mr. Kentish, entitled The moral tendency of the genuine Christian doctrine* (London, 1797). Kentish's *The moral tendency of the genuine Christian doctrine. A discourse, written with reference to Mr. A. Fuller's examination of the Calvinistic and Socinian systems* was published in London in 1796.

3   This is a puzzling reference. A possibility is John Morell (1770–1840), minister at Daventry, Northamptonshire, from 1796 to 1799, and subsequently at Brighton. He was an independent minister who adopted unitarian opinions. A further speculation is raised by the publication in 1799 of the

particular baptist Andrew Fuller's *The discipline of the primitive churches, illustrated and enforced. The circular letter from the ministers and messengers of the several baptist churches of the North-amptonshire association assembled at Olney ... May 21, 22, 23, 1799.* Perhaps the ejected minister was a baptist.

4   See Letter 678. It seems that John Williams Lewis emigrated under a cloud.

5   The arrival at Gravesend of the *Amiable* from Philadelphia was reported in the *Oracle and Daily Advertiser*, 26 Jan. 1799. Joseph Priestley junior arrived in England in the spring of 1799 (although not on board the *William Penn*) and returned to America in the summer of 1800. The overtures of his uncle John Wilkinson (1728–1808) of Castlehead and The Lawns (Brosely) were insufficient to persuade him to remain in England, or to induce his father to return there.

6   John Hollis's *An apology for the disbelief of revealed religion: being a sequel to sober and serious reasons for scepticism, &c* was published (with Hollis's name, but with no publisher identified) in London in 1799. For his previous work, see Letter 631, n. 8.

7   For Wakefield's trial on 21 Feb. 1799, see Letter 673, n. 4. In addition to John Gurney, Wakefield consulted Felix Vaughan (1766–99), a graduate of Cambridge (Jesus College), who is listed under 'counsel' in successive editions of *Browne's law list* in the mid- and late 1790s. He served as defence counsel for several of those accused of sedition, including Thomas Walker of Manchester in 1794, and was a particular friend of John Horne Tooke. It is likely that Lindsey knew him personally, since his address was given as 18 Essex Street, Strand, in *Browne's law list for the year 1796* (London, 1796), p. 41.

8   Wakefield's wife, whom he married in 1779, was Anne, née Watson; they had five sons and two daughters. Possibly the daughter to whom Lindsey referred was Anne (d. 1821), who married the surgeon and chemist Charles Rochemont Aikin (1775–1847), the younger brother of Arthur Aikin.

9   For Joseph Johnson's imprisonment, see Letter 673, n. 3. For his declining health, see Tyson, *Joseph Johnson*, pp. 170–5.

10   *The public characters of 1798*, a collection of short biographical essays, was published in Dublin in 1798. The essays on 'Irish characters' included Henry Grattan and Lord Charlemont. Of particular interest to Lindsey were the essays on Priestley (pp. 304–8) and on George Dyer (pp. 323–9), both of which were broadly sympathetic to their subjects.

11   Lindsey had not previously mentioned this particular work in a surviving letter.

680. To THOMAS EVANS   22 FEBRUARY 1799

Text: NLW, MS 3639C.
Addressed: To/The Rev. Mʳ Thoˢ. Evans/Penpistyll/Brechfa/Caermarthen.
                   Queen head
Postmarked: Postmark missing.

London. Feb. 22. 1799.

Dear Sir,

I do not wonder that you began to think the interval very long since the duty of your last letter to me, especially as you had some just grounds to expect my writing again. But I must say in my defence that I waited for the Duke of Grafton's arrival in Town, which has not taken place till this very week, and I am happy to acquaint you that his health is much better than it was, and that he himself the very first half hour I saw him asked after you and desired I would convey to you his annual present of *ten pounds*; which I propose if the rain permits to pay to morrow to Messʳˢ Champante and Whitrow to the account of Mʳ Ross for him to transmit to you.[1] I shall also add to it *two pounds* from my wife who begs Mʳˢ Evanss acceptance of it for your son Joseph Priestley Evans, to which I shall beg leave to add *one pound* by way of paying the carriage &c of the parcell of books, which now at length I intend to send you.[2]

I hope that this little stranger whom your good wife has brought into the world will live and do good in it, and will be a credit to the name you have given him.[3] No one knows of what infinite service a child brought up in piety and virtue may be in his generation. And this portion, by the divine blessing, you will be able to give to all your children, whatever other advantages for this world, more or less, you may be able to bestow upon them.

I truly rejoice that the heads of the worthy family of Llystyn can retire so comfortably in their old age and live where they have the pleasure of seeing their son treading in their steps. But it gives particular satisfaction that he does not go lazily on in the beaten track of his parents, but looks about him and examines for himself, whether it be the right way or not. This is the only way to become settled on a rock that cannot be shaken. Any of those tracts that I shall send you, which may be useful to him, I beg you will desire his acceptance for his worthy family's sake.[4]

I have not heard from D[r] Priestley since November the 10th. the date of his last letter when he was in perfect good health and happily employed in his various literary pursuits, philosophic and theological: he has many larger works of the latter sort ready for the press, but there is no zeal or curiosity in those southern provinces to encourage the publication.[5] We expect his eldest son over in a few months, who probably will bring over some things that may be put to the press here.

We have just now had the news brought that the brother of the Secretary of State, M[r] Thomas Grenville, who was commissiond to bring over the emperor and k. of Prussia to join in the war against the French is lost at Sea. It will be happy if this disaster may put over rulers on seeking to put an end to the war, which can bring nothing but ruin along with it.[6]

I shall send you a few lines, when I send you the books, which I shall at the same time also send to the two friends you recommended. You will please to let me know when M[r] Ross has received notice of the money paid to his account for you.

My wife joins in all kind wishes for you and yours and in due remembrances to the family of Llystyn and all your old friends who remain firm in the truth.

I remain always your cordial friend

T. Lindsey.

1   For John Ross of Carmarthen, see Letter 668, n. 3.
2   Joseph Priestley Evans, the son of Thomas Evans and his wife Ann (née Davies), was born in 1799. In common with his father, he became a weaver.
3   The 'little stranger' was Joseph Priestley Evans.
4   This refers to the parents of Thomas Evans; see Letter 668. His father, Evan John Evans, was a weaver and although Thomas Evans followed him into this trade, Lindsey praised the younger Evans's interest in theology and willingness to take a critical approach to what he read. In fact, Thomas Evans's father was his intellectual 'mentor' who 'plied him with scriptural material [and] encouraged him to think liberally'; Jenkins, '"Horrid affair"', p. 178.
5   Lindsey almost certainly referred here to Priestley's letter to him, dated Northumberland, 1 Nov. (not 10 Nov.) 1798. The letter is partly printed in Rutt, I, 409–11. In a passage omitted by Rutt, Priestley referred to the preparations of his son, Joseph junior, for a visit to England and added that he would probably follow him, as 'my continuance here appears less and less desirable'; DWL, MS 12.13. In a further passage omitted by Rutt, Priestley lamented 'Nothing that I should print would have any sale, and if I should preach, I should have few hearers, as is evident from my last course of Sermons at Philadelphia.' 'These southern provinces' was Lindsey's (probably ironical) reference to Pennsylvania and the states to the south.
6   Thomas Grenville (1755–1846), the elder brother of the foreign secretary Lord Grenville and a cousin of Pitt, was envoy extraordinary and minister plenipotentiary to Berlin from Dec. 1798 until Aug. 1799. In Jan. 1799, he was dispatched to Berlin with instructions to negotiate an alliance with Prussia, with a view to engaging a Prussian army, financed in part by a British subsidy, to secure the liberation of Holland from the French. His expedition formed part of the process whereby Pitt constructed his second coalition, including Russia, Naples and Portugal, against France. Grenville sailed from Yarmouth on 28 Jan., but his ship was wrecked off Cuxhaven and he barely escaped with his life. He

did not arrive at Berlin until 17 Feb., and in the intervening period nothing was heard from him and he was presumed lost. For the background, and a graphic description of Grenville's adventure, see Piers Mackesy, *Statesmen at war. The strategy of overthrow 1798–1799* (London, 1974), ch. 5. The Holy Roman Emperor was Francis II; the king of Prussia was Frederick William II.

681. WILLIAM TURNER OF NEWCASTLE   1 APRIL 1799

Text: DWL, MS 12.44 (61).
Printed: McLachlan, *Letters*, p. 141 (fourth paragraph); Graham, 'Unhappy country', 152–3 (most of third paragraph; fourth and eighth paragraphs).
Addressed: Address missing.
Endorsed: [Faint pencil endorsement: Lindsey Ap. 1. 99.]
Postmarked: Postmark missing.

London. April. 1. 1799

Dear Sir,

As I do not pass myself off for a regular correspondent, and there was nothing in your letter which demanded an imediate acknowlegement, I have been the more easy under the apparent neglect towards a friend whom I most highly esteem.

I can now in reply to your recomendation of Mr Hood inform you with much satisfaction that we have received much pleasure from the acquaintance of a young person of so amiable a character and so well disposed, and I hope that whenever he is called away he will leave this town not only untainted with its vices, but with such confirmation in good habits and improvements from diligent application to his profession, as will make him useful through life. I may tell You, that he is very much pleased with the manner of our service at the chapel, and with Dr Disney as a preacher, to whom I was careful to introduce him at his first coming.[1]

I confess myself somewhat aukward and ashamed when looking towards the Banks of the Tyne, not only for remissness towards yourself, but for not acknowleging as I ought the very great civilities I received some time since from Mr Bigge, particularly when I once intimated what I thought I could have been able to perform, in furnishing with some aid towards carrying on the Economist. But, my aids, whose names I would mention to you only, Mrs Jebb, and M^r W^m. Belsham failed me. Both greatly equal to the work. But the Lady from imperfect health was incapable for a long time, and the other from too much employ.[2] I should be glad however, if without naming names, you would make my Apology to that most worthy public-spirited character[3] for my silence on this head.

His and Dr Fenwick's judgment concerning the obnoxiousness of Mr Wyvill's pamphlet on the Secession, has been confirmed by no reputable booksellers venturing to undertake the publication.[4] Johnson's fate deters them all, added to the suspension of the Habeas Corpus act, which I do not expect to see removed whilst I remain in the land of the living.[5]

If you wish to see a specimen of the temper of the court and the numberless retainers to it, in Town and country, towards Mr Lockes good principles of liberty civil and religious and towards all good men that hold them, read only the *Shade of Alexander Pope on the Banks of the Thames, written chiefly tho' not entirely on occasion of Mr Grattan, Ex-member of Parliament for the city of Dublin, coming to reside at Twickenham in November 1798.*[6] The parodying and misrepresentation of that Gentleman's words, and assassination of his character throughout is such that

I wonder the Libeller is not afraid considering that it is an Irishman that he attacks. But his vilifying of Mr Fox[7] and incense to Mr Pitt, are all of a piece. This last he calls, Everso juvenis, natus succurrere saeclo.[8]

In his *Pursuits of Literature*, for he professes himself the same author, he had made some proper censure of Mr Godwin, but here he pursues him, and Mrs Wolstoncraft usque ad nauseam; with other sort of men and principles whom you and I have been wont to honour and admire.[9]

I think you would like to see, even after Mr Belsham, Letters to Mr Wilberforce by a Layman. They are written with an unusual civility and unaffected candour, which makes some deem them too tame. But the reasoning throughout is excellent. We have just fished out the author, but woud not wish it needlessly bruited, a Dr Cogan, who now resides at or near Bath. I remember him a physician in Pater noster row, of a club I belonged to, and connected with Drs Price and Priestley, a most chearful ingenious man, after wch he went to Holland, and married there – but upon the disturbances came to England.[10]

Within not many days I received a letter from Dr Priestley, brought as I find by his eldest son, who sent it me by the post, and is gone to see his wife's father and mother and his Sister at Birmingham. The Doctors letter bespeaks him in good health and spirits: referring much to his Son for such particulars as he did not put on paper concerning himself.[11]

I am happy that I can still certifie you of the continuance of my wife's tolerable health. We hope that you and your lovely family enjoy the same. I beg my particular respects may be made acceptable to Mrs Holland.[12] It is a name much and long respected by me. My wife charges me with her kind regards. I am always, Dear Sir, very affectionately Yours

     T. Lindsey.

P.S. I did notice a good *word* in season *for* Christianity, and shall hope, from your promise to see Mr Wood's rebuke of the most conceited self-sufficient coxcomb in vindication of our friends injured character.[13]

---

1   Possibly Mr Hood was a relation of Robert Hood (1749–82), who was Turner's immediate predecessor as minister to the Hanover Square chapel, Newcastle, where he served from 1781 to 1782.

2   Thomas Bigge, the editor of *The Oeconomist; or Englishman's Magazine*; see Letter 672, n. 10. For the career of Ann Jebb as a political writer, see two articles by Anthony Page, '"A great politicianess": Ann Jebb, rational dissent and politics in late eighteenth-century Britain', *Women's History Review*, 17 (2008), 743–65, and '"No effort can be lost": the unitarianism and Republicanism of Ann Jebb (1735–1812)', in *Intellectual exchanges: women and rational dissent*, ed. Gina Luria Walker and G. M. Ditchfield, *E & D*, XXVI (2010), 136–62. No doubt William Belsham was too fully committed to his historical writing to contribute to *The Oeconomist*.

3   Thomas Bigge.

4   John Ralph Fenwick was a medical practitioner in Durham and a supporter of Wyvill's campaigns for parliamentary reform; see Wyvill, *Political papers*, V, 154–6, 159–67. He died aged ninety-three on 11 Jan. 1855; *The Standard*, 15 Jan. 1855. John Debrett declined to publish Christopher Wyvill's pamphlet *The secession from parliament vindicated* (York, 1799; 2nd edn, York; 1799, 3rd edn, York, 1800) and the publisher of each of the three editions was Lucas Lund, of Little Stonegate, York, who also published Wyvill's *Letter to John Cartwright, Esq.* in 1801 (see Letter 724, n. 2). Probably Lindsey used the word 'obnoxiousness' ironically, signifying 'unpopularity'.

5   The Habeas Corpus Act was suspended on 21 Apr. 1798; on 9 Jan. 1799, it was further suspended until 21 May 1799; on 20 May, it was further suspended until Mar. 1800. The suspension ended in 1801. Joseph Johnson's fate was a short period of imprisonment in 1799; see Letter 673, n. 3.

6   *The shade of Alexander Pope on the banks of the Thames. A satirical poem ... occasioned chiefly, but not wholly, by the residence of Henry Grattan, ex-representative in parliament for the city of Dublin, at Twickenham, in November 1798* (Lindsey slightly misquoted the title) was first published

in London in 1799. The author was the satirical poet and Italian scholar Thomas James Mathias (1754–1835).

7   *The shade of Alexander Pope* was indeed a sustained attack upon Henry Grattan. The 'vilification' of Charles James Fox included (p. 33) a jibe about 'the young Wantons' who 'sport on Anna's hill', i.e. Fox's country retreat at St Anne's Hill.

8   'A young man, born to give assistance to an upturned world'; this is an adaptation of Virgil, *Georgics*, I, 500–1. I owe this reference to Mr David Powell. The quotation may be found in the fourth edition of *The shade of Alexander Pope* (4th edn, London, 1799), p. 39, as part of the poem's praise of Pitt.

9   Thomas James Mathias (n. 6, above) was also the author of *The pursuits of literature, or what you will: a satirical poem in dialogue*. It was published in four parts, or 'dialogues', between 1794 and 1796. Its derogatory references to William Godwin may be found in the seventh (revised) edition, which collected the four dialogues into one volume and was published in London in 1798, at pp. 209–15, 352–4, 367–77; they are preceded by a denunciation of 'the contemptible nonsense of William Godwin' (p. 22). In the first edition of *The shade of Alexander Pope* (n. 6, above), the author linked Godwin and Mary Wollstonecraft (p. 54) and located the published works of the latter in 'the vestibule of the Corinthian temple of seduction and adultery' (p. 51).

10 The author of *Letters to William Wilberforce on the doctrine of hereditary depravity, by a layman* (London, 1799, with a second edition in 1806) was Thomas Cogan (1736–1818). Originally intended for the dissenting ministry, Cogan graduated MD from the University of Leiden in 1767 and practised medicine in the Netherlands and Britain. He resided in the Netherlands from 1780 to 1795 and returned to Britain in 1795, to avoid the invasion by the French revolutionary army. He then lived in Bath, was well known for his philanthropy and regularly attended unitarian worship. Eliezer Cogan (see Letters 388, n. 18 and 644, n. 10) was his half-brother.

11 Possibly Lindsey meant Priestley's letter to him of 14 Feb. 1799 (DWL, MS 12.13; partly printed in Rutt, I, 414–15), although it did not refer directly to Priestley's son. Priestley's letter to Lindsey of 21 Mar. 1799, in a passage omitted by Rutt, stated that his son was coming to England, but Lindsey would hardly have received that letter by 1 Apr. 1799; DWL, MS 12.13 and Rutt, I, 415–16.

12 Possibly Esther, née Pilkington, who in 1793 married John Holland (1766–1826), the successor to his uncle Philip Holland as minister of Bank Street chapel, Bolton. John Holland was a cousin of William Turner.

13 It seems that William Wood, of Mill Hill chapel, Leeds, did not publish this work; no publication by him conforms to Lindsey's hope for a 'rebuke' from Wood. The 'injured' friend was Priestley; the 'coxcomb' was, presumably, one of Priestley's many critics.

682. To THOMAS BELSHAM   16 JULY 1799

Text: DWL, MS 12.57 (14).
Addressed: To/The Rev^d. Mr Belsham,/Frystone
Postmarked: Postmark missing.

Richmond. July 16. 1799

Dear Sir,

I have rather chosen to thank you for your most welcome letter and at the same time send congratulations on yours and Miss Belsham's arrival at Frystone, rather than write beforehand to wish you a good journey with some uncertainty of my letter reaching you.[1] And I send my letter away so early, as we are going along with my wife's brother[2] to day to visit Mr Wyvill and shall not return till Thursday, when it might be too late for the post that day, and fridays we have no post goes out.

I have had a letter from Dr Priestley since my last to You, of which I must give you some extracts. It is dated N _____ d May 3.[3] A little tract, which I had sent him on *Universal* Redemption,[4] pleased him exceedingly and awakened that train of ideas concerning his separation from us all and sure prospect of soon meeting again in other scenes if not here, which you know are so familiar to his good mind. He replies to a question of mine, "You ask me why Mr Adams does not silence the person who abuses me so much. He once said to me, *I wonder why the man abuses you*, when a hint from him would have prevented it all. But he is too useful to the party upon the whole; and it answers their purpose to cry down all who are supposed to favour *French* principles.[5] If the French succeed in the war their principles will become more popular here. I rejoice that the war is turning to the East. Read the 19th. *of Isaiah*. The *Turkish empire*, which is doomed to destruction, will not I hope long survive the papal power.[6] The fall of this is an important era, and all the European Monarchies that have supported it, and that are the toes of Nebuchadnezzar's image, must fall with it.[7] Some have fallen, and one stone demolishes the whole. How I long to converse with You or Mr Belsham on these subjects!"[8]

I shd. have sent the letter itself as Mr Milnes would have given leave, instead of quoting so much, but that I have it to shew to a friend in our way to Town.[9]

He afterwards mentions his *Comparison* &c being in the press, but not likely to be finished till the end of summer.[10] This reminds him of perhaps the too strong remonstrances I had put in against making citations that were *too natural*, pleading that the nature of his work demanded them, and that many passages of Scripture might be put in my Index expurgatorius, all which I own I should be for softening, if I had any thing to do with a new Translation.[11] I must honestly confess, that our friend's application of Isaiah xix to the fall of the Turkish power is as little intelligible to me, as Bp. Horseley's of ch. xviii to the restoration of the Jews by some great maritime power, probably the English.[12]

I have lately received a letter from Mr J. Priestley, inquiring if I had happened to have any letter for him from his father, from whom none had come to him since he left America, & only one from his wife, dated May 2.[13] He tells me with much concern some facts that he was informed of while at Cambridge, of D ___ d Jones sitting very loose to any religious principles, which I have long feared was the case.[14]

You would probably see the D of Grafton before you came away. I had a letter from him the end of the last week, in which having mentioned the important deci[is]ive victory over Macdonald, he remarks; "instead of making peace, I fear, we shall be only bent on *re-establishing kingdoms*["].[15]

Mr and Mrs Cappe, as I find from a letter of the latter to my wife, are in great expectation of seeing you at York, where she persuades herself you would come over to see Mr Wellby, whose family at present is at Filey, which he is forced, for want of help, to leave, to officiate in the chapel.[16] Should you go there, you will hear of a very singular society of self-taught Unitarian Baptists.[17] I rejoice most truly in the prosperity and increase of our friends in the west, in their meeting at Warminster and your appointment to be their orator another year.[18] But most of all do I rejoice in the good tidings, that the *Theory of the human mind* is really in the way to be made public.[19] The delay it has received would seem to have been necessary, for your own satisfaction; and your sentiments of such a novel philosophy will not only be acceptable, but instructive to many, and prevent their being imposed upon by these german philosophers, like the famous high-german doctors, who only *verba dant*.[20]

I cannot say my wife's good mother makes much way towards a melioration, as She continues much enfeebled: she does not however leave her alone for the few days we are to be at Burton Hall. Her niece, Miss Blackburne,[21] who is with us here, remains in our absence; much improved in person and accomplishments since you lent her and my wife protection from the mob.[22]

We Shall be for a time, how long we cannot say, stationary here; and from you I must expect directions where and when I may next address you.

With our best compt^s to your Sister, and my wifes affectionate regards, I remain
always, Dear Sir, Your much obliged and affectionate

T. Lindsey

---

1 Fryston Hall, Yorkshire, was the seat of the family of Richard Slater Milnes, MP for York from
   1784 to 1802, and a critic of Pitt's ministry and a supporter of Wyvill. Miss Belsham was Thomas
   Belsham's sister Ann.

2 Francis Blackburne of Brignall, Hannah Lindsey's half-brother.

3 See Rutt, I, 418–19, and n. 8, below.

4 See Letter 676, n. 8.

5 John Adams, president of the United States from 1797 to 1801.

6 In Feb. 1798, French troops entered Rome and proclaimed a republic. Pope Pius VI was captured,
   and after his death in French custody on 29 Aug. 1799, the survival of the papacy itself seemed to
   be in doubt.

7 See Daniel ii. 31–45.

8 Lindsey quoted this extract from Priestley's letter to him of 3 May 1799 (n. 3, above) with almost
   complete accuracy.

9 Richard Slater Milnes, with whom Belsham was staying at Fryston Hall.

10 See Rutt, I, 418. Priestley's *Comparison of the institutions of Moses* was published in Northumberland at the end of 1799.

11 For Priestley's reference to an 'Index Expurgatorius' in his letter of 3 May 1799, see Rutt, I, 419.
   Probably he made it with Lindsey's *List of the false readings* in mind. The 'index expurgatorius' itself
   was a list, promulgated by the catholic church at the Council of Trent, of works which were permitted
   reading if certain passages were expunged or altered. Between 1788 and 1791, Lindsey had been
   involved in Priestley's proposed new translation of the Bible.

12 Isaiah xix describes the destruction of Egypt; Priestley in this letter interpreted the chapter as applicable to the fall of the Turkish empire. Isaiah xviii. 7 prophesies that a people 'scattered and peeled'
   will be brought to 'the mount Zion'. For Horsley's interest in eschatology and his belief that the Jews
   would be restored to their home in Palestine, see Mather, *High church prophet*, pp. 263–6.

13 This letter to Lindsey from Joseph Priestley junior seems not to have survived.

14 David Jones, the 'Welsh freeholder', was admitted as a fellow-commoner to Gonville and Caius
   College, Cambridge, in May 1796. He graduated BA in 1800 and MA in 1803; see *Biographical
   history of Gonville and Caius College 1349–1897. Vol. II 1713–1897*, compiled by John Venn
   (Cambridge, 1898), p. 129. For Jones's subsequent legal career, see Letter 606, n. 8.

15 Grafton's letter to Lindsey seems not to have survived. The 'victory' to which he referred was probably part of the Italian campaign, during which Alexander Suvorov (1729–1800) and his Russian
   army defeated a French army commanded by Jacques MacDonald (1765–1840) at the river Trebbia
   on 17–19 June 1799. By 're-establishing kingdoms', Grafton probably had in mind the Bourbon
   kingdom of Naples, which was briefly transformed into the Parthenopean republic before a short-
   lived Bourbon restoration, and the kingdom of Piedmont.

16 Wellbeloved and his family regularly paid visits to Filey, on the Yorkshire coast, for the benefit of
   their health; see Kenrick, *Memoir of Wellbeloved*, p. 131. Wellbeloved himself was obliged to return
   to York to conduct the services of the St Saviourgate congregation, where he was assistant minister
   to Newcome Cappe, whose ill-health prevented him from preaching.

17 This is a reference to the Unitarian Society founded at York by David Eaton; see Letter 686.

18 By the meeting at Warminster, Lindsey meant the meeting of the Western Unitarian Society in that
   town in 1799 and John Rowe's sermon preached there. It was published as *A discourse delivered
   at Warminster, July 3, 1799, before the Society of Unitarian Christians, Established in the West of
   England, for Promoting Christian Knowledge and the Practice of Virtue by the Distribution of Books*
   (Bristol, 1799). Belsham was nominated as the preacher to the society in 1800. His sermon was
   published as *Freedom of enquiry, and zeal in the diffusion of Christian truth, asserted and recommended in a discourse delivered at Bristol, July 9, 1800, before the Society of Unitarian Christians
   Established in the West of England, for Promoting Christian Knowledge and the Practice of Virtue
   by the Distribution of Books* (London, 1800).

19 Lindsey probably referred here to Thomas Belsham's *Elements of the philosophy of the mind, and of
   moral philosophy. To which is prefixed a compendium of logic* (London, 1801).

20 'Who only offer words.'

21 Lindsey almost certainly referred here to his wife's niece Sarah Blackburne, the daughter of her

half-brother Francis Blackburne of Brignall. A less likely possibility is one of the two daughters of Dr William Blackburne (see Letter 672, n. 2).

22 It is not clear whether this is a literal or a metaphorical reference. Thomas Belsham seems a rather unlikely saviour for potential victims of a tumult. Perhaps Lindsey meant that Belsham's arrival at Lindsey's house in Essex Street had saved him, his wife and his wife's niece from the time-consuming attention of a group of visitors.

683. To THOMAS BELSHAM   13 AUGUST 1799

Text: DWL, MS 12.57 (15).
Addressed: To/The Rev^d. T. Belsham
Postmarked: There is no postmark. The first paragraph of the letter
                  indicates that it was not sent through the regular post.

Richmond. aug. 13. 1799

Dear Sir

My last in reply to your's from Thornes was calculated to meet you on Saturday aug. 3. at your desire, at Warrington, and addressed to you there at Mr Broadbent's.[1] This, I presume from your account of your route, may have a chance of falling into Your hands, free of cost, at our most respectable friend's; if not, it will be conveyed to you at Bedford.

I sent his Grace[2] very lately an extract of a letter I had just received from Dr Priestley, relating to his *Comparison* &c and his intended dedication of it, as I thought what he said about it would satisfy the Duke, as it did me, that there wou'd be nothing improper in it, and therefore we might make ourselves easy in that respect.[3] The Doctor's letter I shall be glad to shew you when we meet in Town. In the mean time, as that is distant and uncertain, I would mention that I have never received a letter from him in which he expressed himself so satisfied and even happy in his present situation, and resolved not to relinquish it; taking it for granted it for granted [*sic*], that his son, from whom he had not heard, will not have any offers made that will induce him to settle in England; and determining beforehand not to [be] prevailed upon by Mr Russell who was coming to pass a fortnight with him, and signified an earnest desire of their spending the remainder of life together, for which purpose he had some proposals to make to him, which he should not listen to if it was to leave Northumberland.[4] I had sent Schleusner's Dictionary of the N.T. with which he is greatly taken, and I do not wonder, styling it a work perfect in it's kind, and of great value indeed.[5] He is not a little pleased, that the French seem disposed to make peace with that country, which he says, is a great disappointment to those who call themselves the *friends of government*, tho' it is so evidently for their advantage.[6] June 6. when the letter was dated, they had printed 200 pages of the *Comparison*, and he expected it to make about 450.[7]

I imagine, that when you wrote to me, you might not have learnt any thing of the last proposals of all, which Mr Wilkinson had intimated a design of making to the Doctor's son [him] on his coming back to settle in England; viz; letting him have his Willey works, and his house at Brosely to live in.[8] This, J. Priestley tells me in his letter from Birmingham, July 31, was quite a new idea, and he was to hear more from him about it.[9]

We shall hope to have a few lines from you, when you get to Bedford, if you make any stay there, and you will not fail to remember us with all respect to your brother.

I see, in the Supplement to the Monthly Magazine, that Dr Aikin, or whoever is the writer is determined not to give up his crimination of the Brunswick historian, wch at the time I thought petulant and wrong, in respect of what was said of Mr Hastings.[10] But your brother will think no more of it. We hear that Mrs Reynolds is at Paxton alone, Mr R. with Mr Nicholson being on a little tour into Kent, and to take up Mr Frend in Town, who was to return with them to Paxton.[11]

My wife's respectable good mother still continues too enfeebled to leave her room or sit up more than an hour, and not often so long, suffering much however in this very weak condition, and desirous of being released from it if it might be the will of heaven. You will believe my wife's must be a very anxious attendance upon her, but I thank God, upon the whole, she bears up under it wonderfully well. She presents you with her affectionate respects. I am always, Dear Sir, Your much obliged and affectionate servant

T. Lindsey.

---

1 Thornes House, near Wakefield, Yorkshire, was the residence of James Milnes (1755–1805), MP for Bletchingley from 1802 to 1805. He belonged to a dissenting family and was a supporter of Fox. For his family, and relationship to Richard Slater Milnes, see Letter 762, nn. 9 and 10. On his death, Thornes House was inherited by Benjamin Gaskell (1781–1856), MP for Maldon from 1806 to 1807 and from 1812 to 1826, and a sympathizer with dissent and with the whig opposition in parliament. For William Broadbent of Warrington, see Letter 640, n. 19.

2 The duke of Grafton.

3 This was Priestley's letter to Lindsey of 6 June 1799; Rutt, I, 419–20. Priestley's *Comparison of the institutions* (see Letter 672, n. 9) was indeed dedicated to Grafton.

4 See Rutt, I, 419.

5 Johann Friedrich Schleusner (1759–1831), professor of theology at the University of Wittenberg , was author of *Novum lexicon Graeco-Latinum in Novum Testamentum* (2 vols., Leipzig, 1792). Priestley expressed his appreciation of this work in his letter to Lindsey of 6 June 1799; Rutt, I, 420.

6 In the first half of 1798, it seemed that France and the United States would go to war.

7 Priestley's *Comparison* (n. 3, above) consisted of 428 pages plus twenty-seven pages of preliminary material.

8 This refers to the iron works of the New Willey company at Willey, near Broseley, Shropshire, owned by John Wilkinson, whose house was The Lawns, Broseley.

9 I have not located this letter, from Birmingham and dated 31 July 1799, from Joseph Priestley junior to Lindsey.

10 In its notice of William Belsham's *History of Great Britain, from the Revolution to the session of parliament, ending A.D. 1793* (4 vols., London, 1798), the 'Supplementary number' of the *MM*, VI (1798), 493–4, had criticized Belsham for his harsh comments on Warren Hastings (made extensively in vol. III) during the latter's impeachment. In particular, it asserted that he should have awaited the outcome of the impeachment before making such judgments. In a letter to the *MM*, VII (Apr. 1799), 182–4, Belsham defended his treatment of Hastings and denied that his work could have influenced the course of the impeachment. In its 'supplementary number' in July 1799 (VII, 509–10), the *MM* included a review of Belsham's *Two historical dissertations, 1. On the causes of the ministerial secession, A.D. 1717. II. On the Treaty of Hanover, concluded A.D. 1725*. In a lengthy footnote to this review, the author replied to Belsham's letter and acknowledged his agreement with Belsham's hostile opinion of Hastings but regretted the virulent tone used by Belsham in expressing it. Dr John Aikin (1747–1822) was the literary editor of the *MM*, which probably explains why Lindsey thought that he was the author of the review. A stronger possibility, however, is Thomas Starling Norgate (1772–1859), who took over the 'half-yearly retrospect of domestic literature' after the death of William Enfield in 1797. See David Chandler, '"A sort of bird's eye view of the British land of letters": the *Monthly Magazine* and its reviewers, 1796–1811', *Studies in Bibliography*, LII (1999), 169–79. I am grateful to Professor William McCarthy for these references.

11 Possibly Mr Nicholson was the merchant Thomas Nicholson (1753–1825) of Gateacre, Liverpool, whose family was related to the dissenting ministers Nicholas Clayton (1730–97), a former tutor at Warrington Academy and minister at Benn's Garden chapel, Liverpool, and William Shepherd (1768–1847), unitarian minister at Gateacre from 1791. See *Memorials of the family of Nicholson of*

Blackshaw, Dumfriesshire, Liverpool and Manchester, ed. Ernest Axon (Kendal, 1928), pp. 83–103. For Mary Catherine Reynolds, see Letter 727, n. 2. The visit to Kent was probably inspired by Frend's family connexions in Canterbury, as well as his close friendship with Richard Reynolds.

684. To JOHN ROWE   5 OCTOBER 1799

Text: JRUL, Lindsey Letters, vol. II, no. 99.
Addressed: [In Hannah Lindsey's hand] Rev^d M^r. Rowe/Bristol
Postmarked: Postmark missing.

London. Oct. 5. 1799

Dear Sir,

We left London on June 20. upon receiving a letter from Richmond in Yorkshire that my wife's aged parent was extremely ill and desirous to see her before she died. We found her however somewhat better tho' greatly enfeebled, and in that state She continued sometimes better, but more often in a very suffering state for two months, constantly relieved and cheared by her beloved daughter's attentions, and happily in the use of all her faculties, in uncomon vigour, till she gently fell asleep in Christ, to awake to that immortal life which is insured to his true disciples and the faithful servants of God.[1]

We have been returned about ten days, being hasten[e]d back as we left town to attend a family of friends, the head of which was seized w^h an apoplectic fit, which at first disabled the body in part, and mind altogether, but is now recovered a little with respect to both, whether he will ever be perfectly restored, is very doubtful.[2]

After this hasty preface, I now turn myself to what is the more imediate business of my letter, and for which this frank was procured, and not knowing your imediate address, your good collegue is troubled, to whom our best respects, to convey it to you.[3]

A few days ago I received a letter from our friend Mr J. Joyce at Chevening, announcing his separation from L^d. Stanhope as fixed for the beginning of January. This is what I have long expected from the strange and fickle behaviour of the said peer, and not from any want of honour, worth or abilities in our friend; who will of course be in want of a situation to employ his powers and good abilities, and to assist in providing for a wife and growing family. A respectable situation as a minister, for he is a christian on the best and truest grounds, is his first Object. But if undue and unreasonable prejudice forbid this, any active useful line, to which a man of strict principle and integrity might turn himself would be acceptable. I am persuaded that You are interested enough in him to take some thought about him. Shrewsbury is the thing that woud accomplish all his wishes, and he would answer any recomendation, but this I fear is not attainable. If you could think or hit upon any thing, I should be obliged to you for a few lines, tho perhaps you may be in the habit of writing to him yourself.[4] But if that be the case, I would beg the favour of hearing from you of yours and Mrs Rowe and your familys health and I will certainly acknowlege the favour more at leisure than I write at present to save the frank from being too late.

My wife unites in kind respects to you and Mrs Rowe and all good wishes, and I remain, Dear Sir, Your obliged and affectionate friend

T. Lindsey.

P.S. Many thanks for a valuable Discourse which I found on my table when we came out of ye north.[5]

1   Hannah Elsworth (née Hotham), the widow of archdeacon Francis Blackburne and the mother of
    Hannah Lindsey, died at Richmond, Yorkshire, on 23 Aug. and was buried on 27 Aug. 1799; *Gent.
    Mag.*, LIX, ii (1799), 726; and NYRO, PR/RM/1/6 (Richmond parish registers). She was aged eighty-
    five or eighty-six; see Letter 641, n. 3.
2   Lindsey almost certainly referred here to the Chambers family and in particular to Christopher Cham-
    bers, who died, after a lengthy illness, on 2 Mar. 1803; *Gent. Mag.*, LXXIII, i (1803), 288. He was
    the cousin of Sophia and Frances Chambers.
3   Rowe's ministerial colleague at Lewin's Mead chapel, Bristol, was John Estlin.
4   After leaving Lord Stanhope's service in Nov. 1799, Joyce did not become minister at Shrews-
    bury nor, at this stage, to any congregation. Instead, he became a successful professional writer and
    popularizer, achieving substantial sales with his *Scientific dialogues*, published by Joseph Johnson
    between 1800 and 1803.
5   This 'valuable Discourse' was probably Rowe's *A discourse delivered at Warminster, July 3, 1799,
    before the Society of Unitarian Christians, Established in the West of England*. It took the form of a
    sermon on Acts xi. 26.

685. To JOHN ROWE   11 NOVEMBER 1799

Text: JRUL, Lindsey Letters, vol. II, no. 100.
Addressed: [In Hobhouse's hand] Bradford November thirteen/The Rev.ᵈ
                   John Rowe/Ashley Place/Bristol[1]
Endorsed: BfreeHobhouse
Postmarked: Postmark missing.

London. Nov. 11. 1799

Dear Sir,

I take the opportunity, as I am writing to M.ʳ Hobhouse,[2] to desire him to forward my letter to you with his signature; and cannot refrain from thanking you, tho' it be a melancholy satisfaction, for mentioning Miss Grignion, for whom we are much concerned, she was always a good and valuable character, but her disinterested friendship for M.ʳˢ Bengough and her family cannot be estimated.[3] If she be still capable of understanding aught and it would be convenient, we should thank you to convey our kind love to her, my wifes in particular, who is very sorry that she missed seeing her when she was last in Town. Very heavy and severe are her's & M.ʳˢ Bengough's sufferings. But Philosophy and Religion leave us without any doubt that her portion of bliss hereafter will be great in proportion to what she has undergone in this trying world, as well as her dying friend's.

I must now thank you for all your efforts to serve our comon friend M.ʳ Joyce, and acquaint you that your future good offices to help him to a situation will not at present be wanted, as he has we think been happy in finding an estabilishment near London, having taken a house of M.ʳ Travers, at Hackney, near London, which tho' of a high rent, it will be in some degree compensated by having fifty pounds a year for the education only of two of his sons, who are to be with him 5 hours a day, and there will be no doubt of his obtaining other boys to educate on the same terms.[4] It will be creditable for him, immediately on leaving Chevely[5] to enter upon such a respectable station, and if Lord Stanhope is wise, he will send his two young sons to finish their education with [him], as they are much attached to him, and will be left destitute without him.[6] One of his talents and industry, will easily find means of acquiring an honourable subsistence in this great metropolis. I am sorry, with you, that no stated employment for him, as a minister presents himself; as I am persuaded, he woud in time, and by correcting some little things in his manner, be useful in it above many.

It seems to have been peculiarly fortunate, that you happened to be present at the meeting relating to the New Academical Institution at Exeter, to prevent any improper connection and interference with the two valuable Tutors that have been set over it.[7] All that remains now to be done, is to provide them with proper subjects, who may enjoy the advantage and benefit of their learned labours and superintendance. We had great satisfaction in learning that M[rs] Rowe and yourself and family were so well, and particularly that your son was in such a fair way in the small pox.[8] Your kind invitation to pay you a visit in your new habitation we are much obliged to you for, and we shall be happy to meet with such friends, if we should have a call that way on any account.

When you do me the favour of writing again, I should be glad to know particularly how M[rs] Finch does. Her brother's last letter bespoke her to have been so much benefited as to be esteemed quite out of danger.[9] And I hope this amendment goes on. We begin to be anxious about hearing from D[r] Priestley, though we hope he is quite out of the way of the infectious fever that makes such ravages.

I dare say you have heard of the picture of Christian Philosophy by the Rev[d] M[r] Fellowe.[10] We prize it exceedingly, and think it among other things peculiarly calculated to silence some fashionable objections to the gospel.

My wife continues, I thank the Almighty, in her best plight, and joins with me in kind respects to M[rs] Rowe and yourself and in wishes of every blessing and improvement to your young folks.

I remain always most truly Yours

T. Lindsey.

---

1   For Rowe's places of residence in Bristol, see Letter 667, n. 11.

2   Lindsey's letter to Benjamin Hobhouse seems not to have survived.

3   Possibly Miss Grignion was Mrs Grignion, or a relative of the Mrs Grignion who kept a school for girls at Whitelands, Chelsea, in the 1780s; see *A history of the county of Middlesex*, ed. Patricia E.C. Croot (*Victoria county history of Middlesex*, vol. XII, Woodbridge, 2004), p. 191. John Disney's daughter Frances Mary attended it; see 'Disney diary', 47 n. 29. Since Rowe had heard of Miss Grignion from Rowe, it is likely that she had moved to Bristol. Probably she was a relative of the Mary Grignion of Clifton, whose will was proved in 1824; TNA: PRO PROB 11/1680, fo. 160r. Possibly, too, she was related to Charles Grignion (1717–1810), who had been employed as an engraver by Hogarth and worked as an illustrator and engraver for Joseph Johnson until the latter's death in 1809. See *Gent. Mag.*, LXXX, ii (1810) 499, and Tyson, *Joseph Johnson*, pp. 46–7. Mrs Bengough was probably Joanna, née Cadell (d. 1821), who married Henry Bengough at Gloucester in 1760. Henry Bengough (d. 1818) was a subscriber to Lewin's Mead chapel, Bristol, in 1797 and a signatory to the invitation to John Prior Estlin to become its joint, as distinct from assistant, minister there in 1792; DWL, box marked 'Lewin's Mead Meeting, Bristol. Letters and papers of historic interest'. He was almost certainly the Henry Bengough, of 5 St James's Square, Bristol, who is listed as a member of the Bristol common council in 1791; see *Universal British directory* (1791), II, 129, and as a subscriber to Joshua Toulmin's *History of the town of Taunton*, unpaginated list of subscribers. Joanna Bengough was probably the Mrs Bengough of Bristol who subscribed to William Enfield's *Sermons on practical subjects*, I, xxix.

4   See Issitt, *Jeremiah Joyce*, p. 72. Benjamin Travers (1752–1817) was treasurer to the Gravel Pit meeting, Hackney, from 1791 to 1796. His family were part owners of a successful grocery business, Smith, Travers and Kemble, of which Travers's twin brother Joseph (1752–1820) and William Smith MP were partners. Smith was a cousin of the Travers twins. See *Chronicles of Cannon Street. A few records of an old firm* (London, ?1957), pp. 10–11 and genealogical table opposite p. 30. No author's name appears in this book. See also Alan Ruston, 'Joseph Priestley at the Gravel Pit chapel, Hackney: the Collier MS', *E & D*, II (1983), 117–19.

5   I.e. Chevening, Kent.

6 Although Joyce had been tutor to Stanhope's children during his employment at Chevening between
   1790 and 1799, he was not tutor to Stanhope's sons thereafter, although he remained on friendly terms
   with them and with Stanhope's daughter Lady Hester Stanhope. Possibly their connexion with Pitt
   (who helped them escape from their eccentric father) deterred Joyce from a closer connexion with
   them; see Issitt, *Jeremiah Joyce*, p. 70.

7 The dissenting academy at Exeter was re-opened in 1799; the two 'valuable tutors' were Timothy
   Kenrick and Joseph Bretland. Lindsey's reference to 'improper connection and interference' probably
   signifies an anxiety about possible attempts to restrain the tutors in their doctrinal opinions.

8 This is probably a reference to Rowe's son John, born in 1798; see Letter 667, n. 8.

9 For Sarah Finch's treatment under the superintendence of Dr Thomas Beddoes, see Letter 687, n. 6.

10 This work was *A picture of Christian philosophy* (London, 1799), by Robert Fellowes (1770–1847).
   An ordained clergyman in the Church of England (though without a parochial living), Fellowes was
   editor of the *Critical Review* from 1804 to 1811. See Letter 731, n. 3.

686. To DAVID EATON   6 JANUARY 1800

Text: David Eaton, *Scripture the only guide to religious truth. A
               narrative of the proceedings of the society of baptists in York,
               in relinquishing the popular systems of religion, from the
               study of the scriptures* (2nd edn, London, 1809), preface, pp.
               xiii–xv; the letter, with very minor variations, is reprinted in
               the 3rd edn of this work (London, 1823), pp. ix–xi, and in
               MR, IV (1809), 683. The first edition, completed in 1799 but
               bearing a publication date of 1800, did not include this letter;
               Eaton waited until Lindsey's death before publishing the letter
               in the second edition. The letter is reproduced in Ditchfield,
               'Unitarianism after the French Revolution', 41–2.

Note: The manuscript of this letter seems not to have survived. The text reproduced here is that in Eaton,
Scripture the only guide (2nd edn, London, 1809), pp. xiii–xv.

Essex Street, Jan. 6, 1800.

DEAR SIR,

   Your obliging thanks for the little assistance I gave in bringing your valuable
work before the public far overpays me, and therefore I shall certainly consider
myself your debtor for the 12 copies you have been so good as to send me, which I
was glad to receive so early, and could not but take your intention very kindly, tho'[1]
I must refuse your kindness.[2] Without entering into particulars, I must say that your
"Narrative", on a deliberate perusal, exceeds the opinion I had entertained from the
recital,*[3] the method and good sense that reigns throughout the whole, with such
strong appearance of sincerity, must recommend it, even to those who may not
agree in sentiment with the writer at first, especially when the whole is considered
as the workings of the human mind upon subjects of the greatest importance. You
cannot easily conceive the satisfaction I had in first putting your "Narrative" into
the hands of some of my most serious and judicious friends, when one of them upon
my next calling upon him, expressed himself so pleased with it, and persuaded of
its tendency to lead to study and value the sacred writings, that he resolved to give
50 copies to a religious society to which he belongs;[4] and from another friend in
the country, I received a letter to order his bookseller to send him down a dozen
copies.[5] I wish it may meet with readers who will know equally how to prize it, and
then this first edition will not be long in hand unsold. I expect you will soon have
an order from Mr. Johnson to send him up some more copies. And I am convinced
you cannot have greater satisfaction than in hearing that your book is likely to be

useful to many in their most important interests respecting a future world, in which light it is viewed by many.

Believe me,

Your much obliged friend and servant,

T. LINDSEY.

---

1 The third edition of Eaton, *Scripture the only guide* (London, 1823), p. x, and *MR*, IV (1809), 683, give 'though' instead of 'tho' at this point.

2 The 'valuable work' was Eaton's *Scripture the only guide*.

3 The second edition of Eaton, *Scripture the only guide,* p. x, has a footnote * at this point, stating 'The last time Mr. and Mrs. Lindsey visited their friends in the North, on their return from Richmond, they staid some days at York, with their old and highly valued friends, Mr. and Mrs. Cappe, and there Mr. Lindsey heard the work read in manuscript, and [this] is the "recital" above alluded to. After which he sent the Author a note, thanking him for the great satisfaction he had derived from it, and begged his acceptance of five pounds towards the expense of printing it. He hoped it would be sent to the press without delay, as it could not fail, in his opinion, of proving highly acceptable, and of doing much service to the cause of rational religion. It was on this occasion, that the Author had the unspeakable pleasure of being first introduced to this great and good man, when his venerable appearance, benevolent cheerfulness of countenance, the simplicity and gentleness of his manners, and his kind attentions, made an impression never to be forgotten; and when that friendship commenced between them, which he cannot but deem the honour and happiness of his life, and which continued with increasing affection till his death.' This footnote is reproduced in the two other published versions of this letter. Lindsey and his wife had visited Richmond from late June to Sept. 1799, at the time of the final illness of Hannah Blackburne; see Letters 682 to 684. That this was indeed Lindsey's last visit to the north of England is confirmed by Cappe, *Memoir*s, pp. 299–300, which also records Lindsey's last meeting with Newcome Cappe, who died the following year. The 'note' from Lindsey to Eaton, with the subsidy of £5, was an earlier (and non-surviving) letter than Letter 686, the opening words of which indicate that Eaton had replied to it. I have not been able to locate that reply.

4 Possibly this friend was Timothy Kenrick of Exeter, or a member of his congregation, to whom, perhaps, Lindsey had given a copy of Eaton's work during a visit to London. On 13 Aug. 1800, Kenrick wrote to Charles Wellbeloved in York, requesting him to inform Eaton that the Western Unitarian Society had authorized him Kenrick to purchase fifty copies of *Scripture the only guide* on its behalf; DWL, MS 24.81 (7).

5 Although Lindsey did not identify this friend in the country who wrote this apparently non-surviving letter, obvious possibilities include John Rowe or John Prior Estlin in Bristol, Joshua Toulmin in Taunton and William Turner in Newcastle upon Tyne.

687. To ROBERT MILLAR   7 JANUARY 1800

Text: DWL, MS 12.46 (17).
Printed: Graham, 'Unhappy country', 153–54 (latter part of first paragraph; second paragraph; first three sentences of third paragraph).
Addressed: Mʳ Robert Millar/Merchant/Dundee
Endorsed: London 7ᵗʰ. Jan 1800/Mʳ Lindsey
Postmarked: Postmark missing.

London. Janʸ. 7. 1800.

Dear Sir,

The first moment I can procure a frank by the return of a most worthy member to Town[1] I sit down to acknowlege and to thank you for your two last favours, the former of which would not have remained unnoticed but from various hindrances which it would be somewhat tedious now to detail.[2] I hasten to thank you as I ought for the most friendly confidence of your last letter in mentioning some private circumstances, which do you great credit, and certainly shall remain with me alone, which make you desirous for the present to forego a certain subscription, and which I am happy to tell may be done for this last and for the present year, without your name being withdrawn from our lists, as a friend of mine wishes to have the advantage of the allotment of books for the two years without putting his name down: so that you may make yourself perfectly easy in this respect.[3] One has just causes of fear that greater calamities may be coming upon these nations than those with which we are now visited, but I trust a kind providence will preserve you from being much involved in them. And I find the stoutest begin to entertain gloomy apprehensions from the particulars that were given us in the different newspapers of yesterday as authentic, that, in answer to the overtures for peace sent over by the French Consul Buonaparte for a peace, in his Letter to the king, and another letter from one in the Government to L^d. Greenville, it was signified to him that we were not disposed to accept any terms or make any treaty but with the king of France, meaning Louis xviii;[4] whence it is concluded that our expedition to the coast of France will not be given up.[5] But, no more of these matters, which I have involuntarily and undesignedly dropped into.

Dr Priestley's son, who came over with Dr Ross is still detained by his attendance on his sister, who is under Dr Beddoes's immediate care at Clifton near Bristol, and is enabled to live with comfort and a prospect of becoming well in time in a Cow-house. It is expected that by the month of June the cure will be perfected.[6] We are all much concerned for Dr Priestley, from having received accounts of all the ships, in number 7, in which all the letters, books and parcells sent him for these last four months have been taken by the French, so that he will be quite in the dark about his son's detention in England and about all his friends, unless he should get some knowlege by other friends, or by incidental means that we know not of.[7]

None of Mr Fyshe Palmer's friends here have lately had any communications from him. And we should be glad to know when you next write, if any thing has come to your knowlege by the way of James Ellis's friends. We think the present year will terminate his exile, and that he will probably be looking towards his native country. He would be grieved to know what you relate of some of the members of your congregation breaking off comunion with their brethren on account of a circumstance so indifferent and rather more eligible one would imagine, as the solemn commemoration of X^{ts} death once a month rather than every sunday. Such narrowness of mind must give concern especially in those with whom one is connected in Society.[8] But these are opportunities of exercising our tempers in bearing with the weaknesses of others. I cannot but honour Dr Small greatly for his christian resolution and firmness in declining to require men to do an Act, which no power upon earth is competent to require of them; and shall be much beholden to you hereafter to be made acquainted with the sequel of this affair at the next meeting of the Assembly.[9]

When you next write, and I shall attend to answer your letters more regularly than your last but one, I shall be glad to be directed how I may send you a small pamphlet. Perhaps you may hear of some one coming to Dundee, who could call and put it in his pocket for you. It is a narrative of a christian Society at York, consisting altogether of Mechanics, most of them journeymen and Shoemakers, shewing by what processes, and laborious inquiries, they emancipated themselves from various popular errors by the study of the Scriptures, and became enlightened and liberal. It is drawn up by one of their number.[10] I promise myself it will give you great satisfaction. I have some copies to dispose of.

We rejoice that you and Mrs Millar enjoy tolerable health. Till within this last fortnight my wife has been extraordinary [*sic*] well for her, but lately confined by an epidemic cold, which has not yet left her. She was greatly supported by the divine goodness in the heavy trial of parting with her good mother who was a great sufferer to the last.[11] She unites in most sincere respects to you both. I hope you will favour me with knowing how you are and how you go on, as we are in such circumstances that the postage of a letter is nothing to us, and as Parl^t. will soon open, I shall have as many covers as I want for my friends.[12]

I am always, Dear Sir, Your much obliged and affectionate friend and servant
T. Lindsey.

1   Probably Benjamin Hobhouse or James Martin.

2   These two letters from Millar to Lindsey seem not to have survived. Lindsey's previous surviving letter to Millar was that of 25 July 1797 (Letter 659); the 'various hindrances' in the second half of 1799 which explained his delay in replying to Millar included his excursion to Yorkshire and his efforts to secure the appointment of Jeremiah Joyce as minister to a dissenting congregation.

3   Miller was excused the payment of his subscription to the Unitarian Society because of his financial difficulties. This state of affairs continued into 1802; see Letter 744.

4   On 6 Jan. 1800, the *Morning Chronicle* and other London newspapers, such as the *Oracle and New Daily Advertiser* and the *Morning Post and Gazetteer*, reported that Bonaparte had offered peace terms to the British cabinet, which had responded with an insistence that it could only deal with France on a secure basis if and when the monarchy was restored. Lord Grenville was the British foreign secretary from 1791 to 1801. Louis XVIII (1755–1824), the younger brother of Louis XVI and previously known as the comte de Provence, had proclaimed himself king of France on the death in captivity of Louis XVI's son, known to French royalists as Louis XVII, in June 1795. From 1798 to 1801, he lived in exile in Courland, as the guest of Czar Paul I of Russia.

5   At the end of Dec. 1799, Napoleon sent a letter to George III proposing peace between Britain and France. The other letter was one from Talleyrand, the French foreign minister from 1797 to 1807, to Grenville. In early Jan. 1800, the British government, on Pitt's initiative, issued a public rejection of the proposal, citing what it saw as the continuing dangers of Jacobin-inspired French aggression, the impermanence of the Consulate in France, and a preference for a return of the monarchy in France as a more reliable negotiating partner. See Ehrman, *The Younger Pitt. The consuming struggle*, pp. 332–43. The British plans for expeditions to Brest, and Quiberon Bay, in support of French royalists in Nov. 1799 to Jan. 1800 are discussed in Piers Mackesy, *War without victory. The downfall of Pitt* (Oxford, 1984), pp. 35–6, 58–68. The plans were abandoned after the collapse of the royalist rebellion at the end of Jan. 1800.

6   Joseph Priestley junior had arrived in England from America, with Dr Andrew Ross, in 1799. Before returning to America in June 1800, he took care of his sister Mrs Sarah Finch, who suffered from a consumptive disorder. The radical physician Thomas Beddoes (1760–1808) had opened his Pneumatic Institute in Dowry Square at the Hotwells, Bristol, in 1799; he specialized in the use of gases in the treatment of lung-related illnesses. For his 'cow-house' treatment, which involved the exposure of his patients to the presence (and breath) of cows, see Roy Porter, *Doctor of society. Thomas Beddoes and the sick trade in late enlightenment England* (London and New York, 1992), pp. 105–7. Although this treatment did not produce a long-term cure for Sarah Finch, she appears to have believed that she benefited from it, declaring 'I am more than ever a friend to the cows' (quoted in Porter, *Thomas Beddoes*, p. 106). For a further discussion of Beddoes's 'cow-house' method, and his patients, see Mike Jay, *The atmosphere of heaven. The unnatural experiments of Dr Beddoes and his sons of genius* (New Haven and London, 2009), ch. 7.

7   Priestley acknowledged the receipt of a letter from Belsham on 14 Nov. 1799 and one from Lindsey on 9 Jan. 1800; Rutt, I, 422, 424. His son did not return to America until the late summer of 1800; see Graham, *Revolutionary in exile*, p. 115 n. 302.

8   There is hardly any surviving evidence for this dispute in the Dundee congregation over the frequency of the communion service. Millar himself probably lacked the authority of an ordained minister in such matters.

9   Dr Robert Small (1732–1808) was minister of St Mary's, Dundee from 1761 and moderator of the general assembly of the Church of Scotland from 1791 to 1792; he held the degree of DD from St Andrew's. In 1800, he was accused of departing from the formularies of the church and also of

refraining from insistence on the subscription by his church elders at Dundee to the confession of faith. He was summoned to appear before the next meeting of the general assembly in May 1800; on 29 May, he was reprimanded, and cautioned to avoid such conduct in future. See *The principal acts of the general assembly of the Church of Scotland, convened at Edinburgh, the 22d day of May 1800* (Edinburgh, 1800), unpaginated summary of the proceedings, under 29 May 1800. See also *Scots Magazine*, LXII (1800), 428–9.

10 This work was David Eaton's *Scripture the only guide*.

11 See Letter 684.

12 Following a recess since Oct. 1799, both houses of parliament resumed business on 21 Jan. 1800.

688. To JOHN ROWE   28 JANUARY 1800

Text: JRUL, Lindsey Letters, vol. II, no. 102.
Printed: McLachlan, *Letters*, p. 16 (part of first sentence of second paragraph).
Addressed: To/The Rev^d. J. Rowe/Bristol./To the obliging care/[of] the rev^d. Mr Estlyn
Postmarked: Postmark missing.

Dear Sir,

We have been greatly edified and affected with your dwelling so much on that worthy creature Miss Grignan, her whole conduct and manner of going out of the world, and thank you much for it.[1] Such examples do the greatest credit to the gospel, and might convince those who unhappily would confine and appropriate all the comforts of a dying hour to those christians who are of their own class, that they belong even to those whom they sometimes reprobate. We feel much satisfaction in having had a place in some of the deceased's kind thoughts, who was always remembered with esteem by us; and we beg you would be so good to acquaint Mrs Bengough that we thank her much for her kind rememberance and trust and pray that the Almighty may support her, we are persuaded he will support her to the end of her journey to that better heavenly country which awaits her.[2]

I reckon it my misfortune, and in some measure my fault, that I have only had the happiness of seeing your most worthy collegue, when he preached at our chapel, and when I afterwards met him at dinner at Mr Serj. Heywoods and we all went afterward together to our Club. It was totally out of my head to press him to take a breakfast with us, and the more as he mentioned his intention to call; and when I was at his lodgings on Saturday he was gone out of town for 2 or 3 days.[3]

I only mention this to excuse myself, as I have a very high esteem for him. I hope we shall be more fortunate in meeting together the next time he comes to the great city; for I hear that he and Mr Barbauld calld upon my wife to day when I was out –

But no more of this. I write these few lines to leave with him to morrow – as he will be engaged all the day I learn, and sets out for Bristol the day after –

I rejoice to hear such particular confirmation from him, of your own and Mrs Rowe's healths, your fine boy, and daughter.[4] May heaven bless and preserve them and you, and give you comfort in them, and then they will be every thing they ought to be both for this world and for another.

I will endeavour to morrow to procure our York Pamphlet, which I am persuaded you will like, the work of honest sensible and painstaking mechanics from diligent thought and study of the Scriptures. We have orderd 150 for our Unitarian Society, that there may be one for each member.[5] I write this in some haste at night after coming home and hearing Mr Estlyn had been here, to be ready to leave at his lodging to morrow when I shall call.

Our kindest respects to Mrs Rowe and yourself, with wishes of all good to [you] and to Your's. I remain, ever Dear Sir,

Your obliged and affectionate servant

T. Lindsey.

London. Jany. 28. 1800.

---

1   For a suggestion as to the identity of Miss Grignon, or Grignion, see Letter 685, n. 3.
2   For an identification of Mrs Bengough, see Letter 685, n. 3.
3   Rowe's 'worthy collegue' at Lewin's Mead chapel, Bristol, was John Prior Estlin. Samuel Heywood's London house was in Bedford Place, Russell Square. 'Our club' was probably the quarterly club of dissenting ministers and laymen to which Lindsey belonged and of which the membership in the 1790s is recorded in Bodl., MS Eng. Misc. e. 334 (Joseph Towers's notebook).
4   For a probable identification of Rowe's son, see Letter 667, n. 8. His daughter was Eliza Clarke Rowe (d.1839).
5   For David Eaton and the 'York pamphlet', see Letter 686. The general quarterly meeting of the Unitarian Society on 16 Jan. 1800 noted that fifty copies of this work had been presented to the society by one of its members and resolved that a further 100 copies should be purchased by the society. It requested Lindsey to convey the thanks of the society to the 'gentleman from whom this donation was received'. See Unitarian Society minute book, p. 68, where the generous member is not identified.

689. To RUSSELL SCOTT   22 FEBRUARY 1800

Text: Scott Coll.
Printed: McLachlan, 'Lindsey to Scott', 124 (short quotations from first and sixth paragraphs; whole of fifth paragraph).
Addressed: Address missing.
Postmarked: Postmark missing.

London. feb. 22. 1800

Dear Sir,

I have been uncomonly engaged with several friends out of the country this week, or I should have acknowleged your letter much sooner. Many things also prevented me volunteering a letter before, which it were bootless now to detail; but that I did not forget you, was manifest by my sending you through Mr Johnson a pamphlet printed at York, which we prize much, and I wished you to see it the first opportunity, but from your saying nothing of it in your letter, I persuade myself you have not received it,[1] and therefore shall send you another copy, together with a curious one just advertised by Mr Frend, at the end of the present month, and shall see all that I can to it's coming certainly to your hands.[2]

I am happy that I can tell You that after having suffered much from repeted colds of the season, and my wife being confined near a month, we are now in as good plight as at any time, and my cough nearly gone.

But we are concerned that You have still so contrary a tale to tell of yourself, and that you have had so heavy and severe a trial to pass through before you could regain that comfortable state in which you now find yourself, and which I trust the Almighty and merciful God will continue to you, without subjecting you any more to such sad reverses, especially with respect to your beloved daughter. Your own reflexions on this whole afflictive dispensation are so edifying as to leave nothing for your friends to add, but that you and Mrs Hawes may enjoy the fullest consolation from them in your own minds.[3]

Who should be now in town, but D^r. Toulmin, brought hither ten days ago on some Law matters where he is an executor in Trust.[4] He preached for Mr Jervis last Sunday, performs that service for Dr Disney to morrow,[5] and think he shall be able to return to Taunton in the following week.

Here is also Mr Walker, that was of Nottingham now at the head of the Academy at Manchester, summoned on some disagreeable Law business by a subpoena, wch he could not decline, tho' ill able to leave his duty.[6] He seems to be much improved by his situation, and is indeed one of the best informed general scholars and pleasantest men, besides his great mathematical excellency.[7]

Here is also Mr J. Priestley, last[?] from Birmingham, having not long before quitted his sister Mrs Finch at Clifton, in a Cowhouse, under Dr Beddoes's care, so far recoverd as to be in better health than before she came there, and in good spirits, but is injoined to remain till the latter end of May or begining of June, to perfect her recovery.[8] Mr Priestley intends to return to his father at Northumberland in about 3 weeks, without any intention of coming back to England. Dr Priestley was very well and very busy in his theological and philosophical pursuits, and perfectly well in health and spirits, save that he longs earnestly to see again his friends and family in England, whom he left behind him.

I write this in some haste, but think I have omitted nothing save my earnest good wishes for Mrs Watson's profiting to a perfect recovery by her removal to Portsmouth, with our respects to her tho unknown, and to Mr Watson and the two most worthy physicians and doers of good at Chichester.[9]

With most kind regards to Mrs Scott and yourself from us both and wishes of health and every thing good to Mrs Scott, I remain, Dear Sir, ever most affectionately Yours

T. Lindsey

I have not time to read my letter over.

---

1   This work was David Eaton's *Scripture the only guide.*

2   This work was William Frend, *Animadversions on the 'Elements of Christian theology', by ... G. Pretyman ... bishop of Lincoln; in a series of letters addressed to his lordship* (London, 1800). See Letter 690.

3   For Scott's daughter, Sophia Russell Scott, see Letter 678, n. 1. Mrs Hawes (Sarah, née Fox, d. 1815) was Scott's mother-in-law and the husband of Dr William Hawes.

4   Joshua Toulmin had evidently come from his congregation at Taunton to London. Probably the purpose of his journey was to deal with a matter affecting a general baptist trust. For his involvement in general baptist affairs, see David L. Wykes, 'Joshua Toulmin (1740–1815) of Taunton: baptist minister, historian and religious radical', *Baptist Quarterly*, XXXIX, 5 (Jan. 2002), 229–30.

5   The previous Sunday, when Toulmin preached for Thomas Jervis at Princes Street chapel, Westminster, was 16 Feb. 1800.

6   George Walker testified as an expert witness in a court action before Lord Eldon, chief justice of the court of common pleas, and 'a special jury of merchants' on behalf of the inventor Edmund Cartwright, who brought a suit against alleged infringements of the patent of a wool-combing machine. See *The Times*, 26 Apr. 1800, and Ditchfield, 'Manchester College and anti-slavery', p. 219 n. 95. Walker had been a partner in the Revolution Mill Company of East Retford, Nottinghamshire, in association with Edmund Cartwright's brother, the reformer John Cartwright.

7   Walker was the author of *A treatise on conic sections* (London, 1794).

8   See Letter 687, n. 6.

9   This is a reference to Thomas Watson of Chichester and his wife Margaret (see Letters 388, n. 12, and 507, n. 14). Lindsey mentioned their therapeutic visit to Portsmouth and the Isle of Wight in Letter

701. The two philanthropic physicians of Chichester who, like Watson, belonged to the Unitarian Society were John Bayly and Thomas Sanden; see Letter 388, n. 12.

690. To ROBERT MILLAR   15 MARCH 1800

Text: DWL, MS 12.46 (18).
Printed: *Unitarian Baptist Advocate*, II, XXIII (Nov. 1838), 248–9
                  (with minor omissions).
Addressed: To/Mr Robt. Millar/Merchant/Dundee
Endorsed: Lond^o 15th Mar. 1800
Postmarked: Postmark missing.

Note: This letter is written on a quarto-sized double sheet. The letter covers three sides; the address and endorsement are on the fourth side. A small section at the foot of the second page (i.e. the third and fourth sides) has been excised. The address is unaffected by the excision, but the last two or three lines of the letter itself, including Lindsey's signature, are missing.

London. March. 15. 1800

Dear Sir,

It was peculiarly unlucky that we should happen to be absent the week your letter came, tho' I take blame to myself in not having left with our servant the book to be delivered when any came from you to inquire about it. It will however only retard a little your having a sight of it, as Dr Priestley's Comparison of the Institutions of Moses and the Hindus &c[1] is just arrived, and as Mr Johnson has orders to present a copy to Dr Ross, and I shall certainly accompany it with another copy from myself for your acceptance, there will be an immediate demand to send a small parcell to you, which I must beg you will point out to me the speediest way in which it may be done with safety, if you know of any vessel soon coming to Dundee.

By your ac[c]ount of so worthy a character as Dr Ross you have added to the esteem I had of him from his being so long an inmate[2] with Dr Priestley in Northumberland, and I congratulate you on such an accession to your acquaintance.[3] I am obliged to you also for bringing me so far acquainted with a character of such respect as Dr Small. What is mentioned will certainly remain with me alone: but it increases the curiosity, not impertinent I hope I may call it, to know how his affair will turn out.[4]

In the parcell intended for you will be a Tract of Mr Frends, just published "Animadversions on the B^p. of Lincoln's Elements of Theology, in a series of letters addressed to him."[5] You may guess the Complexion of the B^p's work, from this circumstance of wch. we were assured yesterday, viz. that the Archb^p. of York has issued a circular Letter to the Clergy of his diocese, forbidding the reading of B^p. Prettyman's book; in the which, among other things obnoxious to High church orthodox men, are a censure of the damnatory clause in the creed of Athanasius, and the giving up the text in 1 John. v. of the three witnesses in heaven as spurious.[6]

I am sorry to conclude my letter with a less favourable account of the state [of] Mrs Finch, Dr Priestley's daughter. Mr Priestley, who has been with me this morning, has written hence to Dr Beddoes of Clifton where his sister is, desiring an answer by the return of post, to know whether the change is so alarming as to oblige him to put off his return to America, which he had fixed to be in three weeks time. As the letter wch mentiond his sister being worse did not come from her to himself, he hopes they that [who] were about her and wrote the acc^t. were more alarmed than necessary.[7]

I have been sorry to write so short an epistle, and in such haste, but I declare I have been interrupted by friends coming in that I have barely had leisure to scrawl what I have done, and I must contrive in future to write when not likely to be interrupted. We hope, as you intimate nothing to the contrary, that Mrs Millar and yourself enjoy tolerable health, and desire to tender our sincere respects and wishes of good to persons we so much esteem.

[The final two or three lines of this letter are missing: see *Note*, above]

1   For the full title of this work, see the list of abbreviations.
2   Lindsey almost certainly intended to write 'intimate'.
3   Probably Dr Andrew Ross; see Letter 659, n. 5.
4   See Letter 687, n. 9.
5   See Letter 689, n. 2.
6   The work of Pretyman which Frend attacked was *Elements of Christian theology ... designed principally for the use of young students in divinity* (2 vols., London, 1799). Pretyman's 'censure' of the clause in the Athanasian creed which stated that those who did not keep the 'Catholic Faith' would 'perish everlastingly' may be found at II, 219–25; his acceptance that much of I John i was spurious may be found at II, 90, n. (c). The archbishop of York was William Markham. I have not been able to confirm the story about the circular letter.
7   For Sarah Finch's ill-health and her experience of the 'cow-house' treatment of Thomas Beddoes, see Letter 687, n. 6. This deterioration of her condition obliged Joseph Priestley junior to postpone his departure for America until June 1800.

691. WILLIAM TURNER OF NEWCASTLE   18 MARCH 1800

Text: DWL, MS 12.44 (63).
Addressed: Rev^d. M^r. Turner/Newcastle/upon Tyne
Endorsed: March 18: 1800
Postmarked: Postmark missing.

> Favour'd of heavn who finds
> One virtuous rarely found,
> That in domestic good combines:
> Happy that house! his way to peace so smooth.

London. March. 18. 1800.

Dear Sir,

The above is the kind salutation, sent me by an excellent person, now no more, little short of 40 years ago, on my happy connection with my present wife; and his salutation has been truly prophetic.[1]

You will permit me, though somewhat late in time, yet with great sincerity, to hail you, as most peculiarly also *favoured* of that Providence which appointeth all things, on the singular felicity of possessing such a domestic treasure and partner of all your cares, after the great loss which you had sustained. May your mutual happiness be as perpetual, as human things can be expected and desired. As I knew and honoured much several of those related to the first Mrs Turner, so have I long entertained a high respect for Mr Willat, and desire you to say for me whatever can bespeak esteem and respect from one who wishes his daughter every thing good, and that may be useful to others in her present situation.[2]

Hoping that this tender of due friendship and civility, tho' so much out of date, may acquit me a little with you for past neglect, I proceed to tell you that Mr Rankin discharged most duly your subscription to our Unitarian Society for the present year 1800, viz £5. 5. 0 for Mr Turner, Mr Doeg, CC, Hanover Square chapel and J.C.

Rankin, and if your present worthy and agreeable messenger, the next year and so on, will take the trouble of delivering the subscriptions to us, my wife will take care to pay them to our new treasurer, and old worthy friend, who is successor to the no less worthy Mr Dodson.[3] I mention my wife, because she is more attentive to these matters and more punctual in them than myself.

Mr Priestley, the worthy eldest son of yours and your father's friend, has just left us, being to return this day, after a stay of ab^t 3 weeks, to Birmingham the residence of his wife's father; to go on after to Clifton where I presume you may know, he conducted his sister, Mrs Finch, the last autumn, prepared a Cowhouse with the Cows for her by Dr Beddoe's orders, and under providence has been the instrument of preserving her life: for since he came to London letters have come from her expressing, that she was quite free from the symptoms of her complaint, and in the most chearful spirits, tho' still by the Doctors order to remain in the Cowhouse, in the same temperature of air, till the latter end of May. If she continues, as there is every hope she will, in tolerable health, he is to set out the middle of the next month to America, the offers wch his uncle had to make him, not being such as to make it prudent to come back to settle in England with his family.[4]

His Father's curious work, so long promised, is recently come to Mr Johnsons, his Comparison of the Institutions of Moses with those of the Eastern nations. I have not yet had time to look into it, but a judicious friend tells me he much approves of it.[5] You will be glad to see a new work of Mr Frend's, Animadversions on the B^p of Lincoln's Elements of Theology, in a series of Letters to him. Conjecture may be made of the complexion of the Bp^s. work, if the report confidently averred, be true; or if there be any foundation for it, "that the Archb^p. of York has issued a circular letter to the Clergy of his diocese, forbidding the reading of the B^p's book".[6] I can have no doubt of your being acquainted, with what we call, the York Pamphlet.[7] A most valuable member of our Unitarian Society so much approved it, that he present[ed] the Society with 50 copies, and at our last meeting we made a resolution to purchase 100 more, that every member of the society might have a copy, our number amounting to near 150.[8] Three days ago, I had a letter out of Wales, signifying a desire, and a sort of intention to translate it into the Welsh languge [sic], particularly as there are so many methodists &c, to whom it may be of infinite use, to read how the unlearnd may interpret the Scriptures and come at the truth for themselves.[9] You will be pleased to know that liberality of sentiment and inquiry into the Scriptures, make their way much, in many parts of Wales, in the West of England &c; and I trust also with you, as well as many other improvem^{ts} for the benefit of Society, in which you are constantly engaged. It will be a pleasure to know that Mrs Turner, yourself and all your family, enjoy the blessing of health and every other blessing desirable for mortals. My wife unites with me in affectionate regards for Mrs Turner and yourself, and I remain always with sincere esteem Dear Sir, most truly Your's

    T. Lindsey.

N.B. I hope you got your books from the Society. I gave your list to our Secretary, Mr Kentish,[10] as soon as it came to hand. I have an apology to make to Mr Prowit for inattention to M^r [word almost illegible],[11] but it was [a] thing unavoidable.

---

1   The quotation is from Milton's *Samson Agonistes*, lines 1046–9; in Milton's text, the final two words are 'is smooth'. The sender of the salutation was almost certainly Archdeacon Francis Blackburne, whose step-daughter Lindsey married on 29 Sept. 1760; Blackburne himself conducted the marriage

ceremony. Blackburne died in 1787; for examples of his well-known admiration for Milton, see Vol. I, Letters 211–16.

2   On 8 June 1799, at Newcastle under Lyme, Staffordshire, Turner married, as his second wife, Jane (d. 1826), née Willets. Her father, William Willets (1697–1779), a dissenting minister of unitarian opinions, had charge of a congregation at Newcastle under Lyme from 1727 until his death. Lindsey had been acquainted with the family of the first Mrs Turner (Mary, née Holland, d. 1797) for many years.

3   Mr Rankin was probably Robert Rankin of Newcastle; see Letter 536, n. 1. For Alexander Doeg, see Letter 491, n. 3. Another contributor to the Unitarian Society was 'C.C.H.' of Newcastle, identified only by his or her initials, whose subscription was forwarded by William Turner; *Unitarian Society ... 1794*, p. 11. Turner also paid a subscription on behalf of Hanover Square chapel, in addition to his personal subscription; *Unitarian Society ... 1791*, p. 14. John Cole Rankin (see Letter 536, n. 1) was a member of the Unitarian Society from its foundation in 1791. He was also a subscriber to George Walker's *Sermons on various subjects* (4 vols., London, 1808, with a second edition later in the same year. This was an extended version of the two-volume edition of Walker's *Sermons* published in 1790). Michael Dodson died on 13 Nov. 1799. His successor as treasurer of the Unitarian Society was the solicitor Godfrey Kettle, a trustee of Essex Street chapel since 1783 and an executor of Elizabeth Rayner's will. He was nominated as treasurer at the general quarterly meeting on 16 Jan. 1800; Unitarian Society minute book, p. 69. He resigned the office on grounds of ill-health in Feb. 1801 and was succeeded by Ebenezer Johnston; Unitarian Society minute book, pp. 69, 73. Kettle died on 6 Apr. 1803; *Gent. Mag.*, LXXIII, i (1803), 389.

4   Joseph Priestley junior returned to America in June 1800; see Letter 696. The uncle to whom Lindsey referred was the ironmaster John Wilkinson.

5   For the full title of this work, see the list of abbreviations. It was published in Northumberland, Pennsylvania, and sold by Joseph Johnson in London.

6   See Letter 690, n. 6. Lindsey presumably heard this story from one of his contacts in York, possibly Catharine Cappe or David Eaton.

7   This is a reference to Eaton's *Scripture the only guide*.

8   Lindsey referred here to the most recent quarterly general meeting of the Unitarian Society, held on 16 Jan. 1800, at which he was in the chair. The meeting expressed thanks to the unnamed gentleman who had presented the society with fifty copies of Eaton's *Scripture the only guide to religious truth* and resolved to purchase a further 100 copies; Unitarian Society minute book, p. 68. Although the minute book offers no evidence (other than that of gender) as to the identity of the donor, the connexion with York prompts the conjecture that Richard Slater Milnes (MP for York from 1784 to 1802) and a member of the Unitarian Society, or a (male) member of his family, might have been the gentleman concerned.

9   This was probably a (non-surviving) letter from Thomas Evans to Lindsey; Evans published a Welsh translation of *The Catechist* in 1796. I have not been able to trace a Welsh translation of David Eaton's *Scripture the only guide*.

10 John Kentish, the secretary of the Unitarian Society.

11 Lindsey's handwriting is uncharacteristically obscure at this point in the letter. Possibly he wrote 'Mufs'. Probably he referred to a friend of Edward Prowitt, although I have not found in the Hanover Square or Pandon Bank records at Tyne and Wear Archives a name which could plausibly be matched to Lindsey's orthography.

692. To ROBERT MILLAR   24 APRIL 1800

Text: DWL, MS 12.46 (19).
Printed: Graham, 'Unhappy country', 154–5
                 (most of third paragraph; seventh paragraph).
Addressed: To/Mʳ Robᵗ. Millar/Merchant/Dundee
Postmarked: Postmark missing.

London. April. 24. 1800

Dear Sir,

Capt. Ross very obligingly called a few hours since and left me your letter, and engaged to call again to morrow forenoon to take the parcel.[1]

I cannot refrain from congratulating with you in the first place on what we trust will be the foundation of better health, the relief obtained by the suppuration, and wish only to suggest a thought whether an issue on the arm on the same side might not in future preserve from an attack upon the chest or any other mischief.[2]

I persuade myself that you have acted most prudently in not spreading the report you heard of our Friend's being on his return to England, as from circumstances it does not appear to be in any way probable. In the latter end of May, the same year, 1799, I and several others received letters then written by him, in which he, to our surprise, makes no mention whatever of his coming back, tho' the time was approaching when he might naturally talk of it, and on the contrary complains of the neglect of his friends, and speaks of many books and various other things which he desires may be sent to him.[3] So that unless some sudden impulse had seized him, on letters rec^d from his relations, for we are by no means certain of his having had intelligence of his brother's death, and of the fortune he bequeathed him, the thing is hardly credible.[4] Whenever he revisists Dundee, should it so please the Divine Providence, I rejoice to know that he will find his flock not diminished, as I am sure it will not be owing to the want of an instructor if they are not advanced in good christian principles and suitable practice. The sight of so many promising young members must warm your heart, as it would mine.

You must let me have my own way in desiring your acceptance from me of the few things I send you; of Dr Priestley's volume, which you will much value, and it is much to be valued, for his sake;[5] of Mr Frend's Animadversions on the B^p. of Lincoln, and of what we call the York Pamphlet, and I do assure you I have a quantity of each which I distribute, and the York sermon is that of a young person, who is one of the most excellent christian ministers I know, formerly Mr Belsham's pupil, and at the same time an eminent teacher of youth, 5 or 6 in his family, with twice that number of day scholars, deep in mathematical as well as classical knowlege, and a more edifying preacher I have scarcely ever heard.[6]

But don't suppose that I send You these things for nothing. Have not you engaged to favour me with some anecdotes of what will probably take place in your national Assembly, where I have no doubt but that Dr Small will well support the cause of religious liberty and the gospel and perhaps there may be some ecclesiastical skirmish exhibited from the pulpit and press which may give information to a stranger.[7]

We I must tell You, are far from being quiet in such respects in this part of the island. So much fostered are the high-church principles, and such increase has there lately been made of Methodists particularly, that it is said to be the design of the legislature, to put a stop to the evil as they call it, by a method which gives alarm to Dissenters in general, that their liberties are aimed at, by the alterations proposed to be made in the Act of Toleration, in lodging a power in the hands of the magistrate to refuse licensing preachers and places, whereas at present they have no such power and are merely official.[8]

Since I last wrote to you Mrs Finch has been worse and better again: but the last acc^t. I had from M^r. J. Priestley, was that Dr Beddoes had declared that his sister might bear a voyage to America, and be much benefited by it; upon wch. he offers to take her along with him – but he cannot prevail with Mr Finch to go or to allow her to go without him: So that probably Mr Priestley will set out on the voyage himself soon, tho' with great concern not to leave his sister as he wished and had laboured to restore her health.[9]

We still have cause of thankfulness for our portion of health, and hope you will now by the divine blessing enjoy a better share than has fallen to your lot. My wife unites with me in kind respects and all good wishes to Mrs Millar and yourself, and I remain always very truly and affectionately Yours

T. Lindsey.

1   Possibly James Ross, a captain in the royal navy captain since 1794; *Royal kalendar ... for the year 1803*, p. 148.
2   Probably this suggestion came from Hannah Lindsey, whose medical knowledge was well known and respected.
3   Although a lengthy letter from Palmer to Disney, dated Sydney, New South Wales, 14 Aug. 1797, and printed in *MR*, XII (1817), 264–6, is annoted by J. T. Rutt as received on 11 Feb. 1799, I have not located the other letters of these dates from Palmer, whose sentence of seven years' transportation was due to end in Sept. 1800.
4   Possibly Jeremy Fyshe Palmer; for his will, see Letter 678, n. 7.
5   Probably this was Priestley's *Comparison of the institutions*.
6   Lindsey probably referred here to Charles Wellbeloved, *The principles of Roman catholics and unitarians contrasted. A sermon; written with reference to the charges brought against those who maintain the doctrine of the divine unity in the strictest sense, by Dr. Horsley. Preached on Tuesday, Nov. 5, 1799, to a congregation of protestant dissenters, in St Saviourgate, York* (York, 1800). Wellbeloved was a pupil at Hackney College between 1787 and 1792, when Belsham was one of the tutors.
7   For the outcome of Robert Small's case before the general assembly of the Church of Scotland in May 1800, see Letter 687, n. 9. According to the *Scots Magazine*, LXII (1800), 428, he made 'a long and able defence'.
8   In Feb. 1800, Michael Angelo Taylor projected a bill in the house of commons to amend the Toleration Act of 1689 with a view to restricting the grant of licences to those dissenting (mainly evangelical) preachers who were not the pastors of settled congregations. The bill was a response to the concerns of some members of the Church of England hierarchy over the growth of itinerant preaching by unlettered persons. Taylor withdrew the bill before it could make any parliamentary progress. For the background, see Watts, *The dissenters. Volume II. The expansion of evangelical nonconformity*, pp. 368–9; there are drafts of the bill in BL, Add. MS 59307, fos. 47–52. In the course of a lengthy parliamentary career, during which he represented seven different constituencies (some more than once), Taylor (?1757–1834) was MP for Aldeburgh from 1796 to Mar. 1800 and Durham from Mar. 1800 to 1802. He was a supporter of the Foxite opposition and his bill received no official support from Pitt's ministry.
9   Joseph Priestley junior returned to America alone, without Sarah and her husband William Finch, in June 1800; see Letter 696.

693. To WILLIAM ALEXANDER   1 MAY 1800

Text: 'Letters of the Rev. Theophilus Lindsey, No. VIII',
                   UH, II, 87 (27 Dec. 1862), 432.

Note: This is the only section of this letter printed by the *UH*; the manuscript seems not to have survived.

London, May 1st, 1800.

I am glad to inform you that the storm is quite blown over for the present, and nothing will be done now by the legislature to alter the Act of Toleration.[1] Some say that this laying aside the design of meddling with that act has been owing to the powerful and earnest solicitation of Mr. Wilberforce and Mr S. Thornton,[2] who have great weight with Mr. Pitt, and who are themselves favourers of the Methodists, who are of late prodigiously increased, and of itinerant preaching, which were supposed to have been what gave immediate umbrage. But others believed that the vast and universal ferment which has been excited among Dissenters of all sorts, and their determined disposition to resist such an attack on their religious freedom, has been the chief circumstance that has had weight with Government to consider twice before they set on foot a religious persecution.[3] I hope, therefore, you may make yourself easy that there will be no disturbance of good men on this account.[4]

1   For Michael Angelo Taylor's unsuccessful bill, see Letter 692, n. 8.
2   Samuel Thornton (1754–1838), MP for Hull from 1784 to 1806 and for Surrey from 1807 to 1812 and from 1813 to 1818, was a prominent banker, evangelical and cousin of William Wilberforce.
3   For the anxiety of the protestant dissenting deputies over Taylor's bill, and their representations against it, see London Metropolitan Archives, MS 3083/3, p. 160 (deputies' minute books). There is no record of any such protest in the minutes of the General Body of Dissenting Ministers: DWL, MS 38.106–7.
4   Alexander's anxiety on this account is explained by the possibility of prosecution for teaching in an unlicensed school which he faced in 1792–3; see Letters 511 and 514.

694. To ROBERT MILLAR   10 MAY 1800

Text: DWL, MS 12.46 (20).
Addressed: [In Hannah Lindsey's hand] To/Mr Robert Millar/Merchant/ Dundee/N:B
Postmarked: Postmark missing.

London. May 10. 1800.

Dear Sir,

Having the easy convenience of a frank by a friend calling in upon us, I make use of the opportunity to write you a few lines.

And first I would wish you to know that the reason I did not send in your parcell by Capt Ross a copy of Dr Priestley's work for Doctor Ross, was, because on inquiry I found it had been sent by Mr Johnson before, and I hope it came safe to him.[1]

Another motive for my writing at present, is to inform you, that I have had sent me by a friend, two very curious pamphlets relating to the business that it is supposed will come on before your General Assembly; one of them, titled, *The New Light Examined; or Observations on the Proceedings of the Associate Synod* &c by *William Porteus DD*.[2] The other, *A defence of the Associate Synod* &c in answer to Dr Porteus by James Peddie, Minister &c Edinburgh, in which the author has replied to him well, particularly to his scandalous charge of Sedition; and I think we should stile the said D.D. if he were in this southern part of the Island, a temporizing High-Churchman.[3] I mention however my being in possession of these two pamphlets, lest you might think them to be of any consequence, and be at the trouble of sending them to me.

I think it proper also to acquaint You, that I am in possession of Mr Rowland Hill's first, and Second Tour into Scotland, and of course know something of the characters of the two brothers, Mr J. Haldane, the Preacher, in particular, and their zeal formerly for the foreign missions, now turned to the propagation of the gospel at home.[4]

We have been here for some weeks past in no small apprehension, that a great Personage might be prevailed upon by his Ministers to make some unpleasant alterations in the Toleration Act, which at his Coronation he swore to keep inviolate:[5] It was believed that one inducement to this was to put a stop to the great increase of Methodists, and itinerant preachers in these southern parts of the isle, and that it was also to be extended to your parts and to give a check to your missions: and it is certain that Mr Rowland Hill for these 3 weeks past has preached in a very bold and vehement stile, against the restrictions given out as intended to be laid, both with regard to Persons to be licensed, and the licensing of Places to preach in: but the Storm is said to be blown over at present.[6] And I should think the Minister has too much business on his hands than to increase it, by meddling with religion, and venturing to disturb the consciences of men in that respect. I have put the letter to M[r] Ellis into the best hands I know to take care of it so as to be sent off the first opportunity.[7] I hope your short excursion to Glasgow will benefit your health. We have for this week past had the weather of July instead of May. I trust it will be for good, for the fruits of the earth, that we may hereafter enjoy them tho' we are so unworthy of them. Thanks for your kind inquiries, we both continue to enjoy our healths, may the like be the portion of yourself and M[rs] Millar. We are going on monday to pass a week with our old friends in Surry. With our joint kind respects to M[rs] Millar and my wifes to yourself,

I remain always very affectionately Yours

T. Lindsey.

---

1   See Letter 692, n. 1.

2   William Porteous, *The new light examined: or, observations of the Associate Synod against their own standards* (Glasgow, 1800). Porteous (1735–1812) was minister to the Old Wynd, or west parish church, Glasgow, from 1770 to 1812. A leading spokesman for the popular party in the Church of Scotland, he was also a prominent philanthropist in Glasgow. But he became a strong critic of the French Revolution, and the work which Lindsey mentioned (and disliked) took the form of an attack on the 'New Light' seceders from the Church of Scotland. Porteous accused the Associate Synod of sectarianism, of pursuing innovation at a time when 'Sedition and Treason were walking about at noon day', and of being 'no less unfriendly to the constitution of this country, than ... to legal establishments of religion' (respectively, pp. 5, 54, 25).

3   James Peddie (1759–1845) was minister to the Associate meeting house at Bristol Street chapel, Edinburgh, from 1783 to 1845. His libertarian principles, inspired by Adam Ferguson and Dugald Stewart at Edinburgh University, led him to express cautious sympathy with the French Revolution. His reply to Porteous was entitled *A defence of the Associate Synod against the charge of sedition: addressed to William Porteous D.D. in reply to his pamphlet 'The new light examined'* (Edinburgh, 1800). Porteous was awarded the degree of DD by the college of New Jersey (from 1896, Princeton University) in 1784. Lindsey identified him, not entirely accurately, with English high church defenders of the existing ecclesiastical and civil constitution.

4   These two works of the Calvinist evangelical preacher Rowland Hill (1744–1833) were his *Journal, through the north of England and parts of Scotland, with remarks on the present state of the established Church of Scotland; and ... some remarks on the prosperity of what is called lay and itinerant preaching* (London, 1799); and *Extract of a journal of a second tour from England to the highlands of Scotland, and the north-western parts of England, with observations and remarks* (London, 1800). James Haldane (1768–1851), formerly an officer on merchant ships sailing between Britain and India, turned from the late 1790s to evangelical preaching tours in Scotland. In 1798, he helped to found the society for the propagation of the gospel at home and in the following year he was ordained as minister of an independent congregation in Edinburgh and thereafter operated outside the established Church of Scotland. His brother Robert Haldane (1764–1842) was his colleague as an evangelical preacher. Both the Haldane brothers had supported Rowland Hill in his itinerant preaching in Scotland.

5   By his coronation oath, George III had promised to maintain 'the Protestant Reformed Religion Established by Law' and to 'maintain and preserve inviolably the Settlement of the Church of England, and the Doctrine, Worship, Discipline, and Government thereof, as by Law Established'. The oath is set out in *The form and order of the service that is to be performed, and of the ceremonies that are to be observed, in the coronation of their Majesties King George III and Queen Charlotte, in the abbey church of St Peter, Westminster, on Tuesday the 22d of September, 1761* (London, 1761), p. 32.

6   This is a reference to Michael Angelo Taylor's bill to restrict the granting of licences to itinerant preachers; see Letter 692, n. 8. The bill had been withdrawn by the time of this letter. During his second tour of Scotland (see n. 4, above), Hill had defended itinerant evangelical preaching such as

his own in a serious of vehement controversies with the general assembly of the Church of Scotland; see Edwin Sidney, *The life of the Rev. Rowland Hill, A.M.* (London, 5th edn, 1861), pp. 251–4.

7   See Letter 696, n. 9.

695. To WILLIAM DAVY   18 JUNE 1800

Text: DWL, Davy letterbook, p. 72.
Addressed: To/William Davy Esqr/Merchant/Philadelphia
Endorsed: Ans^d Sep: 29. 1800 & *Alexander*
Postmarked: Postmark missing.

London. June 18. 1800.

Dear Sir,

Your good brother having kindly undertaken to convey a parcell for Kentucky to you by the Adriana, Capt. John Fletcher of Philadelphia,[1] I take the liberty of addressing it to you and begging your kind care to forward it with the inclosed letter to Mr H. Toulmin at Frankfort. Besides the trouble it will give, I am sensible it must be some expense, and should be most glad to know how to pay my debts on such occasions. The parcell contains some books which the Secretary of state is in want of for his private satisfaction and benefit, and I hope they will come safe to him.[2] Every thing in our own country and even throughout every country continues in a ferment, and in a precarious unsettled State. It is thought the very next mails will bring accounts of Buonaparte's victories over the Austrians in Italy, which may bring the emperor in their consequences to a peace with the French Republic, and so constrain us to come to an accomodation without obtaining our end of placing Louis xviii upon the throne.[3] In the mean time we are in great distress, not only with loads of endless taxes, but at present, the poorer, and even midling ranks thro scantiness and dearness of the necessaries of life. I am sorry to be such a croaker, but I should be glad to have a better account to send. And shall most truly rejoice to do it, when I next take upon me to ask such favours of You, which it would be a pleasure to have pointed out how I might repay.

I remain, always, Dear Sir,
          Your much obliged and faithful servant
               T. Lindsey.

---

1   For William Davy's brother Thomas Davy, see Letter 656, n. 1.

2   Henry Toulmin was secretary of state for Kentucky from 1796 to 1804; see Letter 656, n. 2.

3   Bonaparte defeated the Austrians at Marengo on 14 June 1800. The likelihood of a French victory had been reported in several London newspapers, such as the *Morning Chronicle*, 16 June 1800, and the *General Evening Post*, 17 June 1800, before Lindsey wrote this letter. The Austrian emperor Francis II renewed his alliance with Britain by the treaty of Hohenlinden on 20 June 1800, but further defeats at the hands of the French obliged him to make peace with France by the treaty of Lunéville on 9 Feb. 1801. For Louis XVIII, see Letter 687, n. 4. Contrary to Lindsey's suspicion, the restoration of the Bourbons was not a British priority in the 1790s. Although Louis XVIII, after years of exile in Russian, Prussian and Swedish territory, came to England in 1808, he was kept at arm's length by the British government and was not permitted to live in the vicinity of London.

696. To ROBERT MILLAR   30 JUNE 1800

Text: DWL, MS 12.46 (21).
Printed: Graham, 'Unhappy country', 155–6 (second and third
                 paragraphs; first two sentences of fourth paragraph; second
                 sentence of sixth paragraph).
Addressed: [In Grafton's hand] *London June thirtieth 1800*/To/Mr Robt
                 Millar/Merchant/Dundee/N.B.
Endorsed: Grafton [also endorsed, ?by Millar] Lond^o 30th June 1800/Mr
                 Lindsey [there are a few other, apparently unrelated, pencilled
                 jottings]
Postmarked: FREE JUN 30 1800

Note: The bottom right-hand corner of the second page of the manuscript is torn off, but apparently
without any loss of text.

London. June. 30. 1800

Dear Sir,

The last time I was favoured with a few lines from You, was on the eve of a journey to Glasgow, where you was going to make some little stay, and I hope the exercise w^d. be of service to take away any remains of your rheumatic complaint, from which disorder many of our friends had been sufferers, during the long continued severe and variable weather of the last spring. It will afford pleasure to be assured that this has been your happy lot, and to know that Mrs Millar as well as yourself enjoy the blessing of health.

Since I last wrote and sent Dr Priestley's book[1] for your obliging acceptance by Capt Ross, Mr Joseph Priestley has sailed for America, having had the satisfaction of leaving his sister Mrs Finch so much amended in her health as to be encouraged by Dr Beddoes to take a journey into Wales with a friend: We have not since had any accounts of her, but if she had experienced any reverse, it would certainly have reached us.[2]

I have also of late, once and again had letters from Dr Priestley, the last of so late a date as May 8th. which contains the best account of his health and happiness in his pursuits of philosophy and theological studies, and his desire to see his friends in England if peace would but come that he might take the journey safely; but under apprehensions that this blessed event was still far distant.[3] He mentions also that Mr Cooper had been prosecuted for some writings which were deemed libellous, against the president, and condemned to an imprisonment for 6 months, and a fine of 400 dollars.[4]

I must tell You however that we have entertained hopes, since a confirmation has arrived of Buonaparte's great successes in Italy and Moreau's in Germany, that the Emperor will find himself necessitated to make peace with the French, and the more as Prince Charles and many others have been from the first against the present war.[5] The Stocks certainly have risen within these few days, and it is ascribed to the expectation of peace;[6] and one thing I can tell you, of my own knowlege, that a gentleman and lady of our acquaintance dined no longer ago than Saturday with a relation and M.P. of some note, a frequent speaker and in great connection with the Minister, and he frankly intimated to them that the event was by no means improbable, but that Opposition were much mistaken, as Mr Sheridan threw out in the house on friday, and would be much disappointed, if they imagined that Mr Pitt would turn out for them to come in, and make a peace, for that if there was to [be] a peace, he would certainly make it himself.[7]

I much suspect that your grand General Assembly has met and parted without doing any thing in respect of the Seceders or Dr Small, as nothing has transpired of their doings.[8]

Mr J. Ellis's father's letter to his son was taken care of.[9] We have had no tidings of late from Botany Bay. With our united respects and good wishes to Mrs Millar and yourself

I remain, Dear Sir with sincere esteem

      Your much obliged and affectionate servant

               T. Lindsey

I thank heaven, my wife is in her best plight, and my own lot is amongst the most favoured in that respect.

---

1   This book was probably Priestley's *Comparison of the institutions*.

2   Joseph Priestley junior departed for America in June 1800. For his sister Sarah Finch, a patient of Thomas Beddoes at Bristol, see Letter 687, n. 6; evidently, a brief respite of health permitted her visit to Wales.

3   There is no letter from Priestley to Lindsey dated 8 May 1800 in DWL. Possibly Lindsey referred to Priestley's letter to him of 1 May 1800; Rutt, I, 432–3. Possibly, too, this was the letter to which Lindsey referred in Letter 697, where he attributed to it the date 2 May. In this letter, Priestley did indeed give a favourable impression of his health and happiness ('I have as much *sunshine* as I want') and added 'I want my *friends*, and especially yourself and Mr. Belsham' (Rutt, I, 433).

4   Thomas Cooper became an adherent of the Jeffersonian anti-Federalist party and attacked the administration of John Adams, president of the United States from 1797 to 1801, in his *Political essays* (2 vols., Philadelphia, 1799, with a second edition in 1800) and in the *Northumberland Gazette*. In Nov. 1799, a particularly vehement denunciation of Adams led to Cooper's prosecution for libel under the Sedition Act; eventually he was fined \$400 and imprisoned for six months in Philadelphia jail during the latter half of 1800. Thomas Jefferson referred to these events in his letter to Priestley of 18 Jan. 1800, and Priestley forwarded this letter to Lindsey when writing to him on 29 May of that year. Jefferson described Cooper as 'a rising man in the country', and when he succeeded Adams as president in 1801, he and his party rewarded Cooper with several public offices, including a judgeship; for this correspondence, see Rutt, I, 434–7.

5   The climax of Bonaparte's successes in Italy was the battle of Marengo, 14 June 1800. Jean Victor Moreau (1761–1813) won a series of victories over the Austrians in western Germany in Apr. 1800. Archduke Charles (1771–1847), the younger brother of Emperor Francis II, was the most successful Austrian military commander of the 1790s and (until 1809) of the Napoleonic wars.

6   Between 20 and 30 June 1800, the price of 3 per cent consols increased from 64 to 64$^7/_8$, while that of 4 per cent consols increased from 80$^7/_8$ to 81$^7/_8$; *Gent. Mag.*, LXX, i (1800), 600, 703.

7   Although Lindsey did not identify this MP who was a frequent speaker and in 'great connection' with Pitt, an obvious possibility, under both categories, is George Rose (1744–1818), the secretary to the treasury from 1783 to 1801 and MP for Christchurch from 1790 to 1818, who was one of Pitt's most faithful followers and posthumous defenders. On Friday 27 June 1800, Sheridan moved a motion for a call of the house of commons 'in the present awful conjuncture'. He called for an end to the war and for the removal of Pitt's ministry. His motion was defeated by 124 votes to 27; Cobbett, *Parl. hist.*, XXXV, 393–401.

8   For the assembly's admonition to Robert Small, see Letter 687, n. 9. Lindsey was correct in regard to the 'Seceders'; see *The principal acts of the general assembly of the Church of Scotland, convened at Edinburgh, the 22d day of May 1800*.

9   This letter from James Ellis senior to his son in Australia seems not to have survived.

697. WILLIAM TURNER OF NEWCASTLE   7 JULY 1800

Text:	DWL, MS 12.44 (62).
Printed:	McLachlan, *Letters*, pp. 91–2 (part of last sentence of third paragraph); p. 92 (first two sentences of fifth paragraph); p. 123 (last sentence of third paragraph); Graham, 'Unhappy country', 156–7 (first sentence of third paragraph). Graham wrongly identifies Robert Millar as the recipient of this letter).
Addressed:	To/The Rev^d. M^r. Turner/Newcastle upon Tyne
Endorsed:	July 7: 1800
Postmarked:	Postmark missing.

London. July. 7. 1800.

Dear Sir,

I was much obliged by your packet by Miss Lindsay, who did not fail in delivering it tho' I have been tardy as usual in my acknowlegements.[1] I have satisfaction in finding that I had in very free terms remonstrated to our American friend against those very points which hurt you so much in his late work, and which you so justly in my opinion condemn, as tending to render him and his friends obnoxious to the present powers, and to make him a prophet of evil things upon very precarious and uncertain grounds. But he has ever been too unguarded in things that he has thrown out to the public, with the best meaning in the world, as your good father sometimes observed.[2]

I shall rejoice when his worthy son is returned safe to him, as he is a good judge of propriety in many respects, and by his prudence will be of great service to him, as well as in a thousand other ways.[3]

The report of D^r. P. and all his family having lately been poisoned, may probably have reached you; and certainly something of the kind did take place, whether by some poisonous herb being boiled by mistake or from the copper vessel that was made use of, is uncertain; but the letter, which I saw, and wch was sent by Mr John Vaughan of Philadelphia to his brother M^r. W. Vaughan here, which brought an account of the accident, mentioned that by the use of Emetics &c they were out of all danger.[4] I have lately had a letter from the Doctor from Northumberland of the date of May 2^d. as chearful as any I have had, and bespeaking the writer in the best health and spirits, happy in his situation and preferring it to all others on acc^t of the ease and convenience of pursuing his various studies: and not having the least thought of visiting England till the Storm of war was blown over, of wch. he had not then much expectation.[5]

I am rejoiced to find that he is not at all implicated in what has lately befallen his friend Mr Cooper of Manchester, who for printing what has been adjudged a libel against the President, has been condemned to pay a fine of 400 dollars and to suffer imprisonment for 6 months.[6]

There is some ground of hope that we may be able to see Dr Priestley sooner than he expected, if it be true what was yesterday said, that Buonaparte was returned to Paris with the Preliminaries of a Peace, and that Ulm was also in possession of the French.[7] For surely we shall not continue to carry on the war alone, if the Emperor close with the terms offered him.[8] I write this early in the morning, before any of the papers are out, just in the moment of setting out to pass a few weeks with some old friends in Surrey, but otherwise w[e] shall not take any long journies this year.

You have not called upon us to advance for you any of your payments to our Unitarian Society, or my wife woud have with pleasure done it for You.

The Reports of your Literary Society for the last and present year were very acceptable to me and to one or two friends.[9] M[r] Bowden of Leeds[10] has lately been with M[r] Belsham for a week and sets out with him to morrow to Bristol, where the former is appointed to preach the Annual Sermon of their Unitarian Society in the West.[11] My wife desires to join in kind respects to M[rs] Turner with good wishes to your young folks, and I remain always with a sincere esteem very truly Yours

      T. Lindsey

---

1   Possibly a member of or hearer at Turner's Hanover Square chapel, Newcastle, although I have found no reference to that name in the chapel's records at Tyne and Wear Archives. Another possibility is that Miss Lindsay was a relative of James Lindsay, DD (1753–1821), minister to the Monkwell Street congregation in London from 1783 to 1821, and afternoon preacher at Newington Green from 1787 to 1805.

2   'Our American friend' was Priestley. The 'points' which had 'hurt' William Turner of Newcastle and which tended to render Priestley 'and his friends obnoxious to the present powers' were possibly the attacks on John Adams and the Federalists which Priestley had made in his 'Maxims of political arithmetic', published in the *Aurora*, the pro-Jefferson Philadelphia newspaper, in 1798; see Schofield, *Enlightened Joseph Priestley*, pp. 333–4. Alternatively, those 'points' might have been Priestley's endorsements of the French republic in his *Letters to the inhabitants of Northumberland* (Northumberland, 1799); see Letter 698, n. 20. Lindsey's letter to Priestley on this subject has not survived. Priestley and William Turner of Wakefield had been good friends during the former's pastorate at Mill Hill chapel, Leeds, between 1767 and 1773.

3   See Letter 696.

4   For John Vaughan, a former student of Priestley at Warrington Academy, see Letter 591, n. 1. His brother William Vaughan (1752–1850) was by this time an expert on the London docks, with ambitious schemes for their improvement. For the alleged attempt to poison Priestley and his family, see Letter 704.

5   For this letter from Priestley to Lindsey, see Rutt, I, 432–3.

6   See Letter 696, n. 4.

7   General Moreau's dispatch describing the French victory at Ulm in early June 1800, and Bonaparte's return to Paris at the beginning of July 1800, were both reported in the *Morning Chronicle* on Monday 7 July 1800. Bonaparte's arrival in Paris and the probability (though not the preliminaries) of peace were reported in *Lloyd's Evening Post*, 4 July 1800. On Sunday 6 July, *Bell's Weekly Messenger* quoted a Danish source to the effect that Bonaparte had indeed brought the preliminaries for a 'Continental' peace with him to Paris. In a separate item in the same issue, it reported the French possession of Ulm.

8   The emperor Francis II concluded an armistice with General Moreau in Dec. 1800 and a peace treaty at Lunéville on 9 Feb. 1801.

9   Lindsey referred here to the *Sixth year's report of the Literary and Philosophical Society of Newcastle upon Tyne: with a list of new members and a supplement to the catalogue* (Newcastle, 1799), and the *Seventh year's report of the Literary and Philosophical Society of Newcastle upon Tyne. To which are annexed, a supplement to the catalogue, and a list of new members* (Newcastle, 1800). Turner had forwarded both reports to Lindsey.

10   This refers to Joseph Bowden (d. 1820), a former student of the Daventry Academy, and minister to the dissenting congregation at Call Lane, Leeds, from 1778 until shortly before his death; see *New Monthly Magazine*, XIV (1820), 599, and *MR*, XVII (1822), 196. He was a signatory to the published letter from dissenting ministers at Leeds over the Test and Corporation Acts in Jan. 1790 (see Letter 402, n. 4) and author of *Sermons, delivered to the congregation of protestant dissenters at Call-Lane chapel, Leeds* (Leeds, 1804) and *Prayers and discourses, for the use of families* (London, 1816).

11   Belsham's sermon to the Western Unitarian Society was published as *Freedom of enquiry, and zeal in the diffusion of Christian truth*; see Letter 682, n. 18. Joseph Bowden, who accompanied him to Bristol, had family connexions in that area.

698. To THOMAS BELSHAM   **17 JULY 1800**

Text:	DWL, MS 12.57 (16).
Addressed:	[In Hannah Lindsey's hand] To/The Rev^d. Thos. Belsham/at the Rev^d. M^r. Kenrick's/Exeter
Endorsed:	[By Belsham] Mr Lindsey July: 17: 1800
Postmarked:	Penny Post P^d 1^d Low Mitcham JY 17 800

Mordon. M^{rs}. Chambers's. July. 17. 1800

Dear Sir,

Yesterday, after our post hour, I received your welcome letter from Bristol, containing much which gave us pleasure to know of your travels and the many agreeable and some not unimportant things that came before you in them, of which I remark nothing at present, hastening to give you some account, which you will expect of Mrs Rayner's being taken away from us, of wch you woud read some mention in the Papers.[1] On the Monday forenoon,[2] the day you set out, we called upon her at Clapham, and were conveyed by her as usual to our common friends here. They thought she looked much broken: it did[3] appear at all to us: but she complained of the fatigue in having to return to dinner, and said, she w^d always send the coach for us, but we must not expect her to come herself. She got well home however, tho' much fatigued; and went out an airing the next evening as usual. On the Wednesday,[4] her public day, she had a haunch of Venison, sent by her nephew L^d. Gwydir,[5] and D^r and Mrs Blackburne, Mr Urwick,[6] and other company invited, and she busy and earnest as usual to have every thing in the handsomest way. She had complained to Mrs Blackburne, in the garden, a little before dinner, of being faint, and desired her to fetch her some lavender drops and sugar, which revived her. And she would help her guests with the Venison herself, and some of em more than once; when going to take some herself, she fainted and fell back a little in her chair, which D^r B^l. observing immediately supported, and had her carried into her room: when every medical effort was given to relieve her, and answerd in discharging great quantities of bile &c but nothing of any effect. This was Wednesday evening, when D^r. Bl. was much with her. The next morning Thursday he sent a letter to my wife here, who set out immediately, and found her in such danger, tho' very sensible, that she immediately sent a messenger to inform her favourite niece, Mrs Bennet of Beckenham in Kent about 10 miles off,[7] but the messenger, M^{rs} R's coachman,[8] meeting a few miles off, her niece the Duchess of Hamilton,[9] and telling her his errand, she called upon her aunt, and after staying some time with her, went to London, when she apprized her other relations, and came back in the evening, and stayed the whole time till 4 in the morning, when the scene was finally closed, and she fell asleep without a sigh or groan; and thus went off in that happy easy manner, which she often desired, and said it would crown all the unutterable blessings with which the Almighty had favour her thro' a long life, in which she was the most excellent pattern of true humility, piety, selfdenial, and the most perfect benevolence, I have ever known. Her Executors are two of her relations, Ld Guydir, Mr Bennet, and Dr Disney, Mr Best and Mr Kettle.[10] Amongst other legacies, she has left to me and Dr Disney, each one thousand pounds Stock and her house at Clapham to me, the lease some few years to run, but longer than I am likely to last.[11] And to Dr Priestley, I believe she has left 2 thousand pounds Stock.[12] More particulars you shall know when we meet, wch we look forward to sometime in the next month.

Her[e] we are most happy, but unavoidably much confined. You would make the best use of such leisure; and I earnestly wish you find it and hope you will at your return, during your vacation to furnish the business you have laid out to yourself, and which will benefit the world when you shall have left it, tho' I hope it will be long e'er that day come.[13] I have not had a line from the D. of Grafton since we came here, not any tidings of Locke on Toleration, but shall send him a line in a day or two.[14]

I have a long letter this post from that good creature M[r] Millar of Dundee, with the Sentence of the General Assembly against D[r] Small, and other curious matter of that church. He is there in the very midst of their religious wranglings, and disturbed with the sight. "The longer I live, says he, and the more I know, the stronger satisfaction do I feel, at being intirely free in Religion from human authority, and the dirty puddle of worldly politics in the Religion of Jesus. The best informed are decidedly of opinion that D[r] Small is in the right as to the law about Subscription.[15] –

– "In establishments, what with rigidity ab[t] creeds, carelessness as to vital religion, and the restraints upon free inquiry; there is no wonder that seemingly there sh[d] be so much of the form without the power of real religion; that infidelity should prevail; and many though seriously disposed, yet ignorant and misled, should follow Missionary Teachers, who teach nothing but the highest Calvinism, especially the second Person of the glorious Trinity dying for *a few* of his own creatures. In short what a sad piece of work is made of religion in this world: it is distressing in the extreme to dwell upon it"[16]

I thought for lack of other matter, you would not be sorry to see how low this good creature is made by Mess[rs] Haldane and C[o]. who have their head quarters at Dundee, and the Gen. Assemblys-Squabbles.[17] But he thanks God, their little church goes on quietly.

I cann[t] easily describe to you the joy my wife and I feel in your plain narrative of the good countenance and encouragement given to free inquiry and the doctrine of the Divine Unity in so many appearing for it at Bristol. We are glad that we shall be in the number of of [*sic*] Your hearers.[18] We are however shocked to find our suspicions confirmed w[ch] Miss Barbara Vaughan had raised of some of D[r] Priestleys family. But we still think it was William's wife, not himself, that was so diabolical.[19] Thanks for the sight of the D[r]s letter. We are glad he is in such good spirits himself, and persuaded of his having acted the right part. But it was certainly indiscreet to declare himself so peremptorily w[h] regard to the French Republic.[20] We are rejoiced to have from you such a confirmation of M[r] & M[rs] Rowe's characters, and especially of his being of such usefulness and importance in his place. But the friend and relation under whose roof this will find you, is one who has most boldly stood forth, and will I trust be the most useful character in the West for the support and advancement of true religion and virtue, and my wife begs with me to be most cordially remembered to him as well as your excellent sister.[21] I am sorry we are here quite out of the way of franks, and of every thing of the kind. You will please to direct y[r] letters to me here. I am sorry I can get no frank for You. It must give you pleasure, that your excursion has turnd out so much more than expected for the furtherance of the truth. If you can make it any way convenient to call upon the

Duke, tho' with[t] your brother, and tho but for a day, I hope you will do it.[22] Always your truly obliged & affectionate

T. Lindsey

[On address page] I am highly delighted to find that ther[e] are such apprehensions entertained about the consequences of y[r] present mission.[23]

---

1   Elizabeth Rayner died on Friday 11 July 1800.

2   17 July 1800 was a Thursday; the Monday of the previous week, when Lindsey and his wife visited Mrs Rayner at Clapham, was 7 July.

3   Probably Lindsey unintentionally omitted the word 'not' at this point.

4   Wednesday 9 July 1800.

5   Sir Peter Burrell (1754–1820), of Langley Park, Beckenham, was Elizabeth Rayner's great-nephew. He was MP for Haslemere from 1776 to 1780 and for Boston from 1782 to 1796. Associated with the Portland whigs, he supported Pitt's ministry from 1793 and was created Baron Gwydir in June 1796. Through his wife, the daughter of Peregrine Bertie, 3rd duke of Ancaster, he acquired considerable property and inherited the office of lord great chamberlain.

6   Thomas Urwick (1727–1807), educated at Northampton Academy (under Philip Doddridge) and Glasgow University; assistant minister (1754 to 1764) and minister (1764 to 1775) at Angel Street, Worcester; minister at Narborough, Leicestershire, 1775–9; minister at Grafton Square chapel, Clapham, 1779 to 1807. He died at Balham Hill, 26 Feb. 1807.

7   Elizabeth Amelia (Mrs) Bennet of Beckenham was named in Elizabeth Rayner's will as her great-niece. Richard Henry Alexander Bennet of Beckenham was one of Elizabeth Rayner's executors.

8   In her will, Elizabeth Rayner named her coachman as George Gibbon and bequeathed to him £20; TNA: PRO PROB 11/1345, fo. 271r.

9   Elizabeth Anne (1757–1837), née Burrell, was the sister of Peter Burrell, 1st Baron Gwydir (n. 5, above). In 1778, she married Douglas Hamilton (1756–99), 8th duke of Hamilton in the Scottish peerage. They were divorced in 1794 and on 19 Aug. 1800 she married (as his third wife) Henry Cecil, 1st marquess of Exeter (1754–1804), whose uncle, Brownlow Cecil (1725–93), ninth earl of Exeter, was the cousin of Lindsey's friend William Chambers. She was named in Elizabeth Rayner's will as her great-niece.

10   These were indeed the executors named in Elizabeth Rayner's will. George Nathaniel Best of the Middle Temple is listed as a special pleader in the *Universal British directory* (1791), I, 368. For Godfrey Kettle, see Letter 691, n. 3.

11   Elizabeth Rayner's house was 82 Titchfield Street, Clapham; the lease had approximately fifteen years to run at the time of her death; the original lease was fifty-two years.

12   Lindsey was correct. Elizabeth Rayner bequeathed to Priestley £2,000 in Bank of England four per cent annuities; TNA: PRO PROB 11/1345, fo. 267v.

13   Lindsey probably referred here to Belsham's plan for his *Elements of the philosophy of the mind*, published in 1801; see Letter 682, n. 19. Lindsey's wish for Belsham's longevity was gratified; he lived until 11 Nov. 1829.

14   A new edition of John Locke's *Letters concerning toleration* was published by Joseph Johnson in London in 1800. The unsigned preface is dated June 1800, but there is no clue in the volume itself as to the editorship or sponsorship. In his sermon on Grafton's death, Belsham praised the duke's contribution to 'every temperate and judicious plan for promoting what he conceived to be the interest of truth and virtue'; *Uncorrupted Christianity unpatronised by the great* (London, 1811), p. 50; but made no mention of this edition of Locke.

15   Robert Small had claimed that subscription to the confession of faith should not be a requirement for the ordination of elders in the Church of Scotland, as such subscription was a new practice and not required by any law of the church. For the general assembly's admonition to Small to refrain from such comments in future, see Letter 687, n. 9.

16   This letter from Millar to Lindsey seems not to have survived; Lindsey's reply to it (Letter 699) makes clear that it was dated 14 June 1800.

17   Lindsey referred here to the brothers James and Robert Haldane (see Letter 694, n. 4). Although he was born in Dundee, James Haldane was from 1799 minister to an independent congregation in Edinburgh. Both brothers were extremely hostile to Robert Small and his reservations over subscription (n. 15, above).

18   For this sermon of Belsham at Bristol, preached on 9 July 1800, see Letter 682, n. 18. Probably

Lindsey hoped that Belsham would preach it again, in London, so that he and his wife could be present.

19 Barbara Vaughan (b. 1764) was the daughter of Samuel Vaughan and his wife Sarah, née Hallowell, and the sister of Benjamin and William Vaughan. William Priestley's wife was Margaret, née Foulke; see Letter 640, n. 13.

20 For Priestley's letter to Belsham of 15 May 1800, see Rutt, I, 433–4. In it, Priestley regretted that Lindsey was 'much disturbed' by his *Letters to the inhabitants of Northumberland* (see Letter 697, n. 2). In this work, Priestley defended French principles as republican and therefore the same as American principles, and upheld democracy as the basis of the American constitution: 'Every man, therefore, who is not a democrat is an enemy to this constitution' (pp. 8–9).

21 Timothy Kenrick, who was married to Belsham's sister Elizabeth.

22 Although it is not clear whether or not Belsham visited Grafton on this occasion, the two were on friendly terms; see DWL, MS 12.58 (14), Grafton to Belsham, 1 Aug 1798, a note which reveals Grafton's appreciation of Belsham's company. Belsham visited Grafton at Wakefield Lodge, North-amptonshire, on several occasions and preached a commemorative sermon on the duke's death in 1811; see Williams, *Memoirs*, pp. 491, 611–12.

23 Belsham's 'present mission' signified his travelling and preaching in Bristol and the west country; Lindsey was 'highly delighted' that Belsham's preaching of unitarianism had proved so successful as to raise anxieties among the orthodox there.

699. To ROBERT MILLAR   30 JULY 1800

Text: DWL, MS 12.46 (22).
Addressed: [In James Martin's hand] Westm^r. *Thirty First July* 1800/M^r. Robt. Millar/Merch^t./Dundee/N.B. J^s Martin
Endorsed: London 30 July 1800/Mr Lindsey
Postmarked: JUL 31 1800 FREE   [also postmarked AU 3]

Mordon, Surrey, July 30. 1800

Dear Sir,

We have now been full three weeks at the seat of two respectable gentlewomen, some of our oldest friends,[1] very happy to escape out of the heat and dust of London, which were begining to be very troublesome, and must be now at their height, as there has not been a drop of rain since, wch makes very well for corn, beans, and grain of every kind, but our meadows and pastures are parched up. Soon after we arrived here, within two days, my wife was sent for to a lady, another most excellent friend, who was taken on the sudden dangerously ill, who had only two days before brought us hither in her carriage, on a forenoon visit to our friends with whom she was acquainted, a Mrs Rayner, whom you have heard us name, aunt to some of the first titles in the kingdom, and at the same time one of the most perfect patterns of true humility, genuine piety, and the most pure and enlarged christian benevolence, I had ever known; after a due and decent provision for her station, denying herself every thing to have the more to do good to others. She had every medical assistance, from the moment she was taken ill, wch. was suddenly at dinner, after she had helped her guests, and was going to eat herself; and the applications succeeded in giving a short relief, but the machine itself was worn out at the great age of 87, and my wife stayed with her till the event was over. She was wont often to say, that she could desire, if it pleased God, that to all his other unutterable blessings which she had experienced thro a very long life, might be added that of not lying long on a bed of sickness, and her desire was granted, for it was only the space of 36 hours, from the time of her being seized, till she breathed her last, and fell quietly asleep.[2]

She had been a most true friend to us and to our Society, to Dr Priestley and numberless others; which you will easily conjecture when I tell You, that for the last 23 years of her life, when she became mistress of her fortune,[3] I believe, she gave away not less than two thousand pounds yearly; it being her chearful resolution, frequently repeated, that none of the mammon of this world should stick to her and impede her passage out of it.

I could not refrain from unburdening the mind to such a friend, and acquainting you with our situation here, before I acknowleged and returned my sincere thanks for your welcome letter & pacquett, of the date of June the 14th. which only came to Essex Street since we left it, and have been sent hither to us.[4]

You have indeed, my friend, taken no small pains to gratify me, particularly in respect of the worthy D[r] Small and his prosecution, and I thank you for it. I am quite indignant to see a gentleman of his irreproachable character, great respectability, learning and talents so shamefully treated, for a conduct, which ought and would have crowned him with honour before any other judges but a sett of secular time-serving churchmen, who have no other principle to guide them but the most paltry prejudice and mean self interest.[5] If to this be added, what I have in a letter from a most respectable literary person in the country, that "D[r]. Small was very obnoxious to men in power for his supposed political principles", it not only accounts for the harshness and iniquity of the usage he met with, but he may be reckoned well off, that he was not adjudged by the venerable court to the Lollard's tower, or to Botany Bay.[6]

D[r]. S ___ 's temperate and able defence under such provocation, would expose his adversaries to that just contempt which they deserve, and bring him and good cause great credit. And I am particularly beholden to you for your coment and explanations given in your letter, which have enabled me more easily to understand and become master of the whole business. But I take leave of it for the present, to tell You, the pleasure and satisfaction I felt in your so justly appreciating the tracts sent, especially M[r] Eaton's; and am glad I can add, that I have your judgment of it, in the minute particulars of it confirmed by some most worthy persons and very able hands, in this part of the Island, and also in Ireland.[7]

I had a letter lately from M[r] Belsham, who is gone into the West, during his vacation, being engaged first to preach the annual Sermon of their Unitarian Society at Bristol; where I understand he and his discourse met with a most welcome receptance: and he preached twice the Lord's day after to a very crouded audience, so as to give some umbrage as I am informed to the clergy of the city, what could be the object of his mission, and that such things sh[d] not be allowed, for strangers to come and disturb the minds of the common people.[8] As his sermon is to be printed, I shall have a pleasure in sending it to You.[9] We have been much revived her[e] within these few days with the tidings of a Peace between the French and Austrians, which in the event must certainly restore that blessing to this country. I am the more refreshed with the thought, as I persuade myself, that coming by the channel it does, in the issue and result, tho' nor I nor even you, may live to see it, it will be the means of putting an end to all spiritual dominion and interference of the civil power in religion.[10]

I rejoice with you, that a certain little church goes on quietly, out of it's reach.[11] You will be pleased to know, that my wife as well as myself have seldom at any time enjoyed better health than since we came to these cool and peaceful abodes.

May the blessing be no less shared by Mrs Millar and yourself. My wife joins in the tender of our sincere respects and every good wish for you both.

I remain, Dear Sir, Your very truly obliged and affectionate

T. Lindsey.

1   Sophia and Frances Chambers.
2   See Letter 698. Elizabeth Rayner died at Clapham on 11 July 1800.
3   Elizabeth Rayner had been 'mistress of her fortune' since the death of her husband, John Rayner, in Mar. 1777.
4   Millar's letter and packet of 14 June 1800 seem not to have survived; see Letter 698, n. 16.
5   See Letter 687, n. 9.
6   Lindsey did not identify this 'respectable literary person in the country' and one is reduced to conjecture. A possibility is the antiquary and bibliophile John Croft (1732–1820) of York, author of a work on the wines of Portugal and of several editions of Shakespeare. There is no direct evidence that Lindsey knew him personally, but Croft was a freeman, and sheriff, of York while Lindsey was vicar of Catterick. Possibly, too, he was the gentleman 'out of Yorkshire' to whom Lindsey referred in Letter 700. The Lollards' Tower, at Lambeth Palace, was a prison constructed in the 1430s and used for the incarceration of the followers of John Wycliffe (*c*. 1320–84).
7   It is likely that those in Ireland who approved of David Eaton's pamphlet included Richard Kirwan and Samuel Barber (see Letter 700, n. 12).
8   For Belsham's sermon to the Western Unitarian Society at Bristol, preached on 9 July 1800 and published in the same year, see Letter 682, n. 18.
9   See Letter 697, n. 11.
10   On 22 and 23 July 1800, the *Morning Chronicle* reported that peace between Austria and France was likely. On 29 July, the same newspaper reported that heavy defeats at the hands of the French had obliged the emperor Francis II to agree to an armistice with the French. The *Morning Chronicle* cited as its source 'the Paris Journals', which Lindsey, with his sympathy with the regime in France, was more likely to believe than British ministerial sources.
11   Lindsey referred here to the unitarian congregation at Dundee.

700. To THOMAS BELSHAM   31 JULY 1800

Text: DWL, MS 12.57 (17).
Addressed: [In Hannah Lindsey's hand] To/The Rev^d. Thos. Belsham/at Thos. Smith's Esqr./Bownham House/near Minchinhampton/ Gloucestershire
Endorsed: [By Belsham] Mr Lindsey July 31: 1800
Postmarked: JY 31 800

Mordon. July 31. 1800

Dear Sir

I have still additional reason to congratulate you on the agreeable variety and entertainment you meet with on your western tour as you are so good as to spare time to make us share with you in it. I should have been particularly happy to have been of your party at Lympston to have heard what passed in your theological conversation after dinner, when I think however I should have been inclined to have taken Mr Evanson's side of the question, tho' it woud have depended upon your manner of arguing, and not rejecting the introduction to the book as signifying and teaching an imediate divine interference, and moral instruction to the first of the human race, though not to be literally taken.[1] Your description of M^r and Mrs E. was peculiarly grateful to us and to the ladies our hôtesses, as they know him well and esteem him much, and had seen him frequently when he lived in this neighbourhood and had some of their relations under his care.[2] We are much pleased also with yours and Mr Kenricks diligence and exertions in the kind visit You made to the prisoner at Dorchester, but hope his meagre lank appearance was purely temporary, owing to the heat of the season, joined to his singularities in his diet, and his constant dissatisfaction with the manners of his keepers, all of which will pass away now in a few months.[3] I wonder not at his satisfaction in the thought of the *divine Mill* being set a going, in which I cannot but join with him, and trust it will not cease working till it has thoroughly humbled in the dust and infamy Mess[rs] Pitt & C[o]. so as never to rise again in this system.

I have lately received a curious letter out of Yorkshire from a gentleman who has long known M[r] Wilberforce, and who upon reading his intire defence of the Minister and all his measures, in the Debate on the State of the nation, brought on by M[r] Western, declares he shall not be surprized, if at making his next batch of Peers, and recompensing his friends and adherents, this said gentleman should be one of them, to enjoy his pious exercises and *otium cum dignitate*, out of the way of the brawlings and profane noise of the house of Commons.[4] I canot say I know him sufficiently to give my assent here.

Yesterday I heard from the Duke of Grafton, who seems greatly affected with the situation and troubles of D[r] Priestley, on having heard from you the shocking suspicions which fall on one part of his family; which I am grieved to learn, are still made more probable, if not confirmed, by the manner in which M[r] Davy of Philadelphia speaks of it.[5] I do not perceive, by the Duke, that the *letter* on *Toleration,* is yet much known or called for, though it has been a good deal advertized.[6] I hope however that both will take place before Parliament meets again,[7] because I apprehend, that if the same men are destined to remain in power, they will certainly make an attempt to abridge the *liberty of prophesying*, (forgive me for so classing you,) which such itinerants as you enjoy, in stimulating and promoting unbounded free inquiry, and thereby disturbing the country, as by being brought to *think* seriously on one subject, they may transfer it to others.[8] The Duke is in Northamptonshire, and speaks with great glee of the pleasing prospect of the time to harvest being shortened by the unexpected warmth of the season, w[ch] has caused Corn to fall very considerably at a moment when the utmost distress was expected.[9]

My wife has a letter from M[rs] Stovin, who mentions Frederick having sailed three weeks ago on the secret expedition, and writing to her on shipboard with his arm in a sling, owing to a wrench, or the rheumatism in it.[10] He is in the Iphigenia, Cap[t]. Stackpole,[11] and meets with much kind treatment, a letter or two of good introduction having been of great service. You will know more of M[r] Barber of Ireland from my wife, and how he became a correspondent of M[rs] Cappe's.[12] I sh[d] have sent you another extract from her letter, which shews more the worthy man, and shall put here for want of better materials. "The books were detained in Newry by some relations of mine, till Wednesday last, and from their note, apologising for retaining them. I find they are become disciples. Many thanks to M[r] Wellbeloved for his excellent Sermon: I hope the liberal sentiments it contains will become the religion of the whole world.[13] Unitarian principles have made rapid progress here. Half at least of the Synod of Ulster have embraced them. Emlyn the confessor was one of us.[14] Indeed all our gentlemen and rich merchants are so: but alas many of them have not known where to stop thro the contagion and infidelity of the times"[15]

I had yesterday the pleasure of a letter from M[r] Shore of Meersbrook informing us that M[rs] S. Shore had presented them with another grand daughter, and that the mother and the stranger were doing very well.[16] And added to this, that Sydney's head was now quite well, and that he was wellnigh cured of his lameness by Pond-bathing.[17] On all these accounts I most truly rejoice, as a just concern about them has long occupied one of the worthiest of mankind, and truest patriot in every sense. Mr Wyvill had sent him some strange accounts of the timid, selfish, mercenary spirit wch. manifested itself in many of the gentlemen of the county at their last meeting.[18] Their note may be changed, if the Minister's expected *douceurs* of every kind should fail them. We beg our sincere respects to Mr Smith and his lady, for whom we have an high value and esteem;[19] and to M^r and Mrs Chandler, should you happen to meet with them while in Gloucestershire.[20] Mr Martin sets out to Morrow, having borne his free and honest testimony against the minister, his designs and venal adherents.[21] My wife sends her love, and I remain always, Dear Sir, your much obliged and affectionate

T. Lindsey

---

1   For Belsham's account of this meeting with Edward Evanson, see Williams, p. 494. Evanson moved from Suffolk to Lympston, Devon, in 1799. In the absence of Belsham's letter, it is not clear which theological work was the subject of debate, although it is unlikely that it was one of Evanson's own productions.

2   For Evanson's school at Mitcham, which he kept between 1778 and 1788, see Vol. I, Letter 188. His wife was Dorothy, née Alchorne (1751–1832), the daughter of a London merchant; they were married in 1786.

3   On 30 May 1799, Gilbert Wakefield was sentenced to two years' imprisonment in Dorchester gaol. On 16 June, he left the king's bench prison, where he had been held prior to sentence, and entered Dorchester gaol on 18 June. He was released on 29 May 1801.

4   On 9 July 1800, Charles Callis Western (1767–1844), MP for Maldon and a supporter of the Foxite opposition, introduced a motion in the house of commons for a committee of the whole house to inquire into the state of the nation. He was particularly critical of Pitt's rejection of proposals for peace. Wilberforce spoke strongly in defence of Pitt and against the motion, which was defeated by 148 votes to 26. There is a report of the debate in Debrett, *Parl. reg.*, XII, 299–341 (Wilberforce's speech at pp. 307–10). Wilberforce was not included in the next batch of peerages (in fact sixteen Irish peerages were conferred on 31 July 1800, the date of Lindsey's letter) and never became a peer. Possibly the gentleman 'out of Yorkshire' who wrote to Lindsey was John Croft, the 'literary person' mentioned in Letter 699. 'Otium cum dignitate' may be translated as 'leisure with dignity'.

5   I.e. William Davy; see Letter 695.

6   See Letter 698, n. 14.

7   The session of parliament had ended on 29 July 1800; the next session began on 11 Nov.

8   For the restrictions upon itinerant preachers proposed by Michael Angelo Taylor's bill, see Letter 692, n. 8. Lindsey believed, incorrectly, that Pitt's ministry supported the bill. His designation in this letter of Belsham as an 'itinerant', no doubt arising from the latter's preaching in various parts of the west country, is a rare example of Lindsey's sense of humour.

9   According to the *Gent. Mag.*'s monthly table of the prices of agricultural commodities, the price of a quarter of wheat in Northamptonshire fell from 120s and 4d in July 1800 to 88s 2d in Aug., compared with the overall reduction in England and Wales of 136s 4d to 96s 2d. Grafton had evidently written from his Northamptonshire residence, Wakefield Lodge. The reduction was not maintained, and neither, it seems, was Grafton's optimism (see Letter 703); in Sept. 1800, the price of wheat in Northamptonshire was 119s 4d; *Gent. Mag.*, LXX, ii (1800), 703, 807, 911.

10   Mrs Stovin was Theodosia, née Sparrow (d. 1834), who married James Stovin, JP, of Rossington, Yorkshire, in 1770. Her younger son Frederick Stovin (1783–1865) took part in the unsuccessful British expedition to Ferrol on 25–6 Aug. 1800. He was an army lieutenant in 1801 and subsequently served throughout the Napoleonic wars, received a series of promotions, was knighted in 1815 and ended his life as a general. His eldest son, James Stovin (d. 1833) was rector of Rossington, Yorkshire, from 1783 to 1833; see *Alumn. Cantab.*, II, vol. VI, p. 60. See also Letters 673, n. 6, and 674.

11   The store ship *Iphigenia* (thirty-two guns) was launched in 1780 and accidentally lost through fire at Alexandria in 1801. Hassard Stackpole, or Stacpoole (d. 1814), was its captain. The 'secret expedition' refers to the British attack upon Ferrol (n. 10, above).

12   Samuel Barber (?1738–1811), a member of the presbyterian general synod of Ulster, was minister to a congregation at Rathfriland, county Down, from 1763 until his death. He was a supporter of parliamentary reform, and a delegate of the Irish volunteer movement in the late 1770s and early

1780s. He favoured catholic relief and was increasingly critical of ecclesiastical establishments. In 1797 and 1798, he was imprisoned briefly on suspicion of association with the United Irishmen. His theological opinions leaned more to the Arian than to the Socinian position. There is a brief note about his correspondence with Catharine Cappe in Cappe, *Memoirs*, pp. 271, 273 n. *.

13 See Letter 692, n. 6.

14 Thomas Emlyn (1663–1741) was minister to the presbyterian congregation at Wood Street, Dublin from 1691 to 1705.

15 See above, n. 12; Catharine Cappe's letter to Hannah Lindsey, quoting Samuel Barber's letter, appears not to have survived.

16 This refers either to Lydia or Maria, the younger daughters of Samuel Shore IV (1761–1836) of Norton Hall and his wife Harriet, née Foye (d. 1826). Their youngest daughter, born in 1802, was christened Amelia Theophila, after Lindsey. The girls were the grand-daughters of Lindsey's friend and correspondent Samuel Shore III.

17 Sydney Shore (1790–1827), the son of Samuel Shore IV of Norton Hall.

18 In the early months of 1800, several of Wyvill's friends in Yorkshire cautioned against any suggestion that a county meeting be summoned, and Wyvill himself believed that the time was inappropriate; Wyvill, *Political papers*, VI, 90–7. The propaganda defeat of the reformers at the York county meeting of Dec. 1795 (see Letter 616, n. 6) deterred further efforts for several years thereafter; see Dinwiddy, *Wyvill and reform*, pp. 9–10.

19 Thomas Smith (d. 1822) resided at Bownham House, near Minchinhampton, Gloucestershire. His wife Elizabeth ('Eliza') was the daughter of Richard Chandler of Gloucester (see Letter 516, n. 4 and n. 20, below). His obituary notice described him as a 'well-informed, liberal-minded country gentleman, with a fondness for science'; a student at the Daventry Academy, he was originally trained for the legal profession, but was restricted by a speech impediment from the practice of law; *MR*, XVII (1822), 514. On 1 July 1804, writing to Thomas Belsham, he requested that his 'kindest regards' be conveyed to 'the excellent Mr Lindsey'; DWL, MS 12.58 (18). Belsham visited him at Bownham House, and in 1802 Hannah Lindsey directed a letter to him at that address; see Letter 738.

20 For Richard Chandler, see Letter 516, n. 4. He died in 1810; his wife Mary survived him. See his will, TNA: PRO PROB 11/1515, fos. 64r–65r, which reveals that he left a legacy to the Barton Street dissenting congregation in Gloucester, and that, naming him as his friend, he nominated Benjamin Hobhouse as one of his trustees. His son-in-law was Thomas Smith (see n. 19, above).

21 James Martin spoke in support of Western's motion in the commons' debate on 9 July 1800 (see n. 4, above); *Morning Chronicle* 10 July 1800; Debrett, *Parl. reg.*, XII, 310. However, he is not included in the list of the minority which appeared in the *Morning Chronicle* and several other London newspapers on 11 July, nor in the minority list printed in Debrett, *Parl. reg.*, XII, 341; perhaps he departed for his family's seat at Overbury, Gloucestershire, before the end of the debate.

701. To THOMAS BELSHAM   7 AUGUST 1800

Text: DWL, MS 12.57 (18).
Addressed: [In Hannah Lindsey's hand] To the/Revd Thos Belsham/Grove
                  Place/Hackney/August 7th/Penny Post
Endorsed: [By Belsham] Mr Lindsey Aug^t: 7: 1800
Postmarked: Merton Unpaid Penny Post.   12 o'clock AU 7 1800 NO
                  4 o'clock AU 7 1800 EV

Mordon. Aug. (7)^1 1800

Dear Sir,

Your acceptable and chearful journal was received two hours ago, and I hasten to thank you for it to prevent our anxiety in your having a fruitless walk to Essex Street this hot and dusty season, which our wise men here say is to last a fortnight to come. I may say, that we were almost as glad as yourself at your getting to Bath and having no more to do with those Somersetshire precipices; and were much gratified with your every way favourable account of Mr Broadhurst, and hope he will have health long to enjoy his station, and be an useful minister of the gospel.^2 All of us were exceedingly affected with worthy Mr Simpson's great loss; After so many other heavy trials, we fear he may sink under this: He has been long well-known to the two ladies of this house.[3] We are not unacquainted with M[r] Basnett's worth: he formerly belonged to the Chapel in Essex-Street.[4]

The Scenery from Bownham house we shoud have been happy to have viewed along with you, and thank you for mentioning us to the Master and Mistress and to our friends at Gloucester, where I am afraid you did not find things in such a flourishing way as in other places that you touched at.[5]

The same post-boy which brought your letter, brought the papers, in which is the melancholy account of the fire at Mess[rs] Rutt and Jameson's premises in Rutland Place, at w[ch] I am much dejected. I presume that the former continued to have some share in the business tho withdrawn from the house, and M[r] Jameson struck me much as an amiable and worthy character. I hope however their insurance will help much to indemnify them.[6]

I had a letter a few days since from M[r] Scott of Portsmouth, very kindly claiming a promise of paying them a long visit when we should cease to have a call into the north: but I tell him I am sorry, that, in many unforeseen accounts it will not be in our power to be their guests.[7] He and M[rs] Scott, with M[r] and M[rs] Watson of Chichester, have spent six week[s] happily together in the isle of Wight, from which all the party has experienced great benefit in respect of health, especially the two ladies.[8] M[r] Scott came home to Portsmouth every Saturday, and returned on the Mondays.

I cannot indeed say when we shall leave our present abode, which is so preferable to our own at this season, as well as in every way else agreeable, and our friends so desirous of our stay. My wife has also some work of painting and papering our parlour to the street going forwards, which we are glad to be out of the way of. If you should have no further calls from friends, I hope there will be leisure to put to the press the work you have long promise[d] to D[r] Priestley & and which is much expected by many.[9] I have read over with attention the D[r]'s Essay on the knowlege of a future State among the ancient Hebrews, and persuade myself that it will be of use to have it published, and shall be desirous to engage M[r] Johnson in it as soon as we come to Town.[10]

M[r] Wyvill, after a long silence, sent me a letter this last post, from which it appears that he is at last convinced, to give you his own word, that the patience and mean pusillanimity of the country is at least equal to the tyranny of its ministerial rulers;[11] and tho' our situation be alarming in the highest degree, it is in vain to attempt to make any impression on the people; and we seem to have nothing to[12] but to wait events, and and [*sic*] opening to do something for the public ------

But I really am forced to stop, as I believe I did once before, abruptly,[13] and conclude with my wife's affectionate regards, and that I remain always, Dear Sir, Your truly obliged and affectionate

T. Lindsey.

---

1   The figure 7 in round brackets appears to have been added in another hand.

2   For Thomas Broadhurst, see Letter 653, n. 4.

3   Probably John Simpson of Bath; see Letter 505, n. 1. He was listed as a member of the Unitarian Society in 1791 and 1794; see *Unitarian Society ... 1791*, p. 13; *Unitarian Society ... 1794*, p. 14. Probably his 'great loss' was the death of his only daughter at Bath; see BL, Add. MS 36527, fo. 86r (Joseph Hunter, 'Biographical notices'). His 'other heavy trials included ill-health, although Joseph Hunter detected 'something of the valetudinarian in his appearance' (fo. 86v). Simpson had lived at

Glasgow, Leicester, Nottingham, Walthamstow and Leeds before retiring to Bath; Sophia and Frances Chambers probably came to know him when visiting that city.

4   William Basnett of Bath, whom Belsham had met during his western excursion, was a member of the Unitarian Society and of the Western Unitarian Society; *Unitarian Society ... 1794*, p. 9; list of members appended to Browne, *The necessity of a new version of the sacred writings*, p. 33.

5   See Letter 700, n. 19.

6   John Towill Rutt's wholesale drugs premises were at 239 Rutland Place, Upper Thames Street, Black-friars. The fire was reported in the *Oracle and Daily Advertiser,* 4 Aug. 1800. The *Gent. Mag.*, LXX, ii (1800), 790, estimated the damage caused by this fire at £35,000 and stated that 'there were destroyed six mills for preparing drugs, and one belonging to a mustard manufactory'. Jameson was a business partner of Rutt.

7   Scott's letter to Lindsey seems not to have survived. There is no evidence that Lindsey and his wife visited Scott and his family at Portsmouth.

8   For Thomas Watson of Chichester, see Letter 388, n. 12. The two ladies were Scott's wife Sophia, and Margaret, the wife of Thomas Watson (see Letter 689, n. 9).

9   Probably this is a reference to Belsham's *Elements of the philosophy of the mind*; see Letter 682, n. 19.

10 Priestley's *An inquiry into the knowledge of the antient Hebrews* was edited by Lindsey for publication by Joseph Johnson. It consisted of sixty-eight pages of text, preceded by a 'preface by the editor' (pp. iii–viii) above the initials T.L. The price of the volume was 2s. The title page of the copy in Dr Williams's Library is inscribed in Lindsey's hand 'F: Maseres/Jan: 22, 1801, from the editor'; and the text of this copy contains a few marginal annotations in Lindsey's hand.

11 For Wyvill's pessimism as to the possibility of rousing reforming opinion in Yorkshire, see Letter 700, n. 18. His letter to Lindsey of Aug. 1800 seems not to have survived.

12 Word omitted, probably 'do'.

13 None of Lindsey's previous letters to Belsham end as abruptly as this one; perhaps Lindsey referred to an earlier non-surviving letter.

702. To THOMAS BELSHAM   18 AUGUST 1800

Text: DWL, MS 12.57 (19).
Addressed: To/The Rev^d. Thomas Belsham,/Grove Place/Hackney [in
                   Hannah Lindsey's hand] Penny Post/Monday 18th
Endorsed: [By Belsham] Mr Lindsey Aug^t: 12: 1800
Postmarked: 12 o'Clock AU 18 1800   4 o'Clock AU   1800 EV
                   [postmark otherwise illegible]

Mordon. Aug. 18. 1800

Dear Sir,

I thank you much for your short but most acceptable letter, wch. tells us that you are well, and how you are employed.[1] Tho' there are neither mountains nor seas nor a million of miles to separate us, it is unpleasant to think that we shall not be able to have a sight of You, till your return from the excursion which You intimate that you have in meditation at the expiration of a fortnight, and which we presume will be to Bedford. We do not expect to make a visit to Paxton this year or should have been most happy to have been there in the way of seeing you and your brother, whose society we always value. Frend was to be with Mr Reynolds yesterday, and to hover some weeks in that country, in Cambridge, at his friend Hammond, at Fenstanton, as well as at Paxton.

I have lately received a letter from Mr Davy of Philadelphia, dated July 2^d. 1800, expressing pretty much the same opinion of Dr Priestley & his interfering with the politics of America as you saw in his letter to Dr Toulmin of May. 26, which the D^r has sent me.[2] But he subjoins such facts of the insulting depredatory conduct of our Privateers and Ships of war towards the American vessels and complaints of them, as if they could not be longer endured but must cause a breach between the two countries.

D^r. Toulmin sent me at the same time a short letter to him from that excellent creature Mr Vander Kemp, who desires it may be comunicated to me, together with a long Eulogium on Washington which he delivered to a large audience at the town near wch he lives; wch. contains excellent materials, & marks of a fine genius and of a most independent, enlightened good mind.[3] There are so many *Dutchisms* in his english as makes it not so agreable to read; But, as I presume Dr T. had not rec^d the letter when he saw you, or not mentioned it to You, I shall take the liberty to make an extract from it, which I think will please you.[4]

"My respects to [D^r][5] Lindsey. Ask him, if the miraculous conception should not be of egyptian origin. since – 77 I disbelieved this opinion, and considered it, how pious the intention of these christians may have been, who brought in clandestinely in the disciplina arcana, long before it made it's open appearance in the christian church. I exposed my sentiments more at large in in [*sic*] my *diss. on J.C.* and adduced, in my opinion, a very strong, tho negative proof from the Evang: that his most inveterate enemies never called him a bastard, never sustained the remotest idea injurious of Mary's honour, which undoubtedly would have happened if one of them had suspected the reality, or received the slightest hint of pretensions to a miraculous conception and birth.[6] Then follows a very curious criticism and quotation in Greek, from Plutarch in Numa, explaining the term πλησιαζειυ de coitu, as often used by the best authors."[7]

I have had sent to me the Speech of Dr Brown, Principal of the Marechall College Aberdeen, in the General Assembly May last, on the question respecting the Settlement at Kingsbarns, of D^r. Robt Arnot, Professor of Divinity in St Mary's college St Andrews, in wch. the Doctrine of Pluralities in the Church of Scotland is agitated and decided. You will have pleasure in reading it, but it will keep till we meet.[8]

We are sorry to find from different accounts we have had of this horrid poisoning affair at N _____ nd, that they seem to bear harder upon the husband than the wife. Your report of Dr Aikins being milled over again gives us the greatest joy. We hope he will now far exceede the years of his fathers, and continues his services to literature and good principles.[9]

If you have y^e 8vo Vol of Lowman's Rationale of the Hebrew Ritual &c &c could [you] send it to Essex-Street, to be conveyed to me, I should thank you.[10] Reports concerning your Sermon at Bristol have made [?us] still more anxious to see it, and we are glad you are employed about it; and do not forget the work, which will be κτημα ες αει.[11] We are very happy to be in this quiet cool recess, during these broiling heats of such long continuance. When we think of quitting, of which we have no thought at present, you shall know. Be so good as to remember us properly to our comon Friends, London Field,[12] Old Ford[13] &c &c My wife send[s] you her affectionate regards, and joins in due respects to Miss Belsham.[14] I remain at all times your affectionate and most truly obliged

T. Lindsey.

---

1 Belsham's letter to Lindsey is not among his correspondence at DWL and seems not to have survived.

2 William Davy's letter to Lindsey of 2 July 1800 seems not to have survived, although Lindsey referred to it in his letter to Davy of 3 Feb. 1801 (Letter 713). In his letter to Lindsey of 1 May 1800, Priestley acknowledged Lindsey's concern about his 'taking a part in the politics of this country', but

defended his political involvement by pointing out that he knew more about the local circumstances than did Lindsey; Rutt, I, 432.

3   Francis Adrian Vanderkemp (1752–1829) was a Dutch Mennonite preacher who took a prominent part in the Dutch 'patriot' revolt against the stadholder regime in the 1780s; see Simon Schama, *Patriots and liberators. Revolution in the Netherlands 1780–1813* (London, 1977), 60, 64, 71. After the defeat of the patriots, Vanderkemp emigrated to America. There, according to Belsham, he 'became a sincere and zealous convert to the doctrine of the proper Unity and sole Supremacy of God' as a result of his study of the works of Lindsey and Priestley; Belsham, *Memoirs*, p. 165. Subsequently, he helped to found a successful Unitarian Society at Oldenbarnevelt, in western New York State; see Bowers, *Priestley and English unitarianism in America*, pp. 143–6. Vanderkemp's *Eulogy of George Washington. February 22, 1800* (New York, 1800) was originally published in Dutch.

4   I have not located this letter from Vanderkemp to Joshua Toulmin, although it is clear that the two were on epistolary terms. See *Francis Adrian Van der Kemp 1752–1829. An autobiography together with extracts from his correspondence*, ed. H. L. Fairchild (New York and London, 1903), pp. 6, 16, 199.

5   Lindsey placed 'D^r' in square brackets to indicate that he did not merit that title.

6   This appears to be a reference to an unpublished 'dissertation' by Vanderkemp. It is not a quotation from Lindsey's *Two dissertations* (London, 1779).

7   This is a reference to Plutarch's *Life of Numa*, chapter 4, section 4: 'And yet the Egyptians seem (not implausibly) to make the distinction that it is not impossible for the spirit of a god to have intercourse with a woman and to produce the first stages of generation, but that for a man there is no commingling or association of the body with the divine.' I owe this translation and reference to Mr David Powell.

8   *Substance of a speech, delivered by William Laurence Brown, D.D. ... in the general assembly of the Church of Scotland, on Wednesday, the 28th of May 1800. On the question respecting the settlement, at Kingsbarns, of the Rev. Dr Robert Arnot, professor of divinity in St Mary's College, St Andrews* (Edinburgh, 1800). Brown (1755–1830) was principal of Marischal College, Aberdeen. The parish of Kingsbarns, Fifeshire, was in the presbytery of St Andrews; Robert Arnot (1745–1808) was its minister from 1800 until his death. He was professor of biblical criticism at St Andrews, 1792–1800. On his nomination to Kingsbarns in Dec. 1799, a complaint was made to the general assembly of the Church of Scotland against his holding both offices simultaneously, and Brown's speech expressed this complaint forcibly; it was dismissed; see *Fasti Ecclesiae Scoticanae*, V, 217.

9   Possibly Lindsey referred reprinting of a work by the physician John Aikin (1747–1822), the son of John Aikin, DD (1713–80) and the brother of Anna Letitia Barbauld.

10 This work was Moses Lowman, *A rational[e] of the use of the ritual of the Hebrew worship; in which the wise designs and usefulness of that ritual are explain'd, and vindicated from objections* (London, 1748). It was indeed an octavo volume. Moses Lowman (*c.* 1669–1752) was assistant minister, and subsequently chief minister, of the presbyterian congregation at Grafton square, Clapham, from 1710 until his death. A non-subscriber at the Salters' Hall meeting in 1719, he was a trustee of Dr Williams's trust from 1738, and a prominent biblical scholar.

11 'A possession for all time'; a quotation from Thucydides, *History of the Peloponnesian War*, book 1, chapter 22. I owe this reference to Mr David Powell. For Belsham's sermon, preached at Bristol on 9 July 1800, see Letter 692, n. 18.

12 Probably Lindsey referred here to London Fields, an area of parkland, on the fringes of Hackney.

13 Old Ford was (and is) a district of London adjacent to Hackney.

14 Ann Belsham, the unmarried sister of Thomas Belsham.

703. To THOMAS BELSHAM   **26 AUGUST 1800**

Text: DWL, MS 12.57 (20).
Addressed: To/The Rev^d. T. Belsham/at William Belsham's Esqr/Bedford
Endorsed: [By Belsham] Mr Lindsey Aug^t: 27:1800
Postmarked: AU 27 800 [postmark otherwise illegible]

Tuesday. Aug. 26. 1800
Mordon.

Dear Sir,

Your letter from Hackney of the 22^d was very acceptable, as it informed me that I was right in my conjecture concerning the object of your short visit, and that you had rec^d. Dr Priestleys last.[1] I was also glad that you advised to let the affair of our friend's dining with the ambassador Liston sleep altogether, which however I had determined before it came to hand, for the good reasons you give, and also because it might not have been agreeable to Mr Liston to have his name brought before the public, after so long an interval, and on so trifling an occasion.[2]

Having rec^d. a letter from Mr Thomas Evans, complaining how heavy these hard times lay upon him with his wife and eleven children, and desiring my interest with Dr Disney and Mr Jervis to procure him some help from Dr Williams's bequests to Dissenting Welsh Ministers, I advised him to write himself to the former; who two years ago had been his friend, having mentioned his case myself to Mr Jervis before we left town; but not being certain of their having it in their power to befriend him, I resolved, as I was writing to the D. of Grafton, to make him acquainted with his situation, who by the return of the post most kindly sent me £10 for him, which with some other little matters, will I trust be a needful comfort and encouragement to him.[3] I had not forgotten, in a former letter to him, to inquire whether the sentiments of Mr Davies, whose son accompanied him to Bristol, were the same with his own.[4] My letter to the D. of Grafton, was to thank him for the noble present of half a Buck, which he has been wont to make us for some years past, and which we have always directed him to send to this family of our oldest friends, and to whom we have been and are under continual obligations; but of which we ourselves had never been in the way to partake of till this present year.[5] At the close of his letter, the Duke writes, on Friday last, "This cold, rainy day begins to alarm us for the fate of the Grain": I thought they had been more forward in those parts.[6] I have no doubt of your sending him a copy of your Sermon as soon as it is printed: though he has desired me to tell Mr Johnson to let him have two copies as soon as they are out.[7]

When my wife was in Town for a few hours upon business about ten days ago, she by mere accident saw Mr Frend, who told her he was going down the next day to Paxton, and will I presume for some time continue a visitor to the family there, and to others of his friends in those parts. Had we gone this year into Huntingdonshire, we should not have been sorry to have been there at the same time with him.

I am glad you had not Lowman, for I had found out soon after I had written, that I did not want him, and shoud have mentioned it to you.[8] I trust that you[r] two new Pupils will turn out to your satisfaction as part of your family, and also do credit to their Instructor.[9] I was going to wish you more leisure for other pursuits; but time, precious as it is, cannot certainly be more usefully employed: I only wish you had some more suitable compensation for your labours.

I expect we shall still continue with our friends here for some time to come, wch is every way agreeable to us, and for wch we could feel no sort of regret, but as it debars us of the great pleasure of sometimes seeing you. I thank you for your advice, and will certainly send a letter to Dr Priestley by the New York packet at the begining of this next month, if there sh^d be no ship directly sailing for Philadelphia.[10] What may be future we [?one] cannot say, but it seems to me to be more and more unlikely that we shall see him again in England. A friend lately saw Peter Porcupine, Mr Cobbet,[11] in St James's square, much at his ease, and bien accredité, but a very coarse lout[?] as he appeared to him.[12]

Our respectful comp^{ts} wait upon your brother and sister,[13] and with my wifes affectionate regards, I remain, Dear Sir, always your most truly obliged

T. Lindsey.

1   Priestley's 'last' (i.e. most recent) letter was probably that to Belsham of 5 June 1800, or that to Lindsey of 19 June 1800; see Rutt, I, 437–8, 439–41.

2   For Robert Liston, the British minister to the United States, see Letter 653, n. 7. In Oct. 1799, the *Gent. Mag.* published a letter from 'C.J.M.' claiming that on '17th January 179_ ' Priestley dined as the guest of 'an English gentleman of fortune resident at Philadelphia'. It went on to allege that to prove his 'loyalty' to Britain (17 Jan. was the birthday of Queen Charlotte) he sang 'God save the king' in front of the assembled company; *Gent Mag.*, LXIX (ii), 841–3. The letter made no mention of Liston, whose supposed presence was added by the Philadelphia press. Priestley ridiculed the story in his letter to Lindsey, 18 Jan. 1800; Rutt, I, 437.

3   For Thomas Evans and his family, see Letter 668. For the financial assistance which Evans received from Dr Williams's Trust and from the duke of Grafton, see Jenkins, '"Horrid affair"', p. 183. Disney and Jervis were both trustees of Dr Williams; Lindsey was not.

4   Probably David Davis (1745–1827), 'Arian minister, poet and schoolmaster', who ran a school at Castellhywel, Cardiganshire, from 1782 to *c.* 1820. He was a friend of leading Welsh unitarians, notably Iolo Morganwg and Thomas Evans, although he did not share the latter's Socinian. theology. He and his wife Anne, née Evans, had two sons, David Davis (1778–1846) and Timothy Davis (1779–1860) who both became unitarian ministers in South Wales during the early nineteenth century; the former was a leading founder of the Unitarian Christian Society of South Wales in 1802. See the article on Davis and his family by Robert Thomas Jenkins in *The National Library of Wales: dictionary of Welsh biography*: http://yba.llgc.org.uk/en/s-DAVI-DAV-1745.html. A much more remote possibility is Edward Davies (1756–1831), a schoolmaster at Chipping Sodbury grammar school, Gloucestershire, from 1783 to 1799 and curate of Olverston, Gloucestershire, from the latter year. He shared the interests of Thomas Evans in the ancient language, literature and history of Wales, but unlike Evans, he was a clergyman of the established church, within which he subsequently held several livings in Wales.

5   Lindsey's letter to Grafton does not survive in Grafton's papers at Suffolk RO (Bury St Edmunds) or at Northamptonshire RO.

6   Grafton's letter to Lindsey seems not to have survived. But see Letter 700, in which Grafton was reported to be much more optimistic about the grain harvest.

7   For Belsham's sermon see Letter 682, n. 18. The publisher was Joseph Johnson.

8   See Letter 702.

9   Belsham took a small number of private pupils at his house at Grove Place, Hackney, but it has not proved possible to identify these two individuals. Probably they were the sons of members of his Gravel Pit congregation; Williams, p. 503 refers to the lectures which he gave to the young people of the congregation.

10   The letter which Lindsey intended to send to Priestley at the beginning of Sept. 1800, either via Philadelphia or the New York mail boat, has almost certainly not survived.

11   'Peter Porcupine' was the pseudonym adopted by William Cobbett (1762–1835), and the *Porcupine's Gazette* was the title of his newspaper in Philadelphia. See Letter 704, n. 4.

12   Lindsey's hand is not quite clear at this point; 'lout' in Johnson's *Dictionary of the English language* is defined as 'a mean aukward fellow; a bumpkin; a clown'.

13   Ann Belsham.

704. To THOMAS BELSHAM   **15 SEPTEMBER 1800**

Text: DWL, MS 12.57 (21).
Addressed: To/The Rev[d]. Thomas Belsham/Grove Place/Hackney
                   [in Hannah Lindsey's hand] Penny Post/Sep[tr] 15th
Endorsed: [By Belsham] M[r] Lindsey Sept[r]: 15: 1800
Postmarked: 7 o'Clock SP 15 1800 N.[T]

Mordon. Sept (15) 1800.

Dear Sir,

I make haste to acquaint you, that I yesterday received a Letter from M[r] Joseph Priestley, dated July 25. Philadelphia, apprizing me of his safe arrival at that place after a passage of 60 days, but that M[r] Vaughan being out of the Town, he coud get no satisfactory intelligence of his family, only some information that M[rs]. Priestley was unwell, which made him anxious to be at home, and therefore was setting out the next day, and c[d]. add nothing more, but w[d]. write again the first opportunity from Northumberland.[1]

At the same time I had another letter from D[r] Priestley, dated North __ d June 19. inclosing two printed Letters, one from M[r] W[m]. Priestley, vindicating himself from the atrocious act against his father's life, with which he had been publicly charged in the Reading paper of the 26th April: The other Letter from D[r]. Priestley to his son, dated North ___ nd May. 13. corroborating what he had advanced against such a charge, and attributing to the malignity of party-spirit the Letter in the Reading news paper, whose writer was well known, and his design to add to his affliction &c.[2]

His Letter to me begins with desiring, that if the Reading Letter referred to, shoud make its appearance here in the English News papers as he suspected it would, I should let those sent be inserted.[3] And if Peter Porcupine, now in England, or any body else should publish the Reading Letter, I shall do as he bids me.[4] But I trust there will be no call for the thing. You will judge for yourself, how far it may be proper on this ground to exculpate W. Priestley from the accusation to those friends in the West who laid it home to him. To you I would say it, that tho' I am persuaded the husband w[d] abhor the deed, I cannot say, that the wife stands quite clear in my opinion: But you will better judge when you have the documents before you, which will be now in a few weeks.[5]

His Letter to me is of a most truly pious caste as they ever are, but rather with a gloom of melancholy about them, w[ch]. is unusual. Near the conclusion he says on naming M[r] Finch's behaviour; "At present I am sometimes ready to say with Jacob, that *many things are against me*;[6] but tho' they do not *shake* my faith, they *try* it["].[7] He gives a pleasing account, w[ch] consoles him much, of six young men, who are & have been for some time his constant hearers at North ___ nd, who have made very extraordinary improvements under him in religious knowlege & virtue, and are particularly zealous for the divine Unity: "Four of them, he concludes, are going to work at the Federal city (they are carpenters) and I shall furnish em with books. Wherever they go, they will, I doubt not, make proselytes, and they are strictly virtuous & conscientious".[8]

He mentions his having rec[d]. the box of books in the Washington, w[ch] had been at Lisbon;[9] and lately some Cambridge papers for June & July, so that now he has 1799 compleat:[10] and a parcell of Morning Chronicles for 1797 – but he had not rec[d] the present from M[r] Livius,[11] which you announced some time ago, nor the work of your brother that you mention.[12] If the family of the Vaughans are with you pray make our due respects to them & also to your sister.[13] My wife joins in all affectionate regards with –

Dear Sir, Your most truly obliged

    T. Lindsey.

1   I have not located this letter from Joseph Priestley junior to Lindsey, from Philadelphia, and dated 25 July 1800. Mrs Priestley was his first wife, Elizabeth, née Ryland.

2   Priestley's letter to Lindsey of 19 June 1800 may be found in DWL, MS 12.13 and is partly printed in Rutt, I, 439–41. The copies of the 'two printed Letters' seem not to have survived. For the Pennsylvania newspaper the *Reading Weekly Advertiser* and its attacks on Priestley over the alleged 'poisoning' (n. 5, below), see F. W. Gibbs, *Joseph Priestley. Adventurer in science and truth* (London, 1965), pp. 240–1.

3   Elements of this story from the *Reading Weekly Advertiser* appeared in the British newspaper press only much later, and in an indirect form.

4   William Cobbett's newspaper, the *Porcupine's Gazette*, was published in Philadelphia between 1794 and 1799. Cobbett returned to Britain in 1800. Priestley's anxiety lest Cobbett print this story (n. 5, below) was understandable. In Aug. 1798, Cobbett had denounced him in the *Porcupine's Gazette* as a sympathizer with the French Revolution and a subversive presence in the United States who should be deported. He based these allegations on letters to Priestley and to Benjamin Vaughan from John Hurford Stone (see Letter 574, n. 3) in Paris in 1794, which the British government had intercepted and which had been published in London. The letters gave the impression that Priestley and Vaughan were implicated in a treasonable conspiracy against the British government. Priestley replied to these allegations in his *Letters to the inhabitants of Northumberland* in 1799.

5   William Priestley was accused in 1800 of seeking to poison his father and the rest of the family by the use of arsenic. It appears that his restless and volatile temperament caused difficulties in his relationship with his father. Priestley's biographers suggest that, perhaps while drunk, William added tartar emetic to the family's flour, which produced vomiting but not a threat to life; see Schofield, *Enlightened Joseph Priestley*, p. 406, and Gibbs, *Joseph Priestley*, pp. 240–1. It seems that Lindsey remained suspicious that William Priestley's wife Margaret, née Foulke, was not entirely without blame in this matter. If so, his suspicions had probably been aroused by Priestley's letter to him of 12 Sept. 1799, in which Priestley expressed disapproval of Margaret Foulke's 'malignancy' towards the wife of Joseph Priestley junior; DWL, MS 12.13 (passage omitted by Rutt, I, 421–2).

6   This is probably a reference to Jacob's lament in Genesis, xlii. 36, 'All these things are against me.' Although not an exact quotation from the Bible, Priestley's remark was probably a broader reflection in which he compared his feelings to those of Jacob in adversity. I owe this suggestion to John and Kathleen Court.

7   For William Finch's bankruptcy, see Letter 657, n. 10. Priestley was concerned by Finch's evident inability to retrieve his financial situation, which had damaging implications for Sarah Finch. Writing to Lindsey on 13 Aug. 1800, he enclosed a letter to Sarah Finch, 'to be sent if she be living, otherwise suppress it, as I do not wish it to fall into the hands of Mr Finch'; DWL, MS 12.13 (passage omitted by Rutt, I, 441–2). Sarah Finch died in 1803.

8   Possibly this is a quotation from the section of Priestley's letter to Lindsey of 13 Aug. 1800 which is missing from DWL, MS 12.13; Rutt, I, 441–2, prints part of the surviving section. Washington became the federal capital of the United States, in succession to Philadelphia, in 1800.

9   On 15 Apr. 1800, the London newspaper *The Star* quoted a letter from Lisbon to the effect that the *Washington*, an 'East India ship, Captain Williamson', had suffered damage from an attack by a French privateer, but after repairs had been able to resume its voyage (to America).

10 This almost certainly refers to Benjamin Flower's newspaper the *Cambridge Intelligencer*.

11 In his letter to Belsham of 30 Mar. 1800, Priestley wrote 'I beg my respectful compliment to Mr. Livius, and thanks for his intended present, but I have not yet heard of its arrival. I am interested in every thing relating to the propagation of Christianity in any form, and no sect has done so much in this way as the Moravians; I admire their patience and perseverance'; Rutt, I, 429. Mr Livius was probably George Peter Livius (1743–1816), who was the son of a diplomat of German origin, was born at Lisbon, moved with his family to England and served the East India Company during the 1770s. From 1775 to 1782, he was commissary-general under Warren Hastings in India. On his return to England, he met, and subsequently joined, the Moravians in London and spent his final years with the Moravian community in Bedford. See J. C. S. Mason, *The Moravian church and the*

missionary awakening 1760–1800 (Woodbridge, 2001), pp. 81–3. His intended present for Priestley was probably a book or similar publication or a financial contribution to one of Priestley's last works, perhaps his *History of the Christian church*. I am grateful to Edna Cooper and Robin Hutton for the identification of Livius and for providing me with evidence of his Moravian connexions.

12   This work of William Belsham was probably his *Memoirs of the kings of Great Britain* or his *Remarks on a late publication, styled the history of the politics of Great Britain and France, etc.* (London, 1801). The latter work was part of William Belsham's controversy with Herbert Marsh; see Letter 705, n. 2.

13   Ann Belsham.

705. To THOMAS BELSHAM   3 OCTOBER 1800

Text: DWL, MS 12.57 (22).
Addressed: To/The Rev^d. W^m. Belsham[1]/Grove Place/Hackney
Endorsed: [By Belsham] Mr Lindsey Oct^r: 4: Nov
Postmarked: 7 o'Clock 4 OC 1800 N.T. To be delivered 10 o'Clock

Mordon. Oct. 3. 1800.

Dear Sir,

You are very good, in the midst of so much occupation, to spare time to let us know how you are. We are sorry you have suffered so much, but trust you will now hear no more of your complaint. I am inclined to think almost as well of Mr Marsh, who know him only by hearsay and his writings, as Mr Frend who is his relation and knows him so well, but I was hurt that he shoud engage in the politics of the day, lest he sh^d be diverted from Theology, in which he has been and is capable of being most useful, especially from his acquaintance with German authors, and skill in their language.[2]

I am sensible how much your hours are taken up to have any work cut out for you by others: But all I wished to have done to set off Dr Priestleys Essay with credit to his country woud have been to have had it come out with such an Eloge and testimony as you have given him in a note to your admirable discourse at Bristol, which I think abundant in excellent matter to the purpose as any thing you ever published, suited to the persons and the times; and I do not know, but with your leave, I may steal this said Eloge, and prefix it to the Essay.[3]

I am glad, I can now say, that if all be well, we shall probably return to take up our quarters in Essex Street the latter end of the next week. I shall be glad for the pleasure of seeing you, and likewise of communicating to you the contents of a letter I had from Northumberland 4 days ago, of so late date as August 13. imparting the joy he had rec^d from his son Joseph's arrival, and some other things which must remain intirely with you and ourselves.[4]

He has also sent me "An Attempt to explain the 18th chapter of Isaiah["], occasioned by the perusal of B^p. Horsely on the subject, wch is as probable as any other interpretation I have seen, but does not give much satisfaction on the subject. He mentions a new interpretation of the 53^d of Isaiah, which I should be more curious to have a sight of, and which he has upon the anvil, with Observations on Infant Baptism.[5]

I thank you for kindly engaging to secure Mr W. Christie a vote for allowing him his due allotment of Books at our Unitarian Society's next meeting, if I shoud not be there myself to speak for him.[6]

My wife here comes in, and charges me with her affectionate regards, and to say, that she hopes you will favour us with your company to drink tea next week on the Saturday, or Sunday, as may suit your convenience.[7] We hope your sister is well and desire kind remembrances.

I am always, Dear Sir, most truly Yours

T. Lindsey.

---

1   Lindsey intended to write Thomas Belsham rather than the latter's brother William, who was not a 'reverend' and did not reside at Grove Place, Hackney.

2   Herbert Marsh (1757–1839), biblical scholar and authority on the work of German scriptural critics, was a cousin of William Frend. He was a supporter of Pitt's ministry. His involvement in 'the politics of the day' took the form of several works published in Germany in 1798–9, notably *A history of the politics of Great Britain and France*. This work was also published by Stockdale in London in 1800, and it provoked a reply from Belsham's brother William, entitled *Remarks on a late publication*. Further exchanges between them were published in 1801. Marsh was subsequently Lady Margaret professor of divinity at Cambridge (1807) and bishop of Peterborough from 1819 to 1839.

3   Thomas Belsham's *Freedom of enquiry, and zeal in the diffusion of Christian truth* (see Letter 682, n. 18) included a footnote (p. 6, n. (a)) praising Priestley's *Comparison of the institutions*. In his editorial preface to Priestley's *Inquiry into the knowledge of the antient Hebrews*, p. iv, Lindsey referred to Belsham's *Freedom of enquiry* as an 'excellent Discourse', which showed how usefully Priestley had been employed during his American exile.

4   The manuscript of Priestley's letter to Lindsey of 13 Aug. 1800 is in DWL, MS 12.13, but the latter section of it is missing, evidently cut away; see Letter 704, n. 8. Rutt, I, 441–2, printed part of the surviving section. In the surviving section, Priestley referred to the safe return to America of his son Joseph and mentioned briefly his 'new interpretation' of Isaiah liii, but it can be assumed that the items which 'must remain intirely with you and ourselves' were confined to the missing section – which no doubt explains why it is missing.

5   Priestley sent a copy of this work on Isaiah to Lindsey with his letter of 13 Aug. 1800; Rutt, I, 441–2, suggesting that it might be suitable for the *MM*. With his letter to Lindsey of 30 July 1801, he sent a two-page draft of his 'Notes on Isaiah'; DWL, MS 12.13. Priestley's *Letter to an antipaedobaptist* was published in Northumberland in 1802.

6   At its monthly committee meeting on 13 Nov. 1800, the Unitarian Society resolved that William Christie of Winchester, Virginia, be provided with his arrears of books and that Lindsey be requested to inform him of this resolution. Lindsey himself was not present at the meeting; Unitarian Society minute book, p. 71.

7   Saturday 11 or Sunday 12 Oct. 1800.

---

706. To WILLIAM FREND   **24 OCTOBER 1800**

Text: CUL, Add. MS 7886 (Frend papers), no. 170.
Addressed: [In Hannah Lindsey's hand] To/M[r]. Frend,/Richard Reynolds's Esq[r].,/Paxton near S[t] Neots,/Huntingdonshire
Postmarked: OC 24 800

Dear Sir,

Feeling myself so little capable of giving advice in difficult cases, I believe I should have declined taking any notice of the latter part of your letter till I saw you, had not I imagined you would be disappointed in hearing nothing from me upon it.[1] And therefore you would have received this much sooner, had not M[r] Belsham been hindred calling upon us for a whole week, and I was unwilling to say any thing till I had taken him into consultation, especially as you had desired it.

The terms you propose are exceeding liberal and moderate.[2] M[r] B.[3] says, they cannot be lower. He never gave lectures but one winter to 30 persons, 2 guineas each person: but it was more of a sociable visit from part of his congregation, than any formal lectures.[4] No lectures but medical ones are well attended. The first course of the Aikins did pretty well, as many of their young friends and acquaintance made a point of it: But at the last course there was a great falling off.[5] Still less may be expected from so dry a subject as Mathematics in these days. At a University other things mix, and excite and enliven it. In Town a young man must have a peculiar turn for the subject to attend on purpose. An Advertisement would call attention to your place of residence, and procure you now and then a paragraph from the Porcupine gazette,[6] but would not perhaps draw much attention to the Science you wish to teach. Private recommendation would seem the least objectionable and most effectual way. It is not merely the *odium theologicum*, but *politicum* also, far more pestilential at present, which has marked you out as an infectious person. I am truly mortified to be able to be of so little use to one of such superior talents and abilities, and what is more to be prized, with dispositions to serve both God and man with them. But I live in hope, that with your continued efforts and the aid of friends, there [may be][7] a means of emerging.

Of the above subject you may depend upon my having said nothing to our excellent friends with whom you now are,[8] and I rejoice to hear of your being so happy and chearful; which must be wherever you are, for I know none who has so little gloom, and a more constant fund for variety and entertainment. Never any remarks more truly oracular than those you began with, on the most baneful expedient of the stoppage of the bank and the permission to issue paper money without end, of which as M[r] Morgan of the Bridge[9] was mentioning two days ago, the public in general begin now to feel the effects, and to be quite affrighted; but they will be more so by and by.[10] He is indeed fully persuaded that our's is not a redeemable case. Cash has for some time disappeared. They have received none at the office, nor do they give any at the Bank. As I am writing on Thursday evening to be ready for to morrow,[11] when I shall be obliged to be out most of the day, our neighbour M[r] Joyce steps in to tell us, that there is a report, of the truth of w[ch] he has no doubt, that L[d] Holland is sent to the Tower, on his coming home, and that the cause of his seizure is his going to France without leave of the Privy [Counci]l.[12] If he has done any thing of the kind contrary [MS torn] he is much to be blamed; as[?] he must be certain [the?] [A]dministration would be ready to avail themselves of such a faux pas; and make the worst of it to the Public, especially at this season, when they are glad of any[13] to amuse or to terrify and to turn the nation from looking on them and their measures.[14]

I was with M[rs] Jebb to day and pleased to find her tolerably well, but under some concern for the loss of her Great Nephew, whom she had taken a great affection to, tho he had barely compleated his month.[15] She was mentioning her surprize that M[r]. Tyrwhitt shoud be joined w[h]. D[r] Jowett and M[r] Simeon in a legacy of £800 w[ch] has been left to each of them for any charitable purposes they might think proper.[16] The town in general, and this part of it in particular is at present most empty, but in a fortnights time there will be no lack of company. My wife desires you will thank M[rs] Reynolds for her letter.[17] In no long time I shall pay my respects to the Master of the mansion, and shall be glad to receive any commands that you may have before you leave the country.[18]

My wife sends her best respects, and I am always Dear Sir, very truly Your's

T. Lindsey

---

1   This letter from Frend to Lindsey seems not to have survived.
2   After his banishment from Cambridge University in 1793, Frend lived in London, engaging in radical

activity, conducting an affair with Mary Hays, writing a series of political pamphlets and sporadically taking pupils; see Knight, *William Frend*, ch. 13.

3   Thomas Belsham.

4   The subjects of Belsham's lectures to his congregation and to others interested, in 1800, were meta-physics, 'the positive Institutions of Christianity' and 'the various English Versions of the Old and New Testaments'; see Williams, pp. 495, 501. In later years, he regularly gave lectures after the 6.30 evening service at Essex Street chapel.

5   This refers to the course of lectures on chemistry, beginning in 1799, given in London by Arthur Aikin and his brother Charles Rochemont Aikin.

6   For William Cobbett's *Porcupine's Gazette*, see Letter 704, n. 4. From 1802, Cobbett published a successor, *Cobbett's Weekly Political Register*.

7   The manuscript is slightly torn at this point.

8   Richard Reynolds and his family at Little Paxton.

9   William Morgan, chief actuary to the Equitable Assurance Society, whose offices were at Chatham Place, near Blackfriars Bridge.

10 For the suspension of cash payments by the Bank of England in 1797, see Letter 651.

11 23 Oct. 1800 was a Thursday; 'the morrow' was 24 Oct., the date of the postmark of this letter.

12 The MS is slightly torn at this point and the word 'Council' is almost completely lost.

13 Possibly Lindsey omitted a word (perhaps 'thing') at this point; or perhaps he meant any *faux-pas*.

14 Henry Richard Vassall Fox (1773–1840), 3rd Baron Holland, and his wife Elizabeth, Lady Holland, travelled extensively in Germany between July and Sept. 1800. After a journey through France they arrived at Dover on 11 Oct. 1800; see BL, Add. MS 51735, fos. 176, 178–81, 187–8, 190–1, 192–3, 200–1, 204–5. Shortly thereafter, several London newspapers reported, in an obviously facetious strain, that 'a noble lord' had been committed to the Tower of London for entering the country without a passport; *London Packet, or New Lloyd's Evening Post*, 22–4 Oct. 1800, *General Evening Post*, 23–5 Oct. 1800. The *St James's Chronicle or the British Evening Post*, 23–5 Oct. 1800, added the suggestion that the peer in question was 'a Noble Lord recently returned from the Continent', whose arrest could be 'attributed to his having entered France without authority of our Government'. Because Holland was a leading supporter of the opposition in the house of lords, and the nephew of Charles James Fox, Lindsey and Jeremiah Joyce seem to have assumed that the story was true. It was certainly consistent with their depiction of Pitt's administration as highly repressive. However, the story was soon denied; see, for example, *Albion and Evening Advertiser*, 24 Oct. 1800. In fact, by the time of their arrival at Dover, Holland's party had been provided with passports at short notice; BL, Add. MS 51735, fo. 204.

15 Ann Jebb's maiden name was Torkington. Probably the great-nephew who had died belonged to the Torkington, rather than the Jebb, side of her family; she was not on the best of terms with the Jebbs. Another possibility is the great-nephew of John Jebb's only brother, David Jebb (*c.* 1738–1826), of Slane, county Meath. I owe these suggestions to Dr Anthony Page.

16 Possibly Dr Joseph Jowett (1751–1813), jurist and fellow of Trinity Hall, Cambridge. The evangelical Charles Simeon, minister of the Holy Trinity church, Cambridge, was one of his pallbearers. For Robert Tyrwhitt, see Vol. I, Letter 188, n. 1; and Letter 409, n. 8.

17 I have not located this letter from Mary Catherine Reynolds to Hannah Lindsey, although there is other evidence that they were correspondents (see Letter 425, n. 7). There are surviving letters from Mary Catherine Reynolds to Frend in CUL, Add. MS 7886 (Frend papers).

18 It has not proved possible to confirm that Frend left the country at this time. Evidently he was still in England in Dec. 1800 (or had returned by then); Knight, *William Frend*, p. 231.

707. To JOHN ROWE   10 NOVEMBER 1800

Text: JRUL, Lindsey Letters, vol. II, no. 101
Addressed: To/The Rev^d. J. Rowe/Ashley Place/near/Bristol.
Postmarked: NO 10 800

London. Nov. 10. 1800

Dear Sir,

Early in the month of July we left town to pass three weeks along with some of our oldest friends in Surrey,[1] but did not return for upward of three months, my wife only being obliged to see London twice for part of a day on some business, whilst I remained on the spot, passing the time happily, and with constant cause of thankfulness for the health we enjoyed. In the long interval, we had frequent opportunities of hearing with great pleasure of yourself and your Lady and family, and of your proceedings at Bristol and in the West, especially while our common friend M[r] Belsham was with you and in those parts of whose Discourse at your annual meeting, I had received very extraordinary and favorable reports, but which did not lose its value at all by long expectation when I saw it: for matter more suitable, more seasonable, or more crouded together without losing its perspicuity, I have rarely met with in so small a compass on the like occasion.[2]

If your expectation be in any degree raised like mine, it will give you joy to be informed, that he has within these few days given into M[r] Johnsons hands, his Lectures on the theory of the human Mind, tho' that will not be exactly the title of the Work, which D[r] Priestley so greatly longed to see when in England and urged him to print, which now after much pressing and revising is finished, and will make two volumes in 8[vo]: from which I augur, and not amiss, the youth of the rising generation will reap great advantage. And I shall be happy in living to see such a work out of the Press.[3]

I presume, that as they were plants of a sort of Shrewsbury-growth and connexion, You must have seen good M[r] Orton's Letters to M[r] Stedman; and D[r] or S[r] Ja[s] Stonehouse's to the same gentleman.[4] One cannot but honour the piety of the former, his simplicity, and earnest zeal to make his pupil good and useful, and wish it may have had the desired effect. But the Doctor[5] is so full of himself, and of a censorious intolerant spirit against all that did not come up to his degree of orthodoxy, that his curate[6] could have received little benefit from him, if not a great deal of hurt. I much wonder how a gentleman, who was so near a neighbour of M[r] Tayleur's, and must have probably both seen and known him, could hear such abuse of Socinians and of D[r] Priestley by name, without checking his friend their accuser and setting him right.[7] As to D[r] Stonhouse himself, I will not say as one does that had known him long and well, that his religion was vanity and Self-preaching; but hold his calumnies to be unworthy of notice: And should be glad to know what M[r] Tayleur thought of these two gentlemen, if he happend to know anything of them.

At length I have made up a parcell of books for your acceptance to disperse. I have sent only one hundred Elwall's Triumph of Truth, printed with[t] D[r] Priestley's name, tho' the best he ever printed for its size, and what must by the force of its evidence being a narrative, and a real fact compell every person of any understanding that looks into it, to believe & worship, one God, only even the Father of Jesus Christ.[8] I woud not send you more, at first, of these, for fear of surfeiting, but I have many more hundreds ready to be sent, whe[ne]ver you call for them. I think M[r] Estlyn (to whom our kind respects) as well as yourself will think the Northamptonshire Farmers *Second Caution against Trinitarianism* capable of bringing over even M[r] Andrew Fuller from his strict Calvinism, if he *have an ear to hear*.[9]

But I add no more: when you receive the Tracts, which set out this day in the waggon for you at Ashley Place near Bristol,[10] be so good, at your leisure to tell me that you have received them: that M[rs] Rowe, yourself and amiable family are well: M[r] Estlyn also: and that the truth continues to make its way around you in the midst of many adversaries.

I have time only to add that Mr Belsham has just been with us and desired me to make his comp^ts –

Always very truly & affectionately Yours

T. Lindsey

Excuse this blot.[11]

---

1   These friends were Sophia and Frances Chambers, of Morden, Surrey.

2   For this sermon of Belsham, see Letter 682, n. 18.

3   See Letter 682, n. 19.

4   *Letters from the Rev. Mr. Job Orton; and the Rev. Sir James Stonhouse ... to the Rev. Thomas Stedman, MA, vicar of St Chad's, Shrewsbury* (2 vols., Shrewsbury, 1800). For James Stonhouse (1716–95), see Vol. I, Letter 4, n. 6. He was rector of Little Cheverell, Wiltshire, from 1764 and rector of the adjoining parish of Great Cheverell from 1779, holding both livings until his death, and inherited his family's baronetcy in 1792. He was the author of *Hints from a minister to his curate, for the management of his parish* (Bristol, 1774). Job Orton (1717–83), a pupil of Philip Doddridge at Northampton, was minister to the Presbyterian High Street chapel, Shrewsbury, from 1741 to 1765. The *Letters* were edited for publication by Thomas Stedman, the recipient, himself. Nine years earlier, he had published *Letters to a young clergyman, from the late Job Orton* (Shrewsbury, 1791); he was the young clergyman.

5   James Stonhouse.

6   Thomas Stedman had been curate to Stonhouse at Cheverell; see *Letters from the Rev. Mr. Job Orton; and the Rev. Sir James Stonhouse ... to the Rev. Thomas Stedman*, I, v.

7   Stedman was vicar of St Chad's, Shrewsbury, from 1783 until his death in 1825, and was thus a neighbour of William Tayleur. For Stonhouse's attacks on Socinianism, and his side-swipe at Priestley, which Stedman duly published, see *Letters from the Rev. Mr. Job Orton; and the Rev. Sir James Stonhouse ... to the Rev. Thomas Stedman*, II, 141, 176, 221. Stonhouse took particular exception to the fact that from the 1780s Socinianism was preached at the High Street chapel, Shrewsbury, where the orthodox Job Orton had been minister.

8   *The triumph of truth; being an account of the trial of Mr E. Elwall, for heresy and blasphemy, at Stafford assizes ...to which are added, extracts from some other pieces of Mr. Elwall's, concerning the unity of God. And a few additional illustrations. By the author of an appeal to the serious and candid professors of Christianity, &c* [i.e. Priestley] (Leeds, 1771). A second edition was published in London in 1775. In 1792, Joseph Johnson published in London a further edition of Priestley's *Appeal to the serious and candid*, with Elwall's trial, entitled 'The triumph of truth' appended (pp. 31–8).

9   This work was *A second caution against trinitarianism; or an inquiry whether the system has not some tendency to lead people unto deism and atheism. In a letter addressed to the Rev. Mr. Fuller, Kettering. By a Northamptonshire farmer* (Market Harborough, 1800). The Northamptonshire farmer was probably the baptist minister Edward Sharman; see Letter 630, n. 3. 'Mr Fuller' was the baptist controversial writer Andrew Fuller, minister to a baptist chapel at Kettering from 1782 until his death in 1815. The previous year, the 'Northamptonshire farmer' had published *A caution against trinitarianism*. For Henry Davis, dissenting minister at Wigston Magna, see Letter 630, n. 3. The quotation 'Ear to hear' is (slightly) adapted from Mark iv. 9.

10   See Letter 667, n. 11.

11   At the end of the penultimate paragraph of this letter (after 'adversaries') Lindsey wrote four lines and then crossed them out heavily, rendering them illegible.

708. To ROBERT MILLAR   **13 NOVEMBER 1800**

 Text: DWL, MS 12.46 (23).
 Printed: Graham, 'Unhappy country', 157 (third paragraph).
 Addressed: To/M[r] Rob[t]. Millar/Merchant/Dundee
 Endorsed: London 13th Nov 1800/Mr Lindsey/He has got a legacy
      £1000/Dr Priestley – £2000 [endorsed in a different hand]
      Dr Disney, £1000/All three legacies left by a lady
 Postmarked: Postmark missing.

London. Nov. 13. 1800

Dear Sir,

I seize the very first opportunity of a Member coming to Town[1] to procure a cover for you, not that I should have made any scruple of troubling you with the postage, had I had any real business, but I thought that mine was such as might wait; especially as we had not been long arrived at our winter quarters in Essex-Street.

For tho' we went into the country in July with a view only to be three weeks absent, we remained with our friends betwixt 3 and 4 months, and with some difficulty could get away at the last. Thanks to the divine mercy, hot as the summer turned out, we enjoyed our health unusually well, as also did our friends with whom we sojourned, to which my wife had the great happiness of being very instrumental.[2]

I do not find that any of my friends, who are in the habit of hearing most frequently from him, have lately received any letters from M[r] Palmer, at which they rather wonder; but a friend of our's, only a week ago, met with a gentleman who had just come from Botany Bay, who, at the house where he met him, was giving a most favourable account of M[r] Palmer; ["] that he was in health and spirits; had a good brick house of his own sashed; a large farm in fine cultivation; a sloop ready to sail to Norfolk Island or wherever necessary for articles of food or traffic; that he is upon the best terms with the gentlemen who govern the settlement, and that it is in a very improving state; but he did not intimate any intention to return"[.][3] So far we were glad to get, though it was only so general information: but should have been glad to have inquired how M[r] James Ellis, and particularly, whether M[r] Palmer had found any means of teaching the knowlege of the one true God, and of his goodness to Mankind by Jesus Christ. If I should learn any thing of these things, or any thing further of him, You shall be acquainted.

It will be a pleasure to have it confirmed under your hand; that M[rs] Millar and yourself have found the late summer and autumn as prop[i]tious to the enjoyment of the blessing of health as we have done, and that it has been favourable likewise to the fruits of the Earth, and contributed to remove from you one of the divine scourges of sinful nations with which the nation in general has been threatened, and which nothing but the removal of another scourge under which we have been long suffering can fully take away.[4] At present the happy moment still seems distant. But we must wait to see what the great council of the nation just assembled may bring forth.[5]

I shall take it as a favour to receive a few lines from you, not regarding the postage; for I must tell You that since I last wrote we have been favoured with a legacy of one thousand pounds Stock, 4 per cents. by a lady of our congregation, who has left the like sum to D[r] Disney, and <u>two</u> thousand pounds the same stock to D[r] Priestley, with other kindnesses to my wife: so that our pattern is now by no means narrow.[6] I should be glad likewise to know, whether I named any other Tract wch I wished to send you, besides Mr Flowers account of the proceedings against him.[7] Be so good likewise to mention how the worthy Dr Small does; I trust he is not moved by the iniquity of his adversaries, which others esteem his crown and glory. You will also naturally make mention of your own little church, which I hold to be a respectable branch of Christs own, and persuade myself it will be owned as such by him. Of Dr Priestley I have heard lately & frequently. He is happy in the enjoyment of health, of a calm mind, and chearful towards God in the midst of many trials. His Son Joseph was arrived safe from England, with the acc^t of the recovery of his daughter Mrs Finch, which added greatly to his joy & comforts.[8] My wife unites in all that can bespeak sincerest regards and affectionate esteem for yourself and Mrs Millar, and I remain always

Dear Sir, most truly Yours

T. Lindsey

---

1   The address page of this letter does not have the endorsement of a member of parliament as a mark of the privilege of franking. Probably the MP was Benjamin Hobhouse, James Martin or William Smith.

2   See Letter 707. Lindsey and his wife had been staying with their friends Sophia and Frances Chambers in Morden, Surrey, where Hannah Lindsey had used her medical skills to good effect.

3   Lindsey did not identify the gentleman who provided this report; possibly the friend who conveyed the report to him was Jeremiah Joyce, who had prepared Palmer's *Narrative* for publication in 1795.

4   Lindsey referred to the 'scourge' of food shortages and high prices, from which only the removal of the scourge of war would save the nation.

5   The new session of parliament had opened on 11 Nov. 1800.

6   For these bequests, see Letters 698 and 699, and Elizabeth Rayner's will (TNA: PRO PROB 11/1345, fos. 264r–274v). She did indeed bequeath to Theophilus and Hannah Lindsey £1,000 in Bank of England 4 per cent annuities, and the same sum to John and Jane Disney. She also left many of her household possessions, including a pair of silver candlesticks, and the remaining lease of her house in Clapham, to Lindsey and his wife.

7   This work was *The proceedings of the house of lords in the case of B*[enjamin] *F*[lower] *for a libel on the bishop of Llandaff, with remarks and animadversions on the writings of the bishop of Llandaff ... By the Printer* [i.e. Benjamin Flower] (Cambridge, 1800).

8   There are surviving letters from Priestley to Lindsey, dated 19 June, 13 Aug. and 16 Oct. 1800, in DWL, MS 12.13. That of 13 Aug. mentioned the safe return of Priestley's son Joseph to America; see Rutt, I, 441. Possibly the references to the recovery of Sarah Finch were contained in the missing section of this letter; see Letter 704, n. 8.

---

709. To CHRISTOPHER WYVILL   23 NOVEMBER 1800

Text: NYRO, ZFW 7/2/144/7, Wyvill of Constable Burton MSS.
Printed: Ditchfield, 'Lindsey–Wyvill correspondence', 164–5 (third paragraph); 168 (fifth paragraph); 171 (second paragraph).
Addressed: [In Hannah Lindsey's hand] To/Mrs Wyville,/Burton Hall/near,/ Bedale,/Yorkshire
Postmarked: NO 24 800

London. Novr. 23. 1800

Dear Sir,

I received your kind letter in its due time from Halnaby;[1] and have literally been waiting ever since for something to say in return for it, but am now tired out with waiting. You will probably soon see the Vicar of Brignal, who has been passing a fortnight with his friends here in his way from conducting his eldest son to Cambridge, and who promised us soon to pay you a visit and tell you the state of things here as well as the state in which he had put his father's works, your common care, into the hands of Mr Flower at Cambridge.[2] He left town on Thursday evening last, and we trust got safe home on the Saturday.[3]

We are assured you take a sincere part in any good fortune that befalls us, and accept your kind congratulations on what our kind friend Mrs Rayner has done for us. Her small house at Clapham, of which she has left us the remainder of the lease, long enough for our lives, as well as very ample for us if we had wanted one to live in, but not being able to keep two, we shall certainly dispose of to add somewhat to our income by that means.[4] She bequeathed to us at the same time one thousand pounds Stock 4 per cents. The like sum to Dr Disney. two thousand pounds Ditto to Dr Priestley, to whom it will be very acceptable and seasonable, to Dr Blackburne the like sum in the 3 per cents.[5]

I had the good fortune to see a letter the last week, written by a gentleman who was of a party that spent some days very lately at Mr Whitebreads in Bedfordshire, present Mr Grey and his lady, L^d and Lady Wm Russell, Mr Fox, and some other gentlemen, the D. of Bedford was prevented coming.[6] A more pleasant and agreeable company for wit and chearfulness and information, he never consorted with. It was endeavoured to convince Mr Fox, that now at last the season was come, when it was necessary for him to stand forth in his place in parliament and save the country. But powerful arg^{ts} did he produce, especially with relation to himself individually, that it was better for him to keep at a distance, that instead of being able to persuade him, says one of the ablest of the party, he went very near to the making me a proselyte.[7]

You will excuse me, my good Sir, saying to You, that I think you should take to yourself the consequence that your long services to the County of York and the Public have merited, and by no means to put yourself foremost to call a meeting of the Freeholders, but wait till Necessity and the Times and other persons have brought them together, and then take the place and leading part, which will become you.

I was informed yesterday from very good authority, that there are five thousand regular troops, and canon [sic] lately disposed in the neighbourhood of Birmingham, so as to be easily brought thither should there be a call for them, and that serious apprehensions were entertained of disturbances in that part of the country, as well as in Nottinghamshire and Derbyshire &c where similar precautions had been used.[8]

I had this very morning a few lines from Syon,[9] which mention it being the sentiment of many, that the late speech of the Minister in the house here, will authorize the Chief Consul, if it were not in train before, to compell Count Cobentzel,[10] to sign a peace immediately, or an end will be instantly put to the Truce upon the Continent. "When you write to Mr Wyvill, he concludes, I will trouble you to present my compliments to him, and tell him that I find most people now begin to change their tone, but yet I fear, nothing effectual is likely to happen during this Parliament; which however will most probably end this next year.["][11]

We rejoice to learn that yourself and your Lady are in such good health, and all your amiable family well and improving. Our united respects wait upon you both with wishes of all good to all your young folks present and absent. I leave my wife to direct this letter for me. I remain always Dear Sir, Your much obliged and faithful affectionate servant

      T. Lindsey

---

1   Halnaby Hall, Yorkshire, was the seat of Sir Ralph Milbanke (1747–1825), MP for Durham county from 1790 to 1812, and a supporter of the Foxite opposition in parliament.

2 The vicar of Brignall, Yorkshire, was Francis Blackburne, the eldest son of Archdeacon Blackburne. His edition of his father's works was published by Benjamin Flower in seven volumes in Cambridge in 1804. His own son of the same name matriculated at Sidney Sussex College, Cambridge, in the Lent term 1801 and graduated BA in 1804 (MA 1807). He was vicar of Bellarby, Yorkshire, from 1809 to 1829 and rector of Croscombe, Somerset, from 1826 until his death by drowning in 1829.

3 Thursday 20 Nov. and Saturday 22 Nov. 1800.

4 See Letter 698, n. 11. Theophilus and Hannah Lindsey did not live at Elizabeth Rayner's house at Clapham.

5 For these legacies, see Letter 698. Dr William Blackburne was physician to Elizabeth Rayner, and she did indeed bequeath to him £1,000 in Bank of England 3 per cent annuities; TNA: PRO PROB 11/1345, fo. 269v.

6 Samuel Whitbread (1764–1815), brewer, of Southill, Bedfordshire, was MP for Bedford from 1790 until 1815 and a Foxite whig. Charles Grey (1764–1845), the future whig leader and prime minister, was at this time MP for Northumberland. Lord William Russell (1767–1840) was MP for Surrey from 1789 to 1807; his wife was Lady Charlotte Anne (d. 1808), daughter of George Bussy Villiers, 4th earl of Jersey. Francis Russell (1765–1802), from 1771, 5th duke of Bedford, was a supporter of Fox and the target of Burke's *Letter to a noble lord* (London, 1796). Disappointingly, Lindsey did not identify the gentleman whose letter he had seen; a possibility is Benjamin Hobhouse, MP, at that time a supporter of the parliamentary opposition.

7 For the secession of the Foxites from parliament, see Letter 661. The new session of parliament began on 11 Nov. 1800 and Fox himself returned to the commons in Feb. 1801.

8 In Sept. 1800, after sharp increases in the price of flour and bread, there was a series of attacks on corn dealers, and on at least one mill, in Birmingham. As a result, troops, including a detachment of the seventeenth light dragoons and the Birmingham light horse were brought in; J.A. Langford, *A century of Birmingham life: or, a chronicle of local events, from 1741* (2 vols., Birmingham and London, 1868), II, 101–9. The *Derby Mercury*, 20 Nov. 1800, reported a riot in Derbyshire three days previously.

9 This is probably a reference to a (non-surviving) letter to Lindsey from the 2nd duke of Northumberland at Syon House.

10 Philipp Graf von Cobenzl (1741–1810), was the Austrian vice-chancellor, and, from 1792 to 1793, the chancellor. He was briefly the foreign minister in 1798, and vice-chancellor again in 1800. Pitt's *rôle* in the truce negotiations in the autumn of 1800 is discussed in Ehrman, *The Younger Pitt. The consuming struggle*, pp. 386–8. For the armistice between Austria and France, see Letter 697, n. 8.

11 This parliament was dissolved on 29 June 1802.

710. To WILLIAM ALEXANDER   9 DECEMBER 1800

Text: 'Letters of the Rev. Theophilus Lindsey. No. VIII',
                  UH, II, 87 (27 Dec. 1862), 432.

Note: This is the only section of this letter printed by the *UH*; the manuscript seems not to have survived.

London, Dec. 9th, 1800.

The sermon on the sin of schism is a fine exhibition of the temper of the nation at present, and the retrograde step which many have taken to the days of Sacheverel and good Queen Anne; and I thank you for a sight of it.[1] Dr. Horsley, however, takes a higher flight, and sticks not to accuse all liberal Dissenters and Socinians as Jacobins and Atheists; and one is sorry to find that many are so easy of belief as to take him at his word.[2] This same bishop, however, is much mortified to remain Bishop of Rochester, as he is said to have aimed at crossing the water and going to Armagh, which would have suited him wonderfully, in enabling him to pay his debts, and live in the state that becomes his order.[3]

1 This work was *A serious address from a minister to his parishioners, tending to guard them against the sin of schism, and to excite them to a devout attention to the worship and doctrines of the church, in two sermons. By a clergyman of the establishment* (Louth, 1800).

2 Horsley made this allegation in *The charge of Samuel [Horsley], lord bishop of Rochester, to the*

clergy of his diocese, delivered at his second general visitation, in the year 1800 (London, 1800), pp. 17–21.

3   The archbishopric of Armagh had become vacant with the death of William Newcome on 11 Jan. 1800. Newcome was succeeded not by Horsley but by William Stuart (1755–1822), bishop of St David's, and the fifth son of the former prime minister the earl of Bute. Horsley remained bishop of Rochester until his translation to St Asaph in 1802. For the possibility that he might have been translated to Armagh in 1800, and for his extensive debts (he was insolvent at the time of his death in 1806), see Mather, *High church prophet*, pp. 191, 298–9.

711. To ROBERT MILLAR   12 DECEMBER 1800

Text: DWL, MS 12.46 (24).
Printed: Graham, 'Unhappy country', 158–60 (short extracts from
                  third, fourth, fifth and seventh paragraphs).
Addressed: To/Mr Robt Millar/Merchant/Dundee
Postmarked: Postmark missing.

Dear Sir,

London Decr. 12. 1800

I sit down to acknowlege your most welcome letter,[1] with a disagreeable certainty of doing it very imperfectly, as I have but just rec^d a cover for you, which is dated a day sooner by mistake than I expected, and in expectation every moment of being called on by some persons on unavoidable business.

Yours met one from me on its road, which would give you pleasure from the short tho' defective account of our friend at Botany Bay.[2] No tidings have been since received from that place by any of his friends, or rather, had not been received a fortnight since, when I saw one of the principal of them.[3]

The times and the events of private life will often give a melancholy hue to our thoughts. In such circumstances was your last to me written, but not the less acceptable from the serious and suitable reflections it drew from you.

I was also particularly pleased, that they drew you to speak a little more of that valuable person Dr Ross, who is lately come to reside among you, of whose painful life you make the chief support and comfort, under the apprehension of the loss of such a sister as you describe.[4] Lest I be prevented by company I shall immediately, tho it be rather abruptly transcribe a part of a letter I yesterday rece^d. from Dr Priestley, because I think it will minister satisfaction to that worthy person as well as to yourself. I preface it with mentioning that the Doctor is not only well in health but in some degree of chearful spirits notwithstanding a very great trial he has experienced some month[s] since from the behaviour of his youngest son, William, an ugly affair, of which the less is said the better.[5]

He however enjoys a constant calm and happiness, by being able to be constantly and usefully employed, and by looking always beyond this present scene of things. One of his happy ways of employing himself I am now to transcribe.

"In my last I think I mentioned to you a young man of this place (Northumberland) who is become a zealous Unitarian.[6] By his means chiefly I have now a class of fourteen very promising young men, to whom I have great satisfaction in giving lectures as I used to do in England; and I have also been encouraged to open a place of public worship at a school-room near my house, where I have a growing congregation. Many persons I was told w^d come to hear if I preached out of my own house, and I find it to be so. I principally expound the Scriptures, reading one portion from the O. Testam^t and another from the New. I am now reading Isaiah and the history of the gospel from my Harmony".[7]

So far the extract. I find he intends to pass the present winter, together with his Son Joseph and his family, in Philadelphia, where some farther opportunities of usefulness seem to be opening to him, and prejudices wearing away.

We hope you and Mrs Millar continue to enjoy the tolerable share of the blessing of health as when you last wrote, the same wch we have constant cause to be thankful: but misery & distress, and fearful expectation of worse, increase around us: wch we fear Peace only can remove – Peace which seems far off. Our only and a sufficient support and consolation is, that every event is in the best hands and ordained soon or late for the good & happiness of all. Ever, tho' in haste, y^r truly obliged and affectionate f^d & serv^t.

T. Lindsey.

---

1   This letter from Millar to Lindsey seems not to have survived.
2   This was Lindsey's letter to Millar of 13 Nov. 1800 (Letter 708).
3   Possibly Jeremiah Joyce, the editor of Palmer's *Narrative*.
4   Lindsey seems to have referred here to the death of Andrew Ross's sister, rather than Millar's.
5   After the death of Henry Priestley in 1795, William Priestley was Joseph Priestley's youngest surviving son. For the example of problematical behaviour to which Lindsey referred, see Letter 704, n. 5.
6   Priestley mentioned this self-educated young unitarian, without identifying him, in his letter to Lindsey of 19 June 1800; Rutt, I, 439–40.
7   This is a quotation from Priestley's letter to Lindsey, 16 Oct. 1800, DWL, MS 12.13. It is partly printed, with some inaccuracies, in Rutt, I, 443; for example, Rutt misquoted the last three words as 'from my memory', whereas in the manuscript Priestley wrote 'from my Harmony', referring to his *Harmony of the evangelists, in English* (London, 1780).

---

712. To ROBERT MILLAR   2 FEBRUARY 1801

Text: DWL, MS 12.46 (25).
Addressed: To/Mr Robt. Millar/Merchant/Dundee
Endorsed: Lond^o 2^d Feb 1801/Mr Lindsey
Postmarked: Postmark missing.

London. Feb. 2. 1801.

Dear Sir,

I have for some time been making inquiries of friends who are in the habit of receiving letters from Botany bay, that I might be able to give you some intelligence about our friends in that place, especially as the time of their return from exile, if ever they intend to return, is now very near. In a former letter I acquainted You from a person who was recently come from those parts, and had seen Mr Fysh Palmer, that he did not find that he entertained any thoughts of returning to Europe.[1] But as from what I learned this last, week, his relations in England expect him to come back in no long time, I thought you would be glad to be acquainted with it.

You must know then, that Mr Belsham, our much respected friend, and Dr Priestley's successor in the congregation at Hackney, has a brother who resides at Bedford, where Mr F. Palmers uncle who left him a handsome fortune lately died, and where Mr Fysh Palmer's nephew was lately on a visit, and mentioned among other things, that they expected his uncle Tom, (for so he called our friend an[d] your *quondam* pastor) soon to be in England.[2]

Many things may happen to delay Mr F. Palmers arrival; but I thought I would give you the first notice of the likelihood of his friends seeing him again in England, especially as it costs me nothing but the writing of a few hasty lines, as I easily procure a Frank, now our Imperial Parliament is sitting; tho' to the surprize of many, it is not yet opened, by the King's coming down to the house to open the Parliament.[3]

Various are the causes assigned for this: one and the chief is, that the Duke of York and M[r] Pitt have had high words with respect to the ruined state of the nation during his administration; which has not ended there; but great changes are expected to take place in consequence.[4] One change I shall rejoice in, if it contribute to bring about and accelerate peace.[5] If I sh[d] hear any thing decisive on such an important crisis, before it is necessary to seal my letter, I will give it you.

I think I told you in my last that I was printing a small Tract of D[r] Priestley's on the knowlege of a future state among the antient Hebrews; and I wish you to know that it is printed, and that I wait for y[r] giving me an opportunity to convey such a trifle to you.[6] We have had several letters very lately from the Doctor, informing us in all of them of the continuance of health and success in his various pursuits[7]

P.S. Monday afternoon.[8]

There does not appear to be any ground for the report of any present changes in Administration: But it is generally believed that the Ministers speech to day, when the king goes to the house, will declare the expediency of a measure necessary for the quiet of Ireland, i.e. the emancipation of the Roman Catholics, and in consequence the repeal of all Test-Laws, the latter of w[ch] has been much opposed in the Cabinet: These will be great points, if they pass, altho they are forced by political necessity, and not freely granted.[9]

My wife unites in kind respects and wishes of all good to M[rs] Millar and yourself, and I remain at all times Dear Sir, Your much obliged and affectionate serv[t]

T. Lindsey.

---

1 See Letter 708.

2 The historian William Belsham, like Palmer's family, lived at Bedford. Thomas Fyshe Palmer's uncle, George Palmer 'the elder', died in 1799. One of the witnesses to his will (dated 6 Feb. 1794) was Thomas Fyshe Palmer's brother Jeremy Fyshe Palmer; Thomas Fyshe Palmer himself was not a beneficiary. See TNA: PRO PROB 11/1319, fos. 305v–307r. The nephew of Thomas Fyshe Palmer to whom Lindsey referred was Charles Fyshe Palmer, to whom the former bequeathed £100, 'as a very inadequate reward for his great attention to me', in a codicil to his will, dated 1 Apr. 1794; TNA: PRO PROB 11/1403, fo. 425r.

3 By the 'imperial parliament', Lindsey meant the parliament of the United Kingdom and Ireland which was created by the Act of Union of 1800 (39 & 40 Geo. III, c. 67) and which was regularly referred to at the time as the 'imperial parliament'. Its first meeting took place on 22 Jan. 1801. On 2 Feb. George III formally opened its first session; for the king's speech, see *LJ*, XLIII, 8. The debate on the king's speech and the address of thanks followed immediately thereafter; Cobbett, *Parl. hist.*, XXXV, 887–935. For Pitt's speech (908–18), which did not mention catholic emancipation, see *Parl. Hist.*, XXXV, 908–18.

4 Despite their previous disagreements, in fact Frederick, duke of York, expressed the view that Pitt should not have resigned; see Ehrman, *The Younger Pitt. The consuming struggle*, p. 531.

5 Lindsey referred here to the resignation of Pitt.

6 See Letter 701, n. 10.

7 Lindsey probably had in mind Priestley's letters to him of 16 and 30 Oct. and 6 Nov. 1800, and his letter to Belsham of 26 Nov. 1800; see Rutt, I, 443–48.

8 Monday 2 Feb. 1801.

9 On 2 Feb. 1802, George III opened the new session of parliament. His speech setting out the administration's agenda made no mention of catholic emancipation; *LJ*, XLIII, 8. Pitt, in his speech during the debate on the address of thanks, also did not mention catholic emancipation or the Test Laws, and concentrated instead upon the war, the navy and foreign affairs; Cobbett, *Parl. hist.*, XXXV, 908–18.

713. To WILLIAM DAVY   3 FEBRUARY 1801

Text: DWL, Davy letterbook, p. 73.
Addressed: To/William Davy Esqr/Merchant/Philadelphia
Postmarked: Postmark missing.

London. Feb. 3. 1801.

Dear Sir,

I am sensible of your kind favours of July 2 and Sept. 29 1800, and shall attend to their instructions in any future packages for Mr H. Toulmin with which you still encourage me to trouble you.[1] I have however ventured to go contrary to one piece of information given in your last, that our friend is no longer Secretary of State, in the addressing of my letter and parcell to him, in which I can only wish I may be right and you otherwise: as my account from himself is prior to your's, writing to me June 25. Frankfort "I have the satisfaction of informing you that after a very warm contest, our worthy Governor was re-elected by a large majority of the citizens, in consequence of which I still retain my office".[2]

A few days ago, at the latter end of the last week, there was a rumour which was much credited, that Mr Pitt was to resign his office, which gave a most general satisfaction, and you saw it in every countenance;[3] but unfortunately there was no just foundation for it; and a great personage, notwithstanding the faithful and true state of the country laid before him and the insufficiency of it's present administrators, is said to be determined to abide by them, and the Royal Speech yesterday for the first time to the Imperial Parliament, instead of any promise of peace, declared the necessity of a new naval war and called for the Support of the Country in it.[4] And in the debates afterwards, The Address for complying with his Majesty's desires was carried

In the Lords house ------------- 53
    for an amendment -------- <u>17</u>
               36 majority[5]

In the Comons'
    for the Address ----------- 245
    Amendment --------------- <u>63</u>
               102 majority.[6]

I may mention a piece of intelligence which is well founded, I believe. The beginning of the last week, a dispatch came from Marquess Cornwallis, that something must of necessity be done in the first session of the Imperial Parliament of what had been promised for the emancipation of the Roman Catholics, and for the repeal of all the Test laws whatsoever, or he could not answer for the quiet of Ireland.[7] In consequence, this was debated in the Cabinet, to which the two Archb^{ps} were called, and Mr Pitt pleaded much in behalf of the measure but was in the Minority, being particularly opposed by the Church; but it was added, that he had nevertheless prevailed in a second debate, and the matter was to make a part in the King's Speech, the last night: but not one syllable relating to it; and the tamest and humblest speech the present Ministers have ever yet made for him.[8,5]

I may not forget to add, that the parcell I send to Mr H. Toulmin, consists intirely of Newspapers, and a few monthly Magazines, the value of 15 Shillings.

I would hope, that notwithstanding our present disappointments, peace will certainly come.[9]

You will be so good to alter the direction to Mr H.T. if it be wrong; and intimate to him that his friends in England are most anxious to hear of and from him. I remain at all times, Dear Sir, your much obliged servant

T. Lindsey

---

1   I have not been able to locate these two letters from William Davy to Lindsey.

2   James Garrard (1749–1822) was re-elected for a second term as governor of Kentucky in 1800; a Jeffersonian republican, he served two terms as governor (from 1796 to 1804). A former baptist minister, he came to adopt Socinian opinions as a result of Henry Toulmin's influence. For Toulmin's service as secretary of Kentucky, see Letter 656, n. 2.

3   On Tuesday 3 Feb. 1801 (the date of this letter), Pitt privately indicated his intention to resign, although he did not resign formally until 14 Mar. The end of the previous week meant 29–31 Jan. 1801. Hints that his resignation was likely may be found in several newspapers during those days, for example *Morning Chronicle*, 30 Jan. 1801, and *Morning Post and Gazetteer*, 30 Jan. 1801.

4   See Letter 712, n. 3.

5   For the debate in the house of lords on the address of thanks to the king's speech on 2 Feb. 1801, see Cobbett, *Parl. Hist.*, XXXV, 866–87. An opposition amendment was defeated by 73 votes to 17 (Lindsey omitted the 20 proxy votes from the ministerial total); there is a list of the minority in Cobbett, *Parl. Hist.*, XXXV, 887. The address itself was then carried without a division; *LJ*, XLIII, 8–9.

6   For the debate on the address in the house of commons on 2 Feb. 1801, see Cobbett, *Parl. Hist.*, XXXV, 887–934. An opposition amendment was defeated by 245 votes to 63; Lindsey's report of the voting figures was accurate. There is a list of the minority in Cobbett, *Parl. Hist.*, XXXV, 934–5. The address of thanks itself was then carried without a division; *CJ*, LVI, 9–10.

7   Charles, Marquis Cornwallis (1738–1805), was lord lieutenant of Ireland from June 1798 to Apr. 1801, and favoured catholic emancipation. Possibly the story that Lindsey heard was that reported in the *Morning Chronicle*, 2 Feb. 1801, to the effect that the government's plan for catholic relief had been so diluted that the lord lieutenant 'is said to have declared that he could not present to the catholics such a plan as efficient to the purpose to which the government in Ireland was pledged; and that he conceived a great deal more to be necessary, in order to fulfil the promise given, and to secure the tranquillity of the country. This he is said to have put in strong terms, both in regard to himself, as pledged, and the consequences to the Public if that pledge was not held sacred.' For the background to this question, and for a claim that the catholic issue was not the main reason for Pitt's resignation, see C. J. Fedorak, 'Catholic emancipation and the resignation of William Pitt in 1801', *Albion*, XXIV (1992), 49–64.

8   For the tortuous cabinet meetings over catholic emancipation, and the divisions which they exposed, see Ehrman, *The Younger Pitt. The consuming struggle*, pp. 501–9. The two archbishops were John Moore (Canterbury) and William Markham (York). As Lindsey noted, the king's speech on 2 Feb. 1801 (see n. 5, above) made no mention of catholic emancipation or the Test Laws.

9   Preliminaries of peace between Britain and France were signed on 1 Oct. 1801 and confirmed by the Treaty of Amiens, which was concluded on 25 Mar. 1802.

---

714. To JOSEPH CHADWICK   10 FEBRUARY 1801

Text: DWL, MS 12.80, opp. p. 452.
Addressed: [In Hannah Lindsey's hand] Rev^d M^r. Chadwick/Oundle/ Northamptonshire
Endorsed: To E.M. Esq. from J.C.
Postmarked: Postmark missing.

Note: E.M. in the endorsement probably signifies Edward Martin of Birmingham (see Letter 509). J.C. probably signifies Joseph Chadwick.

London. Feb. 10. 1801.

Dear Sir,

As it is now so long since I had a few lines from You, I write under some apprehension about you and Mrs Chadwick,[1] but still trusting that your usefulness as a gospel Minister continues, and that you are happy in such a valuable helpmate.

I should be glad also to know if you did not receive from me now more than a year since, some copies of Farmer Truman, the York Pamphlet as I called it, which has been much circulated and deservedly prized by many, and some few lesser practical pieces, which you mentioned in your last letter of the date of May 6, 1800.[2] If these have never come to you, for I only know it was intended, but am not absolutely certain about it, I shall see that they are carried as soon as I shall hear from You, to the Parsonage-house of S[t] Mary at Hill, if M[r] Hewson still continue to reside there, to be by him as soon as may be forwarded to you.[3]

I shall be glad also of an opportunity of sending to you a little Tract of D[r] Priestley's, which he sent over to be printed here, upon *the knowlege of the antient Hebrews concerning a future state*, which I am sure you will be glad to see, as I have prefixed to it some account of the excellent author, taken from some letters very lately received from him.[4]

I sh[d] be glad also to know, if I sent you a sermon which your good tutor D[r] Toulmin had preached and printed here on the term *Lord of Hosts*, very ingenious and usefully handled, and which you would much like.[5]

There is a great ferment an[d] much joy in this great city at present upon a report that M[r] Pitt has resigned his places and several of his friends with him, which is expected to lead the way to a termination of this unfortunate war, and to restore to us the longed for blessing of peace, which it is believed his majesty's ministers of late have not been disposed to, but on the contrary have been the authors of prolonging the war.[6]

I shall add no more at present, but that I shall be glad to have a few lines from you at your convenience. My wife and myself, thanks to a kind providence, enjoy the blessing of health and she desires to join with me in wishes for that and every other blessing to you and M[rs] Chadwick:

I am always, Dear Sir, with much esteem, very sincerely Yours

T. Lindsey.

---

1 For Mary Chadwick, see Letter 509, n. 7.

2 For 'Farmer Truman', see Letter 509, n. 6. For David Eaton's 'York pamphlet', *Scripture the only guide*, see Letter 686. Chadwick's letter to Lindsey of 6 May 1800 seems not to have survived.

3 St Mary at Hill was an anglican church in Lovat Lane, off Eastcheap, in Billingsgate ward, Middlesex. A Mr John Hewson is listed at No. 8, St Mary Hill, in *Holden's triennial directory, 1802, 1803 & 1804*, unpaginated list of 'house-keepers, resident in London, and ten miles circular'.

4 This work was Priestley's *An inquiry into the knowledge of the antient Hebrews*; for Lindsey's preface, see Letter 701, n. 10.

5 Joshua Toulmin, *The name, 'Lord of Hosts', explained and improved, in a sermon, preached in the chapels of Princes Street, Westminster, on February 16th, and Essex Street, Strand, on February 23rd, 1800* (London, 1800). Chadwick was educated at South Petherton and at Bridport. However, Toulmin's influence might be evident in Chadwick's reservations about infant baptism which involved him in difficulties during the latter years of his service as minister at Wellington, Somerset; see DWL, MS 12.80, opposite p. 90, Samuel Palmer to Chadwick, 18 Feb. 1786.

6 For rumours in early Feb. 1801 of Pitt's likely resignation, see Ehrman, *The Younger Pitt. The consuming struggle*, pp. 508–9.

715. To WILLIAM WOOD   **19 FEBRUARY 1801**

> **Text:**   Wood, pp. 86–8.

Note: The manuscript of this letter seems not to have survived. The double inverted commas are reproduced as in the printed text.

London, Feb. 19, 1801.

"DEAR SIR,

"I have seldom been more affected and edified than with the perusal of the two
most valuable discourses with which you have favoured me.

"That on the commencement of the 19th century shews the very high advantages
which the constant attendants at Mill-Hill Chapel enjoy in sitting under such a
preacher, who like our great master takes occasion from every circumstance of
time and place, and avails himself of every incident that presents itself to make
his lessons of the sublimest morality sink deep, and take effect in the hearts of his
hearers.[1]

"And in your portrait of Mr. Cappe, you have done to him that justice which
he never did to himself, in exhibiting those great natural and acquired talents and
abilities, and those excellent and continually improving christian dispositions, which
would have fitted him for the most eminent services to mankind, both from the
pulpit and the press, but which were almost entirely lost by an unfortunate modesty
of temper, and the want of opportunity to draw them forth. I cannot help in particular
regretting that, with respect to those serious doubts on the subject of christianity,
which you tell us he entertained on his first thoughts of engaging in the Christian
ministry, and by most diligent study and application happily overcame, that we have
no memorials of what these doubts were, or how he got the better of them, as I am
persuaded the history would have been peculiarly useful in the present day.[2] And I
am the more concerned, as I do not apprehend that any of the manuscripts which he
has left behind him, touch at all upon these points, or the discussion of difficulties
of this sort, but relate chiefly to the right interpretation of particular passages of the
scripture. Instead of complaining, however, we ought to be thankful for what you
have preserved of a character so excellent, which must excite to piety and virtue,
and to a study and esteem for those scriptures which alone can effectually teach
them; and for that interesting and most engaging example of his manner of public
instruction in those discourses on the Providence and Government of God, which
Mrs. Cappe was the happy instrument of giving to the world: of whom, in the
dedication of your sermon, you seem to have laboured how to speak in those terms
that indeed her super-eminent merit called for.[3]

"You make me feel ashamed for the rank you give me in classing me with those
excellent creatures Jebb and Priestley;[4] humbled moreover to find myself cut off
from that usefulness I earnestly wished to retain till the thread of life itself was cut;
happy, meanwhile, if I may but take to myself that consolation of our christian poet -

"They also serve, who only stand and wait."[5]

I remain, &c. &c.
  T. LINDSEY."

---

1   William Wood, *A sermon preached at Mill-Hill chapel, in Leeds, on the commencement of the nine-
    teenth century. Published at the request of the congregation* (Leeds, 1801).
2   William Wood, *A sermon preached ... December 31, 1800, immediately after the interment of the
    Rev. Newcome Cappe; with an appendix, containing brief memoirs of his life* (London, 1801).
3   Newcome Cappe's *Discourses on the providence and government of God* were published in London

(by Joseph Johnson) in 1795. The 'Advertisement' stated that Cappe had delivered these discourses in 1786 and 1787, that he had not intended them for publication and that he was by this time 'disabled by illness'. Although her name was not mentioned, it is clear that Catharine Cappe contributed substantially to preparing the work for publication. A second edition was published at York in 1811 and a third edition (also at York) in 1818; in each of these cases, Catharine Cappe was named as the editor. Wood dedicated his *Sermon* (n. 2, above) to Catharine Cappe, as a 'public testimonial of her watchful care of the deceased', adding that the dedication was made at the request of the surviving children of Newcome Cappe and his first wife.

4   In his *Sermon* (n. 2, above), Wood stated (pp. 12–13) that Newcome Cappe adopted 'nearly the same views of the New Testament as, in different connexions, and under different influences, have been gradually opened to the world by the writings of a Lindsey, a Jebb, a Priestley, and other divines who, for some time have been generally known by the name of Unitarian Christians'.

5   Milton, sonnet 'On his blindness', line 14.

716. To ROBERT MILLAR   21 FEBRUARY 1801

Text: DWL, 12.46 (26).
Addressed: To/Mʳ Robᵗ Millar/Merchant/Dundee
Endorsed: Londᵒ 21 Feb. 1801/Mr Lindsey/Dr Geddes's Bible
Postmarked: Postmark illegible.

London. febʸ. 21. 1801.

Dear Sir,

Our last letters having crossed each other on the road, as I believe I had mentioned to you a rumour of some great changes being expected in the political world, I judged it right to wait their taking place before I wrote again. And I have the pleasure of informing you that Mʳ Pitt is now out of office, the last act of his power as Minister having expired yesterday, when he brought in the budget to provide for expenses of the current year to ease and assist his successor the late Speaker.[1] As Mʳ P. had had the appointment or recomendation of the greater part of those who are to come into office, tho not of all; this change is looked upon by many as a mere juggle, and change of hands for a time, till some points are got over, which he and his collegues coud not do, and then they are to resume their places again. There are those however, who are of a quite contrary sentiment. They believe the late junto who have gone out will admit into offices of trust and power those only who will engage to pursue their measures: but they are persuaded that the two chieftains, Mʳ Pitt and Mʳ Dundas, are and have been both of them, so very little of late acceptable to the king, that he received their resignations instantly and with great pleasure, and will never put them again in such high situations, and it is not probable they will accept inferior ones.[2]

It is our comfort, and that of many, I find, that one change may lead to others, as this was of all things the most unexpected a few weeks past; or weak instruments in the hands of the supreme Ruler, may effect good, and bring the blessing of peace; if we are to be saved.

I must now acquaint you that I was careful to execute your comission with respect to Dʳ Geddes, as soon as I received your letter, when he told Mʳ Johnson who is his bookseller, that he had some other copies to send your way, besides yours and Mʳ Jobson's, and should immediately give orders about them.[3] So that I should think they must be on their way towards you, if he has found a proper opportunity. The Doctor is a most ingenious learned man, and of agreeable and pleasant conversation, and I much fear he will be a loser by this publication, as if all the copies be sold, he will barely indemnify himself, the price of paper and printing being so much risen of late:[4]

But may I mention *to you only*; that I am much disappointed in this Volume. The great respect shewn by our Lord as well as by the writers of the N.T. to the character of Moses, surely sets his mission and authority something beyond that of Lycurgus or Numa, with whom the D[r]. ranks him in a copy of latin verses to J.D. that is to John Disney, my Successor, postfixed to the volume, and in the course of his notes I cannot say that he at all answers my expectations, so that I am surprised he sh[d] take so much pains with a book that he appears to rate so cheaply.[5]

I think you have lost your latin for want of cultivating it: Else Grotius's notes, tho too short, are quite of a different caste, and give light and instruction every where.[6] But I would recomend to you *A Critical and Practical Exposition of the Pentateuch* &c &c, in one volume folio, printed in London in the year 1748, for Knapton, Millar, and all the booksellers of the time, which I think would exceedingly answer your purpose – the author's name is not printed: but in my copy, some possessor of it has written *by D[r]. Jameson*.[7] I value it very much, and remember, some years since I asked D[r] Geddes about it, and as he had not seen the copy, offered to lend it to him. Perhaps you may meet with this book in some of your libraries.

Your method of public instruction I do exceedingly approve, as calculate[d] to improve both the Minister and People, and do not wonder that it attracts and pleases the latter.

I honour your Town for your generous method of relieving your poor at this season; and yourself for engaging in the good work, and for learning that good[8] lesson from it, that true religion is in doing good.[9] I sh[d] thank you, when you write again, to tell me, if the times are mended with You. I have more to say. But am forced to end. You will remember to give me notice, when any one is to call here for a little parcell for you: Or, how I may send it to you. With affection and esteem for M[rs] Millar and yourself in w[ch] my wife desires to unite, I remain ever Dear Sir most truly Your's

T. Lindsey

1   Pitt had determined to resign, partly because of George III's opposition to catholic emancipation, early in Feb. 1801. However, for several reasons, including pressure from some colleagues to remain at his post, and the brief but dangerous illness of the king in the second half of Feb., he did not formally resign until 14 Mar. He introduced the budget in the house of commons on 18 Feb., where its provisions were agreed to without a division; Cobbett, *Parl. hist.*, XXXV, 971–8. Henry Addington, previously the speaker of the commons, was formally appointed in Pitt's place on 17 Mar. 1801.

2   Lindsey was correct in his understanding that relations between George III on the one hand, and Pitt and Dundas (secretary of state for war from July 1794 to Mar. 1801) on the other, had deteriorated during the late 1790s. He also correctly divined that Pitt intended to give his full support to Addington's ministry in its early stages. However, several other cabinet members, notably Lord Grenville (foreign secretary), William Windham (secretary at war) and John George, 2nd Earl Spencer (first lord of the admiralty), also resigned with Pitt and Dundas in Feb. 1801, and Addington's ministry bore a complexion significantly different from that of Pitt. For the background to these events, see Ehrman, *The Younger Pitt. The consuming struggle*, ch. XV.

3   This letter from Millar to Lindsey seems not to have survived. Joseph Johnson was indeed the bookseller of Alexander Geddes (see n. 4, below). Possibly 'Mr Jobson' was David Jobson, the treasurer of the Dundee infirmary; see *Caledonian Mercury*, 18 June 1801. He was married to the sister of Millar's (first) wife, Jean, née Scott; see DWL, MS 12.57 (43), Millar to Lindsey, 8 May 1802. Perhaps, too, he was a member of the family of John Jobson, merchant in Dundee; see *Answers for John Jobson merchant in Dundee, trustee for William Hay ... to the petition of Captain Robert George Bruce of Bunzion* (Edinburgh, 1766).

4   This work of Alexander Geddes's was *Critical remarks on the Hebrew scriptures*. Joseph Johnson is
    named on the title page as one of the two booksellers who sold the book.
5   The Latin verses addressed to 'Amicum mei amantissimum J.D.' (i.e. John Disney), where Moses is
    compared to Numa and Lycurgus, may be found on p. 475 of Geddes's *Critical remarks* (n. 4, above).
6   Possibly Lindsey referred to a work of Hugo Grotius (1583–1645), *The truth of the Christian
    religion. In six books, corrected and illustrated with notes by Mr. Le Clerc* (10th edn, London, 1793).
7   This work was Robert Jameson, *A critical and practical exposition of the Pentateuch, with notes ...
    To which are subjoin'd two dissertations, the first on the Mosaic history of the creation, the other on
    the destruction of the seven nations of Canaan* (London, 1748). J. and P. Knapton of Ludgate Street
    and A. Millar, opposite Katherine-street in the Strand, were indeed among the six London booksellers
    named on the title page.
8   Lindsey's handwriting is not quite clear at this point: possibly he wrote 'great', rather than 'good'.
9   Possibly Lindsey had read, at Millar's suggestion, *Regulations of the society for the relief of the
    indigent sick in the town and suburbs of Dundee. Together with an account of the rise and design
    of the institution* (Dundee, 1797). David Jobson (n. 3, above) and Dr Robert Small, minister of St
    Mary's, Dundee, were among the managers of this charity. It was particularly active during the period
    of exceptionally high food prices in 1800–1. See also Letter 731.

717. To ROBERT MILLAR   19 MARCH 1801

Text: DWL, MS 12.46 (27).
Printed: *Unitarian Baptist Advocate*, II, XXIII (Nov. 1838), 250–1
                 (with minor errors and omissions).
Addressed: To/M^r. Robert Millar/Merchant/Dundee
Endorsed: Lond° 19th Mar 1801/Mr Lindsey

                                                    London. march. 19. 1801.

Dear Sir

Capt. Ross obligingly called here the day before yesterday and left your letter,
and the day after I sent him the parcell, not knowing how soon he might be on the
return, containing D^r. Priestley['s] Essay,[1] a little piece on the fast published by a
friend.[2] Mr Belsham's Sermon at Bristol, to which a reference is made in the preface
to the Essay,[3] and 2 copies of Locke on Toleration, which a friend printed to give
away the last summer, when some new burdens were given out as to be laid on
Dissenters here in England.[4]

Yesterday Mr Pitt was announced in the Gazette to be superseded by Mr Addington
the late Speaker, and Peter Pindar accompanies his fall to day with advertising a
Poem with the Title, *Out at last*, in which I presume he speaks of him what he
durst not do before, as he has always identified himself with the Government and
prosecuted those as against *it*, who only found fault with his measures.[5] As the
new Ministry is wholly made up of men connected with and attached to him and
his measures, it [is] generally believed that he will continue to influence as before
behind the curtain, and when certain Jobs are done, in which it will not so well
become him to engage, will then come forth again in more power than ever, because
Lords Clare[6] and Castlereagh,[7] who have gone all his lengths and are ready to
go further, will join his forces with the whole irish phalanx, whom this country
has bought and paid for.[8] However, as our neighbours speak, L'homme pose, mais
Dieu dispose: the fairest and most plausible plan of ambitious man may easily be
defeated by providence. Would that we were more worthy of such a blessing, and
that peace and along with it plenty might be restored to our suffering; without those
additionall calamities which have been the means and instruments of inflicting on
other countries to gratify views of ambition and gain.

You may depend upon being informed with the first[9] of M[r] Fyshe Palmer's arrival, and also of what you very naturally wish to know further concerning his sentiments on certain matters, in which I should be as curious as yourself. It is a great moral, or as some would wish us to call it, a spiritual disadvantage to be deprived or out of the way of the outward means of religion; and not to lose ground greatly in such situations, a man must deal much privately with himself in the use of such means as are in his power.

The person you mention has certainly great acuteness, and Biblical learning, but his education and habits have warped his judgment, and he is by no means a sound reasoner. I say this the more freely, as it is the sentiment of several of my friends who are more intimate with him than I am.[10]

If you are possessed of D[r] Priestley's answer to M[r]. Paine, and the french politicians and philosophers, w[ch] I published 6 years ago, and if you have it not, I will send it you[;] you will there find a very satisfactory reply to many of the present objections to revelation.[11] And I woud add, that the fashionable attacks upon Moses and other things in the O.T. are continually confuted in his Comparison of Moses and the Hindus; and also in his remarks on M[r]. Dupuis.[12] It is a great pity that he did not put an Index to that work, which contains such a variety of excellent remark[s].[13]

Thanks for the account of the present state of things in your town. Our Governors have not been enough sensible how much they owe to some wise and benevolent Christians for keeping the country in peace which they have brought into such distress. I am not capable of doing much, but my wife is continually employed in going about and doing what good she can.[14] That you and M[rs] Millar are both so tolerably well, as we are thanks to the Giver of all things, is musick to our ears; and it is always such to hear of you or from you. With *our* kind rememberances to you both and sincere wishes of health and every blessing, I remain, Dear Sir

Your affectionate servant

T. Lindsey.

---

1   This was probably a reference to Priestley's *Inquiry into the knowledge of the antient Hebrews*; in Letter 701, Lindsey referred to it as an 'essay'.

2   The fast day in 1801 was 13 Feb. Possibly 'the little piece on the fast' was George Wollaston's *A sermon, preached in the parish church of Richmond, in the county of Surrey, on Friday, February 13, 1801, being the day of the general fast* ('printed but not published', Brentford, 1801). Wollaston (1731–1815) was the youngest brother of Francis Wollaston, author of *The secret history of a private man*; see Letter 607. Although there is no direct evidence of their friendship in Lindsey's surviving letters, they shared many latitudinarian values; George Wollaston had been a contemporary and friend of John Jebb at Cambridge. He was rector of St Mary Aldermanbury in the City of London from 1774 to 1790, when he retired from the ministry and resided at Richmond, Surrey. His fast day sermon delivered the customary denunciations of the profligacy of the age, but probably pleased Lindsey by its explanation for the duration of the 'long protracted war' despite annual days of fasting and prayer. Wollaston suggested (pp. 4–5) that such prayers displeased God by their presumptuous petitioning for military and naval victory, and for 'the aggrandizing of our possessions', rather than for peace, repentance and an abatement of national pride. He also hinted (p. 5) that he favoured a revision of the Church of England's liturgy.

3   For Belsham's sermon, preached at Bristol on 9 July 1800, see Letter 682, n. 18. Lindsey made a complimentary reference to it in his editorial preface to Priestley's *An inquiry into the knowledge of the antient Hebrews*, p. iv. Priestley himself described this work as an essay in a letter to Lindsey which the latter quoted in this preface, p. v.

4   For this edition of Locke's *Letter concerning toleration*, see Letter 698, n. 14. Lindsey's reference to the possibility that 'new burdens' might have been laid upon dissenters the previous year is explained by Michael Angelo Taylor's proposed bill; see Letter 692, n. 8.

5   Lindsey's source was probably the *Morning Chronicle* of 18 Mar. 1801, which reported that 'the

Gazette of last night' contained the news of Addington's appointment. In the same issue, the *Morning Chronicle* advertised the publication of the poem 'Out at last, or, the fallen minister', by 'P. Pindar Esq', i.e. Peter Pindar, the pseudonym of the poet and satirical writer John Walcot (1738–1819).

6   John Fitzgibbon (1748–1802), from 1795 1st earl of Clare in the Irish peerage, was lord chancellor of Ireland from 1789 until his death. A former member of the Irish parliament, and attorney-general for Ireland, he was, like Castlereagh (n. 7, below), a supporter of the Act of Union, but, unlike Castlereagh, a vehement opponent of catholic emancipation.

7   Robert Stewart (1769–1822), Viscount Castlereagh in the Irish peerage, was MP for county Down from 1801 to 1805 and several other constituencies thereafter; he was chief secretary to the lord lieutenant of Ireland (Cornwallis), from 1798 to 1801.

8   This is a reference to the addition of 100 MPs from Irish constituencies to the house of commons, together with twenty-eight lords and four bishops to the house of lords, as a result of the Act of Union with Ireland (1800). For the background, see David Wilkinson, '"How did they pass the union?" Secret service expenditure in Ireland, 1799–1804', *History*, LXXXII (1997), 223–51.

9   Word omitted, probably 'news'.

10   This is probably a reference to Alexander Geddes.

11   For Priestley's *Answer to Mr Paine's Age of reason*, which Lindsey edited for publication, see Letter 602, n. 8.

12   For Priestley's *Comparison of the institutions*, see Letter 672, n. 9. His refutation of the 'fashionable attacks' may be found throughout this work. For his critique of *Origine de tous les cultes, ou la réligion universelle* of Charles François Dupuis (1742–1809), which was first published in Paris in 1795, see pp. 301–64.

13   The manuscript is slightly torn at this point. Priestley's *Comparison* (n. 12, above) did not have an index.

14   There is a note on Hannah Lindsey's relief of 'the poor, and especially of the diseased poor … in the little narrow lanes and alleys of the Essex Street neighbourhood' in Catharine Cappe's 'Memoir of Mrs Lindsey', *MR*, VII (1812), 116–17.

718. To GILBERT WAKEFIELD   14 APRIL 1801

Text: Dr Williams's Library [reference to be confirmed].
Printed: Ditchfield, 'Unitarianism after the French Revolution',
                   42–3.
Addressed: The Rev^d. G. Wakefield/Dorchester Goal
Endorsed: Rev: Theophilus *Lindsey*/(Unitarian Divine)/b:1723/d: 1808
Postmarked: Postmark missing.

Note: In May 2007, this letter was purchased by G. M. Ditchfield from John Wilson Manuscripts Limited, Cheltenham, and presented by him to Dr Williams's Library, London.

London. April. 14. 1801.

Dear Sir,

I do most truly honour and admire those who like you and Dr Priestley are able to sooth and divert private trials and griefs by plans and energies of utility to literature and to mankind, and thence to derive the most honourable support to themselves. And in this view I cannot but wish success to the proposal of Lectures which you have thrown before the public to be read when you are liberated from your long and odious confinement now happily so near an end, and shall do what may lye in my little sphere to promote it, by making it known where it may be likely to be embraced.[1]

It has been a singular satisfaction to me to learn that you have been so usefully and benevolently employed with the poor felons that have been condemned at Dorchester; as I doubt not you would be able to pour some gleams of light and comfort into their minds in their unhappy situation.[2]

I trust the minds of Mrs Wakefield and your amiable daughter,[3] your fellow sufferers, will be softened by degrees for the loss of the sweet innocent to which they were so naturally and tenderly attached, and to whom nothing could happen but for the best.[4]

My wife desires to unite with me in sincerest wishes of every thing truly good for you all, and I remain at all times

Dear Sir, Your truly obliged and affectionate friend and servant

T. Lindsey.

The worthy friend, whose signature conveys this to you, was prevented putting his hand to it or it w[d] have been with you some days sooner.[5]

---

1 Shortly before his release from Dorchester gaol, which took place on 29 May 1801, Wakefield devised a plan for a series of lectures on classical subjects. He delivered the first course of them in June–July 1801 but died on 9 Sept. of that year. See *Memoirs of the life of Gilbert Wakefield*, ed. J. T. Rutt and A. Wainewright (2 vols., London, 1804), II, 259, 283–4; the printed 'proposals' for the lectures may be found at p. 284 n. *.

2 For Wakefield's ministering to his fellow-prisoners in Dorchester gaol, see *Memoirs of Gilbert Wakefield*, II, 241–4.

3 Wakefield married in 1779 Anne, née Watson; they had five sons and two daughters. Possibly the daughter to whom Lindsey referred was Anne (d. 1821), who married Charles Rochemont Aikin (1775–1847), the brother of Arthur Aikin and Lucy Aikin, and the nephew of Anna Laetitia Barbauld; see Wakefield's letter to her, *Memoirs of Gilbert Wakefield*, II, 262.

4 Wakefield's youngest child (a son) died immediately before his release from gaol in May 1801.

5 The 'worthy friend' was probably a sympathetic MP (perhaps Benjamin Hobhouse, James Martin or William Smith) or a peer (perhaps the duke of Grafton) who allowed Lindsey to use his franking privilege for the transmission of this letter.

719. To RUSSELL SCOTT   2 MAY 1801

Text: Scott Coll.
Addressed: To/The Rev[d] Russell Scott/Portsmouth
Endorsed: May 2. 1801
Postmarked: Postmark missing.

London. May. 2. 1801.

Dear Sir,

I make haste to tell you how rejoiced I am to see your hand writing after such a long interval, and the more as it brings such good tidings of the health of M[rs] Scott and yourself and of the addition it has pleased the divine Providence to make to your family in giving you another Son, who I trust will be every way a comfort to his parents.[1]

It is a great pleasure to learn at the close of your letter, that you are likely to be in Town on the 25th if not on the 18th. of the present month. For there has been such a long chasm in our correspondence, that one is affrighted with the thought of filling it up in any way but by conversing together, and therefore I shall look forward to this desireable opportunity of seeing you with great satisfaction. Till that time I shall also defer the discussion of the chapter of yours and M[rs] Scott's most kind renewed invitation to pay you a visit at Portsmouth, where we are intirely persuaded nothing would be wanting that could minister to our ease in all respects.[2]

It was a neglect either of me or M[r] Hunter[3] in not sending you M[r] Belsham's sermon along with his Tract,[4] as I have been accustomed always to let them go together; but it shall be at your service when we meet, and I trust I shall be able to accomodate you with a copy of his Comparison of the Institutions of Moses and the Eastern nations, which I look upon to be a most valuable work and highly useful.[5]

I have heard twice very lately from the excellent author, who is in intire good health, and happy in the midst of many and great trials and afflictions; but I shall say the less on the subject, as I shall be desirous to let you hear him speak for himself in shewing you one of his late letters, with which I thing[6] [*sic*] you will be peculiarly edified.[7]

We also are much edified, and sympathize with you in your reflections on the loss of your dear child, which have surely nothing in them that is not compatible with unfeigned submission to the hand that removed him so soon out of this scene of trial: they are pangs of nature that must long be felt.[8]

I am concerned to find that after having given you so long a truce, your old cruel enemy should renew his attack; but you relieve us by adding that you were already considerably better; and I trust you have outlived the worst of that malady, which generally abates with age, as I can testify of myself: tho' undoubtedly head achs have different causes.[9]

I will not ask you to tell me by letter the story of the proselyte from Methodism, but shall desire not to have it forgotten when you come to Town,[10] as I shall not forget to gratify your inquiry about the story relating to D[r] Priestley, which I should have very unwillingly have put on paper.[11] We presume your amiable daughter is from home, as you do not name her, but hope she is well.[12] My wife desires to unite with me in kind regards to M[rs] Scott, and with her comp[ts] to yourself, I remain at all times,

Dear Sir, your affectionate and obliged friend and Servant
T. Lindsey.

P.S. I shall not give you the trouble of writing again before you come to Town unless any change to be made in the time.

---

1   Scott's second son, Russell, was born on 3 Feb. 1801 and baptized by Lindsey at the house of his grandfather, Dr William Hawes, in Spital Square, London. He was named after Scott himself and after Scott's first son, who died in 1797; Scott, *Family biography*, p. 96. Scott's letter to Lindsey seems not to have survived.

2   Scott was in London on 17 June 1801, the date of Lindsey's will, to which he was a witness: TNA: PRO PROB 11/1488, fo. 213. Lindsey did not go to Portsmouth to visit Scott.

3   Probably Rowland Hunter, an assistant to Joseph Johnson, who continued the publishing business after Johnson's death in 1809. A former pupil of the Barbaulds at Palgrave, he is listed as a bookseller and binder, of 72 St Paul's Churchyard, in *Holden's triennial directory 1805, 1806 and 1807* (3 vols., London, 1807), I, 'London alphabet of businesses, professions &c', unpaginated. See Braithwaite, *Romanticism, publishing and dissent*, pp. 179–80, 181, 214 n. 78,

4   By Belsham's 'sermon', Lindsey probably meant his *A serious caution against popular errors; in a discourse addressed to the young persons who attended the unitarian worship, at the Gravel-Pit meeting, in Hackney* (London, 1801, with a second edition later in that year). By Belsham's 'tract', he probably meant his *Elements of the philosophy of the mind* (see Letter 682, n. 19).

5   Lindsey probably referred here to Priestley's *Comparison of the institutions*, rather than to a work by Belsham.

6   Lindsey evidently intended to write 'think'.

7   Probably these two letters from Priestley to Lindsey were that printed by Rutt, I, 452–3 (undated, but clearly belonging to the early weeks of 1801) and a missing letter from Feb.–Mar. 1801. It is unlikely that Priestley's letter of 8 Apr. 1801 (Rutt, I, 459) had reached Lindsey by 2 May.

8   In his (non-surviving) letter to Lindsey (see n. 1, above), Scott had presumably reflected upon the death of his first child, Russell, aged five years, in 1797.

9   Scott's 'old enemy' was gout and gout-related headaches; see Letters 516 and 630.

10   Disappointingly, the records of the High Street chapel, Portsmouth, for this period (TNA: RG4/564) do not identify this 'proselyte from Methodism'.

11 Probably this was the 'poison' story involving William Priestley; see Letter 704, n. 5.
12 This refers to Scott's only daughter Sophia (1793–1832).

720. To WILLIAM ALEXANDER   28 MAY 1801

> **Text:** 'Letters of the Rev. Theophilus Lindsey. No. VIII', *UH*, II, 87
>   (27 Dec. 1862), 432.

Note: This is the only section of this letter printed by the *UH*; the manuscript seems not to have survived.

London, May 28th, 1801.

You may have heard from London, I presume, or elsewhere, that Dr. Priestley has been in the utmost danger at Philadelphia from a bilious pleuritic fever, in which he was for three days given over by his physicians who attended him. But the Divine Providence has had pity on all that know and love him, and on many others, and has spared him, I trust, for great usefulness to many. A letter from his eldest son, of the date of March 20th, brought an account of his illness, and of all present danger being over; and another letter, of a later date, to a gentleman in town, from his brother at Philadelphia, mentions that Dr. Priestley was so much recovered as to think of going back with his son and daughter-in-law and their family to Northumberland in a few days.[1] We shall wait, however, with some little anxiety for his next letter from Northumberland, under his own hand, to assure us of his perfect recovery. You will have pleasure in being informed that he has acceded to the proposals made to him hence to set about the printing of the continuation of his "Ecclesiastical History", and his "Notes on the whole Scriptures", both of which are ready for the press; when it was engaged to procure him such a number of subscribers as should at least be sufficient to indemnify him for the expense.[2]

---

1 This letter from Joseph Priestley junior seem not to have survived. Possibly the letter 'to gentleman in town' was from William Davy to his brother in Gould Square; see Letter 656, n. 1. For Priestley's illness, during his visit to Philadelphia in early 1801, see William Davy's letter to Lindsey of 14 Mar. 1801, where he referred to Priestley's 'violent disorder, which has proved to be a bilious pleurisy'; Rutt, I, 455, n. ‡. See also Priestley's letter to William Russell, 4 Apr. 1801, and his letter to Lindsey, 8 Apr. 1801; Rutt, I, 458, 459. Priestley returned to Northumberland in Apr. 1801 and although he made a partial recovery, he suffered a series of relapses and never fully regained his former strength.
2 Lindsey referred here to the third and fourth volumes of Priestley's *General history of the Christian church from the fall of the western empire*, and his *Notes on all the books of scripture*. For the subscription to finance the publication of these works, see Letter 736, n. 5.

721. To ROBERT MILLAR   3 JUNE 1801

> **Text:**   DWL, MS 12.46 (28).
> **Printed:**   *Unitarian Baptist Advocate*, II, XXIV (Dec. 1838), 265–6
>   (with minor errors); Ditchfield, 'Quaker–unitarian encounter',
>   211 (first three sentences of third paragraph).
> **Addressed:**   To/Mr Robert Millar,/Merchant/Dundee
> **Endorsed:**   Lond° 3^d June 1801/Mr Lindsey
> **Postmarked:** Postmark illegible.

London. June. 3. 1801.

Dear Sir,

Having an easy opportunity of procuring a conveyance, I am desirous to write and thank you for your last remembrance of April 28,[1] and express our satisfaction at M^{rs}. Millar and yourself being in tolerable health, a blessing for which we both have cause to be thankful.

It is certainly somewhat not a little disheartening to have before one the prospect of the rational and scriptural sentiments of the Divine Being and his pure worship giving way to a narrow and intolerant superstition which indisposes the numerous subjects of it towards their fellowcreatures, and brings undeserved discredit on the gospel, and increases the prejudices of many against it, which are unhappily at this season multiplied from other causes. But so it has been and so it will be. And yet I trust that silently and effectually, the knowlege of the true God, whom Jesus taught and worshipped, is spreading it's beautiful ray, as speaks one who suffered loss and long imprisonment for it about 100 years ago.[2] We have evidence for it from many different districts in the Southern part of the island, and the satisfaction to know that there are not a few sincere labourers at work here as well as in Ireland. But there is one circumstance which has somewhat reviving in it, if it has not reached You: which induces me to say to you, my friend, and to myself in a desponding hour, Let no one be discouraged by the apparent present decline of a good cause, especially that capital one of the Divine Unity: the immediate instruments now employed may fail in seeing the success of their labours, but their zeal should not slacken: the seed may lie long in the ground, but the stamina are unperishable.

A new agent and instrument in this cause has sprung up among the Quakers, and is like to cause a great division among them. Hannah Barnard, a native American, in the neighbourhood of New York, being convinced of this first article of true religion and of many of those connected with or resulting from it, came to England about a year ago to teach it, and her success among the younger part in particular has raised alarm, and she has been silence[d] in the old method, contrary to their own principle that every one is to be heard who speaks from the Spirit of God. She made many converts in Ireland before She came to England, where also she has many serious sensible persons much attached to her, some of whom I have a knowlege of.[3] At their annual meeting, which began on Whitsunday, and is now continuing and nearly at an end, she had appointed to make her appeal upon the justness of her plea, against being restrained from speaking, before the heads of the whole body, who have been summoned from all parts to put a stop to this new doctrine.[4] Her manners are so gentle, her eloquence so persuasive and her knowlege so extraordinary for her rank and situation, with an irreproachable life and conduct, that whatever may be her fate with the vehement and excited body of elders, she has set an inquiry on foot that must be highly useful. As I understand, she had meant much sooner to have returned to her husband and young daughter in America, if this persecution had not constrained her to go back first to Ireland for testimonials of her conduct which were required to be produced on her appeal for her defence, and for the defence at the same time of the doctrine of the gospel as it appears to her.[5]

I have not leisure at present, or should have noticed some other things. But another opportunity will present itself. With <u>our</u> kindest regards to Mrs Millar and yourself I take my leave and remain Dear Sir,

Your affectionate servant
T. Lindsey.

1   Millar's letter to Lindsey of 28 Apr. 1801, which presumably was a reply to Lindsey's letter to him of 19 Mar. 1801 (Letter 717), seems not to have survived.
2   Lindsey referred here to Thomas Emlyn (see Letter 700, n. 14), who was imprisoned in Dublin on a heresy charge from 1703 to 1705.

3   Hannah Barnard (?1754–1825), a self-taught, accredited quaker minister, belonged to the monthly
     meeting of Hudson, New York. In 1798, she obtained permission from her meeting to travel on a
     preaching mission to England and Ireland; she and her companion (Elizabeth Coggeshall) landed at
     Falmouth in July 1798. In Ireland, she became involved with the 'liberal', or 'New Light' element
     among the quakers, which adopted a sceptical approach to several passages of the Old Testament,
     especially those which sanctioned war. On her return from Ireland to England in May 1800, she
     encountered much criticism from the quaker leadership in London, which accused her of departing
     from strict adherence to scripture. She was even called a deist, a Socinian and a disciple of Paine. See
     David W. Maxey, 'New light on Hannah Barnard, a quaker "heretic"', *Quaker History. The Bulletin
     of Friends Historical Association*, LXXVIII, 2 (Fall 1989), 61–5.
4   Hannah Barnard was ordered by the Devonshire House monthly meeting to refrain from preaching;
     her appeals against this ruling to the quarterly meeting of London and Middlesex and to the London
     yearly meeting were unsuccessful. The hostile verdict was communicated to Barnard's own meeting
     at Hudson, New York, which ordered her to desist from preaching and subsequently disowned her as
     a 'heretic'. See Rufus M. Jones, *The later periods of quakerism* (2 vols., London, 1921), I, 299–306.
     Her expulsion was symptomatic of the struggles between the 'liberal' and the 'evangelical' tendencies
     within quakerism at the turn of the century; Lindsey's interest in her case is explained by her associa-
     tion with the former tendency and by his own highly developed sense of identity with a 'persecuted'
     individual. For the same reason, her case received sympathetic treatment in the *Universal Theological
     Magazine*, I (1804), 272–4.
5   Hannah Barnard (née Jenkins) was married to Peter Barnard, a widower with two daughters and a
     son; it seems that she had no children of her own; *Notable American women, 1607–1950*, ed. E. T.
     James, J. W. James and P. S. Boyer (3 vols., Cambridge, MA, 1971), I, 88–9.

722. *To WILLIAM ALEXANDER   10 JUNE 1801

Text: 'Letters of the Rev. Theophilus Lindsey. No. VIII',
                       UH, II, 87 (27 Dec. 1862), 432.

Note: This is the only section of this letter printed by the *UH*; the manuscript seems not to have survived.

June 10th, 1801.

I have nothing particular to reply to your letter, except the pleasure it gave me
to find that our small memorials were not wasted upon unfeeling minds.[1] Loving
myself to have something to look at which had belonged to those whose qualities
or kindness had interested, or caught my affection, after all earthly intercourse had
ceased, I thought others might have the same feeling without being able to have
it gratified, but by a provision *par advance*. This determined me, (not to excite
too tender feelings to which you are prone) but at a period, certainly and happily
appointed by Him who has the issues of life in his own hand, when we are laid to
sleep, you might have something to look at and say, This was theirs.

My mind was cast in a firmer mould than yours, as my kind Maker knew the
lot he had assigned me would require it. Few, very few, indeed, have that perfect
mixture of calm unconquerable fortitude, with all the kind and gentle virtues, which
are so eminent in the dearest friend of my life.[2] I mention this as an excuse for often
saying brisk things to those who may be pained by the manner, however kind the
intention.

I think you had a copy sent you, some time ago, of Mr. Cappe's "Discourses
on the Providence and Government of God". I beg leave to refer you to them, as
the very best thing to reconcile all minds, who are capable of being influenced by
just reasoning, and strong persuasive eloquence, and deep piety. If such views as
are there presented fail to reconcile to all events and circumstances the mind of a
rational being, I despair of any other remedy. The last six, which are the practical
deductions, should be studied, and interwoven into the business of every day.[3]

If you knew how burdensome letter writing is to me, you would never expect me to write; nor should I have done it now, but only for once to show you I understand all your sorrows, and would lead you more and more to the only cure for all human evils, submission to the will of God, with cheerful acquiescence in all his appointments, great and small.[4]

---

1   Alexander's letter seems not to have survived.
2   Theophilus Lindsey.
3   Newcome Cappe's *Discourses on the providence and government of God* consisted of fifteen
     discourses; the last six (X–XV, the practical discourses) may be found on pp. 143–231.
4   Alexander's 'sorrows' included ill-health (although he lived until 1858), vexation at the public
     hostility shown to unitarians and anxiety over 'many of the important social questions of the day',
     including the criminal law. See his obituary in *MR*, NS, XIV (1858), 189.

723. To ROBERT MILLAR   16 JUNE 1801

Text: DWL, MS 12.46 (29).
Printed: Ditchfield, 'Quaker–unitarian encounter', 211 (short quotation
                from first paragraph); Graham, 'Unhappy country', 160–1
                (most of third paragraph; first two sentences of fourth
                paragraph).
Addressed: To/Mr Robt Millar,/Merchant/Dundee
Endorsed: Lond° 16th June 1801/Mr Lindsey [In pencil] D^r & Miss
                Small/M^r & Mrs Thornton/Mr & Mrs Ironside/Mr & Mrs
                [word illegible]/Mr^s Jobson/Miss Scott

Dear Sir,

                                                    London. June 16. 1801.

I am glad to have procured a free conveyance of another letter to Dundee, as my last broke off more abruptly than I intended:[1] but am sorry to begin with acquainting you that Hannah Barnard the quaker, whose case and character I mentioned with much satisfaction, was extremely ill used in her appeal to the society of Friends at their annual meeting, in not permitting her to speak for herself but under great restraints, in refusing her the certificate she had a claim to from their Body, and forbidding her to preach any more on the subjects which they disapproved, especially what related to Jesus not being the supreme God. Many friends however took part with her, and it is expected that the harsh treatment of Hannah will tend to promote that spirit of inquiry, which their leaders have done all in their power to stifle.[2]

I trust that by this time you will have had your property in Russia at liberty, so to have materials to give employment and bread to your manufacturers.[3] Only four days ago a friend of mine on a visit to the Owner of one of the principal Wharfs near London and walking with the Owner in the Rope walk, he observed to the Lady, that he did not know how soon fifteen hundred men might come and make havoc of all he possessed, there being that number at least unemployed for want of materials to work upon, and ready he feared for any mischief.[4]

I am sorry to acquaint you that I this day was informed by a friend who dined two days ago with a gentleman in constant correspondence with many persons at Botany Bay, who related that he was assured that Mr Palmer not only was a great Brewer, but also retailed the Liquor himself not in a very creditable way. Some other disparaging circumstances about him were also mentioned. But tho' I fear the report is true, It may be as well not to propagate it. Only I would not conceal it from You.[5] Nothing whatsoever was said of Mr James Ellis. The friend who gave me this information, remarked, that if the matter was true, it might be done in a kind of freak, as several of our friend's family have been a little flighty.[6] It was added that he had some thoughts of returning soon to England.

You will rejoice in knowing that I have had a letter from Dr Priestley under his own hand, that he was perfectly recovered from his dangerous illness, so as to reckon upon returning to Northumberland in a week or ten days; wch. I may perhaps have spoken of in my last, but am not certain.[7] He adds the increasing satisfaction that Mr Jefferson gives to all parties by his wisdom and moderation in his new office.[8] He also confirms the account of having agreed with a bookseller for printing the continuation of his Ecclesiastical History, and his Notes on the Whole Bible, both Old and New Testament; which I should think must be very valuable: and that he should set about the work without delay.[9] I seldom touch upon political matters with you. But I heard from such certain authority of a conversation which the King had with a person in a very high office, that I cannot refrain from mentioning that I am persuaded from it that his majesty is as well in health, and also in his understanding is as perfect as he was twenty years past, and that he is as likely to live twenty years to come as any one of his Subjects.[10] From this it is concluded, that we shall not soon have peace, as the present men and measures will be continued; and that Mr Pit[t] who brought in his successors will continue to influence them, and in all probability step into his place again.[11] It is a consolation however to think that there is a higher than the highest of them all, in whose disposal are all events, and who directeth every thing for the best, especially for those that reverence and put their trust in him. May He have you both in his good keeping, and preserve and qualifie us all for his heavenly kingdom and presence.

              T.H.L.[12]

---

1   This probably refers to the end of Letter 721.

2   See Letter 721, nn. 3 and 4. For the accusations of unitarianism made against Hannah Barnard, see Maxey, 'New light on Hannah Barnard', 73–4. As Dr Maxey rightly points out, the allegations were exaggerated, and Lindsey, whose unitarianism was based on detailed analysis of the scriptures, rejected Barnard's appeal to the 'inner light' as a reason for doubting Old Testament accounts of warfare or New Testament miracles.

3   Millar's property in Russia probably consisted of the linen and sail-cloth which his business exported; in his letter to Lindsey of 18 June 1791, he referred to the high value of the goods of several Dundee merchants, including himself, at St Petersburg; DWL, MS 12.46 (78). See also DWL, MS 12.57 (43).

4   Possibly Lindsey referred here to the Rope Walk in Sunbury on Thames, near the residence of Elizabeth Rayner, who was perhaps the lady to whom he referred.

5   See Letter 726 for Lindsey's subsequent information and repudiation of this story.

6   For a previous suggestion (in 1794) of insanity in Palmer's family, see Letter 557, n. 2.

7   Lindsey had not mentioned this matter in his previous surviving letter to Millar (Letter 721).

8   Thomas Jefferson (1743–1826) was elected president of the United States in 1800 and inaugurated on 4 Mar. 1801. He served for two terms, until Mar. 1809.

9   Probably this was Priestley's letter to Lindsey, written from Philadelphia, of 8 Apr. 1801, Rutt, I, 459. The final four volumes of Priestley's ecclesiastical history were entitled *A general history of the Christian church from the fall of the western empire* and were published in Northumberland in 1802–3. His *Notes on all the books of scripture* were published in four volumes in Northumberland in 1803–4; the first volume was published during Priestley's lifetime, the other three shortly after his death. His printer and bookseller in Northumberland was Andrew Kennedy.

10   George III lived for another eighteen years and seven months; he died on 29 Jan. 1820.

11   Pitt did not return to office until May 1804, when he succeeded Addington as prime minister. During the early stages of the latter's administration, Pitt gave it his full support. Peace preliminaries between Britain and France were signed on 1 Oct. 1801 and the Treaty of Amiens concluded on 25 Mar. 1802.

[12] This is an unusual example of Lindsey signing a letter with his wife's initial as well as his own; see also Letter 727.

724. To CHRISTOPHER WYVILL   16 JUNE 1801

Text: NYRO, ZFW 7/2/144/15, Wyvill of Constable Burton MSS.
Printed: Ditchfield, 'Lindsey–Wyvill correspondence', 168
                 (third paragraph); 169 (fourth paragraph).
Addressed: [In Hannah Lindsey's hand] To/The Rev^d. M^r. Wyville/Burton
                 Hall/near Bedale/Yorkshire
Endorsed: From The Rev^d. Theophilus Lindsey June 16. 1801
Postmarked: JU 16 801

London. June. 16. 1801.
Dear Sir,

The day after I received your last favour,[1] for such I esteem it, we were engaged to go into the country for the whole week: At our return, finding that nothing was come from Mr Debrett's, I went to Piccadilly, and Mr Debrett being from home, I found your packet for me with several others lying upon the Counter, which I asked for and took accordingly, and inquired of the shopman whether the pamphlet had been advertized, or was to be sold, but he could tell me nothing about it.[2] I shall be sorry if there be any fear or hesitation about vending this small but most valuable, judicious and temperate tract, and most inoffensive as one would think; but there can be no accounting for the apprehensions of Booksellers in these times, nor any blame to be imputed to them.[3]

Having occasion yesterday to write to the Duke of Northumberland, I mentioned your Letter to Major Cartwright in the terms in which I was persuaded, he would think it deserved, but presuming he would have received a copy from you, but if he has not, shall send him one immediately.[4]

It must be of service in the midst of this dead calm with respect to the real state to which the nation has been reduced by its rulers, to hold forth, tho ever so briefly, to those that will see and hear, the liberties and privileges we have lost, and the only way to recover them, if they are recoverable. The contrast of Mr Pitt with Mr Fox, must strike every one. No one perhaps was equally qualified with yourself to delineate the former, and you have done it with a fine hand, but some want some harsher strokes of the pencil.[5] A friend of mine, who is very much with Mr Bosvile, is exceedingly pleased with the wisdom and moderation of what you have laid before the public, and tells me it is the judgment of those with whom he converses.[6]

I must now acquaint you, that on Saturday,[7] we dined at a friend's, where there was much company, particularly of the Law, and one that was present mentioned that he had it from a friend in a very high station, who two days before, passed an hour and half with a great personage; when he could not but observe, with what acuteness, judiciousness, and good sense he delivered himself upon a variety of subjects and characters that came before them: H.M. seemed to be thin and somewhat emaciated, like a convalescent, but also like one that was tending to be plumper and stronger: And the person who mentioned these things, said it appeared to him, that H.M. was as likely to live twenty years to come, saving accidents, as any one of his subjects.[8] From this fact the company concluded; that there was an end of all the expectations, that some had lately, formed under an administration in which Earl Moira,[9] Ld Thurlow, &c were to bear a chief part, under the presumed succession of P.W.[10] to the chief Power, either in a regency or in his own person. It was also concluded, that all hope of the war being ended was to be given up. For that the successors of the late minister were engaged to follow his steps, and to act under his influence; and peace it was known was never his object. And some added, that it was not improbable that he might very soon come in again, as it was rumoured the New Ministry were not able to go on without him.

Many thanks to you, Dear Sir, for your kind invitation to Burton. But we are too old for such long Yorkshire Journies: [one word illegible] certainly will not suit at present, as we happen to have this year much business to attend to which will keep us necessarily in the South. My wife who unites with me in due respects to Mrs Wyvill and yourself, desires me to say how glad we are that Miss Bentham is come back well to you, tho she is also much interested for Miss S.[?] Turner, who has so well supplied her absence and is so amiable and accomplished; as we have heard of you all by Mrs Cappe.[11] And it is our earnest wish that You both may have increasing joy and satisfaction in the health and improvements of your numerous, amiable and promising family.

I remain, Dear Sir, Your much obliged, and faithful affectionate servant
T. Lindsey.

---

1 Wyvill's letter to Lindsey, presumably written in May or early June 1801, seems not to have survived.

2 John Debrett's premises were at 178, Piccadilly. The tract in question was Wyvill's *A letter to John Cartwright, Esq.*, published by Lucas Lund in York in 1801, with a second edition, also published by Lund in York, later in the same year. Wyvill's theme was the need for moderate parliamentary reform which respected property rights and confined the franchise to householders, rather than the universal male suffrage advocated by Cartwright.

3 Lindsey no doubt had in mind Debrett's refusal to publish Wyvill's *The secession from parliament vindicated*; see Letter 681, n. 4.

4 Lindsey's letter to the 2nd duke of Northumberland seems not to have survived in the papers of the dukes of Northumberland at Alnwick Castle. Lindsey evidently undertook to send to the duke a copy of Wyvill's *Letter to John Cartwright*, if Wyvill had not already done so.

5 For Wyvill's contrast between Pitt's abandonment of reform, and the 'manly wisdom and virtue' of Fox, see his *Letter to John Cartwright*, pp. 15–17.

6 Possibly the friend who reported this favourable impression of Wyvill's work was Thomas Brand Hollis. William Bosville (1745–1813), a former army officer, was a political associate of John Horne Tooke, Sir Francis Burdett and other reformers. He was also a well-known host at his London house in Welbeck street.

7 Saturday 13 June 1801.

8 In the spring of 1801, George III made a slow recovery from the illness which in Feb. of that year had threatened to incapacitate him.

9 Francis Rawdon-Hastings (1754–1826), 2nd earl of Moira and (from 1817) marquess of Hastings. In the early months of 1801, he expected to be the head of, or prominent in, a new administration appointed by his friend the prince of Wales in the event of George III's death or permanent incapacity. A successful career soldier, he subsequently served as master-general of the ordnance during the ministry of the talents (1806–7) and was governor-general of India from 1813 to 1821. He was the son of John, Baron Rawdon, 1st earl of Moira, to whom Lindsey wrote eleven (surviving) letters during the 1750s and early 1760s (Vol. I, Letters 35–43, 47, 49). Lindsey had known him as a child, and in 1757, described him and his brother as two 'lovely brats'; see Vol. I, Letter 35.

10 George (1762–1830), prince of Wales; prince regent 1811–1820; reigned as George IV, 1820–30.

11 Possibly Mary Louisa Bentham (1797–1865), the eldest daughter of the naval architect Samuel Bentham (1757–1831) and his wife Maria Sophia, née Fordyce (1765–1858). She was the niece of the philosopher Jeremy Bentham (1748–1832). The initial which Lindsey accorded to Miss Turner is not clear; S is the likeliest reading. It seems certain that she was part of the large extended family of William Turner of Newcastle, which was well known to Wyvill and to Catharine Cappe.

725. To WILLIAM DAVY   **30 JUNE 1801**

Text: DWL, Davy letterbook.
Addressed: To/William Davy Esqʳ/Merchant/Philadelphia
Endorsed: T. Lindsay – [*sic*]/1801

London. June 30. 1801.

Dear Sir,

I was greatly obliged to you for so kindly interesting yourself for me by your favour in March last by acquainting me with Dʳ Priestleys illness, which we are all here full of joy to have taken so happy a turn as to give hope that he may in future enjoy full as good health as he has hitherto done in America, though that has been by no means to be complained of.[1]

I ought and should have sooner thanked you for your letter, had I not continually delayed it in hope of one from Mʳ Harry Toulmin; but I cannot be easy delaying any longer, to desire some kind information from you concerning him.

I have not the letters at present before me to mark the dates; but I well recollect that in the last letter I received from him, he made mention, that his friend had been re-elected Governor of Kentucky, and himself again appointed Secretary of state. But in one which I soon after was favoured with from You, you added that you understood that our friend was not rechosen Secretary, as there had been a determination made, that Place was to be filled by none but native Americans.[2]

The next tidings I had concerning him, was in receiving a draft for fifty Pounds upon me, in his own handwriting as I was persuaded and transmitted as I think in a letter of your's, for I have the letter by me, though I cannot immediately come at it. The draft I accepted, and paid the money.[3] But from that time to this, though I have continued to write as usual, and send some trifling Papers, till very lately, I have never had one syllable from him to say whether he was alive or dead, neither has his worthy father, who cannot but be in the utmost concern at his silence; nor as I understand, has any of his friends in England, or any of his wifes friends and relations, during the long interval, had the least account concerning him or his family.

This circumstance, I confess, rather gives ground to hope, that the great blank relating to him and his family must have arisen from the failure and miscarriage of letters; but still I am filled with anxiety for him, and persuade myself, that if it be in your power to give relief, you will be so good as to do it, the first opportunity.

As war still continues betwixt France, and England, it will be natural, that I should say something to you about it. And I would first observe, that there is something like a peace supposed to be going forwards, with Buonaparte, by means of Mʳ Otto.[4] But it is kept intirely secret, so that nothing transpires. One thing is certain, that nothing will be done, till the fate of Egypt is decided; and that is not yet known, though generally believed that it will fall to us.[5]

There is another event expected, which it is believed will have much effect in regard to peace or war. You are no stranger to his majesty's late illness. It has been given out and generally credited, that he was so well recovered, as to be full as well as he had been for 20 years past. But this has lately lost ground; and I mention it from very high authority, that he is so unsettled, and so little to be depended upon, that there must be a Regency, and the P.W. is at last to be appointed with an estabilishment of £8,000 a year.[6]

I have time only to add my wifes best respects and our wishes of every good to you and Yours. Believe me always, Dear Sir,

Your much obliged and affectionate servant

T. Lindsey.

1   See William Davy's letter to Lindsey of 14 Mar. 1801; Rutt, I, 455 n. ‡.
2   See Letter 713, n. 2. Henry Toulmin was secretary of state of Kentucky from 1796 to 1804.
3   Perhaps unsurprisingly, this draft for £50 sent by Henry Toulmin to Lindsey has not survived. Possibly the letter from Davy to Lindsey to which the latter referred was a part of that of 14 Mar. 1801 (n. 1, above) omitted by Rutt, or an earlier non-surviving letter from Davy to Lindsey.
4   Louis Guillaume Otto (1753–1817) was the French minister plenipotentiary in London for the conduct of peace negotiations in 1800–1, and negotiated the terms of the peace preliminaries which were signed in Oct. 1801, prior to the conclusion of the Treaty of Amiens the following Mar. He was subsequently the French ambassador to the court of Bavaria, and at Vienna, and served as under-secretary of state for foreign affairs during Napoleon's 'Hundred days' in 1815.
5   On 8 Mar. 1801, British troops commanded by Sir Ralph Abercromby made a successful landing at Aboukir against heavy French resistance and on 21 Mar., defeated the French at Alexandria, where Abercromby was fatally wounded. On 30 Aug. 1801, the French capitulated at Cairo and agreed to evacuate Egypt, which was restored to the Ottoman Empire.
6   In fact, George III was well on the way to recovery by July 1801, when he visited Southampton and Weymouth. There was no regency until Feb. 1811. Lindsey omitted two noughts from his estimate of the likely establishment of George, prince of Wales, in the event of a regency in 1801.

726. To ROBERT MILLAR   30 JULY 1801

Text: DWL, MS 12.46 (30).
Printed: Graham, 'Unhappy country', 161–2 (first two paragraphs; first three sentences of third paragraph, with minor errors of transcription).
Addressed: To/Mr Robt Millar/Merchant/Dundee
Endorsed: Londo 30 July 1801/Mr Lindsey
Postmarked: Postmark missing.

Mordon. Surry. July 30
1801.

Dear Sir,

You will have pleasure in reading and I no less in transcribing for you, a letter I lately received from a friend at Portsmouth[1] dated the 25th. ins.

"On monday last I went on board the Buffalo, a sloop of war which was in dock for some repairs, to examine some birds from New South Wales. As I was leaving the ship a gentleman of the yard who was on board, informed me that the man to whom these birds were intrusted had been a convict, and was from Port Jackson.[2] I went to him and interrogated him respecting his knowlege of Mr Palmer, and whether he left him at the settlement when he came away? Two of the officers of the ship hearing me very politely came forward and gave me every information I wished, which I take the earliest opportunity of transmitting to you. These gentlemen spoke of Mr Palmer in the highest terms of approbation and respect, and assured me of his being in great estimation with governor Hunter.[3] The report of his being a Brewer and a Publican is without the least foundation; the officers appeared indignant at such a report and said repeatedly, that never while they were at the settlement, nor before that, had they heard of his having acted in any manner, or in any capacity, that could possibly demean him as a gentleman; and that there was not a better bred man, nor a person who conducted himself more like a gentleman thro' the whole colony.[4] Mr

Palmer dined with them on board the Buffalo the day before she sailed from Port Jackson. I saw also a person on board the Buffalo, who had been in the colony for a considerable time and confirmed the whole of what was told me by the officers. This person had built a vessel called the Matthew, of about 200 tons, I think he said, for Mʳ Palmer, which was employed in procuring skins and conveying them to China. Mʳ Palmer has had another ship built, which is called the Plumer, of 300 tons, commanded by a person of the name of Reed. In this ship, Mʳ Palmer, James Ellis, Mʳ and Mʳˢ Boston and their children are on their passage to England. The Plumer was taking in her ballast when the Buffalo left Port Jackson, and the officers told me they supposed she must be ready to sail in a month or six weeks as the farthest after them. The Buffalo sailed the beginning of October. The Plumer was to touch at the Cape to dispose of part of her cargo, and thence to proceed to Europe: so that in a few weeks we may expect to hear of or to see the living part of her cargo."[5]

You may be assured, my good friend, that I shall diligently inquire after Mʳ Palmer's arrival, and shᵈ I be in London at the time shoud be anxious to see him and have pleasure in comunicating all I see and learn to you. That he has been highly serviceable in civilizing and advancing the welfare of that country one can have no doubt, and will thereby become its great benefactor. That he has endeavoured to spread among them the knowlege of the one true God and the light of the divine truth of the gospel, I should be quite overjoyed to find. *James Ellis's* parents or relations will doubtless rejoice to know that after an exile of so many years he is now drawing towards them.[6] From friends that pass and repass daily to and from the great city, whose pinnacles we behold from some of our downs, we continually hear all that passes. To all appearance Peace was never at a greater distance. It is not pleasing to hear the comon people universally say, that they do not know what harm the french will do, if they invade them: they may fare better, and they cannot be worse. There is the greatest prospect and promise of plenty, but Contractors &c and vermin of that sort will not let it be enjoyed. I think I sent you A Narrative of the Proceedings of a Society of Baptists in York, in relinquishing the popular systems of Religion, from the Study of the Scriptures – by David Eaton.[7] I shᵈ. have been glad to send you his valuable Defence of it in Letters to the Revᵈ Mʳ Graham, a Clergyman in York, were I in the way of doing it.[8] Perhaps you may get a copy by some person [who] passes thro' York.

Having ocasion to write to a friend who is in the house,[9] I have the satisfaction of conveying this through him to You. My wife unites in cordial respects to Mʳˢ Millar and yourself and I am ever, Dear Sir, Your much obliged and affectionate servant

T. Lindsey.

PS. A few lines left at any time in Essex Street will readily find their way to me here; when I shall be glad to learn how your Missions go on. David Eaton, could they be brought to read and inquire, would easily lead them all from their intolerance into the way of peace and truth. Dʳ Priestley I heard from within these ten days. Confirmed in health, he was most busily employed, and happy of course[10]

---

1   The friend at Portsmouth was Russell Scott, whom Lindsey identified as the writer of the letter from which he quoted (see Letter 728).

2   Port Jackson, the modern Sydney harbour, was the place of Palmer's exile.

3   For John Hunter, governor of New South Wales, see Letter 633, n. 4.

4   See Letter 723 for the story of Palmer as brewer.

5   The 'Plumer' was the ship in which Palmer, Boston and Ellis left Botany Bay, hoping to return to Britain via the Cape of Good Hope. Reed was the owner or captain (or both) of the 'Plumer'.

6 The tear in the manuscript means that two words – probably 'the end' – are missing,

7 It is evident from Letters 687 and 699 that Lindsey had sent David Eaton's work to Millar, and that Millar had expressed his approval of it.

8 John Graham, rector of St Mary, Bishophill Sen., and, from Nov. 1796, of St Saviour, York, was author of *A defence of scripture doctrines, as understood by the Church of England; in reply to a pamphlet, 'Scripture the only guide to religious truth'; or, 'A narrative of the proceedings of a society of baptists, in York .... In a series of letters to Mr D. Eaton'* (York, 1800). Eaton's response was *Letters addressed to the Rev. John Graham, in answer to his 'Defence of scripture doctrines', and in vindication of 'A narrative of the proceedings of a society of baptists in York'* (York, 1801).

9 Possibly this friend 'in the house' was James Martin or Benjamin Hobhouse; another possibility is William Mellish (see Letters 728 and 729).

10 Probably Lindsey referred here to his letter from Priestley of 11 June 1801; Rutt, I, 463–4.

727. To WILLIAM FREND   9 AUGUST 1801

Text: CUL, Add. MS 7886, no. 169.
Printed: *Letters to William Frend from the Reynolds family of Little Paxton and John Hammond of Fenstanton 1793–1814*, ed. Frida Knight (Cambridge Antiquarian Records Society, I, 1974), p. 49 (first paragraph).
Addressed: [In Hannah Lindsey's hand] Mr Frend/Inner Temple
Endorsed: Mr Lindsey/1801
Postmarked: Postmark missing.

Morden. Aug. 9. 1801

Dear Sir,

The sight of your handwriting revives us much by delivering us from the anxious suspence we were in with respect to Paxton; but our friend's report at his return from Greatford will relieve us still more:[1] May a kind providence, that watches over all his creatures for good, grant it to be favourable to our hopes of M^{rs} R ___ 's future enjoyment of all those blessings which it has in such abundance poured around her.[2]

You will have heard from Dr Disney, or Mr J. Joyce, or Mr Johnson, or from some other quarter I know not of, concerning the speedy expected return of Mr Fysh Palmer, and some friends along with him, in his own ship from Botany Bay. Had we been in Town I should have not failed to comunicate to you with the first, the notice I had of it, from Mr Scott of Portsmouth.[3]

Mrs Barnard had called in Essex Street, in expectation of seeing us, when I should have heard something of her peculiar sentiments, of which a friend of hers had given me some intimation; but I am more pleased to receive the knowlege from you, and thank you for it. I am sorry for the extreme to which she carries the principle of the quakers, and the erroneous sentiments concerning the divine moral government, which it leads her to embrace; in which she appears to be greatly mistaken: but I do not suppose it would be an easy matter to convince her of this.[4]

In acknowlegement for this kind comunication from you, I have my wife's permission to send you an extract from a correspondent of her's now at Weymouth, which you will say to be from no ordinary hand. The lady has a son a young officer in Egypt, who at the age of 25. will inherit, if he lives, a fortune of two thousand a year at least, and is very promising.[5]

"I am thankful not to be always troubling you with the black catalogue of my sorrows. I have now the comfort of hearing my poor child escaped as well the 21st. as he did on the 1st. dreadful engagement, and he says is quite well, and tho' he seems deeply to feel the sad waste of human blood, writes in good spirits, bids me "not be uneasy as the worst of the business is now over".[6]

"I wish with all my heart Weymouth was as near _____ for I have a comfortable spare room and think we should often laugh at the spectacle this place presents. Among the figurante I own to You, none raises my laughter (shall I add too, indignation) more than the cold, phlegmatic, sharp countenan[c]ed L[d]. Rosslyn (the great lawyer I used to almost tremble before)[7] dress'd as the youngest and gaiest courtier, and his face likewise made to suit the new character, with smiles, with his hat off listening by the hour with delighted attention to the brilliant sallies of the royal party. I actually saw him eagerly devouring for above two hours the *animated* conversation of Prince Adolphus.[8] The royal family is in[?] the water, to the play four times a week: to the rooms sunday evening, to walk other evenings on the esplanade, and in short live in public, which gives little persons like myself the opportunity of hearing so much of their discourse, and to wonder at those who can make the business of their lives, to "watch the looks of beings weak and foolish as themselves".[9] I have just time to add my wife's most kind regards – that we are both very well in this sweet retreat – and always much and truly in haste

Yours

T. H. Lindsey

---

1   This is a reference to Richard Reynolds of Little Paxton; possibly he had just returned from a visit to Greatford, Lincolnshire.

2   Mary Catherine Reynolds, the wife of Richard Reynolds, appears to have suffered from some kind of mental disorder. Writing to Frend on 15 June 1803, Reynolds confided that the mind and person of his wife were greatly altered, 'but in all her wretchedness she is not insensible to kind Treatment, and therefore I don't withdraw entirely from Her' (CUL, Add. MS 7886 (Frend papers), no. 229). According to an obituary of Richard Reynolds, he suffered 'a severe family affliction', under which he 'conducted himself in such a manner as to shew the strength of conjugal affection in the highest degree'. It added that 'he acted towards the unhappy source of his sorrows, whose mind, once of the finest mould, was lost to all feeling, with unparalleled benevolence and attention'; *MR*, IX (1814), 133. Mary Catherine Reynolds died in Jan. 1824; her will, dated 20 Sept. 1799 (with a brief codicil dated 6 Feb. 1807), and proved on 22 Dec. 1824, showed no alteration since the death of her husband in 1814; TNA: PRO PROB 11/1693, fos. 283r–284r.

3   See Letter 726.

4   Possibly the friend of Hannah Barnard from whom Lindsey had heard of her 'peculiar sentiments' was Elizabeth Coggeshall of Rhode Island, an accredited quaker minister who accompanied Barnard on her travels in the British Isles; *Notable American Women*, I, ed. James, James and Boyer, 88–9.

5   Probably the young officer was Frederick Stovin, who was born in 1783. For his family and likely inheritance, see Letter 700, n. 10. His mother, who was almost certainly the writer of the letter to Hannah Lindsey, was Theodosia Stovin, née Sparrow (d. 1834).

6   For these two battles in Egypt, see Letter 725, n. 5. For the likely identity of the writer of this letter, see n. 5, above, and Letter 700, n. 10.

7   Alexander Wedderburn (1733–1805), from 1780, Baron Loughborough and from 1801, earl of Rosslyn, was lord chancellor from Jan. 1793 until Apr. 1801.

8   Prince Adolphus, duke of Cambridge (1774–1850), was the tenth child and seventh son of George III.

9   George III and his wife and younger children, including Prince Adolphus, took their (by this time) customary holiday at Weymouth in the summer of 1801.

728. To RUSSELL SCOTT   **16 AUGUST 1801**

Text: Scott Coll.
Printed: McLachlan, 'Lindsey to Scott', 124–5 (entire letter, except for part of first paragraph, with minor errors of transcription).
Addressed: [?In Mellish's hand] London Eighteen Augt 1801/Revd Russel Scott/Portsmouth/WfreeMellish[?][1]
Postmarked: FREE AUG 18 1801

Mrs Chamber's Mordon Surry
Aug. 16. 1801.

Dear Sir,

Seldom have I been more gratified with a letter from a friend, than with your's of the date of July 25,[2] which brought such an agreeable and authentic account of Mr Fysh Palmer and his movements and expected speedy return from his exile; and I have been much mortified that I have not sooner thanked you for it.[3] But I have been somewhat relieved, in thinking that you would take it as a sort of acknowlegement in receiving since from me, by Mr Johnson, the Letters of David Eaton to a York Clergyman who had thought at once to overwhelm such a puny adversary, but who here sinks very low before him; and I have heard is now very sorry that he stirred him up to write again.[4] In short, I think the work will give both pleasure and satisfaction in the triumph of so good a cause.

Yourself also I trust have been employed in what will essentially and eventually promote it, in being mainly instrumental in the estabilishment of the new Unitarian Society, of which you give me the first notice, confirmed afterwards by Dr Toulmin; of which also I shall be most glad to receive the subsequent regulations &c agreed upon, which you promise me, as I shall surely desire to be admitted a member; but all this at your full leisure.[5]

When the *Plumer* lands its contents at Portsmouth, I have no doubt of your having the first notice of it, and being visited by those to whom You have been constantly ready to do the most friendly offices, and have done them often. If it be in your way, I should wish you would try to discover, though I do not believe they will make any secret of it, whether any great change has taken place in him, or in James Ellis, with respect to the system of Revelation.[6] I do not make the inquiry out of mere curiosity, but because some I highly value and esteem are greatly interested in it. All the particulars of this sort that you remark in them will be peculiarly acceptable, as well as any thing else concerning our friend, his intentions and prospects that you think I should like to know.[7]

I think that when you was in Town, we had some discourse of Mrs Hannah Barnard the female quaker, and her ill treatment from the society of friends, for her strenuous defence of the Divine Unity. She called to see me in Essex-Street, after I left town, for wch. I was sorry, as I sh^d. have been glad to have talked with her, especially as I had been told, what I have since learnt very particularly from a friend who has passed some hours with her; "that she carries the quaker notion concerning war to the farthest extreme, in which I agree with her; but also goes so far as to deny that the supreme being ever gave any countenance to the comands ascribed to him by Moses to extirpate the Canaanites".[8] I am concerned at this, on many accounts, as it will lead her [into] many other errors, and her adversaries will think themselves justified in their intolerance towards her.[9] A letter to day from a quaker of my acquaintance and one of her protectors, says she is setting out to return to America.[10]

I hope M[rs] Scott and your lovely boy and his good sister with yourself, are all in the best plight; as are my wife and your humble servant, tho' the latter not a little the worse for the wear: But we have all cause to be thankful for every thing; myself especially, to have enjoyed and to enjoy so much good in this first state of being. A letter sent as usual to Essex Street, will be sent the next day hither.

Believe me Dear Sir, always your obliged and affectionate

T. Lindsey.

---

[1] This refers to William Mellish MP; see Letter 729.

[2] This refers to the letter from Scott which Lindsey quoted in his letter to Robert Millar of 30 July 1801 (Letter 726).

[3] Evidently, in a non-surviving letter to Lindsey, Russell Scott had conveyed over-optimistic predictions of Palmer's imminent return to Britain.

[4] For David Eaton's reply to John Graham, see Letter 726, n. 8.

[5] This 'new Unitarian Society' was the southern Unitarian Society, founded in 1801.

[6] Lindsey was curious to know whether or not Palmer and Ellis still believed in the Christian revelation. There is no reason to suspect that Palmer had abandoned his belief in it.

[7] This was over-optimistic (see n. 3, above); the *Plumer* and its passengers did not arrive at Portsmouth.

[8] Lindsey did not identify his friend who reported this conversation with Hannah Barnard; obvious possibilities include Thomas Belsham and Jeremiah Joyce. For the biblical commands to Moses to extirpate the Canaanites, see Exodus xxxiii. 2 and xxxiv. 11; Deuteronomy xx.17; and Numbers xxxiii, 51–4.

[9] For Lindsey's concern at Hannah Barnard's theology, see Ditchfield, 'Quaker–unitarian encounter', 211–15.

[10] Possibly this friend among the quakers was William Rathbone of Liverpool (see Letter 500), who subsequently published an account of the controversies within the Society of Friends, entitled *A Narrative of events that have lately taken place in Ireland among the society called quakers* (London, 1804), which was sympathetic to Barnard and those of her persuasions. Barnard left England on her return to America on 31 Aug. 1801.

---

729. To ROBERT MILLAR   26 AUGUST 1801

Text:	DWL, MS 12.46 (31).
Printed:	*Unitarian Baptist Advocate*, II, XXIV (Dec. 1838), 267–9 (with minor errors and omission of the postscript); Ditchfield, 'Quaker–unitarian encounter', 121–3 (most of second paragraph; whole of third paragraph; most of fourth paragraph).
Addressed:	[?In Mellish's hand] London Twenty Nine Aug 1801/M[r]. Rob[t]. Millar/Merchant/Dundee/N B/ Wfree Mellish[1]
Endorsed:	Lond[o]. 26th Aug[t] 1801/Mr Lindsey
Postmarked:	FREE AU 26 1801

Mordon. Surry

Aug. 26. 1801

Dear Sir,

My last letter[2] gave you a very recent account I had received of M[r] Fysh Palmer, and of his being very soon expected in England in his own ship, accompanied by M[r] James Ellis, and M[r] and M[rs] Boston and their family;[3] whether to abide in England, or how they intended to dispose of themselves my information did not reach, but the same friend has engaged to give me the earliest notice of every thing concerning him, if he lands at Portsmouth, which he is fully expected to do.

This letter I perceive has crossed yours on the road,[4] which I am glad to receive, and the more as the interval has furnished me with the means of correcting some mistakes into which my letter had led you, or rather of giving some fuller information concerning the celebrated and worthy Hannah Barnard, the American quaker. Some intercourse had passed between her and myself before I left Lond[on] by means of some of her friends of my acquaintance, and I had presented her with some books that were agreeable to her, particularly the Volume of Haynes, which I had re-published with a Preface, adopted by our unitarian Society.[5] In consequence of this she wished to see me, and actually called in Essex Street some hours after we had left it. Not willing to be disappointed she took the trouble to come down to this place, with three of her friends[6] who brought her along with them in their carriage, the middle of the last week, for which I felt highly obliged to her, and I was glad to observe that the two Ladies, the mistresses of this mansion[7] were no less gratified and even edified by the sight and conversation of so extraordinary a person.

You are at first struck and much pleased with the frankness of her manner, and the ease and good sense with which she enters into conversation and convinces you of her affection for a husband and two daughters she had left behind her and the sacrifice she had made in so doing, but the will of God was to be preferred to every thing.[8] The deep seriousness of her conversation affects you exceedingly, and being possessed of a fine imagination, a most uncommon memory, and having read many of our best moral and religious books, and all our poets, Dr Young[9] in particular, and quoting these occasionally, and the Scriptures continually, gives her great command of the passions and affections of those about her.

But in the course of our conversation, and, I am sorry to remark, in the result of it, tho' managed and conducted with chearfulness and good humour, I was constrained more than once to say, that we must agree to differ. I could perceive from her own conversation and that of her friends along with her, that religion was nothing but a divine philosophy of the mind, in which every thing was to be decided by their own private conviction and feeling. Upon being pressed home with the facts of the divine interposition in the Mosaic history, with much acuteness and civility towards those that might differ from her, she kept aloof, and evaded a direct reply. She [did][10] not allow the supreme Being ever gave the least countenance to war, nor that the commands ascribed to him by Moses to extirpate the Canaanites proceeded from him.[11] Not knowing the Scriptures but according to our english translation, she frequently makes mistakes, of a very essential kind, where a little better information might sett her right. But I tire you. I w^d. only add, that tho' she has been extremely ill used and rejected by the quaker-society, I trust her appearance among them will excite many amongst them to investigate the question of orthodoxy and to relinquish their trinitarian notions to which they seem to be bound by a very slender tye.

Very late letters from Northumberland confirm Dr Priestley's recovery to most perfect health. You may depend upon knowing how he proceeds with his Two Publications.[12]

I hope the crops in your parts will answer the very promising appearances when You last wrote. The harvest here is over, and has been most abundant in all respects. But we shall have no plenty, till peace comes and paper credit is at an end. It is hoped and believed, that the fall of Egypt will make way for peace, and then the other must follow.[13]

I do not allow of any obligations on your side; but my wife, with our joint respects to Mrs Millar and yourself, wishes me to say that she shall be much gratified with your kind intended present of some Scotch honey from your good mother's garden,[14] and rememberance of those it comes from will give it the greater relish.

Believe me always, Dear Sir, y^r much obliged and affectionate

T. Lindsey

I was glad to learn from an intirely new correspondent, a James Smiton of Newburgh, that he has the good principles and discernment to adjoin himself to your Society, when occasionally drawn to Dundee.[15]

---

1   Possibly William Mellish (?1764–1838) of Bush Hill, Edmonton, MP for Great Grimsby from 1796 to 1802 and from 1803 to 1806; for Middlesex from 1806 to 1820. Although usually a supporter of Pitt's second ministry, he voted against it on key issues and gave his backing to the ministry of all the talents in 1806–7. He was an opponent of Sir Francis Burdett at Middlesex in the general election of 1806. Lindsey seems to have used his franking privilege.

2   Lindsey's previous surviving letter to Millar was that of 30 July 1801 (Letter 726).

3   John Boston accompanied Palmer and Ellis in their unsuccessful voyage from Botany Bay, and after Palmer's death at Guam, returned to Botany Bay, where he organized a trading expedition to Canton. On 30 Sept. 1804, he was killed by inhabitants of Tongataboo, where he had landed in search of provisions. His wife and two children predeceased him. See the entry for Boston by George Parsons in *ODNB*, VI, 719–20.

4   This letter from Millar to Lindsey seems not to have survived.

5   For Lindsey's edition of Hopton Haynes, *The scripture account of the attributes and worship of God*, see Letter 406, n. 16.

6   One of Hannah Barnard's three friends whom Lindsey met was probably Elizabeth Coggeshall; see Letter 727, n. 4.

7   Sophia and Frances Chambers.

8   For Hannah Barnard's husband and daughters, whom she had left in Hudson, New York, where they belonged to the Hudson monthly meeting, see Letter 721, n. 5.

9   Edward Young (*c.* 1683–1763), poet, was best known for his 'The complaint, or night-thoughts on life, death and immortality' (1742–6), with which Lindsey was acquainted (see Vol. I, Letter 175). Young held the degree of DCL from Oxford University.

10 The manuscript is very slightly torn at this point: one word, probably 'did', or 'would', is missing.

11 See Letter 728, n. 8.

12 These letters from Priestley from Northumberland were probably that of 11 June 1801 (to Lindsey) and that of 25 June 1801 (to Belsham); see Rutt, I, 463–4, 465–6. In a passage omitted by Rutt from Priestley's letter to Belsham of 25 June 1801, DWL, MS 12.13, Priestley referred to the progress of his *General history of the Christian church* and his *Notes on all the books of scripture*.

13 For the defeat of the French in Egypt, see Letter 725, n. 5.

14 I have not been able to make a positive identification of Millar's mother. However, his obituary in the *Christian Pioneer*, NS, VII (1841), 369, states that he was born in the parish of Inchture (Perthshire) on 27 July 1761. A search via the International Genealogical Index shows that a child named Robert Miller was baptized in that parish on 11 Aug. 1761. Bearing in mind that the names Millar and Miller were often used interchangeably, and the likelihood that baptism took place within three weeks of birth, it is quite possible that the child in question was Robert Millar. The parents of the child were Robert and Isabel Millar; perhaps the latter was the mother of Robert Millar. Although she probably lived in Dundee by 1801, I regret that, other than the reference to honey, I have no information about her garden.

15 Possibly this was the craftsman James Smiton, of Newburgh, Fife, a correspondent of Thomas Palmer, who supplied him with radical literature; see Palmer to Smiton, 20 July 1793, *State trials*, XXIII, 325. The John Smiton of Newburgh, Fife, referred to by Bob Harris was possibly the same person; see Harris, 'Print and politics', in *Scotland in the age of the French Revolution*, ed. Harris, p. 169.

730. To ROBERT MILLAR   **29 SEPTEMBER 1801**

Text:	DWL, MS 12.46 (32).
Printed:	*Unitarian Baptist Advocate*, III, I (Jan. 1839), 15–16 (with minor errors); Ditchfield, 'Quaker–unitarian encounter', 215 (third sentence of third paragraph).
Addressed:	[In Grafton's hand] *Newmarket* ~~September~~ *October first* 1801/ To/M^r. Robert Millar,/Merchant/Dundee/N.B./Grafton
Endorsed:	Lond°. 29 Sep. 1801/Mr Lindsey.
Postmarked:	NEWMARKET 62 OC 4

Mordon. Surry
Septr. 29. 1801.

Dear Sir,

I am sorry it has not been in my power to thank you sooner for your letter; and the acceptable present that accompanied it, and kind directions about it, which have been of use to my wife in writing to our servant to take proper care of it in our absence, as our return home is rather uncertain. My wife desires me to say it will be the more grateful to us to taste it, as it will put upon recollecting such friends and valuable estimable characters from whom it comes, and I that have not even tasted honey of 40 years shall try now if I can eat it without suffering from it.

Your idea seems to me a very good one, of a small liberal publication, adapted to the capacity of the common people, in answer to Mr Haldane's publication.[1] If I were as capable of writing such a piece as your partiality leads you to think, I have not a moment's leisure for such an undertaking. For to tell you what has not yet transpired to Dr Priestley or any other friend, I have been for two years past employed in putting some thoughts together on a very important subject which promised to be of some use if I could be able to give the finishing hand to them; which I rather despaired of this spring from a very enfeebling attack which I met with, and seemed to disable me very much: but the sweet air and quiet, and leisure of this delightful retreat, and above all the kindest attentions of two ladies of our oldest friends, it's hospitable owners, have quite recruited me, so as to encourage me to hope I shall carry up my manuscript with me at our return to town, in such a state as I may venture to produce it before the public with tolerable hope of it being of some use.[2] I shall endeavour however, when we go back to our old quarters in Essex-Street, tho' I cannot offer my own services, to try to procure an ingenious friend whom I have in my eyes, to draw up a small pamphlet that may promote your christian views in bringing those deluded poor people to their senses about their fellow creatures.[3]

I am much pleased with your description of the member of your society, who is likely soon to quit you and join the society of Quakers, for whom he is really a fit subject. Hannah Barnard's abilities and talents and disposition will I trust do some good. Her religion is certainly nothing more or less than a more pious deism, as you take quakerism to be: which I cannot but wish her visit to D^r. Priestley, if she puts it in execution, will help to cure in her, as it is the very disease of the times; and actually rejecting, (for I made some trial of her in that respect) all the interpositions of the deity in the old world, and in the O.T. leads them (and has actually to my knowlege led some) to reject all the miraculous interposition of the N.T. and in short all miracles whatsoever; and those who had been wont to reverence the moral character of Christ, now espy great defects and exorbitances of passion in him.[4]

Your account of James Ellis's father and mother is very affecting. I hope he will have it both in his power and in his heart to make their old age comfortable as may be.[5] You may depend upon being made acquainted with the very first tidings that shall arrive of M[r] Palmer and his vessel's arrival at Portsmouth. Having to write to a character truly christian, whatever he may have been formerly, and member of our society in Essex Street, I take the liberty to inclose my letter for you, to save the postage, which you can better employ.[6] Both our kindest respects attend M[rs] Millar and yourself, and I remain at all times, Dear Sir, Your much obliged and affectionate

T. Lindsey.

---

[1]   By 'Mr Haldane's publication', Lindsey probably meant James Haldane's *Journal of a tour through the northern counties of Scotland and the Orkney Isles* (Edinburgh, 1798), which (pp. 45–6) referred, in fairly neutral terms, to a meeting of Socinians at Banff. Another possibility is Robert Haldane's *Address to the public, concerning political opinions, and plans lately adopted to promote religion in Scotland* (Edinburgh, 1800), in which (pp. 12, 55) the author denied allegations that he was a Socinian. For the Haldane brothers, see Letter 694, n. 4.

[2]   This was Lindsey's last book, *Conversations on the divine government*.

[3]   Lindsey evidently had in mind a London dissenting minister with family connexions in the west country as the potential author of a reply to Haldane; see Letter 731. Obvious possibilities are Thomas Jervis, the successor to Kippis at Princes Street, Westminster, and Thomas Belsham.

[4]   It is unlikely that Hannah Barnard visited Priestley; see Ditchfield, 'Quaker–unitarian encounter', 215–16.

[5]   It is highly unlikely that James Ellis returned to his parents in Dundee; see Letter 768, n. 2.

[6]   This is a reference to Grafton, to whom Lindsey was writing and enclosing a separate letter. Grafton had been first lord of the treasury between 1766 and 1770, and effectively prime minister between 1768 and 1770, and was lord privy seal between 1771 and 1775 and between 1782 and 1783. Lindsey meant that although Grafton been in office when policies disagreeable to Lindsey had been pursued, he had subsequently seen the political (and theological) light.

731. To ROBERT MILLAR   21 NOVEMBER 1801

Text: DWL, 12.46 (33).
Printed: *Unitarian Baptist Advocate*, III, I (Jan. 1839), 13–14 (with minor errors and omissions).
Addressed: M[r] Rob[t] Millar/Merchant/Dundee
Endorsed: Lond[o] 21 Nov 1801/Mr Lindsey
Postmarked: Postmark missing.

London. Nov[r]. 21. 1801

Dear Sir,

Your letter of Oct[r]. 29. which I received two days since, must have crossed one of mine in its way.[1] And I am glad to get so soon a passport from a good man and a good friend to tell You of it.

Whether the friend, whom I thought of for addressing your Missionaries will engage in the work I cannot answer, as he is not yet returned out of the west of England, drawn thither by the unexpected death of a near relation; You have however, I will venture to say, in your letter before me, with great ability drawn an outline, which will be of the greatest use to attend to, in order to avoid urging topics and arguments, which however solid, would be of no service, or not at all minded; and others, that would only irritate and offend. I shall certainly make him acquainted with what you say, which woud doubtless be discouraging to many in such an undertaking, but may not be so to him, as he is not liable [to] take fright at such things.[2]

In the mean while, whether he takes the task upon him or not, I think it very fortunate, that I can put into your hands a Book very recent from the press, which has been sent me by a friend, which I persuade myself will be acceptable to you at this very season. As the worthy author is very much in your situation beset with intolerant Missionaries, or such as have imbibed a large portion of their spirit, and has been prompted to write this work to keep his people and neighbourhood from being infected with it.

The title is, Religion without cant: A preservative against Lukewarmness and Intolerance; Fanaticism, Superstition and Impiety. By Robert Fellowes, M.M.[*sic*] of S[t] Mary Hall, Oxford. Author of a Picture of Christian Philosophy, &c &c. London, printed for J. White, Fleetstreet. 1801.[3] I think I may formerly have mentioned this gentleman's *Picture of Christian Philosophy* to you with comendations.[4] The friend who sends me this work, writes along with it: M[r] Fellowes is a man of great sincerity and piety; is younger brother of a gentleman of good estate, had at first a fortune of about ten thousand pounds, which he mostly spent, or rather lost by being indiscreetly security for other men, but without any vicious indulgences of his own. He is now about 35 years old.[5]

I should now desire to know of you, how I may best and soonest convey this book to you. But having lately received a second letter from M[r] Smiton Newburgh, requesting to have a few more of our Society's books, and the man who brought me his letter being to call again for the books in a couple of days, I have thoughts of engaging him to send M[r] Fellowes's book with those that go to M[r] Smiton, to whom I shall write to desire it may be conveyed to you at Dundee by the first opportunity, and shall seal it up carefully for you.[6]

It is a great satisfaction to learn that the condition of the numerous poor in your town is already so much amended. I trust the benefit of the peace will extend itself to those of upper rank, who have been much brought down, and suffered comparatively not less by war.[7]

The better sort of the nation, as far as I can learn, continue to think well of the peace and of the measures now pursued, and intended to be pursued.[8] And along with this, I am glad to learn that the late Minister and his adherents are looked upon in general as little less than persons insane. I hope this sentiment will continue, as it will be a preservative against ever recurring to the same.

It is my lot to be always pressed for time, by company and intrusions when I have to finish a letter to you – w[ch] is really the case now. My wife and I rejoice in M[rs] Millar and yourself being in the enjoyment of tolerable health as by the blessing of heaven we both continue to be. I had a letter only two days ago from D[r] Priestley.[9] He continues very busy and happy. He had not rec[d] my letter w[ch] gave him the earliest tidings of the peace.[10] I think he will be likely to come to see his friends here, especially his daughter and her family; but not to stay altogether –

Yours w[h] all sincerity & affection

T. Lindsey.

1   Millar's letter to Lindsey of 29 Oct. 1801 seems not to have survived.
2   See Letter 730, n. 3. I have not found evidence that this work was published.
3   The full title of Robert Fellowes' book was *Religion without cant; or, a preservative against luke-warmness and intolerance; fanaticism, superstition and impiety* (London, 1801). Fellowes (1770–1847) held the degree of MA from Oxford (1801), where he had been a member of St Mary Hall;

Lindsey's 'M.M.' for his degree was presumably a slip of the pen. Fellowes was educated for the Church of England ministry and from 1804 to 1811 he was editor of the *Critical Review*. He became the unofficial chaplain (and subsequently heir) to Francis Maseres (d. 1824), baron of the exchequer.

4   Lindsey had praised Fellowes's *A picture of Christian philosophy* in his letter to John Rowe, 11 Nov. 1799 (Letter 685) but had not referred to it in surviving letters to Millar.

5   Born on 15 May 1770, Robert Fellowes was aged thirty-one at the time of this letter. His older brother 'of good estate' was William Fellowes (1766–1835) of Danbury, Essex, who matriculated at Christ Church, Oxford, in 1785; see *Alumn. Oxon.*, II, 455.

6   For James Smiton of Newburgh, see Letter 729, n. 15. His letter to Lindsey has almost certainly not survived.

7   See Letter 716, n. 9. There is an interesting analysis of the medical facilities available to the poor of Dundee in Elizabeth Foyster, 'Life outside the medical centre: health and sickness in early modern Dundee', in *Dundee. Renaissance to Enlightenment*, ed. McKean, Harris and Whatley, pp. 117–20.

8   Peace with France was indeed pursued; the preliminaries had been signed on 1 Oct. 1801 and the Treaty of Amiens was concluded on 25 Mar. 1802.

9   Possibly this was Priestley's letter to Lindsey of 2 Oct. 1801; Rutt, I, 468–70. In a brief postscript to his letter to Lindsey of 14 Feb. 1802, Priestley acknowledged a letter from Lindsey dated 17 Nov. 1801; Rutt, I, 474.

10 This letter from Lindsey to Priestley, concerning the peace preliminaries, has not survived. Perhaps it was Lindsey's letter of 17 Nov. 1801 (see n. 9, above); Priestley's brief acknowledgment of it in his letter to Lindsey of 14 Feb. 1802 did not mention the peace preliminaries.

732. *TO ROBERT MILLAR   20 JANUARY 1802

Text: DWL, MS 12.46 (39).
Addressed: To/Mr Robert Millar/Merchant/Dundee/N:B
Endorsed: Londo 20th. Jan. 1802/Mrs Lindsey/Mr Lindsey's distress
Postmarked: Postmark missing.

Janry. 20th 1802
London.

Dear Sir

Mr Lindsey wishes me to inform you that he sent you a curious publication with a letter, inclosed in a parcel to Mr Smiton, 23 of Novr with a desire that it might as speedily as convenient be conveyed to you:[1] As this is the last letter you will receive from your very excellent and much esteemed friend we hope you will get it. It has pleased God by a paralytic attack to deprive Mr Lindsey of the use of his hands so as he cannot write, tho' otherwise he has recovered strength to feed himself and other comfortable movements, notwithstanding a second & more severe attack about a month ago, when he lost his right side, the leg in particular was a dead log: But by active means and the blessing of the Sovereign Physician he has so far regained his limbs as to walk about alone from room to room, & what has been the greatest mercy of all his senses & speech were never affected, & he can read a little, and injoy the society of his many kind friends, who some of them daily look in upon him.

My dear Husbands strength had been declining all the summer, but his chearful & placid mind made him less sensible of it than I was, and he rather overplied himself to compleat a small work he had planned to promote the good of his fellow creatures as he hopes, and that he might not live quite useless whilst he was continued in existence: That disease has rendered him so, he submits to it as the appointment of a Being who always pursues the happiness of his creatures by the wisest & best means, as alone knowing what will be most advantageous for them through the whole course of their existence, of wch this first infant state is but a span: But the proper temper must be begun here, that heavenly mindedness which adorns your friend, & which teaches as much as Volumn's, all those who have intercourse with him. I rather hope that with the aid of a friend this last work will be published, if no worse disability of mind befall the author.[2]

I am so much occupied by attentions to M[r] Lindsey, and writing to friends either to calm their anxieties, or to close his correspondence by an account of his inability, that I should not have dilated so much to you, had I not known your good & affec[t] temper, & sincere attachment.

M[r] Palmer has never been heard of, it is supposed he may be gone to China with his Cargo.[3] Two letters just rec[d] from D[r] P. are satisfactory:[4] One from his Son intimates that his health declines somewhat:[5] I am the most concerned for him at this distance when he hears of this interruption of any more intercourse with his most beloved friend, who is thus dead to him: But his mind is so truly Christian that he will submit patiently.[6]

M[r] Lindsey desires to join in every good wish to y[r]self & M[rs]. Millar with your sincere f[d] HLindsey

---

1 See Letter 731. The 'curious publication' was probably Fellowes's *A preservative against lukewarm-ness and ignorance*. 'Mr Smiton' was probably James Smiton of Newburgh; see Letter 729, n. 15.
2 This work was Lindsey's *Conversations on the divine government*.
3 Since Palmer and his friends sailed from Botany Bay on 5 Jan. 1801, they had in effect been out of communication with their friends in Britain. See Letter 735, n. 4.
4 These two letters from Priestley were probably those of 2 and 24 Oct. 1801; Rutt, I, 468–70, 470–2.
5 I have not located this letter from Priestley's son; Lindsey probably referred to the eldest son, Joseph Priestley junior.
6 Priestley acknowledged the news of Lindsey's stroke in a letter to Belsham, 18 May 1802, in which he added that he was 'in daily expectation' of hearing of Lindsey's death; Rutt, I, 481.

733. *To ROBERT MILLAR   25 FEBRUARY 1802

Text: DWL, MS 12.46 (40).
Addressed: To/M[r] Robert Millar/Merchant/Dundee
Endorsed: Lond[o] 25th Feb. 1802/Mrs Lindsey/Excellent
Postmarked: Postmark missing.

Feb[ry] 25th 1802

Dear Sir

I fear you will think it long since you heard of your good amiable friend, who thanks to a benign providence, has more perfectly recovered the use of his limbs, and except in not being able to cut his meat, or write letters is in good plight, and full of thankfulness for this repreive [*sic*], which has inabled him to accomplish his work, the printing of which is in great forwardness and will be ready in about six weeks: Correcting the press occupies him pleasantly, the printer he says can make out his pot hook writing:[1] It will please you to hear that to gratify me, and many importunate friends, he has let a Shade of himself be taken to prefix to this new book, it is as like as can be, and in his velvet cap, which he has worn during his illness as most easy to a poor head repeatedly blistered:[2] Neither the season of the year nor the weather tempt him to go out, and he is so well & chearful in his study among his books, and the daily call of some friend or other, that I do not wish him to make any change till the Spring is more advanced.

M[r]. Smiton by a line of acknowledgment for some books he had sent, mentions having been careful to convey your small parcel by a safe hand. If in the course of six weeks you could direct a certain speedy conveyance to y^rself of Mr Lindseys book, intitled "Conversations on the divine Government" he would be glad to send it to you. It holds out very consoling views of the system under which we are placed, and may do good to such as have a well turn'd mind: Others will scoff and cavil, as they do at the Gospel itself.

Mr Lindsey was sorry to hear that you had unusual exertions to make in your business, wishing rather that it should become easier; but these are not times to expect that: He would however encourage you under everything, exertion strengthens the mind, and tho' it be at present for the bread that perishes, the faculties acquired are easily transplanted upon higher objects: We have only to make the most we can of all our powers & faculties, and trust our Maker to find proper imployment, in another, and perhaps not unsimilar but far better world than the present.

Since my last we have heard more than once from Dr Priestley: His health is so much declined that he has given up all thoughts of visiting England which was a favorite design of his whenever there was Peace: But the shock given to his frame by the loss of above thirty ounces of blood in the fever a year & half ago at Philadelphia, and the fits of Ague since, wch has been general in that part of the Country, has made him too much of an Invalid to leave home, & change his mode of living for a Sea voyage.[3] Indeed at near 70 it is not easy to perform such feats; and as his chief object was to see M^r. Lindsey, they are both willing to wait for a reunion till the resurrection of the dead.[4] This previous interruption of intercourse by letter will be very painful to D^r. P. but he really has a mind like his friend which can resign every thing to the Will of God. M^r L: wrote two or three lines at the end of my last letter to him just to express his last & best feelings to his most beloved friend.[5] How differently do men of the world think and act under such circumstances, it is only practical Christians that can look forward with joy.

Mr Lindsey begs his grateful thanks for yours and M^rs. Millars affectionate feelings & solicitude about him, which he can only return by best kindest wishes for all good present and future to you both.

We hear nothing of M^r. Palmer. The delay of the Definitive Treaty creates great anxiety and uncertainty in the Commercial world, nobody dares venture on new channels of trade, tho' there is no doubt as we hear from good authority but that it will be signed.[6]

The power of France is enormous, we have made them Giants and are afraid of them: But Europe must have rest for a time, and we must mend our brok[en] Kettle[7] as well as we can: I wish we had better Tinkers. As wisdom and goodness directs the whole we have no miserable forebodings about what may, or may not happen. Adieu with our joint kind regards to you both I am

Dr Sir Y^r sincere f^d

HL

---

1   A pot hook is defined in the *OED* as a hook placed over a fireplace from which a pot could be suspended; or a metal rod with a hook at the end, for lifting a pot or similar utensil. Hannah Lindsey probably meant that the printer of Lindsey's *Conversations on the divine government* found his handwriting to be legible, despite its hooked appearance caused by the after-effects of his stroke.

2   This (right-hand profile) silhouette is the frontispiece to Lindsey's *Conversations on the divine government*.

3   For a note on Priestley's illness in and after 1801, which necessitated bleedings carried out by Dr Benjamin Rush, see Schofield, *Enlightened Joseph Priestley*, p. 386 and n. 21.

4   Born on 24 Mar. 1733 (new style), Priestley was aged sixty-eight in Feb. 1802.
5   Priestley's response, dated 8 May 1802, to this (non-surviving) letter is addressed to Hannah Lindsey;
     see Rutt, I, 482–3. Priestley wrote that the sight of the few lines written by Lindsey himself in this
     letter 'quite overcame' him.
6   The 'definite treaty' between Britain and France (the Treaty of Amiens) was signed on 25 Mar. 1802.
7   The manuscript is slightly torn at this point.

734. *To ROBERT MILLAR   27 MARCH 1802

Text: DWL, MS 12.46 (41).
Addressed: To/M^r. Robert Millar/Merchant/Dundee
Endorsed: London 27th Mar 1802/Mrs Lindsey
Postmarked: Postmark missing.

London March 27th 1802

Dear Sir

I am again to convey M^r. Lindsey's best thanks for your kind letter,[1] and to inform you, that his little publication is ready for any safe hand you may desire to call for it at Essex House, where it will be packed up with a Shade in a plain frame that you may hang up: This is my own doing as your friend has no notion that anybody can have pleasure in such a representation, which in the Velvet cap it was taken is as perfect a likeness as such a mode can convey: For the mind it must be found in the book.[2]

I have the comfort to say that M^r. Lindsey continues very well, can write a little better, but with more difficulty than is consistent with renewing any intercourse with his friends.

He has had another letter this week, which tho' Dr Priestley does not boast of his health being improved, yet the books he has sent for, and his plans of future imployment chear us with hopes that there is a good deal of vigor left, to be applied for the benefit of mankind.[3]

We begin to fear that something adverse has befallen M^r. Palmer and his little Vessel, as no account whatever is come of him.[4]

Poor Dr Ross seems a thorough hypocondriac [*sic*] I pity him from my heart having been such a grievous sufferer from nervous affections, which exceed all others, & least excite compassion.[5]

But I must have done, having more work on my hands. Pray send a line by Y^r messenger that we may know who to deliver the parcel to.

Mr Lindsey sends all kind regards & wishes to Y^rself and Mrs Millar along with Y^r sincere f^d HLindsey

1   Millar's 'kind letter' has not survived, but in his reply to this letter from Hannah Lindsey, dated 8
     May 1802, Millar acknowledged receipt of Lindsey's *Conversations on the divine government* and
     of the 'shade' of Lindsey prefaced to it.
2   See Letter 733, n. 2.
3   Possibly this was Priestley's letter to Lindsey of 14 Feb. 1802, in which Priestley reported that his
     illnesses had 'shaken and reduced' him, although he was 'now recruiting again'; Rutt, I, 473.
4   See Letter 735, n. 4. Palmer died at Guam on 2 June 1802.
5   In his reply to this letter, Millar noted that his 'friend' Dr Ross was in poor health, 'peevish and apt in
     words (altho' I believe not in heart) to quarrel with Providence'; DWL, MS 12.57 (43). For a possible
     identification of Dr (Andrew) Ross, see Letter 659, n. 5.

735. To ROBERT MILLAR   **20 MAY 1802**

Text:	DWL, MS 12.46 (34).
Addressed:	To/Mr Robert Millar/Merchant/Dundee./By favor of
	Mr Jobson
Endorsed:	Lond^o 20th. May 1802/Mr Lindsey
Postmarked:	Postmark missing.

London. May 20. 1802

Dear Sir,

I have a peculiar satisfaction in learning that my last effort to be of some little use was acceptable to so good a judge, though I am sensible how much I owe at the same time to the partiality of a kind friend. I am glad likewise to hear that you have got the copy from Glasgow, as you think it may be of service to let some other friends see it.[1] And believe me that I shall ever be most highly gratified by any thing that shall contribute to make me live in the remembrance of such highly esteemed friends as yourself and M^{rs}. Millar.

How deeply and sincerely I was affected, I cannot easily say, by the perusal of the latter part of your letter, in which you describe the great and sudden change made in your worldly circumstances by the failures of others with whom you were connected.[2] It is the fate of trade, especially in such difficult times as the present, and will be likely to continue. And I cannot but observed that you make no uneasy remarks on the conduct of others, but seem to ascribe your losses to misfortunes, which it was out of the power of yourself and many other fellow-sufferers to prevent. But I cannot but truly grieve that any thing should happen which so materially affects your situation and ease at a time when you might look for the enjoyment of the fruits of your toil and industry, and not to have the means of usefulness and of assisting your fellow creatures abridged and diminished.

I have a pleasure in this rescript of mine being delivered to you by Mr Jobson, with whom I have to thank you for bringing me acquainted, and who can inform you of the progress I have made since my last attack; which though far from being so much as you kindly hoped, I have the highest reason to be thankful for, and that I am able to enjoy the society of friends and also to walk about and visit them, when the weather permits.

Mr Jobson, when he was with us, had not been able to find out M^r. Patullo,[3] so that we remain still in uncertainty about Mr Fysh Palmer and his companions. Many are inclined to fear they are all lost. But I am told that his relations do not give him [up], but incline to suppose with you that he is pursuing his voyages somewhere to increase his fortunes.[4] My correspondent at Portsmouth[5] sends me no tidings of him.

I am mortified to be able to send you only so very meagre a letter in acknowegement [*sic*] of your's in all respects but one so very welcome to me. But my hand rather tires and forbids me to write any more. I shall rejoice to become a better correspondent. My wife joins in cordial respects to Mrs Millar and yourself, And I remain always very affectionately Yours

T. Lindsey.

---

1   Lindsey had sent to Millar a copy of his *Conversations on the divine government* (see Letter 734, n. 1); 'the partiality of a kind friend' refers to Millar's complimentary remarks upon it in his letter to Lindsey of 2 May 1802. In that letter, Millar confirmed that he had 'just got the other copy from Glasg^w'; it had probably been sent to a member or supporter of the Unitarian Society in that city.

2   A large proportion of Millar's business interests involved trade with Russia conducted via the Baltic, where shipping losses had been particularly high in 1801 and early in 1802. See Letter 773, n. 1.

3   This was almost certainly the 'Ensign Patullo', of Dundee, who was in charge of the convicts on board the *Surprise*, which conveyed Palmer, Muir and their fellow-reformers to New South Wales. Among the copies of letters of Thomas Hardy in TNA: TS/954 is a letter from Hardy to his Scottish allies urging that 'Margarot's friends should make themselves acquainted with Ensign Patullo who has the charge of the Convicts.' Palmer identified 'Pattullo' as William Patullo, an ensign who appeared 'in his regimentals' and abetted Campbell in his ill-treatment of the political prisoners. See, however, Bewley, *Muir of Huntershill*, p. 105, which states that 'the Patullos ... were kind and friendly', and indeed Palmer quoted Patullo's testimony to the effect that he was unaware of the alleged mutiny on board the *Surprise*; Palmer, *Narrative*, Appendix II, pp. 62–5. It appears from Palmer's account that Patullo's wife accompanied him to Botany Bay; Palmer, *Narrative*, pp. 25, 28, 30–1. In his letter to Lindsey of 8 May 1802, Millar provided further information about Patullo, 'who went out in same Ship with Mr Palmer to B. Bay'. According to Millar, Patullo had recently arrived in London with reports that 'Mr Palmer had left the Colony 18 Months previous to his (Mr Patullo's) sailing, with a Cargo of Wood &c for the Cape of Good Hope'; DWL, MS 12.57 (43).

4   At the end of his seven-year sentence, Palmer, with Thomas Boston and James Ellis, obtained a small ship and sailed from Botany Bay on 5 Jan. 1801. Their ultimate intention was to return to Britain after engaging in trade at Cape Town, but their voyage, via New Zealand and Fiji, ended in disaster as they were shipwrecked at Guam. Palmer died of dysentery there on 2 June 1802. See Letter 744, n. 7.

5   Russell Scott.

736. To THOMAS ASTLEY   11 JUNE 1802

Text: Bodl.. MS Eng. lett. c. 352, fos. 21–2 (Astley papers).
Addressed: [In Hannah Lindsey's hand] To/The Revd Mr Astley/
                 Chesterfield
Endorsed: June 1802 [separately, in red pencil] Lindsey
Postmarked: Postmark missing.

June. 11. 1802.

Dear Sir,

I must in my imperfect slow way try to thank you myself for both your very kind letters, and for the loan of a book which came by an unknown hand.[1] This I am glad to have seen, and have been much benefited by the perusal, and edifyed by the honest freedom and great piety of the very worthy author. I knew him when he was a Student at Cambridge, he having visited me at Catterick in company with a friend equally pious and benevolent.[2] They both then leaned strongly to perfect unitarianism; but going on in the Church, and being influenced by the zeal of the methodists with whom they became connected, they could never thoroughly emancipate themselves. Both lived and died exemplary characters, and under friendly feelings for me who could not stop at their point.

The book shall be carefully put up and left for Mr Daintry[3] when he calls, and should be happy to thank him myself for the favour and his kind attentions, but am apprehensive I may be out of town in the month august, Should I continue tolerably well.

I am glad you intend to help good Dr Priestley in his very expensive publication, which he is so earnest to finish, as he says it is his last work, that he has already begun printing it on his own inadequate means, hoping for assistance from friends. We are collecting money for the purpose as fast as we can, in which business my wife uses every effort. Five pounds entitles a subscriber to one copy of both the works, i.e. of the continuation of the Church=History, and the Notes with a Comentary on the Scriptures.[4]

Half of the £500 which is to go to the indemnification of Mr Johnson for printing and importing the work is already subscribed and paid into a Banker's hands; and if the Doctor does not live to finish, after Johnson is indemnified for what he delivers, the residue is to be returned. My wife has put down your name in our list, for one copy.[5]

She desires to join with me in respects to yourself and M[rs] Astley,[6] and I remain, Dear Sir,

Your obliged friend

    T. Lindsey[7]

---

1   Astley's letters to Lindsey seem not to have survived.

2   This Cambridge student was David Simpson (1745–99) of Macclesfield; see Vol. I, p. xlvii. Possibly the 'friend equally pious and benevolent' was William Mason (d. 1797); see Letter 737. The book that Astley loaned to Lindsey was probably Simpson's *A plea for religion, and the sacred writings; addressed to the disciples of Thomas Paine, and wavering Christians of every persuasion* (Macclesfield, 1797, with a second edition published in London in 1797). Lindsey would have approved of Simpson's defence of biblical revelation, if not of the trinitarian interpretations which he drew from it.

3   Possibly a member of the family of Rev. John Daintry (d. 1758), vicar of Leek, approximately twenty-six miles from Chesterfield; see Vol. I, Letter 87, n. 1. One such member was John Daintry of Leek who is listed as a student of Warrington Academy in 1779; *MR*, IX (1814), 597.

4   Priestley's *A general history of the Christian church from the fall of the western empire* was published in four volumes in Northumberland in 1802–3. This work was a 'continuation' of his *General history of the Christian church to the fall of the western empire*. Priestley's *Notes on all the books of scripture* appeared in four volumes in Northumberland in 1803–4.

5   In 1802 and 1803, Lindsey, Hannah Lindsey and Belsham organized a subscription to meet the cost of the publication of two of Priestley's last major theological works (n. 4, above). The initial idea was that 100 individuals should each subscribe £5 in advance, in return for a copy of each of these works. The object was the raising of a fund of £500, half of which was to be paid to the publisher Joseph Johnson. However, the subscription soon exceeded this target. By the end of Aug. 1802, £800 had been raised and by Dec. 1802, £1,200 (see Letters 739 and 744), and according to Belsham, 'upwards of £1300' was raised altogether; Williams, p. 519. The largest single contribution was made by John Law, bishop of Elphin and the son of Lindsey's friend Edmund Law, who gave £100; see his letter to Lindsey, 7 Oct. 1802, Belsham, *Memoirs*, p. 295 n. *. Other contributors included the duke of Grafton (£50) and Lindsey himself (£20). It seems that Thomas Astley, too, intended to become a subscriber. Russell Scott and William Turner of Newcastle also contributed; see, respectively, Letters 741 and 745. See also Priestley, *Works*, IX, iii–iv (preface by J. T. Rutt), and Schofield, *Enlightened Joseph Priestley*, p. 388. For Priestley's appreciation of these efforts on his behalf, see his letters to Lindsey, 28 Aug. 1802, and to Belsham, 24 Sept. 1803; Rutt, I, 490, 517. No list of subscribers was published; indeed, John Law specifically requested that his name be not mentioned in connexion with the subscription. Anxiety at any kind of public association with Priestley evidently remained considerable.

6   Phoebe Astley, née Wilkinson (*c.* 1744–1829), married Thomas Astley at Chesterfield in 1775. She survived her husband by twelve years and died at Chesterfield in 1829; *CR*, XV (1829), 333.

7   This signature is not in Lindsey's own hand. His signature has been excised and his signature copied opposite the excision.

737. To CHRISTOPHER WYVILL   **30 JULY 1802**

> **Text:**   NYRO, ZFW 7/2/157/1, Wyvill of Constable Burton MSS.
> **Printed:**   Ditchfield, 'Lindsey–Wyvill correspondence', 165 (first
>   paragraph).
> **Addressed:**   To/The Rev^d. Christopher Wyvill/Burton-Hall/nea[r] Bedale/
>   Yorkshire
> **Endorsed:**   From the Revd Mr Lindsey/July 30th. 1802
> **Postmarked:**   JY 30 802

July 30. 1802. London.

Dear Sir,

Having performed a great feat for me yesterday by going to Brentford for Sir Francis Burdet, to shew my abhorrence of tyranny, and oppression of the poor and helpless by illegal imprisonment, I congr[a]tulate the country on a ray of its ancient spirit appearing: Not that any great good can be done in such debased state of the Representation, yet every effort is gain.[1]

A thousand thanks for your 4th volume.[2] You have labour'd well and hard, and posterity, (not a late one, I trust) but your own children will see some of the happy consequences of the light thrown out by all your publications and all your efforts for a long series of years.

I have also to acknowlege your £5. draft for D^r. Priestley's works,[3] and to thank your ample testimony to his virtues, talents, and against his cruel and unjust persecution. Alas! he can no more return hither to his native country, however he might be disposed, after being left in such an invalid state by a fever two years ago, in which, at near 70 years he lost as many ounces of blood.[4]

This 4th volume I perceive and anticipate, will be a high treat in many respects. You have indeed adorned the character of our friend Mason. But his moral deserts were great to those who knew him thoroughly. He will however go down to posterity favourably as well as justly in your page.[5]

The biographical brief account of Sir. G. Savile leaves us only thirsting for more.[6]

I own myself particularly delighted with the fine portrait, and justice done to one at large to a most valuable person, still living, which I did not expect to find; pag. 407. 8. Note; which shews what a happy thought the addition of the Notes, was, in this Volume, and how acceptable as well as useful.[7]

But my tired hand forbids to add more at present than to tender <u>our</u> most due respects to Mrs Wyvill and yourself, with most cordial wishes for the health and improvements of your amiable and promising family,

Always, Dear Sir, Your most truly obliged and faithful affectionate Servant
T. Lindsey

---

[1]   The poll book for the county of Middlesex for 1802 shows that in the general election of July of that year Lindsey 'plumped' for the radical libertarian Sir Francis Burdett. By voting for Burdett only, Lindsey withheld his other vote from either of Burdett's rivals, George Byng (the other successful candidate with Burdett) and William Mainwaring. Lindsey was listed as 'Freeholder' of Essex Street, Strand, and under 'Occupier's name' is entered the word 'Self'. After a series of petitions to the house of commons from 1804 to 1806, Burdett was finally unseated and Mainwaring awarded the seat in his place; Thorne, *Hist. parl.*, II, 258–63. Burdett was subsequently MP for Middlesex from 1805 to 1806 and for Westminster from 1807 to 1837.

[2]   This is a reference to the fourth volume of Wyvill's *Political papers*, published in York in 1802.

[3]   For this subscription for Priestley's two works, see Letter 736, n. 5.

[4]   For this illness of Priestley, see Letter 720, n. 1.

[5]   Wyvill's account of William Mason dwelt upon their long co-operation in the cause of parliamentary

reform but referred also to their differences of opinion over the repeal of the Test and Corporation Acts (which Mason opposed) and the policies of Pitt the Younger in the 1790s (which Mason
supported). See Wyvill, *Political papers*, IV, 354–6, n. *. Wyvill (p. 356 n. *) attributed Mason's
more conservative opinions in later life to 'some degree of Cathedral prejudice, and the prevailing
panic of the Times'. Mason, who died on 7 Apr. 1797, had been a prebend and precentor of York.

6   This biographical account, 'communicated in 1802, to the Editor, by one of Sir George Savile's most
     intimate friends', is printed in Wyvill, *Political papers*, IV, 553–8.

7   Lindsey referred here to Wyvill's encomium on the Rev. James Wilkinson (d. 1805) of Broom Hall,
     vicar of Sheffield, 1754–1805, and a magistrate in that town; Wyvill, *Political papers*, IV, 407–8 n.
     *. Wilkinson's house had suffered attacks by anti-enclosure rioters in July 1791; he had also acquired
     a reputation as a somewhat unorthodox dispenser of justice, a reputation fortified by his career as
     a successful amateur boxer. He matriculated at Clare College, Cambridge, in 1748, one year after
     Lindsey became a fellow of St John's, and it is highly likely that they were acquainted at Cambridge.
     See *Alumn. Cantab.*, I, vol. V, 411; R. E. Leader, *Sheffield in the eighteenth century* (Sheffield, 1901),
     pp. 60–1, 238–42; Bohstedt, *Riots and community politics in England and Wales*, p. 199.

738. To THOMAS BELSHAM   25 AUGUST 1802

Text: DWL, MS 12.57 (23).
Addressed: [In Hannah Lindsey's hand] To/The Rev^d. M^r.
                   Belsham,/Thomas Smith's Esqr,/Bownham House,/near
                   Minchinhampton,/Gloucestershire
Endorsed: [By Belsham] Mr Lindsey Aug^t: 25:1802
Postmarked: AU 25 802

Morden. Aug. 25. 1802.

Dear Sir,

I must endeavour to speak a little for myself, my good wife having delated
somewhat too much on a single foolish effort I made rather than return by too long
a round home. I am thankful however that I can walk over the rugged ground of
some parts of this farm, so different from the pavement in London, having gathered
more strength than I expected, and am very sensible of the kind satisfaction you
express at the amendment I am favoured with.

Your history of the opening and full attendance at the New Meeting was very
satisfactory and highly gratifying. I could have no doubt of your getting well
through the arduous task, but am very glad that you did it with so much ease to to
[*sic*] yourself, and shall the less regret not to have had the pleasure of being present,
as I may indulge a hope of sharing in the feast by reading both your discourses.[1]

By a few lines from Plymouth from the good and modest Kentish, we find that
he is not decided to accept the invitation so unanimously and handsomely given
to become the Pastor of this very first-rate Unitarian congregation. I suspect it
is deference to his Father's will which makes him hesitate.[2] Mr Kenrick and he
would accord together most admirably in all respects, and especially as it might
be expected the latter would catch a portion of the animation of his younger friend
which is so necessary in discourses from the pulpit. The union and connection of
two such characters, in such a place, would be a public benefit, and extends itself
not only over the West of England, but to other parts. And I trust it will take place.[3]

We have been made uneasy by an account from York, that M^r. Wellbeloved has
by too excessive an exertion at Cricket brought on a sore throat and fever, the danger
from it I trust will be over before this reaches [you]:[4] but I mention it to apprize you
that his excellent physician and friend Dr Cappe is hardly in a condition to attend
him, being on the eve of trying to go to Naples, for his own restoration, if that be

possible.[5] D[rs] Willan[6] in Town and Corrie[7] and Bostock[8] at Liverpool, are for trying the experiment to be made; and, if he goes, they are to sail from Liverpool. His loss to his friends and to the community at large would be irreparable.

One is quite ashamed of the Leeds people from whom Mr Wood cannot get a single Subscription for D[r]. P ___ y's works.[9] I have had another Letter from him from Northumberland which you will like, and one inclosed to him, very excellent, from the president Jefferson, which you will no less like. It is on the Doctor's dedicating his Ecclesiastical History to him.[10]

I have also just had a letter from M[r] Russell dated from Paris July 18. who begs me to intreat you to write on the particular subject you know; He says, "I am soon going to Abbaye Ardennes pres Caen en Normandie, of which I shall be obliged to you to inform M[r] Belsham["], and adds, that he doubts not of your letter so directed, being safely delivered to him.[11] His whole letter to me is expressive of his approbation of a late little piece, and his solicitude to plan some mode of procuring D[r] Priestley; to be published; of which I should think his son must have told him.[12]

[The latter section of the second and last page of this letter has been excised]

1   Thomas Belsham, *The right and duty of unitarian Christians to form separate societies for religious worship. A sermon preached July 22, 1802, at the opening of the New Meeting-House at Birmingham, erected in the room of that in which Dr. Priestley formerly officiated, and which was destroyed in the riots, July 14, 1791* (London, 1802). Belsham's other discourse published in 1802 was *Reflections and exhortations adapted to the state of the times: a sermon, preached ...1 June 1802; being the day appointed ... for a general thanksgiving to Almighty God, for putting an end to the late bloody, extended and expensive war* (London, 1802).

2   For John Kentish's father, also named John Kentish, see Letter 539, n. 2. According to John Kenrick's 'memoir' of Kentish, as the only surviving child of his parents, he became 'the object of perhaps too intense and concentrated affection and interest' on their part; *CR*, NS, IX (1853), 267. Possibly one reason for Kentish's decision to decline the invitation to Plymouth, and to remain the afternoon preacher at the Gravel Pit meeting, Hackney, and morning preacher at Newington Green and St Thomas's Street Southwark, was a wish to be nearer to his ageing father at St Albans. See Letter 741, n. 14.

3   Kentish became the minister of the New Meeting, Birmingham (Priestley's former congregation) in Jan. 1803.

4   Lindsey omitted a word, almost certainly 'you' at this point. In 1846, an (unnamed) unitarian minister published an account of a visit to Catterick, where he met parishioners who claimed to remember, or to have been told of, Lindsey's incumbency. One of them recalled that Lindsey and his parish clerk broke up a cricket match on a Sunday because of the noise and drunkenness which such games occasioned; *CR*, NS, II (1846), 608.

5   Robert Cappe (1772–1802), the youngest son of Newcome Cappe and his first wife Sarah, née Turner (d. 1773), obtained the degree of MD from Edinburgh University in 1797 and served briefly as physician to the York retreat in 1801. He travelled to Italy in an unsuccessful attempt to improve his health, but died at sea on a journey to Leghorn on 16 Nov. 1802. See Charles Wellbeloved, *A sermon, preached at the chapel in St Saviourgate, York, on Sunday, December 26, 1802, on occasion of the much lamented death of Robert Cappe, MD*, published as an appendix to *Discourses chiefly on devotional subjects, by the late reverend Newcome Cappe. To which are prefixed memoirs of his life, by Catharine Cappe* (York, 1805). Wellbeloved's sermon may be found at pp. 431–62, and his memoir of Robert Cappe at pp. 463–80.

6   Robert Willan (1757–1812), MD (Edinburgh, 1780), was physician, successively, to the public dispensary, the Finsbury dispensary and the fever institution in London. Influenced by quakers but subsequently disowned by the Society of Friends, he was the author of *The history of the ministry of Jesus Christ, combined from the narrations of the four evangelists* (London, 1782).

7   Rather than John Corrie (see Letters 531, n. 4 and 575, n. 2) Lindsey probably referred here to the physician, author and unitarian sympathizer Dr James Currie (1756–1805), whose medical practice was based at Rodney Street, Liverpool. There is an excellent illumination of Currie's intellectual circles in *The diary of Hannah Lightbody 1786–1790*, ed. David Sekers, *E & D*, no. 24 (special supplement, 2008).

8   John Bostock (1772–1846), MD (Edinburgh, 1789), was physician to the general dispensary in Liverpool and belonged to the unitarian community there. He was related to the family of the unitarian minister John Yates (1755–1826). In later life, he was the author of several important works on physiology, Galvanism and infections associated with catarrh.
9   For this subscription, see Letter 736, n. 5. William Wood was Priestley's successor as minister to the Mill Hill chapel, Leeds.
10 In his letter to Lindsey of 26 June 1802, Priestley reported on the progress of his *A general history of the Christian church from the fall of the western empire* and added that it was dedicated to Thomas Jefferson. In his next letter to Lindsey, 3 July 1802, he enclosed Jefferson's letter of 19 June 1802 acknowledging the dedication. This correspondence may be found in Rutt, I, 486–89, with Jefferson's letter at pp. 483–6.
11 William Russell left America for France (via Hamburg) in 1801. His return to Britain, however, was delayed by the renewal of war between his native country and France in 1803. He feared that his having acquired property in France during wartime might amount to a violation of British law, and he therefore remained in France, attending to his property in Paris and his estate in Normandy. He did not return to Britain until the end of the war in 1814. I have not located the letter from Russell to which Lindsey referred.
12 The 'late little piece' was Lindsey's *Conversations on the divine government*. By 1802, Russell was living in Paris and hoped to persuade Priestley to join him there.

739. To ROBERT MILLAR   28 AUGUST 1802

Text: DWL, MS 12.46 (35).
Addressed: [In Martin's hand:] Tewksbr^y. Fourth Sep^r./*1802*/M^r. Robt. Millar/Merch^t./Dundee/N.B. ~~Js Martin~~
Endorsed: Lond^o 28 Aug^t *1802*/Mr Lindsey/Various
Postmarked: TEWKSBURY 107 FREE [postmark otherwise illegible]

                                          August 28. 1802. Morden. Surry.
Dear Sir,
    Although I feel as if I could not write much, I am desirous to return you thanks for your last kind letter, as it bespeaks you to be relieved from some solicitude about the state of your worldly affairs.[1] I cannot but rejoice that a mind of so much sensibility as yours has enough to prevent that over-attention which is apt to divert from better things, in which consists our solace and highest enjoyment.
    As to your subscription to the Unitarian Society, I shall pay it in your name to our Secretary,[2] and be glad to take the allotment myself, as I am never overloaded in that way, and at present really want the books for myself.
    We are raising a Subscription for publishing 2 works of D^r. Priestley's, which he has set his mind upon, as the only way now left for him to be useful: If I live till this business is completed, you may see them: The one is the Continuation of his Church-History; the other, Notes on the Scriptures throughout, and must be very valuable. We have raised £800, which is vested in the funds in the name of four Trustees, to secure the proper disposal of the money for the purposes of the Subscription, as the works are printing, and some progress already made under the Doctor's own eye.[3] My wife, I must tell you, has with her usual energy done the principal part in this business. The Doctor very lately has given us the pleasing news that he feels himself somewhat amended, and his spirits better: still however but precarious.[4]
    You will be glad to read what he says in his last letter to me of Mr Christie, who had acted a very improper part towards him, approaching to insanity, and his account of his amiable wife and family.

"You relieve me very much of [*sic*] in commendation of my behaviour to Mʳ Christie: and now it ceases to give me any concern. His best [word missing: ?friends] say his conduct to me has been ungrateful in the extreme. However we are now on very good terms. His family, which is a pleasing one, are settled here, and are likely to do very well: his two daughters, having opened a school for young women, which promises to bring in more than his Latin School: tho he is a most diligent Schoolmaster, and strictly conscientious in every thing he does: but if he happen to see any thing in an unfavourable point of light, this good property has a bad effect.⁵ He preaches every other Sunday, and I go to hear him, which please him much, tho' he only now and then comes to hear me; and at one time did not come of 16 sundays together. His family received the Lord's Supper, which I lately administred [*sic*], which he did, tho' it was not his day of preaching. He is very well attended and very fluent in preaching and praying without Notes. He will make many unitarians, and do much good in this place.["]⁶

We have been only three weeks yesterday with our excellent kind friends in this place and have found myself my[self] much invigorated.

With kind and respectful regards, and every wish and prayer for every thing good and happy, from us both, to Mʳˢ Millar and yourself, from Mʳˢ Lindsey and myself, I remain ever most truly Yours

T. Lindsey.

---

1 Possibly this refers to Millar's letter to Lindsey of 8 May 1802 (DWL, MS 12.57 (43)), although it is more likely to be a reference to a subsequent (non-surviving) letter in which Millar reported some improvement in his business affairs.

2 Jeremiah Joyce, who succeeded John Kentish as the secretary of the Unitarian Society in 1802.

3 See Letter 736, n. 5. A printed advertisement to raise funds for these two works of Priestley names the four trustees. They were Thomas Belsham; Timothy Brown (d. 1820), of Chiswell Street, London; the attorney Robert Wainewright (d. 1841) of Gray's Inn (and from 1803 a trustee of Essex Street chapel); and Isaac Solly (1768–1853), a merchant in the Baltic trade and the father of the unitarian minister Henry Solly. Their duty was to invest the subscriptions received into 'Public Securities' for transmission to Priestley to cover the costs of publication, and to Joseph Johnson for the cost of reprinting in Britain. Any surplus was to go to Priestley. There is a copy of this advertisement in HMCO, MS WOOD, 1, fos. 9–10, with a letter from Charles Wellbeloved to William Wood of Leeds, 12 Aug. 1802.

4 Priestley conveyed this news of his health in his letter to Lindsey of 3 July 1802; Rutt, I, 489.

5 For William Christie's private school in his own house at Winchester, Virginia, after the end of his employment at the Winchester Academy, see Frank, '"I shall never be intimidated"', 31–2, and *MR*, VI (1811), 198–201. His advertisement for the school offered Latin, Greek and French, and accommodation for boarders at £30 per annum. The school, and a similar venture in Northumberland, Pennsylvania, failed; similarly, Priestley's hopes that Christie would 'make many unitarians' was over-optimistic. Indeed, Priestley had predicted, accurately, in 1801 that 'his Unitarianism would hurt him with us'; Rutt, I, 454. Priestley's letter to Lindsey of 7 Nov. 1801 (DWL, MS 12.13; completely omitted by Rutt) consists of a catalogue of Christie's shortcomings, including the problems he had caused as a guest at Priestley's home; Christie resided at Northumberland from 1801 to Feb. 1806. Christie and his wife had eight children, of whom only three survived to adulthood; two of them were daughters, who conducted a school for girls at Northumberland.

6 This paragraph is an almost exact transcription of a passage from Priestley's letter of 3 July 1802 (see n. 4, above) which was omitted by Rutt; DWL, MS 12.13.

740. To ROBERT MILLAR   **5 SEPTEMBER 1802**

Text:	DWL, MS 12.46 (36).
Addressed:	[In Grafton's hand] *Thetford September seventh 1802*/To/M^r.

> Robert Millar/Merchant/Dundee/North Britain/Grafton

Endorsed: Lond°. 5th. Sep. *1802*/Mr Lindsey/On the death of Mrs Millar
Postmarked: SE 10 81 THETFORD

Dear Sir and my worthy dear friend,

What can I say to you under this heaviest of all afflictions, but that whom the Lord loves he chastises, even as a Father the Son in whom he delighteth?

I have no doubt of your being supported and sanctified by this heavy trial.[1]

You have now the most powerful motive to make light of earthly cares, and follow the deserved object of your affections to a more enduring happy scene, where at the morning of the resurrection, the true disciples of our divine Master will rise with unutterable joy and meet together, rejoicing over those events, which to flesh and blood were so painful and overwhelming.

A temper and conduct so like the Leader of life will assuredly be put at his right hand, and your earnestness to follow so bright an example will be increased by that very loss you now unavoidably mourn as having laid waste all your present comforts.

It is a singular satisfaction to us, that you are not destitute of tender friends, in such a separation, whose qualities are similar to the dear departed object that finished her course so well, and before the days of great infirmity and decay had lessened her powers and means of enjoyment. Time only and the exertion of Christian principles, can soothe your grief, and, as She advised, put you into a capacity of doing all your remaining duties.

At the time of writing my last, the 28. of the last month,[2] which I trust you will have received, I little thought of having so sad an occasion of addressing you again so soon.

I own the shock upon my nerves unfits me either to think or write, but I cou'd not neglect a post to express our sympathy, and earnest prayers for the only effectual consolation to be afforded, being ever your obliged and faithful affectionate friend T. Lindsey

Pray make our kindest remembrances to good Miss Scott.[3]

Luckily I was at the very time writing to the D. of G. which makes this come to you under his cover.[4]

Morden. Surry. Sept. 5. 1802.

---

1   According to Millar's obituary in the *Christian Pioneer*, NS, VII (1841), 377, Millar's first wife, Jean, née Scott, died in 1801.
2   Letter 739.
3   Probably the sister of Millar's first wife Jean, née Scott.
4   The duke of Grafton, hence the Thetford postmark.

741. *To THOMAS BELSHAM   27 SEPTEMBER 1802

Text: DWL, MS 12.57 (33*).
Addressed: To/The Rev^d. Thos Belsham/Grove Place/Hackney/Two^py Post/
                 Sep^br 28th
Endorsed: [By Belsham] Mrs Lindsey Sept^r: 28: 1802
Postmarked: o'Clock SE 28 1802 Two Py Post [postmark otherwise
                 illegible]

Note: The date Sep. 27. 1802 was added in rounded brackets in another hand. But Belsham's endorsement and the postmark establish the date as 27/28 September 1802.

Monday 27th/Morden Surry
(Sep 27. 1802)

Dear Sir

M^r. Lindsey says that if his hand could write ever so well, he should be at a loss to express his admiration of your very excellent discourse, and able just defence of dissent in general, but particularly of the right, duty and obligation of Unitarian Christians to stand fearless in their worship of the one only true God: And he hopes many will be both informed, & incouraged by this valuable publication: Your elevated & just introduction of D^r. Priestley's character talents & labors gave him great delight, but your Elogium upon himself has humbled him to the ground:[1] Here I must take up the cudgels, defend your sincerity in saying what you think, and in which you are not alone, tho' few would, or could have expressed their feelings so happily, & drawn the Christian in his present advanced state.

I was much alarmed on Friday last by the appearance of great returning debility in Mr Lindsey during his evening walk, we were happily got near the House when he fell down, and I got the assistance of the Gardener to raise him up, after sitting a while & taking a dose of a restorative medicine he recovered his limbs, & passed the evening as usual: However I sent for Dr Blackburne whose opinion was, that this was occasioned only by too great, & repeated exercise both in a carriage & on foot during this very hot & debilitating weather, & that perfect rest & quite [*sic*] would restore him, which thank God has been the case, and this morning on his second visit the D^r. found him so well, as to want nothing but care, & more prudence for the future.

Wednesday next compleats forty two years since this precious creature became the object of my fixed affection, my monitor, guide, and example in the best things, knowledge & virtue, and not the least blessing of this union, a sharer in his exalted friendships, with such men as y^rself & D^r. Priestley: Advantages these that will last for ever, and are above all price.[2]

The sword still hangs over the heads of our worthy, aged, & infirm friends: Their brother is struggling (by an original strong frame) from his late attack, but with less powers of every kind:[3] A termination of life would be a blessing to himself, but would probably involve them in a removal from this place, which long habit has indeared, and in addition, a place made comfortable, and adorned by the skill and industry of the younger sister, every tree & shrub being of her own raising: These ideas however painful they will submit to with all the fortitude wch. becomes christians, but they are too unable to sustain such a change without great detriment to their nearly worn out bodies.[4]

We have had a letter from Thos Evans, who is in good health, with his wife & children, the under Sheriff, a quondam friend of his, conducted the Pillory business very advantageously, legally & well, suffered only himself and constables to be within the ring, & two of the innocent Culprits oldest daughters: The multitude without shewed nothing but compassion.[5] There is however in Tho[s] Evans an unsubdued resentful mind, not only against his Judge & persecutors, but against those who would not stand forward & protect him, as a Unitarian: All his letters to M[r]. Lindsey since he wrote to him on his first commitment seem to have cancelled in his mind, all the kindness w[ch] first gave rise to his exertions, and since his imprisonment has been by himself & friends his chief support.[6] This high conceit of himself his talents, & title to distinction was very prominent at the Unitarian meeting two years ago at Bristol, as was apparent by a letter he wrote after his return to M[r]. Lindsey, whose meek & unaspiring mind could only wonder what the man would be at. Unjust as his treatment has been, this long discipline may do him moral good, & his frailties will not lessen our efforts to help him & his innocent family.[7]

I have got 5[ll] more by M[r]. Scot for D[r] Priestley from some society:[8] That worthy man has been a Month or more in town attending his wife in a dangerous fever, she is recovered, & they were to set out last Saturday for Portsmouth.[9]

Whilst the weather continue fine, & all goes well with us, we shall remain with our good friends, but I have all ready at home to receive us instantly, if that be necessary. But M[r]. L. is so happy, comfortable & f[MS torn] that he hopes for a few more walks on [MS torn] a nice smooth lawn, where he can go [MS torn] alone, & not alarm me he says.[10]

I have had a charming letter from Geneva f[rom] M[rs] Clyfford, who is on the remove to Florence: Her invalid Son has atchieved wonders, been carried up to near Mount S[t] Bernard: His mind will carry him anywhere, but his disease has not yet suffered any diminution.[11]

M[r] Frend has sent us some anecdotes of the visiters at Tunbridge Wells, where he has been with a sick sister:[12] he returns this week by Riegate [sic] to pass a few days with the disconsolate Baron Maseres, who has lost his only Brother & relative, whose chief residence was with the Baron, and a very amiable ingenious well principled man he was, and an able balance against such a man as Cobbet, who with a french noble-man (that was) is poisoning the Baron's better principles, & will make a prey of him, by their adulation & falsehoods.[13]

I wonder we have not heard from M[r] Kentish, his Father will shackle him to an advanced age and then leave him a fortune, when its principal use is lost: If he had been my Son, I w[d] have given him half my fortune, near 1000 p[r] ann, sent him to Birmingham where he w[d] have been most useful, & where he might have married his very nice cousin Mary Kettle & been as happy as mortals ever can be.[14]

D[r] Toulmin has sent to you five names & the money for copies of D[r] P's works, so his last letter said he would.[15] I have heard no more of D[r] Cappe or his journey, & fear my poor friend his Mother is not well, as she is a most punctual correspondent.[16] You will pray indulge us with a letter at y[r]. leisure, till a personal intercourse is renew[ed]. I think I told you that our worthy friend M[r] Millar of Dundee is in the depth of sorrow for the loss of a most excellent wife.[17] Our ladies desire their respects, greatly approve your superexcellent Sermon.[18]

M[r]. Lindsey joins in best regards & most affec[t] esteem with y[r] obliged f[d] HL.
What is become of y[r] Brother? His talents s[d] not lye idle.[19]

---

1   This work was Belsham's *The right and duty of unitarian Christians to form separate societies for religious worship* (see Letter 738, n. 1). In a lengthy footnote (p. 40 n. *), Belsham paid tribute to

Priestley and added that Lindsey's name 'cannot be pronounced by his numerous friends, but with sentiments of veneration and affection, which can hardly be conceived by those who are not intimately acquainted with his truly primitive and apostolic character'.

2   Theophilus and Hannah Lindsey were married on 29 Sept. 1760.

3   Christopher Chambers, merchant, of Mincing Lane, Tower Street, London, and the brother of Sophia and Frances Chambers, died on 2 Mar. 1803, aged seventy; *Gent. Mag.*, LXXIII, i (1803), 288.

4   Sophia and Frances Chambers did not move from Morden. The latter was the younger sister.

5   In Aug. 1801, Thomas Evans was convicted of sedition, following allegations that he had taken part in the singing of a disloyal song at Brechfa, Carmarthenshire, the previous Mar. He was sentenced to two years' imprisonment in Carmarthen gaol and was made to stand in the pillory in each of those years. For the public sympathy for him at and after his trial, see Jenkins, '"Horrid affair"', pp. 178–86.

6   Evans's resentful letters to Lindsey seem not to have survived. On 17 Sept. 1803, Hannah Lindsey wrote to William Frend 'Thoˢ Evans is very poor & unhappy by his wifes misconduct, & in utter dispair where to turn him for bread for his nine children: The sureties he depended upon, have also failed him: This family grievance has swallowed up all ideas of indignity about the Pillory'; CUL, Add. MS 7886 (Frend papers), no. 141. His conduct during (and after) his imprisonment alienated many of his friends, including his fellow-bard and fellow-radical Edward Williams (Iolo Morganwg). Evans and his wife Ann were both involved in marital infidelities; two of their eleven children had died in infancy. See Jenkins, '"Horrid affair"', pp. 192–6.

7   At the time of his trial, Evans received moral, legal and possibly financial support from the unitarian congregation at Lewin's Mead, Bristol, notably from its minister, John Estlin. Evidently he visited this congregation in 1800, the year before his trial; Jenkins, '"Horrid affair"', pp. 189–91.

8   See Letter 736, n. 5. Possibly Hannah Lindsey meant that Russell Scott had collected £5 from a society in Portsmouth or – bearing in mind the elevated social status of some of the contributors – she meant some persons of high social status in Portsmouth.

9   Russell Scott and his wife.

10 In each of the instances in this paragraph where the manuscript is slightly torn, it seems that one word is missing.

11 For Eliza Maria Clifford, see Letter 588, n. 2. Her son was Morgan Clifford of Perrystone.

12 Probably this is a reference to William Frend's unmarried half-sister Mary Frend, who was in delicate health for most of her life.

13 John Maseres, the younger brother of Francis Maseres, died in London on 12 Sept. 1802; *Gent. Mag.*, LXXII, ii (1802), 885. William Cobbett, while rejecting the unitarian beliefs of Maseres, was in fact on friendly terms with him, visited his home at Reigate and in later years wrote warmly of him; see Cobbett, *Rural rides* (Everyman edn, London, 1973, with introduction by Asa Briggs), pp. 270–6. At the same time, Cobbett sneered at the unitarians and their 'old and original warehouse and manufactory, Essex Street, in the Strand' (p. 270).

14 See Letter 738, n. 2. John Kentish's father, also named John Kentish, of St Albans, died in 1814. It has been claimed that the death of his father, and of his uncles, allowed Kentish to improve his material and intellectual standard of living and gave him 'the power of contributing more largely to objects of public and private charity'; John Kenrick, 'Memoir of Kentish', *CR*, NS, IX (1853), 279. In Jan. 1803, Kentish moved from his ministerial commitments in London and became minister of the New Meeting in Birmingham, in succession to John Edwards. On 28 Oct. 1805, he married his second cousin, Mary Kettle (1775–1864); she was the daughter of John Kettle of Birmingham.

15 Joshua Toulmin, who was still minister at the Mary Street congregation, Taunton, immediately before his move to New Meeting, Birmingham, in 1803, had raised subscriptions towards the publication of Priestley's *General history of the Christian church*, and his *Notes on all the books of scripture*; see Letter 736, n. 5.

16 For Robert Cappe, see Letter 738, n. 5. Catharine Cappe was his step-mother.

17 See Letter 740.

18 For the two sermons which Belsham published in 1802, see Letter 738, n. 1. Hannah Lindsey probably referred to *The right and duty of unitarian Christians to form separate societies for religious worship*; see n. 1, above.

19 In 1802, William Belsham still lived at Bedford. He was engaged on a new and extended edition of his *History of Great Britain from the Revolution, 1688 ... to the termination of the regency, A.D. 1820*, which was published in four volumes in London between 1805 and 1824. In 1802, he also published a pamphlet entitled *Remarks on the late definitive treaty of peace, signed at Amiens, March 25, 1802*, and pursued his controversy with Herbert Marsh (see Letter 705, n. 2).

742. To ROBERT MILLAR   **8 OCTOBER 1802**

Text: DWL, MS 12.46 (37).
Addressed: London October fifteen 1802/M^r. Robt Millar/Merchant/
                Dundee/N. Britain
Endorsed: [Word illegible] [Also endorsed] Lond^o. Octo. *1802*/Mr
                Lindsey
Postmarked: OC 15 802

Morden, Surry, Octr. 8. 1802.

Dear Sir,

I feel much obliged to you for letting us know how you do, as we have often wished it, and are happy to hear that your health of body is not too much impaired, and also your headach gone: but we rejoice more in your resigned state of mind, which alone fits poor mortals either for living with advantage or dying, if such be the will of God. You have been enabled to sustain well the most painful separation that an affectionate mind is capable of, and which brings you forcibly to lean upon that great omnipresent being whose we are, and whose condescending command is to love him above all other things, and this we can only learn first to do by the exercise of our earthly affections upon good and amiable objects, his favourite children; and in this prime duty of all you are happily exercising yourself.

We are now grieving over the sudden loss of a most dear and intimate friend, who in the last month of her tenth pregnancy, from apparent perfect health, was dead in a few hours and left her excellent astonished husband and only two sweet children to deplore her loss, never to be repaired to him or his. It is supposed that she died of the rupture of some large blood-vessel near the heart. She was like your dear wife as perfect as a human creature could be: beautiful without vanity, pious and benevolent without show, and her temper and manners so gentle and kind, that you had only to see her to love her. To us both, to Mrs Lindsey especially, her attachment was that of a child to a Parent; and at the early period of 30 years she had attained the perfect christian character.[1] My wife knew her most intimately, and is persuaded you will be edified with the account.

Such is the will of God; that her tryal should cease, and her husband's begin, for his greater good no doubt, as. hithert[o] no sorrow had ever approached him: For under the even tenour of a virtuous useful life in his profession of the Law, of high character and unblemished integrity, and a very ample private fortune, his road had been smooth and uninterrupted, and such a wife, nearly of his own age, and the object of his first affection, was every thing to him. May this aweful event be sanctified to him.[2]

As the period for sending out this year's books is past, and your's can only be obtained by favour of the Society, I would advise you to let it pass; and if you are in want of any of our Tracts to give away, I must beg you to permit me to supply them out of my ample stock. There is a valuable new edition of Mason's tract of Self-knowlege,[3] by our Secretary which I should be glad [to] present you with. I am also endeavouring to get leave of the Bishop of Elphin[4] to republish his father's (B^p. Law) life of Christ,[5] as we want much treatises of piety on rational principles.

I have not heard since I wrote last of Dr Priestley, but have the best hope that he is health [*sic*], fulfilling the purposes of his two intended important publications, for which a Subscription of upward of one thousand pounds is already in hand, though he has has [*sic*] not yet been apprized of it, that we know of it.[6]

I beg you will never mind postage in writing [to u]s.[7] It is all the money we spend in pleasure to [one word overlaid by the seal]

Pray commission some safe hand to call upon us at Essex house in a month's time, when [we] expect to be at home; and mention by what hand or Ship any parcell may be conveyed to You.

I have rather tired my hand, and can only add <u>our</u> best kindest wishes of all good to yourself,

from your affectionate friend,

T. Lindsey.

Pray remember us most kindly to Miss Scott.

---

1   The *Gent. Mag.*, LXXVII, ii (1802), 980, reported the death at Brompton on 1 Oct. 1802 of the wife of Samuel Yate Benyon of King's-road, Bedford-row. It stated that she died 'in childbed, of a rupture of the uterus'. She was Elizabeth, née Mason, originally of Shrewsbury, who married Samuel Yate Benyon on 26 Oct. 1789; see Letter 517. Benyon (d. 1822), born at Ashe, Shropshire, was educated at Warrington Academy, and Jesus College, Cambridge. In the early 1780s, he undertook legal training at Lincoln's Inn and attended Essex Street chapel, where Lindsey came to know and like him; see Vol. I, Letters 239, 241–3, 246, 249 and 254. In common with John Lee, he was a rare example of a dissenter who obtained high legal office, serving as recorder of Chester and vice-chancellor of the duchy of Lancaster. See his obituary, *MR*, XVII (1822), 377. He and Elizabeth Benyon had two surviving children, of whom the eldest, also named Samuel Yate Benyon (d. 1864), followed a legal career and served as chairman of the Newmarket bench of magistrates. On 22 Dec. 1803, Benyon married, as his second wife, Constance, née Wroughton; she died in 1836, *CR*, NS, III (1836), 292. See *Familiae min. gen.*, I, 414.

2   Samuel Yate Benyon (n. 1, above).

3   John Mason (1706–1763) was an independent minister at Cheshunt. His *Self-knowledge. A treatise, shewing the nature and benefit of that important science, and the way to attain it* was first published in London in 1732 and went through numerous subsequent editions. On 13 May 1802, the monthly committee meeting of the Unitarian Society requested Jeremiah Joyce, the secretary of the society from 1802 to 1816, to prepare a new edition of Mason's *Self-knowledge* for the press; on 7 Oct. 1802, Joyce reported to the committee that the edition was printed and ready for sale. In June 1804, the edition was reprinted. See Unitarian Society minute book, pp. 80–1, 93.

4   John Law (1745–1810), bishop of Elphin from 1795 to 1810, was the second son of Edmund Law, bishop of Carlisle.

5   Edmund Law's *A discourse upon the life and character of Jesus Christ* was first published in Cambridge and London in 1749. It was subsequently appended to several editions of Law's *Considerations on the theory of religion* (first published in Cambridge in 1745), including the fourth, fifth, sixth and seventh editions, which were published, respectively, in 1759, 1765, 1774 and 1784. Although the Unitarian Society did not immediately adopt this work, Law's *Reflections on the life and character of Christ* was re-published in London in 1807 and 1818, and in Philadelphia in 1808.

6   See Letter 736, n. 5.

7   The manuscript is slightly torn at this point.

743. *To THOMAS BELSHAM   **26 OCTOBER 1802**

    Text: DWL, MS 12.57 (24).

    Addressed: To/The Rev^d. T: Belsham/Grove Place/Hackney/Post Two^py/

                    Wednesday 27th. Oct^r

    Endorsed: [By Belsham] Mrs Lindsey Octr. 27. 1802 [in a different hand]

                    Oct. 27. 1802

    Postmarked: 7 o'Clock 27 OC 1802 N^T   Two Pen[ny] POST 206 Strand

Tuesday Evening
Morden 20th

Dr Sir

A thousand thanks to you for your communications by letter this day: As we are to remove hence to Essex Street tomorrow, I write this to put into the Post on our arrival at home.[1]

The damp weather prevents all farther improvement in M^r. Lindsey, but I think you will find him considerably improved upon the whole. We feel some regret in leaving our excellent friends & this happy retreat, probably for the last time,[2] as altho' their Brother is better his life is in a most precarious state.[3]

All things pleasant & otherwise come to an end, long injoyment of them indears, but does not prevent the knowledge that all changes are for good.

Dr P. has written in low spirits.[4]

Adieu M^r L: joins in affec^t esteem with y^r obliged f^d

                              HL

1   This no doubt explains the seven-day gap between the date of the letter and the postmark.

2   In fact Lindsey and his wife visited Morden again in 1803; see Letters 748 and 753–4.

3   For the death of Christopher Chambers in Mar. 1803, see Letter 741, n. 3.

4   In his letters to Lindsey of 3 July and 28 Aug. 1802, Priestley had referred to the precarious state of his health and his sense of the proximity of death. He was all the more anxious to complete the final volumes of his *General history of the Christian church from the fall of the western empire* and his *Notes on all the books of scripture*. See Rutt, I, 488–90.

744. **To ROBERT MILLAR   **4 DECEMBER 1802**

    Text: DWL, MS 12.46 (42).

    Addressed: To/M^r. Robert Millar/Merchant/Dundee/N:B

    Endorsed: Lond^o. 4th. Decr 1802/Mrs Lindsey/Moral, Relig^n, &

                    Mr Palmer

    Postmarked: Postmark missing.

London Decr 4th 1802

Dear Sir

M^r. Lindsey desires me to thank you for your letter of Novr 15th. It gave us great satisfaction to hear that you have been inabled to struggle so manfully under your great shock & irreparable loss, and that altho' weak yet your bodily health is rather improving, which considering this trying season of the Year is as much as can be expected. We trust that your removal into your own house will not too much increase those melancholy feelings, which a natural low tone of spirits under the late great change renders in some degree unavoidable: But you greatly excede our other friend in bearing patiently and acting firmly under your severe trial: His mind is more afloat by living in the world, and attending to the advice of men of the world, which bewilders, & turns the mind from looking to, & putting its trust wholly upon that Being who wounds and makes whole.[1]

M[r]. Lindsey is particularly gratified by the effort you have made to recall the wandering sheep to their old fold, and most useful Pastor, whatever your amiable diffidence may suggest of incompetence for the work, nobody would do it better, or have half the influence you have: And nothing is so difficult to get as a voluntary teacher where little or no profit can attach, even for a bare maintenance:[2] The Methodists have large funds and many very wealthy adherents, and their regulations oblige all their followers to contribute if it is but 1[d] a week: This attaches them & gives them consequence in their own eyes, & a great deal of money is raised in this way. Go on D[r] Sir and your happy moments will increase, & your spirits revive to that calm chearful point, w[ch] insures the greatest portion of injoyment that such a probationary state as the present permits.

M[r] Lindsey recommends you to buy a work of D[r] Payley's lately published intitled "Natural Theology" the subject is treated in a new and superior way & contains a great deal of natural history to inforce and illustrate his design of proving beyond all doubt *One* great intelligent cause of all things.[3]

As to our Society books M[r]. Lindsey would advise you to wait till Jan[ry]. as the little practical pieces he has proposed to print of the late B[p] Laws will be ready for the list for 1803, and he is sure you will like to have half a dozen of them:[4] He is quite disinclined to select books for you, as he knows not which will be most useful: Neither do we know what your arrears are, the last time your name stands in my private list as paid, was in 1799: But I will try to get the Treasurers[5] books looked into, the present Treasurer lives at Hackney & we have no intercourse with him.[6]

The last satisfactory account, (because true) of M[r] Palmer was brought by a Cap[t] Wilson about five weeks ago: We had it by a private friend from him, but to prevent trouble by inquiry at the Cap[t] lodging Arundel Street near us, he got it inserted in the Morning Chronicle.[7] The general facts were these that above 2 years ago M[r]. Palmer, James Ellis, M[r] & M[rs]. Abbot & children,[8] who had always lived with M[r]. P. with three or four orderly convicts who were to work their way home, all sailed in a small Vessel from the Bay, meaning to take wood to the Cape of good Hope, & there to exchange it for merchandise, & then procede to England. After many delays & difficulties, for they had not one Mariner on board, but were to navigate, by the skill they had acquired by Coasting in a Vessel of their own building, this Quixote headed party was met by Cap[t] Wilson at New Zealand, the Ship leaky, & in want of every thing, Cap[t] W: gave them all the help he c[d] to repair, & a barrel of Pork, & left them all in good health & spirits: A friend of ours wishing to know when they might be expected home call [*sic*] at Cap[t] Wilsons lodging, but missed him, but his 1st Mate said, he thought they must return to the Bay as the wisest & safest plan.[9]

Of D[r] Priestley we had last week a much better account of his health in a letter he wrote Sep[r] 25 for the preceding fortnight he had been quite free from Fever, Ague, & the extreme languor w[ch] had so long subdued his strength; that his natural ardor was returned, and if he continued as well as he was, he hoped certainly to be able to accomplish his two great works, 3 Volumn's of Church History, and four or five of Notes on the Scriptures: The 2nd Vol. of the History w[d] have been finished, if his Printer & man, had not with the whole neighborhood been laid up with the Fever & Ague, w[ch] this year prevails to an extent unknown before.[10] The Subscription here for these works tho' D[r]. P. knows not yet the extent, has cheared him under his labors

& great expence, and it has exceded our expectation much, being now about 1200£, wch is vested in the funds, & not figuring on paper as most Subscriptions are.[11]

You will rejoice with us that Peace is at present the order of the day, may it please the Almighty to preserve it to this undeserving Nation. The inclosed excellent little piece came out the day before Parliament met, & was sent to the Ministers & several Members, & will let [you] into the real causes of the late outcry by [one word overlaid by the seal] papers for a renewal of War, horrid War.[12]

I must now say a few words respecting ourselves tho' I am tired with writing, as you may be with reading, but we wanted to amuse & inform you of what you wished to know & M^r. Lindsey's hand was not equal to the detail. After twelve weeks of comfort & retirement at our second home,[13] we returned in as good health & strength, as age and infirmities permit, & expect bad colds & coughs for a fortnight, have only to be as thankful as we ought, that limbs & senses are continued sufficient for moving about in a quiet way, & injoying the calls of our many kind friends. Pray remember us kindly to Miss Scot, we hope she will sometimes break in upon your solitude: Do not live intirely by yourself: A Niece you might instruct more by example than books & an object of attention is worth something with our joint kindest regards Y^rs T: & HL

---

1 Probably 'our other friend' was the bereaved lawyer, Samuel Yate Benyon; see Letter 742, n. 1.

2 Millar had been the lay organizer and effective leader of the unitarian congregation at Dundee since Thomas Palmer's arrest and subsequent transportation in 1793 and 1794.

3 William Paley's *Natural theology: or evidences of the existence and attributes of the deity collected from the appearances of nature* was published in London in 1802. Nine editions of this work had appeared by the time of Paley's death in 1805.

4 See Letter 742, n. 5.

5 Hannah Lindsey first wrote 'Secretary's', then crossed the word out and wrote 'Treasurers' above.

6 The treasurer of the Unitarian Society from 1799 to 1803 was the solicitor Godfrey Kettle, who lived at Gower Street, Bedford Square. Perhaps Hannah Lindsey meant 'the present secretary' (n. 5, above), John Kentish, who was the afternoon preacher at the Gravel Pit meeting, Hackney, from 1795, and morning preacher at nearby Newington Green from 1799 to 1802. He resided at Hackney during these years. Kentish was secretary of the Unitarian Society from 1796 until 1802, when he was succeeded by Jeremiah Joyce.

7 On 28 Oct. 1802, the *Morning Chronicle* published the following report: 'Some accounts have lately been received respecting the fate of Mr. Fysche Palmer, who our readers will recollect was sentenced by the Judiciary Court of Scotland to be banished to New South Wales, on account of his political principles at an early period of the late war, and the other persons who in March 1801 sailed from that Settlement on their return to England. – These accounts are communicated by Captain Wilson, of the Royal Admiral transport, who fell in with them at New Zealand. They had touched there to purchase spars and timber, which, together with the ship, they meant to dispose of at the Cape of Good Hope. This was about the middle of June, and they had been on their passage to that place from the middle of March 1801. Most of the crew were very indifferent, the vessel was leaky, and ill supplied with provisions. – Captain Wilson very kindly gave a supply of whatever he could spare, and they then resolved to touch at some of the South Sea Islands to get a farther supply. In case by any unforeseen accident they should be detained at New Zealand, Captain Wilson had, by his solicitations, prevailed on Governor King, to send them provisions, which would reach them about February last. – The vessel they sailed in was about three hundred tons burthen, and was the joint purchase of Mr. Palmer, Mr. Boston, and two other persons in the settlement. – At the time Captain Wilson left them, Mr. Palmer and his companions were in good health'. Captain Wilson was possibly Alexander Wilson, who had been a royal navy captain since 1795; see *Royal kalendar ... for the year 1803*, p. 149. The naval officer Philip Gidley King (1758–1808) succeeded John Hunter as governor of New South Wales in 1800 and served in that capacity until 1806. He had previously been the lieutenant-governor of Norfolk Island.

8 Probably a family of free settlers, rather then convicts or persons transported.

9 See Letter 735, n. 4.

10 For Priestley's letter to Lindsey of 25 Sept. 1802, see Rutt, I, 492.

¹¹ For this subscription, see Letter 736, n. 5.

¹² This 'excellent little piece' was a sixteen-page pamphlet by John McCreery, entitled *Observations on the present relative situation of Great Britain and France. November the 16th, 1802* (Liverpool, 1802). Arguing strongly against the renewal of war, the author claimed that after the peace of Amiens, 'a disappointed and sanguinary party' retired from government and, 'disappointed in their hopes of exciting internal commotions in France, they raised the cry of war'; in doing so, they were supported by the 'licentiousness of the press' (pp. 11, 12, 14). Several newspapers, if not clamouring for a renewal of war, drew attention to Bonaparte's plans for aggression; see, for example, the *Morning Post and Gazetteer*, 1 and 2 Nov. 1802. The new session of parliament began on 16 Nov. 1802.

¹³ By 1802 Lindsey and his wife regarded the residence of Frances and Sophia Chambers at Morden, Surrey, as their 'second home'.

745. *To WILLIAM TURNER OF NEWCASTLE   4 JANUARY 1803

Text: LPN, MS 59 (r).
Printed: Nicholson and McLachlan, pp. 162–3 (brief references to the
                  first two paragraphs; most of fifth paragraph; sixth to tenth
                  paragraphs, inclusive).
Addressed: To/The Revᵈ Mʳ Turner/Newcastle/upon/Tyne
Postmarked: Postmark missing.

Dear Sir,

Mʳ. Lindsey wishes he could write himself to thank you for your kind communications by Mʳ. Bigge:[1] He cannot find words to express the high approbation he feels both of the design of the new Institution, and the talents shewn by yourself for executing and fully accomplishing the very valuable ends and objects of it: And hopes more ample assistance will be given by the Gentlemen of Fortune in the District of the North, for so noble a design.[2] He enters also with pleasure into your views & wishes for a Coadjutor in a few years.[3]

We thank you also for the assistance you have lent to Dʳ. Priestleys Subscription, neither I not Johnson have yet received the draft for 25~[4] which you say would be sent in a few days: I only mention this because the little things relating to Mʳ. Prowitt never came to hand, & in your hurry you forgot to inclose one.[5]

No other modes of receiving Subscriptions for Dʳ Priestley are now admissible, nor would anything but receiving the money, and having it funded been at all equal to the purpose; as names only give ten times the trouble in collecting at a distant period when the promise is either forgotten, or reluctantly complied with: I have had enough of this work on other occasions, & been no little out of pocket by it.

By a letter from Dʳ. P. a few weeks ago we felt much discouraged, as he described himself as having the symptoms of an advanced Liver disease,[6] & that this is his ailment I have no doubt as he had fits of Gall stones above ten years ago, & was relieved by a vegetable diet wᶜʰ he persisted in for near two years: By a letter just recᵈ by Mʳ. Belsham, he speaks of himself as getting better by a return to nearly the same regimen, altho' his flesh and strength are greatly diminished, but that with care he hopes to live to accomplish his two works wᶜʰ. will take about a year & half.[7]

By the favor of God, Mʳ. Lindsey continues free from any fresh attack, and his health and looks as well as before: His general frame is more tottering, but he still can walk out a little when the weather suits, and sees his friends with pleasure, but his books are his most lasting resource, & his eyes continue good. For so many blessings we can never be enough thankful.

Of M[r]. Cappes works M[r]. Lindsey can form no judgment, not being strong enough to enter sufficiently into new Disquisitions;[8] of the temper and ingenuity there can be no doubt: such of his friends as have read them, declare themselves not so much inlightened as they expected: D[r]. Priestley often urged him above twenty years ago to publish, & let the subjects be canvassed when he was able to reply & defend.

M[r]. Lindsey desires me to tell you of a recent Publication by M[r] Evanson intitled "Reflections on the State of Religion in Christendom", written in his own bold & manly way, which must give great offence to the Hierarchy.[9]

We have been very uneasy for the last fortnight on D[r] Disneys account who has suffered greatly by a fever & great debility: it is now happily subdued but his return to health strength, & flesh must be very slow: He is not careful of himself and sadly overplies both mind & body in various sorts of secular business, w[ch]. he executes with a harrassing [*sic*] rapidity.

M[r]. Joyce whose useful Scientific Dialogues your handsome notice, has much gratified, has done the Duty at this Chapel for a year in the afternoons, and taken the whole during the D[rs] confinement.[10]

M[r] Lindsey desires to join in the be[st] wishes of this and all seasons for y[r]self M[rs]. Turner, and family, with

D[r] Sir your obliged & sincere f[d]

HL

Jan[ry] 4[th] 1803.

London

---

1   Probably Thomas Bigge, the co-founder and editor of *The Oeconomist; or Englishman's Magazine*.
2   Turner's 'noble design' was the 'New Institution for public lectures in natural philosophy in Newcastle upon Tyne', founded in 1802; see Harbottle, *William Turner*, ch. 8.
3   Turner's need for a coadjutor at Hanover Square chapel, Newcastle upon Tyne, was occasioned by the death of Edward Prowitt on 3 July 1802. He did not have a formally constituted assistant during the remainder of his ministry (which ended with his retirement in 1841), although he was assisted from time to time by other ministers, including his eldest son William Turner (1788–1853).
4   Hannah Lindsey left a characteristic squiggle (see also Letters 756, 758 and 768) after the figure 25; presumably it signified a £ sign.
5   See Letter 736, n. 5. Edward Prowitt of Newcastle had died on 3 July 1803.
6   This letter from Priestley to Hannah Lindsey, dated 16 Oct. 1802, may be found in DWL, MS 12.13 and is partly printed in Rutt, I, 493–4 (with the reference to Priestley's digestion at 494). In a passage omitted by Rutt, Priestley described the symptoms concerning his liver and gallstones to which Hannah Lindsey referred.
7   Priestley's letter to Belsham, dated 30 Oct. 1802, may be found in DWL, MS 12.13 and is partly printed in Rutt, I, 497–8. In a passage omitted by Rutt, Priestley wrote 'My health, I thank God, is much better than it has been. I got rid of the gall stones by the regimen I used to have recourse to for the same complaint … I am, however, thin and weak, but that is usually the effect of years.'
8   This is probably a reference to Newcome Cappe's *Discourses chiefly on devotional subjects*; see Letter 738, n. 5.
9   The full title of Evanson's book was *Reflections upon the state of religion in Christendom; particularly in the countries situated within the limits of the western Roman empire at the commencement of the XIX century of the Christian era*. It was printed in Exeter, and published in London, in 1802.
10 Jeremiah Joyce's *Scientific dialogues intended for the instruction and entertainment of young people: in which the first principles of natural and experimental philosophy are fully explained* were published in six volumes by Joseph Johnson in London between 1800 and 1803. There were many subsequent editions. See Issitt, *Jeremiah Joyce*, pp. 121–5. From the retirement of Lindsey in 1793 until 1804, Joyce was assistant minister at Essex Street chapel, and frequently conducted the afternoon service, and deputized for Disney during the latter's illnesses.

746. To TIMOTHY KENRICK   18 JANUARY 1803

Text: The Sharpe papers, UCL Library Services, Special Collections
                 (Kenrick papers), 178/66
Printed: 'The Kenrick letters', *TUHS*, V, 1 (Oct. 1931), 83–4
                 (with minor errors).
Addressed: Address missing.
Postmarked: Postmark missing.

Dear Sir,

London. Jan. 18. 1803.

Your letter yesterday revived me much by leading me to hope that you are inclined to accept what is right and honourable for yourself in the invitation from Birmingham; and allowing for the differences, which prevent an unanimity, always desireable, but seldom attainable in so large a Society. Your judgment respecting the causes of fewer names is perfectly just; we know from the best authority that very few are really disinclined, and that in the midst of all the toil, some new and additional subscriptions have been made, which augurs well, that when you and M[r]. Kentish are once settled all will be harmony, and great increased usefulness be the result of your joint labours.[1] This is my sincere opinion and view of things, and I am much interested in its accomplishment.

As to an Academical Institution being formed, it must be the work of time and favourable events. If the Manchester Pupils are removed to York, which is now in agitation, their small funds must go there: London and Exeter funds might possibly be united.[2] But I trust you will not fail to finish the education of the promising students you have at present. Except to the Welsh men the distance will not be inconvenient, and they may be helped at the long Vacation in their travelling expences. As I am yet spared in life, I will add 20£ this year for you to use as you shall judge best.[3]

It is the utmost effort of weak hand to have written thus much this cold weather.[4] Your friends at Birmingham wait anxiously for your decision, good Kentish above all.[5] With best regards from us both, to yourself and M[rs] Kenrick,[6] I remain, Dear Sir
Most truly your's,
T. Lindsey.

---

[1]   Timothy Kenrick did not move from Exeter to the New Meeting, Birmingham, where John Kentish became the minister on 23 Jan. 1803.

[2]   Manchester College was moved to York in Sept. 1803, with Wellbeloved as principal and theological tutor. The London fund consisted of the remnant of the Hackney College funds after the closure in 1796; see HMCO, MS MNC Miscellaneous fo. 47, and MS Misc. fos. 272–89. The Exeter fund consisted of the fund surviving from the second Exeter Academy (1760–71). Kenrick's Academy, which was closed on his death in Aug. 1804, was the third Exeter Academy. The first, founded by Joseph Hallett (1656–1722), existed from 1690 to 1722. I am grateful to Dr David Wykes for guidance on this question.

[3]   Kenrick and Joseph Bretland re-opened the dissenting academy at Exeter in Oct. 1799. Kenrick himself taught a wide range of subjects, including the New Testament, the evidences for natural and revealed religion, and logic. The academy suffered a severe blow with Kenrick's sudden death in Aug. 1804, and closed the following year; see the entry for Kenrick by A. Gordon, revised by S. J. Skedd, in *ODNB*, XXXI, 309–10.

[4]   This is the last surviving letter in Lindsey's own hand.

[5]   Kenrick's decision was to remain at Exeter; see n. 1, above.

[6]   Elizabeth (1743–1819), née Belsham, was Kenrick's second wife; they were married in 1794.

747. *To ROBERT MILLAR   **12 MARCH 1803**

Text: DWL, MS 12.46 (43).
Addressed: To/M^r. Robert Millar/Merchant/Dundee
Endorsed: Lond^o 12 Mar 1803/Mrs Lindsey
Postmarked: Postmark missing.

March 12th 1803

Dear Sir,

We were glad to hear that you had recovered from your indisposition, under wch your solitary situation would necessarily be very painfully impressive: Everything tends to send us more to our kind Maker, whose favor & support exceeds all earthly help & comfort.

Your parcel lies here ready for any safe messenger you send for it: I have added for your half guinea what Mr Lindsey thought you would like, & a few small pieces besides. Your excellent amiable friend has been in the greatest danger from a violent attack of the Influenza that prevails universally here.[1] It began with fever, pulse 100, an incessant Cough, wheesing, & pain in the eye balls, wch in a few days moderated, & we hoped w^d have subsided, but an unfortunate relapse by efforts to get well too soon, aggravated the disease & made a blister on the Chest, & small doses of James's powder necessary, but all did not do, till by cupping on the Chest, & taking blood in this safest way, it has pleased God to give a favorable turn to this sad disease: The fever is gone, & the cough nearly, and he can now take a little food & wine, and is recruiting slowly, as both strength & flesh have suffer'd a great diminution by an attack of fever beyond any of a do^z years, and what it c^d not previously have been supposed with nervous debility at fourscore his frame had been capable of:[2] But nothing is too hard for the Almighty to accomplish, & his goodness has also been manifest in preserving me from this disorder, & our two faithful servants who attend day & night on their kind and beloved Master.[3]

There is scarcely a family here that are not afflicted more or less, & whole families fall down altogether under it, tho' it is not infectious, but a disease of the air, & weakness & intire wakefulness attend in most cases.

Added to this Visitation, we have had a sudden & quite unexpected alarm of War, the very steps for precaution will much burden this impoverished Country, but at any rate we must be on our Guard against a bold & enterprizing enemy, whose ambition never sleeps, & who has availed himself of the suspension of fifteen Months War, to do what might secure his own power, settle the affairs of Germany, & strengthen himself by the Countries he has conquered, and their resources.[4] But M^r. Lindsey says, he can do nothing but what is the Will of Omnipotence and we must submit with all the fortitude we can to whatever is appointed.

M^r. Belsham had a letter yesterday dated late in January from Dr Priestley which is chearful, and as he says nothing of his health, and has been writing a small piece on the Comparison of Socrates with Jesus, wch shews him in vigor: He says also that 3 Volumn's of the 4 of his Church History are packing up to go to Philadelphia with his son & daughter to be shipped for England by the first good Vessel.[5]

We have very severe cold weather with snow, but it is better now, than in May. Mr Palmer & his company are much too adventerous [*sic*] to trust their passage home in such a crazy Vessel & ill man'd: They are not likely to escape safe thro' such dangerous Seas, & it can, or ought to be no object to save or get money, in comparison of probable safety, & comfort.[6] But we land folks who sit snug at home, have no notion of the vigor & efforts, which those can with ease exert, who have surmounted so many great difficulties for a course of years.

M[r] Lindsey is sorry for the defection of your old useful friend in the congregation,[7] begs you will be discouraged with nothing, but do what little you can, & be satisfied with acting with faithfulness in the cause of God & truth even if alone, and thereby meet with his approbation who knows best, when, & by whom good is to be done.

Adieu with our joint kindest regards and best wishes for every support & comfort to you, I am always

Y[r] faithful f[d]

HL

P.S.

Our Comp[ts] to Miss Scot.

---

1   On 4 Mar 1803, the *Morning Chronicle*, reporting on 'the Influenza which is so prevalent at this time', recommended 'the real *James's Powder*' as a 'particularly efficacious' remedy. See also *Ipswich Journal*, 12 Mar. 1803.

2   Lindsey reached the age of eighty on 1 July 1803.

3   The rate books of the parish of St Clement Danes do not include the names of these servants; probably 'my good Mary' (see Letter 761) was one of them.

4   Britain declared war on France on 18 May 1803; during the previous six months, France had secured a territorial and constitutional re-arrangement in Germany, which included the secularization of the former ecclesiastical electorates and the abolition of the rights of most of the free cities. The 'suspension of fifteen months' refers to the period between the signing of the Treaty of Amiens on 25 Mar. 1802 and the renewal of the war fifteen months later.

5   For this letter from Priestley to Belsham, dated 22 Jan. 1803, see Rutt, I, 501–3. Priestley's *Socrates and Jesus compared* was published in Philadelphia in 1803 and reprinted by Joseph Johnson in London in the same year.

6   For Palmer's fate, see Letters 735, n. 4, and 744, n. 7.

7   The surviving evidence does not permit the identification of this member of Millar's congregation.

748. **To THOMAS BELSHAM   5 JULY 1803

Text: DWL, MS 12.57 (25).
Addressed: To/The Rev[d]. Tho[s]. Belsham/Grove Place/Hackney. Mordon
                 Surry./Two[py] Post/Friday July 5th./2 o'clock
Endorsed: [By Belsham] M[rs] Lindsey July 5: 1803
Postmarked: 7 o'Clock AU 5 1803 N.[T]   Two Py Post Unpaid
                 [postmark otherwise illegible]

Morden Surry
M[rs] Chamber's
July 5th 1803

Dear Sir

Thinking it would gratify you very much after your arrival at Hackney to send you the inclosed from D[r]. Priestley M[r]. Lindsey wished me to do it. His accident is a serious one, & the consequences may be felt during his life, he should not have thrown away his Crutches so soon, as he feels pain in walking with a stick: It is most happy that he has so much imployment that he likes, & has health sufficient to do it.[1]

You will please to return the letter in your first packet to Morden.

We arrived here on Tuesday Evening[2] and I have already found benefit from the air & quiet, & M[r]. Lindsey also: Our kind excellent friends are as much Invalids as ourselves, but we have so long been used to comfort & be comforted by the same Society that we try to remember better days, and make the best of these.

M[r] Frend found M[rs]. Reynolds worse than he expected, but she has lucid intervals, & has joined in writing a letter to me, along with a few lines from M[r]. Reynolds, who is laid up with the Gout; & Frend has added his mite, by sending a history of somebody we do not know, as the name is omitted: As he says nothing of his lame leg, w[ch] [he] suffered by travelling we hope he is in a mending way again.[3] M[r] Hoare & Son, & other neighboring Gentlemen, are busy raising & training men, for the defence of the Country, so that we have good hope from the general energy of success.[4]

Best regards to y[r] Brother, &[c] accept the affec[t] esteem y[r]self of T: & HL

1   In his letter to Lindsey of 4 June 1803, Priestley explained that as a result of a 'dangerous fall', he had suffered a damaged hip and 'a strain of the muscles of that thigh'; Rutt, I, 512–13.
2   5 July 1803 was a Tuesday; the previous Tuesday was 28 June 1803.
3   This letter from Richard and Mary Catherine Reynolds to Hannah Lindsey seems not to have survived. However, a letter from Richard Reynolds to Frend, dated 15 June 1803, most of which was written by Mary Catherine Reynolds, may be found in CUL, Add. MS 7886 (Frend papers), no. 229. In it, Reynolds referred to his improvement of health after a series of accidents and noted that Frend had experienced only a slow recovery from the lameness of his leg. He also commented on his wife's mental condition; see Letter 727, n. 2.
4   This is probably a reference to Henry Hoare, Esq., of Grove House, Mitcham; see *Holden's triennial directory, 1802, 1803 & 1804*, unpaginated 'directory … of housekeepers resident in London and Ten Miles circular, in private life'. Though part of the landed gentry by 1803, Hoare and his son were related to the celebrated banking family of Hoare. The training of men in this context denotes the militia or, more likely, the volunteer force, which by 1804 numbered some 400,000 troops in preparation for a possible French invasion.

749. **To CHRISTOPHER WYVILL   11 JULY 1803

Text: NYRO, ZFW 7/2/159/8, Wyvill of Constable Burton MSS.
Printed: Ditchfield, 'Lindsey–Wyvill correspondence', 170 (most of second paragraph; whole of third paragraph; first two sentences of fourth paragraph); 172 (most of seventh paragraph).
Addressed: To/The Rev[d]. M[r]. Wyville/Burton Hall/near Bedale/Yorkshire
Endorsed: From Rev[d] M[r] Lindsey July 11th. 1803
Postmarked: JY 11 803

July 11th 1803 London

Dear Sir

M[r] Lindsey had just desired me to thank you for your first most acceptable letter which relieved many anxieties we were under for yourself and dear family, who had been under so much disease and trial; and I must confess that we felt very uncomfortable for the effects of the Influenza which hung so long upon Y[r]self not having your Magnanimous mind, and great Equanimity, which my brother D[r]. B. admires, praises, and envy's.[1]

Your second letter demands immediate notice: M[r]. Lindsey is highly gratified by your wishes to exhibit him in so hon[ble] a way as a friend & correspondent of yours, and has not the least desire, but of leaving his letters intirely to your good judgment & discretion, if they can be of the least use.[2]

He rejoices in your confirmed health and active exertions for putting before the

Public additional valuable information to rouse our depraved Countrymen to a sense of the valuable rights, wch. are still possessed, tho' neglected.

We are glad you will attend the Meeting at Northallerton, it is only by active & judicious measures, that we can hope to extricate ourselves out of this premature & unnecessary War.[3] We are sorry that with you, as well as here, there is so little sense of the danger of having roused a Tyger accustomed to Victory, & who singly we can do little to annoy, and he everything, by only threats of Invasion. The break at the Newcastle bank, will ruin many besides themselves, their speculations in every way have been unbounded, and unpardonable: Mr Burdon was warned above a Year ago against the ruinous plans they had adopted: The deficit we here [sic]is two Million, if half be true it is enough.[4] We were told yesterday from pretty good authority that Government had been applied to for aid, and had ingaged to lend three hundred thousand pounds on the security of all the Lands & property of the House.

Ld Eldon who married a daughter of old Surtees's is come forward in a considerably [sic] way to assist her family.[5]

The Duke of Northumberland was going to Alnwic to raise men, but is stopped again by a return of the Gout.

On Friday July 1st. M^r. Lindsey entered on his 81st. year, a wonderful period considering the infirmities and disease of the last two years. His health is now very good, but the feebleness of the limbs is not amendable, but he can still walk to Johnson's & back after resting.[6] He is sorry not to be able to use his pen to you, but his right hand had two strokes the side & leg but one. I am at present under a long bad fit of Gallstones and bilious misery, but hope it is giving way. We with you join in thankfulness to the giver of nothing but good, for all his mercies to us all.

We are under some concern about Dr Priestley, who by a letter from his Son to M^r. Johnson, has had a bad fall by reaching a book from the top shelf of his high Library, and is now upon crutches, and Joseph says recovering.[7] Three out of four Vol^s of the Church History are arrived, & the box with the 4th Vol: is at Philadelphia to be put on board the 1st ship for England: And half of the Notes on the Bible will be printed by Christmas.[8]

We trust that the Sea air and bathing, & your recess from business will chear, restore, & purify you all from every remaining atom of disease, and this glorious weather give plenty of everything.

With our joint kindest regards & wishes to Y^rself, Mrs Wyville and family, we are Dr Sir

Y^r obliged & affec^t f^ds

    T: & H. Lindsey

---

1   No letter from Wyvill to Lindsey from 1803 appears to have survived.

2   See n. 1, above. Wyvill's 'second letter' evidently requested permission to quote from Lindsey's letters in an encomium on Lindsey which he wished to include in his *Political papers*, V. That volume was published at York in 1804 and Wyvill printed (pp. 10–17) extracts from an exchange of letters between himself and Lindsey in Apr.–May 1792. Lindsey's two letters in this exchange are included in this edition (Letters 494 and 497). Wyvill added a panegyric on Lindsey (p. 12 n. *), in which he recalled a friendship dating from the time of the Feathers Tavern petition in 1772. He praised Lindsey's 'virtuous zeal' and 'the boldness of his Unitarian doctrine', adding, in adaptation of Pope's 'Epilogue to the satires', lines 131–2, the couplet 'Let modest Lindsey, if he will, excel /Ten Metropolitans in preaching well'. For the background to these exchanges, see Ditchfield, 'Lindsey–Wyvill correspondence'.

3   Hannah Lindsey referred here to the general meeting of the lieutenancy and magistracy of the north riding of Yorkshire, at Northallerton on 13 July 1803. Wyvill was present; the meeting authorized

measures for defence throughout the riding following the renewal of war between Britain and France on 18 May 1803. See *York Herald*, 16 July 1803.

4   In June 1803, the Exchange Bank in Newcastle upon Tyne collapsed and was wound up; Hannah Lindsey's estimate of the deficit was broadly accurate. The partners of the bank included Rowland Burdon (see Letter 394, n. 3), Aubone Surtees junior (d. 1827) and his brother John Surtees (1757–1849). The process of repaying the creditors of the Exchange Bank was not completed until the 1830s, when Burdon, declared bankrupt in 1803, restored himself to solvency. See Maberly Phillips, *A history of banks, bankers and banking in Northumberland, Durham and North Yorkshire, illustrating the commercial development of the north of England, from 1755 to 1894* (London, 1894), pp. 385–90.

5   For John Scott, 1st Baron Eldon (1751–1838), see Letter 499, n. 4. He eloped in 1772 with Elizabeth Surtees (1754–1831), the daughter of the Newcastle banker Aubone Surtees (1711–1800), whose sons were partners in the failed Exchange Bank (n. 4, above) and to whom Hannah Lindsey referred as 'old Surtees'. Although the Surtees family initially disapproved of the marriage, Eldon subsequently gave them financial support.

6   Lindsey could walk from Essex Street to Joseph Johnson's premises at 72 Paternoster Row.

7   This letter from Joseph Priestley junior to Joseph Johnson seems not to have survived. For Priestley's fall and injury, see Letter 748, n. 1.

8   For these two works of Priestley, see Letter 736, n. 4.

750. **To THOMAS BELSHAM   16 JULY 1803

Text: DWL, MS 12.57 (26).
Addressed: To/The Rev^d. Thos. Belsham,/~~Rev^d. M^r. Kenrick's/Exeter.~~
                   [added, in another hand] Hackney/London
Endorsed: [By Belsham] Mrs Lindsey July 16: 1803
Postmarked: JY 803 [postmark otherwise illegible]

July 16th 1803
London

Dear Sir

As you kindly desired a few lines, I cannot neglect your friendly request altho' I have nothing new to tell you.

Your Venerable friend by the cool weather of the last three or four days was braced, & able every day to walk out with advantage, and more vigor. As far as a gradual remove of the bilious obstruction, I am also better, and by the greatest temperance, part of the irritability of the stomach is also abated, so that I am better on the whole certainly.

So much for ourselves about whom you kindly interest yourself.

I think you heard before you went of Dr Priestley's fall in reaching a book & his being upon Crutches. This week a Ship being to sail for Philadelphia, Mr Lindsey put forth all his powers, & wrote one side of a folio sheet to his dear friend, and I filled it up; with some account of his daughters near approach to dissolution [*sic*], of which I rather apprehend he is quite ignorant, which is not right.[1]

We have rec^d a new Subscription to the D^rs work, I shall keep the money till we see you, only leave a direction with Mr Johnson to send a Copy of the Corruptions, if they should be sent out, before we return from Morden, whither we think of going in a fortnight, having luckily by means of the Apothecary at Mitcham, only a mile off, heard of an incomperable [*sic*] Shaver[?]: which has removed all that difficulty.[2]

On Thursday the Unitarian Society met and Mr Lindsey attended to make the third, and all the business was done respecting M^r. Vidlers having the books to sell to his Country Bookseller, to whom 25 p^r Cent is allowed, by raising the price of the books 7^d a piece.[3]

Mr Jarvis and Dr Disney were at the Meeting, the latter was going the next day to M^r. Brand Hollis's being quite unable to do any duty.[4] Mr Joyce changes with Mr Barbauld tomorrow, so I may have the pleasure of hearing him once.[5] Mr Jarvis was setting out for the West of England, as his Meeting is shut up for a repair of the dry rot, wch that new built place is under.[6]

We hear that warlike preparations go on vigorously, & that we have an Expedition is [sc. in] Contemplation: some think to Holland, if so, our Ministers should be sure of the Dutch joining heartily with us, or we had better be quiet.[7]

M^r. Pitt comes forth with much contempt & raillery again[st] the Premier who is feeble in the Contest.[8]

We hope that your journey and exertions have done you good, this occupation in the good cause, & meeting others ingaged in the same is cheering. You will indulge us with some account of yourself and progress, & where you are likely to be found, if my feeble head & hands can give you another letter.

Pray make our kind respects to M^r and M^{rs}. Kenrick, and accept y^{r}self of the kindest regards & best wishes of y^r affec^t friends T: and HL

1   See Rutt, I, 516, for Priestley's response, dated 12 Sept. 1803, to this (non-surviving) letter from Lindsey, and his pleasure at the sight of Lindsey's own handwriting. According to the *Derby Mercury*, 8 Sept. 1803, Priestley's daughter Sarah Finch died on 1 Sept. 1803; her date of death is given as June 1803 in Toulmin, 'Descendants of Priestley', 13.

2   For the subscription to Priestley's work, see Letter 736, n. 5. Possibly the apothecary was John Parrott, listed as surgeon and apothecary, Lower Mitcham, Surrey, in *Holden's triennial directory, 1802, 1804, & 1804*, unpaginated list of trades people. Hannah Lindsey's hand is not quite clear at this point; 'shaver' is defined, with admirable succinctness, in Johnson's *Dictionary of the English language*, as 'a man that practises the art of shaving', an art which Lindsey perhaps found beyond him after his paralytic stroke.

3   At its monthly meeting on 14 July 1803, with Lindsey in the chair, the Unitarian Society resolved that William Vidler be appointed to sell the society's books, and that he be allowed a discount of 25 per cent, 'upon the presumption that he settle his account at Christmas & Midsummer in every year'; Unitarian Society minute book, p. 89. According to the minute book, this was the last meeting of the society which Lindsey attended. It is not clear to which of Vidler's country booksellers Hannah Lindsey referred.

4   Jervis and Disney were indeed present at the monthly meeting of the Unitarian Society; minute book, p. 88. Disney visited Thomas Brand Hollis, at the Hyde, Essex; he inherited Brand Hollis's estate on the latter's death in 1804.

5   'Tomorrow' was Sunday 17 July 1803. On that day, Rochement Barbauld, who had been the morning preacher at Newington Green since 1802, preached for Joyce at Essex Street chapel, while Joyce preached for Barbauld at Newington Green. Hannah Lindsey found Barbauld's sermon difficult to follow; see Letter 751.

6   Jervis was minister at Princes Street chapel, Westminster; his journey to the west of England probably took the form of a visit to his brother John Jervis, minister to a dissenting congregation at Lympstone, Devon. The new building for the Princes Street chapel was opened on 2 June 1799. The problems caused by dry rot, and the surveyor's reports on the state of the chapel, may be found in DWL (to be catalogued), vestry minute book of Princes Street chapel, fos. 47–51.

7   After the British declaration of war against France on 18 May 1803, Bonaparte prepared an invasion of England and sought the support in this enterprise of his rather reluctant ally the Batavian republic. There was no British expedition to Holland in 1803, although the British used their naval superiority to launch several successful attacks upon some of the Dutch colonies, including Surinam.

8   Hannah Lindsey clearly intended to write 'against the Premier', Henry Addington. Pitt resumed office as prime minister on 10 May 1804.

751. **To THOMAS BELSHAM   23 JULY 1803

Text: DWL, MS 12.67 (27).
Addressed: To/The Rev^d. Thos. Belsham/Rev^d. M^r. Kenrick's/Exeter
Endorsed: Mrs Lindsey July 23: 1803
Postmarked: JY 23 803

London July 23rd 1803

Dear Sir,

Your pleasant letter gave us great satisfaction as it ascertains your health & courage under your Sea expedition, and in particular that your services will certainly be of use to excite inquiry.[1]

Mr Dalton is an old acquaintance of ours, used to visit M^r. Lindsey frequently and was very liberal for an Oxonian and a Church man, & always subscribed for free publications on Theological subjects; & is a decided Unitarian, with all his own explanations in other points. We have understood that he became an alarmist on affairs taking such a turn in France: And he is, & ever was, incapable of adopting your sweeping creed; so that the fear he shewed of meeting you is not to be wondered at.[2]

We are sorry you are disappointed in not meeting M^r. Kenrick, but you will highly gratify your Sister by your visit: Mr Kenrick will be sorry not to have been at the closing scene of his Father.[3]

By a letter from Mrs Cappe we learn that Mrs Welbeloved is safe in bed of her third pair of twins, in succession, a boy & a girl each time:[4] It is hoped the Mother will continue to do well, & leave him at liberty & without anxiety to go on his important business to Manchester next week.[5]

We are sorry for your account of the want of sailors, it seems incredible so soon after the Peace, nobody can tell what is become of those numerous brave fellows, who were too hastily, & harshly (as Capt Gifford told us) dismissed from the service, merely to make a reduction of expence; & this disgusted many.[6] The Country seems rousing at last, and if our Ministers had the necessary talents, and vigor, & could put matters in any train for execution, as easily as they form crude plans, & pass bills, the Country w^d soon be competent to resist effectually any invasion: it must be done M^r. Joyce says by Parishes under the Lord Lieutenants, as ours is now ready & able to raise their quota for the army of reserve, and the en masse too, & can do it in a fortnight but cannot get leave, or an answer from the proud ignorant Secretary at War, & they are now applying to the Solicitor Gen^rl.[7]

We were pleased by a declaration of Genl Moores, a first rate Officer & who has the command in Kent: "I know said he the French Officers well, and what they will do, they will Land in the face of any army of ours that can be opposed to them, but never with the population of the Country at their back."[8]

The Bishop of London carried all the City of York to the Minster to hear him preach on Sunday sen'night, upon Slander, & it is said that the sermon was very appropriate and striking, & his manner impressive: What can have carried him into Y'shire.[9]

I am doing all my *possible* in writing you this second letter, but my husband says you are worthy of any effort, he continues as well as this excessive hot weather will permit: which also adds something to the debility ~~from~~ which disease occasions in me: If kind wishes would relieve me, yours would operate powerfully, but if by these painful processes, my way to *Life* is marked out by my wise and benevolent

Maker, I would not by resistance, and repining turn sorrows into crimes, but with patience & fortitude, & increasing trust, hold on to the end.

We have now fixed Tuesday the 2nd of August for our removal to Morden: Dr. B:[10] lays great stress upon fresh air, now the bile seems moving, at least air & quiet are good things, if we do not too much incomode our kind friends by adding two more Invalids to their crowded house.

Tho' you will arrive soon after we are gone, you will not be stationary at Hackney, and we hope will let us hear of your movements. We wish yr. discerning brother[11] would neither despond himself nor lower your spirits, dispair makes everything worse, the course of events are in the hands of Omnipotent Goodness, who can in a moment turn the heart of a Tyrant, or an Ideot, & the fate of Nations with them.

Mr Barbauld preached last Sunday here for Mr. Joyce, he was ingenious & pious, but could not be followed, or understood from his singularity of voice & accent. I found the Duke[12] was desirous to speak to Mrs Barbauld when going down stairs, so I introduced her: He said next day here when he came to take leave, that he was always gratified by seeing the person of any one of eminent talents.

Adieu, present our joint kind regards to your good Sister, and accept the best wishes & affect regards of yours truly

T: & HL

---

1   This letter from Belsham to Theophilus and Hannah Lindsey is not among Belsham's papers in DWL and seems not to have survived. Possibly his 'sea expedition' was a visit to the Isle of Wight, where he might have met (but evidently did not) Thomas Dalton (n. 2, below).

2   Thomas Dalton, of Queen's College, Oxford, where he graduated BA in 1757, was vicar of Carisbrooke, Isle of Wight, from 1782 until his death in 1822. He was a subscriber to the *Works* of John Jebb in 1787 and became a member of the Unitarian Society on its foundation in 1791. See Vol. I, Letter 291, n. 3.

3   Timothy Kenrick's father John, a landowner, died at the family estate of Wynn Hall, Denbighshire, on 15 July 1803. Belsham's sister Elizabeth (d. 1819) was Kenrick's wife.

4   Charles Wellbeloved and his wife Ann, née Kinder, had four sons and three daughters, including three sets of mixed twins; see David Wykes, 'Wellbeloved, Charles', *ODNB*, LVII, 998–9.

5   Wellbeloved's 'important business' at Manchester concerned his invitation to succeed George Walker as principal of Manchester College; he accepted the invitation, and the college moved to York, where it remained under his superintendence until its return to Manchester in 1840.

6   The number of seamen voted by parliament for the navy in 1803 was 130,000; in 1804, it was 100,000. See W. M. James, *The naval history of Great Britain, during the French revolutionary and Napoleonic wars* (new edn, 6 vols., with introduction by Andrew Lambert, London, 2002), III, 164, 215. Captain Gifford was probably James Gifford the younger (1768–1853), a serving naval officer who in 1803 was acting captain of the frigate *Braave*; he was promoted to the full rank of captain in 1812. The son of Lindsey's friend James Gifford the elder (see Letters 433, n. 12, and 493, n. 2), he followed his father's example and converted to unitarianism. See the entry for James Gifford the younger by J. K. Laughton, rev. Roger Morriss, in *ODNB*, XXII, 144.

7   For these parish- and county-based quotas for raising the militia in 1802 and 1803, see Western, *The English militia in the eighteenth century*, pp. 246–7, 449–50. For an estimate of the numbers involved in the *levee en masse*, see Letter 752, n. 3; those numbers included approximately 30,000 soldiers who were recruited for the army of reserve. 'Our' parish was St Clement Dane's, London. The secretary of state for war and the colonies from 1801 to 1804 was Robert Hobart (1760–1816), 4th Baron Hobart, and, from 1804, 4th earl of Buckinghamshire. The solicitor-general from 1802 to 1805 was Thomas Manners Sutton (1756–1842), MP for Newark and subsequently lord chancellor of Ireland.

8   General Sir John Moore (1761–1809) commanded a brigade based at Shorncliffe, near Folkestone, Kent, between July 1803 and Dec. 1804. He was subsequently in command of the defences of the southern district and based at Canterbury. Well known at the time for his infantry training, he is best remembered for his defence of, and death at, Corunna in a battle against the French in Jan. 1809.

9   23 July 1803 was a Saturday. 'Sunday sen'night' was 10 July 1803. The bishop of London was Beilby Porteus. His sermon on slander, preached at York Minster, was not published at this time.

10   William Blackburne, Hannah Lindsey's step-brother.

11   William Belsham.

12   The duke of Grafton.

752. **To ROBERT MILLAR   29 JULY 1803

Text: DWL, MS 12.46 (44).
Addressed: To/Mr. Robert Millar/Merchnat/Dundee./N.B.
Endorsed: Londo 29th July 1803/Mrs Lindsey
Postmarked: Postmark missing.

29th of July London

Dear Sir,

for the last three or four Months I have been so afflicted with obstructed bile ducts, and irritability of the stomach, my natural infirmity, that I have not been able to write a letter, to which I was not driven by necessity; I am now I hope getting a little better, and that you may not think yrself wholly forgotten, I write you a few lines before we go into the Country, to our old friends 10 miles off at Morden in Surry, for air & quiet which are thought to be of absolute necessity to prop me up again: Tho' a merciful providence has inabled me all along to assist my dear Husband in all that is necessary to his comfort: And you will be happy to hear that your venerable friend is compleatly recovered from all the bad effects of the Influenza, and has had no more nervous attacks, but is able to walk about a little, & sometimes a mile in the streets on a cool day, or in an Evening.

We were concerned to find by yours of the 19th of April[1] that you was not benefitted by a change of House: Where the tender impressions on the mind are strong such changes do little good: Journies and new scenes have a better effect, & we were glad to hear that you had been at Glasgow and Edenburgh [sic], & had heard at least of some small beginnings of Unitarianism:[2] This pure system will make its way slowly, and not till the great calamities, that are hastening on this ungodly & devoted Country, bring on general repentance, for such great & neglected means of knowing, and serving that great Being on whom all depends. It is happy for those who have graciously been led by milder measures & in times of quiet to see the truth, and to be brought even by affliction nearer to God, the only refuge & trust for his poor frail creatures: We may be soothed and comforted, & aided by kind friends, and are so to a degree, but it is only to our wise powerful & good Maker, that we can look for inward support under all circumstances.

This sudden, & apparently unnecessary, return of War is most dreadful, and in all its probable consequences the most aweful state ever experienced in this Country, and its issue quite out of human ken. Great preparations are making to repel the ferocious Invader, who has been permitted to overrun & subdue so great a part of Europe:[3] Yet we dare not put our trust in man, but look with trembling hope that Britain may again be saved, & become a regenerated people.

Dr Priestley's works are come safe, at least three out of the 4 Volumn's of Church History, and the fourth we think is coming having been shipped some time: He is now printing his Notes on the Scriptures three or four Vols. These works as I told you are subscribed for here to the amount of 1200£ wch will barely pay the expence.[4]

Mr Lindsey would be glad to send you a little piece of the D^{rs} just printed intitled "Socrates and Jesus compared" which is a very useful thing, & calculated to make Christians value their religion still more, by seeing in comprehensive view all that the very wisest, & best of the Heathens could attain to, & which the superior light of the gospel presents to everyone that can read the Scriptures.[5] Dr Priestley's health was considerably improvd by his journey with his Son & daughter to Philadelphia where he staid a Month: He returned home in vigor to print the "Notes" & has now even plans for other works, if his health & life is spared.[6] He is happily out of the reach of the toils & miseries of Europe, but will be an anxious inquirer after the fate of his friends in England, especially his aged best beloved friend, who on the 1st of July compleated fourscore Years.[7]

You cannot inclose to Mr Martin who is so long absent from London,[8] but you may occasionally send a letter for M^r. Lindsey under cover to Thomas Darch Esqr, Admiralty.[9] By his kind means I get this sent to you free. The time of our stay in the Country depends on health, and those various circumstances which may arise in these disastrous times: We mean not to fly, but be at our post, to wait & trust; the appointments of Almighty God must be the best, either for the present or the future, & our sand is run so low, that where it runs out is of little importance. May your health, spirits, & fortitude be equal to every call of duty, you can only now suffer for yourself, your better part was taken away from the evil to come.

Pray remember us kindly to Miss Scot, and accept yourself the affec^t regards & best wishes of y^r sincere f^{ds}

T: and HL

---

1 Millar's letter to Theophilus and Hannah Lindsey of 19 Apr. 1803 seems not to have survived.

2 There is a short account of Millar's travels in the *Christian Pioneer*, NS, VII (1841), 376–7. For the development of unitarianism in Scotland more generally, see L. Baker Short, *Pioneers of Scottish unitarianism* (Narberth, n.d.), chs. 7–9; Archibald MacWhirter, 'Unitarianism in Scotland', *Records of the Scottish Church History Society*, XIII (1959), 101–43; and Andrew Hill, 'The successors of the remnant: a bicentenary account of St Mark's unitarian church, Edinburgh, I: before 1776 until 1822', *TUHS*, XVI, 3 (Sept. 1977), 102–23.

3 Britain declared war on France on 18 May 1803, after several months of provocation on both sides. The fear of a French invasion led to an unprecedented level of recruitment to the armed forces. It has been estimated that by the end of 1803, some 800,000 men (approximately one fifth of the able-bodied male population of military age) was engaged in some form of military or naval service; J. E. Cookson, *The British armed nation 1793–1815* (Oxford, 1997), p. 95.

4 See Letter 736, n. 5.

5 For Priestley's *Socrates and Jesus compared*, see Letter 747, n. 5.

6 This is a reference to Priestley's letter to Belsham, dated Northumberland, 2 Apr. 1803; see Rutt, I, 507. It contained the information which Hannah Lindsey conveyed to Millar, and which she had no doubt acquired from Belsham.

7 1 July 1803 was indeed Lindsey's eightieth birthday.

8 James Martin MP spent an increasing proportion of his time at his estate at Overbury, Worcestershire; aged sixty-five in the summer of 1803, he found parliamentary attendance increasingly burdensome and did not seek re-election for his constituency of Tewkesbury at the general election of 1807. Hence he could no longer provide franking privileges, or act as a forwarding base for letters to Lindsey and his wife.

9 Thomas Darch was first clerk in the naval works department of the admiralty from 1796 to 1800; extra clerk from 1800 to 1804; junior clerk from 1804 to 1816; and first class clerk from 1816 until his retirement in 1832. See *Office-holders in modern Britain. IV. Admiralty officials 1660–1870*, comp. J. C. Sainty (London, 1975), p. 120. In 1805, Hannah Lindsey sought his advice about ways of helping Millar in his business concerns; see Letter 773.

753. **To CHRISTOPHER WYVILL   8 AUGUST 1803**

Text: NYRO, ZFW 7/2/160/5, Wyvill of Constable Burton MSS.
Printed: Ditchfield, 'Lindsey–Wyvill correspondence', 170
                  (first paragraph); 171 (first section of third paragraph);
                  p. 172 (fourth paragraph).
Addressed: To/The Rev^d. M^r. Wyvill/Hartlepool,/County of Durham
Postmarked: AU 8 803

Morden Surry
August 8th 1803

Dear Sir,

M^r. Lindsey was delighted with your very excellent Letter, and the various laudable great & truly Constitutional efforts which you have made almost alone in these degenerate times;[1] which however are so alarming as to make one hope that every latent spark of patriotism will be kindled into a flame, which under the course of events now in embryo may produce reform of every kind: We trust that a merciful Providence will preserve us from the fangs of French Despotism, & leave us to struggle for the attainment of the many valuable blessings which sloth, increasing luxury, & the insidious principles which the last forty years have introduced, & the oppressions of the last ten confirmed: Go on and prosper in your great line of duty, no human effort was ever lost.

We are made very happy by the good account of the confirmed health of yourself and dear promising family, and have no doubt but the dips in old Ocean will quite purify every particles, if any can remain of former disease, and make you all strong for the future.

On Tuesday last the 2nd. we removed to this friendly Mansion, & delectable spot, which for upwards of twenty years has so often recovered us from sickness and made life more desirable: It was never more necessary to me than at present, after a bilious obstruction of near four Months, wch has wasted both flesh & strength, joined to a natural irritability of stomach & diseased sensations, the worst of all; I am already somewhat better, and M^r. Lindsey also, as much as his feeble aged frame is capable of: The quiet & fresh air are great soothers after the very extreme heat & military bustle of London, and the constant attention to the falsehood, fears & direful forebodings which distress many. The Duke of Grafton left town very low, both on account of the public danger, and the sufferings of his daughter, now of three years standing & her total loss of voice,[2] besides the recent loss of another who was particularly useful to him, as a sort of Librarian, & entering more into his literary attentions:[3] He called to take leave, & had previous on the 1st of July when Mr Lindsey compleated his eigthieth [sic] year, sent him a present of three bottles of super excellent wine to treat a very few friends who met on this occasion: He is a most amiable friendly character, and what is the best part, truly turned to piety & benevolence.

By a letter last week from Dr Priestley we are sorry to find that by a fall in reaching a book from the top of his Library he has injured his right hip & leg, & has been upon crutches, tho' now with pain uses a stick; but this does & must suspend his experiments: But his health is sufficiently improved & his mind so active, that he is going on with printing his Notes on the Scriptures, and making a biblical Concordance much wanted, on subjects, not words meerly.[4]

A relation of our friends dined here yesterday, Mr Sargent, first Clerk of the

Treasury,[5] from him however we learnt nothing, but that he with the Premier & a large party, all in health & high spirits had the day before visited the West India Docks, & were amazed at the greatness & utility of the works. From a friend at Woodbridge in Suffolk we had the following interesting anecdote: "The Camp at Bromeswell commanded by S[r] Eyre Coote is so near, that we can distinctly hear the music in our house.[6]

S[r] Sidney Smith often comes ashore from his Ship in Hollesby Bay[7] about nine miles off, and visits the Camp: Within a few days S[r] Sidney & his men are to personate Bonaparte & his legions; & attempt a landing, & the whole force from Camp, & I believe from Woodbridge are to go & oppose him". This may not be an unuseful thing, as S[r] S: is versed in these matters, & may shew our inexperienced men how to attack boats. S[r] Sidney vows to run his ship on shore wherever the French Consul lands, & with his own crew fight him.

Gen[l] Moore a very good officer who commands in Kent, says that he knows what French officers will do as well as what himself would do, that they will all Land in the face of any army that can be brought against against [sic] them, but *never* with the population of the Country at their back.[8]

Berthier,[9] who is to command the Invasion told a gentleman, who personated a Gentman[?][10] that he had no doubt of Landing, & making his way to the Capital, where he & his army would probably be cut to pieces["].

Such are the things we hear, w[ch] I relate as they may gratify you, & are not the tittle tattle of the day.

M[r] Lindsey desires me to express his most grateful & affec[t] feelings for all Y[r] distinguished kindness: Accept the best regards & wishes for all good & happiness to you & y[rs] from yours T: HL.

---

1   This letter from Wyvill to Lindsey seems not to have survived. For Wyvill's perseverance in York-shire on behalf of the cause of parliamentary reform in 1803, see Dinwiddy, *Christopher Wyvill and reform*, pp. 12–14.

2   Hannah Lindsey referred here to one of the five daughters of Grafton and his second wife, Elizabeth, née Wrottesley, namely Charlotte, Elizabeth (d. 1839), Augusta (d. 1839), Frances (d. 1866); only Charlotte and Isabella were unmarried in 1803.

3   See n. 2, above. Georgiana, the only daughter of Grafton and his first wife Anne, née Liddell, whose death on 17 Jan. 1799 was reported in *Gent. Mag.*, LIX, i (1799), 167. She was married to John Smyth of Heath, Yorkshire.

4   For Priestley's *Notes on the scriptures*, see Letter 736, n. 4. His *Index to the Bible* was published in London by Joseph Johnson in 1805.

5   John Sargent (1750–1831), MP for Queenborough, from 1802 to 1806, was joint secretary to the treasury from 1802 to 1804. He was the son of Lindsey's friend of the same name, of Halstead Place, Kent.

6   Sir Eyre Coote (1759–1823), a major-general in 1803, was a highly experienced soldier who had served in North America, the Caribbean, Egypt and the Netherlands. In 1803, he was based at Bromeswell, near Woodbridge, Suffolk. He subsequently served in Ireland, Jamaica and in the Walcheren campaign of 1809. He was MP for Queen's County, Ireland, from 1802 to 1806 and for Barnstaple from 1812 to 1816. His uncle of the same name had been a highly successful British general in India. Probably this correspondent from Woodbridge was William Alexander; Woodbridge is between two and three miles from Bromeswell.

7   Hannah Lindsey referred here to Hollesley Bay, Suffolk. The British naval officer Sir William Sidney Smith (1764–1840) was the victor over Napoleon at Acre in 1799. In the summer of 1803, he was in command of a squadron charged with the blockade of the Flemish coast. He was promoted to rear-admiral in 1805 and was MP for Rochester between 1804 and 1806.

8   For Sir John Moore, see Letter 751, n. 8.

9   Alexandre Berthier (1753–1815), marshal of France, Napoleon's chief of staff and war minister.

10 Hannah Lindsey's handwriting is not quite clear at this point: possibly she wrote 'German'.

754. **To THOMAS BELSHAM   **2 SEPTEMBER 1803**

Text: DWL, MS 24.107 (15).
Addressed: To/The Rev^d. Thos. Belsham/Grove Place/Hackney
Endorsed: [By Belsham] Mrs Lindsey Sept: 2: 1803
Postmarked: Postmark missing.

Morden September 2nd 1803

Dear Sir,

Not knowing when a letter would certainly meet you on y^r. rambles into Essex, I delayed writing till near the end of the week when we conclude that you will be at your Post.

I return Dr Priestley's letter, and also inclose one to M^r. Lindsey rec^d since: Our friend has taken fright at hearing that Mr Lindsey had changed the future destination of his books: Cowper has (as he always will) be busy in what he has nothing to do with, & the Doctor is too communicative to such a loquacious man.[1] You will however as I guess join in the wish to have them sent to America, & M^r. L: says he will consider farther about it: But in these tumultuous times, & the great expence & trouble wch will attach to their conveyance, with the probable insecurity of their safe arrival, he does not feel the confidence necessary to determine him what it is best to do. However there is time enough I hope for this business to be setled [*sic*] for the best.

Detesting this War & all its consequences we endeavor to think about it as little as possible; tho' we have now no fear of an Invasion being successful, but expect that Bonaparte may find business at home: But such are the weakness's & blunders of our present Government, that they may contrive to weaken our means of defence, and offend so great a proportion of the Volunteers, & all the English Catholics, that help may not be ready & sufficient in the day of danger.[2] As Christians we have only to follow our Lords advice, and in patience possess our souls, & leave events to the Great Ruler of the World, & all its affairs down to a Atom to his Sovereign disposal. We have rather better accounts from Paxton, Mr Frend has been of use to the unhappy Invalid, by ingaging her attention, & getting her to walk & ride out with him: His leg is much mended, so as to promise soon to do its usual business, as M^r. Reynolds tells us, who is also recovered from a fit of the Gout, & writes chearfully, & under the best frame of mind.[3] Mr Frend is now on a visit to the Duke of Grafton at the Lodge, near the Forest, & the Duke told us, he had invited him for not less than a fortnight.[4]

Notwithstanding the fatigue, your excellent Brother is better imployed at Bedford than anywhere else, his various talents there have scope for the good of mankind, tho' as a States man he could at present be more extensively useful:[5] But whilst such a character as Mr Fox, is laid by useless, any one else need feel no offence in being overlooked:[6] Indeed their principles are quite out of fashion with this degenerate age: altho' some are roused a little to think & act nobly, especially in the North, where Messrs Wyville, Fawkes,[7] & Lord Mulgrave[8] &^c have distinguished themselves: Mr Welby told Mrs Cappe that their eloquence & energy at the County Meeting could not be excelled and the effect was prodigious. The speeches were taken down, printed & thousands dispersed all over the Country, & the sale of the York Herald, the only free paper, was increased to 4000 a week.[9]

All this gives pleasure & hope to your venerable friend in his peaceful retirement.

He has stood the change of the season vastly well, & is the stoutest of the Invalid Groupe, who advance but slowly to health or strength: The Mistress of the Mansion[10] is still confined to her room with the Rheumatism but we hope daily getting a little better. I am almost arrived at my ne plus ultra, having also experienced a check, by an attack of Cholera Morbus, the disease of the season, but Dr Blackburn's gentle treatment, has carried it off, without any great diminution of strength, & I have got again to eat animal food: Morbid sensations are my natural inheritance, & they must go thro' this system with me, but not I trust into the next, if properly improved.

Pray did you see, or hear anything of worthy Eaton at Mr Rutts, or how he goes on, both as to worldly, & spiritual matters.[11]

Thomas Evans has written to beg assistance on leaving his Prison, wch M^r. L. has sent, his last exhibition in the Pillory was not attended with the least insult: His health is so much injured that he intends going to the Sea coast to recruit: I should have hoped that air & exercise would soon have restored him, without that expence: He says nothing of his future plans for providing for himself & family, who have been supported during his confinement by what will now cease, the bounty of others: David Jones said, he had better try for a School, as his habits of idleness & literary turn, w^d not suffer his return to Weaving.[12]

Adieu, pray remember us kindly to Y^r sister. Our Ladies desire their Comp^t to you: I have put forth all my strength to write thus much, & can only add the best regards & wishes for y^r noble self of

Dr Sir Your obliged & affec^t f^{ds}

T: and HL

1   Writing to Belsham on 10 Mar. 1803, Priestley complained of Joseph Johnson's lack of punctuality and dispatch in sending him books and other published items from England. He expressed further anxiety over the non-receipt of books and periodicals in his letter to Belsham of 4 June 1803, adding 'I am happy in receiving the Monthly publications from Liverpool. Could not every thing else also be sent in the same manner?' Both letters may be found in DWL, MS 12.13. On 3 July 1803, he expressed relief to Belsham at the arrival of a box of books, with an account, from Johnson and expressed the intention of retaining Johnson as his bookseller; DWL, MS 12.13. 'Cowper' is almost certainly a reference to Thomas Cooper.

2   For the volunteer movement, see Letter 748, n. 4. Hannah Lindsey meant that the denial of emancipation in 1801 meant that the national defence would not be able to draw upon the services of patriotic English catholics.

3   In his letter to Frend of 15 June 1803 (see Letter 748, n. 3), Richard Reynolds wrote in fairly optimistic terms about his health. He added that 'the establishing a News Room at St Neots has been very agreeable to me and I ride over to it three or four times in a Week'; CUL, Add. MS 7886 (Frend papers), no. 229. The 'unhappy invalid' was his wife Mary Catherine Reynolds.

4   Lindsey probably referred here to Wakefield Lodge, near Whittlewood Forest, Whittlebury, Northamptonshire.

5   William Belsham at Bedford was 'imployed' as a historian of recent British history, which he presented from a dissenting viewpoint. Hannah Lindsey evidently believed that he could have embarked on a successful political career.

6   Hannah Lindsey meant that Fox was out of office and therefore unable to serve the nation.

7   Walter Ramsden Hawkesworth Fawkes (1769–1825), of Farnley Hall, Yorkshire, and MP for Yorkshire from 1806 to 1807, was an opposition whig, a supporter of Wyvill and an associate of Sir Francis Burdett.

8   Henry Phipps, Baron Mulgrave (1755–1831), of Mulgrave castle, Yorkshire, was MP for Totnes from 1784 to 1790 and for Scarborough from 1790 to 1794, when he was created Baron Mulgrave. From 1812, he was earl of Mulgrave. A member of Pitt's second ministry, he was foreign secretary from Jan. 1805 to Feb. 1806.

9   The proceedings of this county meeting, including the speeches of Fawkes and Mulgrave, were reported in *Proceedings of the county meeting at Yorkshire, held on the 28th of July, 1803, at the*

Castle of York ... For the purpose of addressing His Majesty on the present state of the country (York, 1803). This small and cheap pamphlet was published by Alexander Bartholoman (d. 1811), the proprietor and printer of the *York Herald* and a common councillor of the city. The *York Herald* began publication on 1 Jan. 1790; one of its subsequent editors was the Shakespearean forger William Henry Ireland (d. 1835).

10 Sophia, the elder sister of Frances Chambers.

11 In 1802, David Eaton of York moved to London, where he was immediately befriended by John Towill Rutt. Through Rutt's help, he served briefly as assistant minister to a dissenting congregation at Billericay, Essex, and then succeeded to the bookselling business of William Vidler at 187 Holborn. See *MR*, NS, III (1829), 357.

12 For the imprisonment of Thomas Evans, see Letter 741, n. 5. After his release, rather than become a schoolteacher, he continued to preach at Brechfa, Carmarthenshire, and became minister to a unitarian congregation at Aberdare in 1811. He had been brought up to the weaving trade in Carmarthenshire and it has been suggested that he first encountered unitarianism while selling his produce in Glamorgan; see David Russell Barnes, *People of Seion. Patterns of nonconformity in Cardiganshire and Carmarthenshire in the century preceding the religious census of 1851* (Llandysul, 1995), p. 105. David Jones, the 'Welsh freeholder', was acquainted with Evans through their common origin in Carmarthenshire.

755. **To ROBERT MILLAR   26 DECEMBER 1803

Text: DWL, MS 12.46 (45).
Addressed: To/Mr Robert Millar,/Merchant/Dundee/N:B
Endorsed: Lond° 26th Decr 1803/Mrs Lindsey
Postmarked: Postmark missing.

Dec^br. 26th 1803

Dear Sir,

I have been intending to write to you for a Month past, but waited from day to day & week to week for some authentic information respecting Mr Fysh Palmer which was promised to us, but not obtained till yesterday: a more inlarged account will be given in the Monthly Magazine for this Month if it can be got ready, & if not it will be in the next.[1]

The following we believe you may depend upon, M^r. T:F. Palmer was wrecked in coming home in his own Ship Plumer off the Island Guam, he and all the Passengers escaped to the Island: Soon after he was taken with a Dysentery which ended in a mortification.[2] He left his papers to James Ellis, who with Boston is now carrying on a large Distillery at Manilla.[3]

This Boston & his wife were sent out by Government to make Salt to cure Fish, in the same Ship with Mr Palmer, and being too honest to swear against M^r P on their arrival, & examination on the many accusations against poor Palmer during the voyage before the Govenor [*sic*], he was never suffered to work for Government, but thrown upon his own hands pennyless in that strange Country, was taken and supported by Mr P. and was very useful to him in his various plans & building a small Vessel wch went coast wise & brought food &c wch was very beneficial, & himself wife & children were all returning to England with our worthy friend who was taken away, by a disorder to wch he had often been liable.[4] The Ship was certainly not fit for the Voyage as he was told by Capt Wilson who met them in great distress above a Year & half ago & helped them all he could.[5]

A Brother of Mr Palmers was at our Chapel today, came to town on purpose to learn what he could about him, says he last Year sent him 600£ the accumulation on his share of some joint property, but never heard whether it reached him.[6]

We thank you much for the Inscription on your beloved, & excellent wife's tomb stone, you might without ostentation have said a great deal more, but her Virtues live in your tender remembrance to the best purpose, of copying the fair example, and preparing to join her in the regions of uninterrupted bliss.[7] As it would be a great pleasure to us to comfort you in any degree pray do not refrain from writing what you feel as occasion offers, you have no friends who more sympathize in your loss and afflictions: Only our wise and benevolent Maker knows what trials are best for us to fit us for himself, and he can supply to us every blessing he withdraws, and inable us to say "His will be done" and you are struggling for that point of acquiescence and will arrive at it, as by the very frame of our minds, sorrow dies away, not intirely but so as to pass out of the region of pain.

M[r] Lindsey passed a tolerable Summer in the Country, & could walk in and out on a lawn quite alone, & bore riding ten or twelve miles in a Carriage twice a week, till the first attack of sudden cold weather after so much heat, pinched & infeebled him, and the very irregular weather, & the rain & damp of the last Month, has rather added to it: A blister to his head was very beneficial to him about six weeks ago, as his head had been shook a little before, by an accidental fall from his chair w[ch] struck his eye against a table but happily did not hurt the sight, tho' it swelled and inflamed the [word illegible] externally very much. His general health is comfortable & he can read & walk yet from room to room, a great blessing to us both: His temper blessed calm and submissive temper under all circumstances never forsakes him, nor his feelings for others, with a placid chearfulness & injoyment of his friends who call upon him. Yet I see him gradually going and can only say in the fine language of D[r] Watts

"He stands yet, but with his starry pinions on,
drest for the flight & ready to be gone[8]

Indeed with his sickly frame it is only to be wondered at that he has lasted to fourscore & near six months. I was very poorly for some months with a bad stomach complaint the disease of my life, but have lately been much better, at least not so nervous, the worst part of the Story.

D[r] Priestleys Church History is come & delivered to the Subscribers: It has gratified M[r] Lindsey much to have seen it, as also a Volume of his Notes on the Scriptures, w[ch] came this week to M[r] Lindsey alone:[9] The D[r] has had a bad fit of Gallstones but is getting better, but his health is very uncertain.[10] Adieu be of good courage the state of the Country is aweful, but the Lord God Omnipotent ruleth over all, there let us look & trust: and without fearing what is to come, injoy the present hour with chearful & grateful hearts for the innumerable blessings we have all rec[d]. Pray, remember us kindly to Miss Scot, & accept the kindest wishes & regards of Y[r] affec[t] f[ds]

T: and HL

1   The *MM*, XVI (ii) (Nov. 1803), 357, reported that Palmer, although 'much broken in health and constitution' had reached Manila safely on his homeward journey. The Dec. 1803 number of the same magazine carried (p. 481) a brief report of Palmer's death. The 'more inlarged account' of Palmer's life was published in the *MM* of Feb. 1804 (XVII (i), 83–5) and took the form of a laudatory obituary, comparing Palmer to the whig heroes William Russell and Algernon Sidney, both of whom were executed in 1683 in the aftermath of the Rye House plot.

2   Palmer died at Guam on 2 June 1802, following an attack of dysentery; for his bequests to Ellis, see his will, proved on 2 Jan. 1804; TNA: PRO PROB 11/1403, fos. 424v–425v.

3   The *MM* obituary of Palmer (see n. 1, above) reported (p. 85) that James Ellis and John Boston were 'carrying on a large distillery, under the protection of the Spanish governor' of Guam.

4   For John Boston, see Letters 566, n. 4, and 729, n. 3. At Botany Bay he had helped Palmer in various

commercial enterprises, including the sale of rum. He had not been allowed to work directly for the government because of his reputation for outspoken republican opinions.

5 For a possible identification of Captain Wilson, see Letter 744, n. 7. For Palmer's voyage, see Letter 735, n. 4.

6 Thomas Fyshe Palmer's brother, Jeremy Fyshe Palmer, who died in 1798 (see Letter 678, n. 7), named in his will three brothers in addition to Thomas as his joint legatees; they were Charles, Edward and John Palmer. Probably the visitor to the chapel to whom Hannah Lindsey referred was one of them. Another possibility is James Fyshe Palmer, an older brother of Thomas, who was rector of Borough Green, Cambridgeshire, from 1760 to 1806.

7 This refers to the death of Millar's wife Jean, née Scott, in 1801. I have not located the inscription.

8 This is a slightly adapted quotation from the closing lines of Isaac Watts, *An elegiac essay upon the death of the Reverend Mr. Thomas Gouge* (London, 1700). The lines themselves were written as a tribute to John Howe (1630–1705), ejected minister, and subsequently pastor to a presbyterian congregation in London. Thomas Gouge (*c.* 1665–1700) was minister to a meeting of dissenters in Thames Street, London, and should not be confused with the better-known Thomas Gouge (1605–81), an ejected minister who features in the *ODNB*. See Thomas Gibbons, *Memoirs of the Rev. Isaac Watts, D.D.* (London, 1780), pp. 154–5.

9 For Priestley's *Notes on all the books of scripture*, see Letter 736, n. 4.

10 In his letter to Lindsey of 4 Nov. 1803, Priestley wrote that he had made a partial recovery from an attack of gallstones the previous year; DWL, MS 12.13 (passage omitted by Rutt, I, 519).

756. **To ROBERT MILLAR   5 MARCH 1804

Text: DWL, MS 12.46 (46).
Addressed: To/M^r. Robert Millar,/Merchant,/Dundee, N:B
Endorsed: Lond^o 5th Mar 1804/Mrs Lindsey/Dr Priestley/Mr Vidler &c
Postmarked: Postmark missing.

March 5th 1804 London

Dear Sir,

Nothing but a load of occupations added to a continual attention to my dear feeble Invalid, would have prevented my thanking you before, for your good letter, and acceptable communications to M^r. Joyce, who altho' he wanted facts principally yet he has made out an interesting account from yours, and it is published in the Universal Theological Magazine, & Impartial Review, a new shilling Monthly publication,[1] by a most zealous and popular Unitarian Minister in London, who having been long a Baptist teacher and very diligent inquirer after truth, now he has found it, is by his labors here & also in the neighboring Counties leading many to imbrace it, not merely individuals but Societies in different parts; he has a grave persuasive manner, with great good sense, and a ready elocution as an extempore preacher: His audience are all of the midling class, who will go on a rainy as well as a fine day to attend divine worship: He first gained attention by the doctrine of the final salvation of all men, & was himself a convert of M^r. Winchester, an American, who has written much on this point.[2] His name is Vidler, he has a small shop as a bookseller in the Strand, and our Unitarian Society have ingaged him to inlarge the circulation of our books, by sending them to his country customers: This, and many other beneficial things is owing to the zeal and activity of our present Secretary M^r. Joyce, a very excellent young man, not enough estimated: He has been the afternoon preacher above a year & half at our Chapel, since D^r. Disney's health has been but indifferent. He has sent your books here ready to be called for, and I will inclose Mr Vidler's Magazine wch has the article about M^r. Palmer.[3]

I think I told you of the imminent danger Dr Priestley had been in, from a difficulty of swallowing food to support life, & of the little he could get down, returning again, owing as was supposed to a schirrous[4] in the Oesophagus; Providentially an eminent Physician, a Quaker crossing the Country on his travels, at this critical juncture called upon the Doctor, & staid three days, and happily discovered, that the obstruction was only spasmodic, owing to flatulence from vegetable food, and the last letter a Month ago says that by living on animal juice, in broth & jelly he was recovering, had no difficulty in swallowing liquids, or even Oysters, but his legs & feet were swelled from debility.[5] We are solicitous to hear again: His mind however partook not of the weakness of his body, he was going on with printing his second great work, "Notes on all the Scriptures" for the use of Churches & families; and another new work, a continuance of a comparison of all the Heathen Moralists with Jesus, in the manner of Socrates & Jesus, w[ch] comes from M[r] Lindsey in your parcel.[6]

Having under age & sickness had 200 p[r]. ann of his income withdrawn, a loss he can ill sustain, his friends here are raising it by a 5[-7] subscription from forty friends to continue for his life, & this is nearly accomplished: By M[r] Lindsey's individual influence, we have raised half ourselves:[8] So that he does not live in vain, tho' he regrets sometimes his uselessness. As if such an example of patience & chearfull fortitude under debility was nothing of itself.

I wish we could incourage you to think more justly of the efforts you make to teach the little flock, and by an example of unswerving principle in the cause of Gods true worship was not of singular use, even tho' almost alone in it: And especially under that heavy affliction which has added to your natural diffident temper: Also oppressed with many worldly cares, which these uncertain times & prospects increase. Be comforted, the conflict is well known to the Sovereign Appointer, who will never leave his faithful servants without support, and power to accomplish all his purposes of good for them, & final happiness as the end of it.

The Country seems in a most hazardous state by the incapacity of the Chief Majestrate [sic] under a considerable return of his old dreadful malady: Parliament seem dispose[d] to enter into an examination as to his real state, w[ch] has not very satisfactorily been stated yet to the public:[9] Some think the French will take advantage of the difficulties this has thrown us into, but we are inclined to think the contrary: Bonaparte certainly wished to keep the Peace, and expects that even under a Regency that object is more likely to be attained: And as his plan of Invasion is not very likely to add to his Military Glory, he may wish to watch the course of events & wait.[10]

He has done by his threats, what never can be undone, changed the manners and views of this Country from Commerce merely, to a Military cast: The result of it all must be left to Providence, who may bring strange things to pass, out of this Chaos, quite out of mortal ken, but for general good, and individual moral discipline, if not national. In the hand of omnipotent Goodness all is safe, and without regretting what is past, or fearing what is to come, we injoy the present hour with thankful & chearful hearts.

I have written my old blind eyes quite down: we are both as well as age & infirmities permit. M[r] Lindsey's health is good, his limbs feeble, but eyes and faculties remain to him.

Adieu send soon for y[r] parcel, remember us kindly to Miss Scot, keep up your spirits, and believe us ever your sincere and affec[t] f[ds]
                    T: and HL

1   This almost certainly refers to the obituary of Thomas Fyshe Palmer, which was published in the *Universal Theological Magazine and Impartial Review*, I, 2 (Feb. 1804), 108–10. The author of the article was not named, but there is no reason to doubt Hannah Lindsey's attribution of it to Jeremiah Joyce. Millar had evidently supplied Joyce with information concerning Palmer's work for unitarianism in Scotland.

2   For Elhanan Winchester, see Letter 630, n. 6. After his return to America in 1794, he was briefly the minister of the universalist church, Philadelphia, where he allowed Priestley to preach in 1796; see Letter 641, n. 7, and Rutt, I, 266, 333, 344. William Vidler had been converted to unitarian universalism by reading Winchester's *The universal restoration: exhibited in a series of dialogues between a minister and his friend* (London, 1788), and the two were collaborators at the universalist chapel at Parliament Court, London, between 1792 and 1794. Winchester died at Hartford, Connecticut, on 18 Apr. 1797.

3   See n. 1, above. William Vidler's premises for his bookselling business at this time were at 349 The Strand; *Holden's triennial directory 1802, 1803, & 1804* (London, 1804), unpaginated section; *Kent's directory for 1804* (London, 1804), p. 203.

4   I.e. a scirrhus (or scirrhous), a hard swelling or tumour.

5   There is an account of Priestley's final illness, written by his eldest son Joseph Priestley, in Rutt, I, 526–31. I have not been able to identify the quaker physician.

6   For Priestley's *Notes on all the books of scripture*, see Letter 736, n. 4. For his *Socrates and Jesus compared*, see Letter 747, n. 5.

7   Hannah Lindsey wrote a squiggle alongside the figure '5'; possibly she intended to write '£'. For other examples, see Letters 745, 758 and 768.

8   This subscription for Priestley, to be distinguished from the subscription towards the publication of his last two major publications, was necessitated partly by his inability to realize the investments in the French funds which had been made for him by his brother-in-law John Wilkinson, by the bankruptcy of his son-in-law in England, William Finch. On 4 June 1803, Priestley wrote to Lindsey 'My philosophical benefactors are all dropped off'; Rutt, I, 513. See Gibbs, *Joseph Priestley*, p. 232.

9   George III experienced a further visitation of his illness (probably porphyria, but widely interpreted as insanity) in Feb. and Mar. 1804, following the more serious outbreaks in 1788–9 and in 1801.

10 Hannah Lindsey implied that Napoleon believed that the prospect of peace with Britain would be increased under the regency which would have been necessitated had George III failed to recover his mental faculties.

757. *To ROBERT MILLAR   7 MARCH 1804

Text: DWL, MS 12.46 (47).
Addressed: Mʳ Millar/Dundee
Endorsed: Londᵒ 7ᵗʰ Mar 1804/Mr Lindsey
Postmarked: Postmark missing.

March 7ᵗʰ 1804

Dear Sir

Mʳ Lindsey has added these few little pieces[1] to amuse you at some solutory [*sic*][2] hour & take you out of yʳself; It is the prime remedy for all earthly grievances.
                    Yʳˢ sincerely
                        HL
        Essex House.

1   Probably small items, mainly sermons, published by the Unitarian Society in 1803 and 1804.
2   Hannah Lindsey probably intended to write 'solitary'.

758. **To TIMOTHY KENRICK   31 MARCH 1804

Text: The Sharpe papers, UCL Library Services, Special Collections
                (Kenrick papers), 178/73.
Printed: 'The Kenrick letters', *TUHS*, V, 2 (Oct. 1932), 192–4 (minor
                errors).
Addressed: Rev^d M^r. Kenrick/Exeter.
Endorsed: M^rs. Lindsey 1804
Postmarked: Postmark missing.

March 31st 1804
London

Dear Sir

I am afraid that you will have thought me tardy in not answering your letter soon, and the more as your kind and affec^t notice of Mr Lindsey was so gratefully felt by him.[1]

The truth is that being too old to do much ourselves in any very active way, we depended upon Mr Joyce for getting "Newcomes Ezekiel" now very scarce, & illness having confined him at home some weeks it is not many days since the Commission was executed and the books sent off.[2]

Inclosed is a List of them to the amount of 5.[3]

Mr Lindsey is glad to hear of a new Pupil of such a promising character as M^r. Madge, and desires that if necessary to his progress that he may afford him a little help at any future period, if life be spared.[4]

It is to be regretted that M^r. Belshams excellent Sermon may have diverted that attention to y^r Institution wch it was intended to promote: But my excuse for him was, that on such a subject as this so few opportunities can occur of producing such subjects before the public, that a zealous friend to academical learning may easily be forgiven.[5]

Dr Priestleys last letter dated Jany 16th was remarkably consolatory after the very alarming ones we had rec^d. which almost excluded the hope of his recovery: He only now mentions extreme weakness & increased deafness, the first of wch. time with renovating quality of Spring air, will we trust remove. His Alphabetical Index to all the books of the Scriptures he has sent to the Booksellers at Philadelphia, hopeing [*sic*] some of them will print it, as he desires nothing for his labor: And his Comparison of all the Grecian Philosophers with Jesus, in the manner of Socrates &c which compleats the scheme, is also ready for the press.[6]

His next new work is a Bible collating all the new Versions of seperate [*sic*] books by various hands and smoothing & collating where he can the whole of both Testaments so as to make a Version considerably better on the whole than any preceding one, wch will be highly useful, altho' from his rapid manner of executing it will not be so perfect as could be wished, but wonderful to be designed & done at all at 71 and under considerable bodily infirmities.

The great success we have had in raising the D^r. a life Annuity will chear & animate him, and inable him to print gradually the works he has now ready,[7] when the Notes on the Scriptures by the first Subscription are finished, which they hope will be soon after Midsummer.[8]

I have set my Heart upon having an ingraving to prefix to this last great work from a Painting sent to Mr Lindsey of the Doctor in his own grey hair, so different from any former exhibition of him: The Artist is at work upon it, to be ready when the books come: I wish it may be executed well & convey what the picture does, the calm philosophic mind of that dear extraordinary [*sic*] man & practical Christian: We have got 12 Guineas towards 20 for the expence.[9]

M[r] Lindsey (thank God) continues much as when you saw him, except a recent cold & cough, w[ch] affects most persons this variable weather.

We hope y[r]self & M[rs]. Kenrick, continue well. Of public affairs there is nothing incouraging to relate: We are comforted by the persuasion that the Government of the world is in the best Hands that is the unfailing sheet anchor.

With our joint respects & best wishes to you both, we are D[r] Sir your obliged f[ds]

T: and HL.

P.S

M[r] Edwards late of Birmingham is quite recovered, & his mind turned to promote truth, by a Sunday night Lecture at Monkwell Street Meeting: And a Morning Service with a Liturgy at Edmonton, in his brothers house to accomodate some Church people who can learn nothing from the regular Minister: They have a small organ, which his Sister is to shew her fine hand upon, if they can get it Licenced.[10]

We hope M[r] Vidlers Thursday Lecture at Leather Lane will also excite attention.[11]

---

1 Evidently Timothy Kenrick had referred in kindly terms to Lindsey in a (non-surviving) letter to Hannah Lindsey.

2 William Newcome's *An attempt towards an improved version, a metrical arrangement and an explanation of the prophet Ezekiel* was published in Dublin in 1788. For Newcome, see Vol. I, Letter 226, n. 7, and Letter 655, n. 11. During his controversy with Priestley a mutual respect was sustained.

3 Hannah Lindsey placed an indecipherable squiggle after the figure 5; probably she meant £5. In 'The Kenrick letters', *TUHS*, V, 2 (Oct. 1832), 192, it is rendered as [li].

4 Thomas Madge (1786–1870) became a pupil at Kenrick's Academy at Exeter in 1804. He subsequently studied at Manchester College and served as minister at Bury St Edmunds and at the Octagon chapel, Norwich. He was assistant to Belsham at Essex Street chapel from 1825 to 1829, succeeded Belsham as minister in 1829 and continued in that capacity until 1859.

5 With the possibility that Manchester College might be closed, Belsham suggested that its remaining funds might be combined with those of the now-defunct Hackney College and those of Timothy Kenrick's Academy at Exeter to finance a new dissenting academy at Birmingham, with Kenrick and John Kentish as tutors. However, Manchester College survived and was moved to York in 1803, and Kenrick refused to leave Exeter. Hence Belsham's suggestion came to nothing. However, Kenrick feared that Belsham's intervention had drawn money and support from his academy at Exeter. See Williams, pp. 522–7, and Letter 762.

6 For Priestley's *Index to the Bible*, see Letter 753, n. 4; for his *Socrates and Jesus compared*, see Letter 747, n. 5. In his letter to Lindsey of 16 Jan. 1804, Priestley explained that he had sent the text of the former work to 'the booksellers in Philadelphia' and did not seek payment for it; Rutt, I, 523.

7 See Letter 756, n. 8.

8 The works which Priestley had 'now ready' included his *Index to the Bible* and *The doctrines of heathen philosophy, compared with those of Revelation* (Northumberland, 1804). For his *Notes on all the books of scripture*, see Letter 736, n. 5.

9 This portrait of Priestley was painted by the American artist Gilbert Stuart (1755–1828) in *c.* 1803. It depicts Priestley without a wig, and with his grey hair centre-parted. The original is now privately owned. It was sent to England, where William Artaud (see Letter 574, n. 6) made at least three full-sized, and several smaller copies, of it. Several engravings made from it were published, such as that which forms the frontispiece to the *MR*, X (1815), and it is also the frontispiece to Rutt, I. By Priestley's 'last great work', Hannah Lindsey meant his *Notes on all the books of scripture*. An engraving by an unknown artist from what was evidently a different painting was prefixed to Vol. I of this work. While it shows Priestley with grey hair (and wigless), it is a left-hand profile, whereas the Stuart painting and the engravings made from it were full-face depictions of their subject. See John McLachlan, *Joseph Priestley, man of science 1733–1804. The iconography of a great Yorkshireman* (Braunton, Devon, 1983), pp. 31–4, 43.

10 For John Edwards, see Letter 608, n. 7. In 1802, he moved from Birmingham to become minister to the Old Jewry congregation in London, and to a dissenting congregation at Edmonton, as well as

lecturer at the Monkwell Street meeting. There is a brief note on his family in his obituary, *MR*, III (1808), 517. The vicar of the parish priest of Edmonton from 1795 to 1839 was Dawson Warren.

11 The minister of the dissenting congregation at Leather Lane, Holborn, from 1803 to 1805 was Nathaniel Philips; see Letter 619, n. 7. In the spring of 1804, William Vidler began a series of lectures there on Thursday evenings, 'assisted by the subscriptions of a few friends who had formed themselves into an "Unitarian Evangelical Society"'; *MR*, XII (1817), 197. However, the attendance was disappointing and Vidler did not continue the experiment after the first year.

759. **To ROBERT MILLAR   14 APRIL 1804

Text: DWL, MS 12.46 (48).
Addressed: To/M^r. Robert Millar/Merchant/Dundee/N:B
Endorsed: Lond^o. 18 Ap. 1804/Mrs Lindsey
Postmarked: Postmark missing.

Dear Sir

You[r] last excellent letter gave us singular pleasure: I have ordered M^r. Vidlers Magazine to be sent by some of the Dundee Vessels.[1]

I write thus soon a few short lines, to relieve your kind heart from anxiety about your venerable friend under the heavy shock of the loss of his most beloved friend, the good & eminent, D^r. Priestley:[2] This is borne with the same piety and resignation to the divine will which has marked his character through life. His wakeful nights at first, and intermitting pulse, gave me great apprehension of another nervous attack, but these symptoms went off, and it has pleased God to preserve him from any material injury to his health, only a great increased general debility, which at his age and shattered frame can never be repaired.

The very exemplary decline & exit of our invaluable friend has been very consoling: It first appeared in several of the Newspapers as an article from the Philadelphia Gazette which we hope you may have seen, or you soon will, with additions in Vidlers next Magazine.[3] The truth of wch is ascertained by many more particulars in a long letter from the D^{rs} eldest son which M^r. Lindsey rec^d on Tuesday last, & from wch letter the extract at Philadelphia was made to counteract some idle rumors which existed there by a comon friend.[4]

The whole account will be given in some proper way ere long: It must do good to see how Unitarian Christians can die, & it was a providential thing that this great champion of truth was so supported to the last: Even the short detail in the papers has affected many, & in the upper ranks has impressed some orthodox persons with more favorable ideas of Dr Priestley than they had formerly had: so that tho' dead he yet speaketh.[5]

Mr Belsham, Mr Jarvis, Dr Disney, Mr Joyce have all paid a just tribute from the heart to the memory of this extraordinary man, & it is very gratifying to see the interest that is generally taken in that event.[6]

Our house is often like a fair, regret for our friend, and solicitude for Mr Lindsey brings us many inquirers, who all learn something from the aged Saints calm and chearing fortitude.

His Annuity money will in part be applied to printing two very valuable posthumous works left ready for the press.[7] But I must have done, to prevent you unnecessary suffering, I have in great hast[e] scribbled these lines, and to assure you once more of the affec^t regards of

T: and HL

April 14th 1804

Essex House.

Every honor is intended in America to be given by all the public Societies.[8]

---

1 This letter from Millar's letter to Theophilus and Hannah Lindsey seems not to have survived. Vidler's magazine was the *Universal Theological Magazine and Impartial Review*.

2 Priestley died at Northumberland, Pennsylvania, on 6 Feb. 1804.

3 News of Priestley's death reached Lindsey through a notice, based on 'a Communication in the *Philadelphia Gazette*', which set out the details of his final illness and which appeared in the *Morning Chronicle*, 7 Apr. 1804, and in several other newspapers, including the *Caledonian Mercury*, 23 Apr. 1804. The *Universal Theological Magazine and Impartial Review*, I, 4 (Apr. 1804), 171–89, carried a substantial memoir of Priestley.

4 Possibly this was the letter from Joseph Priestley junior to Lindsey to which Belsham referred in *Memoirs*, pp. 257–8. 'Tuesday last' was 10 Apr. 1804. The 'common friend' was probably Thomas Cooper, who was present at Priestley's deathbed; Lindsey was evidently concerned about potential inaccuracies in Cooper's account of Priestley's last days.

5 For this 'short detail' in the *Morning Chronicle*, 7 Apr. 1804, see n. 3, above. 'Tho dead he yet speaketh' is a slight adaptation of the last words of Hebrews xi. 4.

6 Of these commemorative sermons, I have been able to identify two: Thomas Belsham, *Zeal and fortitude in the Christian ministry illustrated and exemplified. A discourse ... on occasion of the death of the Rev. Joseph Priestley ... to which is annexed, a brief memoir of Dr. Priestley's life and writings, and a letter from his son, Mr. Joseph Priestley, containing the particulars of his last sickness* (London, 1804); and John Disney *A sermon* [on Rev. xiv. 13] *... on occasion of the death of Joseph Priestley* (London, 1804). There is no evidence that the sermons on this subject preached by Thomas Jervis and Jeremiah Joyce were published.

7 For Priestley's annuity, see Letter 756, n. 8. The two posthumously published works of Priestley to which Hannah Lindsey referred were his *Notes on all the books of scripture* and his *Index to the Bible*.

8 On 29 Dec. 1804, the American Philosophical Society held a memorial service in Priestley's honour; Schofield, *Enlightened Joseph Priestley*, p. 401; for some of the other honours accorded to him, see Edgar F. Smith, *Priestley in America 1794–1804* (Philadelphia, 1920), pp. 166–71.

---

760. **CHRISTOPHER WYVILL   12 MAY 1804

Text:	NYRO, ZFW 7/2/164/10, Wyvill of Constable Burton MSS.
Printed:	Ditchfield, 'Lindsey–Wyvill correspondence', 169 (fifth paragraph).
Addressed:	To/The Rev^d. M^r. Wyvill/Burton Hall,/near/Bedale,/Yorkshire
Endorsed:	From the Revd Theophilus Lindsey, May 12th 1804
Postmarked:	MA 12 804

May 12th 1804

Dear Sir,

Various unavoidable things have prevent'd me from acomplishing [*sic*] M^r. Lindsey's wish to congratulate you in the first place, on your safe return home, and finding all your dear family in health.

Your kind short visit was like a shadow that passes away leaving however a pleasing impression.[1]

But your early and very gratifying communications of a very important nature deserves Mr Lindsey's grateful acknowledgements.

You do not seem to have laboured in vain with respect to strengthening M^r. Fox in the best and setled [*sic*] principles of his own mind, when not operated upon by the less interested, as well, as weaker judgment of those who continually surround him.[2]

That he is out of this wicked & magical combination against good of any sort to this Country we rejoice.[3] The Queen, M^r. Pitt and their faithful allies Ld Melville & the Chancellor will govern this illfated Nation as long as they can, and by making a raree [*sic*] shew of the poor Thing, expect to deceive the people into a belief of his competency to fill his office of chief Magistrate.[4] On his Chariot passing the top of our Street yesterday a friend of ours was standing there & saw him grinning indeed as if happy, but with a countenance expressive of his real state, and the passengers saying one to another, dear me! how mad he looks.[5]

M^r. Fox seems to be much increasing in favour with many of those men, who heretofore were devoted to M^r. Pitt: They say Mr Fox's councils w^d have led to Peace: This may not procede from any change or amendment of their own principles, but as considering war as destructive to the pecuniary welfare of England. Major Cartwright wrote to a friend saying, the only thing that can reconcile me to Pitts Administration is, that he will force every man to be a Soldier and then they will chuse for themselves.[6]

We hear that the Prince intends taking a public part in Politics, to concenter his friends about him, by two public days, & says as his Mother & Pitt keep no decent bounds, he will lye by no longer: If this be true, he acts probably from advice.[7]

Haveing in a short way told you what is passing here, I cannot sufficiently express the perfect approbation your venerable friend feels at the whole of your manly, judicious, and zealous indeavours for public good, and come what may, under the frightful picture before us, you have the best of all comforters, the approbation of unsullied integrity and an unremitting zeal and labors to do good to others.[8]

A friend just come in tells us that what was just hinted at in the papers & hon^{ble} to Mr Pitt, is true, viz. M^r P: offered M^r. F: 5 seats in the Cabinet & to content himself with 4, and as it was impossible to conquer the Kings repugnance to M^r. F: *at present* if he w^d take the situation offered, and in the course of three months, he could not bring the King to consent to M^r F's coming into power, he would resign himself.[9] This we believe to be fact.

Another thing wch passed between the K: and M^r P, when quite competent, as he sometimes is, "That upon proposing the emancipation, the K, he said, no man he believed ever came to offer to a Monarch, first to request him to break his Coronation Oath, & then to take into his councils again the very man (F) who himself had advised his dismission from the Privy Council as an enemy to the Constitution of the Country. This must have baffled M^r. P: with all his art & dexterity, & shews he did not dispair by some influence or other, in time to overcome the K.[10]

Nothing of all this may be new to you, but Mr Lindsey desired it might be communicated as his authority was good.

This return of cold weather does not quite suit my invalid, but he is not much otherwise than when you saw him: And if we live to the proper season, we have provided a retreat in the Country during the hot weather.

I have been so often interrupted you will please kindly to excuse all defects of the old womans letter, and accept the best esteem for y^{r}self & the kindest wishes for you & all Yours of Dr Sir

Your obliged & affec^{te} f^{ds}

T: and HL.

---

1   Wyvill had been in London to meet Fox on 27 Apr. 1804 and during this visit evidently called upon Lindsey, presumably at Essex Street.

2   See NYRO, ZFW 7/2/164/2, Wyvill's memorandum (dated 29 Apr. 1804) recording his conversation with Fox in the morning of 27 Apr. 1804. Wyvill urged Fox to maintain his principles and not to make compromises in order to secure inclusion within Pitt's newly formed second ministry. Wyvill had sent Lindsey copies of this and other related documents.

3   Fox and his followers did not join Pitt's new ministry, despite Pitt's wish that they should; see n. 9, below.

4   In Feb. 1804, George III suffered a brief recurrence of the illness which had afflicted him in 1788–9 and 1801. He made a slow recovery in the spring and summer of 1804. Henry Dundas, from 1802 Viscount Melville, took office as first lord of the admiralty in Pitt's second administration; John Scott, 1st Baron Eldon, had been lord chancellor since Apr. 1801.

5   This story, although indicative of Hannah Lindsey's hostility to George III, is not without plausibility. On 12 May 1804, the *Morning Chronicle* reported that 'yesterday', George III and his seventh son, Adolphus, duke of Cambridge (1774–1850) 'took an airing through Mary-le-Bone by Islington and the neighbouring villages, and entered the City by Whitechapel, proceeding through Cornhill, Cheapside, Fleet-street, and the Strand to the Queen's house [Buckingham palace], where His Majesty arrived about three o'clock'. The top of Essex Street adjoins the Strand.

6   I have not found this precise reference, but Cartwright expressed similar sentiments in a letter to Charles James Fox in Dec. 1803, where he advocated arming all tax-payers, as well as some persons 'of an inferior description', to whom arms should be provided at public expense; *The life and correspondence of Major Cartwright. Edited by his niece F.D. Cartwright* (2 vols., London, 1826), I, 316–18. His book *England's Ægis; or the military energies of the constitution*, published in two parts (London, 1804 and 1806) was a plea for rearmament. Cartwright himself was a major in the Nottinghamshire militia.

7   George, prince of Wales, concerned about the renewal of his father's illness (n. 4, above) and regretting that Pitt's second ministry had taken office without Fox and his followers, became more actively involved with the Foxites immediately thereafter. The *Hampshire Telegraph and Sussex Chronicle*, however, reported on Monday 7 May that the Prince 'is expected to re-enliven Brighton with his presence in the course of the present week'. The prince's mother was Queen Charlotte (1744–1818).

8   Wyvill's work 'for public good' consisted principally of campaigns for parliamentary reform; see Dinwiddy, *Christopher Wyvill and reform.*

9   For the negotiations whereby Pitt sought unsuccessfully to strengthen his new ministry by the inclusion of leading Foxites, see Ehrman, *Pitt the Younger. The consuming struggle*, pp. 653–60, and Mitchell, *Charles James Fox*, pp. 211–14. Hannah Lindsey probably referred to the report in the *Morning Chronicle*, 4 May 1804, that Pitt had told the king that he could not form a credible administration without the participation of Fox. On 8 May, it reported, as 'no inconsiderable disappointment', that Fox was to be excluded from the new ministry, and on 9 May, it noted that Fox's friends had insisted that they would not take office without him. The friend who confirmed the story of Pitt's offer was possibly William Smith, who was present at a meeting of the whig club on 8 May (*Morning Chronicle*, 9 May 1804). Another possibility is Samuel Heywood, who became a friend of Fox and in 1811 published a *Vindication* of Fox's *History of the early part of the reign of James II* (London, 1808).

10   George III believed that had he assented to catholic emancipation he would have broken his coronation oath to protect the Church of England; see Letter 694, n. 5. Hence, quite apart from his personal detestation of Fox, he was reluctant to accept into the cabinet any politician who favoured its immediate introduction. On 1 May 1798 at a meeting of the whig club, Fox raised a toast to 'the sovereignty of the people'; eight days later George III struck off his name from the list of privy councillors. Pitt, by contrast, while sympathetic to catholic emancipation, had undertaken not to bring it forward during his second ministry, which began in May 1804.

761. **To THOMAS BELSHAM   **24 JULY 1804**

Text:	DWL, MS 12.57 (29).
Addressed:	To/The Revd Thos. Belsham
Endorsed:	[By Belsham] Mrs Lindsey July 24: 1804
Postmark:	Postmark missing.

Clapham
Balam Hill
July 24th. 1804

D^r. Sir

Your welcome account of yourself is only this minute arrived, the irregularity of this pretended 2^py Post w^d fret me if trifles were worth the concern of an old woman, who assumes to a bit of Philosophy.[1]

Here after many exertions (and my good Mary still sick[2]) we are setled [*sic*] in great comfort as far as the main object, my precious invalid is concerned, now he has got into the habits of a new dwelling, with stairs to mount, and absent from his dear Study; He is nicely accomodated with a barber, gentle & punctual to a q^r before 8 o'clock every morning.

We have not seen a creature but M^r. Frend, our domestic circle is aided & inlivened by my charming Niece, who is devoted to her Uncle and reads to, & amuses him very much, she admires that aptitude to be pleased with everything at fourscore & with nervous disease, for which Mr Lindsey is so eminently distinguished with vigorous wishes for public & private good.[3]

We have had six copies of Notes on the Scriptures Vol 1st. but know not whence they came, or whither they are to go: One copy of Vol 2nd folded but not stitched apparently as it came from America, but not a line with it.[4] How could M^r. Travers be so scanty of the Advertisement as only to send thirteen when we want to send twenty to our Subscribing friends? I must send him a line to beg a few more.[5]

In looking over a mass of letters to find all we have of Dr Priestley a good job will be accomplished of committing to the flames many precious morsels, of various excellent men, correspondents of Mr Lindsey's most of them gone to sleep, and so peculiar to himself & detached from general use, that he chuses not to leave them behind him, least those who think better of him than he does of himself should give them to the public.[6]

In this rumage the inclosed was found, wch we have often mentioned to you, and desire you will put into your safe pocket book to return, when you have amused y^rself, and the noble family you are with[7] by this picture of what struck, a very amiable [word illegible] man: Who if this vain world, high office, and a great Church Establishment had not bewitched from better things would have borne his testimony to truth and a purer worship.[8]

How much are those to be honored, praised and loved, who have nobly overcome the world, & its censures, to worship and publicly acknowledge Jehovah, the sole God of the Universe as their God, & who will acknowledge and hereafter approve them before men & angels.

So the Pope is forced to attend at the Coronation of the arbitrary Emperor of France: be it so for the edification of Roman Catholics, by seeing how their sacred things are brought low.[9]

We are sorry you c^d not see this quiet pleasant dwelling just suited to its present inhabitants, & in better culture that Y^r friend Mr Urwicks[?], tho' I have no objection to his Cocks & Hens wandering over his grass plot, as ours do not. He has never called, we do not regret his absence, as we learn, that age has much diminished his mental powers, & makes him say the same things twenty times over: It is what we talkers may all come to.[10]

M^r. Lindsey desires to present his best respects to the Duke,[11] & laments he s^d not have had the pleasure of personally offering his thanks for the gracious remembrance of his birthday,[12] when his Grace was so kind as to call in Essex Street, and the more as an opportunity was lost of putting before the Duke the state of the Unitarian Chaple [*sic*] at Boston: Whether he would hear or forbear, the application was the bounden duty of M^r. Lindsey, being one of the small efforts left for him to make.[13]

Adieu I am called to this Letter sorting business. Accept the joint affec^t regards & esteem of T: & HL.

P.S.

D^r B: & his Niece are both in town.[14]

---

1 The two penny post, between 1801 and 1839, allowed for the conveyance of letters in London for a charge of 2d. It was the immediate predecessor of the penny post, introduced in 1840.

2 See Letter 747, n. 3.

3 This niece was Sarah Blackburne, who married William Frend in 1808. The uncle to whom she read was Lindsey himself.

4 See Letter 736, n. 4.

5 Probably Benjamin Travers or his twin brother, Joseph, both of Clapton; see Letter 685, n. 4. There is no 'advertisement' to any of the four volumes of Priestley's *Notes on all the books of scripture, for the use of the pulpit and private families*, published in Northumberland by Andrew Kennedy (see Letter 760). Probably Hannah Lindsey referred to a newspaper advertisement (which I have not been able to find), or to a separate single-sheet advertisement, or flyer.

6 This intention on Hannah Lindsey's part to preserve her husband's modesty no doubt helps to explain the non-survival of so many letters to Lindsey.

7 I.e. the family of the duke of Grafton, with which Belsham was on friendly terms, and with which he stayed at Wakefield Lodge on several occasions; see Williams, p. 570.

8 Possibly this is a reference to William Mason; see Letter 737, n. 5.

9 Napoleon Bonaparte was crowned as emperor at Notre Dame cathedral on 2 Dec. 1804. Although Pope Pius VII had come to Paris to perform the ceremony, Napoleon famously seized the crown from him and crowned himself as emperor (and Josephine as empress).

10 Born on 8 Dec. 1727, Thomas Urwick was aged seventy-six in July 1804. He was minister of the Grafton Square chapel, Clapham, from 1779 until his death on 26 Feb. 1807.

11 The duke of Grafton.

12 1 July 1804, Lindsey's eighty-first birthday.

13 Lindsey was anxious to secure the maximum possible help for James Freeman and his unitarian congregation at King's chapel, Boston. For his awareness of the resistance to unitarianism in New England, see Belsham, *Memoirs*, pp. 164–75.

14 See n. 3, above.

762. **To THOMAS BELSHAM   6 AUGUST 1804

Text: DWL, MS. 12.80, opp. p. 524.
Addressed: To/The Rev^d M^r. Belsham/Revd Mr Broadbents,/Latchford
                     near/Warrington[1]
Endorsed: Mrs Lindsey Aug^t: 6: 1804
Postmarked: AU 6 804

Balam Hill
August 6th 1804

Dear Sir

Your journal was a great amusement & pleasure to us:[2] We had begun to wonder what was become of you. The curious free conversation with the Duke, shews that no honest well-intentioned characters can ever do any good to this devoted Country, & that we are fast tending by more recent events to destruction as a free people.[3] The Contest in Middlesex will end as all efforts of the sort must under such paramount influence, tho' the Agents & Actors thoroughly disgrace themselves in the eyes of all honest men.[4]

Should I regret that so pure & peaceable a character is wearing out fast? My dear Invalid has suffered a great diminution of the active movements he exercised, only this day week when he walked with pleasure a quarter of a mile & seemingly unfatigued: The next two excessive hot days quite overcame the feeble system brought on pain from the Os Sacrum down the lame[?] side, & a general debility, & wakefulness. He was too unable to be moved to try the effect of a blister on the part, & happily the application of strong salt & water with a towel has so far aided the diseased leg, that the pain is trifling when not in motion, & he can now stand with hold of anything, or be led once round the Garden: His health & vigor of mind & chearfulness still continue, to wch my charming Niece with her attentions and lively sallies, not a little contributes.[5] I wish you could have seen us, before you went as the picture of comfort, & every convenience we injoy here, would have soothed your feeling heart, under this unexpect'd reverse of our wishes.

The old woman cannot boast much of herself having besides great fatigue day & night our good useful Mary confined to her room, & often bed by an inflamation of the Liver, wch Leeches & a blister have removed, but the Chronic[?] disease of this Organ resists everything but Mercury rubbed in, and wch process is now begun, as the only chance for a cure. I have got a person from town, competent to help in household matters, as Hanah is quite occupied with her sister, & so dispirited as to be of little use to me, or her Master.[6] This discipline is for good no doubt to us all, & my spirit is willing but the body weak.

Mr Lindsey is much occupied in reading the Life of Sr Wm Jones, & only laments that a methodist is the Editor: Not that the reader of any disernment [*sic*] is at a loss to find out the great, liberal, & rationally pious mind of S^r. William, but the ply given by Ld Teignmouth will operate upon many.[7]

Mr Travers could send me no more Advertisements but refers me to you; so I must wait till y^r. return, & leave our friends in ignorance of our joint proceedings till then.[8]

A few days ago I felt a pang at Y^r distance from us, but Almighty God is near, & of what should I be afraid?

Friston without its late owner would unavoidably occasion painful and melancholy sensations: We rejoice that the Widow & Fatherless are supported, they were gradually weaned, and M[rs] Milnes has a calm steady mind, & will we hope use her power well, or she will revolt her hitherto over indulged sons, who have a proper self government to learn.[9] M[r] Milnes of Thornes House wants somebody to rouse him, and take off the cumbrous load of wealth, & a great establishment to w[ch] his mind never was equal: The loss of his wife is irreparable.[10]

D[r] Toulmin is again gone out for a Month into the West with his wife & daughter to keep their Son in Law (M[r] Sweet) in temper, whose wife is now unwell.[11] M[r] Kentish is returned from Cheltenham and taken the labouring oar, at their pu[?]lpit] [MS torn: one or two words missing]: together amount before & after service [to] 160. M[rs] J[?]: Mansell[12] is my informant; she laments the very small collection for M[r] Kenrick's Academy: But himself much more in a letter lately, & blames you for damping the ardor of the rich Merchants in & near town: I have told him that no efforts of yours could have drawn money to such a distant Establishment as theirs or York:[13] He is now with his sister near Wrexham.[14] By Miss Mansells account the most powerful Oratory of M[r]. Hall, could get but little for the Baptists Charity children who have 500 taught by the young persons of the Congregation every Sunday to be sure £35: 4: 0[d] from above a thousand hearers was but small: M[r] Simpson did much better for them.[15] She adds "I sh[d] have been much more hurt for the Preacher had it been any other but M[r] Hall, but he appears one who would never have an idea that defect could act upon him, nor did it indeed upon his matter, but his manner was extremely rapid & very unpleasing, tho' the latter taken in the connectedness of his discourse is surely very wonderful, but his voice is so weak he was not heard half over the Meeting". "M[r] Kentish wants more relaxation from business I believe he never has a moment unoccupied; however his whole heart is in his business, & in return he is almost idolized among us".[16] M[r] W[m] Wilkinson has been at Birm[m] – seems anxious about M[rs]. Finch's family, can make nothing of Finch, who has now about 200 p[r] ann to keep his family & will do nothing himself.[17] M[r] Brand Hollis lives on, the weather infeebles him, but the viscera is perfect: D[r] D: is just come from thence.[18] A second letter is arrived from M[r]. Priestley who with his wife & Joe are at Philadelphia for a week, he is sending off 2nd Vol: of Notes, the 3rd nearly finished: Is beginning the Alphabetical Index with new types & good paper: Wants Y[rs] & M[r] L's opinion advice, & help about the life: Disowns any general Commission to Philips to send books.[19] Adieu I can write no more: our kindest affec[t] regards

Sarah sends her best respects.

Y[rs]   T: &HL

Vidler has Let his house & sold his fixtures, & has now a chance of doing well, this will give you pleasure.[20]

---

1   For William Broadbent, minister of the Cairo Street chapel, Warrington, see Letter 640, n. 19. The (then) village of Latchford is approximately one mile from the centre of Warrington.

2   Belsham's letter to Theophilus and Hannah Lindsey, with the account of his conversation with Grafton, is not among Belsham's papers in DWL and seems not to have survived.

3   In his later years, Grafton, although no longer an active participant in debates of the house of lords, shared Fox's criticisms of the renewal of war with France and what both saw as the attendant threat to civil liberty.

4   For the outcome(s) of the Middlesex by-election of 23 July 1804, occasioned by the ruling that Burdett's election in 1802 (Letter 737, n. 1) was invalid, see Letters 763, n. 4, and 764, n. 12.

5   Probably the niece was Sarah Blackburne.

6   Han[n]ah was presumably the sister to 'my good Mary' (Letter 761). The only servant named in

Hannah Lindsey's will was Elizabeth Catlow, who inherited all her mistress's 'wearing apparel', together with a modest financial legacy; TNA: PRO PROB 11/1529, fos. 235r–235v.

7 *Memoirs of the life, writings and correspondence of Sir William Jones*, by John Shore (1751–1834), from 1798 Baron Teignmouth, was published in London in 1804. A fervent evangelical, he was associated with the Clapham sect and from 1798 to 1834 he was president of the British and Foreign Bible Society. His immense experience in India, which included service as governor-general of Bengal from 1793 to 1798, qualified him to undertake the life of Sir William Jones (1746–94), the puisne judge of the Bengal court of judicature from 1783 to 1794.

8 For Travers and the advertisements for Priestley's *Notes on all the books of scripture*, see Letter 761, n. 5. By 'our joint proceedings', Hannah Lindsey meant the efforts made by herself, Belsham and other sympathizers to forward the publication of Priestley's works.

9 Richard Slater Milnes of Fryston Hall, Yorkshire, died on 2 June 1804. He had been MP for York from 1784 to 1802. His wife Rachel, née Busk, died in 1835. They had two sons, namely Robert Pemberton Milnes (1784–1858), MP for Pontefract from 1806 to 1818, and Richard Rodes Milnes (1785–1835), together with seven daughters.

10 James Milnes (1755–1805), of Thornes House, near Wakefield, Yorkshire, was MP for Bletchingley from 1802 until his death on 21 Apr. 1805. He married in 1778 Mary Ann, née Busk, the sister of the wife of Richard Slater Milnes (see n. 9, above). She died on 10 Nov. 1802.

11 The daughter of Joshua Toulmin and his wife Jane (d. 1824) was Lucinda, who married David Sweet in 1791. Toulmin's other daughter who accompanied him to the west country was possibly Sarah Emma Toulmin, who is named as a legatee in his will; TNA: PRO PROB11/1572, fo. 283v.

12 Possibly Judith Mansell; see Letter 639, n. 17, for an identification of the Mansell family of Birmingham. It is not clear whether Lindsey wrote 'Mrs' or 'Miss'.

13 See Letter 758, n. 5. Timothy Kenrick died suddenly near Wrexham (presumably during the visit mentioned in this letter) on 22 Aug. 1804 and his academy closed in Mar. of the following year.

14 This is a reference to Timothy Kenrick's youngest sister Martha (1762–1853), who subsequently married the dissenting minister James Parry (d. 1848); they ran a school at Wrexham. See Kenrick, *Chronicles of a nonconformist family*, pp. 67, 159, and genealogical table inside the end-cover.

15 The 'Baptists charity children' were probably the children who attended the Sunday school of the Cannon Street Memorial baptist church in Birmingham. The congregation was founded in 1737 and the Sunday school flourished, with over 1,000 scholars, in the 1790s. Mr Hall was probably Robert Hall, minister of St Andrew's baptist church, Cambridge (see Letter 428, n. 6), who was already famed for his pulpit eloquence. I am grateful to the Rev. Dr Roger Hayden for advice over this charity.

16 This letter from Miss Mansell (n. 12, above) to Hannah Lindsey seems not to have survived. Possibly it was one of her letters which were destroyed at her own request immediately after her death; see Catharine Cappe's memoir of Hannah Lindsey, MR, VII (1812), 114.

17 William Wilkinson (1744–1808), Priestley's brother-in-law and the younger brother of John Wilkinson; the cause of his concern was the bankruptcy of William Finch, the wife of Priestley's daughter Sarah, who had died on 1 Sept. 1803.

18 Thomas Brand Hollis died on 9 Sept. 1804 at the Hyde, Ingatestone, Essex, which he bequeathed to Disney.

19 Mr Priestley was Joseph Priestley's eldest son who shared his father's name; 'Joe' was Joseph Rayner Priestley, the son of Joseph Priestley junior. The 'Alphabetical index' refers to Priestley's *Index to the Bible*, which was published by Joseph Johnson in London in 1805. For the radical bookseller Richard Phillips, see Letter 640, n. 5.

20 This refers to Vidler's house and premises at 349 The Strand; see Letter 756, n. 3.

763. **To THOMAS BELSHAM   **12 AUGUST 1804**

> **Text:**   DWL, MS 12.57 (30).
> **Addressed:**   To/The Rev^d. Thos. Belsham,/at the Rev^d. John Yates's,/
>   Liverpool
> **Endorsed:**   Mrs Lindsey Aug^t: 12: 1804
> **Postmarked:** AU 13 804

Sunday morning
August 12th.
1804

Dear Sir

I hasten to tell you that your precious friend has by divine permission returned to the best state he is probably capable of: His health, & appetite are improved, the general debility lessened, & except the hip wch. cripples him in walking he is comfortable, & sleeps better: Altho' he is always content & happy, yet the sight of his friends exhilirates [*sic*] his spirits, and he passed a pleasant day yesterday by M^r. Frend dining with us, who related many anecdotes of the vile procedings [*sic*] of the late ill terminated Election in which he had been busily imployed: He sunk my fond hopes, when saying that I hoped the spirit wch had appeared so universally would lead to good, Yes, it may be so, or it may be the expiring flame, when you consider the system of venality & corruption under wch we live, and the unprincipled ardent mind of the man who is at the Helm. There is little doubt but the change of conduct in the Sherriffs took place after a consultation in Downing Street.[1]

Shaw is the man who drank Pitts health at a City feast, and was so properly corrected by Mr Sheridan, who gave M^r. Fox directly: He is in the high road to be Lord Mayor, and to be made a Baronet, what is right & justice, with such dazzling objects before a vain man.[2]

Perry has exhibited facts all through the contest fairly & well, and has increased the sale of his paper between three & four hundred copies daily.[3] What an impudent Advertisement is Manwarings to say with only 5 Majority that the sense of the County is with him;[4] but Tom Melish can write, & make him sign anything: I knew that intrepid ministerial tool, in his Mothers arms: He was bred to the Law, prompt in vice, & by the death of his Father made very rich (as all the family are) and with great talents, and an fruitful immagination, & means to gratify every wish, is the instrument of evil wherever he comes: Yet he has latent good points that calamity may draw out to future good. He was the best tool for Pitt to work with on such a being as was pushed forward, in contempt of all respect & comon decency on the County.[5]

Mary is mending gradually, so that all present fear, that she was rapidly going off, is averted: She must be in her room, & long useless, but such things do not fret, only inconvenience me:[6] And indeed the whole of this large new system, has set me to learn the toils & cares of a larger family, now I am too old to do my business well, and with an unimbarrassed clear head, that could once, have done anything. The diminution to my comfort, is not additional bodily labor, wch does not hurt my health, but that bewildered state of mind, which leaves no calm moments to retire within itself & converse with better things: Your certain glorious prospects I believe in, but they do not animate my dead nervous stomach, or anything give pleasant sensations: But I trust to tread the rugged road perseveringly, and reach the Goal at last. This world has not one thing in it, that I desire & do not possess, but still feel myself an ungrative[*sic*] Catiff, for such unceasing bounty. You my Father Confessor will not I know impose any hard penance, knowing the human mind too well, to feel any addition necessary.

We are glad that you found the good Shores well, M^r S: is so absorbed in his Military imploy, as to forget writing to me, on a business he set me to do & wch. must be very inconvenient to the person concern'd if yet ignorant of his intentions concerning her.[7] Somebody told us M^r. Aspland w^d. take Norton, I think it was M^r. Eaton, who admires him greatly:[8] Last Sunday after preaching at Leather Lane for Dr Philips,[9] who sent to him late on Saturday night saying he was taken ill on the road home, poor Eaton fagged hither, & came too late to eat our dinner, as we conform to the habits of this place on account of public worship, wch some of our family attends: Sarah likes the Church preacher best Mr Venn, because Trinity, & Atonement is not so bad in classical hands, as the same sad stuff is at the Meeting: The Church is too much crowded to admit servants, or anyone, unless befriended, & there is empty space enough at the Meeting.[10] Mr Urick has called once: He preached a funeral sermon for one of his quondam rich flock, two Sundays ago:[11] And is accused of great unfeelingness, when called up at 3 o'clock in the morning to give the Sacrament to this truly miserable man who died in horrors from an inflamation of the bowels neglected, who begged to know if he might not hope to meet his beloved wife in heaven, to wch. M^r. U: replied he did not know that, & left the sufferer in very deep dispair. Why not console the man with the only idea that could reconcile him to dying.

Thanks for your agreable history in meeting with so many pleasant friends: We hope your farther progress will be equally chearing, & we shall be glad to partake with you at second hand. Pray remember us to all our friends at Birmingham: Accept the kind respects of D^r. Blackburne & my good Niece, and the most affec^t regards & wishes of

Your ever faithful & obliged f^ds

T: & HL

P.S

Good Mr Walker can never do at Norton, his habits cannot be changed, tho' Mr Lindsey says adversity will change anybody.[12] Pray present M^r. L's Comp^ts to your Host.[13]

---

1   Frend had been a strong supporter of Sir Francis Burdett at the controversial Middlesex by-election in July 1804 (see n. 4, below). Burdett himself was much admired by, and on social terms with, Frend's family until the 1830s.

2   James Shaw (1764–1843) was MP for London from 1806 to 1818. He was sheriff of London from 1803 to 1804 and lord mayor from 1805 to 1806. He was created a baronet in Sept. 1809.

3   James Perry (see Letter 449, n. 7), who had been the sole proprietor and editor of the *Morning Chronicle* since 1793, covered the Middlesex election of 1804 in considerable detail, from a pro-Burdett point of view. For the increase in the *Morning Chronicle*'s sales and profits between 1802 and 1806, see Ivon Asquith, 'Advertising and the press in the late eighteenth and early nineteenth centuries: James Perry and the *Morning Chronicle*, 1790–1821', *HJ*, XVIII, 4 (1975), 703–24.

4   At the Middlesex by-election of 23 July 1804, caused by the invalidation of Burdett's election in 1802, William Mainwaring was elected with 2,828 votes to the 2,823 votes for Burdett. The advertisement to which Hannah Lindsey referred appeared in the *Morning Chronicle*, 11 Aug. 1804.

5   The special pleader Thomas Mellish was a supporter of Mainwaring in the Middlesex election; see *Morning Chronicle*, 25 July 1804. The previous day, Mellish published a notice in that newspaper denying that George Byng (1764–1847), the other MP for Middlesex, supported Burdett in the by-election of 1804 and asserting that Byng took a neural stance between Burdett and Mainwaring. Probably he was related to William Mellish MP; see Letter 729, n. 1.

6   See Letters 747, n. 3, 761, n. 2, and 762, n. 6.

7   The 'military employ' of Samuel Shore III took the form of the raising of a company of volunteers
    from his tenants in the region of Meersbrook House; see Lady Stephen, 'The Shores of Sheffield and
    the Offleys of Norton Hall', , 10–11. Disappointingly, the 'business', or commission, which Shore
    had given to Hannah Lindsey remains obscure, as does the identity of the lady concerned. Samuel
    Shore's second wife Lydia, née Flower, was still alive at this time, and it is highly unlikely that he
    was thinking of re-marriage. Perhaps he had in mind a governess for his younger grandchildren, in
    whom he took a sustained and detailed interest.

8   Robert Aspland (1782–1845), educated as a baptist, became a unitarian partly through the influence
    of Thomas Belsham, and served briefly as minister to the Shores' congregation at Norton, Derbyshire,
    in 1804–5, in succession to John Williams (see Letter 413, n. 9). David Eaton appears to have been
    Hannah Lindsey's informant. In 1805, Aspland succeeded Belsham as minister to the Gravel Pit
    meeting, Hackney, and continued in that capacity until his death. He was one of the leading unitarian
    preachers and organizers of the early nineteenth century, and helped to found the *Monthly Repository*
    in 1806.

9   Nathaniel Philips (see Letter 619, n. 7) was minister to the Leather Lane dissenting congregation from
    1803 to 1805. For Vidler's lecture there, see Letter 758, n. 11. 12 Aug. 1804 was a Sunday; 'Last
    Sunday' was 5 Aug. 1804.

10 John Venn (1759–1813) was rector of Clapham from 1792 until his death and a central figure in the
    evangelical 'Clapham sect'. His father was Henry Venn (see Vol. I, Letters 39, 90 and 91). Hannah
    Lindsey implied that trinitarian orthodoxy was more acceptable when preached by an educated cler-
    gyman than by an unlettered dissenting or methodist preacher.

11 Although Thomas Urwick retired from his ministry at Clapham shortly before his death in 1807, he
    still preached there on occasion. His former 'rich flock' was probably the congregation at Narbor-
    ough, Leicestershire, where he was minister from 1775 to 1779, and where, according to his obituary,
    'a new and handsome house was erected for him, to the expense of which he himself contributed';
    MR, II (1807), 161. Urwick did not publish this funeral sermon. 'Two Sundays ago' was 29 July 1804.

12 George Walker did not become minister at Norton. Born in 1734, he was seventy in 1804, which
    helps to explain Hannah Lindsey's comment that 'his habits cannot be changed'. From 1798 to
    1803, he had been principal of Manchester College, where his period of office ended in an acrimo-
    nious financial wrangle between him and the college trustees; see Ditchfield, 'The early history of
    Manchester College', 86–90. After his retirement from the college, Walker resided in Manchester and
    subsequently in Liverpool, but did not undertake any further congregational duty.

13 Belsham's host, as indicated by the address to which this letter was directed, was John Yates (1755–
    1826), minister of the unitarian congregation at Paradise Street, Liverpool, from 1791 to 1823. From
    1777, he had been minister to that congregation at its previous location at Kaye Street.

764. **To ROBERT MILLAR   **20 AUGUST 1804**

    Text: DWL, MS 12.46 (50).
    Addressed: To/Mr. Robert Millar/Merchant/Dundee/N:B
    Endorsed: Londo. 20 Augt 1804/Mrs Lindsey
    Postmarked: Postmark missing.

Clapham

Balam Hill

August 20th 1804.

Dear Sir,

I wish much to acknowledge your kind letter of July 5th.[1] and to inquire after
your own health with something like the same solicitude exercised towards your
venerable friend and his old wife: I trust that you did not let the Bile prevail over
you to any extent, as on its first approach, it so easily gives way to a small potion
Miss Scot can give you, wch is two drams (viz a quarter of an ounce) of the comon
bitter purging Salts, dissolved in a tea-cupfull of small camomile tea, & taken every
morning, or every second morning, according to its operation, wch should bring two
easy motions a day, till the enemy is dislodged: Your gentle spirit may cast a slight

remark why this was not told you before: And if a vast & almost overwhelming mass of business had not then occupied me, I certainly should have sooner been your Physician.

But the obligation we were under to [have] provided a summer residence for ourselves & to take a House, and inlarge our establishment to double its numbers, with all the preparations necessary to accomodate my Invalid, & make things run as smoothly as may be, fill'd up my time every hour: And altho' we have been five weeks here, the like occupations have continued, especially with the distressing addition of our old valuable Mary, being even dangerously ill with an inflamation of the Liver, in addition to a Chronic disease of that organ.[2] This my main instrument becoming a great anxiety and to be waited upon in her bed & room for a Month. Happily my brother Dr Blackburn's house being at liberty, by his wife & childrens absence in Yorkshire with her Mother,[3] we have taken that, & have him with us to sleep almost every night, & this lessened my anxiety both for poor Mary; and even more on M^r. Lindseys account to whom a few very hot days we had proved to a great degree debilitating to my dear Invalid, & brought on pain in the back & hip on the weak side so as quite to disable him from standing alone or walking, wch previous to this attack he had great pleasure in doing in our pretty little garden: By the use of Salt & Water every morning with a towel to the back & hip, by the blessing of God, he is again recruited so as to walk alone across a room, & round the Garden with help, & this is the utmost to be expected in his very feeble state: His health & spirits, & tranquil mind, & ability to read, are still continued, a rare privillege [sic], wch demands unceasing thankfulness.

You will now feel satisfied as to us: We have heard twice from M^r. Priestley, who is going on with all expedition to compleat the Notes on the Scriptures, two Vols of which are arrived & delivered in part to the Subscribers:[4] The Posthumous works are also put in hand, and the residue of the money raised for D^r P's life, wch this first Year amounted to 452£ will pay the expence of printing, when 200£ is paid to the Gentleman who took up the Draft of the good D^{rs}. wch was not honrd by his unworthy brother in Law, & to make up wch deficiency in his income, this life Annuity was set on foot.[5] But it did not please God, to continue his valuable labors, or even to hear of this bounty of his friends; but took him to his rest & reward, before age & inability came on: which I hold a blessing, when granted.

We are very sorry you have so troublesome an Appointment as Commissioner to the property tax, not very easy to execute, but y^r integrity and caution makes you a very proper person, and you judge well in not giving way to ease, so as not to fill up a station of great use to Society.[6]

We are glad that M^r. Vidlers Magazine furnishes you with agreable information: He is a most zealous and able advocate for the final salvation of all mankind: How anyone who loves his fellow creatures as he ought can feel reluctance to this most consolatory doctrine I cannot conceive.[7]

Dr Payley published about a Year ago, a most capital work intitled "Natural Theology" Mr Joyce our good Secretary, has by making an Analysis of an expensive book brought it within a more reasonable price & size: It contains every argument to prove that one single intelligent Being is the Author of everything, and that he brings about by natural causes, the greatest possible good of his rational creatures, as also of those below them, & that happiness was, & is the object of all his works: The price is 3^s. published by Conde [MS torn] Bucklerbury, & Rees Paternoster row, & Flow[er] late of Cambridge, now Harlow in Essex.[8] The prospect of a good

Harvest is not at present flattering here, but we trust that t[he] promising bounty of Heaven on this sinful land will not be withdrawn: But bread rises rapidly by some means or other, & all other provisions are uncomonly high.[9] Peace there is no chance of with our present governers [sic], who are again send [sic] out an alarm of Invasion, to cover other things, but this is too stale to have any effect:[10] A certain great Personage is laid by as useless, & Pitt is sole Actor:[11] The Middlesex Election makes a noise at present, & we hope such a grose [sic] violation of the Elective Franchise will not be suffered to pass unpunished, and reversed even under so daring a patron as the Premier himself.[12]

Your sorrows are all working to your greater good, whether your life be short, or long: I have been under the same impression as you have, about 45 years, & am still toiling on with the same infirmities, & may even toil to old age: God knows what is necessary to make us anyway fit, for his munificent gift of a happy immortality. Adieu accept the affec^t regards of your ever sincere f^{ds} T: & HL.

Exercise on horseback is an excellent remedy for bilious diseases.

Comp^{ts} to Miss Scot. Letters as usual to Essex S^t.[13]

1   Millar's letter of 5 July 1804 seems not to have survived.

2   For 'our old valuable Mary', see Letters 747, n. 3, 761, n. 2, and 762, n. 6.

3   Dr William Blackburne's wife was Hannah, née Wilson; for their children, see *Familiae min. gen.*, II, 770. Hannah Blackburne's family lived at Ayton in the north riding of Yorkshire. Her father was William Wilson; I have not been able to identify her mother. William Blackburne's house was 23 Spring Gardens, London.

4   These two letters from Joseph Priestley junior seem not to have survived. For the works of Priestley to which they referred, see Letter 736, n. 4.

5   In addition to the *Notes on all the books of scripture,* the posthumous works of Priestley to which Lindsey referred included the final volumes of the *General history of the Christian church* and *The doctrines of heathen philosophy.* Priestley's 'unworthy brother-in-law' was John Wilkinson; possibly the 'gentleman' was William Vaughan. For Priestley's annuity, see Letter 756, n. 8.

6   See the *Caledonian Mercury,* 25 Feb. 1804.

7   William Vidler had moved from a particular baptist congregation at Battle and came to hold the universalist view that all men will ultimately be saved. His magazine was the *Universal Theological Magazine and Impartial Review.* For the background to this type of thought, see Geoffrey Rowell, 'The origins and history of universalist societies in Britain, 1750–1850', *JEH,* XXII, 1 (1971), 35–56.

8   Jeremiah Joyce's *A full and complete analysis of Dr. Paley's natural theology; or evidences for the existence and attributes of the deity: collected from the appearances of nature* was published by Benjamin Flower in Cambridge in 1804. The booksellers for whom it was printed are listed on the title page as T. Conder, Bucklersbury; Longman, Hurst, Rees and Orme, Paternoster Row, London; and J. Deighton, and J. Nicholson, Cambridge. For a further note on Deighton, see Letter 475, n. 6. The price of the book was indeed 3*s.* Joyce had already published *An analysis of Paley's view of the evidences of Christianity* (Cambridge, 1795, with a second edition in 1797).

9   See Letter 765, n. 6.

10   See, for example, *Morning Post,* 1, 8 Aug. 1804.

11   For George III's illness and recovery in the early months of 1804, see Letter 760, n. 4. Although his eyesight was deteriorating, it was a considerable exaggeration to state that he was 'laid by as useless'; on 31 July 1804, he was able to come to Westminster to prorogue parliament in person; *LJ,* XLIV, 699–701.

12   Mainwaring's election for Middlesex in July 1804 (see Letter 763, n. 4) was overturned by a commons' select committee on 5 Mar. 1805, in response to a petition from Burdett's supporters. Burdett was then reinstated in the seat which he had first won in 1802. On 10 Feb. 1806, however, a petition from Mainwaring led the committee to reverse its verdict and install Mainwaring as the MP.

13   Hannah Lindsey wrote the two lines of this postscript at right angles to the main text, opposite the opening paragraph dealing with Millar's health.

765. **To THOMAS BELSHAM   **24 AUGUST 1804**

Text: DWL, MS 12.57 (31).
Addressed: To/The Rev^d. Thos. Belsham,/at Richard Chandlers Esqr,/
                  Gloucester[1]
Endorsed: Mrs Lindsey Aug^t: 24: 1804
Postmarked: AU 25 804

Dear Sir,

Your letters are a great treat, both as very interesting, and as an assurance to us, that your time is spent pleasantly, profitably and usefully; such are the reciprocal consequences of social intercourse with intelligent virtuous minds, and a small specimen of what may be expected when all are new cloathed: I judge of others by myself whose perfect injoyment is only obstructed by terrene concretions.

How I envy M^rs. Rathbone her successful exertions to make other happy: By so doing if she is not baffled by "diseased sensations" she must be happy herself.[2]

Poor Martin: has not studied the "Art of happiness" he recommended to others in his little printed piece, wch has lately fallen into my hands among other papers: The eager pursuit of wealth is a most debasing thing, and of a Miser nothing is ever to be expected but perishable dust: I hope however that as he has a tender affection for his most amiable wife, that she may counteract this dreadful propensity.[3]

Your venerable friend is much as when I wrote last, much feebler on his feet than when you saw him, but can creep round our little garden without hold: And on Monday last when he exerted himself to go & see Mrs Chambers our Widow friend and her daughter at Beckenham which is near miles,[4] & return'd in the Evening & slept well after all: Finding our friends in better plight than we had been led to expect, and charmingly situated in a Parsonage House which they rent at 300 p^r ann, the like to which we have never seen, M^r. Lindsey seemed to feel no fatigue so called out & excited by the company of his friends, & the novel scene.[5]

It is reported that London is a desart, the quietude which has succeded the bustle of the Election, must be considerable at the West end of the town: It is only in the City where business excites both one class and another, either to get, or save money, that toil never ends. The advanced price of bread is by the comon people attributed to S^r F: Burdetts not being the Member for Middlesex, so skillful are they in cause & effect: he was too hon^le & just to urge the price of grain, to increase his popularity as he was urged to do: No says he, I will not try to deceive I can neither make Corn dearer or cheaper, nor increase a popular outcry against Government, for any acts of theirs where the injury is not clear.[6]

Mr Frend is gone into Kent with Mr Bosville,[7] from thence to the Duke of Grafton's, and, then to Paxton: The accounts from thence are not at all comfortable, it is now a confirmed disease for life, with regular periods of greater or lesser irritation: Our most worthy friend bears his sorrow as heroically as he can, alone, & on the Verge of fourscore.[8]

Our friends in town seem all to have forgot their promises of calling as they pass by, at Balam Hill: M^rs. Dodson who is mopeing in town hesitates about coming, tho' she has got rid of her blue devils and is well & in good spirits for her.[9]

Dr Disney is tied to the Chapel by Mr Joyces absence at Worthing, where after all other remedies failed to recruit his wife he was obliged to take her: he called one Sunday after service before he left town finally; said he had provided for the afternoon service w^(ch) was all he had to do with.[10]

We are very barren of news or anecdote here, know no more of Clapham than if fifty miles off, except one kind friend M^(rs). Crompton, who would be very good to us, if her health & limbs would permit her to move, in any degree equal to the activity of her mind: You would hear of her sons severe illness at Cheltenham, when you was at Birmingham; that anxiety for him has quite overcome his Mother, by adding to an old disease.[11]

You would see in the Papers that Mr Wm Smiths Mother was dead here: Now he has got all that death can bring him: Mr Urick told me she died quite unexpectedly both by herself & all about her, altho' attended by Dr Lister.[12] He is a queer old man, wonders what can have become of you, as he knows your Pupils must be coming back.[13] We hope to see you soon after your return whenever it is, but beg a line the day before lest we should be flitted to Morden, or elsewhere: Letters with all sorts of directions do find us sooner or later, but Dr Blackburn's Balam Hill Clapham come most certainly.

I have neither light, eyes, or time to bore you any longer, w^(ch) is lucky for you. Pray make our kind Comp^t to M^r & M^(rs). Chandler,[15] also to M^r & M^(rs) Smith[14] when you see them: The D^(r16) and Sarah desire theirs to you: Accept the best wishes & affec^t regards of

    T: & HL

P.S.

Mary is comfortably about again, tho' not quite cured.[17]

    August 24^(th) 1804

---

1   For Richard Chandler of Gloucester and his wife Mary, see Letters 516, n. 4, and 700, n. 20.

2   Hannah Mary Rathbone (1761–1839) was the wife of William Rathbone of Liverpool (see Letter 500), whom she married in 1786. She was the daughter of the quaker ironmaster Richard Reynolds (1735–1816).

3   'Poor Martin' was probably Thomas Martin, until 1797, minister at Great Yarmouth. I have not located the item of ephemera which he evidently produced.

4   Hannah Lindsey omitted the number of miles (approximately six) from Balham to Beckenham.

5   'Our widow friend' was the widow of Christopher Chambers; the parsonage house at Balham was her residence after the death of her husband on 2 Mar. 1803.

6   The price of a quarter of wheat in Middlesex rose from 51s 11d in May 1804 to 66s 10d in Aug. In the same period, the price in England and Wales rose from 51s 7d to 60s 1d, see *Gent. Mag.*, LXXIV, i (1804), 394, ii, 798. On 7 July, *Jackson's Oxford Journal* reported that fifty bakers had been convicted within the previous month for selling bread which was deficient in weight. On the other hand, according to *Cobbett's Weekly Political Register*, 21 July 1804, the price of a quartern loaf fell from 1s in Feb. 1802 to 8d and one farthing in July 1804. Cobbett used these figures to assert that the fall had been the result of a succession of good harvests and not to the Addington ministry's peace treaty with France in 1802. Hannah Lindsey referred to the aftermath of the Middlesex by-election of July 1804, in which Burdett was narrowly defeated; see Letter 763, n. 4.

7   Probably William Bosville; see Letter 724, n. 6.

8   According to *MR*, IX (1814), Richard Reynolds, at his death on 10 Jan. 1814, was in his eighty-seventh year. This is consistent with his recorded admission to St John's College, Cambridge, in 1717 at the age of fifteen; *Admissions to the College of St John the Evangelist. Part III*, pp. 106–7. Hannah Lindsey referred also to the mental state of Mary Catherine Reynolds (see Letter 727, n. 2).

9   Elizabeth Dodson was the widow of Michael Dodson, who died in 1799; after his death she was nominated as a member of the Unitarian Society as a tribute to his memory; Unitarian Society minute book, p. 68. She died in 1811. 'Blue devils' are defined in the *OED* as 'despondency, depression of spirits, hypochondriac melancholy'.

10   Jeremiah Joyce's wife, whom he married in 1796, was Elizabeth, née Harding (1776–1847). In the event, despite this concern over her health, she outlived her husband for more than thirty years.

11 For Mrs Sarah Crompton, see Letter 483, n. 7. Probably her son to whom Lindsey referred was Samuel Crompton (1785–1848), of Wood End, Yorkshire, subsequently MP for East Retford, Derby and Thirsk, and, from 1838, Sir Samuel Crompton, baronet.

12 On 23 Aug. 1804, the *Morning Chronicle* reported the death at Clapham, 'a few days ago', of Mrs Smith, the widow of Samuel Smith, Esq., 'and mother-in-law to Wm. Smith, Esq. M.P. for Norwich'. A similar report appeared in the *Gent. Mag.*, LXXIV, ii (1804), 789. In fact Ann Smith (née Manning, and the widow of Robert Prockter) was the step-mother of William Smith MP, whose father Samuel Smith (1727–98) had married her, as his second wife, in 1772. In her will, proved on 10 Oct. 1804, she bequeathed to William Smith all her plate, her carriage and horses, and to Smith's wife Frances, née Coape (1758–1840), £100 together with household goods; TNA: PRO PROB 11/1416, fos. 249v–251v. See J. Handley and H. Lake, *Progress by persuasion. The life of William Smith 1756–1835* (Hazel Lake, no place of publication stated, 2007), pp. 6–7, 186, 376. Dr Lister was William Lister MD (1756–1830) of Clapham, a physician who, according to his obituary in *MR*, NS IV (1830), 555, was 'a true friend of civil and religious liberty'. He was a subscriber of £50 to Hackney College in 1786; DWL, MS 12.90 (1). Perhaps his appearance belied his age (forty-eight) in 1804. In her will, Ann Smith left him a legacy of £50.

13 This refers to William Urwick; see Letter 761, n. 10. Belsham at this time taught a small number of pupils at his house in Grove Place, Hackney.

14 See n. 1, above.

15 This refers to Thomas Smith and his wife Eliza, of Bownham House; see Letter 700, n. 19.

16 Dr William Blackburne and his niece Sarah.

17 See Letters 747, n. 3, 761, n. 2, and 762, n. 6.

766. **To THOMAS BELSHAM   1 SEPTEMBER 1804

Text: DWL, MS 12.57 (28).
Addressed: To/The Rev^d. Thos. Belsham/Grove Place/Hackney/2p^y Post/
                   Saturday Sep^tr1^st
Endorsed: [By Belsham] Mrs Lindsey ~~July~~ Sepr 1:1804
Postmarked: 4 o'Clock SP 1 1804 E

Note: Although Hannah Lindsey dated this letter 1 July 1804, she altered the date to 1 September on the address page; and the latter date is confirmed by the postmark and by Belsham's endorsement. The date of the death of Timothy Kenrick on 22 Aug. 1804, to which the letter referred, eliminates the possibility of 1 July as the date of the letter.

July [*sic*.]1st 1804
Balam Hill

Dear Sir,

Your last letter brought us ill news, if we may be permitted to use language wch. conveys ill to us, & shocks our feelings and makes inroads upon tender affections. M^r. Lindsey was much hurt by an event so singular & unlooked for: Many die as sudden, not as safe:[1] The loss to his children is irritreviable [*sic*], & to his poor pupils whom by every exertion he was training up to piety and future usefulness as teachers of truth. It is the Lords doing, that is the only consolation: But an instrument so able, zealous and competent will not easily fill his place, & that district will long lament the Pastor & Friend.[2]

Yours is also a great loss in many ways, and on your Sisters account many difficulties may arise: She is so good and excellent that whatever is right to be done, she will do, when the first most painful impressions of this severe blow have a little subsided.[3]

The loss of both M^r. Kenrick & D^r. Toulmin[4] will leave our cause in the West much weakened, but other instruments are in the hands of omnipotent goodness. Your views of this event are so perfect & consolatory that if they could be always acted upon, we should be able to rejoice in all events alike, prosperous & adverse, but this is not to be fully attained to, in our present state.

We shall be truly glad to see you on Tuesday next[5] to dinner at 4 o'clock, but the sooner it suits you to be here, the better we shall like it; and as your old friend M[r]. Ur[w]ick will be out on a journey for a week in Essex, his bed he says is at your service: I do not lament his absence as it gives us more of your company uninterrupted, as the poor man is so odd & dafling (as the Y[r]shire people say) & so misunderstands, & misrepresents, what he hears, that his lady friends are evermore repeating & detailing fiction, not to the advantage of their innocent unoffending neighbors:[6] What mischief this sort of temper occasions: What happiness from the mild candid heavenly mind of old age, in y[r] venerable friend: Whom the older Cadell always called the Apostle John.[7] Yet both have their use in the general system.

We have a very incouraging letter from M[r] Frend as to the French coming, he has been at Dover with M[r]. Bosville,[8] and also visited all the Camps, Barham Downs, Shorn cliff &c saw the Commander in chief very busy, & expending much useless money on inadequate defence.[9] The people all on the coast have not an idea of any attempt being intended: And we rest quite easy as to this matter, w[ch] is now a general bugbear, and imbitters the comfort of many timid persons, till we have notice from the Admiralty that a Landing is effected: M[r]. Lindsey is in his best fashion, hopes to be permitted to meet you so. D[r] B: was sorry he c[d] not stop to speak to y[r] Sister[10] yesterday in the street, desires his Comp[ts] with us to her: Sarah[11] adds hers to you, with the best affec[t] regards of T: & HL

1   This is a quotation from Edward Young, 'The complaint; or night thoughts on life, death and immortality, night the first', line 384. Lindsey had quoted it in his obituary of William Chambers in 1777; see Vol. I, Letter 175.
2   Timothy Kenrick of Exeter died on 22 Aug. 1804. His surviving children included the prominent unitarian minister and scholar John Kenrick (1788–1877).
3   Kenrick's second wife, and from 1804 his widow, was Thomas Belsham's sister Elizabeth (1743–1819). She was the second daughter of Belsham's parents.
4   In Jan. 1804, Toulmin moved from his ministry at the Mary Street general baptist congregation at Taunton to become minister to the New Meeting, Birmingham, where he became the colleague of John Kentish.
5   Tuesday 3 July 1804.
6   A sympathetic obituary of Thomas Urwick gently hinted at some of his eccentricities, noting that 'he maintained a cordial intercourse with those Christians by the progress of whose opinions he too often suffered his mind to be disturbed'; *MR*, II (1807), 216. The Christians to whom the obituary referred were those who denied the divinity of Christ as well as the doctrine of the Trinity.
7   The 'older Cadell', was Thomas Cadell (1742–1802), who retired from his bookselling and publishing business in 1793. His son, the younger Thomas Cadell (1773–1836), inherited the firm and conducted it, at first in conjunction with William Davies (d. 1820), until his death.
8   Probably the reformer William Bosville, see Letter 724, n. 6.
9   The commander in chief of land forces in Britain between 1795 and 1809 was Frederick (1763–1827), duke of York, the second son of George III.
10   Probably this refers to Belsham's unmarried sister Ann (d. 1824), who lived with him in Hackney.
11   Sarah Blackburne, the niece of Dr William Blackburne and the future wife of William Frend.

767. To **ROBERT MILLAR   29 NOVEMBER 1804

Text: DWL, MS 12.46 (51).
Addressed: To/M^r. Robert Millar/Merchant,/Dundee
Endorsed: Lond^o. 29th. Nov. 1804/Mrs Lindsey
Postmarked: NO 30 804   DE 3 1804   Temple

Novr 29th 1804
Essex House

Dear Sir

Many adverse things respecting my own state of nerves has befallen me since your truly welcome letter arrived, wch has made writing most uneasy to me, neither is the debility removed:[1] But as any thing is better to you to conjecture than neglect or indifference of you or your welfare and happiness, I send you this line, to convey our ardent vows for a projected union, so likely to contribute to your greatest human comfort: It is a wise measure & has been brought about with that proper attention & those right dispositions of mind which have marked your conduct thro' life: May Almighty God please to preserve you in this new connection & every thing else.[2]

Mr Lindsey continues as comfortably well as can be expected, and hopes it may please God to restore my ability to write again or rather to indite[?] wch is my greatest defect, not for want of limbs but feebleness of mind. The inability of writing or thinking has been coming on some months: Blisters & cupping has done my speach & head much good, but the nerves of the stomach continue so affected as to make me good for little, except helping my precious Invalid wch is a great blessing to us both.

I can add no more but our best wishes & affec^t prayers, & that if all intercourse must cease in this world we may meet again in that better one where imperfection will be done away.

Y^r sincere friend
HLindsey.

1   This letter from Millar to Theophilus and Hannah Lindsey seems not to have survived.
2   On 26 Nov. 1804 Millar married, as his second wife, Augusta Barclay; she died in 1837, four years before Millar's death; see *Christian Pioneer*, NS, VII (1841), 377.

768. **To ROBERT MILLAR   13 DECEMBER 1804

Text: DWL, MS 12.46 (52).
Addressed: To/M^r. Robert Millar/Merchant/Dundee/N:B
Endorsed: Lond^o 13 Decr 1804/Mrs Lindsey/On my Marriage
Postmarked: Postmark missing.

Decr 13th 1804
Essex S^t.

Dear Sir,

Your letter this Morning[1] shews as usual your affec^t and good, but too depressed and over delicate mind, too much so for the reasonable injoyment of the present life, wch has many blessings if we indeavor to make them such: You see I am yet competent to admonish you to get over useless & painful scrupulosities, which imbitter comfort, make us ungrateful to our bountiful Maker, & abridge the happiness of those connected with us & who have a right to our affections & to feel them: There is no reason to be riotous to injoy life, but to be chearful is of absolute necessity. You talk justly of the example of your invaluable friend, pray follow it, neither age not infirmities have made a mope of him, nor shorten'd his duties; go & do likewise.

The letter from James Ellis is a painful account of our poor friend but not more than we have had before heard, in a catholic country nothing better could be expected as to his burial, & among Pirates his property was sure to be taken, either with or without Law: Similar things are happening every day.[2] James Ellis has his bread to seek again, & cannot help his poor Father, pray give him the inclosed 1 Note.[3] Adieu accept our joint kindest regards to Y^rself & amiable wife & believe us ever y^r sincere f^ds T: HL

---

1 This letter from Millar, presumably written in early Dec. 1804, seems not to have survived.
2 It is most unlikely that James Ellis returned to Britain. Although he was Palmer's principal legatee, he died shortly after Palmer's death and the residue of Palmer's estate passed to Ellis's sisters in Dundee; see *Dundee celebrities of the nineteenth century*, comp. Norrie, p. 13, and Bewley, *Muir of Huntershill*, p. 184.
3 Palmer died on 2 June 1802 and was buried near the shore on the island of Guam, a territory under the control of Spain, a catholic power. In 1804, an American ship conveyed his body to Boston, Massachusetts, where he was re-buried. Probably the reference to the 'inclosed … note' indicates a bank note for Millar to give to the father of James Ellis. Hannah Lindsey placed an indecipherable squiggle (another example may be found in Letter 745) immediately after the figure 1. Probably she meant a £ sign.

769. **To ROBERT MILLAR   n.d., post-7 APRIL 1804

Text: DWL, MS 12.46 (49).
Addressed: To Mr Robert Millar/Dundee
Endorsed: London 1804/Mrs Lindsey
Postmarked: Postmark missing.

Note: This letter could only have been written after the arrival in London of the news of Priestley's death; see Letter 759, n. 3. It is an editorial assumption that it was written towards the end of 1804, shortly after the publication of the two commemorative sermons (n. 1, below) which Hannah Lindsey forwarded with this letter to Millar. Both sermons had appeared before the end of 1804.

Dr Sir

Mr Lindsey sends you the only two Sermons yet published, as it will give you pleasure to see how his Illustrious friend is exhibited.[1]

I am so overplied in writing, in addition to attendance to my dear tottering invalid, that I can only say, that we continue as well as can be expected, and always
                    Y^r sincere f^ds
                    THL

---

1 These were the commemorative sermons for Priestley, published by Belsham and Disney; see Letter 759, n. 6.

770. **To THOMAS BELSHAM   5 APRIL 1805

Text: DWL, MS 12.57 (32).
Addressed: To/The Rev^d. Thos. Belsham/Grove Place/Hackney./Friday
                  5th/10 o'clock Post
Endorsed: [By Belsham] Mrs Lindsey April: 5: 1805
Postmarked: 4 o'Clock AP 5 1805 Penny Post Unpaid 206 Strand

Friday April 5th
[added in pencil] 1805

My dear Sir,

Will you pardon me for suggesting to you after your apparent resolution to decline accepting the afternoon service at Hackney for reasons hon^bl to y^rself, and to set that Society at full liberty: That some of your friends who affect to know your mind & intentions declared as late as yesterday that they were sure of your acceptance, and worse than that, you considered our Trustees as having no claim upon your ingagements to them, and that without a conference or explanation you would determine for yourself: Of this we know you are incapable, but others know you not so well, nor your habits of proceding towards all you are in connection with: And therefore naturally having heard these strange rumors, feel disatisfied at not being previously made acquainted with your wishes. This to me very irksome communication tends only to caution you against any decisive ingagement, but what you are under here, till the matter is truly understood by all parties.[1]

We hope you are busy in forwarding Y^r Sermon, which not merely affects this Congregation, but the world at large who will scan & critisicise [*sic*] what you advance upon entering this theatre of great notoriety.[2]

By a letter from Mr Shore yesterday we find they expect Mr Aspland, who set out as he proposed on Tuesday & sent a letter to a Mr Rolland (I think) one of the Hackney Committee declining all offers from them but through the mediation of M^r. Shore very rightly. His wife & children remain with her Father in town, till his destination is ascertained.[3]

Mr Shore says, "They have just had a great loss at Sheffield Mr Nayler has resigned as their Pastor, & is going to enter into Commercial Business".[4]

He thinks that if Mr Edwards were as steady as heretofore he might suit at Hackney;[5] so has certainly no idea of Aspland at present. He wants to hear of us, but I cannot write whilst things are so unsettled, as he expects the free communications we have always been accustomed to make to him: And of all creatures I can hid[e] nothing wch concerns my known & steady friends. We are in usual health, and in all circumstances your devoted & affe^ct f^ds

T. & HL

---

1   In Mar. 1805, Belsham resigned as minister of the Gravel Pit meeting, Hackney, where he had served as Priestley's successor since 1794, and accepted an invitation from the trustees of Essex Street chapel to become the minister there in succession to Disney. He preached his first sermon as minister of Essex Street chapel on 31 Mar. Theophilus and Hannah Lindsey had been the main promoters of the appointment. However, Belsham's departure from Hackney caused distress to his Gravel Pit hearers, and he hoped initially to remain as the afternoon preacher there even after his assumption of the Essex Street ministry, especially as he still lived in Hackney and did not move into Essex House until the death of Hannah Lindsey in 1812. The Lindseys disapproved of this suggestion as a distraction from his principal commitment and Belsham soon abandoned it. See Williams, pp. 540–54.
2   For Belsham's sermon, see Letter 771, n. 5. 'This theatre of great notoriety' was Hannah Lindsey's ironical description of the theology of Essex Street chapel, which she had helped to forward.

3   In Apr. 1805, on his way to Norton, Derbyshire (see Letter 763, n. 8), Aspland was invited by
    Belsham to preach at the Gravel Pit meeting, Hackney. Shortly afterwards, he was appointed as
    Belsham's successor there. 'Mr Rolland' was probably Francis Ronald of 1, Highbury Terrace, who
    is listed as 'Esq.' in *Holden's triennial directory, 1802, 1803 & 1804*, unpaginated list of 'house-
    keepers resident in London, and ten miles ciruclar'. He was a member of the committee of the Gravel
    Pit meeting, Hackney, and was admitted as a member of the Unitarian Society on 12 Nov. 1801; see
    Williams, p. 549, and Unitarian Society minute book, p. 74. Samuel Shore III, of Norton Hall, had
    been a trustee of Essex Street chapel since 1783.

4   Benjamin Naylor (1761–1846) was minister at Upper chapel, Sheffield, as co-minister (from 1780
    to 1798) and minister (from 1798 to 1805). In 1805, he resigned his ministry and removed to
    Manchester. See Vol. I, Letter 303, n. 4.

5   This is probably a reference to John Edwards (see Letters 608, n. 7, and 758, n. 10). He did not
    become minister at Hackney and in 1806, moved to a congregation at Newport, Isle of Wight. From
    1806 until his death in 1808 he was minister at Crediton, Devon. In the spring of 1805, Robert
    Aspland was still minister at Norton; on 5 May 1805, Belsham preached his farewell sermon at the
    Gravel Pit meeting, Hackney, and Aspland succeeded him as minister there the following month.

771. **To THOMAS BELSHAM   15 APRIL 1805

   Text: Williams, pp. 550–2.

April 15, 1805.

DEAR SIR,

"I do not know when I have suffered more than on Saturday morning by the
communication I made to you, for which I have blamed myself, as nothing official
has past, nor even any personal communication from the Serjeant (Heywood) to Mr.
_____ whom we saw on Saturday night.[1] I hope you have not acted upon such a mere
expression of the *then* mind of *one* Trustee; it would be very wrong and precipitate,
as you are connected with a body of persons.

"I have been an unlucky agent all through this business, by too great eagerness
and injudicious zeal; and I fear have done more harm than good, and am suffering
in proportion: for my diseased sensations admit of no calm reasoning, no principles
becoming a Christian, and the philosophy which belongs to it, 'that there is but
one will in the universe', and that will must take place, and is always for the best.[2]

"If I have not contributed to your unhappiness, or abridged your usefulness, my
first object being to promote both for the good of others, and actively to accomplish
my very excellent husband's wishes, what happens to my individual self is as
nothing.

"Mr. Lindsey is persuaded that something favourable to your views will take
place, when the parties can meet in a fortnight's time and confer; the thing which
has unavoidably been wanting all along in this business; and nothing has been made
plain to you for want of this at an early period. Single and detached representations
are not the proper way to judge and act well, especially on important permanent
points.[3]

"The great satisfaction to us both, and to many, many others, is, that we have
you here; whether single or divided would not grieve us if your happiness, ease, and
usefulness are but promoted. And previous to what has happened, I believed that
your course was as clear and unembarrassed as a human being's could be, connected
with men of long-known liberality, generous minds, and friendly hearts. Of their
legal obligation, to such an extent, I was not aware, as nothing before had called it
into action: your peculiar previous connexion has now made the difficulty.[4] But I
must have done; my weak mind is too much impressed. My pen was only taken up

at your venerable friend's desire to express, in the fullest manner, his delight and entire approbation of your first discourse, which arrived late on Saturday, and which so charmed me in the reading, that eyes and voice, so often faltering, were quite perfect whilst I read your sermon, and which was conned again and again by Mr. Lindsey yesterday.[5] My zeal for *you* and our cause can never suffer but a momentary suspension: it is interwoven into my very nature, and can only cease with the powers of mind or body, or jointly. Our best, cordial wishes and affectionate regards are yours.

T. and H. LINDSEY"

---

1 Samuel Heywood had been a trustee of Essex Street chapel since 1792; 'Mr ___' was probably a committee member of the Gravel Pit meeting, Hackney, perhaps Francis Ronald (see Letter 770, n. 3).

2 By her 'too great eagerness', Hannah Lindsey meant her efforts to secure Belsham's nomination as successor to Disney as minister of Essex Street chapel.

3 The outcome of these consultations was that Belsham relinquished all his ministerial duties at the Gravel Pit meeting and preached his farewell sermon there on 5 May 1805. See Williams, pp. 556–60.

4 The legal obligation of the trustees of Essex Street chapel, stated in the deed of foundation and re-affirmed in the minutes of the trustees on 4 Mar. 1805, was embodied in the stipulation that services at the chapel were to be conducted 'according to the liturgy of the Church of England reformed'. The trustees noted that 'It has been also customary for the Minister to wear such a Gown as is worn by the Ministers of the Established Church'; see Peter B. Godfrey and G. M. Ditchfield, 'The Unitarian Archives at Essex Hall', *Archives. The Journal of the British Records Association*, XXVI, 104 (Apr. 2001), 65–6. Belsham, the successor to Lindsey and Disney, was the first minister of Essex Street chapel to have been educated as a dissenter and to have served as a dissenting minister; this was his 'peculiar previous connexion'.

5 This was Belsham's inaugural sermon as minister (in succession to John Disney) of Essex Street chapel. Entitled *The progress of error concerning the person of Christ. Represented in a sermon delivered at the unitarian chapel, in Essex Street, March 31, 1805* (London, 1805), it was dedicated to the trustees of the chapel and included (pp. 28–9) a warm tribute to Lindsey.

772. **To ROBERT MILLAR   1 MAY 1805

Text: DWL, MS 12.46 (53).
Addressed: To/M^r. Robert Millar,/Merchant/Dundee,/N:B
Endorsed: Lond^o 1 May 1805/Mrs Lindsey
Postmarked: Postmark missing.

May 1st 1805.
Essex House

Dear Sir,

My inability of writing is greatly shortened by a late violent attack of inflamation in my eyes, very prevalent here, called the Egyptian Opthalmia, because imported into this Country by our troops who returned in a truly miserable state of their eyes, & by which many became totally blind:[1] And being communicated to their families, (children especially) has spread about at intervals ever since, & much increased by the cutting East winds: I caught it of a tradesman in the street without having any fear of infection, nor should I have attributed it to that cause, if unfortunately Mr Lindsey had not been afflicted in a few days with the same, to such a degree that he could not see to cut his meat: By blisters to myself & Leeches to his temples we are both getting better, but he yet cannot read, and this privation (besides the pain) has been more grievous than all his other infirmities, as it is his principal source of amusement & comfort. However the absence of this blessing, as it often happens,

& is designed, makes us value it the more. We sympathize cordially with you, & your amiable patient wife in her long illness & rejoice in her amendment, and trust it will please God to restore her to perfect health & comfort for both your sakes: Her youth and the Spring coming on is much in her favor.[2]

As there is no probability of your having what you call an able Minister, we rejoice in the good you are willing, & actually do, and the absence of many when you cannot attend shews a steadiness of Principle highly commendable, and must give you the incouragement your diffident temper wants.

I wish I could send you by a private hand Mr. Belshams inauguration Sermon; it is a capital, short, & satisfactory statement of the "Errors concerning the person of Christ".[3]

The House of Commons have done their duty nobly, and rendered Ld Melville infamous for life in the eyes of all honest men: But there are so many hundreds who partake of similar crimes, and he has so overpowering a friend and patron in our abominable Minister Pitt, that if art, & insolence joined with power can whitewash such villany, this great culprit will be acquitted & brought into office again some where.[4] In every department a like inquiry is wanted, but no substantial good can be done for this poor abused Country whilst we are so governed.

There are three of Mr Lindsey's small pieces now printing by the Unitarian society, which will make a neat Volumn they begin to wonder his works have been so long neglected, who was the original promoter & support of the Society.[5]

But my weak eyes will hold out no longer, in health we are (bless God) as usual: Hope this will find Mrs Millar recruiting, and your gentle spirit soothed which is the sincere wish of hers & your sincere & affec{t} f{lls}

T: & HL.

P.S. I have found & sent you Vidlers bill & receipt.[6]

---

1   A legacy of the Egyptian campaign of 1801; on the day on which Hannah Lindsey wrote this letter, the *Morning Chronicle* carried an advertisement placed by the committee for managing the fund for the relief of the widows, wives and children of the troops killed or wounded in the Egyptian expedition; it was one of many such.

2   For Millar's marriage to Augusta Barclay in 1804, see Letter 767, n. 2. I regret that I have not discovered her age.

3   See Letter 771, n. 5.

4   On 8 Apr. 1805, the house of commons determined, on the speaker's casting vote, that Henry Dundas, Viscount Melville, the first lord of the admiralty, should face charges of corruption arising from his period of office (1784–1800) as treasurer of the navy. He was subsequently impeached before the house of lords and, although acquitted on 12 June 1806, never held public office again. He remains the last person in Britain (to date) to be impeached.

5   On 12 Feb. 1805, the committee of the Unitarian Society resolved that Lindsey's *Conversations on Christian idolatry*, his *Conversations on the divine government* and his *Farewel address* should be reprinted by the society and bound together to form one volume. This was done, and the volume was published in London in 1805. On 6 June 1805, the committee decided to present Lindsey with twenty-five copies; Unitarian Society minute book, pp. 95, 97.

6   On 14 July 1803, the committee of the Unitarian Society appointed William Vidler to sell the society's books and to allow him a discount of 25 per cent on those which he sold; Unitarian Society minute book, p. 89. Vidler had supplied Millar with the society's publications for 1805 and Hannah Lindsey forwarded his receipted bill to Millar.

773. **To ROBERT MILLAR   20 DECEMBER 1805

Text: DWL, MS 12.46 (54).
Addressed: To/Mʳ Robert Millar/Merchant/Dundee/N:B
Endorsed: London 20ᵗʰ. Decr 1806/Mrs Lindsey/Govᵗ Contract
Postmarked: Postmark missing.

Decʳ 20ᵗʰ. 1805
Dear Sir,

I have been using every effort to get proper information, where & how you can apply with prospect of success to Government as a person capable of serving them faithfully & well in the Sail cloth, & Linnen way: But have not been able yet to find the right channel. Mʳ Darch knows nothing at all of that branch no more than ourselves: Every office has its own proper department: Could not you learn from your neighbors who have got shares in Government business, how or to whom they applied, most probably to some Agent who acts by Commission to some of the great Merchants who undertake to furnish these articles, wᶜʰ pass through & are divided into many hands, great Manufacturers imploying others as is the case at Manchester & that district.¹ We think this must be the only way for you to get orders, and get your money in any safe & reasonable time: The Navy board to whom this branch probably belongs, Pay in Navy bills only and at long dates, & difficult often to get payment: So that before the articles get into use, so much interest must be allowed for, that the price is doubled to the Country who pay enormusly [*sic*] for everything, & only the great Contractors get rich.² But let not this discouragement prevent your making efforts to increase Yʳ business as others do, by getting into new channels, & if you can find anybody whom we know, or any of our friends, you may depend upon any assistance or recommendation we can give or procure: Nothing can be done without labor and inquiry.

We have applied to a most worthy intel[l]igent friend who is in the victualing office for any information he can give, & I have delayed writing sooner to you waiting his answer, but he is subject to the Gout, lives at Deptford, and under a vast hurry of business in sending stores out with, & for our army gone to foreign service.³

I write therefore merely to urge you to get all the information you can, and to exert Yʳself to the utmost, & not sit down passive because Mʳ Darch can't help you: I have left no stone unturn'd to try to help you, & several have promised to inquire, who are more in the way of knowledge & business of all kinds than us.

Mʳ B's Sermons & a book you will like to see, have been packed up ever since your letter came, but nobody has called.⁴

Mʳ Lindsey would be obliged by the report of the Last General Assembly: An intimate friend of ours (Baron Masere⁵) has told us of Mʳ Professor Leslies unjust accusation, excited by his superior talents, & eager wish to make him ineligible to the Professors chair in the only way his opponents cᵈ devise.⁶

We both continue as usual, and with best regards & wishes to your good wife and self ever your sincere fᵈˢ

            T: & HL

---

1   The provision of sail cloth was one of Millar's business concerns; he was probably the 'Rob. Miller [*sic*]', listed as a 'linen & Baltic merchant', under Dundee, in Holden's *Annual London and country directory* (3 vols., London, 1811), unpaginated. Lindsey referred to Millar's Russian transactions (conducted presumably via the Baltic) in Letter 723. For Thomas Darch of the admiralty, see Letter 752, n. 9.

2   Navy bills were promissory notes issued by the Navy Board in lieu of cash payments. The Navy

Board itself was an administrative branch of the British navy. It was merged with the admiralty in the naval reforms of 1832.

3   This friend in the victual office was William Joseph Porter; see Letter 602, n. 1.

4   Possibly this refers to the two separate sermons which Belsham published in 1805. They were *The progress of error concerning the person of Christ* (see Letter 771, n. 5); and *Adherence to Christian truth, recommended in a discourse, delivered to the unitarian congregation at Hackney, May 5, 1805* (London, 1805). Possibly the other book was the bound volume of Lindsey's three tracts, commissioned by the Unitarian Society; see Letter 772, n. 5.

5   Francis Maseres (1731–1824), cursitor baron of the court of exchequer from 1773.

6   John Leslie (1766–1832) was elected to the professorship of mathematics at Edinburgh University in Mar. 1805. However, some of his scientific publications led to allegations against him of atheism and to a move in the general assembly of the Church of Scotland in May 1805 to condemn his works and deprive him of his chair. Although this move was narrowly defeated, it reflected the disquiet of the 'Moderate' party in the Church of Scotland over Leslie's advanced theological opinions and his strong political commitment to whiggism. These were the very qualities which endeared him to radical dissenters in England, including Theophilus and Hannah Lindsey. See *Report of the proceedings and debate in the general assembly of the Church of Scotland, respecting the election of Mr Leslie to the mathematical chair in the University of Edinburgh* (Edinburgh, 1805; 2nd edn, 1806). Hannah Lindsey acknowledged receipt of Leslie's *Case* in Letter 774. In 1819, Leslie moved from the chair of mathematics to that of natural philosophy at Edinburgh University. See J. B. Morell, 'The Leslie affair: career, kirk and politics in Edinburgh in 1805', *Scottish Historical Review*, LIV, 1 (1975), 63–82.

774. **To ROBERT MILLAR   19 FEBRUARY 1806

Text: DWL, MS 12.46 (55).
Addressed: To/Mʳ Robert Millar/Merchant/Dundee/N:B
Endorsed: Londᵒ. 19 Feb 1806/Mrs Lindsey/[Word illegible] £105 ---
Postmarked: Postmark missing.

Febʳʸ 19ᵗʰ 1806
London

Dear Sir,

Mʳ Lindsey sends his best thanks for Mʳ Leslie's Case which is curious, & does no credit to those who upon such a frivolous question in the eighteenth Century, can call out such matters into notoriety: Not that Mʳ Leslie was without blame, & will lose estimation by it.[1]

Your parcel was delivered on Sunday was a fortnight during divine service when we were all in the Chapel, the pewkeeper heard the house bell ring repeatedly & went down to Yʳ messenger, who asked for no parcel in return, but demanded half a crown wᶜʰ he recᵈ & went off: I was very sorry that your parcel wᶜʰ has laid ready many weeks missed this messenger: when you send your orders for the books of the Unitarian Society this small thing may come with it, if you mention it to the Secretary Mʳ Joyce:[2] And as you have such efforts to make to keep your little flock together, Mʳ Lindsey begs you will accept of this years Subscription of books to aid & amuse some of your leisure hours.

We cannot help hopeing that the great change in the Administration will be produced of good, by which we mean Peace, after shewing ourselves prepared for War. Nothing but the Providential removal of Mʳ Pitt, could have made way for such a prospect, if we are to be saved at all.[3] We hope also that you & others not benefitted by the War will fare better, and recover some of your losses.

We hear of some comfortable progress in our cause from various quarters, it is at present the grain of Mustard seed, slow in its growth but sure to flourish at last:

Do not be discouraged, your efforts to rouse your sleeping flock was worthy of you; and at least the Shepherd will not be unnoticed by his Master.

By letters from America we are informed that light is springing up by means of an excellent Dutchman, not far from New York banished some years ago from Holland into the Wilderness after making his escape from prison in his wifes cloaths, for the grand fault of seeing more truth than his neighbors: His fine library & all his property not small, was imbezzeled by the friend of his heart; & himself wife & four children has been digging for their daily bread for years, & not yet in ease & comfort, except that which the world, can neither give nor take away: Mʳ Lindsey has known him by name many years, & sent him books and trifling aid: with these he has unceasingly labored to convert those near him, & his piety & virtue has won some very respectable friends, & they others, so that now they have collected a congregation, & found a Minister self-taught by the Scriptures & some of Dʳ P's works, Mʳ L's, & Dʳ Toulmins by whose means this Mʳ Vanderkempt was first known to Mʳ Lindsey, his last letter would delight you to tears: He consoles himself with the hope that we shall all know each other in the kingdom of our great Master.⁴

We go on very well with our excellent Pastor Mʳ Belsham, and trust by the divine blessing upon his pious and judicious labors that some will be inlightened, and many saved from scepticism, & all be called to a holy life: Converts from Calvinism are not wanting, a few will do good especially two young Ministers who were educated at the orthodoxy [*sic*] Dissenting Academy, one has resigned his congregation tho' much beloved by them, as he could no longer hold their creed.⁵

In the East Indies many are becoming Christians from the Hindoos, this a beginning ray.⁶ Even the late changes in Germany has given a preponderance to the Protestant interest:⁷ And the efforts in France to restore the mummery of Popery does not succede: where all are free to worship as they please, & equally patronized by the Government, nonsense & blasphemy must die away.⁸

Be you cheared, look upon the large scale of things, under the benevolent & all powerful Governor, whose councils cannot be frustrated by all the weak & erring creatures who seem to withstand truth & his pure worship: Let us be thankful in having been brought to it.

The inclosed is too true a picture of the late Premier, & meant to ridicule his intended Monument makers.⁹ As a private man we know he had virtues, wᶜʰ. may lessen the crimes of an arrogant & ambitious mind the scourge of this vain & ungodly Nation. Adieu accept our kind best wishes for Yʳself & Mʳˢ Millar, being always

Yʳ affecᵗ fᵈˡ
T: & HL

PS
We are both in tolerable plight as to health.

---

1   See Letter 773, n. 6. By suggesting that Leslie was 'not without blame', Hannah Lindsey probably had in mind his reputed scepticism in religion and the way in which 'personal feuds' had helped to motivate his attacks upon his critics; see Morell, 'Leslie affair', 79–82.

2   The surviving Essex chapel archives, now at DWL, do not permit the identification of the pewkeeper. Jeremiah Joyce was the secretary of the Unitarian Society.

3   Pitt died on 23 Jan. 1806. His administration was succeeded by the 'ministry of all the talents', which consisted of some of Pitt's former followers in coalition with the leading Foxites. Lord Grenville was prime minister and Fox foreign secretary.

4   For Francis Adrian Vanderkemp, see Letter 702, nn. 3 and 4.

5   The reference to Calvinism suggests the possibility that the 'orthodox' dissenting academy was that

of the countess of Huntingdon's connexion, founded at Trevecca, Brecknockshire, in 1768 and based from 1792 at Cheshunt, Hertfordshire. Hannah Lindsey did not identify the two 'converts'.

6   Probably Hannah Lindsey's source of information for this report was Lord Teignmouth's *Memoirs* of Sir William Jones, a work which Lindsey had read; see Letter 762, n. 7. Teignmouth noted (p. 364) the pleasure which Jones would have derived from 'the conversion of the Hindus to the Christian religion'.

7   By 'the late changes in Germany', Hannah Lindsey referred to the Peace of Pressburg (Dec. 1805), following the French defeat of Austria at Ulm and Austerlitz, which deprived (catholic) Austria of substantial territory and led directly to the end of the Holy Roman Empire; see Letter 776, n. 4.

8   In 1802, Napoleon as first consul negotiated a concordat with the catholic church in France, whereby the church hierarchy and parochial system were restored, albeit in a far more limited form than that of the pre-1789 period, and with far more control on the part of the state. The 'Organic articles' which immediately followed the concordat outlined the duties of the clergy and placed very severe limitations upon their freedom of action. Bishops were to be appointed by the state and invested with spiritual authority by the pope. After Napoleon's coronation as emperor on 2 Dec. 1804, there was something of a catholic revival, with a substantial increase in the numbers and membership of confraternities and the re-establishment of some of the female religious orders. Hannah Lindsey based her optimism on the concordat's guarantee of freedom of worship for protestants and Jews, and on the unambiguous and permanent removal of the catholic church's status as the first estate in France, together with the confirmation that there would be no reversal of the confiscation of its lands and other endowments. These developments are set out with admirable lucidity in Aston, *Religion and revolution in France*, ch. 12.

9   This squib took the form of a one-sheet, caustic, denunciation of Pitt's ministries, entitled *An inscription for the proposed monument to Mr PITT, respectfully dedicated to the subscribers to his statue* (London, 1806). It appeared above the name 'Wilks, Inv'. It would have been relatively easy for Hannah Lindsey to enclose a copy in her letter to Millar.

775. **To ROBERT MILLAR   28 JULY 1806

   Text: DWL, MS 12.46 (56).
   Addressed: To Mr Robert Millar/Merchant/Dundee
   Endorsed: London 28th. July 1806/Mrs Lindsey
   Postmarked: Postmark missing.

                                                    London.
                                                    July 28th 1806

Dear Sir,

   Although writing letters is now become very burdensome to me, owing to the increase of diseased nervous sensations from my long sadly diseased stomach which I fear is now become permanent: Yet when I look at your last letter and the painful state you were in, on account of your good wifes illness, & being obliged to leave her with her Sisters at Edinburgh, I cannot help wishing that I had as formerly been able to afford you a little consolation, under these new circumstances of sorrow which her ill health occasioned, and to say how little we are capable of knowing what events will best contribute to our greater comfort, or become fresh trials to our trust and submission to the Will of God.[1]

   Long before this time we hope & believe that Mrs Millar is returned home, and in that health & strength which we wish her: And that you are not in any additional trouble on account of business, rendered more precarious & difficult by the discouraging state of our Country, and the restless spirit, talants [*sic*], and enormous power of our opposite neighbour.

   We have been flattering ourselves of late with a shew of Peace, which M^r. Fox in particular has been laboring to obtain, in the midst of great debility of body by a severe illness:[2] But the News of today that a seperate Peace has been established between France & Russia has overthrown all our hopes, by leaving us alone to contend with France, & depriving this Country of many necessary valuable articles of Commerce which was furnished by Russia, and wch we also furnished to them.[3] Our Enemy is too cunning for us, & means to humble us to his own terms. Happily for the World that there is a wise and good Governor without whose permission nothing can happen either to Nations, or Individuals, and in whose hands every thing will be good finally: And happy are they who look to that only source of consolation.

Your excellent aged friend now in his 84th Year, continues by the divine blessing in comfortable health, although much infeebled in his lower limbs: He can still read, and injoy the society of kind friends; and preserves his tranquil calm mind: Not indifferent to what is befalling the World, or his Country, but not dismayed at the singular events which have taken place in Europe. He is able still to be carried up to Chapel & rejoices in meeting many who revere & love the old Pastor. Our Congregation is very flourishing, and we trust improving in knowledge & Virtue under their able instructor.

We are glad your little Society are not imbroiled in any of the unworthy contests of their angry neighbours about Church-Government, never with Christians worth any strife and all.[4]

We have had a small pamphlet sent from America ascertaining the Institution of a Unitarian Society in the State of New-York, wch. is much opposed & written against by the Orthodox, which may make the cause better known.[5] By information from friends in Essex & Suffolk we are assured our cause gains ground, & that there is nothing but a want of vigor in declaring themselves, that hinders many from openly professing the truth: The Harvest will come when we are all asleep, as the Seed is sowing.[6]

By the inclosed you will see that our Unitarian Society are not idle: A new translation of the New Testament if It can be accomplished will do good.[7]

Adieu we are all out of heart with the next to certainty of losing M^r. Fox in a very short time, and in this critical state of the Country: The Seperate Peace now concluded between France & Russia, has quite made his case hopeless.[8]

Accept the best wishes for you both of everything that is good for you, from Y^r affec^t friends

        T: and HLindsey.

---

[1] This letter from Millar seems not to have survived; his wife Augusta lived until 1837.

[2] Fox was appointed foreign secretary in the 'Ministry of the talents' in Feb. 1806. The illness from which he suffered during the final months of his life was probably a form of dropsy; he died on 13 Sept. 1806. His attempts to negotiate peace with France were unsuccessful, partly because of his over-optimistic assumptions as to Napoleon's pacific intentions.

[3] By 'the news of today', Hannah Lindsey meant the report in the *Morning Chronicle*, 28 July 1806, that a treaty had been concluded between France and Russia. Several London newspapers had raised this possibility on 26 July 1806; see *Morning Post*, and (for a more cautious report about the prospect of peace), *Morning Chronicle*, of that date. In the event, peace between France and Russia was not concluded until the Treaty of Tilsit on 7 July 1807.

[4] Hannah Lindsey referred to disputes with the (established) Church of Scotland between moderates, evagelicals and the 'popular' party over patronage, parochial appointments and the licensing of chapels.

[5] I have not located this pamphlet.

[6] These friends in Essex included William Smith MP, whose country residence was Parndon Hall, near Harlow and Francis Stone, rector of Cold Norton. A friend and correspondent of Theophilus and Hannah Lindsey in Suffolk was William Alexander.

7 Probably the 'inclosed' was a list of the Unitarian Society's publications.
8 See above, nn. 2 and 3.

776. **To CHRISTOPHER WYVILL   8 OCTOBER 1806

Text: NYRO, ZFW 7/2/197/4, Wyvill of Constable Burton MSS.
Printed: Ditchfield, 'Lindsey–Wyvill correspondence', 173 (most of
                 third paragraph).
Addressed: To/The Rev^d. M^r. Wyvill/Burton Hall,/near Bedale./Y^rshire
Endorsed: From The Revd T. Lindsey Oct. 8th 1806
Postmarked: OC 8 [806]

Oct^br 8th 1806

Dear Sir,

M^r. Lindsey wishes me at this first moment of ability to send you his cordial thanks, and congratulations on the contents of your interesting letter:[1] He rejoices in the great satisfaction of mind which must arise from this effort of integrity & testimony to divine Truth: He only prays it may contribute to that temperate Reform in the Church so long wanted, & of which Denmark is now setting a noble example in a Reformation of the established Liturgy now in hand by the Bishop of Soland & Falster, and Commissioners are appointed to revise & improve his plan, to fit it for the Royal approbation before the end of December next. The particulars of this article are to be found in the last "Monthly Repository of Theology & General Literature".[2] Published by Vidler 187 high Holborn.[3]

The changes which Napolian [sic] is making in Germany is a very chearing prospect as to religious tolerance, & a beginning for the emancipation of the human race, hitherto in chains of darkness, which virtuous minds must rejoice in:[4] Many particulars of these changes are also in the above article & we know the integrity of the Editor, who is Mr Belshams successor at Hackney, who has printed an excellent Sermon, on the "fall of eminent men" in which our greatly lamented illustrious statesman is well pourtrayed.[5]

We rejoice in the health & happiness of Y^rself & family, long may it continue & your usefulness in various lines: We are worn out, Y^r venerable friend declines both in body & mind, in a slow & not unpainful way: I have been much afflicted of late with bile & gravel, & this adds much to my worst sufferings diseased sensations which makes writing & everything quite burdensome. But the Will of God must be done, and we would submit with patience & chearful resignation to it: Y^r dear placid friend will I trust wear out under the same mind to the end, and I trust to be supported under all circumstances.

Our united cordial respects & affec^t wishes & prayers are ever yours.

T: & HL.

1 Wyvill sent to Lindsey and to John Disney letters, dated 28 Sept. 1806, informing them of his resignation of the rectory of Black Notley, Essex, where he had been the non-resident clergyman since 1763;
   NYRO, ZFW 7/2/197/2. His letter of resignation to Beilby Porteus, bishop of London, dated 22 Sept.
   1806, may be found in NYRO, ZFW 7/2/189/8. Lindsey had mildly teased Wyvill for remaining a
   parish clergyman (see Letter 494).
2 The *Monthly Repository of Theology and General Literature* is usually known by the first two words
   of its title. The Sept. issue of its first volume (1806), p. 498, carried a short report to the effect that the
   bishop of Soland and Falster, P. O. Boisen, had initiated a programme of reform of public worship in
   the established church of Denmark. Its purpose was the accommodation of the liturgy to 'the liberal
   and enlightened principles of the 19th century'. The report claimed that the reforms were due for

presentation to the king by the end of Dec. 1806. The king of Denmark, Christian VII (1749–1808, reigned 1766–1808), was mentally incapacitated, and the government was in the hands of his son, the future Frederik VI (1768–1839).

3   The *MR* was the successor to William Vidler's *Universalists' Miscellany*. The title page of its first number in 1806 stated that it was printed by C[aleb] Stower, of Paternoster Row, for Longman, Hurst, Rees and Orme, also of Paternoster Row. Caleb Stower (who died at Hackney, aged thirty-seven or thirty-eight, in 1816) was the author of several works on the technicalities of printing; see C. H. Timperley, *A dictionary of printers and printing, with the progress of literature, ancient and modern* (London, 1839), p. 864. He was also a unitarian, and he and William Vidler were admitted as members of the Unitarian Society on 19 Apr. 1804; Unitarian Society minute book, p. 92.

4   In its issue of Sept. 1806 (see n. 2, above), the *MR* included (pp. 477–81) a letter from 'W.H.R.' describing the French-imposed arrangements in Germany following the defeat of Austria in 1805 and the abolition of the Holy Roman Empire in Aug. 1806. It drew attention to the creation of the confederation of the Rhine, praised the secularization of much ecclesiastical property and claimed that, with the overthrow of papal power in Germany, 'universal toleration – a complete and unlimited liberty in matters of conscience and modes of thinking' (p. 477) would follow.

5   Belsham's successor as minister to the Gravel Pit meeting, Hackney, was Robert Aspland, who served there from the summer of 1805 until his death forty years later. Aspland was also the editor of the *MR*. His sermon to which Hannah Lindsey referred was entitled *The fall of eminent men in critical periods a national calamity. A sermon preached at the Gravel-Pit meeting, Hackney, on Sunday, Sept. 21, 1806, on occasion of the recent death of the Right Hon. C.J. Fox* (London, 1806).

777. **To ROBERT MILLAR 10 APRIL 1807

Text: DWL, MS 12.46 (57).
Addressed: To/M^r. Robert Millar/Merchant/Dundee/N:B
Endorsed: Lond 10 Ap. 1807/Mrs Lindsey
Postmarked: Postmark missing.

London April 10th 1807

Dear Sir

You thought right that disease had arrested my pen, and I now write a few night lines with one eye shut & the other dim, owing to a violent attack in my head & face, above two months ago wch from the inflamation being also much on the internal membranes has affected the nerves of my eyes, wch our great Occulists say will in a long time be restored as the sight of the eyes is not essentially injured, and will amend with the strength of my general frame much debilitated: May it please God to grant it, if it be good for me: My precious charge was in his best state during my worse, never so bad as to hinder my helping in his essential wants: But a fortnight ago after a good nights sleep in a moment he quite lost his speech, but was not otherwise affec^t either in body or mind: He now speaks intelligebly [*sic*] & injoys the society of his numerous kind friends. Hopes your labors will not cease altho' an assistance is not likely to be easily found greatly approves y^r advice not to try to make a figure about the place you meet in.

Our money is all expended as the inclosed will shew you on this grand plan of a new Version of the New Testament wch delights Mr Lindsey beyond measure, & the printing will be begun in a fortnight, as we do not doubt of raising the money, wch to finish all well should be 1000£ the first calculation was too moderate.[1]

Adieu I can write no more but thought you w^d like my own story best. May heaven preserve you & Mrs Millar in tolerable health & restore me to that portion wch will best fit me for the favor of God, & let my dear husband gently down, with all his unchangeable good patient & heavenly mind. Of the public there is little to hope but we are all in the hands of omnipotent goodness. Accept always the sincere affec^t regards of

T: &HLindsey

---

1   This work was published as *The New Testament, in an improved version, upon the basis of Archbishop Newcome's new translation: with a corrected text, and notes critical and explanatory. Published by a society for promoting Christian knowledge and the practice of virtue, by the distribution of books* (London, 1808). Probably the 'inclosed' was a prospectus in advance of its publication.

778. **To ROBERT MILLAR   10 AUGUST 1807

Text: DWL, MS 12.46 (58).
Addressed: To/M^r. Robert Millar/Merchant/Dundee/N:B
Endorsed: Lond° 10 Augt 1807/Mrs Lindsey
Postmarked: Postmark missing.

August 10th 1807

Dear Sir

Your letter of the 16th of July arrived a few days ago, & having a favorable opportunity to get a frank by the last Member belonging to our Chapel I coaxed him to write one for you,[1] just to tell you that your aged friend has borne the late uncomon hot weather, & the rain and damp debilitating fortnight since full as well as apparently stouter persons: His health is tolerable, but his limbs & movements with the help of two persons is very feeble indeed. The mind & temper sweet placid & resigned as usual, & his great delight is in knowing that the New Testament copy is going on as expeditiously as the Printer, & such a work can do.[2] Thank you for y^r Subscription of two Guineas towards this work, wch I will advance for you as we take no names without money; and have now in hand 1200: So that you need not fret that your poor flock are not able to add their mite to this good work.[3]

I cannot persuade you to give over repining at your insufficiency & calling for other laborers when none are to be found of our sort: We must patiently wait the Will of the Lord of the harvest & each do the little we can: If the grain of Mustard seed is but sown by you, the reward will be the same to you as if you had hundreds in crowds about you altho' not so incouraging.

We rejoice that you & Mrs Millar are in tolerable health, a blessing not permitted me to injoy altho' I am better as to sight: Indeed my diseased Stomach is not capable of amendment so as to pass one day free from pain & diseased nervous sensations, but my benevolent Maker knows what is best, & I try only to desire that I may not suffer in vain, & that his Will may become mine. The prospect of public affairs is but gloomy, Peace might be had, if there was not such an arrogant mind in our rulers: But we consider this Country as under a judicial Blindness wch leads to the Chastisement we deserve, and final good under the Divine Government will be the result: Under this persuasion we do not dis-quite[4] ourselves: It is thought that matters will be made up with America, their President is a judicious man:[5] When Bonaparte puts in his scikel [*sic*] he will get an end to this presumptious [*sic*] claim of the Sovereignty of the Sea, which is no more ours than the air we breath[e], exclusively.[6]

Pray know you anybody at Bamff, I have a poor woman called Catherine Douglass & want to know if she is really living & in the suffering necessitous state described (by a taylor I believe) of the name of Duff & to whom I send her money: If you have an opportunity to inquire I should be obliged to you.[7]

Our Chapel goes on most prosperously, & well attended by strangers now most of our own people are gone into the Country [for the[8]] Summer. Adieu accept the cordial best wishes to y^{r}self & Mrs Millar of

Y^r sincere old f^{ds}

T: & HLindsey.

---

1 Millar's letter of 16 July 1807 seems not to have survived. The MP who provided the frank (the 'last Member belonging to our chapel') was probably Benjamin Hobhouse; James Martin had retired as MP for Tewkesbury at the general election of May 1807. There is no franking signature on the address page.

2 For the Unitarian Society's *The New Testament, in an improved version*, see Letter 777, n. 1.

3 *The New Testament, in an improved version* did not print a list of subscribers. The preface stated (p. v) that the level of subscriptions had 'far exceeded the most sanguine expectations', but that the subscribers, not seeking 'honour from their fellow creatures', preferred the 'sacrifice of grateful odour to that Being who is witness to all that passes within the temple of the heart' to 'human applause'. Accordingly, they were too modest to wish to see their names in print. In the event, more than £1,200 was raised in subscriptions for the work, including £100 from the duke of Grafton; see Belsham, *Memoirs*, pp. 306–7.

4 I.e. disquiet.

5 Thomas Jefferson.

6 Probably Hannah Lindsey referred here to Bonaparte's attempts to blockade the British Isles and exclude British goods from European ports through his 'continental system', enunciated in the Berlin decree (Nov. 1806) and Warsaw decree (Jan. 1807). Her confidence in British command of the seas, drawing on much eighteenth-century tradition, was enhanced by the British naval victory at Trafalgar on 21 Oct. 1805.

7 I have not been able to identify Catherine Douglass of Banff, although from Letter 779 it is clear that Millar enquired after her, as requested. Successive issues of *Holden's directory* have not revealed a tailor named Duff in that town. Hannah Lindsey's sympathetic interest in Catherine Douglass is evidence of her concern and practical help for the poor, as noted by Catharine Cappe in her memoir of Hannah Lindsey, *MR*, VII (1812), 116–17.

8 At this point two words in the manuscript are overlaid by the seal.

779. ** To ROBERT MILLAR   25 NOVEMBER 1807

Text: DWL, MS 12.46 (59).
Addressed: To/M^r. Robert Millar Merchant/Dundee/N:B
Endorsed: Lond^o 25 Nov 1807/Mrs Lindsey
Postmarked: Postmark missing.

Novr 25th 1807

Dear Sir

I am very sorry that it has not been in my power to write you a line of thanks for your letter & receipt of £2: 2s: 0d for the Testament which we with you hope will be of singular use to inlighten many by a better understanding of the scriptures: It is printed as far as Galatians & will be compleated by early next Year.[1]

We hope that Mrs Millar will go on well, and give you along with a new care a new blessing, and that your good amiable wife will be inabled to perform all the tender duties of a Mother with advantage to her own health. If a Christning [*sic*] should be called for, why not yourself use the form in our Liturgy either in public or private as we do constantly: The Parents standing for the child: With a Certificate of its birth signed by two or three of the persons present at the birth wch is now allowed legal evidence: we have two copies the parents keep one, & the other is registered in a book for the purpose, at Dr Williams Library belonging to Dissenters.[2]

I cannot give you any pleasant account of ourselves: My dear aged invalid grows feeble, but what is worse has short intervals of alienation of mind, very frightful to me, they arise from immovable pressure upon the brain, & have hitherto been removed by cupping and blisters, but this has only been successful for a short time: At all other seasons he is his own happy self, full of love to his great Maker, & the whole human race, & injoys the sight of his many friends who call upon him. The season & my diseased sensations, admit of no relaxation of my nervous sufferings, and the daily & nightly attentions to my excellent husband confines me so intirely to the house & the same scene that I have no remedy, nor chance of alleviation in this life. May I submit with more patience & resignation to the Will of a merciful & powerful Being who alone knows what is best for his frail & erring creatures thro' the course of their existence, & can support them under all circumstances.

Pray does not your headach arise, as it often does from bile, if Y^r bowels are at all dry empty them with any physic you are used to: If the bowels are too much relaxed, warm cordials with bark will do better.

Adieu dear Sir may heaven preserve you & yours, and support us all under the trials allotted to us, painful as many of them are, & fit us at last for his heavenly kingdom is the sincere wish of Y^{rs} & Mrs Millars sincere & affect^t friends

T: & HLindsey.

Thank you for inquiring after Catherine Douglass of Bamff.[3]

---

1   See Letters 777, n. 1 and 778, n. 3.
2   I have not been able to identify this child born to Robert and Augusta Millar in 1807. An edition of Lindsey's revised *Book of Common Prayer* was used as a baptism and burial register for Essex Street chapel during the early years of Belsham's ministry; see George Eyre Evans, 'Essex Street chapel register (1814–1827)', *TUHS*, III, 1 (Oct. 1923), 64. Eyre Evans noted that the title page of the volume was missing, and speculated that it was the fifth edition of Lindsey's *The Book of Comon Prayer reformed*, edited by Belsham and published in London in 1805. He added that the volume was forwarded to the commissioners of registration in 1837. These registers of Essex Street chapel may be found at TNA: RG4/4488 (baptisms, 1814–27; burials, 1814–22), but they do not cover the year of the birth of Millar's child. The service for infant baptism in the fifth edition of Lindsey's *Book of Common Prayer reformed* may be found at pp. 64–71.
3   See Letter 778, n. 7.

---

780. **To SARAH WYVILL   28 DECEMBER 1807

> **Text:**   NYRO, ZFW 7/2/197/13, Wyvill of Constable Burton MSS.
> **Printed:**   Ditchfield, 'Lindsey–Wyvill correspondence', 173.
> **Addressed:**   To/M^{rs}. Wyvill/Burton Hall/near/Bedale/Yorkshire
> **Endorsed:**   From Mrs Lindsey for the Rev^d. Theo. Lindsey Dec. 28th. 1807
> **Postmarked:** DE 28 807

Decr 28th. 1807

Accept for Mr Wyville & yourself[1] our best united thanks for your ample kind supply of Christmas fare which arrived safe.

Mr Lindsey begs his best acknowledgements to M^r. Wyvill for his letter & the Bishops answer: The resignation was a right step for him to take & will satisfy his own mind, whoever approves or not.[2]

The Prosecution of Mr Stone for his Visitation Sermon however injudicious in the subject,[3] will do no credit to B^p Porteus nor, the way bitter & unjust in wch the

Court carries it on:[4] His letter to the B[p] just published is written with an excellent temper, & the reasoning will not easily be refuted: it is printed by Eton Bookseller 187 High Holborn & is well worth reading: Their object can only be to beggar a conscientious (tho' too hasty man) with nine children.[5]

Miss Blackburne[6] intended to send her thanks to Miss Wyvill[7] for her very kind letter, & to have saved my half blind eyes, but she is called out upon business. We were glad to find that in a short time you will all be in town, and if it please God that M[r] Lindsey should be spared till then, to shake his dear friend by the hand will give him as much pleasure as his now debilitated mind permits. I cannot boast of either bodily or mental strength, but God knows what is good for us all. Accept of our best cordial wishes to M[r] W: Y[r]self & the dear happy groupe of children f[t] Y[r] obliged T: &HL

1   Sarah, née Codling, was the second wife of Christopher Wyvill.
2   Wyvill forwarded to Lindsey, Disney and Samuel Shore the papers relating to his resignation of the rectory of Black Notley in 1806; his letter to Lindsey, dated 14 Dec. 1807, is in the possession of Mr George Cockman and I am grateful to him for providing me with a copy. For the correspondence between Wyvill and Beilby Porteus, bishop of London, over this matter, see NYRO, ZFW 7/2/1971–6. Although relinquishing his living, Wyvill did not resign from the church.
3   Francis Stone's visitation sermon was published as *Jewish prophecy, the sole criterion to distinguish between genuine and spurious Christian scripture; or, an humble attempt to remove the grand and hitherto insurmountable obstacles to the conversion of Jews and Deists to the Christian faith, affectionately submitted to their serious consideration: a discourse preached before the Rev. Dr. William Gretton, archdeacon of Essex, at his visitation holden at Danbury, on Tuesday, the 8th of July, 1806* (London, 1806, with a second edition later in 1806, and a third edition in 1808).
4   Stone was rector of Cold Norton, Essex, from 1765 until his deprivation in 1808. As a result of his visitation sermon (n. 3, above), he was prosecuted in the bishop of London's consistory court on 13 May 1808. He was sentenced to deprivation of his living unless he withdrew his views, which he declined to do. His appeal to the court of arches was unsuccessful. The bishop of London from 1787 until his death on 14 May 1809 was Beilby Porteus. For Lindsey's sceptical comments on Stone's pamphlet, *A call to the Jews* (1783), see Vol. I, Letters 267 and 268.
5   This work was Francis Stone's *A letter to the Right Rev. Dr. Beilby Porteus, on the subject of his citation of the writer before the spiritual court; on an unfounded charge respecting certain doctrines contained in his visitation discourse, preached before Dr. Gretton, archdeacon of Essex, at Danbury, July 8th, 1806* (London, 1807). The publisher was Caleb Stower (see Letter 776, n. 3) of Paternoster Row, for David Eaton, of 187 High Holborn. On his death in 1813, Stone left a widow, Ann Stone, and, according to his will, eight children; TNA: PRO PROB 11/1554, fo. 207r.
6   Probably this was Sarah Blackburne, the daughter of Francis Blackburne of Brignall and niece of Dr William Blackburne; she married William Frend on 16 Jan. 1808.
7   Probably Elizabeth-Anne Wyvill (b. 1789) the eldest daughter of Christopher and Sarah Wyvill.

781. *To RUSSELL SCOTT   8 MARCH 1808

Text: Scott Coll.
Printed: McLachlan, 'Lindsey to Scott', 125–6 (entire letter except the opening words of the first paragraph).
Addressed: [To] Russell Scott/[Ports]mouth
Endorsed: March 9 –
Postmarked: MR 8 808

Note: A few sections of this letter are obscured, possibly by ink. These sections are indicated by square brackets, and an indication of the number of words which are probably missing, or the probable words themselves, are inserted.

March 8ᵗʰ 1808

My dear Sir

In compliance to [your] request of hearing from me, I write [three words obscured], being so unwell from disease in [two words obscured] head, owing to my long stomach disease [word obscured] that writing a letter goes nearly beyond the ability now left to me, altho' by a blister upon the head I am somewhat better than last week: I feel this increased incapacity the more, as I can less help my precious invalid, but Gods Will is best for us all. His feebleness increases but he still continues to have pleasure in seeing his friends who call, & in general injoys his own placid & angelic mind, except towards evening when a painful irregularity of ideas makes him want to go to his own house, & blames me for his confinement: This is only cured by going to bed & having a mild opiate draft wᶜʰ keeps him quiet happily all night, a great blessing to us both: Cupping has now ceased to remove this wandering as it used for a Month or more but the arterial system is yet so strong that his head must be emptied to prevent worse. My diseased sensations are now constant & add mainly to other trials, but I mean not to complain but to submit: Yʳ Brothers is a more lamentable case & you had nothing to lose.¹

We admire & applaud Yʳ zeal about the New Testament, the copy is finished, & the small Edition put to the press, we want more money, but shall not stop:² The good Duke of G: has given another 50£ to that before.³ Adieu may heaven support & bless you & yours, & make the trials of this life contribute to that wᶜʰ is to come: So prays yʳ affecᵗ fᵈ

HLindsey.

My dear Niece Miss Blackburne is married to Mʳ Frend, a union to our hearts content, & they live near us, at the [Rock] Assurance Office of wᶜʰ he is Actuary in Bridge Street.⁴

---

1 Russell Scott's only surviving brother in 1808 was Samuel Scott (1753–1836), Russell Scott's senior by seven years. Possibly Hannah Lindsey referred to Scott's brother-in-law John Taylor, Scott's brother-in-law, who died in 1817, and whom Lindsey had regarded as 'lost' as far as unitarianism was concerned since as least 1791; see Letter 445, n. 5.
2 For the different editions (two-volume octave and four-volume duodecimo) and the small (pocket) editions of the unitarian New Testament, see Issitt, *Jeremiah Joyce*, p. 85
3 The duke of Grafton.
4 See Letter 780, n. 6.

782. **To THOMAS BELSHAM   20 AUGUST 1808

Text: DWL, MS 12.57 (33).
Addressed: To/The Revᵈ. Thoˢ. Belsham/at Thoˢ. Smith's Esqʳ./Easton
                 Gray/near/Tetbury
Endorsed: [By Belsham] Mʳˢ Lindsey Augᵗ 20: 1808
Postmarked: AU 20 800

Saturday/August 20ᵗʰ./1808

My dear Sir,

Thanks for your letter: Miss Belsham¹ had informed us of yʳ arrival at Exeter & of the good health & spirits of yʳ excellent Sister, we lament her increased deafness:² Mʳ Lindsey could spare her some of his acute hearing wᶜʰ is more than usual: He is less able even to be led about, but his health not impaired since you saw him, but you will see a change at yʳ return from a diminution of chearfulness wᶜʰ has taken place after a long heavy sleep of 13 hours wch alarmed both me & even M^rs. Cappe, whose mind like that of my precious charge is full fraught with placidity & hope: He was waked gently & in the full possession of his mind & has so remained.

We trust you are injoying y^rself in perfect health with your most amiable friends M^r & Mrs Smith, to whom in their new situation we wish every blessing that virtue and a useful life can bestow in this first stage of Being.[3]

At last we have heard of the Frends by a letter from my Brother Blackburne who speaks capitally of the health & activity of his visitors especially of Mrs Frend & intimates that they are beginning to look Southward, wch I am glad of on Mrs Cappes account to whom the heat & damp has done no good with her rheumatic frame.[4]

We were delighted yesterday with a message we rec^d from the Duke of Graftons Porter by a letter he had just rec^d from Whittlebury from his brother. "The Duke he says had not been 24 hours here, before we saw a change for the better, he is now so far recovered as to ride on horse back three or four hours every day."[5]

Mrs Cappe begs her respects & thanks for your account of Madge. Hopes he will cease to incur debts he cannot pay, as his relation has two heirs already & may have two more to exclude all ideas of his own Heirship.[6]

We have not one of our usual kind visiting friends left in town, & should be quite solitary but for Mrs Cappe, and Dr Blackburne when he is at leisure to eat our dinner, now at 3 o'clock as Mr Lindsey grows very languid for want of food by that hour, & if he eats anything before it spoils his best meal.

There was a moderate congregation on Sunday morning last, but so many ask Robert & send here to inquire if you will be at home, that we shall be thin enough by the time you return.[7]

I hear that Mr Edward Foss is got much better:[8] Also that there has already been 8 Candidates talked of for Princes Street.[9]

All the town divines are gone, and nobody but poor Davies the schoolmaster to supply.[10]

Mr Eton has a violent swelled face & is under the operation of a blister.[11]

Of myself I shall say nothing, neither body nor mind are at ease or tranquillity: May the discipline be effectual for brighter scenes.

Adieu pray write again, and in the days of absence believe you have our best wishes & the most affec^t regards

of Y^r ever affec^t f^ds

T: and HL

1 Ann Belsham.
2 This is a reference to Belsham's older sister Elizabeth, the widow of Timothy Kenrick of Exeter. She died in 1819.
3 For Thomas Smith and his wife, see Letter 700, n. 19. Their 'new situation' signified their removal from Bownham House, near Minchinhampton, to Easton Grey, near Malmesbury; see *MR*, XVII (1822), 514.
4 Mrs Frend was Sarah Blackburne, the grand-daughter of archdeacon Francis Blackburne and the niece of Dr William Blackburne; 'my Brother Blackburne' was Hannah Lindsey's half-brother Francis Blackburne, rector of Brignall. The newly married Frends were staying with him and his family in Yorkshire before their return 'southward'.
5 This probably refers to the brother of Grafton's porter; the duke's only brother to survive childhood, Charles Fitzroy (1737–97), Baron Southampton, died on 21 Mar. 1797. For Whittlebury, Northamptonshire, see Letter 754, n. 4.
6 For Thomas Madge, see Letter 758, n. 4. His 'relation' was the surgeon Thomas Hugo, of Crediton, who died in that town 'at an advanced age' on 9 Feb. 1844; *Gent. Mag.*, NS, XXI, i (1844), 329. In his will, dated 9 Dec. 1843, he bequeathed his property to his four sons and his daughter, and made

no mention of Madge; TNA: PRO PROB 11/1995, fos. 66r–69v. Possibly he disapproved of Madge's commitment to unitarianism; from 1804 to 1809, Madge was a student at Manchester College, York, training for the unitarian ministry. See the entry for Madge by Alan Ruston in *ODNB*, XXXVI, 84–5.

7   Hannah Lindsey presumably meant that there had been a moderately sized audience at Essex Street chapel on the previous Sunday (14 Aug. 1808). Robert was presumably a servant of Theophilus and Hannah Lindsey, or a servant of the chapel.

8   Possibly Edward Foss of Gough Square, London, who is listed as a member of the Revolution Society in 1790; BL, Add. MS 64814, fo. 62v.

9   In the summer of 1808, Thomas Jervis, who had been minister to the dissenting congregation at Princes Street, Westminster, since 1796, became the minister of Priestley's former chapel at Mill Hill, Leeds, where he succeeded William Wood. His successor at the Princes Street congregation was Pendlebury Houghton, who served there from 1808 to 1811.

10 Possibly David Davis (1745–1827); see Letter 703, n. 4.

11 This is a reference to David Eaton.

UNDATED LETTER

783. *To THOMAS CADELL   **14 SEPTEMBER**[1]

> **Text:**   JRUL, English MS 370, fo. 76.
> **Addressed:**   [In Hannah Lindsey's hand] Mr Cadell/Strand
> **Endorsed:**   There are several columns of figures, evidently monetary
>   calculations, on the address page.

Mr Lindsey presents his Comp^{ts}. to M^r. Cadell, and begs to pay for the books wch. have been so long detained by his absence in the North, and which he has also promised to bestow on a friend to whom they will give both amusement & information.

    Essex Street Sep^{tr} 14th

Absence from town prevented this being done last week.

---

1   I owe my awareness of this letter to the kindness of Dr David Wykes. The only clues as to its date are 14 Sept. and the fact that it was sent from Essex House, which indicates that it must have been written in or after 1778. It must also have been written in a year during which Lindsey had visited the north of England, which he did in approximately half the years between 1788 and 1799 inclusive. The implication, however, is that the recipient of the letter was Thomas Cadell, senior, who relinquished his publishing firm to his son in 1793. Probably, therefore, the letter was written between 1778 and 1793.

APPENDIX I

LETTERS OF THEOPHILUS LINDSEY FROM 1747 TO 1788 NOT INCLUDED IN VOLUME I

69.   To WILLIAM TURNER OF WAKEFIELD   10 NOVEMBER 1770

Text:	DWL, MS 12.57 (1) (copy).
Printed:	Rutt, I, 72 n. ‖ (fourth and fifth paragraphs).
Addressed:	Address missing.
Endorsed:	(Lindsey to Turner S^{nr}) (Ex. VII. 14. 30)
Postmarked:	Postmark missing.

Note: The letter is copied on to the blank reverse of a printed sheet; the latter is headed 'Draft of Proposed Resolutions' concerning a public subscription for Mr Buckingham's 'commercial intercourse with the countries of the Eastern World'.

Note for Volume II. In Vol. I, only the first section of this letter was published, since the editor was not then fully convinced of the accuracy or authenticity of the remaining section could be guaranteed. These reservations overcome, the full text of the letter is reproduced here; the section omitted from Vol. I appears below the broken line.

Catterick Novr. 10 1770

Dear Sir

I was much gratified, by your letter of Sepr. 10, which Mr Zouch[1] was so good, as to send up from the inn in our village,[2] & I found upon my return that morning from a ride out. I was told he did not make any stay in Catterick.

A worthy & learned acquaintance, such as you describe, & I believe this gentleman to be, would be a desirable acquisition; but the distance of fifteen miles puts us quite out of each others neighbourhood, &, I suppose, he will be much confined, as he has already one pupil, & it is reported is to have one or two more in his house with him.[3] However, I may, probably have the pleasure of meeting him at Mr Archdeacon Blackburne's, where he has been several times; and Richmond, being his market town, my wife's mother has had several little commissions to do for him. Mr Blackburne also, & his eldest son[4] went over, about a fortnight ago, to induct him, & stayed to dinner with him.[5] He is well spoken of by every one, as a scholar, & a gentleman, but the report also is, that he is most thoroughly orthodox, both in church & state, which account does not seem much to differ from another sent to me.

His sister, I am sure, from description, must be a most amiable & deserving person;[6] though one is sorry to see the good influence of such a character locked up by such narrowness; but these are a misfortune, not a fault, in most cases. And how rare to see any one forego an advantage, out of religious principle, like this lady.

Your letter announced to me our friend Dr Priestley's piece on church discipline, which I have since received from him, & like many things in it, but, as I have told him, there are others, that might have been either left out, or altered for the better.[7] I do not, at present, think it will become the subject of much controversy, as real, practical religion, to which his plan of discipline leads, is not much an object at present, &, I suppose, the great part will not be forward to attack an author, who has already shewn himself so ready, & so able to give an answer when called upon.[8]

But, however called out, I hope he will not be prevailed on wholly to cashier the religious observance of one day in seven.[9] Its observance is low enough, already in the nation. Others wish it were more attended to. I must own, I never met with any parish or family, that had any real religion, where this day was spent as other days, the attendance on public worship excepted. As to the morality of such an observance, all must allow, that much may be said for it, if much may be said in disproof of it, from ye Bible.

I know not whether you have heard of an affair at Cambridge, which makes some noise, & is likely to have some good consequences, I hope. You are at liberty to mention the matter, without naming your author.

M^r. Jebb, formerly Fellow of Peter-house, but lately married & settled in the University, where he had many pupils whom he assisted in their academical Studies, & others, to whom he explained the scriptures of the N. Testament.[10] This gentleman, having occasion, the last year to go to the AB.P of Canterbury, for a dispensation, to hold two little contiguous preferments in Suffolk, his constant residence in the summer, found that there had been an accusation preferred against him to the ABP as a teacher of heresy in the University; his accuser, the worthy & orthodox B^p of Gloucester;[11] the bishop's informer unknown or unnamed. The ABP, upon hearing M^r. Jebb's defence, & his engaging to send his Grace a sketch of his plan of lecturing, gave him the dispensation he desired.[12]

Soon after his return to Cambridge, M^r. Jebb sent the promised plan, (an admirable one, I once had a sight of it,) to the ABP. who sent no note of his disapprobation. But, being prevailed upon to send it also to his Diocesan the pious bishop of Norwich, his Lordship sent word to him, that, though no heresy in the plan sent him, he might teach heresy from it, & therefore M^r. Jebb must justify himself to the University, i.e. to Dr Rutherforth &c &c his most violent enemies.[13]

Here the matter rested, during the vacation, till lately, that the Arabic professorship being vacant, M^r. Jebb, who had been long encouraged to offer himself for it, found that this accusation of heresy had hurt him with many of the Heads, who had been before willing to give him their votes. Upon which, he wrote to the B^p. of Gl___r to know the particulars of his crime, & who were his accusers; & also wrote at the same time, to y^e ABP.[14] But his letters written with great freedom, were so resented, that it is said, it is determined to make him feel their resentments, & particularly to hinder his continuing his lectures. A letter, the last post, told me that his Diocesan had ordered him to residence upon his living. But a letter from Cambridge to-day, says, he has already got four pupils to attend him, & proposes to open his lectures very soon. As far as I can judge or learn from others, such excellent lectures, on a plan so scriptural, were never read in ours, scarce in any University.[15] But, I fear this will succeed in demolish [*sic*] [gap: at least two words missing] gentleman, as they did the excellent [gap: at least one word missing]. The B^p. of Gl. is all in all with the Minis[?try] [gap: at least two words missing] Mansfield his patron, whom he has [gap: at least three words missing] is determined to carry him to the head [gap: at least two words missing] church.[16] And L^d. M___ ld [MS torn: word missing] do wha[t] [gap: at least two words missing] at present. Excuse the haste in which I am obliged to write this. My wife thinks herself much honoured by, & happy in the least testimony [word illegible] of your approbation. She joins with me in sincere regards to M^{rs}. Turner & yourself, with every good wish for your two fine boys.[17]

I assure you, Sir, I think myself honoured in the appellation, & therefore shall gladly subscribe myself, with a most sincere esteem

Your affectionate brother & most humble servant

T. Lindsey

For The Rev^d M^r. Turner, Wakefield

---

1 Thomas Zouch (1737–1815), clergyman and antiquarian, educated at Trinity College, Cambridge, and rector of Wycliffe, on the river Tees in the north riding of Yorkshire, 1770–93. Wycliffe is approximately ten miles from Catterick. The usual number of his pupils at any one time was three.

2 Possibly the George Inn at Catterick Bridge.

3 I.e. Thomas Zouch.

4 Francis Blackburne, at that time of Peterhouse, Cambridge; he became a fellow of St Catharine's College in 1772 and vicar of Rudby, Yorkshire, in 1774.

5 Zouch was inducted at Wycliffe in October 1772.

6 Zouch had two surviving sisters in 1770, namely Elizabeth Dorothea (d. 1792), the wife of William Graeme of Halifax, and Anne, the wife of Sir William Lowther, rector of Swillington, Yorkshire.

7 Joseph Priestley, *A free address to the protestant dissenters, on the subject of church discipline; with a preliminary discourse concerning the spirit of Christianity, etc* (London, 1770).

8 On 4 Nov. 1770, Priestley wrote to Lindsey 'I am glad you approve of anything in my *Essay on discipline*, notwithstanding the faults that I doubt not you justly find with it': DWL, MS 12.23, fo. 23.

9 Priestley's *Free address to the protestant dissenters*, pp. 22–3, condemned what he believed was the 'pharisaical' observation of the sabbath in some quarters, and argued that Sunday observance from mere habit not only diminished respect for the Sabbath itself but also lessened 'the power of conscience in general'.

10 John Jebb married Ann Torkington (1735–1812) on 29 Dec. 1764.

11 The bishop of Gloucester from 1760 until his death in 1779 was William Warburton. Jebb's 'two little contiguous preferments in Suffolk' were the rectory of Homersfield and the vicarage of Flixton, both near Bungay, Suffolk.

12 See Anthony Page, *John Jebb and the enlightenment origins of British radicalism* (Westport, CT, and London, 2003), p. 60. The archbishop of Canterbury from 1768 to 1783 was Frederick Cornwallis.

13 For Jebb's plan for reform of the educational system at Cambridge, see Page, *John Jebb*, pp. 130–5. The plan included a broader intellectual curriculum, reflecting Jebb's reading of Locke and Hartley, together with annual examinations. It aroused opposition on the ground that it would infringe the autonomy of the colleges as well as promote heresy. The bishop of Norwich from 1761 to 1783 was Philip Yonge, Jebb's diocesan. Thomas Rutherforth (1712–71) was regius professor of divinity at Cambridge from 1756 until his death on 5 Oct. 1771.

14 The professor of Arabic at Cambridge from 1678 to 1770 was Samuel Hallifax, who resigned the office in the latter year on his nomination as professor of civil law in the university. His successor was William Craven (d. 1815), who held the professorship of Arabic from 1770 to 1795; he was master of St John's College from 1789 to 1815.

15 Joseph Price, vicar of Brabourne, Kent, a 'ten-year man' at Peterhouse during the 1770s, recorded much academic gossip about Jebb in his diary. He noted that Jebb's lectures 'had made so much noise, and he had been charged with propagating Socinianism and Fatalism', that Warburton 'complained to the Archbishop of Canterbury of the strange notions advanced by Jebb, and said, what was worse, he was countenanced by one of the Bench, meaning Law'. See *A Kentish parson: selections from the private papers of the Revd Joseph Price, Vicar of Brabourne, 1767–1786*, ed. G. M. Ditchfield and Bryan Keith-Lucas (Stroud, 1991), p. 71. Edmund Law was bishop of Carlisle and master of Peterhouse, Jebb's college.

16 Although Warburton was on friendly terms with William Murray, from 1756 baron, and from 1776 earl of Mansfield, lord chief justice of the court of king's bench from 1756 to 1788, he owed his promotions to Thomas Pelham, duke of Newcastle, and Philip, 1st earl of Hardwicke.

17 The wife of William Turner of Wakefield was Mary, née Holland (1724–84); his two sons were William Turner of Newcastle, Lindsey's friend and correspondent, and his younger brother John Turner (1765–1816).

89. To JOHN JEBB   **MAY 1772**

>   **Text:**   DWL, MS 12.58 (20) (copy)
>   **Printed:**   Joyce, 'Brief account', 447.

Note: In this letter, although only a brief extract survives in print and the manuscript not at all, Lindsey evidently berated Jebb for disparaging the dissenters for what he perceived to be their lack of support for the clerical petition. Writing to Thomas Belsham on 2 Dec. 1808, less than a month after Lindsey's death, Jeremiah Joyce noted that his 'Brief account' of Lindsey in the *MM* had provoked a complaint from Jebb's widow Ann, to the effect that Jebb 'ever entertained the smallest prejudice against the Dissenters'. Joyce added 'I shall answer her by Mr Lindseys own letter to Mr Jebb: in which he writes', and gives the extract from Lindsey's letter set out below. The manuscript of the letter, which was evidently in Joyce's possession, appears not to have survived. It was probably the same letter as that from Lindsey to Jebb in May which Joyce quoted in the 'Brief account', 447 (Letter 89), in which Joyce noted that Lindsey vindicated the dissenters from Jebb's criticisms. The extract below should probably have been included in Volume I, Letter 89. The words in square brackets are Joyce's.

You injure them exceedingly, let who will whisper to the contrary, in believing that the Dissenters have not been our most active friends from the first of our affair. To my certain &c &c [see Memoir. Farther on he says] I beg you will correct this great error, for a great one it is &c &c

155. To WILLIAM TURNER OF WAKEFIELD   12 DECEMBER 1775

In addition to the text in Lindsey's hand printed in Volume I, pp. 219–21, there is a copy of this letter in DWL, MS 12.57 (39).

244. To WILLIAM TURNER OF WAKEFIELD   2 APRIL 1782

In addition to the text in Lindsey's hand printed in Volume I, pp. 352–3, there is a copy of this letter in DWL, MS 12.57 (40).

374A. To NEWCOME CAPPE   **n.d. 1788**

>   **Text:**   DWL, MS 12.57 (41) (copy)
>   **Addressed:**   Address missing; the letter carries the endorsement
>   'Endorsed/To Mr Cappe, about 1789. Literary Works'/Ex^d.
>   xi.3.36'

Note: The original manuscript of Lindsey's letter appears not to have survived. Although this copy is endorsed '1789' on the first page, internal evidence indicates that the letter was written in mid-July 1788. Its place, therefore, is between Letters 374 and 375, and is here numbered 374A. The references to Frend's letters in the press, and Kipling's attack, may be found in Volume I, Letters 373 and 374. One suspects that the copyist used the comma on a more extensive scale than did Lindsey.

Dear Sir & my much esteemed friend,

By the signature which convey[s] this, you will perceive that our friend, whom you apprehended a month ago, to have been leaving this town, has not yet turned his back upon it. Indeed, not being disposed to attend to business, nor, strongly to anything, as the season has been pleasant, the parliament sitting, & many acquaintance remaining he has amused himself, agreeably enough, & now that almost every one is decamping, he would have marched off, I believe, this week, but for a little indisposition of Mr Lee's, which, however, will not prevent their departure the next week.[1] Sometimes, he appears perfectly well, but flags a little, at others, Saturday, for instance, & Sunday, when our weather was quite sultry, he was not so well, but, to-day, is recruited, again.

I had a very singular satisfaction, in the degree of approbation, with which you spoke of the Vindiciae; but was more pleased, with the just remarks you made, on what was not so correct, as it ought to be, or might be amended. The *Reasonableness of Christianity*, certainly, should not have been so indiscriminately commended, nor, perhaps, the *Theory*, though, in the last edition of all, it has undergone many corrections, & been made much less exceptionable.[2] And I would certainly make some limitation, with respect to the former, should the piece come to a new edition and, though not with an *immediate* prospect, yet with some hope of that, I should take it as a favour, to receive any remarks, with respect to stile or matter, which you made, in running[?] it over.[3]

Your would see, about a fortnight ago, M[r] Frend of Cambridge's statement of his case, in contradiction to some misrepresentations of it, which I was the means of handing to the press for him.[4] You would, also, see, in the Morning Chronicle last week, in the Whitehall Evening Post, & perhaps in other papers, a most curious account of the low, abusive insults, & accusations of D[r] Priestley, in particular, by the deputy Divinity Professor, D[r]. Kipling, at the late Commencement, at Cambridge,[5] D[r]. Edwards, who writes the letter, is the son of a gentleman of the same name, who some years ago, published a valuable pamphlet, on irresistible grace &c.[6] He is married, but still continues a member of the University, & lives in the town; is most liberal, & of a noble independent spirit, & one of the great supports of a good cause against the powers of the world in that University.[7] *Hints* &c to *the New Association*, by a Layman, which has been sent me, by the unknown author, shews that there are serious members of the Established Church, who are in earnest for a reformation, however the Heads of it oppose it.[8] I am told that the small tract, well drawn up, *A Letter to the Bishop of London, on the abolition of Slavery*, is by M[r]. Holmes master of Scorton School, who, with a growing family of 8 or 9 children can accept of no church-preferment to mend his situation.[9]

The closing number of the Theological Repository is intended to be published, the beginning of August. It will contain three pieces of D[r]. Priestley's, which I have seen & much like. An answer to Eubulus, on the Sabbath; Some reply to the abuse of the late M[r]. Taylor, Ben Mordecai's son, in the preface to his father's posthumous work, published, a few months since; & a concluding short, but seasonable address, to the public; with a word to M[r]. Gibbon, with which you will be much pleased.[10]

I presume ere this, you will have seen the first number of the Analytical Review.[11] We are much displeased with a paragraph, in the review (too diffuse) of Rutherforth's work, which could only come from an unbeliever, relating to the history of Saul. D[r]. Priestley has been reported to have, but really has nothing whatsoever to do with the work.[12] I know none[?] concerned, but M[r]. Christie of Montrose, who has the Unitarian congregation, & who is the author of the first article, the very sensible & learned account of De Rossi's collations.[13] I think, also, I have heard, that D[r]. Beddowes, a very sensible able man has engaged to give an account of some things, as his leisure serves, relating to natural philosophy. He is chemical professor at Oxford, & a friend of D[r] Priestley.[14] I might have been able to have given you, a full & exact account, if I had lately seen young Christie, but he [is][15] so busy & studious, & I have been so occupied, that we have not, I believe, of these two months.[16]

M[r]. Bruce has been in town. His Memoirs are said to be printed, & wait, only, for the plates, to be laid before the public, but these will not be ready before the winter.[17] There is such great delay, as M[r]. Cadell tells me, in sending every sheet, to D[r]. Campbell to be corrected, that his work could not, possibly, be ready, this year.[18] Hardly any bookseller, besides, could have procured such a succession of franks to send each sheet, & members, here to whom they might be conveyed back.[19]

I have not been wanting to procure you Jones on the Canon of Scripture, though, hitherto, without success.[20] If you are in immediate need of it, the loan of my copy is much at your service.

I hope your rheumatic complaint is relieved. I have been a fellow-sufferer, that way, for a weak [*sic*] past, but not in a very great degree. I beg my best respects to M[rs] Cappe, & compts & good wishes to all your family, but, particularly, to be remembered to M[r]. Cappe, if he be with you, or when you write to him.[21]

I am, always, your obliged &affectionate

      T. Lindsey

---

1   Mary Lee and her husband John Lee, MP.

2   In his *Vindiciae* Lindsey had praised John Locke's *The reasonableness of Christianity, as delivered in the scriptures*, which was first published in 1695 as an 'admirable tract' (p. 37). He also expressed admiration for Edmund Law's *Considerations on the theory of religion* and for its author (pp. 258–60). By 'the last edition of all' Lindsey referred to a final draft, not a separate edition; there was only one edition of the *Vindiciae*.

3   Lindsey did not publish another edition of the *Vindiciae*. Instead, he followed it up with *A second address to the students of Oxford and Cambridge, relating to Jesus Christ, and the origin of the great errors concerning him: with a list of the false readings of the scriptures and the mistranslations of the English Bible, which contribute to support those errors* (London, 1790).

4   Frend's 'statement of his case' took the form of his letter published in several newspapers, including the *Morning Chronicle*, 21 June 1788; for the details, see Vol. I, Letter 373, n. 3.

5   This letter from Thomas Edwards, criticizing the attack on Priestley made by Thomas Kipling was published in the *Whitehall Evening Post*, 5–8 July 1788, and in the *Morning Chronicle*, 8 July 1788; it also appeared in the *Public Advertiser*, 9 July 1788. For Kipling, see Vol. I, Letter 374, n. 3.

6   For Thomas Edwards of Jesus College, Cambridge, see Vol. I, Letter 282, n. 17. His father, also named Thomas Edwards (1729–85), was a fellow of Clare College, Cambridge, and from 1770 until his death, vicar of Nuneaton, Warwickshire. He was the author of *The doctrine of irresistible grace proved to have no foundation in the writings of the New Testament* (Cambridge, 1759).

7   Mary, the wife of the younger Thomas Edwards, outlived him; see TNA: PRO PROB 11/2026, fo. 278 (will of Thomas Edwards).

8   For this work, entitled *Hints &c. submitted to the serious attention of the clergy, nobility and gentry, newly associated, by a layman* (London, 1789), see Letter 384, n. 3. The author was the duke of Grafton, and evidently he submitted a draft for Lindsey's comments before publication.

9   This work was *A letter to the Right Honourable and Right Reverend Beilby, lord bishop of London, on the abolition of slavery* (London, 1788). Edward Holmes (d. 1799) graduated BA from Cambridge (Magdalene College) in 1762 and MA in 1766. He was a fellow of his college before serving as assistant master at Harrow, and in 1767, succeeded John Noble (see Vol. I, Letter 62) as headmaster of Scorton Grammar School, near Richmond, Yorkshire. According to an obituary, he became a 'decided Unitarian' as a result of reading Lindsey's works; *Gent. Mag.*, LXIX, ii (1799), 720–1.

10 The sixth and final volume of the *Theological Repository*, published in the summer of 1788, contained thirty-five essays. They included three essays by Priestley, 'On the observation of the Lord's Day' (pp. 113–35), 'On the Elijah foretold by Malachi', a reply to Henry Taylor, and a brief note 'To the public' (pp. 491–3) in which he criticized Gibbon for declining to make 'a public defence of what he has advanced' (pp. 492–3). Priestley also contributed a short tribute (pp. 217–24) to John Palmer (1742–86), dissenting minister and contributor to the *Theological Repository*.

11 The first number of the *Analytical Review*, published in London by Joseph Johnson, appeared in May 1788. It continued publication until Johnson's imprisonment in 1798. See Helen Braithwaite, *Romanticism, publishing and dissent. Joseph Johnson and the cause of liberty* (Basingstoke, 2003), p. 88.

12 The fifth article in the first number of the *Analytical Review* took the form of a review of William

Rutherford's *A view of antient history; including the progress of literature and the fine arts. Volume I* (London, 1788; the second of the two volumes appeared in 1791). Rutherford was master of the academy at Uxbridge. The paragraph to which Lindsey objected may be found at p. 45. The review defended Saul, the Old Testament king of Israel, against Rutherford's allegation that he was 'rejected … on account of his imbecility and misconduct'. It added that 'the former part of his reign … was splendid', and the rest of it would have been equally so had not Saul possessed 'a disposition to mercy … which rendered him, in some respects, unfit to rule over a barbarous people, in barbarous times'.

13 The first article in the first number of the *Analytical Review* was a lengthy review of *Variae Lectiones Vet. Testamenti, ex immense MSS … Opera as Studie Joan. Bernardi De Rossi, STD* (4 vols., Parma, 1784–87). It may be found at pp. 1–12, and a continuation of it appeared (pp. 269–86) in the number of the *Analytical Review* for July 1788. Giovanni Bernardo De Rossi (1742–1831) was professor of oriental languages at the University of Parma. William Christie (1750–1823), the founder of a Unitarian Society at Montrose in 1784, was the author of *Discourses on the divine unity* (Montrose, 1784).

14 Thomas Beddoes (1760–1808) was appointed reader in chemistry at Oxford University in the spring of 1788. For his attempts to cure Priestley's daughter Sarah, a sufferer from consumption, at Bristol in 1800, see Letters 687, 689, 690, 692 and 696.

15 The word 'is' was placed in square brackets by the copyist; perhaps Lindsey in the original letter omitted the word.

16 'Young Christie' was Thomas Christie (1761–96), the nephew of William Christie of Montrose.

17 This is a reference to James Bruce (1730–94) and his *Travels to discover the source of the Nile* (5 vols., Edinburgh, 1790). An abridged version in one volume, edited by Samuel Shaw, also appeared (in London) in 1790.

18 For George Campbell, and his *The four gospels, translated from the Greek*, published in two volumes in 1789, see Letter 383, n. 7.

19 The parliamentary session of 1787–8 lasted from 15 Nov. 1787 to 11 July 1788. During parliamentary sessions, peers and MPs were able to use their privilege of franking letters.

20 Possibly this is a reference to William Jones, *A course of lectures on the figurative language of the Holy Scripture, and the interpretation of it from Scripture itself … to which are added, four lectures on the relation between the Old and New Testaments, as it is set forth in the Epistle to the Hebrews* (London, 1797). Jones (1726–1800) was perpetual curate of Nayland, Suffolk, from 1777 until his death, and a leading high churchman.

21 Mrs Cappe was Catharine Cappe, the second wife of Newcome Cappe; Mr Cappe was probably one of Newcome Cappe's sons from his first marriage, namely Joseph Cappe (d. 1791), or his younger brother Robert Cappe (d. 1802); they graduated in medicine, respectively, from the Universities of Edinburgh and Leyden. For a further note on Robert Cappe, see Letter 738.

APPENDIX II

A LIST OF LETTERS TO THEOPHILUS LINDSEY, 1751–1807

The purpose of this appendix is twofold: to illustrate the extent of Lindsey's correspondence and the range of his contacts in a way that the non-survival of so many of his own letters does not permit; and to provide a convenient means whereby scholars can consult them. It includes letters to Lindsey where a text, in manuscript or in print, survives and is available for consultation. It does not include letters to Lindsey to which reference is made, usually by Lindsey himself, or in the diary of Thomas Hollis, and for which no text of any kind survives. For example, writing to William Tayleur on 7 Mar. 1796 (Letter 624) Lindsey referred to 'a very agreeable letter' from Henry Toulmin, in Lexington, Kentucky, but the letter itself seems not to have survived. Belsham, in his *Memoirs* of Lindsey (p. 80) mentioned 'many anonymous libels' immediately after Lindsey's resignation of Catterick in 1773, but, perhaps disappointingly, did not print any of them.

Where possible, a manuscript reference is provided. Otherwise, a printed copy, complete or incomplete, is listed. Most of Priestley's letters to Lindsey which are now in Dr Williams's Library were printed, although with inaccuracies and omissions, by J. T. Rutt in his *Life and correspondence of Joseph Priestley*. Priestley's letters to Lindsey between 1769 and his departure for America in April 1794 (DWL, MS 12.12) are available on-line via the Centre for Dissenting Studies website, where they are thoroughly annotated by Dr Simon Mills.

1751 (all old style)

Date	Sender	Source
9 July	Frances, duchess of Somerset	DWL
23 July	Frances, duchess of Somerset	George Cockman
29 Sept.	Frances, duchess of Somerset	Belsham, *Memoirs*
13 Dec.	Frances, duchess of Somerset	Belsham, *Memoirs*
n.d. 1751	Frances, duchess of Somerset	Belsham, *Memoirs*

1752 (all old style)

14 Mar.	Frances, duchess of Somerset	Belsham, *Memoirs*
19 Mar.	Frances, duchess of Somerset	Belsham, *Memoirs*

1754

5 Mar.	Frances, duchess of Somerset	Belsham, *Memoirs*

1756

2 Jan.	Francis Blackburne	DWL
6 Jan.	Francis Blackburne	DWL

8 Jan.	Francis Blackburne	DWL
20 Jan.	Francis Blackburne	DWL
10 Feb.	Francis Blackburne	DWL
1 Mar.	Francis Blackburne	DWL
19 Mar.	Francis Blackburne	DWL
26 Mar.	Francis Blackburne	DWL
13 Apr.	Francis Blackburne	DWL
2 May	Francis Blackburne	DWL
21 May	Francis Blackburne	DWL
4 June	Francis Blackburne	DWL
14 June	Francis Blackburne	DWL
18 June	Francis Blackburne	DWL
20 July	Francis Blackburne	DWL
23 July	Francis Blackburne	DWL
2 Aug.	Francis Blackburne	DWL
19 Sept.	Francis Blackburne	DWL
1 Oct.	Francis Blackburne	DWL
19 Oct.	Francis Blackburne	DWL
9 Nov.	Francis Blackburne	DWL
30 Nov.	Francis Blackburne	DWL
21 Dec.	Francis Blackburne	DWL
26 Dec.	Francis Blackburne	DWL
29 Dec.	Francis Blackburne	DWL
n.d., ?1756	Francis Blackburne	DWL

1757

9 Jan.	Francis Blackburne	DWL
14 Jan.	Francis Blackburne	DWL
25 Jan.	Francis Blackburne	DWL
28 Jan.	Francis Blackburne	DWL
?1 Feb.	Francis Blackburne	DWL
12 Feb.	Francis Blackburne	DWL
14 Feb.	Francis Blackburne	DWL
18 Feb.	Francis Blackburne	DWL
20 Feb.	Francis Blackburne	DWL
22 Feb.	Francis Blackburne	DWL
25 Feb.	Francis Blackburne	DWL
8 Mar.	Francis Blackburne	DWL
11 Mar.	Francis Blackburne	DWL
15 Mar.	Francis Blackburne	DWL
18 Mar.	Francis Blackburne	DWL
? Mar.	Francis Blackburne	DWL
14 Apr.	Francis Blackburne	DWL
18 Apr.	Francis Blackburne	DWL
29 Apr.	Francis Blackburne	DWL
? May	Francis Blackburne	DWL
? May	Francis Blackburne	DWL
? June	Francis Blackburne	DWL
16 Oct.	Francis Blackburne	DWL
27 Oct.	Francis Blackburne	DWL
27 Oct.	Francis Blackburne	DWL
15 Nov.	Francis Blackburne	DWL
16 Nov. [?1757]	Frances, duchess of Somerset	George Cockman

| 27 Nov. | Francis Blackburne | DWL |
| 20 Dec. | Francis Blackburne | DWL |

1758

| 27 June [?1758] | Elizabeth, countess of Northumberland | Belsham, *Memoirs* |

1759

5 Jan.	Francis Blackburne	DWL
21[?] Jan.	Francis Blackburne	DWL
22 Jan.	Francis Blackburne	DWL
? Jan.	Francis Blackburne	DWL
6 Feb.	Francis Blackburne	DWL
23 Feb.	Francis Blackburne	DWL
23 Mar.	Francis Blackburne	DWL
? Mar.	Francis Blackburne	DWL
5 June	Francis Blackburne	DWL
17 June	Francis Blackburne	DWL
25 June	Francis Blackburne	DWL
3 July	Francis Blackburne	DWL
25 July	Elizabeth, countess of Northumberland	Belsham, *Memoirs*
14 Aug.	Francis Blackburne	DWL
21 Sept.	Francis Blackburne	DWL
30 Oct.	Francis Blackburne	DWL
2 Nov.	Francis Blackburne	DWL
15 Nov.	Francis Blackburne	DWL
18 Dec.	Francis Blackburne	DWL

1763

1 Feb.	Francis Blackburne	DWL
25 Feb.	Francis Blackburne	DWL
1 Mar.	Francis Blackburne	DWL
?8 Mar.	Francis Blackburne	DWL
15 Mar.	Francis Blackburne	DWL
22 Mar.	Francis Blackburne	DWL
22 Mar.	Francis Blackburne	DWL
29 Mar.	Francis Blackburne	DWL
3 Apr.	Francis Blackburne	DWL
12 Apr.	Francis Blackburne	DWL
12 Apr.	Francis Blackburne	DWL
30 Apr.	Francis Blackburne	DWL
9 May	Francis Blackburne	DWL
10 May	Francis Blackburne	DWL
17 May	Francis Blackburne	DWL
22 May	Francis Blackburne	DWL
4 June	Francis Blackburne	DWL
13 June	Francis Blackburne	DWL
24 June	Francis Blackburne	DWL
1 July	Francis Blackburne	DWL
5 July	Francis Blackburne	DWL
10 July	Francis Blackburne	DWL
n.d., ?1763	Francis Blackburne	DWL

n.d., ?1763	Francis Blackburne	DWL
n.d., ?1763	Francis Blackburne	DWL
n.d., ?1763	Francis Blackburne	DWL

1764

| 27 Mar. | Hugh Percy, earl of Northumberland (draft) | Alnwick |

1766

| 26 July | Thomas Hollis | Rutt |
| 18 Oct. | 'Pierce Delver' [Thomas Hollis] | Belsham, *Memoirs* |

1767

| After 3 Aug. | 'Pierce Delver' [Thomas Hollis] | Belsham, *Memoirs* |

1768

2 Feb.	'Pierce Delver' [Thomas Hollis]	Belsham *Memoirs*
11 Oct.	Thomas Hollis	Rutt
10 Nov.	Thomas Hollis	Rutt

1769

9 Mar.	'Pierce Delver' [Thomas Hollis]	Belsham, *Memoirs*
16 May	Thomas Hollis	Rutt
26 Oct.	Thomas Hollis	Rutt
After Oct.	Joseph Priestley	Rutt
18 Dec.	Joseph Priestley	DWL

1770

13 May [?1770]	Francis Blackburne	DWL
18 Jan.	Joseph Priestley	DWL
21 Feb.	Joseph Priestley	Rutt
Before 30 May	Joseph Priestley	DWL
30 July	Joseph Priestley	DWL
? Aug.	Francis Blackburne	DWL
30 Aug.	Joseph Priestley	DWL
1 Nov.	Joseph Priestley	DWL
4 Nov.	Joseph Priestley	DWL
6 Dec.	Joseph Priestley	DWL
23 Dec.	Joseph Priestley	DWL

1771

8 Jan.	Joseph Priestley	DWL
27 Jan.	Joseph Priestley	Rutt
4 Feb.	Joseph Priestley	DWL
11 Feb.	Joseph Priestley	Rutt
17 Feb.	Joseph Priestley	George Cockman
After 17 Feb.	Joseph Priestley	DWL
?Apr.	Joseph Priestley	Rutt
14 June	Joseph Priestley	Rutt

6 July	Caleb Rotheram	Rutt
23 Aug.	Joseph Priestley	Rutt
12 Nov.	Hans Stanley	Belsham, *Memoirs*

1772

2 Mar.	Joseph Priestley	DWL
9 Mar.	Joseph Priestley	DWL
3 Apr.	Joseph Priestley	Rutt
20 Apr.	Joseph Priestley	DWL
21 Apr.	Joseph Priestley	Rutt
?Apr.	Joseph Priestley	Rutt
23 May	Joseph Priestley	Rutt
May	Joseph Priestley	DWL
19 June	C. Rotheram	Rutt
n.d. [1772–3]	Joseph Priestley	DWL

1773

14 Jan.	William Tayleur (copy)	JRUL
1 Nov.	Newcome Cappe	Belsham, *Memoirs*
6 Nov.	Grey Cooper	Belsham, *Memoirs*
16 Nov.	William Markham, bishop of Chester	Belsham, *Memoirs*
Nov.	Hugh Percy, duke of Northumberland	Belsham, *Memoirs*

1774

4 June	Joseph Priestley	Rutt
11 June	Samuel Badcock	Belsham, *Memoirs*
21 Oct.	Joseph Priestley	Rutt
n.d., 1774	'An eminent leader among the associated clergy'	Belsham, *Memoirs*
n.d. ?1774	Barnard Turner	Belsham, *Memoirs*

1775

26 Jan.	John Jebb	Rutt
25 Mar.	Joseph Priestley	DWL
Before 5 Aug.	William Tayleur (draft)	JRUL
29 Aug.	John Jebb	DWL
13 Oct.	Francis Blackburne	DWL
19 Nov.	Francis Blackburne	DWL
6 Dec.	William Turner	DWL

1776

Before 14 May	William Tayleur (copy)	JRUL
19 May	William Chambers	Rutt
8 July	Joseph Priestley	Rutt

1777

May 1777	William Tayleur	Belsham, *Memoirs*
13 Nov ?1777	William Tayleur	Belsham, *Memoirs*
14 June	William Turner of Wakefield	Belsham, *Memoirs*

20 Nov.	Joseph Priestley	Rutt

1778

11 Feb.	William Tayleur	Rutt
11 Mar.	William Turner of Wakefield	Rutt
17 Jan.	William Tayleur (?draft)	JRUL
Mar.	William Tayleur (copy)	JRUL
5 Apr.	William Robertson	Belsham, *Memoirs*
27 Apr.	William Robertson	Belsham, *Memoirs*
'Summer'	William Tayleur (copy)	JRUL

1779

n.d., ?1779	William Tayleur (copy)	JRUL

1780

2 Apr.	William Tayleur (also draft)	JRUL
20 Sept.	William Tayleur	JRUL
22 Nov.	William Tayleur	JRUL
25 Nov.	William Tayleur	JRUL
n.d., ?1780	William Tayleur (draft)	JRUL

1781

31 Jan.	William Tayleur	JRUL
10 Feb.	William Tayleur	JRUL
14 Mar.	William Tayleur	JRUL
20 May	William Tayleur	JRUL
31 July	William Tayleur	JRUL
25 Sept.	William Tayleur	JRUL
11 Dec.	William Tayleur	JRUL

1782

5 Dec.	Edward Harries	Lindsey, *Historical view*

1783

23 Sept.	Edmund Law	Belsham, *Memoirs*

1784

26 Feb.	William Tayleur	JRUL
26 Mar.	William Tayleur	JRUL
29 Mar.	William Hopkins	Belsham, *Memoirs*
29 Apr.	William Hopkins	Belsham, *Memoirs*
1 May	William Tayleur	JRUL
21 May	William Tayleur	JRUL
17 June	William Tayleur	JRUL
28 July	William Tayleur	JRUL
11 Sept.	William Tayleur	JRUL
3 Oct.	William Tayleur	JRUL
23 Dec.	William Tayleur	JRUL
1784	W. Hopkins	Rutt; Belsham, *Memoirs*

| n.d. | William Tayleur (?draft) | JRUL |
| n.d., ?1784 | William Tayleur (draft) | JRUL |

1785

| 29 Sept. | Pierre-François Courayer | Belsham, *Memoirs* (mis-dated by Belsham, *Memoirs*, p. 354, as 29 Sept. 1875; Le Courayer died on 17 Oct. 1776) |
| 17 Dec. | William Hopkins | Belsham, *Memoirs* |

1786

28 Feb.	William Tayleur	JRUL
27 Apr.	William Tayleur	JRUL
25 May	William Tayleur	JRUL
17 May	Joseph Priestley	DWL
30 May	Joseph Priestley	Rutt
5 July	Joseph Priestley	DWL
7 July 1786	James Freeman	Belsham, *Memoirs*
14 [?20] July	Joseph Priestley	DWL
10 Aug.	William Tayleur	JRUL
11 Dec.	William Tayleur	JRUL
25 Dec.	William Tayleur	JRUL

1787

20 Mar.	Joseph Priestley	Rutt
24 Mar.	Joseph Priestley	Rutt
10 Apr.	William Tayleur	JRUL
6 May	Joseph Priestley	DWL
21 June	William Tayleur	JRUL
11 June	Joseph Priestley	DWL
17 June	Joseph Priestley	DWL
June	William Tayleur	JRUL
14 July	Joseph Priestley	DWL
27 July	Joseph Priestley	DWL
26 Aug.	Joseph Priestley	DWL
29 Aug.	Joseph Priestley	DWL
9 Sept.	Joseph Priestley	DWL
28 Oct.	Joseph Priestley	DWL
19 Nov.	James Freeman	DWL
27 Nov.	Joseph Priestley	DWL
7 Dec.	Joseph Priestley	Rutt
n.d., 1787	Joseph Priestley	Rutt

1788

Feb.	William Tayleur	JRUL
20 Mar.	Joseph Priestley	DWL
29 Mar.	James Freeman	DWL
3 Apr.	William Tayleur	JRUL
20 May	William Tayleur	JRUL

26 May	Richard Price	Belsham, *Memoirs*
2 June	Richard Price	DWL
Aug.	William Tayleur	JRUL
18 Sept.	William Tayleur	JRUL
29 Sept.	Joseph Priestley	DWL
15 Oct.	James Freeman	DWL
17 Oct.	J. Smith	DWL
17 Oct.	James Freeman	DWL
20 Oct.	Joseph Priestley	DWL
16 Nov.	Joseph Priestley	Rutt
22 Nov.	James Freeman	DWL
27 Nov.	William Tayleur	JRUL
Nov.	Joseph Priestley	Rutt
14 Dec.	Joseph Priestley	Rutt
1788	James Freeman	Belsham, *Memoirs*
1788	James Freeman	Belsham, *Memoirs*

1789

26 Jan.	Joseph Priestley	DWL
27 Jan.	Joseph Priestley	Rutt
5 Feb.	Joseph Priestley	Royal Soc.
7 Feb.	Joseph Priestley	DWL
9 Mar.	Joseph Priestley	DWL
3 Apr.	Joseph Priestley	DWL
Apr.	Joseph Priestley	DWL
4 May	Joseph Priestley	DWL
14 May	Joseph Priestley	DWL
4 June	Augustus Henry, duke of Grafton	DWL
June	James Freeman	Belsham, *Memoirs*
11 July	J. Smith	DWL
22 July	Joseph Priestley	DWL
14 Aug.	Joseph Priestley	DWL
After 14 Aug.	Joseph Priestley	DWL
31 Aug.	Joseph Priestley	DWL
7 Sept.	Joseph Priestley	DWL
21 Sept.	Joseph Priestley	DWL
8 Oct.	Joseph Priestley	Rutt (also Belsham, *Memoirs*, p. 363, where the letter is mis-dated 3 Oct. 1789)
12 Oct.	Joseph Priestley	DWL
21 Oct.	Joseph Priestley	DWL
29 Oct.	Joseph Priestley	DWL
10 Nov.	Joseph Priestley	DWL
18 Nov.	Joseph Priestley	DWL
25 Nov.	Joseph Priestley	DWL
29 Nov.	Joseph Priestley	DWL
4 Dec.	Joseph Priestley	DWL
10 Dec.	Joseph Priestley	DWL
19 Dec.	Joseph Priestley	DWL

1790

22 Jan.	Joseph Priestley	DWL
26 Jan.	Joseph Priestley	DWL
27 Jan.	Joseph Priestley	DWL
11 Feb.	Joseph Priestley	Rutt
?26 Feb.	Joseph Priestley	DWL
11 Mar.	Joseph Priestley	DWL
12 Mar.	Joseph Priestley	DWL
14 Mar.	Joseph Priestley	DWL
22 Mar.	Joseph Priestley	DWL
29 Mar.	Joseph Priestley	DWL
6 Apr.	Joseph Priestley	DWL
9 May	Joseph Priestley	DWL
11 May	William Tayleur	JRUL
14 May	Richard Price	William Morgan, *Memoirs of the life of the Rev. Richard Price, DD, FRS* (London, 1815)
13 May	Joseph Priestley	DWL
24 May	Joseph Priestley	DWL
27 May	Joseph Priestley	DWL
11 June	Joseph Priestley	DWL
21 June	Joseph Priestley	DWL
24 June	Joseph Priestley	DWL
26 June	Joseph Priestley	Belsham, *Memoirs*
2 July	Joseph Priestley	DWL
6 July	Joseph Priestley	DWL
13 July	Joseph Priestley	DWL
16 July	Joseph Priestley	DWL
22 July	Joseph Priestley	DWL
18 Aug.	Joseph Priestley	DWL
22 Sept.	Joseph Priestley	Rutt
30 Sept.	Joseph Priestley	DWL
13 Oct.	Joseph Priestley	DWL
14 Oct.	William Tayleur	JRUL
n.d. [?15 Oct.]	Joseph Priestley	DWL
17 Oct.	Joseph Priestley	DWL
18 Oct.	Joseph Priestley	DWL
27 Oct.	Joseph Priestley	DWL
2 Nov.	Joseph Priestley	DWL
25 Nov.	William Tayleur (with draft)	JRUL
26 Nov.	Joseph Priestley	DWL
4 Dec.	Robert Millar	DWL
18 Dec.	Mr Edwards	DWL
23 Dec.	Joseph Priestley	DWL
27 Dec.	Joseph Priestley	DWL

1791

9 Jan.	Joseph Priestley	DWL
Before 10 Jan.	Joseph Priestley	DWL
17 Jan.	Joseph Priestley	DWL

8 Feb.	Joseph Priestley	DWL
13 Feb.	Joseph Priestley	DWL
18 Feb.	Joseph Priestley	DWL
23 Feb.	Joseph Priestley	Rutt
24 Feb.	Joseph Priestley	DWL
28 Feb.	Joseph Priestley	DWL
7 Mar.	Joseph Priestley	DWL
9 Mar.	Joseph Priestley	DWL
11 Mar.	Joseph Priestley	DWL
14 Mar.	Joseph Priestley	DWL
25 Mar.	Joseph Priestley	Rutt
Apr.	Joseph Priestley	Rutt
2 June	Joseph Priestley	DWL
18 June	Robert Millar (copy)	DWL
29 June	Joseph Priestley	DWL
15 July	Joseph Priestley	Rutt
30 Aug.	Joseph Priestley	DWL
5 Sept.	Robert Millar	DWL

1792

7 Jan.	William Morgan	NYRO
26 Apr.	William Tayleur	JRUL
27 Apr.	Christopher Wyvill	NYRO
21 May	James Freeman	Belsham, *Memoirs*
28 May	Christopher Wyvill	NYRO
May	William Tayleur (?draft of letter of 14 June)	JRUL
14 June	William Tayleur	JRUL
1 July	William Tayleur	JRUL
18 July	William Tayleur	JRUL
25 July	James Freeman	DWL
26 July (?or 1793)	William Tayleur	JRUL

1793

Jan.	John Lee	Rutt
13 Mar.	Christopher Wyvill	NYRO
May	Trustees of Essex Street chapel	Belsham, *Memoirs*
?May	Trustees of Essex Street chapel	Belsham, *Memoirs*
16 June	James Freeman	DWL
24 July	Joseph Priestley	DWL
5 Aug.	Joseph Priestley	DWL
23 Aug.	Joseph Priestley	DWL
7 Sept.	Joseph Priestley	DWL
1 Oct.	Frederick Montagu	DWL

1794

10 Jan.	Joseph Priestley	Univ. of Birmingham Library
7 Apr.	Joseph Priestley	DWL
9 Apr.	Joseph Priestley	APS
11 Apr.	Joseph Priestley	DWL
5 June	James Freeman	DWL

6 June	Joseph Priestley	Rutt; also Belsham, *Memoirs*
15 June	Joseph Priestley	DWL
24 June	Joseph Priestley	DWL
5 July	Joseph Priestley	DWL
21 July	Joseph Priestley	DWL
15 Aug.	Joseph Priestley	Dickinson College, Pa.
24 Aug.	Joseph Priestley	Dickinson College, Pa.
28 Aug.	Henry Wansey	Belsham, *Memoirs*
14 Sept.	Joseph Priestley	DWL
16 Oct.	Joseph Priestley	Rutt; also Belsham, *Memoirs*
5 Nov.	Thomas Jenkins	DWL
12 Nov.	Joseph Priestley	DWL
12 Dec.	William Christie	DWL
20 Dec.	Joseph Priestley	DWL
1794, n.d.	James Freeman	Belsham, *Memoirs*

1795

19 Jan.	Joseph Priestley	DWL
After 7 Feb.	Robert Millar (copy)	DWL
10 Feb.	Joseph Priestley	Rutt
22 Feb.	Joseph Priestley	Rutt
5 Apr.	Joseph Priestley	Rutt
17 May	Joseph Priestley	DWL
17 June	Joseph Priestley	Rutt
6 July	Joseph Priestley	Rutt
12 July	Joseph Priestley	DWL
12 Aug.	Joseph Priestley	DWL
14 Sept.	Joseph Priestley	DWL
15 Sept.	Thomas Fyshe Palmer	Belsham, *Memoirs*
9 Nov.	Joseph Priestley	DWL
6 Dec.	Joseph Priestley	DWL
17 Dec.	Joseph Priestley	DWL

1796

12/15 Feb.	Joseph Priestley	Rutt
8 Apr.	Joseph Priestley	DWL
3 May	Joseph Priestley	DWL
5 May	Thomas Fyshe Palmer	HMCO, Shepherd MS, vol. X, no. 12
24 May	James Freeman	Belsham, *Memoirs*
12 June	Joseph Priestley	DWL
14 July	Thomas Muir (copy)	Mitchell Library, Sydney
28 July	Joseph Priestley	DWL
1 Aug.	Joseph Priestley	DWL
11 Sept.	Joseph Priestley	Rutt
16 Sept.	Thomas Fyshe Palmer (copy)	HMCO, Shepherd MS, vol. X, no. 11
19 Sept.	Joseph Priestley	DWL
29 Oct.	Joseph Priestley	Rutt

| 3 Dec. | Joseph Priestley | DWL |

1797

13 Jan.	Joseph Priestley	DWL
20 Feb.	Joseph Priestley	DWL
3 Apr.	Joseph Priestley	Rutt
30 Apr.	Joseph Priestley	Rutt
29 May	Joseph Priestley	DWL
18 June	Joseph Priestley	DWL
27 Aug.	Joseph Priestley	DWL
14 Sept.	Joseph Priestley	DWL
4 Nov.	Joseph Priestley	DWL
16 Nov.	Joseph Priestley	DWL
30 Nov.	Joseph Priestley	DWL
c. 1797	Edward Williams (Iolo Morganwg) (draft)	NLW

1798

1 Jan.	Joseph Priestley	DWL
18 Jan.	Joseph Priestley	DWL
8 Mar.	Joseph Priestley	DWL
17 May	Joseph Priestley	DWL
16 June	Joseph Priestley	DWL
2 Aug.	Joseph Priestley	DWL
6 Sept.	Joseph Priestley	DWL
1 Nov.	Joseph Priestley	DWL
23 Dec.	Joseph Priestley	DWL

1799

14 Feb.	Joseph Priestley	DWL
21 Mar.	Joseph Priestley	DWL
3 May	Joseph Priestley	Rutt
6 June	Joseph Priestley	Rutt
25 June	Joseph Priestley	DWL
12/19 Sept.	Joseph Priestley	DWL
14 Nov.	Joseph Priestley	DWL
25 Nov.	Robert Edward Garnham	DWL

1800

9 Jan.	Joseph Priestley	DWL
13 Jan.	Christopher Wyvill	Wyvill, *Political papers*, VI, 81–2 (this is a variant on a letter sent to several of Wyvill's supporters, including Lindsey)
16 Jan.	Joseph Priestley	DWL
6 Mar.	Joseph Priestley	DWL
10 Apr.	Joseph Priestley	DWL
1 May	Joseph Priestley	Rutt
29 May	Joseph Priestley	DWL

19 June	Joseph Priestley	DWL
13 Aug.	Joseph Priestley	DWL
16 Oct.	Joseph Priestley	DWL
30 Oct.	Joseph Priestley	Rutt
16 Dec.	Joseph Priestley	DWL
25 Dec.	Joseph Priestley	DWL
1800	Joseph Priestley	R. B. Aspland, *Memoir of the life, works and correspondence of the Rev. Robert Aspland* (London, 1850)

1801

18 Jan.	James Freeman	DWL
14 Mar.	William Davy	Rutt
Before 16 Mar.	Joseph Priestley	Rutt
8 Apr.	Joseph Priestley	Rutt
28 May	Joseph Priestley	DWL
11 June	Joseph Priestley	Rutt; also Belsham, *Memoirs*, p. 265
22 July	Joseph Priestley	DWL
30 July	Joseph Priestley	DWL
2 Oct.	Joseph Priestley	DWL
24 Oct.	Joseph Priestley	Rutt
7 Nov.	Joseph Priestley	DWL
19 Dec.	Joseph Priestley	APS
1801	John Hurford Stone	Rutt

1802

14 Feb.	Joseph Priestley	DWL
Mar.	Christopher Wyvill	Belsham, *Memoirs*
8 May	Robert Millar	DWL
8 May	Joseph Priestley to Hannah Lindsey	Rutt; Belsham, *Memoirs*
26 June	Joseph Priestley	DWL
3 July	Joseph Priestley	DWL
28 Aug.	Joseph Priestley	DWL
31 Aug.	William Winterbotham	Belsham, *Memoirs*
25 Sept.	Joseph Priestley	Rutt; Belsham, *Memoirs*
7 Oct.	John Law, bishop of Elphin	Belsham, *Memoirs*, p. 295 n. * (extract); Priestley, *Works*, IX, iv (shorter extract)
16 Oct.	Joseph Priestley to Hannah Lindsey	DWL
11 Dec.	Joseph Priestley	DWL

1803

1 Jan.	Joseph Priestley	DWL
1 Mar.	Joseph Priestley	Rutt
5 Mar.	Joseph Priestley	Rutt
15 Apr.	Joseph Priestley	DWL
23 Apr.	Joseph Priestley	Rutt; Belsham, *Memoirs*

4 June	Joseph Priestley		DWL
11 July	Joseph Priestley		DWL
12 Sept.	Joseph Priestley		DWL
4 Nov.	Joseph Priestley		DWL
27 Aug.	Joseph Priestley		APS
19 Dec.	Joseph Priestley		Rutt; Belsham, *Memoirs*
1803	Joseph Priestley		Priestley, *Works*, II, 64 and Rutt, I, 361 n. †

1804

| 16 Jan. | Joseph Priestley | | University of Birmingham |
| 17 Apr. | William Rathbone | | University of Liverpool |

1805

| 15 Apr. | Thomas Belsham | | Williams |

1806

| 28 Sept. | Christopher Wyvill | | NYRO |

1807

| 5 Nov. | Frederic Adrian Vanderkemp | | Belsham, *Memoirs* |
| 14 Dec. | Christopher Wyvill | | George Cockman |

Undated letters to Lindsey

'Pierce Delver' (Thomas Hollis) (?1760s)	Belsham, *Memoirs*
Samuel Heywood	DWL
Mr [Timothy] Hollis 'Tuesday morn^g'	DWL
Joseph Priestley (? to Lindsey)	DWL
Unidentified sender, 18 Oct. 90	DWL
Francis Blackburne	DWL
The president and fellows of Harvard College	Belsham, *Memoirs*
James Freeman	Belsham, *Memoirs*

There are also in DWL three letters whose senders can be identified but whose recipients cannot; possibly Lindsey was the recipient in each case

Francis Blackburne to unnamed recipient, ?1757	DWL, MS 12.52 (106)
Francis Blackburne to unnamed recipient, n.d.	DWL, MS 12.52 (107)
Joseph Priestley to unnamed recipient, n.d.	DWL, MS 24.86 (3)

Letters to Lindsey from unidentified correspondents

16 June (no year) (from New York)		DWL
25 Dec. 1801	unnamed recipient in Paris	*MR*, XI (1816), 642–3
n.d.	?copy of letter to Lindsey	Rutt, I, 509 n. ‡

Index to volumes I and II

Following the practice of Dr Sarah Brewer in her edition of *The Early Letters of Richard Hurd*, the introduction to each volume, the letters themselves, the accompanying notes, and the appendices have all been indexed. References to the introductory sections are to page numbers (lower case roman numerals); references to the letters, notes and appendices are to letters numbers (Arabic numerals). Theophilus Lindsey is denoted in the index as TL and Hannah Lindsey as HL. References to Hannah Lindsey (HL) are not indexed when they are conventional forms whereby Lindsey conveyed her good wishes to his correspondent, as he did with most of his post-1760 letters. Where two persons of the same surname and first name are indexed, they are distinguished from one another, as far as possible, by their dates of birth and death.

The entries under 'London: specific locations' include all locations in the city of London and the adjacent area to which Lindsey refers, and the same applies to the city of Westminster. These locations are not indexed separately, with the exceptions of Essex Street and Essex Street chapel. Locations in the headings to Lindsey's letters are not indexed.

For a work of this length, considerable cross-referencing in the index has been necessary. Every effort, however, has been made to avoid excessive duplication of entries. Hence, for example, the substantive entry for Essex Street chapel includes every reference, of whatever kind, to that institution, but where Essex chapel features as a sub-entry under Lindsey, Theophilus, it contains only those references which are directly concerned with Lindsey's own role as its minister. Sub-entries for published works are provided under the author's substantive entry, and not under the cross-referenced title entry. Titles of key sub-entries appear in bold.

Bristol, bishop of, *see* Bagot, Lewis; Butler, Joseph; Madan, Spencer; Newton, Thomas; Wilson, Christopher

Bristol county (Massachusetts), II, 582

Bristol, 4th earl of, *see* Hervey, Frederick Augustus

British and Foreign Bible Society, II, 762 n. 7

British and Foreign Unitarian Association, II, xxxii

British linen company, II, 598 n. 7

British Museum, I, lviii, 194 and n. 10, 223, 374 n. 8

Brittany, II, 527

Broadbent, Rebecca, II, 640 n. 19

Broadbent, Thomas Biggin, II, 640 n. 19

Broadbent, William
death of his wife, II, 640 n. 19
dissenting minister at Cairo Street, Warrington, II, 640 n. 19, 683, 762
pupil of Thomas Belsham at Daventry, II, 640 n. 19

Broadhurst, Thomas
student and tutor Hackney college, I, 354
dissenting minister, I, 354 n. 21
minister at Taunton and at Halifax, II, 653 n. 4
minister at Trim Street, Bath, II, 653 n. 4, 667, 701
possibility that he might become minister at High Street chapel, Shrewsbury, II, 667
TL's favourable opinion of, II, 667, 701
and Richard Price, I, 354

Brocklesby, Richard
physician to Samuel Johnson, I, 310 n. 21

Brome (Suffolk), II, 426 n. 4

Bromeswell (Suffolk), II, 753

Bromsgrove (Worcs)
John Corrie minister at, II, 575 n. 2, 639 n. 18, 640 n. 6, 673 n. 5
Williams Wells minister at, II, 604

Brooke, John
under sheriff of Warwickshire, II, 474 and n. 7
and Priestley riots, II, 474
and church and king club and Association for the Preservation of Liberty and Property against Republicans and Levellers, II, 474 n. 7
and Pitt and Henry Dundas, II, 474 and n. 9

Brooksbank, George, stockbroker, I, lx, lxi, 241 n. 3
and Essex Street chapel, I, lxv, 225, 313 n. 18
his contribution of £200 stock to Essex Street chapel, I, 237, 255 and n. 8
a subscriber to Essex Street chapel, I, 170, Appendix I
and mortgage for Essex Street chapel, I, Appendix I
a trustee of Essex Street chapel, I, 170 n. 20, 271 n. 10

Broome, Ralph
his hostility to Edmund Burke, II, 648 n. 9

his 'Simkin letters', II, 648 n. 9
Works: *Strictures on Mr Burke's two letters, addressed to a member of the present parliament on the proposals for peace with the regicide directory of France, and upon the proposal for funding the navy debt*, II, 648 n. 9

Broseley (Shropshire), II, 683 n. 8

Brothers, Richard
millenarian prophet, II, 601
and Nathaniel Brassey Halhead, II, 601 n. 6
Works: *A revealed knowledge of the prophecies and times*, II, 601 n. 6

Brough Hall, Catterick (Yorks), I, xliv

Browne, Anthony, 6th Viscount Montagu, I, 37

Brown, Elizabeth
widow of John Brown (q.v.), I, 380 and n. 9
legacies to TL and John Disney, I, 380 and n. 9

Browne, Isaac Hawkins
MP for Bridgnorth, I, 340 n. 18
and repeal of Test and Corporation Acts (1787), I, 340 and n. 18

Browne, James, I, 84 n. 5, 90 n. 6

Browne, John
pupil of Abraham Rees at Hackney college, II, 676 n. 8
and Sidney Sussex college, Cambridge, II, 676 n. 8
and Middle Temple, II, 676 n. 8
Works: *An essay on universal redemption; tending to prove that the general sense of scripture favours the opinion of the final salvation of all mankind*, II, 676 and n. 8
publishers of, II, 676 and n. 8
TL's praise for, II, 676
Joseph Priestley pleased by, II, 682

Browne, Wade, II, 488 n. 6

Brown, John, druggist, of Holborn, I, lxi, 241 n. 3
subscriber to Essex Street chapel, I, 170 and n. 9, Appendix I
death of, I, 378
TL funeral sermon for, I, 378 n. 4
his legacies to Essex Street chapel and Hackney college, I, 378, 380
his legacies to TL and Disney, I, 378 n. 5, 380

Brown, Timothy, trustee of subscription fund for Priestley's later works, II, 739 n. 3

Brown, William Lawrence
principal of Marischal college, Aberdeen, II, 702 n. 8
and dispute over Robert Arnot's nomination to parish of Kingsbarns, II, 702
his published speech to general assembly of Church of Scotland, II, 702 and n. 8

Bruce, James, II, 374A n. 17

Bruce, Lady Mary, I, 33 n. 8

Bruce-Brudenell, Thomas, Baron Bruce, from 1776 earl of Ailesbury, I, 29, 30

supported by William Heberden, I, l, 186

supported by Henry Hinckley, I, 170 and n. 23, 217, Appendix I

supported by Barnard Turner, I, 132, 134

supported by Michael Dodson, I, 197

supported by William Basnett, II, 487 n. 2, 701

supported by William Buller, I, 354

supported by Henry Duncombe, I, Appendix I and n. 16; II, 634

supported by Francis Maseres, II, 498

supported by earl of Surrey, I, 218; II, 387

earl of Surrey ceases to attend, I, 293

supported by Sir George Savile, I, 153–4, 159, 170, 195

supported by Samuel Pipe-Wolferstan, I, lxv, lxix; II, xx, xxiii–xxiv, xxxvii, 660 n. 3

supported by Robert Smith, I, lxv, 154 and n. 1, 178 n. 2, 249; II, 639 n. 14

supported by Christopher Wyvill, I, 218, Appendix I

Sir John Pringle's coolness over plans for, I, 117

attempts to discourage, I, 118 and n. 1

never visited by William Tayleur, I, lxxxv, 178 n. 5

supported by Elizabeth Rayner, I, lx, lxxxvi, 177, 194, 255 n. 1, 256 n. 3, 311 n. 2, Appendix I; II, 699

Elizabeth Rayner's gift of £500 to, I, 193 and n. 1, Appendix I

Brand Hollis pledge of £100 for, I, 159

John Hett's pledge of £100 for, I, 159

John Lee's pledge of £100 for, I, 159

Fox's pledge of £100 for, I, 159

Shelburne's (unfulfilled) pledge of £100 to, I, 159 and n. 4, 171 n. 5

John Lee a subscriber to, I, 170; II, 529

John Brown a subscriber to, I, 170 n. 9, 378, 380, Appendix I

John Brown's legacy to, I, 378, 380

lawyers and, I, lxv, 176, 239, 262, 293

William Wilberforce attends, I, lxvi, 293; II, xvii n. 6

and Samuel Yate Benyon, I, 239, 241–3, 245–6, 293; II, 742 n. 1

and Benyon family, II, xxv

William Congreve's gift to, I, 194 and n. 3

Richard Kirwan a member of, I, 181, 184, 260

and James Martin, II, 436

and Thomas Whitmore, I, lxv, 218, 219 n. 1, 220–1, 232, 238, 293

and Owen Salusbury Brereton, I, 219 and n. 4

and Sir Francis Charlton, I, 246, 293

and George Rogers, II, 427

hearers at, their social composition, I, lxv

social respectability of, II, xxv

membership of, I, 132

conveyed to trustees, 1782–3, I, lxi, lxii, 164 n. 4, 167 n. 2, 255 and n. 2, 262

trustees of, I, lxxxv, 164 nn. 4 and 5, 177 and n. 5, 217 n. 9, 262; II, 525, 528, 530, 531 535, 691 n. 3, 770

George Brooksbank a trustee of, I, 170 n. 20, 271 n. 10

supported by George Brooksbank, I, lx, lxi, lxv, 170, 225, 237, 313 n. 18, Appendix I

James West a trustee and benefactor of, I, 282 n. 33; II, 570 n. 5

Robert Wainewright a trustee of, II, 561 n. 6, 739 n. 3

'the head-quarters of Unitarianism, the great mother- church' (Priestley), I, liii; II, xxii

praised by Priestley, I, 229

Disney TL's co-minister at Essex Street chapel, I, xxiii, xxxv, xlvii, liii, lxi–lxiii, lxvii n. 284, lxxiv, 42 n. 13, 148, n. 4, 252 and n. 4, 254–6; II, xvii, xix, 408

Disney's remuneration at, I, 148 n. 4, 255

Disney sole minister at, in succession to TL, II, xlvi, 525, 528, 530, 531, 681

attacked by John Randolph, I, lxx

attacked by Lewis Bagot, I, 193 and n. 12

TL as preacher at, I, lxvi, xlvii, lxviii, lxix, lxxvii, 159, 186; II, xxiii–xxiv, xxv, 475

Boswell on TL's preaching at, I, lxix

Samuel Pipe-Wolferstan on TL's preaching at, I, lxix; II, xxiii–xxiv, xlvi

Mary Nicholson on TL's preaching at, II, xxv

Thomas Belsham preaching for TL at, II, xxiii

William Enfield preaching for TL at, I, 160, 206, 223

John Prior Estlin preaching at, II, 239 n. 2, 688

Joshua Toulmin preaching for TL at, I, lxiv, lxv, lxxxvi, 219, 234 n. 6, 369; II, xxiii

Joshua Toulmin preaching for John Disney at, II, 564 n. 7, 567, 574, 689, 714 and n. 5

George Walker preaching for TL at, I, lxiv, 198; II, xxiii–xxiv

John Calder preaching for TL at, I, lxiv, lxxix, 245 n. 2

Priestley preaching for TL at, I, lxiv, 209–10, 234 n. 6, 289 and n. 7, 316, 331 and n. 1, 367; II, xxiii, 407 and n. 9, 409–11, 450, 451, 455, 475–6

Sir Henry Trelawny preaching at, I, 220

Samuel Curwen on, I, lxiii, lxix, 234 n. 6, 239 n. 1, 243 n. 3, 245 n. 2, 250 n. 4, 289 n. 7

TL's 'fatigue' at two services per Sunday (1775), I, 151

TL avoids excessive fatigue at (1778), I, 191

Giovanni Fabbrioni at, I, 187 and n. 7

and duke of Grafton, I, lxx; II, xxii, 529, 730, 751, 761

and Edward Williams (Iolo Morganwg), II, xxxiv

and Paul Henry Maty, I, 199

and heterodoxy, I, lxxi

provost of Trinity college, Dublin, II, 427
MP for Cork, II, 427 n. 4
death of, at Buxton, II, 427 n. 4
Hemington, Robert, I, xxix–xxxi, 2, 22 nn. 11
and 21, 26A, 28, 57
Hemlingford (Warwicks), II, 493 n. 7
Henley, Esther, I, 20 n. 9
Henley, John, I, 20 n. 9
Henley, Phocion, I, 15 and n. 8, 17, 20
Henley, Robert, 1st earl of Northington, I, 15 n.
8, 59 and n. 9
and George III, I, 59
Henley (Oxfordshire), I, 67
Henry IV of France, I, 229 and n. 7
Henry VII, I, xxii n. 41
Henry VIII, I, 9, 37, 65
Henry, Matthew, I, 64; II, 521
presbyterian minister at Chester and at
Hackney, II 521 n. 2
Works: *Exposition of the Old and New
Testament*, I, 64; II, 521 n. 2
Herbert family, earls of Pembroke, I, 37 n. 7
Herbert, Elizabeth, *née* Spencer, Lady Pembroke,
I, 29 and n. 15, 30 n. 20, 37 and n. 8
Herbert, Henry, 9th earl of Pembroke, I, 24 n. 7
Herbert, Henry, 10th earl of Pembroke, I, 29, 30,
37 n. 8, 191 n. 4
Herbert, Mary, *née* Fitzwilliam, Lady Pembroke,
I, 24 and n. 7
Hereford, bishop of, *see* Beauclerk, James;
Hoadly, Benjamin
Hereford, city of, I, 262
Hereford, diocese of, I, 252 n. 5
Herodotus, I, 22
Hertford, II, 458 n. 3
Hertford college, Oxford, I, 276 n. 20
Hertford, Lord and Lady, *see* Seymour Conway
Hertfordshire, I, 324; II, 604 n. 7
Hervey, Frederick Augustus, 4th earl of Bristol,
bishop of Cloyne and of Derry, I, 268, 276
n. 13; II, 521 n. 4
heterodoxy, I, 37
Hetherington, William
his charity for the blind, I, 310 and n. 5
Hett, John, I, lxv
master in chancery, I, 167, 305
pledge of £100 for Essex Street chapel, I, 159
subscriber to Essex Street chapel, I, 170 and n.
17, Appendix I
and purchase of Essex house, I, 167
a trustee of Essex Street chapel, I, 164 n. 5,
262 n. 5
advice to TL over presentation to Chew
Magna, I, 305
Heveningham (Suffolk), II, 476 n. 4
Hewley, Lady Sarah, I, 161 and n. 7
Lady Hewley's trust, I, 161 and n. 7; II, 536
n. 4
trustees of, I, 161 and n. 7
Hewson, John, II, 714 and n. 3

Hey, John
and the latitudinarian tradition, II, xx, 524 n. 3
Heyrick, Tobias,
hostility to Feathers Tavern petition, I, 92 and
n. 2
hostility to dissenting bill (1772), I, 92 and
n. 2
Heywood family, of Liverpool, II, 433 n. 8
Heywood, John Pemberton, I, 217
a trustee of Essex Street chapel, I, 217 and n.
9; II, 433 n. 8
a special pleader, II, 433 n. 8
Heywood, Samuel, I, 260, 357 and n. 6; II, 399,
433 n. 8, 459 n. 12, 508 n. 4, 511 n. 7
and Essex Street chapel, I, lxv, 217, 310
a trustee of Essex Street chapel, I, 217 and n.
9; II, 771 n. 1
family of, and Essex Street chapel, II, xxv
student at Warrington academy, I, 310; II, 404
n. 5
serjeant at law, II, 587, 688
and lord mayor of London, II, 587 and n. 10
attorney on the northern circuit, I, 340 n. 10;
II, 404
his services to dissent, II, 404
and quarterly club, II, 688
his house at Bedford Place, Russell Square,
London, II, 688 n. 3
Joseph Johnson his publisher, I, 340; II, 482
at Brighthelmstone, II, 394
and Samuel Horsley, II, 429 n. 9
and unitarian petition, II, 449, 488
and Thomas Fyshe Palmer, II, 538 n. 3
and Charles James Fox, II, 760 n. 9
his *Vindication* of Fox's *History*, II, 760 n. 9
Works: *High Church politics: being a
seasonable appeal to the friends of the
British constitution, against the practices and
principles of high churchmen*, II, 429 n. 9,
482–4; *The right of Protestant Dissenters to a
compleat toleration asserted*, I, 340 n. 10; II,
429 n. 9
Hickling (Notts), I, 105 n. 16, 282 n. 18
Hicks, Sir Baptist, I, 126 n. 2
Higham Ferrers (Northants), I, lxxxii, 128 n. 14,
182 n. 12, 200 n. 3; II, lviii, 514 n. 7, 634 n. 4
'high churchmen', *see* Church of England
*High Church politics: being a seasonable appeal
to the friends of the British constitution,
against the practices and principles of high
churchmen* (Samuel Heywood), II, 429 n. 9,
482–4
Hildyard, Sir Robert, II, 634
his estates, II, 634 n. 12
Hildyard, Robert D'Arcy, I, 105 and n. 5
Hill, George
professor of divinity and principal of St
Andrews, II, 457 n. 10
moderator of general assembly of Church of
Scotland (1789), II, 457 n. 10

and French revolutionary and Napoleonic wars

TL deplores prospect of, I, lxxi, II, 480, 498, 510, 512–13

TL critical of, I, lxx; II, xv, 524, 529, 536, 541, 545, 553, 572, 578, 588, 598, 602, 604–5, 607, 610, 616, 650, 655–6, 662, 664, 687, 695, 699, 708, 711, 717 n. 2

TL regards it as 'the cause of the ruin of England's greatness', II, 612

TL calls it 'this cruel, wicked and unchristian war', II, 636

TL on impoverishment caused by, II, 669, 695

TL's admiration for Vicesimus Knox's *Antipolemus*, II, 577

TL's admiration for Robert Miln's fast day sermon (1794), II, 578

TL and rumours of peace (Nov. 1794), II, 588

TL's fear of French invasion of England (1794–5), II, 590, 603

TL and rumours of peace (1796), II, 539, 541–2

TL's hostility to Pitt's 'Triple Assessment' bill, II, 664–5

TL's hopes for peace (1797), II, 659

TL and rumours of peace negotiations (1800), II, 687

TL welcomes prospect of peace (July 1800), II, 699

TL's pessimism over prospect of peace (Dec. 1800, June and July 1801), II, 723, 726

TL's hopes for peace (1801), II, 712–14, 716–17

TL on 'Contractors &c and vermin of that sort' exploiting the war, II, 726

TL and HL and renewal of war with France, from 1803, II, 749

TL and HL deplore prospect of renewal of war, II, 747

a 'premature and unnecessary War' (HL), II, 749, 752

and Bonaparte's ambition, II, II, 747

HL thinks Britain changed 'from a Commerce merely, to a Military cast', II, 756

HL on 'the fangs of French Despotism', II, 753

HL on inadequacies of defence (1803), II, 754

HL on need for Catholic emancipation as aid to defence, II, 754

HL on high food prices (1804), II, 764–5

HL blames Pitt for continuation of war (1804), II, 764

TL and HL hopes for peace, following death of Pitt (1806), II, 774, 778

HL distinguishes between Pitt's private virtues and his public policies, II, 774

TL and HL attitude to Napoleonic War, II, xlviii, 778

TL and HL and politics, 1790s and early 1800s

TL's political contacts, II, xxi

TL's opinions of William Pitt the younger, I, lxxvii, 285; II, xv, xxxviii, 595, 616, 664, 673, 700, 706 n. 14, 714, 723, 724, 731

TL critical of ministry of Pitt the younger, II, xv, xxxviii, 595, 616, 628, 650–1, 657, 664, 673, 706,

TL condemns Pitt's ministry for increase in postal rates, II, 674

TL's hope that Pitt's 'system' would be humbled, II, 700

TL's pleasure at Pitt's resignation, II, 712, 714

TL expects Pitt's return to office, II, 717, 723, 724

TL compares Pitt unfavourably to Fox, II, 724

TL claims Pitt and his adherents 'little less than persons insane', II, 731

TL critical of Henry Dundas (1797), II, 650

TL claims to have avoided taking part in politics, II, 617

TL claims that he 'seldom' mentions political matters in his letters, II, 723

TL's political disillusionment after 1789, I, lxx

TL and extra-parliamentary radicalism, II, xxxviii

TL deplores Burke's *Reflections*, II, xvi, 428–30, 432, 452, 454

TL deplores Burke's *Appeal from the New to the Old Whigs*, II, 469

TL's admiration for Thomas Christie's reply to Burke, II, 454–5

TL regards Burke as a Tory, II, 407, 428, 469

TL credits Burke with 'no more knowledge than a horse' of Christianity, II, 429

TL describes Burke as 'an high-church declaimer', II, 452

TL describes Burke as 'a mere political sophist', II, 494

TL's admiration for Charles James Fox, II, xvi, xxx, xxxviii, 529

TL wishes Fox were in power (1793), II, 539

TL and Foxite Whigs, II, xxxviii, 539, 661–2

TL's favourite newspaper the *Morning Chronicle*, II, xxxviii, xliii

TL disapproves of George III but not a republican, II, xxxviii, 659

TL admiration for Benjamin Flower and *Cambridge Intelligencer*, II, xxxviii, 490, 535, 541, 546

TL admiration for Flower's *The French constitution*, II, 490–2, 535

TL a member of revolution society, II, xxxix, 418

TL and revolution society's anniversary celebration (14 July 1790), II, 418 and n. 19

TL and revolution society's anniversary celebration (4 Nov. 1790), II, 430 and n. 8

TL and revolution society's anniversary celebrations (14 July 1791), II, 461 and n. 10

TL regards him as 'too unguarded in things he has thrown out to the public', II, 697

TL's anxiety over his involvement in American politics, II, 702

sends TL a draft of his work on Isaiah, II, 705 and n. 5

TL and HL raising subscriptions for later volumes of his *General history of the Christian church*, II, xv, xxviii, 672 n. 8, 720, 736 n. 5, 739 n. 3, 741–2, 744–5, 750, 752

TL and HL raising subscriptions for his *Notes on all the books of scripture*, II, 672 n. 8, 720, 736 n. 5, 739 n. 3, 741–2, 744–5, 750, 752, 758, 761–2

HL and TL and subscriptions for Priestley's annuity, II, 756 and n. 8, 758, 764

William Wood compares Priestley to TL, II, 715 and n. 4

other references to, by TL, II, 447, 718, 730

Priestley expecting TL's death, II, 732 n. 6

TL and death of Priestley, II, xlvi, xlix, xlvii–xlviii, 759

destruction of TL's letters to, I, lxxii; II, lxvii

his letters to TL, I, lxxii, lxxvi, 73, 102, 105, 132, 140, 141 n. 9, 166, 188, 194, 209–10, 238, 271, 295, 322, 378 n. 11, 379; II, xli, 417, 427, 443 and n. 3, 459 and n. 2, 462, 534 n. 4, 536, 563–5, 568, 587 and n. 7, 594, 595–6, 600, 602, 604 and n. 8, 605, 607, 609, 612–14, 621, 622, 624, 626, 627, 629–31, 636 n. 8, 639, 640–4, 646, 648–50, 652–9, 663, 666, 669, 680, 681 and n. 11, 682–3, 696–7, 703 n. 1, 704–5, 708 n. 8, 711–12, 719 and n. 7, 723 and n. 9, 726 and n. 10, 729 and n. 12, 731 and n. 9, 732 and n. 4, 733 and n. 5, 734 and n. 3, 738 and n. 10, 739 and nn. 4 and 6, 743–5, 748, 758

TL's non-surviving letters to, I, 88, 93; II, xlviii, 429, 434, 443 and n. 3, 477, 564, 571, 639 and n. 13, 642 n. 5, 649, 687 n. 7, 703 and n. 10, 731 and n. 10, 733 and n. 5, 750 and n. 1

TL's letter to: I, 555

and William Tayleur

and Tayleur, I, 275, 284; II, 452, 487, 506

admiration for Tayleur, I, 199; II, 477 n. 6

and Tayleur's proposal for a public address to unitarians, I, 199

Tayleur's letters to, I, 271; II, 492 n. 3

Priestley and TL hope to visit at Shrewsbury, II, 459

visits to Tayleur at Shrewsbury, I, 282, 378 and n. 11; II, 391, 421, 487 n. 5

Priestley and TL visit to Tayleur at Shrewsbury, II, 421

Priestley and TL unable to visit Tayleur at Shrewsbury (July 1791), II, 461 n. 12, 469, 472, 477 n. 6

Tayleur's support for his experiments, I, 291

Tayleur's financial support for, I, lxxxv, 352; II, 477 and n. 6

Tayleur's support for new translation of the Bible, II, 413 and n. 4

Tayleur's disagreement with his view of eternal life and happiness for the wicked, II, 413 n. 10

his letters to Tayleur, II, 430, 492, 612

sending Tayleur *A view of revealed religion; a sermon, preached at the ordination of the Rev. William Field ... with a charge ... by the Rev. Thomas Belsham*, II, 430 n. 15

sending Tayleur *Letters to a young man, occasioned by Mr Wakefield's essay on public worship*, II, 492 n. 3

hopes to meet Tayleur 'in still better scenes', II, 643

controversies

controversy with Benjamin Dawson, I, 74 n. 14, 87 and n. 10, 97, 102

Evanson's letter to (1774), I, 132

attacked by John Shebbeare, I, 139 and n. 11

controversy with Thomas Balguy, I, xxiii, 146

dispute with Cornish and Towgood over the doctrine of necessity, I, 209–10

and necessarianism, I, 180, 182; II, 428 and n. 3, 520 n. 4

friendly controversy with William Newcome, I, 226, 250; II, 758 n. 2

Horsley's attack on his *History of the corruptions of Christianity*, I, 270

controversy with Horsley, I, 186 n. 4, 271, 274, 276, 296–7, 299, 311, 331, 337, 368; II, 398

Price thought him 'overcivil' to Horsley, I, 298, 305

TL and Priestley see Horsley in London (1790), II, 409

Horsley's 'execration' of him (1793), II, 514

TL describes Horsley as Priestley's 'great Opponent', II, 429

attacked in the *Monthly Review*, 276–7, 280, 286, 300

hostile *Letter to Dr Priestley*, I, 300 n. 6

controversy with Samuel Badcock, I, 280,nn. 8, 10 and 12, 288, 300 and n. 7

controversy with Thomas Howes in *St James's Chronicle*, I, 346 and n. 7

his critique of Joseph White, I, 324 and n. 15

and Edward Whittaker, I, 336

and George Horne, I, 336 n. 3, 338 n. 5, 339, 345, 350, 357, 360

attack on, in *The conference*, I, 339 and n. 4

exchanges with Jews in London, I, 334 and n. 5, 368–9

William, duke of Gloucester, brother of George III, II, 496 and n. 3

William III, I, xxiii, 377; II, 445 and n. 8
  attacked by John Shebbeare, I, 139 and n. 11

Williams, Benjamin
  dissenting minister at Salisbury, I, 270

Williams, Daniel, Trust and Library of, I, lxxi; II, 434, 599 n. 9, 779
  at Red Cross Street, London, I, 141, 155, 354
  TL not a trustee of, II, 703 n. 3
  John Coates a trustee and librarian of, II, 481 n. 3
  John Disney a trustee of, II, 703 and n. 3
  Thomas Jervis a trustee of, II, 703 and n. 3
  George Lewis a trustee of, II, 606 n. 6
  Moses Lowman a trustee of, II, 702 n. 10
  Thomas Morgan a trustee and librarian of, II, 609 n. 6
  John Williams curator of, II, 501 n. 7
  financial support for Thomas Evans, II, 703 and n. 3

Williams, Edward (Iolo Morganwg)
  and Essex Street chapel, II, xxxiv
  and Thomas Evans (Tomos Glyn Cothi), II, lvi, 703 n. 4, 741 n. 6
  and unitarianism, II, 703 n. 4

Williams, Helen Maria
  and William Godwin, I, 328 n. 9
  TL a subscriber to her poems, I, 328
  in Paris with John Hurford Stone, II, 549
  her 'Letters from France', II, 549 and n. 6
  imprisonment in Paris (1793), II, 549, 549 n. 6
  Works: *The poems of Helen Maria Williams*, I, 328 and n. 9

Williams, John (1727–98)
  student at the Cambrian academy, Carmarthen, II, 501 n. 6
  dissenting minister at Sydenham (Kent), II, 501
  curator of Dr Williams's Library, II, 501 n. 7
  his biblical scholarship, II, 501 n. 7
  contributor to *Theological Repository*, II, 501 n. 7
  and Thomas Evans, II, 501 nn. 7 and 8

Williams, John (1768–1835)
  educated at Carmarthen, Hoxton and Daventry academies, II, 413 n. 9
  minister at Uffculme (Devon), II, 413 n. 9
  and western unitarian society, II, 413 n. 9
  minister at Norton chapel (Derbyshire), II, 413 n. 9, 549, 583, 597 n. 10, 763 n. 8

Williams, John Henry, II, xx, 602
  vicar of Wellesbourne, II, 602 n. 10
  Works: *War the stumbling block of a Christian; or, the absurdity of defending religion by the sword. A sermon on the public fast, February 25, 1795*, II, 602 n. 10

Williams, Peter
  preaching against socinianism in Oxford, I, 367

Works: *Sermon preached before the University of Oxford, at Christ Church, on Ascension day, 1786*, I, 367

Williams, Thomas
  prosecution of, II, 642 n. 10, 673 n. 7
  and Proclamation Society, II, 673 n. 7
  and Thomas Erskine, II, 673 and n. 7
  convicted of blasphemy in court of king's bench, II, 673 n. 7
  imprisoned in Newgate, II, 673 n. 7
  sentenced to one year's imprisonment and required to give surety, II, 673 n. 7

William V, stadholder of the United Provinces, II, 430 n. 11
  overthrown and exiled, II, 590 n. 8

Willis, Thomas, I, 8,

Wills, Thomas, 64 n. 4

Wilmot, Ann, II, 433 n. 8

Wilson, Captain
  possible identification of, II, 744 n. 7
  and Thomas Fyshe Palmer, II, 744, 755

Wilson, Christopher, I, xxii

Wilson, James
  minister at High Street chapel, Stockport, II, 488 and n. 9
  his Glasgow and Edinburgh degrees, II, 488 n. 9
  minister in the Church of Scotland, II, 488 n. 9
  his exchange with Gilbert Wakefield, II, 488–9
  Works: *A defence of public or social worship; in a letter, address to Gilbert Wakefield. In answer to the latter's "Enquiry"*, II, 488 and n. 9, 489

Wilson, John, I, xxvi n. 65

Wilson, William, II, 764 n. 3

Wilton (Wilts), I, 354, 359 n. 5; II, 381 n. 4

Wilton House (Wilts), I, 37, 191 n. 4

Wiltshire, I, 288; II, 428, 490 n. 10, 491 and n. 8, 565 n. 6, 678 n. 7
  price of estates in, I, 40
  Deptford Club, I, 30 n. 25

Wimbledon (Surrey), II, 673 n. 2

Wimborne St Giles (Dorset), I, 37

Wimering (Hants), II, 547 n. 1, 678 n. 4

Wimpole (Cambs), I, 324

Winchester, I, xxiii, lvii, 5 n. 7, 37, 85 n. 8, 235 n. 4
  troop encampment at, visited by George III, I, 191 n. 4

Winchester, Elhanan, II, 630
  visit to England, II, 630 n. 6
  and universalist church, Philadelphia, II, 630 n. 6, 641 n. 7, 756 n. 2
  and Richard Price, II, 630 n. 6
  Joseph Priestley preaching for, II, 630, 631 n. 6, 756 n. 2
  and William Vidler, II, 756 and n. 2
  and universalist chapel at Parliament Court, London, II, 756 n. 2
  death of, II, 756 n. 2

PUBLICATIONS

Forthcoming Publications

THE DIARY OF JOHN BARGRAVE, 1644–1645. Ed. Michael Brennan, Jas' Elsner and Judith Maltby

THE 1669 RETURN OF NONCONFORMIST CONVENTICLES. Ed. David Wykes

THE SERMONS OF JOHN SHARP. Ed. Françoise Deconinck-Brossard

THE CORRESPONDENCE OF FRANCIS BLACKBURNE (1705–1787). Ed. G. M. Ditchfield

THE LETTERS AND PAPERS OF WILLIAM PALEY. Ed. Neil Hichin

THE CORRESPONDENCE, DIARIES AND PERSONAL MEMORANDA OF CHARLES SIMEON. Ed. Andrew Atherstone

THE DIARY OF AN OXFORD PARSON: THE REVEREND JOHN HILL, VICE-PRINCIPAL OF ST EDMUND HALL, OXFORD, 1805–1808, 1820–1855. Ed. Grayson Carter

THE JOURNAL OF DANIEL WILSON, BISHOP OF CALCUTTA, 1845–1857. Ed. Andrew Atherstone

ANGLO-CATHOLIC COMMUNICANTS' GUILDS AND SOCIETIES IN THE LATE NINETEENTH CENTURY. Ed. Jeremy Morris

THE CORRESPONDENCE OF ARCHBISHOP LANG WITH BISHOP WILFRID PARKER. Ed. Garth Turner

Suggestions for publications should be addressed to Professor Stephen Taylor, General Editor, Church of England Record Society, Department of History, University of Reading, Whiteknights, Reading RG6 6AH, or at s.j.c.taylor@reading.ac.uk.

Membership of the Church of England Record Society is open to all who are interested in the history of the Church of England. Enquiries should be addressed to the Honorary Treasurer, Professor Alec Ryrie, Department of Theology and Religion, Durham University, Abbey House, Palace Green, Durham DH1 3RS.